D0926953

THE CAMBRIDGE HISTORY OF CLASSICAL LITERATURE

THE CAMBRIDGE HISTORY OF CLASSICAL LITERATURE

II
LATIN LITERATURE

Edited by
E. J. KENNEY
Fellow of Peterhouse, Cambridge

Advisory editor
W. V. CLAUSEN
Professor of Greek and Latin
Harvard University

CAMBRIDGE UNIVERSITY PRESS
CAMBRIDGE
LONDON NEW YORK NEW ROCHELLE
MELBOURNE SYDNEY

Published by the Press Syndicate of the University of Cambridge
The Pitt Building, Trumpington Street, Cambridge CB2 1RP
32 East 57th Street, New York, NY 10022, USA
296 Beaconsfield Parade, Middle Park, Melbourne 3206, Australia

First published 1982

Printed in Great Britain at the University Press, Cambridge

Library of Congress Cataloguing in Publication Data

Main entry under title:

Latin literature.

(The Cambridge history of classical literature; 2)

1. Latin literature—History and criticism

I. Kenney, E. J. II. Series.

PA6003. L3 870'.9 79–121

ISBN 0 521 21043 7

CONTENTS

CONTENTS

CONTENTS

CONTENTS

PART V: EARLY PRINCIPATE

PLATES

(*between pages* 30 *and* 31)

PREFACE

The Cambridge History of Classical Literature is intended to make available to the widest possible public the results of recent and current scholarship in this field. Its emphasis is critical: material relating to biography, chronology and bibliography is presented for the most part in the Appendix of Authors and Works at the end of the volume, leaving contributors free to concentrate on discussion of the literary texts themselves. The introductory section 'Readers and Critics' is also designed to provide a background to these individual critical examinations, by sketching a general picture of the main features of ancient literary culture, which remained in most essential ways unchanged during the period covered by this volume.

The plan of the History is traditional, in that it consists of chapters on individual authors or genres within a broadly chronological framework. It has been left to each contributor to treat his author or topic as he sees fit. The inconsistencies and disparities that have inevitably arisen in these circumstances are such, it is hoped, as will not seriously inconvenience or mislead the reader. In a history of literature even more than most histories strict chronological sequence is hardly to be looked for. The only obtrusive anomaly under this head, the appearance of Apuleius in final place, represents an aesthetic rather than a historical decision on the part of the Editor.

For the most part it has not been possible for contributors to take account of secondary literature later than 1975, but the Appendix of Authors and Works includes important items published subsequently.

It is an agreeable duty to make acknowledgement to all those who have aided the production of this volume. On behalf of the contributors to be mentioned the Publishers and Editors offer cordial thanks for valuable assistance to (E. J. Kenney) Mr M. H. Bräude, Miss A. Duke, Dr Salvatore Lilla, Professor A. M. Snodgrass, Dr Sebastiano Timpanaro, Mr L. P. Wilkinson, Dr M. Winterbottom, Professor J. E. G. Zetzel; (J. C. Bramble) Professor R. G. M. Nisbet; (F. R. D. Goodyear) Miss S. French, Professor H. D. Jocelyn; (W. V. Clausen) Professor G. W. Bowersock, Professor J. P. Elder, Professor H. C. Gotoff,

Mr A. G. Lee, Sir Roger Mynors. A special tribute is owed to Mr Martin Drury, who as redactor of the Appendix of Authors and Works skilfully reduced to order a vast and diverse mass of material. He also composed the Metrical Appendix and compiled the Index.

Finally the Editors have a particular obligation to express their deep appreciation of the patience and courtesy extended to them by both Publishers and contributors during a prolonged and occasionally difficult period of gestation.

E.J.K.
W.V.C.

ABBREVIATIONS

Anth. Lat.	A. Riese–F. Bücheler–E. Lommatzsch, *Anthologia Latina Latina* (Leipzig, 1894–1926). (Cf. *CLE*)
ANRW	H. Temporini, *Aufstieg und Niedergang der römischen Welt* (Berlin, 1972–)
Bardon	H. Bardon, *La littérature latine inconnue* (Paris 1951–6)
BT	Bibliotheca Scriptorum Graecorum et Romanorum Teubneriana (Leipzig & Stuttgart)
Budé	Collection des Universités de France, publiée sous le patronage de l'Association Guillaume Budé (Paris)
Bursian	Bursian's *Jahresbericht über die Fortschritte der klassischen Altertumswissenschaft* (Berlin, 1873–1945)
CAF	T. Kock, *Comicorum Atticorum Fragmenta* (Leipzig, 1880–8)
CAH	*The Cambridge Ancient History* (Cambridge, 1923–39)
CAH[2]	2nd ed. (Cambridge, 1961–)
CC	*Corpus Christianorum.* Series Latina (Turnholt, 1953–)
CGF	G. Kaibel, *Comicorum Graecorum Fragmenta* (Berlin, 1899)
CGFPap.	C. F. L. Austin, *Comicorum Graecorum Fragmenta in papyris reperta* (Berlin, 1973)
CIL	*Corpus Inscriptionum Latinarum* (Berlin, 1863–)
CLE	F. Bücheler–E. Lommatzsch, *Carmina Latina Epigraphica* (Leipzig, 1897–1930). (= *Anth. Lat.* Pars II)
CRF	O. Ribbeck, *Comicorum Romanorum Fragmenta*, 3rd. ed. (Leipzig, 1897)
CSEL	*Corpus Scriptorum Ecclesiasticorum Latinorum* (Vienna, 1866–)
CVA	*Corpus Vasorum Antiquorum* (Paris & elsewhere, 1925–)
Christ–Schmid–Stählin	W. von Christ, *Geschichte der griechischen Literatur*, rev. W. Schmid and O. Stählin (Munich, 1920–1924) 6th ed. (Cf. Schmid–Stählin)
DTC	A. W. Pickard-Cambridge, *Dithyramb, tragedy and comedy.* 2nd ed., rev. T. B. L. Webster (Oxford, 1962)
DFA	A. W. Pickard-Cambridge, *The dramatic festivals of Athens.* 2nd ed., rev. J. Gould–D. M. Lewis (Oxford, 1968)

DK	H. Diels–W. Kranz, *Die Fragmente der Vorsokratiker*. 6th ed. (Berlin, 1951)
EGF	G. Kinkel, *Epicorum Graecorum Fragmenta* (Leipzig, 1877)
FGrH	F. Jacoby, *Fragmente der griechischen Historiker* (Berlin, 1923–)
FHG	C. Müller, *Fragmenta Historicorum Graecorum* (Berlin, 1841–70)
FPL	W. Morel, *Fragmenta Poetarum Latinorum* (Leipzig, 1927)
FPR	E. Baehrens, *Fragmenta Poetarum Romanorum* (Leipzig, 1886)
FYAT	(ed.) M. Platnauer, *Fifty years (and twelve) of classical scholarship* (Oxford, 1968)
GLK	H. Keil, *Grammatici Latini* (Leipzig, 1855–1923)
GLP	D. L. Page, *Greek Literary Papyri* (Cambridge, Mass. & London, 1942–)
Gow–Page, *Hell. Ep.*	A. S. F. Gow–D. L. Page, *The Greek Anthology: Hellenistic Epigrams* (Cambridge, 1965)
Gow–Page, *Garland*	A. S. F. Gow–D. L. Page, *The Greek Anthology: The Garland of Philip* (Cambridge, 1968)
Guthrie	W. K. C. Guthrie, *A History of Greek Philosophy* (Cambridge, 1965–81)
HRR	H. Peter, *Historicorum Romanorum reliquiae* (Leipzig, 1906–14)
HS	J. B. Hofmann, *Lateinische Syntax und Stilistik*, rev. A. Szantyr (Munich, 1965)
IEG	M. L. West, *Iambi et Elegi Graeci* (Oxford, 1971–2)
IG	*Inscriptiones Graecae* (Berlin, 1873–)
ILS	H. Dessau, *Inscriptiones Latinae Selectae* (Berlin, 1892–1916)
KG	R. Kühner–B. Gerth, *Ausführliche Grammatik der griechischen Sprache: Satzlehre*. 4th ed. (Hannover, 1955)
KS	R. Kühner–C. Stegmann, *Ausführliche Grammatik der lateinischen sprache: Satzlehre*. 3rd ed., rev. A. Thierfelder (Hannover, 1955)
Leo, *Gesch.*	F. Leo, *Geschichte der romischen Literatur*. I *Die archaische Literatur* (all pubd) (Berlin, 1913; repr. Darmstadt, 1967, w. *Die römische Poesie in der sullanischen Zeit*)
Lesky	A. Lesky, *A History of Greek Literature*, tr. J. Willis–C. de Heer (London, 1966)
Lesky, *TDH*	A. Lesky, *Die tragische Dichtung der Hellenen*, 3rd ed. (Göttingen, 1972)
LSJ	Liddell–Scott–Jones, *Greek–English Lexicon*, 9th ed. (Oxford, 1925–40)
Loeb	Loeb Classical Library (Cambridge, Mass. & London)
MGH	*Monumenta Germaniae Historica* (Berlin, 1877–91)
OCD[2]	*Oxford Classical Dictionary*, 2nd ed. (Oxford, 1970)

OCT	Scriptorum Classicorum Bibliotheca Oxoniensis (Oxford)
Paravia	Corpus Scriptorum Latinorum Paravianum (Turin)
PIR	E. Klebs–H. Dessau, *Prosopographia Imperii Romani Saeculi I, II, III* (Berlin, 1897–8), 2nd ed. E. Groag–A. Stein (Berlin & Leipzig, 1933–)
PL	J.-P. Migne, *Patrologiae cursus completus* Series Latina (Paris, 1844–)
PLF	E. Lobel–D. Page, *Poetarum Lesbiorum Fragmenta* (Oxford, 1963)
PLM	E. Baehrens, *Poetae Latini Minores* (Leipzig, 1879–83), rev. F. Vollmer (incomplete) (1911–35)
PLRE	A. H. M. Jones–J. R. Martindale–J. Morris, *The prosopography of the later Roman Empire* (Cambridge, 1971–)
PMG	D. L. Page, *Poetae Melici Graeci* (Oxford, 1962)
PPF	H. Diels, *Poetarum Philosophorum Graecorum Fragmenta* (Berlin, 1901)
Pfeiffer	R. Pfeiffer, *A history of classical scholarship* (Oxford, 1968)
Powell	J. U. Powell, *Collectanea Alexandrina* (Oxford, 1925)
Powell–Barber	J. U. Powell–E. A. Barber, *New chapters in the history of Greek Literature* (Oxford, 1921), 2nd ser. (1929), 3rd ser. (Powell alone) (1933)
Preller–Robert	L. Preller, *Griechische Mythologie*, 4th ed., rev. C. Robert (Berlin, 1894)
RAC	*Reallexicon für Antike und Christentum* (Stuttgart, 1941–)
RE	A. Pauly–G. Wissowa–W. Kroll, *Real-Encyclopädie der klassischen Altertumswissenschaft* (Stuttgart, 1893–)
ROL	E. H. Warmington, *Remains of old Latin* (Cambridge, Mass. & London, 1935–40)
Roscher	W. H. Roscher, *Ausführliches Lexicon der griechischen und römischen Mythologie* (Leipzig, 1884–)
SEG	*Supplementum Epigraphicum Graecum* (Leyden, 1923–71; Alphen aan den Rijn, 1979–)
SVF	H. von Arnim, *Stoicorum Veterum Fragmenta* (Leipzig, 1903–)
Snell	B. Snell, *Tragicorum Graecorum Fragmenta* (Göttingen, 1971–)
Schanz–Hosius	M. Schanz–C. Hosius, *Geschichte der römischen Literatur* (Munich, 1914–1935)
Schmid–Stählin	W. Schmid–O. Stählin, *Geschichte der griechischen Literatur* (Munich, 1929–1948)
Spengel	L. Spengel, *Rhetores Graeci* (1853–6); I ii rev. C. Hammer (Leipzig, 1894)
Teuffel	W. S. Teuffel, *Geschichte der römischen Literatur* (Leipzig & Berlin, 1913–1920)

TGF	A. Nauck, *Tragicorum Graecorum Fragmenta*, 2nd ed. (Leipzig, 1889)
TLL	*Thesaurus Linguae Latinae* (Leipzig, 1900–)
TRF	O. Ribbeck, *Tragicorum Romanorum Fragmenta*, 3rd ed. (Leipzig, 1897)
Walz	C. Walz, *Rhetores Graeci* (Stuttgart, 1832–6)
Williams, *TORP*	G. Williams, *Tradition and originality in Roman Poetry* (Oxford, 1968)

I

READERS AND CRITICS

1

BOOKS AND READERS IN THE ROMAN WORLD

For half a millennium the printed book has been the primary means of communicating ideas in the Western world. Now, with the development of film, radio, and television, together with alternative means of storing and retrieving information, the old empire of the printed word is under threat and has indeed already suffered some erosion. Nevertheless, for contemporary Western man the book, in the shape in which he has known it for centuries, still stands firmly at the centre of his literary and scientific culture. This shape is so familiar that it requires a considerable effort of the imagination to grasp the essential differences between the book as it is now and as it was in classical antiquity. In the following pages an attempt is made to sketch the conditions under which books were composed, copied, circulated, preserved, studied and used during the period covered by this volume. In this way it is hoped that the modern reader – who inevitably approaches this subject with certain preconceptions as to what a 'book' should look like and how it is to be read – may be helped to form an idea of some of the fundamental differences between ancient and modern literary culture, and hence achieve a clearer appreciation of the books and authors discussed in the body of the work. In some respects, as will emerge, the literary life of Greece and Rome retained the characteristics of an oral culture, a fact reflected in much of the literature that has come down to us. The modern reader, who is accustomed to taking in literature through the eye rather than through the ear, cannot be too frequently reminded that nearly all the books discussed in this history were written to be listened to.

Any attempt to discuss this subject must begin with a number of caveats, which arise from the extent and character of the evidence available to us. In the first place, whereas the remains of Greek books written in classical antiquity (dating predominantly from the first to the third centuries A.D.) are reasonably plentiful, few Latin papyri survive, and many of them are non-literary.[1] Inferences from the Greek to the Latin book, though in the circumstances inevitable, must be made with great caution.

Secondly, within the span of time covered by the phrase 'the Roman

[1] Texts at Cavenaile (1958) 7–142. See also Plate III.

world' – here taken to embrace the period from the third century B.C. to the early fifth century A.D. – only certain select periods, persons and types of literary activity are illuminated by the surviving evidence. This limitation must be patiently accepted and the temptation to generalize resisted. In the effort, for example, to construct a picture of the Roman book trade, much has been made of the well-documented relationship of Cicero with Atticus; but this procedure can be extremely misleading (see below, section 4). It is admittedly reasonable to assume a good deal of continuity in this, as in many other areas of ancient life, during the period under review: so far as our evidence takes us, it seems true to say that the conditions under which Latin books were written, copied, 'published' and read did not in essentials differ (when the effects of the introduction of the *codex* are allowed for) in the time of St Jerome from what they had been in Cicero's day.[1] Even so, general inferences about authorship or the book trade based, for example, on what Martial says about his own work must be recognized for what they are: hypotheses offered *faute de mieux*.

Thirdly, far too much implicit reliance has in the past been placed on arguments from analogy with modern literary and publishing practice. To style Atticus a 'publisher', as is still done in more than one current treatment, is to import into the reconstruction of his activities an entirely modern and obtrusive concept belonging in the world of the printed book.[2] In so far as analogies in this field are valid at all, they should rather be sought in the Middle Ages, and more especially in the last century of the Renaissance (that is, from about 1350 to 1450), when there recurred for the first time since classical antiquity the phenomenon of a highly developed and intensive literary and scholarly culture (which we can document in considerable detail) propagating itself through the medium of the manuscript book.

In the light of these considerations the evidence relating to specific cases must be interpreted with circumspection and not made the basis for superstructures of speculation which it is unequal to bearing. Much of what at present passes for the history of scholarship in the Roman world needs close and sceptical re-examination.[3] The results of such an analysis would no doubt be a less coherent and indeed in some ways less intelligible picture than that presented by some standard works of reference; but not least among the virtues of a student of this branch of scholarship ought to be, in Quintilian's words (*Inst.* 1.8.21), *aliqua nescire* – to accept the necessity to be ignorant of some things.

[1] Arns (1953) *passim*.
[2] Sommer (1926) 422; cf. for instance the highly tendentious title chosen by Kleberg (1967).
[3] Zetzel (1972); id. (1973) 239–43.

1. GREEK AND ROMAN LITERARY CULTURE

Graecia capta ferum uictorem cepit 'captive Greece led her rough conqueror captive' (Hor. *Epist.* 2.1.156). The history of Roman literature effectively begins with Ennius. Plautus in his comedies had reproduced his Greek models in metres in which the influence of native Latin verse is apparent. Ennius, by choosing to naturalize the Greek hexameter as the metre of his national epic, the *Annales*, declared an allegiance which was never thereafter shaken off. Literary dependence on Greek models was part of a general (if not universal and unquestioning) acceptance of contemporary Greek culture by the Romans of the second century B.C.[1] Thus the nascent Roman literary tradition found itself almost overnight the inheritor, not only of the riches of Greek literature itself, but also of a copious and highly developed body of critical, grammatical and rhetorical theory and practice.

The assimilation of this huge mass of intellectual nourishment was a prodigious undertaking, never completely achieved. To take two examples from the extremities of our period: it seems doubtful whether even Cicero's first-hand knowledge of Greek poetry and philosophy was as considerable as his allusions, taken at their face value, appear to suggest;[2] and Claudian was evidently exceptional among his contemporaries for his erudition in both languages.[3] It may be questioned whether a truly unified Graeco-Roman literary culture ever existed; if it did, it was short-lived and precarious. Juvenal and Lucian (especially in his *De mercede conductis*) illuminate the mutual dislike of Greeks and Romans and, more especially, the one-way nature of the cultural traffic. Ammianus Marcellinus and Claudian, whose native language was Greek but who wrote in Latin, are quite untypical. What can safely be asserted is that the Latin poets from Catullus and Lucretius onwards assumed in their readers an acquaintance with – or at all events an awareness of – a wide range of Greek poetry. The educational curriculum also subscribed, in theory, to a similar ideal (see below, section 2). Moreover the criticism and exegesis of Latin literature was conducted through 'the application and misapplication of Alexandrian methods'.[4] In this sense the Roman consumer of literature may indeed be said to have been the prisoner of Greek culture.

2. EDUCATION

Roman educational institutions, predictably, followed Greek models. Indeed, down to the time of Augustus Roman education essentially *was* Greek: that is to say, it was Greek poetry and Greek oratory that formed the staple of study and imitation. 'Latin poetry came into existence so that teachers should have

[1] Marrou (1956) 243–7; Momigliano (1975) 17–21.
[2] Jocelyn (1973); cf. Marrou (1956) 426–7.
[3] Cameron (1970) 305, 348.
[4] Zetzel (1972) 272.

something to argue about': it was not until there was a native literature that could challenge comparison with Greek that Latin texts could become central in Roman education.[1] Cultivated Romans were conscious of the need for a literature of their own and eager to exploit it as it came into being. In the field of oratory Cicero's speeches were studied as exemplary in his own lifetime (*Att.* 2.1.3, 4.2.2), and his treatises *De oratore*, *Orator* and *Brutus* breathe a conviction of authority, a consciousness that their author had laid the foundations of a truly Latin school of eloquence. In the field of epic the *Aeneid* was acclaimed, even before publication, as a work of classical status (Prop. 2.34.65–6); a fact officially recognized, as it were, by the decision of the grammarian Q. Caecilius Epirota in about 25 B.C. to lecture on 'Virgil and other modern poets'.[2] From now on Latin literature could occupy its rightful place in the scheme of education.

This education was almost entirely linguistic and literary, and it served with almost complete single-mindedness the end of perfecting self-expression. Lip-service is paid by Quintilian to the need to study philosophy, natural science, history and law; but in the grand design of his work these recommendations have all the air of an afterthought.[3] For him the aim of the pre-rhetorical stages of education is summed up in the phrase *recte loquendi scientiam et poetarum enarrationem* 'the understanding of correct speech and the interpretation of the poets' (*Inst.* 1.4.2).[4] The methods used to this end were slow, thorough, and relentlessly pedantic. Under his elementary schoolmaster (*litterator*, *magister ludi litterarii*), from about the age of seven, the child practised writing and reciting the letters of the alphabet in every possible combination before repeating the procedure with syllables and then complete words. No short cuts were permitted. 'There is no short way with syllables', says Quintilian: 'they must be learned thoroughly, and the difficult ones must not (as usually happens) be left until they are encountered in actual words' (1.1.30). That is to say, attention to form is to precede attention to sense; and that is the order of priority expressly commended by the Greek critic Dionysius of Halicarnassus (writing under Augustus) at the beginning of his treatise *On composition*.[5] The whole process was taken over entire from Hellenistic primary education.[6]

[1] Marrou (1956) 251–2.

[2] Suet. *Gramm.* 16.2 *primus dicitur... Vergilium et alios poetas nouos praelegere coepisse.* The word '*nouos*' here means 'modern'; it does not of itself connote the existence of a particular school of poets.

[3] 12.2–4; cf. also 1.4.4 (music, astronomy, science), 1.10 (music, geometry); Marrou (1956) 281–2. Treatment of these topics in school would be even more perfunctory; Servius' commentary on Virgil indicates the level of instruction provided.

[4] This was taken over from Greek: Dion. Thrax 1 on judging poetry, as the end of grammar; cf. Varro *ap.* Diomed. *GLK* 1 426.

[5] Dion. Hal. *Comp.* 3; cf. Guillemin (1937) 47.

[6] Marrou (1956) 150–3, with examples of school-exercises from the papyri. If the recommendations of Quintilian may be taken to represent general practice, children would seem ordinarily to have begun the systematic grammatical study of Greek before that of Latin (1.1.12). However, it is clear that Quintilian himself was much better read in Latin than in Greek, and it may be guessed that these were counsels of perfection.

The same dependence, and the same emphasis on literal and verbal *minutiae*, were evident in the next stage, under the teacher of literature (*grammaticus*), begun usually at the age of eleven or thereabouts. The reading (*praelectio*) and interpretation (*enarratio*) of texts was conducted on a predominantly technical level. An example of the relentlessly pedantic methods employed may be found in Priscian's *Partitiones* ('Distinctions') on the first twelve verses of the *Aeneid*: they occupy some fifty-five large octavo pages in Keil's edition.[1] Exposition of content (*enarratio historiarum*) formed part of the process but was almost entirely an affair of factual erudition. Literary criticism as it is now understood – concern with larger social and aesthetic values – was virtually unknown at any level of scholarly activity and certainly formed no part of the school curriculum. A paradoxical feature of the system, but one which had important implications for literature, was the concentration in the schools on poetical texts, given that the ultimate aim was to produce the *perfectus orator* – a man consummately well trained in the art of effective extempore speech in prose.[2] On the face of it this emphasis was beneficial. The range of authors recommended by Quintilian for school reading in both Greek and Latin (1.8.5–12) is quite extensive and offers an excellent foundation for a literary education. In point of fact his list (like nearly all such lists) reflects a traditional view of what is ideally desirable rather than current reality.[3] However, even when allowance is made for the normal discrepancy between theory and practice, it seems clear that the choice of authors regarded as classical in the highest sense and so especially suitable to form the basis of the curriculum gradually narrowed during the later Empire. For the late fourth-century grammarian Arusianus Messius four authors had come to represent the preferred sources of classical Latin usage, Virgil, Sallust, Terence and Cicero.[4] Again, of these four it was the two poets who predominated in the school curriculum and who attracted most attention from grammarians and commentators. So it is that Virgil and Terence enjoy the best protected traditions of all Latin writers – that is to say, they have been largely immune from the casual and arbitrary alterations that in varying degrees have affected the texts of other authors (cf. below, section 5). But there was no question of studying them, or any other author, for their own sake. The role of poetry in education was always ancillary to the overriding rhetorical purpose of the system. When Quintilian commends the older poets of Rome (1.8.10–12), it is as a source of authority and embellishment for the orator.

1 *GLK* III 459–515.

2 Cf. Quint. *Inst.* 1.4.4, 2.5.1–20, suggesting, rather apologetically, the *praelectio* of orators and historians by the *rhetor* as part of the first elements of rhetorical instruction (*prima rhetorices rudimenta*).

3 This is even more true of his famous conspectus of the reading of the orator in Book 10: on its sources in Alexandrian and later literary tradition see Peterson (1891) xxviii–xxxix.

4 *GLK* VII 449–515; Cassiodorus (*Inst.* 1.15.7) refers to 'Messius' foursome', *quadriga Messii.* Cf. Marrou (1956) 277–8.

The formal education of many boys no doubt finished with the *grammaticus*. Some moved on, usually at the age of puberty but in some cases several years earlier, to the third, and for most Romans final, stage of their education under the teacher of rhetoric (*rhetor*). Rhetorical teaching in Latin was comparatively late in developing and did not become securely established until early in the first century B.C.[1] What is significant for literature is that its establishment coincided in time with the rise to power of Octavian, later Augustus, and the gradual disappearance of real political liberty at Rome. The main practical element in the education of the Roman boy who was destined (as all Romans of good family were traditionally destined) for public life was declamation: formal speeches on specified topics. At Rome this exercise may have originally tended to resort more often to real life for its choice of themes – contemporary legal and political issues – than its Greek counterpart.[2] Under the Principate there was, for obvious reasons, a shift away from realistic and contemporary subjects to those founded on premisses ranging from the improbable through the romantic to the frankly grotesque. Some of the subjects can be seen to have been derived from literature, especially the New Comedy, rather than from life.

Declamation, which began as a purely private exercise, quickly became a public spectacle in which even accomplished speakers and prominent men of affairs did not think it beneath them to participate. Quintilian (10.5.14) recommends declamation as of practical use for the speaker who is already fully perfect in the art and celebrated in the courts, *consummatus ac iam in foro clarus*. A notable example of the adult practitioner was the Emperor Nero (Suet. *Nero* 10). Two types of exercise were in vogue: the *suasoria*, in which the speaker advised some famous character of history or fable on his proper course of action in a difficult situation; and the *controversia*, in which the speakers argued on opposite sides of a case, usually of a legal or quasi-legal nature. Of these types the *controversia* was in general more popular as being more directly competitive. Given the emphasis on competition and the unreal premisses of the arguments, the aim of the adepts was not so much to convince as to astonish their auditors. To this end they employed all possible resources: vivid descriptions, striking turns of phrase, paradox, point, sententious epigram, and emotional extravagances of the most extreme kind. Above all they relied on what were technically known as *colores* 'colours': the ingenious manipulation, often to the point of standing things on their heads, of words and ideas, with the object of putting a new and unexpected complexion on the data of the case. In all this probability was hardly regarded; the aim was less to persuade than to outdo the previous speaker.

[1] For the political background to the process see Gwynn (1926) 60–9, Clarke (1953) 11–15, Marrou (1956) 252–3.

[2] Cf. on the anonymous treatise *Ad Herennium* Marrou loc. cit.; Bonner (1949) 25. Cicero's early *De inventione* may, however, give a more typical picture.

Such were the characteristics of declamation.[1] The danger that these exercises, designed as subordinate to the practical ends of oratory, might become an end in themselves was recognized very soon, and the literature of the first century A.D. abounds in criticisms of the excesses and abuses of the schools. But the thought of any alternative form of training was never seriously entertained; Quintilian's belief in the value of declamation when properly controlled is clearly unshakeable (2.10). For Pliny, Quintilian's star pupil, the cultivation of eloquence was a life-long pursuit; and he in turn instructed his juniors in the pleasure and utility of the exercises on which it depended (*Epist.* 7.9, esp. sections 12–14). Only to Tacitus did it occur to question, and then only implicitly, in his *Dialogus*, the *raison d'être* of this ceaseless activity. For Pliny and his circle, as for most others, its necessity and virtue were self-evident.

The effects on literature of this mass conditioning, as it must be accounted, of writers and public alike can be traced already in the work of Ovid, and it is conspicuous in the poets of the Silver Age. However, one reservation must be made: women, who formed a not inconsiderable part of the literate public, did not go through the whole course of education just described. There is some evidence to show that some girls, probably from less well-to-do families, attended elementary schools;[2] but most of those who received any education at all must have received it at home. There is ample testimony to the existence of cultured women in the poetry of Catullus, Propertius and Ovid, and in Pliny's letters;[3] and Juvenal's tirade against bluestockings must have had some basis in fact to be effective satire. Little literature written by women has survived or is known to have existed;[4] but the purity of the Latin spoken by ladies of good family is remarked by both Cicero and Pliny.[5] In attempting to form an idea of the Roman literary scene, therefore, some allowance should be made for the existence of a class of readers who had not been through the mill of contemporary rhetoric.

The most striking feature of ancient education is its extreme conservatism and effective resistance to change. In essentials the Roman schools of the fifth century A.D. were still patterned after those of Hellenistic Greece; the main difference, language apart, was that the emphasis on rhetoric was even more concentrated. Efforts by Cicero and – such as they were – Quintilian to impart

[1] They are best understood through study of the elder Seneca's *Controversiae* and *Suasoriae*; cf. Bonner (1949) 51–70; Winterbottom (1974) vii–xv.

[2] Guillemin (1937) 85 n. 4, citing Martial 8.3.15–16, 9.68.1–2; Friedländer (1908–28) I 230–1, IV 410–11.

[3] Sherwin-White (1966) 347 on Plin. *Epist.* 5.16.3.

[4] There seems to be no good reason to doubt the authenticity of the poems ascribed to Sulpicia in the Tibullan corpus, though the patronizing remarks of an older generation of critics about 'feminine Latinity' will not bear examination: Smith (1913) 80.

[5] *Brut.* 211, *De or.* 3.45, Plin. *Epist.* 1.16.6; cf. Cameron (1970) 317 n. 1.

a more liberal cast to school studies failed. The emphasis remained verbal, grammatical and rhetorical; and the fact is reflected in the critical and exegetical tradition as well as in the literature itself.[1]

3. AUTHOR AND PUBLIC

No quantitative estimate of the extent of literacy at any period in the Roman world is possible.[2] What can be said with some assurance is that the literature with which this discussion is concerned was from first to last the preserve of the relatively small élite in which high culture flourished. To this rule drama and oratory, which were necessarily directed to the wider public, constitute the only exceptions of importance. The other literary genres, along with Hellenistic standards of technical refinement and curious learning in poetry, took over the assumption that the poet wrote for a select group of readers who shared his ideas of how poetry should be written and were competent to judge his work. From the first Latin literature was an affair of groups and coteries. The fact is intimately connected with the largely informal way in which books were 'published' and circulated (see below, section 4). This situation was not altered by the spread of Roman power and the development of Rome into a cosmopolitan capital. Latin literature took on the characteristics of a world literature: Ovid and Martial purport to be conscious of a public extending from Britain to the Black Sea. But most literary activity was concentrated at Rome, and it was to Rome that provincial writers made their way.[3] In spite of the huge and heterogeneous population of the capital, the literary public must have been relatively small: Martial's epigrams give an impression of a closed society whose members were mostly well known to each other. The analogy of, say, eighteenth-century London suggests that this is what might be expected. Literary circles of course existed in the provinces, such as that at Naples, with which Statius was connected,[4] but it was Rome that offered the best opportunities to writers, whether amateur or professional.

Though the idea of a mass audience was rejected by the poet who was conscious of his traditional status, writers were acutely alive to the need to please if their works – and hence they themselves – were to survive. That this idea of survival through one's works was, in a pagan culture, extremely powerful is shown by such affirmations as Horace's Ode *Exegi monumentum* (3.30) and the conclusion of Ovid's *Metamorphoses*. But before submitting himself to a verdict from which there could be no appeal, an author would often try out

[1] For a good general survey see Bonner (1977).

[2] Cf. Guillemin (1937) 78–84, arguing that literacy was widespread.

[3] Most Roman writers hailed from the provinces; there is no proof that any was born at Rome, though Lucretius and Caesar may have been: Watts (1971) 97.

[4] Vessey (1973) 44–6.

his work on a smaller circle. There were good practical reasons for this, founded in the character of ancient publication. Once a book was in full circulation, there was no effective means of correcting it, let alone recalling it. Second thoughts therefore were likely to be unavailing; a corrected second edition could not be guaranteed to supersede the first. Horace puts the matter in a nutshell when he warns intending authors to show their work to competent critics and to keep it by them for revision for nine years before launching it into the world: *nescit uox missa reuerti* 'the word once uttered cannot be recalled' (*A.P.* 386–90). Some at least of the poets who died leaving their work to be published by their executors – Lucretius, Catullus (?), Virgil, Persius – may have been actuated by a desire to postpone the irrevocable moment as long as possible. The feelings of Virgil on the subject were indeed so acute that he tried to ensure that his uncompleted *Aeneid* should perish with him (*Vit. Donat.* 39).

It was, then, even more important than it is today for a writer to submit his work to the test of critical opinion before publication. For the younger Pliny and his friends – though his circle cannot be taken as entirely representative – this became almost an obsession: 'la précaution a dégénéré en tic'.[1] This is where the coterie might assume considerable importance. Books or portions of books were read aloud to a small audience of friends, who were invited to criticize freely what they heard. The origins of this custom go back at least to Hellenistic Alexandria: the variations on the same themes that we encounter in the epigrams of Callimachus and Asclepiades represent a critical as well as a creative activity, practised for a small audience of cultured friends round the dinner-table. About literary coteries at Rome before the age of Cicero we are ill informed. The so-called 'Scipionic circle' – the literary friends of Scipio Aemilianus Africanus Numantinus (185–129 B.C.), who included Terence and Lucilius – cannot on the basis of the extant evidence be shown to have represented any shared artistic position.[2] Similarly the poets who towards the end of the second century B.C. were writing Latin epigrams on the Hellenistic pattern – Valerius Aedituus, Porcius Licinus, Q. Lutatius Catulus – cannot be proved to have formed a group with common aims.[3] It is with Catullus that we first encounter clear evidence of something like a full-blown literary circle, wedded to the Callimachean idea of a poetic programme and a doctrinaire view of poetry.[4]

Under the Principate the sort of private and informal criticism that must have played a part in shaping many of Catullus' poems and that still flourished among Pliny's acquaintance began to yield pride of place to a more public kind

[1] Guillemin (1937) 37; cf. Burr (1959) 59.

[2] Astin (1967) 294, affirming that the term is 'essentially an invention of modern scholarship'.

[3] Ross (1969*b*) 142.

[4] Guillemin (1937) 36, Clausen (1964) 189. On the possible connexion of the grammarian Valerius Cato with Catullus and the 'Neoterics' cf. Crowther (1971) 108–9.

of occasion. The institution of the *recitatio*, the public or semi-public reading aloud by an author of his work, appears (Sen. *Contr.* 4 *praef.* 2) to be due to the historian Asinius Pollio (76 B.C.–A.D. 4). Virgil, as is well known, read (under some compulsion) Books 2 (1?), 4 and 6 of the *Aeneid* to Augustus and members of his family; and it is also recorded that he would on occasion read to larger audiences passages which he felt might benefit from criticism (*Vit. Donat.* 32–3). In the first century A.D. the *recitatio* became a regular feature of the literary life of Rome, as numerous contemporary references indicate.[1] Some of these occasions were private and were genuinely intended to elicit criticism before final publication. However, for writers who were in any sense professional – i.e. who depended on writing for their living (see below, p. 21) – the *recitatio* was primarily a form of advertisement or puffing.

Preliminary publication of this kind, as the *recitatio* must be accounted, undoubtedly influenced the way in which literature was written. In general it may be taken for granted that throughout antiquity books were written to be read aloud, and that even private reading often took on some of the characteristics of a modulated declamation.[2] It might be said without undue exaggeration that a book of poetry or artistic prose was not simply a text in the modern sense but something like a score for public or private performance. This consideration must have been present from the start to the writer who dictated his work (as many did) as part of the process of composition; the next and logical step was obviously to assess the effect on others by experiment. However, the writer who was more concerned to puff his book than to invite criticism of it was apt to study primarily to please his audience – to carry over into the recitation hall the declaimer's ambition to impress by astonishing. So Cestius, quoted by the elder Seneca (*Contr.* 9.6.12): 'Much of what I say is said, not because it pleases me, but because I know that it will please my hearers.' Many of the characteristics of Seneca's tragedies and Juvenal's satires, to take the two most obvious examples, stem from the writer's consciousness of an audience present and waiting, more eager for immediate gratification than attentive to larger questions of proportion and balance or desirous of food for thought. For this feature of Silver Age Latin literature the *recitatio* must bear considerable responsibility, as contemporary opinion, represented most vividly in the first Satire of Persius, clearly recognized.

Connected with the literary coterie is the role of patronage. In the absence of a developed system of publishing as we now know it an ancient writer could not live on the sale of his books (cf. below, section 4). If he lacked sufficient private means he required financial subvention of some kind; moreover, if he

[1] Sherwin-White (1966) 115–16 on Plin. *Epist.* 1.13; Juv. 7.36–47.

[2] Bibliography of the question at Allen (1972) 10 n. 25. It is not true that silent reading was unknown, only that it was unusual: Knox (1968). The Roman ear clearly relished sound and rhythm. For the use of the verb *cantare* 'sing' of reading aloud see Allen (1972) *passim.*

was of humble or non-citizen status he might well need protection in case his writings gave offence. Again, more especially in the period down to the end of the Republic, when literary culture was less unified and organized than it later became, his work would in the first instance make itself known only through the channels of personal recommendation: patron to friends, friends to their friends, and so on. Accordingly it is not surprising to find patronage playing a prominent part in the lives of Republican writers such as Ennius and the dramatists.

Under the centralized and autocratic administration of Augustus it became possible to think of using literary patronage as an effective instrument of policy. To what extent this actually happened is disputed.[1] It certainly cannot be assumed that all 'Augustanism' in Augustan literature represents a 'party line' laid down from above; Livy, who belonged to no coterie and had no patron, wrote a history which in many of its fundamental characteristics is quite as 'Augustan' as the *Aeneid*. However, there are clear signs in the literature of the period that poets such as Virgil, Horace and Propertius were aware of an expectation on the part of the Princeps and his lieutenants that literature had a part to play in the establishment of the new order, whether through straightforward celebration of the achievements of the Princeps or more subtly by canonizing, so to say, the Augustan myths. The frequency in contemporary poetry of the motif of the *recusatio* – the formal, courtly rejection of certain epic or official themes – is sufficient evidence of these pressures. Among the myths seeking poetical recognition may perhaps be reckoned that of Maecenas as typifying the golden age of liberal and disinterested patronage; but the evidence of Horace's *Satires* and *Epistles* is enough to show that the legend of the 'mécénat', though it was exaggerated and embellished during the Neronian and Flavian periods, had a substantial core of truth.

After Augustus Roman emperors displayed little constructive interest in literature. The most important exception was Nero, under whom there occurred something approaching a minor renaissance of Latin poetry, characterized by a neo-Augustan effusion of pastoral. Private patronage, which under Augustus had still flourished in the 'opposition' circle of writers round M. Valerius Messalla Corvinus, which included Ovid and Tibullus, deteriorated during the first century A.D. into a relationship of dependence and degradation: 'Le "mécénat" fit place à la clientèle.'[2] As seen from the writer's point of view the position is vividly depicted in Juvenal's first, fifth and seventh Satires. The letters of Pliny suggest at first sight a more roseate picture, but they refer in the main to the activities of learned amateurs such as Pliny himself, the motto of whose life might have been Horace's *strenua inertia* 'busy idleness'. Between the worlds of Juvenal and Pliny, though they were contemporaries, there is

[1] André (1967) 102.

[2] Guillemin (1937) 96; cf. Vessey (1973) 16–17.

little sign of contact. The professional writer – the writer, that is, with a genuine vocation and a conception of literature as offering a complete and exclusive career (an idea relatively late in developing at Rome)[1] – received very little encouragement after the Augustan period. What the system of patronage as it existed under the early Empire seems to have been designed to foster was ephemeral, amateur and courtly writing. Notable examples are Martial's epigrams and Statius' *Silvae*, released to entertain the world at large, it would seem, only when they had served their first purpose of engaging favour through recitation or private presentation.[2] That not all the literature of the Silver Age falls into these categories says something for the professional conscience of at least some writers.

Patronage apart, what further pressures were brought to bear on literature and how far they were effective can only be considered in specific cases, and the answer is rarely unambiguous. That the emphasis of the *Aeneid* as actually written was due to the promptings of Augustus rather than to Virgil's own sense of artistic fitness seems highly improbable.[3] Nor is it by any means clear what part Augustus played in the rescue and posthumous publication of the poem in despite of the poet's expressed wishes (*Vit. Donat.* 39). If his intervention on that occasion was really decisive, it was not always so. After banishing Ovid the Princeps banned his work from the public libraries, but his action cannot be shown to have had any effect on their survival. Conversely the attempt of the Emperor Tacitus (if the *Historia Augusta* may be believed) to revive interest in his namesake the historian by placing and renewing copies 'in all the libraries' did not save him from total eclipse in the second and third centuries A.D.[4] Signs of remarkable independence are found in literature published when the Principate was at its most absolute: the seventh book of Lucan's *De bello civili* contains passages of bitter satire that astonish in a poem dedicated – apparently in all seriousness – to Nero.

That it might be dangerous under the Empire to write tragedies glorifying Brutus or Cato we are reminded by the opening chapters of Tacitus' *Dialogus*; but that same work ends with a passage purporting to show that eloquence, as stemming from political faction, has become redundant, in which it is difficult not to discern irony. The reticences and ambiguities of the surviving evidence interpose an almost impenetrable barrier. Even the best-documented episode of all, the disgrace and exile of Ovid, is still surrounded in mystery. Read with attention the poems of his exile are highly, even bitterly, critical of Augustus. That we still have them shows that they were not suppressed; but how widely they were circulated in Augustus' lifetime we do not know – still less whether Augustus ever saw them. As an instrument for arousing public opinion literature

[1] Bardon (1956) 318–19.
[2] White (1974).
[3] Bardon (1940) 71–2.
[4] *Hist. Aug. Tac.* 10.3; cf. Syme (1958) 503, 796.

remained relatively powerless in large centralized societies until the coming of the printing-press. Once again consideration of the effects of literature returns us to the questions of its physical medium: the book itself, and the circumstances under which it was copied and circulated.

4. BOOKS AND PUBLICATION

By 'book' in this section is meant papyrus roll; the change to the *codex* and its implications are considered below, section 5. The manufacture of papyrus and the make-up of the book in roll form have been described in Volume I,[1] and what is said there applies for the most part, *mutatis mutandis*, to Roman books. Something must be added, however, on the subject of terminology. The ordinary Latin word for book, *liber*, originally meant 'bark'. Whether it was used as the equivalent for Greek βιβλίον because it already meant 'book', *sc.* book written on bark (the existence of such books being entirely a matter of inference from the name), or whether because bark was the native substance most closely resembling papyrus (which is not indigenous to western Europe) it is impossible to determine. The specifically Roman word for book, to which Greek offers no analogue, was *uolumen* 'roll'. This remained the term proper to the book as a physical object; whereas *liber* might mean (i) 'roll' (= *uolumen*); or (ii) a 'book' of a work written to occupy more than one roll, e.g. a 'book' of Virgil or Livy; or (iii) a 'book' in the sense of a work of literature, e.g. the *Aeneid*. This last sense is rare, and in most of the passages taken by lexicographers and others to represent it, there is at least a tinge of senses (i) or (ii).[2] For a work consisting of more than one *liber* (sense (ii)) the normal designation would be *libri*, as when Cicero refers to his *De re publica* as his 'books on the Constitution' (*Fin.* 2.59 *in nostris de re publica libris*) or Quintilian to his 'books on the teaching of oratory' (*praef.* 1 *libros quos...de institutione oratoria scripseram*).[3] Use was also made of such variants as *opus* 'work' (Ovid, *Amores epigr.* 2, referring to a work in three or five *libelli*), *charta*, properly 'papyrus, paper' (Lucretius 3.10 *tuis ex...chartis*); and of descriptive terms such as *uersus*, *carmen*, *poemata*, *commentarii*, *epistulae*; or paraphrases with words such as *scribere*, *dicere*, *canere*, and the like. The use of these periphrastic expressions is connected with the lack of a universally accepted convention for the identification of books in the modern manner by title. A convenient alternative to *liber* was its diminutive *libellus*, properly 'small book', used particularly of poetry (Catullus 1.1, Ovid, *Amores epigr.* 1, Martial 1 *praef.*, 1.3, Statius, *Silvae* 1 *praef.*, etc.).

On the continuous strip of papyrus forming the book the text was written

[1] *CHCL* 1, ch. 1.

[2] See below, Excursus 1, p. 30.

[3] Contrast Vitruv. 1 *praef.* 3 *his uoluminibus*.

from left to right in columns, *paginae*. Thus to read a book the user held it in both hands horizontally, rolling it up with the left hand and unrolling with the right as he read. The common terms for this process were *explicare* 'unfold', *euoluere* 'unroll', and variants of these verbs.[1] It seems probable that the ends of the roll were commonly reinforced against wear and secured to wooden rollers, the ends of which were often fitted with ornamental knobs called *umbilici* 'navels', or *cornua* 'horns':[2] hence the expression *ad umbilicos* (or *cornua*) *explicare* (or *uenire*), and the like, meaning 'to read to the end' (Mart. 4.89.2, 11.107.1, *al.*). Books were supposed to be kept rolled with the beginning outwards, and on coming to the end of a book a considerate user would re-roll it for the next reader.[3] This thoughtful action was, we may surmise, frequently neglected; which may help to explain why (so far as the Greek evidence goes, at all events) the author and title (or other identification) of the book were often given at the end of the roll.[4] Titling indeed seems to have been something of a difficulty. There was no place on a papyrus roll corresponding to the fore-edge or spine of a modern book; for quick identification the reader must have had to depend on the tag of parchment (*titulus*) which was glued to the outside of the roll and hung down as it lay on the shelf or projected if the roll was stored upright in a box.[5]

All in all, it will be clear that in comparison with a modern book the papyrus roll was impractical and inconvenient to use and to store. It also called for extravagant use of material, since only the inner, protected side was normally written on. As a measure of economy the back of a roll was sometimes used also ('opisthograph'), but for obvious reasons this was an inconvenient expedient. To read a *uolumen* needed two hands, which made note-taking difficult; and when it was not in use it was liable to be crushed unless protected by such devices as parchment wrappers (*membranae*) or book-boxes (*capsae*, *capsulae*). To find a given book in a large library, even if all the books were duly equipped with *tituli* (which were apt as a matter of course to come off), must have been a tiresome business; and to verify a reference quickly next to impossible – hence the notorious inaccuracy in citation by ancient authorities, who tended to rely on memory and to cite from the beginnings of books. Nor was the text itself as a rule equipped with much in the way of aids to the reader of the kind that the user of modern books takes for granted. In professionally written copies the writing would be a handsome and regular majuscule; but on the analogy of surviving

[1] This terminology survived the transition from roll to *codex*: cf. esp. the common formula in medieval manuscripts 'Liber I Explicit. Incipit Liber II', where *Explicit* is probably an abbreviation of *Explicitus* '(fully) unrolled'.

[2] But see below, Excursus 2, p. 31.

[3] Mart. 1.66.8, 10.93.6, seem to suggest that during this process one end (?) of the roll was tucked under the chin.

[4] Wendel (1949) 24, Turner (1971) 16.

[5] Examples at Turner (1971) 34. On titling see below, Excursus 3, p. 31.

Greek papyri we should expect that there also existed many privately made copies in cursive or documentary handwriting.[1] There were considerable variations in format as well as in legibility. The width of the columns of writing bore no relationship to the sheets out of which the roll was formed (*chartae*, *schedae/scidae*; also, confusingly, *paginae*, *plagulae*), since the joints between these were carefully smoothed down and offered no obstacle to the pen. Their width therefore varied greatly, though there is some evidence that the average length of a hexameter verse, about 35 letters, might on occasion serve as a norm. There were also wide variations in the number of lines in the column, size of margins, and all other aspects of get-up. In these matters, as in everything else connected with book-production, standards depended on circumstances: whether the copy in question was a regular one produced for trade sale, a *de luxe* exemplar intended for presentation, or an amateur effort for personal use.

The few surviving examples of early papyri, taken together with the evidence of contemporary inscriptions, offer some evidence, by no means conclusive, that down to the second century A.D. the words in Latin books were divided in writing by the use of a conventional sign and that punctuation was in use; though such evidence as does exist is not enough to show that there was any generally accepted system.[2] Seneca notes a difference between Greek and Roman usage in this respect.[3] In the second century, in a curious fit of what seems to have been cultural snobbery, the Romans adopted continuous writing without word-division (*scriptura continua*) on the Greek model; and if punctuation had previously been in common use, it too was rejected. Behind this decision may perhaps be sensed a feeling that to make literature more accessible by providing aids to the reader somehow devalues it; the preservation of certain anomalies in English spelling offers an analogy, though admittedly a very incomplete one. It should however be remembered that the best Latin writers impose the required punctuation on the reader's mind and ear by their phrasing, and it must always have been tacitly accepted that the onus was on the author to do this, whatever aids might or might not be provided in the written text. A writer who neglected this duty would be liable to puzzle his readers: Jerome complains that he cannot tell where Jovinian's sentences begin and end (*Adv. Jovin.* 1.2).

[1] Roberts (1956) xi–xii.

[2] Cavenaile (1958) nos. 20 (Cicero, *Verr.* 2.2.3–4; 20 B.C.)*; 41 (anon. on Servius Tullius; 2nd c. A.D.); 43 (hist. fragment; A.D. 100)*; 45 (philos. fragment; before A.D. 115). Not in Cavenaile: *Carmen de Bello Actiaco*; before A.D. 79*. (* = with punctuation.) Cf. Wingo (1972) 50–63. A few later papyri, e.g. Cavenaile 47 (4th–5th c. A.D.), 65 (2nd–3rd c. A.D.) have word-division with interpuncts.

[3] *Epist. mor.* 40.11; but the word *interpungere* may refer either to word-division or to sense-punctuation or possibly (the distinction between them not being hard-and-fast) to both: Wingo (1972) 15 n. 10. For a different interpretation, denying the existence of punctuation in Latin books, Townend (1969) 330–2.

Whatever the reasons for the change, it threw an added burden of interpretation on the individual reader, especially when confronted with a brand-new copy of a text. In that case he was obliged to divide the words and supply any punctuation that he required for himself.[1] As a rule he would indeed have to do a good deal more, for a newly-copied text would normally be full of copying errors. A reader who took textual accuracy at all seriously had virtually to make his own edition of his book by correcting slips of the pen (and sometimes graver corruptions), where possible by comparison with other, putatively if not actually, more reliable copies (*emendare*); by dividing the words and punctuating (*distinguere*); and – if he chanced to be of a scholarly turn of mind – by equipping his text with critical signs (*adnotare*). These routine operations should not be magnified into genuinely philological procedures. The word *emendo* in practice usually meant no more than to correct obvious minor errors.[2] All users of books would have been habituated to do this from their schooldays, since it seems likely that the texts used in schools were copied and corrected by the pupils themselves from the master's dictation.[3] Since it is a matter of common experience that few men are competent textual critics and that the average reader is all too ready to tolerate nonsense in what he reads, there must have been very many bad copies of literary texts circulating in antiquity.

Papyrus was supplied by the trade in various lengths and widths, but a roll could be as long or short as was required, since papyrus is very easy to cut and join (Plin. *N.H.* 13.78–9; Cic. *Att.* 16.6.4). However, very short or (even more) very long rolls were unmanageable: for Greek books a maximum of about 10·5 metres seems to be established.[4] In certain genres, notably epic, the *uolumen* became an accepted literary unit. Ovid refers to the *Metamorphoses* as a work in fifteen *uolumina* (*Trist.* 3.14.19). Thus the architecture of the *De rerum natura* and the *Aeneid* may be said to have in some sense arisen out of the exigencies of ancient book-production.[5] In these cases an artistic virtue has been made out of necessity – or at all events convenience. From Augustan times onwards the average length of a 'book' of poetry became established as about 700–900 lines; we find Martial (1.16) frankly acknowledging the occasional need for an author to pad so as to eke out his book to the minimum which could decently be offered to the public as a *liber*. Even in the totally different modern context authors are to some extent limited by comparable preconceptions as to propriety of length and format.

[1] Such punctuation as is found in ancient *codices* is generally the work of a second hand; the text was written in *scriptura continua* and without aids to the reader (Wingo (1972) 23 n. 11). Scholiasts not infrequently discuss problems of punctuation: for Servius cf. Mountford–Schultz (1930) 55 s.v. 'distinctio'.

[2] Zetzel (1972) 2 n. 8; cf. on the *subscriptiones* below, p. 28. The word did not have the specifically textual connotations that it has acquired in modern technical usage: Zetzel (1972) 6.

[3] Cf. Marrou (1956) 154–5. [4] Kenyon (1951) 54. [5] Cf. Birt (1882) 141–50.

In antiquity there were no copyright laws and no legal safeguards against unauthorized copying and circulation of books: therefore there was no such thing as publication in anything like its modern sense. In practice it was often possible for an author to confine the circulation of his work in the first instance to a limited number of friends;[1] but sooner or later the decision would have to be taken, if it had not already been taken by events,[2] to authorize or at least acquiesce in general circulation. Publication in this sense was less a matter of formal release to the public than a recognition by the author that his work was now, so to speak, on its own in the world: the word usually translated 'publish' (*edere* = Greek ἐκδιδόναι) connotes the resignation of rights and responsibilities.[3] Publication might on occasion operate as a protection in that it served as a formal claim to authorship and constituted some sort of a safeguard against plagiarism.[4] It did not necessarily connote the making of arrangements for the multiplication of copies. That might happen on occasion, but a work once relinquished by its author was public property, and in that sense published, whether or not a bookseller was employed to copy and put it into circulation. What mattered was the author's intention.

Once a book was released in this way the author had no rights in it whatever (even before publication what rights he had were moral rather than legal), no control over its fate, and no secure prospect of being able to correct it.[5] As Symmachus put it: 'Once a poem has left your hands, you resign all your rights; a speech when published is a free entity' (*Epist.* 1.31; cf. Hor. *Epist.* 1.20, Mart. 1.3). Thus it was open to any private individual to make or procure for himself a copy of any text to which he had access; and if he could command the services of a trained scribe the result would be indistinguishable from a copy obtained through trade channels – and, according to the quality of the exemplar used, might well be textually superior. The earliest evidence for the existence of a trade in books at Rome dates from the Ciceronian period;[6] before that time the circulation of books must have been almost exclusively a matter of private enterprise – as indeed it continued in large measure to be down to

[1] van Groningen (1963) 9, Dziatzko (1899*b*) 978; cf. Plin. *Epist.* 1.8.3, accepting the offer of a friend to read and criticize one of his compositions and remarking that even when he had corrected it he could withhold it or publish it as he pleased: *erit. . . et post emendationem liberum nobis uel publicare uel continere.*

[2] As was evidently the case with Cicero's speech *In Clodium et Curionem*, which he thought he had succeeded in suppressing (*Att.* 3.12.2), and with his juvenile *De inventione* (*De or.* 1.94); similarly with the rhetorical treatises of Quintilian (1 *prooem.* 7, 3.6.68). Fronto, *Epist.* pp. 111, 137 N.

[3] van Groningen (1963) 5.

[4] Cf. Plin. *Epist.* 2.10.3, Mart. 1.29, 1.66, 2.20.

[5] van Groningen (1963) 7. The best expedient was to include the correction in some later work: Quint. 3.6.64.

[6] Cic. *Phil.* 2.21 refers (incidentally) to a *taberna libraria* 'bookshop'; and Catullus mentions certain contemporary poets as likely to be found on the shelves of the booksellers, *librariorum scrinia* (14.17–19). The word *librarius* meant both 'copyist' and 'bookseller'; for the latter the Greek loan-word *bibliopola* also occurs.

the end of antiquity and in the Middle Ages. Indeed, as one of Cicero's letters to his brother Quintus (*Q.Fr.* 3.4.5) illustrates, many of the books, especially Greek books, which a scholar or amateur might need for his library, were not commercially available. Many well-to-do Romans must have had in their possession one or two slaves trained as clerks, who could be used as copyists of books when not otherwise employed and so build up the libraries of their employers and on occasion their employers' friends. This was how Atticus assisted Cicero; and his further services in copying and disseminating Cicero's own writings represent an extension of the same activity. His services, however, were given in friendship, not in a commercial way, and the picture of him still to be met with in modern handbooks as a 'publisher' on a large scale is quite wide of the mark, being based on anachronistic presuppositions rather than consideration of the contemporary evidence.[1] What Atticus did on a large scale and in a way that happens to be well documented, many others must have done to the extent that their more limited resources allowed. Essentially, however, there was no difference except one of scale.

That a book trade existed is undeniable. What cannot be established even in the sketchiest way is its extent and its economic basis, let alone the details of distribution, remuneration of authors (if any), and the like. From the time of Augustus we begin to hear of named *librarii*; the Sosii, mentioned by Horace, and Tryphon, to whom Quintilian entrusted the *Institutio oratoria* and who is referred to, along with Atrectus and others, by Martial. Rome was clearly the main entrepôt; in the early second century Pliny appears to be surprised to learn that there was a bookshop at such an important provincial centre as Lyons (*Epist.* 9.11.2). Gellius, writing towards the end of the same century, reports having found Greek books for sale at Brindisi, but he does not say that he found them in a bookshop, and the episode may in any case be a figment of his imagination.[2] In the time of Augustine there were bookshops at Carthage and Hippo (*Retract.* 2.58, *Epist.* 118.2.9). By the time of Pliny and Martial Latin literature was widely disseminated in the Western Empire,[3] but we know almost nothing of the channels through which it travelled. How many bookshops there were at any time, what stock they carried, how they acquired their exemplars for copying, whether nearly all their work was done to order, whether the copying and selling of books was generally a sideline, how large a proportion of the trade was in new books and how large in antiquarian – these and many other pertinent questions are matters of speculation.[4]

[1] By (e.g.) Kleberg (1967) 23–5, Burr (1959) 604. See Sommer (1926) for a full discussion and analysis of the evidence of Cicero's letters.

[2] Zetzel (1972) 64. In any case, the inference drawn by Kleberg (1967) 45 that there was a flourishing book trade at Brindisi is far too sweeping.

[3] Sherwin-White (1966) 490.

[4] For a brief and admirably sceptical discussion see Zetzel (1972) 255–7.

We are on slightly, though only slightly, firmer ground when we turn to consider what inducements may have existed for an author to entrust his work to the booksellers. They can hardly have been predominantly financial. When Horace refers to the profits from his writing, it is those likely to accrue to the Sosii, not to himself, that he means (*A.P.* 345). Similarly Martial implies that the rewards earned by his pen are virtually non-existent and that (like Juvenal) he is dependent on the client's daily dole for subsistence (10.74.7; Juv. 1.134). More explicitly he remarks elsewhere that it is nothing to him financially that his books are read in distant Britain. For him and for Juvenal poetry is synonymous with poverty.[1] If he, or any other writer, did receive payment from the booksellers it must have been in the form of a lump sum for an exemplar of which the bookseller was to have exclusive use (for the limited time during which the book was not in general circulation) as source for his trade copies. But Martial illustrates again the danger of generalizing. His work was slight, modish, occasional;[2] it would have been a rash man who dared to prophesy at the time that it would outlive the elegies of Gallus and Ovid's *Medea*. For the booksellers any profit to be made from such writing must have come from a quick sale. Martial is not entirely disinterested, it would appear; he refers satirically to those who read his poetry only if they can do so for nothing (5.16.9–10). His interest may have lain in the fact that he could command a respectable price for the authorial exemplar of his latest *libellus*, for immediate publication in a comparatively large edition, with little or no expectation of a continuing sale, in Rome at all events, once copies were widely available. The success of such an arrangement would naturally have been threatened if free copies were available at the same time. Martial sometimes gives friends his own poems as presents, and there may have been provision for a limited number of author's copies.[3] Here too we are thrown back on speculation.

Martial was a special case. Even for the well-to-do writer, professional or amateur, there were advantages other than financial in using the services of a bookseller. It would have suited Horace, for instance, to arrange for his poems, once released for publication, to be distributed initially by the trade, for more than one reason. (Whether it suited the trade would be very much a financial matter.) It was convenient to have somewhere to refer importunate friends in search of a copy (cf. Mart. 1.117). To provide the bookseller with an authorized exemplar, corrected by the author, offered some sort of safeguard, at all events in the early stages of dissemination, that reasonable textual accuracy would be maintained. Here much would depend on the quality of the bookseller and his staff of copyists. The inaccuracy of trade copies was

[1] Mart. 11.3.5–6; 3.38.7–10, Juv. 7.74–97. Cf. Tac. *Dial.* 9.1.

[2] As was that of the poets mentioned by Catullus (above, p. 19, n. 6); cf. Sommer (1926) 392.

[3] Birt (1882) 355.

notorious;[1] probably the Sosii and a handful of other *librarii* had a reputation to lose. For a wealthy amateur like Pliny, with a good conceit of himself, these inducements were probably sufficient in themselves. However, the number and tone of the references to booksellers in Pliny's letters and Martial's epigrams also suggest that by the end of the first century A.D. the book trade in Rome had developed to the point where it was normal for new books to be made available through trade channels, as had certainly not been the case in the days of Cicero and earlier.[2]

The size of editions[3] and the arrangements for distribution are also subjects for speculation. In Cicero's day, before the growth of the book trade, the 'edition' of a book was the handful of copies that passed from the author and his coadjutors, if he had any, into the hands of his friends.[4] Even in the time of Martial and Pliny there was no need for the bookseller to keep a large stock of most books on hand. Access to an exemplar was all that was needed; a short *libellus*, such as a book of Martial or Statius' *Silvae*, could if necessary be copied while the customer waited, and no doubt sometimes was (cf. Mart. 2.8.3–4). For distribution in the provinces (a subject about which nothing is known) a single exemplar for each centre of distribution was all that was needed, to serve as source for the copies to be sold. But the demand for books through trade channels must have been quite haphazard and unpredictable; it would have been absurd to lock up capital in the shape of ready-written books.[5] It is therefore not surprising to find that such information as exists about prices is both scanty and conflicting.[6] It must have been entirely a matter of supply and demand. The inflated prices quoted by Gellius for antiquarian books need not detain us; the subject belongs to the history of forgery and bibliomania.[7]

[1] Cic. *Q.Fr.* 3.5.6; Strabo (writing probably under Augustus) 13.1.54 *fin.*; Mart. 2.8.3–4. Trustworthy copyists were clearly not easy to find: Cic. *Q.Fr.* 3.4.5.

[2] Sherwin-White (1966) 91: 'Pliny indicates...that the distribution of his books was entirely in the hands of the *bibliopolae*.' It probably was; but his text does not actually prove the fact.

[3] What Birt (1882) 351–2 has to say on the subject is guesswork pure and simple. The case of Rufus' life of his son (Plin. *Epist.* 4.7.2) throws no light on normal practice.

[4] Cf. Sommer (1926) 412–14.

[5] That booksellers held stocks which sometimes had to be 'wasted' may be suggested by references to the use of discarded books as wrapping paper (e.g. Cat. 95.8, Hor. *Epist.* 2.1.269–70, *al.*); but it is hazardous to press the significance of what was clearly a literary *topos*.

[6] Mart. 13.3: a copy of the *Xenia* (Book 13) for 2 or 4 sesterces; 1.117.15–17: a finely produced copy of Book 1 for 5 denarii. In Martial's time a denarius was the price of a day's labour. Statius, *Silv.* 4.9.9, 21: a book of the *Silvae* (?) for a decussis (10 asses = a denarius, old value), contrasted with Brutus' orations for an as; but the context warns us against taking all this literally. On the tariff for copyists laid down in Diocletian's Edict see Birt (1882) 208–9.

[7] Zetzel (1972) 239–43.

5. THE 'FATA LIBELLORUM'

What has been well described as 'the casual and fluid nature of publication in the ancient world'[1] is just as characteristic of what happened to books after publication. The paucity of our evidence for the activities of the book trade must not be pressed to the point of denying that it played some part in keeping literature alive. But it is inherent in the nature of the manuscript book itself that the propagation of texts in antiquity must have been very largely an affair of private enterprise. The fate of any individual book – in basic terms, its physical survival – depended on a number of factors, among which, with a few outstanding exceptions, systematic scholarly and critical activity played a remarkably small part. Changes of public taste, coupled with the gradual narrowing of the educational focus mentioned above, had considerable effects on survival, but sheer hazard must probably be accounted the most potent force at work. That Gallus died under a cloud did not necessarily entail that his works must have perished with him,[2] any more than the *Ars amatoria* perished with Ovid. It seems reasonable to believe that Quintilian would not have recommended Gallus to the budding orator a century later if his poems were not still available; but his inclusion in the catalogue of best books does not prove that Quintilian himself had ever set eyes on a copy of his *Amores*. The disappearance of the first (five-book) edition of Ovid's *Amores* is not to be ascribed to 'respect for his wishes on the part of those responsible for the transmission'[3] so much as (from the poet's point of view) good luck. Nobody was 'responsible' for anything once the book was published. Nor will it do to explain Cicero's failure to suppress the first edition of the *Academica* by the suggestion that in his day things were less well organized than in Ovid's.[4] In that sense they were never at any time 'organized'.

The main, and perhaps the only, element of stability in the process of transmission and conservation of literature was that contributed by the public libraries; though here too intelligent guesswork must form the basis of discussion. There never existed at Rome any real parallel to the huge royal collections of Pergamum and Alexandria, still less to the scholarly and critical activity associated with the Museum. From the second century B.C. Greek books began to enter Italy in quantity as part of the spoils of war; the transition from looting to collection may be observed in the figure of L. Licinius Lucullus (Plut. *Lucull.* 42). These private collections offered a valuable resource to the scholar, of which we find Cicero and Cato availing themselves.[5] As a national Latin literature grew, it too was collected. Under the Empire it became the normal

1 Reynolds–Wilson (1974) 23.

2 As suggested by Büchner (1961) 340.

3 Büchner (1961) 326.

4 Büchner ibid.

5 Cic. *Fin.* 3.7–8, *Att.* 4.10.1, 4.14.1; cf. Plut. loc. cit.

thing for rich men to equip their houses with libraries, often less for use than for ostentation.[1] These collections must have been very numerous, and the total number of volumes extant at any one time huge; but they could not provide the permanency and the organization that were necessary to ensure that copies of what was most worth preserving – if possible carefully written and corrected copies made from the best available exemplars – were accessible to all accredited comers in known places. The role of public collections in the preservation of literature, as well as their often precarious existence, is illustrated indirectly by the report that when libraries at Rome were destroyed by fire, Domitian sent to Alexandria to procure fresh copies of the lost books (Suet. *Dom.* 20).

The first public library at Rome was founded by C. Asinius Pollio in 39 B.C., and his example was followed by Augustus and subsequent emperors. By the time of Constantine there appear to have been twenty-eight in the City. That founded by Augustus in the temple of the Palatine Apollo served as a prototype for several later foundations. It was on the Greek model, but the plan was double, since Greek and Latin books were separately housed; this segregation of the two languages was, it would seem, the rule throughout antiquity.[2] The fact is another reminder that Greek and Latin culture were never in any real sense integrated. The annexation of the library to a temple was also a recurrent feature, though some library buildings were purely secular. In the provinces local benefactors often endowed their communities with libraries; the example of Pliny's library at his native Comum is well known, since he took pains to record it himself (Plin. *Epist.* 1.8.2). Evidence as to the financing and staffing of libraries is scanty; at Rome they seem to have come under the supervision of the imperial civil service.[3] The Theodosian Code contains details of the *antiquarii* (in this context not 'antiquarians' but 'scribes') employed in the Constantinople library in A.D. 372 in the care and conservation of books,[4] and it is a reasonable guess (no more) that most libraries had copying departments (*scriptoria*) attached to them, in which new copies were made and – if the librarian were a scholar – existing copies corrected.[5] Generally it may be surmised that readers consulted books in the library, but loans were evidently permitted on occasion.[6]

It was notoriously difficult to get accurate copies of books in antiquity; as has already been remarked, the first task of a reader with a new book was to correct it, *emendare*. The life of a papyrus roll kept in a library under ideal

[1] Sen. *De tranqu. an.* 9, Lucian, *Adv. indoct. passim*; cf. Petron. 48.4.

[2] Suet. *Aug.* 29.3; Ihm (1893) 514–18, Callmer (1944) 159; cf. Petron. 48.4.

[3] Ihm (1893) 522–6.

[4] *Cod. Theod.* 14.9.2; Ihm (1893) 529. Cf. the reference to a MS written 'ab eo . . . Theodoro antiquario qui nunc Palatinus est' in a *subscriptio* to Book 3 of Boethius' *De syllogismo hypothetico* in MS Orleans 267 fol. 51r (Zetzel (1972) 233).

[5] Wendel (1954) 267–8.

[6] Gell. 11.17.1, 13.20.1, 16.8.2; 19.5.4, Fronto, *Epist.* p. 68 N; cf. Clift (1945) 37.

conditions – as ideal as might be in the climate of western Europe, which does not really suit papyrus – might be considerably longer than the 200 years mentioned by Pliny or even the 300 mentioned by Galen.[1] Thus if a good copy of a book – ideally one corrected by the author – had been placed in a library soon after publication it might serve as a standing check on the accuracy of current copies, which would have a relatively short life and need replacement at more frequent intervals than library copies. Unfortunately losses by fire were frequent; of all the libraries founded by earlier Roman emperors only Trajan's Bibliotheca Ulpia seems to have survived unscathed down to the fifth century A.D.[2] Nevertheless it seems probable that the transmission of Latin literature as it has come down to us was to some degree dependent on copies conserved in libraries. The textual quality of the average copy in general circulation in antiquity can be inferred from the evidence of surviving papyri and other ancient fragments, citations in grammarians and similar sources, and from the complaints of contemporaries: it was not high. Yet the medieval tradition of many Latin authors is not nearly as corrupt as we should expect if our earliest surviving *codices* are the lineal desendants of such generally current copies.

The simplest way of accounting for this fact is to suppose that the early monastic and cathedral libraries in Italy built up their stocks of books by acquiring or copying from manuscripts in the old pagan public libraries of Rome, some of which might have been of great age and most of which were likely to have been textually superior to copies in general circulation.[3] This hypothesis may also help to account for the survival in corpus form of certain collections of poetry such as the so-called *Corpus Tibullianum*. Individuals would copy or have copied for them Tibullus or 'Lygdamus' in separate rolls according to their own requirements; the collection as we have it was brought together by somebody connected with the literary coterie from which the various poems sprang, soon after the time at which they were written, and lodged in a library as a corpus of separate but related rolls, which was subsequently incorporated in a *codex*, from which our tradition originates.[4]

The other dominant factor, both conservative and destructive, in the transmission of Latin books was the replacement of the roll by the *codex*, the form of book with pages that is in use today. This change was going on at the same time as, though it did not completely coincide with, the replacement of papyrus as the usual writing material for books by parchment or vellum.[5] Parchment had in fact been in use for various purposes since Hellenistic times, and note-

1 Plin. *N.H.* 13.83, Galen 18.630 K; cf. Roberts (1954) 183, Birt (1882) 364–6, Lewis (1974) 59–60.

2 *Hist. Aug. Aurel.* 1.7, 10, etc., *Prob.* 2.1 – for what this testimony is worth.

3 Cf. Ihm (1893) 531, Knowles (1958) 139, Callmer (1944) 191.

4 Cf. Clift (1945) 25–6; Büchner (1961) 324–5; and below, pp. 193–7, on Catullus.

5 'There is no essential connexion between format and material' (Roberts (1954) 183); cf. Turner (1968) 8.

books made of it were already common in the first century B.C. It was merely a question of time before this handy combination of format and material was applied to book production. In the event the time was curiously slow in coming. In a well-known group of poems Martial refers to presents in the form of parchment *codices*, evidently miniatures, containing literary texts.[1] It seems a commendable innovation, but it was not generally taken up. The change from roll to *codex*, when it did come, was connected with the eventual triumph of Christianity in the Roman empire. For reasons which are not entirely clear Christian literature, especially the Bible, was from the first, whether written on papyrus or parchment, circulated in *codex*-format.[2] By the middle of the fourth century the *codex* had for all literary purposes ousted the roll and parchment had ousted papyrus. Again the reasons for the general change are neither simple nor entirely clear;[3] though in the light of hindsight it is obvious that for both durability and convenience the old, classical, kind of book could not begin to challenge comparison with the new.[4]

The triumph of the *codex* had important consequences for the transmission and preservation of literary texts. On the credit side the parchment *codex* was a far more robust and durable article than the papyrus *uolumen*, so that a text once transcribed into *codex*-form had a decent chance of survival through the cultural and political collapse of ancient civilization and the subsequent Dark Ages. A text on papyrus had almost none. But survival of a particular text depended on whether it was selected for transcription into *codex*-form. This selection in turn depended on a number of factors. Design and system played little part; no person or agency passed the whole of classical Latin literature in review at this time, allowing some books through the barrier and turning others back. Nor was the whole of classical literature by now available to be reviewed. Substantial losses must have occurred as early as the Silver Age. Already in the first century A.D. the Republican poets were alluded to more often than they were read, and even an actual citation by no means proves first-hand knowledge of the text cited. Gellius' appeal to 'a truly ancient manuscript' of Livius Andronicus 'in the library at Patras' as authority for early Latin spelling must be taken with a pinch of salt.[5] What his testimony does show is that by the end of the second century A.D. it was becoming difficult to find copies of Republican authors; they had to be searched for. Whether Gellius ever visited a library at Patras or found an old manuscript there is less important than the implication that this was the sort of place where at that date an enquirer might be expected

[1] Mart. 2.1, 14.184, 186, 188, 190, 192; cf. Roberts (1954) 177–80. Pliny, *N.H.* 7. 85, mentions a complete *Iliad*, small enough to fit into a nutshell, supposed to have been attested by Cicero.

[2] Roberts (1954) 186–91, Turner (1968) 10–12.

[3] Roberts (1954) 203–4.

[4] On the final triumph of parchment in the time of Jerome cf. Arns (1953) 23–5.

[5] Gell. 18.9.5; Zetzel (1972) 65–6.

to look. Even writers such as Macrobius and Servius are unlikely to have taken their citations of early Republican writers direct from the texts themselves. By the time of Augustine texts even of Cicero were hard to come by in Africa (*Epist.* 118.2.9).

For educational and rhetorical purposes epitomes and abstracts were increasingly in vogue; Marcus Aurelius asks Fronto for excerpts from Lucretius and Ennius (Fronto, *Epist.* p. 105 N). Such habits threatened more expecially lengthy works such as Livy's history, but were also generally inimical to the survival of all books not central to the standard school programme. The purpose for which a book was read had an important bearing on its textual fortunes. Literary authors, especially those used as grammatical texts, were respectfully treated. Books which were read for content rather than form – grammars, manuals such as Cato's *De agri cultura* or the cookery book ascribed to Apicius – were abbreviated, expanded, and generally altered at will.

In spite of temporary and local revivals of interest in this or that period or author, as when Juvenal suddenly became popular in the aristocratic circles of Rome in the fourth century – revivals which tended to be offset by a corresponding neglect of other areas[1] – a steady process of attrition had been at work for many years before the roll was finally superseded by the *codex*. *Quod latet, ignotum est* 'what is hidden, is unknown' (Ov. *Ars Am.* 3.397); even those texts which still survived somewhere[2] were effectively lost unless they satisfied two requirements. Their existence had to be known, and they had to be deemed worth the trouble (and expense) of recopying. Texts which failed to pass this double test were doomed to disappearance. Further losses of course were to occur during the Dark and Middle Ages, but they must have been relatively small in comparison with what failed to survive the end of classical antiquity. A text that had been copied into a *codex* and lodged in a monastic or capitular library was by no means out of the wood; but it had a better than sporting chance of coming through.[3]

6. SCHOLARSHIP AND CRITICISM

Roman scholars took over the traditions of Alexandrian literary scholarship along with the rest of Hellenistic culture.[4] An early exercise in the collection and determination of authenticity of texts was conducted by Cicero's contemporary M. Terentius Varro, who established the canon of Plautus' plays

[1] Wessner (1929); cf. Cameron (1964) 367–8 on the general neglect of Silver Age literature in the later Empire.

[2] At least one complete text of Ennius' *Annales* was still extant as late as the fifth century: Norden (1915) 78–86.

[3] Cf. Knowles (1958) 143–7.

[4] On Hellenistic scholarship see Pfeiffer (1968) 123–251, Turner (1968) 97–126, Fraser (1972) I 447–79; *CHCL* I.

which became and remained authoritative: only the twenty-one plays (including the fragmentary *Vidularia*) accepted by Varro are transmitted in the medieval tradition.[1] In general, however, there is little evidence for systematic scholarly preoccupation with texts, and to predicate the existence in classical antiquity of textual criticism in anything like its modern sense of orderly recension and emendation is mistaken. Even Probus, whose activities are described in apparently circumstantial detail by Suetonius, was not in any strict sense of the word a critic, and his dealings have left little impression on the texts with which we are told he occupied himself.[2]

In this connexion a recurring and fundamental misconception must be dealt with, concerning the so-called *subscriptiones*. These are notes surviving in the manuscripts of certain authors which testify to the fact that a named individual 'corrected' (the word used is *emendo*) a particular copy of the text in question, with or without the help of a mentor or another copy.[3] Most of these notes can be dated to late antiquity. The *subscriptiones* offer valuable information about particular texts: who was reading such and such a book at such and such a time, where and in association with whom, and so on. Thus the Juvenal *subscriptio* of Nicaeus, who read his text 'at Rome with my master Servius' (the well-known grammarian and commentator on Virgil) helps to illustrate the revival of interest in Juvenal which took place in the fourth century.[4] They are not, as has often been assumed, evidence for the production of critical editions of Latin texts – except in so far as every copy of any text was an edition, being different from every other copy, and in so far as any reader who cared to take the trouble had always been accustomed to correct, punctuate and annotate his own books using whatever resources were open to him. They represent a few documented cases of a practice that went on throughout Roman antiquity. The activity which they represent was essentially a private one and, regarded from the philological point of view, uncontrolled and irresponsible.[5]

The authors of the *subscriptiones* tinkered at their texts for the most part by the light of nature. Scholars such as C. Julius Hyginus, Palatine Librarian under Augustus, and Valerius Probus (end of first century A.D.), as heirs to the Alexandrian tradition, were in theory committed to a code of practice which incorporated stringent safeguards against unauthorized alteration of texts. The text itself was reproduced from the best available copies (however 'best' might be defined); conjectural readings were not admitted. They belonged in the com-

[1] Gell. 3.3.3; cf. Zetzel (1972) 19, 76–8. It should be noted that Varro's canon was based, not on an independent appraisal of the evidence, but on the general consensus of existing scholarly opinion.

[2] Suet. *Gramm.* 24; Zetzel (1972) 44–58.

[3] First comprehensively listed by Jahn (1851*b*) 327–72; cf. Büchner (1961) 355–7. A new provisional corrected and augmented list at Zetzel (1972) 225–42, 308–9.

[4] Cf. Cameron (1964) 369–71.

[5] Zetzel (1972) 253. On irresponsible 'correction' of texts by amateurs cf. Quint. *Inst.* 9.4.39.

panion volume of commentary, in which critical and exegetical problems were discussed. A battery of critical signs was used in the text itself to signal the nature and existence of the particular problem.[1] Given the technical limitations of the ancient book and the character of ancient publication, the plan was perfectly sound. In point of fact few traces of the systematic application of these methods have survived, even in Greek papyri;[2] and in the Roman world 'pure' scholarship was hardly known. Such critical discussions as figure in extant Latin commentaries and collections of *scholia* (detached notes of varying age and provenance that have accumulated in the margins of medieval copies) can be seen to represent a by-product of grammatical interpretation rather than a scientific concern with the problem of textual sources and their use.[3]

As to the character of this interpretation, it is of a piece with the educational and rhetorical system which had given it birth and which it existed to serve. There is the same preoccupation with minute, and often absurd, details; there is the same blindness to what we should account the larger issues of literary criticism.[4] Even in the technical sphere of language, metre, and rhetoric, standards are sometimes surprisingly low. Again and again Servius and the other Virgilian commentators betray a fundamental lack of understanding of Virgil's poetry. That the prevailing standard of critical judgement in the face of unquestioned prejudice was low can be seen from the general readiness to accept the ascription of certain poems in what is now called the Virgilian Appendix to the young Virgil.[5] The most striking feature of this situation, which has not received the attention that it deserves, is the discrepancy between the quality of literary appreciation which, on the evidence of the literature itself, the great writers and in particular the learned poets of Rome expected from their readers, and the almost complete failure of the professional exegetes to respond to these standards. This is especially noticeable in the preoccupation with overall economy, balance, symmetry and related questions of structure and scale displayed by (for instance) Lucretius, Virgil, Livy and Tacitus, and the total indifference to these things evident in our critical sources, who almost never allow their attention to stray from the individual word, phrase or verse.

In itself their concentration on details and on rhetorical techniques was by no means misplaced. Again, the literature itself, read with attention and in consciousness of the rhetorical conditioning discussed above, offers ample evidence that it was not only on the large scale that poets and artistic prose-writers took pains. From Virgil onwards Latin poetry was profoundly influenced by rhetoric, and a style of literary criticism that fails to take account of this

1 For these signs, listed in a Paris MS, see *GLK* VII 533–6, Büchner (1961) 329–30.
2 Reynolds–Wilson (1974) 11; cf. Turner (1968) 116–17.
3 Cf. on Servius Zetzel (1972) 87–158 *passim*.
4 Cf. Guillemin (1937) 49–54; and on Fronto's preoccupation with single words Grube (1965) 321.
5 Cf. *Vit. Donat.* 17–18; and in general Speyer (1971) 112–28.

fact will miss much that is essential to the poetry.[1] But the style of interpretation favoured by most ancient critics and commentators was conditioned by a basic premiss which a modern critic cannot accept, though he must be aware of it, that literary studies were a part of rhetoric and subservient to its social, political and moral ends. Of all the ancient critics whose works have survived the only one who transcended these limitations was the author of the treatise *On the sublime*, who was concerned exclusively with Greek literature.

The student of Latin will find that the most valuable guidance to the appreciation of Latin literature is that which emerges from close study of the texts themselves. The insistence by the poets that they wrote for a restricted and specially qualified readership, mentioned earlier in this discussion, was not a conventional pose. To read Latin literature so as to extract from it the greatest possible profit and enjoyment is a very demanding undertaking. It calls for a combination of detailed knowledge, linguistic and factual, and educated sensibility, that can only come from laborious application. The books in which we read our Latin authors are much more convenient than those which a Roman reader had, and our texts are probably purer than his often were. In other respects, even after allowing for the fact that Latin was his native language, we are not at such a disadvantage as might be thought. Literary Latin was an artificial dialect, quite distinct from the spoken idiom. Moreover a Roman reader must have been to a considerable extent the prisoner of his own age. To a Roman of the second century A.D. the language of Lucretius must have presented many puzzles to which solutions were not easily available even to a scholar with access to a good library. The main advantage that we enjoy, the ready availability of a vast apparatus of accurate scholarship in the shape of commentaries, dictionaries, reference books and other secondary literature, can be attributed directly to the invention of printing and what it made possible in the way of cooperative effort. If we try to imagine ourselves without these aids to understanding of literature we may begin to comprehend something of the situation of the reader in the world of the hand-written papyrus book.

Excursus I. THE SENSE OF 'LIBER' (P. 15)

Sense (iii) of *liber* and also of βιβλίον was denied by Birt (1882) 29–34. Unambiguous examples of this sense are indeed not easy to find. At Gell. 18.9.5, cited both by Dziatzko (1899*a*) 940 and Wendel (1949) 51, the predominant sense is (i), almost = 'copy'. At Juv. 3.41–2 *librum | si malus est, nequeo laudare et poscere* 'I am incapable of praising and asking for a bad book', the sense 'work of literature' is uppermost; but even this passage does not prove that Juvenal would have described (e.g.) the *Thebaid* of Statius as a *liber*. Similar reservations are in order when considering the other examples cited at *OLD* **liber**[4] 2a. Cicero twice refers to his *De gloria*, a work in

[1] Cf. on (e.g.) Lucan's rhetoric Getty (1955) xliv–lxvi.

I Rome, Museo Nazionale Romano. Fragment of Christian sarcophagus of ?third century A.D. showing philosophers in discussion. These were the ordinary ways of handling a papyrus *uolumen*, open or rolled. See p. 16.

II Rome, Museo Nuovo Capitolino. Tombstone of Q. Sulpicius Maximus, who distinguished himself at the Capitoline poetry contest (cf. Suet. *Dom.* 4.4) in A.D. 94 with the Greek poem here inscribed and died aged eleven. Shows how an open roll might be managed with one hand, leaving the other free for gesture. By a common convention the writing is incorrectly shown as running across the width of the roll, presumably to make it easier to read. For an example of the same convention in Greek vase-painting see *CHCL* I Plate I*a*.

III PQaṣr Ibrîm L 1/2. Part of a papyrus roll written between *c.* 50 and (probably) *c.* 20 B.C. containing elegiac verses by Gallus (see pp. 410–11). Before the discovery of this papyrus in 1978 all that survived of Gallus' work was a single pentameter (*FPL* 99). See Anderson, Parsons and Nisbet (1979).

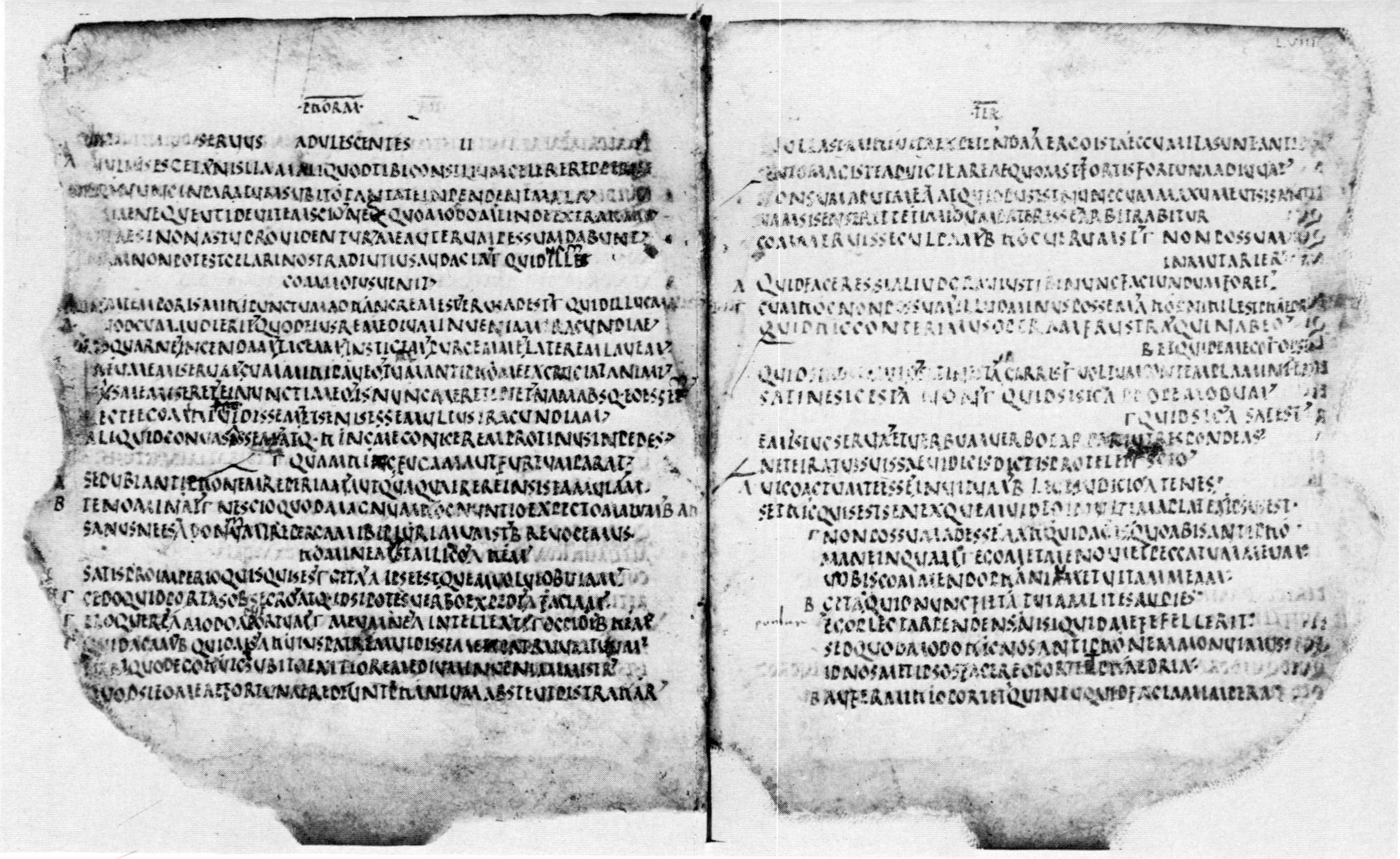

IV Biblioteca Apostolica Vaticana MS Latinus 3226 (Bembinus), foll. 57ᵛ–58ʳ. A vellum codex written in the fourth or fifth century A.D. containing most of Terence. The photograph shows *Phormio* 179–223. Whereas in the Gallus papyrus (Plate III) the words are separated by dots (interpuncts), the copyist here has followed the fashion that became normal after the second century A.D. of continuous writing without word-division (*scriptura*

two books, as a *liber* (*De or.* 2.31; *Att.* 15.27.2, 16.6.4). This however has been explained in the light of 'a last-minute change in the form of the work before publication' (Shackleton Bailey (1965–70) VI 289). The second example cited by Dziatzko, loc. cit., is from the fourth-century grammarian Charisius, who refers to Varro's *De poematis*, a work in three books, as *liber* (1.53, p. 66 Barwick). From these admittedly inconclusive data it seems to emerge that sense (iii) was late in developing and slow to make headway. In this sense *uolumen* is also found: cf. Plin. *N.H.* 3.58, Vell. 1.14.1, 2.131 (Wendel loc. cit.). The definition of a 'book' might be of some legal importance: cf. *Dig.* 32.52, Dziatzko (1899*a*) 941.

EXCURSUS 2. THE SENSE OF 'CORNUA' (P. 16)

The explanation given in the text is that usually accepted, and analogies such as the use of *cornu* for the tip of a yard-arm seem to lend support to it (*OLD* **cornu** 7e). However, Birt (1882) 299 argued strongly that *cornua* were the ends of the roll itself. In this connexion it is also relevant to consider the meaning of the word *frons* ('front, side, forehead') as applied to a book. The *frontes* are usually taken to be (i) the long edges of the roll (Birt (1882) 365, id. (1913) 304–5, *TLL* VI 1362.84). It has, however, been argued that they were (ii) the ends of the roll (*OLD* **frons**[2] 8b, but 'flat ends' is unclear; Luck (1968) on Ov. *Trist.* 1.1.8 (supporting this as the sense in the singular, sense (i) in the plural); Schubart (1921) 105). The *frons* or *frontes* were smoothed with pumice as part of the process of finishing the book (Ov. *Trist.* 1.1.11, Mart, 1.66.10) and were apparently, with the *titulus*, what showed when the book was shelved (Sen. *De tranqu. an.* 9.6). The emphasis on the appearance of both *frontes* at (e.g.) Mart. 3.2.8 suggests that sense (i) is the more likely, since when the book was properly rolled only the outside end would be visible, whereas both edges would be. The relationship of the *cornua* to the *frons* or *frontes* still remains somewhat obscure, especially since the poets tend to indulge in word-plays of an obvious kind when referring to the external appearance of the *libellus*: cf. Ov. *Trist.* 1.1.8. A much-cited but very difficult verse in this connexion is [Tib.] 3.1.13 *inter geminas pingantur cornua frontes* 'let the *cornua* between the twin *frontes* be coloured'. When the book was rolled, each *cornu*, if taken = knob, would stand out in the centre of its *frons* (sense (i)); but *inter* is not good Latin to express this idea (cf. Luck, loc. cit.; Erath (1971) 29). Ov. *Pont.* 4.13.7 shows that the tag (*titulus*) which identified the book when it stood on the shelf was attached to the *frons*, presumably meaning 'edge' rather than 'beginning of the book' (Erath, loc. cit.). Cf. on these tags Cic. *Att.* 4.4a.1, 8.2 and Shackleton Bailey (1965–70) ad locc.; Turner (1971) 34. On the whole problem see Besslich (1973).

EXCURSUS 3. TITLING (P. 16)

On the analogy of the modern book it might be expected that the author and title of a work would be given at the beginning of the text; the handful of surviving (Greek) rolls in which this is the case are all of late date (Turner (1971) 16). This is not in itself conclusive, since the beginning of a roll is the most vulnerable part of it, and the odds against survival into modern times of a roll complete with its beginning were large. Nor is the indirect evidence clear. Martial writes of the '*Epigramma*' of Book 9 of his poems being placed *extra ordinem paginarum* 'outside the sequence of columns' (9 *praef.*; cf. 2 *praef.*). Since the columns were not numbered, and their *ordo* could begin as close to the beginning of the roll as convention and the taste of the copyist dictated, it is difficult to see what exactly the phrase means. There is more than one possibility: (i) The two passages in Martial (and possibly, for instance, the *Epigramma* to the three-book edition of Ovid's *Amores*) refer to an addition made to the clean copy of the book just before it left the author's hands; it was an easy matter to add another sheet of papyrus to the left-hand end of the roll (cf. above, p. 18). But nothing is specifically said about *adglutinatio*, and in the copies made from the original exemplar peculiarities of this kind would not have been reproduced: the scribe would simply have copied the text as it now stood, starting at the normal place on his clean roll. (ii) The *ordo paginarum* was a matter of scribal differentiation. Martial is distinguishing between the text of the book proper, written in regular columns, and the prefatory matter, set off in some way from the rest and differently treated, thus appearing to stand to the left of a notional line from which the *ordo* began. (iii) The *Epigramma* was written at the beginning of the roll on the *outside*. This last is the solution favoured by (e.g.) Birt (1882) 142, id. (1913) 301, Wendel (1949) 26–7; a few examples of Greek rolls so titled have survived (Turner (1971) 16, 125). Wendel suggests that such matter came to be transferred to the inside of the roll, and then to occupy a separate page in the *codex*-form (ibid. 27, citing Aug. *Epist.* 2.40.2 for the phrase *in liminari pagina* 'on the threshold page'). If Wendel's hypothesis is correct, then both solutions (ii) and (iii) would be correct, but for different periods. Certainly, if an *Epigramma* such as these could stand outside the roll, so *a fortiori* could a shorter inscription, giving merely author and title (or contents: cf. on the question of how books were identified Nachmanson (1941), Koep (1954) 674). But are we to take it that such prefatory matter as (e.g.) Quintilian's letter to Tryphon or the letters introducing the individual books of Statius' *Silvae* (as apparently suggested by Birt (1882) 142 n. 3) regularly stood on the outside of the roll? If so, it is miraculous that they have survived or that their authors expected them to. Indeed it seems unlikely that an *Epigramma* or the like would have been allowed to encroach even on the inside of the roll on the length of papyrus normally left blank for protection at the beginning, for that also would have endangered its survival; the text as a whole, including *Epigrammata* and the like, would start precisely where it normally started, in terms of distance from the left-hand end of the papyrus. It seems preferable to accept solution (ii), i.e. to believe that Martial's reference to the *ordo paginarum* represents a *façon de parler*. This may ultimately go back to a time when identifying details were regularly written outside the roll (Wendel (1949) 24–5); but it strains credulity to think that such a practice can have been followed with textual matter, even when it was of a merely prefatory character.

2

LITERARY CRITICISM

Literary critics today fall into two broad categories. There are the academics, out to impress their colleagues and instruct their pupils. And there are, in the great tradition of Dryden, creative writers meditating on their craft. In the Roman world, academics, or their nearest equivalents, practised on literature something that they called *kritikē* (*iudicium* 'judgement'), but at an infinitely lower level of sophistication than has now been reached. The creative writers might comment on their trades, but they did it less systematically than Dryden or Eliot, and in response, rather, to the feuds and challenges of the moment. Neither teachers nor writers give us anything as abstract and theoretical as Aristotle's *Poetics*, or anything with as perceptive a treatment of cited passages as 'Longinus'. Cicero, Horace and Quintilian, authoritative and influential though they were, not only rank inferior to the best Greek critics: they are not competing in the same field.

I. THE 'ACADEMICS'

Grammatici

Horace, registering the judgement that Ennius was a second Homer, adds *ut critici dicunt* 'as the critics say' (*Epist.* 2.1.51). What, for the Romans, was a *criticus*?

In Greece scholars seem to have been called *kritikoi* before they took over the term *grammatikos*.[1] Even when *grammatikos* was in vogue, the exercise of judgement was regarded as an important part of a scholar's task; and Crates of Mallos, the wheel having come full circle, claimed to be critic rather than, or as well as, grammarian.[2] For Crates a critic was a superior being, 'skilled in the whole science of language'.[3] But we do not know that the great Alexandrians, such as Aristarchus and Aristophanes ('judges of poets', as Quintilian called them: *Inst.* 10.1.54), took their judgements very far. One of their activities was the establishment of an *ordo* or 'ranking' of approved writers in each genre.

[1] Pfeiffer (1968) 157.
[2] Pfeiffer (1968) 238.
[3] Sext. Emp. *Adv. math.* 1.79.

Another was to decide whether a work, or a portion of a work, was genuine. Both of these functions, of course, involved the making of value judgements; and we know that Aristophanes judged Archilochus' iambi best (Cic. *Att.* 16.11.2), though three writers were 'received' in this genre (Quintilian 10.1.59). But it was the stern textual procedures, as applied especially by Aristarchus to individual lines or passages of poetry, that attracted most lay attention.

It is accordingly a sort of athetesis (diagnosis of spuria) that is most often mentioned in connexion with such Romans as were explicitly called *critici* – which may mean no more than *grammatici* exercising their function of judgement. In his commentary on Virgil, Servius eleven times[1] uses the term, always in a context of blame. Typically, on *Aen.* 8.731 the critics are said to 'censure' (*notant*) the whole verse 'as having been added superfluously'. It is true that this sort of phrase does not seem to carry the implication that Virgil did not actually write the line or word censured: merely that he would have done better not to write it. Thus, very clearly, *Ecl.* 2.65 is 'censured for giving this sentiment to a rustic in contravention of the law of pastoral poetry' (*supra bucolici carminis legem*). Servius' *critici* apply Zenodotus' obelus with realistic regard to the difference between Homer and Virgil. But the grounds for their censure are very similar to Zenodotus'.

Elsewhere we can find close Roman parallels to Greek concern for the genuineness of whole works.[2] Accius' work on the chronology of Roman drama was precursor to the properly 'critical' activity of Varro on Plautus. According to Gellius (*N.A.* 3.3.3) Varro added to the twenty-one comedies commonly attributed to Plautus others that he felt on stylistic grounds – 'swayed by the texture and humour of their language' – to be genuine. And Gellius adds that his own teacher Favorinus employed the same criterion: 'even this one verse can be proof enough that this play is Plautine' (3.3.6).

Nor did Roman scholars shirk the task of establishing, in the wake of the Greeks, an *ordo* of the best Latin writers. The classic case of this, in Quintilian, will have to be discussed further below; but the tendency goes back much earlier. Volcacius Sedigitus' verses ranking the comic authors allude to the many who 'dispute to whom they should award the palm' (Gellius, *N.A.* 15.24). Moreover, Quintilian's concern to match Latin authors with Greek – Virgil with Homer, Livy with Herodotus, and the rest – finds, as we have seen, an earlier counterpart in Horace. It may be Varro who lies behind the docketing of Ennius as a second Homer; in that case, Varronian too will be the succeeding parallels drawn between Afranius and Menander, Plautus and Epicharmus, and the schoolmasterly distinction between the art of Terence and the gravity of Caecilius. Varro certainly extended his interest in literature beyond Plautus,

[1] *Ecl.* 2.65; *Aen.* 1.71, 2.668, 8.291 and 731, 9.81, 10.157 and 861, 11.24 and 188, 12.83.

[2] A concern that still weighed with writers on rhetoric: see e.g. Dion. Hal. *Isaeus* 2 and *Dem.* 13.

for we find him assigning Pacuvius, Lucilius and Terence to the three types of style, and incidentally cutting across genres as he did so.[1]

We have seen that in the terminology of the Servian scholia *critici* is used of those who found fault with certain aspects of Virgil's poetry. It has been argued[2] that the phrase refers especially to the early *obtrectatores* or 'disparagers' of the poet, one of whom wrote a distich to make fun of the rusticity of *cuium pecus* in *Ecl.* 3.1[3] Whatever the truth, the Servian *critici* behave little differently from other carpers, who were certainly full-blown *grammatici*. Thus Probus remarked on *Aen.* 4.418 that 'if Virgil had omitted this verse, he would have done better'.[4] And we see the same distinguished grammarian at work in more detail in Gellius (9.9.12–17), who reports his robust discussion of the comparison of Dido with Diana in *Aen.* 1.498–502. The simile, for Probus, is by no means appropriate (*nequaquam conueniens*), Diana's quiver far from functional and her joy far from unconfined. We may well quarrel with the judgement; but the importance of the passage is that it juxtaposes Virgil with his Homeric model (*Od.* 6.102–8) and attempts an aesthetic valuation. This scrap of Probus' scholarship, and others like it, should prevent us from assuming too readily that the Servian commentary, with its reluctance to comment helpfully on, or often even to mention, Virgil's models, is typical of Roman dealings with this most traditional of poets. On the contrary, we can see from the enormous discussion in Macrobius (*Saturnalia* 5–6), where not only tracts of Homer but also many passages of earlier Roman poets are cited *in extenso*, that the ancients took this task as seriously as modern commentators. It did not, fortunately, take long to outgrow the attitude that 'imitation' was no more than 'borrowing' or 'theft'. Where Perellius Faustus 'collected thefts' (*Vita Donati* 44) and drew the pained comment of the poet that it was easier to steal his club from Hercules than a line from Homer, Macrobius regards such transference as a subject for muted congratulation (*Sat.* 5.3.16). Many a Victorian commentator was less sophisticated than that.

But the general run of the scholia on Virgil is less impressive. These commentaries are designed largely to instruct – and to instruct the young; and though their sources are often very learned, they themselves rarely sound very adult. They will (to take examples from a familiar book of the *Aeneid*) identify the Hesperides (4.484), give us a snippet of information on the habits of the planet Mercury (239), put Aulis on the map (426); this is what Quintilian's enthusiasm for knowledge of mythology and astronomy at the grammar school

[1] Gell. 6.14.6. Cf. Charisius p. 315, 3 Barwick (= Varro fr. 40 Funaioli), where Caecilius and Terence are contrasted in the matter of the rousing of emotion.

[2] Ribbeck (1866) 102, 107; Georgii (1891) 2.

[3] For him and others see *Vita Donati* 43–5.

[4] Georgii (1891) 560–7 has a helpful table showing the various grounds on which Virgil was criticized in the Servian commentary.

must usually have meant in practice.[1] Then, because grammarian and *rhetor* had always overlapped and tended more and more to fuse,[2] there are rhetorical analyses of speeches, usually very sketchy; the remarks on Anna's speech at 31 as a *suasoria* are fuller than most. There are portentous pronouncements on religious practice, with Aeneas and Dido forced into a mould of priest and priestess (374, etc.). There are occasional hints at allegory (so at 114), a common fate for poetry from Crates to Tiberius Claudius Donatus. Figures are occasionally identified (276, etc.), riddles propounded and solved (262: why did Aeneas wear a bejewelled sword to supervise the building of Carthage?). This, with the pabulum of explication, leaves little room for anything we should regard as literary criticism.

But that is perhaps too hasty a judgement. The occasional condescending pat on the back for Virgil – *bene*... – sometimes prefaces a shrewd point. Thus at 403 the commentator remarks on the 'sublimity' lent by military metaphor to the description of ants. There are modern critics who would be proud to have connected the wounded stag in the Dictaean woods (73) with the herb dittany (*dictamnum*) that was reputed to heal the wounds of wild beasts, as we know that Virgil knew (*Aen.* 12.414). And suggestive recent work on 'multiple-correspondence' similes in Virgil[3] finds firm roots in the remarks of the commentator at 442–5.

We should bring this sort of balance to our judgement on Macrobius, who after all makes Servius participate in the conversation that forms the *Saturnalia*, and who was clearly drawing on largely grammatical or antiquarian sources. There are the same weaknesses. Where *grammatici* are criticized, it is for failing to raise a *quaestio* of their own kind (as at 5.18.3). To prove his own enthusiasm for the fray, one speaker proudly produces the recondite information that Euripides was reproved by Aristotle for saying it was the left foot rather than the right that Aetolians kept unshod (5.18.16–20). And there is a tendency to see Virgil as always right: 'there is another way of *defending* the use of the word *inlaudatus*', someone significantly remarks (6.7.16). At the same time, Macrobius had a certain feel for the relativity of critical judgements: 'let no one think old poets worthless just because their verses seem rough (*scabri*) to us' (6.3.9) – and this at a day when men did not care for the archaic (6.4.1; cf. 6.9.9). There is nothing to be ashamed of in the appraisal of Homer as a poet who showed 'not only grandeur but also simplicity, vividness (*praesentiam*) of language, and silent dignity' (5.13.40). And when it came to detailed assessment, modern studies of the catalogue in *Aeneid* 7[4] do not go far beyond the remarks in 5.15–16, where Homer's catalogue is compared, with due comment

[1] Quintilian 1.8.18 (with Colson's note) and 1.10.46–8.

[2] For early instances, Suet. *Gramm.* 4.6, 7.3. For later, Marrou (1958) 10 n. 2.

[3] West (1969).

[4] E.g. Williams (1961). Macrobius doubtless had his sources, here as elsewhere.

on the prominence of the Boeotians, and where the variety of Virgil is contrasted with Homer's repetitiousness which 'somehow supremely suits him, is appropriate to the genius of an ancient poet, and is the right way of conducting an enumeration' (5.15.16). At their best, the *grammatici* did look carefully at passages, not just as strings of words to be glossed but as wholes with literary predecessors, and make judgements on them that have stood the test of time.

Parallel to commentaries on Virgil were similar works on other distinguished poets. Thus Aelius Donatus commented on Terence as well as on Virgil, Acron on Terence and Horace. Asconius Pedianus, author of a lost work 'Against the disparagers of Virgil', bridged the gap between commentators on prose and poetry; for he produced impressive historical comments on speeches of Cicero. He elucidates allusions with economically phrased erudition, and explains in elaborate prefaces the circumstances of each speech. This is one side of what Quintilian was later to call for; he was to point out the desirability of teachers of rhetoric providing *enarratio* for the great orators as the grammarians did for the poets (2.5.1), stressing the need to give details of the case a speech is written for (ibid. 7).[1] But the rest of what Quintilian looked for (ibid. 7–9), close observation of the use made by great masters of rhetorical devices of all kinds, is lacking in Asconius and rarely apparent elsewhere. It was a matter, perhaps, that fell between the stools of *grammaticus* and *rhetor*. The Bobbio scholia on Cicero give an idea of the possibilities in this direction. Yet here, though great attention is properly devoted to detail, there is neglect of the equally vital view of the speech as a whole. The monograph rather than the commentary, or a combination of the two, would have been, then as now, the right vehicle.

Declamation

When he stepped over the frontier dividing grammarian from rhetorician, the Roman school-boy was faced by declamation rather than by oratory; and Quintilian gives the impression of fighting a losing battle in an attempt to widen the syllabus to include constant and detailed reading of prose masters at this stage (2.5.1–2). Declamation looms large, too, in first-century criticism. But much of what is said of it is generalized and polemical. There is the view put by Petronius at the (present) start of the *Satyricon* (1–2), and less vividly but equally forcefully in a mutilated chapter of the *Dialogus* of Tacitus (35), that declamation, with its parade of stepmothers and pirates and plagues, is too divorced from reality to make a satisfactory training for the lawcourts; and that when the unfortunate pupil arrives in the real world of interdicts and ancient lights he is thoroughly out of his depth. There is the balanced reply of

[1] Cf. Asconius 54, on the desirability of reading Cominius' prosecution speech as well as Cicero's defence of Cornelius, with Quintilian 10.1.22–3.

Quintilian (2.10). On the one hand, declamation did need some reform: it would help to introduce real names and jokes, and avoid the more unreal sort of theme. On the other hand, declamation was, in its way, a form of display oratory and could hardly avoid excursions into territory more agreeable and fanciful than the average law suit. Quintilian clearly was not prepared to envisage the abolition of declamation; and those who made fun of it seem to have had no alternative to offer. Nor indeed was it abolished; it was still going strong in the time of Ennodius, on the very verge of the early Middle Ages.

Alongside this generalized debate, we do have an occasional glimpse into the detail of declamation. It is here most profitable, perhaps, to study the *sermones* of the pseudo-Quintilian, the introductory remarks of a schoolmaster prefaced to model treatments of the themes he set. The form militates against anything very much like criticism; but there is at least an attempt to guide declamation into practical and useful paths, to show what the aims of a speaker in a given speech were, and how they were best pursued. Look, for instance, at the *sermo* to *Decl.* 270. 'It is easy to argue the case of this old man as far as emotion and equity are concerned. But unless he is also defended with legal arguments, there is danger that he may be condemned by the judges for all his tears.' And there follows a polemic on those who leave out the tougher parts of a speech, leaving flesh lacking bone and sinew. There are certain points to be proved. Only when we have proved them can we proceed to say the things to which most declaimers nowadays restrict themselves. This is in Quintilian's tradition, perhaps even his actual teaching. It shows us a rhetorician conscientiously trying to make the best of his educational tool. It is not unimpressive: more impressive, in a way, than the bitty and anecdotal treatment of the elder Seneca. In his collection of *Controversiae* and *Suasoriae* we have a vast array of fragments of declamation; from Seneca, more than from any other ancient author, derives the surely exaggerated view that declamations consisted of little but epigram. It is true that Seneca normally gives us the 'division' that Latro or some other declaimer applied to a case (e.g. *Contr.* 1.1.13), but he only once (2.7) set himself to give a declamation in full, so enabling us to judge how a speech related to its bare scheme; and on that one occasion, by an irony of fate, a lacuna in our manuscripts cuts the speech short (and deprives us of the division). But in general Seneca was interested in detail, and especially in the epigrams and 'colours', the more or less ingenious slants put on a case. And Seneca's own comments on these matters will hardly be thought of as serious criticism. He ridicules Junius Otho for over-using dreams to supply colours (2.1.33). Epigrams are on occasion – and rather arbitrarily, one feels – picked off as 'very stupid' (5.2) or 'nicely put' (7.1.26), or 'with its own kind of insanity' (9.2.28). Style is characterized as corrupt, Asianic, *kakozelos* ('in bad taste'). The prefaces to individual books attempt a more rounded view of some distinguished declaimers, and include more penetrating assessments of their styles. As for the practice of declamation[1] in general, Seneca's standpoint is sane, and he recounts with some relish the vigorous protests of Cassius Severus against the whole system (3 *praef.*). But he is a magpie rather than a critic; he makes no attempt to see declamation, or even any individual declamation, as a whole. No need to dwell on the incidental judgements on other authors that are scattered through the book. It is in the manner of the *grammaticus* that a description of Cestius' is placed alongside two lines of Virgil and their model in Varro of Atax (7.1.27). And Cicero is declaimed about, not assessed (*Contr.* 7.2; *Suas.* 6 and 7).

Quintilian

Seneca was not himself, it would seem, a practising rhetorician, merely an old man recalling past glories to enthusiastic sons. With Quintilian we come to a professional *rhetor*, well qualified, as well as inclined, to assess Cicero as well as praise him. Yet the part of the *Institutio* that is most widely read, perhaps the most familiar example of ancient literary criticism, is markedly in the tradition of the grammarian. In Alexandria, as we have seen, scholars established lists of selected writers, and laid down orders of merit within genres. Quintilian's famous survey of Greek literature (10.1.46–84) draws on listing of this kind,[2] and his treatment of Roman authors (85–131) provides a rival list for the rival language. Thus on the one hand he tells us that among the elegists Callimachus is 'regarded as leader, while most agree that Philetas took second place' (58); and on the other Virgil is placed first among Roman writers of hexameters (85–6), while Cornelius Severus 'could lay good claim to the second place if he had completed his *Sicilian War* to the standard of his first book' (89). The whole treatment of the Latin authors is consciously modelled on that of the Greeks: 'I must keep to the same order in dealing with Roman writers also' (85). Further, every effort is made to pit Roman against Greek. Virgil is praised as second only to Homer (85); 'I should not be afraid to match Sallust with Thucydides, and Herodotus should not be angry to find Livy put on a par with him' (101). We have seen the same tendency earlier. And where Cicero had in the *Brutus* constructed a 'canon' of Roman orators culminating in himself, in conscious rivalry with the Greeks, Quintilian takes equally open pride in the Roman achievement. 'And perhaps *we* make up by Virgil's good general level for the inferiority our champion shows to Homer's heights' (86). *We* – that is Cicero as opposed to Demosthenes – are victorious in wit and pathos (107). 'As for satire, it is completely ours' (93).

[1] Which, thought Seneca (*Contr.* 2 *praef.* 3), 'equips even those whom it does not train for its own ends'.

[2] Explicitly enough: see sections 52, 54, 58–9, 72–3.

All the same, reminiscent of the *grammaticus* though Quintilian's list is, it is quite clearly directed towards the training of the orator. The reading of all these authors is part of the process of producing a *hexis*, a soundly based ability to speak (10.1.1). 'I am not talking here about how an orator should be trained (I have already expressed myself on that topic enough – or at least as well as I could); now I am dealing with an athlete who has already learnt all the tricks from his teacher: by what kind of exercise is he to be prepared for combat?' (4). Just as in Lucian (*Lexiph.* 22) a progression is envisaged from the best poets through the orators to the heights of Plato and Thucydides, so Quintilian has given a graded course of reading: Homer and Virgil, tragedy, and selections from lyric at the school of the *grammaticus* (1.8.5), Cicero and Livy in the early stages of the *rhetor's* education (2.5.19–20), and then finally, in the last years of the rhetorical training, a whole range of Latin and Greek literature. The list may seem optimistically long; but the intention is to point to the authors available, and to suggest as briefly as possible what elements in them should be imitated and can contribute to the 'strengthening of the faculty of oratory' (10.1.44). And Quintilian is not all-inclusive: 'if I miss people out, that does not mean I have not heard of them... But to those lesser poets we shall return once our strength is complete and established' (57–8). Pisandros, Nicander, Euphorion, Tyrtaeus can wait; meanwhile 'we must get used to the best; our minds must be formed, our style developed, by much reading rather than the exploration of many authors' (59). Only when real maturity is reached can we safely read Seneca, one of whose virtues is that he can exercise the reader's judgement – for him and against him (131).

'Few, perhaps none, can be found, among those who have worn well, who would not have something useful to offer to readers prepared to exercise judgement' (40). And even though Quintilian claims to pick out only the most eminent (45), his list remains long. This fits in closely with Quintilian's view of imitation. Even if there were a supreme model for an orator – and Cicero comes close to being that – our human weakness would prevent us being able in practice to reproduce him whole (10.2.25–6). 'A prudent man should, if he can, make his own what he sees to be best in every author... We should put before our eyes the good points of a number of orators, so that one thing may stick from one source, one from another, and so that we can fit each in at the right place' (26). Nor does this apply only to the reading of orators; there is grist for the mill to be found everywhere. The reading of poetry has its advantages for the orator as well as its dangers (10.1.27–30). Hence the attention Quintilian pays to poets in his list, but hence too his constant care to define how far they can be of use to the orator. On the smaller scale, we see Alcaeus as a poet who is 'often similar to an orator'[1] though he 'also wrote trivia, and

[1] Similar phrases in 65 (comedy), 74 (Theopompus); cf. 90 on Lucan.

descended to erotica' (63); Euripides (67) is by general consent more useful to the budding advocate[1] than Sophocles – their merits as *poets* are expressly left out of account. So too on the negative side. Propertius is docketed with the remark that some prefer him (93) not because Quintilian disapproves of him but because he sees nothing in him for the student, not even the terseness and elegance he has just attributed to Tibullus. And on the large scale, when Quintilian discusses Homer, he adopts an elaborate series of rhetorical schemata to catalogue his virtues. He is pattern for forensic and deliberative oratory, not to speak of panegyric (47); he is master of emotion, both gentle and violent (48); he knows how to handle proem, narration, argument, and epilogue (48–50). This is not so much an unhistorical attribution to Homer of rhetorical skills of which he was innocent[2] as a careful directing of the pupil towards the aspects of the great poet to which he needs to pay attention.

All this had to be read *carefully*. 'Everything should be scrutinized – but not merely a little at a time; a book should be read right through, and then taken up again from the beginning' (20). Authors should be masticated, for proper digestion (19). This too cohered with Quintilian's view of imitation. The pupil should not be like those misguided persons who 'imagined that they had reproduced the style of the superhuman Cicero beautifully if they had put *esse uideatur* at the end of the sentence' (10.2.18).[3] Imitation is not just a matter of aping verbal mannerisms. The point was not new.[4] Dionysius of Halicarnassus (*Din.* 7) contrasts two sorts of imitation, one which depends on slavish adherence to rules and results in 'something contrived and unnatural', while the superior kind is 'natural and the outcome of prolonged instruction and familiarity'. 'Longinus', as usual, saw it more grandly: imitating is a matter of being taken over by a spirit, so that, like the priestess at Delphi, you give utterance to sublimities not your own (13.2). Quintilian, in his practical way, places his emphasis on a dogged analysis of oratorical texts.

> We must concentrate on the sense of fitness that those great men show in adapting themselves to circumstances and personalities; on their strategy, their arrangement, the way in which everything – even things that seem to be put in merely for entertainment – has victory as its aim. We should note what the proem is designed to do; what sort of tactics are adopted in the narration, and how various they are; what powers of proof and refutation are displayed, what skill in arousing all kinds of emotion; how even public popularity is turned to advantage...If we see all this clearly, we shall be able truly to imitate. (10.2.27)

[1] And Menander would help not only the orator (69) but the declaimer (71).

[2] As Quintilian observes (49), 'even writers of rhetorical handbooks look to this poet for very many of their examples': an instance (like the Servian commentary) of the cross-fertilization of rhetorical and grammatical precept; Cicero and Quintilian, too, mix prose and verse examples.

[3] Cf. Tac. *Dial.* 23.1, where Cicero's love of this version of a favourite clausula is maliciously exaggerated. For similar remarks on purely verbal imitation, see Seneca, *Epist.* 114.17–19.

[4] 'The true imitator of Demosthenes is one who speaks in the manner of Demosthenes, not one who speaks words of Demosthenes' ([Dion Hal.] *Ars Rhet.* 10.19).

It is clear from this passage, and from that in 10.1.22–4 on the need to acquaint oneself with the historical background of a speech, that Quintilian knew how literary criticism of oratory should be conducted; and it is a mark of his sophistication that only recently have scholars approached Cicero in this wide and unprejudiced way.[1] Quintilian saw that orators did not write in slavish compliance with rhetorical precept,[2] and that they should not be judged by using those precepts as a Procrustean bed to limit them. The pity is that the scope of the *Institutio* did not require him to put these principles into practice. We have seen them applied to some effect by Asconius on the historical side, and by the Cicero scholia on the rhetorical side. But we can only judge the quality of Quintilian's analysis by scattered comments; the sophistication of the *enarratio* by which he had hoped (2.5.1–2) to guide his pupils' reading of their oratorical texts can only be glimpsed.

We may take as an example Quintilian's treatment of a speech he much admired and frequently cited, Cicero's for Milo. Much of what he has to say about it is merely classificatory. *Facere enim probus adulescens periculose quam perpeti turpiter maluit*[3] (*Mil.* 9) is an example of *epiphonema* or exclamation (Quint. 8.5.11). The emotional appeal to the hills and groves of Alba (*Mil.* 85) is used five times, to illustrate apostrophe (9.2.38), luxuriance of style (11.1.34) and grandness (12.10.62), and to comment on the gestures (11.3.115) and tone of voice (11.3.167) that must have accompanied the words. But far more perceptive than these are the passages where Quintilian remarks on the 'design' (*consilium*) of the orator: 'He refused to give his narration before freeing the defendant from the effect of all preceding verdicts. He turned the invidious charge of ambushing against Clodius, even though in fact the fight had been fortuitous. He praised the deed – and yet at the same time denied that Milo intended it. He would not put prayers into Milo's mouth, but took them upon himself' (6.5.10). It is with a similar alertness that Quintilian analyses the technique of narrative that makes Clodius rather than Milo seem the aggressor: the celebrated description of Milo getting ready to leave Rome, pottering about while his wife dressed, is seen for what it is, a careful manipulation of the hearer's reactions: 'Milo seems to have done nothing in a hurry or of set purpose. The great orator produced this effect not only by the content – his stress on the delay and the detail of the prolonged setting forth – but by his common-or-garden, everyday wording and by hiding his art' (4.2.58). And Quintilian sees as a virtue what others might have felt to be a defect, Cicero's bending of the rhetorical rules: usually narrative should directly follow upon the proem, but Cicero was quite right to delay the narrative of the *Pro Milone* by placing

[1] I think especially of Neumeister (1964), to whom this account owes much. Compare the remarks of Douglas (1973) 99.

[2] See especially his sane comments on rhetorical precept in 2.13.

[3] 'The upright young man preferred dangerous activity to disgraceful passivity.'

before it three preliminary questions which had to be settled in the defendant's favour before the exposition of the facts could profitably be undertaken (4.2.25). Quintilian anticipated the best modern work on Cicero's speeches by seeing them as instruments of persuasion where every touch might have its effect. The orator, for Quintilian, had to be a good man (12.1.1), and the very definition of rhetoric had to stress moral values rather than persuasiveness (2.15.38:[1] contrast 2.15.3); but when it came to analysing a speech, Quintilian knew, from practical experience (for he was lawyer as well as teacher), that technique is what gets results, and that, as his despised predecessor Celsus remarked, 'the reward is not a good conscience but victory for one's client' (2.15.32).

2. THE CRAFTSMEN ON THEIR CRAFTS

Oratory

Cicero himself only gives us tantalizing scraps of comment on his own speeches, and there in the vaguest of terms. Thus on the *Milo*:

> but as for those who think that it would have been fitting for the speech for Milo to have been made (at a time when the army was in position in the forum and all the temples round about) in the same tone as if I had been speaking about a private case before a single judge: such people are measuring the force of eloquence by their own capabilities, not by its potentialities. (*Opt. gen.* 10)

And when he quotes it is for technical analysis (thus of rhythm at *Orat.* 225) or with a brief condescending glance at his own juvenile excesses (*Orat.* 107 on *Rosc. Am.* 72). Cicero's enormous practical experience is poured into an abstract form in the great dialogue *De oratore* and in the sketch of a perfect speaker, the *Orator*. He gives us the Greek rhetorical rules, modified not only by the demands of the genres he adopts but also by the restrictions he knew that real life imposed on theory. But in one extended passage of the *De oratore* he brings us into the orator's workshop, and shows vividly how the politician got his effects in the Roman court (2.197–203). The speaker in the dialogue is the great orator Marcus Antonius, who died during the Marian troubles; he is made to tell us of the celebrated speech in which he contrived the acquittal of his former quaestor Gaius Norbanus on a charge of *maiestas* or treason. Everything was in favour of the accuser, Sulpicius. There was need of *ars aliqua*, an element of craft. The rules of rhetoric could supply little more than hints on the arguing of the legal issue: in what did treason consist? Antonius argued that point very briefly, though naturally in such a way as to favour his client. He relied instead on two things 'by no means elaborately treated in the handbooks', the rousing of sympathy and indignation: sympathy by playing on his

[1] The whole of the previous discussion makes it clear that *bene* contains a moral element.

own record as an advocate and his obligation to defend his former quaestor, indignation by stirring old emotions in the equestrian jury against the cowardice and ineptness of Caepio, whom Norbanus had had convicted. These emotional arguments, used to back up a specious defence of civil strife as the mother of constitutional improvement, carried the day against the odds. Antonius, who has earlier in the dialogue been represented as distrustful of the wisdom of the handbooks, says slyly: 'You will, if you please, find some place in your theories for my defence of Norbanus.' And indeed this is the sort of *exemplum* that, as Quintilian remarks (10.1.15), is more effective than the textbooks. Together with Sulpicius' wry comments on Antonius' simulated hesitation at the beginning of the speech and his inexorable rise to the heights of emotional appeal, these sections give us a perfect example of the criticism of oratory, cunningly disguised behind the urbanities of Cicero's dialogue.

Cicero brought to the theory of oratory a width that it had never known before and was rarely to know again. He thinks often of an ideal orator, who shall have all the qualities of Cicero himself and more besides. The theories of the handbooks are only a beginning, to be supplemented and modified by the lessons of experience and the exigencies of particular circumstances. Furthermore, the orator must have the widest of educations; not only is a detailed knowledge of law an essential, but philosophy will give him the ability to expound the general principles that lie behind individual cases. He will be master of all the styles, grand, middle and plain, and capable thereby of fulfilling all the duties, to move, to please and to instruct. He will be in the best sense eclectic.

But all this, however admirable, is theory rather than criticism; and it is not often to Cicero's point to pass judgement on orators. When he does so, it is sometimes with a casualness that is reminiscent of the *grammaticus*: labelling[1] rather than analysis. Nor are his discussions of Greek literature improved by their normal tendency to argue a general case.[2] Thus in *De oratore* 2.93–5 the Greek orators are paraded by generations to demonstrate the doubtful proposition that each age had a particular manner of speaking and that this similarity was due to the habit of imitation of a single model. They are paraded again in *Orator* 28–32 to show how different they all are, how various the Attic orators whom modern 'Atticists' wished to force into a single pattern. And even the fullest survey, in *Brutus* 25–51, is over-generalized. There is little feel of personal assessment; instead, metaphors that give bloom and blood to the Attic orators before Demetrius turned aside to cloying sweetness. A similar tendency to label and catalogue is forced upon the *Brutus* as a whole by its vast aim –

[1] A familiar feature of Roman critical writing: see e.g. Quintilian 12.10.11, Tac. *Dial.* 25.4 (poking grave fun?), and, most absurdly, Fronto pp. 113–14 Naber (= II 48 Haines).

[2] The same is true of Ovid's eccentric demonstration in *Trist.* 2.363–470 that all literature can be regarded as erotic.

to survey oratory from its Roman beginnings to the present day. Many of the orators mentioned are only names to us, and what Cicero finds room to say of them cannot bring them to life. Even when he launches, occasionally, into a full-dress portrait, little comes across. Thus his picture of the elder Cato (*Brut.* 61–76) is purposely exaggerated in the interests of the Atticist controversy; Cicero does not mean too seriously his analogy between Cato and Lysias (again the *grammaticus*' trick!), and Atticus duly demolishes it later (293–4). Here as elsewhere Cicero relies on schematism and metaphor. Cato was a little uncouth, yet used figures lavishly; he is nearer a Canachus than a Polyclitus.[1] 'Pick out the passages deserving especial notice and praise: you will find all the qualities of an orator there' (65). That is just what Cicero does *not* do. Doubtless the form of his dialogue made it impossible; and doubtless too Cicero was capable of it. His discussion of the Norbanus case, even without quotation from Antonius' speech, shows us what he could have done in the way of oratorical criticism; it is our loss that he did so little.

In the exciting days of the 50s, when Cicero and Calvus were fighting their unequal battle for the primacy in Roman eloquence (Sen. *Contr.* 7.4.6), it was easy to see oratory as the universal art, the key to political as well as literary eminence. Hence the width of the *De oratore*. Once Caesar came to power, the field narrowed; and its narrowness is reflected in the *Orator*'s preoccupation with a somewhat academic controversy, the quarrel of Atticists and Asianists. Cicero, at the very end of his career, found the presuppositions of his emotional, expansive and rhythmical oratory challenged; and in the grave proem to the *Brutus* (6) he senses further the passing of oratory itself as a means to action: 'if Hortensius lived today...his particular regret would be to see the Roman forum...despoiled of any educated voice, any worthy of Roman or Greek ears'. And in fact, as the Empire was consolidated, political oratory, that had been the lifeblood of Cicero, lost importance; forensic speeches rarely swayed wide emotions, and there was more and more call for flattering panegyric. The consequent loss of prestige sustained by oratory was called its decay and corruption; and the phenomenon aroused widespread speculation.[2] The elder Seneca, for instance, under Tiberius, attributed it to 'some grudge on nature's part' (*Contr.* 1 *praef.* 6): perhaps it was the effect of the luxury of the age, perhaps big business had become more attractive than oratory, perhaps it was just an instance of the rule that 'things that rise to the top sink back to the bottom, faster than they rose' (7).[3]

Something like the first of those views would have been taken by the philosopher Seneca, whose 114th letter is the classic statement of the doctrine

[1] The parallel with the fine arts is common in ancient criticism: see Quintilian 12.10.1–9 with Austin's notes.

[2] Texts are conveniently assembled and discussed by Caplan (1970) ch. 8.

[3] Cf. also Velleius 1.17.6.

that 'le style est l'homme même'. 'Licentious speech is a sign of public luxury' (2). Maecenas was a striking case in point: 'Is not his style as lax as the man himself was dissolute?' (4). The man who, as Augustus' deputy in Rome, gave the watchword for the day without bothering to put on a belt was the man who indulged in the wildest extravagance of word order and conceit. And, more generally, styles go by fashions, swinging abruptly from the over-archaic to the over-novel, and 'wherever you see that a corrupt style of speech finds favour, you may be sure that morals too have gone astray' (11).

Seneca was thinking purely of style. 'Corrupt' style for him meant an extreme of verbal manipulation. And that is probably what Quintilian concentrated on in his lost 'On the causes of the corruption of eloquence'. He reserves, ironically enough, his longest and sternest criticisms in his review of literature for Seneca himself:

> I am supposed to condemn Seneca, and even hate him. This is the result of my attempt to recall a corrupted style of oratory, enervated by every vice,[1] to more rigorous standards: and at the time when I did this, Seneca was virtually the only reading-matter of young men... If he had not scorned the straightforward and yearned for the corrupt, if he had not loved all his own work, if he had avoided breaking up his weighty pronouncements into the briefest possible epigrams, he would be approved by scholars generally, not merely by enthusiastic youth. (10.1.125, 130: text uncertain)

As to oratory as a whole, Quintilian was not convinced that it was dead. He gives praise to several orators of his own century, and 'later writers on oratory will have great scope for sincere praise of those who flourish today' (122) – men, no doubt, like Quintilian's own pupil Pliny. Furthermore, the whole weight of his twelfth book, and his advocacy of Ciceronian standards of education and aspiration, rested on a conviction that there was a role still available to the 'good man, skilled in speaking' (12.1.1). There was room for improvement in style – Quintilian had laboured that point for twenty years, trying to bring a new sanity to the declamation-schools. But oratory was alive and kicking.

It was just this that was challenged by the *Dialogus*. It is generally accepted nowadays that this was given a 'Ciceronian' style because of its Ciceronian genre. Yet that daring innovator, Tacitus, may not have been so fettered by the *lex operis* as we imagine. It is at least a by-product of the old-tyme manner of the work that the whole topic is made to seem a little remote. Aper and Messala and Maternus talk in the grave cadences of a bygone era – and they talk about an oratory that has had its day. Aper – and even he is hinted to be no more than an *advocatus diaboli*[2] – praises the pleasures and practical rewards of

[1] Again the moralizing. Sexual metaphor in pejorative literary criticism was common (e.g. Tac. *Dial.* 18.5 with Gudeman's notes).

[2] See 15.2 and note the general agreement expected at 28.1.

forensic oratory. He says to his friends: 'Go on brightening this age of ours with beauty of speech as you can, and as you do' (23.5). Modern eloquence is brilliant and entertaining; contrast the symptoms of the old manner as seen in, say, Caelius: 'shabby language, disjointed rhythm, and lack of periodic structure' (21.4). Cicero developed his style towards something more flowery and epigrammatic, and in doing so showed the way for what was to come. And when Cassius Severus took the decisive step into a new era, it was with the conscious intention of adapting oratory to the requirements of a new age and more sophisticated audiences. Aper's speech uses Ciceronian arguments to deflate Cicero's claims to supremacy; for the *Brutus* (e.g. 68), like, as we shall see, the critical poems of Horace, has a consistent sense of the inevitability of progress from crude to polished.

Messala proffers an educational viewpoint not unlike that of Quintilian: the old wide education has given way to the absurdities of declamation. At the same time, some of what he says is redolent of the moral outlook of the Senecas; for he contrasts the old austerities with the vices of modern youth and even modern children.[1] The new element comes with the final speech of Maternus. Earlier he had seemed to accept the view of Aper that eloquence had influence in modern Rome, while rejecting all that it stood for. Now, as though moving from the Flavian age in which the dialogue is set to the principate of Trajan during which Tacitus was probably writing, or perhaps rather from forensic to political oratory, Maternus cuts the ground from under modern eloquence. Cicero had had interesting things to say about the influence of audiences on orators. It is for the ordinary listener that the orator speaks as much as for the educated critic – perhaps more (*Brut.* 183–200):[2] and the elegant taste of Athens fostered Attic oratory as surely as the uncultivated Carians attracted Asianic (*Orat.* 24–7). But Cicero did not try to think out the effect of a political system on oratory. He connects the rise of oratory in Sicily, and by implication in Greece as well, with the peace following the removal of the tyrants, not with the rise of democracy (*Brut.* 45–6). And he points out the lack of a Spartan orator to take up the terse tradition of Menelaus without any attempt to explain it (50). Maternus picks up that trick. Great eloquence does not arise in well-ordered communities (those, that is, with a king or aristocracy), and the many Athenian orators were the natural product of a city where 'everything was in the power of the people...everyone, you might almost say, had a hand in everything' (40.3). Conversely the Rome of the Empire, where for better or for worse 'the deliberations of state are not left to the ignorant many – they are the duty of one man, the wisest' (41.4), left no room for great oratory. For Maternus his friends are 'as eloquent as our day requires'

[1] Though it is true that Quintilian was strong on this point also (e.g. 1.2.6–8).

[2] Compare the intelligent remarks of Dion. Hal. *Dem.* 15.

(41.5). They would have reached the heights of oratory if they had lived a century before; as it is, they have the blessings of the imperial peace to console them.

Between them, two exponents of the art of oratory, Cicero and Tacitus, said much of what can profitably be said about oratory in general. And Cicero gives us, in the most urbane form possible, the Greek precepts for rhetoric as well. It was rarely to Cicero's point, and never to Tacitus', to apply their insights to the task of criticizing individual speeches. And when we turn finally to Horace and the criticism of poetry, we find ourselves again in the company of one who, reacting to the controversies of the time, gives us memorable labels and influential generalities rather than the particularities of a 'Longinus'.

Horace and poetry

Horace's *Satires* 1.4 and 1.10 together give us the poet's programme for satire. His father's method of moral education had been to point to concrete instances of vice – 'don't be like Scetanus' (1.4.112). Horace therefore does the same in his poetry, acting as the 'frank friend' (132) to whom he says he owes any improvement in his own character during adulthood. Those who criticize him for malicious back-biting are wide of the mark. And Horace implicitly contrasts himself with his great predecessor and model Lucilius, who, in a freer age, pilloried 'anyone worthy of being represented as a bad man and a thief, as an adulterer or murderer or some other type of criminal' (3–5). Horace deals only with minor vices, and in any case he does not publish his satires – he only recites to his friends, when he cannot avoid it.

In the course of these two poems Horace has much to say of Lucilius, whom he represents as a diffuse and disorganized writer, flowing along 'like a muddy river' (1.4.11; cf. 1.10.50), mixing Latin and Greek words with no sense of propriety, and producing verse that stops in artistic pretension at the point of ensuring that each line has its six feet. Horace makes no exaggerated claims for his own poems; with whatever irony, he disclaims the very title of poet in this genre. But he emphasizes the need for a style 'now sad, now gay, keeping up the role sometimes of a declaimer or poet, sometimes of a wit who purposely spares his strength' (1.10.11–14), for care in composition, and for use of the eraser. Lucilius was better than his predecessors, and in his turn, 'if fate had made him a contemporary of ours, he'd be cutting a lot out of his own works, deleting everything that goes on after the point is made' (68–70). Those who regard poets as no more than *personae*, and as portraying lives that bear no relation to anything but books, can see all this as merely the taking up of a literary stance. But Horace represents the poems as being reactions to criticism – of Horace's own satirical malice, and of his claim to improve on Lucilius. And to judge from the pointed hostility he displays towards *grammatici*[1] – among them, it seems, 'the pretty Hermogenes' (1.10.17–18; cf. 1.4.72) and 'the well-known ape whose learning extends only so far as singing Calvus and Catullus' (1.10.18–19) – Horace had been genuinely nettled by academics' attempts to laugh off the new satire as inferior to Lucilius', just as, maybe, they saw the *Odes* as inferior to the Neoterics. And he falls back on the favour of a few friends, Varius, Maecenas, Virgil, and some others ('it's *their* approval I want': 1.10.82) because those who formed literate taste in the schoolroom were unready to be favourable. Poets after all can hardly welcome being read by the few, even if, in face of the fact, they make a virtue of it.

This conclusion is reinforced by the observation that a similar defensiveness underlies the famous letter to Augustus. Unlike Augustus, Horace says, poets are not appreciated till they are dead. The Greeks had launched out, after their wars, into a period of inventiveness and experiment, and it is natural that the Romans, after theirs,[2] should do the same. Yet as far as popular taste goes there is a stubborn reluctance to approve higher standards; if Plautus was of inferior quality, the modern theatre is corrupt beyond redemption. We know that Augustus himself enjoyed the theatre, and we may speculate that he cannot have agreed with all that Horace says here. But Horace was surely casting his net wider. He was trying to influence, even to annoy, the philistine Roman public, whose tastes were formed by having Livius Andronicus and the other antique classics beaten into them, as they were into Horace, at school: the sort of people who formed the juries to which Cicero habitually quoted passages from poetry no more recent than Plautus and Terence, and in front of which he had to spend most of a speech defending Archias for being, purely and simply, a modern poet. Horace pleads that the latest generation should not be left out of account. They are trying to improve on the past, and to introduce new standards of craftsmanship. And in any case, a point Cicero made about Archias, poets have their patriotic uses.

Against this background we can also set the most famous of all Horace's critical pronouncements, the so-called *Ars poetica*. There is perhaps no hope of finding in this poem a structure on which all will agree; here, more than elsewhere, Horace makes transitions of bewildering abruptness or subtlety, circling around points and reverting to them with no apparent plan. Nor, maybe, does the structure matter unduly; more important, rather, to decide where the emphasis should lie.

The celebrated parts of the poem, those that have exercised an almost accidental but nevertheless profound influence on later theory and practice,

[1] In *Epist.* 1.19.39–41 Horace attributes his lack of popular acclaim to his refusal to 'canvass the tribes of grammarians' (see also *Epist.* 2.2.103).

[2] This is, I think, the implication. This may be another Aristotelian view; compare Aristotle's doctrine on the rise of oratory, used by Cicero in *Brut.* 45–6 (above, p. 47).

largely concern the theatre. Aristotelian and sub-Aristotelian principles, themselves largely inferences from actual Greek tragedy, are here given enduring expression: there should be no violent action on stage, plays should have five acts, gods should rarely intervene, chorus should sing relevant and morally satisfactory odes; myths should be given new twists rather than be entirely discarded; language should be appropriate to character and to the emotion presented. All this had its relevance to the present day: Horace has already alluded to the current pre-eminence of Fundanius as an exponent of 'New Comedy' and Pollio in tragedy (*Sat.* 1.10.40–3). And presumably Horace concentrates on tragedy[1] partly because the Pisones whom he is addressing were interested in the genre: just as in the Epistle to Augustus he spends much space on the theatre. But just as in that poem Horace's true interests lay elsewhere, or rather in the poet generally, so here, in a way, the parts on drama are not at the core of the poem.

Crucial, surely, is what the *Ars poetica* has in common with the other poems we have examined. The Roman public is over-inclined to praise the old favourites: Accius, Ennius, Plautus have technical imperfections to which licence has been granted for long enough. Moreover, the Romans are too materialistic: though, even judging by practical criteria, poets have always had their uses. But far more important than that is the stress Horace places on the craft of the poet. Not everyone can be a poet, though nowadays everyone writes poetry. One has to be a professional, and that means taking pains. 'If you do write something some day, let it find its way to critic Maccius' ears...and be stored up for eight years in your notebooks at home' (386–9). The poet Quintilius was the ideal critic of his friends' work: no room for flattery there, but an insistence on high standards.[2] 'A wise and good man will censure flabby lines, reprehend harsh ones, put a black line with a stroke of the pen beside unpolished ones, prune pretentious ornaments, force you to shed light on obscurities, convict you of ambiguity, mark down what must be changed. He'll be an Aristarchus' (445–50).

This reminds us that for the Romans literary criticism was practised mostly in private. It was a part of *amicitia* to look at your friends' work and help them to improve it for what we have to call publication.[3] The practice clearly left room for insincerity and flattery, but Quintilius will not have been the only one to bring integrity and thoroughness to the task. The literary productions to which we can properly apply the term 'literary criticism' are very few in Latin. But that critical standards existed is abundantly proved by the craftsmanship that, at their best, Romans demanded of their friends and of themselves.

[1] His remarks on satyr plays remain mysterious even on this view.

[2] For less rigorous critics see e.g. *Epist.* 2.2.87–101. A little later in that poem (109–25) Horace gives a truly Roman colour to the critic's task by invoking the office of censor.

[3] References are collected by White (1974) 53–4.

II

EARLY REPUBLIC

3

THE GENESIS OF POETRY IN ROME

I. THE PRE-LITERARY BACKGROUND

If blatantly historicizing reconstructions, like that of Livy,[1] are excluded, our knowledge of a literature written in Latin begins abruptly in 240 B.C. with the reported performance of a play (probably a tragedy) by Livius Andronicus.[2] This is curious; for knowledge of the history of the Roman people extends back at least three centuries before that, and, with the help of archaeology, much further. Was there no artistic composition in the Latin language before 240 B.C.? The proposition is incredible. For centuries the Romans had achieved considerable political sophistication, and that involved public debates with carefully composed speeches. Roman religion was a series of highly organized cults, with complicated ritual. Roman law had in the far past been codified, and was continually needing – and receiving – well-considered amendments and additions of great complexity. But of all this, little remains to antedate 240 B.C., and what there is has been carelessly preserved, for ulterior purposes, by late authors (mainly grammarians). Yet it is here that scanty and riddling indications must be sought of the background to the literature which seems suddenly to have sprung full-grown into existence in 240 B.C. This can only be done by a series of different approaches, all of them incomplete and uncertain.

Carmina

The word *carmen* (etymologically related to *canere* 'sing') was adopted by Augustan poets as the generic term for their own compositions. But this meaning of 'poem' and 'poetry' was a specialization imposed on a word whose meaning was originally much wider. An earlier meaning appears when Cicero recalls his schooldays:[3] he and his companions had to study the *Twelve Tables* as a *carmen necessarium* to be learnt by heart. The *Twelve Tables* themselves legislated against the use of 'spells': the word used is *carmen*.[4] An early treaty is described by Livy as a *carmen*;[5] so also a sentence of execution[6] and an oath.[7]

[1] 7.2.3–12. [2] Cicero, *Brutus* 72. [3] *De legibus* 2.59. [4] Pliny, *N.H.* 28.18.
[5] 1.24.6. [6] 1.26.6. [7] 31.17.9.

Elsewhere the word means a prayer or the words of a covenant. There was clearly no limitation to the content of a *carmen*; its characteristic must have been its form.

Typical of the compositions described as *carmina* is the formula under which the investigating tribunal (*duumuiri*) was set up to try Horatius for murdering his sister:[1] *duumuiri perduellionem iudicent; si a duumuiris prouocarit, prouocatione certato; si uincent, caput obnubito, infelici arbori reste suspendito, uerberato uel intra pomoerium uel extra pomoerium* 'let the tribunal of two judge the issue of treason; if he shall appeal from the tribunal, one must argue the case on appeal; if tribunal shall win, one must cover his head, one must hang him by a rope from a barren tree, one must scourge him either within the city-boundary or without the city-boundary'. The language here is not genuinely archaic; it has been modernized. But its essential accuracy is guaranteed by the similar quotation in Cicero's speech for Gaius Rabirius,[2] and one characteristic is clear which is common to all reports of ancient *carmina*: it is not metrical. It is rhythmical prose, with balanced cola, rhyme and alliteration. It is, to this extent, 'artistic': the composition is deliberate and contrived for a particular purpose. The intention is to produce a solemn and measured formality of language, suitable to a ceremonious occasion. This motive, involving particular interest in the sound of the language, explains the style of all surviving *carmina*.

The most extensive surviving *carmen* is a prayer quoted by the elder Cato (writing about 180 B.C.); it was prescribed for performance at the annual fertility ceremony of *lustratio agri* (purification of the land).[3] Here the rhythmical structure depends on parallelism of clauses which have the two basic patterns of dicolon and tricolon, the latter always in the special form of 'tricolon crescendo' (*mihi domo familiaeque nostrae*, *agrum terram fundumque meum*, or *prohibessis defendas auerruncesque*). It is especially notable that these structures often depend on pleonasm (a similar pleonasm fulfils a similar rhythmical function in the Psalms). Thus all three verbs in the last quoted tricolon have the same meaning ('ward off'); so also among dicola there are found *precor quaesoque*, *uolens propitius*, *uiduertatem uastitudinemque*. Formal devices, like anaphora, alliteration and assonance, are used to link the elements in the cola. It becomes clear on a reading of such a hymn that rhythm and structure were not the only relevant stylistic motives: there was evidently considerable solemnity and literary satisfaction to be won from the exhaustive expression of an idea (this is particularly important in religious utterances). The same motive can be seen also in the use of 'polar' expressions like *uisos inuisosque* 'seen and unseen' and in the very frequent use of *figura etymologica* (e.g. *facinus facere* 'do a deed'), the use of which in later Latin always marks a desire for impressive speech (it is never used in ordinary prose).[4]

[1] 1.26.6. [2] *Pro C. Rab.* 13. [3] *De agri cultura* 141.2–3. [4] Cf. Haffter (1934) ch. 1.

The linguistic satisfaction and emphatic solemnity which can be achieved by these methods of expression must be stressed, for it explains their influence on all later artistic writing in Latin, especially in poetry, where their frequent occurrence marks off the style even of a poet like Virgil from that of any of his Greek models. These were devices of expression on which a Roman could draw when he wished to speak (for whatever purpose, in verse or in prose) in an impressive way. The occurrence of the same devices in Umbrian (especially on the *Iguvine Tablets*)[1] suggests that their use was not confined to Latin but may have been common to all speakers of Italic dialects. The style survived intact into the very late period, and easily recognizable *carmina* can be found in the fifth-century medical writer Marcellus.[2]

These *carmina* had clearly been composed in Rome from the earliest times,[3] and the artistic forms of expression which had been devised for them were ready to be used by the earliest literary artists in Rome.

Heroic lays

Early in the nineteenth century, the great German historian Niebuhr, anxious to give a basis to his reconstruction of the early Roman tradition, revived the theory[4] that legends such as that of Horatius or Verginia had been preserved by oral tradition in great families in the form of heroic lays. Cicero reports Cato as describing performances of these *carmina* at banquets; the story is repeated with variations by Varro. But it is clear from Cicero's report that the lays, if they ever existed, had perished long before Cato's time. Their existence was given vigorous and romantic life by Macaulay in the introduction to his *Lays of Ancient Rome*.

Unfortunately the evidence is totally inconclusive[5] as far as Roman sources are concerned. But the widespread evidence for the existence of such lays in human societies at all times and in all places (excellently gathered by Macaulay) makes it attractive to posit their existence in Rome too. The difficulty lies in the fact that Roman historians of the second century B.C., who were responsible for formulating the early traditions of Rome, have successfully obliterated all traces of the sources they used. Furthermore, they were apt to invent a Roman pre-history for literary genres on the basis of Greek models. One fact mitigates scepticism: it was precisely those families that would have preserved the lays who were open to the influx of Greek literary culture in the third century B.C., and the new literary standards might well have bred contempt for the rude balladry of their forefathers; such a chronology would fit well with Cato's reported setting of the custom some generations before his own time.[6]

[1] Devoto (1954) and Poultney (1959).
[2] *De medicamentis* 15.11; 20.78.
[3] See the collection of Thulin (1906).
[4] Cf. Momigliano (1957) 104ff.
[5] Cf. Dahlmann (1951) and Momigliano, op. cit.
[6] See also p. 59 below.

Versus quadratus[1]

Porphyrio, commenting on Horace,[2] quotes a children's rhyme:

–́ ⏑–́ – –́ – ⏑́⏑– –́ – ⏑́⏑– –́ ⏑–́
rex erit qui recte faciet: qui non faciet non erit

He shall be king who shall act correctly: who shall not so act, shall not be king.

This is analogous to 'I'm king of this castle: get down you dirty rascal', with its play on the etymology of *rex*, *regere*, and *rectus*. It has a memorable metrical form: a trochaic septenarius, with coincidence of syntactical units and metra. Petronius (about A.D. 60) quotes a riddle:[3]

–́ – –́ – –́ – ⏑́⏑– –́– ⏑́⏑– –́ ⏑ –́
qui de nobis longe uenio late uenio: solue me

I am one who comes out from us in great length, in great depth: solve me.

(The answer is probably 'hair'.) The pattern is the same, and there are many similar examples belonging to the spheres of popular sayings, witticisms and obscenities; for example:

–́ – –́ – –́ ⏑ –́ – –́ ⏑ –́ – –́ ⏑–́
postquam Crassus carbo factus, Carbo crassus factus est

After Crassus became a cinder, Carbo became dull,

that is, the enmity between the two men was the only thing that kept them at all sharp.[4]

Both the metrical pattern and the uses to which it was put suggest a pre-literary or non-literary origin. There are many lines of the early Roman dramatists which, without slavishly following it, clearly show the influence of the pattern. The technique is quantitative and related closely to Greek practices. There are, further, quite a few examples of oracular sayings, witticisms and lampoons in Greek which display the same metrical pattern, and it is very significant that these (no less than the Latin analogues) differ in certain precise technical features from the norm established for trochaic septenarii by Archilochus and followed by all later Greek poets and tragedians. The simplest hypothesis is that the metrical form was picked up by Romans in early contacts with Greek culture in Italy at a sub-literary level; this would be just one of very many ways in which Roman culture was indebted to Greek in its earliest stages of growth. A similar hypothesis, which does not involve the assumption of direct imitation at a literary level, would give a satisfactory explanation of certain persistent differences in technique between the iambic senarius and the Greek trimeter[5] which are hard to explain on the hypothesis that Roman dramatists directly imitated the metrical techniques of their Greek models.

[1] Cf. Fraenkel (1927). [2] *Epist.* 1.1.62. [3] *Sat.* 58.8.
[4] Sacerdos in *GLK* VI 461.26ff. [5] Cf. Klotz (1947).

This argument could be followed further, but it establishes at least the possibility of the existence of Greek metrical patterns in Rome at a sub-literary level, ready to be used by literary artists when they arose.

Saturnian verse

What may be the earliest poetry in Latin (if the *carmen Arvale* is excepted) is a pair of epitaphs on L. Cornelius Scipio Barbatus, consul in 298 B.C. and his son L. Cornelius Scipio, consul in 259 B.C.[1] The ancient Roman custom was to set a man's *titulus* (his name and, perhaps, a mention of important offices) over his grave: both Scipios have this, painted in red. But both also have epitaphs in Saturnian verse; these are cut in stone on the sarcophagi and that on the son is distinctly earlier than that on the father. The inscribing of a poem over a tomb represents clear Greek influence, and this origin is underlined by one sentiment in the father's epitaph: *quoius forma uirtutei parisuma fuit* 'his physical perfection was the absolute match of his courage'. This translates into Latin the Athenian ideal of καλοκἀγαθία, and significantly the adjective ἀγαθός is given its early-fifth-century sense of 'brave'.

The name of the metre expresses the view that it was native Italic, but basic uncertainty about its true nature and origin persists as strongly now as in the ancient world. Was it Greek in origin and quantitative? Or was it constructed on syllabic principles or principles of stress quite alien to Greek? No certainty can be reached[2] (largely because of the poor textual state of the surviving lines – preserved mainly in quotations by late grammarians who had not the slightest understanding of, or interest in, the metre). But a Greek origin seems the more coherent hypothesis for three reasons: (*a*) the context in which the metre is first found in the Scipio epitaphs suggests a grecizing milieu; and elements of the metre are also found in the *carmen Arvale* which goes back to the fifth or sixth centuries B.C. and certainly contains recognizable Greek religious elements.[3] (*b*) The two poets, Livius Andronicus and Naevius (the one a Greek slave, the other from a region of Greek culture), who first took up the metre in Rome, were both trained in Greek metrical techniques and wrote their other works with an astonishing mastery of those techniques in Latin. (*c*) The detailed statements of Caesius Bassus about the Greek background to the Saturnian can be verified in Greek,[4] and, in particular, a non-literary Greek cult-hymn, displaying the same metrical form, has been preserved.[5] When these facts are put together with the widespread evidence for Greek cultural influence on Rome from the sixth century B.C. onwards, both in customs and in language (and also in metres), it is hard to see the Saturnian as a purely Italic metre.

[1] *CIL* I 2.6–9.
[2] Survey and bibliography in Cole (1972).
[3] Cf. Norden (1939) 109ff., 236–78.
[4] Hephaestion cap. XV; Caesius Bassus in *GLK* VI 265f.
[5] Fraenkel (1951*b*).

The various approaches above have tried to examine what can be discovered about elements which might have contributed to a literary culture and which existed in Rome prior to 240 B.C. The evidence is meagre and indicates a practical culture: that is, one of compositions designed for specific public occasions. But there is evidence of a certain stylistic sophistication and certainly of acquaintance with Greek techniques: in both these respects, the earliest literary culture in Rome displays features which characterize all later literature composed in Latin.

2. THE EARLIEST EPIC POETRY

It is symptomatic that the first poem (as distinct from drama) in Latin should have claimed to be a translation of Homer's *Odyssey*. Yet the *Odyssia* of Livius Andronicus[1] was far more than a Latin translation; the word used for 'translate' was *uortere* 'turn', but 'adapt' or 'recast' would more truly represent the fact that, even in the wretched fragments (at most forty-five, of which only four exceed one line in extent and only one reaches three lines),[2] one is conscious of reading a genuinely Latin poem. The genius of Livius lay in finding Roman equivalents for Greek ideas:[3] so *Camenae* (a plurality of fountain-goddesses who had a shrine outside the Porta Capena) for Μοῦσαι (Muses); or for the impossible Homeric concept of (*Od.* 3.237–8) ὁππότε κεν δὴ | μοῖρ' ὀλοὴ καθέλῃσι τανηλεγέος θανάτοιο 'whenever the fatal destiny of death which lays low may destroy him...', he wrote *quando dies adueniet, quem profata Morta est* 'when the day comes which Morta has ordained...', where, in a quite different way, the Roman sense of *dies*[4] and the ancient Italic goddess of Fate[5] catch the tone of solemnity in a moving way that is specifically Roman. Homeric metaphors must have been difficult, and here too Livius has happy touches: for the odd Homeric idea of (5.297) λύτο γούνατα καὶ φίλον ἦτορ 'his knees and heart were loosened' he substituted *cor frixit prae pauore* 'his heart froze for terror', and something of the way in which Livius' genius influenced later writers can be seen in Virgil's combination of both metaphors (*Aen.* 1.92) *soluuntur frigore membra* 'his limbs were loosened by the chill (*sc.* of fear)'. In fact, what Livius most conspicuously seems to have missed was the simplicity and grace and speed of Homeric language; for these he substituted solemnity (to be seen, for instance, in an un-Homeric use of patronymics – e.g. 4.557 νύμφης ἐν μεγάροισι Καλυψοῦς 'in the halls of the nymph Calypso' became *apud nympham Atlantis filiam Calypsonem* 'in the house of the nymph Calypso daughter of Atlas'). He also legislated for all later Latin poetry by the way in which he used archaisms as one element in the creation of a specifically poetic language.

[1] Bibliography in Mariotti (1952).
[2] *FPL* pp. 7–17.
[3] Cf. Mariotti (1952) 14–72.
[4] Cf. Fraenkel (1922) 107–10 = (1960) 101–4.
[5] Cf. Latte (1960) 53.

Despite a larger number of extant lines (about sixty, but no fragment exceeds three lines),[1] it is harder to get a real sense of Naevius' *Bellum Poenicum*.[2] This is largely due to the absence of any such help as the Homeric source gives to the appreciation of the *Odyssia*. But Naevius, writing in his later years,[3] contributed a feature that was to dominate Roman poetry and had already been exploited by Roman dramatists: this was the conflation of Greek and Roman material into a unity that constructed a world of ideas which was neither Greek nor Roman but gave hitherto unknown freedom to the play of poetic imagination. Stylistically Naevius depended much on Livius,[4] but he went beyond him in direct imitation of Homeric compounds. However, since the fragments happen to be largely historical in matter, there is a stronger impression of prosiness in Naevius. But this should not be mistaken: it represents, in contrast with Greek historical epics, the Roman poet's emphasis on factual accuracy in recounting a war in which he himself took part (and said so in the poem[5]). Contemporary history and Greek mythology (chiefly the mythical and prehistorical background to Rome and Carthage) were united for the first time and in an exemplary way in the *Bellum Poenicum*. This was probably accomplished (to some extent following Homeric models) by a series of appropriate digressions from the historical narrative.[6] This was a technique often used by Virgil, on whom this work had a profound influence – an influence which can be traced in a most interesting way even on the evidence of the meagre remaining fragments.[7]

The chief disadvantage under which both Livius and Naevius laboured must have been the Saturnian metre, with its jerky combination of iambic and trochaic rhythms that broke each line into predictable halves; it was no match for the easy flow of the hexameter. The choice of that metre for epic must have been forced on them by Roman conditions – a fact which adds to the evidence for the existence of a type of epic balladry in earlier Rome.

[1] *FPL* pp. 17–27.
[2] Bibliography in Barchiesi (1962).
[3] Cicero, *De senectute* 50.
[4] Fraenkel, *RE* Suppl. B. 6.622ff.
[5] Gellius 17.21.45. Cf. Mariotti (1955) 11–83.
[6] Cf. Strzelecki (1935) and Rowell (1947).
[7] Bibliography in Barchiesi (1962).

4
ENNIUS' *ANNALES*

I. THE SCOPE AND CONTENTS OF THE 'ANNALES'

Ennius went further than Naevius in Hellenizing the form of Latin epic, shaping it in books which were to have aesthetic unity and casting it in Homer's hexameter. (The *Bellum Pœnicum* was divided into seven books not by its author Naevius but by Octavius Lampadio, a contemporary of Accius, whose sense of decorum on this point was learnt from Hellenistic poets in general and Ennius in particular (Suet. *Gramm.* 2).) The scale of the books was between about 1,000 and 1,700 lines each; the fragments amount to barely half such a book, and represent less than a twentieth of a poem which in its final form had eighteen books. Most fragments are assigned to their books, and grammarians and others allude to the contents of some: hence, and also because the subject matter was historical, narrated chronologically (though at very varying pace), attempts at reconstruction are saved from utter futility. Ennius appears to have organized his poem as five triads of books, each covering a coherent period of Rome's story.[1] These fifteen books spanned almost or exactly one thousand years in the contemporary reckoning (1184/3 B.C. – 187/184 B.C.), and this may be relevant to the architecture of the poem; see pp. 63–4. A sixth triad, which circulated separately, was added by Ennius in the last years of his life (d. 169 B.C.).

The first triad covered the mythical era from the fall of Troy to the end of the regal period. As is usual with fragmentary authors, the first book is the best represented. It began with an invocation of the Muses. Ennius narrated a dream, formally recalling famous prooemia of Hesiod (*Theogony*) and Callimachus (*Aetia*), in which he told how Homer's spirit appeared and revealed that he, Homer, was reincarnated in Ennius. This stupendous claim asserted the unique importance of Ennius' theme, but it is not clear how literally Ennius meant it. Allegory, though not yet literary allusion, was familiar to the public through tragedy; at the same time, Ennius himself was seriously interested in sub-Platonic astral mysticism and Pythagorean ideas of reincarnation, beliefs which were enjoying some fashion at Rome in the 180s and 170s B.C.[2] The narrative began with the

[1] See F. Skutsch, *RE* v 2610, O. Skutsch (1968) 28 n. 4, Jocelyn (1972) 1005f.

[2] See Boyancé (1955) 172–92.

sack of Troy, Aeneas' escape, his arrival in Italy, his alliance with Latinus, and his death. Thus in less than half of the first book Ennius covered more ground than Virgil in the whole *Aeneid*. Ilia, whom Ennius represented as Aeneas' daughter, had a prominent part in the sequel. She narrated a strange dream presaging her future,[1] and bore to Mars the twins Romulus and Remus, who in this version were therefore Aeneas' grandsons.[2] By telescoping the twins' ancestry, Ennius put Ilia at the centre of the stage, as it were, and he evidently presented her in tragic manner, as if she were one of his dramatic heroines. This emphasis on female character and psychology was typically Hellenistic. The rest of the book told the story of the twins, apparently following the usual version as recorded some years earlier in Greek by Fabius Pictor, and the climax of Book I was the foundation of the City. An important fragment ((I) 77–96 V = *ROL* 80–100)[3] describes the taking of the auspices with precise regard for modern Roman ritual, and the silence of the onlookers is strikingly compared to that of the people at the games as they wait with bated breath for the consul to signal the start of the chariot-race.[4] These anachronisms characteristically imply the tradition, continuity, even timelessness of Roman public institutions. Somewhere in this book there was a Council of the Gods in Homeric style, at which the deification of Romulus was discussed as if at a meeting of the Senate. This was later parodied by Lucilius and Seneca. Books 2 and 3 are badly represented. Somehow they narrated and filled out the regal period; but on any view there is a chronological problem. An unassigned fragment makes some orator state that 'it is now more or less seven hundred years since Rome was founded' ((*lib. inc.*) 501f. V = *ROL* 468f.). If 'now' were the poet's own time, the foundation of Rome would fall early in the ninth century B.C.; it is, however, probable that Ennius followed Eratosthenes on the date of the fall of Troy (1184/3 B.C.), and since as we have seen Romulus and Remus are Aeneas' grandsons in this version, this implies a date around 1100 B.C. for the foundation of Rome, coeval that is with the Return of the Sons of Heracles (the Dorian invasion) in mythological history. In this case, the fragment belongs in the mouth of someone like Camillus, and the occasion might be the Gallic invasion (390 or 387 B.C.).[5] On either view, of course, it remains unclear how Ennius reconciled his chronology with the usual story of only seven kings, the last of whom, Tarquin the Proud, fell just when the Athenian democracy was being established (*c.* 510 B.C.).

[1] (I) 35–51 V = *ROL* 32–48; Leo (1913) 178f.; G. W. Williams (1968) 689f.

[2] So also Naevius (Serv. auct. *Aen.* 1.273); Eratosthenes made the twins grandsons of Aeneas through Ascanius, not Ilia (ibid.). These versions contradict Timaeus (cf. Lycophron, *Alex.* 1226ff. with the Scholiast) and Fabius Pictor (Plut. *Rom.* 3), whose account is the dominant one.

[3] References to Ennius' *Annales* are given with the numeration of Vahlen (1928) (= V) and Warmington (= *ROL*). The figure in parentheses indicates the book number.

[4] Williams (1968) 684ff., 698.

[5] Skutsch (1968) 12f.

Book 4 covered events from the foundation of the Republic to the Gallic invasion, Book 5 came to the end of the Samnite Wars (*c.* 295 B.C.). Each therefore covered about a century, and both are badly represented. Book 6 was devoted wholly to the war against Pyrrhus (281–271 B.C.), i.e. only ten years: it will have been here for the first time that Ennius had occasion for a more thoroughgoing 'annalistic' presentation in the manner of Naevius. Pyrrhus was one of the earliest figures about whom there was available relatively copious and reliable information, and Ennius presents him in a very magnanimous light.[1] With Pyrrhus, Ennius had reached a point only just beyond living memory, and it is interesting that the gods still participated in this book in Homeric style; there is no certain sign of them later in the poem ((6) 175f. V = *ROL* 207f.).

In the third triad, the centrepiece of the original poem, Ennius entered the period of living memory. We do not know whether he regarded this second half of his work as a *maius opus* (cf. Virgil, *Aen.* 7.45), but it certainly presented extra problems. There was the question what to do with the gods, and the wider problem of maintaining epic dignity without sounding ridiculous when speaking of the recent past.[2] Besides, there was from here on ever less scope for pure fiction, and ever more need both for the historian's methods and acumen, and the diplomat's tact to avoid giving offence by omission or distortion. On the other hand, the example of Naevius' *Bellum Pœnicum* was available. The seventh book opened with an important introduction (Cic. *Brut.* 76; (7) 213ff. V = *ROL* 231ff.).[3] Ennius proposed not to deal with the First Punic War, since 'others', i.e. Naevius, had done it 'in verses which the Fauns and bards used to chant'. He dissociated himself from the ranting bards (*uates*), with whom he unfairly classed Naevius: Ennius was a *poeta*, a 'maker', and he proclaims that no one before himself had been *dicti studiosus* 'keen on the "word",' a loan-translation of the appellation of the scholar-poets of Alexandria, φιλό-λογος.[4] True, he was an 'inspired' poet, but his *sapientia*/σοφία, 'wisdom', was not like that of the seers, oracular and unaccountable; his was a knowledge of the Muses, a religious γνῶσις which was the hard-won result of practice and lucubration ((7) 218f. V = *ROL* 229f.). Here speaks not Homer reincarnated, but the Latin Callimachus. The narrative of 7 took events to the invasion of Hannibal (218 B.C.), an expansion of scale compared with 6 no doubt due to the summary treatment of the First Punic War (264–241 B.C.). The book included a remarkable description of a Roman commander's 'good companion', a *parasitus* seen favourably,

[1] Williams (1968) 254f. Cicero knew what passed as a genuine speech of Ap. Claudius Pulcher dissuading the Romans from making peace with Pyrrhus, and quotes the beginning of Ennius' poetic version (*Sen.* 16; (6) 202f. V = *ROL* 194f.), which is directly copied from Homer (*Il.* 24.401). The prose-speech was probably an amplification of Ennius' fiction.

[2] Cf. Hor. *Sat.* 1.10.54 *uersus Enni grauitate minores.*

[3] Cic. *Brut.* 76, cf. Suerbaum (1968) 249–95, Williams (1968) 253, Jocelyn (1972) 1017f.

[4] Jocelyn (1972) 1013 n. 262; an observation made independently by several scholars.

which was later thought to be a portrait of the artist (Gell. *N.A.* 12.4; Enn. *Ann.* (7) 234–51 V = *ROL* 210–27).[1] Books 8 and 9 described the rest of the Second Punic War (218–201 B.C.), a return to the scale of Book 6.

Very little survives of the remainder. Book 10 began with a fresh invocation of the Muses and described the war against Philip of Macedon (201–196 B.C.); 11 and 12 brought the narrative to the eve of war against Antiochus III of Syria (192/1 B.C.). The narrative was becoming very dense, and it was even slower in the final triad 13–15. This covered the war against Antiochus (13, 191 B.C.), the Scipios' victory at Magnesia and the naval war (14, 190 B.C.), while the last book dealt with the deeds of Ennius' patron M. Fulvius Nobilior in Aetolia, Cephalenia, and Ambracia.[2] It is particularly unfortunate that we know so little of this book, for, as we shall see, its ending has an important bearing on the shape and unity of Ennius' *Annales* as a whole. As for Books 16–18, see below, p. 66.

2. ENNIUS AND THE MUSES: THE UNITY AND COMPOSITION OF THE 'ANNALES'

The cult of the Muses was introduced by M. Fulvius Nobilior, who built a *Templum Herculis Musarum* to house statues of Hercules Musageta and the Nine Sisters taken with much other booty from what had once been Pyrrhus' palace in Ambracia.[3] Nobilior and Ennius saw this institution as a Greek Μουσεῖον, 'house of the Muses', and naturally enough they saw the province of the Muses as it was understood at the most famous 'Museum', the one at Alexandria. There the scholars and poets formed a nominally religious group under the presidency of the 'priest of the Museum', who, however, was never as distinguished for learning or poetry as the Royal Librarian.[4] This post had been occupied by Apollonius and after him Eratosthenes, who died between 196 and 193 B.C., while Ennius was making a name as a teacher and dramatist. The province of the Muses as defined by their activities and interests included not only the writing of poetry and literary studies but also science, geography, and history, rather than philosophy and rhetoric: the name φιλόλογοι which was specially theirs implicitly distinguishes them from φιλόσοφοι.

Nobilior composed and deposited in his Templum a work described as *fasti* which included etymological explanations of the months' names.[5] This was evidently more than a bald chronicle: it was a piece of chronological investi-

[1] Leo (1913) 178, Skutsch (1968) 92–4, Williams (1968) 691–3, Joycelyn (1972) 993ff.

[2] Jocelyn (1972) 1006. Macrobius, *Sat.* 6.2.30 and 6.3.1 wrongly assigns some passages of 16 to 15.

[3] Badian (1971) 151–95; Cancik (1969) 323–8, (1970) 7–17; Nash (1961/2) 471 (site of the temple). The statues: E. A. Sydenham, *CRR* nos. 810–23 (silver denarii of Q. Pomponius Musa, *c.* 68–66 B.C.); *CIL* I² 615 (the base of one of them). The *aedicula* of the *Camenae* was transferred to the temple from the temple of Honos and Virtus (Serv. *Aen.* 1.8).

[4] Pfeiffer (1968) 96f.; Fraser (1972) I 312–35.

[5] Macrobius, *Sat.* 1.12.16; 13.21.

gation and as such it is important, for it is the earliest known example of specifically Latin 'research', and it reminds one in its field, if only humbly, of the famous and important *chronographiae* of Eratosthenes. In these Eratosthenes presented in summary form a continuous chronology of the Greek world from the fall of Troy (which he put in the equivalent of 1184/3 B.C.) to the death of Alexander (323 B.C.), and popularized the Olympiad-system for Greek dating. This greatly facilitated the composition of the kind of universal history at which Polybius aimed, and gave a more exact perspective and depth to Greek history as a whole by linking the mythical age to the modern by measured steps. Fabius Pictor's Greek history, composed probably in the 190s, used the Olympiad-reckoning where appropriate (809 F 3b Jacoby).

The title of Ennius' poem looks immediately to the priestly *Annales*, 'year-books', instituted by the Pythagorean king Numa Pompilius and kept by the *pontifices*.[1] But, from a different point of view, here were *chronographiae* of a new kind, indirectly made possible, like Fabius' history, by Alexandrian scholarship. The epic form had been used in modern times in Greek for poems about the foundation of cities (e.g. the 'foundation' poems of Apollonius Rhodius), the chronicles of a people (e.g. Rhianus' *Messeniaca*, Euphorion's *Mopsopia*), and the praise of living kings (e.g. Simonides of Magnesia's poem about Antiochus III, and Leschides' about one of the Attalids of Pergamum: see the Suda under these names). The conception of Ennius' verse-history of the Roman People was on a grander and more consciously ambitious scale than anything before, or, it can be argued, since. His practical debt to Fabius Pictor was probably great, and Ennius was not a scientific historian in our sense or the Alexandrians' or even Cato's. In the prose *Origines* Cato made a point of referring to officers on active service simply as 'the consul', 'the praetor', without naming them: in this, he followed the tradition of the priestly *annales*, and implicitly asserted the subordination of the individual to the community (Nepos 24.3.4, cf. Gell. *N.A.* 3.7).[2] Whether conscious or not, this was a reaction against the individualism of Ennius, who praised not only famous men by name, but also adapted Homer to celebrate the bravery of 'other ranks', e.g. a lone stand by a tribune whose name is now, ironically, corrupt ((15) 401–8 V = *ROL* (16) 409–16; *Iliad* 16.102–11, on Ajax; Macrob. *Sat.* 6.3.1).[3] Ennius receives short measure in accounts of Roman historiography: this is unfair, for two reasons. His poem remained until

[1] Jocelyn (1972), 1008–23; published only in the 120s B.C. by P. Mucius Scaevola Pontifex (Serv. auct. *Aen.* 1.373, Cic. *De or.* 2.52).

[2] See Leo (1913) 292, 296f. It is usually assumed (as by Leo) that Cato did not name the heroic tribune whose story is reported by Gellius, loc. cit., just as Caesar left unnamed the brave *signifer* who led the way on Caesar's first British expedition (*Bell. Gall.* 4.25.3). There must be some doubt about this, however, since Gellius' narrative reads as though he had the name Caedicius from Cato's text, and Nepos (loc. cit.) refers to *bellorum duces* only, which does not necessarily mean that no one was named.

[3] G.W. Williams (1968) 687–9.

Virgil's time a central set-piece in Roman education and as such it was a common store of facts, stories, attitudes, and *exempla*, and deeply affected, indeed defined, the Roman consciousness. Again, by dwelling as *exornator rerum* on moral example, Ennius established an enduring trait of Roman historiography.

It has been suggested that Book 15 of the *Annales* ended with the inauguration of the cult of the Muses at Rome: 'In you my beginning, in you my end.'[1] If this is so, the narrative must have gone beyond 188 B.C. (when Nobilior's campaign ended). Nobilior's right to his booty was disputed by Cato and others, his triumph was postponed until summer 187 B.C., and his votive games took place in summer 186 B.C. Meanwhile Roman confidence had been shaken by internal crises – the disgrace of the Scipios (187 B.C.), the Bacchanalian 'conspiracy' (186 B.C.), and the loss of a consular army in Liguria (186 B.C.). The inauguration of a cult and the erection of a temple take time, and analogy suggests that the cult of the Muses will have been inaugurated in 185–183 B.C. or later, certainly not earlier.[2]

There are two separate considerations affecting the content of 15. Ennius cannot have passed over the great crisis of confidence which succeeded the liberal and optimistic spirit of the censorship of Flamininus and Marcellus (189/8 B.C.) and which brought his old patron Cato to the censorship for 184/3 B.C. Cato was elected at a time when in the opinion of his supporters 'Rome was tottering to her fall', and he 'saved the state by his wise measures', as it said on the base of a statue of Cato later erected in the Temple of Salus (Plut. *Cat. maj.* 19.4). The composition of the *Annales* belongs to the 170s B.C. and it is improbable that Ennius began earlier than the late 180s. In retrospect, Cato's censorship stood out as a memorable moral *exemplum*, which could be seen as marking the end and beginning of epochs in Roman history. Here was an appropriate end for the poem, both on private and public grounds. Nor was it only in retrospect that the censorship of the new Lycurgus might be seen as climacteric. It can hardly have escaped the attention of contemporaries that Cato became censor 1,000 years after the fall of Troy. It may be suggested that the Pythagorean Ennius and others saw some significance in this, and that Ennius' poem covered exactly this millennium. If the cult of the Muses was officially inaugurated in or about 184 B.C., as seems probable, there was another fitting personal as well as public conclusion to the epic which proclaimed Rome a full and equal member of the Hellenistic world. Ennius could thus do honour to both the great men who had helped him in his career, in spite of their political divergences.

These speculations – for that is all they are – about Book 15 at least raise important questions about the unity, composition, and publication of the poem.

[1] Skutsch (1968) 20, going beyond Leo (1913) 170; cf. Jocelyn (1972) 1006 n. 183.

[2] Eumenius, *Pan. Lat.* 5.7.3 appears to suggest 179 B.C., but that is not supported by Livy 40.51.

Lucilius refers to the *Iliad* and the *Annales* as examples of *poesis*, 'poetry', as opposed to *poemata*, 'books' (like Lucilius' own) (Lucil. (9) 340–4 M = *ROL* 403–7); they each have *una* θέσις 'one subject', and make ἔπος *unum*, 'one epic'.[1] There is, however, an obvious difference between the poem which deals with the consequences of Achilles' anger over a few weeks, and the poem which spans a thousand years and has many heroes. Ennius himself treated the *Annales* as extendible. After completing 1–15, he 'added' 16–18, which described events of the Istrian War down to 171 B.C. (Pliny, *N.H.* 7.101). Somewhere in 12 Ennius mentioned that he was 67 years old, i.e. that at the time of writing, or publication, which is not the same thing, it was 172 B.C. (Gell. 17.21.43, quoting Varro). The apparent implication is that Ennius wrote 13–15 and then added 16–18 all after 172 B.C., but before 169 B.C. Scholars have been reluctant to accept that a third of the whole therefore belongs to the last three years of the poet's life. This line of thought, however, begs important questions. We may not assume that the books were simply composed in the order in which they are numbered, nor do we know how they were presented to the public, e.g. whether the books came out singly, in triads, or as a complete work. It is too often assumed that Ennius began at the beginning and went on to the end, publishing as he went along. But Ennius was no Lucilius, and allusions in Augustan poets to what they saw as his lack of polish tell us more about Augustan taste than about Ennius. No doubt he worked faster than Virgil, but it is probable that for years his *scrinia* and notebooks were filled with notes, ideas, and 'bits' which had yet to be integrated or which anticipated the narrative. One among several possibilities is that the first fifteen appeared together in 172 B.C. as a complete work. In this case, the various personal appearances which Ennius makes throughout in his assumed poetical guise as *sacerdos musarum*[2] will be, so to speak, simultaneous, not successive. The composition of the *Annales* belonged to the late 180s and 170s: a fragment of Book 9 refers to Cornelius Cethegus (d. 196 B.C., Livy 33.42.5) as one whom 'those who were then alive' admired for his oratory. 'Then' means 215–200 B.C., and would hardly be intelligible if the poet's 'now' were earlier than 180 B.C. The hexameters of the *Hedyphagetica* (see Appendix) were experimental, and it has been shown that this poem must date from after 188 B.C. (see p. 156).

3. ENNIUS THE HELLENISTIC POET: EPIC DICTION AND VERSE

It is typical of Ennius' authority that after him no one attempted extended composition in Saturnians. The latest public inscriptions in that metre date from

[1] Ennius himself refers to the *Annales* as *poemata*, (1) 3–4 V = *ROL* 2–3.

[2] It is arguable, but cannot be proved, that Ennius really was *sacerdos musarum* at Nobilior's temple. Someone must have been; who more appropriate than Ennius? This would give a practical reason for Ennius' registration as a citizen.

the Gracchan era, and the Ennian hexameter and elegiac couplet were being used for public and private dedications and epitaphs within a generation of the poet's death. He may himself have set the fashion:

> — ⁄ — ⏑́ ⏑ — ⏑́⏑— — ⁄⏑⏑ ⁄—
> ṇẹmo mẹ dacrumịs decorẹt neu fụnera flẹtu
> ⁄— ⁄ ⏑́⏑— ⁄⏑ ⏑ ⁄⏑ ⏑́—
> fạxit. cụr? uolitọ uịuo' per ọra uirụm.
>
> (*Epigrams* 17–18 V = *ROL* 9–10)

Let no one honour me with tears or attend my obsequies with weeping. Why? I live flying through the mouths of men.

> — ⏑́⏑ — ⁄— ⏑́⏑ ⁄ ⏑⏑ ⁄⏑⏑ ⁄ —
> ạspicit(e) ọ ciuẹs senis Ẹnni imạgini' fọrmam;
> — ⁄ — ⁄ — ⁄⏑ ⏑ ⁄⏑ ⏑́ —
> hịc uestrụm panxịt mạxuma fạcta patrụm.
>
> (*Epigrams* 15–16 V = *ROL* 7–8)

Behold, fellow-citizens, the form of the image of the aged Ennius: he unfolded the marvellous deeds of your forefathers.

The authenticity of these noble epigrams need not be doubted. Whether or not they reached their respective destinations, the one was intended for Ennius' tomb, and the other for a statue of Ennius to be set in a prominent public place in Rome. The site of Ennius' tomb was later forgotten, and in Cicero's time there was a tradition that a statue of Ennius had been set up in the tomb of the Scipios.[1] That, however, is hardly a public place, and by rejecting that tradition one does not necessarily disprove the view that the busts and representations of Ennius which existed in Cicero's time represent an authentic iconographical tradition.[2] The natural setting for such a statue, actual or intended, would be the Templum Herculis Musarum, where Accius' likeness was placed within his own lifetime.[3] One notes the proud address *o ciues*, alluding to the fact that Ennius himself had been made a Roman citizen by a special grant through the influence of the Nobiliores in 184/3 B.C., i.e. before Ennius began serious work on the *Annales*, and presumably with the tacit consent of Cato the censor. The *Annales*, then, was the work of a full *ciuis Romanus*, not of an alien or of an entertainer who had acquired second-class citizenship through manumission. The language of the epigram is strikingly simple and unadorned in comparison with the first. In this it is like, say, the epitaph of Scipio Barbatus (*CIL* I^2 6–7), whose *gesta*, services, are their own eloquence. Ennius has but one service to record. Others might be censors, consuls, aediles; he, as author of the *Annales*, has performed his service through poetry as an historian. His work mattered not because of its literary qualities, but because it was true and morally important.

1 Suerbaum (1968) 210ff.
2 See Hafner (1968).
3 See Cancik (1968, 1970) (Lucil. (28) 794 M = *ROL* 844, Pliny, *N.H.* 34.19).

This to the Roman people as a fellow-citizen. As an individual Ennius makes a different claim in the tomb-epigram. It is personal and pointed. A paradox is stated, the reader's query is made explicit, and the explanation is given, as in Catullus 85 *odi et amo*... The claim that a poet's name and his poetry (all of it, not just the *Annales*) will live, and therefore the poet himself, was later a commonplace in Latin poetry. Here it appears to be new; for, perhaps surprisingly, no Greek poet made this claim or had it made for him. It goes beyond the observation made by Callimachus on the poetry of his friend Heraclitus of Halicarnassus (Callim. *Epigr.* 2). Moreover, in Ennius' case there is the complication that he was a Pythagorean. The tone is engagingly cheerful, and the three strong alliterations are nicely contrasted. This commemorates the private artist rather than the public historian.

The elegiac couplet was introduced by Ennius as an epigrammatic form. It was apparently only towards the end of the second century B.C. that it began to be used, e.g. by Q. Lutatius Catulus, for the amatory subjects with which in Latin it is particularly associated (Gell. 19.9.12, 14; cf. Callim. *Epigr.* 41, *Anth. Pal.* 12.73). When Plautus alluded to lovers' *graffiti* as *elegea* (*Merc.* 409) he had in mind what was as yet a Greek, not a Roman expression of affection (cf. *CIL* IV 585 for a later Latin example). The first line consists of a hexameter of six quantitative feet which must be dactyls (– ⏑ ⏑) or spondees (– –); in the last foot, only a spondee was admitted, though, as in drama, the final syllable might be heavy or light (⏓), and hiatus was permitted between lines. The second line, the 'pentameter', was made of two members of the form – ⏖ – ⏖ – and – ⏑⏑ – ⏑⏑ ⏓. Problems analogous to those which had been satisfactorily solved for drama (see pp. 86–93) arose with the relation of word-accents and the flow of the verse, the *arses* in this metre being the invariable (–) and the *theses* being the variable places (⏖). Ennius established for the hexameter what proved to be definitive patterns of normal rhythm:

Musae quae pedibus magnum pulsatis Olympum...
(*Annales* (1) 1 V = *ROL* 1)

Muses, you who shake great Olympus with your steps...

As in *nemo me dacrumis*..., there is here a clash of movements in the middle of the line, resolved at line-end. Conversely, the preferred cadence for the second colon of the so-called pentameter involved a strong clash at line-end, secured by making the last word a disyllable. Four of Ennius' five extant epigrams have this rhythm, which, as versifiers will know, does not occur with an easy spontaneity. These characteristic rhythms differ significantly from those favoured by Greek poets, for whom the placing of the word-accent in relation to the quantitative movement was an irrelevant consideration (see pp. 86–93).

The rhythm of the Ennian hexameter was quite new in Latin, for although anapaestic lines were used in drama, their technique was quite different. In particular, Ennius did not permit himself to scan words ending with a cretic pattern (– ⏑ –) as if they ended with dactyls (– ⏑ ⏑), as did Plautus. This severely restricted the available vocabulary: words like *cīuĭtās* or *făcĭnŏră* were automatically ruled out. Iambo-trochaic verse was more accommodating. This imposed and encouraged artifice, particularly in the exploitation of archaic forms drawn from the formulae of ritual and law (e.g. *īndŭpĕrātōr* for *īmpĕrātōr*) and in the coining of more or less bizarre expressions calqued from Homer (e.g. *endo suam do* 'into his house' ~ *Od.* 1.176 ἡμέτερον δῶ). The epic style subsumed all the resources of the tragic, but differed in two ways: as it was still 'grander', it could accommodate archaisms avoided by tragic dramatists; and as it was based on Homer, whose dialect is mixed, anomalies and alternative forms were admissible in a manner not permitted in the more homogeneous and economical language of the stage. Final *-s* after a short vowel might be dropped or kept before an initial consonant not (as in drama) according to linguistic but purely metrical rules. Words like *patrem* might be syllabified as *pāt-rēm* (with Homeric precedent) as well as in the natural Latin way, *pă-trēm*. Some final syllables (*-at*, *-or*) might be scanned heavy in *arsis* and light in *thesis*. Iambic shortening was given up (see p. 87). Elision and synaloepha were admitted less freely than in drama. Unfortunately, we have no idea how Ennius would 'declaim' his verse; these technicalities all point away from a conversational delivery, and there is only one point in which Ennius seems more 'naturalistic' than the language of drama: he is much less fond of end-stopping his lines, and favours no particular punctuation-points within the line.

In drama, the separation of an epithet and its noun was normally significant, i.e. emphasis was thus laid on either or both words. Ennius was responsible for an important innovation in Latin poetic diction which has no real precedent in either Greek or earlier Latin practice. We frequently find epithets and nouns separated in his hexameters, e.g. *magnum...Olympum*, *ueter...Priamus*, *pium...Anchisen*, *teneras...auras*, *tremulis...artubus*, *caerula...templa*, *calido ...sanguine*, *miserum...homonem*, *crudeli...sepulcro*, *densis...pinnis*, without emphasis falling on either word. The obvious explanation, that this facilitated scansion in this 'difficult' metre, will not suffice; for, as in the examples quoted, it is always the adjective which comes first, whereas when adjectives and nouns stand next to each other, the order is free.

–́ ⏑ ⏑ – –́ – ⏑́ ⏑ – – –́ ⏑ ⏑ –́ –
uụlturus ịn spinịs *miserụm* mandẹbat *homọnem*;
–́ – – –́ – – –́ – –́ ⏑ ⏑ –́ –
hẹu, quam *crụdelị* condẹbat mẹmbra *sepụlcro*.

(*Ann.* (2) 138f. V = *ROL* 141f.)

A vulture was gobbling a poor wight amidst the thorns; alas, in what a cruel tomb did it lay his limbs!

The epithets are qualitative, emotional, and subjective; a riddle, as it were, is posed in mid-line, which is solved by the corresponding noun at the end. In

hic *uestrum* panxit **maxuma facta** *patrum*

(see above) two adjectives precede two nouns. This is rare in Ennius' *Annales*, but it is simply a duplication of the principle described, an elaboration of a very common Ennian trait. It became a mannerism of the neoteric poets, and remained a very important device in all Latin hexameter poetry. That here too Father Ennius was the ultimate source has not been sufficiently recognized.[1]

While Ennius established the norms of Epic rhythm, diction, and word-order without which there would be no Latin hexameter poetry, he also experimented widely with rhythms and stylistic devices which were later restricted or avoided e.g. the shortening rather than elision of a final long vowel in ... *Ēnnĭ ĭmāgĭnĭ' fōrmām* (cf. Hom. *Od.* 1.241), the lengthening in *arsis* of a light syllable (*quōm nĭhĭl hōrrĭdĭūs ūmquām...*, (5) 170 V = *ROL* 474), and Greek 'epicisms' like *ēndŏ sŭām dō* (see above). Some of these, e.g. *Mēttōeŏquĕ Fūfĕtĭōeō* (Quint. *Inst.* 1.5.12), 'of Mettius Fufetius', modelled on the Homeric genitive -οιο, suggest that Ennius thought of Latin as a much-corrupted Greek dialect, and here overstepped the bounds of decorum with a spurious archaism. Others, e.g. (*lib. inc.*) 609 V = *ROL* Enn. *spuria* 13...*saxo cere- comminuit -brum*, an absurdly literal and violent tmesis, seem scarcely credible and may only be schoolmasterly jokes. Ennius sometimes played on words in a manner hardly appropriate to the majesty of the epic form. He 'seems to have been joking', we are told, when he wrote *inde parum* [...] *ulabant* ((*lib. inc.*) 524 V = *ROL* 544); evidently there was a pun on *parum* 'too little' and *Parum* '(to) Paros' or 'Pharos'. Again in a line referring probably to the building of the via Flaminia in 220 B.C. we read ((7) 260 V = *ROL* 255) *sulphureas posuit spiramina Nāris ad undas* 'He set blow-holes by the sulphurous waters of the river Nar'; here the nonce-word *spiramina*, literally 'things by which one breathes', is nothing but a synonym of *nāres* 'nostrils'; the unfortunate pun was presumably meant to imply that the river was so called because of its pungent smell (cf. Vitruv. 7.4).

These and other blemishes offended the taste of the Augustan age. However, it would have pained Ennius to learn that although his *ingenium* was acknowledged by such as Propertius and Ovid, they could not repress an amused smile when contemplating his *ars*, his technique – an aspect of his work in which Ennius took pride. Indeed, the romantic view of Ennius, current in Ovid's time, as an untutored and therefore artistically hirsute genius has still not entirely evaporated. He deserves to be judged more analytically and against less

[1] Patzer (1955) 77–95 cites Euphorion fr. 9.10–15, Hermesianax fr. 7.21–6 Powell in connexion with Catullus' practice. There is nothing similar in Apollonius or Callimachus. Norden (1926) 391f. and Pearce (1966, 1968) are concerned with poets of the first century B.C., not with Ennius.

anachronistic criteria; and it should be borne in mind that where others followed, he led the way. Space prevents more than a cursory survey of his diverse techniques.

In Book 6 Ennius described the felling of trees, probably for a funeral pyre, in the following words:

> Incedunt arbusta per alta, securibu' caedunt.
> percellunt magnas quercus, exciditur ilex;
> fraxinu' frangitur atque abies consternitur alta;
> pinus proceras peruortunt. omne sonabat
> arbustum fremitu siluai frondosai.
>
> (*Ann.* (6) 187–91 V = *ROL* 181–5)

They pass among the tall groves, they hew with axes. They hack down great oaks; the holm is chopped; the ash is broken and the tall fir is laid low; they overturn high pines. The whole glade echoed with the noise of the leafy forest.

This recalls the passage in Book 23 of the *Iliad* where Meriones is sent with mules and carts to Mount Ida to cut wood for Patroclus' pyre, in particular lines 118–20:

> αὐτίκ' ἄρα δρῦς ὑψικόμους ταναήκεϊ χαλκῷ
> τάμνον ἐπειγόμενοι · ταὶ δὲ μεγάλα κτυπέουσαι
> πῖπτον.

Then straightway they set to with a will and started cutting the high-leafed oaks with long-edged bronze, and the oaks fell crashing mightily.

The whole passage in Homer is an excellent illustration of his rapid, plain, and elevated narrative-style. Ennius in emphasizing the latter qualities sacrifices the first altogether; his description is massive and slow. He has five variations on the theme δρῦς ὑψικόμους . . . τάμνον, strung together with bald parataxis and end-stopping. The vocabulary is simple and his expression direct. The only qualitative adjectives are variations on the idea 'tall', all simplifications of ὑψικόμους. The solid strength of each phrase is loudly, even crudely, proclaimed by the contrast of its special alliteration with that of the neighbouring phrase. The only subtlety in the enumeration is the variation of active and passive and of plural and singular. The effect is to focus our attention upwards: we see not the sawyers hard at work but the great trees toppling one after another. Homer's ταὶ δὲ μεγάλα κτυπέουσαι πῖπτον lies behind Ennius' superb *omne sonabat arbustum fremitu siluai frondosai*, but is transmuted; for *fremitus* is not (as in Homer) the sound of the trees crashing to the ground – that would be *crepitu*, *strepitu* – but the more continuous murmuring rustle of the leaves (*frondosai*) of the forest, commenting, as it were, on the destruction of the great lords (*proceras*) of their community. The august character of the ancient forest is implied by the slow, spondaic line-end with its (even for Ennius) archaic genitives in -*āī*, a trick used elsewhere by Ennius to achieve a suitably Homeric *grauitas* and solemnity:

> ǫ́lli rẹspóndịt réx Ạlbáị longáị (*Ann.* (1) 33 V = *ROL* 31)
>
> *To him replied the king of Alba Longa...*

olli is also archaic, for *illi*; this is Ennius' version of the much lighter Homeric formula τὸν δ' ἀπαμειβόμενος προσέφη 'X addressed him in answer...'. Ennius was here evidently seeking with his massive spondees and his archaisms to mark the importance and majesty of the king's words to the Trojan exiles.

Virgil imitated Ennius' tree-felling passage twice in the *Aeneid*; on both occasions it is a question of preparing a funeral-pyre.

> Itur in antiquam siluam, stabula alta ferarum.
> procumbunt piceae, sonat icta securibus ilex
> fraxineaeque trabes cuneis et fissile robur
> scinditur; aduoluunt ingentes montibus ornos. (*Aen.* 6. 179–82)
>
> *Progress is made into an ancient forest, the full-grown dens of the wild. Pitch-pines topple, the holm echoes struck with axes, beams of ash and fissile oak are split with wedges; they roll huge rowans from the mountains.*

> ferro sonat icta bipenni
> fraxinus, euertunt actas ad sidera pinus
> robora nec cuneis et olentem scindere cedrum
> nec plaustris cessant uectare gementibus ornos. (*Aen.* 11. 135–8)
>
> *The tall ash echoes under the iron axe, they overturn pines aimed at the stars, nor do they cease from splitting oaks and the fragrant cedar with wedges, or from conveying rowans on groaning carts.*

Virgil here takes some things directly from Homer – most important, his speed and economy – and he tones down Ennius' alliterative emphases. In Book 6 he uses the same variation of active and passive and of singular and plural as Ennius; in Book 11 *euertunt actas ad sidera pinus* is an exaggerated and therefore not wholly felicitous rendering of Ennius' blunt *pinus proceras peruortunt.* It is instructive to see how Silius Italicus (*Punica* 10.527–34) and Statius (*Thebaid* 6.90–127) elaborate still further the basic Ennian theme.

It would be wrong to infer that Ennius always wrote in this powerful, static style:

> concurrunt ueluti uenti quom spiritus Austri
> imbricitor Aquiloque suo cum flamine contra
> indu mari magno fluctus extollere certant...
> (*Ann.* (17) 443–5 V = *ROL* 430–2)
>
> *They* [two warriors or armies] *run together as when the breath of Auster the rain-starter* [i.e. the South Wind] *and Aquilo* [the North Wind] *with his blast strive in opposition to raise billowing waves on the great sea...*

This is inspired by *Iliad* 9.4–7:

> ὡς δ' ἄνεμοι δύο πόντον ὀρίνετον ἰχθυόεντα
> Βορέης καὶ Ζέφυρος, τώ τε Θρῄκηθεν ἄητον
> ἐλθόντ' ἐξαπίνης· ἄμυδις δέ τε κῦμα κελαινὸν
> κορθύεται...

As when two winds, Boreas and Zephyr, stir up the fish-filled sea; they both come sudden, blowing from Thrace, and at once the dark billow raises its crest... (cf. Virg. *Aen.* 2.416–19).

Here Ennius has achieved the rapidity of Homer by using a mixture of dactyls and spondees quite different from that in his tree-felling passage, and by keeping Homer's enjambments, essential to the impetus of a passage describing great and uncontrolled natural forces at large. But he is essentially un-Homeric in calling the South Wind *spiritus Austri imbricitor*: that is Hellenistic baroque.

Ennius had an ear for effective rhythms, as in:

> rẹges per regnụm statuạsque sepụlchraque quạerunt:
> ạedíficạnt nómẹn, súmmạ nitụ́ntur ópụm uí...
> (*Ann.* (16) 411f. V = *ROL* 393f.)

kings through kingship seek statues and sepulchres: they build their names, they strive with all the force of their resources...

The strength of these lines comes from the paradox of the tangible and intangible in *aedificant nomen* and from the rhythm: verse-ictus and word-accent wrestle to the end of the second line without resolution. *Summa nituntur opum ui* is repeated here from *Ann.* (4) 161 V = *ROL* 164, *Romani scalis summa nituntur opum ui* 'the Romans strive on the ladders with all the force of their resources', where 'resources' means 'strength', not 'wealth'. By such judicious repetition and adaptation Ennius created the impression of Homer's formulaic diction; once again Virgil paid him the compliment of imitation at *Aen.* 12.552 *pro se quisque uiri summa nituntur opum ui* 'each for himself the men strive with all the force of their resources'.

A more harmonious exploitation of the hexameter is seen in such lines as these:

> pọ́ste recụ́mbite uẹ́straque pẹ́ctora pẹ́llite tọ́nsis...
> (*Ann.* (7) 230 V = *ROL* 245)

Lean back and beat your breasts with the blades...

> lạ́bitur ụ́ncta carị́na per ạ́equora cạ́na celọ́cis...
> (*Ann.* (*lib. inc.*) 478 V = *ROL* (8/9?) 442)

The oiled keel of the cutter glides through the hoary levels...

The un-Homeric care of the *dicti studiosus* manifests itself in other ways too. The elaborately broken punctuation of Ilia's invocation of Venus is intended to express her breathless agitation:

> te nunc, sancta, precor, Venu', te, genetrix patri' nostri,
> ut me de caelo uisas, cognata, parumper...
>
> (*Ann.* (1) 52f. V = *ROL* 49f.)

Holy one, thee now I pray, Venus, thee, who didst bear my father, that thou look down on me from heaven, kinswoman, a little while...

After the appropriately liturgical language of the first line, *cognata*, though logically prepared for by *genetrix patris nostri*, comes as a mildly prosaic shock. 'Grandmother' would have been absurd; 'kinswoman' is a typically Hellenistic conceit. The passage narrating Ilia's frightening dream begins

> excita quom tremulis anus attulit artubu' lumen...
>
> (*Ann.* (1) 35 V = *ROL* 32)

When the old woman was awoken and had brought a lamp with trembling limbs...

The detail *tremulis* effectively paints the eery scene: the lamp gutters in her unsteady grasp, the shadows leap and flicker. That is the economical precision of Callimachus. Ennius sometimes wrote single lines or couplets in which he used rhetorical figures in epigrammatical comments as editor on individuals who display *uirtus* or deserve sympathy; these are eminently quotable and were clearly intended to be quotable as 'tags'.[1] That is Hellenistic, not Homeric. On the other hand there are harshly 'unpoetic' lines such as

> ...nonis iunis soli luna obstitit, et nox...
>
> (*Ann.* (4) 163 V = *ROL* 166)

On the Nones of June the moon blocked the sun, and night...

Such lines are criticized as tasteless; it would however be prudent to suspend judgement on this, for the contexts are unknown and one cannot tell how the severe, annalistic manner evoked here fitted into the texture of a style which was evidently richly various and avoided a monotony of either Hellenistic elaboration or jejune simplicity.

In his essay *On translating Homer* Matthew Arnold identified four characteristic qualities of Homer – his rapidity; his plainness and directness in evolving and expressing his thought; the plainness and directness of the substance of his thought; and his nobility, i.e. his σεμνότης or *grauitas*. Ennius regularly hits the Homeric mark in two or three but rarely in all four respects at once. The tree-felling fragment is plain and direct and noble, but it is anything but rapid; his

[1] *uirtus*: (10) 338 V = *ROL* 330 (Flamininus), (12) 370–2 V = *ROL* 360–2 (Fabius Maximus); (*lib. inc.*) 500 V = *ROL* 467 (the Roman state). Pathos: (*lib. inc.*) 519f. V = *ROL* 499f.; (*lib. inc.*) 472f. V = *ROL* 501f.; (2) 138f. V = *ROL* 141f.

wind-simile is noble and rapid and direct in thought but not in expression (*spiritus Austri imbricitor*); his play on *nares* is ignoble and indirect in expression. But Ennius was not really aiming to translate Homer; he was a highly original and eclectic poet. He may pose as Homer in his claim to be the medium of the Muses, in the general form and texture of his narrative, in the anthropomorphic presentation of the gods, in his touches of formulaic diction,[1] and in his similes drawn from Nature; but these were all common coin current among Hellenistic poets who used the form and expression of Homeric verse for new purposes. Ennius' frequent editorial comments, direct and indirect, his didactic tone, the arbitrary pace of the narrative, his stylistic self-consciousness, his exploitation of pathos and his gratuitous interest in female psychology are all features which emphasize the importance of the *poeta* as the organizer of his material in an un-Homeric way. He is, as it were, a master of ceremonies, the priest of the Muses who has both exoteric and esoteric lore to impart. The first line of the poem (quoted above, p. 68) is constructed of Homeric tags and has as its literal meaning 'Muses, you who shake great Olympus with your steps'; but there is also an allegorical meaning, 'Muses, you who make the great sky vibrate with your steps', an allusion to the theory of the harmony of the spheres. The Hellenistic poet at play would tell a tale perhaps trivial or preposterous with a straight face, and with irony and display. The difference with Ennius is that his subject was of the highest seriousness and he addressed not only the *cognoscenti* who knew Callimachus and Greek philosophy, but also the many.

4. ENNIUS THE ROMAN CITIZEN: HIS VALUES AND APPEAL

The *Annales* cannot have been an imperialistic poem like the *Aeneid*. Ennius died two years before the defeat of Philip of Macedon at Pydna in 167 B.C.; his adult life did not quite span the whole of that period of fifty-three years, from 220 to 167 B.C., during which Rome rose from obscurity to world power. As Polybius noted at the beginning of his *History*, written at Rome in the next generation, this was one of the most remarkable facts in history (Polyb. 1.1.5); Polybius already looked back to that time as an age of heroes. Ennius wrote his *Annales* in the wake of wars which had caused changes more rapid than was comfortable or even comprehensible to the Romans: no one in 202 B.C. could have predicted or looked for the phenomenal successes which Rome had experienced in world-politics by 188 B.C. It was not the intention or policy of the Senate to create new provinces or take on commitments outside Italy, and it was still far from clear during the years when Ennius was writing the *Annales* what Rome's precise relationship to the other Great Powers was to be.

[1] E.g. *olli respondit*...(1) 33 V = *ROL* 31, (2) 119 V = *ROL* 124, *caelum*...*stellis fulgentibus aptum* (1) 29 V = *ROL* 59, (3) 159 V = *ROL* 162 (Macrobius, *Sat.* 6.1.9).

Ennius' view of history was moral, individualistic, and aristocratic: *uirtus* was all; the safety of the common weal depended on individual *uirtus*; and *noblesse oblige*...

> unus homo nobis cunctando restituit rem.
> noenum rumores ponebat ante salutem;
> ergo postque magisque uiri nunc gloria claret...
>
> (*Ann.* (12) 370–2 V = *ROL* 360–2)
>
> *One man restored us the commonwealth by delaying;*
> *he would not put grumbling before our safety;*
> *therefore his fame shines now the more in retrospect...*

These famous lines on Fabius Maximus Cunctator express this attitude. Ennius admired Rome like Polybius, but had no sophisticated analysis of its constitution or society, other than to praise *uirtus* where he saw it, and to honour and emphasize the antiquity of Roman institutions. He did this at a time when society was faced with great internal and external changes. The *Annales* celebrated and defined what the Romans of that time liked to think were the qualities which had made them what they were, explained their place in the world, and implied how they should continue. By linking myth to remote history, remote to recent, and recent to the present, Ennius strengthened the community's sense of continuity, hence its identity and purpose, and provided patterns of excellence to which the young should aspire. The success of the poem was immediate and remarkable. We are told that it was declaimed in public not long after Ennius' death, as rhapsodes performed Homer, and for a century and a half it continued to provide the classic definitions and examples of Roman attitudes and values. It had a central place in the school curriculum. But epics, except Homer's, become superannuated. They lose directness, for tastes in style and assumptions about values change. Virgil displaced Ennius in the classroom, and, although the antiquarians of the second century A.D. read Ennius, his manuscripts must have been very rare by A.D. 500. His fragments were first printed in 1564; Scaliger wrote of him 'Ennius, poeta egregius, magnifico ingenio. utinam hunc haberemus integrum et amisissemus Lucanum, Statium, Silium, et tous ces garçons-là...quamquam interdum alium olet, tamen optime animatus est' 'Ennius, an outstanding poet of great genius. If only we had him [i.e. the *Annales*] whole, and had lost Lucan, Statius, Silius Italicus *et tous ces garçons-là* ...Although he sometimes smells of garlic, he has an excellent spirit.' Without wishing ill to 'all those adolescents', we may agree with Scaliger that the loss of Ennius' *Annales* is the most regrettable in all Latin literature.

5

DRAMA

I. THE ORIGINS OF ROMAN DRAMA

The Hellenistic theatre and Italy

After Menander's death (292 B.C.) the Greek theatrical profession, which had been primarily Athenian, became Panhellenic. Many Greek cities built or renovated theatres on a grand scale, and it is the remains of these, not of theatres of the classical period, that the traveller sees at such sites as Delos or Epidaurus. In the generation during which the scholar-poet Callimachus worked at Ptolemy's new 'Museum' in Alexandria, when the Sicilian Theocritus was composing his pastorals, and when the future father of Roman literature, the Greek Andronicus, was still a boy at Tarentum, the acting profession was acquiring a new prestige, even political power. The actors, musicians, and writers of tragedy and comedy were organized into 'chapels' or 'conventicles', θίασοι or σύνοδοι, and they called themselves οἱ περὶ τὸν Διόνυσον τεχνῖται 'the Artists in the service of Dionysus'. Four 'Guilds' of the Artists emerged, each corresponding to a region of the Greek world; apart from regulating terms and rules for dramatic competitions, these organizations even behaved in some ways like independent states, and would negotiate rights of safe passage for their members with a city or federation. Thus the acting profession came to depend and to thrive on a 'circuit' of musical and dramatic festivals among which Athens was only one of several centres. New plays were still produced, but the emphasis shifted to a repertoire of classics – in comedy, Menander, Philemon, and Diphilus; in tragedy, Sophocles, Euripides, and the latter's imitators.

Our knowledge of these developments of the years 290–250 B.C. is largely due to archaeological discoveries, and, as is the nature of such evidence, it is detailed (e.g. for Delphi and Delos) and patchy (e.g. for Sicily and South Italy).[1] We hear first of the Artists at Rome only in the 180s B.C. (Livy 39.22.2, 10), when a Roman drama based on their repertoire was already two generations old. In spite of the absence of direct evidence, it is likely that the Artists

[1] Sifakis (1967), *DFA* (1968).

did visit such centres as Syracuse and Tarentum in the third century B.C., and it is certain that their example lies behind the vigorous growth of the Roman theatre after the middle of that century.

However, it is clear that the practice of the Artists and the presentation and style of their Attic repertoire were not the only models on which the earliest Latin drama was based. Unfortunately, even the scholars of the Gracchan period (Aelius Stilo, Accius) and of Cicero's time (Varro) knew very little for certain about the beginnings of Roman drama. They tried to provide a pedigree to match the teleological histories of Greek drama prepared by scholars of the Peripatetic school. Accius seems to have regarded Naevius as the first important Roman dramatist, and gave a chronology for Andronicus which seems impossibly late, in spite of modern attempts to vindicate it.[1] Varro claimed the authority of 'old records' to show that Andronicus was the 'first inventor' of Latin drama, and that he produced a play in 240 B.C. at the end of the First Punic War (Cic. *Brut.* 72f.). The remains of accounts of the early theatre which were current in the first century B.C. are entirely worthless with respect to tragedy, and virtually so for comedy.[2] The objective value of the surviving summaries is only to illustrate the dubious methods of inference, synthesis, and invention which scholars like Accius had learnt from the school of Pergamum rather than Alexandria. As such, and since this is what passed for the truth, it is instructive. A source used by Horace (*Epist.* 2.1.139–63) alleged that the extempore joke-capping of harvest-home, the so-called Fescennine ritual which featured also in the celebrations of Roman weddings and triumphs and which was intended to avert malign spirits, led to an equivalent of the uproarious Old Comedy of Athens; this was curbed by law because of its slanderous content. Another account, summarized by Livy (7.2) and Valerius Maximus (2.4.4), is more speciously historical. According to this, Andronicus was indeed a 'first inventor' in that he was the first to present an entertainment with a story-line; it is very strange, however, that the author of this version did not think it interesting or important that the story was taken from a Greek play. The source refers to a dramatic *satura*, 'medley', before Andronicus; this had a written libretto, a prominent part for the musician (*tibicen*), and was acted by professional *histriones*, 'actors', a word borrowed from the Etruscan name for masked dancers of apotropaic rites, who, in their magic capacity, had been known in Rome since at least the early fourth century. The writer regarded these *histriones* with dislike and disdain, and he contrasts them unfavourably with the amateur performers (apparently young Romans of respectable birth) of an extempore kind of farce, borrowed from Oscan Atellae, and hence known as Atellane. He concludes by alluding in a muddled way to mime in an aetiological

[1] Suerbaum (1968) 2 n. 2, 297–300; Waszink (1972) 873f.

[2] Duckworth (1952) 4–17.

story in which he confuses first-century B.C. forms of that unmasked entertainment with the presentation of Andronicus' drama: according to him, Andronicus acted and sang in his own productions, but one day, straining his voice, passed his singing part over to a convenient *puer*, while he himself mimed the appropriate actions.

Etruscan dancers, Atellane farce, *tibicines*, mime, and Fescennine exchanges are relevant in various ways to Roman drama as we know it, but it is striking that this source and others seem determined to mention nothing Greek in connexion with early Roman drama. Yet the long-established prose- and verse-comedies of Sicily, the vigorous Doric verse-comedies of South Italy, and the farces of Rhinthon (*phlyakes*, *hilarotragoediae*), not to mention the repertoire of the Artists, must have had direct and important influences. Roman drama was an adaptation of Hellenic drama. Why was it adopted at Rome so fruitfully in the middle of the third century B.C., rather than much sooner or much later?

It would be a mistake to oppose Greek and Italian elements in the implicitly chauvinistic manner of the sources reviewed above. Nor is it enough to acknowledge the importance of the theatrical traditions of South Italy and Sicily. To answer the question posed, one must look at Italy in its Hellenistic setting. The Roman people had no hermetic or racial self-consciousness. Their foundation-myths showed that they were a mixed people and their unusual law of manumission made freed slaves members of the body politic, so that potentially anyone of any race might be a *ciuis Romanus*. They were open to Greek influences in all spheres, and their political and military contacts with the Greeks of Epirus, South Italy, and Sicily, in particular, the war against Pyrrhus and the First Punic War, came at a time when Greeks, for their part, were ceasing to think of 'Hellenism' as racially exclusive. As we have seen, it was at just this time that a particularly vivid expression of Hellenism, the Attic drama, was being disseminated more widely than ever before. Under Eratosthenes, the second generation of scholars at the Alexandrian Library were directing their attention outside the Greek world as traditionally defined, and were translating into Greek law-codes, technical manuals, and records in other languages. The most famous of these is the version of the Hebrew Pentateuch which lies behind the Septuagint.[1] It is a striking accident, if it is only an accident, that Andronicus and Naevius should have embarked in this very generation on what is in a sense the counterpart of this activity at Alexandria. Theirs, however, was the more ambitious and difficult task. The works to which the Alexandrians directed their attention were factual; the contents mattered, not the style. The merely factual content of the *Odyssey*, which Andronicus 'translated', or of an Attic play is less important than its presentation: the form and style of a literary

[1] Jellicoe (1968) 47–58; Pfeiffer (1968) 152–70; Fraser (1972) 305–35.

work is part of its meaning. Andronicus is a major figure in the history of literature as the first to tackle the problems of literary translation. His approach was crucial for the subsequent development of Latin literature; it was a matter of adaptation rather than of translation of the letter or even of that chimerical aim, fidelity to the spirit. The *Camena* whom Andronicus invoked at the beginning of his *Odyssey* was not Homer's μοῦσα (Muse) relabelled, but an Italian nymph who could inspire the *uates*, the bard. Homer and the Attic dramatists were the foundation of Greek education, and Andronicus was providing his fellow Roman citizens – he was an ex-slave, therefore a *ciuis* – with the works which, as a Greek, he must have seen as essential for a proper education. That a people might be civilized, even Hellenized, yet not speak Greek was a paradoxical idea, characteristic not of the age of Callimachus, but of his successor in scholarship Eratosthenes; its most striking manifestation was the emergence of Roman literature, in particular the drama, in the years after 240 B.C. For more detail of the manner in which the earliest *poetae*, 'makers', went about the business of adaptation (*uertere*, 'turning', as they called it), and how adaptation and free invention merged, see pp. 84ff. on the form of Roman drama, 93ff., 127ff. on light and serious drama, and pp. 58–76 on epic.

The organization of the acting profession at Rome

There was no permanent theatre at Rome until 55 B.C.; plans afoot in 179 and 174 B.C. failed.[1] The tradition at Rome had always been that the entertainers went to the festival, not the festival to the entertainers. Prefabricated wooden stages, presumably like those depicted on South Italian vases, were erected on the various sites of festivals.[2] These and other paraphernalia belonged to actor-*impresari* like T. Publilius Pellio, associated over a long period with Plautus,[3] and L. Ambivius Turpio, who produced, managed, and acted for Terence and Caecilius. There is a persistent belief that the Roman theatre in its early period was the province of the obscure and poverty-stricken. This is questionable. However Pellio and Turpio came to sport such aristocratic-sounding names,[4] they were men of substance and consequence, acquaintances of the élite in politics through their constant trade with the aediles, the future praetors and consuls. Ambivius presents himself in Terence's prologues (of the 160s B.C.)

[1] Livy 40.51.3, cf. 41.27.5, *periocha* 48. Pompey's theatre (55 B.C.): Tac. *Ann.* 14.20, cf. 13.54.

[2] Beare (1964) 176ff., 256ff., 335ff.; Trendall (1967).

[3] Plaut. *Men.* 404 (*Pellionis*, not *pellionis*); 'Pellio's gear' is the wooden stage. An early play. *Pseud.* didascalia (Nov./Dec. 192 B.C. Julian). *Bac.* 215 (Pellio is probably acting Pistoclerus' part), 185/4 B.C.

[4] It was still unusual for any but prominent families to have cognomens of pure Latin attributive (usually derogatory) character, e.g. Balbus, Verrucosus, rather than ethnics (P. Terentius Afer) or foreign personal names (L. Livius Andronicus), which implied servile origin. Most people had just two names (C. Laelius).

not only as a great actor, proud of his craft, but also an artistic patron who can afford to back unpopular work and vindicate it (*prol.* Ter. *Hec. passim*). There was plenty of money in Rome in the years following the Punic and Eastern Wars, and Pellio and Turpio belong to the class of men who became rich by taking state-contracts from the aediles. By the 170s a remarkable 'social season' had developed. The religious festivals were preceded by a number of days devoted to entertainment, financed and run by the aediles. Races (*ludi circenses*) and shows (*ludi scaenici*) might be accompanied by 'fringe' events, e.g. boxing matches or tight-rope-walking. The season opened with the *ludi Megalenses* (*Megalesia*) (early April); there followed the *ludi Cereales* (late April), *Florales* (early May), *Apollinares* (mid-July), *Romani* (mid-September), and *Plebeii* (early November). Thus in theory it ran from spring to autumn. In practice, owing to the omission in the 190s of the biennial intercalations, the calendar was seriously out of step with the seasons – by nearly four months in Plautus' heyday, an error only reduced to two and a half months by Terence's time.[1] Thus in the 180s the *Megalesia* was falling in mid-winter, and the *ludi Plebeii* in high summer. The festivals had been instituted one by one, the *ludi Romani* being by far the oldest. The main period of growth was 230–190 B.C., years of great strain and anxiety, when the Senate saw such entertainments as a useful way to sustain public morale. The drama benefited greatly, and by the 180s it is probable that Plautus and Ennius had about fourteen official days for production, hardly less than the time available at Athens for dramatic competitions. That was not all. There were productions at occasional votive or funeral games given at private expense; and when a defect was noted in the ritual, the whole festival, plays and and all, had to be repeated, until things went right.

The prologues to Plautus' *Poenulus* and Terence's *Hecyra* show that audiences were mixed as to class, age, and sex, and that they could be unruly. From 194 B.C., the best seats were reserved for senators (Livy 34.44.5), a reform not welcomed by the people. The audiences of the Greek Artists at great festivals like the Delphic *Soteria* had read the authors of the repertoire at school and could be expected to be knowledgeable and discriminating. At Rome, although there were apparently revival-performances already in Plautus' time (cf. *Bac.* 214f.), most plays, light or serious, were new, and most of the audience would neither know nor care about the models; if they were bored, they would vote with their feet. The cultural levels of the audiences could hardly be more different.[2] There was a competitive aspect to productions at Roman festivals, but it is unclear what exactly was being judged, or by whom, or how central this element was; nor do we know whether or how strictly tragic and comic

[1] For the festivals, see Taylor (1937) 284–304; on the disruption of the calendar, see Michels (1967) 102, 170–1, Derow (1973) 345–56.

[2] See Cèbe (1960) 101–6.

offerings were segregated at a festival. Roman production-notices, unlike Greek, only record whether a play 'pleased' or not, and that only sometimes. A large cash prize awarded to Terence for his *Eunuchus* was unusual (Don. *praef. Eun.* p. 266 W).

The real financial competition came earlier, when the *impresario* approached the aediles with his offering. Whether the aediles paid 'standard' rates, or were permitted to supplement public moneys out of their own purses, is unclear. They would be interested in the political success of their festivals rather than in artistic merit, experiment, or social comment, and one can see that the work of a known success, such as Plautus or Ennius around 190 B.C., might be at a premium, whereas an unknown like Caecilius might experience difficulty without the patronage of a successful manager and friends in the nobility. Indeed, a successful actor or playwright enjoyed a peculiar opportunity to make contacts. Unlike a physician or tutor in the *clientela* of a particular family, which might be in political eclipse, e.g. the Julii Caesares of Plautus' time, the actor-manager's *exclusive* business was with the rising stars of politics. That alone explains why after Naevius Roman drama was usually only indirectly political or controversial. It was in the dramatist's interest to avoid offending families whose younger members might be next year's aediles. Clearly, these are all circumstances far removed from those of the contemporary Artists of Dionysus. By the 180s Rome, unlike any one Greek city, was maintaining her own internal and self-sufficient 'circuit'. The theatre was to the politician a convenient means of winning popular favour; to the entrepreneur it was a lucrative business; and to the public it was part (only part) of an enjoyable day off work. The Artists, by contrast, had long-standing traditions; they travelled far and wide to perform the classics before cultured audiences in fine stone theatres financed out of civic pride; artistic competition was central, and the rules and financial terms were minutely regulated by the Guilds.

The Roman acting-profession differed from the Greek also in several points which emphasize that the Artists' organization and tradition was not the exclusive model (cf. p. 78). In Greece, tragedy and comedy were strictly separate professions. The argument at the end of Plato's *Symposium* whether the same man might not try both genres is as speculative as whether a woman might make a good general. At Rome, Andronicus and Naevius developed a similar dramatic form for both light and serious plays, and they were supposed to have acted in their own productions (Festus p. 448 L, Livy 7.2). Specialization came in gradually. Plautus kept to comedy, though he was technically capable of writing serious drama; Ennius was the last to try both kinds. In Terence's time Q. Minucius Prothymus apparently acted tragic as well as comic parts, as later did Roscius (Don. p. 26 W, p. 266 W; Cic. *Orat.* 109). All kinds of Roman drama were far more musical and 'operatic' than Greek. Roman production-notices regularly record the name of the *tibicen* and technical details of his wind-instrument, the double pipe: the musician never figures in the *didascaliae* of Greek plays. The 'three-actor' rule of Greek drama was unknown to Plautus and Terence; the former sometimes has as many as six full actors simultaneously present in one play (*Poenulus*); the latter has up to four (*Heauton timorumenus*). There is no evidence at all for the doubling of roles which was a necessity and a point of pride in the Greek acting profession. However these radical differences of presentation and technique are to be explained, they clearly have nothing to do with the tradition of the Artists. It is here that the weakness of ancient accounts of the development of Roman drama is specially regrettable.

And yet, the Artists' influence is clear. It was their repertoire that was adapted. The iambo-trochaic quantitative verse of Roman drama represents a compromise between the more divergent styles of Greek tragedy and comedy. Latin plays were from the start presented in the contemporary costume of the Greek theatre. This was considered so characteristic a feature that later at any rate (for the terms cannot be traced earlier than Varro) comedies from the Greek repertoire were called *fabulae palliatae* 'Cloak plays' (from *pallium* = ἱμάτιον, 'cloak') and tragedies were called *fabulae crepidatae* 'Buskin plays', with allusion to the high-soled boot of Hellenistic tragedy. Lastly, although certain evidence on this point is lacking, it is unlikely that women ever acted in Roman productions. After all, these were dramas, not mimes, in spite of the confusion in Livy's source (see above, pp. 78–9).

This brings us to the question of masks. The ancient sources are confused as to whether and when Roman actors began using them. The consensus seems to have been that at first they did not, i.e. that the 'actors' were not really *histriones* but *mimi*, 'imitators'.[1] It is hard to believe this. It is not as if masks were alien to the Romans as they are to us. The Etruscan dancers who gave the name *histriones* were certainly masked; the word *persōna* 'mask' is also probably borrowed from Etruscan (it has nothing to do with *per-sŏnare* 'sound through'); the actors of Atellane farce, professional and amateur, had always used masks for the stock characters Bucco, Pappus, Manducus, etc. It seems incredible that a profession which took the names *histrio* 'masked ritual performer' and *artifex* 'artist' (~ τεχνίτης; see below) could have borrowed the plots, verse-form, and costume of the Greek tradition, but not its masks. Arguments against the Roman use of masks have sometimes been adduced on the basis of allusions to changes of expression in the scripts, e.g. the observation that someone is weeping or pale or blushing. These are of course valueless, since they occur also in Greek scripts; and anyway, who can blush at will? It is true that plays like *Menaechmi*, *Amphitruo*, and *Gemini Lenones*, all involving important parts for 'doubles', could be staged without masks, like *Twelfth*

[1] See Beare (1964) 184–95, 303–9.

Night or *The Comedy of Errors*. One must, however, wonder about the feasibility of an unmasked *Trigemini* (pseudo-Plautus) or *Quadrigemini* (Naevius).

Another sign of the influence of the Greek acting profession on the Roman is that the Romans adopted and characteristically adapted the idea of a 'Guild'. A decree of the Senate passed in 207 B.C. permitted actors and *scribae* 'writers', meaning playwrights and notaries, to belong to a conventicle which, like the Artists' organization, was nominally religious.[1] Actors and writers might meet (*consistere* ~ συνοδεύειν) and make offerings (*dona ponere* ~ δῶρα ἀνατιθέναι) in the temple of Minerva on the Aventine, in honour of Livius Andronicus, not as *poeta*, 'maker', because of his plays or his *Odyssey*, but because as *uates*, 'bard', he could be represented as having appeased Juno's anger by the composition and successful performance of a *carmen*, 'spell', for an expiatory rite. Luckily for Andronicus this took place not long before the Roman victory over the Carthaginians at the Metaurus. Roman actors and writers thus avoided association with Dionysus/Bacchus, whose cult was private and increasingly disreputable, and were associated with Minerva/Athene, the general goddess of the *artes*/τέχναι 'skills'; but since none of the festivals was in her special honour, the association was superficial and the secularization of the profession all but complete. Roman theatre-folk – actors, writers, and all – seem to have been known as *artifices scaenici* 'scenic artists', a partial loan-translation of the Greek appellation τεχνίτης Διονύσου. The association with Minerva was therefore to the logical Roman mind an obvious one.

It is unclear how this 'Athenaeum' on the Aventine related to the more successful 'Museum', the Templum Herculis Musarum founded in the 180s and associated with Ennius. Nor is the position of the *collegium poetarum*, the college of poets, fully clear. This body later at least met in the Templum Herculis Musarum, and is first mentioned as such in an anecdote set *c*. 90 B.C. (Val. Max. 3.7.11). By Terence's time there existed some formal procedure at the scrutiny and sale of plays by which hostile parties might be present and raise objections to another's offering on technical grounds (Ter. *Eun*. 19f.). What is certain is that in Rome the 'guild(s)' of actors and writers were never permitted to enjoy the degree of control and influence that the Greek Guilds exercised. That remained in the hands of the capitalist *impresari* and their clients, the nobility.

The form and verse of Roman drama

(i) *Speech, song, and recitative*. There were three modes of presentation in Greek tragedy. Iambic trimeters

– – ∪ –|∪– ∪ –|– – ∪–
ὦ κοινὸν αὐτάδελφον Ἰσμήνης κάρα

[1] Festus p. 466 L. On this, and the *collegium poetarum*, see Horsfall (1976) 79–95.

declaimed without musical accompaniment, were the normal medium for speeches, dialogue, and debates. Trochaic tetrameters catalectic[1]

— ◡ — | — — ◡ — | — — ◡ — | ◡ — ◡ —
ὦ τέκνον, χαῖρ'· ἡ γὰρ ἀρχὴ τοῦ λόγου πρέπουσά μοι

longer lines using the same diction and articulation as iambic trimeters,[2] were 'chanted' in some way to a musical ground, and indicated a rise in the emotional temperature. Lastly there was polymetric song, of two kinds. Choral odes were normally strophic in construction, i.e. written in pairs of 'stanzas' (strophe and antistrophe, 'turn' and 're-turn') which corresponded to the choreography of the dance. One also finds passages of polymetric lyric without strophic construction, a style used for highly emotional monodies, duets, and exchanges between a character and the chorus.

New Comedy was very different. The chorus no longer participated in the action, and there was virtually no lyric song. Only iambic trimeters, freer in structure than those of tragedy, and 'recitative' in trochaic and also iambic tetrameters catalectic, accompanied by the musician, were used. The rhythms and diction of tragedy and comedy were distinct, formal and elevated in tragedy, freer and more prosaic in comedy. In both, especially in comedy, spoken iambic trimeters were the norm.

The earliest Roman dramatists composed both light and serious plays, and they developed a dramatic form and medium for both which in some ways was a compromise between the two Greek styles, and in others was new. In comedy they dropped the chorus altogether; as its only function in New Comedy had been to mark the *entr'actes*, a consequence of this was to obscure the main aesthetic articulations, the 'acts', normally five. More than two-thirds of Plautus is divided between the equivalent of iambic trimeters (referred to in Latin as *senarii* 'sixers') and the equivalent of trochaic tetrameters catalectic (trochaic *septenarii* 'seveners'). The rest consists of iambic tetrameters and anapaests (if they are anapaests) written by the line, and lyric songs for up to four parts, which may be polymetric, or written by the line in cretic (– ◡ –) or bacchiac (◡ – –) tetrameters, or in a mixture. The analysis of these songs is still far from fully understood.[3] Everything except senarii was musically accompanied by the *tibicen*. This style of presentation involved three basic modes (like Greek Tragedy), which we may denote as *S* (= speech, the senarii),

[1] 'Cut short by one place.'

[2] Trochaic tetrameters catalectic may be analysed as iambic trimeters with a cretic element – ◡ – (bridged or unbridged) at the head: (*Sōcrătēs*) *bĕātŭs ĭllĕ quī prŏcŭl nĕgōtĭīs*..., cf. Marius Victorinus in *GLK* VI 131.17, Fraenkel (1928) 91. Whether or not it is historically justified, this analysis has the advantages that it works, and that it enables one to use the same terms to describe both metres.

[3] Leo (1897*a*), Lindsay (1922) 274–316, Drexler (1967) 67–78, MacCary and Willcock (1976) 219–32.

R (= 'recitative', the septenarii), and *O* (= 'Opera', i.e. all the other metres, including iambic septenarii and anapaests). It is immediately striking that Plautine comedy was more musical not only than its model, the prosaic New Comedy, but also than Greek tragedy; for the three styles of presentation are about equally represented overall, so that one cannot call any one of them the norm.

It is supposed that Plautus inherited this presentation from Andronicus and Naevius, who are presumed to have extended to comedy the tripartite manner natural enough for their versions of tragedy; and there are among their fragments lines which appear to be lyric.[1] But even so, there remain severe problems, for the techniques of metre and music established by the early dramatists correspond only very roughly to Greek practice. There is no sign of strophic construction either in Plautus or in Roman tragedy: the chorus of serious drama normally expressed itself in blocks of iambo-trochaic recitative, or in anapaests. This implies a quite different style of choreography. Again, the cretico-bacchiac tetrameters so important in Plautus and attested for Andronicus and Naevius have no obvious counterpart in the astrophic lyrics of Greek tragedy, while, on the other hand, the excited dochmiac rhythms of Greek monody and duet do not figure in Roman drama at all. What songs the Romans sang before Andronicus seems beyond conjecture, and we cannot even offer reasonable guesses as to how strange the early dramatists' music and quantitative polymetric lyrics sounded to audiences familiar with Saturnian verse and the cadences of the *tibicines* whose art was ultimately Etruscan.

Although the three styles are fairly evenly distributed overall in Plautus, the proportions vary greatly between plays. *Epidicus* oscillates between *O* and *R*, descending to *S* for only a fifth of the whole. The musician's stamina was a practical consideration. His first rest in *Epidicus* comes at l. 305. On the other hand *Poenulus* moves between *S* and *R* and there are only two complex *cantica mutatis modis* 'songs with altered modes'. The *Miles gloriosus* is written wholly in stichic verses, without polymetric songs. No linear pattern of development can be established either towards or away from a more musical style. The normal sequence, and indeed the main dramatic articulation, in Plautus is (*S*)*OR*(*S*)*OR*..., or *SRSR*... The modulations *SO*, *SR*, *RS* mark entries and exits; the transition *OR* is less dramatically important, and *OS* is very rare.

(ii) *Excursus on the nature and art of Latin quantitative verse* The most important metres were the iambo-trochaic.[2] In many ways these were direct imitations of general

[1] Andronicus (?), *TRF* 20–2 = *ROL* 20–2 (*Equos Troianus*), Naevius, *TRF* 5 = *ROL* 10f. (*Danae*), Fraenkel (1960) 327ff., 436, *RE* Suppl. VI 633. Andronicus, *CRF* 4f. = *ROL inc.* 4 *affatim edi bibi lusi* looks more like cretic than iambo-trochaic or Saturnian verse.

[2] General accounts: Lindsay (1922), Nougaret (1943, 1948), Raven (1965), Drexler (1967), Questa (1967). Greek iambo-trochaics: Maas and Lloyd-Jones (1962).

Greek practice. The quantitative principles of both will be examined below. The Romans used the same line-lengths as the Greeks and no others. At line-end a light syllable might do duty for a heavy (marked ⌢), and hiatus was permitted between lines even when there was enjambment. On the other hand the Romans also imitated (in time, with increasing strictness) the strange Greek convention by which elision or synaloepha was obligatory (at least on paper) even across punctuation and changes of speaker within the line. The same restrictions, purely metrical in character, applied in Latin as in Greek to pairs of light syllables occupying one place of the verse – they might not be split between independent words, nor be constituted by the final pair of a polysyllabic word. In other points Roman dramatic verse looks like a compromise between the more divergent styles of Greek tragedy and comedy. Menander was freer than Euripides, for example, with respect to enjambment and pairs of light syllables. Light and serious Latin dramatic verse is more uniform; it is more like Greek tragedy with respect to enjambment, and more like Greek comedy with respect to pairs of light syllables. Again, the jaunty iambic tetrameter catalectic was a species of verse which occurred in Greek comedy. Its Latin equivalent was also admitted in tragedy. This relative unity of verse-style is usually and plausibly attributed to the earliest dramatists, who developed both light and serious drama; and one might also attribute to them certain innovations in prosody which took account of un-Greek features of Latin pronunciation. In speech, a run of syllables ...⏑–⏋́...could be heard as...⏑⏑⏋́..., and this is reflected in versification. Thus *ăpū́d mē* (*me* unemphatic) 'at my house' scans as one would expect, but *ăpŭd mḗ* (*me* emphatic) 'at *my* house', does not; here the necessary conditions for so-called 'iambic shortening' apply.[1]

The Latin word-accent is involved in this merely secondary feature; it was also the key factor in a more radical difference between the Latin and Greek brands of iambo-trochaic verse. The minimal rhythmical characteristic which they shared was the predictable alternation of two kinds of place defined not, as in English, by the presence or absence of stress, but by the quantities of the syllables, light or heavy. The sequence of expectation was a segment from a series of places occupied by syllables conforming to the pattern '...never light, maybe light, never light, maybe light...'; iambic sequence began 'maybe light...', and trochaic 'never light...'. A light syllable has a short vowel and is open (*mă-rĕ*, *fă-cĕ-rĕ*) or closed by one consonant (*uĭr*); all others were heavy (*sphīnx*, *prāē*, *rēs*), including those like *uir* when placed before another syllable beginning with a consonant (*uīr-tūs*, *uīr bŏnŭs*). The marks – and ⏑ are thus used to denote both the length of vowels and the weights of syllables, and versification exploited such differences as there are between *lívĭd* and *límpĭd*, *béddĭng* and *béd-tīme*, words which having the same stress pattern may be interchanged in English metric.

[1] Lindsay (1922) 35ff., Drexler (1969), Allen (1973) 179–85, 191–9. 'Iambic shortening' and '*brevis brevians*' ('short (syllable) shortening (the next)') are misnomers for a sandhi-phenomenon which involves not only a preceding *brevis* but also a following word- or phrase-accent; not merely verse-ictus, which may or may not coincide with the accented syllable. Besides e.g. *uŏlŭptā̧tem* one may have *uọlŭptā́tēm* and *uŏlūptā́tẹm*. Even in an intentionally extreme case such as *ūxṓr mĕă mḗăqu(e) ămṓenĭtās, quīd tú ăgĭs?::ā́b(ĭ) ătqu(e) ā́bstĭnĕ mắnūm* (*Cas.* 229), where there are two successive examples, *ābstĭnē* becomes *ābstĭnĕ* not because of the second-last verse-ictus, but because of the last word-accent. The irregularity here is metrical not prosodical. A true dactyl (e.g. *ābstrăhĕ*) would have been equally ungainly, for a resolved place may not be occupied by the last syllables of a polysyllable. Substituting *ā́ufēr mắnūm* one normalizes the rhythm – and ruins the effect.

A light syllable counted as one 'time' (*mora*), a heavy as two. Hence a more positive formulation of the rhythm '...never light, maybe light...' would be 'two *morae*, one *or* two...'. In Latin the first kind of place ('never light' = two *morae*) was called the *arsis* 'rise', and the other ('maybe light' = one or two *morae*) the *thesis* 'fall', by a vocal metaphor;[1] for one might underline the quantitative opposition of these places by what the Roman grammarians called 'raising' and 'lowering' the voice at these places in recitation; in fact, they probably meant 'stressing' and 'relaxing' the voice. Another dynamic expression of the quantitative movement would be tapping the foot or a stick to mark the *arses*. It is important to note that either means of marking the 'beat', the ictus of a line, was extrinsic and adventitious, for it was not *necessary* to tap the foot or stress the voice to provide the rhythm. It is therefore strictly wrong to speak of 'ictus-places' in Latin verse, as if ictus were an essential component of the verse; that is to confuse the phenomenon, quantitative alternation, with its epiphenomenon, stressing or tapping. On the other hand, it is hardly less wrong to deny the existence of ictus altogether, for that is to deny that the phenomenon might have its secondary manifestation.[2]

This movement was shared in essence by Greek and Roman iambo-trochaic verse, but it was only one facet of the rhythm. The molecule of Greek verse was a sequence not of two but of four places, the metron (measure); it is only necessary to consider the iambic version ⏓–⏑–, the places of which we denote as A B C D, since the trochaic version (–⏑–⏓ B C D A) works the same. In tragic style the *arses*[3] B and D were occupied by heavy syllables *B* and *D* occasionally resolved as pairs of light syllables *bb* and *dd*. Taken by itself, then, – = ⏑⏑. More rarely, one finds *aa* for the usual *A* or *a* of the first *thesis*. Substitution of *cc* for *c* was a very rare licence permitted in proper names. Comic verse was much freer with these resolutions and substitutions, most strikingly in the case of *cc* for *c*, which is thoroughly current coin. In both genres, there was an essential double aspect to the rhythm with respect to the ear's expectation of true heavy and light syllables:

	A	B	C	D
		Tragedy		
Heavy?	maybe	mostly	never	mostly
Light?	maybe	never	always	never
		Comedy		
Heavy?	maybe	maybe	never	maybe
Light?	maybe	never	maybe	never

Thus there was, as it were, a left hand and a right to the movement, fully described only over recurring sequences of four places. The question arises, why, if the comic

[1] There are no accepted alternatives to these terms in English (German *Hebung* = French *temps fort* for *arsis* as defined, *Senkung* = *temps faible* for *thesis*); 'definite' 'indefinite' would serve well. Unfortunately the places where one might 'raise' the voice are also the places where one 'drops' the foot in tapping time, and vice versa; in Greek, it was in this exactly opposite sense that the terms *arsis* and *thesis* had been originally used. See Nougaret (1948) 7; Drexler (1967) 10; Allen (1973) 276–9, 431–6.

[2] Contrast, e.g., the lines taken by Drexler (1967) 9–11, and Questa (1967) xi–xii.

[3] We use the term in its usual Latin sense as defined above; cf. above, n. 1.

poets freely admitted *cc* for *c*, did they not also admit a true heavy syllable *C*? The reason is apparent from the pattern of expectation in comedy with respect to *true* heavy syllables which *in sequence* were not simply equated with pairs of light. If *C* were admitted, the pattern for heavies would have become 'maybe, maybe, maybe, maybe', which is not a rhythm at all; the only quantitative movement would have been the binary expectation of 'maybe, never' with respect to light syllables. This is exactly what Roman dramatists did, both in comedy and in tragedy.

This is a startling and apparently gratuitous discontinuity between Greek and Roman practice, not adequately explained by the observation (true in itself) that Latin is less rich than Greek in light syllables. The derogatory inference has been drawn that Andronicus, or whoever did legislate for Latin iambo-trochaic verse, did not understand the essential double movement of the Greek, and that the Latin version is essentially cruder than its model. This is a mistake. It is here that the Latin word-accent is crucially important. If one takes any number of similarly articulated Greek verses, e.g.

...οἰῳνὸν ⋮ ἕ̣θετο ⋮ κᾀ̣κέλε̣υσ' ἄλλο̣ν ⋮ νέο̣ν
κρατῆ̣ρα ⋮ πλη̣ροῦν· ⋮ τὰ̣ς δὲ πρὶ̣ν σπονδὰ̣ς ⋮ θεο̣ῦ
δίδῳσι ⋮ γα̣ίᾳ ⋮ πᾶ̣σί τ' ἐ̣κσπένδε̣ιν ⋮ λέγε̣ι...

(Euripides, *Ion* 1191–3)

it is apparent that they will not necessarily have similar patterns of word-accents. In fact, the Greek accent, which was of musical pitch, had nothing to do with the rhythm of the line at all. On the other hand, similarly constructed Latin lines necessarily share a single accentual pattern. We mark *arses* with a point below the line, and accents with an acute above:

⏓ –́ – –́ – –́ ⏑ – –́ – ⏑́ –
...exọrat, ạufert; dẹtulịt rectạ domụm... (Plautus, *Casina* 43)

– ⏑́ ⏑ – –́ – –́ ⏑ – ⏑́ ⏑ – ⏑́ ⌒
...non pọtero fẹrr(e) hoc, Pạrmenọ; periị misẹr...

(Terence, *Hecyra* 133)

– –́ – ⏑́ ⏑ – –́ ⏑ – –́ – ⏑́ –
...mi gnạt(e), ut uẹrear ẹloquị porcẹt pudọr...

(Pacuvius 67 R³ (*Atalanta*))

The reason is that in Latin the word-accent was strictly regressive (*rḗcta*, *dŏ́mum*) and in long words its place determined by the quantity of the second-last syllable; if heavy, it took the accent (*Parmenṓnem*); if light, the accent retreated to the third syllable (*Pármĕnō*) or in cases like *fắcĭnŏră*, *Phĭ́lŏlăchēs* to the fourth-last (cf. cápitalist). In very long words like *Pyrgopolynī́ces*, *índecorabĭ́lĭter* there is good reason to suppose that there was a secondary accent on the initial syllable; on the other hand, the case for believing that there was a secondary accent on the last syllables of words like *Pármeno*, *éloqui*, *détulit* is very weak.[1] In Greek the accent was not necessarily regressive, and other factors, grammatical and semantic, might determine its placing.

[1] Lindsay (1922) 56 n. 1, Enk (1953) 97. Drexler's theory (1932/3) of 'cretic accentuation' is based on circular argument.

It is immaterial whether the Latin accent was of stress, musical pitch, or both: its placing was a direct function of quantity, and therefore an audible expression of the arrangement of words in a line; if accents fell on *arses* (or their first elements if resolved), the essential sequence '. . . never light, maybe light, never light, maybe light. . .' was reinforced; if accents fell on *theses*, there was a contradiction. These opposed articulations are respectively represented by the first and second halves of the above lines. Too much of the first articulation would be motonous and flabby, as if the poet were apologizing for using a verse-medium at all; too much of the second would be artificial. It is on the blending of these two opposed articulations that an important aspect of the art of dramatic and indeed all Latin quantitative verse depends. The working hypothesis formulated by Bentley that 'Roman dramatists sought to reconcile ictus and accent as far as possible' is a mistaken inference from the fact that the first articulation is in the majority.[1] On the contrary, the second articulation is the salt to the meat, and attempts to explain away as many as possible of the apparent cases of clash as actual reflections of prose-pronunciation start from a false premiss; not but what there are many cases where a clash is only apparent and a linguistic explanation is right – as, for example, when enclitic particles are involved (*uirúm quidem*, like *uirúmque*).

The vital relationship between word-accentuation and quantitative progression is that the opposed articulations are subject to opposed prosodical treatments which emphasize their characters. In a sequence like *exọ́rat, ạ́ufert. . .*, the unaccented *theses* may be light, heavy, or double light (subject to the general rule given above, p. 87), as long as the *thesis* in question is next to an accented *arsis*. This is where Roman metric is fundamentally different from Greek. The freedom is extreme; the verse-form as such yields to the flow of the phrase, and the only quantitative pattern is '. . . maybe light, never light. . .', a binary movement quite properly analysed in 'feet'.

On the other hand, the treatment of *theses* was highly determined in sequences like *. . . dẹ́tulịt. . .*, where an unaccented final syllable falls in *arsis*, and like *. . . réctạ dómụm*, where in addition word-accents are falling in *theses*. To formulate the rule, is best to regard the senarius as a trimeter A B C D/A B C D/A B C D, since it applies over a sequence of four places: if an unaccented word-end falls in an *arsis* D, the cadence should run *. . . c D*, not *. . . cc D* nor *. . . C D*; conversely, if unaccented word-end falls in the last B-place, the cadence should run *. . . A B* or *. . . aa B*, not *. . . aB*. The latter principle, 'Luchs's law', is a mirror image of the first, and its effect is to impose a strongly quaternary quantitative rhythm at line-end, '. . . never light, never light, ⁝ always light, never light'. That is stricter even than in Greek tragedy. Luchs's law does not apply earlier in the line – so lines may begin *a B*/– but the other
a a B / c D A B / c D a B/
principle does. Hence lines may begin e.g. *lepido seni*. . . or *duro seni*. . . but not *seni*
c c D a B / C D
lepido or *seni duro*, unless an enclitic follows (e.g. *quidem*), in which case the word-accent is in harmony with the *arsis*, and we have moved into the 'free' articulation. The principle also applies strongly in the middle of the line; here, however, there is

[1] Bentley (1726) xvii–xviii, cf. Meyer (1886) 10–18. The hypothesis has been fundamental to virtually all Anglo-German study of early dramatic verse, notably Fraenkel (1928), Drexler (1932/3), and is still widely taken to be axiomatic (Allen (1973) 153f.).

a well-defined but unexplained exception: lines might run out with the rhythm . . . *plebeio piaculumst*, . . . *despiciunt Euripidem*, where a single word follows the irregularity without breathpause. This 'limping' effect was sometimes deliberately used to express emotions, as in Pamphilus' lines about his estranged wife:

> quae nụmquam quịcqu(am) ergạ-me cọmmeritạst, patẹr,
> quod nọll(em), et sạepe quọd uellẹm : meritạm sciọ;
> amọqu(e) et lạud(o) et uẹmentẹr : desịderọ.
>
> (Terence, *Hecyra* 488–90)

She never did anything to displease me, father, and I know that she often did things in order to please me – I love and praise and oh, so badly miss her.

This licence is so rare in Terence that two consecutive cases are certainly deliberate. Statistical tests show that combined with breathpause or change of speaker the licence is a strong departure from the norm, as in

> T. non dạt, non dẹbet. D. nọn debẹt? : T. ne frịt quidẹm.
>
> (Plautus, *Mostellaria* 595)

TRANIO *He's not paying, he owes nothing.*
MONEYLENDER *He owes* nothing*?*
TRANIO *Not a bean . . .*

To 'correct' this by reading *nọn dabịt* ('Won't he pay?') would be to throw away what is a deliberate dragged rhythm intended to mark the speaker's outrage (cf. Ter. *An.* 767 for a similar effect).

Roman dramatists established norms of rhythm for tragedy and comedy the parameters of which, as with the diction, overlapped; within the genres, individual playwrights had their own norms and idiosyncrasies,[1] the ground against which their departures and their irregularities are highlighted. These were delicate matters of more or less, i.e. of style; we must listen to Plautus, as he would say, *perpurigatis auribus*, with clean ears. By varying the rhythms between the poles of the harmonious free style and the dissonant strict style, and by exploiting the quite separate resource of resolution and contraction, a playwright could render a passage fast, slow, pleasant, ugly, monotonous, or surprising. Here is Pseudolus at the very moment of *Die Entführung aus dem Serail*:

[1] Clash of word-accent and verse-movement is distributed thus in the senarii of Plautus and Terence, with negligible mean deviations between plays:

	1st foot	2nd	3rd	4th	5th
Plautus	10%	3%	½%	15%	30%
Terence	10%	7%	½%	8%	25%

These figures denote a basic difference between Plautus' and Terence's styles.

nunc ịn metụ sum mạxumọ, triplicị modọ:
prim(um) ọmniụm i(am) hunc cọmparẹm metuọ meụm,
ne dẹserạt med ạtqu(e) ad họstis trạnseạt.
metu(o) ạutem, nẹ eru' rẹdeat ẹtiamd(um) ạ forọ,
ne cạpta prạeda cạpti prạedonẹs fuạnt;
qu(om) haec mẹtuo, mẹtuo n(e) ịll(e) huc Hạrpax ạduenạt,
priu' qu(am) hịnc hic Hạrpax ạbierịt cum mụlierẹ.

(Plautus, *Pseudolus* 1024ff.)

Now I am in the greatest fear, in a triple way; first of all I fear this accomplice of mine, lest he desert me and cross to the enemy; besides I fear lest Master be even now returning from the market; while I fear these things, I fear lest that [real] *Harpax comes here before this* [fake] *Harpax gets away from here* [Ballio's house] *with the girl.*

This bald version fails to bring out the rhythmical quality of the original. It is spoken verse, yet its movement could be the choreography of the stage-business. The first two and a half verses are written in the strict style, *tríplicị módọ*; the spaces separate the 'metra'. The tension of the verse suits the sense well. Then Plautus changes to the harmonious style (*ad họ́stis trạ́nseat*) without exploiting its freedom; the same quantitative pattern ––⏑– ends the third line. The next three and a half lines are in the harmonious style too (except as usual the line-ends); note how the heavy lugubrious line *nē cạ́ptā*... contrasts with the panicky resolutions of its neighbours. The coda of the passage *ạ́bĭĕrịt cūm mụ́lĭĕrē* returns to the strict style, this time with rapid resolutions. This is virtuoso writing; for much more off-hand Plautine stuff see p. 99; and for Terence, p. 124.

Andronicus is not named by any ancient source as *primus inventor* of Roman iambo-trochaic verse, and if he had a claim, it was forgotten or disputed by the first century B.C. (on the *carmen* attributed to Appius Claudius Caecus, see p. 138). The medium appears fully developed in Andronicus, and because of this, some modern scholars would posit a period of experimental development before 240 B.C.; they suppose, among other things, that one articulation of the trochaic septenarius, the *versus quadratus* ('square verse'), e.g.

uọs scelẹsti, uọs rapạces, uọs praedọnes:: pẹriimụs

(Plautus, *Menaechmi* 1015)

represents an ancient Italian metre, on the ground that in later days it was favoured in the popular songs sung at triumphs, and in children's ditties.[1] It is, however, hazardous to infer that the Fescennine verses and children's songs of the fourth century B.C. were not in Saturnians; and what was the subject matter of the 'experimental' verse,

[1] Immisch (1923) 29–34; Fraenkel (1927) 357–70; Drexler (1967) 29.

and who were its audience? The origin of the Roman brand of iambo-trochaic verse remains a mystery, but whoever did invent the form, and in particular the principles respecting word-accent and prosody, was a genius; for analogous principles were naturally followed in all other forms of quantitative verse borrowed from the Greeks. Perhaps we might understand the matter better if more were known of the Saturnian verse (see p. 57) and if we could trust Livy's allusion to a pre-dramatic '*satura*' (see pp. 160–2).

2. LIGHT DRAMA

Andronicus and Naevius

Volcacius Sedigitus did not even mention Andronicus in his list of the ten best (i.e. funniest) comic poets, but gave Naevius third place after Caecilius and Plautus, reversing their chronological order. Cicero did not think Andronicus' plays worth a second reading, and it was his fate even more in comedy than in tragedy to suffer invidious comparisons with his successors. Plautus was later supposed to have borrowed a good deal from Andronicus and there was a tradition that at *Eun.* 426 Terence was satirically quoting a line of Andronicus, *lepus tute es: pulpamentum quaeris?* 'You are a hare: are *you* looking for tasty meat?'[1] This has been compared with a favourite Plautine form of expression in which riddles (not, however, epigrams like this) are posed with a more or less bizarre identification followed by an explanation with no connecting or causal conjunction; e.g. *Pseud.* 747 'What when he's caught red-handed?' *anguillast: elabitur* 'He's an eel: he slips away'; *Mer.* 361 *musca est meus pater: nil potest eum clam haberi* 'My father is a fly: you can't keep anything private from him.'[2] The influence of Naevius on Plautus is very evident from the titles and the style of the fragments. If one early dramatist deserves the credit for establishing the form and stabilizing the diction of Roman comedy, it is he.[3] There is some suggestion that Plautus worked with him or revised some of his scripts.[4] Titles such as *Lampadio*, *Stalagmus*, *Stigmatias*, *Technicus* denote leading slaves; the titles of New Comedy very rarely denote a slave, and hardly ever name him. It seems that Naevius, not Plautus, was responsible for the promotion in Roman comedy of the clever slave. On the other hand plays called *Testicularia*, *Apella*, *Triphallus*/*Tribacelus* imply a more bawdy approach than we find either in New Comedy or Plautus. Naevius freely renamed the plays which he adapted, and added material involving Italian allusions or dramatic ideas suggested more or less specifically by other Greek plays. Plautus followed Naevius in these points and we may draw

[1] Wright (1974) 24–7.

[2] Fraenkel (1960) 35ff.

[3] Wright (1974) 33–85.

[4] *Carbonaria*, *Colax*, *Fretum*, *Nervolaria* are titles rightly or wrongly assigned to both; cf. Ter. *Eun.* 25.

the important inference that they did not invite or expect their audiences to enquire after the originals or measure excellence in terms of fidelity either to the letter or the spirit. The allusions in one fragment to Praeneste and Roman diet (*Ariolus*, *CRF* 22–6) have been taken to show that Naevius invented the *togata* ('Toga-play') on domestic Italian themes;[1] he certainly invented the *praetexta* ('Hem'- or 'Robe-play'), the genre in which Roman themes, ancient and modern, were presented in the form and style of the *fabula crepidata* ('Buskin-play'), as representations of Greek tragedy were known in later times. However, it is at least as likely that the *Ariolus* was a *fabula palliata* ('Cloak-play') representing New Comedy, and that Naevius was already exploiting the essential ambiguity of the genre, that apparent Greeks in a domestic setting should speak orotund and zestful Latin verse, to create a Graeco-Roman setting. This too is a central feature of Plautine comedy. Naevius had a reputation among scholiasts for political outspokenness. He was supposed to have got into trouble with the Metelli by naming them in an ironic line on the stage, but whether others of his extant fragments should be related to this seems questionable.[2]

Contemporary allusions in Plautus are for the historian frustratingly elusive. Nevertheless, it would be wrong to regard his plays as wholly unpolitical; he was simply more careful than Naevius (cf. p. 162). He is supposed to have died in 184 B.C., an inference from the absence of later dated production-records. It is possible that Plautus was one of those who attracted the censor Cato's attention in that year of moral correction. The *Poenulus* of 188/7 B.C., though a slap-dash piece of work, is remarkable for its liberal and cosmopolitan premisses. The lover is a Carthaginian by birth and an Aetolian by adoption; thus he represents the two states most detested and least trusted by contemporary Romans. Yet he is portrayed sympathetically like any other Plautine lover. It is as if a play dealing sympathetically with the Germans *and* Japanese had been staged in Britain in the early fifties. The title-figure, the 'poor Carthaginian' Hanno, is presented with a bizarre mixture of traits, now those of a *senex lepidus*, a gay old dog, now of a *servus callidus*, a crafty slave, and now of one who displays the very virtues of an Aeneas – steadfastness and piety. The portrayal is wholly (if disparately) sympathetic, and there is no trace of xenophobia, although the play was certainly produced within Hannibal's lifetime (d. 183 B.C.). It is difficult to imagine a supporter of Cato's financing this play as aedile; that Plautus should even have envisaged its successful production tells us something of his authority in the theatre and of the openmindedness of his audience.

[1] Leo (1913) 92.

[2] Jocelyn (1969) 32–47; Wright (1974) 33f., 56f.

Plautus

(i) *The authenticity of the plays.* Plautus is represented by the twenty-one so-called *Fabulae Varronianae*; our manuscripts descend from a collected edition assembled *c.* A.D. 100.[1] It is as if a distant posterity were to know Shakespeare from copies made from a folio edition compiled from available acting scripts of the various plays in the 1920s. *Vidularia*, the last, is all but lost, and others have more or less serious gaps (*Cistellaria*, *Amphitruo*, *Bacchides*, *Aulularia*). Some plays were available only in revival-scripts (*Casina*) or incompatible versions (*Poenulus*) or drastically cut (*Curculio*).[2] Any signs used by the editors to clarify the status of interpolations, alternative versions, and dislocations have been lost. The plays are divided into scenes and present a dilettante mixture of archaic and 'modern' spelling. The act-divisions in modern editions derive from mistaken inferences by Renaissance scholars from Horace's prescription at *A.P.* 189f.; the same applies to Terence. The manuscripts in which Plautus became known to the Renaissance and from which he was first printed partly neglected the line-division; hence an academic justification for prose as a medium in Italian and Elizabethan comedy. No canon of Plautus' works existed in or near his own time. In the 160s B.C. Terence could at least plausibly allege that he had not known that a certain play had been 'turned' by Plautus (*Eun.* 25–34), and a generation later Accius even denied the Plautine origin of another comedy which Terence had thought genuine (*Ad.* 7, Gell. 3.3.9). Accius' contemporary Aelius Stilo reckoned only twenty-five scripts authentic out of some 130 going under Plautus' name (Gell. 3.3.11). The so-called *fabulae Varronianae* are the twenty-one which Varro grouped as authentic 'by everyone's agreement' (Gell. 3.3.3), i.e. the plays which no one had impugned, and it is virtually certain that these are the twenty-one which our MSS preserve. The plays which really deserve the title *Varronianae* are those which had been suspected by such as Accius and Stilo but which Varro judged Plautine on stylistic grounds, apparently another nineteen (see Appendix).

In view of the precarious nature of the transmission, doubts might be entertained as to the unity of the corpus and the quality of the text. Statistical analysis shows, however, that we have the work of one hand, and that under the circumstances it is remarkably well preserved. Features such as the normal distribution of clash of ictus and accent or the details of prosody, e.g. the treatment of final *-s* after a short vowel before an initial consonant, reveal distinctive internal regularities. Criteria like these are valuable, because they are unnoticed by the listener or reader and are subconsciously determined by the writer;

[1] Leo (1912) 1ff., right in essentials against Lindsay (1904).

[2] See Leo's note on *Cur.* 454 in his edition.

hence they are more reliable than the features of surface style recognized by Varro and used by him for the vindication of disputed plays. Mythological identifications, typical nonce-formations, characteristic turns of phrase (cf. p. 103), etc., are precisely those features which a careful reader will notice, and which any competent imitator or forger would reproduce.

(ii) *Plautus and his models*. Plautus does not care whether we know the name of an original or its author; we may be told either, neither, or both, and only in one case (*Alazon* 'Big talker' = (*Miles*) *gloriosus*) is it certain that the information comes from the original script. Only one or two have translation-titles (*Mercator* = *Emporos* 'Merchant') and most are disguised. Five have *-aria* titles, on a Naevian pattern. Three are named after leading slaves against New Comedy practice: thus Epidicus, Pseudolus, Stichus are implicitly given the status of an Ajax or Agamemnon. Several titles are jocosely misleading or even perverse. *Truculentus* 'Grumpy' has nothing to do with the famous *Dyskolos* of Menander; *Trinummus* 'Threepence' is a *Thesauros* 'Treasure'. The titles of Menander, Philemon, and Diphilus fall into well-defined categories which Plautus following Naevius plays with and explodes. Evidently the plays are to stand in their own right. An important corollary for us is that knowledge of the originals as such is irrelevant to the evaluation of Plautus, for he did not expect it in his spectators; or rather, it would be, if we knew more about the precise circumstances and presentation of Plautine comedy. As it is, we have hardly any first-hand information, and the scholiastic tradition as regards historical matters is the narrowest and feeblest attaching to any ancient dramatist. In the circumstances we cannot afford to ignore the archaeology of the plays. By looking into Plautus' workshop we may illuminate his assessment of his audience's taste and discover terms appropriate for his dramatic criticism. For a most disconcerting aspect of Plautus' drama is that instead of trying to reproduce or emulate the special features of the New Comedy – economical and internally consistent plot-construction, subtle characterization, irony, pathos – he utterly subverts them. This is so pervasive and marked that it cannot be regarded as mere negligence, but as the assertion of a comic style quite alien to the naturalism of a Menander or a Terence and the consequent European tradition of the Comedy of Manners.

Three plays are known for certain to be based on Menander (*Cistellaria* 'The casket comedy' = *Synaristosai* 'Ladies at lunch', *Stichus* 'Sketch' = first *Adelphoi* 'Brothers', *Bacchides* 'The Bacchis girls' = *Dis exapaton* 'The double deceiver'). Two are from Philemon (*Mercator* = *Emporos*; *Trinummus* = *Thesauros*) and three from Diphilus (*Rudens* 'The rope'; *Casina* 'Passion-flower' = *Kleroumenoi* 'The lot-takers'; *Vidularia* 'The hamper comedy' = *Schedia* 'The raft' (?)). One is from Alexis (*Poenulus* 'The poor

Carthaginian' = *Karchedonios* 'The Carthaginian') and another from the otherwise unknown Demophilus (*Asinaria* 'The ass comedy' = *Onagos* 'The muleteer'). Plautus' taste in authors centred on the three who dominated the Artists' repertoire, but was evidently catholic. These plays have a uniform surface-style in which wildly hyperbolical comparisons, nonce-formations, bizarre identifications, asyndetic riddles, military imagery, jokes exploiting formulae and concepts of Roman law, and mythological comparisons are prominent.[1] None of these is particularly characteristic of any New Comedy writer, nor of Terence, and it is rightly inferred that they are specially Plautine traits, though one would like to know how markedly Plautus differed here from Naevius. The plots of all Plautus' plays are distorted considerably by the re-casting of their musical and metrical form and by the running together of act-divisions of the originals; this allowed, the two Philemon plays preserve their plots relatively intact. Other plays like this are *Aulularia* 'The jar comedy' (possibly from Menander), *Captivi* 'Prisoners', and *Menaechmi* (from unknown authors). It is significant that Cicero actually quotes only from *Aulularia* (once) and *Trinummus* (several times), that *Menaechmi* was particularly popular in the Renaissance, and that Lessing thought so highly of the *Captivi* that he called it the best play ever written. In these cases Plautus happens to have kept well-wrought New Comedy plots more or less intact, and the dramatic critic familiar with the theory of comedy as a 'mirror of life' has therefore felt more at home with these plays than with others. Plautus is sometimes praised for the characterization of Euclio in *Aulularia* and for having preserved the well-oiled plot of the *Menaechmi*. This praise is in fact misplaced, for his adjustments of the Euclio-figure were such as to simplify and categorize a complex character, and in the *Menaechmi* he has gone out of his way to upset the formal balance of the original. These plays, which are not necessarily to be associated in date,[2] perhaps represent a treatment of plot more characteristic of Caecilius Statius, whom Varro praises for his *argumenta*, but whom nonetheless Gellius found very wanting by Menandrian standards (Gell. 2.23).

Plautus is usually more actively disruptive. The *Stichus* (from Menander; 200 B.C.) begins with a delicate musical vignette depicting two sisters whose father wishes to have them divorced from their absent husbands. The spectator is invited to expect a complex and various family-drama, and that no doubt was the main theme of the original. He might two or three years earlier have seen the *Cistellaria* (also from Menander), which began with a technically similar operatic tableau for female characters. Plautus was already fully himself in the *Cistellaria*; the story-line was prominent, though stretched here, telescoped

[1] A comprehensive account of Plautine style in English remains a *desideratum*. See Lejay (1925), Haffter (1935), Fraenkel (1960), Wright (1974).

[2] Among dating-studies Schutter's (1952) is the best.

there, and lopped at the end. In *Stichus* Plautus all but discards the main action of the *Adelphoi*, and the play turns into a balletic *satura* of joyous home-coming – the Punic War was not long over – in which the opposed fortunes of the resident parasite and of the below-stairs characters amount to a theme, hardly a plot. In *Casina* (from Diphilus; after 186 B.C.) Plautus has cut the return of the young lover, the recognition of Casina, and their betrothal (*Cas.* 65). Papyri published in the late nineteen fifties and sixties provided important direct evidence, previously all but lacking, of the great freedom with which Plautus treated the plots of his models. An extensive fragment of Menander's *Dis exapaton* shows that Plautus has cut a scene of this, the original of his *Bacchides*, and has re-cast dramaturgy radically at an act-break of the original, though not without trace.[1] In the *Poenulus* (from Alexis; 189–187 B.C.) Plautus has seriously distorted the dramatic structure of the original (*Karchedonios*) both by episodic expansions (e.g. 330–409) and more importantly by the insertion of a 'second trick' (1086–110; see below). Terence appeals to the example of Naevius, Plautus, and Ennius when defending himself for making alien additions which are not merely episodic in character (Ter. *An.* 15ff.), and he adds to his version of Menander's second *Adelphoi* a scene of Diphilus' *Synapothneskontes* 'Partners in death' which, he says, Plautus had left out in his version of that play (Ter. *Ad.* 9f.). Another addition of a scene containing a dramatic idea, gravely distorting the structure as a whole, occurs in *Miles gloriosus*.[2] It used to be maintained, on a partial and imperfect statement of the problems of these plays, that here and elsewhere Plautus had taken all or most of two Greek originals, and joined them end to beginning. There is no external evidence for this method of composition, and the internal evidence alone, if correctly stated, proves that it was not used in these two cases, which Leo regarded as certain.[3] As an illustration of Plautus' workmanship, and incidentally of his less flamboyant style, it will be convenient to look in more detail at the case of the *Poenulus*.

The central peculiarity of this play is that it contains two tricks which cause it to fall into unsatisfactory halves. The first three acts are devoted to a deception which is sufficiently comprehensive to put the procurer Lycus in a very difficult position. He has been successfully 'framed' thanks to the slave Milphio's wiles, so that Milphio's master Agorastocles can threaten Lycus: 'Either you allow me access to my beloved Adelphasium, or I shall prosecute you for theft; you will be condemned to pay me compensation so huge that all your property, including the girls, will be mine.' The threat is less immediate than Plautus makes out, since 'today' is a holiday and the courts will only be open 'tomorrow', but Plautus, magnifying Milphio, puts no emphasis on this

[1] See Handley (1968), Gaiser (1970) 51–87, Questa (1970) 183–228, Wright (1974) 138–41, Arnott (1975) 38–41.

[2] G. W. Williams (1958) 79–105.

[3] Leo (1912) 170.

(Alexis may have). Lycus' response is adequate for the moment – he absconds (795). Only after this do Milphio and then Agorastocles discover that Adelphasium, and her sister Anterastilis, are freeborn Carthaginians (iv.1, v.2 *init.*). By a cleverly economical stroke, the girls' father Hanno is introduced just as they are discussing the implications of the news (v.1–2). Plautus makes out that it provides a separate way of attacking Lycus: simply prosecute him. The Plautine law provides that whether Lycus is acting in good faith or not, the proof that the girls are *ingenuae*, freeborn, will ensure their release, and that since Lycus knows the truth, he will be punished (963ff., cf. 905ff., 919; 1226ff., 1344ff., 1391ff., 1402). Later on (1086ff.) Hanno is invited by Milphio to pretend that he is their father and prosecute Lycus; this is simply an elaborate means of establishing that Hanno really is the girls' father:

MIL. Nunc hoc consilium capio et hanc fabricam apparo,
ut te allegemus, filias dicas tuas
surruptasque esse paruolas Carthagine,
manu liberali causa ambas adseras,
quasi filiae tuae sint. iamne intellegis?
HAN. Intellego hercle. nam mi item gnatae duae
cum nutrice una sunt surruptae paruolae.
MIL. Lepide hercle adsimulas iam in principio: id mihi placet.
HAN. Pol magis quam uellem. MIL. eu hercle mortalem malum,
⟨senem⟩ catum crudumque, Aeolidam subdolum!
ut adflet, quo illud gestu faciat facilius!
me quoque dolis iam superat architectinem!

MIL. (*Self-importantly*) *Now I commend this counsel and I provide you this patent device: that we commission you to say that they are your daughters kidnapped as children at Carthage, and that you lay hands on both of them in a suit for liberty. Do you get it yet?*
HAN. *Indeed I do: my two daughters were kidnapped just like that along with their nurse when they were children.*
MIL. *That's good acting right at the start! I like it!*
HAN. *More than I would wish.*
MIL. *Aha, here's a crafty cove, a tough old trickster, a shifty Sisyphus! Tears to order, to make his performance the more effective! He even beats me the master-builder in deceit!*

Reflection will show that Plautus' legal assumption cannot possibly have been made in Alexis' original; hence this episode cannot have figured at all. The scene is Calydon, the girls are Carthaginian, Lycus did not kidnap them, he bought them long ago from their abductor in Anactorium. Alexis went out of his way to arrange a situation in which precisely the absence of adequate international law was an important theme. The girls are not even Greeks – they are Hellenized barbarians. The law can provide no redress. The best that the slave might suggest at the place equivalent to 964 in the original would be not 'assert their rights at law', but simply 'seize them'. For it was the dramatic, not the legal situation, that was changed in Alexis. Agorastocles is now required by a well-known convention of New Comedy to marry his beloved, not simply have her as his concubine; that implies finding her family – and, ironically, Father has just arrived and is listening. Secondly, and more urgently, it is now vital to prevent either of the girls from returning to Lycus' house. Earlier in the play we saw them depart for the festival of Venus at which they are to dedicate themselves before beginning their professions as *meretrices*. At the festival an unpleasant soldier has seen and taken a fancy to the younger Anterastilis; he is now in Lycus' house waiting for her to return, and he is an immediate threat to her chastity. As long as Agorastocles and Milphio had thought that the girls were mere slaves, this had not mattered; the truth has changed that. This is the organic reason for the soldier's role in Alexis' play: Plautus' adjustments incidentally render the soldier all but irrelevant.

The dénouement which Alexis had in mind seems clear. First, a recognition-scene between Hanno and Agorastocles; next, as in Plautus, the return of the daughters; then, the emergence and pacification of the disgruntled soldier; finally, the return of Lycus, who capitulates not simply because Father has come offering a ransom, still less threatening a lawsuit, but in virtue of the threat posed by the first trick. This is a well-balanced and unitary action, and its emotional interest lies precisely in the absence of any simple legal remedy. There is no room for the proposal of a second trick such as Plautus includes as an elaboration of the recognition and which will only work on premisses which ruin the point of Alexis' play.

On this view, the whole episode in which the 'second trick' occurs must be a Plautine addition, substituting for and expanding on a very brief transition by Hanno to the subject of his daughters after the recognition of Agorastocles: 'What were you saying just now about two Carthaginian girls who have been kidnapped? How old are they? Have they a nurse?' The passage in question is 1086–1110, and examination shows that it presents a number of dramatic and dramaturgic flaws. Most strikingly, Agorastocles has nothing to say or do from 1086 on, and is only brought back at 1136, with what in the circumstances is an ineptly surprised question. In the closely-knit recognition which ends at 1085, Agorastocles has been an excited protagonist: Plautus has simply omitted him in his insertion, the purpose of which is to enhance the dwindling role of Milphio. This alone is insupportable as homogeneous dramatic composition. Next the transitions to and from the inserted episode are abrupt and illogical. The change of subject at 1085/6 from Hanno's liberality and Agorastocles' inheritance to Milphio's 'clever idea' is arbitrary; at 1110/11, Hanno has not been told that the supposititious Carthaginian girls have a nurse, and therefore cannot logically ask about her. Thirdly, Milphio's brief explanation of the dramatic situation (1090ff.) is unsatisfactory: he ought to mention that Lycus had at least been put on the defensive. In fact, the relationships, situation, and language which he uses are calqued straight from the prologue and earlier lines of the play; Plautus is thus guilty of a dramatic anachronism: Milphio's description is out of date. Lastly, by describing the girls to Hanno as *meretrices seruolae* (1094) 'working girls', rather than as *Carthaginienses ingenuae*, 'freeborn Carthaginians', as would now be natural, Milphio makes it seem to Hanno that not only is he to pretend to be their father, but also that it is a fiction that the girls are Carthaginian at all.

The dramatic objection to any second trick in the play, its particular legal absurdity, Agorastocles' abrupt disappearance, and the other technical faults mentioned are characteristic of Plautus' neglect of realism. His intentions were to make his Milphio another Epidicus or Pseudolus, and to present Hanno in his readiness to participate (1086ff.) as a 'crafty Carthaginian'. It is significant that he does not balk at seriously distorting the plot of his original in the attempt, and that 'craftiness' is essentially incompatible with what in the original was undoubtedly a wholly serious and high-minded presentation of the alien.

In the opinion of the present writer, the source of Plautus' insertion was a passage of Menander's *Sikyonioi* 'The Sicyonians' known to us from papyrus fragments first published in 1964. Plautus certainly knew this famous play: he borrowed its hero's name Stratophanes and used it for the soldier in his *Truculentus*, a play produced about the same time as *Poenulus* (189–187 B.C.). It is therefore unreasonable to suppose that the episode in question occurred in other plays and that one of these, and not the *Sikyonioi*, provided the model. In any case, we are not dealing with a simple *locus communis*, like the entrance motif of the soldier who sees his beloved embraced by a brother or father and mistakes the situation (e.g. Menander, *Perikeiromene init.*, *Misoumenos* 208ff., *Poen.* 1280ff.) but with a very specific dramatic situation which (as Plautus shows) cannot easily be transplanted – daughter and faithful retainer taken long ago by pirates; ignoble but well-meant proposal of a legal deception to establish the girl's identity;[1] misinterpretation, praise, tears. Here, then, we have the first documentary example of the kind of 'contaminatio' which Terence practised and which he attributed to Plautus (see above, p. 95):

ΚΙΧ. οὐκ εἰς τὸν ὄλεθρον – ΘΗΡ. χαλεπὸς ἦσθα.
ΚΙΣ. – ἀποφθερεῖ
ἀπ' ἐμοῦ; Κιχησίαν σὺ τοιοῦθ' ὑπέλαβες
ἔργον ποήσειν ἢ λαβεῖν ἂν παρά τινος
ἀργύριον ἀδίκου πράγματος; ΘΗΡ. †Κιχησίαν

[1] In the *Sikyonioi* this makes sense, because it is a question *in Attica* of the rights of an Athenian.

Σκαμβωνίδην γενόμενος† εὖ γὰρ ὑπέλαβες·
τούτου με πρᾶξαι μισθὸν αὐτοῦ, μηκέτι
ὧν ἔλεγον ἄρτι. ΚΙΧ. τοῦ τίνος; ΘΗΡ. Κιχησίας
Σκαμβωνίδης γε πολὺ σὺ βέλτιον λέγεις·
ποεῖν τι φαίνει τὸν τύπον τοῦ πράγματος.
οὗτος γενοῦ· καὶ σιμὸς εἶ γὰρ ἀπὸ τύχης
καὶ μικρός, οἷον ἔλεγεν ὁ θεράπων τότε,
γέρων. ΚΙΧ. ὅς εἰμι γέγονα. ΘΗΡ. πρόσθες, θυγάτριον
Ἁλῆθεν ἀπολέσας ἑαυτοῦ τετραετὲς
Δρόμωνά τ' οἰκέτην. ΚΙΧ. ἀπολέσας; ΘΗΡ. εὖ πάνυ·
ἁρπασθὲν ὑπὸ λῃστῶν. ΚΙΧ. ἀνέμνησας πάθους
τὸν ἄθλιόν με καὶ φθορᾶς οἰκτρᾶς ἐμοί·
ΘΗΡ. ἄριστα. τοῦτον διαφύλαττε τὸν τρόπον
τό τ' ἐπιδακρύειν. ἀγαθὸς ἄνθρωπος σφόδρα.

(Menander, *Sikyonioi* 343–60)

KICHESIAS *To hell with you –*

THERON *(Good!) You're being awkward!*

KICHESIAS *– Damn you! Do you imagine that Kichesias would do such a thing or would take money from anyone for a wicked act?*

THERON *Yes – You've got Kichesias of Skambonidai exactly! Charge me money for just that, not for what I was saying just now.*

KICHESIAS *For what?*

THERON *As Kichesias of Skambonidai you're speaking much better. You seem to have got the hang of the matter. Be that man; for as it happens you are a snub-nosed little old fellow just as the servant said that time.*

KICHESIAS *I am the person I was born.*

THERON *Add 'who lost his four year old daughter and Dromon the servant at Halae'.*

KICHESIAS *Lost?*

THERON *Very good – 'kidnapped by pirates'?*

KICHESIAS *You remind me in my sorrow of my tragedy and a spoliation piteous for me.*

THERON *Excellent! Keep that style going and the accompanying tears. The fellow's really very good!*

There are hardly any verbal echoes in Plautus' version (*adflere* ~ ἐπιδακρύειν; *lepide hercle adsimulas* ~ εὖ πάνυ; *intellegere* ~ νοεῖν τι...); even when turning iambic trimeters into senarii, Plautus seems to work from memory and from the occasional glance at his model rather than from close scrutiny. Menander's old gentleman has been offered money (unlike Hanno, who is implausibly slave-like in his willingness to participate in a good wheeze, 1086ff.): part of his supposed 'acting' is his outrage at the very suggestion. Plautus drops this, as well as the subtle change to tragic tones when Kichesias breaks down (ἀνέμνησας... ἐμοί). The passages of *Bacchides* which correspond to trimeters of the *Dis exapaton* have been inflated into trochaic septenarii with much verbal fol-de-rol: this passage by contrast is in Plautus' most off-hand style, and yet the verse obtrudes as verse far more than in Menander. It is end-stopped, and Menander's excited chopping of phrases (which makes the division of parts uncertain) has been simplified. Yet even in this bald style there are characteristically Plautine touches absent in Menander. Alliteration marks Milphio's self-importance (1099) and admiration. Menander's ἄριστα... σφόδρα (359f.) becomes a triadic phrase (*eu hercle... Aeolidam subdolum*) which (if the emendation *Aeolidam* be accepted)[1] involves a typical Plautine mythological identification: *fabrica* and *architectinem* are metaphors from a favourite Plautine stock; *superare aliquem* is a characteristic Plautine turn of phrase in exaggerated comparisons.

The view of the *Poenulus* sketched above is new. Even if it is wrong, it has (besides economy) two virtues as an *exemplum*. If Menander, *Sik*. 343ff. is not the model which Plautus had in mind at this point, something very like it was, and characteristic Plautine traits are still well shown by the comparison. Again, the arguments used above are a good example of the kind of diagnostic analysis which we have described (p. 96) as the 'archaeology' of Plautus' plays. This is an intricate matter, and concentrates on traits and clues in Plautus' text which the audience is not invited or expected to notice. For that very reason, this approach must not be thought itself to be dramatic criticism of Plautus, yet it is often mistaken for it. While such analysis is itself of interest for the history of New Comedy, it is for Plautus only an indispensable preliminary to dramatic criticism, an indirect method, which, since we cannot intuitively share the values and assumptions of Plautus' audience, helps to define what Plautus thought important. It is, for example, startling to discover that he values imbroglio and deception for its own sake *so* much more than plot-structure, realistic dialogue and characterization. His plays are in an evidently only very attenuated sense 'translations': many critics from Gellius on have felt that a Menander should not be used thus, and condemned this approach to comedy. Plautus is not even trying to capture Menandrian qualities: he positively rejects them, and therefore cannot be any good. But the comparison of chalk and cheese is not profitable. Where then is the grace and charm of Plautine comedy, if any? It lies in quite different aspects of his drama, to which we now turn.

(iii) *Character and presentation.* Plautus has as strong an aversion from the central repertoire of *persona*-names of New Comedy as from their titles.

[1] A new suggestion for the corrupt *crudumque est ollidum* of the MSS; *crudumq· ęolidam* would have been mistaken for *crudumq··e·olidam* (*·e· = est*, *ę = ae*, *q· = que*). The allusion is to 'Sisyphos Aiolides, who was the most crafty of men' (*Iliad* 6.153), and specifically the type of the *aged* trickster (see Roscher *s.n.*) as opposed to Odysseus/Ulysses, himself an Aeolid. Hence support for Leo's *senem* at the line-beginning, where there is a separate corruption.

Chrysalus sings

non mihi isti placent Parmenones Syri
qui duas aut tris minas auferunt eris (*Bacchides* 649f.)

I do not like your Parmenoes and Syruses who steal (a mere) two or three minae *from their masters.*

In the *Dis exapaton*, Chrysalus was himself a Syros. Plautus only rarely kept a name, e.g. Lydus in the same play. His stage-population are given individual names varying in formation from the possible but unattested (Agorastocles) to the absurd (Pyrgopolynices). Only very few are borrowed from New Comedy. The young man Charinus and old men Callicles, Demipho, Charmides, Simo are allowed to appear in two plays each, but that is the extent of Plautine duplication. Some others known in New Comedy appear once each,[1] but most are kept at bay, down the street, in the house, in the past, in imaginary lists (e.g. Davus, Dromo, Chaerea). Most, however, do not receive even that ghostly tribute (Gorgias, Sostratos, Pythias, etc.). Plautus plays many games in naming his *personae*. The aged Laches of New Comedy makes his only appearance as the second element of the young man's name Philolaches. The Menaechmi twins are named after the mathematician of Syracuse (*fl.* 350 B.C.) who had evolved a method for duplicating regular solids by conic sections; the cook is called Cylindrus. Characters whose names end in *-io* (Acanthio, Ballio, Milphio, Olympio, etc.) and *-lus* (Toxilus, Chrysalus, Dordalus, etc.) are slaves or otherwise disreputable: the patterns seem to be Scipio and Attalus.

Most of Plautus' audience will have had only a vague second- or third-hand acquaintance with New Comedy practice as to names, and for them the more striking contrast will have been with the Atellane farce in which the names of the stock-characters were fixed. By giving his characters individual names, Plautus was drawing a sharp line between the extempore farce and his own entertainments with their fixed scripts and complex musical structure. For us, the contrast with New Comedy practice is the more obvious, and we, who are used to the idea (then new) that a dramatist might invent all his characters' names, might draw the conclusion that the pimps Ballio, Dordalus, Lycus, Labrax, and Cappadox for example are intended to be individual characters each with special traits of his own. This would be wrong. For all the apparent individuation by names quirky and fantastical, the same Atellane-type troupe in fact appears in every play. It is a mistake to look for individual characterization in Plautus, or to regret its absence. At the same time, we must not leave the matter there, for aspects of what we mean by characterization are the very essence of Plautine comedy.

[1] Bacchis, Cario, Lydus, Myrrina, Philaenium, Sosia, Strobilus, Stratophanes; not many among about 150 named inhabitants of Plautinopolis.

Characterization is not a category in its own right. It is a function of five others: the plot, the typology, the musical and metrical form, the diction and the dramatic illusion. In New Comedy, a dramatist began with the germ of a dramatic idea; this involved certain roles. The action, as it was worked out in greater detail, determined which of the traditional stock of named masks – the *dramatis personae* 'masks of the action' – would be suitable; Daos, Laches, Myrrina, etc. It was the same in tragedy, and it is in this context that one should understand Aristotle's assertion of the primacy of the 'story' over 'character' (Arist. *Poetics* 1450a20–2). In proceeding thus New Comedy playwrights were like Goldoni writing for masked Italian *commedia* types rather than, say, Jonson or Molière, whose typology was derived not from appearance, the outer shell, but from a theory of humours, the categories of inner disposition. A playwright might commission a special new mask for a particular purpose, for example the grumpy Knemon of *Dyskolos* or the Carthaginian Himilkon of *Karchedonios*, both Menandrian inventions; these might be used by someone else, and, if popular, join the 'stock'. Essentially, however, New Comedy writers began with a plot and selected the necessary chessmen for their game from a simple typology based on appearance, age, and class as denoted by the named masks. Daos appears in at least eight of sixteen better-known Menander-plays. No doubt he looked the same in each and the Athenian audience knew who he was without being told and how he differed in physiognomy from his fellow-slaves Parmenon, Getas, and Tibeios. This, however, did *not* determine his ethos, at least in the hands of a master like Menander. In one play he is deftly sketched and has a tiny role; in another he is drawn more fully and carefully, and quite differently as a 'character'. So the old bottles might be filled with different wines. The importance of plot and typology of the masked drama being defined thus, the other factors, diction, metrical form, and dramatic illusion were developed in New Comedy to sustain a quiet and relatively prosaic naturalism. This was essential for the subtle and realistic depiction of ordinary contemporaries, the 'mirroring of life' which came to be seen as characteristic of the genre, and towards which Terence sought to bring the reluctant form of comedy as inherited from Plautus and Caecilius.

Plautus' approach to characterization will be understood best if we review in turn the five aspects of the term as defined above. First, as to plot. He did not approach his task like a Menander or his own Pseudolus, who, 'like a poet when he has opened his notebook seeks for what is not, yet finds it' (*Pseud.* 401ff.). The plot is given, and is not the real substance of his plays. He cuts, stretches, squashes, and amplifies. Dramaturgically, all Plautus' plays are far simpler than the early yet complex and finely-handled *Dyskolos* of Menander. The comings and goings have been simplified, and with them, the action. The motive for alteration and expansion is generally Plautus' desire to amplify the farcical aspects of the play at the expense of the pathetic, and in particular to increase in volume and apparent importance the role of the leading slave and of his deception. The plays of known derivation are fairly characteristic of the *œuvre* as a whole in this respect. Love is the *primum mobile*, but not married love; a *Hecyra* would not have attracted Plautus as a model. The lover is represented sympathetically, but farcically; the pathos of his frustration or dejection as depicted by a Menander or Theocritus is shunned entirely. If he loves a *meretrix*, she is a delightful gold-digger; if she returns his affection or is a virgin in distress, money must be had by deceiving Father or a wicked *leno* or *lena* who has richer clients in mind. The slave is promoted to be master-builder or general in devising and administering a trick to outwit the blocking character. If the girl is a wronged citizen, the young man does not know this at first; her separation from her family is explained by themes of exposure or kidnapping, and after the recognition – only sometimes played 'straight' for pathos – she will be betrothed to her lover. Plautus is less fond than Terence of sub-plots and exploration of the relationship of father and son except in its farcical aspect when they are rivals in love; but the ludicrous lust of the *senex amans* never prospers, for Mother finds out and produces her rolling-pin. Thus the same broad themes of love, misapprehension, and deception are as central in Plautus as in New Comedy. Comparison of Plautus with Terence and New Comedy, however, show that a very imperfect impression of the themes, tone, variety, and emphases of New Comedy would be had from Plautine comedy alone. He seeks farce, promotes deception, simplifies relationships, categorizes themes, and is not interested in ethos, social commentary, or the exploration of motives. In adjusting a plot he does not mind loose ends, dramatic anachronism, implausibilities, or minor obscurities, and sometimes he omits the expository prologue even in a recognition play (*Epidicus*, *Curculio*). The plot is treated as an excuse, not as an end in itself. We turn now to the typology.

Plautus simplifies ethos drastically according to the doctrines of a comic catechism, an absurd catalogue of appropriate behaviour. The central members of the troupe are the *adulescens amans* and his clever slave, most characteristically represented in *Bacchides*, *Epidicus*, *Miles gloriosus*, *Mostellaria*, *Pseudolus*, and (less successfully) *Poenulus*. The slave is unswervingly loyal to his master, though his own definition of the love of *meretrices* is *damnum merum* 'a dead loss'.[1] The volume and apparent importance of his deception are much inflated. He is *doctus* 'clever', *astutus* 'sophisticated', *malus* 'bad', *nequam* 'good for nothing', and is given to self-glorification, arrogating to himself the status and rights of a citizen, reversing roles with his betters and giving the orders, and, as master-builder and military expert, comparing his

[1] E.g. *Cur.* 49, *Poen.* 199, *Men.* 133 (where the lover is speaking with the slave's voice: see below, p. 107).

exploits and strategy with those of kings and epic heroes.[1] The slave is the most internally consistent of Plautus' types, and he has the power to address the audience confidentially without disrupting the dramatic illusion. He is at once a member of the audience and of the cast, the director of the action, and the intermediary between us and the more exotic characters. There is, as it were, no actor behind the mask of the slave.

By contrast the lover is the most schizophrenic of Plautus' characters. His ruling humour as lover is *immodestia*, a lack of a sense of proportion (cf., e.g., *Bac.* 612ff.), and *in propria persona* he will dither, rush, express without warning extravagantly incoherent joy or zestfully indulge in a show of despair (Charinus, *Mer.*), speak impiously of his parents or the gods (Calidorus, *Pseud.*) and beat his slave for no offence (Agorastocles, *Poen.*). The reason is that he is in love, a self-sufficient excuse for anything, for love is represented not as Plato's divine madness but plain if amiable lunacy. The sentiment expressed at Plautus, *Mil.* 1252 and *Poen.* 140f. is a travesty of the generous idea reproduced from Menander by Terence at *Eun.* 880f. The nearest that the lover comes to reflection and ratiocination are the immensely prolix and exuberant arias at *Most.* 84ff. and *Trin.* 223ff.; pathos is entirely avoided.[2] The soliloquy of Mnesilochus at *Bac.* 500–25 is characteristic. This represents two speeches of Sostratos in *Dis exapaton*, one before, the other after an interview with his father which Plautus has dropped in his version (*Dis exapaton* 18ff., 89ff. Sandbach). Sostratos is represented as suffering a turmoil of emotions – disappointment in his friend and bitterness towards the *hetaira*; he is of course mistaken on both points. The tone and means of expression are exactly those of Catullus. He uses short phrases and colloquial language; he turns from apostrophe through reflection to self-address, and at the end of his second speech he is inclined to blame the girl rather than his apparently faithless friend. In all these points one is reminded of Demeas' fine speech at Menander, *Samia* 325–56, elements of which Plautus absurdly echoes at *Asin.* 140ff. (cf. *Sam.* 326, 377ff., 390f.). The actual verbal echoes of Menander in Mnesilochus' speech are minimal, as in Caecilius' operatic version of a father's entrance-speech from Menander's *Plokion.*[3] Mnesilochus begins *in propria persona* as if he were to propound a thesis, 'Which is my worse enemy, he or she?', to be worked out in the manner of Hamlet's 'To be or not to be...?' In fact, he decides at once that the girl is to blame, and forgets all about his friend. In what follows (503ff.) we are not listening to a sad lover – there is no such thing in Plautus – but rather to a *servus* addressed as an *amans* who cracks jokes which being in the first person defeat expectation; put in the third person, they are simply the Plautine slave's

[1] Fraenkel (1960) 223–41 and *passim.*

[2] Menandrian lovers also fail to know what is appropriate, but the gentle humour of, e.g., Men. *Dysk.* 52ff., 76ff. is different from anything in Plautus – or Terence.

[3] Gell. 2.23; G.W. Williams (1968) 363–6, Wright (1974) 120–6, Traina (1970) 41–53.

axioms about love and lovers' behaviour. This is the other aspect of the lover's personality: the Plautine lover is ever and again presented as really being a Plautine slave *ornatus*, dressed up, and saying those things which he and we agree in this comic world to be ineptly appropriate for lovers to say. Thus there is a certain depth to Plautus' typology: behind the mask of the *amans* there is not simply an actor, but another *servus callidus*. In this way the domination of the stage by the *servus callidus* is rendered even more extreme than it appears; for *non iucundum est nisi amans facit stulte* 'it isn't funny unless the lover acts stupidly' as the lover Calidorus says (*Pseud.* 238). When *servus* and *amans* merge again (*Bac.* 513), it is to express offended pride in a long, weighty sentence; but no pain or regret with respect to the friend Pistoclerus. That is reserved for a long and sententious intrusion of *flosculi* on the nature of friendship which has no counterpart in the swift and laconically eloquent encounter of the two friends in Menander. It could not have been inferred from the Plautine text that this sententiousness had no direct equivalent in Menander, a salutary proof that Plautus can 'look Greek' even in his own embroidery.

Fathers in Plautus are *anxii* rather than *duri* – Caecilius' harsh fathers were famous (Cic. *Cael.* 16.37) – and their comic office is not willingly to part with a penny. Father is no pantaloon: he is a formidable opponent for the slave. The *senex amans*, on the other hand, a Plautine favourite,[1] is a buffoon in whom both aspects of the young lover appear. The *senex lepidus* has escaped marriage and is Epicurean in outlook, without the parasite's selfishness and greed. For him to love is *facere sapienter* 'do act wisely', the counterpart of the normal idea that it is *facere stulte* 'to act foolishly': and he honours Plautus' favourite deities, Venus and Pietas.[2] The *leno* is extravagantly villainous and mercenary. His task is perfidy, his one aim in life is *lucrum*, profit, and he takes pleasure in telling us so.[3] By implicitly exploiting aspects and features of Roman law Plautus makes him more wicked than perhaps intended by the Greek dramatists. For example in the *Pseudolus*, Ballio is represented as breaking a solemn Roman contract (*sponsio*) in accepting a higher offer for his girl from a rival; in Greek custom it was open to a vendor to accept a higher bid even when a deposit had been paid.[4] Most notably in the *Poenulus*, but also in the *Rudens*, *Curculio*, and *Persa* Plautus implies that a *leno* is breaking the law merely by owning girls whom he knows to be 'freeborn' without specification of the girls' origin. Greek dramatists took care to arrange things so that a former citizeness of

[1] *Asinaria*, *Bacchides*, *Casina*, *Mercator*, *Amphitruo* – a quarter of the *corpus* – have *senes amantes*.

[2] *facere sapienter*, *Amph.* 289. *Poen.* 1092, inverting the usual definition (Publilius Syrus A 15, 22 *amare et sapere uix deo conceditur*). The sympathy (*Mil.* 638), piety (675, 736f.), and liberality of Periplecomenus are the opposites of the *leno*'s qualities (contrast, e.g., *Poen.* 449ff., 746ff. with the passages cited).

[3] E.g. *Pseud.* 264ff., *Poen.* 746ff., *Rud.* 727, *Persa* 689f.

[4] G. W. Williams (1956) 424–55.

City One is, through exposure or kidnapping, in the power of a *leno* in City Two which has no reciprocal arrangement regarding civil rights with One, precisely to prevent the mere demonstration of the truth about the girl's origin from seeming sufficient to ensure her release and her owner's punishment. Like the *amans*, whose arch-enemy he is without the need of detailed motivation, the *leno* sometimes appears to be a character who is being acted by another *servus callidus*, so zestful is his self-incrimination. You cannot really blame him, it is his job to be like that (e.g. *Pers.* 479, 688; *Pseud.* 351–77; *Rud.* 1343ff.). The hungry parasite is the most explicitly Italian of all the types. The most specifically Italian allusions occur in parasite scenes,[1] not only in respect of food;[2] his language and imagery are gaudy;[3] he is an accomplished rhetorician, but he takes no interest in the *res publica*,[4] for all that he may expound his way of life as a philosophy or an honourable ancestral profession.[5] If he is faithless to his patron, his outrageous parody of self-sufficiency leads from initial complacency to frustration and rejection. Technically he is a free man, but is in fact the spiritual slave, the very opposite of the loyal *servus callidus*. For this reason, we rarely hear the voice of the slave-commentator from behind the parasite's mask, his narrow-spirited dedication to food matches that of the *leno* to profit, and he is consequently an ambiguous figure. The helpful parasite Curculio is an important exception: here Plautus has invested the role with the gusto of a Pseudolus or a Pyrgopolynices. The flattering parasite (*colax*) is represented in Plautus only by Artotrogus in the *Miles gloriosus* (*init.*), and, fleetingly, in scenes where other characters don and doff the role as part of Plautus' play with the typology.[6] The professional soldier (Greek, not a Roman) is presented as vainglorious, selfish, and deluded; it is remarkable that Menander's military characters seem to have been presented in a far less formulaic way.[7] Females in Plautus are 'other' and their psychology as women does not interest him. Apart from Alcumena, presented powerfully as a tragic

[1] E.g. *Cap.* 90 (*porta Trigemina*), 158ff. and 877ff. (Italian towns), 489 (*Velabrum*), 492ff. (cf. *Stich.* 193f.) (*mores barbari*), 790ff. (cf. *Cur.* 280ff.) (praetorian edict).

[2] E.g. *Cap.* 818, 847, 901ff., *Men.* 208ff. (the words are the parasite's), *Cur.* 323ff. On butchers and pork-cuts in Plautus, almost absent from the gourmet-lists of fish-dishes and sweet confections of New Comedy, see Fraenkel (1960) 109, 124f., 141, 408–13.

[3] Bizarre imagery: *Cap.* 153 (*edendi exercitus*), 187 *calceatis dentibus* 'teeth with boots on'; Latin puns: *Cur.* 316 (*uentum*), *Persa* 103 (*Essurio*); mixed metaphors: *Cur.* 318 ('teeth full of rheum, blind jaws'), *Cap.* 109 ('inebriated with repletion'), cf. *Boeotia* fr. 1.9 ('parched with starvation'); prosopopoeia: *Cur.* 338ff., *Cap.* 479ff., *Stich.* 185ff., *Mil.* 61–5; rhythmical effects: *Cap.* 309f.; sub-Stoic paradoxes: *Men.* 95.

[4] *Men.* 451ff., *Persa* 75ff.

[5] *Cap.* 69ff., *Men.* 79ff., *Persa* 53ff., *Stich.* 155ff.; Leo (1906) 441–6.

[6] E.g. Mercury (*Amph.* 515ff.), the *aduocati* in *Poen.*, Romans in disguise.

[7] Pyrgopolynices (*Mil.*), Stratophanes (*Tru.*), Cleomachus (*Bac.*), 'Antamoenides' (*Poen.*), Therapontigonus (*Cur.*), Harpax (*Pseud.*) are all treated with the same brush; in boasting of their prowess, they remind one of the *servi gloriosi*. Plautine soldiers are Macedonians, not Romans; see Shipp (1955) 193–52.

heroine in *Amphitruo*, the *matrona* in her housewifely setting is kept behind doors as much as possible, and appears only in plays where her husband is unfaithful (*Men.*, *Asin.*, *Cas.*) and is severely restricted in her musical presentation. The *virgo* is the opposite of the *amans*, being self-consistent, *modesta*, and given to *docta dicta.*[1] The *meretrix* is exotic, extravagant, and amoral rather than immoral. She is presented as the intellectual equal of the clever slave, being *docta*, *astuta*, *callida*, *faceta*, *mala*, *nequam*, and taking the same detached view of love as he. He never aims his tricks at her, and she sometimes helps or herself sustains deceptions (*Mil.*, *Tru.*).

When Plautus had to deal with complex characters in his models, he thought in terms of this simple Atellane-style typology, and mixed traits which are strikingly incompatible by Menander's or Terence's standards. Hanno in the *Poenulus* is perhaps the most extreme case, in whom are the violently disparate elements of *pater pius*, *senex lepidus*, and *servus callidus*. In the same play Adelphasium is dressed as a *meretrix* but is in fact a *virgo*; in her first appearance, the mere fact that she is dressed as a *meretrix* is exploited by Plautus in his episodic expansion of the scene to allow her to behave as a *meretrix*, even though this is incompatible with her role as a whole and involves contradictions and loose ends.[2] Euclio in *Aulularia*, Therapontigonus in *Curculio*, Truculentus in his eponymous play, and many others have had their roles simplified in this way. A character will sometimes explicitly adopt another's characteristic role, e.g. Mercury's inept imitation of the *parasitus* at *Amph.* 515ff.

So much for Plautus' treatment of plot and typology. As we have seen (pp. 85f.) there is a particularly violent contrast between the musical and metrical forms of New Comedy and Plautus. Each of the three modes, speech, recitative, and opera affects the presentation of character. The scale of time and space in the spoken parts (iambic senarii) is closest to the audience's real world. Addresses 'on the doorstep', remarks 'aside', and meetings here are usually reasonably brief; but even in this mode Plautus happily offends against plausibility when telescoping acts (*Cist.* 630/1, *Men.* 880/1) or recasting the dramaturgy (*Poen.* 707ff.) or preparing an episodic insertion (*Poen.* 975ff.). The worlds of recitative (trochaic septenarii) and of song (all the other metres) are much more spacious and elastic. A character on stage will fail to notice a lengthy canticum sung by someone entering (*Bac.* 925ff., *Men.* 966ff.). Running slaves deliver long harangues out of all proportion to the size of the stage.[3]

[1] *Persa* 336–89, *Poen.* 284–312.

[2] *Poen.* 210–329 is integral to the action of the play and based on an episode of the original, but the sequel 330–409 is formless Plautine farce intended to promote Milphio's role. Fraenkel (1960) 253ff. wrongly regarded the whole of 210–409 as lifted from another play.

[3] *Bac.* 832 *tris unos passus* implies a stage about fifty feet wide, if we assume three doors and symmetrical arrangement. Vitruvius, the size of theatres of the imperial era, and the lengths of many harangues by running slaves are misleading evidence.

Ballio's entrance in *Pseudolus* is a memorable expansion of a brief doorstep address, introducing the Roman idea that it is his birthday and presents must be given him (*Pseud.* 133ff.). The imbalance of *Men.* 110ff. and 466ff., 603ff. and 700ff. is due to the different musical presentations. Plautus likes to spin out that split second when two people notice each other,[1] and keeps surprising the audience with his variations of musical form.

Female characters (played by boys) are given highly operatic parts in proportion to their charms: the Bacchis sisters, Palaestra and Ampelisca (*Rudens*), Adelphasium and Anterastilis (*Poenulus*), and others such never merely speak senarii. When women do, e.g. the girl in *Persa*, it is because the mode has been established for the scene by an unsympathetic male character. *Matrona* in *Menaechmi* is a significant exception: she has the initiative at 559ff. and 701ff., but she chooses senarii, a formal hint that we are not to feel too sorry for her. The flowery language of Phoenicium's letter (*Pseud.* 46ff.) in senarii is, as it were, a canticum in reported speech. Conversely, villains like Cappadox (*Cur.*) and Lycus (*Poen.*) or unsympathetic characters like the tutor Lydus in *Bacchides* live in the worlds of senarii and septenarii. It is part of Ballio's outrageous charm in *Pseudolus* that, very unconventionally for a *leno*, he bursts on us in song at his first entrance. Even he spends most of his time in the more prosaic modes. Pivotal characters, the lovers and their slaves, are equally at home in all three modes, e.g. Pseudolus and Calidorus, Tranio and Philolaches (*Mostellaria*). It is important that the mere reader be careful to allow for bold, unpredictable changes of mood and pace which are an expression of the musical structure. The plot is not only distorted by truncations and additions, there is a certain variable geometry of space, time, and mood, a more than Elizabethan variety of tone. In *Poen.* iii.3 we may almost be persuaded that we are eavesdropping on an internally stylized but self-consistent representation of a street-scene; there is no question of that in v.4 of the same play, where we are assaulted by a kaleidoscopic mixture of the most varied emotions and impressionistic presentation. The metrical presentation of a *persona* is thus not an insignificant element of his characterization and is a major aspect of the dramatic experience.

Plautine diction, the fourth aspect of characterization, is not intended to sustain the prosaic realism of a Menander. In canticum and recitative Plautus was normally embroidering and filling out trimeters in the prolix and alliterative manner evident at *Bac.* 496–500 ~ *Dis exapaton* 11–16. Even his senarii are by comparison with Menander's trimeters emphatically a verse-diction, not a mere analogue for prose. Here he is like Naevius. End-stopping is the norm; the movement and weight of the verse are elements of the meaning;

[1] *Bac.* 534ff. (contrast *Dis exapaton* 101), *Amph.* 292ff. (recitative); *Persa* 13ff. (canticum); *Poen.* 975ff. (senarii).

obsolescent forms are artificially exploited at line-end to facilitate scansion (e.g. *siem* = *sim*, *laudarier* = *laudari*). Word-order and syntax however relate directly to contemporary speech, so that, e.g., hyperbaton is significant when it occurs. Contrary to a common opinion, Plautus' language is not in any sense vulgar. In vocabulary, for example, *lumbi* 'bottom' occurs, but not *culus* 'arse', and words like *fabulari* which disappear from polite diction after Terence but survive in Romance (> Fr. *faibler*, Sp. *hablar*) were stylistically neutral in Plautus. Greek borrowings and 'neat' Greek are admitted, the latter (like obscene jokes) only just enough to make one wonder why there is not more; this Greek is sub-literary Doric and is attributed almost exclusively to the lower orders.[1] Here is an example of the internal social differentiation of the stage-language, and it is a question that would reward investigation whether the greater variety of Plautine syntax relative to the classical language is also to some extent socially determined.[2] Plautus was quite capable of writing well-sustained complex sentences (e.g. *Amph.* 1ff., the longest in Plautus[3]) and could affect an almost Terentian telegraphic style (*Mer.* 562ff., *Trin.* 1078ff.); normally, however, when he wishes to express emotion in any of his modes, he does so not by those means which would convey the impression of real life overheard, for example, studied brevity, broken utterance, and baldness of expression, but rather a bludgeoning prolixity, exuberance of imagery, verbal inventiveness, bizarre identifications, and elevation of the tone to that of tragic discourse; borrowing elements of archaic and public diction, with festoons of alliteration and assonance. Lastly, Plautine diction is characterized by its great variety of resources. Any one of these, e.g. the use of riddle-jokes, of legal terms and ideas, of particular diminutive or adverb formations, etc., will be found by itself to be less common overall than anticipated. Terence's three main alterations of the inherited stage-diction were to loosen the movement of the verse, to reduce but not eliminate the aural exuberances of a Plautus, and to exploit a smaller number of resources but with greater internal variety and absolute frequency.

The last and most remarkable feature of Plautine comedy bearing on the question of characterization is its setting and dramatic illusion. There was no point in inviting a Roman audience to 'imagine that this is Phyle in Attica', as Menander's Pan (*Dysk.* 1ff.); the evocations would be lost. Plautus' plays are nominally set in 'Athens', 'Epidamnus', even 'Aetolia', but in fact we are always in the same *ciuitas graecoromana*, a universal city as large as the civilized world, the contemporary *oecumene*. Celts, Scyths, and Spaniards are

[1] Shipp (1953) 105–12, (1955) 139–52. For example *Pseud.* 483ff. ναὶ γάρ is a combination of affirmative particles never found in written Greek, and a word like *thermipolium* 'bistro, café' is borrowed from a Greek word which no doubt existed in southern Italy, but is unrecorded in literature.

[2] Arnott (1972) 58–64 broaches the question of linguistic characterization in Plautus.

[3] A parody of the *exordium* of a magistrate's speech, cf. Cic. *Pro Murena init.*

mentioned as outsiders, but the inhabitants of Plautinopolis have never heard of Rome and Italy, only of *barbari* and *barbaria*. Romans are mentioned explicitly only once in a passage of vigorous Plautine quality but of doubtful authenticity, a jokingly uncomplimentary allusion (*Poen.* 1314), as are all veiled allusions to sections of the audience.[1] There is no praise or celebration of the city as was traditional in Attic comedy. The stage-city is remarkably objective and cosmopolitan. The caricature of a Greek sketched by Curculio (280ff.) is not at all chauvinistic, and characteristically the humour is that a *persona* dressed as a *Graecus palliatus* is made to deliver a parody of a praetorian edict against *Graeci palliati*. We have alluded (p. 94) to the remarkably sympathetic treatment of Carthage and Aetolia in *Poenulus*; Aetolians are again treated with sympathy in *Captivi*.

The dramatic time is the present, and the place is an ambiguous 'here'. Plautus does not mechanically reproduce unintelligible allusions from his models, or simply keep situations which depend on alien assumptions, customs or laws. Either he explains them (*Cas.* 68ff., *Stich.* 446ff.), or, more commonly, he assimilates and adjusts the material to Italian usage. Thus Ballio is supposed to be celebrating his birthday in *Pseudolus*; his demand for gifts gives the opportunity for the famous tableau i.2. But the giving of presents on annual birthdays was a Roman, not a Greek custom. Exotic Greek pastries such as abound in Athenaeus' citations of New Comedy are supplemented and supplanted by Italian hams and pork-cuts. First-cousin marriages do not appear in Plautus or Terence at all, yet marriages of this degree of kin were commonplace in upper-class Athenian society and therefore in New Comedy. Plautus implicitly exploits concepts and formulae of Roman law in jokes of all kinds[2] and sometimes he exploits Roman legal assumptions which may distort the plot of his model (*Poen.*, *Pseud.*). Plautus inflates the Roman law to fill his comic city so that it is a basic rule that a manumitted slave is supposed to become a citizen of 'Athens' by virtue of the manumission. That is Roman law disguised.[3] Plautus similarly represents 'freeborn' persons held as slaves in this city as having an absolute legal right to freedom, if they have been kidnapped; this too is inflation of the Roman law, and thus by accident, for the first time in history, freedom and free birth are represented as legal absolutes which need not be defined in terms of the citizenship of this or that city. As the first popular

[1] Often marked by *iste* and/or *ubi sunt...?*, cf. Fraenkel (1960) 136ff.

[2] For example, slaves claim a pedigree (*Amph.* 365), the right of *quiritatio* (*Amph.* 375), of making sacrifice (*Pseud.* 108), of owning property (*Pseud.* 108, cf. Ter. *H.T.* 86, Cic. *Rep.* 2.59, *Att.* 9.6.3 for the amusing anticlimax), of mancipation (*Men.* 1077), of making *sponsiones* (*Pseud.* 114–18). They and others pun (*Mil.* 611), joke (*Trin.* 267 – the divorce formula, applied to Love), and develop conceits (*Tru.* 141ff., *Trin.* 1037ff.) in ways that show Plautus' audiences were well acquainted with quite technical aspects of the law. See Watson (1971) *passim*.

[3] *Persa* 474ff., *Poen.* 372, where the promise that Adelphasium will become a *ciuis Attica atque libera* is merely a fancy way of saying that on manumission she will be a *ciuis libertina*.

writer to represent the idea of free birth as a practically enforcible legal universal, Plautus deserves a modest note in the history of ideas in the immediately post-Eratosthenic world. These uses of Roman assumption, custom, and law are means by which Plautus focuses his plays in the *hic et nunc* of his audience. On the other hand he avoids identifying the scene too explicitly as the *real* Rome, except in prologues and *entr'actes*. We are not to think of his *ciuitas* as fluctuating between Greek and Italian poles. It is homogeneous. A festival takes place in honour of Venus, but its occasion is not the native Vinalia but exotic Aphrodisia. *Praetores*, *comitia*, *senatus* may be mentioned alongside *dicae*, *agoranomi*, *strategi* because in contemporary usage they also denoted Greek institutions as well as Roman; not, however, consuls, censors, quaestors, flamens or the like. There are contemporary allusions in Plautus, probably more than we can detect, for those that can be grasped are always fleeting (*Cas.* 980), indirect (*Tru.* 75), and even deliberately garbled (*Men.* 407–12, *Poen.* 663–5).

The plot, typology, musical presentation, diction, and dramatic illusion of Plautine comedy are designed to subvert the regularities and realism of New Comedy. The real substance of Plautine drama is the 'play' which he constantly maintains with us as to whether we are unseen observers of real life or not. Many a scene, especially in senarii, is set up to invite us to suppose a Menandrian or Terentian mode of presentation, in which a glass wall separates us from the characters, who act, suffer, and discuss as if we were not there. Plautus delights in breaking this illusion in different ways. Here the characteristic presentation of lover, slave, and *leno* are important. Besides straightforward ruptures of the dramatic illusion there are confidential asides from characters who acknowledge our presence but seem to think we are Greeks (*Poen.* 597–9, contrast *Cur.* 288ff.). Plautus' most salient characteristic is his variety, an un-Hellenic trait picked up and sustained in satire. This is so marked that it should not be seen merely as a failure of Terentian art, but as a positive principle, alien to what was to become the main European tradition. Plautus deliberately commits all those errors which Hamlet condemns in bad actors.[1]

Hamlet's theory of comedy as a 'mirror of life' with paradigmatic value can be traced through Gellius, Quintilian, Horace, Cicero, and Terence to the practice of Menander, of whom Aristophanes of Byzantium, Plautus' contemporary, wrote 'O Menander and Life, which of you imitated the other?' The theory is implicit in the Hellenistic tags which call the *Odyssey* a fine mirror of human life and liken the *Iliad* to a tragedy, the *Odyssey* to a comedy. Plautus was not unaware of the view that comedy might have an educational as well as an entertaining function. At the end of the uniquely womanless *Captivi* he sententiously recommends the play to the audience on the ground that 'poets make few comedies like this, by which the good become better'.

[1] Shakespeare, *Hamlet* III ii *init.*

He lists several objectionable themes and *loci* which are absent from the play: the joke is that these are the normal material of his *œuvre* at large. The irony here and Plautus' disruptive treatment of New Comedy show that he put no weight on the alleged educational value of comedy: and if he needed an academic justification, he might have quoted Eratosthenes' view that the end of poetry was not moral improvement but the involvement of the audience in the entertainment.[1] From Plato's time we find in discussions of imaginative or fictional art the loaded terms ψεῦδος 'lie' and ἀπάτη 'deceit' which can imply that the artist's task is to trick or deceive his audience. Plautus might be said to apply this in a new way. The plots of his plays are not to be seen as coherent wholes, but as series of episodes of unpredictably various pace, mode, and tone and ambiguous presentation. His characters are not intended to deceive us uniformly into imagining that they are real or credible. There is a constant 'play' between the author and his audience on this point. The characters – or is it the actors? – know that we know that they are not real. As double and triple deceivers, they take pleasure in pretending to be what they seem, ever and again catching us out by reminding us that they are not, but never quite frankly admitting in the course of the action that they are really Romans like you and me.

Caecilius Statius

Caecilius (d. 168 B.C.) dominated the comic theatre between the ages of Plautus and Terence. His first efforts, perhaps put on around 190 B.C., had been failures, but success came through the support and persistence of L. Ambivius Turpio, who proudly recalls this when speaking on behalf of Terence's *Hecyra*. Caecilius was also a friend of Ennius, and these two playwrights were the first to benefit from the activities of literary scholars: there was no doubt about the number and authenticity of their productions; earlier playwrights, especially Plautus, were less fortunate. The scripts of Caecilius and Ennius soon found a place in the school syllabus; Cicero assumes that his jurors and correspondents have read them as well as seen them on the stage (cf. *Opt. gen. orat.* 6.18).

Volcacius Sedigitus (*c.* 100 B.C.) counted Caecilius as the funniest Roman playwright; yet he is also praised for his *grauitas*, moral earnestness (Hor. *Epist.* 2.1.59), his emotional power (Varro *ap.* Charis. in *GLK* I 241.28), and the quality of his plots (Varro, *Sat.* 399). Cicero criticizes his Latinity (*Att.* 7.3.10, *Brut.* 258); Gellius compares several passages of his *Plocium* with the corresponding passages of Menander in an important and carefully thought out essay (*N.A.* 2.23), much to Caecilius' discredit. The fragments are too brief to enable us to recognize, let alone to reconcile, the various points for which Caecilius is praised; and they are certainly not characteristic of the *Plocium*-

[1] Pfeiffer (1968) 166f.

fragments. These are thoroughly Plautine. A Menandrian monologue has been converted into a farcical canticum, while other exchanges quoted by Gellius have been vulgarized with jokes that recall the tone of Plautus' *Asinaria*. Unfortunately we have no means of knowing whether the *Plocium* was an early or late work, or whether it is representative, or whether and in what directions Caecilius' style developed over the years. Nevertheless, and with all due caution, one can point to a number of features of his work taken as a whole which suggest an intermediary position between Plautus and Terence, not only in time, but also in technique.

At least a third of his output – probably upwards of fifty plays in about twenty-five years – represents Menander. The titles of his plays fall more easily into the well-defined categories of New Comedy than Naevius' or Plautus'; most are simply the Greek title retained, or simply Latinized. Terence, Turpilius, and others followed this example. It is an aesthetically significant change, for it implies the identity of the Latin play and its model, and invites comparisons of the kind made by Gellius in a way avoided by Plautus. The slave appears to have been demoted from the prominent status with which Plautus and Naevius had endowed him. None of the plays is named after him (*Davos* is a corrupt title). Caecilius also gave up Plautus' freedom in naming his characters and apparently kept exclusively to the main stock names of New Comedy. While in most points, e.g. word-formation and articulation of the verse, Caecilius is like his seniors, he favours the line-cadence ... ⏑⏑ ⏑ ⏓ significantly more often than they. In these points he anticipates Terentian traits. Terence omits Caecilius' name when he appeals to others' example to defend his own interference with the dramatic structure of a model (*An.* 18), but it would he hazardous to combine this with Varro's praise of Caecilian plots, or the trimmed role of the slave, to infer that Caecilius kept specially close to his models. To judge from the fragments in general, even the late Caecilius can have contributed little to the revolution in style represented by Terence's *Andria*, which, according to a dubious story, was read and approved by the aged Caecilius.

This revolution was abortive. The old, full-blooded style represented by Caecilius was at least as influential as Terence's in the work of Sextus Turpilius, the last important writer of *palliatae*, and in the *togatae* of Afranius; and this exuberant style was still the only one favoured in the scripted mimes and Atellane farces of the first century B.C.

Terence

(i) *Terence's aims and models.* Terence regarded Plautus, Caecilius, and his own adversary Luscius Lanuvinus as old-fashioned; it was a fault that they did not even try to imitate the direct, accurate, and charming qualities of

Menander, but distorted the mirror of life by indulging on the one hand in any old comic business, and on the other in tragic bombast (cf. Gellius on Caecilius, Gell. 2.23.12). Terence cites from Luscius the case of a rumbustious running slave as an example of the one, and an overdone mad scene for the other.[1] Terence did not wish to eliminate such things, but to tame them (*An.* 338ff., a running slave; *Ad.* 789f., anger). He wanted to make plays without 'faults' (*H.T.* 29), and he probably would have approved of Hamlet's advice to the Players in respect of technique, theory, and the distinction of the judicious and the vulgar spectator.

Terence's first play, the *Andria* of 166 B.C., is conventional in theme – pregnancy, recognition, marriage – but strikingly new in treatment and ambition. That Terence should have interfered extensively with the plot of Menander's *Andria* was not in itself new. As he pointed out he was following Naevius, Plautus, and Ennius. Luscius Lanuvinus had evidently given up the freedom of older writers to add themes, scenes, and characters; *contaminari non decere fabulas*, one ought not to 'spoil' plays (*An.* 9–21). Otherwise, Terence could have retorted *tu quoque*. In fact, he criticizes Luscius (and, implicitly, Menander) for not changing the legally (but not necessarily dramatically) illogical order of a pair of speeches in Menander's *Thesaurus* (*Eun.* 10ff.). The term *contaminatio* has been coined from this passage and *H.T.* 17 and used by modern scholars as if it had been a current technical term for the addition of alien material from a particular Greek source to a main original, or even the joining of two whole Greek plays.[2] We have direct evidence that Plautus did sometimes write in the former manner (see p. 101), but there is no proof external or internal that comedians welded whole plays. In fact, *contaminare* is merely the quotation of Luscius' abusive description of Terence's particular procedure. If *contaminatio* as a technical term is to be used in future, it should be redefined to denote all those ways in which a Roman playwright might 'mess about' with his model.

Terence's arguments were not intended to be fair, but successful. Half-truths were adequate material. While there are superficial similarities between Plautus' and Terence's procedures, the motives and execution of the two playwrights differed fundamentally, and Terence (though he does not admit it) disliked what he called the negligence of a Plautus.

The first scene of the *Andria* is a dialogue between a father and a trusted freedman. This relationship, unique in comedy, is depicted in a humane and liberal manner as interesting in itself. The dramatic function of the freedman, however, is merely to listen to the suspicions and intentions of the father. In

[1] Ter. *H.T.* 31ff., cf. Plaut. *Amph.* 984ff., *Cur.* 280ff., *Mer.* 111ff.; Ter. *Pho.* 6ff., cf. *Men.* 835ff.

[2] See Ludwig (1968) 169ff.; Beare (1964) 96–108, 310–12.

the original *Andria* the father was alone and narrated all this in a long monologue. But in the *Perinthia*, a play of Menander which Terence alleges was virtually identical in plot but different in 'style', the first scene was a conversation between mother and father. Terence says that he has taken 'what suited' from the *Perinthia*, and he makes it sound as though this was the source of all the alterations which Luscius criticized. Terence's commentator Donatus was hard put to it to find any material or ideas specifically from the *Perinthia*, and attributes to it the idea of a dialogue. Even so Terence's substitution of a freedman for the wife is a substantial independent change. The scene as a whole, although the first, is among the best of all those where Terence can be seen to differ from his models; and yet, even here, the integration is not quite perfect. The father wants Sosia to counteract his slave Davus' influence on his son (50, 168f.), but nothing comes of this; and the integration of the scene with its sequel is not quite right.[1]

The other major change in the *Andria* was the introduction of a young man Charinus and his slave Byrria. In Menander the man called Simo by Terence (he rings the changes quite pointlessly on Menander's names) tried to force Pamphilus' hand with respect to his unadmitted liaison with the girl next door by pretending that Pamphilus shall marry a friend's daughter 'today'. The girl next door, who was delivered of Pamphilus' baby during the play, was in fact an Athenian citizen, and so could marry Pamphilus; the friend's daughter was left unmarried at the end of the original. Neither girl actually appeared on stage. Charinus' role is to be the friend's daughter's suitor and to marry her at the end, after misapprehension as to Pamphilus' intentions. Thus a considerable sub-plot is added to the action. It is Menandrian in character – Charinus' misapprehensions are like those of Sostratos in the *Dis exapaton* (see p. 107) – but the material in question cannot derive from the *Perinthia* in any simple sense, unless Terence's allegation about the similarity of the plays is wholly misleading. Terence's main reason for the addition was 'that there should not be an element of sadness in the rejection of the girl without a husband and Pamphilus' marriage to another' (Don. *ad An.* 301); that is an aesthetic reason, and as such interesting: Terence thought that he could improve on Menander in Menander's own terms – ethos and structure – and this is the earliest known straightforward case in Roman literature of *aemulatio*, competition with Greeks on their own terms. A secondary reason may have been a certain lack of confidence on Terence's part in the simple and unadorned plot of Menander's *Andria*. We may question Terence's success in both taste and execution. His main motive reveals some sentimentality and the confusion of artificiality with structural neatness. Again, although we never see Glycerium, she matters to us because of what we are told about her, because she has her baby in our hear-

[1] *sequor* or *sequar* at 171? cf. 204, 404.

ing, and because of the faithful Mysis' concern; it was dramatically right in Menander that the other girl and her father should have been relegated to an address 'down the road', for out of sight is out of mind, and if the girl had any real emotional presence, Terence's point might have been valid. In fact, her Menandrian function was simply as a threat to Pamphilus and Glycerium. Terence has kept this arrangement, but by giving the girl an admirer he has complicated matters. Something must be done to make us take an interest in the girl; the rather empty exclamations of the colourless Charinus are not good enough. A single appearance would have sufficed. The additions can be isolated from the main composition fairly easily, and their technical execution falls short of the Menandrian excellence emulated here by Terence. One example must suffice. Charinus and Byrria enter at 301, Pamphilus being 'left over' from the previous scene. He is given no proper reason for failing to observe the newcomers, and his integration into the conversation at 318 is unmotivated and arbitrary.[1] Menander did not compose thus – but Plautus did.

There are no substantial Terentian additions to the plays turned from originals by Menander's admirer Apollodorus of Carystus, *Hecyra*, 'The mother in law', Terence's second play, unsuccessfully staged in 165 B.C., and only given a fair hearing at its third showing, in 160 B.C., and *Phormio*, his fifth, a version of *Epidikazomenos*, 'The suitor' (161 B.C.). The complex and tightly-knit *Heauton timorumenus*, 'The self-tormentor', his third play (163 B.C.) is the only Menander-original which has not been filled out. The *Eunuchus*, staged very successfully in 161 B.C., is from a Menandrian original in which a sympathetic *hetaira* Chrysis was obliged to accept the unwelcome attentions of an admirer – much to her lover Chairestratos' chagrin – because he was in possession of a young girl who had been brought up by Chrysis' deceased mother and who, as Chrysis believed, was really an Athenian citizen. Her problems were to play along with the suitor until she might gain custody of the girl; to restrain Chairestratos' consequent jealousy; and to find the girl's relatives. Chrysis having achieved the first two objects and nearly accomplished the third, the girl is raped in Chrysis' house by Chairestratos' nasty young brother, who has gained access by disguising himself as a eunuch; this débâcle was resolved by the marriage of the two on the establishment of the girl's identity. It may be conjectured that Chairestratos' rival was not a wholly unsympathetic figure. Menander would have been characteristically economical and subtle if he had made the rival the mysteriously deceased merchant of Terence's play; he brought Chrysis from Samos to Athens and set her up there in luxury (*Eun.* 119ff.). If he had some claim on our sympathy, the arrangement at the end of the play by which the courtesan shares her favours between the two lovers would be less unsatisfactory than it appears in Terence. For Terence has

[1] The dramaturgy at 404–31 is again rather crude.

substituted for Menander's rival a vainglorious soldier Thraso and his parasite Gnatho; this is not only an addition but also a substitution of alien material, and is more firmly integrated than the Charinus-theme of *Andria*. Terence claims as his only alteration that he has taken these characters from Menander's *Colax*, 'The toady' (*Eun.* 30ff.), but this is a gross oversimplification. His purpose was to enliven the action, and he has exploited perceptibly more various features of the traditional stage-language and business than in his previous work.[1]

These features represent a successful concession to the public which had rejected *Hecyra*, for his soldier and parasite are quite strongly drawn. However there is no technical improvement; for example, the advice which Gnatho gives Thraso at 439ff. would be strictly logical only if the girl were still in their possession, and the entry at 454 of Thais (Menander's Chrysis) is poorly motivated.[2] Terence's addition of a scene from Diphilus' *Synapothneskontes*, 'Companions in death', to his version of Menander's second *Adelphoi*, his last play (161 B.C.), is similar in intention and execution, though less ambitious; the scene in question represents the forcible abduction of a girl from a protesting *leno*, another stock-figure evidently beloved of the public. All the same, Terence does not represent him in a farcical Plautine manner, dedicated to *lucrum*, but as the victim of a robbery for which he is duly and justly compensated. Again the scene is not perfectly integrated; it represents as happening 'now' the consequence of what at 88ff. was represented (as in Menander) as having happened some time since; Sannio is 'spare' in ii.3–4; the theme of the girl's alleged freedom at 191ff. is dramatically irrelevant and illogically handled; we ought to be made aware earlier that Aeschinus is seizing the girl not for himself but for his brother. Evidently such things did not worry the Roman public. The end of the play has been rendered more farcical than in Menander, as in the *Eunuchus*: the liberal Micio is represented as a comic butt and unwilling bridegroom, as if good sense were on the side of the neurotic and authoritarian Demea.[3]

Thus a certain development may be discerned in Terence's treatment of plot. He began with ambitious notions of presenting and improving on Menander in his own terms by making alien additions for aesthetic reasons (*Andria*), and changing the emphasis of the *palliata* in the direction of psychological realism (*Hecyra*). He never gave up these ideals, but was obliged to make compromises with the groundlings. The *Heauton* was to be a play without aesthetic faults, and was, like the failed *Hecyra*, a quiet play (*stataria*) without parasites, soldiers, and *lenones*; but its plot was much more various and complex,

[1] E.g. *Eun.* 270f., cf. Plaut. *Pseud.* 457, *Epid.* 126f.

[2] It would be better if she entered wondering 'Where can Chremes be?', cf. 204f. The 'asides' in the siege-scene are awkward by Menandrian standards (1053–60).

[3] Rieth (1964), Martin (1976) 26–9.

and even spectacular – Bacchis' entrance is excellent theatre. Nevertheless this was not enough; those who deserted the *Hecyra* may have yawned at *Heauton*. The *Phormio* is taken from a sparkling and lively piece, and, unlike Terence's other plays, is dominated by a single strong character.[1] It is noteworthy that Terence felt the need to justify his change of the title of the original by pointing this out; the play could be seen in the Roman tradition of a *motaria* like *Pseudolus*, where the dominion of the slave was due to the Roman dramatist. In his *Eunuchus* and *Adelphoe* his alien additions and his adjustments of the final scenes show no technical improvement. This did not matter, for his purpose was to strengthen the variety and farcical element to please a conservative public unconcerned with niceties of structure.

(ii) *Techniques and tone.* Plautus had sometimes dropped an expository prologue (*Trinummus*), even in recognition plays (*Epidicus*, *Curculio*); Terence made this a rule, for the models of all five of his recognition plays as well as the *Adelphoe* had expository prologues identifying persons to be found, and explaining circumstances: thus the audience was able to appreciate ironies arising from their superior knowledge. Terence's departure from Greek practice has imposed re-casting of material in all the plays, particularly in the early scenes, and while it affords Terence the opportunity for some clever foreshadowing (*An.* 220ff.), it also introduces surprises of questionable dramatic merit – the arrival of Crito in *Andria*, Phormio's knowledge of Demipho's double life, the discovery that Ctesipho is the lover in *Adelphoe*. The omissions also lead to un-Menandrian obscurities, for example the unexplained detective-work by which Thais (Menander's Chrysis) had found Chremes and identified him as the likely brother of her protégée in the *Eunuchus*. Again, Terence follows Roman practice in running together and adjusting the act-divisions of his originals, and though Terence is more careful about this than Plautus, here too he fails to hide his traces (*H.T.* 170f., *Ad.* 511ff.). Terence has only a very small amount of non-iambo-trochaic canticum (*An.* 481ff., 625ff., *Eun.* 560, *Ad.* 610ff.), a significant shift towards the more prosaic voice of New Comedy away from the styles of Plautus and Caecilius; but the fact that there is any canticum at all, that only half the dialogue is in spoken iambic senarii, that the rest is in longer iambo-trochaic metres, often used in a new way and certainly 'sung' – these contrast Terence as strongly with New Comedy practice as with his Roman predecessors, within whose firmly established tradition he remains. He evidently followed his predecessors in regularly working up a good deal of trimeter-dialogue into longer, musically-presented Roman metres. These exhibit a somewhat more prolix and decorated manner than his senarii, and this too is an inheritance. On the other hand, he could be far more faithful over

[1] Arnott (1970) 32–57.

longer passages than any that can be confidently cited from Plautus. Thais' discovery that Chaerea has raped Pamphila is such a passage.[1] Sometimes he would implicitly Romanize a detail for the sake of comprehensibility or immediacy,[2] but never with the gusto of Plautus. Sometimes he remodelled a passage with a rather pusillanimous eye to Roman *decorum* : a dialogue between a respectable wife and a prostitute is reported, not presented; a disappointed lover contemplates not suicide but flight.[3] Terence avoids themes involving aged or middle-aged lovers, and none of his Syruses or Parmenos steals even those two or three *minae* which Plautus' Chrysalus regarded as such small beer. From the few brief lines that can be compared directly with their originals and from general comparison, it is clear that Terence often enfeebled the specific quality of Menander by generalization, even where this was unnecessary: the midwife at *An.* 483–5 gives her instructions in general and rhetorical form, whereas her Menandrian counterpart spoke with a properly crone-like intimacy and recommended the new mother to take 'the yolk of four eggs' (*Men.* fr. 37 K–Th). At *H.T.* 64, on the other hand, it was essential to give up the allusion to the setting of the play in Halai; but it is a weakness of all Terence's plays that they take place nominally '*in his regionibus*', i.e. an undefined 'Athens'. Terence avoids the means which Plautus used to specify his plays and actually goes beyond Menander in isolating his cast from contact with the audience. He never solved the problem which his rejection of the older style involved: Afranius, who greatly admired Terence (Macrob. 6.1.4), may have done better here. An epigram of Julius Caesar praises Terence as *puri sermonis amator* 'a lover of refined diction', but criticizes him as 'half-Menander' (*o dimidiate Menander*) because of his lack of drive (*uis*, not *uis comica*).[4] This is a fair point. Terence's alterations do not compensate for his failure to focus and particularize adequately.

It is certainly mistaken, in the present writer's opinion, to interpret any of the alterations reviewed as having deep spiritual significance, or to credit Terence with the communication, even the invention, of a new conception of reason, reasonability, and relationships (*humanitas*) that differed essentially from ideas already present in Menander and widely diffused in the post-Eratosthenic *oecumene*.[5] Plautus and Ennius do not use *homo*, *humanus* in the

[1] *Eun.* 817–922, cf. Men. *Dysk.* 233–81 for the dramaturgy.

[2] *Eun.* 255ff., an Italian market complete with butchers (cf. p. 109, n. 2); 319, the praetorian edict.

[3] Ter. *Hec.* 816–40, *Ad.* 275, Don. *ad loc.*; Ludwig (1968) 176.

[4] Suet. *Vita Terenti* 7. The tag *vis comica* 'comic strength' is a mistake deriving from false punctuation: *lenibus atque utinam scriptis adiuncta foret uis, | comica ut aequato uirtus polleret honore | cum Graecis neue hac despectus parte iaceres*; as if Caesar meant that Terence failed in *uirtus* compared with the Greeks rather than *uirtus comica*.

[5] Too much has been made of this alleged aspect of Terence, especially by Italian writers since Croce. See Ludwig (1968) 169f., 175, 178.

loaded sense which we find in Terence, but that does not mean that they were unaware of the concept of the community of the wise and good; indeed that is an essential aspect of their cosmopolitan outlook. The inference to be made is rather that the usage had become fashionable in the 170s and 160s in the upper-class philhellene circles in which Terence grew up, and that it was a loan-translation of ἄνθρωπος, ἀνθρώπινος 'human(e)' as long since used in Greek, not least in Menander, whom the Roman pupils of such teachers as Chilon (Plut. *Cat. Maj.* 20.5) will no doubt have been reading as part of their syllabus. Since the nearest Latin translation of φιλανθρωπία would have to be something clumsy like *studium hominum*, the abstract corresponding to *humanus* came to be used instead, *humanitas*. Terence was not leading but reflecting contemporary polite usage and the most that could be attributed to him is the popularization of the usage.

We have used the terms 'upper-class philhellene circles' and 'polite usage' advisedly. Scholars have questioned the existence of the so-called 'Scipionic Circle' and pointed out that that phrase was only coined by Bernhardy in 1850 to denote Scipio Aemilianus' cultured friends (cf. Cic. *Amic.* 69).[1] There is some danger here of over-emphasis. Of course there never was an exclusive club or *salon* called the 'Scipionic Circle' (if anyone should think that), but nevertheless Scipio Aemilianus did count C. Laelius and C. Lucilius, who were his social equals, and the philosopher Panaetius and the historian Polybius, his inferiors, as personal friends on an equal footing. Polybius describes his relationship as respected teacher and friend of Aemilianus in a moving passage (Polyb. 32.9). From the intellectual point of view *humanitas* cut across social divisions and required that all of merit should be equal citizens in the Republic of Letters. Terence himself had friends in high places who took this view; whether these included or centred on Scipio is unimportant. *Humanitas*, of which a Greek education was an essential part, was admired by young Romans destined for high things in Terence's time, and, after Pydna, the practical advantages to the ruling class of a cosmopolitan education were becoming more than ever obvious.

(iii) *Language and style: Terence's achievement.* Luscius criticized Terence for having a 'thin' style, from which it may be inferred that he himself composed in the full-blooded traditional manner. This 'thin' style was, however, Terence's most remarkable and important achievement, for it was, together with his new and less insistently varied musical presentation, the essential medium for realistic characterization. Even Plautus' most consistent characters, Euclio (*Aul.*) and Hegio (*Capt.*), fail to convince us that they are real because they are writ too large, and thoroughly enjoy all their emotions indiscriminately.

[1] See Astin (1967) 295–306.

The noisy prolixity of the older style is such that there is no scope for fleeting and ironic retrospective verbal allusion as there is in Terence (e.g. Ter. *H.T.* 919/70; *An.* 586/503; *Ad.* 934/107). Terence's achievement is the more remarkable, as his medium is fashioned by numerous small adjustments, some in this direction, some in that, within a traditional and homogeneous stage-language which had been developed for different purposes.

Terence preserves this homogeneity and even emphasizes it, so that slaves do not speak with an accent different from that of their betters. Rhythm is still used as a component of the meaning of a verse (e.g. *Pho.* 429f., *An.* 767, *Eun.* 190), but generally Terence seeks to make his medium more Menandrian by under-emphasizing its movement. This is achieved in a number of ways; there is a significant overall reduction in clash of ictus and accent, and such clashes are distributed more evenly inside the verse than in Plautus; enjambement of sense from line to line and change of speaker are exploited more freely and variously. Some forms archaic already for Plautus, e.g. *-ĕrunt* as a line-end, are given up in the diction of the plays, but others, e.g. the line-end type ...*nullu' sum*, are relatively commoner in Terence, and, what is significant and characteristic, are exploited with greater internal variety. Consequently the texture of his verse is more complex than his predecessors'.

SIMO Ị́bi tum fị́liụs
cum illị́s qui amạ́rant Chrýsidem ụ́na aderạt fréquẹns;
curạ́bat ụ́na fụ́nus; trị́stis ị́nterịm;
nonnụ́mquam cọ́nlacrumạ́bat. plạ́cuit tum ịd mihị;
síc cọgitạbam: 'hic pạ́ruae cọ́nsuetụ́dinịs
causa hụ́ius mọrtém fẹrt[1] tam fạ́miliạ́ritẹr:
quid si ị́pse amạsset? quịd hic míhị faciẹt pátrị?'
háec ẹgo putạ́bam esse ọ́mnia hụmáni ị́ngenị
mansuẹtíque ạ́nimi offị́cia. quid múltịs mórọr?
egomẹ́t quoque ẹ́ius cạ́usa in fụ́nus prọ́deọ,
níl sụspicạns etiạm máli. SOSIA. Hẹm quíd id ẹst? SIMO scíẹs:
ecfẹ́rtur; ị́mus. ịntérea ịnter mụ́lierẹs

[1] Only verbs are freely admitted as monosyllabic forms at line-end not involving elision in Plautus and Terence; so Ter. *H.T.* 461 ...*ómnẹs sollị́citos hạ́bui – ạtque haec ụ́na nọ́x!* 'I distributed *all* (my wines) – and that was just *one* night!' is intentionally and effectively anomalous in this (and its hiatus), expressing Chremes' horror at Bacchis' effects on his cellar. It follows that full coincidence of ictus and accent in the last place was strongly avoided, and that monosyllabic verb-forms were sentence-enclitic, as once all verb-forms in Latin had been, acquiring an accent only at sentence-head. In the above presentation word-accents have been also omitted in certain verb-collocations where dramatic emphasis suggests that the phrase-accent was stronger than the word-accent which, at least in later Latin, would be the verb's prerogativc – *ụ́na aderạt fréquẹns*, *síc cọgitạbam*, *si ị́pse amạsset*, *quịd hic míhị faciẹt pátrị*, *níl sụspicạns etiạm málị*, *únam ạspicio ạ́dulescẹ́ntulạm*, *sorọ́rem esse ạiunt Chrýsidịs*, perhaps *quịd multịs morọr*, *prạ́eter cẹ́terạs/uisạst*, *ad sepụ́lchrum uẹnimụs*, *in ị́gnem impọsitast*. The phenomenon is so common that an interesting question arises as to the accentual status of verb-forms in general in pre-Classical Latin; was the old rule about verbal accent still operative to the extent that verbs tended to stand, as it were, in the accentual shade?

quae ibi ạ́derant fọrte únam ạspicio ạ́dulescẹ́ntulạm
fórmạ – SOS. Bónạ, fortạ́sse? SIMO Et uọ́ltu, Sọ́siạ,
ádeọ modẹ́sto, ádeọ uenụ́sto, ut nị́l suprạ.
quị́a tụm mihi lạ́mentạ́ri prạ́eter cẹ́terạs
uísạst, et quị́a erat fọ́rma prạ́eter cẹ́teras
honẹ́sta ac lị́berạ́li, accẹ́do ad pẹ́disequạs,
quáe sịt rógọ: sorọ́rem esse ạiunt – Chrýsidịs!
percụ́ssit ị́lico ạ́nimum: attạ́t họ́c ị́llud ẹst,
hị́nc ịllae lạ́crumae, hạ́ec ịllast mị́sericọ́rdiạ!
SOS. Quam tị́meo quọ́rsum euạ́das! SIMO fụ́nus ị́nterịm
procẹ́dit; sẹ́quimur; ad sepụ́lchrum uẹ́nimụs;
in ị́gnem impọ́sitast; flẹ́tur. ịntérea hạec sórọr... (*Andria* 101–29)

SIMO *Then my son began spending a great deal of time with those who had been Chrysis' lovers; he organized the funeral with them. He was gloomy all the while, and sometimes he would burst into tears. 'Good', I thought.* (110) *'He's taking the death of this slight acquaintance very personally: what if he had fallen in love with her himself? How deeply he will feel for me, his father!' I thought these were all the proper manifestations of a warm disposition and a well-trained character. Well, to be brief, I myself also went to pay my respects at her funeral,* (115) *not yet suspecting any trouble.*

SOSIA *Trouble? What?*

SIMO *I'll tell you. The body was brought out, and the procession set off. As we went along, among the women who were assisting I happened to spot a particular young lady. Her figure –*

SOSIA *– was good, perhaps?*

SIMO *– and her features, Sosia,* (120) *were so classic, so lovely that it was perfection. As her grief seemed to be deeper than the others', and as she looked more decent and lady-like than the others, I went up to the servant-women and asked who she was. 'The sister', they said, 'of –* Chrysis!' (125) *It hit me at once. Aha,* that's *what it meant,* this *was the cause of those tears, the cause of that 'compassion'.*

SOSIA *I don't like the way your story is going!*

SIMO *Meanwhile the funeral-procession went ahead; we followed; we came to the tomb; she was placed on the pyre; general weeping. Meanwhile the sister...*

Simo had thought, rightly, that there was nothing between his son Pamphilus and the deceased Chrysis; this was the more fortunate, since Simo had plans for a good match for his son, and these were well advanced – without Pamphilus' knowledge. Simo claims somewhat rhetorically – note the *prosopopoeia* and argument *a fortiori*, 110ff. – that it was a father's sympathy for his son's feelings that brought him, an embarrassed outsider, to attend the funeral of the socially dubious Chrysis; and so it was, but Simo does not add that he was concealing something from Pamphilus. The sequel is described with freshness, irony, economy, and considerable unobtrusive art. It is fresh, for this is a real death and a real funeral such as one never finds in Plautus. It is ironical in the presentation of Simo's character. He likes to think of himself as enlightened in his relationship to his son, yet as soon as he learns the truth

attạ́t hóc ị́llud ẹst

that his own inferences have been mistaken, and, worse, that his plans are threatened anew and more seriously than by Chrysis, the understanding sympathy which he has claimed for himself runs out. Autumn was himself attracted by Spring, and he can understand all too well why his son should be in love with her. It is economical, for Simo says more about himself than he intends. These traits are Menandrian, and Terence has successfully conveyed them by adapting the traditional language and rhythms of Roman comedy. His originality and art lie here. The first spectators of this scene, the first of Terence's first play, were familiar only with the full-blooded manner of Plautus and Caecilius and Luscius. Whether they approved or not, they must have been struck by the lightness, rapidity, naturalism, and complexity of writing such as this. The alliteration, neologism, and prolixity of the 'full' style have gone. Terence makes Simo quote his own and others' words for vividness, and favours pungent and economical strings of verbs for rapid narrative. At the same time he freely admits very long words, not (as in Plautus) in order to increase the weight of a particular line, but simply as they occur as the *mots justes*; elision is very frequent; and he is much less insistent than his predecessors on the line as a sense-unit. These traits have the effect of complicating considerably the relation of word-accent and the flow of the verse. The passage above begins with familiar movement, but from 111 to 114 it is more complex; at 115 it is simple, in 116 complex, in 117 simple, in 118–20 complex, and from there to 125 essentially simple, effectively highlighting the famous couplet 125f.; normality of movement is restored in 127–9. However Roman actors delivered 'difficult' lines where elision across changes of speaker and breathpause was involved, or where the natural pattern of word-accents did not coincide with the flow of the verse, we may be certain that there was a contrast between them and 'easy' verses, and the *poeta* Terence was well aware of the importance of this aspect of composition. The reader may easily check for himself how effectively Terence varies the rhythms of this passage, and in particular, how 'difficult' rhythms correspond to emphasis and emotion in Simo's speech.

Terence's diction in longer metres is somewhat more ornate than in senarii, but here too he aims at a more various, naturalistic tone than his predecessors. It is precisely because of this that some inherited features of his language seem awkward when compared with Menander's more fluid usage, for example Terence's rather wooden use of what had become in the *palliata* fixed formulae of intention and entrance (e.g. *An.* 796–800, Crito's arrival).[1]

[1] See Gomme (1937) 255f.

Terence had a difficult theatrical career, not only because of Luscius Lanuvinus, but also because of his trouble in reconciling the tastes of a discriminating minority and a conservative majority. His reforms of theatrical technique all lie within the tradition of the *palliata*, but were mostly centripetal and negative. In particular, he eschewed the means by which older writers had established *rapport* with the audience without being able to focus his 'Athens' satisfactorily. He concentrated on a narrower spectrum of experience than Menander or his own seniors, but, on the other hand, he did this well: for example, his interest in the relationship of parents and children and in education, and his realistic, consistent, and sympathetic representation of character, particularly female, which were new to Roman audiences. He inadvertently damaged the *palliata* as a dramatic form, for the logical setting for such realistic characters as he presented was not his colourless 'Athens', but the real Italy; with him there opens a permanent rift between 'higher' and 'lower' literary tastes. The broad public did not like Terence much, and he did not like them. The spirit of the older comedians survived in the mime and farce, while Terence's interest in character was maintained by Afranius in his *togatae*. *Ea tempestate flos poetarum fuit* 'that age was the flower of poets', said the reviver of Plautus' *Casina* with reference to the pre-Terentian period; he may well have included Terence and Luscius in his condemnation of the moderns. However, Terence's unique and most important success was to become *Menander Latinus* in the library and classroom rather than on the stage, and as such he was very important in establishing the taste and diction of the classical period.

3. SERIOUS DRAMA

Praetextae *and* crepidatae

Grammarians drew a distinction between *tragoediae* (*fabulae crepidatae* 'Buskin-plays'), modelled on Greek tragedy, and *fabulae praetextae* 'Hem-' or 'Robe-plays', on Roman themes, ancient and modern. This is parallel to the distinction of *comoediae* (*fabulae palliatae*) and *fabulae togatae* (*tabernariae*).[1] There is no certain evidence for *fabulae togatae* before the time of Terence and Afranius, and no light dramatist is known to have written both kinds of comedy. The case is different in serious drama. All the known dramatists except Andronicus wrote the occasional Roman play and they seem to have used the same style and form, chorus and all, as in their *tragoediae*. Aeschylus' *Persians* belongs to the genre tragedy no less than his other plays, and Naevius' *Clastidium*, cele-

[1] The grammarians' classifications are worthy of Polonius, but the use of such terms as *crepidata*, *praetext(at)a*, *togata*, *tabernaria*, *mimus*, *Rhinthonica*, *palliata*, *Atellana*, *mimus* was not altogether self-consistent. Only *tragoedia* and *comoedia* and *fabula* are attested for the creative perod. The definitions implied in the text may not be strictly correct, but the terms are commonly so used. See Beare (1964) 264–6.

brating M. Claudius Marcellus' winning of the *spolia opima* in 222 B.C., was not really different in genre from his other *tragoediae*. However, apart from the obvious matter of costume, there were two special aspects of the *praetexta*. The playwright had to organize his dramaturgy and plot wholly for himself, using motifs and ideas transferred from tragedy.[1] Again, the *praetextae* were distinguished by their obvious *utilitas*, their 'importance', their 'relevance'. Cicero defended the poet Archias in 62 B.C. before an aristocratic jury by making much of the argument that the poet's highest task was to celebrate the deeds of famous men. Of course, by then the argument was obsolescent; Catullus would have sniggered.[2] At the beginning of the Hannibalic War, however, the successful production of the *Clastidium* must have seemed an important demonstration to the nobility of the high seriousness and political utility of the theatre. A generation later Fulvius Nobilior took Ennius with him on campaign, as Hellenistic kings had taken poets to celebrate their deeds, and the result, the *Ambracia*, was probably a *praetexta* rather than a narrative poem, produced in 187 or 186 B.C.; Fulvius was the object of political attacks when he returned, and such propaganda was really useful. The long if intermittent survival of the tradition begun by Naevius – Accius was still writing *praetextae* in the 130s B.C., and perhaps later – suggests that noble patrons, if not the dramatists, found this form congenial. The real vigour and popularity of the serious theatre, however, was in its Greek mythological aspect.

A survey of the writers of tragedy

Varro dated Andronicus' first production, probably a tragedy, to 240 B.C., and Naevius' first, which was certainly a tragedy, to 235 B.C. Another tradition was that 'the Muse', whether tragic or epic is not clear, 'arrived' in Rome during the Second Punic War (223–202 B.C.; Porcius Licinus *ap.* Gell. *N.A.* 17.21.45); a third states that it was after the Second Punic War that Romans turned to tragedy (Hor. *Epist.* 2.1.161ff.). Both the latter views seem to follow the mistaken chronology propounded by the scholar-tragedian Accius in his *Didascalica*, that Andronicus was junior to Naevius; the third even ignores him, and regards Ennius (*fl.* 203–169 B.C.) as the first real Roman tragedian. Whatever the truth about Andronicus, the plays of Plautus strongly imply in various ways that tragedy was in fact a well-developed and popular genre well before the end of the Punic War. The work of the pioneers, particularly perhaps Naevius, was crucial in establishing the form, style, and emotional province of serious drama. The titles of Andronicus and Naevius (see Appendix) suggest an interest in the Trojan Cycle, and in the fortunes of suffering heroines.

[1] Jocelyn (1972) 1004f.; Leo (1913) 179f., 398f.
[2] G.W. Williams (1968) 31ff.

The Argonautic saga and those parts of the Theban Cycle involving Dionysus and Bacchantes were also used; Oedipus himself is a strikingly rare figure in Roman tragedy. Andronicus is known to have used Sophocles (*Aiax Mastigophorus* and *Hermiona* (?)), while Naevius may have used originals as different in character as Aeschylus' *Lycurgus* and Euripides' *Iphigenia in Tauris*.[1]

Even the names of the rivals and lesser imitators of Ennius (who wrote between *c.* 202 and 169 B.C.) are forgotten. It was he who made the composition of tragedy an unequivocally respectable activity for the leisure of gentlemen who did not depend on the theatre. Among these his nephew the painter Pacuvius (*fl.* 154 B.C., according to Jerome) and Accius (who wrote between *c.* 145 and *c.* 100 B.C.) stood out and all but monopolized the attention of subsequent generations. Ennius was particularly fond of Euripides, though he was far from faithful to the true spirit of his author. Pacuvius, whose *œuvre* was small, used all three of the classic Athenian dramatists, and also the imitators of Euripides. There are almost as many titles of plays by Accius as there are of all the others together. Like Pacuvius, he was eclectic in his choice of models. In his case, as we shall see, the question arises whether he did not sometimes compose tragedies 'from scratch', exactly as a contemporary Greek might; in exploring the by-ways and sequels of the famous stories of Troy, Thebes, and the Argonauts, the scholar-poet would know and study not only the Masters' versions and others', but also the remarks of the commentators, and might take things 'even from a Latin', as Afranius in the contemporary *togata* (*CRF* 28, Macrob. *Sat.* 6.1.4).

Accius' latest-known play was a *Tereus* of 104 B.C., and fresh tragedies were still being composed, apparently for stage-performance, in the 90s B.C.[2] Throughout Cicero's lifetime, there were revivals (as of comedy) of what were now regarded as the classics of Pacuvius, Accius, and Ennius (this seems to have been their order of esteem)[3] before large audiences, who might interpret passages with reference to contemporary politics[4]. The acting profession bade fair to win the social prestige which it enjoyed in Greece; orators admired, befriended, and learnt from great actors such as Aesopus and Roscius. It is likely that the composition of tragedy had become a literary exercise already

[1] On Andronicus, *TRF* 16 = *ROL* 16 ~ Soph. *Aj.* 1266f., see Traina (1970) 22, 42. Of the others' work the Greek models exist in whole or part for: Ennius, *Eumenides* (Aesch.), *Hecuba*, *Iphigenia in Aulis*, *Medea exul* (all Eur.); Pacuvius, *Antiopa* (Eur.); Accius, *Bacchae*, *Phoenissae*, *Telephus* (all Eur.). See Mette (1964) 5–212.

[2] Marius Victorinus in *GLK* VI 8 implies that the *Tecmessa* of C. Julius Strabo (*fl.* 100–90 B.C.) was for stage-performance.

[3] Cic. *Opt. gen. orat.* 1.2, Hor. *Epist.* 2.1.55; later Accius was more favoured (Vell. 2.9.3, Quint. *Inst.* 10.1.97).

[4] *Eurysaces*, 57 B.C. (Cic. *Sest.* 120); *Clytemestra*, 55 B.C. (Cic. *Fam.* 7.1.2); *Tereus*, 44 B.C. (Cic. *Phil.* 1.15.36, *Att.* 16.2.3).

before 100 B.C. The three classic Roman authors were read in Cicero's time (Cic. *Fin.* 1.2.4), and probably figured in the school syllabus. Quintus Cicero wrote several tragedies, including four which he dashed off in sixteen days of leave while he was serving with the army in Gaul in 54 B.C. (Cic. *Qu. Fr.* 3.5(6).7).

The appeal and scope of Roman tragedy

The province of Roman tragedy was firstly the celebration of contemporary aristocratic ideals through myth, with concessions neither to the Athens of Pericles or Cleon, nor to the distant mythical past; next, the stimulation not of the intellect but of the emotions; thirdly, the cultivation of rhetoric; lastly, to a limited extent, the retailing of current philosophical-scientific views.

The 'Corinth' or 'Mycenae' of the setting was (as in comedy) a blend of Greek and Italian elements; though naturally Italian allusions were generally less quotidian and specific than they could be in comedy, the values and value-terms were quite frankly Roman.

uirtus praemium est optumum
uirtus omnibus rebus anteit profecto
libertas, salus, uita, res et parentes,
patria et prognati
tutantur, seruantur;
uirtus omnia in sese habet, omnia adsunt
bona quem penest uirtus.

(Plautus, *Amphitruo* 648–53)

Manliness is the best prize; manliness in truth precedes all things; (by it) are protected and kept freedom, safety, life, property and parents, fatherland and children; manliness has all things in itself, and he has at hand all good things, in whose charge is manliness.

So Alcumena ends a tragic aria, in which it is wrong to see any parody. The highest function of tragedy was the celebration of *uirtus* in war and counsel in terms which were essentially those of contemporary politics. *Virtus* denoted physical fitness, endurance, bravery, initiative, piety, versatility, even eloquence. From it come the stability of the community and personal honour and fame. Thus *uirtus* far from being a coherent moral virtue was a collection of competitive skills put to good use in the service of the community (cf. Ennius, *TRF* 160f. = *ROL* 200 f.). It was through Stoic philosophy that in the second century there was added but not substituted the notion of moral purity. The cardinal Greek virtue of moderation is subordinate in Roman tragedy, and appears as such only as a woman's '*uirtus*', or as the criterion to be respected when the individual's thirst for glory endangered the common interest. Thus the moral concern of Roman tragedy, and its conception of a tragic hero, was narrow and unsystematic, but very relevant to the political battles of the second century.

There was much ferment in the religious life of the Romans in the years following the Punic War. The Senate sanctioned some alien cults, e.g. Magna Mater, Venus of Eryx, Hercules and the Muses, and inaugurated others, e.g. Pietas, while private enthusiams as diverse as the cult of Bacchus and a sub-Platonic astral mysticism were fashionable, though curbed eventually by law. From at least the 180s the teachings of the Epicurean and Stoic schools were becoming known at Rome. For all that, traditional public and private Roman religion and rites were more deeply ingrained and valued than is sometimes suggested. Thus by the time of Pacuvius, there co-existed many different levels and kinds of religious sophistication. Polybius, one of the very many educated Greeks who settled at Rome in the 160s, was amazed at the superstitious punctiliousness of the audiences of Ennius and Pacuvius (Polyb. 12.56.6), and suggested that the ruling classes deliberately fostered traditional religion to keep the lower orders in their place. It was nothing so Machiavellian. The theological and cosmological *loci* which one finds in Ennius and Pacuvius (not, it seems, in Accius) reflect contemporary teachings, particularly of the Stoics, and no doubt tragedy played some part in disseminating such ideas among the unlearned. Roman religion was not dogmatic; when Ennius makes Telamo express the Epicurean view that the gods exist, but take no interest in human affairs, for otherwise the good would prosper and the wicked suffer (Cic. *Div.* 2.104 = *TRF* 269–71 = *ROL* 328–30), no article of a creed was directly attacked; the Roman spectator was no doubt impressed, but he will not therefore have ceased his pious Roman observances. An Ennian Neoptolemus expressed what was and remained a typical Roman view, that one must philosophize, but briefly; for systematic philosophy was uncongenial.[1] Stoic opinions are reflected and introduced by the dramatists as and when they coincided with traditional aristocratic ideas about self-discipline and service to the state.

Non uentus fuit sed Alcumena Euripidi (Plaut. *Rud.* 86) 'That was no gale, it was the Alcmene of Euripides', says Plautus, alluding to the razmataz of a recent Roman production about 190 B.C. Storms, shipwreck, torture, riddles, augury, dreams, portents, snakes, solitude, want, exile, ghosts, battle-narratives, madness, bacchantes, martial heroes, and ladies in reduced circumstances are prominent in the remains of Roman tragedy, and Euripidean themes of recognition, deception, and revenge are particularly favoured. The musical presentation and highly elaborate diction of tragedy were to stimulate the audience emotionally, not intellectually. The demotic realism, the social criticism, the

[1] *TRF* 340 = *ROL* 400. 'Briefly' probably restricts 'philosophy' to the wisdom of Delphi – 'know thyself', etc.

direct challenge to received opinion characteristic of Euripides have boiled away in the decoction.

The rhetorical aspects of tragedy were popular, and, as the second century progressed, increasingly prominent. There had always been divergent tendencies in Latin eloquence. The one was laconic and compressed, and derived from the nature of the language: a single word, a verb, may express a quite complicated sentence; a major part of the nouns and adjectives in Latin are formed from verbal stems; and words may readily be 'understood'. Different facets of this tendency may be seen, for example, in some epitaphs and *elogia* of the second century, in Cato's speeches and *De agri cultura*, and in Terence's plays (not his prologues). The other tendency was towards elaboration, a fullness and decoration effected by alliteration, anaphora, assonance, antithesis, and the like. This may be seen in the epitaphs of the Scipios, the fragments of some of the annalists such as Coelius Antipater, and in the prologues (not the plays) of Terence, as well as in the 'full-blooded' style of Plautus and, above all, in tragic diction. Very roughly, these inherent tendencies correspond to the divergences between the 'Attic' and the 'Asiatic' schools of Greek rhetoric. In the two generations following the Second Punic War the relations of Rome and Pergamum were close, and the leading exponent of the Asiatic style of oratory was the head of the school there, Crates of Mallos. He visited Rome and lectured there on rhetoric while recovering from an accident in 167 B.C.; Terence's prologues, written over the immediately following years, are striking proof of the popularity of this style, which for us is perhaps most familiar in the Epistles of St Paul, himself an 'Asiatic' writer. The Romans discovered, as it were, in the theories and systems and patterns of Greek rhetoric, particularly Asiatic, that they had been speaking prose all the while; the strained antitheses and the almost painfully correct partitioning of Terence's prologues reflect a popular taste for euphuistic excess in judicial rhetoric. This did not go unchallenged. Cato's famous remark *rem tene, uerba sequentur* 'hold to the subject, the words will follow' was directed against this artificiality, and the satirist Lucilius in the 120s B.C. scoffed not only at the contortions of Pacuvian *exordia* (*ROL* (29) 879) but also at the 'tessellation' (*ROL* (2) 84–6) and 'childishness' (*ROL* (5) 186–93) of the Pergamene style.

Accius visited 'Asia', i.e. Pergamum, in the 130s B.C., and he was an adherent of that school both in rhetoric and in scholarship. When asked why he did not plead cases in court, Accius is said to have replied that whereas he (not his Greek author!) controlled what his characters might say, he could not control what an opponent might (Quint. *Inst.* 5.13.43). The story is *bien trouvé*: Accius was of the same age and social class as Afranius, the writer of *togatae*, who did plead cases (Cic. *Brut.* 167).

For all its extreme elaboration, the grand manner of tragedy was directly related to the real-life practice of judicial and forensic rhetoric, especially, no doubt, in Euripidean debates and monologues. Unfortunately no really extensive fragment survives. The figure of thought called by the schoolmen the *dilemma* ('Whither now shall I turn? To *A*? No, because...; then to *B*? No, because...', etc.) occurs at Ennius, *Medea exul*, *TRF* 231f. = *ROL* 284f., translating Euripides, *Medea* 502–4. It occurs again in C. Gracchus fr. 58 Malcovati (Cic. *De or.* 3.214), a fragment of his famous and final speech on the Capitol before being murdered (121 B.C.). Cicero used it in the peroration of his *Pro Murena* (Nov. 63 B.C.), and not much later Catullus again used it (with Ennius in mind) in Ariadne's lament (Cat. 64.177ff.). This intimate relation between the rhetoric of political oratory and of elevated poetry, and the fact that such stylization appealed not to the few but to the many, is very hard for the modern sensibility: our assumptions about the art of persuasion, the place of rhetoric in poetry, sincerity, originality, spontaneity, and so on, are so very different.

Tragic style

The best evidence for the tone and style of early tragedy is in Plautus, who alludes to well-known productions and assumes a considerable knowledge of mythology which will have been disseminated most widely by tragedy. He himself is a master of what was already a fully developed tragic style. He uses this not only for parody and burlesque,[1] but as a normal medium for cantica and as a way of elevating the emotional temperature, e.g. the inquisition in *Captivi* (659–767, senarii), the shipwreck scene and presentation of Ptolemocratia in *Rudens* (185–289, lyric melodrama), the gnomic quality of such passages as *Bac.* 534ff. (septenarii), *Persa* 341ff. (senarii), and above all the *Amphitruo*, the 'tragicomoedia' with its messenger-speeches (186ff., 1053ff., monodies in iambic octonarii) and Alcumena's polymetric song in praise of *uirtus* (633ff.).

As in comedy, a playwright will often have modulated 'upwards' by changing from senarii (representing Greek trimeters) to recitative or canticum also representing trimeters of the original on the arrival of a new character: far less was presented in senarii in a Roman tragedy than in trimeters in a typical Euripidean model. About 70% of the *Iphigenia in Aulis* is in trimeters, but only 30% of Ennius' fragments are in senarii. With the increasing popularity of rhetoric, this spoken element made a considerable recovery in Pacuvius (45%) and Accius (55%), but even so it was never as prominent as in Greek tragedy. On the musical form of Roman drama, see pp. 84–6; in Ennius, all the certain cases of song are solo arias, while all the certain cases of what

[1] Plaut. *Pseud.* 702ff., a messenger; *Mer.* 842ff., departure; *Men.* 831ff., a mad scene. All these in trochaic septenarii.

had been strophic songs in the originals for the chorus have been rewritten as recitative in the long trochaic metres.

This radical change of form naturally affected presentation and character. Ennius makes Medea enter with an operatic libretto in which the subtleties and density of the corresponding trimeter-speech in Euripides are lost (*TRF* 219–21 = *ROL* 266–8 ~ Eur. *Med.* 214ff.). Instead the Roman dramatist makes Medea express sentiments and use language which evoke Roman ideas about honour and service in the *res publica*, with the result that we seem to be listening to a Roman magistrate rather than a Medea.[1] Earlier in the same play Ennius used senarii for the trimeters of the nurse's opening speech (*TRF* 205–13 = *ROL* 253–61 ~ Eur. *Med.* 1ff.), comparison of which is instructive,[2] and for the ensuing dialogue (also in trimeters in the original) between the paidagogos and the nurse:

παλαιὸν οἴκων κτῆμα δεσποίνης ἐμῆς,
τί πρὸς πύλαισι τήνδ' ἄγουσ' ἐρημίαν
ἕστηκας αὐτὴ...; (Euripides, *Medea* 49–51)

Ancient chattel of my mistress' house, why standest thou alone before the doors, keeping this solitude...?

– –́ ⏑–́– –́⏑ –́ – –́ ⏑⁀
antịqu(a) erịlis fịda cụstos cọrporịs,
– –́ – –́ – – ⏑⏑ –́ – –́ ⏑ –
quid sịc t(e) extr(a) ạedes ẹxanimạt(a) elịminạs?
(Ennius, *Medea exul*, *TRF* 214f. = *ROL* 262f.)

Ancient faithful guardian of the mistress' person, why dost thou breathless unthreshold thyself from out the palace...?

As in Euripides, Ennius has a heavy, five-word line, varied in vowels, for the formal address. *Erile corpus* is calqued from such expressions as μητρῷον δέμας 'maternum corpus', as it were, 'the lady my mother' (Aesch. *Eum.* 84), which is far from natural Latin, but which had been 'naturalized' by Naevius:

–́ –́ – –́– –́ ⏑– – –́⏑–
uos quị regạlis cọrporịs custọdiạs
⏑⏑–́⏑
agitạtis... (Naevius, *Lycurgus*, *TRF* 21f. = *ROL* 27f.)

Ye who exercise guardianships of the royal person...

where the poetic plural is also a Grecism. One notes also the tragic compound *e-liminare*, literally 'to unthreshold', the contrived assonance and alliteration of the Latin, and the regrettable exaggeration (*exanimata*) absent from the original. All these traits are characteristic not only of Ennius but all the Roman

[1] G.W. Williams (1968) 359–61.
[2] Leo (1912) 98.

dramatists. Perhaps most striking of all, the address by itself might have seemed a more 'literal' version of another context in Euripides altogether:

γύναι γεραιά, βασιλίδος πιστὴ τροφέ...
(Euripides, *Hippolytus* 267)

Aged woman, faithful nurse of the queen...

Clearly it is a fruitless task to infer details of lost Greek texts from even what appear to be 'literal' Latin translation. Ennius had that line at the back of his mind when he was turning the *Medea*, and has promoted the 'ancient chattel' unnecessarily.

The establishment of a suitably elevated diction for tragedy was not an easy matter. There was a definite upper limit. Epic admitted certain very archaic forms drawn from the language of ritual and law which were avoided in tragedy, e.g. *indu-*, *endo* for *in*, and tragedy could exploit forms from the same sources avoided in comedy, e.g. *quaesendum* for *quaerendum* in *liberum quaesendum causa* 'for the begetting of offspring'.[1] Formulae of the law such as this were used as patterns for analogical extensions and revivals of obsolescent forms (the genitive *-um* for *-orum* is a case in point). Words like *ciuis*, *lex*, *ius*, *arx*, *pater*, *matrona*, *uxor*, *liberi*, *honos*, *gloria*, *laus* were often loaded with emotional Roman connotations. The solemnity and rich diversity of Attic tragic diction were also echoed by analogical formations within living Latin patterns. Thus *e-liminare*, *con-glomerare* were typical tragic inventions, of which a surprising number now lead prosaic lives in English derivatives. On the other hand a formation **ipsi-uentralis*, a 'literal' translation of αὐτάδελφον 'same-wombed' (Soph. *Ant.* 1) would have sounded too bizarre, as there are no *ipse*-compounds in Latin to correspond to the common αὐτο-compounds of Greek. Naturally neologisms attracted the attention of scoffers like Lucilius and grammarians, and for that reason may be over-represented among the fragments: words like *ampl-are* 'enlarge', *clar-ere* 'be famous', adverbs in *-im*, *-atim*, *-itus*, long adjectives (often negated with *in-*) formed with *-bilis*, *-ficus*, *-osus*, *-bundus*, compound adjectives like *alti-uolans*, *tardi-gradus*, *tauri-genus*, *flex-animus*, which correspond to types much more freely formed in Greek. The same striving after variety within the morphology of spoken Latin is to be seen in the coining of abstract nouns in *-tudo* for *-tas*, *-tia* (and the reverse), and of verbal derivatives in *-men(tum)*, *-io*. These are often used as if they were personifications, as the subjects of the sentence, against the grain of the language. Alliteration, assonance, homoeoteleuton, and all the figures which tend to an expansive rather than a laconic eloquence were exploited – anaphora, polyptoton, *figura etymologica*, climax, tricolon, and the multiplication of synonyms. These artifices as well as antitheses, quibbles, etymological and

[1] Ennius, *TRF* 97, 120 = *ROL* 126, 136; see G.W. Williams (1968) 371.

epigrammatic points, the clothing rather than the substance of a sound rhetoric, were favoured, the more so when the influence of Pergamum lent them academic support; but their over-use sometimes detracted from sense and precision.

tú̦ m(e) amǫ́ris mą́gis qu(am) honǫ́ris sẹ́ruauịsti grā̦tiạ.
(Ennius, *Medea exul*, *TRF* 233 = *ROL* 286)

You saved me for love rather than for honour.

So Ennius' Jason to Medea; but it is clear from the context (Eur. *Med.* 530f.) that *honoris* is Ennius' addition, for the sake of a jingle; it is in fact illogical, for *honos*, the reward of the public man, is irrelevant here; at the back of Ennius' mind there is the axiom that *amor* is the province of comedy, the passive condition of an idle soul.[1] In his version of Euripides' *Bacchae* Accius made Tiresias allege that 'neither antiquity nor death nor "huge-agedness"' (*grandaeuitas*) was to prevent Thebans from dancing in honour of Dionysus. Euripides had more reasonably said that the god made no distinction between young and old (Accius, *TRF* 245 = *ROL* 210 ~ Eur. *Bacc.* 206f.), without absurdly mentioning 'death'.

Originality

Cicero was misleading when he alluded to *fabellas Latinas ad uerbum ex graecis expressis* 'entertainments in Latin literally translated from the Greek' (*Fin.* 1.2.4). He had in mind Ennius' *Medea exul* and Pacuvius' *Antiopa*, of which sufficient survives in Greek and Latin to show that *ad uerbum* is an exaggeration. He only meant that in these cases, to which may be added Accius' *Bacchae*, the adaptor had kept the same scenes in the same order as in his original. Elsewhere (*Acad.* 1.10) Cicero says that Roman tragedians expressed the 'feel', not the words (*non uerba sed uim*) of the originals. Not even that is true: the Euripides who appears in Ennian or Accian guise has been transmogrified, especially with respect to his intellectual 'bite'.

Dramatists not only interfered with the musical, metrical, and stylistic presentation of Greek plays, but also changed their emphases and substance in all sorts of ways. The soldier-chorus of Euripides' *Iphigenia in Aulis* become girls in Ennius' version. Pacuvius toned down Ulysses' lamentations in his version of Sophocles' *Niptra* (Cic. *Tusc.* 2.21.48). He introduced a philosophical *locus* inspired by a passage of Euripides' *Chrysippus*, quite un-Sophoclean in tone, into Sophocles' *Chryses*. As Cicero noted (*Div.* 1.131) it is imperfectly integrated, both logically and dramatically. Accius changed the arrangement in Euripides' *Phoenissae* by which Polynices and Eteocles were to share power, thus altering the balance of sympathies (Eur. *Phoen.* 69ff., cf. Accius,

[1] G.W. Williams (1968) 362f.

TRF 590, 591–3 = *ROL* 589, 594–6). If his *Antigone* represents Sophocles' play, Accius changed the guard's famous narrative into dramatic action.

These alterations are like those known in Roman comedy, where, as we know, they gave rise to a controversy in Terence's time about the role of the adaptor and his fidelity to an original. Whether something similar was argued over by tragedians is unknown. Perhaps not; for since Naevius, tragedians had appeared as original authors of *praetextae*, and anyway, it was open to them to take the line that they were not dealing with works of fiction in the same sense as a comic poet. The tragedian was a poetic historian, a scholar, the interpreter of a complex source-material which included not only the Attic drama but Homer and Pindar and the commentators. He was as entitled to reinterpret, to cut, and to add, as a contemporary Greek dramatist. Ennius might have written tragedies without any particular model, but did not go so far. Free addition and complete independence came later. It is hard to imagine any Greek original for the laboured, academic rhetoric of Pacuvius' lines on Hellenistic Fortune (*TRF* 366–75 = *ROL tr. inc.* 37–46, Auct. *ad Her.* 2.23.36),[1] and Accius' plays *Nyctegresia* 'The night-sortie' and *Epinausimache* 'The battle at the ships' sound like direct dramatizations of the corresponding episodes of the *Iliad*. If these had no originals in the Attic drama, it is possible that other plays of his with more conventional tragic titles were also free compositions, the result of much reading, not only of the texts of the Attic dramatists, but also Greek literature in general, the commentators too, and the handbooks of rhetorical theory.

Accius, the polemical scholar, the Pergamene rhetorician, the authority on orthography, the head of the college of poets, the historian of the Greek and Roman theatre, and the Hellenistic tragedian evinces a new self-confidence and artistic awareness.[2] He, Afranius, and Lucilius were children in Terence's time; all were Roman citizens by birth, and had no need to earn their living by the pen. In this generation we see a thorough blending of the Greek and the specifically Roman (as opposed to Italian) traditions. It is unfortunate that the Greek intellectual influences to which Accius and his contemporaries were most open were those of Pergamum, rather than of Alexandria; Roman scholarship got off to a bad start from which it never recovered; it was the poets of Alexandria, rather than the rhetoricians of Pergamum, who had most fruitfully stimulated Ennius, and who were to do the same again for the poets of the classical period.

[1] Pacuvius quotes, as a lecturer might, the tenets of various *philosophi* (among whom he counts artists, like himself). The image of Fortune standing on a ball was modern; it occurs first in Greek literature in Cebes, *Pinax* 7.

[2] Leo (1913) 384ff.

6

PROSE LITERATURE

1. THE RANGE OF OLD LATIN PROSE: CATO AND FLAMININUS

'Manios made me for Numasios'; 'Let no one violate this grove nor cart or carry away what is in the grove nor cut wood except on the day when the annual sacrifice takes place.' The oldest use of the alphabet had been to record particular facts and prohibitions like these; and we need not doubt that from a very early date people wrote lists, recipes, letters, etc. on more perishable surfaces than stone or bronze. Of these all trace is lost, as there is no Roman Oxyrhynchus. Prose literature, as opposed to mere writing, may be said to have begun when men began to exploit the fact that their views on important matters could be disseminated by means of the *liber* or *uolumen* which could be multiplied. That was in the Hellenistic period, after the Romans came into contact with the Greeks of southern Italy and Sicily. Before then the Romans had been like most ancient peoples – for example, the contemporary Spartans or Carthaginians, or the Athenians down to Socrates' time – in using the alphabet for specific, 'one-off' purposes in writing prose. While men knew that to speak well was a necessary *uirtus* in politics, the pen was not regarded as a potential source of authority or glory in the affairs of the city, or any other sphere of life. As to what is implied by the 'multiplication' of copies of a book, the very notions of 'publication', 'book-trade', and 'reading public', as well as of reading itself – for listening was just as important – the reader is referred to Chapter 1, 'Books and Readers': the points made there have an important bearing on the styles, the range, and the order of the expansion of Latin prose literature.

From at least the 130s B.C. the Romans themselves believed that the father of Latin prose was Appius Claudius Caecus, a contemporary of Philemon, Ptolemy I, and Pyrrhus. Cicero refers to a letter of Panaetius (resident at Rome in the 130s B.C.) in which the Stoic philosopher praised a *carmen* – the word does not necessarily imply a verse-form – which he took to be by Appius Claudius Caecus and which was of apparently Pythagorean character (Cic. *Tusc.* 4.2.4).[1]

[1] Other ancient references to this supposed work of Appius are given by Schanz–Hosius (1927) 41f. Cato's *Carmen de moribus* was a collection of moralizing reflections quite certainly in prose (Gell. *N.A.* 11.2). It should not be lightly assumed that Cato put it together at all, though it is clear that collections of Cato's real or alleged *dicta* were already circulating in Cicero's time (cf., e.g., Cic. *Off.* 2.25).

Cicero himself accepted as genuine a speech in which Appius opposed peace with Pyrrhus (*Sen.* 16, *Brut.* 61, cf. p. 62 n. 1), and in the second century A.D. the jurist Pomponius refers to an alleged work of Appius, *De usurpationibus*, which, however, was no longer extant (*Dig.* 1.2.2.36). Morals, oratory, the law: it is significant for our appreciation of the Roman attitude to prose that it should have been works of this kind that were attributed to the venerable elder statesman. It is, however, at best doubtful whether any of them were authentic.

In the generation before Cicero the kinds of writing which were either already flourishing as distinct genres or still acquiring 'their own nature' ranged down in grandeur from oratory – forensic, judicial, commemorative – through history, memoirs, letter-writing, to technical treatises on practical subjects such as farming, the law, or the calendar. Besides, now that a Hellenizing Latin poetry had existed for a century and more, there were the beginnings of a scholarly literature directed to its mapping and explanation. This was naturally the business of the poets themselves and of educated freedmen or freedmen's sons like Accius, Aelius Stilo, Octavius Lampadio, and Lutatius Daphnis (cf. Suet. *Gramm.* 1ff.). All other kinds of prose writing, however, were developed by Roman senators, not for art's sake, but as ever more carefully honed weapons directly or indirectly useful in their political lives. M. Porcius Cato the Elder was the most important of them all. In the preface to his *Origines* (see p. 149) he remarked that the great and famous should give an account not only of their public lives but also of their *otium*, their relaxation (fr. 2 Peter).[1] He wrote history not to thrill nor to philosophize, but to persuade the reader of the rightness for the present and the future of certain moral and political values – Cato's own, of course – as he saw them in the *exempla* of the past, and so confirm what he saw as the true Roman identity in the minds of his readers.

Cato reached the consulship in 195 B.C. at the age of thirty-nine, a remarkable achievement in itself for a *nouus homo* at this time, but this was only the beginning of the eventful period in which his long literary career belongs (see Appendix). As consul he campaigned in Spain; in 191 B.C. he was sent on an important diplomatic mission to Athens, where he spoke in Latin through an interpreter, and served with distinction under M'. Acilius Glabrio (whom he later prosecuted) at Thermopylae. In 189 B.C. he was an unsuccessful competitor for the censorship when the liberal and philhellene aristocrats T. Quinctius Flamininus and Marcellus were successful: Flamininus' brother was also the victim of a prosecution by the litigious Cato.

Flamininus, some six years younger than Cato, had fiery ambition in common with him, but in most other respects of background and temperament was very different. His early career had brought him into close contact with the Greek

[1] We cite the *Origines* from Peter (1914), the speeches from Malcovati (1955), and the other fragments from Jordan (1860).

culture of Tarentum, and, thanks to military and diplomatic skill as well as to his excellent connexions, he reached the consulship three years before Cato, and received charge of the war against Philip of Macedon, which he duly won (197 B.C.).[1] The spirit of his and Marcellus' censorship was optimistic and liberal. Wars were ending, and at last there was the prospect of lasting peace. Armies and navies were returning with vast booty and new tastes. Rome was now the diplomatic focus of the *oecumene*. Five years later, however, the mood had changed entirely. The Scipios had been disgraced in a series of trials which Cato himself had promoted; the scandal of the Bacchanalian affair had shaken domestic confidence, and a consular army had been lost in Liguria. Cato was elected censor for 184/3 B.C. at a time when it seemed that every facet of Roman life was subject to momentous and uncontrolled forces which (Cato thought) threatened to destroy the character of the Roman institutions. His censorship was never forgotten for its severity.

He championed what he saw as the true *mores maiorum*, ancestral customs, in which a vision (perhaps even then romantic) of the simple life was central. He presented himself as the hard-headed, commonsensical peasant, with no time for Hellenistic fol-de-rol: Greek doctors are death, *poetae* and expert chefs are a sign of decadence (cf. *or. fr.* 217).[2] Cato's son Licinianus was born about 192 B.C., and Cato took his role as educator seriously, even preparing a book of improving stories 'written in big letters' to teach the boy to read (Plut. *Cat. Maj.* 20). From this time until his death in 149 B.C. Cato used his pen to attack, to defend, to judge, and to instruct with a verve, originality, and directness that would be remarkable in a man half his age and in any era. His blunt and contentious manner involved him in many prosecutions of leading men; he himself was prosecuted forty-four times, though he was never convicted of anything: that is at least as much a tribute to his own eloquence as to his honesty.[3]

It would be an over-simplification to suppose that Flamininus and Cato were respectively simply 'for' and 'against' the tide of Hellenistic culture. In particular one must beware of irrelevant modern ideas of cultural nationalism if one is to understand Cato, who was a great deal more versed in things Greek than, say, Marius two generations later, and whose very eclecticism was Hellenistic. He recommended that one should dip into Greek literature, not soak oneself in it; and the once widespread idea, that he did not learn the language until he was an old man, has been recognized as a mistake.[4] Like

[1] On Flamininus see Badian (1970).

[2] *Ad Marcum filium* fr. 1 Jordan (Pliny, *N.H.* 29.7.14, *Cat. Maj.* 23); *carmen de moribus* fr. 2 Jordan (Gell. *N.A.* 11.2).

[3] On Cato see Kienast (1954) *passim* with his bibliography, 167f.

[4] See Helm, *RE* XXII 145.33ff., Gelzer, ibid. 110.43ff., Fraenkel (1968) 130, against Leo (1913) 283.

Flamininus, whose interest in Greek literature as such may even have been exaggerated, he will have learnt the language as a young man in southern Italy. A fragment of his Athenian speech, *Antiochus epistulis bellum gerit*, *calamo et atramento militat* 'Antiochus wages war with letters, he fights with pen and ink' (fr. 20 Malcovati), has been identified as an echo of a disparaging remark of Demosthenes about Philip of Macedon, a clever ploy in a speech delivered through an interpreter.[1] As Plutarch noted (*Cat. Maj.* 12), Cato could have used Greek if he had wanted: he used Latin for a political reason (see p. 149). Although Cato made a point of praising the collectivism of the good old *res publica* (cf. e.g. frs. 18, 149, 206) and of ridiculing the adoption of Greek customs (frs. 95, 115), he himself was an example of the drive and individualism of Hellenistic *uomo universale* dedicated to the active life. The dictum from the preface of the *Origines* quoted above (p. 139) is an adaptation of the first sentence of Xenophon's *Symposium*. Xenophon was the kind of Greek that Cato could admire as a man of action and as a writer: for he if anyone among Greeks 'held to the subject and let the words follow' (see p. 143).

It may surprise the student of literature that the spectrum of prose-writing described above did not include the novel, the short story, or *belles lettres* of any kind. This would have seemed less strange to a Panaetius or a Polybius; for Greeks as for Romans, what we would call fiction and expect to find in prose was properly a lower part of poetry. At Rome this meant *saturae* (see pp. 156–71). Nor was there any prose philosophy, theology, or sociology. The theory that Ennius' *Euhemerus* was a prose work, although widely accepted today, is questionable on this and on more particular grounds (see pp. 157–8). In the age of the Gracchi, Latin prose was a medium for facts, instruction, argumentation, exhortation, persuasion, and propaganda, not merely for entertainment, artistic experiment, or speculation, which, nevertheless, might have their places as means to more serious ends.

Before we survey the prose of the second century more closely, three general points must be made. Firstly, it is appropriate enough at almost any other stage of Latin literature's development to adopt a strict approach by genre; but here if we were to confine our attention to that which is in Latin and in prose, we should seriously restrict and misrepresent the horizons of our subject. Latin prose of the second century B.C. is even worse represented by fragments than poetry; in historiography a quite false picture would emerge if we ignored the works of Fabius Pictor, Aulus Albinus, and Polybius and others, all written in Greek and belonging equally to the history of Hellenistic literature; in oratory, the prologues of Plautus and Terence and the Greek diplomatic correspondence of, for example, Flamininus are important evidence for the practice of the art of persuasion in the earlier second century B.C., while the fragments of tragedy,

[1] Fraenkel (1968) 130 compares fr. 20 with Dem. 4.30.

Ennius' *Annales*, and Lucilius' *Satires* are in various ways important for the theory and practice of rhetoric.

Next, the ancient theory of genres was teleological; modern critics following ancient often discuss early Roman writing on the implicit premiss that what came first was necessarily crude, but prepared the way for later developments, which culminate when the genre 'achieves its own nature', after which there is a decline. There are some dangers in this model; see p. 154. We have dismissed the ancient claim made for Appius Claudius Caecus that he was the father of Roman prose-literature; but we do not therefore imply that when he addressed the Senate all he could do was grunt. There were strong men before Agamemnon, and there were eloquent Romans before Cato: Ennius called M. Cornelius Cethegus 'choice flower of the People, the marrow of Persuasion' (*Ann.* (9) 303–8v = *ROL* 300–5), and he died in 196 B.C., before the consulship of Cato.

Thirdly, and most important of all, it was the same men, active politicians all, who practised all the as yet imperfectly differentiated kinds of prose enumerated earlier. Among these Cato is most important, and the tones of voice which he used in any writing, even sometimes the technical, were naturally those which he used in the Senate and the courts. Oratory therefore, the highest of our categories, was crucially important for the style of prose-writing on any but the most mundane topics.

2. TECHNICAL WRITING

Only the least pretentious kind of prose is represented by a more-or-less complete surviving work. Cato's *De agri cultura* was written about 160 B.C., when Italy as a whole was beginning to recover from the worst effects of the Punic War and when radical changes in land-use were taking place. In the brief preface we hear the didactic voice of Cato the statesman and orator; his purpose is protreptic, and he is addressing the man with money to invest. Having briefly compared the profitability and security of farming with those of banking and trade and commended the farming way of life, 'So much for eloquence', Cato seems to say; 'now down to business.' In what follows we have a pot-pourri of principles, notes, recipes, instructions, and advice salted with apophthegms. Cato does not attempt a systematic treatment. The work altogether lacks the kind of structural organization that we find even artificially imposed in, say, Varro's *Res rusticae* (37 B.C.) or the anonymous *Rhetorica ad Herennium* (*c.* 80 B.C.). It is a work to dip into, not to read as a continuous whole, and except superficially it lacks the character of a Greek technical manual, a humble but well-established genre to which Hellenistic mathematicians, philosophers, and *philologoi* had contributed. Cato can be very precise in giving quantities for a recipe or the exact magic formula for a ritual or spell, but when he attempts the description of an oil-press he is less successful; for although he gives precise dimensions for the parts, he omits to explain adequately all his technical terms, and he does not use (as he might) lettered diagrams in the manner of an Archimedes or a Philon Mechanicus. For us, and for later generations of Romans, a remarkable quality of the book is the vivid impression of its editor's personality – his provocative directness (e.g. his advice on how to pick and control a bailiff and what to do with an old slave, 2–3), his idiosyncratic enthusiasms (e.g. for cabbage as a panacea, 156), his blend of sharp worldliness and credulous superstition, his authoritarian outlook, and his respect for the *mores maiorum*. The lack of formal organization can only to a very limited extent be explained as due to the vicissitudes of transmission and interpolation, and in several ways one is reminded of the characteristics of the *satura* of the poets.

This was only one of several monographs or treatises on practical subjects of social relevance that Cato wrote (see Appendix). Some of these were addressed as more or less open letters to his son Cato Licinianus, born *c.* 192 B.C. One on rhetoric contained the definition *orator est, Marce fili, uir bonus dicendi peritus* 'The statesman, Marcus my boy, is a gentleman experienced in speaking' (fr. 14 Jordan, Sen. *Contr.* 1 *praef.* 9), and the famous precept *rem tene, uerba sequentur* 'Hold to the subject, the words will follow' (fr. 15, Julius Victor p. 374 Halm). It is probably misleading to think of these works as a collection, constituting a kind of encyclopaedia; apart from the fact that they were certainly unsystematic and eclectic and quirky, there is no evidence at all to suggest that Cato himself collected or edited them as a body, whatever their *fortuna* may have been.[1]

The one and only example of the Senate's patronage of 'literature' was the commission given to D. Silanus after the destruction of Carthage in 146 B.C. to translate into Latin the twenty-eight books of the farming manual of the Carthaginian Mago (Pliny, *N.H.* 18.22). Other researches of which we hear include the chronological and calendaric studies of M'. Acilius Glabrio and M. Fulvius Nobilior, *c.* 190 B.C. (see p. 63), and the astronomical work of C. Sulpicius Galus (cos. 166 B.C., Pliny, *N.H.* 2.53, 2.83, Livy 44.37.5), who, however, is unlikely to have known, let alone understood, the researches of his great contemporary, Hipparchus of Bithynia. As mentioned above, poets and freedmen-scholars inaugurated the study of the history of Latin literature in the Gracchan period; unfortunately for the quality of their work it was the school of Pergamum rather than the tradition of Alexandrian scholarship which most influenced them (see pp. 78, 137). Much more important was the study of Roman law, to which the methods of Peripatetic classification and definition were directly appropriate, and this suffered less from the dogmatism and speculation

[1] The important growth-point for *florilegia* which ultimately lie behind the collections of *dicta Catonis* so well known in the Middle Ages (cf. F. Skutsch, *RE* v 358–70) will have been in Imperial times, when the memory of Cato the Elder and Cato Minor, the Stoic sage, was confused.

characteristic of Crates of Mallos and his Pergamene followers. The earliest important work was the *Tripertita* of Sex. Aelius Paetus Catus (Pomp. *Dig.* 1.2.2.38), written probably in the 190s B.C.[1] This included a text of the Twelve Tables, a commentary on their interpretation, and an account of the appropriate procedures at law. It is noteworthy that Aelius was the first jurist who was not himself a *pontifex* or *augur*. Neither was Cato; he himself, or his son, wrote commentaries of some kind on the civil law (Festus p. 144 L, cf. Cic. *De or.* 3.135, 2.142), while Licinianus certainly wrote fifteen or more books identical with or including a *De legis disciplina*, in which theoretical propositions appeared (Gell. *N.A.* 13.20(19).9). C. Sempronius Tuditanus (cos. 129 B.C.) wrote thirteen or more *libri magistratuum*, a work combining historical research and legal interpretation. Pomponius (loc. cit.) describes P. Mucius Scaevola Pontifex (cos. 133), M. Junius Brutus, and Manius Manilius (a friend of Lucilius) as the 'founders' of civil law. He ascribes to them respectively ten, seven[2] and three books. P. Mucius Scaevola Pontifex in some sense also published the *annales* of the pontifical college; these filled eighty books (Cic. *De or.* 2.52, Serv. auct. *ad* Virg. *Aen.* 1.373). What exactly 'publication' implies is not clear; the records had certainly been available to earlier historians. His son Q. Mucius Scaevola Pontifex (cos. 95) composed eighteen authoritative books on civil law, as well as a monograph, the title of which, Ὅροι 'definitions', itself implies the Peripatetic nature of the treatment. M. Junius Brutus' three genuine works are of interest as they were the first in dialogue form in Latin, with dramatic settings at Privernum, Albanum, and Tibur; this of course is the literary form used with such grace and nostalgia by Cicero in the last years of the Republic. Although virtually nothing specific can be cited from these legal studies of the second century B.C. they collectively represent an important contribution to the history of ideas, for these jurists went far beyond Greek achievement in this area by combining empirical studies of precedent with theoretical abstraction; from which emerged such important legal concepts as the *ius gentium* and the *liber homo*.

3. THE PEN IN POLITICS

The intended readers of the kind of technical works reviewed above were influential Romans professionally interested in the subjects treated. The authors, themselves rich men, will have seen to the multiplication and circulation of copies in the first instance; there was no 'copyright', and the very idea that an author might make some money, let alone a living, by writing prose would have seemed odd to all and to many perhaps wrong (cf. pp. 19–22). These circumstances naturally hindered the development of a prose literature addressed to a

[1] See Watson (1971) 9.

[2] Cicero emphasizes that only three of these were authentic (*De or.* 2.224).

wider audience on topics less specialist in character or of more ambitious appeal than the technical. The subject of potentially greatest interest and widest appeal was Roman history and contemporary politics: the whole cast of Roman thought, the character of the constitution, and the kaleidoscopic nature of the history of the past century precluded for the generation of the Gracchi the neat separation of the study of the past and the present into distinct genres. Even by the end of the century, the various strands which make up the rope of Roman historiography were still only strands. While certain themes can be seen to have been shared by writers as different as Ennius and Cato, Fabius and Coelius Antipater, for example an emphasis on the individual and his proper relation through *uirtus* to the extended family which was the *res publica*, fundamental questions of approach, emphasis, and presentation remained open at the end of the second century B.C. Thus, in discussing 'History' (pp. 149–52), we shall in fact be dealing with strands; and in order that we should appreciate their texture, it will be necessary first to discuss some kinds of writing which are best described as political manifestos or memoirs.

In the Greek world it had long been the custom of authors to address poems, histories, and technical works to a patron or friend, so that the work might take on the appearance of a private letter of didactic character. In the later second century we find the same in Latin literature. Lucilius addressed several of his poems to friends as verse-epistles; Accius' *Didascalica* was nominally addressed to one Baebius, Coelius Antipater's History of the Second Punic War was addressed to Aelius Stilo. Written during the last decades of the second century, this was the first prose-history in which the author sought to sweeten his instruction with the charms of rhetorical presentation. He seems to have followed the example of the worse sort of Hellenistic historian, and his style involved the disruption of the natural order of words in order to achieve rhythmical effects later, and rightly, condemned (cf. Auct. *ad Her*. 4.12.18 *has res ad te scriptas Luci misimus Aeli*, with a hexameter-movement, cf. Cic. *Orat*. 229). Clearly Coelius had a wider audience in mind, and his dedication to Aelius Stilo is only a literary device. In other works, however, the use of the letter-form or dedication was not so simply a convention. As we have seen, several of Cato's shorter works were addressed to Cato Licinianus, among them 'letters' on rhetoric (see p. 143), on medicine (Pliny, *N.H*. 29.14), and even several books on agriculture (Serv. *ad* Virg. *Geo*. 2.412). A century later the *Commentariolum petitionis* attributed rightly or wrongly to Marcus' brother Quintus Cicero is in the form of a private letter giving Marcus Cicero advice on the occasion of his standing for the consulship of 63 B.C. From the 120s B.C. there are excerpts of a similarly political letter written by Cornelia to her son Gaius Gracchus dissuading him from his plan to stand for the Tribunate in 123 B.C. The authenticity of the document has been much disputed, for no good reason at all.[1] It is of special interest that, if genuine, this is the earliest extant prose-writing in *any* language by a woman:

Verbis conceptis deierare ausim, praeterquam qui Tiberium Gracchum necarunt, neminem inimicum tantum molestiae tantumque laboris quantum te ob has res mihi tradidisse, quem oportebat omnium eorum quos antehac habui liberos [eorum] partis tolerare, atque curare ut quam minimum sollicitudinis in senecta haberem, utique quaecumque ageres, ea uelles maxume mihi placere, atque uti nefas haberes rerum maiorum aduersum meam sententiam quicquam facere, praesertim mihi quoi parua pars uitae superest. ne id quidem tam breue spatium potest opitulari quin et mihi aduersere et rem publicam profliges? denique quae pausa erit? ecquando desinet familia nostra insanire? ecquando modus ei rei haberi poterit? ecquando desinemus et habentes et praebentes molestiis insistere? ecquando perpudescet miscenda atque perturbanda re publica? sed si omnino non id fieri potest, ubi ego mortua ero, petito tribunatum: per me facito quod lubebit, cum ego non sentiam. ubi ego mortua ero, parentabis mihi et inuocabis deum parentem. in eo tempore nonne pudebit te eorum deum preces expetere, quos uiuos atque praesentes relictos atque desertos habueris? ne ille sirit Iuppiter te ea perseuerare nec tibi tantam dementiam uenire in animum! et si perseueras, uereor ne in omnem uitam tantum laboris culpa tua recipias, uti nullo tempore tute tibi placere possis.

'uerba ex epistula Corneliae Gracchorum matris ex libro Corneli Nepotis de Latinis Historicis excerpta.' (Nepos, frag. 2 Winstedt)

I would take a solemn oath that apart from those who killed Tiberius Gracchus no one has given me so much trouble and so much pain as you in this matter, who ought to undertake the part of all the children I have ever had, and to make sure that I should have as little worry as possible in my old age, and that, whatever your schemes might be, you should wish them to be agreeable to me, and that you should count it a sin to take any major step against my wishes, especially considering I have only a little part of life left. Is it quite impossible to cooperate for even that short space of time without your opposing me and ruining our country? Where will it all end? Will our family ever cease from madness? Can a bound ever be put to it? Shall we ever cease to dwell on affronts, both causing and suffering them? Shall we ever begin to feel true shame for confounding and destroying the constitution? But if that is quite impossible, when I am dead, then seek the Tribunate. Do what you like as far as I am concerned, when I am not there to know it. When I am dead, you will sacrifice to me and invoke me as your hallowed parent. At that time will you not be ashamed to seek the intercession of those hallowed ones whom alive and present you treated with abandonment and desertion? May Jove above not let you persist in this nor let such lunacy enter your mind! But if you do persist, I fear that through your own fault you will encounter so much trouble throughout your whole life that at no time will you be able to rest content.

Cornelia wrote from Misenum, whither she had retired from Rome after Tiberius' assassination (133 B.C.). It is precisely because she is in deadly earnest that she addresses Gaius as if he were a public meeting, and it is remarkable that

[1] Cicero knew a collection of her letters, *Brut.* 211; cf. Leo (1913) 304f.

she is able to write so forcefully in Gaius' own language: no Roman lady ever had the opportunity or occasion to practise public oratory. Cornelia was an exceptional character: Plutarch comments on her culture (*C. Gracchus* 19) and Cicero recognized in her letters the same pure Latin as he admired in her son's speeches (*Brut.* 211, cf. Quint. *Inst.* 1.1.6, Plut. *C. Gracchus* 13). The style is virile, and it is noteworthy that Cornelia avoids diminutives even where they might have been appropriate (*pars* not *particula uitae*, *breue* not *breuiculum spatium*). The grammarian might criticize the loosely strung clauses of the opening sentence and the change of construction at *praesertim mihi* as well as the superabundance of Cornelia's rhetorical questions starting *ecquando...?*. These features, however, show that we are dealing not with a carefully revised and elaborate composition but with a spontaneous outburst, and it is therefore the more striking to note how naturally come the figures of speech which Cornelia uses – antithesis (*quam minimum...maxume*, *mihi aduersere*, *rem publicam profliges*), anaphora (*quantum...quantum*), hendiadys (*quos uiuos atque praesentes relictos atque desertos habueris*). This is a good example of Cato's precept *rem tene, uerba sequentur* observed. In fact, he could not have done better himself, and the Latinity and directness are precisely his (see below, p. 152). Although this has the appearance of a private letter intended for Gaius' guilty eyes alone, Cornelia's forensic vigour suggests that she may have intended to 'play dirty' by circulating copies at Rome to embarrass Gaius. In this case the ostensibly private letter would, like the *Commentariolum petitionis*, also be a political broadsheet.

Gaius himself wrote a memoir addressed to one M. Pomponius (Cic. *Div.* 1.18.36, Plut. *Ti. Gracchus* 8) which was clearly intended as an 'open letter' and contained information about his own and Tiberius' experiences. The autobiographical memoir is well attested in the period 120–90 B.C. Aemilius Scaurus wrote three books *De vita sua* to L. Fufidius (Cic. *Brut.* 112), Rutilius Rufus wrote five, and Q. Catulus one *De consulatu et de rebus gestis suis*, addressing the work to the poet Furius and affecting Xenophon's style (Cic. *Brut.* 132). All these men were considerable orators, and the forensic manner will naturally have coloured their writings. One can judge by analogy with the popularity in our own times of politicians' memoirs how such compositions would find a reading public not only among senators but also among many of lower degree who would otherwise have little interest in 'literature'.

This kind of prose-work was the special product of the Roman nobility at a particularly contentious period. Among Hellenes, as far as we know, only King Pyrrhus (possibly) and Aratus of Sicyon had written political autobiographies intended for the public and posterity. The later books of Cato's *Origines* included lengthy quotations of the author's own speeches, and undoubtedly had some of the character of political autobiography (see p. 150). Scipio Africanus (father of Cornelia) wrote a policy statement in Greek and addressed it to Philip V of Macedon (Polyb. 10.9.3) – and, no doubt, the world; none of his Latin speeches were preserved (cf. Cic. *Brut.* 77, *Off.* 3.1.4; Livy 38.56.6 and Gell. *N.A.* 4.18 derive from someone's imaginative concoction, not from Scipio).[1] Scipio Nasica Corculum wrote a Greek account of the Pydna campaign of 167 B.C., giving his own version of events, and addressing it to a Hellenistic prince (Plut. *Aem.* 15), no doubt to influence Greek opinion in general.

There survive from the 190s and 180s a number of decrees in the form of letters drafted in Greek and addressed to Greek communities by the Senate or individual Roman commanders. One by Flamininus to the lords and citizenry of the small town of Chyretiae in Perrhaebia illustrates the eager thirst of a Roman noble for χάριτα καὶ φιλοδοξίαν, i.e. *gratiam atque gloriam*. It is plausibly supposed that Flamininus wrote this rather flowery piece himself (*Syll.*[3] 593 = Sherk (1969) no. 33); while criticism of Flamininus' Greek as Greek is certainly mistaken,[2] the letter may fairly be faulted as over-elaborate, as diplomatese so often was and is. Flamininus overdoes the intensifying adverbs, and used the same kind of strained antithesis as is characteristic of Terence in his prologues. Nevertheless it is interesting and significant that at this comparatively early date a Roman should be seen taking such pains over phrase-length and sentence-structure. The passage turns easily into Latin, and the result will look if not like Cicero, then like C. Gracchus. How then did Flamininus speak when he addressed the Senate? And what kind of oratorical style underlies the very long and complex sentence with which Plautus makes Mercury greet the audience of *Amphitruo* (*c.* 189 B.C.: ll. 1–16)? We must beware of too simple a teleological model in describing the development of style in Latin oratory.

A quite different impression is given by the laconic but legally precise note scribbled by Aemilius Paullus in Spain in September 190 B.C. (Julian):

L. Aimilius L. f. inpeirator decreiuit utei quei Hastensium seruei in turri Lascutana habitarent leiberei essent. agrum oppidumque quod ea tempestate posedisent, item possidere habereque iousit, dum poplus senatusque Romanus uellet. act. in castreis a. d. xii k. febr. (*CIL* 1^2 614)

> *L. Aemilius (Paullus) son of Lucius, victorious general, decreed that the slaves of the Hastenses who lived at* Turris Luscitana *should be free. The land and the township which they possessed at that time he ordered they should likewise possess and own as long as the Roman People and Senate wished. Transacted in camp twelve days before the kalends of February.*[3]

[1] See Malcovati (1955) 6–8.

[2] The criticisms made by Sherk (1969) 199 are mistaken, and Badian's verdict that Flamininus' Greek is 'harsh and unidiomatic' is unkind (1974: 54). Neither takes account of the sentence structure.

[3] The calendar was out of true at this time (see p. 81), and the date in fact denotes September. The inscription is usually assigned to 189 B.C., after Paullus' victory over the Lusitanians (Livy 37.57.5).

When Cato spoke in Latin at Athens in 191 B.C. (see above, p. 141) it struck the listeners how much longer the interpreter seemed to take than Cato in making a point; and Cato could have got by in Greek if he had chosen (Plut. *Cat. Maj.* 12). It looks as though Cato was making a deliberate point here. By using Latin in his own pithy way, Cato was asserting the new importance of the language in international diplomacy, and implicitly rejecting the attitude and the Greek rhetoric of a Flamininus.

4. HISTORY

The earliest prose-histories of Rome were written in Greek by Q. Fabius Maximus and L. Cincius Alimentus, probably in the 190s B.C.; their aim will have been to explain and publicize the history of their relatively obscure πόλις, city, to the Hellenistic world at large.[1] Naevius and Ennius addressed a domestic audience in verse with quite another aim (see pp. 59–76). The sources theoretically available to them all included the *annales* kept by the Pontifex Maximus, treaties (e.g. with Carthage, Polyb. 3.22.3), *elogia*, family records and traditions, funeral laudations, the Greek historians Hellanicus, Hieronymus of Cardia, Antigonus, Timaeus, Silenus, Chaerea, Sosylus, the chronographical and geographical studies of Eratosthenes, and last but not least, personal experience; for all of them played some part in the events which they describe. Greek continued to be a medium for history right through the second century. P. Cornelius Scipio (the adoptive father of Scipio Aemilianus, Cic. *Brut.* 77), A. Postumius Albinus (whom Polybius called a windbag (32.29.1) and whom Cato mocked for his apologizing in advance for any stylistic shortcomings in his Greek, Gell. *N.A.* 11.8.2), C. Acilius (Liv. *per.* 53 *ad ann.* 142 B.C.), and Rutilius Rufus (Ath. 168d) all wrote in this tradition. It was Cato who founded Latin historiography as such with his *Origines*.

This was a work of his old age begun not earlier than 170 B.C. when he was sixty-five (cf. fr. 49 Peter and Leo (1913) 291); its general character is summarized in Cornelius Nepos' *Life of Cato* (24.3.4). The first book dealt with the Greek *Aborigines* of Italy, Aeneas and his Trojans, Lavinium, Alba, the foundation of Rome (752/1 B.C. in Cato's reckoning, fr. 17), and the reigns of the kings. The second and third books described the origins, customs and characters of Italian cities and peoples; it is only to the first three books that the

This would conveniently explain *inpeirator*, but it seems not to have been noticed that Polybius says that the Commissioners for the Eastern Settlement (of whom Paullus was one) left Italy just as Regillus' fleet was returning to Brundisium (21.24.16–17); Regillus hurried to Rome and triumphed *kal. feb.* 189 B.C. (Livy 37.59), i.e. early in September. Either Paullus must have missed the boat, or in fact the inscription belongs to September 190 B.C.: the fact that Paullus had suffered a heavy reverse that year (Livy 37.46) is not incompatible with his also having won a victory in virtue of which he had been hailed as *imperator*.

[1] See Badian (1966) ch. 1.

title *Origines* (κτίσεις 'foundations') properly applies. Probably what later passed as Books 4 to 7 were only published after Cato's death; these were a separate work as regards content and approach, and Cato omitted altogether the early Republic. According to Nepos Books 4 and 5 dealt with the Punic Wars, and he adds that here and subsequently Cato described wars *capitulatim* 'in summary form', or 'by topics', not like, say, Thucydides, or Polybius. There must be some over-simplification here, since Cato included a long quotation from his own speech *Against the Rhodians* (167 B.C.) in Book 5, which might imply that Philip, Antiochus, and Perseus also came in these books.[1] Book 7 ended with the misbehaviour in Spain of the praetor Servius Galba (151 B.C.) and Cato's own prosecution of him (149 B.C.), this last only months before Cato's death. Whatever the precise interpretation of *capitulatim* and the content of Books 4 and 5, the narrative evidently became slower and denser in the last books. Nepos ends by noting that Cato did not name the leaders in these wars, but referred to them simply by their military titles ('the consul', 'the praetor', etc.), that he narrated the *admiranda*, marvellous or surprising phenomena, to be seen in Spain and Italy, and that in the whole work there was a great deal of careful research and no small learning.[2]

Cato's motives for writing history were moral, didactic, and political. The elder statesman who had served and saved his country from enemies external and internal 'had no desire to write what can be found in the records of the Pontifex, how often corn was dear, how often an eclipse or whatever had obscured the light of the sun or moon', but to teach useful lessons (cf. frs. 2, 3). This might imply an indifference to detail and complexities; in fact ancient sources are unanimous in their praise of Cato's careful research, and his critical sense seems to have been a great deal better than, say, Accius'. He used the *annales* as the basis of his chronology (frs. 17, 45, 49) along with Eratosthenes (fr. 17); he appreciated the importance of documentary evidence (fr. 58); he recognized the limits of possible knowledge (frs. 40, 45); he had a thoroughly Alexandrian interest in the characteristics of peoples (frs. 31, 34, 51, 73, 76) and geography (fr. 38) and the *admiranda* to which Nepos alludes as a special feature are also represented in the fragments (frs. 17, 69). Besides Fabius Pictor (frs. 15, 23) it is likely that Cato will have consulted Timaeus, and Greek political theory lies behind his account of the constitution of Carthage (fr. 80). It would be quite wrong to see Cato simply as an Italian chauvinist (see p. 140): his Aborigines are Greeks from Achaia (fr. 6), Latin is a Greek dialect, the Sabines are of Spartan stock (fr. 50), the Arcadian Catillus founded Tibur (fr. 56).

[1] So Leo (1913) 294f.; but there are other possibilities.

[2] Nep. *Vitae* 24.4 *ad fin. in quibus multa industria et diligentia comparet, nulla doctrina* is beyond reasonable defence: read *nonnulla doctrina*.

To be truly Roman was not a matter of race but of service rendered to the *res publica*, and Cato's practice of leaving commanders anonymous is an affirmation of a view of society quite unlike that implicit in, say, Ennius' *Annales*. Unfortunately it is not clear how Cato spoke of himself in episodes where he himself was involved. His quotations from his own speeches (frs. 95, 106) certainly imply that the later books will have had some of the characteristics of the memoirs and autobiographies which were an important feature of political life in the next generation. Cato did not follow the convention of Greek historiography by which speeches might be invented to summarize issues dramatically or for appropriate occasions such as a meeting of Hannibal and Scipio before Zama. It is also to to his credit that his account of ancient Italy is based without speculative elaboration on what he found to be current local traditions, and he avoided the enigma of what might be called Rome's 'mediaeval history' by omitting the Early Republic altogether, beginning Book 4 with the First Punic War.

The quality of Cato's *Origines* is highlighted by comparison with the work of his immediate successors who seem, by and large, to have been less critical and reliable, and who were not above inventing where sound evidence was lacking. Cassius Hemina's five books of *Annales* attempted a more continuous account of Roman history than Cato's: Books 2 and 3 dealt with the period which Cato had 'skipped', the early Republic, and, as in Cato, Book 4 began with the First Punic War. Cassius' style is clearly influenced by Cato; he shows an interest in etymologies (frs. 2, 3, 4, 6), 'firsts' (frs. 15, 26), aetiology (frs. 11, 14, 15, 20), moral points (fr. 13), and, what is new, imaginative description – the image of Aeneas leaving Troy as described by Cassius may owe something to Naevius (fr. 5 *ad fin.*). The *Annales* of L. Calpurnius Frugi was in seven books; he too dealt with the early Republic in Books 2 and 3, and wrote in a more jejune and less idiosyncratic manner than Cato, possibly with a Greek model such as Xenophon in mind as well as the pontifical records themselves. He quotes a *bon mot* of Romulus (fr. 8) and had a penchant for anecdotes of no real historical import (frs. 27, 33). The *Annales* of Cn. Gellius were on a scale that can only have been achieved by massive invention: he only reached 389 B.C. in Book 15 (fr. 25) and 216 B.C. in a book numbered at least 30 (fr. 26). Charisius quotes from a ninety-seventh book, which is perhaps not quite beyond credibility considering the scale of the *Annales* as published by Scaevola pontifex (Serv. auct. *ad* Virg. *Aen.* 1.373). The retreat from Cato's original and critical if quirky style of historiography into the mainstream of second-rate Hellenistic rhetoricizing narrative seems to have been completed by L. Coelius Antipater, the first to write on a single theme (the Second Punic War) (see p. 145), and C. Fannius, cos. 122 B.C., who included fictitious speeches (Cic. *Brut.* 81). Lastly Sempronius Asellio shows the influence of Polybius in his reflections on the nature of true history (fr. 1), but seems in his large-scale work (at least fourteen books) to have dealt with a subject which he knew at first hand, the Numantine War (fr. 6), thus fulfilling in prose a role which the satirist Lucilius declined to fulfil in verse (see p. 169).

5. CATO ORATOR

The following is from a speech *De sumptu suo* made by Cato in his own defence: in the extract he is presenting himself and his secretary as preparing the defence which he is now making:

Iussi caudicem proferri ubi mea oratio scripta erat de ea re quod sponsionem feceram cum M. Cornelio. tabulae prolatae: maiorum benefacta perlecta: deinde quae ego pro re publica leguntur. ubi id utrumque perlectumst, deinde scriptum erat in oratione: 'numquam ego pecuniam neque meam neque sociorum per ambitionem dilargitus sum.' 'attat, noli noli scribere inquam istud: nolunt audire.' deinde recitauit: 'numquam ego praefectos per sociorum uestrorum oppida imposiui qui eorum bona liberos ⟨uxores⟩ diriperent.' 'istud quoque dele: nolunt audire, recita porro.' 'numquam ego praedam neque quod de hostibus captum esset neque manubias inter pauculos amicos meos diuisi ut illis eriperem qui cepissent.' 'istuc quoque dele: nihil eo minus uolunt dici; non opus est recitato.' 'numquam ego euectionem dataui quo amici mei per symbolos pecunias magnas caperent.' 'perge istuc quoque uti cum maxume delere.' 'numquam ego argentum pro uino congiario inter apparitores atque amicos meos disdidi neque eos malo publico diuites feci.' 'enimuero usque istuc ad lignum dele.' uide sis quo in loco res publica siet, uti quod rei publicae bene fecissem, unde gratiam capiebam, nunc idem illud memorare non audeo, ne inuidiae siet. ita inductum est male facere impoene, bene facere non impoene licere.

(*Or. fr.* 173 Malcovati (Fronto p. 92 N))

I called for the book to be produced in which was written my speech on the subject of the contract which I had made with M. Cornelius. The records were produced, my ancestors' services read through, then what I had done for the community was read out. When each reading was over, the next item written in my speech was this: 'Never did I hand out sums of money, neither my own nor the allies', in bribery.' 'Aha! No, no, don't write that', says I; 'they don't want to hear that.' Then he read out: 'Never did I billet officers on your Allies' townships to ravage their property, children, and their wives.' 'Score that out too: they don't want to hear that: read on.' 'Never did I divide plunder, neither what had been taken from the enemy nor the cash from its sale, among my little circle of friends, in order to defraud those who had taken it.' Score that out too; there is nothing they want said less; no need to read that out.' 'Never did I automatically dole out travel-vouchers so that my friends could get large sums of money with the seals.'[1] *'Go on, score* that *out too as hard as you can.' 'Never did I distribute cash instead of the wine-ration among my staff and friends, nor did I enrich them at the public expense.' 'Yes, score* that *out right down to the wood.'*[2] *Just see*

[1] Precisely what racket is implied by *per symbolos* is not clear.

[2] We are to understand that Cato's *codicilli* were the kind in which the writing surface was a layer of beeswax on wood.

what a position our country is in: the service which I have rendered the community and from which I won favour is now the very thing that I dare not mention, lest it be the source of envious spite. So the new order is the freedom to do mischief and get away with it, and to render useful service but not get away with it.

Cato composed this remarkably lively, witty, and ironic piece when he was seventy, in 164 B.C., that is in Terence's heyday; and a comparison and contrast of their styles is instructive. Cato was among the first to keep *codicilli* recording the texts of his speeches; his reasons were of course professional, as this extract shows. By the 160s he will have had a considerable library. Cicero tells us that he revised some of his speeches in his old age (*Sen.* 38), and we have seen that he used some in his *Origines*. How, when, and in what sense Cato's speeches were published and circulated after his death is obscure, but they will have been of interest to a potentially wide public as a political testament, as a historical source, and as oratory. Thus without intending it Cato made oratory a literary genre, as Demosthenes had at Athens: his speeches might be closely conned as examples in the teaching of the art of rhetoric, and evaluated by connoisseurs, both politicians and professors. By the end of the second century B.C. it was unusual for a prominent statesman such as M. Antonius *not* to circulate copies of his major speeches or keep them with an eye to his memoirs and his reputation (Cic. *Cluent.* 140, Val. Max. 7.3.5).

The directness of Cato's manner survived into the Gracchan era. The fragments of Gaius Gracchus show as many similarities to Cato as differences; such passages as Cornelia's letter (p. 146) and the Hogarthian description of the behaviour of Roman *iudices* in a forceful passage of C. Titius cited by Macrobius (*Sat.* 3.16.4) are genuinely Catonian in tone and expression. However, perhaps already in Flamininus' time, and certainly by the 160s B.C., more self-consciously showy and formalized rhetoric was coming into favour; the prologues of Terence's plays are miniature specimens of the Asiatic style of Pergamum; see pp. 233–6 on the whole question of this and the Attic manner in Roman rhetoric before Cicero. In Cicero's time Cato was little read by aspiring orators, an omission much regretted by Cicero, who had managed, apparently with some difficulty, to trace 150 speeches by the old master. His commendation of Cato's attitude and style (*Brut.* 63–5) shows some historical perspective rare in Roman literary criticism, and it is probable that an edition of the speeches was prepared by Atticus. Thanks to this Cato's speeches continued to be read and admired well into the second century A.D.

The conventional view of the development of Roman oratory is summed up by Tacitus (*Dial.* 18): *Catone sene C. Gracchus plenior et uberior, sic Graccho politior atque ornatior Crassus, sic utroque distinctior et urbanior et altior Cicero* 'Gaius Gracchus is proportionately as fuller and richer than Cato the Elder as Crassus is more polished and ornate than Gracchus and as Cicero is more harmonious and civilized and sublime than either.' There are dangers in such pat summaries. The individual's qualities will be over-simplified, and the first in such a series is almost bound to appear by implication as less sophisticated and various than he was. An Andronicus, an Ennius, or a Cato were naturally especially liable to this kind of treatment in Roman literary criticism, which was often quite crudely teleological. It puzzled and surprised Fronto, a frank admirer of Cato's work, that the extended example of the figure of παράλειψις (omission; our cliché 'not to mention...') which he quotes from the *De sumptu suo* seemed unparalleled in his experience and better handled than in any writer that he knew, Greek or Latin. This is typical of Cato. His rhetoric could not be neatly pigeon-holed according to the rules of the manuals and *exempla* (Gell. *N.A.* 6.3.52) which made teleological criticism easy.

Cato's style,[1] both in his speeches and in his *Origines*, was essentially paratactic, reflecting the same speech-patterns as we hear in Terence's narrative and dialogue rather than in his prologues. Sentence-connexion is simple, and Cato shows no desire to avoid repetition of words in linking sentences. A Crassus or Antonius would probably have regarded the brief narration at the beginning of the passage cited as marred by the repetitions 'read through' (*perlecta... leguntur...perlectum*) and 'written in the speech' (*oratio scripta erat...deinde scriptum erat*). On the other hand Cato took more care over phrasing in his speeches than in his *De agri cultura*: *tabulae...leguntur* is a modestly rising tricolon, and some of the attention to the rhythmical cadences of phrases and sentences so characteristic of later Roman oratory is already apparent in Cato. A small but clear sign of the different levels of diction which Cato felt appropriate to his speeches and to his technical works is the fact that the weighty *atque* is the normal word for 'and' in the speeches (so too in Cornelia's letter), but the lightweight *et* in the *De agricultura*. When Cato is being self-consciously didactic, this becomes a noticeable mannerism, as in the beginning of the speech against the Rhodians (Gell. *N.A.* 6(7).3, fr. 95 Malcovati).

Cato's language is remarkably various. He would not have agreed with the precept of the purist Julius Caesar that one should avoid an unknown word as one would a reef. Cato enjoyed something of the freedom of the older Comedians in exploiting the resources of morphology to make a striking phrase or to find the *mot juste*, e.g. *pauculos amicos* in the *De sumptu suo*. The exclamation *attat* is borrowed not from life but from comedy, and aptly, for Cato is here presenting himself as a character in a tragicomedy, where true moral values have been stood on their heads. Frequentatives (*futare* = *fu-it-are* = *saepius fuisse*), analogical formations (*pulchralia* = *bellaria* 'desserts', fr. 107), new adjectives (*impudentiam praemiosam*, 241), expressions like *cloacale flumen* (126) 'a sewery stream', *uecticulariam uitam uiuere* (246) 'to live a crowbarious life', nouns like

[1] See Leo (1913) 273f., 286ff., 299f.; Till (1936) *passim*.

plebitas, *duritudo* (cf. Gell. *N.A.* 17.2.20), *pelliculatio* (243), from **pelliculare* from *pellicere* 'enticement', a phrase such as...*ridibundum magistratum gerere, pauculos homines, mediocriculum exercitum obuium duci*...(44) '...to exercise a laughful magistracy, that a handful of men, a standardlet army be led to face...' (cf. *tuburcinabundus*, *lurcinabundus*, 253) – all these mark one who is not the servant but the master of a language in which the kind of decorum observed by Terence has not yet become the rule. Anaphora, tricolon and the multiplication of synonyms are used to render a passage formidable (δείνωσις): *tuum nefarium facinus peiore facinore operire postulas, succidias humanas facis, tantam trucidationem facis, decem funera facis, decem capita libera interficis, decem hominibus uitam eripis indicta causa, iniudicatis, incondemnatis* 'You expect to hide your foul crime with a worse crime; you cause human butchery, you cause such slaughter, ten pyres you cause, ten free persons you kill, ten men's lives you steal, their case unstated, themselves untried and uncondemned' (fr. 59, *In Q. Minucium Thermum de decem hominibus*, 190 B.C.); and paronomasia and vigorous puns (*M. Fulvius Mobilior*, 151; *eam ego uiam pedetemptim temptabam*, 45) also have their place in a style characterized by Cicero (*Orat.* 152) as *horridula* 'rather hirsute', and more fully and paradoxically by Plutarch (*Cat. Maj.* 7) as εὔχαρις ἅμα καὶ δεινός... καὶ ἡδὺς καὶ καταπληκτικός, φιλοσκώμμων καὶ αὐστηρός, ἀποφθεγματικὸς καὶ ἀγωνιστικός 'charming and at the same time formidable, simple and surprising, jocular and dry, full of quotable passages and tight argument': 'Now they say that there are fine crops in the meadows and the fields. Don't put too much trust in that. I have often heard it said that a lot can happen between the dish and the mouth. But between the dish and the field, that really is a long way' (fr. 217); 'That man can be hired for a crust of bread to keep quiet or to speak' (fr. 112); 'Thieves of private property spend their lives in jails and in fetters: public thieves in gold and purple' (fr. 224); 'It is difficult, citizens of Rome, to address bellies: they don't have ears' (fr. 254); 'I spent my whole life as a young man right from the start in thrift and in toughness and in hard work, cultivating the farm – making meadow out of Sabine stones and flint and sowing seed on them' (fr. 217, cf. Men. *Dysk.* 1ff.); *iure lege libertate re publica communiter uti oportet: gloria atque honore quomodo sibi quisque struxit* 'all should equally enjoy justice, law, liberty, and the constitution: glory and public office, as each has built for himself' (fr. 252).

7

THE SATIRES OF ENNIUS AND LUCILIUS

I. THE MINOR WORKS OF ENNIUS

Ennius was not only a major dramatist and the author of the most ambitious Roman epic. He also extended the range of Latin poetry in a series of compositions in the *genus humile*, the low key, some based on Greek models, and others original. In these the poet had a prominent part, sometimes as himself, more pervasively as arbiter, editor, and commentator. Ennius' aim was sometimes to instruct, sometimes to amuse, and most often to do both. Right from the start, 'to tell the truth with a smile' and 'to mix the useful with the sweet' were characteristics of what fifty years later in Lucilius emerged as an important and specially Roman genre, satire. Let us review the content and tone of these minor works.

Ennius' *Sota* was a Latin version of a bawdy poem by Sotades, an Alexandrian of the third century B.C. It was written in the species of ionic tetrameter named after Sotades, a rhythm intended to call to mind the salacious dance-style of *cinaedi* and fit for comic treatment (cf. Plautus, *Pers.* 826, *Stich.* 769ff.; Petronius, *Sat.* 23):

ille ictu' retro reccidit in natem supinus...

(*Sota* 5 V = *ROL* 5)

Knocked backwards, he fell square down on his bum...

This was a linguistic and metrical experiment on Ennius' part. Even the few fragments extant show that he admitted low language and themes carefully avoided in the *palliata*. *Nates*, 'bum', occurs only once in Plautus, in the mouth of a vulgarian (*Pers.* 847): and Ennius used dialect words, e.g. *tongent* 'they ken' (*ROL* fr. 4) where the normal *callent* 'they know' would have done.

The *Hedyphagetica* was also experimental. We have some fragments of its model, the *Gastronomia* of Archestratus of Gela, enough to show that this was not simply a translation but an adaptation like Plautus' or Ennius' plays. One addition to Archestratus' catalogue of succulent fish implies that the poem was not written until after Ennius' visit to Ambracia (189/8 B.C.).[1] As in the *Sota*,

[1] Skutsch (1968) 38f.

Ennius kept the metre of the original, the dactylic hexameter,[1] proper to martial and didactic themes:

> Surrenti tu elopem fac emas glaucumque ἀπὸ Κύμης.
> Quid scaru'? Praeterii, cerebrum Ioui' paene supremi!
> Nestoris ad patriam hic capitur magnusque bonusque...
> (*Hedyphagetica*, *ROL* 6ff. = Apul. *Apol.* 39)

See you get sturgeon at Surrentum and blue shark from Cumae. What about wrasse? I missed that – nearly the brain of majestic Jove, it is! A good one and a big can be taken in the land of Nestor...

Here the expressions *fac emas* and the 'neat' Greek ἀπὸ Κύμης[2] as well as the pretence of spontaneity in *praeterii* are colloquial and stand in absurd contrast to the tone of *Nestoris ad patriam* and the use of the connectives ...*que*...*que* which are traits of a much more pretentious diction.[3]

Others of Ennius' minor works were more serious. A work called *Scipio* praised Africanus and included separate poems in trochaic septenarii and in hexameters; the style of the extant fragments corresponds to that of the tragedies and of the *Annales*. Moral instruction and entertainment were mixed in the *Protrepticum* (perhaps identical with a work called *Praecepta*), the *Euhemerus* or *Historia sacra*, and *Epicharmus*. In the last Ennius is supposed to have translated or adapted a didactic work which passed as that of Epicharmus; in it Ennius recorded how he dreamt that he was dead, and how he learnt, presumably from Epicharmus himself, the theory of the four elements and related ideas referred to also in the Tragedies and the *Annales*.[4] The dream is likely to be an Ennian invention, and Cicero may have taken the setting of the *Somnium Scipionis* from here. The *Epicharmus* and the *Protrepticus* are thought, probably rightly, to have been all in trochaic septenarii. The *Historia sacra* was modelled on the 'Ιερὰ ἀναγραφή of Euhemerus of Messene (b. *c.* 340 B.C.),[5] a philosophical 'novel' in which the gods and heroes were explained as mortals whose deeds had been magnified and distorted by the poets. Lactantius preserves quite lengthy extracts in a strikingly bald prose; he thought that he was quoting Ennius verbatim (cf. *Div. inst.* 1.14.1, where Ennius' words are opposed to those of 'the poets'). It has been the fashion to regard these fragments as our earliest extant literary Latin prose; Ennius, it is alleged, experimented here with a deliberately naive style intended to match the manner of logographers like

1 On unusual features of the verse-technique, see Lindsay (1922) ch. 1.

2 The text here is uncertain, however.

3 Fraenkel (1960) 199f.

4 The ideas of 'Epicharmus' and Empedocles of Acragas are not to be nicely distinguished in this connexion; cf. e.g. Ennius, *Thyestes TRF* 351, *Annales* (*lib. inc.*) 522 V = *ROL* (8) 261, Menander fr. 614.

5 Note that Archestratus, Epicharmus, and possibly also Euhemerus were Sicilian.

Hecataeus of Miletus in his *Historiae* or *Heroologia*, whom it is supposed – there is no direct evidence at all – Euhemerus himself will have imitated.[1] This is an elaborate theory with an important link missing, and one may ask what was the point of a poet's choosing such a peculiar style for a first extensive essay in Latin prose. There is in fact more probability in the older theory that the *Historia sacra* was, like Ennius' other expository works, presented in iambo-trochaic verse. There are constant echoes of the rhythms and diction of septenarii in Lactantius' citations and these become specially obvious when one compares the prose-version of the fable of the Crested Lark and its Chicks quoted by Gellius at *N.A.* 2.29.3ff. This, from Ennius' *Saturae*, was certainly written in septenarii. The prose citations of the *Euhemerus* are best seen as belonging to the same class of paraphrase. The extreme simplicity of the phrasing and syntax suggest that Lactantius' immediate source was a prose version intended for use as a school-book.

Porphyrio (*ad* Hor. *Sat.* 1.10.46) states that Ennius left four books called *Saturae*;[2] the manuscripts of Donatus *ad* Ter. *Pho.* 339, where a passage is cited from a sixth book, are probably corrupt. While it is likely that the title *Saturae* does derive from Ennius, it does not follow that the book arrangement or even the contents of the edition known to Porphyrio were due to Ennius himself. Each book, one *Satura*, contained miscellaneous poems, mainly in the iambo-trochaic metres and diction of comedy, but also some in hexameters and perhaps Sotadeans.[3] The subject matter was very diverse: fables (the Crested Lark; the Piper and the Fish (*Sat.* 65 V = *ROL* 20, cf. Hdt. 1.141)), moral criticism of types (a glutton, *Sat.* 1 V = *ROL* 1; busybodies, 5 V = *ROL* 5; slanderers, 8f. V = *ROL* 8f.), exhortation (2 V = *ROL* 2), proverbs (70 V = *ROL* 27), quasi-dramatic encounters implying dialogue (6f. V = *ROL* 6f.), an etymological point (69 V = *ROL* 23, *simia/similis*), a parasite's monologue (14–19 V = *ROL* 14–19) in good comic style, and a debate between Life and Death (Quint. *Inst.* 9.2.36). The poet himself is never far away – 'I never poetize but when I'm gouty' (64 V = *ROL* 21); 'Ennius the maker, greetings, you who pass to mortal men a cup of flaming verses drawn from your marrow' (6f. V = *ROL* 6f., a particularly fine pair of lines); '. . . from there I contemplate the clear and columned shores of Aether' (3f. V = *ROL* 3f.). It is probable that the *Saturae* are the source of some of the anecdotal and personal details that we have about Ennius, for example, an amusing story at Ennius' expense about an encounter with Scipio Nasica (Cic. *De or.* 2.276), that he lived on the Aventine with only one servant to 'do' for him, that he was a *contubernalis*, close

[1] Laughton (1951) 35ff., Fraenkel (1951*a*) 50ff.; followed by Waszink (1972) 106, 351, and Jocelyn (1972) 1023.

[2] For the meaning of this term, 'Salad-dishes', see below, p. 161.

[3] *Sat.* 28–31 (an enthymeme involving much repetition of the word *frustrari*) is in a species of ionic tetrameter, certainly not Saturnians (so Warmington).

associate, of Caecilius Statius, that he was a neighbour of the Servilii Galbae (Cic. *Acad.* 2.51), and that he had three personalities (*tria corda*) because he could speak Greek, Latin, and Oscan (Gellius, *N.A.* 17.17.1).[1]

The *Saturae* thus had elements and themes moral, paraenetic, reflective, comic, narrative, and autobiographical, and were based mainly on the stage-medium. The low language and tone of *Sota*, the mixture of colloquial and elevated in the hexameters of *Hedyphagetica*, the use of different metres in a single work (*Scipio*), the evident importance of the poet's *ego* in *Epicharmus*, and the paraenetic and didactic character of the other minor works – these features complement and agree with the tone and content of the fragments transmitted as belonging to the *Saturae*, and are all to be found in later Satire. It has been maintained that some of the works known by individual titles are really part of the *Saturae*. *Scipio*, for example, has been claimed as part of *Satura* III (cf. 10f. V = *ROL* 10f.), and *Epicharmus* might be part of *Satura* II (cf. 3f. V = *ROL* 3f.). Now in view of the complexities which can arise in the transmission of *libelli* consisting of collections of short works – Lucilius and Catullus are examples – it is prudent not to be dogmatic about this in any way. Such arguments as have been adduced in recent studies for separating the *Saturae* from the named minor works are not conclusive, since we know too little about the early transmission of any of the works in question.[2] It is in any case a rather serious mistake in tracing the history of the genre satire to draw a qualitative distinction between those works of Ennius referred to as *Saturae* and all the rest, and to focus attention on the former; for, however and *sub quocumque nomine* they circulated there is no essential difference between the poems referred to as from the *Saturae* and the rest, and by attending mainly or exclusively to the *Saturae*, one may beg the question 'What is the nature and origin of Latin satire?'

One characteristic of later satire is definitely absent from Ennius. He has no personal invective or specific social criticism. On the contrary, when Ennius names someone, it is to praise him (Scipio), or to tell a pleasant tale (Galba, Nasica). *Non est meum*, says he (63 V = *ROL* 22), *ac si me canis memorderit* 'It's not my way, as if a dog had bitten me...'; an attitude quite unlike Lucilius': *inde canino ricto oculisque inuolem...* 'from there let me fly (at him/them) with a dog's grin and eyes' (Lucil. (30) 1095–6 M = *ROL* 1001).[3] The one rejects, the other accepts gladly the κυνικὸς τρόπος, the cynic role and the accusation of hydrophobia.

[1] See in general van Rooy (1965) 30–49; Waszink (1972) 99–147; Coffey (1976) 27–32; Badian (1971) 168ff.

[2] Waszink (1972) 101–7, Jocelyn (1972) 1023. Van Rooy (1965) 39 only mentions the minor works in passing and does not raise the issue; Coffey (1976) 31 over-simplifies it; none of them sufficiently recognizes the homogeneity of the *Saturae* and the named minor works.

[3] See below, p. 163 n. 1.

In fact, Ennius' minor works as a whole remind one of many features of low-key, unpretentious Alexandrian poetry and moralizing literature. A judicious modern account of fourth- and third-century Greek literature as it relates in style, intent, and variety to *all* of Ennius' minor works remains a *desideratum*.[1] It is clear that Ennius' *Saturae* cannot possibly have been intended as a new genre of *poetry* 'untouched by the Greeks' as Horace puts it (*Sat.* 1.10.66). The Σωρός 'Heap (of grain for winnowing)' by Posidippus offers an analogy for a *Satura*, a 'Salad-dish' of σύμμεικτα or ἄτακτα, 'miscellanies', 'bits and pieces' in a variety of metres. The *Chreiai* 'Exercises' of Machon are a collection of anecdotes about parasites, playwrights, and courtesans, written in the medium of New Comedy, and hitting the same note as Ennius with his stage-language and iambo-trochaics. The moralizing of Cercidas of Megalopolis, the *Silloi* of Timon, and the exoteric writings of the Cynics are all relevant to him; and the *Iamboi* of Callimachus, although not themselves a direct pattern for Ennius' *Saturae*, are perhaps the best-known example of the kind of Greek poetry to which Ennius' *Saturae* may be compared.[2]

2. SATURA BEFORE ENNIUS?

According to the unreliable source used by Livy at 7.2.4–10, the last stage in the development of Roman drama before Andronicus (see p. 78) had been a dramatic *satura*, a show with music and a libretto, but no consecutive plot; and it was a received opinion in Imperial times, possibly deriving from Varro, that satire was a specially Roman genre. 'Grant that Lucilius is more polished', says Horace (*Sat.* 1.10.66), *quam rudis et Graecis intacti carminis auctor* 'than the unsophisticated originator of a poetry untouched even by the Greeks...'; he means Ennius in his *Saturae*, and is alluding to, though not necessarily embracing, an evidently well-known view that Ennius was *primus inventor* of the genre literary satire, to which Greek example allegedly contributed nothing.[3] In the course of a discussion of the relative merits of Greek and Latin literature by genre Quintilian (*Inst.* 10.1.93) remarks *satura quidem tota nostra est* 'but satire is all ours'; he has just finished discussing elegy, where he reckons the honours even, and, after a characteristically sensible and pithy evaluation of Lucilius and his successors, he proceeds to the Greek *iambus*, since Archilochus the form *par excellence* for Greek invective. Two interpretations of Quintilian's

[1] Geffcken's articles (1911) are useful, but our knowledge of Hellenistic literature is now much extended.

[2] It misses the point to debate how closely Ennius' *Saturae* resembled the *Iamboi*: his *Medea* is hardly faithful to Euripides in letter or spirit. See Waszink (1972) 119ff. for some account of the gradual acceptance over the last thirty years of the influence of Callimachus' *Iamboi*; we should add *id genus omne*.

[3] See Rudd (1960*a*) 36ff.; van Rooy (1965) 45 n. 6; Waszink (1972) 123.

remark are current. The minority view, first proposed by W. Rennie (1922) 21 is that he means 'but in satire we Romans win easily'; the older and alternative, that he means 'but satire is an exclusively Roman genre', has been reasserted in recent studies.[1] Rennie's basic point is that Quintilian's discussion is not about origins but evaluations; on the other hand, it is argued, the passage of Horace cited above can be taken to support the other view; and there is the consideration that alone among the genres listed by Quintilian, satire does not have a Greek name. The grammarian Diomedes (*GLK* I 485) defines *satyra* (*sic*) as *carmen apud Romanos, nunc quidem maledicum et ad carpenda hominum uitia Archaeae Comoediae charactere compositum, quale scripserunt Lucilius et Horatius et Persius; sed olim carmen quod ex uariis poematibus constabat satyra uocabatur, quale scripserunt Pacuuius et Ennius* 'poetry with the Romans, now vituperative and composed with the *timbre* of Old Comedy, such as Lucilius, Horace and Persius wrote; but once poetry which consisted of different (kinds of) poems was called *satyra*, such as Pacuvius and Ennius wrote'. Diomedes proceeds to list various suggested etymologies for the word, starting with the one which he himself thought (certainly wrongly) the most probable: *satyra autem dicta siue a Satyris, quod similiter in hoc carmine ridiculae res pudendaeque dicuntur, uelut quae a Satyris proferuntur et fiunt* '*satyra* is so called either from Satyrs, because ridiculous and shameful things are likewise said in this poetry as are delivered and done by Satyrs...'. There lies behind this an allusion to the satyr plays of Attic and Hellenistic drama such as Sophocles' *Ichneutae*. Among other serious objections to this evidently popular and widespread theory there are the points that in that case the name should be *satyrica* (n. pl.), not *satura* (*-yra*, *-ira*) (f. sing.); and that since there is no feminine nominal suffix *-ŭra* (*-yra*, *-ĭra*) in Latin, we must be dealing with the adjective *satur* in the feminine, with a noun left understood. That is indeed Diomedes' second suggestion, ...*siue satyra a lance quae referta uariis multisque primitiis in sacro apud priscos dis inferebatur*... 'or *satyra* is named after a *lanx* (f.), dish, which filled with many different first-fruits was offered to the gods in a religious service in olden times'. This is generally agreed to be the right explanation.[2]

These passages have given rise to an enormous amount of speculation, and in particular to the theory that Ennius' *saturae* with their dramatic elements somehow represent a literary development of pre- or sub-literate dramatic performances by a *cantor* and *tibicen*, which, on the evidence of Livy, will have been called *saturae*; and support for this has been found in the passages cited from Horace and Quintilian as interpreted by the majority, not without the aid of certain unhistorical prejudices of the late Romantic period about popular

[1] In particular van Rooy (1965) 117–23, followed by Coffey (1976) 3.

[2] For Diomedes' other suggestions, and modern elaborations, see van Rooy (1965) 1–27, Coffey (1976) 12–18, Waszink (1972) 103.

culture and nationalism and the originality of Roman literature vis-à-vis Greek. However, as Ennius said (*Sat.* 70 V = *ROL* 27), *quaerunt in scirpo soliti quod dicere nodum* 'As the common saying is, they are looking for a knot in a bulrush.' Livy's dramatic *satura* is plausibly explained as a confused and confusing attempt by Livy's source to include in the pedigree of Roman comedy an equivalent to the satyr plays of Greek drama, just as we find a rough Italian counterpart earlier in his account for the Old Comedy of Athens.[1] He or some other cultural nationalist may have patriotically derived literary satire from that source. There is indeed something specially Roman in Lucilius' (not Ennius') satire: the combination of his caustic tone, his impudent disregard for the decorum of literary theory, his use of his own experiences and encounters, and his variety are unique, not but what each separate trait can be found somewhere in Greek literature. It does not follow, however, that critics in the first century B.C. or the earlier twentieth A.D. were justified in inferring the existence of a lively native Italian tradition of satirical character passing back through Ennius to a hypothetical form of popular drama.

The only evidence for Latin satire before Ennius is in fact a single quotation of 'Naeuius in Satyra' (Festus p. 306 L); the line is a Saturnian, and therefore cannot come from a play called *Satura* 'The Pregnant Woman' (cf. Plautus. *Amph.* 667 and the title of an *Atellana* by Pomponius and a *togata* by Atta). With all due caution one may reckon with the possibility that Naevius did write occasional poems; his supposed epitaph (Saturnians: Gell. *N.A.* 1.24.2, from Varro), the line *fato Metelli Romae fiunt consules* (ps.-Asconius *ad* Cic. *Verr.* 1.10.29) cited as a senarius, but possibly a saturnian matching the reply *malum dabunt Metelli Naeuio poetae*, and the naughty story in iambic septenarii about the young Scipio Africanus (Gell. *N.A.* 7.8.5) might belong here. However, even if Naevius did write and circulate occasional poems in various metres, it does not follow that he issued a collected 'edition', still less that he himself called the collection a 'Salad-dish' or 'Medley'.

3. LUCILIUS

Nothing is known of the *saturae* of Ennius' nephew Pacuvius, and it is only by chance that we hear of the letters written at Corinth in 146 B.C. by Sp. Mummius *uersiculis facetis*, in witty verse, and sent to his *familiares*, his private friends (Cic. *Att.* 13.6*a*). There may have been much more of this domestic *lusus*, verse-play, than we know: Lucilius himself refers to a comic verse-edict regulating behaviour at banquets, the *Lex Tappula* of one Valerius Valentinus ((*lib. inc.*) 1307, 1316 M = *ROL* 1239–40), and in an early poem Lucilius implies that if his were the most notorious occasional verses, they were not the only ones

[1] Waszink (1972) 107–9; Coffey (1976) 18–22. See p. 78.

((30) 1013 M = *ROL* 1091).[1] His earliest traceable works date from the late 130s B.C., when he had returned to Rome after war-service as a cavalryman in the entourage of Scipio Aemilianus at the siege of Numantia in Spain. Lucilius belonged to the Latin (not the Roman) aristocracy; a senator Manius Lucilius may have been his brother, and he was great-uncle to Pompeius Magnus. He was rich and independent, owning an important house in Rome and large estates in southern Italy and Sicily; the family seat was at Suessa Aurunca on the borders of Campania and Latium Adiecticium. Thus, like Sp. Mummius, he was a grandee, superior in status to his contemporaries in letters L. Accius and L. Afranius. He was a friend of Scipio Aemilianus ((6) 1132–42 M = *ROL* 254–8; (11) 394f. M = *ROL* 424f., Hor. *Sat.* 2.1.71 and schol. ad loc.), Decimus Laelius and the young Iunius Congus ((26) 595–6 M = *ROL* 632–4), Gaius Laelius, and probably C. Sempronius Tuditanus ((30) 1079–87 M = *ROL* 1008–15 may be addressed to him). The sceptic philosopher Clitomachus as head of the Academy at Athens dedicated a work to Lucilius (Cic. *Acad.* 2.102), and it is likely enough that he knew the Stoic Panaetius and Polybius, also friends of Aemilianus. A salient feature of Lucilius' work in the eyes of posterity was his outspoken criticism of famous men, and he was compared with Archilochus (whom he had himself read, (28) 698 M = *ROL* 786) and the writers of the Old Comedy. It was Lucilius' privileged position in society that made it possible for him to mount and to sustain such attacks. Even the fragments attest an impressive series of the great as his victims: Q. Caecilius Metellus Macedonicus (*RE* no. 94), cens. 131 B.C. (schol. *ad* Hor. *Sat.* 2.1.72, (26) 676ff. M = *ROL* 636ff.); L. Cornelius Lentulus Lupus (*RE* no. 224), cens. 147 B.C., *princeps senatus* 131–126 B.C. (Hor. *Sat.* 2.1.62ff., schol. *ad* 67 and 72, Persius 1.114, (28) 784–90 M = *ROL* 805–11 and *lib.* 1 *passim*, Serv. *ad Aen.* 10.104); Macedonicus' son C. Caecilius Metellus Caprarius (*RE* no. 84, Supplbd. III 222), praetor 117 B.C. ((5) 1130, 210–1 M = *ROL* 232–4, schol. *ad* Hor. *Sat.* 2.1.67); C. Papirius Carbo (*RE* no. 33), tr. pl. 131 B.C., pr. 130 B.C., cos. 120 B.C. (*lib. inc.* 1312–13 M = *ROL* 1138–41); L. Opimius (*RE* no. 4) cos. 121 B.C. ((11) 418–20 M = *ROL* 450–2); Q. Mucius Scaevola Augur (*RE* no. 21), pr. 121/120 B.C. (*lib.* 2 *passim*); and others. A rather muddily-written passage defining *uirtus* is addressed to one Albinus; this may have been intended ironically for the benefit of A. or Sp. Postumius Albinus after their disgraceful showing in the Jugurthan War (110/109 B.C.) (*lib. inc.* 1326–38 M = *ROL* 1196–1208). Although some of those mentioned had been *inimici*, personal enemies of Aemilianus (d. 129 B.C.), Lucilius, who may or may not have been a Roman citizen, was not a party politician. As a Latin and a landowner, he must have had views about the major questions of his time, the proper relation of Rome and the Italian cities, and the effects of

[1] Here and *passim* in references to Lucilius the bracketed figure denotes the book number. As to how it is that a fragment of *lib.* 30 can be called 'early', see below, p. 168.

capitalism and large-scale plantation and ranch-style farming on the traditional peasant society of the countryside; yet he only mentions these things, if at all, fleetingly. Neither do we hear anything for certain of the Gracchi or of Marius. Lucilius' *ludus ac sermones* 'playful chats', *schedia* 'improvisations' – the term *satura* is not directly attested for him – were not the satire of a social reformer with a consistent standpoint and a long-term plan. Prose was the medium for a manifesto, see pp. 144–7. His targets were what he claims as notorious examples of arrogance, folly, delusion, incompetence, inhumanity, pretension, unworthiness, or greed whether in high places or low – in politics, in the tragic theatre (Pacuvius, *lib.* 26 and 29; Accius, *lib.* 30, 9 and 10), in trade ((20) 1181f. M = *ROL* 609f., an auctioneer, Q. Granius, cf. Cic. *Brut.* 160–1), or in the bedroom whether with the girls (Cretaea (29) 817 M = *ROL* 897, Collyra, *lib.* 16, among others) or the boys (Gentius and Macedo (7) 273–5 M = *ROL* 308–10). In view of this explicitness, it is amusing to read that Lucilius himself lost a case which he brought against an unknown comedian (auctor *ad Her.* 2.19, cf. 1.24), who had named him on the stage.

Facit indignatio uersum: but Lucilius was not monotonously shrill or self-righteous. He had a stronger and broader sense of humour than any other Roman satirist, and he presents himself with ironic detachment, warts and all. His opponents have their say: for them, he is *improbus* 'unfair' and no gentleman ((30) 1026 M = *ROL* 1077 where *formonsi fortes* = καλοκἀγαθοί), *improbus ille Lucilius* 'that bounder Lucilius' ((29) 821f. M = *ROL* 929f.); he consciously adopts the role of the cynic dog ((30) 1095f. M = *ROL* 1000–1), and accepts the part of the muck-raking σκατοφάγος: *hic in stercore humi stabulique fimo atque sucerdis* 'he (grubs about) in the dung on the ground, in the filth of the byre and the pig-shit' ((30) 1018 M = *ROL* 1081). Moreover, his voice is direct and intimate: he speaks to you and me, not to an audience of connoisseurs in a declamation hall. It is noteworthy that politicians in Lucilius' time were giving a new validity to the literary convention by which a Greek tract intended for the public at large would be addressed to an appropriate individual: Gracchus, Rutilius Rufus, and others of course intended to influence the public in their political memoirs, but by causing them to be circulated in the guise of letters addressed to a sympathetic friend, they created the impression that the reader was being admitted to an inner circle, and thus was getting a more authentic account of affairs (see p. 145). Lucilius seems to have made quite extensive use of the letter-form:

> Quo me habeam pacto, tam etsi non quaeri', docebo,
> quando in eo numero mansi quo in maxuma non est
> pars hominum...
> ut periisse uelis quem uisere nolueris cum
> debueris. hoc nolueris et debueris te

si minu' delectat, quod ἄτεχνον et Ἰσοκράτειον
ληρῶδέςque simul totum ac sit μειρακιῶδες,
non operam perdo, si tu hic... ((5) 181–8 M = *ROL* 186–93)

I shall tell you how I'm keeping, even though you don't ask, since I have remained in the number in which the greatest part of mankind is not; (not that I think you dislike me so much) that you would wish him dead whom you have not sought when seek him you ought. If you don't much fancy that 'sought' and 'ought', as being sans art *and* Isocratique *and* bavard *and altogether* puéril, *I'm not wasting my time on it, if you are...*

In a relatively early satire Horace comments thus on that kind of writing:

Nam fuit hoc uitiosus: in hora saepe ducentos
ut magnum uersus dictabat stans pede in uno;
cum flueret lutulentus, erat quod tollere uelles:
garrulus atque piger scribendi ferre laborem,
scribendi recte: nam ut multum nil moror... (*Sat.* 1.4.9ff.)

For Lucilius was faulty in this: he would often stand on one foot and dictate two hundred verses an hour, as if that were something great; whenever he flowed muddy, there was always something that you would want to cut: he was garrulous and unready to bear the work of writing, I mean writing properly: for I've no time for it as (mere) bulk...

Later, however, he came to appreciate qualities in Lucilius which are a function of this unmannered style:

ille uelut fidis arcana sodalibus olim
credebat libris, neque si male cesserat usquam
decurrens alio, neque si bene: quo fit ut omnis
uotiua pateat ueluti descripta tabella
uita senis... (*Sat.* 2.1.30ff.)

Lucilius used to entrust his secrets to his books as to faithful friends, not swerving off to another theme if he had come out of something badly or well: and the result is that all *his later life lies exposed as if written down on a votive tablet...*

Lucilius is not confessional in the sense that St Augustine is: he expresses no serious regrets and is too much of a jester.[1] His real subject was nevertheless himself and his reactions and experiences and acquaintances, and this was something new in Latin literature, without which it is difficult, for example, to imagine some of Catullus' characteristic poetry.

[1] Fraenkel's excellent appreciation (1957) 150–3 does not do full justice to the complex character of Lucilius' self-portrait. He is at times not only himself, the bluff Roman with an eye for a horse or a girl, but also the cynic preacher, the man of the world, and a buffoon. We meet a *persona*, as in Pliny's or Seneca's letters, not a person, as in Cicero's.

In a very early work this individualism is expressed in the often-quoted lines:

publicanus uero ut Asiae fiam, ut scripturarius
pro Lucilio, id ego nolo, et uno hoc non muto omnia
((26) 671f. M = *ROL* 650f.)

That I should become a tax-gatherer in Asia, an assessment-man instead of Lucilius, that I refuse, and I would not exchange everything merely for this.

On the other hand he does not mind being a damned nuisance:

...at libertinus tricorius, Syrus ipse ac mastigias
quicum uersipellis fio et quicum commuto omnia...
((26) 669f. M = *ROL* 652f.)

But a triple-hided freedman, a very Syrus and a whipping post with whom I swap my skin and with whom I exchange everything (e.g. *is mihi cordi est* 'he is congenial').[1]

The language here is redolent of comedy; and it is Plautus who provides the best commentary of what *uersipellis* implies:

uorsipellem frugi conuenit esse hominem
pectus quoi sapit: bonus sit bonis, malus sit malis
(*Bacchides* 658f.)

A useful fellow with any sense will be a turnskin: let him be good to the good, and bad to the bad.

The philosophy of Chrysalus (Syrus in Menander's original, see p. 104) is an appropriate motto for the writer of σπουδογέλοια, enjoyable but thought-provoking tales and discourses.

Lucilius, who was probably born in 180 B.C.,[2] grew up in the generation when once and for all *Graecia capta ferum captorem cepit et artes | intulit agresti Latio* 'captive Greece caught her fierce captor and introduced the arts to rustic Latium' (Hor. *Epist.* 2.1.156). Carneades (accompanied among others by the young Clitomachus) visited Rome in 155 B.C., when Lucilius will have been about twenty-five, and made a great impression in a series of lectures intended to show the inadequacies of traditional moral assumptions. He argued convincingly on both sides of ethical questions, for example, whether a cavalryman in a rout

[1] On 671f. M = *ROL* 650f., see Williams (1968) 449f. The interpretation offered here for 669f. M = 652f. is new: commentators suppose that 669 M = *ROL* 652 denotes someone whom Lucilius dislikes, e.g. a dishonest agent or taxman; how that is compatible with the next line I do not see and they do not explain.

[2] He died and was honoured with a public funeral at Naples 'at the age of 46' according to Jerome, *ad ann.* 1869 (? 1870) = 103 (? 102) B.C. There are no sufficient grounds for accepting the emendation in Jerome *LXVI* for *XLVI*, which would put his birth in 169/8 B.C. The consuls of 148 B.C. had names very similar to those of 180 B.C., and this is the probable cause of the confusion in Jerome.

should risk his own life to rescue a wounded comrade or abandon him to save himself (Lact. *Div. inst.* 5.16.10, quoting Cicero, *Rep.* 3 (Ziegler pp. 85–96)). Cicero describes Lucilius as *homo doctus et perurbanus* 'an educated and thoroughly civilized man' (*De or.* 3.171), and Lucilius himself said in an early programmatic poem that he wrote neither for the ignoramus nor the expert ((26) 592–3, 595–6 M = *ROL* 632–5). His writings constitute an important document of the thorough blending of Greek and Roman culture in Aemilianus' generation; for the fragments not only display but also assume a knowledge of Ennius' *Annales*, Roman drama, the main authors of the Greek *paideia* – Homer, of course, whom Aemilianus was apt to quote, New Comedy, Euripides, Plato, Xenophon, Demosthenes among others. Similarly it is assumed that although we may not be experts we have some knowledge of the Academy and its teachings, of Peripatetic doctrines, of Epicureanism, and of Stoicism, some comments on which point to Panaetius ((27) 738 M = *ROL* 749, cf. Cic. *Off.* 1.51); and that we can take the technical language of philosophy and still more of rhetoric 'neat', in the original Greek, or only half assimilated into Latin. It would be a mistake to identify Lucilius from his fragments as a Stoic, or as a serious adherent of any ism: Stoic ideas are parodied at *lib. inc.* 1225f. M = *ROL* 1189f., and terms comically misapplied at (28) 784–90 M = *ROL* 805–11, while the somewhat dourly Stoic Q. Mucius Scaevola Augur, whose trial for alleged peculation during his governorship of Asia was the subject of Book 2, seems to have come off little better than his Epicurean prosecutor T. Albucius, whose silly mannerisms of Asiatic rhetoric are held up to ridicule.

Lucilius' style (described as *gracilis*, 'thin', by Varro *ap.* Gell. *N.A.* 6.14.6, Fronto p. 113 N) is itself an affront to the elaborate theory and practice of Asiatic rhetoric. One sympathizes with his attitude to artificiality in prose oratory and in the tragic diction of Pacuvius and Accius. Lucilius *primus condidit stili nasum* 'was the first to establish a nose for style', i.e. to practise literary criticism (Pliny, *N.H. praef.* 7). A discussion of the distinction of *poesis* and a *poema* ((9) 338–47 M = *ROL* 401–10), and of the nature of the unity of large-scale examples of *poesis* like the *Annales* or the *Iliad* draws on some current ideas of Hellenistic theory; this possibly came in the course of a defence by Lucilius of his already considerable *œuvre* against the charge that it ignored blatantly the proprieties advocated by Accius (*Didascalica lib.* 9 *ap.* Charis., *GLK* I 141). In the same book he advocated a number of spelling rules. Some of these are sensible enough, but others so intrinsically absurd that it is hard to believe that we are meant to take them seriously. In particular, Lucilius' prescriptions for the 'correct' use of the spellings *ei* and *i* ((9) 358–61 M = *ROL* 384–7) are a ludicrous alternative to a quite practical proposal of Accius (Warmington, *ROL* II xxii–xxiv).

In 123 B.C. or later[1] Lucilius arranged a collection in five books of the poems which, privately circulated, had brought him notoriety over the last ten years. These were arranged in roughly chronological order; and he wrote an important programmatic poem to serve as preface to the earliest book. Thus when the 'edition' was launched some, though not all, of those with whom Lucilius had crossed swords were dead (Lentulus Lupus and Pacuvius). Whether Lucilius himself called these (or any) of his works *Libri saturarum* or *Saturae* cannot be shown, and it is noteworthy that our major source for these earliest works, Nonius Marcellus in his *De compendiosa doctrina*, regularly cites these books by their number alone, whereas he refers to later books in the typical form *Lucilius in sexto satyrarum* (*sic*). The five earliest books were known to grammarians not as 1–5, but as 26–30: they counted as a separate part of a large collected edition in which 1–21 were all hexameter-poems and 22–5 (of which hardly anything remains) were wholly or partly elegiac. This arrangement is at least as old as Varro (*Ling. Lat.* 5.17) and has been attributed to C. Valerius Cato (b. 100 B.C.), cf. Hor. *Sat.* 1.10.1ff. The metres of 26–30 are principally iambo-trochaic; the arrangement of the *œuvre* into three sections, hexameters, elegiacs, and iambo-trochaics reflects ineptly enough in Lucilius' case the standard doctrine about the relative grandeur of those metres. Horace deals with them in this order in *Ars poetica*. Books 1–21 were arranged chronologically, as far as we can tell. Book 1 was possibly written as early as 126/5 B.C., that is, before 26–30 were presented as a group. Books 1, 2, and 3 seem to have consisted of one long composition each, so that it is here for the first time that the term *satura* might be applied (whether by Lucilius or his editors) to a single poem. This in turn affected the denotation of the term: if one calls a *libellus* containing one poem a *satura*, one no longer has in mind the Ennian meaning 'medley'[2] but the qualitative characteristics of that poem. It is not until Horace (*Sat.* 1.1.1) that we find *satura* used generically to designate a certain kind of poetry, and what Horace means is the kind of poetry that Lucilius wrote.

Reconstruction of individual books of Lucilius is extraordinarily hard. There is no connected theme, and with Book 4 Lucilius reverted to his original practice of including several poems in a book. Lucilius' language is often difficult and obscure, and it is often a question whether a remark belongs in the mouth of the satirist or someone else. Horace is helpful: the programmatic poem of the earliest book, 26, can to some extent be elucidated from Hor. *Sat.* 2.1, where the poet meets the charge that his previous work is excessively

[1] Cichorius (1908) 72ff., 84ff. pointed out that (26) 671f. M = *ROL* 650f. (quoted above) alludes to a consequence of the *Lex Sempronia* of C. Gracchus (123 B.C.), that the right to farm taxes in the province of Asia would belong to Roman *equites*.

[2] It cannot be shown that Lucilius himself called any of his *ludus ac sermones* or *chartae* or *schedia* specifically *saturae* (cf. (30) 1039 M = *ROL* 1039, 1084 M = *ROL* 1014, (*lib. inc.*) 1279 M = *ROL* 1131).

cruel by asking a friend how then, and what, he should write; reasoned rejection of the friend's advice amounts to a positive assertion of the poet's stance against humbug. Lucilius seems to have done something similar, and this is the context of his definition of his ideal reader ((26) 592–3, 595–6 M = *ROL* 632–5), his assertion of his identity ((26) 671–2, 669–70 M = *ROL* 650–3, cf. 675 M = *ROL* 647), and his refusal of the suggestion that he should confine himself to the uncontroversial Ennian role of *praeco uirtutis*:

hunc laborem sumas, laudem qui tibi ac fructum ferat:
percrepa pugnam Popili, facta Corneli cane
((26) 620, 621 M = *ROL* 713, 714)

You should undertake this labour, which would bring you fame and profit: boom out the battle of Popilius Laenas [against the Numantians, 138 B.C.: Livy, *epit.* 55], *sing the deeds of Cornelius* [Scipio Aemilianus, again against the Numantians, 134/3 B.C.][1]

Book 3 of Lucilius, a verse-epistle (cf. (3) 94–5) in which he described a journey from Rome to his estates in Sicily, provided the framework of Horace's 'Journey to Brundisium' (*Sat.* 1.5), and an anecdote about Aemilianus and an unwelcome hanger-on in Book 6 was the model for 'Horace and the Bore', *Sat.* 1.9. In Book 1 Lucilius felicitously exploited the conjunction of the death of Lentulus Lupus and a disastrous storm which hit Rome in 126 B.C. (cf. Julius Obsequens 29 (89)). Lucilius reported a meeting of the gods at which the questions were debated whether Rome could be allowed to continue to exist and what was to be done with Lentulus Lupus, who though convicted of extortion had become censor and *princeps senatus*. In the end, a condign punishment was no doubt fixed for Lupus and it was decided to send the prodigious storm as a warning to Romans to mend their ways. Thus Lucilius could pose as didactic *uates*, explaining the cause of the gods' anger, and he modelled his council of the gods on a famous episode in the first book of Ennius' *Annales* at which the deification of Romulus was ratified. The vein of parody was rich. The gods were made to observe the etiquette and procedure of the Senate; in their speeches they used mannerisms and clichés of contemporary earthly rhetoric ((1) 33–5 M = *ROL* 30–2, an *enthymema*; (1) 26–9 M = *ROL* 19–22, the hackneyed exordium 'I wish that *X* was not the case; but since it is...'); a confused Neptune doubts whether even Carneades (d. 129 B.C.) could help on some baffling point if he were released from Hades ((1) 31 M = *ROL* 35). A god, probably Romulus, complains about the mercenary attitudes of modern Rome ((1) 10 M = *ROL* 10), contrasting the old simple ways with fashionable exquisiteness in diet and dress; why, says he, even our language is being destroyed; what we used to call 'bed-feet' and 'lights' are now *pieds de lit* and

[1] A task for which he would have been well qualified: he served with Scipio at Numantia, Vell. 2.9.3.

lumières. It is part of the joke that Romulus himself uses a bizarre Graeco-Latin *franglais* to express this ((1) 15f. M = *ROL* 15f.). Lucilius clearly enjoyed clothing his provocatively demotic language in the heroic hexameter. This was important, for he never reverted to the iambo-trochaics of his earliest work, in which the contrast of form and style was less preposterous and pointed; and consequently the slackly-written hexameter became the form *par excellence* in Latin satire.[1]

The language and form of those earliest works were those of drama, as was only natural, since Ennius had established the iambo-trochaic metres and diction of the form as the ordinary medium for any poetry of less than heroic pretensions; including in Lucilius' time even epitaphs (*CIL* 1^2 1529). The question to be asked is not why Lucilius should have used iambo-trochaics at first instead of hexameters, but why and how he came to use hexameters. The earliest hexameter-poem was in Book 28: only seven lines survive (794–801 M = *ROL* 844–51); Accius is mentioned and two lines (795 M = *ROL* 845; 799 M = *ROL* 848) have the characteristic rhythms and alliteration of the epic style. Book 29 also included one hexameter poem (851–67 M, 1297 M = *ROL* 910–28), a mock-didactic disquisition on sex and whores. Book 30 consisted entirely of hexameter poems on a variety of themes – a barrack-room story telling how one Troginus acquired the nickname 'Pintpot', a debate between Lucilius and his adversaries, a letter addressing a marshal (Tuditanus?) in honorific terms can be distinguished. The hexameter *a priori* excluded common word-configurations, e.g. *cīuĭtātēs*, *făcĭnŏră*, *ēxpōstŭlānt*, unlike the iambo-trochaic metres, to which most of the vocabulary could be accommodated; thus it was in itself less λεκτικόν, appropriate for ordinary speech. There was, then, in spite of Horace's stricture (see p. 165), a certain cleverness in the ability to rattle off prose which conforms to the metrical rules of the hexameter, and the comic possibilities even included the confession:

seruorum est festus dies hic
quem plane hexametro uersu non dicere possis
((6) 228f. M = *ROL* 252f.)

There is a slaves' holiday here which you cannot possibly name in hexameter verse

(cf. Hor. *Sat.* 1.5.87, Porph. ad loc.).

It was a noted feature of Lucilius' diction that he drew directly on 'the technical words in every art and business' (Fronto p. 62 N), and among these

[1] The best accounts of the contents of Lucilius' works are those of Leo (1913) 411ff., and Coffey (1976). It was a regrettable decision of Krenkel (1970) 63–103 to give a detailed reconstruction, for he provided the German public with no means of distinguishing in his reconstruction what is certain, probable, possible, and worse. His edition represents a retreat from the critical standards of Warmington's *ROL* (1957), an edition itself only the best available, not the best possible, of this very difficult author.

Greek words are very prominent (cf. Hor. *Sat.* 1.10.20). Rhetoric, philosophy and science, medicine, the *cuisine*, and the *boudoir* are the main sources. There is a contrast here with Plautus, whose Greek expressions are fewer in number, and sometimes drawn from sources in southern Italy so colloquial and sub-literary that his borrowings are not attested in written Greek at all (*graphicus* 'clever', *thermipolium* 'bistro', the combination ναὶ γάρ 'yes'); and with Terence, who was more selective than either. Lucilius' use of Homer represents another and often witty kind of Greek borrowing: in the satire in which Scipio was plagued by a hanger-on, someone, perhaps Scipio, wishes

nil ut discrepet ac τὸν δ' ἐξήρπαξεν 'Απόλλων
fiat ((6) 231f. M = *ROL* 267f.)

that it be no different than if 'Apollo snatched him away' [*Il.* 20.443] *should happen*

(cf. Porph. *ad* Hor. *Sat.* 1.9.78 *sic me seruauit Apollo*, imitated from here). With such allusiveness, we are but a step from the world of Cicero's letters.

III

LATE REPUBLIC

8
PREDECESSORS

The short poems of Catullus, which he himself calls *nugae* 'trifles' (1.4), confront the critic with a paradox: poetry of obviously major significance and power which belongs formally to a minor genre. Only poems 11 and 51, written in the metre associated with Sappho herself, were entitled to lay claim to real lyric status; Catullus' preferred metres – the elegiac couplet, the hendecasyllable, the scazon (limping) iambus – belonged outside the grand tradition. Narrative elegy had of course been written by Callimachus, Philetas and Hermesianax; and Propertius in particular (3.1.1) acknowledged Callimachus and Philetas as his masters.[1] It was, however, the short elegiac epigram that first served Roman poets as a model for a new kind of personal poetry, as it eventually became. Aulus Gellius and Cicero have preserved five short epigrams by a trio of accomplished amateurs, Valerius Aedituus, Porcius Licinus and Quintus Lutatius Catulus. These are freely adapted from Hellenistic Greek originals, most of which can be identified in the Greek Anthology. This trio may have been writing as early as 150 B.C.; the fact that they are cited as a group by Gellius does not prove that they formed a literary coterie,[2] but at least it shows that there existed in the latter part of the second century B.C. a class of Roman *literati* who were actively interested in exploiting the short personal poem in Latin. That this was not a flash in the pan and that this sort of piece continued to be written during the first century is shown by the fragments of nine similar, though less polished compositions unearthed among the Pompeian graffiti.[3] There must have been also continuing stimulation from Greece. More than one anthology of Greek epigram was circulating in Italy during the century or so before Catullus; one of the most influential must have been the Garland (Στέφανος) of Meleager, whose own poems flaunted many of the ideas and images singled out for attack by Lucretius in his famous polemic against false manifestations of love.[4]

More original than such adaptive exercises was the highly experimental Muse

[1] The extent of his debt to Philetas is obscure: Ross (1975*a*) 120 n. 2.

[2] Ross (1969*a*) 140–2 and n. 61.

[3] Ross (1969*b*), (1969*a*) 147–9.

[4] Kenney (1970*a*) 381–5.

of Laevius, who appears to have written in the early part of the first century B.C. At first sight the nearly thirty fragments which survive seem to have a good deal in common with Catullus in subject matter, metre and diction, and Laevius has been conventionally counted among the predecessors or harbingers of the 'new' poetry. Closer analysis reveals important points of difference; and though it must remain probable *a priori* that Catullus and his contemporaries knew Laevius, direct indebtedness is difficult to demonstrate.[1] 'That Laevius provides a link with the neoterics cannot be denied, but that Catullus owed more to him than a vague suggestion of certain possibilities is unlikely.'[2]

Cicero, it is generally agreed, was no poet. He is, however, a more important figure in the history of Latin poetry than is commonly acknowledged. No Roman writer was more keenly alive to the rhythmical and sonorous properties of the Latin language; and it is only to be expected that Cicero should have had something to contribute to poetry also in the sphere of technique – even if, as must be admitted, he had nothing to say in his own poetry that posterity much wanted to hear. For it is the surviving fragments of his translations from the Greek that are of most interest to the historian of Latin literature, especially his version of Aratus' *Phaenomena*. This was a work of his youth (*Nat. D.* 2.104),[3] the first Latin version of this much-translated and (to modern ways of thinking) unexpectedly popular work; and it seems probable that it enjoyed a considerable circulation. Certainly it was known to and indeed imitated by Lucretius. What is perhaps less to be expected is that it shows Cicero to have been, in spite of his apparent reservations about the 'new' poetry – or about certain of its characteristics and practitioners at all events[4] – what might be called a pre- or proto-neoteric poet himself, much more so than Laevius. For one of the hallmarks of the 'new' school of poets was their (Callimachean) insistence on careful and exact craftsmanship; and Cicero's hexameters, flat and lifeless as they read, are technically much more like those of Catullus than those of Ennius or even Lucretius. In part the resemblance is due to stricter metrical observances, especially in the matter of caesuras and the treatment of the end of the verse. This process of self-discipline, however, goes hand in hand with and contributes to an increased awareness and realization of the artistic possibilities of word-order in the verse-sentence structure, such as are normally associated with Catullus and the Augustans.[5] The precise part played by Cicero in the development of Latin poetry is bound to remain obscure, given the fragmentary nature of the evidence; but the 'modern' character of his hexameters is unmistakable

[1] Ross (1969*a*) 155–60.
[2] Ibid. 160.
[3] On the dating see Ross (1969*a*) 134 n. 48.
[4] Below, pp. 178–9.
[5] Ross (1969*a*) 133–4; for analyses of the Ciceronian hexameter see Ewbank (1933) 40–71, Duckworth (1969) 37–45.

even to a twentieth-century reader and must have leapt (so to say) to the ear of his contemporaries. No account of the genesis of the 'new' poetry of Catullus and his school should omit mention of Rome's greatest orator. If Catullus himself was conscious of any debt, he does not own it. A reader of poem 49 ignorant of the *Aratea* would not readily guess that the poet might have had any reason to be grateful to Cicero other than the one so carefully not explained in that enigmatic poem.

9
THE NEW DIRECTION IN POETRY

I. THE NEW POETS AND THEIR ANTECEDENTS

The New Poets, as they are conventionally and conveniently called, were so called by an older poet who disliked them, at least some of them. Cicero, *Orat.* 161 (46–45 B.C.), observes that the suppression of final *s* was, at one time, a characteristic of refined speech but that now it seems somewhat countrified, *subrusticum*; and the new poets now shun it, *nunc fugiunt poetae noui*. 'We used to talk like this', he adds, quoting from Ennius' *Annals* and Lucilius. A year or so later, *Tusc. disp.* 3.45 (45–44 B.C.), he again refers to these poets while extolling the virtues of Ennius. *O poetam egregium! quamquam ab his cantoribus Euphorionis nunc contemnitur* 'What an outstanding poet! although he is despised by these choristers of Euphorion.' Who were these poets, *cantores Euphorionis?* Not Catullus certainly, who had been dead for nearly a decade. Probably his friend Cinna, a sedulous imitator of Euphorion,[1] and contemporary poetasters who imitated Cinna; possibly Cornelius Gallus, now in his mid twenties, who 'translated' Euphorion.[2]

It is a mistake, often made, to speak of 'Cicero's poetry' as if it were a body of work in which a consistent development might be traced from beginning to end. Cicero was serious about poetry, whenever the mood seized him. To an exceptional degree, and at a very early age, he mastered poetic form, and produced, in his youthful version of Aratus' *Phaenomena*, the first elegant hexameters written in Latin. That one unfortunate verse, written years later, should be forgiven him and forgotten:

> O fortunatam natam me consule Romam!
>
> *O happy Roman state born in my consulate!*

Neither as a poet nor as a critic of poetry is Cicero to be ridiculed: he was a shrewd and knowledgeable critic, and as good a poet as a highly intelligent man who has never experienced the sacred rage can be.

[1] See below, pp. 186–7.
[2] Servius on *Ecl.* 10.50–1; Ross (1975*a*) 40–3.

In 50 B.C. Cicero begins a letter to Atticus with a playful reference to a mannerism of the New Poets, the spondaic hexameter. *Brundisium uenimus VII Kal. Dec. usi tua felicitate nauigandi; ita belle nobis 'flauit ab Epiro lenissimus Onchesmites'. hunc* σπονδειάζοντα *si cui uoles* τῶν νεωτέρων *pro tuo uendito* 'We arrived at Brundisium on 24 November, as favoured in the crossing as yourself. "Softly, softly, from Epirus blew the Onchesmitic breeze." There! vend that spondaic as your own to any of the Neoterics you like.'[1] Cicero's witty fabrication (the verse must be his own) is perfect of its kind, closing with a 'learned' geographical allusion to an insignificant port on the coast of Epirus. The spondaic hexameter is as old as Homer, but in Homer infrequent and casual; in the Hellenistic poets – Aratus, Callimachus, Apollonius, Euphorion, and others – and in their Latin imitators it becomes frequent and designed.[2] Cicero was well aware of this device, for he had taken pains to avoid it, with a single exception that could hardly be avoided, in his version of Aratus.[3]

The New Poets were a group of young and impressionable poets in the generation after Cicero's who shared a literary attitude relating even to stylistic minutiae, of which Cicero chose to notice two. They wished to change Latin poetry, and to a considerable extent they succeeded in their purpose. The only one of their small number who survives, all but entire, is Catullus; of the others there are meagre remains.[4] It is easy and safe to assume that Catullus survives because he was their best: ancient readers, who were in a position to judge, evidently thought so. At the time, however, Calvus may have seemed the more imposing figure: a poet like Catullus, an accomplished orator, whose attacks on Caesar's henchman Vatinius were still read and studied in Tacitus' day (*Dial.* 21.4), and a Roman noble. Catullus was a provincial, but of a family that must have been prominent in Verona and well connected; otherwise Caesar would not have been a guest in his father's house. Caesar complained of the 'permanent scars' inflicted on his reputation by Catullus' pungent lampoons (poems 29 and 57?). The son apologized: that same day Caesar invited him to dinner and continued to enjoy the father's hospitality.[5] In one of his latest poems Catullus made amends, on a grand scale:

siue trans altas gradietur Alpes,
Caesaris uisens monimenta magni,
Gallicum Rhenum, horribile aequor ulti-
   mosque Britannos... (11.9–12)

or whether he [Catullus] shall traverse the lofty Alps to view great Caesar's monuments, the Gallic Rhine, the rough strait, and the utmost Britons...

1 *Att.* 7.2.1; adapted from Shackleton Bailey (1965–70) III.
2 A survey in Norden (1916) 441–6.
3 *Oriona* in line 3. In the corresponding lines of Aratus there are 66 spondaic hexameters.
4 Collected in *FPL* 80–91.
5 Suet. *Div. Iul.* 73; Gelzer (1968) 134.

That Calvus and Catullus were intimate friends appears from several poems (14, 50, 53, 96); and their names are coupled by later writers. Cinna was another friend, a fellow-Transpadane; Catullus' praise of his *Zmyrna* could scarcely be warmer (95). It is odd that Catullus nowhere alludes to Calvus' *Io*. Perhaps it was written after Catullus' death; if so, then Cinna was the first of the trio to write an epyllion, a miniature epic in the new style; and hence Catullus' enthusiasm. Catullus and Cinna were members of the cohort or entourage that accompanied the propraetor Memmius to Bithynia in 57 B.C. Cinna brought home some sedan-bearers and Aratus' *Phaenomena* copied on mallow bast;[1] Catullus only an abiding sense of outrage (10 and 28).

And there were others, shadowy figures, about whom very little is known. There was Cornificius, like Calvus a poet and an orator; to him Catullus addresses an amusingly rueful little poem (38). Furius Bibaculus was older and lived a long while; he was to be remembered for his lampoons on Caesar, with Catullus, and Octavian (Tac. *Ann.* 4.34.8). Two slight, affectionate poems of his are preserved on the bankrupt old age of the renowned teacher (*grammaticus*) and poet Valerius Cato, 'the Latin siren, who alone reads and makes poets' (Suet. *Gramm.* 11) – and who was not, perhaps, too dignified to be the recipient of Catullus 56. (Ovid, *Trist.* 2.436, cites Cato for his indecent verse in company with Catullus, Calvus, Ticidas, Memmius, Cinna, Cornificius.) A *Dictynna* is praised by Cinna, a *Lydia* by Ticidas. Ticidas composed an epithalamium in the metre of Catullus 61, as did Calvus. Caecilius is known only from Catullus 35: a native of nearby Novum Comum whom Catullus invites to visit Verona, if ever he can disentangle himself from the embrace of that girl who so passionately loves his poetry. The wit of Catullus' poem lies in the repetition *incohatam* (14)...*incohata* (18), the last line:

est enim uenuste
Magna Caecilio incohata Mater. (17–18)

The beginning of Caecilius' Magna Mater *is indeed lovely.*

In circumstances so time-beguiling Caecilius may never have finished his *Magna Mater*. It is not unlikely that Catullus followed Caecilius' progress, or lack of it, with special interest because of his own poem on the subject (63).

The New Poetry cannot be understood simply as issuing from the Latin literary tradition – almost no new form of Latin poetry can: the impulse comes from Greek, in this case later Greek, poetry. Of Hellenistic poets the one who meant most to the New Poets was Callimachus – Callimachus 'the chief classic of an unclassical art';[2] although to Catullus writing his epyllion (64) Apollonius was

[1] *FPL* 89; Tränkle (1967) 87–9.

[2] Wilamowitz (1924) I 170.

as important, and to Virgil, a second-generation New Poet, writing his *Eclogues* Theocritus necessarily more important. Still, Callimachus remained the type and ideal of Alexandrian elegance; but for his poetry and the aesthetic attitudes professed or implied in it much of what they wrote – as indeed much of Latin poetry after them – could not have been written.

In Alexandria Callimachus had been a dominant personality; an incredibly learned and industrious scholar of the library, and court poet. A dominant personality, but no literary dictator: Callimachus' position is at once polemical and defensive. Towards the end of his life he made an apologia for his poetic career; he had been attacked – and vehemently attacked, to judge from the vehemence of his retort – by Posidippus and Asclepiades and some others. Callimachus' famous refusal to write an epic suggests a widely held opinion that poets ought to write epics, and some expectation, possibly, on the part of those in high places. Callimachus had no decisive effect on Greek poetry either during his life or, though he was read for centuries, after his death. Epics continued to be written: epics about monarchs or war-lords, epics on mythological themes, epics concerning the history of a people or a region.

Callimachus' idea of poetry is expressed most fully in his apologia, a fastidious and beautiful denunciation of his enemies – the Telchines, as he dubs them, ill-natured literary dwarfs. (The text is defective here and there.)

The Telchines, who are ignorant and no friends of the Muse, murmur at my poetry because I have not made a single song, unbroken, of many thousands of verses about kings and heroes. But I roll my poem forward just a little, like a child, yet the decades of my years are not a few...(The short poems of Philitas and Mimnermus are better than their long.) Let the crane delighting in Pygmies' blood fly far, from Egypt to the Thracians; and let the Massagetes shoot their arrows far, at the Mede: shorter poems – 'nightingales' – are sweeter. Away, deathly brood of Envy! Henceforth judge poetry by its art, not by the Persian surveyor's chain. Don't expect me to produce a great rattling song: thunder is not my job, but Jove's.

καὶ γὰρ ὅτε πρώτιστον ἐμοῖς ἐπὶ δέλτον ἔθηκα
  γούνασιν, Ἀ[πό]λλων εἶπεν ὅ μοι Λύκιος·
'.......]...ἀοιδέ, τὸ μὲν θύος ὅττι πάχιστον
  θρέψαι, τὴ]ν̣ Μοῦσαν δ' ὠγαθὲ λεπταλέην·
πρὸς δέ σε] καὶ τόδ' ἄνωγα, τὰ μὴ πατέουσιν ἅμαξαι
  τὰ στείβειν, ἑτέρων ἴχνια μὴ καθ' ὁμά
δίφρον ἐλ]ᾶ̣ν μηδ' οἶμον ἀνὰ πλατύν, ἀλλὰ κελεύθους
  ἀτρίπτο]υ̣ς, εἰ καὶ στεινο̣τέρην ἐλάσεις.' (21–8)

For when first I set a writing-tablet on my knees, Lycian Apollo spoke to me: 'poet, feed your victim as fat as you can, but your Muse, my good fellow, keep her thin. And I tell you this besides: where no wagons pass, walk there; don't drive your cart in the tracks of others or along a wide road, but on ways unworn, even a narrower one.'

Then follow the poignant, wistful lines on the poet's old age. This 'testament' Callimachus placed before the original proem to his *Aetia* ('Causes'), which he had written as a young man: the Hesiodic dream of initiation by the Muses on Helicon. Even in this personal retrospect, literary allusions abound, to Homer, to Herodotus, to Mimnermus, so fearful of growing old, and to Euripides' *Mad Heracles*, written when the tragedian was an old man, as Callimachus the scholar would have known.

It is impossible to read much of Callimachus – his epigrams apart – without being impressed, or depressed, by his multifarious learning; but it would be perverse to wish that his poetry might be dissociated from his pedantry. Callimachus was not a poet and a scholar; he was a poet, or rather could be a poet, because he was a scholar, a γραμματικός, a man whose business was with literature. The earlier literature of Greece being now collected in the great library at Alexandria, men discovered the exquisite pleasure of writing books from books. Now a scholar-poet could scan and compare texts, delicately modify an admired metaphor or simile; follow an obscure variant of a myth or legend while deftly signalling an awareness of the usual version; join an old word with a new in a telling arrangement; choose a unique or rare word or form out of Homer or some other poet and locate it, perhaps with polemical intent, in a context of his own making. As, for instance, Callimachus does at the beginning of the story of Acontius and Cydippe:

Αὐτὸς Ἔρως ἐδίδαξεν Ἀκόντιον, ὁππότε καλῇ
  ἤθετο Κυδίππῃ παῖς ἐπὶ παρθενικῇ,
τέχνην – οὐ γὰρ ὅγ᾽ ἔσκε πολύκροτος – (*Aetia* 67.1–3)

Eros himself taught Acontius, when the youth was burning for the fair maid Cydippe, the craft – for he was not clever – . . .

In line 3 there is an allusion to the opening of the *Odyssey:* Ἄνδρα μοι ἔννεπε Μοῦσα, πολύτροπον . . . 'Speak to me, Muse, of the man . . .'; πολύκροτον is a rare variant. Earlier Greek poets supposed a sizeable group of auditors; Callimachus and his like only a few readers, learned or almost as learned as themselves.

That these umbratile poets were drawn to the composition of didactic poetry is not surprising; for in such poetry they could everywhere display their erudition and artfulness, and please themselves with a performance that owed little or nothing to the subject. Hence their choice of inert or seemingly intractable subjects. They wished to shine, not to persuade: in Nicander's *Theriaca* there breathes no Lucretian fire. The exemplar of such poetry appears to have been Aratus' *Phaenomena*. In one of his epigrams (27) Callimachus hails the subtle, Hesiodic quality of Aratus' verse; so might he have hailed his own *Aetia*.

The attitude of Callimachus to Hesiod and Homer has occasionally been misunderstood: for Callimachus Hesiod was imitable, Homer beyond imitation. Callimachus did not condemn Homer, he condemned Homer's imitators, those who copied whole phrases and tried to reproduce the epic form, not realizing it was by now empty and outworn. Hesiod's poems were relatively short, as, in Callimachus' judgement, poems should be, and told no long tales of kings and heroes. The *Theogony* interested Callimachus especially. It dealt with the true causes or wherefores of things (αἴτια); it was learned, if naively so – but its very naivety would appeal to Callimachus' sophistication; above all, Hesiod's was a personal voice. Hesiod provided Callimachus with the means of describing his own source of inspiration, a matter of deep concern to a late and self-conscious poet. While keeping his flock under Helicon, Hesiod met the Muses, who gave him a laurel branch (the living symbol of poetic inspiration) and breathed into him the divine power of song. While still a young man, Callimachus dreamed that he had been wafted to Helicon and there met the Muses. (Details are uncertain, for only a fragment of the text survives, and the scene cannot be reconstructed with any confidence from Latin imitations – notably that of Propertius 3.3.) The old bard of Ascra[1] seems to describe an actual encounter – strange things happen to shepherds by day in lonely places; but there is some intimation of night and darkness, and the passage was later interpreted allegorically, as a dream. And Callimachus, in Alexandria, could only dream of the Muses of Helicon.

Ennius, who knew so much, knew something of the poetry of Callimachus; he alluded to the famous dream – for reasons now not easy to grasp – at the beginning of his *Annals*, a long epic about kings and heroes. But Callimachus had little or no influence on Latin poetry until the generation of the New Poets. Some time, perhaps a long time, before he was forced to commit suicide in 87 B.C., Lutatius Catulus rendered one of Callimachus' epigrams (41: *FPL* 43); but this, the diversion of an idle hour, should not be taken as evidence of any serious interest in Callimachus' poetry or his aesthetic views. Catulus was a Roman noble with a taste for Greek poetry, an elegant amateur. He would have read many Greek epigrams: one, by Callimachus, caught his fancy and he made a version of it. Meleager's *Garland* had been published a few years before Catulus' death; he could have read the epigram there, or elsewhere; or it might have been shown him by his Greek friend Antipater of Sidon, a fluent epigrammatist who died about 125 B.C. In all probability, Catulus had never read any of the *Aetia*; had he attempted to do so, he would have found the literary polemic and philology either incomprehensible or distasteful. There is, moreover, no

[1] Virgil identifies his *Georgics* as belonging to this tradition, 2.176 *Ascraeumque cano Romana per oppida carmen* 'I sing the song of Ascra through Roman towns'.

reason to suppose that Catulus felt any aversion to old-fashioned epic: his circle included a certain Furius, a writer of such poetry, *Annals*.

Callimachus' poetry was brought to Rome by Parthenius of Nicaea, a zealous Callimachean; and arrived there with all the charm and force of novelty. Not that Callimachus had been altogether unknown in Rome; rather that Parthenius introduced him to some young and aspiring poets there, and made him an active part of their education. According to the biographical notice in the Suda, Parthenius was taken prisoner when the Romans defeated Mithridates, becoming the property or prize of Cinna (not further identified); and was later freed because of his learning, διὰ παίδευσιν. Therefore Parthenius arrived in Rome sometime after 73 B.C., the year the Romans captured Nicaea; possibly not until about 65 B.C., when Mithridates was finally defeated. It may be that literary young men in Rome were minded to read Callimachus without prompting; but then the suddenness and intensity of their interest would be difficult to explain; and it is doubtful whether a Cinna or a Calvus or a Catullus could have begun to appreciate Callimachus without a Parthenius at his elbow.

Cinna laboured for nine years to be as obscure as Euphorion, and succeeded brilliantly: his *Zmyrna* required an exegetical commentary.[1] Catullus greeted the publication of Cinna's epyllion with an enthusiasm truly Callimachean (95):

Zmyrna mei Cinnae nonam post denique messem
  quam coepta est nonamque edita post hiemem,
milia cum interea quingenta Hortensius uno
...
Zmyrna cauas Satrachi penitus mittetur ad undas,
  Zmyrnam cana diu saecula peruoluent.
At Volusi Annales Paduam morientur ad ipsam
  et laxas scombris saepe dabunt tunicas.

My Cinna's Zmyrna *is finally out, nine summers and nine winters after it was conceived, while in the meantime Hortensius... five hundred thousand... in one...* Zmyrna *will be sent all the way to the Satrachus' curled waves, grey centuries will long peruse* Zmyrna. *But Volusius'* Annals *will perish at Padua itself, and often supply loose wraps for mackerel.*

The technique of the poem is minute. There are, or were, eight lines, divided into two sections of four, each section beginning with the name of Cinna's poem. In the second section two rivers are mentioned, the Satrachus and the Po (Padua was a mouth of the Po, Latin *Padus*): *Satrachi* stands immediately before the caesura, or pause, of the first hexameter, *Paduam* immediately after that of the second, and both hexameters close with similar phrases: *mittetur ad undas*,

[1] By the grammarian Crassicius: Suet. *Gramm.* 18, with an ingenious parody of Catullus 70.

morientur ad ipsam. Nor is it fanciful to hear an echo of the first pentameter in the second:

> Zmyrnam cana diu *sae*cula peruoluent.
> et laxas scombris *sae*pe dabunt tunicas.

A polemical poem in the Callimachean style was not merely a confutation; it was, simultaneously, a demonstration of how poetry ought to be written. Catullus wrote another such poem vilifying the wretched Volusius and his *Annals*, 36 *Annales Volusi*, which has not quite been recognized for what it is.[1] Volusius must have been a neighbouring poet; otherwise there would be no point to the emphatic reference, *Paduam . . . ad ipsam*; and the name is attested on inscriptions from that part of Italy. Catullus pays Cinna an artful compliment: his poem will be read even by that far distant river which it celebrates. But there is a piquancy, also, in the oblique comparison of the two rivers: the broad, familiar Po with its mud and flotsam, the exotic Satrachus, swift and clear – this seems to be the implication of *cauus*; Lucan 2.421–2 applies the adjective to the Tiber and the Rutuba where they rush down from the Apennines. Callimachus had used a similar metaphor for long and short, or bad and good, poetry at the end of his second *Hymn*: Envy (Φθόνος) sidles up to Apollo and whispers an anti-Callimachean opinion into his ear; Apollo gives Envy a kick and replies:

> 'Ἀσσυρίου ποταμοῖο μέγας ῥόος, ἀλλὰ τὰ πολλά
> λύματα γῆς καὶ πολλὸν ἐφ' ὕδατι συρφετὸν ἕλκει.
> Δηοῖ δ' οὐκ ἀπὸ παντὸς ὕδωρ φορέουσι μέλισσαι,
> ἀλλ' ἥτις καθαρή τε καὶ ἀχράαντος ἀνέρπει
> πίδακος ἐξ ἱερῆς ὀλίγη λιβὰς ἄκρον ἄωτον.' (108–12)

'Great is the flood of the Assyrian river, but it drags much filth of earth and much refuse on its water. No common water do the bees bring to Demeter, but that which seeps up pure and undefiled from a sacred spring, a tiny rill, the crest and flower of water.'

What was the subject of Cinna's poem? The incestuous passion of Zmyrna (or Smyrna or Myrrha) for her father Cinyras, her metamorphosis into a tree, and the subsequent birth of Adonis from her trunk. Precisely the kind of tale Parthenius approved of – erotic, morbid, grotesque – as may be conjectured from the fragments of his poetry and from the poetical handbook Περὶ ἐρωτικῶν παθημάτων 'Tales of passion', which he compiled for the use of Cornelius Gallus. One of these (11) tells of the incestuous passion of Byblis for her brother Caunus, on which Parthenius himself had written a poem. And so he quotes, for example, some of his own lines:

> ἡ δ' ὅτε δὴ ⟨ῥ'⟩ ὀλοοῖο κασιγνήτου νόον ἔγνω,
> κλαῖεν ἀηδονίδων θαμινώτερον, αἵ τ' ἐνὶ βήσσῃς
> Σιθονίῳ κούρῳ πέρι μυρίον αἰάζουσιν.

[1] See below, pp. 200–1.

καί ῥα κατὰ στυφελοῖο σαρωνίδος αὐτίκα μίτρην
ἀψαμένη δειρὴν ἐνεθήκατο · ταὶ δ' ἐπ' ἐκείνῃ
βεύδεα παρθενικαὶ Μιλησίδες ἐρρήξαντο.

And when she knew her brother's cruel mind, she wailed more loudly than the nightingales that in the groves make myriad-lament for the Sithonian boy. And from a sturdy oak she straightway tied her head-scarf, and therein laid her neck: for her the virgins of Miletus rent their garments.

Six hexameters, divided into two sections of three, the third and sixth hexameter being a spondaic: the phrase ἡ δ' ὅτε δή ῥ' ὀλοοῖο (1) is echoed by καί ῥα κατὰ στυφελοῖο (4); θαμινώτερον (2) is metrically equivalent to ἐνεθήκατο (5), and both words are followed by similar phrases: αἵ τ' ἐνὶ βήσσῃς, ταὶ δ' ἐπ' ἐκείνῃ. There are two proper names, carefully disposed: Σιθονίῳ at the beginning of the third hexameter, and Μιλησίδες immediately after the caesura of the sixth.[1] The relative dates of Parthenius' poem and Catullus 95 cannot now be determined; or Catullus may not have been thinking of these lines in particular as he composed 95: yet the technique of 95 evidently owes a good deal to the example of Parthenius.

The Satrachus (or Σέτραχος) 'surfaces' at only three places in Greek poetry: Lycophron 448, Nonnus 13.459 with an allusion to Myrrha, and Parthenius frs. 23 and 24 – a recondite river for a young Latin poet to find without an experienced guide. It is entirely probable that Parthenius suggested this subject to Cinna for an epyllion, as he later suggested subjects to Gallus for epyllia and elegies.

It remains to characterize Euphorion, *Callimachus dimidiatus*. Euphorion had Callimachus' interest in philology, mythology, geography, aetiology, and more than his interest in the epyllion, a form that Callimachus invented but did not exploit. Callimachus' *Hecale* has almost every feature of the later epyllion, including an αἴτιον (the establishment of the Hecalesian festival) at the end. But one feature is conspicuously absent: a histrionic woman at centre-stage. It is doubtful whether Callimachus was capable of representing a woman's feelings, or cared to: his Cydippe is a sort of wax figurine,[2] an artifact manipulated by the poet, whose concern is for the male attractiveness of Acontius (*Aetia* frs. 68 and 69). Berenice suffers a similar disregard. Callimachus' *Lock of Berenice* is an elegant and frigid poem that allows no emotion whatever to the bereft queen and bride; only in Catullus' hands does she come alive, all the tender feminine touches having been added, apparently, in his translation (66).[3] Medea, by contrast, seems to acquire a vitality and will of her own: the confused girl smitten with

[1] Rohde (1914) 102n. failed to appreciate the symmetry of Parthenius' lines or the delicacy and restraint of his narrative and supposed that some words had been lost after ἐνεθήκατο. Eurydice's death is presented in the same elliptical style, *Georg.* 4.457–61. Parthenius was Virgil's tutor in Greek, and Virgil imitated – in effect, transcribed – one of his lines; Clausen (1976*a*).

[2] Wilamowitz (1924) I 188; contrast the Cydippe of 'Ovid', *Heroides* 21.

[3] Putnam (1960).

love becoming the impassioned, masterful woman – her sentimental education is the achievement of Apollonius in his *Argonautica*. And Euphorion, as did Catullus and Virgil after him, learned from Apollonius. An instructive fragment is preserved.[1] Apriate, while being hotly pursued along a precipice by the hero Trambelus, unburdens herself of an erudite and disdainful speech, and then – in a single hexameter – throws herself into the sea: the occasion of an αἴτιον. Euphorion is not interested in narrative, he is interested rather in obscure mythological allusion and the emotional state of his heroine: his procedure consequently, like that of Catullus in his epyllion (64), is elliptical and abrupt.

2. 'THE MARRIAGE OF PELEUS AND THETIS'

An epyllion was more or less expected of the complete New Poet;[2] and Catullus would have been eager to emulate Cinna, whose *Zmyrna* he so extravagantly admired. *The Marriage of Peleus and Thetis*, as 64 is usually called, is Catullus' longest and most ambitious poem, undoubtedly his intended masterpiece; a beautiful poem only partially successful but necessary to an understanding of Catullus. Catullus did not spend nine years working on it (is there a note of banter in his compliment to Cinna?); but he did not write it in a single mood of excitement, nor easily. 64 is learned and laborious, a specimen of strictly premeditated art.

Formality is established at the outset, and a sense of remoteness from experience:

Peliaco quondam prognatae uertice pinus
dicuntur liquidas Neptuni nasse per undas
Phasidos ad fluctus et fines Aeeteos... (1–3)

On Pelion's crest once long ago pine-trees were born, and swam (men say) through Neptune's liquid waves to Phasis' waters and the borders of Aeetes...

In these lines there is nothing of the apparent easiness with which, for instance, 50 begins: *Hesterno, Licini, die otiosi*... 'Yesterday, Licinius, at our leisure...'; so might Cicero have begun a letter to an intimate friend, the rhythm of the hendecasyllable being so close to that of ordinary cultivated speech.

It is of the essence of this poetry that there should be no dissimulation of the means by which its effect is attained. Certain features would have been recognized immediately by an ancient reader:

Peliaco quondam: an ornamental adjective with an adverb to summon up the dateless past; a formula invented by Callimachus for the beginning of his *Hecale* and then imitated by Theocritus and Moschus.[3]

[1] Easily accessible in Page (1940) 495–7. The tale is essentially the same as that of Britomartis (Dictyna) and Minos, told by Callimachus, *Hymn* 2.189–200, which Valerius Cato probably used for his *Dictynna*.

[2] Furius Bibaculus and Ticidas appear to have been exceptions; Cornificius wrote a *Glaucus*.

[3] Bühler (1960) 47.

prognatae: a word antique even in Plautus' day, here alliterating with *Peliaco* and *pinus* in the high archaic style of Ennius; this entire period (1–7) is in fact reminiscent of the opening of Ennius' famous tragedy, the *Medea exul*.

dicuntur: echoed in lines 19 *fertur*, 76 *perhibent*, 124 *perhibent*, 212 *ferunt*. Callimachus never tires of reminding his reader that whatever he tells him is true, that it can be found (he means) somewhere in a book: ἀμάρτυρον οὐδὲν ἀείδω 'nothing unattested sing I'.[1] Callimachus was that rarity – an original imagination almost wholly nourished on books. Catullus was not an immensely learned man; his scholarly gestures are affected therefore, and are to be taken rather as indications of the kind of poem he aspired to write.

Line 3 has been carefully fabricated from pieces of adjacent lines in Apollonius, *Arg*. 2.1277–8 ῥέεθρα | Φάσιδος 'the waters of the Phasis' and 1279 Αἰήταο 'of Aeetes'. A truly exquisite hexameter results: chiastic, alliterative, spondaic, and enclosed with two Greek names of which the first has a Greek ending.

All this – and these three lines are typical of the poem throughout – might seem but an absurd confusion of Hellenistic artifice, with Ennius doubling for Homer; yet the voice of Catullus does emerge, powerfully if obliquely.

64 is, in many ways, a bewildering poem, a maze difficult to penetrate without a plan of some sort. (It may be that Catullus constructed one for his own guidance while writing.)

1–30: the Argonauts set sail, the Nereids rise from the sea, and Peleus immediately falls in love with Thetis.

31–49: their marriage at Pharsalus; the mortal guests arrive.

50–264: the story of Theseus and Ariadne, the suicide of Aegeus, Adriadne's rescue by Bacchus on the isle of Dia – figures on a tapestry draped over the marriage bed.

265–302: the marriage again; the mortal guests depart, the immortal arrive.

303–81: the Parcae – tremulous crones with bits of wool adhering to their withered lips – weave a strange and fateful wedding song in praise of Achilles, the destined son.

382–408: then and now; Catullus reflects bitterly on the godlessness and degeneracy of his own times.

There is an undeniable awkwardness about the structure of the poem, a ponderosity vaguely sensed. The movement of the hexameter itself is noticeably heavy, with the same rhythmic pattern recurring again and again after the main caesura: *prognatae uertice pinus*. No doubt Catullus managed as best he could; but his skill seems to have been as yet unequal to a composition so relatively large and intricate. (His one other attempt of the kind (68), though shorter, is even more perplexed.) The beauty of 64 is intermittent, showing here and there – in 86–93: the sudden onrush of a first love; in 132–201: 'Ariadne passioning for Theseus' perjury and unjust flight' (Shakespeare), a speech Virgil apparently

[1] Fr. 612 Pf.; Norden (1916) 123–4.

knew by heart;[1] in 268–75: the simile of the west wind rippling the sea at dawn; in 278–84: Chiron, down from Pelion's crest, bringing huge bunches of wildflowers to the bridal pair (Catullus' own invention?).

The story of Peleus and Thetis was immemorially old; it is depicted on the François vase[2] and was already familiar to Homer's audience (*Il.* 24.534–40): Peleus, dear to the gods above all other men from birth, to whom they gave a goddess for wife – a splendid paradigm of mortal happiness, but overshadowed by sorrow: the goddess was unwilling, and their only son foredoomed. The story became, with variants and elaboration, a favourite subject of art and poetry. The last Greek poet of consequence to make use of it was Apollonius, whose *Argonautica* Catullus studied with care, taking from it whatever he could use for his own poem. The form, or idea, of 64 is due ultimately to Callimachus, much in its content and manner, however, to Apollonius. Callimachus' epyllion, the *Hecale*, ends with an αἴτιον, as, presumably, did the *Zmyrna* and the *Io*; but Catullus' epyllion has none, at the end or elsewhere. (The suicide of Aegeus offered an opportunity; but that would have been merely a distraction.) For this singular lack Catullus had a double precedent: Callimachus' story of Acontius and Cydippe has no αἴτιον, though it seems to invite one, nor does Apollonius' story of Jason and Medea, though Books 1, 2, and 4 of the *Argonautica* are replete with such.[3]

sed quid ego a primo digressus carmine plura
commemorem...? (116–17)

But why should I digress from the first of my song to recount more...?

Catullus is referring not to the marriage of Peleus and Thetis, as the reader might, for a blurred moment, suppose, but to the story of Theseus and Ariadne (52–75). Now, after embroidering as much of it as pleased him – Ariadne's fearful emotions as she watches Theseus struggling with her brute half-brother, the simile of the storm-felled tree (in both of which passages Catullus is indebted to Apollonius) – Catullus breaks off, in the manner of Apollonius:

ἀλλὰ τί μύθους
Αἰθαλίδεω χρειώ με διηνεκέως ἀγορεύειν; (1.648–9)

But why should I tell the tales about Aethalides straight through?

Thus Catullus underlines his own adroit description of the labyrinth and, in so doing, prepares for Ariadne's entrance and great speech (132–201).

[1] Compare 132–3: *Aen.* 4.305–6; 141: 4.316; 154: 4.365–7; 171–2: 4.657–8; 175–6: 4.10; 181–2: 4.21; 201: 4.629. Allowing for the scale and decorum of epic, *Aen.* 4 may be read as an epyllion.

[2] Dated 'about 570 B.C.' by Beazley (1951) 26–9; also depicted on it are Theseus and Ariadne.

[3] Fraser (1972) I 726–7, 627.

It has been objected that the inflated role of Ariadne impairs the economy of the poem. The incidental story or digression[1] from the main story – if it was that for Catullus – is longer than any other of its kind, and does seem excessive; but so do other features, small as well as large, of this strained and oddly personal poem. The two stories are inversely parallel: the voyage of Peleus ends in love and marriage (in the normal version Peleus is married before the voyage begins), the voyage of Theseus and Ariadne in forgetfulness of love, betrayal, and separation – themes that haunted Catullus' imagination.[2] A happy marriage with a suggestion of sorrow to come: an unhappy marriage (so to speak), with an unexpectedly joyous conclusion; the mortal Peleus in love with the immortal Thetis: the immortal Bacchus in love with the mortal (as then she was) Ariadne – all this Catullus contrived, and wished his reader to notice. Notice, for example, the obvious similarity of the references to Peleus and Bacchus in love:

tum Thetidis Peleus incensus fertur amore... (19)

Then Peleus is said to have been aflame with love of Thetis...

te quaerens, Ariadna, tuoque incensus amore... (253)

seeking you, Ariadne, and aflame with love of you...

Ornate, purposeful description of a work of art is a very old device of poetry, as old as Homer's description of the shield of Achilles (*Il.* 18.478–608); and has a long history.

What men or gods are these? What maidens loth?
What mad pursuit? What struggle to escape?
What pipes and timbrels? What wild ecstasy?

Inanimate scenes and figures are stirred briefly to life by the poet's voice; then left to quietness.

O Attic shape! Fair attitude! with brede
Of marble men and maidens overwrought...

talibus amplifice uestis decorata figuris
puluinar complexa suo uelabat amictu. (265–6)

With such figures richly wrought, the tapestry covered the bed, embracing it in its folds.

Thus, with quiet formality,[3] the turbulent episode of Ariadne concludes.

[1] Or ἔκφρασις, the technical term; Friedländer (1912) 1–23.

[2] The forgetfulness of Theseus had become proverbial (Theocr. 2.45–6, where the scholiast puts the blame on Dionysus), but Catullus stresses it as a personal fault leading to his father's death: lines 58, 123, 134–5, 148, 208, 209, 231, 248.

[3] Bühler (1960) 108.

Catullus knew several examples of such description in Hellenistic poetry. In Apollonius 1.721–67: Jason's elaborately figured mantle. In Moschus 2.43–62: Europa's golden flower-basket; in this poem, for the first time, an intimate relationship is established between the ἔκφρασις (the story of Io) and the main story. And, especially, in Theocritus 1.27–56: the goatherd's promised gift to Thyrsis for a song. (Catullus seems to have modelled his song of the Parcae – the deliberate irregularity of the refrain, to suggest in hexameters the form of a song, and the shape of the refrain itself – after the song of Thyrsis.[1]) The gift is a deep wooden cup, washed with sweet wax, two-handled, newly made, still smelling of the knife; and handsomely chased without and within. Within are three scenes. A woman, a divine creature, and two suitors hollow-eyed from love, passionately arguing in turn – but their complaints (unlike Ariadne's) go unheard; the woman is unconcerned, now smiling upon one, now shifting her attention to the other. Hard by, an old fisherman on a sea-cliff, eagerly gathering his great net for a cast with all the sinewy strength of youth. A little apart, a fine vineyard laden with purplish clusters, a boy sitting on a dry-wall to guard, and two foxes, one busily ravaging the ripe grapes, the other eyeing the boy's wallet; meanwhile the boy – careless sentinel – is plaiting a pretty cricket-cage of rush and asphodel. Through reading and studying such lavish, self-delighting passages Catullus was enabled to depict the variety and movement of the wedding reception at Pharsalus (267–302), the wild canorous rout on the isle of Dia (251–64).

A tapestry as a vehicle of the story of Theseus and Ariadne may have been suggested to Catullus by Apollonius, 4.421–34: the murder of Medea's brother Apsyrtus – in Apollonius a grown man who has tracked down the fugitive pair. They lure him to his death with gifts of specious friendship, among them Hypsipyle's crimson robe, fashioned by the very Graces on sea-girt Dia for Dionysus, who gave it to Thoas, and he to Hypsipyle, and she to Jason:

τοῦ δὲ καὶ ἀμβροσίη ὀδμὴ πέλεν ἐξέτι κείνου
ἐξ οὗ ἄναξ αὐτὸς Νυσήιος ἐγκατέλεκτο
ἀκροχάλιξ οἴνῳ καὶ νέκταρι, καλὰ μεμαρπώς
στήθεα παρθενικῆς Μινωίδος, ἥν ποτε Θησεύς
Κνωσσόθεν ἑσπομένην Δίῃ ἔνι κάλλιπε νήσῳ. (4.430–4)

And out of it came forth ambrosial sweetness, after the time Nysa's lord himself lay down upon it, high with wine and nectar, and clasped the lovely breast of Minos' virgin daughter; her Theseus once (for she followed him from Cnossus) left behind on Dia's isle.

Earlier, in Colchis, Jason had told Medea of Ariadne, of how she saved Theseus in his hour of peril; and hinted (for he badly needed Medea's magical aid) that she might elope with him.

[1] Gow (1952) II 16; Wilamowitz (1924) II 303.

ἀλλ' ἡ μὲν καὶ νηός, ἐπεὶ χόλον εὔνασε Μίνως,
σὺν τῷ ἐφεζομένη πάτρην λίπε· τὴν δὲ καὶ αὐτοί
ἀθάνατοι φίλαντο, μέσῳ δέ οἱ αἰθέρι τέκμωρ
ἀστερόεις στέφανος, τόν τε κλείουσ' Ἀριάδνης,
πάννυχος οὐρανίοις ἐνελίσσεται εἰδώλοισιν. (3.1000–4)

But she, when Minos' wrath was lulled, boarded ship with Theseus, and left her country. Even the gods loved her, and in mid-sky a sign, a starry crown that men call Ariadne's, wheels all night among the heavenly figures.

A seductive paradigm, with a considerable adjustment and a significant omission. The wrath of Minos remained vigilant and unsleeping,[1] nor is there a word about the forsaken Ariadne. The gods loved her...Apollonius' version (or perversion) of the story is a poet's: Jason persuades the foreign girl with his sweet Hellenic speech.

Perhaps Catullus was emboldened by the example of Apollonius. All other accounts agree:[2] Thetis was a most reluctant bride. (In a fit of rage she left Peleus soon after the birth of Achilles: Apollonius 4.865–79 – an inconvenient detail and so omitted by Catullus.) But Catullus twice insists to the contrary, with all the force and elegance of rhetoric at his command:

tum Thetidis Peleus incensus fertur amore,
tum Thetis humanos non despexit hymenaeos,
tum Thetidi pater ipse iugandum Pelea sensit. (19–21)

Then Peleus is said to have been aflame with love of Thetis, then Thetis did not scorn a human marriage, then the father himself of the gods deemed that Peleus should be joined to Thetis.

And again, in the wedding song:

nulla domus tales umquam contexit amores,
nullus amor tali coniunxit foedere amantis,
qualis adest Thetidi, qualis concordia Peleo. (334–6)

No house ever sheltered such love, no love ever joined lovers in such a compact, such a harmonious compact as that of Thetis, of Peleus.

Why did Catullus make so drastic a 'correction' in so venerable a story? In part, his reason must have been that of Apollonius, a poet's: to satisfy the logic of his poem as he conceived it; for Catullus is an uncompromising artist. But the peculiar emphasis can be related only to the intensity of his own awareness and desire.

For Catullus, then and now, *quondam* and *nunc*, were starkly opposed – an

[1] Clausen (1976*b*).

[2] With the curious exception of Alcaeus 42 (Lobel–Page), a poem that Catullus could hardly have known.

ideal past and the present, void of innocence and miserable. This emotional perspective recurs in the poems to or about Lesbia, in 8, 11, 58, 68.67–76, 72, 76.

Miser Catulle, desinas ineptire,
et quod uides perisse perditum ducas.
fulsere *quondam* candidi tibi soles... (8.1–3)

Poor Catullus, stop playing the fool, and what you see is lost, consider lost. Bright suns once shone upon you...

fulsere uere candidi tibi soles.
nunc iam illa non uolt... (8.8–9)

Bright suns truly shone upon you. Now she no longer wants it...

In the luminous, mythical world Catullus envisions, the felicity of Peleus must be pure and undisturbed:

talia praefantes quondam felicia Pelei
carmina diuino cecinerunt pectore Parcae. (382–3)

With such glad and solemn song the Parcae sang for Peleus once from their divining hearts.

Now earth is imbrued with crime and guilt, horrible desecrations of kinship, faith, love. A reference to Hesiod (*Works and Days* 177–201) will not suffice to explain the powerful, dark conclusion of this poem.[1] Few poets can have felt so painfully the pollution and remorse of time. *Peliaco quondam*: at the beginning *quondam* is traditional, at the end it is personal as well. The poem is both.

3. 'CATVLLI VERONENSIS LIBER'[2]

Cui dono lepidum nouum libellum
arida modo pumice expolitum?
Corneli, tibi; namque tu solebas
meas esse aliquid putare nugas
iam tum, cum ausus es unus Italorum
omne aeuum tribus explicare cartis
doctis, Iuppiter, et laboriosis.
quare habe tibi quidquid hoc libelli,
qualecumque quod, o patrona uirgo,
plus uno maneat perenne saeclo.

To whom shall I give this pretty new book, just polished with dry pumice-stone? Cornelius, to you; for you thought my trifles worth something even then, when you

[1] As Wilamowitz understood (1924) II 304: 'In der Seele des Dichters nicht in seiner Handbibliothek ist die Antwort zu suchen.'

[2] This section appeared originally in *Class. Philology* 71 (1976), and is reprinted in a somewhat revised form by kind permission of the University of Chicago Press.

dared, alone of Italians, to unfold all the world's history in three volumes – learned volumes! and laborious! So have this for yours, this little book; and such as it is, may it, o patron Muse, last more than one age.

With this brief and unobtrusive poem, for which almost no precedent exists, Catullus introduces himself and his book. Commentators cite Meleager:

> Μοῦσα φίλα, τίνι τάνδε φέρεις πάγκαρπον ἀοιδάν,
> ἢ τίς ὁ καὶ τεύξας ὑμνοθετᾶν στέφανον;
> ἄνυσε μὲν Μελέαγρος, ἀριζάλῳ δὲ Διοκλεῖ
> μναμόσυνον ταύταν ἐξεπόνησε χάριν... (*Anth. Pal.* 4.1.1–4)

Dear Muse, to whom do you bring this rich harvest of song? or who was it arranged this garland of poets? It was Meleager, and he fashioned this present as a keepsake for glorious Diocles.

The Muse, the poet and his book, and a receptive friend: there is a similarity, apparent and superficial. Catullus knew Meleager's poem, and may even have had it in mind as he was composing his own. But what, finally, has the studied simplicity of Catullus to do with Meleager's long and implicated conceit? Catullus' poem is personal and Roman. Publication of Nepos' *Chronica* furnished the pretext. Not that Catullus feigned a gratitude he did not feel, rather his gratitude cannot have been altogether literary. Cornelius Nepos was a fellow-Transpadane, considerably older than Catullus, with important friends in Rome, notably Cicero and Atticus; and, as an established author, had bestowed words of praise or encouragement on the younger man. It is not likely that Catullus admired so unreservedly the chronological survey Nepos had compiled, or that he much valued his literary judgement. Some twenty years later Nepos was to maintain that L. Julius Calidus (it is perhaps suggestive that Nepos gives the name in full) was by far the most elegant poet the age had produced after the death of Lucretius and Catullus: *L. Iulium Calidum, quem post Lucretii Catullique mortem multo elegantissumum poetam nostram tulisse aetatem uere uideor posse contendere.*[1] Had Nepos forgotten Catullus' friends Calvus and Cinna? Was he too old to appreciate Cornelius Gallus or Virgil, whose *Eclogues* had just been published? Only one conclusion is probable: like his friend Cicero, Nepos did not care for the *cantores Euphorionis*. But, like Calidus and other worthies, he was an amateur of verse, risqué verse according to Pliny, *Epist.* 5.3.6; fit recipient therefore of a small book of short poems, mostly in hendecasyllables, in which there was little or nothing overtly neoteric.

Was this *libellus* – a papyrus roll – substantially the same as the *liber* – a *codex* or book in the modern sense – that miraculously appeared in Verona towards the end of the thirteenth century? No doubt there is a delicate irony in Catullus' disparagement of his own book; but no *libellus* would contain so many

[1] *Att.* 12.4, a biography begun about 35 B.C. and finished after the death of Atticus in 32 B.C.

lines of poetry, nor could the long poems be described, even playfully, as *nugae*, in particular not *Peliaco quondam*, which must originally have formed a *libellus* by itself, like the *Culex* (of about the same length) or the *Ciris* (somewhat longer), or the *Zmyrna* or the *Io*.

Any effort, however subtle or elaborate, to prove that *The Book of Catullus of Verona* is an artistic whole, arranged and published by the poet himself, founders on an obvious hard fact: the physical limitation of the ancient papyrus roll. And for Catullus, as for writers before and after him until the supervention of the *codex*, the papyrus roll was the only 'book'. Too much is now known about the Greek roll, and too much can be inferred about the Latin, to leave room for doubt or special pleading. Book 5 of Lucretius, although shorter than Catullus' putative book by a thousand lines or so, is still extraordinarily long (some 1,457 lines). An ordinary roll would contain a book of Virgil's *Aeneid*, of Ovid's *Amores* or *Ars amatoria*, of Statius' *Thebaid*, of Juvenal, of Martial; a roll, on average, of between 700 and 900 lines.[1]

What, then, did the *libellus* dedicated to Nepos contain? No precise answer can be given; but a poem by Martial, a frequent imitator of Catullus, and the dedicatory poem itself indicate an answer.

'Tis the season to be jolly, the Saturnalia. Martial invites Silius Italicus, serious epic poet and constant imitator of Virgil, to unbend and read the poetry he has sent him, books of it 'steeped with racy jests':

nec torua lege fronte, sed remissa
lasciuis madidos iocis libellos.
sic forsan tener ausus est Catullus
magno mittere Passerem Maroni. (4.14.11–14)

So mayhap sweet Catullus dared to send
His 'Sparrow' book to Virgil, his great friend.

So mayhap sweet Catullus...A fancy highly agreeable to both parties. It is clear from the context that Martial refers to a book like his own (a *libellus* of 680 lines, not allowing for interstices) and not to a poem or two; and he does so, after the use of antiquity, by quoting the first word of the first poem – in this case, of the first poem after the dedicatory poem, which he may have regarded as belonging to the whole collection.

In metre as in manner the dedicatory poem is consonant with the poems that follow, 2–60, or more exactly, fifty-seven poems and two fragments, 2*b* and 14*b*. Of these, forty-five are in hendecasyllables, a pretty verse (6.17 *lepido...uersu*) in a pretty book, and favoured by the New Poets. In this part of the collection artistic design is discernible. Thus, two similar poems will be separated by a

[1] Exact figures in Birt (1882) 292–3.

poem dissimilar in subject or metre: 2 and 3, Lesbia's sparrow, by *2b*; 5 and 7, Lesbia's kisses, by 6; 34 and 36, a hymn and a parody of the hymnic style (36.11–16), by 35; 37 and 39, Egnatius and his gleaming teeth, by 38. The arrangement of 37, 38, 39 and 41, 42, 43 seems especially careful. 37 and 39 are longer poems of almost the same length (20 and 21 lines) in choliambics separated by a short poem (8 lines) in hendecasyllables; both 37 and 39 end with a word of the same meaning: *urina* and *loti*. Conversely, 41 and 43 are short poems of the same length (8 lines) in hendecasyllables separated by a longer poem (24 lines) in the same metre; the three poems are attacks on prostitutes, 41 and 43 directly, 42 indirectly. Such evidence is not sufficient to prove that the *libellus* contained all the polymetric poems; but probable cause for believing that it contained most of them, and in their present order.

If Catullus did not edit his 'collected poems', who did, and when? A member of his circle, a close friend perhaps – in any case, a *homo uenustus* like himself, and shortly after his death when it would still be possible to do so. The editor (so call him) collected all the poems he could find, poems in Catullus' papers whether at Rome or Verona, poems in the hands of friends, poems...[1] How did he go about putting them together? To begin with he had the *libellus*: to it he could add any unpublished polymetric poems. An easy, mechanical decision that would not disturb the already published order. If the *libellus* ended with 50[2] – and 50 would be, for several reasons, the perfect ending – then the position of 51, which should precede 11, as 2 precedes 3 and 5 precedes 7, or at least stand closer to it, is explicable. The fourth stanza of 51 is somehow unsatisfactory, and no ingenuity of interpretation will make it seem otherwise.[3] May it be that this famed poem of passion did not quite satisfy its author? That Catullus left it out of his *libellus*; and that the editor, connecting the first line of 50 (*otiosi*) with the last stanza of 51 (*otium*, *otio*, *otium*), added it? 53 and 56 are amusing squibs, 52 and 59 less so; 57 is as elegantly obscene as 29, 58 extremely moving. Catullus may have omitted these poems (reasons why can be invented), or he may have written them after he had published his *libellus*. It need not be assumed that he died immediately thereafter, or that he gave up writing in these congenial metres. Very little can be made of 54; 55 reads like a failed metrical experiment; *58b* must be unfinished; and 60 is a mere scrap. Would Catullus end his *libellus*, his pretty book of poems, this way? No; but the editor, more concerned to preserve than to present, would.

The second *libellus*, the editor's, begins with 61, an epithalamium, for a reason simple enough: it is in virtually the same metre as most of the poems in

[1] Naturally he missed a few; Mynors (1958) 106.

[2] A *libellus* of 772 lines, not allowing for the lacuna in *2b* or *14b* or for interstices.

[3] See below, pp. 198–9.

Catullus' *libellus*. Next, the editor put the other epithalamium (62); and next, the *Attis* in galliambics (63) to separate the two poems in hexameters, so that the epyllion (64) enjoys pride of place at the end.

At some point the editor had decided to keep all the elegiac poems, of no matter what length, together. Again, an easy, mechanical decision. (The editor must not, however, be imagined as a man without taste; an occasional artfulness of arrangement may be owing to him.) The third *libellus* begins with a suitably long elegiac poem, 65–6; perhaps the editor thought it appropriate initially because of the reference to the Muses in the opening lines:

Etsi me adsiduo confectum cura dolore
  seuocat a doctis, Hortale, uirginibus,
nec potis est dulcis Musarum expromere fetus
  mens animi... (65.1–4)

Although I am so wearied with constant sorrow, Hortalus, that grief keeps me from the learned maids, and my inmost soul is unable to produce the sweet fruits of the Muses...

Three rolls, *tres libelli*, the first containing poems 1–60, or 863 lines, not allowing for the lacuna in 2*b* or 14*b* or for interstices; the second, poems 61–4, or 802 lines, allowing for the lacuna in 61 but not for that in 62 or 64 or for interstices; the third, poems 65–116, or 644 lines, not allowing for the lacuna in 68 (after line 141) or 78*b* or for interstices – or 2,309 lines in all.[1]

Another consequence of the size of the roll is that collected editions of an author's work could not exist, except in the sense that the rolls containing them could be kept in the same bucket...Volumes containing the whole corpus of an author's work only became possible after the invention of the codex, and especially of the vellum codex.[2]

In late antiquity, probably in the fourth century, these three rolls, or rather rolls copied from them, were translated into a *codex* with the first poem now serving as a dedication to the whole collection. From such a *codex*, by a long and hazardous route, descends *The Book of Catullus of Verona*.[3]

[1] The first three books of Horace's *Odes* were published together, *tres libelli*: the first containing 876 lines; the second, 572 lines; the third, 1,004 lines – or 2,452 lines in all, not allowing for interstices.

[2] Kenyon (1951) 65.

[3] Additional documentation of this argument in Clausen (1976*c*).

4. LESBIA, SIRMIO, CALVUS

51

Ille mi par esse deo uidetur,
ille, si fas est, superare diuos,
qui sedens aduersus identidem te
  spectat et audit
dulce ridentem, misero quod omnis
eripit sensus mihi; nam simul te,
Lesbia, aspexi, nihil est super mi
...
lingua sed torpet, tenuis sub artus
flamma demanat, sonitu suopte
tintinant aures, gemina teguntur
  lumina nocte.
otium, Catulle, tibi molestum est,
otio exsultas nimiumque gestis
otium et reges prius et beatas
  perdidit urbes.

He seems to me the equal of a god,
He seems, if that may be, above the gods,
Who sitting opposite looks again and again
At you and hears

Your sweet laughter – and misery strips me
Of all my senses; for once I have seen you,
Lesbia, nothing remains to me,
No voice...

But my tongue grows numb, a thin flame
Flows through my limbs, with their own sound
My ears ring, my eyes are covered
With double night.

Idleness, Catullus, is your trouble,
Idleness – you're wild, beyond restraint:
Idleness has ruined kings of old
And prosperous cities.

This is commonly taken as Catullus' first poem to 'Lesbia'. Catullus watches jealously – so the scene is imagined – as another man converses with Clodia: his senses waver, he nearly faints, he recollects an old and passionate[1] poem by Sappho: Φαίνεταί μοι κῆνος ἴσος θέοισιν 'He seems to me the equal of the gods'. Hence, from an altered point of view, this translation; and hence the pseudonym

[1] And well known, an 'anthology piece'; Russell (1964) on 10.2 and Ross (1969*a*) 149–50. Catullus had not read through the *opera omnia* of Sappho.

Lesbia. But Lesbia no more wanted explaining than did Cynthia or Delia or the others; and she had already been introduced, in hendecasyllables, to the reader of the *libellus*, 5.1 *Viuamus, mea Lesbia, atque amemus* 'Let us live, my Lesbia, and love.' A less romantic aspect is ignored. This is indeed a first poem, the first Latin poem written in Sapphic stanzas: a bold and not altogether successful literary experiment. The Hellenistic poets, although they were given to renovating old forms, did not attempt this one; perhaps they knew better. Catullus' poem may plausibly claim to be the first Sapphic after Sappho.

It is by no means an inert translation: Catullus was concerned to modernize Sappho, to bring her poem up to date. To a close rendering of her first line he adds a second entirely his own, importing a note of Roman solemnity.[1] Lines 5 and 6 exhibit him enveloped in his own misery, *misero...mihi*; his general condition preceding a diagnosis of individual symptoms. Sappho's symptoms have been so re-ordered by Catullus that sight falls last: it was, in the first instance, the vision of Lesbia that all but unnerved him. Here in his third stanza, Catullus the New Poet has most carefully shaped and refined Sappho. There is a detail of Hellenistic technique – the postposition of *sed* – at the beginning; a verbal sophistication – *gemina...nocte* – at the end. In each line the caesura occurs at the same point, coinciding with the end of a clause; and each clause is discrete. With this stanza Catullus' direct emulation of Sappho ends (he disregards her fourth stanza); but his poem does not.

For many readers, however, it will always seem to end – as Landor maintained it did – with the beautiful cadence *lumina nocte*; a sort of premature success that Catullus cannot have intended. Sappho's 'congress of emotions' (so termed by 'Longinus': παθῶν σύνοδος) apparently concluded with a brief moralizing soliloquy: 'But all is endurable...' (The first line of a fifth, and probably final, stanza is preserved partially corrupt in 'Longinus'.) Catullus designed a similar conclusion, but with a larger reference, Roman in sensibility. At this juncture his poem fails: the added stanza is abrupt and inconsequent, and the mechanism of effect – *otium*, *otio*, *otium* – too obvious. The poet's erotic trouble appears as contingent, as hardly related to the downfall and perdition of empires.

58

Caeli, Lesbia nostra, Lesbia illa,
illa Lesbia, quam Catullus unam
plus quam se atque suos amauit omnes,
nunc in quadriuiis et angiportis
glubit magnanimi Remi nepotes.

[1] Fedeli (1972) 276; to his examples add Suet. *Div. Aug.* 98.

Caelius, my Lesbia, the *Lesbia,*
Lesbia, the one Catullus loved
more than himself and all his own,
now, in cross-roads and alleys,
'peels' great-souled Remus' sons.

The iteration of Lesbia's name is extremely moving. The nearest equivalent in Latin is, perhaps, the anguished cry with which Cicero begins a letter to his brother, 1.3.1 *Mi frater, mi frater, mi frater* 'My brother, my brother, my brother'; in English, David's lament for his son: 'O my son Absalom, my son, my son Absalom'. The poem consists of a single sentence of unrelenting intensity culminating in the stark juxtaposition *glubit magnanimi*: a low word, out of the gutter, and a high heroic word; with such force can Catullus – as only he, of Roman poets, can – bring the weight of the fabled past to bear on his own enormous sense of injury and disgust.

36

Annales Volusi, cacata carta

'*Annals* of Volusius...' This drastic line, the first and last of the poem,[1] defines its subject: poetry, the old and outmoded as opposed, implicitly, to the neat and new: the poetry of Catullus and Cinna and their friends, of which this poem is meant to be, as it is, an elegant specimen.[2]

Lesbia had made a naughty vow to Venus and Cupid: if Catullus should be restored to her and cease hurling his fierce 'iambs', then she would donate the choicest verse of the worst poet (meaning Catullus) to the slow-footed god of fire. Catullus assents: let her charming vow be paid, and into the fire with – the *Annals* of Volusius! Lesbia, like the inamorata of Caecilius in the poem preceding, is a *docta puella*, a witty, seductive woman whose taste in poetry and poets is impeccable. This peculiar involvement of poetry (or pedantry, as occasionally it becomes) with passion is not easy to comprehend, not even with the help of Catullus' 'explication' (68.1–40).

The amusing little comedy of Lesbia's vow serves as a pretext for Catullus' prayer to the goddess of love and the sea – an exquisite passage of literary and personal geography:

nunc, o caeruleo creata ponto,
quae sanctum Idalium Vriosque apertos,
quaeque Ancona Cnidumque harundinosam
colis quaeque Amathunta, quaeque Golgos,
quaeque Durrachium Hadriae tabernam... (11–15)

Now, o thou created of the sky-blue sea,
that dost dwell in holy Idalium and wind-swept Urii,
in Ancona and reedy Cnidus,
in Amathus, in Golgi,
in Dyrrachium, Adria's tavern...

[1] Like 16.1 and 57.1, lines equally drastic.

[2] See above, p. 185.

Hadriae taberna: sailors' slang picked up by Catullus on his Bithynian tour? Here it functions to reduce the heightened tone of the invocation to the conversational level of the rest of the poem (1–10, 16–20). Idalium, Urii, Ancona,[1] Cnidus, Amathus, Golgi, Dyrrachium – all names of places where the goddess of love was worshipped, with scant ceremony, as may be surmised, at Dyrrachium.

A line in *Peliaco quondam*: *quaeque regis Golgos quaeque Idalium frondosum* 'that dost rule Golgi and leafy Idalium' (64.96) indicates that Catullus had read and remembered Theocritus: Δέσποιν', ἃ Γολγώς τε καὶ Ἰδάλιον ἐφίλησας 'Lady, that dost love Golgi and Idalium' (15.100). Catullus would have read of Cnidus too, and probably visited it on his sight-seeing cruise down the coast of Asia Minor (46.6); for it was a tourist attraction, and he seems to have gone as far south as Rhodes (4.8). Golgi, Idalium, and Amathus were towns in Cyprus – towns Catullus had never seen – and all three connected with the legend of Adonis. At Amathus, according to Pausanias 9.41.2, was an ancient sanctuary of Adonis and Aphrodite. But Amathus is not now to be found, whether in prose or poetry, before Catullus. Where did Catullus find so rare a name? Most likely in Cinna's *Zmyrna*;[2] and he employs it here as he employs *Satrachus* in 95: to flatter a poet-friend and point the contrast between the New Poetry and the old. Three names remain: Dyrrachium, Urii, Ancona – names of the three stopping-places on Catullus' voyage through the Adriatic in the spring or summer of 56 B.C.[3] From Dyrrachium he crossed over to Urii, a small harbour on the northern side of Monte Gargano, then sailed up the coast to Ancona before a following wind,[4] then into the Po (by the Padua mouth?) – and home at last to Sirmio.

31

Perhaps no poem of Catullus has been so persistently misread or, for all its brevity, so incompletely read. The subject of the poem, home-coming, is likely to occasion diffuse sentiment; but 31 is not a sentimental poem. Whatever the emotions Catullus felt as he arrived at Sirmio, they were not – not, certainly, as expressed in his poem – 'the simplest and most natural...plainly expressed' (Kroll, and others similarly). Catullus' delight is exactly reflected in the wit and complicated play, the 'happiness', of his language.

The poem commences with a flamboyant conceit, *uterque Neptunus*: Neptune

[1] That Venus had a temple at Ancona is known from another poet, Juvenal 4.40. To make poetic a place obscure or previously unsung, as here by associating it (Urii) with illustrious names, is in the Alexandrian tradition; cf. 64.35–6 (Cieros).

[2] And *Amathusia* (68.51)? Similarly, Parthenius in his *Aphrodite* (fr. 3) calls the goddess 'Acamantis' after Acamas, an obscure promontory in Cyprus. It is surely no accident that nearly all of Parthenius' fragments are preserved in geographical authors.

[3] Wiseman (1969) 42–5.

[4] Cf. 4.18–24. Dante, *Purg.* 28.19–21, heard the south wind, the scirocco, stirring among the boughs of the pine-wood at Chiassi (Ravenna), past which Catullus would have sailed.

in his either capacity, that is, sweet or salt. (A dim memory of an old Italic god of lakes and rivers may have lingered on in the region of the Po.)

Paene insularum, Sirmio, insularumque
ocelle, quascumque in liquentibus stagnis
marique uasto fert uterque Neptunus... (1–3)

Gem[1] *of all-but-islands and islands, Sirmio, which either Neptune bears in clear, quiet lakes and the vast sea...*

Obviously, Catullus was glad to be home:

quam te libenter quamque laetus inuiso (4)

how glad and how happy I am to see you

– a plain statement, but immediately qualified with a playfully erudite geographical allusion in the manner of Callimachus (or Parthenius):

uix mi ipse credens Thyniam atque Bithynos
liquisse campos... (5–6)

scarce myself believing I have left behind Thynia and the plains of Bithynia...

The Thyni and Bithyni were in fact adjacent but distinct tribes (Herod. 1.28), as Catullus would have learned in Bithynia. But he cared nothing for the ethnic differentiation, and even shows a fine indifference to the rough terrain of the province.

o quid solutis est beatius curis,
cum mens onus reponit ac peregrino
labore fessi uenimus larem ad nostrum
desideratoque acquiescimus lecto?
hoc est quod unum est pro laboribus tantis. (7–11)

O what more blissful than cares resolved, when the mind lays down its burden, and, weary from effort abroad, we come to our own household and rest on the bed we have longed for. This, this alone makes up for efforts so great.

Again, a plain statement, ampler and occupying the centre of the poem, with only a hint of deliberate rhetoric in the contrast *peregrino*/*nostrum*; but again qualified, in a final exuberance of expression:

salue, o uenusta Sirmio, atque ero gaude,
gaudete uosque, o Lydiae lacus undae,
ridete quidquid est domi cachinnorum. (13–15)

Hail o lovely Sirmio, and be glad for your master, and you, o Lydian waves of the lake, be glad, laugh with all the noisy laughter you own.

[1] See p. 206 n. 1.

o uenusta Sirmio: *uenustus* belongs to the same range of feeling as *ocellus* (2 *ocelle*). Only one other writer uses both these words of lovely places, Cicero – of his villas, *Att.* 16.6.2 *ocellos Italiae*, of the sea-shore at Astura (?), *Att.* 15.16*b*.1 *haec loca uenusta.* (On the language of Catullus in his polymetric poems the most informative 'commentator' by far is Cicero in his letters.) But the vocative here is unique, and all but personifies Sirmio. The tone is further heightened by the second apostrophe *o Lydiae lacus undae*; an example of enallage or 'transferred epithet', a figure appropriate to the highest style of poetry. Earlier critics therefore, persuaded that Catullus should be simpler in his shorter poems, wished to rid the line both of its figure and its too erudite allusion (by emendation, *limpidi*, *lucidae*, or the like): plainly they were reading, or fancied they were, a quite different poem.

85

Odi et amo. quare id faciam, fortasse requiris.
nescio sed fieri sentio et excrucior.

I hate and love. Why do that, perhaps you ask. I don't know, but I feel it happen and am tormented.

The pathos of ordinary speech: fourteen words, a poem. The reader may be strangely moved, and perhaps ask why. There is no ornament of language, no learned allusion, no very striking word. For too much, probably, has been made of *excrucior* in this context: while *excrucior* can signify the deepest distress, it is Plautine and colloquial, like *discrucior* in 66.76 or Plaut. *Cas.* 276 *ego discrucior miser amore* 'I am wretchedly distracted by love'; the metaphor is scarcely felt. The whole effect of a poem only two lines long, a couplet, must depend rather, or as well, upon the compression and exactness of its form. The hexameter is active in sense (*faciam*), the pentameter passive (*fieri*); the initial phrase of the hexameter (*od*(*i*) *et amo*) is balanced by the final phrase of the pentameter (*senti*(*o*) *et excrucior*); and the pentameter is so articulated that a rhythmic emphasis falls on *nescio* and *sentio*: I don't know, I feel. The poem defines not so much the feeling as the fact of feeling.

109

Iucundum, mea uita, mihi proponis amorem
hunc nostrum inter nos perpetuumque fore.
di magni, facite ut uere promittere possit,
atque id sincere dicat et ex animo,
ut liceat nobis tota perducere uita
aeternum hoc sanctae foedus amicitiae.

You promise me, my life, that this love of ours will be pleasant, and will endure. Great gods, make her able to promise truly, and say this sincerely and from her heart, so that we may extend, our whole life through, this everlasting compact of sacred friendship.

The poem rises, as it were, from the bland elegance of the first couplet through the prayerful earnestness of the second to the solemn conclusion of the third. Why, then, does the final, climactic line fall flat? Or rather, why does it seem to? Lesbia proposes love (*amor*), Catullus opposes friendship (*amicitia*): the structure of the poem, and of the last line in particular, requires that 'friendship' be the stronger, the weightier term. No English reader can hope to have a contemporary Roman's sense of *amicitia*, much less of its absolute rightness here. *Amicitia* was basically a political term, well understood and capable of accurate definition.

amicitia in politics was a responsible relationship. A man expected from his friends not only support at the polls, but aid in the perils of public life, the unending prosecutions brought from political motives by his personal enemies, his *inimici*, his rivals in the contest for office and for the manifold rewards of public life. Friendship for the man in politics was a sacred agreement.[1]

Catullus 'abuses' the phrase *foedus amicitiae* to define the unusual nature of the relationship he wants to have with Lesbia. *Aeternum hoc sanctae foedus amicitiae*: the intertwining word-order is Hellenistic,[2] the sentiment pure Roman.

The second couplet depends mainly upon adverbs for effect – more precisely, two adverbs and an adverbial phrase. Catullus remembered a passage in Terence's *Eunuchus* (a young man speaking to a prostitute):

utinam istuc uerbum *ex animo* ac *uere* diceres
'potius quam te inimicum habeam'! si istuc crederem
sincere dici, quiduis possem perpeti. (175–7)

How I wish you said that from your heart and truly, 'rather than have you for an enemy'! If I could believe that was said sincerely, I would be able to endure anything.

In these two passages, and in these two only, are these three adverbs combined. *Potius quam te inimicum habeam*: did *inimicus*, in this context, suggest the erotic possibilities of a political vocabulary to Catullus? However that might be, Catullus discovered this potent metaphor and made it his own; the Augustan elegists neglect it.

50

Hesterno, Licini, die otiosi
multum lusimus in meis tabellis,
ut conuenerat esse delicatos:
scribens uersiculos uterque nostrum
ludebat numero modo hoc modo illoc,
reddens mutua per iocum atque uinum. (1–6)

[1] L. R. Taylor, quoted by Ross (1969*a*) 84. On Catullus' metaphorical use of this political vocabulary – *amicitia, foedus, fides, fidus, iniuria, pietas, pius, officium, bene facere, bene uelle* – see Reitzenstein (1912); Ross (1969*a*) 80–95. Most enlightening in this regard is a letter written by Cicero to M. Licinius Crassus in 54 B.C., *Fam.* 5.8: note especially *amicitiae fides* (2), *foederis, sanctissime* (5).

[2] And for that reason objected to by Reitzenstein (1912) 28–9, who preferred to read *aeternae hoc sancte* after the Oxford MS.

Licinius, yesterday at Leisure
We in my tablets took much pleasure,
As either of us then thought fit
To Versify, and deal in Wit;
Now in this sort of verse, now that,
As Mirth and Wine indulg'd the Chat.[1]

Catullus and Calvus had passed an idle day together drinking and making extempore verses; a 'wit-combat' had been stipulated: *ut conuenerat esse delicatos*. (*Delicatus* is practically untranslatable. It is one of those words used by Catullus and, presumably, Calvus and the others – *deliciae*, *lepor*, *lepidus*, *illepidus*, *facetiae*, *infacetus*, *uenustus*, *inuenustus*, *iucundus*, *elegans*, *inelegans*, *ineptus*, *ludere*; ordinary words, frequent in Plautus and Terence, and yet, as used by the New Poets, intimating a special sensibility.) Catullus went away so fired by the charm and wit of Calvus – *tuo lepore incensus*, *Licini*, *facetiisque* (7–8) – that he could neither eat nor sleep; at last, half dead with fatigue, he made this poem as a means of quenching his ardour.

One of Cicero's letters[2] was written under similar circumstances, a brief letter to his lawyer-friend Trebatius Testa which begins: *Illuseras heri inter scyphos* 'You made fun of me yesterday over our cups'. At issue had been an abstruse point of testamentary law. On returning home 'well liquored and late', Cicero looked out the pertinent chapter, found that he had been right, and wrote to Trebatius in the morning to tell him so, closing with a graceful compliment to the younger man. Cicero's letter and Catullus' poem have this in common, that each was prompted by an occasion; but there is a crucial difference. Cicero's letter was intended for Trebatius only; Catullus' poem, though it is addressed to Calvus, was intended for publication. Calvus, after all, did not need to be told what he and Catullus had been doing only a few hours earlier, but other readers would, for the poem's sake.

The poem seems to be an effusion of sentiment; and it is – while being also, as might be expected, a meticulous composition. It is composed of three sections: six lines (1–6) on yesterday's conviviality, seven lines (7–13) on Catullus' emotional reaction, and eight lines (14–41) divided into two subsections (the form is as calculated as the term implies) of four lines each: the making of the poem (14–17), and a playful warning to Calvus:

nunc audax caue sis, precesque nostras,
oramus, caue despuas, ocelle,
ne poenas Nemesis reposcat a te.
est uehemens dea: laedere hanc caueto. (18–21)

[1] An anonymous translation published in 1707: Duckett (1925) 103.
[2] *Fam.* 7.22, cited by Fraenkel (1956) 281–2.

Now don't be over-proud, and don't, I beg you, despise my prayers, dear friend,[1] *lest Nemesis require penalties of you. She is a vehement goddess: offend her not.*

By convention Nemesis punished any overweening speech or act, but her wrath might be averted by spitting, preferably three times. This quaint custom is hinted at in *despuas* (here first in this sense) and the triple caveat: *caue*, *caue*, *caueto*, the archaic form being put last for a mock-solemn emphasis.

This poem has, finally, a unique feature: Calvus is addressed not once but four times, once in each section and subsection of the poem. He is twice addressed by name: *Licini* (1), *Licini* (8), and twice – to match the intensification of mood – with increasing warmth and affection: *iucunde* (16), *ocelle* (19). So apt is Catullus' response to the passionate and fiery nature of his dearest friend.[2]

[1] *ocelle*: a diminutive term of endearment which English is helpless to render.

[2] There is a vivid 'portrait' of Calvus in Seneca the Elder, *Contr.* 7.4.6–8.

10

LUCRETIUS

The *De rerum natura* of Lucretius represents one of the rarest of literary accomplishments, a successful didactic poem on a scientific subject. Few great poets have attempted such a work, and many critics, from Aristotle on, have argued that the contradictions which are implicit in the genre, and indeed in all didactic poetry, can never be fully reconciled. 'Didactic poetry is my abhorrence', wrote Shelley in the preface to *Prometheus Unbound*, 'nothing can be equally well expressed in prose that is not tedious and supererogatory in verse', and Mommsen dismissed the greater part of the *De rerum natura* as 'rhythmisierte Mathematik'. What, then, is the relationship between Lucretius the poet and Lucretius the philosopher? To what extent do they come together to form a successful unity? Otto Regenbogen called this the 'central question' in Lucretian criticism,[1] and in his famous essay 'Lukrez: seine Gestalt in seinem Gedicht' he attempted to answer it in three ways: by examining the background of the poem, the personality of the poet, and the structure and quality of the work itself. Most Lucretian criticism falls under one or other of these headings and it will be convenient to consider each in turn.

I. BACKGROUND

One might imagine that a didactic and moralizing work like the *De rerum natura* would have deep roots in the society which produced it. Yet there is a wide disparity of views about the purpose of the poem and the character of the audience for which it was composed. Ostensibly it was written for the poet's aristocratic patron Memmius, but, since literary convention required that a didactic poem be addressed to some particular person, we may suppose that behind Memmius stands the general reader. Both are linked, rather awkwardly, in the famous programmatic passage about the poet's mission.

> ...quoniam haec ratio plerumque uidetur
> tristior esse quibus non est tractata, retroque
> uolgus abhorret ab hac, uolui tibi suauiloquenti
> carmine Pierio rationem exponere nostram... (1.943–6 ~ 4.18–21)

[1] Regenbogen (1932) 2.

> *...since my philosophy often seems too bitter to those who have not tasted it, and the crowd shies away from it, I have desired to set out for you, Memmius, an explanation of our system in the sweet language of the Muses...*

This passage does not explicitly state that the poem is intended for ordinary men, but it does imply a wider audience than might have been attracted by a purely technical treatise.

We should not, however, exaggerate the popular nature of the poem. There cannot have been in the first century, any more than there is today, a large number of people interested in the indivisible magnitudes of the atom or in the weaknesses in Anaxagoras' theory of *homoeomeria*. In spite of Lucretius' reference to the 'crowd', he has clearly in mind an audience which is prepared to follow a long and complex argument. Granted that the poet simplifies and that some of his arguments are addressed more to the emotions than to the intellect, the *De rerum natura* is nevertheless a serious attempt to explain the principal doctrines of Epicurean physics and it requires the reader's cooperation and concentration. This is true not only of the argument but also of the poetry itself: recent critics have rightly stressed the sophistication of the poet's literary technique and his ability, when he wished, to adopt the allusive manner of his neoteric contemporaries. That Lucretius is a distinctly 'literary' author can be seen from the long list of his debts to earlier writers, both Greek and Latin. To mention only Greek authors, and to exclude the philosophers, there is evidence that he knew Homer, Euripides, Thucydides, parts of the Hippocratic *corpus*, Callimachus, some of the writers of epigram, and probably also Hesiod, Sappho, Aeschylus and Aristophanes. The list is significant not only for its length, but also for the range of its intellectual sympathies.

It is instructive to compare the *De rerum natura* with the philosophical dialogues which Cicero was writing about the same time and with the same general aim, to make the message of Greek philosophy available to his countrymen. In Cicero the manner is less intense: he is constantly aware of his Roman audience and always ready to adapt the argument to the needs of practical men. Lucretius by contrast makes far fewer concessions, and the Roman elements in the poem are outbalanced by those which are clearly Greek. Lucretius' subject is 'the dark discoveries of the Greeks' (1.136) and Epicurus is hailed as 'the glory of the Grecian race' (3.3). The setting is frequently Greek: Book 6 begins with the praise of Athens and ends with an account of the Athenian plague. Greek place-names are ten times as common in the poem as Roman. Apart from a reference to Etruscan scrolls (6.381), to the habit of covering the head during prayer (5.1198–9) and possibly to the *parentatio* (3.51), specifically Roman religious practices are never mentioned in the poem. It is difficult to explain why one who appears so obsessed with religion should have neglected the experience of his own people. Did he consider, as Schmid suggests, that references to Roman ritual would have been out of place in a scientific poem written in the Alexandrian tradition?[1] Or did he prefer to speak indirectly to his countrymen through a polemical treatment of Greek ideas? Whatever the explanation, this apparent reluctance to deal directly with Roman religious practices says something about the audience for which Lucretius wrote.

It is against this background that we must assess Lucretius' attitude towards the events of his own time. It was an age of dangerous instability and violent factional strife. In his childhood and youth Lucretius had lived through the fierce conflict of the Social War, the reign of terror organized by Marius and Cinna and the proscriptions of Sulla. The period which followed Sulla's retirement was hardly less tense, and although the years during which the *De rerum natura* was being written were quieter by contrast with what had gone before, there was continued rioting in the streets and the danger of civil war was coming closer. All this must have had its effect on a sensitive mind and it may account for the intensity with which Lucretius condemns political ambition in the prologue to Book 2 and elsewhere in the poem. Yet he does not drive home the lesson himself, though it would have been easy to reinforce his moral strictures with examples from his own time. The nearest he comes to pointed contemporary comment is in the following lines on the subject of human greed:

sanguine ciuili rem conflant diuitiasque
conduplicant auidi, caedem caede accumulantes. (3.70–1)

They mass a fortune through the blood of fellow citizens
and greedily multiply their wealth, heaping death on death.

Lucretius' contemporaries could hardly have read these lines without thinking of the crimes and confiscations which made the revolution profitable for the strong. But passages of this sort are rare in the poem; for the message of Lucretius was not national regeneration, but personal salvation. In adopting such an attitude he was following the orthodox teaching of his school. Yet, when Epicurus counselled his followers to avoid the political struggle, he did not intend that the state should wither away or lapse into anarchy. Epicurean political theory always implied a distinction between what is right for the philosopher and what is right for the mass of men, and in practice the good life would hardly have been possible without the stability of law.[2] Certainly there were Epicureans at Rome like C. Velleius and L. Manlius Torquatus who managed to reconcile their beliefs with an active public life. But Lucretius was not a man for compromise and his acknowledgement in the first prologue (1.41–3) that, if war comes, Memmius will have to do his duty, is doubtless not so much a statement of principle as a recognition of the inevitable.

[1] Schmid (1944) 98–9.
[2] R. Müller (1969) 63–76. See also Momigliano (1941) 149–57.

It is therefore only in a special sense that the *De rerum natura* can be called a 'tract for the times'. It is not a political poem, and there is no stress on contemporary themes. Even the account of the development of government in Book 5.1105–60 is surprisingly theoretical and it is hard to square what Lucretius says on the subject with what the Romans believed about their own constitutional history. Marxist critics in particular have overemphasized the political relevance of the poem. It is unlikely, for example, that Lucretius' attacks on religion were aimed at the wealthy and powerful whose authority rested in part upon the dignity of established custom. The last century of the Republic offered a rich field for a writer of Lucretius' satiric gifts and there was much which he could have said, had he wished, about the cynical exploitation of religion for political ends. But clearly this was not his purpose. Lily Ross Taylor puts it well: 'His poem on the Nature of Things was not directed to the common man at the mercy of the men who manipulated state cult to suit their own ends. If it had been, Lucretius would not have failed to show up the shocking religious abuses of his day.'[1]

The use which Lucretius made of his philosophical sources raises another issue about the contemporary significance of his poem. Epicureanism was the most conservative of the Hellenistic philosophies, but it was not immune to change and modification. While Lucretius was writing, Epicurean philosophers like Philodemus were busy developing the master's doctrine and attempting to answer the objections of their philosophical opponents. Yet it cannot be established that Lucretius was familiar with Philodemus or was in any way influenced by his work. More significant is the poet's relationship with contemporary Stoicism. The Stoics, along with the members of the New Academy, constituted the principal opposition to Epicureanism, but they are never mentioned in the poem. It is true that much of Lucretius' argument might be interpreted as a direct challenge to Stoic teaching; but Furley has argued convincingly that, when the poet attacks rival schools, the target is always the Presocratics, or the Platonists and Aristotelians.[2] If this is correct, it is a conclusion of some importance: not only is it a significant clue to the understanding of Lucretius' sources but it implies also a somewhat distant attitude on the part of the poet towards the philosophical controversies of his own time. Lucretius must have been aware of the relevance of many of his arguments to current debate, but he was not at pains to point it out or to insist upon his philosophical modernity.

The most crucial problem in relating the *De rerum natura* to its contemporary background concerns the attitude of the poet towards religion. The attack on *religio* is one of the central themes of the poem and it is pressed with such force that Lucretius, like Epicurus himself, has sometimes been considered an atheist.

[1] Taylor (1949) 96.
[2] Furley (1966) 13–33; for a contrary opinion see De Lacy (1948) 12–23.

This verdict cannot be correct and there is little reason to doubt his Epicurean orthodoxy. Not only does he accept the doctrine of the existence of gods in the distant spaces between the worlds, but it is clear from an interesting passage in the prologue to Book 6 about the 'tranquil images of the gods which strike the minds of men' that he was aware of the deeper side of Epicurus' religious teaching. Nevertheless, in spite of his orthodoxy in matters of doctrine, Lucretius' references to religious practice are nearly always hostile and it is difficult to decide where he would have drawn the line between what was acceptable and what was not. We know that Epicurus took pleasure in the public ceremonies and even urged his followers to participate in the sacrifices in spite of the dangers of absorbing false beliefs (Philodemus, *De piet.* 2, col. 108, 9, p. 126 Gomperz). Lucretius, on the other hand, showed little interest in such matters and, like Empedocles, he was repelled by animal sacrifice (5.1198–202).

Epicureans at Rome were often criticized for exaggerating the terrors of religion. The attack on superstition had become a commonplace of the school, and Cicero knew of 'whole books of the philosophers full of discussions of such matters' (*Tusc. disp.* 1.11). What, then, are we to say of the relevance of Lucretius' polemic? Was he flogging a dead horse and attacking beliefs which, as Cicero suggests (*Tusc. disp.* 1.48), troubled no one any longer? To this question two answers have generally been given: either that the real situation was more complex than Cicero admitted, or that Lucretius was not writing for the educated but for the men of the provinces, or even for the 'man in the street'. The second line of argument cannot be correct; for, apart from the fact that scientific epic is not the favourite reading of unsophisticated men, Lucretius makes it clear that superstitious fears affect all men, even kings:

> non populi gentesque tremunt, regesque superbi
> corripiunt diuum percussi membra timore...? (5.1222–3)
>
> *Do not peoples and nations tremble and proud kings*
> *crouch in terror, struck by fear of the gods?*

The other response is more plausible; for it is not difficult to show that in the last years of the Roman Republic, even among the educated classes, there was a wide variety of religious beliefs and practices. Against the wavering rationalism of Cicero and the hostility of Lucretius we can set the religious conservatism of men like Appius Claudius Pulcher or the popular teaching of the Pythagorean astrologer Nigidius Figulus or the growing support of foreign cults which prompted the Senate to take action four times during the decade 58–48 B.C. Cicero's own evidence is ambivalent: his *De divinatione* was intended to combat an increasing interest in religious prophecy and it ends with an eloquent attack on superstition, which is described as 'spreading throughout the world oppressing the minds of almost everyone and seizing on the weakness of men' (2.148).

It is important to realize that the criticisms of Epicurean exaggeration refer to one topic only, the old stories about the torments of the damned. When Cicero says that legends of this sort were not generally believed, we should take his word for it. These stories are described as 'the marvels of poets and painters', that is to say, they are part of the literary tradition and belong to a different theology from that of the old Roman notion of the *di Manes*. Professor Jocelyn Toynbee, after surveying the literary and epigraphic evidence, concluded that in the late Republic and throughout the Empire, 'views on the nature of the life that awaited the soul beyond the grave were, in the main, optimistic'.[1] It follows that to rescue men from a belief in eternal torment cannot have been a serious part of Lucretius' intention. In fact, the underworld theme is not prominent in the poem, nor in the extant writings of Epicurus is there a single reference to the legends of the damned, although the topic is discussed by Democritus (DK II 207, B 297) and by later Epicurean writers. Lucretius mentions the fear of the underworld in the prologue of the poem, but the long *consolatio* about death in Book 3 is mainly about man's general fear of extinction and not about the terrors of the underworld. The legends of the damned are introduced in one section only (987–1023), but here the poet's interest is in contrasting these ancient stories with the ethical doctrines of Epicurus.

It should now be clear that Lucretius' poem is not to be interpreted simply as an attack on popular religion. If he refers sometimes to fading beliefs and old superstitions, it is as symbols of a more persistent misconception. His target is larger and more important: he is attacking a whole way of looking at the world in theological terms, of explaining its movements and its mystery as evidence of the working of a higher power. *Religio*, as Lucretius conceived it, was not just a source of vulgar superstition: it could also deceive more serious and reflective minds. It was *religio*, for example, which inspired belief in the divinity of heavenly bodies (5.110–21), a view which had impressive philosophical support and was accepted by Aristotle. What Lucretius found humiliating about the theological mode of thought was that it made men slaves. The universe, which ought to inspire wonder, became arbitrary and inexplicable, and men suffered as the victims of their own imaginings. For Lucretius the scientific materialism of Epicurus was a liberating doctrine: it made it possible to see the world as it really was, to understand not just its surface appearance, but its inner workings as well. Sellar may have exaggerated in claiming for Lucretius a 'genuine philosophic impulse and the powers of mind demanded for abstruse and systematic thinking';[2] but there is no mistaking the

[1] Toynbee (1971) 38.

[2] Sellar (1889) 335.

genuine excitement, the *diuina uoluptas atque horror*, which the poet feels in the understanding of nature. It is here that we should seek the clue to the meaning of the poem. The pervasive influence of Empedocles proves that Lucretius thought of his poem as belonging to the Presocratic tradition. This does not mean that he would have claimed for his work a philosophical originality – he was the first to acknowledge his debts – but in the physical doctrines of Epicurus he had found a system which gripped his imagination and satisfied his reason. It was this revelation which the poem attempts to describe, and it could not be understood by simple or unsophisticated minds.

2. POET AND PHILOSOPHER

If the central question in Lucretian criticism is the relationship between poetry and philosophy, then it is important to understand the extent to which Lucretius accurately reflects the spirit of Epicurus. The poet clearly thought of himself as an orthodox Epicurean and there can be no doubt about the intensity of his devotion to his philosophical mentor. Yet the *De rerum natura* is very different in tone and character from the writings of Epicurus. How are these differences to be accounted for? One way in which this question has commonly been answered is through an examination of the poet's personality: the *De rerum natura* differs from the writings of Epicurus because Lucretius himself was different. The biographical approach to literature is always hazardous and in the case of Lucretius it is particularly so because it is biographical criticism without a biography. Almost nothing is known about the poet's personal life and we are forced therefore to draw inferences about his personality from the poem itself. Of the external testimony the most influential is that of Jerome. In the additions which he made to Eusebius' *Chronicle* he noted under the year 94 or 93 B.C.: *T. Lucretius poeta nascitur; qui postea amatorio poculo in furorem uersus, cum aliquot libros per interualla insaniae conscripsisset, quos postea Cicero emendauit, propria se manu interfecit anno aetatis XLIIII.* (Titus Lucretius, poet, is born; afterwards, he was driven mad by a love potion, and when, in the intervals between bouts of madness, he had written several books, which Cicero later corrected, he died by his own hand in the forty-fourth year of his age.) Every detail in this sensational sentence has been contested: the dates can hardly be right (see Appendix); Cicero's editorship has been denied on account of his hostility to Epicureanism and defended because of his interest in literature; love potions are not likely to have produced the dire medical consequences which Jerome's statement suggests, though some ancient doctors believed that they did;[1] and the story of madness and suicide, unsupported by any other ancient testimony, may be the result of historical confusion or Christ-

[1] See, e.g., Caelius Aurelianus, *Chronic diseases* 1.5.147 (Drabkin).

ian malice. Nevertheless, brief and controversial though it may be, Jerome's statement has done much to set the mould of Lucretian criticism.

Those who have stressed the temperamental differences between Lucretius and Epicurus have often sought confirmation of their view in the poet's pessimism. 'The Epicurean comedy of Nature', wrote Giussani, 'almost changes into tragedy in Lucretius.' The whole question of the poet's pessimism has been discussed at enormous length and widely different verdicts have been reached, ranging from gentle melancholy to morbid depression. It is unlikely that the subject would have bulked so large in Lucretian criticism if Jerome had not written about the poet's madness and suicide and thus challenged critics to find in the poem evidence of mental instability. Such an approach has no doubt been encouraged by the poet's own interest in medical and psychological matters. He is the most Freudian of Latin poets: not only does he discuss, as his subject demanded, the working of the human mind, but he concerns himself also with the explanation of dreams, human sexuality and the psychological effects of fear and insecurity. For all of these interests he could claim respectable Epicurean precedents, but the emphasis which he places on psychological factors is his own. In discussing dreams, for example (4.962–1036), he first makes the orthodox and commonplace point that dreams reflect the pattern of one's waking life, but then he proceeds to discuss sex dreams and wish-fulfilment dreams which cannot be so readily accounted for on the theory which he has presented. Such interest in psychological matters is typical, but in none of the relevant passages is it easy to find evidence of a mind in conflict with itself. The attitude throughout is scientific and rational, not morbid or obsessive. One must be on one's guard therefore against overemphasizing the darker side of Lucretius' personality. It is true that there are sombre pages in the *De rerum natura* and that Lucretius never softens the tragedy of human suffering or human ignorance, but to compare him with Leopardi or to write, as Sellar does, of the 'grandeur of desolation' is to go beyond the evidence of the poem. Moreover the bleaker passages do not necessarily reflect a bias in the man himself. As Seneca recognized (*Vita beata* 13.1), there was an austere side to Epicureanism, and much of what has been interpreted in Lucretius as pessimism is in fact orthodox doctrine.

The same may be said about the internal conflicts which some have seen in the poem. Here too we should look first at the poet's sources. The view of Lucretius as a man divided against himself received its classic statement in the essay which Patin published in 1868. Patin's thesis of an 'Antilucrèce chez Lucrèce' is no longer so influential as it once was, but in various modified forms it has become embedded in the tradition of Lucretian criticism.[1] It rests on the belief that there are contradictions within the *De rerum natura*, and that

[1] Patin (1883) I 117–37.

these can be explained only by supposing that in the deepest parts of his nature Lucretius was unconvinced by the doctrine which he expounded. There may be some truth in this assessment, but before one presses it too far, it should be recognized that Epicureanism itself had its own contradictions – between freedom and law, for example, and between detachment and involvement[1] – and it is not easy to reconcile the optimism of its ethics with the neutrality of the atomic world. Such conflicts are implicit in the system itself and it is natural that they should have left their mark on Lucretius' poem. There is another, and more important, factor to be taken into account. Lucretius was not simply summarizing Epicurean physics: he was writing a poem, and poetry sharpens and intensifies the emotional impact of a subject. Epicurus believed that the world is decaying and will one day perish, but when Lucretius (not without a hint of irony) describes the old ploughman shaking his head over the declining fertility of the earth (2.1164–7), the effect is immediate and memorable. Another example of how the emotional involvement of the poet places an essentially orthodox argument in a different light is provided by the satiric passage about love at the end of Book 4. As Kleve has shown,[2] what Lucretius says on the subject is perfectly in accord with the teaching of Epicurus so far as we can reconstruct it; yet the ironic tone of the writing and the violence of the language are likely to leave the reader with a somewhat exaggerated impression of the Epicurean position. To conceive an idea poetically is to modify its shape.

The view that poetry subtly distorts or at least transforms the thought which it expresses would have been familiar to Epicurus. There has been much discussion, especially since Giancotti published his *Il preludio di Lucrezio*,[3] about the extent of the philosopher's opposition to poetry. Giancotti believed that Epicurus wished to discourage only those kinds of poetry which were based on mythological subjects or which appealed to the passions, and that a genuine philosophical poetry would have escaped his censure. But this is not a conclusion which emerges readily from the small number of texts which bear upon the subject, and it is difficult to see how Epicurus could have held it. 'In practice the wise man will not compose poems' (Diog. Laert. 10.121) is the philosopher's unambiguous assertion and he does not modify it with any qualifying phrase. Epicurus' opposition to poetry was not a matter of taste or temperament: it was founded on a serious conviction that the proper language of truth should be free from the glitter of poetry and the exaggerations of rhetoric and related as closely as possible to the objects of sense experience. Such a view would seem to exclude philosophical poetry, though it might leave room for unpretentious forms of verse which made fewer claims upon the reader's mind. We know that Philodemus defended – and composed – poetry of this kind, but

[1] The point is well argued by De Lacy (1957) 114–26.

[2] Kleve (1969) 376–83.

[3] Giancotti (1959) 15–90.

he too insisted that, whatever may be the excellence of individual poems, they are not to be judged by veridical or moral standards. All the evidence suggests that the Epicureans, though they may have differed in their attitude to poetry in general, were unanimous in holding that it was not a suitable medium for philosophic thought. Epicurus and Philodemus both seem agreed on this and the Epicurean Colotes wrote a celebrated work attacking Plato's use of poetic myth. Cicero took it for granted that Epicurus could find 'no solid value' in poetry (*Fin.* 1.72) and in his own dialogues he is generally careful to avoid poetical allusions when Epicureans are speaking, though such references are relatively common elsewhere in his philosophical works.[1] There seems no means of escaping the conclusion that, when Lucretius decided to describe the physical doctrine of Epicurus in verse, he was doing something which, from the point of view of his school, was strictly unorthodox.

Almost certainly Lucretius himself was aware of the dilemma. One would not expect much discussion of the function of poetry in a poem about nature, but in fact Lucretius was very conscious of his position as a philosophic poet and there are more than a dozen references to poetry in the *De rerum natura*. From the Epicurean point of view the most striking claim which he makes for poetry is that it lends clarity to an obscure subject (1.933–4 ~ 4.8–9). The emphasis on clarity is certainly Epicurean, but the idea that this might be achieved by writing in verse would have been rejected by Epicurus and indeed by most ancient theorists. It was because of its ambiguity that Aristotle judged the poetic style of Empedocles unsuitable for scientific thought (*Rhet.* 1407a31), and when Philodemus attempted to define obscurity (*Rhet.* 1.158–9 Sudhaus), he listed among its principal causes metaphorical language, digressions and archaisms, all prominent features of Lucretian style. The confident statement therefore that poetry can shed light on dark places sounds like a direct challenge to Epicurean belief. Whether or not Lucretius intended it as such, he must surely have been aware that he was following an unorthodox and difficult course. In spite of a revival of interest in scientific poetry there was nothing in contemporary Latin literature which would have made him confident of success. Lucretius must have been aware that, if philosophy and poetry were to be brought into some kind of creative harmony, he had first to solve a number of difficult problems: in particular he had to find a satisfactory structure for his material and he had to develop a suitable style for poetic argument which would combine the clarity upon which Epicurus insisted with that special excitement of language without which there can be no poetry at all. In the remainder of this discussion we shall examine the solutions which Lucretius sought for these difficulties and we shall deal in turn with the structure, style and imagery of the poem.

[1] Jocelyn (1973) 69.

3. THE POEM

Structure

Like Virgil's *Aeneid*, the *De rerum natura* never received its final revision. But although unrevised, it is not substantially incomplete and there is no compelling reason to believe that Lucretius would have continued beyond the present ending except perhaps to add some identifying lines such as Virgil appended to the *Georgics*. We have the poet's own statement (6.92–5) that Book 6 was designed to conclude the work and its impressive final section on the Athenian plague is the longest descriptive passage in the poem and must surely have been written for its present climactic position. As it stands, the poem has a rational and satisfying structure. It is divided into three parts, each consisting of two books. The first and third parts deal with physical doctrine, the microcosm of the atom in Books 1 and 2 and the macrocosm of the universe in Books 5 and 6. Between these two outer panels the central section describes the Epicurean doctrine of the soul, the senses, the mind and the will. Each of the six books begins with a formal prologue and ends with an extended passage of particular interest or striking poetry. The first book in each pair is more systematic in argument, the second is generally more relaxed and discursive. Each book has a number of clearly articulated sections and within each section there is usually a neat pointing of the argument. This 'klare, harmonische Gliederung der Form' is considered by Büchner an archaic feature of Lucretius' style;[1] and undoubtedly the effect would be monotonous if there was not a considerable variety in the length and tone of the different sections. By means of this careful articulation of the argument, Lucretius creates an impression of logical exactness and sweeps the reader on with an imposing array of balanced proofs. To some extent this impression of a systematic progression is misleading: for if we attempt to follow the argument closely, we soon discover a number of passages where the logical connexion is elusive, and not all of these can be blamed on the inadequacies of the textual tradition or the incompleteness of the poem. But in spite of these difficulties the general impression which the work creates is of great structural simplicity and strength.

So far as we can tell, the broad plan of the *De rerum natura* is the poet's own. No known work of Epicurus appears to be exactly parallel to Lucretius' poem in the order in which the subject matter is presented. The capacity to organize material in a logical and coherent fashion was not one of Epicurus' strong points and critics in antiquity found fault with the looseness and repetitiveness of his most important work (Diog. Laert. 10.7). It is not likely, therefore, that anything which he produced would have anticipated the balanced structure of the *De rerum natura*. It may be, of course, that Lucretius' immediate source

[1] Büchner (1936) 15.

was not Epicurus, but his persistent claims to be treading in his master's footsteps and the closeness of many of his arguments to the surviving Greek text suggests that his main debt was to the philosopher himself.[1] If this conclusion is correct, then Lucretius must have undertaken a considerable reorganization of his philosophical material. The problem which he faced was not simply that of the expositor who must present his argument in the most logical manner possible. As a poet he needed also to create a feeling of unity and to direct and condition the reader's response. To achieve this larger purpose, Lucretius concentrated on the anti-theological elements in Epicurean thought and put them in the forefront of his poem. The process begins in the opening prologue. This contains two programmatic passages separated by about seventy lines which between them summarize the contents of the work. The first (54–61) mentions the atoms and the working of the heavens and the second (127–35) stresses the nature of the soul. Some commentators have thought that these two passages represent different stages in the composition of the prologue and this may be so; but in fact both are necessary to indicate the scope of the poem. The *De rerum natura*, as Lucretius presents it, is a work about the soul and about the heavens. It is significant that Aristotle traced the origin of belief in the gods to these same two factors, τὰ περὶ ψυχήν and τὰ μετέωρα, 'the experiences of the soul' and 'celestial phenomena' (fr. 10 Rose). This is the clue to the structure of Lucretius' poem; after the first two books have laid the necessary theoretical foundation, Books 3 and 4 deal with the soul and the senses and Books 5 and 6 with the heavens and the gods. The whole concept of the poem is determined by its theological position. Once this is clear, not only the general outline of the work but also some of its details fall into place. For example Book 4, after the brilliant satiric passage about the nature of love, ends rather quietly with two paragraphs, the first on sterility and the second about the unattractive woman. At first reading they may appear something of an anticlimax; but there is nothing arbitrary or makeshift about them. In the first Lucretius shows that sterility is not caused by the gods and that prayers to heaven will be of no avail. The second passage is designed to show that improbable unions are not the work of heaven and that the shafts of Venus have nothing to do with the matter. Both are part of the anti-theological argument of the poem.

This preoccupation with religion may correspond to something deep in Lucretius' nature. It is possible to argue, as many have done, that the attack on superstition was the main motivation for the poem. But the critic should also be aware of the importance of the religious polemic as an organizing device. It is this which holds the argument together and gives it its emotional force. One may suspect that Lucretius sometimes exaggerated this aspect of Epicurean

[1] On Lucretius' sources see Giussani (1896) 1–17.

teaching. The prologues, for example, often draw attention to theological issues which are subsequently lost sight of or passed over without emphasis in the text which follows. The opening of Book 4 is particularly revealing. In the syllabus we are told that one of the main themes of the book will be false beliefs in the ghosts of the dead. This subject was first announced in the preface to Book 1 and is recalled near the beginning of Book 5. With such widespread advertisement one might imagine that belief in ghosts would occupy a major section of the poem. In fact, Lucretius devotes to the subject only a single short paragraph (4.757–67). It is true that these lines could not be understood if separated from the longer discussion of dreams and visions. But that discussion is carried on in a purely scientific manner and is not related particularly to the ghosts of the dead. What this suggests is that in the prologues Lucretius is deliberately directing the attention of his readers to the theological implications of his work even when his own interests lay elsewhere. By stressing this element in Epicurean doctrine, he is guiding and conditioning the reader's emotional response and giving to his scientific account of the world a far-ranging and profound human interest. It was a brilliant solution to the problem of unity.

Style

Something must now be said about style, though in a brief survey it is not possible to do more than touch on a few of the more important points. We may begin with the problem of vocabulary. Three times in the poem Lucretius complains of the poverty of the Latin language, always in relation to the translation of unfamiliar ideas, and he was clearly aware of his pioneering role in the development of a philosophical vocabulary. There was no difficulty with simple concepts like the 'void' which could be turned directly into Latin; but where there was no obvious Latin equivalent or where a more complex idea had to be expressed, it was necessary to adapt an existing word to a new context or invent a new term on the analogy of the Greek original. One solution which Lucretius rejected was simply to transliterate the Greek term. A few Greek words for scientific notions are to be found in the poem, particularly in botanical and astronomical contexts, but it is probable that many of these had already been naturalized in the Latin language. When it came to translating unfamiliar concepts, Lucretius almost never used a Greek word: *harmonia* and *homoeomeria* are two exceptions, but both are used ironically to dismiss an opponent's theory. Lucretius is often credited, along with Cicero, with the invention of a philosophical vocabulary for the Latin language and there is some truth in the claim. But if we follow the poet's innovations through the later history of the language, it is surprising how few of them survived. Words like *clinamen* (for the Greek παρέγκλισις 'swerve') and *adopinari* (for προσδοξάζεσθαι 'to add to evidence by conjecture') have no subsequent history in philosophical Latin. The fact is that Lucretius managed to operate to a remarkable extent without a technical vocabulary. It is instructive to compare his account of the Athenian plague with that of Thucydides. Both deal with the medical symptoms in some detail, but whereas Thucydides in a single chapter (2.49) uses almost seventy words which are either technical medical terms or are commonly found in medical authors, Lucretius manages very largely with the regular vocabulary of epic poetry. There is obviously some loss of precision in such a method and scientific discussion can hardly proceed without accepted definitions and a technical vocabulary. But the Latin of Lucretius' day lacked such resources and the poet had to grapple with the problem as best he could. Paradoxically the absence of a philosophical language may have helped him as a writer; for he was compelled to adopt a more concrete mode of expression. What the philosopher lost in precision, the poet gained in clarity and vividness of style.

Didactic poetry always involves compromise. Lucretius' aim was to be both impressive and intelligible, to do justice to the *maiestas rerum* while preserving the lively spirit of a philosophical debate. For this purpose he combined the dignified language of Roman epic with the spirited manner of the popular diatribe and both traditions affected his style. The influence of epic can be seen in the Ennian diction, in the frequency of alliteration and assonance, and above all in a pervasive archaism, both in metre and language, which admirably suited the antique dignity which he wished to impart to his theme. The popular tradition contributed other features to his style, a tone of biting irony, the occasional use of a more colloquial language, and a habit of dramatizing the argument. The result of this combination is a highly individual style which cannot be mistaken for anything else. Its principal characteristic is a feeling of energy, a quality which Baudelaire called 'la grâce littéraire suprême'. There is a robust vigour in the very sound of his verse, which, though it lacks Virgil's metrical subtlety, had a wider range of verbal effects than Augustan taste found acceptable. The piling up of arguments, the use of doublets, a sentence structure which seems to tumble over itself in its eagerness to reach a conclusion, a fondness for word-play ranging from simple locutions like *innumero numero* to complex puns, all helped to produce that feeling of exuberance which is so characteristic of his style. Only an artist of great self-confidence would have attempted to create a unity out of such varied elements.

The peculiar texture of Lucretius' writing is in part the consequence of his fondness for repetition. No other major Latin poet repeats himself so frequently. Phrases, sentences, and indeed whole passages recur, sometimes more than once. In a seventeen-line paragraph about the origin of the world (5.416–31) not a single verse is wholly new and several are borrowed without alteration from earlier parts of the poem. The function of these repetitions has been much discussed. 'What is right may well be said twice', wrote Empedocles (DK I 322, B 25), and doubtless part of Lucretius' purpose was to drive home his message with repeated emphasis. This explanation will account for the repetition of such key passages as that on the conservation of matter, which appears four times in the poem (1.670–1 ~ 792–3, 2.753–4, 3.519–20). But it will not explain the repetition of unimportant and incomplete sentences or of decorative passages which have no significance for the argument. The longest of all the repeated passages in the poem is the brilliant prologue to Book 4 which first appears in an almost identical form at the end of Book 1 (926–50). Editors generally suppose that one of these two passages would have been removed in the final revision and they are probably right; but with Lucretius one cannot be certain because of his willingness to repeat passages of memorable poetry. Pedagogical considerations may have been a factor in the poet's use of repeated phrases, but the main explanation is almost certainly stylistic. The nearest parallels are in Homer and Empedocles and these are among the poet's principal literary models.

Every reader of the *De rerum natura* is aware of a considerable difference in the level of poetic excitement between the great set pieces and the passages of technical argument. The former contain some of the finest poetry in Latin, while the latter are marked by a deliberate prosiness which serves to underline the didactic purpose. The existence of such contrasts has given rise to the doctrine of 'two styles' in Lucretius, but perhaps it would be better to think of 'differences of tone' rather than 'differences of style', since the disparity which the reader feels is less the result of any significant change in the basic ingredients of Lucretius' language than in the intensification of emotion and the concentration of imagery. In fact it would be impossible to draw a sharp line between what is poetic in the poem and what is expository. Lucretius' aim is to 'touch all with the charm of the Muses' (1.934), and when he describes his poetry as honey on the lip of the cup, he is not thinking of the purple patches only. It is a mistake, therefore, in attempting to understand the poet, to concentrate too much upon the 'poetic' passages; for the total effect of the *De rerum natura* depends upon the balance of its lyrical and expository elements. For the same reason it is difficult to demonstrate Lucretius' quality as a writer from a single extract; but perhaps the following lines, which fall somewhere between the grand manner of the prologues and the austere writing of the more technical sections, will illustrate some of the points which have already been made about the poet's style.

quod superest, ne te in promissis plura moremur,
principio maria ac terras caelumque tuere;
quorum naturam triplicem, tria corpora, Memmi,
tris species tam dissimilis, tria talia texta,

una dies dabit exitio, multosque per annos
sustentata ruet moles et machina mundi.
nec me animi fallit quam res noua miraque menti
accidat exitium caeli terraeque futurum,
et quam difficile id mihi sit peruincere dictis;
ut fit ubi insolitam rem apportes auribus ante
nec tamen hanc possis oculorum subdere uisu
nec iacere indu manus, uia qua munita fidei
proxima fert humanum in pectus templaque mentis.
sed tamen effabor. dictis dabit ipsa fidem res
forsitan et grauiter terrarum motibus ortis
omnia conquassari in paruo tempore cernes.
quod procul a nobis flectat fortuna gubernans,
et ratio potius quam res persuadeat ipsa
succidere horrisono posse omnia uicta fragore. (5.91–109)

To proceed and not to put you off with promises,
first look upon the seas, the lands, the heavens:
their threefold nature, Memmius, their three bodies,
three forms so different in appearance, three such varied textures,
a single day will destroy, and the immense contrivance of the world,
upheld for many years, will collapse in ruin.
I am not unaware how strange and novel
is this doctrine of the future disappearance of earth and sky
and how hard it is to prove my proposition in words;
it is always thus when one brings to men's ears some unfamiliar fact
which cannot be set before the eyes
or touched with the hand (for touch is a paved road
which leads directly to the human heart and the precincts of the mind).
But yet I shall speak forth. Perhaps the event itself
will bring belief to my words and shortly amid the shock of earthquake
you will see everything shattered.
May guiding fortune pilot this fate from us
and may reason, rather than experience, convince us
that the whole world may fail and fall with a dread-sounding crash.

These lines, which impressed Ovid so deeply that he cites them no less than four times, follow immediately upon the long prelude to Book 5. They introduce the first important argument of the book, but the supporting proof does not begin until line 235, since Lucretius characteristically 'suspends the thought' and inserts a long polemical passage to show that the universe is not divine (110–234). In spite of the length of this insertion there is no loss of momentum or confusion of thought because the 'digression' is closely related to the main subject of the book, and both it and the basic argument have been anticipated in the prologue. This feeling of unity is further assisted by Lucretius' typically formular style: nearly a dozen phrases in this short paragraph are repeated elsewhere in the work and some, like the brisk opening formula, appear several times. The passage is simple in structure and the writing is direct and straightforward. There is little of that interweaving of words and phrases which Augustan writers employed to add tension to their verse. Enjambment is kept to a minimum and in general the thought is accommodated to the units of the hexameter verse. This is not Lucretius' invariable way of writing: there are passages, for example in the prologues, where he creates a strong sense of forward movement by allowing the thought to spill over from one line to another (over a quarter of the lines in the poem are enjambed); but here an important statement is enunciated in measured phrases and the shape of the verse adds clarity and point to the argument.

Many of the formal features of Lucretius' style can be seen in these lines: archaism (*indu*), periphrasis (*oculorum uisu*), dignified poetic diction (*effabor*), the occasional telling use of a compound adjective (*horrisono*), and most obviously, alliteration and assonance. But what makes the passage impressive is the energy and fullness of the writing. Much of that energy resides in the use and placing of the verbs (*sustentata ruet*, *conquassari*). Although the *De rerum natura* is a great descriptive poem, it depends far more for its effect upon the choice of verbs and participles than upon picturesque adjectives or decorative epithets. Lucretius' style is above all functional and the commonest adjectives in the poem are colourless quantitative words like *magnus* and *paruus*. In fact Lucretius is seldom content simply to describe: he wants to explain what is happening behind the surface appearances of things and for this words of action are needed. They impart to his style a tremendous vigour and strength. Alliteration contributes to the same result. Grammarians warned against its over-use and sometimes Lucretius, like the older poets whom he imitated, may be guilty of excess. But the device is effective when it is employed, as here, to point a striking phrase like *machina mundi* or to draw attention to a new and important subject. It can also underline and punctuate the meaning: the first sentence, for example, divides into three parts of approximately equal length and each is marked off with its own alliterative sequence. The musical effect of alliteration is particularly pleasing when it involves the blending of different sounds: lines 104–5 provide a good example with their interweaving of the consonants *d*, *t*, and *f* and their strong assonantal pattern, *ta- -tīs -tan -ter ter- -ti- -tīs*. In trying to account for the characteristic energy and amplitude of Lucretius' style, one should also mention his use of doublets (*noua miraque*) and his habit of piling up nouns within a single verse (*principio maria ac terras caelumque tuere*, 92). Like Milton, Lucretius is fond of such 'catalogue lines' and employs them with a wide range of effects: impressiveness and majesty in 5.115: *terras et solem et caelum, mare, sidera, lunam* 'lands and sun and sky, sea, stars and moon'; lyrical beauty in 5.1190: *luna dies et nox et noctis signa seuera* 'moon, day and night and the night's solemn constellations'; and irony in 4.1132: *pocula crebra, unguenta, coronae serta parantur* 'cups in abundance, perfume, crowns, garlands are made ready' (note in this last example how the mocking tone is supported by the rhythm: in all six feet there is coincidence of ictus and accent).

But there are hazards in this manner of writing; for amplitude can easily degenerate into bombast. At first sight lines 93–4 may seem an excessively ponderous way of making the simple point that earth, sea and sky are three bodies which differ in appearance and texture. Yet the sentence is not mere padding; for 'appearance' and 'texture' are key themes in the poem. The reference to texture in these lines recalls a passage in Book 1 (238–49) in which Lucretius argues that it is on account of their different textures that the objects of our experience do not suddenly disintegrate at a single stroke. Here by contrast a more sinister point is being made: that in the final cataclysm the varied textures of sea, earth and sky will not prevent their simultaneous destruction. The emphasis on the complex texture of the world is not, therefore, simply rhetorical: it is part of the argument itself. This is typical of the best of Lucretius' writing; his success as a didactic poet lies in his total absorption, both emotionally and intellectually, in the message of his poem. The passage which we have been examining is a good example of this capacity to transmute argument into poetry. Clearly the Epicurean doctrine of the eventual destruction of the world captured the poet's imagination, as it captured that of Ovid, and inspired him to a solemn and impressive statement. Such an emphatic manner of writing would not have suited more tender or commonplace writers, but it was admirable for Lucretius' purpose. For him the majesty of his theme demanded and justified an impressive rhetoric. This does not mean that he is uniformly solemn. He could turn an epic phrase to mock-heroic effect, as when he describes a goose as *Romulidarum arcis seruator candidus anser* 'the white goose, saviour of the citidal of the children of Romulus' (4.683), and he could stand back and smile at the very force and vigour of his own dialectic (see, e.g., 1.410–17).

Image and symbol

One important feature of Lucretius' style which has been neglected in this analysis is his use of imagery. According to Epicurean theory all knowledge is ultimately based upon the evidence of the senses and what cannot be known from direct observation must be inferred by analogy from observed fact. This stress upon the importance of visual experience was grist to Lucretius' mill and it may help to explain the astonishing richness and vitality of his imagery. Few Latin poets can rival him in this and none can equal his range. Like Empedocles, he extended the field of imagery beyond the traditionally 'poetic' subjects: not only did he borrow from arts and crafts, but also from war, politics, law, and public ceremonial. There is nothing like this in the writings of Epicurus; in spite of the philosopher's insistence on the value of the senses, he rarely attempted to clarify an argument with an apt illustration. Other philosophers, both inside and outside the Atomic school, were less austere, and some of Lucretius' most celebrated pictures are derived from the philosophical tradition: the motes in the sunbeam go back at least to Democritus (Aristotle, *De anima* 404a1–6); the torch race and the famous image of honey on the lip of the cup are both anticipated by Plato in the *Laws* (776b and 659e); the illustration of the worn ring was used by Melissus of Samos (DK I 274, B 8.3); the image of the road in the passage which we have just discussed is derived from Empedocles (DK I 365, B 133); and the important comparison of the atoms to the letters of the alphabet appears in two passages of Aristotle which deal with the atomic theory of Leucippus and Democritus (*Metaph.* 985b15–19 and *De gen. et corr.* 315b9–15).

Illustrations of this sort are part of the dialectic of the poem. They are employed not simply to add a decorative veneer, but to clarify the argument or to provide the evidence on which it is based. But 'the function of imagery in poetry is never that of mere illustration'.[1] A good image should do more than engage the reader's mind through the aptness of the comparison: there should be some element of surprise, something to stir the imagination. In fact the more logical and exact an illustration may be, the less effectively will it work as poetry. What is impressive about Lucretius' use of imagery is the skill with which he goes beyond mere illustration or analogy. Even a commonplace picture like that of drying clothes (a favourite with Lucretius) can be changed into poetry: a crack of thunder is compared to the flapping of clothes in a fresh breeze (6.114–15) and the sea, evaporating into the air, is like washing spread out on the green (6.617–19). In these examples the image does more than bolster the argument: it also adds a touch of imagination and quickens science into poetry. Much of the special feeling of the *De rerum natura* is generated by its imagery. There is a characteristic sensuousness about the column of air which 'brushes through the pupil of the eye' (4.249); and there is wit in the description of cosmetics as the 'backstage business of life' (4.1186) or of the cock 'chasing the night off the stage with the applause of his wings' (4.710). Above all, it is through imagery that Lucretius heightens and intensifies the emotional quality of his writing. Sometimes this concentration is achieved by boldly mixing metaphors, as in the magnificent lines about the insatiability of love:

> ...quoniam medio de fonte leporum
> surgit amari aliquid quod in ipsis floribus angat... (4.1133–4)

> *...since from the centre of the fountain of enchantment*
> *bitterness rises up to choke delight even amid the flowers...*

[1] Brooks and Warren (1960) 556.

Is it possible to go further and see in the poet's imagery some clue to the larger meaning of the poem? It is easy enough to recognize the obvious symbolism in Lucretius' equation of darkness and light with ignorance and truth, if only because such secondary meanings are implicit in the language itself. But other cases are not so plain, and because of the Epicurean insistence on clear and simple language it is hazardous to impose upon Lucretius' text a conscious and complex symbolism. The most difficult passages to interpret are the great set pieces and the mythological parts of the poem. The very existence of myth in an Epicurean poem is itself surprising, and in the treatment of such passages, if anywhere, one might expect some concessions to the traditions of epic poetry in order to enlarge and deepen the meaning of the poem. The problem of interpretation is complex and it is not possible to do more than illustrate its complexity by examining briefly two passages, those which close and open the poem.

The account of the Athenian plague at the end of Book 6 is introduced ostensibly as an example of the sort of pestilence which Lucretius has explained in the previous lines. The illustration serves no purpose in clarifying the argument and in fact little is said about the causes of the disaster. The passage is elaborated beyond the immediate needs of the context and it brings the poem to a stark and dramatic conclusion. It is natural to suppose that such a passage in such a position must have some special significance for the poem as a whole. Lucretius' emphasis throughout on the psychological effects of the disaster, and the frequent use in the poem of the imagery of disease in reference to moral sickness both suggest that the poet saw the plague as a symbol of man's tragic predicament. But such an interpretation, attractive though it is, involves an uncomfortable corollary. For the plague, as Lucretius describes it, knows no cure. It is true that some of its victims recovered (though this fact is barely hinted at), but recovery was as unpredictable as the onset of the disease. Medicine could do nothing but 'mutter with silent dread'. The plague at Athens, sudden in its attack and undiscriminating in its victims, is not a satisfactory symbol for the moral degeneracy which Lucretius saw around him, and if it were, it would be a strange point on which to conclude a poem which proclaims the victory of man over fear and circumstance. Surely we cannot imagine that, as Lucretius approached the conclusion of his great task, he suddenly lost his nerve and chose to end in a mood of uncertainty and gloom. The victory of Epicurus dominates the poem and must guide our understanding of its final pages. We shall distort the poet's meaning if we insist on reading his account of the plague as a coded statement about man's spiritual blindness. But if the passage is not to be interpreted symbolically, it is nevertheless at a deeper and more emotional level an entirely satisfactory ending to the poem. What was needed was a passage which would suit the subject matter of Book 6 and which would at the same time produce an effective cadence to a long and emotional poem. The poet has found a solution which satisfies both of these requirements. The account of the Athenian plague, which depends heavily on material set out earlier in the work, forms a fitting climax to a book which deals with striking natural events; and the tragic story is told in such a way as to recapitulate some of the principal themes of the poem: the bitter consequences of ignorance, the almost universal fear of death, man's crippling anxiety and his hopeless dependence on divine powers. In this long description of a terrible disaster Lucretius appears once again in his characteristic role as the scientific observer of natural causes, the ironic critic of man's folly and the sympathetic poet of human misery.

Let us turn, in conclusion, to the prologue to Book I, perhaps the most difficult passage in the poem. Here there can be no question of a literal interpretation; for, although Epicurean theology conceded the possibility of some form of communion with the gods, the sort of prayer which Lucretius addresses to Venus, that she endow his poem with 'undying grace' and bring peace to Rome by clasping Mars in her arms, goes far beyond the decent limits of Epicurean piety. Clearly the poet had something else in mind and we naturally look for some secondary meaning in his words. But what? The difficulty here is not so much to find some suitable equation for Lucretius' goddess as to know where to stop, how to determine the limits of the poet's symbolic imagination. Is Venus here simply the power of love or the generative force of nature? Or is the main emphasis on the concept of peace? Or should she be interpreted at a more philosophical level and equated with one or other of the two types of pleasure which Epicurus defined in his ethics? As Bignone has shown, there is ample precedent among Greek writers for this sort of philosophical allegory.[1] The idea of introducing the old Homeric myth of Venus and Mars may in fact have come to Lucretius from Empedocles, who is said to have used it for the two great forces of love and strife which control the Empedoclean universe.[2] The world which Lucretius describes, though it differs from that of Empedocles, is also dominated by an unending cycle of birth and decay. Some idea of this sort may have been at the back of Lucretius' mind when he introduced the story of Mars and Venus, but this cannot be what the myth *means*. For the Mars of the Lucretian prologue is not presented as a grim symbol of destruction and decay, but as a sensual being with the instincts of the elegiac lover. Mars is not in fact a potent figure in the poem at all and after the prologue his name never reappears except as a more or less conventional synonym for war.

What then does Venus stand for in the prologue? Whatever answer is given

[1] Bignone (1942–50) II 434–9.

[2] Heraclitus, *Alleg. Hom.* 69; Eustathius, *ad Od.* 8.367. Cf. Empedocles, DK I 317, B 17.24.

to this question must take into account the poet's attitude to myth and allegory. The term 'allegory' is often loosely applied in Lucretian criticism in contexts where it does not properly apply. There is certainly allegory in the Magna Mater passage (2.600–60), but it should be noted that half of Lucretius' allegorical interpretations of the myth are inconsistent with his own beliefs and are clearly not intended to be taken seriously. The description of the tortures of the damned in 3.978–1023 comes close to allegory, but even here one should hesitate. What Lucretius says could be paraphrased like this: 'Nowhere is there a Tantalus numb with fear because a huge rock hangs over him; but in this life men fear the blow of fate...' This is not allegory in the strict sense. No attempt is made to reinterpret the myth or find a deeper meaning in it. Rather the purpose is to deny the validity of myth and to contrast the punishments of the underworld with realities of a more pressing and credible kind. Other mythological passages are even clearer: their function is almost always polemical and they lack that quality of reverence which genuine allegory requires. If this is correct, then we should not expect to find Lucretius saying important things about his own philosophy in mythical terms. In particular the equation of Venus with the Epicurean concept of 'static pleasure' is not likely to be right. Nor does so sophisticated a notion emerge readily from what Lucretius actually says. A complex symbol of this sort, if it is to be understood, needs a context and the opening of a poem has no context.

A good poem always means more than it says. It would be wrong therefore to limit in too arbitrary a fashion one's response to so complex a piece of writing as the prelude to Lucretius' poem. One should, however, be clear where the main emphasis is to be placed, and for this the poet has given us the help we need. The first two words of the poem, *Aeneadum genetrix*, echo the *Annals* of Ennius and the phrase which follows, *hominum diuumque uoluptas*, is used again in Book 6 in an address to Calliope. Lucretius could hardly have made it plainer that we are here in the realm of the imagination rather than of truth and that Venus is being invoked as the poet's Muse. In this context the reader is likely to think of a different range of symbols from those we have been considering before. As Classen has pointed out, Venus and Aphrodite and ἡδονή, the Greek equivalent of the Latin *uoluptas*, are all associated in the literary tradition with grace and ease of style.[1] Lucretius' prayer to Venus is for *lepos*, for beauty of words and persuasiveness of speech; and Venus is invoked as the embodiment of that beauty which manifests itself throughout the whole Nature of Things. In the opening prayer Lucretius is careful not to reveal the scope and purpose of his poem. We are still in the world of poetry and have not yet been told what the real subject of the poem will be. To seek in such a passage for a complex network of philosophical symbols is to approach

[1] Classen (1968) 103–5.

poetry in too cerebral a manner. The main function of the prologue is to indicate the beauty and majesty of the world and the magnitude of Lucretius' task. As C. S. Lewis says of the opening of *Paradise Lost*: 'The ostensible philosophical purpose of the poem...is here of secondary importance. The real function of these...lines is to give us the sensation *that some great thing is now about to begin*.'[1]

One final observation about the prologue will bring us back to the question which we posed at the start. If we compare the manner in which Lucretius begins with the opening of Empedocles' poem *On nature* (so far as it can be reconstructed from its fragmentary remains), we become aware of an important difference of tone. Although Empedocles had the reputation in antiquity of being a braggart and there is a strain of dogmatism in his work, he began his poem rather tentatively, stressing the shortness of life, the limitations of human knowledge and the dangers of presumption and he called on his white-armed Muse only for 'such knowledge as it is lawful for creatures of a day to hear'. Where Empedocles is tentative, Lucretius is full of confidence and joy. The colour and excitement of the long opening sentence underline the magnificence of the subject and the importance of the message. Lucretius never doubts that reason will prevail if only the right words can be found. It is the poet's task to set forth the *diuina ratio* in the most persuasive language possible. The difficulties – both of convincing the timid and of mastering a difficult literary form – are not to be concealed; but the ultimate message is of victory and hope and joy. It is the poet's confidence that the doctrine of Epicurus can explain the whole of life and set the mind at peace which makes the task possible. For Lucretius the philosophy of Epicurus was something which could be conceived both intellectually and emotionally, that is to say, it was something which could be conceived poetically. The problem of matching poetry and philosophy was on its way to being solved.

[1] Lewis (1942) 40.

11

CICERO AND THE RELATIONSHIP OF ORATORY TO LITERATURE

I. CICERO'S ATTITUDE TO CULTURE

Marcus Tullius Cicero (106–43 B.C.) has been endlessly studied as a character and as a politician, and certainly these aspects of him are of absorbing interest; but his chief historical importance is as a man of letters. Deeply conscious of the philistinism of most Romans, this 'new man' with no ancestors adopted as his spiritual ancestors the younger Scipio and his friends of the second century, the disseminators, under the guidance of the Stoic Panaetius, of Hellenism, who were also exemplars of Roman patriotism, *decorum* and *humanitas*. 'I am more than others a philhellene and known to be', he says to Atticus, though his admiration was for the literature, philosophy and art of the great Greeks of the past rather than for the shifty modern 'Greeklings' (*Q. Fr.* 1.2.2). In his dialogues, composed in the beautifully situated villas he had acquired at Tusculum (above Frascati) and down the west coast of Italy, which he sometimes also used as their *mise en scène*, he seems concerned to portray a particularly courteous society (like Shakespeare in *The Merchant of Venice*): no one is allowed to be rude, unlike some of the Sophists in Plato. His characters have that tolerance which is one of his own characteristics.

When he was eighteen Philo of Larissa, head of the 'New' Academy at Athens, visited Rome and made a deep impression on him. Philo stood for hearing every side in a debate before making up one's mind. Holding that nothing could be known for certain, he deplored dogmatism and insisted that all conclusions were provisional. So when Cicero later visited Athens to study, he chose to join the Academy.[1] His own philosophy of life was eclectic and unsystematic, adapted to his temperament. He was no real philosopher, and knew it, though fascinated by philosophy. He welcomed criticism, and claimed the right to change his mind. In a passage in the prologue to his dialogue *On the nature of the gods* (1.10) that won Voltaire's admiration he deplored the Pytha-

[1] Now under Antiochus of Ascalon, however, it had become eclectic rather than sceptical – drawing ideas from Peripatetics and Stoics as well as Academics; but Cicero remains true to Philo's undogmatic spirit of discussion. Philo had also introduced courses in rhetoric, alongside those in philosophy, which would attract Cicero.

gorean formula 'The Master said...' (*Ipse dixit*): 'Those who ask what I think myself are unnecessarily curious. In a discussion what is to be sought is not so much weight of authority as force of argument. Indeed the authority of professed teachers is often a positive hindrance to would-be learners.'

Such openmindedness was also encouraged by the rhetorical exercise, recommended by Aristotle, of arguing both sides of a question. How deeply this conditioned Cicero's way of thinking is shown by a letter he wrote to Atticus in his agony of indecision two months after Caesar crossed the Rubicon in 49 (*Att.* 9.4). He says he has been debating a series of 'theses' (discussions of general principles) relevant to the situation, first in Greek and then in Latin, and proceeds to list the topics in Greek. He says he is doing this partly to distract his mind, partly to give relevance to his exercise.

The prologues to his dialogues and treatises form collectively an interesting corpus of intellectual autobiography, in which the defence of cultural studies as an occupation for an ex-consul consonant with '*otium cum dignitate*' is a recurrent theme. (He makes the Muse Urania praise him for this in his poem on his consulship: *Div.* 1.17.) Deploring utilitarian values, he remarks sarcastically in the *Brutus* (257) that, while no doubt it was more important for the Athenians to have watertight roofs over their heads than to possess that ivory statue of Athena, he would rather be Phidias than a master-roofer. In his famous Dream of Scipio (see p. 261), at a time when he was in eclipse as a statesman, he made Africanus reveal that there is a place in heaven reserved for benefactors of their country, including not only men of action but (remarkable for a Roman) others who have devoted their genius to divine pursuits (*Rep.* 6.19). The debate that began among Aristotle's followers as to whether the life of contemplation was better than the life of action was continued intermittently in Cicero's soul. Normally the life of action prevailed.

Naturally he was drawn to men who needed no conversion to culture; to Atticus, with his hospitable library, his propagation of books and his historical interests, who bought works of art for him at Athens; to Cato and Brutus, who, even if at times he did not see eye to eye with them, were likewise lifelong students of philosophy; even to Caesar, politically his arch-enemy, whose keen critical interest in literature and language provided them with safe topics of discourse. But he aimed at reaching a wider circle, with special hopes of influencing the rising generation. All his life he was concerned to promote humane education. It was unthinkable at Rome that higher education should be anything but rhetorical in basis; but in the *De oratore* (55 B.C.) he put forward the view that the perfect orator should be a 'full man', and propounded accordingly an unprecedented scheme of liberal education, *politior humanitas* (*humanus*, a word embracing both culture and human-kindness, meant something like our 'civilized' as applied to people). His letters provide ample evidence that he was himself a 'full man', well versed in Greek and Latin literature, and in philosophy, history and law. (It must not however be assumed that quotation by Cicero from a Greek poem means that he had read it. Some of his quotations in his philosophical works seem to have been lifted from his sources; some, there and elsewhere, may have been commonplaces in conversation; and he makes tell-tale slips.[1])

In philosophy he was a moralist with hankerings for the transcendental. He therefore went back to 'that god of mine Plato', whose statue stood on the lawn of his town house. Of the Hellenistic philosophies Stoicism attracted him most, again as a moralist: he encountered Posidonius at Rhodes, and the domestic philosopher he kept was a Stoic, Diodotus. Epicurus he praised as a good man. He appealed to Memmius to preserve his ruined house at Athens (*Fam.* 13.1), and Jerome says he 'corrected' (*emendauit*) the *De rerum natura* of Lucretius. But he dismissed the hedonistic Epicurean philosophy with a contempt softened only by indulgence for some of its practitioners.

Books meant a great deal to him. He begs Atticus not to resell a library he has bought, in the hope that he himself will find the resources to buy it for his new Tusculan villa. 'Now that Tyrannio has arranged my books', he says after returning from exile to his wrecked property, 'my house seems to have acquired a soul.' We find him reading books relevant to his situation, and using Aristotle's library, which Sulla had brought to Italy. When his public life was shattered, he wrote to Varro: 'I must tell you that...I have made it up with those old friends of mine, my books...They have forgiven me, and invited me to resume our former intercourse' (*Fam.* 9.1.2). Even in his speeches he quotes sometimes from the old Latin poets (as did some of his contemporaries), especially in the period during which he composed the *De oratore*. Usually it was from plays which might be familiar to his audience from stage revivals. In the *Pro Caelio* (37–8) he adroitly solicits tolerance for the young man's peccadilloes by contrasting an unattractively stern father in Caecilius with an attractively lenient one in Terence. But he was careful not to alienate his hearers by transcending their ignorances and prejudices.

His historical sense was also exceptional: 'to be ignorant of history is like remaining a child for life'. He tried to see not only external events but himself also in its perspective: just as, when appealing to Caesar the Dictator for Marcellus, he urged him to think what posterity would say about him, so he was concerned about what people would be saying about his own conduct a thousand years hence. His *Brutus* and Book 2 of his *De re publica* are notable pieces of historiography, his account of himself at *Brutus* 313–36 a landmark in the history of autobiography. And in other dialogues besides the *Brutus* he makes the continuity of Roman history felt. Cato in the *De senectute*, whose dramatic

[1] Jocelyn (1973) 77ff.

date is 150 B.C., had known Duillius, commander in the First Punic War (260) and met people who remembered the war against Pyrrhus before that. He was talking there to the younger Scipio, who in the *De re publica* transmits Roman and family tradition to the younger generation, including the sons-in-law of his friend Laelius. In the *De amicitia*, set in the same year (129), Laelius in turn is entertaining his sons-in-law; while in the *De oratore* Crassus, initially in the presence of Laelius' son in-law, the now aged Scaevola the Augur, is represented as discoursing in 91 to a distinguished gathering, one of whom, Cotta, could be represented by Cicero as later describing the occasion to himself.[1] In the Prologue to *De finibus* 5 (1–8) he recalls his youthful explorations of Athens with his brother, his cousin, Atticus and another friend: 'wherever we step, we are treading on history'.

It must be admitted however that Cicero sometimes compromised with his principles. In politics he was bad at seeing opponents' points of view and dogmatic in formulating his own. He was capable of soliciting Lucceius to waive the strict veracities of history when he came to deal with his own consulship (*Fam.* 5.12). With specious chauvinism he even once asserted that the Latin language, far from being poor, as was popularly supposed, was richer than the Greek (*Fin.* 1.3.10). He was as ready in his speeches as any other advocate, if it suited his brief, to disparage the law and lawyers, laugh at Stoics, insinuate that an Epicurean must be a libertine, suggest that you could not trust a Greek or a Gaul, and call Judaism a barbarous superstition (see p. 252). Only in defending the Greek poet Archias, where there was little case to answer, did he feel he could speak out in court for culture. His studies, highly though he valued them, were in truth a second best to political activity: 'I see nothing else I can do now.' He suggested that Scipio, the philosophic man of action, had the edge over Socrates and Plato. Writing after Caesar's murder, when he was once more at the helm, to his son, then a student of philosophy at Athens, he said, 'one should know what the philosophers recommend, but live as a man of the world (*ciuiliter*)'.[2] However, as with Seneca, it is the ideals he so eloquently proclaimed, not the extent to which he lived up to them, that have mattered in the cultural history of the world.

2. ORATORICAL THEORY AND PRACTICE AS CICERO FOUND IT

Not only higher education but literature in general at Rome was founded on oratory. For its early history we have to rely on Cicero's account in his *Brutus*. Though he shapes this in such a way that it culminates in himself, there is no evidence, at least in our fragments of previous speeches,[3] to gainsay him.

[1] Rambaud (1953) 104–7.

[2] Lactantius, *De fals. sap.* 3.14.

[3] Assembled by H. (= E.) Malcovati (1955).

Tradition, represented by Ennius, celebrated the eloquence of Appius Claudius the Blind, who persuaded the Senate not to compromise with Pyrrhus, and of M. Cornelius Cethegus in the Hannibalic War; but the first real figure in the story was the elder Cato (234–149 B.C.). Before his time the scope for rhetoric was limited. Apart from funeral orations (buried in family archives) there were speeches to the Senate; but its decisions would often have been pre-empted behind the scenes by groups of noble families. A magistrate would sometimes address the popular assembly, a general exhort his troops. But there was none of the 'epideictic' (display) oratory of Hellenistic Greece; and the 'formulaic' system of the praetorian law courts lent itself more to argumentation and cross-examination.

Things changed in the second century with the establishment of larger juries, as in the centumviral court and the standing tribunals (*quaestiones perpetuae*). Henceforward the chief theatre of eloquence was to be the law courts, where many of the cases tried were really political. Trials were held publicly, in the Forum or an adjoining basilica, and amid a ring (*corona*) of bystanders. At the same time the revolutionary activities of tribunes such as the Gracchi were furthered by rhetorical harangues to the inflammable popular assembly. (Mark Antony's in *Julius Caesar* plausibly conveys the effect.)[1]

Coincidental with these changes of circumstance was the influx of Greeks and Greek ideas. Under the Hellenistic monarchies eloquence had had less political scope than in such milieus as democratic Athens of the fourth century. It concentrated on display, and at the same time established a scholastic discipline of definition and classification, on Aristotelian principles, which was inculcated into the young by catechism and repetition in unison. In Roman pupils the Greeks found at last a political outlet for their skills; conversely the Romans were captivated by the rhetorical virtuosity of Greek embassies, increasingly frequent as the empire grew, notably that of the three philosophers from Athens in 156–155, which so excited the young and incensed Cato. Expelled by the Senate in 161, the Greek rhetoricians crept back, first perhaps as tutors in private houses. One difference the Greeks will have found at Rome was the persuasive power of *auctoritas*, the prestige of the speaker. Advocacy was much more personal: your advocate was called your *patronus*, and he might say more about himself than about you.

Romans were predisposed in two quite different ways in their attitude to rhetoric. On the one hand the image of themselves cultivated by Romans favoured a pithy, laconic, unadorned directness. In this they were abetted by the Stoics, to whom any oratorical device was meretricious and the only permissible rhetoric was dialectic – argument aimed at persuading by truth. The most famous example was that of P. Rutilius Rufus (consul 105), condemned on a

[1] Kennedy (1972) 7–21.

trumped up charge because, according to Cicero, he declined the help of the most eloquent advocates of the time: 'Why, none of his defenders even stamped his foot, for fear, I suppose, that the Stoics might hear it.' On the other hand the Italian character could be highly emotional, witness Cicero's own letters. Aristotle had emphasized the importance of emotion in rhetoric; and Cicero was clear that it was by moving, more than by pleasing or convincing, the jury that verdicts were obtained. *Flectere uictoriae est.* Hence he preferred to speak last of the several advocates who were retained. Servius Sulpicius Galba (consul 144), when vigorously impeached by the elder Cato for cruelty and treachery to the Lusitanians, obtained a monstrous acquittal by producing his weeping children in court and commending them, with added tears of his own, to the protection of the Roman people. The dullness of his speeches when read after publication was in itself testimony to the emotional power of his performances. He was also the first Latin orator consciously to employ the resources of rhetoric, seeking to charm and to move his hearers and enlarging on his theme with exaggeration, generalization and ornamental digressions.

But the pivotal figure was the elder Cato. He was the first to publish his speeches, and Cicero unearthed more than 150 of them. Some displayed schemata of rhetoric such as 'rhetorical question' and anaphora. The one 'On his own expenditure' contained a most elaborate exploitation of the figure *praeteritio* (mentioning things by saying you will not mention them). He certainly owed more in general to Greek influence than he pretended, but whether or not in rhetoric is a moot point.[1] All rhetorical schemata are systematizations of nature. Yet although anaphora (repetition of a word or words at the beginning of successive clauses), for instance, might seem a spontaneous feature, it is noteworthy that it is almost completely absent from Homer, the few instances seeming intended for expressive effect. Its use in literature becomes much more marked after the formulation of rhetorical schemata by Gorgias. Though Cato's own encyclopaedia contained a section on rhetoric (Quint. *Inst.* 3.1.19), if the famous dictum *rem tene, uerba sequentur* ('stick to the matter and the words will follow') came from it, it may have been a sort of anti-Rhetorica. What he lacked that he could have learned from the Greeks was *concinnitas* – the elegance of clarity, smoothness, artistic weighting and disposition of clauses (*membra*), and the quantitative rhythm conspicuous at cadences, in fact the art of the rounded Isocratean 'period'. The first Roman to display the Isocratean virtues, the '*stilus artifex*', was M. Aemilius Lepidus Porcina (consul 137); but the first to equal the Greeks, in Cicero's opinion, were the leading orators of his youth, L. Crassus and M. Antonius. Crassus was careful of euphony; and his periods, though he preferred to break them into smaller members, were rhythmical.

[1] Norden (1898) held the former view (I 165f.), Leo (1913) the latter (I 286). Clarke (1953) 40–2.

Hellenistic criticism recognized three styles, the grand, middle and plain. Cicero in the *Orator* (69) associated these with the three aims of oratory, to move, to please and to convince respectively. The grand style was forceful, weighty, spacious, emotional and ornate, carrying men away: it was what we understand by 'rhetorical'. Galba was its first notable practitioner in Latin, Gaius Gracchus a gifted exponent, who strode up and down, bared his shoulder, and employed a backstage piper to keep his pitch right.[1] This style prevailed over the plain for decades, despite the inclination of Stoicism to plainness. It was akin to the 'Asianic', represented by Hortensius, leader of the Bar from Antonius' death in 87 until the young Cicero's triumphant prosecution of Verres in 70. 'Asianic' was an ambiguous, not very helpful term. As late as 46 B.C. Cicero still felt obliged to define it (*Brut.* 325; cf. 51). It covered two styles prevalent in Asia Minor; (1) the epigrammatic and brilliant (*sententiosum et argutum*), relying on neatness and charm (*concinnum et uenustum*); (2) the swift and impetuous (*uolucre et incitatum*), but lacking in Isocratean refinements. These clearly differ widely, though Cicero alleges that Hortensius excelled in both. Generally the latter seems to have been meant. A detailed comparison between Hortensius and himself forms the climax of Cicero's *Brutus* (317–30).

3. ORATORICAL THEORY AND PRACTICE IN CICERO AND HIS CONTEMPORARIES

The ambition to be an orator probably came to the boy from the hill-town of Arpinum, south-east of Rome, through his being entrusted by his father to the care of Rome's leading orator, Lucius Crassus. While still in his 'teens he embarked on the composition of a full-scale Rhetorica; but he completed only the first section, preserved for us under the title of *De inventione*. Some idea of what the whole would have been like may be obtained from the anonymous *Rhetorica ad Herennium*, composed about the same time, possibly with the help of notes from the same teacher.[2] Some thirty years later, when Cicero came to compose the *De oratore*, it was partly in order 'to efface that crude, unfinished stuff that slipped out of my boyhood or adolescent notebooks'. In his oratorical, as in his philosophic, studies he favoured eclecticism, comparing the painter Zeuxis (*Inv.* 2.1–8).

Ancient criticism and pedagogic concentrated on artistry, as being susceptible of analysis; the genius of the artist, though no less essential, was not reducible to rules, so more cursorily treated. Cicero reversed the priority. He set out to describe the perfect orator, defined by his Crassus as 'a man who can speak with fulness and variety on any topic'. His spiritual ancestor was Isocrates.

[1] Plut. *Tib. G.* 2.2; Cic. *De or.* 225.

[2] Kennedy (1972) 106–11; 126–38. On Cicero's style the standard work is Laurand (1907/1936).

However much he might revere Plato, to him, as to Plato's rival, 'philosophy' meant culture, not dialectic. Philosophy was 'all knowledge of the best subjects and practice in them' (*De or.* 3.60). (Plato and Aristotle had claimed the term for dialectic, and despite Cicero they ultimately won.) Isocrates, the refiner and consummator of sophistic culture, had given his pupils a fairly wide education in the humanities, as a basis for eloquence and success in statesmanship. Cicero believed that it was his own general education that had enabled him to outshine other orators (*Brut.* 322). Further, the formal artistry which Cicero considered essential was another legacy from Isocrates, 'the father of eloquence', whose style had by 350 B.C. become the norm for Greece, though he brought to it also something of the fire of Demosthenes.

The essence of Isocrates' style was what the ancients called 'rhythm', in Latin *numerus* (with verse in mind, though prose must never fall into actual verse) – any construct of words which could somehow be measured by the ear. This covered 'length' of syllables as well as of members, and artistic disposition of members. These might, for instance, be balanced, and the balance pointed by antithesis or anaphora, or they might be arranged in threes (*tricola*) or in fours (*tetracola*), of ascending length so as to round off the period. The whole should be easily grasped, with no syntactical inconsequences or loose ends (such as we find in the speeches in Thucydides, for instance), and comfortably utterable in one breath. As to what we more narrowly distinguish as 'rhythm', the disposition of long and short syllables, this should be controlled, certain effective combinations being reserved for the cadence (*clausula*).[1] The various figures of speech should also be suitably exploited. Further, the Isocrateans were careful of smoothness, avoiding 'jaw-breaking hiatus' (R. L. Stevenson's phrase) between final and initial vowels and tongue-twisting juxtapositions of consonants.

Peripatetic critics, developing Aristotle, *Rhetoric* 3.8–9 and Theophrastus' lost book *On speech*, analysed such refinements. Cicero gives a fuller account of them, he claims, than any predecessor.[2] He expresses surprise that early orators, when they produced a good period by accident, did not realize the effect and consciously cultivate the art; and he credits even the uneducated multitude with

[1] Lacking the modern signs for 'long' and 'short', the ancients tended to borrow from verse the terminology of 'feet'. As applied to prose this encouraged excessive schematization in criticism. Cicero's rhythm exercised scholars from about 1900 to 1930. His likes and dislikes have been diagnosed, and compared with what occurs in prose that does not try to be rhythmic. They are naturally more marked in exordia, perorations etc., though they are characteristic of all his serious prose, even his more carefully composed letters. But he himself emphasized that he did not work strictly to rule (*Orat.* 220); and his seven favourite clausulae account for only 56·5% of his period-endings (as against 28% for their occurrence in non-rhythmical prose). The pioneer of modern investigation was Th. Zieliński (1904). See Wilkinson (1963) 156–60; and for a survey of literature on the subject, 237–42.

[2] *De or.* 3.171–98; amplified at *Orat.* 134–9; 149–236.

an instinctive feeling for rhythm. The skilled orator will organize a period as soon as he knows what to say, his mind disposing the words with lightning rapidity in appropriate order and rhythm relative to a foreseen ending.[1] But to avoid monotony there must not be excessive regularity, and the sword-sweeps of long sentences must be varied by stabs with the short dagger.

An example from the speech *Pro lege Manilia* of 66 B.C. (2) will show how quite a long sentence can be controlled and kept intelligible through balance emphasized by correlatives and anaphora. (To translate for the Latinless would be pointless here.)

Nunc cum
et auctoritatis *in me tantum* sit
quantum uos honoribus mandandis ēssĕ uŏlŭīstĭs,
et ad agendum facultatis *tantum*
quantum homini uigilanti ex forensi usu prope
cotidiana dicendi exercitatio pŏtŭĭt ādfērrĕ,
certe
et si quid auctoritatis in me est,
apud *eos* utar *qui eām* mĭhĭ dĕdērŭnt,
et si quid in dicendo consequi possum,
iis ostendam potissimum *qui ei* quoque rei
fructum suo iudicio tribuendum ēssĕ dūxērŭnt.

We note how *nunc cum* and *certe* mark off the subordinate and main clauses, how nearly the two parts are parallel in the length of their corresponding members, and how this parallelism is emphasized even by corresponding clausulae of types that Cicero favoured.[2]

In chapter 43 of the same speech (a speech which Cicero himself chose to exemplify the *middle* style at *Orat.* 103) the grand, impetuous manner, throbbing with emotive words, is in full swing:

Quod igitur nomen unquam in orbe terrarum clarius fuit? Cuius res gestae pares? De quo homine uos, id quod maxime facit auctoritatem, tanta et tam praeclara iudicia fecistis? An uero ullam unquam oram tam desertam putatis quo non illius diei fama peruaserit, cum uniuersus populus Romanus foro completisque omnibus templis ex quibus hic locus conspici potest unum sibi ad commune omnium gentium bellum Gnaeum Pompeium imperatorem depoposcit?

We note how the short rhetorical questions build up to the longer one, and how the period ends with a resounding *clausula*, the 'Asiatic ditrochee' (– ∪ – ∪), which was among Cicero's favourites. (He recalled (*Orat.* 213–14) how, when

[1] *De or.* 3.195–8; *Orat.* 199–200.

[2] In terms of feet, the tribrach 'pŏtŭĭt' counts as a resolution of a trochee, and is thus rhythmically equivalent to 'ēssĕ'.

he was sixteen, he heard Carbo end a stirring period with *temeritas fili comprobauit*: 'It was marvellous what a shout arose from the crowd at this ditrochee.')[1]

Such however was Roman subservience to Greek precepts that Cicero, regardless of the differences between the two languages, is found recommending some rhythms which in practice he markedly avoided. He even begins to prescribe that bugbear the avoidance of hiatus, but is for once pulled up by the glaring discrepancy with what happens in Latin. (He himself has just written *legendo oculus*.) For whereas in Greek the occurrence of a final long vowel before an initial vowel was avoided, in Latin such vowels were fused together by 'synaloepha', as in Italian, 'even by rustics'.[2] So he withdraws (without however deleting) what he has just said, with 'But we can leave that to the Greeks: we cannot gape between vowels even if we want to.' And analysis makes it almost certain that synaloepha does in fact operate in Latin prose rhythm. Again while he despises the formalism of Greek teaching, Cicero is loth to shake it off: his *Partitiones oratoriae*, a handbook in the form of a catechism of himself by his son, is conventional school stuff.

In practice Cicero cultivated the Isocratean manner. Though he recognized that it was primarily suited to the oratory of display, he allowed that it could be used in the exordium, peroration and other heightened passages of both political and forensic speeches, provided it was not so obtrusive that the hearer suspected he was being beguiled against his better judgement. Indeed it became his normal prose style, characteristic of his discourses as well. He also tended in his speeches to the vehemence and ornament of the grand manner. Up to the age of twenty-five he declaimed throughout with voice and body at highest tension, so much so that he endangered his health. A visit to Rhodes during his peregrination not only restored him but enabled him to learn restraint from a rhetorician called Molo (whom he had already met at Rome), though his style still remained what we should call 'rhetorical' and, as it seemed to others, inclined to the Asianic. He had the actor's ability to live his part and to feel for the moment the emotions he expressed: 'that supreme manipulator of men's hearts', Quintilian called him.[3] He cultivated the acquaintance of the great actors, Aesopus and Roscius, who gave him hints on dramatic delivery (Plut. *Cic.* 5). The element common to the ornate periodical and the grand emotional styles was, that both sought to appeal to irrational instincts in the hearers. Cicero's success was due to a combination of faculties, including wit and humour (he lists them in a mock-modest *praeteritio* at *Brutus* 322), none of them new, but exploited with such flair that the difference from his predecessors, and even his contemporaries,

[1] A molossus (– – –) was often the ditrochee's springboard, as here; more often a cretic (– ⏑ –).

[2] Laurand (1907/1936) 124 cites a passage from the *Verrines* (4.117) in which there are 9 hiatuses in 47 words. For Latin practice in this matter see Allen (1973) 142–6.

[3] *Summus ille tractandarum animarum artifex*: *Inst.* 11.1.85; cf. 8.3.4.

amounted to one in kind, so that Caesar could flatteringly call him 'almost the pioneer and inventor of eloquence (*copia*)'.

For some twenty years after the *Verrines* he remained the undisputed master of oratory. Then began a predictable reaction, probably less coordinated than some have supposed, towards a chaster style. There were always Stoics and characters such as Brutus who were temperamentally allergic to the passionate and the ornate. When Brutus wished to publish the speech he made to the people after Caesar's murder, he submitted the text to Cicero for criticism; but Cicero had to tell Atticus he could do nothing with it, it was so dispassionate; he himself would have handled the whole thing differently.[1] (This is the speech represented by Shakespeare in *Julius Caesar* III ii; it fell flat.) Then there were the self-styled 'Atticists', led by Catullus' poet-friend Calvus (d. 47), who affected a dry, unadorned style and claimed Lysias among the fourth-century Attic orators as their master. Calvus had at least one great success, against Vatinius, celebrated in a snatch of verse by Catullus (53). About the year 50 the young Virgil, leaving Rome for Naples and the Epicurean philosopher Siro, dismissed with relief the 'futile paintpots of the gaudy rhetoricians, words inflated with un-Attic hot air'.[2] Dionysius of Halicarnassus wrote of the recent return, within a short period, everywhere save in a few cities of Asia, to the old, temperate style of oratory. This he attributed to the political influence of Imperial Rome, the chief agents being members of her ruling class, 'highly cultivated men of refined taste'.[3]

As to historical writing, Caesar, besides being rationalistic by temperament, wrote his commentaries on his campaigns in plain style because he wanted to give an impression of unvarnished truth; and Cicero himself praised them as 'naked, regular and beautiful, stripped of all oratorical ornament'. Sallust's reaction against the Ciceronian style was more positive: in emulation of Thucydides he affected an abrupt, asymmetrical, arresting style prefiguring that of Tacitus.

Cicero defended himself with spirit against the Atticists in two treatises, the *Brutus* and the *Orator*, composed in the year 46, by which time both the chief exponents of Asianism and Atticism, Hortensius and Calvus, were dead. Rightly championing the Panaetian principle of appropriateness (*decorum*), he maintained that an orator should be master of all the styles. Lysias was too narrowly plain to be a general model, and Calvus, in following him with painful scrupulosity, had become jejune and too fastidious for the common man to appreciate. The consummate Greek orator, with no less right to the title 'Attic', was

[1] *Att.* 15.1*a*.2. Brutus should not be bracketed with the Atticists, though in some respects they agreed: Portalupi (1955); Douglas (1966) xiii–xiv.

[2] *Catalepton* 5.1–2 (reading '*rhoezo* non Achaico' with K. Münscher).

[3] *De antiqu. or.*, proem 3; Rhys Roberts (1901) 34–5. Dionysius resided at Rome from about 30 to 8 B.C.

Demosthenes; and he instanced speeches of Demosthenes and of his own to illustrate the stylistic range of both, which included variation within speeches as dictated by *decorum*.[1] As for 'rhythm', no orator capable of making use of it neglected to do so.

The plainness of Lysias may have sufficed at that moment, when under Caesar's dictatorship political oratory was dumb; but Demosthenes' style came into its own again when freedom was for a few months restored, in Cicero's *Philippics*, pointedly named after his. Yet Cicero himself was not unaffected by the movement in taste. In his mature speeches the style tends to be less Asianic, less Isocratean, less elaborated with figures of speech and cluttered up with redundant synonyms, more disciplined and muscular. This can be seen even in the Ninth *Philippic*, from the last year of his life, a panegyric proposing public honours for his dead friend Servius Sulpicius. On such a subject he would, in his young days, have pulled out all his organ-stops. But he realized now that that style was at best only consonant with youth (hence the decline in the reputation of Hortensius: *Brut.* 325).

Finally, there was the question of language. The 'genius' of a language is something real, but elusive and subtle. Why, for instance, should Latin be less tolerant of compound words than Greek (see *Orat.* 164), English than German? The influx of foreigners into Rome in the second century B.C., most of them slaves, of whom many would be freed by their masters and thus automatically become citizens, inevitably affected the purity of the Latin tongue. The younger Scipio called the Roman *plebs* 'the stepchildren of Italy'. He himself and his friends spoke pure Latin by heredity. It is not surprising that people alleged they had a hand in the plays of their protégé, the African slave Terence, whom Caesar saluted in retrospect as 'lover of pure language'; for Cicero noted that no such purity was to be found in the language of two playwrights contemporary with him, Pacuvius from the 'heel' of Italy and Caecilius, an Insubrian Gaul. Equally important, there was a Roman accent and intonation. An empire of many peoples needed a common Latin (corresponding to the 'common' Greek of Alexander's empire), and Roman aristocrats were concerned that it should be that of the capital. Grammar and syntax, vocabulary and pronunciation, were all involved.[2] There had been similar movements in Greek lands in defence of pure 'Hellenism', and latterly, of pure 'Atticism'.

In the matter of grammar and syntax the purists sought to standardize: there should be a 'correct' form for every word, e.g. for 'old age' *senectus*, not *senecta*. There should also be a correct construction for each syntactical relationship. Standardization raised a question which had exercised the Greeks: should

[1] He claimed that he used the plain, middle and grand styles in the *Pro Caecina*, *Pro Lege Manilia* and *Pro Rabirio perduellionis reo* respectively, all three in the *Verrines* and *Pro Cluentio* (*Orat.* 102–3).

[2] *De or.* 3.44; on language in general, 149–70; *Brut.* 170–2. Meillet (1948) 205–17.

language be governed by rules ('analogy') or by usage ('anomaly')? The Alexandrian scholars had sought to identify underlying rules, whereas the Stoics, champions of Nature, accepted what was produced by evolution. At Rome the encyclopaedic scholar Varro (116–27 B.C.) in his partly extant *De lingua Latina*, while leaning towards analogy, made ample concessions to usage. A stricter analogist was Caesar, whose efficient and systematic mind wished to correct the language just as he corrected the calendar. His treatise *De analogia* was a scholarly work, dedicated, like most of the *De lingua Latina*, to Cicero.

Strict analogy was associated with the Atticists, and as such it comes under attack in the *Orator*. Cicero's position was a sensible compromise. Thus he did not wish to alter phrases hallowed by tradition, nor to suppress exceptional forms which Nature had introduced for the sake of euphony. Though aware that it is incorrect to introduce an *h* into certain words such as *pulcer* and *Cartago*, 'after a while – a long while – I allowed correctness to be forced out of me by what was dinned into my ears'. There were even fifty-four instances in his writings (half of them in letters) of the indicative mood in indirect question, which Caesar shunned and every modern schoolboy is taught to shun. Nevertheless he repeatedly enjoined correctness in his rhetorical works; he taunted Mark Antony in the senate with using the superlative form *piissimus*, 'a word which does not exist in Latin'; and he took both his son and his secretary to task in letters for solecisms.

As to vocabulary, the purists sought to establish a 'proper' word for every thing or idea. In public speeches it was obviously important to make your meaning clear and not to give your hearers a sense of ignorance or inferiority. It may have been in this context that Caesar gave his famous warning, 'Avoid like a reef the unfamiliar or unusual word', but his taste was certainly fastidious. He held that selection of words was the beginning of eloquence, and in the *Brutus* Cicero makes Atticus say that Caesar 'speaks purer Latin than almost any orator'.[1] That 'almost' leaves room for Cicero himself. In his speeches Cicero was careful to use only good, established words still in general use. But he also insisted that they should be select words with some body and sonority. We find no instance of anything that looks like a new coinage, and only three instances of Greek words (all in the *Verrines*, about Sicily, and all carefully explained). Even naturalized Greek words occur only in one speech, *In Pisonem*, and there with ironical nuance. Aper in Tacitus' *Dialogus* singles Cicero out as one who applied selection to language, and *Tulliana puritas* is a phrase of St Jerome.

Languages do need some defence, and Latin was particularly vulnerable in the conditions of the late Republic. Cicero remarked to Brutus, 'When you

[1] 252. Gell. 1.10.4.

became Governor of Cisalpine Gaul you must have come across words that are not familiar at Rome. These can be unlearnt and replaced. More important is the fact that our orators' pronunciation has a timbre and accent that is somehow more metropolitan (*urbanius*).'[1] Archaic words had to be weeded out. Even we can tell that one like *topper* ('forthwith') would be a misfit in classical Latin. There were also rusticisms to be eradicated, like dropping final *s* and the incorrect aspiration for which Arrius was pilloried by Catullus (84). And there were vulgarisms (which must be distinguished from the colloquialisms of educated speech): Cicero criticizes two Epicurean writers for using *sermo uulgaris*. Modern composers of classical Latin prose, thumbing their dictionaries, are made aware of words which are not found in Cicero or Caesar but are common in Plautus and in late Latin (vulgarisms), or in Virgil (archaisms, traditional poeticisms, poetic licences). We are not in a position to judge how far purification was necessary for the defence of Latin. Was a language admittedly poor being further impoverished merely in the interests of snobbery? Reflection on modern parallels may well make us hesitate. The French have an official Academy to protect their language and control immigration. De Gaulle instituted a special campaign to expel foreign words from common speech. The English, more empirical, have only the unofficial *Oxford English Dictionary*, the still less official *Fowler's Modern English Usage*, and the erratic example of the British Broadcasting Corporation; while the Americans follow popular usage to a degree dismaying to the more fastidious among the English. The reaction against chaste classicism, associated with the name of Sallust, included the use of archaic and poetic words in prose as well as the deliberate flouting of the Isocratean elegances.

In his careful letters to important personages Cicero is linguistically on his best behaviour; but when addressing Atticus or other familiar friends he relaxes into colloquial Latin, perhaps consciously enjoying such truancy from the Forum. He even asks Paetus, 'What do you make of the style of my letters to you? Don't you find that I use plebeian language?' In these more intimate letters, by contrast with the speeches, he uses about 850 Greek words, especially to Atticus, who was, by choice and residence, almost an Athenian.[2] They clearly came quite naturally to him. Again, for Atticus he alludes freely to Greek literature, whereas in the cautious letters referred to above he was as chary of this as in his speeches.

When he came to philosophic writing, as a sexagenarian in 45–43 B.C., he was faced with difficulties inherent in Latin, which lacked not only the terminology

[1] *Brut.* 171. One such cisalpinism may have been *basium*, the Veronese Catullus' favourite word for 'kiss', otherwise found only in his imitator Martial. On *Latinitas, urbanitas, rusticitas* see Marouzeau (1928/1949) 7–25.

[2] It is noteworthy that Greek words were freely admitted into Roman comedy, never into tragedy or other serious poetry. Meillet (1928/1948) 109.

but the syntactical flexibility of the Greek he found in his sources.[1] Thus lack of the definite article made it hard to deal in abstractions.[2] *Omne bonum* has to serve for *to agathon*, 'the Good'. Sometimes however a neuter adjective alone would do – *honestum*, *uerum*. Lack of a past participle active (except in deponent verbs) sometimes drove him to clumsy periphrasis. But terminology was a more serious problem. The Romans had not dealt much in ideas. Cicero realized that existing words in the two languages were not complete equivalents, translating *physis* sometimes as *natura*, sometimes as *ingenium*. He might use an old word in a new sense, as *decreta* for *dogmata*. *Euidens*, a word not found in the speeches, does duty for *enarges*. We find him groping for the *mot juste*. Thus *pathos* is rendered by *motus animi* or *commotio* or *perturbatio*; but the ultimate rendering *passio* that has come down to us dates only from Augustine. He did however make some lasting coinages, such as *moralis*, *prouidentia*, *qualitas*, *quantitas*, and perhaps *essentia*. Sometimes he tells us he is inventing; but he was inhibited by his innate respect for the Latin language. He shrank from overfeeding it with indigestible neologisms or straining it with unfamiliar constructions. Thus he could not bring himself to countenance the word *medietas* ('middle position'), only going so far as to say, 'take it *as if* I had said that'.[3] (Others coming later had no such scruple; and from their use of *medietas* came the Italian *metà* and the French *moitié*.) He even apologized for venturing *beatitudo*, though *beatus* was a good Latin word found in his speeches, and *-itudo* a recognized suffix for producing an abstract word: 'whether we call it *beatitudo* or *beatitas* (both sound utterly harsh; but we should soften words by use)'.[4] Despite this last concession he seems never to have used either again. It is going too far to say that he created a supple philosophical language: he strove, as far as his fastidiousness would allow him, to enlarge his meagre linguistic patrimony, and to make philosophy comprehensible to the common reader;[5] in his own words, 'to teach Philosophy Latin and confer Roman Citizenship on her' (*Fin.* 3.40).

One means of enrichment to which he did have recourse was metaphor, which he rightly held to be a natural factor in the evolution of languages (*De or.* 3.155). A letter to Atticus gives us a glimpse of his workshop. Taking a hint from Lucilius, he had used *sustinere* to represent Carneades' Greek word for suspending judgement. Atticus had suggested instead *inhibere*, a metaphor from rowing. But now Cicero writes: 'I thought that sailors, when ordered *inhibere*,

[1] We possess translations by him which enable us to appreciate his problems: of a large part of Plato's *Timaeus*, and passages from his *Phaedrus* embedded in the *De oratore* and *De republica*. Unfortunately his translations of Aeschines' speech *In Ctesiphontem* and Demosthenes' *De corona* are lost; we have only the introduction, which goes by the name of *De optimo genere oratorum*. His translation of Plato's *Protagoras* (*Fin.* 1.7) is also lost.

[2] For 'the conquest of the abstract' in Latin see Marouzeau (1949) ch. v.

[3] *Tim.* 7.23. For Cicero's philosophic language see Meillet (1928/1948) 215–17. Glossary and discussion of renderings of technical terms in Lişcu (1937).

[4] *De nat. deor.* 1.95.

[5] Poncelet (1957); conclusions, 363–75.

rested on their oars; but yesterday, when a ship put in at my villa, I found this was not so: they don't rest on their oars, they back water. So *inhibere* involves action of a fairly strenuous kind.' He therefore asks Atticus to restore *sustinere* in the master-copy of the *Academica* he has for copying.

But while realizing that metaphor was in this respect a function, not an ornament, of speech, he also appreciated that it could be a transcendent ornament. His discussion of the subject at *De oratore* 3.155–70 is of exceptional interest. Here, as elsewhere, we may note that he considers language largely with poetry in mind, as his illustrative quotations show, forgetting the puritanism of his theory and practice as regards oratorical prose.

Latin has two outstanding qualities, sonorous gravity and conciseness. One of Cicero's great services was to reveal, following precursors such as Ennius, the possibilities of the former. Though he could also be admirably concise, it remained for Sallust, for Horace in his *Odes*, and finally for Tacitus, to exploit the latter to the full.

4. VERSE

According to Plutarch (*Cic.* 2) Cicero was considered the best poet as well as the best orator of his time, and his poetry was now neglected only because many superior poets had since appeared. This statement is less surprising when we recollect that there was a sag in Roman poetry before the emergence, roughly in the years 60–55 B.C., of Catullus and the other 'Neoterics' and of Lucretius. He may well have surpassed Hortensius in poetry as well as oratory, let alone such poetasters as Volusius, whose *Annals* Catullus derided. Even schoolboys down the ages have been taught by Quintilian and Juvenal to laugh at his line

O fortunatam natam me consule Romam

O Rome most blest, established in my consulship!

By Quintilian's time the historical context may have faded from memory; it was rather the jingles, one may suspect, that offended ears refined by Virgil and the rhetoricians. Whether or not they should so offend, is a matter of taste. After all, another master of verbal sound-effects, Tennyson, began a poem to Queen Victoria with

O loyal to the royal in yourself...

Cicero's verse is full of alliteration and assonance, a feature inherited from earlier Roman poetry which Virgil and his successors were to reserve for special purposes. The lines of Ennius that evoked his enthusiastic outburst, 'O excellent poet!' at *Tusc.* 3.44 are remarkable for this:

haec omnia uidi inflammari,
Priami ui uitam euitari,
Iouis aram sanguine turpari.

Better to forget that controversial line, remember historical perspective, and re-examine the surviving fragments, which at least testify that his poems were still remembered by some people centuries after his death.

What we can gather of his early poems (*Halcyones*, *Pontius Glaucus*, *Uxorius*, *Nilus*), varied in metre and subject, suggests an experimental precursor of the Neoterics; and it is significant that he chose for translation Aratus, the third-century astronomical poet whose *Phaenomena* and *Weather-signs* aroused among the Callimacheans of Alexandria and their Roman followers an enthusiasm that is hard for us to understand, even granted that they were nearer to people who regulated their life by the stars. But here, as elsewhere, his impulse to Latinize Greek works had an element of patriotism; and he also celebrated, likewise in hexameters, the hero of his native Arpinum, Marius the saviour of Rome.[1] His chief original poems were in this epic-panegyric hexameter tradition derived from his favourite Ennius. Others had written autobiographical apologias in prose; but it was a novelty when Cicero, disappointed in his hopes of a panegyric from his protégé the Greek poet Archias (for whose services there was a queue of nobles), composed one in Latin hexameters *On his consulship*, followed after his exile by one *On his experiences* (*tempora*). Of the former we possess a 78-line piece because he quoted it, as well as a dozen lines of his *Marius*, in the *De divinatione*.

The first thing that strikes one about his hexameters is that the position of caesuras and the limitation of metrical word-forms at the end of lines are already practically regularized as we find them in Virgil.[2] This is far from being the case in the extant fragments of his predecessors or in Lucretius. What Virgil and his successors approved (probably for reasons concerned with adapting quantitative Greek metres to the un-Greek accent of Latin[3]), it is not for us to criticize; and it may well have been the master of Latin prose rhythm himself who realized and regularized what had been only a half-conscious tendency in Ennius. But we should also be struck by the fact that the master of Latin prose *period* did not appreciate (as Virgil was to do) how his art could here also be applied to verse; for he falls into monotony. The lines are largely self-contained units of sense: the varied enjambment which imparts infinite variety and expressiveness to Virgil's verse is no more found in Cicero's than in the *Peleus and Thetis* of Catullus. There are also, as in Catullus, too many lines built round a word of three long syllables following a 'strong' caesura, such as

Principio aetherio flammatus Iupiter igni.

[1] The *Marius* was probably written after his return from exile in 57: Malcovati (1943); Büchner (1964) 302.

[2] For a detailed analysis of Cicero's versification see Ewbank (1933), introduction 40–74.

[3] For exposition of this theory, and criticism of other ones, see Wilkinson (1963), chapter 4 and appendix I. For general discussion of the reading of Latin hexameters see Allen (1973) appendix.

Lines of similar structure too often occur in close proximity; and in that long piece from the *De consulatu suo* 18 out of 19 successive lines (47–65) end in a trisyllable or quasi-trisyllable.

In celebrating his own deeds Cicero followed the ancient convention of sticking to the tradition of the genre. He incongruously adopted the whole epic paraphernalia of Ennius. Ennius had told of the apotheosis of Romulus, received into the Council of the Gods. Cicero apparently described the *Dichterweihe* of Cicero, welcomed to Olympus by Jupiter and taught the arts by Minerva. Further, he adopted the grand manner we have seen to be characteristic of at least his earlier oratory, along with archaisms of language which are also features of his verse translations. Ancient critical opinion was in any case inclined to consider grandiloquence, the *os magnum*, an essential of real poetry (e.g. Horace, *Sat.* 1.4.44). The passage referred to above, put into the mouth of the Muse Urania, is monotonously 'rhetorical', and we may suspect that the rest was similarly inflated. Post-Virgilian critics who belittled him as a poet may not have been mistaken absolutely, though they may not have realized the advance he represented as a versifier. All his life he wrote verse as a gentleman's pastime, like other contemporaries, including his brother Quintus, who while serving in Britain polished off four tragedies in sixteen days. Under Caesar's dictatorship he 'amused himself', Plutarch says (*Cic.* 40), by sometimes composing up to five hundred lines in a night. Clearly he lacked that respect for poetry as an art which led the neoteric Cinna to spend nine years over his short epic *Zmyrna* and Virgil seven years over his *Georgics*. Yet he produced not a few fine lines; and his incidental verse translations of Homer and Greek tragedy in his philosophical works are at least dignified (they include a precious 28-line passage from the lost *Prometheus unbound* of Aeschylus: *Tusc.* 2.23–5).

It is worth comparing Aratus' text with Cicero's free translation, of which we possess 581 lines, half as much as the original. This youthful work, occasionally archaic in metre as in vocabulary, has some errors; but it exhibits, in Munro's words, 'much spirit and vivacity of language'. In the *Weather-signs* we may detect touches not in Aratus – rhetorical intensification, 'onomatopoeic' expressiveness, hints of personal observation, and the ascription of human feelings to animals and of animation to the inanimate, all of which presage, if they did not actually prompt, the Virgil of the *Georgics*.[1]

5. LETTERS

The letter became a literary-rhetorical form in the Hellenistic age. Timotheus employed Isocrates to compose his despatches on campaign. Artemo published Alexander's letters. Epicurus, following Plato, used letter form and Isocratean

[1] Malcovati (1943) 248–9; G. B. Townend in Dorey (1965) 113–16.

style to embody philosophy. In rhetorical schools models of socially useful letters were purveyed, and imaginary ones from mythical or historical personages composed. Rhetoric came naturally to educated letter-writers.[1] St Paul's impassioned appeal for charity in his First Epistle to the Corinthians (13) teems with its figures.

Book 13 of Cicero's letters *Ad familiares* consists entirely of seventy-nine letters of recommendation. Most of the people recommended are mere names: his secretary Tiro, or whoever arranged the corpus after his death for publication, clearly envisaged these letters as serving as models. Cicero had been at pains to vary them to suit the recipient; thus a short one to Caesar (15) contains six quotations from Greek poets, and concludes, 'I have used a new style of letter to you, to convey that this is no ordinary recommendation.' Book 4 consists mainly of letters of condolence (*consolationes*), and includes the famous one he received from Servius Sulpicius on the death of his daughter Tullia (5). He recognized three kinds of letter, the serious, the informative, and the gossipy (*familiare et iocosum*). One of his complaints against Antony was that he had violated the etiquette of social intercourse by publicizing what he had said in a private letter.[2]

Some of his letters he did however expect to be read by more than the addressee. Thus he was glad to hear that an important one he had addressed to Caesar had got around, having himself allowed several people to make copies of it: he wanted his view of the political situation to go on record (*Att.* 8.9.1). The seventy letters or more he was hoping, three months after Caesar's murder, to revise for publication (*Att.* 16.5.5) were probably selected political ones, though possibly the collection of recommendations (*Fam.* 13). How carefully he composed his serious ones can be seen in the collection of those to Lentulus Spinther, which Tiro put in the forefront of Book 1.[3] They abound in periods which would not have sounded out of place in a formal speech. The very first sentence is an elaborate antithesis:

Ego omni officio ac potius pietate erga te
        ceteris satisfacio omnibus,
        mihi ipsi nunquam satisfacio;
tanta enim magnitudo est tuorum erga me meritorum ut,
        quod tu nisi perfecta re de me non conquiesti,
        ego quia non idem in tua causa efficio,
                uitam mihi ēss(e) ăcērbām pŭtĕ̽m.

[1] For letter-writing at Rome see Peter (1901); pp. 38–100 are on Cicero. Many of his letters are lost, including most of the collection *Ad Brutum* and all of those to Octavian, the future Augustus. (Nor have we any *from* Atticus.) Most of those that survive date from the last nine years of his life.

[2] *Fam.* 2.4; *Flacc.* 37; *Phil.* 2.7.

[3] Significantly, his letters from exile show much less care. He admits himself that his grief has bereft him of *huius generis facultatem* (*Att.* 3.7.3).

In letter no. 9, long enough to be a political manifesto, the clausulae of his rhetoric are ubiquitous (the first being his hallmark *ēssĕ uĭdĕātŭ̽r*). Take section 5. The first sentence contains a balanced antithesis, *aut occulta nonnullorum odia aut obscura in me studia*, the second is reminiscent in its construction of the opening period of the *Pro Archia*, famous for its elegance; the third again contains balanced clauses; and all three end with a clausula from among Cicero's favourites. In 7 there is a miniature 'tricolon crescendo' with anaphora: *de ui, de auspiciis, de donatiōnĕ rēgnōrŭ̽m*. A comparison with portrait-painting occurs in 15 and is elegantly expressed, with enough variation for relief and with a favourite clausula to each member:

nunc
ut Apelles Veneris caput et summa pectoris politissima
ārtĕ pērfēcĭ̽t,
reliquam partem corporis incohatām *rĕlīquĭ̽t*,
sic quidam homines in capite meo solum ēlăbōrā̽nt,
reliquum corpus imperfectum ac rŭdĕ *rĕlīquērŭ̽nt*.

In 19 six lines are quoted from Terence's *Eunuchus*.

Letters of this kind are literature. So are Cicero's letter to Marcus Marius consoling him for missing Pompey's games, and that to Lucceius asking for his own consulship to be given special treatment in his history, which he himself described as 'a very pretty piece of work (*ualde bella*)'.[1]

But the great collection of letters to Atticus is wholly spontaneous, with only so much of rhetoric as Cicero had in his blood. Clearly he never intended that these outpourings, full of indiscretions, should be published, and they appear not to have become available until Nero's reign, though the historian Cornelius Nepos, who was privileged to see eleven volumes of them in 34 B.C., realized that anyone who read them would have a practically continuous history of those times by a man whom he credited with uncanny foresight (*Life of Atticus* 16). These letters show us how educated Romans talked. Some of those to his brother Quintus and to other friends with whom he was wholly at ease, to Papirius Paetus in *Fam.* 9, for instance, have the same quality. But they were to have no true parallel in general until quite modern times, and are one of the greatest legacies of Latin writing – a record of the experiences, in unusually stirring times, of a remarkable personality who was in the thick of things, and who was fortunately also exceptionally witty and a spontaneous master of literary expression.

[1] *Fam.* 7.1; 5.12; *Att.* 4.6.4.

6. SPEECHES

It is primarily on his speeches, perhaps, that the literary reputation of Cicero has depended in recent times, though to the present generation the style of '*o tempora! o mores!*' seems fustian and we are more stimulated by the unguarded self-revelation of the letters. He himself could joke to Atticus about his own pomposity: 'You know those paintpots of mine', and again, 'You know how I can thunder on about all that; it was so loud you probably heard it over there in Greece.'[1] But how did the spoken word become literature?

Although shorthand writers might operate when a speech was delivered in court, the Romans were well aware that the published speeches they read were not verbatim records. It was exceptional when Hortensius, who had a remarkable memory, delivered one in a state fit for publication, or when Cicero read out a speech, *Post reditum in senatu*, for the record. We know from Quintilian that Cicero normally wrote out beforehand the exordium, peroration and other vital passages (which incidentally show special care for rhythm) and learned them by heart, the rest being preconceived in outline only, though apparently he used notes (10.7.30–1). Everyone knew that his second *Actio* against Verres, published in five books, had never been delivered because the opposing counsel, Hortensius, threw up his brief after the first one and Verres went into voluntary exile; that the *Pro Milone* as delivered fell far short of the polished form in which we have it because he lost his nerve under heckling from Clodius' gangsters, whom the presence of Pompey's soldiers did not intimidate; and that the *Second Philippic* was not delivered on the ostensible occasion, with Antony menacingly present in Rome, but published some weeks later, after he had left, as a gauntlet thrown down. The *Catilinarians*, published more than two years after the events concerned, betray by their defensiveness (Book 4 especially) his anxiety now that he was under attack for having put Roman citizens to death without trial. (Not that publication was normally so long delayed, as is indicated by signs of haste in some other speeches; for instance, too many apparently redundant passages are left in, such as might have been helpful to hearers but are tiresome to readers.) Nor would two long passages in the *Pro Sestio* on the true nature of 'Optimates' (96–105; 136–43), a politician's apologia, have been relevant enough for even a Roman speech in court.[2] It has also been shown, from a reconstruction of Roman legal procedure, that Cicero's forensic speeches, published in the form most effective as literature, could not have been delivered in that form in court.[3] They are essentially pamphlets.

[1] For Cicero's speeches see, besides Laurand (1907/1936) and Büchner (1964), Clarke (1953) chh. VI and VII, R. G. M. Nisbet's chapter in Dorey (1965), and Kennedy (1972).

[2] Nisbet in Dorey (1965) 66.

[3] Humbert (1925); Douglas (1968) 14–15.

We may surmise however that the nature of Roman legal procedure did promote Cicero's oratorical development; for it differed from that of Athens in that the set speeches were delivered before, not after, the calling of witnesses. (The normal difference is highlit by the *Pro Milone* of 52 B.C., whose organization does approximate to that recommended by Greek handbooks because Pompey's emergency rules, designed to limit the effect of pathetic oratory as well as judicial bribery, had assimilated Roman procedure to Greek.) This meant that the speaker was more free to range, expatiating on generalities and personalities and indulging in excursuses and extended narrative; and more important, that he was less tempted to rely, with Roman deference, on the prescriptions of Greek handbooks, whose arrangement would not tally. So we find Cicero tailoring his speeches to suit the needs of the occasion. Thus in the *Verrines* he forwent the preliminary speech, since the defence was playing for delay and an adjournment till the next year, when its leader Hortensius would be consul, and went straight to the revelation of his devastating evidence. He thus sacrificed to winning his case a seductive opportunity for competitive oratorical display. Again, Greek forensic speeches were composed 'in character' to be delivered by the litigant. At Rome the advocate's own personality and prestige counted for much, and he could speak of and for himself as well as his client. In his early speeches Cicero sought to win sympathy as a courageous young man, and a 'new' man at that, in his later ones, to impress with his consular prestige (*auctoritas*). We know of 139 speeches of his out of a doubtless much larger number (speeches in civil suits were generally not thought worth publishing, Cicero's *Pro Caecina* being an exception). He won 74 of these cases and lost 16, the result of the remaining 49 being unknown.[1]

Of the 58 speeches of his which survive whole or in part the most famous are probably the *Verrines* (70), the *Catilinarians* (63) and the *Philippics* (44–43). The *Verrines* have come to life again particularly wherever there has been resistance to an oppressor of provincials or colonials, the *Catilinarians* in times of privy conspiracy and rebellion, the *Philippics* where republican freedom has been threatened by autocracy. Together they have created a rather one-sided impression of Ciceronian oratory. They are all vehement, not to say ranting, whereas many of the other speeches are relaxed. Thus the *Pro Murena*, composed amid the *Catilinarians* in the year of Cicero's consulship, has amusing passages at the expense of Sulpicius' legalism and Cato's philosophy (all the judges laughed, and even Cato forced a wry smile). Not that the invective characteristic of the *Verrines*, *Catilinarians* and *Philippics* is absent elsewhere: we meet it in the *In Pisonem*, which was soon being studied in the rhetorical schools as a model, and counter-attack was often the better part of defence. It was regarded as an art form (Ovid's *Ibis* is a counterpart in verse). No holds

[1] Granrud (1913) 241.

were barred. A man might be mocked for his banausic origins or his physical features. We have all heard of modern briefs marked 'no case: abuse plaintiff'. Brutus indeed deprecated the unbridled abuse of Antony by Cicero in *Philippic* 2. Professing however to prefer defending to prosecuting, Cicero maintained it was wrong to prosecute a man you thought innocent, though not wrong to defend someone who *might* be guilty, unless he was otherwise vicious.

Patriotic he certainly was, and courageous too as a young man attacking the powerful, and when in those supreme crises he nerved his naturally hesitant will; but it is distressing to see him tamed after his return from exile, putting his unique talents at the service of Caesar or Pompey. And while it may be too sweeping to say that 'he championed unworthy causes for short-term results in front of audiences he despised',[1] it is certainly true that, while we may admire from outside the way he handled his briefs and sometimes made political capital out of them, it is rarely that we can identify ourselves whole-heartedly with his cause, as we can in the *Verrines*, the *Catilinarians*, and (some would say) the *Philippics*. And it is disturbing to learn from a letter to Atticus (1.2.2) that he even thought of defending Catiline when they were rivals for the consulship, reasoning that, if he were acquitted, Catiline might feel obliged to pull his punches, and if condemned, he would be out of the way. But even Panaetius held that, while it is the business of the judge to find out the truth, it is sometimes the business of the advocate to maintain what is plausible even if it is not strictly true (Cic. *Off.* 2.51). In the rhetorical schools you were advised, if need be, to 'pepper your case with fibs' (*causam mendaciunculis aspergere*: ib. 59). In the *Pro Cluentio*, highly praised in antiquity and considered by the younger Pliny to be Cicero's masterpiece, he 'threw dust in the eyes of the jury', as he afterwards boasted. In this attitude to advocacy he would have had plenty of supporters, ancient and modern; but it was an awkward one to maintain in the high-minded atmosphere of philosophy, as we shall see.

A history of literature is not concerned with politics or even morality except insofar as they affect readabilility. But insincerity is a flaw which lowers our response from the level of sympathetic interest to that of cynical appraisal. In this respect our reaction may be the opposite of Petrarch's when he rediscovered the letters to Atticus in 1345. Petrarch was shocked to find that the philosophic master he had envisaged was a man of human weaknesses; whereas we can take a sympathetic interest in the self-revealing man while we can give only grudging admiration to the accomplished hypocrite. The most interested readers of Cicero's speeches in modern times are likely to be historians, for whom they provide a mass of sidelights on Roman life and institutions. This much said, we may turn to their literary qualities other than those already considered.

[1] Nisbet in Dorey (1965) 78.

Exordia, in Cicero's opinion, should be moderate and ingratiating in tone, spacious and periodic in style, but pointed with apophthegms designed to commend yourself or discredit your adversary (*Orat.* 125). He conformed to this doctrine unless he had reason to do otherwise, as in the most famous case of all when, no doubt in order to startle the Senate into a sense of crisis, he began: *Quousque tandem abutere, Catilina, patientiam nostram?* 'How much longer, Catiline, are you going to abuse our patience?' Generally the impassioned climaxes would be more effective after a temperate opening.

A considerable portion of the speeches naturally consists in narrative. If Cicero had written history ('a particularly oratorical genre', as he called it), his style would no doubt have largely displayed the 'milky richness' that was attributed to Livy. But in court the first essential was clarity: the jury must grasp and remember the facts as represented. Hence in the story of Sopater of Halyciae in *Verrines* 2.68–75, extending to about 875 words, the average length of a sentence is only fourteen words. Narratives must also be unadorned, almost colloquial: they must give 'a most clever imitation of simplicity', in the words of Quintilian, who especially admired the account of Clodius' murder in the *Pro Milone*, perhaps the most perfect of Cicero's speeches:[1] 'Milo, after attending the senate on that day until the end of the sitting, went home, changed his shoes and his clothes, hung around a little while his wife got ready, the way wives do, and then set out at an hour when Clodius, if he had really wanted to get back to Rome that day, could already have been there...'

The Second *Actio* of the *Verrines*, in five books, was designed from the start to be read. Cicero must have been aware that, while he must refer to all possible crimes of Verres, there was a certain sameness about them that would pall. By the fifth book he was therefore particularly concerned to be readable. Verres had been Governor of Sicily from 73 to 70, his tenure prolonged because the serious slave revolt of Spartacus broke out on the mainland in 73, and Sicily, as the scene of previous revolts, was considered precarious. In fact it did not spread to the island, and Cicero had to anticipate that this would be credited by his opponents to the Governor's military efficiency. He marshalled all his powers of telling detail and innuendo in a devastating account that presages Tacitus (1–101). Even a summary may give some impression.

Hortensius, he says (3), would no doubt compare Verres with his predecessor Manius Aquilius, who had put down the slave rising in Sicily in 101. When he was impeached for extortion, Aquilius' counsel had dramatically secured his acquittal by tearing open his tunic before the jury and the Roman people to show the honourable scars he bore on the front of his body. (This is a time-fuse whose detonation comes only at 32: 'Are you going to ask Verres to stand up, bare his breast, and show the Roman people his scars – the records of women's lascivious love-bites?') Aquilius' measures had secured

[1] *Inst.* 4.2.57–9; *Mil.* 28.

that slaves were disarmed throughout Sicily. This gives occasion for a decorative story. A successor of his, Domitius, admiring a huge boar, had asked who killed it. When a proud shepherd was produced who said he had done it with a hunting spear, Domitius had him crucified for being armed. He may have been cruel, but at least he was not lax (7). This prepares for a scene in which Verres, having duly bound to the stake some slaves convicted of rebellion, suddenly released them and returned them to their master (10f.). 'I will not ask', says Cicero, 'how much money changed hands.' No less surprisingly, Verres had suddenly released, after eighteen months of imprisonment, a rich Sicilian whose slave foreman had got up a revolt. 'I have no ready cash', the poor man had pleaded as he was haled off at his trial.

As to military tours of inspection, laborious but essential, Verres made admirable arrangements (26ff.). He chose Syracuse for his headquarters because of its mild climate and spent his winters there, the short days in feasting, the long nights in sexual indulgence, rarely seen out of doors, or even out of bed. When the appearance of roses on his table informed him that spring had come, he began his tour. On horseback? No. Like the old kings of Bithynia, he rode in a litter with eight bearers, resting on a delicate Maltese pillow stuffed with rose petals. On arrival at any assize town he went straight to bed, where he heard and decided cases for an hour or two before devoting the rest of his visit to Venus and Bacchus. The wives of local notables were entertained, the more brazen at dinner, the discreet at later assignations. His dinner parties were riots; for although he never obeyed the laws of Rome, he scrupulously observed the rules of drinking-parties (26–8).

At midsummer, when the inspection of harvest labourers and corn-threshing, so important for Governors of Sicily, fell due, Verres left the old palace of King Hiero and set up summer headquarters with his cronies in marquees in the loveliest part of Syracuse, at the mouth of the harbour, where he and his young son received only those connected with their pleasures, including his favourite mistress Tertia, whose presence (since she was the daughter of a ballet-dancer whom Verres had enticed away from her Rhodian fluteplayer) was resented by the higher-class wives who shared his favours with her. The law-courts were deserted – but in this case that was a mercy (29–31).

If Hortensius really tried to present Verres as a military commander, baring those scars, Cicero would be obliged to reveal his previous exploits. This introduces an elaborate extended metaphor, the campaigns of love (later dear to elegists like Ovid). It is true that no slave rising occurred. Did he then also put down piracy? Here come in (42) his relations with the city of Messana, the only one that had sent a deputation to eulogize him at his trial. He had publicly received from it a fine cargo vessel for his private use, to bring home his plunder, for which the town was a convenient depot – or was it to remove it later, when he was sent into the exile he must anticipate? In return he exempted Messana not only from the corn levy but also from providing a warship. Its eulogy was thus worthless. Verres also altered the practice by which pay for the fleet was channelled through commanders. Channelling it through himself, he pocketed not only the bribes from the men he exempted but also the pay they would have got. The pirates were well aware of this. One pirate ship was indeed brought in. It proved to be full of silver, fabrics and attractive young people. Verres, though drunk when told, was not too drunk to leave his women and hurry down to it.

He executed all the prisoners who were not goodlooking, and distributed the remaining loot to his friends and hangers-on, sending six musicians to a friend at Rome. But nothing was seen again of the pirate captain. Would-be spectators of his being led in chains and beheaded were fobbed off. A man who was presumably a substitute was kept, not in the famous Syracusan quarries, where the imposture would have been detected, but in comfortable circumstances in an inland town which had never seen any sort of pirate but Verres' agent. Meanwhile he did have others beheaded, not all together (since he knew there were Syracusans who would count them) but in driblets. Yet some did keep a count, and demanded to see the rest of them. So Verres substituted some Roman citizens he had casually imprisoned on trumped up charges. Their friends recognized them though they were hooded, and protested in vain. But provoked in court, Verres lost his head: he admitted he had not beheaded all the pirate captains, but had kept two imprisoned in his own house – *because* he knew he would be charged with receiving bribes for not having executed the real pirate captain. No one doubted that he had in fact been so bribed, and that these two were in reserve in case that other substitute died or escaped (32–79).

Cicero now returns to the lunch parties at those summer quarters by the bay. Verres and his young son were the only men present – if you could call them men – except that his freedman Timarchides was occasionally invited. Apart from Tertia, the women were all wives of Syracusans. Among them was Nike, wife of Cleomenes, said to be very goodlooking. Even Verres would have felt uncomfortable if her husband had been around; so he put this Syracusan Greek in command of Roman naval forces, though there were plenty of Romans, up to the rank of quaestor, on his staff. And why, when so many Sicilian cities had always been loyal, choose a citizen of Syracuse, so suspect a city that ever since its capture by Marcellus no citizen had been allowed to live on its strategic island of Ortygia? Cleomenes' squadron of seven vessels set sail with skeleton crews only, most of the sailors having paid Verres for immunity from service. The Governor, unseen for days past, turned out to watch it, in a purple Greek cloak and a long, skirted tunic, leaning on a woman's arm. After four days at sea the ships put in at Pachynus because he had kept them so short of provisions; and while Cleomenes enjoyed himself in Verrine fashion, the sailors were reduced to grubbing up the roots of palm trees to eat. News then reached the inebriated captain that there were pirates at Odyssea. He had hoped to fill up the crews from the land garrison, but that too proved to have been depleted by Verrine exemptions. His flagship, far superior for action to those of the pirates, was the fastest, and got away. The last two ships were picked off, and the rest, having put in at Helorus following him, were burnt by the pirates when darkness fell (80–91).

Verres meanwhile had returned to the palace with his train of women. So strict was his discipline, that his orders that no one should disturb him were obeyed even in this crisis, while poor Cleomenes found no wife at home to comfort him in his troubles. Alerted however, not by any official beacon but by the glare of the burning ships, a fiercely hostile crowd gathered. Finding the Governor himself obviously dazed and only half awake, they encouraged each other to arm themselves and occupy the forum and island. The pirates, anxious no doubt to take their only chance of viewing Syracuse and its splendid fortifications, put to sea again next day and with their four ships entered the Grand Harbour, the heart of the city, passing Verres' deserted pleasure-camp; and it was only after, not frightened but sated, they had sailed out again that people began to ask themselves what was responsible for such a disaster (92–101).

Cicero was famous for his wit, which sparkles through his letters to Atticus. He complained that everyone's sallies were attributed to him – even those of Sestius; but he was flattered when he heard that Caesar not only collected his *bons mots* but claimed to be able to distinguish the spurious from the authentic.[1] Three books of them were published after his death by the faithful Tiro. In *De oratore* 2 he makes Caesar Strabo, after mocking the idea of classifying humour, proceed to do so for seventy-five chapters (216–90), a repertoire of jokes which throws considerable light on Roman mentality.[2] Wit and humour were naturally characteristic of the plain style, which eschewed emotion,[3] but they were also valuable in the middle style, which sought especially to please. Cicero's command of them was one of the things that enabled him to speak effectively, as he claimed, in whatever style was appropriate to his subject.

In his own speeches we may note a progress from the rather crude puns and sarcasms of the earlier ones, not completely outgrown even in the *Verrines*, to the more delicate irony of his maturity in the *Pro Murena*, *Pro Caelio* and *Pro Ligario*. The climax of his defence of Caelius was a brilliant piece of ridicule, of the implausible story of how one Licinius, allegedly sent by Caelius to deliver a casket of poison to Clodia's treacherous slaves at the Senian Baths, of all places, gave the slip to her agents, who lay in wait to catch him in the act (61–9). Even if there were something in the story, what the jury would retain would be an impression of farce. Indeed Cicero himself had suggested to them that it was more like a Mime than a play with a coherent plot.

7. DIALOGUES AND TREATISES

Cicero had always hoped, so he says, that after his consulship he would be free to enjoy leisure and esteem and to devote himself to literary pursuits. Instead he had to endure six years of trouble and anxiety, and it was only the leisure with greatly diminished esteem forced upon him by the Triumvirs in 56, after he had tried to take an independent line in politics, that brought him to embark, as a compensation, on two manifestos he had always wanted to write, about the things that mattered to him most, the *De oratore* on his oratorical ideals and the *De republica* on his political ideals. He was consciously setting out to inaugurate for Rome something she lacked, a prose literature worthy of the Latin tongue.

[1] Sen. *Contr.* 7.3.9; Quint. *Inst.* 6.3.5; Cic. *Fam.* 7.32.1.

[2] His own irony and humour have been exhaustively catalogued and analysed by Haury (1955).

[3] Grant (1924).

As his primary form he chose dialogue – not the Platonic dialogue in which conclusions emerge from discussion (the *Symposium* is exceptional), but the Aristotelian,[1] more congenial to an orator, in which the various characters express, in speeches that may be lengthy, opinions already formed. Indeed the speeches may be complementary, as they mainly are in the *De oratore*, which therefore approximates to a treatise; or they may express differing views, as in the *De natura deorum*, to encourage the reader, in the spirit of Philo, to make up his mind for himself (1.10). In either case he would be able incidentally to portray humane intercourse. We are spoiled by Plato's excellence; but anyone who belittles Cicero's skill in the dialogue should read Varro's *Res rusticae*.

The *De oratore* was begun in 55 and completed next year. For its dramatic occasion Cicero chose three days during a crisis over the Italian allies in September of 91 B.C., when the Senate had adjourned for the Roman Festival. The setting is the villa at Tusculum of that Lucius Crassus who had been his mentor in boyhood. Another of Cicero's old mentors is present at first, Scaevola the Augur, now old and infirm. Cicero is, in fact, escaping into his youth, and though he could hardly introduce himself, as a boy of fifteen, into that company, he probably remembered that house. One feels his involvement. In the prologue to Book 3 he tells his brother that he has wanted to do for Crassus what Plato did for Socrates, and indeed Plato is never far from his thoughts. Scaevola plays the part of Cephalus, the old man who is present for a while at the beginning of Plato's *Republic*. A fine plane tree reminds him of the one at the beginning of the *Phaedrus*, and he suggests they sit under it. And as Socrates at the end of the *Phaedrus* prophesies a great future for the young Isocrates without mentioning Plato, so Crassus at the end of the *De oratore* prophesies a great future for the young Hortensius, who in that year made his debut as an orator, without mentioning Cicero – a graceful compliment whose irony however would not be lost on the reader. As in the *Phaedo*, the occasion is described to the author by a survivor. But it is the *Gorgias* that haunts the dialogue, as we shall see. In the prologue to Book 3 Cicero bitterly recalls how within four years, of those seven courteous participants, Crassus and Scaevola had soon died, both after brave resistance to threatened tyranny, Catulus had killed himself, and Antonius, Caesar Strabo and Sulpicius had been murdered, either by Marians or Sullans. Only Cotta survived to tell the tale. The heads of those three had been spiked on the Rostra, including, to Cicero's especial horror, that of the orator Marcus Antonius, whom he admired almost as much as Crassus. For us there is an added poignancy in the thought that twelve years later his own head and hands were to be displayed there by Antonius' grandson and namesake.

[1] Aristotle's 'exoteric' works, admired in antiquity for their 'golden eloquence', are unfortunately lost (*Acad.* 2.119; Quint. *Inst.* 10.1.83).

The main theme is *paideia*, cultural education, or more widely, *humanitas*. Cicero claimed that he owed his oratory to the spacious Academy, not to the rhetoricians' workshops (*Orat.* 12). Crassus, who in general represents Cicero's views, deplores narrow specialization and the utilitarian approach, claiming that the ideal orator must be highly educated in all subjects, able to speak with fullness and variety on any topic. That, we remember, was what Gorgias claimed to teach; and throughout the dialogue Cicero is haunted by the spirit of the Platonic Socrates.[1] For if Socrates was right, oratory was a mere knack, morally neutral at best and potentially pernicious, and he himself has been living all along 'the unexamined life'. Right at the beginning Crassus mentions the *Gorgias* only to dismiss it with a quibble (cf. Catulus at 3.29), and he castigates people who gibe at orators, *ut ille in Gorgia Socrates* (3.129). In effect Cicero is tacitly renewing the great debate between Isocrates the pupil of Gorgias and Plato the pupil of Socrates; and as we saw (p. 237) he is, for all his veneration of Plato, an Isocratean. He was bound to be: his own life of practical politics conducted through the influence of oratory, the source of his fame and self-respect, committed him irrevocably to that camp. His clever and plausible defence, perhaps suggested by a thesis of Posidonius, consists in reproaching Socrates with having split the *logos*, divorced thought from speech, philosophy from rhetoric, the contemplative life from the active, so that some have even come to exalt the former above the latter (as Aristotle did at the end of his *Ethics*). He puts into Catulus' mouth at 3.126–30 an encomium of the *paideia* of the old Greek Sophists, whom he calls 'orators', and defines the ideal orator in such wide terms that he might seem to have stolen the thunder of the Platonic philosopher. In contrasting this 'full man' with the narrow rhetoricians he is choosing ground on which Plato and Isocrates were united, and thus avoiding a head-on collision. The fact that he is so much *engagé* imparts to the work an intensity of intellectual passion. It is his *apologia pro vita sua*. The greatest heir of the Sophists is grappling in his soul with the spirit of Socrates.

Into this, his first literary work, he pours all the riches of his own fullness. His remarkable grasp of cultural history, his sense of period and his fund of anecdotes and quotations enable him to diversify the work with such passages as Caesar Strabo's disquisition on wit (2.216–90). Book 3 alone contains passages on correct Latin speech (43–6), on the relation between philosophy and oratory down the ages (56–73), on the actor Roscius' voice-control (101–2), on metaphor (155–69), on artistic functionalism (178–80), on the sensitivity of Roman audiences to style and rhythm (195–8), and on delivery (the orator as the actor of real life; 215–27).

[1] The inevitability of this conflict had been recognized by his brother (if indeed he was the author) when he said to him, in the brochure of advice on electioneering (*Comm. Pet.* 46), with reference to the necessity of time-serving, 'But it will probably be rather hard to persuade a Platonist like you of this.'

Yet the *De oratore* is in some ways an exasperating work. The great issue is repeatedly sidestepped. Scaevola at the outset suggests that oratory may have done more harm than good and puts forensic eloquence in a cynical light (35–41), but no one takes up the challenge. We are fobbed off with 'it's all a matter of nomenclature' (1.47; 3.142–3); as if it made no difference whether *philosophia* denoted dialectic or cultural knowledge! There is too much repetition. Nor is there any real tension of argument: for Antonius, the purely utilitarian orator, after acting as a foil to Crassus in Book 1, is made to confess next day that he was only arguing for the sake of arguing (2.40), and thereafter is merely complimentary to him. Moreover Cicero tries to do too many things at once. In his eagerness to portray Crassus, whom he considers to be misconceived by his contemporaries, he blurs the distinction between him as speaking in character and as mouthpiece of himself (compare Plato and Socrates). Books 2 and 3 are a '*technologia*', as he himself calls it, to supersede the *De inventione* (*Att.* 4.16.3). Sending a copy to Lentulus, he says he hopes it will be helpful to his son (*Fam.* 1.9.34). It is true that, by a salutary innovation, *ars* is subordinated to *artifex*; also that the textbook is camouflaged as literary *sermo*, the underlying subdivisions being disguised (compare Horace's *Ars poetica*), and the *disiecta membra* wrapped up in words of philosophic discourse. Yet the bones do sometimes obtrude. Thus Antonius, after saying that panegyric needs no rules, proceeds to give some (2.44ff.); Caesar Strabo ridicules the idea of analysing wit, then analyses it (2.217–18; 235ff.): and strangest of all, in Book 3 Crassus is constrained to do what all along he has protested against doing – to go into technical details of style of the most scholastic kind (200ff.) (Cicero himself would never have belittled the importance of style; and in the *Orator* he made amends nine years later for what he must have felt to be inadequate treatment.) Like other Romans, Cicero could not shake off the framework of the rhetoricians with their pigeon-holes, Graeculi whom he represents his Crassus as despising.[1] He does not start from his own experience, any more than Horace does in the *Ars poetica*.

In the summer of 54 we find Cicero deep in a dialogue on his other interest, politics, which he thought would be well worth all the labour involved, if he could bring it off. The prologue to *De re publica* 1 movingly expresses his bitterness at what has given him leisure to write, his being excluded from active participation after all his services to the state. For the dramatic occasion he chose the Latin Festival of the winter of 129, and as his spokesman the younger Scipio. As in the *De oratore*, the conversation purports to have been retailed by a survivor: Cicero reminds his brother, the dedicatee, how on their youthful tour they heard about it at Smyrna from the exiled Rutilius Rufus. The choice of a

[1] Clarke (1953) ch. v gives a fair critique of the *De oratore*.

moment when Scipio, like Crassus in the *De oratore*, was shortly to meet his death may have been suggested by the situation of Socrates in Plato's *Phaedo*, for again Plato was much in his mind, though Aristotle also had written a *Republic* in dialogue form. A friend nearly persuaded him to downdate the occasion and take the leading part himself, as Aristotle had done; but he reverted to his original plan, partly because he wanted to depict the period which seemed to him to show the Republic at its best, partly to avoid giving offence to living people (notably, of course, the Triumvirs).[1] Contemporaries could draw their own conclusions.

The *De re publica* was a broader and better organized work than the *De oratore*, but unfortunately it has come down to us only in fragments, though these were greatly increased in 1822, when Cardinal Mai published what may amount to nearly a third of the whole, which he had discovered in a Vatican palimpsest. Of the six books every other one had an external prologue. Book 1 conceives of the state as based on common interest and common rights (39). It reviews, as Greeks had done ever since Plato's *Republic*, the three constitutions of democracy, aristocracy and monarchy, and like Polybius (6.3–18) favours the composite, best seen in the Roman Republic (1.70). Book 2 traces Rome's early development towards the attainment of this equilibrium, *optima re publica*, in the second century. In 3 Philus consents to play devil's advocate, arguing that justice depends on expediency, and Laelius replies as a Stoic (his eloquent eulogy in 33 of Natural Law, god-given, above all man-made laws, is famous), Scipio reinforcing his opinions. 4, very fragmentary, was apparently on education, moral and physical as well as intellectual, probably with emphasis on the family, and on culture in general in the context of the community. 5 and 6, on the ideal statesman and his reward, are also very fragmentary except for the celebrated conclusion, the Dream of Scipio, preserved with the Neoplatonic commentary of Macrobius (*c.* A.D. 400).

Remarking that it would be easier to show how the Roman Republic came about than to invent an imaginary state like Plato's Republic, Cicero makes Scipio give (2.1–63) an account of her early history (the first indeed that has come down to us). Though the nearest approach to a political theorist that Rome produced, he is an empiricist: he follows Cato in believing that the Roman constitution is superior because it was evolved, not created.[2] The virtue of composite states was supposed to be stability, a subject highly relevant for Romans talking in 129, when Tiberius Gracchus, Scipio's own brother-in-law, had just broken it. Cicero's ideal was not an equilibrium of forces, of tensions, but a concord like harmony in music (and one thinks at once of the concord of

[1] *Q.Fr.* 2.12; 3.5.1–2. For a full discussion of the *De re publica* see the introduction to Sabine and Smith's translation (1929). Boyancé (1970) 180–96 gives a critical survey of work done on it down to 1964.

[2] 1.45; 69.2.41–3; 57.3.41.

Senate and Equites which he secured in the Catilinarian crisis and wanted to perpetuate).

The *De re publica* is naturally of great interest to historians. In it Greek ideas of the ideal state encounter the practical wisdom of the Roman *mos maiorum.* Thus Book 3 broaches the question of the basic justice or injustice of the Roman empire. The Romans had long recognized, with their Foreign Praetor and their Law of Nations, that justice transcended national boundaries. The meeting of this practical tradition with Greek (Stoic) ideas of the brotherhood of man and of Natural Law gave impetus to both.

Cicero's Scipio flirts in Book 1 with the idea of monarchy as an element in his composite state. (Plato's philosopher-king would be in mind.) There has been endless discussion as to whether the '*rector*' or '*moderator*' or '*princeps*' of Books 5 and 6 is envisaged as a particular person – Scipio as he might have been if he had not been murdered (see 6.12), or Pompey, or even himself; or, as seems more likely, an ideal *politicus* like that of Plato or Aristotle holding no constitutional position of autarchy. Again, did this dialogue in any way mould or colour the Augustan image of the *princeps*?[1] For us there is a pathetic irony, parallel to that we noted in the *De oratore*, in the thought that among the last of the young men Cicero was so eager to influence was one who was to consent to his proscription, the future Augustus.

The relevance of the *De re publica* to its time lay in its insistence that all men had a duty to serve their country, that no one should put his personal *dignitas* before her interests, and that private morality was applicable to public affairs. We can imagine the impact of this widely read work on the Rome of 52–1, which had just seen, amid Epicurean apathy on the part of many who should have been leaders, rioting between the rival gangs of Clodius and Milo, and a state of emergency such that Pompey had had to be made sole consul. And Cicero meant what he said. In a moral crisis for him soon after, when, as Governor of Cilicia, he decided not to countenance financial oppression of Cypriots by his friend Brutus, he commented to Atticus: 'I prefer to be on good terms with my conscience, especially now that I have given bail for my conduct in the shape of six volumes' (*Att.* 6.1.8).

As literature, what matters in the remains of the *De re publica* is Scipio's dream (see p. 231). To match the Myth of Er at the end of Plato's *Republic* Cicero invented an effective climax. Scipio tells his friends how, as a young man, he stayed with the Numidian king Massinissa, who was devoted to the memory of Scipio Africanus and talked of him far into the night. Africanus had then appeared in a dream to his adoptive grandson and had unfolded to him, from a heavenly vantage-point in the Milky Way, a (mainly Platonic) view of the universe, a presage of Anchises' revelation to Aeneas in

[1] On these debates see Boyancé (1970) ch. IX.

Aeneid 6.[1] 'The starry spheres far surpassed the earth in size. Indeed the earth itself now seemed so small to me that I was disappointed with our empire, no bigger than a spot, as it were, on the surface' (16). The message is, that while you are on earth it is your duty to serve your country, but that human glory is transient *sub specie aeternitatis*; you should set your affection on things above, for there is a reward of immortality in heaven, amid the harmony of the spheres; and that not only for men of action, but for all who have already caught that harmony and reproduced it for mankind. *Mens cuiusque is est quisque* 'the mind is the true man', and that mind is immortal. Nothing in Cicero was to prove more congenial to Christians down the centuries than this vision.

If the *De oratore* is Cicero's *apologia*, the *De re publica* is his *consolatio*. He planned the *De legibus* to follow it. This again was on the analogy of Plato; but whereas Plato in his *Laws* was creating a construct unrelated to the *Republic*, Cicero gives, after a discussion of the nature of law, an account of the actual laws of Rome, with only occasional, if sometimes important, amendments, an appendix in fact to the *De re publica*.[2] The setting is idyllic, and again intentionally reminiscent of Plato's *Phaedrus*. Cicero and his brother, at their native Arpinum in the hills, are talking to Atticus on his first visit there, walking along the bank of the Liris till they come to an island that splits the cold, swift Fibrenus before it plunges into the larger river. There are interesting discussions in Book 3, which deal with magistrates, of the institution of the tribunate (19–26), and of whether voting should be open or secret (33–9). But the dialogue form is purely *pro forma*: indeed the brothers make a joke about this (3.26). The composition of the work was interrupted by Cicero's governorship and the subsequent civil war, and it may not have been published in his lifetime. Out of at least five books only the first three, and they with gaps, have survived.

In 46, when, after the defeat of the Pompeians, Cicero had been finally allowed by the Dictator Caesar to return to Rome, he reverted to the subject of oratory, apparently in reaction to growing criticisms of his style (see p. 240). In the treatise *Orator* he depicted the perfect orator, and also elaborated the rather hurried precepts his Crassus had deigned to vouchsafe in *De oratore* 3; and in the dialogue *Brutus* he traced the history of oratory at Rome up to its culmination in himself. Both are dedicated to Brutus, most promising of the young friends he sought to mould. The following year, 45, was one of great misery for him. He had divorced his wife Terentia after thirty years of marriage, he had for some time been estranged from his much loved brother, and worst of all,

[1] For Cicero's sources and originality see Harder (1929).

[2] His tenor is reactionary. On religion in Book 2 he seems concerned to re-establish even the obsolete, on politics in 3 to reinforce the nobles, priests and censors. Rawson (1973) 342–55.

his daughter Tullia, the apple of his eye, died that February. In an attempt to assuage his grief for her he composed a *Consolatio*, novel in being addressed to himself. Then, encouraged by Brutus and Matius, he conceived the idea of seeking an anodyne in philosophical writing, in presenting Greek philosophy to Latin readers. The result was momentous for Europe. All his life, though more keenly when he was excluded from politics, he had, as he insisted (*Nat. deor.* 1.6–7), been interested in philosophy. This was uncommon at Rome; indeed at one time, he says, there was no statesman apart from Cato who shared this interest with him. He defended it in the prologue to his *De finibus*. Some were against it altogether; some thought it should be studied only in moderation; some could see no point in translating what any interested person could read in Greek. Cicero replied, that not all could read Greek who pretended they could; that if tragedy was worth translating, so was philosophy; and that in any case he did not merely translate, but arranged and criticized the arguments. He wanted to convert people to philosophy. His lost protreptic dialogue was named after a participant who had been in need of such conversion, Hortensius (d. 50). Particularly he hoped to convert young people who might become influential in the state (*Div.* 2.4–5).

We know a good deal about his motives, programme and progress from his letters and his prologues. In most of these works he makes himself a participant. Not being greatly interested, as a practical Roman, in metaphysics, he dealt mainly with ethics. The philosophers whose views he reproduced were mainly Hellenistic ones interested in the soul of man who was no longer primarily citizen of a *polis*; but his claim (*Acad.* 2.3) to go back to Socrates was justified, in view of his sceptical method of enquiry and his emphasis on ethics.[1] His scheme may be described in his own words, from the prologue to *De divinatione* 2, completed shortly after Caesar's murder:

In my *Hortensius* I exhorted my fellow citizens as earnestly as I could to the study of philosophy, and in the four books of my *Academics* I expounded the philosophical system I thought least arrogant and most consistent and refined.[2] And since philosophy rests on the determination of the ultimate good and evil, I clarified that topic in five books (*De finibus bonorum et malorum*), so that readers might understand how the various philosophers had argued against each other. There followed, also in five books, the *Tusculan disputations*, dealing with the essentials of the happy life, the first on despising death, the second on bearing pain, the third on relieving sickness, the fourth on psychological disturbances, and the fifth on the crown of all philosophy, the (Stoic) contention that virtue is in itself sufficient for the happy life. Thereafter I completed

[1] A. E. Douglas, in his sympathetic account in Dorey (1965) 137.

[2] The attempt of Hunt (1954) to show that Cicero's philosophical works are a critical edition in logical order of the lectures he had heard Antiochus (see p. 230) give at the Academy is interesting, but there are too many pieces that do not fit in. The best introduction to these philosophical works is that of Süss (1965).

three books *On the nature of the gods*, comprising all the arguments on that topic, followed by these two books *On divination*; and if, as I intend, I add a work *On fate*, I shall have fully treated this branch of study.

Of the *Hortensius*, which changed Augustine's life and turned him to God (*Conf.* 3.4–7), we have only fragments (about 100). The *Academica*, on the epistemology of the Academy, appeared in two versions, in two and four books respectively. We possess Book 2 of the '*Priora*' and part of Book 1 of the '*Posteriora*'. Cicero also mentions the *De senectute* or *Cato maior*, on old age, and the eulogy (lost) of the younger Cato; but not the lost *De gloria*, in two books, nor the *De legibus*; nor the *De amicitia* or *Laelius* on friendship, and the *De officiis*, which were yet to come. The *De senectute* and *De amicitia*, imaginary discourses by Cato and Laelius rather than dialogue, both short and both dedicated to Atticus, enshrine the quintessence of Ciceronian humanism, and with the *De officiis* were chiefly to represent Cicero for such readers as he had in the Dark and Middle Ages.

Cicero wrote by night and day, since he could not sleep (*Att.* 13.26.2). In twenty months he composed five or more major and several minor philosophical works. Naturally these, apart from the *De senectute* and *De amicitia*, have not the degree of originality, springing from personal experience, of the *De oratore* and *De re publica*, and Cicero is more scrupulous than most ancients in acknowledging his debts. But they are far from being mere compilations from the Greek; without years of meditation behind him he could never have mastered the material so quickly. Their success appears to have been immediate: there were so many other souls at this time who longed to escape into a spiritual world. As philosophy they deal with problems that still beset human beings, even if they have ceased to preoccupy philosophers except perhaps for the post-Aristotelian problem of freewill and that of cognition. But Cicero cannot be said to interest historians of philosophy so much as original thinkers like Plato and Aristotle do.

There is however historical interest in the *De natura deorum* and *De divinatione*, for example, where religion is no more exempt than any other subject from the Academic practice of hearing all sides. Cicero's mentor Scaevola the Pontiff had pragmatically distinguished three kinds of religion, that of the poets, the statesmen and the philosophers. In his poems Cicero introduced that of the poets, in his *De legibus* that of the statesmen, in these later works that of the philosophers. In spite of the cloak of dialogue in some, his views do emerge. Thus in *De divinatione* 2 this augur appropriates to himself, in answer to his brother, the role of demolishing, with Lucretian relish, superstitions he treated with solemn respect in *De legibus* 2. 'But we are alone' he says to his brother, 'so we can search for the truth freely' (*sine inuidia*, 2.28). Augustine commented that what he proclaimed so eloquently in this discussion he would not have dared to breathe in a public speech (*Civ. Dei* 2.30). Cotta in the *De natura deorum* is a pontiff who adheres scrupulously in public to the traditional cults but is largely sceptical about them in private (1.61) – like some Renaissance Pope, and no doubt like Cicero himself. Nevertheless Cicero was careful to distinguish between superstition and true religion (*Div.* 2.148). Again, at the end of the *De natura deorum*, despite his disclaimer at 1.10 (see p. 230), he briefly intimates *in propria persona* that he himself considers the Stoic view put by Balbus in Book 2 'most like the semblance of truth'. Yet he has reservations: although 'the argument from design' convinces him of the existence of a providential deity (indeed outright atheists were very few in antiquity), and he takes his conscience as evidence that the soul is divine and comprehends the divine law (though 'no one has ever owed his virtue to god'), he rejects the (inconsistent) Stoic doctrines of divine interference and determinism because of his predisposition to believe in freewill and the reality of moral choice.[1] The *Tusculans* in particular, though ostensibly a detached exposition of various views, betray by their tone his own commitment to belief in the immortality of the soul. Books 1 and 5 are really emotional declamations. Pain and death were particularly topical subjects at that time.

As literature these works are perhaps not exciting by modern standards. Their significance lies in their having become the medium by which the substance of Greek philosophy was transmitted to the West and kept alive until Greek works were studied in the original again. They are enhanced by the illustrations, literary, historical and anecdotal, that came so readily to Cicero's pen, and by the mastery of language that never failed however fast he wrote. His last and most influential work, astonishing considering that he was now in the forefront of the struggle with Mark Antony, was not a dialogue but a treatise ostensibly addressed to his student son, the *De officiis* (*On moral obligations*). This has therefore a special status as representing his own views, though the first two books are avowedly based on Panaetius; and for once he deviates into dogmatism. Though he incidentally criticizes Caesar (without sparing Pompey), approves of his assassination, and deplores the flouting of the republic by Antony, that is not sufficient reason for supposing the work to have been politically motivated. It carries on from the *De finibus*. Books 1 and 2, somewhat encumbered by repetitions but relieved by Cicero's perennial abundance of illustrations, deal with right (*honestum*) and expediency (*utile*) respectively. Book 3 examines cases of apparent conflict between the two. (There could be no real conflict, for the advantages of expediency are short-term; by doing wrong you harm your own soul.) Book 1 introduces, *à propos the* cardinal virtue of

[1] In the partially extant *De fato* (31ff.). The extant *Paradoxa Stoicorum* shows his interest in Stoicism. It is a rhetorical elaboration of the paradoxes, composed in the spring of 46, probably as an intellectual exercise, and dedicated to Brutus.

temperance, the interesting moral-aesthetic Panaetian doctrine of 'propriety' (*decorum*). Doing what was appropriate to nature in every sphere of life included being true to your own individual nature, insofar as that did not conflict with universal natural morality, and acting consonantly with your own age and status (107–51). The subject of Book 3, casuistry, had for some reason been left aside by Panaetius, but Cicero finds other Hellenistic philosophers to exploit. Though it is less carefully composed, and the problems sometimes recall the fantastic ones beloved of the rhetorical schools, it has a certain interest in airing ancient ideas about many of the practical problems of daily life, such as business ethics.

From the philosophic point of view the work rests on insecure foundations.[1] Nature is assumed to be good. The conflict between the springs of altruism and self-regard is superficially assumed to be easily reconcilable (as in the case of private property and common interest: 1.92). Nevertheless, in its independence of external sanctions for morality, it foreshadows modern ideas of evolutionary ethics; and from the practical point of view its emphasis on strict morality must have been as salutary in its age as it has been since. Cicero proclaims a very high standard based on the brotherhood of man. The *De officiis* laid the foundations of liberal humanism for Europe and the world.

8. LITERARY INFLUENCE IN ANTIQUITY

In dedicating the *De officiis* to his son Cicero said:

> As to the subject matter, use your own judgement (I will not impede you). But by reading my writings you will certainly extend the range of your Latin. . . So I earnestly urge you to read not only my speeches but also my philosophical works, which are now almost as extensive; for while the former have a more forceful style, yet this equable and restrained style is also to be cultivated. (1.2–3)

Nothing could illustrate better how much greater relative importance the ancients attached to style than we do; and historically it has been primarily by his manner that Cicero has won readers, and through this that he has then obtained a hearing for his matter.

Livy advised his son to read Cicero and Demosthenes first and then the authors nearest to them – presumably to form his oratorical style. Though the Augustan poets do not mention Cicero, his memory, as of the opponent and victim of Augustus' last enemy, was allowed to survive in the rhetorical schools. His style too was still admired by some, including the elder Seneca, but not by the *avant-garde*, probably the majority, who preferred the terse and epigrammatic manner which came to be associated with the name of Seneca. The debate

[1] For severe critiques see Hunt (1954) 163–78, and Süss (1965) 351–69.

features in Tacitus' *Dialogue on orators*, Ciceronian in form, at the end of the first century A.D. (Messalla *vs.* Afer). Quintilian could say at that time that Cicero was popularly thought to be '*durus et ineruditus*' (? dry and unsophisticated, unadventurous in language), whereas to him he was '*perfectus*' and 'no longer the name of a man but a synonym for eloquence'. It was his advocacy that established Cicero as the model for Latin prose.[1] The letters also won admirers, such as the younger Pliny and Marcus Aurelius' mentor Fronto. His rehabilitation was permanent but his influence patchy, now in one department, now in another. The great educational ideals embodied in the *De oratore* and Quintilian's *Institutio oratoria* were too ambitious for human weakness. Ironically, it was the *De inventione*, which Cicero had repudiated, and the *Rhetorica ad Herennium*, falsely attributed to him until 1492 ('*Rhetorica prima et secunda*') that kept his reputation as a rhetorician alive in the schools. Between A.D. 800 and 1500 these occur 148 times in extant library catalogues, the *De oratore* only 12 times.[2] By his example however Cicero greatly influenced the style of some of the Christian Fathers, notably Lactantius, whose *Divinae institutiones* (304–13) were called by Jerome 'a river of Ciceronian eloquence', and whom Pico was to dub 'The Christian Cicero'.

[1] *Inst.* 8 *praef.* 26; 10.1.105–12; 2.25; 12.10.45–8.
[2] Bolgar (1954) 396, summarizing M. Manitius' researches.

12

SALLUST

Of Sallust's early life, education, and allegiances we know nothing, except that he embarked on a political career. Limited information becomes available for the years 52–45 B.C., when he was in the thick of the tumults of the period. He appears first in 52 B.C. as a tribune bent on trouble-making. He may already have been an adherent of Caesar. Certainly, when he was expelled from the Senate in 50 B.C. on moral grounds (a convenient pretext for settling political scores), it was to Caesar he turned and whom he served, with little success until 46 B.C., when he distinguished himself in organizing supplies for the African campaign. He was appointed the first governor of Caesar's new African province. There, it is alleged, he speedily acquired a vast fortune, and, on his return to Rome, faced charges of extortion, but, thanks to bribery or connivance, was never brought to trial. In 45 B.C. or not much later he withdrew from public life, and, desiring to occupy his leisure in a befitting way, set about writing history. In his first work he claims that he abandoned politics in disgust at the wholesale corruption in which he had been enmeshed (*Cat.* 3.3–4.2). In all his three works he passes stern and lofty judgements upon standards of conduct. His detractors were not slow to remark on the apparent hypocrisy of an adulterer and peculator transmuted into a custodian of public and private morality (e.g. Varro *apud* Gell. 17.18, *Invect. in Sall. passim*, Suet. *Gramm.* p. 112 R). The discrepancy still troubles a few modern critics. Others, the majority, dismiss the matter one way or another. The stories about Sallust, some say, are wholly unreliable, nothing more than echoes of the virulent personal abuse conventionally exchanged between politicians of his time. Again, we are told, even if the stories are true, they are immaterial: a man whose own behaviour is deplorable may yet make an excellent observer and moralist. Witness Francis Bacon. These arguments have their force, but do not expunge all doubts. Can we brush aside the allegations against Sallust, insecure though they are, when we enquire into his honesty as a historian?

Sallust's first two works, which survive entire, are monographs concerned with limited themes of special interest. His own statements (*Cat.* 4.2–3) suggest that he had written nothing of moment before the *Bellum Catilinae* (commonly known as the 'Catiline'), published after Caesar's death and probably after Cicero's. The *Bellum Iugurthinum* (commonly known as the 'Iugurtha') followed within about two years, if we assume slow but consistent progress in writing. Then Sallust moved to history on a larger scale, starting his narrative in 78 B.C. He had reached 67 B.C. by Book 5, which remained incomplete at his death. The loss of his *Histories* is grievous indeed, but enough fragments have come down to us, including speeches, letters, and important parts of the prooemium, to permit a reasonable understanding of the work's scope and character.

Evidence of the lively interest which Sallust provoked is afforded by three spurious writings, all concocted in the rhetorical schools a generation or two later. The *Invective against Cicero*, like its companion piece against Sallust, ascribed to Cicero, is a clumsy imposture, designed to make schoolboys titter, but the *Epistles to the aged Caesar on the state*[1] are quite accomplished fabrications. The author (or authors) made a tolerable, if imperfect, attempt to catch Sallust's historical style, forgetting that no one with the slightest taste would have used this style in letters. The *Epistles* have some slender interest as sources for the political thought of the early Principate, and they contain some pointedly expressed maxims of statecraft, still occasionally quoted, but otherwise they are only worth perusal as exercises in imitation. Surprisingly some scholars of repute have considered them genuine.

Sallust was the first recognized classic amongst Roman historians, avidly read, admired and abused, immensely influential on many diverse writers, and cited more often than any Latin prose author, Cicero alone excepted. But he was not in any obvious sense a pioneer. Romans had been writing history for over a century, and the main types were firmly established. Annalists, like Gellius and Piso, had long since begun to put flesh on the bare bones of tradition. A few at least, for instance Valerius Antias, were not punctilious about the truth, if lies would better reinforce a case or divert the reader. These men took Rome's whole history for their subject, as did Livy who used and antiquated them. Others chose particular topics, notably Coelius Antipater, who wrote of the second Punic War, or, like Rutilius Rufus and Cornelius Sisenna, related contemporary events and their own experiences. An appreciable range of interests is evident from the start, for Cato the Elder, the father of Latin historiography, accommodated in his *Origins* both speculation about the remote past and outspoken comment on recent history. Altogether there are few areas into which Sallust's predecessors had not boldly ventured. And they did not write casually. Even that bare, repetitive, and seemingly artless phraseology found in fragments of the earlier annalists may have been cultivated as appro-

[1] This title is incredible in itself, but, being of uncertain date, cannot be used as an argument against authenticity.

priate to the dignity of theme and narrator. Others, notably Coelius and Sisenna, preferred distinct and colourful styles. Sisenna, for whom Sallust has some regard (*Iug.* 95.2), was an innovator in language (he clearly fascinated the grammarians) and perhaps no mean historian. Sallust did not attempt to treat again the social and civil wars which Sisenna had narrated, but took up the story where he had left off. Acknowledged veneration for Cato (*Hist.* 1.4) should not obscure Sallust's likely debts to predecessors nearer in time. For adventures in expression, if for nothing else, Sisenna provided a precedent and example.

Oratory at Rome reached its maturity a generation or more before history. That simple fact largely explains why Cicero's remarks about history (*De or.* 2.51ff., *Leg.* 1.6ff., *Fam.* 5.12) are prejudiced and condescending. He sees the further development of Latin prose only as a modification of the oratory which he has perfected: hence for him history is an orator's task, and it must be couched in a style much resembling his own. In *Fam.* 5.12, anxious as always to have his consulship celebrated, Cicero outlines the attractions for a historian of a circumscribed period or topic, and explains to Lucceius how effectively a unified, varied and elaborate work may be centred upon an individual. Ironically it was Sallust, not Lucceius, who took up the challenge, displaced Cicero from the pre-eminent importance in the Catilinarian affair which he claimed, and devised a viable style which was utterly alien from Cicero's. In *Leg.* 1.6ff. Cicero observes that talented Romans had devoted themselves to political and forensic oratory, at the expense of history. Sallust, no modest man, was ready to redress the balance, but he still felt obliged, in his prooemia, to justify his decision. As yet historians were little esteemed.

The prooemia of Sallust's three works, together with his digression at *Iug.* 41–2, have engendered endless debate. Quintilian (*Inst.* 3.8.9) affirmed that in the *Catiline* and *Iugurtha* Sallust *nihil ad historiam pertinentibus principiis orsus est* 'began with prooemia not at all appropriate to history', in other words more suited for oratory or philosophy.[1] That is unfair. Greek historians, if not Roman, had often enough wandered into general discussion or generously sketched a background or praised history as a worthwhile avocation. Sallust may more fairly be criticized, in his *Catiline* at least, for the disproportionate bulk of introductory matter in a comparatively short composition. Whether or not the prooemia accord with any preconceived notions of the historical genre, they certainly raise some problems. Are the ideas expressed relevant to the narrative? And have these ideas any intrinsic interest, either through originality or as commonplaces which illuminate the intellectual preoccupations of Sallust's time?

We find in the prooemia a texture of loosely related themes. On the most general level Sallust assesses the value and scope of human activity, labouring

[1] Some consider (implausibly) that Quintilian means 'irrelevant to his narrative'.

over distinction between body and soul and physical as opposed to mental achievements. He proceeds to ask how men's talents may best be employed in the service of the state, accepting without question conventional Roman views on discipline, moderation, and honour. He leaves us in no doubt of the standards by which he will pass judgement in his narrative. But first, since he agrees with Cato that prominent men must render account even for their leisure, he must justify himself and defend the writing of history. In the *Catiline* he is still apologetic, but in the *Iugurtha* he takes an aggressive stance and dares to claim that historiography is quite as useful to the state as anything which politicians do. Of the purport of the prooemium to the *Histories* we can only speculate. It may have been cooler and more assured, though it contained some biting remarks (e.g. 1.5, 1.13). Sallust seems to be concerned with much the same matters in all three prooemia, and one theme at least, thanks to the preservation of certain fragments of *Hist.* 1, we can follow right through. It is the decadence of Rome, Sallust's obsession or (to speak more politely) the firmest nexus of his thought.

Sallust begins to talk directly of general moral decadence at *Cat.* 5.8, where something more than innate depravity is needed to explain Catiline's behaviour. He then (*Cat.* 6–13) offers a summary account of Rome's social and political history. While honour and patriotism directed the conduct of individuals, the state flourished (*Cat.* 7). Latterly, however, the Roman commonwealth, once so admirable, had become utterly corrupt (*Cat.* 10.6: cf. *Hist.* 1.16, Liv. *praef.* 7–10). Ambition, greed, and luxury (with, or resulting from foreign influences) had undermined the old virtues, and fortune, always wilful (*Cat.* 8.1), had grown positively malevolent (*Cat.* 10.1). Removal of external threats, completed by the destruction of Carthage in 146 B.C., permitted Roman degeneration to proceed unchecked (*Cat.* 10.1, *Iug.* 41.2–3). Before that turning-point there had been discipline and concord. These generalizations, even on cursory inspection, seem a little ramshackle: Sallust has thrown together, but not reconciled, several different ideas. For instance, he employs *fortuna* ('fortune', 'chance') only as a transient motif, dramatic and vague: the thought is not worked out. Again, he reflects the confusion of his sources and contemporaries when they sought to establish an exact time for the beginning of Rome's moral decline. Some authorities set it well before 146 B.C., others as late as Sulla's return from the East (cf. *Cat.* 11.4–8). We may easily perceive that all these views are over-simple and unhistorical, and perhaps Sallust began to realize the fact himself. At *Hist.* 1.11 he admits that many bitter dissensions existed from the beginning of the state, and at *Hist.* 1.7 ascribes such dissensions to a basic flaw in human nature. Very little weight can be given to fragments divorced from a context, but these fragments may show that Sallust's opinions (or sources) had changed for the better.

Many of the ideas found in Sallust's prooemia can be traced a long way back, to Plato, Xenophon, and Isocrates amongst others, but his immediate sources are not easily fixed. Several later Greeks had discussed the development and decline of states. Polybius saw in a balanced constitution the foundation of Rome's success, and foresaw what would happen if this balance were lost: disorder and a scramble for power. Sallust probably read Polybius, though he must have found Polybius' flat and colourless writing very uncongenial. Posidonius, historian, philosopher, and teacher, may well have appealed more strongly.[1] Two items particularly suggest a connexion with Posidonius, Sallust's quasi-evolutionary view of society, with idealization of primitive life (*Cat.* 2.1, 9.1), and his notion of the self-sufficiency of the mind (*Iug.* 2.3). And Sallust shares with Posidonius a belief in the salutary effect of external constraint upon Rome (cf. Diod. Sic. 34.33), as well as his generally moralistic approach (cf. Diod. Sic. 37.2). But Posidonius favoured the *optimates*: here at least Sallust parted company from him. Again, Stoic elements in his thought do not prove that Sallust was an adherent of that school, for other elements can equally well be used to suggest obligation to the Epicureans. If anything he is an eclectic, though he probably never thought about the matter. One important contemporary influence, Cicero, can too readily be neglected: antipathy does not preclude exploitation. Sallust probably knew Cicero's published writings extremely well, and Cicero must have been a major source of information for the *Catiline* and *Histories*. Again, in his *De re publica* and elsewhere, Cicero, like Sallust, touches upon the political problems immediately confronting Rome. They have some common ground: both, for instance, consider that parts of the second century B.C. were good periods, morally and politically.

As essays in historical analysis the prooemia are far from admirable. Sallust talks too much in extremes and makes many unwarranted assumptions. He is sometimes precipitate and heated in his opinions. But one must respect the forthrightness, indeed courage, of a man who, writing under the second triumvirate, castigated in scathing terms the pernicious effects of concentration of power in a few hands (*Iug.* 3). Again, while Sallust often rambles haphazardly, several ideas debated in the prooemia relate closely to the narrative. One instance is the idea that terminology, as well as standards, can be perverted (*Cat.* 12.1, 52.11, *Hist.* 1.12, 3.48.13), borrowed from Thucydides' discussion of the dissensions at Corcyra (3.82), a passage by which Sallust was deeply fascinated. Another is provided by Sallust's incessant concern to define and appraise virtue. At *Cat.* 7.5 *uirtus omnia domuerat* 'virtue had conquered all' summarizes the idealized picture of early Rome which Sallust too unquestioningly accepted. Where, he wants to know, may such qualities be found in

[1] We should, here as elsewhere, equally resist the current tendency to discount Posidonius' influence and the earlier tendency to magnify it.

recent history? An answer is supplied at *Cat.* 53, where Sallust compares Caesar and Cato, the two statesmen whom alone of their contemporaries he regarded as cast in heroic mould. Others then, including Cicero, fell short. The same question is posed repeatedly in the *Iugurtha*, and more searchingly debated. The nobles had counted honour and esteem as their inherited perquisites, but Marius' achievements had finally shattered the illusion: only individual virtue could secure pre-eminence.

At the outset (*Cat.* 4.2) Sallust planned to write *carptim* 'selectively', rather than attempt continuous history. It is not his declared aim to look for new facts. Indeed *Cat.* 4.3–4 may be taken to suggest that he was avid to redeploy familiar and, in particular, sensational material. How far his conception of his task broadened or matured is hard to assess. The *Iugurtha* certainly covers a much longer period than the *Catiline*, but the coverage is arbitrary and patchy. In his *Histories* Sallust had presumably to handle the whole history of the period, and could no longer select freely. If that is so, the change of form from the monograph reflects a different, arguably more serious approach. But the larger scope of his narrative in the *Histories*, while it brought obligations, also allowed much latitude. Sallust could embark on digressions, with good precedent (Herodotus for instance): his descriptions of places and peoples, particularly those around the Black Sea (*Hist.* 3.61–80), were celebrated and prompted imitation. Again, he seems to have coped with major and protracted stories (notably Sertorius and Mithridates) without anxiety over tight adherence to an annalistic framework based on the consular year at Rome.

Sempronius Asellio (fr. 1 P) had long since asserted that mere narration is not enough: a historian must lay bare causes and motives. Cicero elaborated the same point (*De or.* 2.63), adding that much attention must also be paid to personality. Sallust tries to meet those requirements. He wants to know the truth, he is alert, trenchant, and spiteful, and, like his model and inspiration Thucydides, he is interested in the realities, not the façades, of political history, in underlying as well as immediate explanations. But a resolve to probe and question is in itself of little use: insight and penetration are essential. Sallust is but modestly endowed with these qualities, and detachment, the best of Thucydides' virtues, he can hardly claim at all. The Roman critics were not wholly misguided in making a comparison between the two historians, but they failed to draw a just conclusion, unfavourable to Sallust, from it.

Some modern writers regard Sallust as primarily a literary artist. They argue, for instance, that he conceived of the *Catiline* as a tragedy: it presents the inevitable fall of a man of heroic calibre, vitiated by a moral flaw, who bravely sustains a hopeless cause to the end. The work admits such interpretation, but we cannot appraise it in these terms alone. Indeed Sallust himself prescribes the terms in which he must be judged, as a historian who solemnly declares that he will try to tell the truth (*Cat.* 4.3). At *Iug.* 95.2 he says that Sisenna, for all his merits, did not speak freely. Does Sallust then speak without bias, prejudice, or distortion? Does he represent men and events honestly?

It has been alleged that Sallust's picture of the late Republic is gravely distorted, in selection and treatment of material, by intense bias against the *optimates*. Others go further and maintain that the *Catiline* is a partisan tract, designed to exonerate Caesar from complicity in the Catilinarian affair and generally to show him in a good light. Others again believe that the *Catiline* is a riposte to Cicero's *De consiliis suis* 'On his courses of action', released after the author's death. In this work Cicero may have revealed embarrassing ramifications of Catiline's conspiracy which he had for long been obliged to suppress, but Sallust would not leave Cicero's account unchallenged. In reply to these and other criticisms Sallust's defenders assert that he is fair and impartial, or that, if he is biased, bias is not the same as falsification or an intention to mislead, or again that incompetence rather than bias is the charge properly to be directed against him.

That Sallust is hostile to the majority of *optimates* cannot be denied: he commonly describes them as arrogant, venal, and useless. Further, he appears to consider the whole political system utterly rotten. Men strove for their own selfish ends, not the good of the state. Sallust does not applaud or whitewash any party, but looks for merit in individuals, of whatever affiliations. We need not give great weight to the virulent attacks on the ruling oligarchy found in certain speeches, notably those of Lepidus and Macer (*Hist.* 1.55 and 3.48). They are aptly contrived for the speakers and occasions, like the letter of Mithridates (*Hist.* 4.69). Sallust could not draw a sharp and consistent distinction between corrupt *optimates* and virtuous *populares*, since several major figures would simply not fit any such scheme, amongst them Cicero, Caesar, and Cato. Cicero showed that talent could still find a way to the top, and Sallust notes (*Cat.* 23.5–6) that, though the nobility loathed new men, they had to back this one in a time of crisis. But Cicero's sympathies were or became optimate, and to many who held other views he was a *bête noire*. Nevertheless Sallust treats him perfectly fairly, without warmth indeed (Cicero's self-praise quenched that), but with all due acknowledgement of his services. Sallust may seem to disregard Cicero's speeches against Catiline, but for this there is a special reason. The speeches were available and well known (cf. *Cat.* 31.6) and could not appropriately have been adjusted to the fabric and compass of Sallust's monograph. Caesar obtains special prominence at *Cat.* 49 and in the senatorial debate which Sallust proceeds to record (*Cat.* 50–2), but he is not made out to be a commanding figure generally. And in the memorable comparison of Caesar and Cato which follows the debate (*Cat.* 53–4), Cato arguably comes off better. *Esse quam uideri bonus malebat* 'he preferred to be rather than to seem good' is high praise of the man whom Caesar most detested, and it would be incongruous in a work intended as an apologia for Caesar.

In chapters 18–19 of his *Catiline* Sallust sketchily records an abortive attempt at revolution two years before the main conspiracy. Catiline and various others are alleged to have been involved. As Sallust narrates it this 'first conspiracy' is a flimsy tissue of improbabilities. Straightforward interpretation of the evidence we have suggests that in 65 B.C. Catiline was still seeking power by normal, constitutional means. He resorted to force only when these means had finally failed him. If Sallust has a bias here, it is against Catiline. But that is improbable, for he presents Catiline as a man of ability and courage, albeit catastrophically misdirected. The truth is rather that he saw Catiline's career only with the narrow vision of hindsight. Catiline must play the role of villain from first to last: thus he will better point a moral and adorn a lurid tale. Gullibility, not bias, explains the inadequacies of chapters 18–19. Having no reliable material relating to an earlier conspiracy, Sallust collects some half-remembered rumours from the political warfare of the 60s and makes a patchwork of hearsay.

Chapter 25 of the *Catiline* presents no less of a problem. Why is it there at all? In 24.3–4 Sallust mentions various types of people induced to join the conspiracy, including several women of bad character. Then (in 25) he says that one of these women was Sempronia, and gives her a full-scale characterization, comparable with that of Catiline himself (5). She was high born, cultured, witty and fascinating, but also wanton, unscrupulous, and extremely dangerous. The sketch is superb, and justly admired. But Sempronia, who has not appeared in the narrative before, will only once appear again. The extraordinary oddity of this fact protrudes inescapably. We cannot well argue that Sallust wanted a female counterpart for Catiline, and count that a justification. A historian should only make use of a 'female lead' if she belongs to the story, as Tacitus, masterfully imitating Sallust's sketch (*Ann.* 13.45), accords Poppaea the prominence which she merited or may be claimed to have merited historically. There are only two reasonable explanations of Sallust's Sempronia. He may have been so enamoured of the characterization that he would not cut it out, although it impaired the unity of his monograph. Alternatively, realizing that his contemporaries would know of Sempronia's reputation and be titillated by a colourful portrait, he obligingly provided one, indifferent to the example of Thucydides who attempted to write for all time, not for the gossipmongers of his day. In a work clumsily planned as a whole Sempronia is the worst blemish.

The *Iugurtha* unfolds more simply than the *Catiline*, but still has enough complexities. In particular Sallust must simultaneously keep track of events in Africa and political developments in Rome, and explain their interrelation.

There is here much risk of confusion over chronology or between cause and effect. Again, Sallust cannot or does not entirely centre his narrative upon one person. His focus shifts and, though Iugurtha holds his interest for considerable periods, fixes in the end on Marius. Once Iugurtha has at last fallen into Roman hands, no more is said about him: we do not hear how he was dragged in the triumphal procession and then ignominiously strangled by the public executioner. That would have been a fittingly melodramatic conclusion, if he had conceived of the *Iugurtha* as a self-contained entity, a story in its own right. Since he chose to conclude with reference to the imminent peril from northern invaders and the hopes pinned on Marius, he evidently regarded his monograph as concerned with an integral segment of Roman history, to be related to the whole.

In the *Iugurtha* praise and censure are meted out equally freely. Metellus, a great aristocrat, is duly commended for his distinguished services to the state. On the other hand, Marius is by no means glorified. While his achievements obtain full recognition and we are left in no doubt that his career presages the end of the old order, he appears as brash, conceited, and selfish, a demagogue rather than a statesman. Again, when he briefly talks of the Gracchi (42), Sallust mixes criticism with approval,[1] suggesting that they were rash and over-confident, and proceeds to damn party strife generally. As far as individuals are concerned, the *Iugurtha* seems to give a dispassionate, if selective, record of a controversial period. But, when Sallust deals with wider matters, his judgement can be singularly obtuse. He supposes, for instance, that the Senate of the late second century B.C. was corrupt and venal, and finds in this venality the main reason for delay of decisive measures against Iugurtha. That view was doubtless much fostered by the *populares*. Sallust should have weighed another explanation against it. Further entanglement in Africa and the dissensions of Massinissa's dynasty would bring Rome trouble, expense, and no very certain profit. And Rome had no binding obligation to intervene. The Senate's long hesitation can be imputed to good sense and statecraft. Instead of canvassing such possibilities, Sallust opted for a crudely biased or, at least, unduly simple account. One wonders how many sources he used and suspects that they were very few.

The elder Cato excluded the names of Roman leaders from his narrative: honour and glory, he contended, belonged to the people as a whole. That view, unrealistic even in Cato's time, had been utterly antiquated by events. Those who had seen Marius and Sulla, Pompey, Caesar and Octavian could not doubt the immense importance of individuals. Naturally, then, the shift of power from an oligarchy to a succession of dynasts is directly reflected in historical writing. Detailed characterization becomes indispensable and history

[1] The interpretation of this passage, particularly 42.3 *sed bono...uincere*, is very problematic.

moves closer to biography. Sallust was exceptionally good at depicting character, both directly, by means of introductory sketch (cf. Sen. *Suas.* 6.21) and supplementary comments, and indirectly, by means of speeches, report of the opinion of others, and revealing items of behaviour included in his narrative. But, since his approach was strongly moralistic, we sometimes find overlap, even confusion, between description of individual traits of personality and exemplification of the predictable qualities of certain types of men in certain situations, be they reactionaries, liberals, or revolutionaries. Let us revert, for illustration, to his treatment of Catiline.

Catiline is introduced (5.1–8) in a sketch of monumental gravity, abruptly and harshly phrased, censorious in tone, brief and ponderous. Antithesis supports and enlivens the description: great physical and mental power opposed to depravity of disposition, greed to acquire opposed to profusion in spending, adequate eloquence opposed to deficiency in sense, and so on. No doubt Catiline had some or all of these characteristics, but he also represents for Sallust a type of person allegedly to be found all too often in the aftermath of Sulla, in that he was unprincipled, self-seeking, and insatiable. Three features stand out in Sallust's sketch: determined courage, truculence verging on megalomania, and acceptance of perverted values. Catiline shows conspicuous powers of leadership, by holding together a motley following in face of great odds, and makes a good end, in traditional Roman manner (60.7). But ferocity and incipient dementia are recorded at the start (5.7), and the notion of madness is developed at 15.4–5, a good instance of supplementary direct characterization. According to Sallust, madness finally drove Catiline to desperate measures. That is questionable: Catiline struggled long to win the consulship legitimately (26.1), and his later conduct, desperate perhaps, was hardly mad. To the last he claimed to stand for a cause and could calculate what might be to its advantage: thus he rejected the enrolment of slaves (56.5). Sallust contradicts himself, or at least his efforts in psychological analysis are ill attuned with his narrative. If, as he would have us believe, Catiline is a criminal lunatic, he ought to be shown behaving as such. No doubt Sallust drew on the stock-in-trade of political invective, which included accusations of fury and insanity, as well as lust for regal power (5.6). But truculence is a quality which Catiline really seems to have possessed: he displayed it before the Senate in confrontation with Cicero (31.9) and retained it in death (61.4). As to perversion of values, Catiline is made to assert that right is on his side, that he is a victim of enmity and faction (35.3). Hence he feels obliged to defend his dignity and honour. It was to dignity and honour that Caesar was later to appeal, as justification for a greater civil war. How much better then was Caesar than Catiline? Sallust hardly intended us to make this comparison, but it is there to be made.

Sallust determined to forge a prose style for history unlike anything Rome had known before, and he succeeded where Sisenna, who was led by the same ambition, had failed. Wanting to be different, Sallust reacted not only against the style of Cicero, periodic, expansive, and rhythmical, but also against the movement, dominant in his day, towards standardization of vocabulary, grammar, and syntax. For such a rebel the end justifies the means. Provided he can write excitingly and colourfully, Sallust cares little what sources or devices he resorts to, except that he does not, as some have supposed, readily employ colloquialisms. Ancient critics recorded the most distinctive features of his style: archaism, brevity, abruptness, and novelty (see, e.g., Suet. *Gramm.* p. 108 R, Quint. *Inst.* 4.2.45, 8.3.29, 10.1.32, Gell. 4.15.1). One might add pure idiosyncrasy, for there is much of that. And he seems willing to admit or affect Grecisms, from which his contemporaries were shying away. Altogether he offers a daring pastiche, outlandish and grotesque, pungent and arresting.

Archaism appears not only in Sallust's choice of words, but also in variety of construction, where one construction had become normal, and in loose, paratactic sentence-structure, best paralleled in authors of the earliest period (e.g. Cato). Since Sallust is writing about recent and nearly contemporary history, he is plainly not attempting to find archaic clothing for archaic themes, as Livy may be said to do. His purpose cannot be explained simply. No doubt he seeks to enhance his expression, to lend it special dignity: the Romans believed (and we have no reason to doubt) that archaism could have that effect. Again, he wants to show that he at least will use the abundant riches of older Latin, which others were increasingly denying themselves. But above all, by employing parataxis and avoiding the rhythmical patterns beloved by orators, he would fain appear straightforward and honest, like the most artless of the old annalists. The trappings of rhetoric do not become a man who professes to tell the truth bluntly and briefly.

The brevity which Sallust pursued and often attained made a great impression on Roman readers, to judge by the numerous references to it. For this quality in particular he was thought to rival Thucydides (see, e.g., Sen. *Contr.* 9.1.13–14). Of course brevity takes several forms. There is compression of much thought into few words: Sallust, like Thucydides, can be admirably pregnant. Then there is haste to tell what has to be told, which results in selective use of material and excision of detail. In this Sallust is only too adept, but an imitator, Velleius, surpassed him in precipitancy. Again, there is economy of expression proper, which consists in omission of connectives, ellipse of auxiliary verbs, and so on. Sallust is economical, but he does not reject every superfluity. Indeed certain features of his style make for pleonasm, particularly the asyndetic lists and alliterating combinations in which he so much delights.

Many asyndeta do not effect brevity as such, but rather an impression of jerkiness and spontaneity. The words seem to pour out uncontrolled, and often an afterthought will be loosely appended. These aspects of brevity are closely allied with the abruptness of sentence-ending and switch of construction which still astonishes those who are habituated to smoothly articulated and inevitably rounded periods. Sallust clearly liked to surprise his readers and keep them wide awake: his staccato phraseology, highly conducive to point and epigram, was ideally suited for the purpose. And so too was his aversion from balanced phrases and clauses and his distaste for certain conventional terms, which he paraphrases, varies, or turns back to front. The results of his tortuous manipulations of word and phrase must have jarred horribly, as he intended, on many contemporary ears.

That Sallust should be an innovator as well as an archaizer is perfectly explicable: he claims the same freedom to develop and experiment with his medium as was exercised by the early writers. Hence he coins words, extends usage, and assimilates unfamiliar idiom. In his mixture of archaism and novelty he may be compared with Lucretius. But, while Lucretius is often compelled to experiment by his subject matter and metre, Sallust's innovations are largely a matter of free choice. He was anti-suggestible in the extreme and spurned convention. Hence his aggressive and tetchy style reflects the very nature of the man.

Sallust's outspokenness and self-will commanded the attention of contemporaries and posterity. He puts over his personality, real or assumed, very forcefully: witness the violent opening words of the *Iugurtha*. A man who writes in so striking a manner is not readily ignored, and Sallust was being blunt and provocative at a time when most people were beginning to temper their words. Again his language and style, being pointedly, indeed contemptuously, opposed to the main fashion of his age, could not fail to be exciting. He was hated by some, enthusiastically imitated by others (see Sen. *Epist.* 114.17–18). And he posed an embarrassing problem for teachers, like Quintilian, who could neither pass him by nor easily reconcile his writing with the ideals of style they tried to inculcate. Quintilian finds a convenient way out by commending Sallust for advanced pupils, but not beginners (*Inst.* 2.5.19). Most of the critical comment on Sallust which survives from antiquity relates to his expression, not his thought. But some writers, and those the weightiest, believed that he had much to say of moment. Tacitus adopted his sceptical and disenchanted view of Roman political life, and Augustine found in his observations on the nature and causes of Rome's decadence congenial material to employ in argument over the reasons for the city's final collapse. Again, Sallust has largely contributed to determining the way in which the history of the later Republic is conceived of in modern times.

Sallust has faults, some serious, some venial. His prooemia are pretentious, but for the main part barren of new ideas. In his narrative we can detect inconsistency and inaccuracies. Again, his selection of material is often wilful, occasionally inexplicable. Further, while extreme bias or partisanship may be discounted, he can fairly be convicted of lack of detachment and historical perspective. He is no Thucydides, and only Roman literary jingoists would dream of placing him in that rank. Pollio and others derided him for plagiarism (Suet. *Gramm.* p. 108 R, Quint. *Inst.* 8.3.29), a conventional jibe, but perhaps not so wide of the mark, if we consider not merely borrowing of words from Cato but also use of ideas pillaged from Greek sources. Sallust was outrageous and irrepressible, a humbug and an egotist, resolved to make his mark on Latin literature. Whatever his faults, his achievements were solid and enduring. By his fierce individualism he won a firmer place in the Roman educational tradition than the temperate and compromising Livy ever attained. He, more than anyone, prevented the style and attitudes of Cicero from becoming canonical for prose-writing in general, he enriched the Latin language at a time when it was most in danger of impoverishment, and he secured the continuation at Rome of the stern and uncompromising tradition of historiography, created by Thucydides, which rhetoricians and romantics alike would happily have discarded.

13

CAESAR

C. Julius Caesar's surviving output comprises seven books on the Gallic Wars (*Commentarii rerum gestarum*) and three on the Civil Wars. They are remarkable not only for the light which they throw on the man and on the history of the time, but as works of art.

The Commentary, as a form of literature, had a long history. Its Greek precursor was the *hypomnema* (or memoir), a term applied to official dispatches, minutes, administrative reports, private papers or even diaries. It was a narrative statement of facts for record purposes. It was distinct from History which was composed within a moralistic framework and with conscious literary art. Cicero, for instance, offered to submit *commentarii* of his consulship of 63 B.C. to L. Lucceius to turn into a history (Cicero, *Fam.* 5.12.10). The Romans, however, had a much greater interest in biography, as can be sensed from their funeral masks and inscriptions, from their portraiture and from the popularity of books dealing with historical examples of good and bad conduct; and Roman statesmen developed the Commentary into a factual account of their achievements which was to be published for their own self-justification and for the benefit of their descendants. We know of such works written in the generation before Caesar by M. Aemilius Scaurus, Q. Lutatius Catulus, P. Rutilius Rufus, and, above all, the dictator Sulla.

This is the literary background to the *Commentaries* on the Gallic Wars and on the Civil Wars. The seven books on the Gallic Wars cover the years 58 to 52 B.C., a period which witnessed Caesar's systematic subjugation of the whole of Gaul. Book 1 deals with the defeat of the Helvetii and, separately, of the German Ariovistus, 58 B.C.; Book 2 with the revolt of the Gallic tribes and his desperate encounter with the Nervii; Book 3 with the suppression of the Veneti, a coastal tribe of west Gaul; Book 4 with invasions across the Rhine and operations against rebel Gallic leaders, Indutiomarus and Ambiorix; Book 6 with continued action against Ambiorix, and Book 7 with the full-scale revolt of Vercingetorix, culminating in his siege and capitulation at Alesia in 52 B.C. The work was published some time the following year and this fact is important in understanding its nature. At that time Caesar was anxious to secure the consulship of 49 B.C. but under Roman law he was required to lay down his command before he was eligible to stand for office. During that period, however, he would no longer have been immune from prosecution, and he had many enemies anxious to foil his ambition. So in 51 B.C. he proposed to the Senate that as an exceptional measure his proconsulship should be extended to cover that period and thus shield him from attack. The publication of the *Commentaries* was timed to assert his claim on the gratitude of his fellow-countrymen and to display his *dignitas*, the Roman quality of achievement which merits recognition by high office. It will also have appealed, as did Tacitus' *Agricola*, to the imagination of an educated public fascinated by the remote and the unknown, as Gaul then was.

The work must then have been completed quickly, and we know that Caesar was a very fast writer. But it is disputed whether the whole work was composed in one year or whether it had been written year by year and was only put into final form for publication in 51 B.C. Various indications make the latter more probable, especially since one would in any case expect war-diaries and dispatches to be written up as each campaign took place. In Book 3.17–27 Caesar recounts the operations of his lieutenant, Q. Titurius Sabinus, in a way that seems based on a detailed discussion between the two men. Sabinus was killed in 54 B.C. Each of the books is self-contained, dealing with one year's action, and no book contains a forward reference to a later book. Finally, there are significant differences in style between Book 1 and Book 7, which suggests the passage of years. Word-usage changes (e.g. *ab imo* 'from the bottom' gives way to *ab infimo* (7.19.1, 73.5)), the syntax becomes less stereotyped and freer, direct speech is introduced instead of the formalized reported speech. Evidence of Caesar's editorial activity in preparing the work for publication can be found in the insertion of several digressions of a geographical kind (notably 4.1–3 on the Suebi, 5.12–14 on Britain, 6.11–28 on the Hercynian Forest). The Caesarian authorship of these has been doubted on the grounds that they contain information that was not known until after Caesar's time but this is mere speculation, and it is more likely that Caesar drew on a written scholarly source to add background information to his narrative.

The *Gallic Wars* was a statement of Caesar's achievements. That he had detractors is beyond doubt (at one point he alludes to them (*Bell. Gall.* 1.44.12); some of Catullus' poems are far from favourable, and criticism, even scandal, is preserved in Suetonius' *Life*), and Asinius Pollio alleged that Caesar had made many mis-statements in his *Commentaries*. But Caesar had no need to distort the facts to enhance his reputation: indeed he would have been too easily refuted if he had tried. So far as the actual events are concerned, his account of what happened is sober and factual. There is only one passage where a real conflict of evidence exists. In *Bell. Gall.* 1.12 Caesar described his defeat of the

Tigurini on the river Arar, making no mention of his lieutenant Labienus. Subsequently Labienus, who ultimately deserted Caesar in the Civil Wars, claimed the credit for the victory (Plutarch, *Caesar* 18.1). Scholars have attempted to find other falsifications or distortions but with more ingenuity than success. Did Caesar, for instance, cross the Thames with an elephant – a detail supplied by Polyaenus (8.23.5), but not mentioned by Caesar himself? Where there is obscurity or uncertainty, it may usually be attributed to the difficulty which Caesar will have had in finding out the facts or understanding in such a fluid type of guerrilla warfare what was actually going on. Also, it is easy to be misled by the convention, which Caesar adopted from Xenophon's *Anabasis*, of always referring to himself in the third person. This gives an air of objectivity to what is a personal, autobiographical account.

The overwhelming impression of the book is its clarity and precision, a quality which Cicero, no friend, instantly recognized when he wrote of it: *nihil est pura et inlustri breuitate dulcius* 'nothing is more pleasing than unaffected and lucid brevity' (*Brutus* 262). He had had the same literary tutors as Cicero – the perfectionist grammarian M. Antonius Gnipho (Suetonius, *Gramm.* 7) and the most famous rhetorician of his time Molon (Plutarch, *Caesar* 3). The effect is achieved in two main ways. Firstly, the style is one of great simplicity. Set phrases are used over and over again because they do their duty adequately – *certior factus est* 'he was informed', *quae cum ita essent* 'since this was so', *his rebus cognitis* 'when this had been found out', and so on. The syntax is equally clear-cut and formal. Whereas Livy enjoys variety of language, Caesar dispenses with synonyms. Thus Livy uses *gradum referre* and *pedem referre* 'to retreat' interchangeably, Caesar only uses *pedem referre*. Livy has *ad ultimum*, *ad extremum* and *ad postremum*, all in the sense of 'finally', Caesar only has *ad extremum*. There are a number of comparative expressions in Latin meaning 'as if' – *uelut (si)*, *perinde ac (si)*, *haud secus quam (si)*, *tamquam si* – which Livy employs indiscriminately; only *uelut si* is found in Caesar. In the same way Caesar only writes *flumen* for 'a river', never *fluuius* or *amnis*. There is little connotative difference between the words (*amnis* may carry more power and grandeur) and Livy calls the Rhône, for instance, *flumen* thirteen times, *amnis* six times. Caesar chooses one word for one thing and adheres to it. His motive is principally simplicity, but the comparison with Livy shows that he is also influenced by concern for purity or propriety of diction. Language had always been a study of interest to him. During early 54 B.C. he had written two volumes entitled *De analogia* which were concerned with purity of diction as a counterblast to current trends, favoured by Cicero, who relished a rich and florid vocabulary. In the first volume he states a fundamental principle: 'as the sailor avoids the reef, so should you avoid the rare and obsolete word' (Aul. Gellius, *Noctes Atticae* 1.10.4). And probably at the same period he wrote his only surviving verses, on the comic poet Terence, perhaps in reply to some verses by Cicero. In them, summing the poet up as a half-Menander (*dimidiate Menander*), he praises his refined style (*puri sermonis amator*) but deplores his lack of intensity (*uis*). But it is not only rare and obsolete words which are conspicuous by their absence. Usages which are very common in Livy, such as *super* as an equivalent to *de* 'about', are not accepted by Caesar, presumably because they are loose and incorrect: it is to be noted that *super* in this sense occurs only three times in Cicero, always in letters. Adjectives followed by a genitive (e.g. *capax imperii*, *inops animi*, etc.) occur occasionally in Cicero, commonly in Livy, never in Caesar.

But Caesar's own simplicity, unlike Terence's, does not lack intensity. The pace of the narrative is never monotonous, always exciting. His battle-scenes are models of clear, fast-moving description with critical moments dramatically emphasized and the climax often told in breathless, clipped, staccato phrases. The outstanding example is his account of the battle against the Nervii (*Bell. Gall.* 2.18–27). First of all the battle-ground is sketched; then the Roman dispositions are described in a matter-of-fact style, suitable to a military communiqué. The first stage of the battle is told in a series of long, subordinate clauses, which convey the complexity of events until Caesar's Gallic cavalry, from the tribe of Treveri, panic. That moment is one of stark simplicity: 'they despaired of our cause and galloped for home; they reported that the Romans were routed' (*desperatis nostris rebus domum contenderunt; Romanos pulsos superatosque...renuntiauerunt*). The next word is *Caesar*, and Caesar's dramatic intervention saves the day. The account is rounded off by praise for the heroic fight which the Nervii put up, culminating in a movingly rhetorical tricolon – *ausos transire latissimum flumen, ascendere altissimas ripas, subire iniquissimum locum* 'they dared to cross a very wide river, to climb very tall banks and to approach a very impregnable position'. We do not know the quality of the writing of Caesar's predecessors, but Caesar certainly elevated the Commentary into a literary form in its own right. It was no longer merely raw material for history. Secondly, although, in line with convention, the *Commentaries* are no document of self-awareness and tell us little of Caesar's personal life but much of diplomacy and warfare, they reveal at every turn the masterful character of their author, his sharp decision, his courage in the face of daunting perplexities and disloyalties and his brilliant tactical sense. To conquer Gaul was a major undertaking whose true dimensions we only appreciate as we read the work.

The *Civil Wars* consist of three books, the first two dealing with the events of 49 B.C. and the third with 48 B.C. The time and purpose of composition are uncertain. Book 3 is formally incomplete since it does not deal with all the events of 48 B.C. and the work as a whole is more sketchy and less accurate than the *Gallic Wars*. Indeed it was criticized by the scholar Asinius Pollio a few years later for these deficiencies (Suetonius, *Iulius* 56.4). This suggests that it too was compiled in a hurry, perhaps in 47 B.C. at a time when Caesar thought that the Civil War was over and that his side of the case needed to be heard if a stable society was to be restored. The accuracy of the work can be checked much more closely because there are a number of independent witnesses to the events (notably Cicero in his letters, and authorities ultimately derived from Asinius Pollio and Livy) but it is fair-minded in the treatment of opponents (Pompey, Labienus, Domitius Ahenobarbus, etc.) and objective in the handling of fact. The style and presentation follow the pattern of the *Gallic Wars*. The same simplicity is in evidence. A fine example can be seen in the account of the emergency debate of the Senate at which Pompey tried frantically to mobilize his side (*Bell. Civ.* 1.6). Short sentences in asyndeton tumble over one another.

Both in the *Bell. Gall.* and the *Bell. Civ.* there are a few self-contained passages of more elevated writing, characterized by direct speech or general reflection, the use of the historic infinitive, unusual word-order and uncommon vocabulary. The most conspicuous is the account of Curio's campaign in *Bell. Civ.* 2.34–44, but the same phenomena can be recognized also in *Bell. Gall.* 5.26–52 (the battle for the winter quarters), 7.44–52 (Gergovia), 7.69–95 (Alesia) and *Bell. Civ.* 3.86–96 (Pharsalus). Scholars have claimed that Caesar wrote up these events, which did not reflect particular credit on his generalship, in order to distract attention from his shortcomings, but such episodes do no more than reflect the strength of Caesar's emotions. He had, for instance, great affection for Curio.

Four other works survive in the corpus attached to Caesar's name. The first (Book 8 of the *Gallic Wars*) is a completion of the history of Caesar's command written by his subordinate in Gaul, A. Hirtius (consul in 43 B.C.). The three others are brief accounts, by Roman officers, of the campaigns during the Civil Wars in Egypt, Africa and Spain. Their interest lies not only in the facts that they record but in the difference of their style from the easy command which Caesar developed. In particular the *Bellum Hispaniense* is one of the very few works written in a predominantly *un*-literary Latin, and is, therefore, a very valuable source for our knowledge of the language.

14
PROSE AND MIME

I. VARRO

Varro towered over his contemporaries: in literary output, range of achievement and posthumous influence even Cicero – who admitted as much – does not compare. He wrote some 620 books, more than any other Roman, more than most Greeks: they range from satire to theology, from etymology to navigation. Augustine marvels that he read so much yet had time to write and wrote so much as to defeat any reader.[1] This same man was a distinguished admiral and general, decorated for personal bravery at fifty; he administered rich estates, served numerous magistracies, reaching the rank of praetor, and acted both as land commissioner and as state librarian. Fate has dealt unkindly with his survival: we have a complete treatise on agriculture and six damaged books out of twenty-five 'On the Latin language'. Yet paradoxically, the loss of so much Varro constitutes a tribute to his achievement, for his systematization of so much earlier Greek and Roman scholarship made him wholly indispensable as a factual source for later writers and he has perished by absorption: from Virgil and Ovid to Ausonius, from Columella to Suetonius and Isidore of Seville his influence, not always at first-hand, was all-pervasive. One slight but characteristic example may be given: an annalist about 100 B.C. wrote about the boomerang (*cateia*) of the invading Teutones. He was in all probability excerpted by Varro, whom Virgil later consulted for learned detail in *Aeneid* 7. This boomerang-lore passed on, perhaps through Suetonius' *Prata*, to surface in Isidore of Seville and, desperately garbled, in the commentators on Virgil, as late as the ninth century A.D.[2] On a wider front, the *trivium* (grammar, rhetoric and dialectic) and *quadrivium* (geometry, arithmetic, astronomy and music) of medieval education descend ultimately from Varro's *Disciplinae*, a work of his eighties; indeed traces of Varronian systematization still lurk in modern university syllabuses.

Characteristic methods, of research and of disposition, can be detected in widely scattered areas: they serve to reveal the Roman polymath at work and

[1] *Civ. Dei* 6.2.

[2] Cf. *De gente Populi Romani* fr. 37 Fraccaro, Virg. *Aen.* 7.741 and Horsfall (1969) 297–9.

to explain how, in a full life, one man's output could be so colossal. Varro worked at speed: 'If I had had time, Fundania, I would be writing to you more agreeably what I shall now expound as I can, thinking I should hurry because, as it's said, "if a man's a bubble, an old man's more so"' is how he begins the *Res rusticae*. He never allowed didacticism to crush his markedly 'folksy' humour. Nor was he unaware of the niceties of Latin style, but in his prose-works there was rarely time to display them; if pronouns and conjunctions got postponed, relative clauses mislaid, verbs omitted and concords of number and gender violated, they were casualties of the clock. Facts and interpretations were set down as they came to hand. Varro lacks the massive elegance of Cicero because he never sought it. The arrangement of accumulated facts fell regularly into a simple pattern: people, places, periods and things (*de hominibus*; *de locis*; *de temporibus*; *de rebus*). It is discernible even in the long and delightful fragment of the Menippean satire 'You don't know what the late evening may bring' preserved by Gellius.[1] A preoccupation with numerology – under Pythagorean influence – contributed to excessive rigidity: agriculture has four divisions (*partes*) each with two subdivisions (*species*);[2] that scheme is not fully worked out, but clearly such arrangements could provide a long row of convenient pegs from which to suspend appropriate quotations and observations.

The focus of Varro's interests altered with time; periods of relatively restricted concentration assisted composition: the Menippean satires are early, the antiquarian treatises and cultural histories largely late; only the history and nature of the Latin language retained his attention throughout, from the *De antiquitate litterarum*, dedicated to the tragedian Accius in the early 80s, to *Disciplinae I*, *De grammatica*, over half a century later. Material, once accumulated, could be re-used indefinitely: the formal procedure for concluding treaties was, for instance, discussed early in the *Res humanae*, in the *De vita Populi Romani*, in the *De lingua Latina* and probably in the *Calenus*; this was a *Logistoricus*, a kind of philosophical and historical dialogue, probably not unlike Cicero's *De amicitia* and *De senectute*.

The working method may be reconstructed from internal evidence and by comparison with what we know of the elder Pliny's. From reading and from personal observation Varro made innumerable notes, with, doubtless, the help of expert *notarii*, carrying a supply of small tablets, *pugillares*. On campaign, he recorded, e.g., the statue of a lion on Mt Ida and the effects of the pirates' sack of Delos in 69 B.C.; travelling in Italy, he recorded inscriptions at Tarracina and Praeneste; on his estate at Casinum (mod. Cassino) there was evidently a magnificent library and Varro read hugely. Excerpts must somehow have been indexed, but haste shows up even in his library work;[3] study of Varro's

[1] *N.A.* 13.11.

[2] *Rust.* 1.5.4.

[3] Skydsgaard (1968) 64–88.

use of Theophrastus shows him reluctant to verify excerpts against a continuous text, and in consequence prone to error, to distortion and to misrepresentation of his original. Varro, one must never forget, wrote as a gentleman amateur, primarily for his peers. The *Res rusticae* is selective, muddled and at times inaccurate; it is not a practical manual for daily consultation by bailiff or overseer; depending in part on such manuals, it served rather to inform a readership of prosperous landowners, to entertain them with jokes, digressions and erudition, to charm them with precise and vivid observation,[1] to create, in effect, an agreeable illusion that there was mud on their boots.

It is particularly important not to think of Varro, with his numerous obsessions and lack of critical judgement as a scholar in anything like the modern sense. He gives five explanations for the name 'Palatine' without expressing any preference; all are now rejected. Stoic influence gave him a passion for etymology, which he used to provide evidence for his theories of Italian pre-history. Yet even here a sharp awareness is revealed that cultural and linguistic history are indivisible and the language is examined minutely for the light it can shed on the life of old Italy, which Varro loved so dearly. Social history and agricultural lore in a work on language should surprise us no more than etymologies in a work on agriculture; '*Panis* "bread" because originally they used to make it in the shape of a *panus* "cloth" '[2] is characteristic.

Varro was not an easy man: he enjoyed the friendship of Atticus and Pompey and there was a certain mutual respect between him and Caesar. But Cicero thought him strange, devious and irascible; dislike struggled with admiration.[3] A remarkable personality begins to emerge and one that was susceptible to a very wide range of influences. Varro was a romantic conservative, passionately devoted to the harsh Sabine countryside, to its simple pieties and onions-and-water life-style: 'when I was a boy I had a single adequate shirt and toga, shoes without straps, a horse without caparison, no daily bath, an occasional tub'.[4] His lifetime had witnessed vast social and political upheavals and the changes did not please him: in the Menippean satire *Sexagesis* he represents himself as a kind of Rip Van Winkle, who fell asleep for fifty years and woke about 70 B.C.; nothing was the same; piety, trust and decency, austerity and purity were all gone and Rome was a vice-ridden shambles.

In his admiration for the simple and natural life, as in his rejection of greed, luxury and intellectual pretentiousness Varro, the Roman reactionary, came unexpectedly close to the moral outlook of Hellenistic popular preaching. He was no Cynic; their rejection of social and cultural values, like the earnestness and coarse mockery of their diatribes, can only have repelled him. But he

[1] 2.10, for instance, on herdsmen.

[2] *Ling.* 5.105.

[3] See below for the great tribute in *Acad. Post.* 1.9.

[4] 'On the education of children', *Logistoricus Catus*, fr. xix Riese.

found in Menippus, a third-century Syrian freedman writing under Cynic influence, a model for profitable imitation and his 150 *Menippeae*, combining prose and verse, humour and moral improvement, dominated the literary output of his active public life. The Levantine exuberance of the form and the Sabine solidity of the ideas interact most successfully: Varro revels in the variety permitted; some three-quarters of the fragments are verse and in a wide range of metres (hendecasyllables, sotadeans, glyconics, limping iambi, etc.). Seneca's *Apocolocyntosis* – the only complete specimen of the genre that survives – seems almost fettered by comparison. Varro displays a remarkably wide range of characters and scenes, from Roman life and from myth. The tone is personal and vigorous, the language endlessly inventive, revelling in puns, vulgarisms, archaisms and snatches of Greek and moving rapidly through the whole scale of stylistic levels.

In the *Sesculixes*, Varro describes himself with engaging self-mockery as 'chewing over antiquities' (*ruminans antiquitates*).[1] The fully digested product, the *Antiquitates*, was his masterpiece.

Your books [wrote Cicero] have so to speak brought us home, for we were like visitors, wandering and straying in our own city; now at last we can tell who and where we are. You have revealed our country's age, the periods of its chronology, the laws of its rituals and priests, its civil and military institutions, the topography of its districts and localities, the names, divisions, duties and causes of all our affairs, both divine and human.[2]

The *Res humanae* were composed first, because divine affairs are the creation of mankind: there was an introduction and six books each on the familiar people, places, periods (i.e. the calendar) and things; Varro was concerned primarily with Rome as she actually was; Rome as she had been he described in the *De vita Populi Romani* ('On the life of the Roman People'), written at about the same date on the model of Dicaearchus' famous 'Life of Greece'. Fragments of the *Res humanae* tell us little of the work's detailed structure and content and even less of its general character.

The *Res divinae*, a central target of Christian polemic, notably St Augustine's, comes far more vividly alive. It was dedicated to Caesar as *pontifex maximus*, an office to which he attached the greatest importance, at a time when he was undoubtedly interested in religious reform. Caesar's descent from Venus through Aeneas and Iulus was being emphasized in all forms of propaganda and Varro's argument that it was useful for states that their chief men should draw inspiration for performing great deeds from a conviction, however ill-founded, of their divine ancestry, will have given parts at least of the *Res divinae* a strong contemporary relevance.

[1] *Sat. Men.* 505 Bücheler.

[2] Cic. *Acad. Post.* 1.9.

Towards the old Roman religion, Varro's attitude was complex and paradoxical: he was afraid lest the gods perish not by enemy invasion but by Roman neglect; it was his mission to save them and this would be a greater service even than that of Aeneas when he saved the Penates from the sack of Troy.[1] The cults and traditions that he described so minutely belonged to the *theologia ciuilis*, the religion of states. For Varro, it was by no means a perfect system, but he insisted that in an old city one must adhere to tradition: the populace should worship the gods, not despise them, for the growth of Rome had depended upon her religious observance. This emphasis upon the national and traditional value of the state religion was to be expected from the patriotic antiquary. But Varro's susceptibility to the influences of Antiochus of Ascalon's Platonism and Posidonius' Stoicism – not to mention his fashionable but deep-rooted acceptance of Pythagorean ideas – made him intellectually critical of the traditional pieties and it was from the standpoint of the philosophers' natural theology that he criticized Roman religion and still more the mythical theology of the poets – to conclude that in a state, religion was useful, even when untrue. Varro tried to integrate the state religion into a philosophically acceptable cosmic theory: Roman polytheism had to be explained as representing divisions (*partes*) or powers (*uirtutes*) of a universal Jupiter and the wish to reconcile the religions of Numa and Cleanthes led Varro into remarkable misrepresentations of early Roman worship. We cannot tell how far his programme for the purging of religion from accretions and improprieties will have gone and indeed how Caesar reacted. But his achievements as recorder dwarf his waywardness as reformer.

2. CORNELIUS NEPOS

Nepos is an intellectual pygmy whom we find associating uneasily with the literary giants of his generation. Atticus, whom Nepos called friend and to whom he dedicated his biographies, shared jokes with Cicero at Nepos' expense. Nepos wrote a large biography of Cicero, helped publish his letters and paid eloquent posthumous tribute to Cicero's contribution to the development of Latin style and philosophy, yet declared Cicero's own favourite works not worth reading and told him bluntly that philosophy was a pernicious waste of time. Cicero's collected letters to Nepos may well have made choice reading! Catullus dedicated his *libellus* to Nepos, himself a writer of risqué short poems and a fellow Cisalpine, yet the honour was tempered by mockery, however gentle, of Nepos' pedantic learning in the *Chronica*. Varro, whom Nepos must have known through Atticus, can have found little to admire in a man of slight scholarly talents, who pursued no public career. The elder Pliny condemns Nepos' credulity; Aulus Gellius alone praises him, faintly, for his industry.

[1] Varr. *ap.* Aug. *Civ. Dei* 6.2.

Nepos' shallow learning was exercised upon fashionable topics. The *Chronica*, indebted to the renowned verse *Chronica* of the second-century Athenian scholar Apollodorus, was largely concerned with synchronisms: were, for example, the Greek poet Archilochus and the Roman king Tullus Hostilius contemporaries? The warmth of Nepos' tribute to Atticus' thorough and comprehensive *Annales*, with their accurate genealogies, suggests an acknowledgement of scholarly inferiority: one may also wonder how he stood in comparison with the great Varro's *Annales*. The moralizing didacticism of his biographies ('I'm not sure how to set out [Pelopidas'] *uirtutes*...'[1]) was to be expected from a writer who made possibly the first formal collection of moral *exempla* – the stock-in-trade of the orator and the ethical essayist; the freedman Hyginus, active as a scholar and librarian under Augustus, was soon to produce another such convenient handbook.

Nepos' sole importance to us lies in the accident of his survival as the earliest Latin biographer. In his day the genre was popular and Nepos' models for the conception and arrangement of the *De illustribus viris* are easily conjectured: Varro, Santra, Nepos and Hyginus are named by Suetonius as the founders of Latin biography. The *Imagines* or *Hebdomades* of Varro shortly preceded Nepos' work: seven hundred portraits of famous men, with explanatory text. Like Nepos' biographies, Varro's collection was international in scope, whereas Atticus' collection of portraits with appended epigrams seems to have been limited to Romans. Nepos arranged his sixteen (or more) books in pairs, non-Romans first, by fields of eminence: pairs *de imperatoribus*, *de regibus*, and *de historicis* (on generals, kings and historians) are firmly attested. A comparable arrangement seems to have prevailed in Varro's *Imagines*.

Nepos and Varro diverge sharply from the narrow traditions of Roman and familial pride, which constitute the origins of Roman biography. In Nepos' case, the purpose of his internationalism is clear: a desire to provide the materials for *synkrisis*, comparison between the eminent men of Rome and those of other nations: 'to make it possible, by comparing the deeds of both, to judge which men should be assigned pre-eminence'.[2] This desire to compare and contrast both individuals and cultures is equally evident at this time in Posidonius, in Varro and in Cicero, notably when he is writing literary history, or considering the relative virtues of Greek and Latin as languages.

Nepos has a humble notion of the status of biography: he prefaces the 'Foreign generals' by conceding that many readers will consider it a trivial (*leue*) kind of writing and unworthy of the personalities of great men and in the *Pelopidas* he is at pains to assert that he is not writing history. Nor is he writing for historians, but for the general public (*uulgus*).[3] He does not expect of his readers any real knowledge of Greek history or literature and assumes that they will be shocked

[1] 1.16.1. [2] 23.13.4. [3] 16.1.1.

by pederasty, sister-marriage, dancing, acting, and other non-Roman *mores* displayed by his subjects. This audience will have been not appalled but comforted by references to temples of Minerva (i.e. Athena) at Sparta and Jupiter Optimus Maximus (i.e. Baal) at Carthage, or to a Spartan senate and magistrates (i.e. gerousia and ephors)!

The 'Foreign generals' are arranged in rough chronological sequence; it seems likely that the three non-Greeks (Datames, Hannibal, Hamilcar) were added in a second edition, which will, it seems, have required a larger papyrus than any single Latin book hitherto. There is no uniformity of length or treatment; the *Agesilaus* and *Epaminondas* stand out as formal eulogies. The remainder are in the 'Peripatetic' tradition, employing anecdote as moral illustration in the manner of Aristotle's successors. Nepos cheerfully admits to irrelevant digression in the *Pelopidas*,[1] to show 'what disaster usually results from excessive confidence'.

In merit, the *Cato* and *Atticus*, which are all that survive of the 'Latin historians', clearly come highest. The *Cato* is an abbreviation of a longer life written at Atticus' request; the *Atticus*, whose manner is closer to the eulogies, displays intermittently personal knowledge and understanding. The *Alcibiades* recaptures a little of its subject's variety and energy. But it is hard to speak well of the 'Foreign generals'. Their wide and abiding popularity as a schoolbook is owed more to their morality and simplicity that to any historical value or stylistic merit. Nepos names many Greek historical authorities, but his knowledge of Greek was demonstrably poor and it is likely that much of his scholarly plumage was borrowed. To his credit, though, he did recognize the historical value of Cicero's works. Yet admiration is promptly cancelled by the grossest of Nepos' many absurd exaggerations: Cicero not only predicted events in his own lifetime but *quae nunc usu ueniunt cęcinit ut uates* 'sang like a seer events that are now being experienced'.[2] Inaccuracies are startling and innumerable: Miltiades is confused with his uncle of the same name; Lemnos is placed among the Cyclades; the battles of Mycale and the Eurymedon are confused; the narrative of Hannibal's crossing of the Alps was a travesty – and Nepos was a native of Pavia! Nor will it do to palliate the deficiencies of Nepos' style by arguing that the Latin language was as yet undeveloped: the 'Lives' postdate the whole corpus of Cicero's work. His periods are not sustained, his excessive alliteration and strivings for antithesis annoy, his archaisms and colloquialisms are used without apparent purpose.

Nepos' scheme was ambitious and influential (for Plutarch, evidently), yet the execution often fell regrettably short.

[1] 16.3.1.

[2] 25.17.4.

3. THE LITERARY MIME

About 90 B.C. Pomponius and Novius gave some semblance of literary form to the *Atellana fabula*, a type of *commedia dell'arte* imported from Campania; a generation later Decimus Laberius and Publilius Syrus took the lead in effecting a similar development in the mime, which seems originally to have reached Rome from Sicily during the third century B.C., and the mime now took over from the *Atellana* as the *exodium* (epilogue) to comedies proper. The changes brought about cannot be defined with confidence, beyond saying that the role of improvisation in the mime was reduced, though not eliminated, and the place of verse, usually iambic, sometimes trochaic, was consequently increased. Improvised mime had made for notoriously slight and trivial plots (reversals of fortune, the marital triangle), with abrupt endings when inspiration failed; some consequence and credibility were now injected and the range of plots grew wider, while the role of slapstick was modified under the influence of comedy, both Greek-based and Roman-based. We even find the assumptions of Hellenistic popular philosophy both exploited and criticized. But the mime's appeal never rested upon sophistication. Its aim was laughter and nothing was done to refine it; moralists' condemnations continue ineffective and unabated into the Byzantine period. Parody of religion and myth, ripe obscenity and double meanings are all attested. Cicero acknowledges with embarrassment his pleasure in the mime's humour.[1]

There were other attractions: songs, striptease,[2] live sex and live animals on stage, imitations of beasts and humans, both by voice and by movement, and topical, personal and satiric allusions; Cicero recognized performance and audience reaction as valuable barometers of public opinion.[3] No masks or shoes were worn, staging and costume were simple and performers normally few. Yet the mime bred a certain wit and grace: Sulla was the first of Rome's rulers to relish the company of mimic actors: female roles were played by real women, and actresses – Tertia, Arbuscula, Cytheris – feature prominently in the scandal of the late Republic. The orator Cassius Severus and the philosopher Seneca were understandably surprised at finding in Publilius finely expressed moral maxims and it is ironic that we owe our fragments of a great popular entertainer to his moments of sententious virtue.

Laberius and Publilius must be differentiated sharply: Laberius revelled in neologisms and vulgarisms; Publilius wrote pointedly but plainly. Laberius, as a Roman knight, might not himself act, while Publilius, a Levantine and the freedman of a freedman, regularly performed in his own plays and rapidly

[1] *De or.* 2.173.

[2] Val. Max. 2.10.8: the younger Cato once left the theatre on hearing that his presence was inhibiting the crowd from telling the girls to strip.

[3] Cic. *Att.* 14.2.1, 3.2.

earned great popularity throughout Italy. Towards Caesar, Laberius was notoriously disrespectful; his gibes clearly reached a wider audience than Catullus' and the Dictator reacted less graciously. Events at the *Ludi Victoriae Caesaris* in July 46 (?) are confusingly recorded: Caesar induced Laberius to act in person and he lamented his loss of civil status – automatic for a mimic actor – in a moving and dignified prologue: well-received iambics on tyranny followed. Publilius probably performed on the same occasion – competitions are attested elsewhere – and was declared victorious; Laberius was restored to equestrian rank at once, but the humiliation was itself a tribute to the mime's importance.

IV

THE AGE OF AUGUSTUS

15

UNCERTAINTIES

Cicero was murdered by the soldiers of Antony and Octavian in December of 43 B.C. In the following year, according to the ancient tradition, Virgil began to write the *Eclogues*. A new age, in both politics and literature, had begun.[1] The period between Virgil's début and the death of Ovid was one of extraordinary and unprecedented literary creativity at Rome. Perhaps no other half-century in the history of the world has witnessed the publication in one city of so many unquestioned masterpieces of enduring significance in so many different fields. Between them Virgil, Horace and Ovid imparted to most of the major genres of poetry what might appear their mature, even definitive, shape. Epic, lyric, elegy, bucolic, didactic, satire, all underwent this magisterial discipline. In prose one monumental undertaking, Livy's history *Ab urbe condita*, survives (in part) to uphold Ciceronian canons of historiography against the influence of Sallust and to leave a permanent mark on the tradition. Only drama and oratory languished in a society in which free speech, at least among the upper classes,[2] was confined within increasingly narrow limits.

In some such manner, simplified by hindsight and the selective operations of taste and chance, what is conventionally called the Augustan Age of Latin literature tends to be presented. Contemporary reality was considerably more complex. The record of lost and fragmentary literature,[3] added to the explicit testimony of our sources, provides evidence of much diversity and experiment, conducted to a counterpoint of sometimes fiercely outspoken criticism and controversy. All the best work of Virgil, Horace and Ovid was experimental and a good deal of it, in the eyes of their contemporaries, controversial. Vilification of Virgil began, we are told (*Vit. Don.* 171–9 B) immediately with the publication of the *Eclogues*. The poet's deathbed wish to have the *Aeneid* destroyed (ibid. 143–53) may well have been due to a more fundamental uneasiness than that arising from its unfinished state. This was, after all, and Virgil must have been well aware of the fact, the most original epic ever

[1] Cf. Du Quesnay (1976) 39–43.
[2] Cf. Cameron (1976) 173.
[3] See below, pp. 476–9, 483–93.

written, not at all what many people would have been expecting after reading the proem to the third book of the *Georgics*; and in spite of Propertius' famous eulogy (2.34.65–6) its success can at the time have seemed by no means secure to the poet.[1] Horace's literary epistles afford vivid, if not always unambiguous,[2] insights into the literary dissensions of the age. Even Ovid, whose earliest poetry (he tells us) took the town by storm, had encountered critical hostility (*Rem. Am.* 387–98) some years before incurring the much more damaging displeasure of the Princeps.

In these respects, then, the Augustan Age did not differ materially from the ages that preceded and followed it. It is in the domain of technique that it may lay claim to a unique status. In the period of almost exactly two centuries which separates the literary début of Virgil from that of Livius Andronicus the Latin language and its native modes of expression had been, by fits and starts as genius came on to the scene, and not without friction,[3] assimilating itself to the metres and forms of Greece. In the work of Virgil and Horace it seems that the process of assimilation has achieved a happy equilibrium: the most characteristic monuments of Augustan poetry display a formally and aesthetically satisfying fusion of new and old, native and alien elements. For the first time since the classical age of Greece the competing claims of technique (*ars*) and inspiration (*ingenium*) were again harmonized. The balance which Callimachus (Ov. *Am.* 1.15.14) and Ennius (Ov. *Trist.* 2.424) had missed, Ovid – and by implication those contemporary writers approved by educated taste – had triumphantly compassed.

As in human affairs in general, so in art, equilibrium is a transitory thing. In the longer perspectives of later literary history Ovid himself, like his contemporary Livy, is a transitional figure, documenting – to use a familiar though fundamentally misleading stereotype – the waning of the 'Golden' and the waxing of the 'Silver' Ages of Latin letters. In Ovid's verse we find consummated the technical legacy of the Augustans to their successors: a common idiom, a poetical *koine*, with affinities to current prose, in which anything could be expressed with ease and elegance by anybody with an ear and the necessary training. Respect for the generic boundary-lines and restraint in the exploitation of the abundant technical resources, subordination of means to ends, self-control: the area in which technique shades into taste, and taste into morals – that was a bequest with less appeal to poets eager to astonish and surprise. Already in the *Controversiae* and *Suasoriae* of the Elder Seneca, whose memories went back to the age of Cicero (*Contr.* 1 *praef.* 11), the incipient domination of the rhetoric which in the view of Wilamowitz was principally to blame for

[1] Cf. Kidd (1977), on Hor. *Odes* 1.3 as referring to the boldness of Virgil's attempt.

[2] See, for instance, the interpretations of *Epist.* 1.19 by Fraenkel (1957) 339–50 and G. W. Williams (1968) 25–8.

[3] Cf. on Lucilius above, pp. 167, 169–71.

the decline of civilization[1] is clearly perceptible. Even before the fall of the Republic, that is to say, the pursuit of rhetorical brilliance for its own sake was tending to obscure the practical ends of public speaking,[2] and the infection was spreading to literature.

After the elimination of Octavian's last rival at Actium in 31 B.C. the Roman world entered on an unexampled period of peace and prosperity. Naturally the official author of these blessings expected his achievements to be reflected in contemporary literature. A tradition of court poetry going back through Theocritus and Callimachus to Pindar and beyond[3] offered obvious models; and in his friend and first minister Maecenas Augustus could call on the services of an intermediary who could bring to bear on the irritable brood of poets (Hor. *Epist.* 2.2.102) an unrivalled combination of tact and munificence – so much so that he still stands for later ages as the type of literary patron. Very little surviving Augustan poetry, however, can be described as court poetry: comparison with Statius' *Silvae* is enough to make the point. Certain poets, notably Ovid and Tibullus, were attached to patrons other than Maecenas; and even Virgil, Horace and Propertius obstinately resisted all inducements to celebrate Augustus and the régime in ways which they could not reconcile with their literary (i.e. Callimachean) consciences. Dissent and reservations may go deeper than that. Although some poems – the 'Roman' odes and the *Georgics* spring to mind – appear to align the poet solidly with current official attitudes and aspirations, it is rarely appropriate to talk of propaganda. The message of the *Georgics* is moral rather than political;[4] and even the *Aeneid*, a poem undertaken, we are told, expressly in order to bring past and present into harmony,[5] strikes a note of resignation rather than of confidence. To what extent signs of disillusion can be detected in the poetry of Horace and Propertius is more problematical.[6] In the case of Ovid, goaded by a cruel and vindictive persecution, resentment finally broke out into overt protest – if irony may be so bitter as to justify the phrase.[7] It would indeed be odd if the political and social stresses and strains of Augustus' long reign[8] were not reflected in the literature of the period, even in the work of writers not basically disaffected. Even if common prudence had not imposed discretion, Virgil and Horace were heirs to a poetical tradition in which a wink was as good as a nod, in which nuance and innuendo were preferred to explicit statement. The hints of independence, of emancipation from officially-approved values, in their work take different forms.

[1] Wilamowitz (1928) 73.

[2] Cf. Winterbottom (1974) I viii–ix.

[3] Gow (1950) II 305–7, 325.

[4] Wilkinson (1969) 49–55.

[5] *Vit. Don.* 77–8 B '...et in quo, quod maxime studebat, Romanae simul urbis et Augusti origo contineretur'.

[6] Johnson (1973).

[7] See below, pp. 449–52.

[8] Syme (1939) *passim.*

In Horace uneasiness perhaps expressed itself by what would now be called politely opting out;[1] in Virgil it issued in tortured and ambiguous literary guise. Only Ovid was finally pushed into what bordered on defiance. Paradoxically, the result was some of his sincerest and finest poetry. There is a negative as well as a positive patronage.

[1] Johnson (1973) 174.

16

THEOCRITUS AND VIRGIL

Theocritus of Syracuse, who invented the pastoral, was a Hellenistic poet, a contemporary of Callimachus and Apollonius. Disappointed perhaps in an earlier appeal to Hiero II of Syracuse (*Idyll* 16,[1] a brilliant display-piece), Theocritus migrated 'with the Muses' (16.107) to the great new capital of Egypt, whose lord, Ptolemy Philadelphus, was renowned for his liberality to poets and men of letters. It is evident from *Idyll* 15 that Theocritus was familiar with the city of Alexandria; and from *Idyll* 17 that he gained Ptolemy's favour. He was familiar too with the Aegean island of Cos, Ptolemy's birthplace and home of his tutor Philitas, the coryphaeus, as it were, of the Alexandrian school of poetry. There Theocritus had good friends, Eucritus, Amyntas, the brothers Phrasidamus and Antigenes, all mentioned in *Idyll* 7, the setting of which is Cos; and there he probably met Nicias, the love-sick physician and minor poet to whom *Idyll* 11 is addressed: the Cyclops in love, no longer Homer's blood-curdling monster but '*our* Cyclops, old Polyphemus' (7–8), an enamoured country bumpkin. It is tempting to imagine Theocritus in Alexandria, Alexander's city, a city composed of all sorts and conditions of men, Greek and barbarian, with no history, no common traditions, no intimate relationship to the countryside – to imagine him there cultivating a special nostalgia by writing of the Sicilian herdsmen of his youth: a landscape of memory, for it is not known that he ever returned to Sicily.

Theocritus' poetry, or rather his pastoral poetry (for he wrote much else besides), is nostalgic, exquisitely so, as any urbane reflection on a simpler, now remote existence will be. But it is saved from sentimentality by the elegance of the poet's language and his apparent – at times his too apparent – erudition. (Pastoral poetry was never quite to lose this character of learning, except perhaps in its most attenuated derivation from Virgil.)

Here, for example, is a passage from Theocritus' first *Idyll*: the beginning of Thyrsis' lament for the cowherd Daphnis, mysteriously, ruthlessly, dying of

[1] Theocritus' poems are indiscriminately called 'idylls', εἰδύλλια – an all but meaningless term having none of its English connotations.

love; a passage imitated by Virgil in his tenth *Eclogue* and by Milton (after Virgil) in his *Lycidas*:

> Ἄρχετε βουκολικᾶς, Μοῖσαι φίλαι, ἄρχετ' ἀοιδᾶς.
>
> Θύρσις ὅδ' ὡξ Αἴτνας, καὶ Θύρσιδος ἁδέα φωνά.
> πᾷ ποκ' ἄρ' ἦσθ', ὅκα Δάφνις ἐτάκετο, πᾷ ποκα, Νύμφαι;
> ἦ κατὰ Πηνειῶ καλὰ τέμπεα, ἦ κατὰ Πίνδω;
> οὐ γὰρ δὴ ποταμοῖο μέγαν ῥόον εἴχετ' Ἀνάπω,
> οὐδ' Αἴτνας σκοπιάν, οὐδ' Ἄκιδος ἱερὸν ὕδωρ.
>
> ἄρχετε βουκολικᾶς, Μοῖσαι φίλαι, ἄρχετ' ἀοιδᾶς.
>
> τῆνον μὰν θῶες, τῆνον λύκοι ὠρύσαντο,
> τῆνον χὠκ δρυμοῖο λέων ἔκλαυσε θανόντα. (64–72)

Begin, dear Muses, begin the pastoral song.

Thyrsis of Etna am I, and sweet is the voice of Thyrsis. Where were ye, Nymphs, where were ye, when Daphnis was wasting: in the fair vales of Peneius or of Pindus? for surely ye kept not the mighty stream of Anapus, nor the peak of Etna, nor the sacred rill of Acis.

Begin, dear Muses, begin the pastoral song.

For him the jackals howled, for him the wolves; for him dead even the lion of the forest made lament.

This translation[1] fails, as any translation will, because it does not represent qualities inherent in the original, of which three may be briefly noted:

Poetic reminiscence: Ἄκιδος ἱερὸν ὕδωρ 'the sacred water of Acis' (69). The Acis is a small stream that rises under Etna and flows into the sea. Theocritus would have known it as a boy; no doubt is pleased him to ennoble it with a phrase out of Homer.

Doric dialect: an artificial dialect largely adapted from previous poetry, though Theocritus' own speech may be involved to a degree; certainly not the 'boorish dialect' Dryden took it for (*The dedication of the Pastorals* (1697); but Dryden rightly sensed 'a secret charm in it which the Roman language cannot imitate'). Given the linguistic sophistication of the poet and, presumably, of his audience, it is probable that some effect of rusticity was intended.

Rhetorical structure: lines 71–2 form a highly stylized period composed of three clauses (a tricolon), the last being the longest; in this case each begins with the same word, an added refinement (anaphora).

This passage, as indeed most of the first *Idyll*, is remarkably elaborate; of the pastoral *Idylls* only the seventh compares with it. Still, even Theocritus' lesser efforts, those that seem closer to the realities of peasant experience, are not at bottom dissimilar. Theocritus' pastoral style or mode, though varying greatly in intensity, is nevertheless consistent: his most penetrating critic – to judge from the catholicity of Virgil's imitation[2] – found it so.

[1] By Gow (1952) I 9.

[2] But Virgil did not particularly care for *Idylls* 6, 9, 10; see Posch (1969) 17.

The *Idyll* begins with Thyrsis complimenting an unnamed goatherd on the sweetness of his music:

> ʽΑδύ τι τὸ ψιθύρισμα καὶ ἁ πίτυς, αἰπόλε, τήνα,
> ἁ ποτὶ ταῖς παγαῖσι, μελίσδεται, ἁδὺ δὲ καὶ τύ
> συρίσδες.

Sweet is the whispering music of that pinetree, goatherd, the pinetree by the springs, sweet too your piping.

Casual rustic speech (such is the fiction) is apprehended and, with beautiful precision, fastened in the rhythm of the hexameter.

'Sweet is the whispering music of that pinetree...' Landscape is necessary to this poetry: in Theocritus description is accurate and frequently luxuriant, in Virgil sparse and suggestive. The pastoral landscape is capacious: strange and oddly assorted figures may be accommodated; it is static, a perpetual décor or background against which these figures are set off, and thus it serves to unify what might otherwise seem a discordant collocation of speakers and topics. In this environment of rural fantasy the sophisticated, city-bred poet, poet-scholar in the guise of poet-shepherd, is able to speak with a kind of obtrusive simplicity: he may speak of country things, oftener (in Virgil) he speaks of political events, of love, of poetry. And, meanwhile, goats will continue to behave in their goatish way:

> αἱ δὲ χίμαιραι,
> οὐ μὴ σκιρτασῆτε, μὴ ὁ τράγος ὔμμιν ἀναστῇ.

You she-goats, don't be so skittish, the he-goat will rouse himself.

So ends the first *Idyll*, almost abruptly: after the prolonged elevation of Thyrsis' lament for Daphnis, a moment of earthy humour – and a reminder of the confines of this poetry.

I. VIRGIL AND THEOCRITUS

> Prima Syracosio dignata est ludere uersu
> nostra neque erubuit siluas habitare Thalia. (*Ecl.* 6.1–2)

My Thalia first condescended to amuse herself with Syracusan verse nor did she blush to dwell in the woods.

A proud claim, made with all the delicate force of which pastoral rhetoric is capable: the claim, that is, of being the first Latin poet to imitate Theocritean pastoral; and made at the beginning of an eclogue which owes little or nothing overtly to Theocritus. Hence two questions: was Virgil indeed the first? and what was the nature of his imitation?

Virgil's imitation of Theocritus is restricted mainly, and not surprisingly, to the pastoral *Idylls* (1, 3–11), with the notable exception of *Idyll* 2, Simaetha's incantation, a most unpastoral song which Virgil managed to translate into a pastoral setting (*Ecl.* 8.64–109). Virgil may be thought of as a Roman poet appropriating a province of Greek poetry, formed late and not, as he gracefully insinuates, highly prized. Indications of a Theocritean presence in Latin poetry, or what remains of it, before Virgil are meagre and elusive. So erudite a poet as Parthenius could hardly have been ignorant of Theocritus, a famous Alexandrian who had, moreover, sided with Callimachus against his critics.[1] (Parthenius nowhere uses Theocritus in his Περὶ ἐρωτικῶν παθημάτων, but that instructive booklet had a very limited purpose.[2]) Catullus apparently modelled the refrain in his epyllion (64) on that in *Idyll* 1, and adapted, perhaps after Cinna, a single verse from *Idyll* 15.[3] And there is the curious remark of Pliny the Elder (*N.H.* 28.19) to the effect that Catullus, like Virgil, imitated Simaetha's song; the imitation has not survived. Perhaps Parthenius possessed only a few of the idylls; perhaps his first pupils were not interested in pastoral poetry.

For Catullus and his friends, young poets concerned to be fashionable, to be urbane, 'of the city', the country had no charm; it represented rather the very qualities they despised, in poetry as in manners, the inept, the uncouth, the out-of-date. So the ultimate dispraise of Suffenus, witty and delightful fellow that he is, is this: let him but touch poetry and he becomes country clumsy, clumsier (Catull. 22.14 *idem infaceto est infacetior rure*); and of the superannuated *Annals* by the disgusting Volusius: that they are a mass of country clumsiness (Catull. 36.19 *pleni ruris et inficetiarum*). Not for such poets idealized peasants and pastoral sentiment – even had they read Theocritus.

Virgil was different, as, somehow, Virgil always is. He was born in a rural district not far from Mantua; his father was a farmer, though hardly so poor as the ancient Life (*Vita Donati*) would have him be; more likely a country entrepreneur (a type not uncommon in Italy today) with ambition and money enough to send a gifted son away to school, first to Cremona, where Virgil assumed the *toga uirilis*, the garb of manhood, then to Milan and shortly thereafter to Rome. In later years Virgil owned a house in Rome, on the Esquiline near the gardens of his patron Maecenas. (Why does Maecenas not figure in the *Eclogues*? For it is now clear that Virgil became a member of his 'circle' several years before the Book of *Eclogues* was published.) Most of the time, however, Virgil lived in peaceful retirement at Naples or in Sicily. Unlike Catullus, miserable in Verona (Catull. 68.1–40), Virgil did not long for Rome; he very rarely went there, and when he did he shunned public notice. So far from seeming urbane, he had the look of a countryman about him (*Vita Don.* 8 *facie*

[1] *Id.* 7.45–8; cf. Gow (1952) II ad loc.

[2] See above, pp. 184–6.

[3] See above, p. 191.

rusticana). Of course Virgil's biography will not explain why he wrote pastoral poetry; or why he wrote the ten pastoral poems he did; or why he wrote poetry at all. Still, a serious writer of pastoral poetry must have some affection for the country; and Virgil's deep and abiding affection is evident in all his poetry, even his latest. So it is that a reader will encounter, with the surprised pleasure of recognizing the familiar in a strange place, a passage in the *Aeneid* which puts him in mind of the young poet of the *Eclogues*. *Aen.* 12.517–20, for example: Menoetes, a young Arcadian, a fisherman once, who died in the fields of Laurentum, to whom the doors of the rich and powerful were unknown, whose father was a poor farmer tilling rented land.[1] It is not difficult to understand why Virgil was attracted to Theocritus' pastoral *Idylls*. Were these poems then new in Rome? Or new for Virgil?

From a prefatory epigram it appears that Artemidorus of Tarsus, a grammarian more or less contemporary with Parthenius (but having no known connexion with him), published a collection of pastoral poems:

> Βουκολικαὶ Μοῖσαι σποράδες ποκά, νῦν δ' ἅμα πᾶσαι
> ἐντὶ μιᾶς μάνδρας, ἐντὶ μιᾶς ἀγέλας. (*A.P.* 9.205)

The bucolic Muses, scattered once, are now together, all in one fold, in one flock.

Did Virgil use this comprehensive edition? Or a separate edition of Theocritus? In any case, he used an edition that contained – by one of the happiest accidents in literature – ten pastoral *Idylls* 'of Theocritus'.[2] To Virgil, a Latin poet after all, it would matter little that Bion and Moschus or other Greek imitators of Theocritus had written pastoral poetry; or that there were pastoral moments, if in fact there were, in the elegies of Gallus: he, Virgil, was indisputably the first Latin poet to make whole poems, *Bucolica*, after the example of Theocritus.

> But Theocritus may justly be preferr'd as the Original, without injury to Virgil, who modestly contents himself with the second place, and glories only in being the first who transplanted Pastoral into his own country; and brought it there to bear as happily as the Cherry-trees which Lucullus brought from Pontus.
> (Dryden, *The dedication of the Pastorals*, 1697)

Whether Virgil was modestly content with second place may be questioned. Very likely he felt some diffidence at the start (when writing the second and third *Eclogues*, as they were to become), but did he by the time he had almost finished with the pastoral Muse, when he could write:

> Prima Syracosio dignata est ludere uersu
> nostra neque erubuit siluas habitare Thalia?

[1] Cf. Clausen (1976*d*).

[2] *Id.* 8 (which Virgil admired) is probably, and *Id.* 9 certainly, spurious; but Virgil could not have known.

It may be questioned too whether the transplanting was quite so easy as Dryden's pretty simile – very pretty, and thoroughly Roman in sensibility – suggests: it required some seven or eight years to accomplish.

The relationship of Virgil and Theocritus is extraordinary, a literary symbiosis unparalleled in Graeco-Latin poetry. Comparison as usually proposed, between the *Eclogues* and the pastoral *Idylls*, is unequal and tends to Virgil's disadvantage. Nor can Theocritus' poetic achievement, which is of the highest order, be appreciated as it should be if attention is confined to his pastoral *Idylls*. If such a comparison must be made, then it should be between the whole of Theocritus, on the one hand, and the *Eclogues* and parts of the *Georgics*, at least, on the other.

Virgil was a young poet when he started the *Eclogues*. Much, far too much, has been written (echoes of which still, incredibly, are heard) about the adolescent Virgil, the supposed author of the *Culex* and several other bad or indifferent poems; much less about the young poet of the *Eclogues*, his problems, his successes, his failures. The reason is the *Aeneid*: the lustre of that august and splendid poem has been reflected on to the *Eclogues*, so that the young poet is very hard to see. (If only it might be given to read the *Eclogues* in perfect innocence of the *Aeneid*...) A few perceptive comments have been made about him, not by a professional scholar but by a professional poet, Paul Valéry,[1] who had been persuaded by a friend to translate the *Eclogues* – 'cette œuvre illustre', as he justly terms it, 'fixée dans une gloire millénaire'. By a wilful act of sympathy, by recalling himself to himself as a young poet, Valéry was able to see in Virgil another young poet and speak personally, as it were, of him at a critical phase in his development and that of Latin poetry:

> L'homme était jeune; mais l'art des vers à Rome en était au point ou il devient si conscient de ses moyens que la tentation de les employer pour le plaisir de s'en servir et de les développer à l'extrême, passe le besoin vrai, primitif et naïf de s'exprimer. Le goût de produire l'effet devient cause...(p. 214)

> Les *Bucoliques*, me tirant pour quelques instants de ma vieillesse, me remirent au temps de mes premiers vers. Il me semblait en retrouver les impressions. Je croyais bien voir dans le texte un mélange de perfections et d'imperfections, de très heureuses combinaisons et grâces de la forme avec des maladresses très sensibles; parfois, des pauvretés assez surprenantes, dont je montrerai quelqu'une. Je reconnaissais dans ces inégalités d'exécution un âge tendre du talent, et ce talent venu à poindre dans un âge critique de la poésie. (p. 216)

Virgil's second *Eclogue* is generally considered his earliest: apart from lines 45–55, a somewhat overfull description of flowers, fruits, and sweet-smelling trees, which may have been added later, it is mostly derived from Theocritus'

[1] Valéry (1962).

eleventh *Idyll*. Here, if anywhere, some infelicity of expression, some awkwardness or incompetence might be looked for.

The love-sick Corydon, denied the favours of the petulant boy Alexis, his master's darling, boasts that he too is somebody:

> despectus tibi sum, nec qui sim quaeris, Alexi,
> quam diues pecoris, niuei quam lactis abundans.
> mille meae Siculis errant in montibus agnae;
> lac mihi non aestate nouum, non frigore defit. (19–22)

I am despised by you, nor do you ask who I am, Alexis, how rich in herds, how abundantly supplied with snowy milk. A thousand ewes of mine roam the Sicilian hills. Fresh milk I lack not, neither in summer nor winter.

Now Polyphemus, Theocritus' old neighbour (and rather too close for the comfort of Virgil's reader here), may preen himself on his pastoral riches:

> ἀλλ' οὗτος τοιοῦτος ἐὼν βοτὰ χίλια βόσκω,
> κἠκ τούτων τὸ κράτιστον ἀμελγόμενος γάλα πίνω·
> τυρὸς δ' οὐ λείπει μ' οὔτ' ἐν θέρει οὔτ' ἐν ὀπώρᾳ,
> οὐ χειμῶνος ἄκρω. (*Id.* 11.34–7)

Yet, such as I am, I graze a thousand sheep, and from these I draw and drink milk, the very best. Cheese I lack not, neither in summer nor autumn, nor in midwinter.

But Corydon... Corydon is a poor slave. Comment on this passage is somewhat embarrassed, and excuses are made.

Polyphemus proceeds:

> συρίσδεν δ' ὡς οὔτις ἐπίσταμαι ὧδε Κυκλώπων,
> τίν, τὸ φίλον γλυκύμαλον, ἁμᾷ κἠμαυτὸν ἀείδων. (38–9)

I can pipe as no other Cyclops here, singing to you, my sweet honey-apple, and of myself.

And Corydon partially follows:

> canto quae solitus, si quando armenta uocabat
> Amphion Dircaeus in Actaeo Aracyntho. (23–4)

I sing as Amphion used to sing when calling the cattle home, Dircaean Amphion in Actaean Aracynthus.

Verse 24 – over which grown men have puzzled their brains – is beautiful nonsense of the most precious Alexandrian sort: 'Le goût de produire l'effet devient cause.'

Corydon continues:

> nec sum adeo informis: nuper me in litore uidi,
> cum placidum uentis staret mare. (25–6)

Nor am I so very ugly: for recently I saw myself on the shore, when the sea was calm and still.

This passage is imitated from Theocritus' sixth *Idyll*, a singing-match between Daphnis and Damoetas,[1] Damoetas impersonating Polyphemus:

καὶ γάρ θην οὐδ' εἶδος ἔχω κακὸν ὥς με λέγοντι.
ἦ γὰρ πρᾶν ἐς πόντον ἐσέβλεπον, ἦς δὲ γαλάνα... (34–5)

Indeed I am not so bad looking as they say. For I gazed into the sea recently, it was calm...

Again, comment is somewhat embarrassed.[2] The phrase *nec s(um) ade(o) informis* is itself very ugly with its harsh elisions: technical incompetence? or deliberate artifice? like the description of 'shepherd Polyphemus' (*pastorem Polyphemum*) in the *Aeneid*: *monstr(um) horrend(um) inform(e) ingens*...'a monster horrible, ugly, huge...' (3.658), where the elisions are obviously expressive. On a note of irresolution this soft impeachment may well conclude.

Intentional imitation (as distinguished from reminiscence, of which the poet may not have been aware) was not looked down on in antiquity, it was looked for; and where found admired, thoughtfully, critically, as the poet intended it should be. The body of literature that might be referred to was not large, and the poet knew very well for whom he was writing – not for the crowd, whose ignorant praise he scorned, but for the discerning few, friends and others who shared his idea of poetry:

Plotius et Varius, Maecenas Vergiliusque,
Valgius, et probet haec Octauius, optimus atque
Fuscus, et haec utinam Viscorum laudet uterque!
ambitione relegata te dicere possum,
Pollio, te, Messalla... (Horace, *Serm.* 1.10.81–5)

May Plotius and Varius, may Maecenas and Virgil, Valgius, may Octavius approve of these poems, and the excellent Fuscus, and may both the Viscus brothers praise them. Flattery aside, I can name you, Pollio, you, Messalla...

For the Alexandrian poets and for their Roman derivatives, imitation involved emulation, poetic rivalry, with no implication of disability or want of inventive-

[1] These pastoral names are mostly borrowed from Theocritus and have no hidden significance, except that Tityrus and Menalcas seem occasionally to represent Virgil. The pastoral masque belongs to the later tradition: in Virgil Pollio is Pollio, Varus Varus, Gallus Gallus.

[2] 'It is just possible that a Mediterranean cove might be calm enough to mirror a giant, not possible that it should be calm enough to mirror Corydon' Conington (1881) ad loc. Cerda (1608) ad loc. argues very learnedly to the contrary; but his advice to doubters – that they should go look in the sea for themselves – betrays some exasperation. Marvell diminishes and intensifies the conceit:

Nor am I so deform'd to sight,
If in my Sithe I looked right;
In which I see my picture done,
As in a crescent Moon the Sun. (*Damon the Mower* 57–60)

ness on the part of the imitator. So understood, imitation may be taken as evidence both of a poet's confidence in himself and of his esteem for the poet he has chosen to imitate: his aim was not to reproduce but to improve on the original. Virgil's imitations of Theocritus occasionally result in something inferior, rarely, if ever, in anything equivalent; usually the result is something quite different. It is not sufficient to notice places where Virgil uses Theocritus, as commentators routinely do, without enquiring further how or for what purpose he uses Theocritus. These imitations or allusions (a better word, perhaps, as hinting that quality of playful elegance which Horace detected in these poems: *molle atque facetum*[1] | *Vergilio adnuerunt gaudentes rure Camenae* 'To Virgil the Muses who rejoice in the country granted grace and wit' (*Serm.* 1.10.44–5)) – these allusions, then, are not discrete elements: they are, allowing for some failures, fused into Virgil's own composition.

'The title of his first book was Fragments.'[2] The paradox of the Book of *Eclogues* is, that it should contain so many fragments and yet not seem fragmentary. Whoever reads it through will be left with a sense of completeness, Virgilian completeness.

2. THE BOOK OF 'ECLOGUES'

Not only did Virgil compose the *Eclogues*, he also, and to some extent simultaneously, composed the Book of *Eclogues*,[3] a poetic achievement scarcely less remarkable. Virgil was not the first Latin poet to arrange his own poems for publication: Catullus had already done so.[4] But the Book of *Eclogues* differs essentially from Catullus' book of occasional poems: in Virgil's book the design of individual poems has been adjusted to the design of the book as a whole.

The chronology of the ten *Eclogues* had become a subject of learned speculation in late antiquity. Three apparent dates could be extracted from the text: 42 B.C., the land-confiscations (*Ecl.* 1 and 9), 40 B.C., Pollio's consulate (*Ecl.* 4.11–12), and 39 B.C., Pollio's campaign against the Parthini (*Ecl.* 8.6–13). It has recently been demonstrated,[5] however, on historical grounds, that the reference in the eighth *Eclogue* is not to Pollio but to Octavian, not therefore to the year 39 but to the year 35: this year – and not 38 or 37 as heretofore – must now be accepted, with certain literary consequences, as that in which the book of *Eclogues* was published.

[1] It will be noticed that Horace associates with the country the very quality (*facetum*) that Catullus denied to it.

[2] Robert Frost (1946), of the apprentice poet, in 'The constant symbol'.

[3] The title *Bucolicon liber* is found only in the explicit of the Medicean MS (fifth cent.). Virgil apparently called his poems (and his book) *Bucolica*, cf. Quint. *Inst.* 8.6.46, 9.2.3, 11.1.56, Suet. *Gramm.* 23, *Vita Don.* 19, 25, 26, 43.

[4] See above, pp. 193–7.

[5] By Bowersock (1971).

The second and third *Eclogues* may well be the earliest Virgil wrote: both are studiously imitative of Theocritus and both exhibit some technical immaturity. Near the end of the fifth *Eclogue* Virgil refers, in the ancient fashion, to the second and third by quoting part of the opening line of each:

hac te nos fragili donabimus ante cicuta;
haec nos 'formosum Corydon ardebat Alexin',
haec eadem docuit 'cuium pecus? an Meliboei?

This delicate pipe I will give you first; this taught me 'Corydon burned for the fair Alexis', this same 'Whose flock? Is it Meliboeus'?'

When Virgil had written several eclogues, he decided that *Cur non, Mopse* 'Why not, Mopsus' would be the fifth; and having so decided, added or substituted a few lines to produce a summary effect, an effect of cadence, and thus to define, as will be argued below, the first half of his book.

From line 60 onwards the third *Eclogue* is occupied with a singing-match between two rival shepherds, Damoetas and Menalcas. There is nothing strange about the form of their song, granted the amoebaean convention: couplet responds to couplet with strict partiality; nor, for the most part, about its content: the attitudes struck, the emotions vented are such as seem suitable to imaginary shepherds. But suddenly, rather disturbingly, the real Pollio is intruded into the scene:

D. Triste lupus stabulis, maturis frugibus imbres,
arboribus uenti, nobis Amaryllidis irae.
M. Dulce satis umor, depulsis arbutus haedis,
lenta salix feto pecori, mihi solus Amyntas.
D. Pollio amat nostram, quamuis est rustica, Musam:
Pierides, uitulam lectori pascite uestro.
M. Pollio et ipse facit noua carmina: pascite taurum,
iam cornu petat et pedibus qui spargat harenam.
D. Qui te, Pollio, amat, ueniat quo te quoque gaudet;
mella fluant illi, ferat et rubus asper amomum.
M. Qui Bauium non odit, amet tua carmina, Meui,
atque idem iungat uulpes et mulgeat hircos.
D. Qui legitis flores et humi nascentia fraga,
frigidus, o pueri (fugite hinc!), latet anguis in herba.
M. Parcite, oues, nimium procedere: non bene ripae
creditur; ipse aries etiam nunc uellera siccat. (80–95)

D. A wolf is harmful to the folds, rain to the ripened wheat, a high wind to the trees, to me Amaryllis' ire.

M. A shower is delightful to the crops, the arbutus to the weaned kids, the tender willow to the gravid flock, to me only Amyntas.

D. Pollio loves my Muse, rustic though she be: Pierian maids, feed a heifer for your reader.

M. *Pollio himself makes new poems: feed a bull that now will butt with his horn and scatter sand with his hooves.*

D. *Let him who loves you, Pollio, come where he gladly sees you too have come; may honey flow for him, and the rough bramble bear spikenard.*

M. *Let him who loathes not Bavius love your poems, Mevius, and may the same yoke foxes and milk he-goats.*

D. *You who pick flowers and the low-growing strawberries, a cold snake, children (run away!), lurks in the grass.*

M. *Don't go too far, my sheep: it's no good to trust the bank; the ram himself even now is drying his fleece.*

Lines 84–91 are unrelated to those which precede or follow and would not be missed were they absent. (Let the reader try the experiment of reading the third *Eclogue* through without these lines: perhaps he will find that it gains as a poem by their absence.) Why then are they present? Because Virgil inserted them when he was shaping his book, after he had decided that *Dic mihi, Damoeta* 'Tell me, Damoetas' would be the third *Eclogue* and the one which honours Pollio, *Sicelides Musae* 'Sicilian Muses', the fourth. Line 89:

mella fluant illi, ferat et rubus asper amomum

was designed to 'anticipate':

occidet et serpens, et fallax herba ueneni
occidet; Assyrium uulgo nascetur amomum. (*Ecl.* 4.24–5)

The snake shall die, and the herb that hides its poison shall die; Assyrian spikenard shall spring up everywhere.

Virgil nowhere else mentions this rare spice-plant.

Individual eclogues must have been shown or given to friends as they were written, the fourth to Pollio in 40 B.C. surely; but since all ten were published together in 35 B.C., all ten are, in a sense, contemporaneous; and any attempt to determine the exact order of their composition will be illusory. Until Virgil finally relinquished his book, he was free to make changes in it – reworking, adding, deleting – where and whenever he pleased.

The main design of Virgil's Book of *Eclogues* is obvious because Virgil took pains to make it so. (Lesser or partial designs are not however precluded: Virgil is a poet of labyrinthine complexity.[1]) The book is divided into two halves of five eclogues each: 1–5, 6–10,[2] the first containing 420, the second

[1] For a description and criticism of the various designs that have been discovered see Rudd (1976) 119–44.

[2] Horace adverts to the design of Virgil's book in his own first book, published about the same time, *Sat.* 1: ten satires, the first of which begins *Qui fit, Maecenas* 'How comes it, Maecenas', the sixth *Non quia, Maecenas* 'Not because, Maecenas'. The impression made by Virgil's book must be the reason why subsequent poets – Horace, Tibullus, Ovid – composed books of ten (or multiples of ten or five) poems.

410 (or 408) lines. The two longest eclogues, the third (111 lines) and the eighth (110 or 108 lines) are symmetrically placed, each being the centre-piece of its half; and in each eight lines have been inserted to flatter a patron who is praised for his poetry: 3.84–91 (Pollio), 8.6–13 (Octavian).

The first word of the first line of the first *Eclogue* and the last word of the last line of the fifth is a poet-shepherd's name, in the vocative case: *Tityre*... *Menalca*. Tityrus and Menalcas, Virgil's *personae*: such precision of form cannot be accidental. The two names define the first half of the book as tersely as the name Alexis, in the accusative case, rounds off the second *Eclogue*, the first line of which ends... *Alexin*, as does the last... *Alexin*. Did Virgil expect his readers to notice – or, rather, would a Roman reader notice details of this sort? Probably: for he read aloud, slowly, and had been trained from boyhood up in the discipline of rhetoric. However, artifice need not be noticed to be effective, and may be the more effective for not being noticed.

The opening line of the sixth *Eclogue*:

Prima Syracosio dignata est ludere uersu

suggests a fresh start, and some ancient critics (so Servius affirms) wished to put the sixth *Eclogue* first. Tityrus' name in line 4 (*Tityre*) and especially line 8:

agrestem tenui meditabor harundine Musam

I will meditate the rural Muse on a slender reed

were meant to recall the opening lines of the first *Eclogue*:

Tityre, tu patulae recubans sub tegmine fagi
siluestrem tenui Musam meditaris auena.

Tityrus, you lying there under the covert of a spreading beech, you meditate the woodland Muse on a slender reed.

Virgil, or for that matter any poet schooled in the Alexandrian tradition, rarely repeats a line intact or even slightly varied; and if he does, he does so with a special purpose in mind. Virgil's purpose here is obviously to define the first half of his book and, at the same time, connect it with the second half.

It will be enough to add – although much more might be added to this brief and necessarily superficial description – that as Gallus the erudite Alexandrian is the chief figure of the sixth *Eclogue*, so Gallus the love-sick elegist is the chief figure of the tenth. Again, Virgil's purpose is obvious: to define the second half of his book.

But why a book of ten pastoral poems? a book in which each of the ten is enhanced somehow in its place? in which the ten, taken together, have a collective beauty and sense? The marvellous fact of the Book of *Eclogues* defies explanation. As to the number ten, however, a conjecture is probable: Virgil got the idea from the edition of Theocritus he used, in which there happened to be ten pastoral poems; and this original idea, vague and inchoate as it must have been, he eventually realized, by patient labour, by a slow process of refinement,[1] in the Book of *Eclogues*.

The peculiar charm of Virgil's book is immediately felt but not so readily accounted for: elegance of phrase, a harmony of meaning and music so that the one reinforces the other, artifice evident and unabashed – these and suchlike impressions can be summed up, perhaps, in a single word: style, style in its larger significance, style as displayed by no poet before Virgil. The publication of the Book of *Eclogues* is an epoch in Latin poetry.

3. THREE ECLOGUES

The first

Two shepherds are talking, but not of country things; they talk rather of civil discord and violence, of a possible reconciliation, of the infinite sadness of exile. Meliboeus has lost his farm; as he is driving off the pitiful remnant of his flock he espies Tityrus, canopied from the heat under a beech-tree and carelessly meditating his thankful Muse:

> Tityre, tu patulae recubans sub tegmine fagi
> siluestrem tenui Musam meditaris auena:
> nos patriae finis et dulcia linquimus arua.
> nos patriam fugimus: tu, Tityre, lentus in umbra
> formosam resonare doces Amaryllida siluas. (1–5)

Tityrus, you lying there under the covert of a spreading beech, you meditate the woodland Muse on a slender reed: we are leaving our country and these dear fields. We are fleeing our country: you, Tityrus, easy in the shade, teach the woods to echo fair Amaryllis' name.

This seemingly artless statement consists of two sentences or periods, each a tricolon (the rhetorical structure would be clearer with a comma after *fagi* and *umbra*); and has in fact been contrived with much art:

Line 2: the two adjectives before the main pause or caesura, *siluestrem tenui*, are completed and balanced by the two nouns after the caesura, *Musam...auena*; the implicated word-order is suggestively Alexandrian in technique.

[1] Virgil was a laborious finisher. When he was writing the *Georgics*, he would dictate a very large number of verses every morning, then spend the whole day reducing these to the fewest possible – like a she-bear, he said, licking his poem into shape (*Vita Don.* 22). 'When he was writing the *Georgics*' – that is, when the *Eclogues* had made him famous and his work-habits an object of curiosity.

Lines 3–4: the iteration is extremely pathetic, *nos patriae finis... | nos patriam...* The contrasting arrangement of the personal pronouns, *tu...nos*, *nos...tu*, adds to the intensity of the effect.

Line 5: the two last words echo (*resonare*) to the sense, *Amaryllida siluas.*[1]

No Roman reader had ever heard music quite like this before.

The first *Eclogue* is, in several ways, a strange poem, recognizably Theocritean in manner and yet very different from anything Theocritus wrote: Theocritus excludes the profanity of war and politics from his pastoral demesne. It is a beautiful poem, however, about a harsh and ugly experience that Virgil had suffered with his fellow-countrymen, but only as may be surmised: the first *Eclogue* is not, in any useful sense, autobiography. Virgil's paternal farm, not quite fact and not quite fiction, bears no resemblance to Horace's Sabine villa.

'O Meliboeus', Tityrus answers (the tone deepening):

O Meliboee, deus nobis haec otia fecit,
namque erit ille mihi semper deus, illius aram
saepe tener nostris ab ouilibus imbuet agnus. (6–8)

O Meliboeus, a god has given me this ease. For he *will ever be a god to me, often will a tender lamb from my fold stain* his *altar.*

Who is the benevolent young god to whom Tityrus owes his pastoral ease?

sed tamen iste deus qui sit da, Tityre, nobis. (18)

But tell me, Tityrus, who is this god of yours.

Meliboeus is not told; Tityrus changes the subject: *urbem quam dicunt Romam, Meliboee*...'The city they call Rome, Meliboeus...' (19). Ancient readers noticed, and were puzzled: 'The question is why does he, on being asked about Octavian, describe Rome' (Servius). Virgil's poetic tact is here most politic.[2]

The first *Eclogue* cannot have been written, as generally supposed, about 40 B.C. In that year Octavian was a young man of twenty-three, but a young man hated and feared for the depredations in the Po valley and the massacre of Perugia, and more or less openly despised in comparison with Antony. Furthermore, in that year, as may be inferred from the fourth *Eclogue*, Pollio was Virgil's patron (perhaps they met when Pollio was governing Cisalpine Gaul for Antony); and Pollio and Octavian were not then, nor were they ever to be, friends.

The first in an ancient book of poems was usually the last or one of the last written, and served to introduce those which followed.[3] Only on the assump-

[1] Cf. Catull. 11.3–4; a similar effect can be heard in *Geo.* 1.486.

[2] See Clausen (1972) 204–5.

[3] *Ecl.* 1 appears to have been designed so as to conform with the design of the book itself: Meliboeus begins with *5* lines, Tityrus answers with *5* = *10*; then M. 8, T. 7 = 15; M. 1, T. 9 = 10; M. 4, T. 6 = 10; M. 13, T. *5* = 18 (a slight variation characteristic of Virgil's mature style); M. 15,

tion that it was written in 35 B.C. (or at the very end of 36 B.C.) does the first *Eclogue* become intelligible. In early September 36 B.C. Pompey's son Sextus was utterly defeated at Naulochus, and peace at last seemed secure in the West. In the grateful municipalities of Italy Octavian's statue was set up beside the statues of the customary gods: he became, in Hellenistic style, an 'additional' god. Virgil's first *Eclogue* may be taken as a personal expression of a public attitude; and in this respect compared with his fourth, written in a mood of hope and euphoria after Brundisium.

Time is a relation of experience, and much had happened in the few urgent years during which Virgil was meditating his book. His consulate over, Pollio had gone off to govern Macedonia for Antony; Virgil came to know Maecenas and, somewhat later it would seem, Octavian. Whether imperceptibly or dramatically his position changed – supposing a previous allegiance of some kind had existed. To confound past experience with present is only human; yet Virgil does not forget the anguish of that earlier time. Now, finally, he can represent that experience in pastoral terms and contemplate, in the person of Tityrus, Octavian as saviour and god.

The fourth

By a small irony of history the one eclogue that can be related to a historical event was related to a historic event, and consequently misunderstood for centuries. The modern reader of course understands that the fourth *Eclogue* has nothing to do with the advent of Christ and the peaceable kingdom; he may find, however, that hallowed error is not so easily dispelled, and that it is all but impossible not to overhear, as he reads, the dominant tones of Isaiah 11.6: 'And the wolf shall dwell with the lamb, and the leopard shall lie down with the kid; and the calf and the young lion and the fatling together; and a little child shall lead them.' Something of its grand and sombre repute clings to this brilliant little poem still.

For such it is, exuberantly imaginative, allusive, elusive; serious, tender, playful – a virtuoso performance by a very self-confident young poet, finely calculated, but bewildering with its sudden intensities. The poem was excited by the pact of Brundisium, a political settlement between Antony and Octavian which soon receded into insignificance but which, for the moment, appeared bright with promise. Negotiations were concluded in late September or early October 40 B.C. with the consul Pollio acting on Antony's behalf. Hence:

teque adeo decus hoc aeui, te consule inibit,
Pollio, et incipient magni procedere menses. (11–12)

While you, while you are consul, Pollio, shall enter this glorious age and the great months begin their state.

T. *5* = 20. In *Ecl.* 2 Corydon's 'disordered' utterance (4 *haec incondita*) is introduced with 5 lines and ends with 5 lines of self-reproach. To secure this symmetry Virgil amputated the last 3 lines of Polyphemus' complaint in *Id.* 11 (77–9); thus he relates *Ecl.* 2 formally to *Ecl.* 1.

This poetical annunciation seems curiously remote from the political fact: such extravagant reference is typical of the poem and makes it difficult to interpret. And yet, at whatever remove, political fact must be reckoned with.

The poem begins with oracular solemnity: the last age of the Sibyl's spell is now come, a great ordinance of time is born anew (*nascitur ordo*) and with it a wonder-child:

> tu modo nascenti puero, quo ferrea primum
> desinet ac toto surget gens aurea mundo,
> casta faue Lucina. (8–10)

Lucina, chaste goddess, bless the boy, at whose birth the iron age shall first cease and the golden rise up throughout the world.

As this son of time grows slowly to manhood, so will the golden age (for a few traces of aboriginal sin remain) be purified.

The pact of Brundisium was consummated, after the high Roman fashion, with a dynastic wedding: Antony took Octavian's sister, the blameless Octavia, to wife. For contemporary readers of Virgil's poem the vexed question 'Who is the boy?' would not arise. They would know who was meant: the son of Antony and Octavia, and heir to Antony's greatness (17) – the son that never was, a daughter was born instead.[1] Antony claimed descent from Hercules as proudly as Julius Caesar claimed descent from Venus;[2] thus the boy would have been descended on his father's side from Hercules, on his mother's from Venus: a symbol incarnate of unity and peace. Like Hercules[3] (the poem implies) he will be exalted to heaven, there to see gods mingling with heroes (15–16, among them the recently deified Julius?), to banquet with gods and share a goddess's bed (63).

In the year 40 B.C. – on earth – Antony, not Octavian, was the commanding figure; and of this their contemporaries, spectators to the mighty scene, would have no doubt. The modern reader, under the disadvantage of hindsight, must constantly remind himself that Octavian was not yet Augustus nor Virgil yet the poet of the *Aeneid*; that both eventualities were as yet latent in an unimaginable future. Failure of historical perspective distorts much of what is written about the fourth *Eclogue*.

The epithalamium is a potentially embarrassing form of composition. That Virgil conceived of his poem as in some sort an epithalamium is indicated by lines 46–7:

> 'Talia saecla' suis dixerunt 'currite' fusis
> concordes stabili fatorum numine Parcae.

'Speed on such ages' to their spindles the Parcae sang, unanimous by fate's established will

[1] All this was forgotten with the years, until Asinius Gallus (Pollio's son) could assert that he was the child. What would his father have said!

[2] App. *Bell. civ.* 3.16, 19; also Plut. *Ant.* 4, 36.

[3] The type and model of heroic virtue; the word *heros* occurs 3 times in *Ecl.* 4, but nowhere else in the *Eclogues*. This divine connexion was later appropriated to Augustus even though he was not descended from Hercules, cf. Hor. *Odes* 3.3.9–12, 14.1–4.

– an allusion to Catullus 64, to the song the Parcae sang at the wedding of Peleus and Thetis, whose son was to be the great Achilles.[1] When, some five years later, Virgil decided to publish his 'epithalamium' as an 'eclogue', he prefixed a brief pastoral apologia (1–3); at the same time – hope having been disappointed, circumstances altered – it is likely that he made certain other adjustments. Hence something of the mystery, or mystification perhaps, which readers sense in the fourth *Eclogue*.

The sixth

cum canerem reges et proelia, Cynthius aurem
uellit et admonuit: 'pastorem, Tityre, pinguis
pascere oportet ouis, deductum dicere carmen.'
nunc ego (namque super tibi erunt qui dicere laudes,
Vare, tuas cupiant et tristia condere bella)
agrestem tenui meditabor harundine Musam. (3–8)

When I was singing of kings and battles, Cynthian Apollo tweaked my ear and warned: 'A shepherd, Tityrus, ought to feed fat sheep, but sing a fine-spun song.' Now I (for there will be poets enough wanting to tell your praises, Varus, and recount war's grim story), I will meditate the rural Muse on a slender reed.

This passage can now be understood for what it is: not an autobiographical statement, as ancient scholiasts thought, but a literary allusion, Virgil's pastoral rendering of Callimachus' famous rejection of epic:[2]

καὶ γὰρ ὅτε πρώτιστον ἐμοῖς ἐπὶ δέλτον ἔθηκα
γούνασιν, Ἀ[πό]λλων εἶπεν ὅ μοι Λύκιος·
'.......]... ἀοιδέ, τὸ μὲν θύος ὅττι πάχιστον
θρέψαι, τὴ]ν Μοῦσαν δ' ὠγαθὲ λεπταλέην. (*Aet.* 1.1.21–4)

For when first I set a writing-tablet on my knees, Lycian Apollo spoke to me: poet, feed your victim as fat as you can, but your Muse, my good fellow, keep her thin.

Agrestem tenui meditabor harundine Musam: no attentive reader can fail to hear the echo of the first *Eclogue*: *siluestrem tenui Musam meditaris auena.* There the adjective *tenui* is ornamental, necessary rather to the balance of the line than to its meaning. Here, however, the adjective is no mere ornament: it involves a concept of style, the Callimachean concept, and is the Latin equivalent of λεπταλέος (or λεπτός). His pastoral poetry, all of it, Virgil thus obliquely asserts, is Callimachean in nature.

Silenus is a stranger to Theocritean pastoral; an intractable character whom Virgil hardly confines within a pastoral frame of reference (13–30, 82–6).

[1] See especially Slater (1912); more generally Tarn (1932) 151–7, Syme (1939) 216–20; and above, p. 193.
[2] See above, pp. 181–2.

Traditional features[1] remain: he is the ancient drunkard still, the lover of nymphs and music, gifted with arcane wisdom. Yet Virgil's Silenus – and the Silenus of the sixth *Ecologue* is largely Virgil's – is wondrously changed: he has undergone a Callimachean metamorphosis from forest seer to literary critic.

Virgil's song of Silenus (31–73) originates in Apollonius' song of Orpheus, as Virgil wished his reader to notice: Silenus sings more enchantingly than even Orpheus himself (27–8, 30).

> Ἤειδεν δ' ὡς γαῖα καὶ οὐρανὸς ἠδὲ θάλασσα,
> τὸ πρὶν ἔτ' ἀλλήλοισι μιῇ συναρηρότα μορφῇ,
> νείκεος ἐξ ὀλοοῖο διέκριθεν ἀμφὶς ἕκαστα·
> ἠδ' ὡς ἔμπεδον αἰὲν ἐν αἰθέρι τέκμαρ ἔχουσιν
> ἄστρα, σεληναίης τε καὶ ἠελίοιο κέλευθοι·
> οὔρεά θ' ὡς ἀνέτειλε, καὶ ὡς ποταμοὶ κελάδοντες
> αὐτῇσιν νύμφῃσι καὶ ἑρπετὰ πάντ' ἐγένοντο.
> ἤειδεν δ' ὡς πρῶτον Ὀφίων Εὐρυνόμη τε
> Ὠκεανὶς νιφόεντος ἔχον κράτος Οὐλύμποιο. (*Arg.* 1.496–594)

He sang how earth and sky and sea had of old been fitted together in one form, but separated, each apart, the result of a deadly quarrel; and how forever in heaven the stars and the paths of the moon and sun have their steadfast place; and how the mountains rose up, and how plashing rivers with their nymphs and all creeping things came to be. He sang how first Ophion and Eurynome, daughter of Ocean, held sway over snowy Olympus.

Like Orpheus, Silenus begins with the creation of the world, the emergence of living things, primeval figures, Pyrrha, Prometheus; and his song is similarly articulated: 31 *namque canebat* 'for he sang', 41 *hinc* 'hereupon', 43 *his adiungit* 'to these he joins', 61 *tum canit* 'then he sings', 62 *tum* 'then', 64 *tum canit* 'then he sings'. But whereas Orpheus 'stayed his lyre and ambrosial voice' (512) with Zeus still a child in the Dictaean cave, still thinking childish thoughts, Silenus continues on, singing as if there were to be no end of song, singing until 'the evening star advanced in the unwilling sky' (86). He sings distractedly, as it seems, touching on various subjects; in fact, his song is by way of being a neoteric *ars poetica*, artfully concealed, with but a single subject: poetry, as defined by Callimachus (and poets after Callimachus) and as now exemplified by Gallus. That Pasiphae's ἐρωτικὸν πάθημα – Virgil's perfect miniature of an epyllion – and the recondite praise of Gallus' aetiological poem occupy most of the song can only be a reflection of contemporary taste, Virgil's and that of his friends.

Although the sixth *Eclogue* is addressed ostensibly to Varus, the chief figure is obviously Gallus; and readers have therefore sensed an awkwardness or disunity in the poem. The failure of sensibility is not Virgil's, it is the modern

[1] Cf. *OCD* s.v. 'Satyrs and Silenoi'.

reader's, unschooled in Callimachean poetics. The refusal to write an epic poem necessarily involved writing a different poem since the refusal was always made in a poem. Apollo's magisterial rebuke to the poet and the poet's initiation on Helicon: these two scenes are complementary, the one explicitly, the other implicitly, programmatic; and the two occurred together at the beginning of the *Aetia*.

One of the Muses conducts Gallus to the summit of Helicon, where the divine singer-shepherd Linus (pastoralized by Virgil for the occasion) gives him Hesiod's pipes, with these words:

> 'hos tibi dant calamos (en accipe) Musae,
> Ascraeo quos ante seni, quibus ille solebat
> cantando rigidas deducere montibus ornos.
> his tibi Grynei nemoris dicatur origo,
> ne quis sit lucus quo se plus iactet Apollo.' (69–73)

'These reeds the Muses give you (come, take them), the reeds they gave of old to Ascra's poet, with which he used to sing and draw the stubborn ash-trees down from the mountains. With these tell the "cause" of the Grynean grove, so that there be no wood in which Apollo glories more.'

Apollo will be pleased with Gallus' poem about his sacred grove: at this point the reader may recall how displeased Apollo was with a poem about kings and battles. Now with a conclusive *quid loquar...?* 'Why should I speak of...?' at the beginning of line 74, Virgil hurries Silenus' song and his own to a pastoral close. The abrupt phrase has the effect of underlining what immediately precedes; and the poet speaks again in his own person, as he did at the outset: *cum canerem reges et proelia.*

That the same poet who wrote *cum canerem reges et proelia* wrote, years later, *Arma uirumque cano* is one of the considerable surprises of literature. The sixth *Eclogue* is an appropriately oblique – but uncompromising – declaration of adherence to the aesthetic principles of Callimachus; no reader at the time could have anticipated that its author would one day write an epic – a didactic or aetiological poem possibly, but not an epic. The *Aeneid* so imposes upon the imagination that Virgil's poetic career is seen as an orderly progression from the lesser to the greater work; it requires a corresponding effort of the imagination to see that it cannot have been so.

17

THE *GEORGICS*

I. POLITICAL BACKGROUND

By 39 B.C. Virgil had joined the circle of Octavian's right-hand man Maecenas. But Antony was still the dominant Triumvir. It was only with the defeat of Sextus Pompeius in 36 and the consequent lifting of the threat of starvation from Italy that Octavian, the man on the spot, brushing Lepidus aside, began to outshine his other colleague, absent in the East. From then on the final showdown, at Actium in 31, became inevitable. The misery of the years following Julius' murder are recalled in Virgil's next work, the *Georgics*, in the magnificent rhetoric of the finale of Book 1, 466–514, which represents the chaos as continuing and the young Octavian as the only hope. But by the time the proems to Books 1 and 3 and the epilogue were composed Octavian has emerged as sole leader, a triumphant candidate for divinity. One major misery had been the ruin of agriculture: small-holders were conscripted for war or evicted to accommodate veterans, many of whom would be less competent farmers even if minded to cultivate land at all.

To what extent was there already an 'Augustan' policy? As to agriculture, we hear of no legislation concerning land-tenure apart from the settlement of veterans. The development of large slave-run estates (*latifundia*), favoured by the geography of Italy and the economic trends of the times, continued. But there was a feeling abroad among thinking people, reflected also by Horace, that a simple, Sabine-type, peasant life was happier and morally healthier, at least for others. It is this that the *Georgics* advocated, its idealism signalized by the astonishing absence of any reference to slavery; and the districts Virgil knew best, the Po valley and the surroundings of Naples, happened to be ones in which the small-holder (*colonus*) still flourished. The attunement of the *Georgics* to future Augustan policy was more moral than agricultural. Nor need we press the words 'your behest, no easy one, Maecenas' (3.41):[1] whatever encouragement may have come from the statesman, its inspiration is clearly literary and personal: it was a labour of love – *singula dum* capti *circumuectamur* amore 'while enthralled by love we are transported from one thing to another' (3.289).

[1] See van de Woestijne (1929) 523–30.

The poem deals with husbandry in four books – on Crops, Trees, Beasts and Bees. It occupied Virgil till 29 B.C. The set pieces with which it is diversified, though integral to the overall poetic design, seem mostly to have been worked up last. Thus the proem (1.1–42) addresses Caesar (Octavian) as now supreme; the epilogue (4.559–62) and the encomium of Italy (2.136–76) refer to his eastern campaign during the winter of 30/29 (2.170–2); the proem to Book 3 anticipates his triple Triumph of August 29 (ll. 26–36); the encomium of country life (2.458–540) has references that would be topical then (ll. 495–8), and the description of the Corycian's garden (4.116–48) proclaims itself as late in its opening lines. Suetonius tells how Virgil, aided by Maecenas, read the completed poem to Caesar on his return to Italy in the summer of 29.[1]

2. LITERARY ANTECEDENTS

In the *Eclogues* Virgil had established himself as the Roman Theocritus. He had shown an interest in country life to be expected of the son of the Mantuan farm, a concern for evicted peasants in 9 and 1, and for the revival of agriculture in 5. But his singing herdsmen are inhabitants of a 'soft primitive' Arcady of the imagination. He next aspired to be the Roman Hesiod, Hesiod being another poet who had appealed to the Alexandrianizing 'modernists',[2] to 'sing a song of Ascra through Roman towns' (2.176). There are in Book 1 some obvious superficial reminders of Hesiod's *Works and days*, but otherwise his chief relevance is more general, by his insistence on the moral value of relentless hard work performed by the small farmer *ipse manu*.

Another favourite of the Alexandrians and their 'neoteric' followers was Aratus. Virgil, always adept at transfiguring what was suggestive in inferior poets, made much poetic capital out of his *Weather-signs* in 1.351–468. More generally, his attribution of phenomena to divine providence may owe something to Aratus. There is further evidence of specific influence at 2.536–42; the onset of the Iron Age is marked, as in Aratus (*Phaenomena* 127, 132), by the departure of Justice (in Hesiod it was Aidos and Nemesis) and the impious innovation of eating meat (oxen). Even the dry Hellenistic versifier Nicander is laid under contribution, his extant work at 3.391 and 425; and Quintilian (10.1.56) is our authority for thinking that more was owed to his *Georgics* (of which his poem on *Bee-keeping* may possibly have been a part).

But by far the greatest poetical influence, directly and indirectly, was

[1] Suet. *Virg.* 25, 27. We may suppose that Virgil began to study for the *Georgics* well before 36, even if we do not accept J. Bayet's theory (1930) that he composed Book 1 as a Hesiodic entity in 39–37, and then added 2–4 under the stimulus of Varro's prose treatise in dialogue *Res rusticae*, which appeared in 37/6.

[2] '*Neoteroi*'. At *Eclogue* 6.64–71 Gallus, consecrated as poet by Linus, receives as a gift from the Muses of Helicon the pipe they had once given to Hesiod.

Lucretius, whose *De rerum natura* appeared when Virgil was at school. Lucretius would show him how a didactic poem could be moving by its descriptive power and its moral-philosophic fervour. Many passages show specific influence, whether they agree, as in detestation of war, or disagree, as on Stoic providence against Epicurean fortuity in the universe.[1] The attraction of poet for poet is stronger than any difference of mentality and temperament:

> felix qui potuit rerum cognoscere causas...
> fortunatus et ille deos qui nouit agrestis. (2.490, 493)

Happy the man who has been able to find out the causes of things... Fortunate too is he who has found the gods of the countryside.

Scientific sources

As for agricultural lore, many of Virgil's possible sources are lost.[2] But he clearly used Theophrastus for Book 2, Aristotle for 3 and 4. No Roman would disregard Cato's extant *De agri cultura*, of which we find traces. But paramount was Varro's *Res rusticae*, which appeared in 37/6, just when he was starting work. This dialogue had literary pretensions, and may have suggested certain literary features, such as the opening invocation to twelve gods (cf. Varro 1.4–6). It certainly influenced some technical passages. But above all it is a standing reminder that for any Roman farmer who, *ignarus uiae*, needed technical advice there were real handbooks available, far fuller than the *Georgics*. Those who praise Virgil's knowledge of husbandry should recollect that, while he gives the impression of being a keen countryman, his knowledge may always be second-hand, and that he sometimes gives advice which first-hand knowledge would have precluded. This opens the whole question of the intention and nature of the poem.

3. INTENTION AND NATURE OF THE POEM

Seneca (*Epist.* 86.15) said pertinently that Virgil was interested in what could be said most gracefully (*decentissime*), not most truthfully (*uerissime*), and wrote not to teach farmers but to delight readers. Even Hesiod had tempered didactic with descriptive as well as narrative set-pieces (e.g. winter and summer, *Works and days* 504–35, 582–96) and endowed it with moral import. In Lucretius the scientifically didactic had to be exhaustive to validate his message, but it is blended with descriptive and moral-philosophical elements to form a whole of cosmic imagination. In Virgil the technically didactic matter is eclectic, yet it forms too large a part of the poem for it to be taken as purely symbolic. Addison may supplement Seneca: 'this kind of poem addresses itself wholly to the

[1] See also *Ecl.* 6.33ff.; *Aen.* 6.724ff.

[2] On Virgil's sources, scientific and literary, see Büchner (1955) 305–9.

imagination...It raises in our minds a pleasing variety of Scenes and Landskips whilst it teaches us...We find our Imaginations more affected by the descriptions than they would have been by the very sight of what he describes.' Hellenistic writers had delighted in passages of description (*ekphrasis*), and Hellenistic landscape-painting was ubiquitous in Roman houses. The *Georgics* can be seen as the first poem in which the descriptive element (largely embodied in precept form) is the prime source of pleasure. Yet it is much more; for it uses teaching about husbandry to convey the essence of a way of life, hard and sometimes tragic, but regular and often rewarding. In the shameful darkness of contemporary Rome and Italy it shines a ray of hope and pride. But it is also representative of human life in general, with its rewards as well as its toil and with intimations of divine presences and paternal providence. Selective variety, another Hellenistic trait, and ingenious artistic structure sustain the whole.

4. STRUCTURE

In the case of a poem whose excellence depends on a variety of features the best, perhaps the only, way of doing justice to it is by a running commentary, in terms of structure. To several sensitive critics the *Georgics* has suggested a musical composition, a symphony with four movements and various themes enunciated and then harmoniously interwoven.[1] It falls into pairs of books, each pair having an 'external' proem. The first and third books emphasize the struggle against degeneration, disease and death and are generally sombre in tone; the second and fourth deal by contrast with work that is easier, are mainly cheerful, and end happily. But these are only crude generalizations: the modulations of mood are much subtler.

After a neatly economical summary of contents, addressed to Maecenas, the proem bursts into a breathless, grand-style invocation of agricultural deities (twelve, a canonical number), followed by a balancing invocation, in the exaggerated 'baroque' style of Hellenistic adulation, of the coming god Caesar (1–42). (Modern readers may find this distasteful; but ancient ones, familiar with the convention, and at that historical moment, will have taken it in their stride.) Then begins, with spring, a long section on field crops (43–203). At once the Hesiodic theme of hard work emerges. Ploughing slips insensibly into study of local differences of soil, thence to the picturesque variety of products of foreign lands, and so, by 'ring composition', a device as old as Hesiod, back again to ploughing in early spring (of rich land only – poorer must be ploughed in autumn: 63–70). So far, in twenty-eight lines since the proem, we have had four precepts only, but a vivid, pictorial impression of continual work. The

[1] The structure of the *Georgics* has been given a new dimension in the criticism of Burck (1929), Büchner (1955), Klingner (1963) and Otis (1963). See further Wilkinson (1969), Ch. IV.

mention of poorer soil leads into soil-improvement. The foreign lands theme is heard again, and two new ones emerge – religion (prayer for good weather and Ceres' help for him who helps himself) and the military metaphor of subduing the fields (71–117).

Injurious birds, weeds and shade, which impose a constant struggle, are the cue for an important and controversial philosophic passage (188–59), a theodicy. 'The Father himself did not want the path of husbandry to be easy, and introduced the skills of agriculture, sharpening the wits of mortals by cares.' The 'soft primitivism' of Golden Age mythology is rejected in favour of a Stoic solution of the problem of evil and justification of the ways of God to men. Rapidly Virgil reviews the consequent achievements of man's inventiveness, in a passage which ends with the famous words

labor omnia uicit
improbus, et duris urgens in rebus egestas. (145–6)

Wicked toil has mastered everything, and the pressure of pinching poverty.

Improbus is always a pejorative epithet, and some critics take this conclusion to be wholly pessimistic.[1] But does it represent Virgil's reaction or that of the toiler? The recital of man's achievements is reminiscent of Prometheus' recital in Aeschylus (*Prom. Bound* 458–522) of the inventions he has taught man, but Virgil has boldly transferred Prometheus' role to Jupiter himself. One may feel that to him, as to Lucretius also (5.1361–78, 1448–57), the arts that give variety to life are worth the struggle involved. (*Varius* is a key-word that constantly recurs throughout the poem, see p. 323.) This passage, thus placed early, separates Jupiter from the conventional agricultural deities of the proem as the monotheistic Zeus of the Stoics, and sets the philosophical tone of the whole. With the passing of the easy Golden Age, the institution of ploughing, and more about the invasion of birds, weeds, and shade, the paragraph is rounded off – 'ring-composition' again.

The metaphorical warfare requires arms, which follow (160–75), some implements merely listed, some dignified with epithets recalling the mystic agricultural rites of Eleusis, with the making of a plough finally described in Hesiodic detail (*uariatio*). Divers detailed precepts follow (176–99), with a discernible train of thought-association, till the vivid simile (199–203) of a man rowing against the current and only just managing not to be swept away sums up a section whose theme has been relentless toil. It is a law of nature that everything tends to degenerate; but Virgil slips in at 168 a reminder of the reward for defeating the tendency – *diuini gloria ruris* 'the glory of a divine countryside'.

'Days' follow 'Works': a balancing section (204–350) deals with the

[1] E.g. Altevogt (1952).

farmer's calendar. Passages on the rising and setting of constellations as signals to him, and on the five zones of the earth, raise incidental thoughts (*idcirco* 231, *munere concessae diuum* 238) of the Providence that has ordered the universe for man with such signals and two habitable zones (204–58). Miscellaneous precepts follow for making good use of every moment, even winter nights and days of religious festival – though these give relaxation also (259–310). A spectacular descriptive passage of a storm at harvest-time is here introduced, ostensibly to remind the farmer to observe the signs and seasons and to propitiate the gods – a festival of Ceres (a synthetic one, it seems[1]) affords relief (311–50). The storm provides a natural lead into the next section, the Weather Signs, established by 'the Father himself'. Virgil draws freely on Aratus, though with much more picturesque detail; but he reverses his order so that the sun comes last as a sign-giver (351–463). He is thus able to lead, by way of the portents allegedly shown by it at the time of Julius Caesar's murder, into a tremendous rhetorical finale on other portents of that time, and an appeal to the old indigenous gods of Rome to allow the young Caesar to rescue an age careering to ruin (463–514).

Book 2 opens contrastingly with a short, cheering invocation to Bacchus, god of all trees but especially the vine (1–8). (The address to Maecenas, which every book contains, is deferred to 39–46.) The first main section (9–258) illustrates, and is sustained by, variety, with special reference to trees[2] – variety in methods (nine) of tree-propagation (9–82), variety of trees, and of vines in particular, which give occasion for a connoisseur's list of Greek and Italian wines (83–108). A passage on the different products of various lands (109–35) prepares for a rhetorical encomium of the all-producing land of Italy (136–76; cf. Varro 1.2.6), a famous passage in which pride in the (somewhat idealized) fertility, variety and beauty of the 'Saturnian' land (Saturn ruled in the Golden Age) mingles with pride in the men of Rome and their achievements. (This Romano-Italian patriotism, dating from the end of the Social War sixty years before, was to be an essential part of Augustanism, as in the latter part of the *Aeneid*.) The passage is in key with Book 2 by contrast with the finale of Book 1, where *squalent abductis arua colonis* 'the fields are unkempt, their tillers taken away' (508).

Abruptly, so as not to blur his climax, Virgil restarts at ground level, giving technical details about various soils and what they are suited for (177–258), with glimpses (surprisingly rare in the *Georgics*) of particular localities, notably ones familiar to him near Mantua, Naples or Tarentum, in the Italy just comprehensively praised. The next section (259–457) is on planting and care of trees, especially vines. The precepts, picturesque in themselves, are diversified

[1] Bayet (1955).

[2] The book can be seen as comprising three main parts, 9–258, 259–457, 458–542; alternatively, with Richter (1957), four: 9–126 variety in the production of trees; 177–345 nature and testing of soil, and planting; 346–457 work for the growth and protection of the plants; 458–542 finale.

by the simile of a legion drawn up for battle (279–85), the description of a great oak (291–7), and of a plantation fire (303–11), and the soaring paean on spring (322–45). The damage done by the goat, for which it is sacrificed to Bacchus, gives occasion for a description of the festival of Compitalia (380–96), corresponding to that of Ceres in Book 1 but in this case idealized by the introduction of Greek elements (for this is literature, not documentary).[1] It is important to realize that religion in the *Georgics* is more Greek than Italian.[2] (To see their life-scene in the light of their knowledge of Greek life and literature was peculiarly exciting to Romans, just as post-Renaissance Europeans loved to invest the present with classical trappings.) Other trees need less care than vines, and are treated in a light-hearted passage that ranges far and wide over the world (420–57).

The tone is thus set for the famous finale, the encomium of country life (458–542), which consummates the optimism of Book 2 by contrast with the finale that consummates the pessimism of Book 1. It is fine rhetoric on a conventional theme, even if the idyllic and Golden Age colouring belies the emphasis in Book 1, and particularly in the theodicy there, on the necessity for unremitting toil. Lines 495–512 are Lucretian-style satire on the hectic, immoral life of the metropolis, juxtaposed most effectively, through the sudden, asyndetic peace of the spondaic line, *agricola incuruo terram dimouit aratro* 'the farmer has gone on cleaving his land with the curved plough', to an enthusiastic description of the regular, moral life of the country, with its constant round of produce and pleasures, the life that in the past made Rome great.

Book 3 opens with a proem (1–48) in which Virgil speaks of his poetic intentions. The central portion (10–40) reveals a remarkable symbolic vision. Apparently with Pindar in mind, he imagines himself as both victor and master of ceremonies at games to be held at his native Mantua, whither he has led the Muses in triumph from Helicon. There he will build by the Mincius a temple to Caesar, with his cult-statue placed in the midst. (No doubt he was thinking of the temple of Divus Iulius which Caesar, who must here be Octavian, was shortly to dedicate, as well as the temple of Zeus by the Alpheus at Olympia and the Pindaric metaphor of building a temple of song.) Then, adopting another Pindaric metaphor, that of the chariot of song, already introduced at the close of the previous book, he says he will cause a hundred chariots to race by the river, and divert all Greece from Olympia and Nemea to these Mantuan competitions. He himself will lead the procession to sacrifice and also stage plays (a feature of Roman, not Greek, games). On the doors of the temple (here he may have had in mind another temple then rising, that of Palatine Apollo) he will have carvings descriptive or symbolic of Caesar's victories in the East, and there will be statues of the Trojan ancestors of Rome and Apollo the founder of

[1] Meuli (1955).

[2] Wissowa (1917) 98–9.

Troy. Caesar himself has now become the Triumphator, as he was shortly to be in reality. At 41, dropping the symbolism, Virgil intimates that he means to finish the *Georgics* and then soon gird himself to immortalize Caesar's battles. The most astonishing thing about this passage is the way in which the shy son of a Mantuan farmer, emboldened by Pindar, dares to represent himself as triumphant in poetry just as Caesar is in war, already the laureate of Augustanism. The quasi-deification of Caesar in the present is a feature of the enthusiasm of the first year or two after Actium (cf. 1.42; Horace, *Odes* 1.2 fin.): later Caesar himself was to enjoin more caution.

Seu quis Olympiacae – the train of thought from the proem to horses is clear in the opening of the first of two roughly-equal parts that constitute Book 3 – 49–283 on horses and cattle, the rest on sheep and goats. The pessimistic lines 66–8 on the swift fading of youth set the tone: as in Book 1, toil and trouble are again the burden. Sex and death emerge as dominant themes, with disease and age between (49–156). We read of the selection of breeding-stock in cattle and horses and the rearing of their young (157–208). There follows a passage on the power of sex, something that Virgil clearly regards as dangerous and debilitating, however necessary for procreation (209–83). The description of the battle between two bulls for a beautiful cow and the the come-back made by the defeated rival (215–41) moves us as Virgil's anthropomorphism so often does. Lust is indeed a madness (*furor*) common to all living things; and in a passage of headlong intensity (242–83) he instances its ravages, with humans represented by 'the youth' (Leander, but he is not named, thus seeming representative of all) who to come to his love set out even on a night of terrible storm to swim a strait, to his destruction and hers.

From the horror of this climax Virgil recalls himself to a new section, on the care of sheep and goats in winter and summer (284–338), humdrum matters which he resolves nevertheless, as a pioneer inspired by Lucretian enthusiasm, to dignify in verse (284–94). It is graced by an idyllic passage on pasturage at the first coming of spring (322–38), and a sketch of the nomad shepherds of Libya (339–48) and a longer one by way of contrast, on life in the frozen north (349–83). All this is descriptive poetry at its best. After further precepts (384–413) we come to the prevention and treatment of diseases (414–69), and hence to a great Lucretian-style finale (470–566), corresponding to the climactic passage on sex that ends the first part, and on a larger scale to the finale of Book 1 – a horrific description of a plague in the Nordic lands beneath the Alps which involved humans ultimately as well as animals in desolation and death. The horror is heightened by the fact that here, by contrast with other passages, the idea of providence is forgotten. Indeed the plague robs the gods of their rites. Once again, overall balance and poetic effectiveness seem to mean more to Virgil than consistency.

Book 4 transports us from this miasma to the 'heavenly gifts of airy honey' and the wonderful spectacle of the bees' world (1–7). A mock-heroic note is struck immediately with *magnanimosque duces* 'great-hearted leaders', and 'this play of great and small' is a feature of the first section of the book (8–115), especially in the battle-scene (67–85), which is brought to an end with the ironical curtain-lines, 'These upheavals of heart and these prodigious contests the throwing of a little handful of dust will reduce to quiescence.' The battle is between two kings (few ancients realized that the leader is queen, and also mother, of the hive) and their supporters, and the contrast between the superior and the inferior (88–102), both vividly described – the latter to be killed that the former may rule alone – is highly reminiscent of what was being said about Caesar and Antony by Caesarian propaganda at the time when the *Georgics* was being completed. Critics are divided as to whether any such application is intended.

In this section, dealing with settling, swarming, fighting, selection and swarming-fever, the bees are treated thus in an almost patronizing, half-humorous way. Apparently to mark off a change in approach Virgil here inserts a sketch for a garden Georgic he has no time to write, a description of a flourishing garden with apiary he once saw near Tarentum, made out of a small piece of unwanted land by an old immigrant from Corycus in Cilicia (166–48). The next section (149–227) deals with the peculiar *mores* of bees, a special gift to them from Jupiter – communism even as to children, loyalty to their homes and its laws, pooling of gains and division of labour, propagation without sexual intercourse (another vulgar error), readiness to sacrifice their life for the community, and finally, utter devotion to their ruler. It is clear that, to some extent, they are now being idealized. The passage is the obverse of those on anti-social behaviour at Rome in the finale of Book 1 and sexual lust in Book 3. It breathes the purer air of Augustan idealism. The section culminates (219–27) in a reference to a theory held by some, that bees have a share in divine intelligence, which merges into a wider theory, that of Platonic–Stoic pantheism Here Virgil only attributes this to 'certain people'; but that he was sympathetic to it himself is suggested by the fact that at *Aeneid* 6.729ff. he makes Anchises state it as fact.

Further precepts, about harvesting honey, are followed by short passages on pests, diseases and their remedies (239–80). This leads us on into the method of replacing an extinguished hive known as *bugonia*, a vulgar error countenanced by all ancient authorities known to us except Aristotle: from the carcase of an animal rightly treated, bees would appear by spontaneous generation. Virgil's version prescribes shutting up a bull-calf in a small specially constructed chamber amid aromatic branches and beating it to death without breaking the hide, then blocking up the natural orifices – presumably to keep in the life principle, which could thus pass into the emergent bees (281–314). Varro began his account of bees with *bugonia* (3.16.4); Virgil kept it till last, both logically and to prepare for the grand finale of the poem, an *aition* attributing its origin to the hero Aristaeus (315–558). The episode constitutes what we know as an epyllion (other extant examples in Latin are Catullus' 'Peleus and Thetis' and the pseudo-Virgilian *Ciris*), a short epic with a different, but in some sense relevant, story inset. Aristaeus, for the crime of causing Eurydice's death (she trod on a snake while fleeing from his embraces), lost all his bees. He had recourse to his divine mother Cyrene, who advised him to consult Proteus (315–414). Proteus when finally captured explained that he was being punished, and why, telling him also how Orpheus went down to the underworld and was retrieving Eurydice when he lost her again through disobediently looking back at her (415–527). Cyrene is then able to instruct him how to placate Eurydice's companions, the Nymphs, by sacrificing four bulls. He does so, and nine days later new bees are born from their carcases (528–58).

What function has this epyllion, a superb masterpiece in itself, in the poetic scheme of the poem (assuming that it was not a later substitute: see Excursus below)? Certainly the miracle of *bugonia* would have seemed a suitable climax to bee-lore. A finale was then needed, a set-piece to surpass even those that concluded the other books. *Aitia* (origins) were a favourite subject, and epyllia a favourite form of the Alexandrians in whose tradition Virgil was reared. Aristaeus, famous as pioneer of beekeeping, would be the obvious originator. It may be that there is no more to be said. But some modern critics are naturally loth to believe that Virgil, so careful over the structure of the rest of the poem, would have ended with a passage of some 244 lines that had little relevance to it. And what of the inset Orpheus story? So far as we know, Virgil was the first to connect Orpheus with Aristaeus, and the first to make him lose Eurydice through looking back because of overpowering love. He must have had some reason. These critics have therefore advanced symbolic interpretations of various kinds extending from the epyllion to the whole work (see Excursus). How convincing these are found, must depend on the individual reader's sense of probability in the context of what we know of ancient modes of thought. The propounders in turn may understandably be dissatisfied with the sceptic's explanation, or lack of one.

EXCURSUS

Servius twice indicates that the finale of Book 4 was, all or in part, a substitute: on *Eclogue* 10.1 he says that Book 4 from the middle to the end contained the praises of Gallus, which afterwards Virgil changed at the bidding of Augustus to the story of *Aristaeus*; while on *Georgics* 4.1 he says that the praises of Gallus stood in the place now occupied by the story of *Orpheus* (the inset portion ll. 453–527), which was inserted after the anger of Augustus led to Gallus' death. (Gallus, made first Prefect of Egypt in 30, was accused in 27 of treason and committed suicide.) 'Orpheus' here must surely be a slip for 'Aristaeus'; but Servius can often be convicted of fallacious concoction, and the story, mentioned by no one else, is dubious. For this is a public poem, and Gallus, though a close friend of Virgil, was less important than his patron Maecenas, let alone Caesar. How, with either political or poetic propriety, could it have ended with some 250 lines in his praise? The weight of scholarly opinion, despite some authoritative exceptions,[1] seems to have shifted towards accepting the original presence of the Aristaeus epyllion, and it has been assumed here. Nevertheless the origin of Servius' story remains a puzzle. Eight lines on Egypt (287–94) as the scene of bugonia occur in the transitional passage. Our text has been dislocated here, and a few lines about its new Prefect Gallus may have been removed through *damnatio memoriae*. Some tradition about this may have misled Servius or a predecessor to concoct the more drastic story.

As to possible applications of the Aristaeus epyllion to the poem as a whole, some have concentrated on the Orpheus episode. Orpheus figures as the enchanter of nature by his song, and also as centre of mystery cults of agrarian origin (Scazzoso, 1956, 5–28). The Mysteries *may* lie behind this episode, but the connexion of Orpheus with Aristaeus and of the epyllion with the rest of the poem is still not clearly explained. Some have suggested that Orpheus stood for Gallus, or that the epyllion was a substitute as a poem about tragic love of the kind he wrote, and so a veiled tribute to him (Coleman (1962) 55–71). But would this not have been seen as a reprehensible breach of *damnatio memoriae*?

J. Bayet (1930, 246–7) suggested that, whereas the theme of Book 3 was love and the Triumph of Death, that of 4 was chastity and the Triumph of Life; while Duckworth (1959, 225–37) characterized the ends of the four books as emphasizing respectively war, peace, death and rebirth. More comprehensive theories were put forward in 1963 by F. Klingner and B. Otis. Klingner (234ff.) interpreted the epyllion as a unity of opposites expressing Virgil's deepest intuitions, integrating two stories of newly granted and ever renewed life and of life passionately resought, almost regained, and then lost with utter finality. The life of the individual was fraught with pain, tragedy and death; but life is also the all-pervading and joyfully stirring spirit of life, which gives and takes back all individual life, so that, universally speaking, 'there is no room for death'. Klingner is, in fact, connecting the epyllion with the pantheistic views attributed to *quidam* (pl.) at 4.219–27. Disease and death for man and beast, represented in Book 3 without redemption, are redeemed and absorbed into a higher divine order (cf. Anchises' speech at *Aeneid* 6.724–51). Otis (186) also sees in ll. 219–27 'a theological idea to be set against the death-dealing nature of the second half of III'. To him the myth of the epyllion is the ultimate synthesis (in a different mode) of all the poet has been saying. 'We cannot understand the poem finally until we have understood the actual conclusion, its conception of the moral *cause* and *origin* of resurrection' (189). All the antitheses in the poem are resolved 'when man, exercising his full moral powers of control, work, self-sacrifice and devotion to his *patria*, finds himself sup-

[1] The case against Servius was revived in modern times notably by Anderson (1933) and independently Norden (1934). His more recent supporters include Büchner (1955) 294–7, de Saint-Denis (1956) and Richter (1957). Büchner suggests that Gallus was praised here as the elegiac poet of love. Richter (12–13) deduces that the *Georgics* cannot have been published until 26/5, after Gallus' death, so that the original Gallus passage was never published.

ported by the *logos* and indwelling spirit of the whole cosmos' (213). Otis well observes that the Orpheus section contrasts with the rest in that Virgil deals 'empathetically' with him, objectively with Aristaeus. C. Segal (1966), starting from this contrast, carried the symbolical interpretation to more complex depths. The Aristaeus episode is *necessary* to complete the *Georgics* because

> it ties together...the delicate and complicated relations between human activism and nature's resistance or acquiescence, between human destructiveness and nature's creativeness (or the reverse), between man's power over nature and nature's power over man. Human life, framed between the two figures (Aristaeus and Orpheus) is *essentially* tragic. And here emerges the significance of the first half of the Book, the bees: instead of collectivity selflessly devoted to the *genus immortale* we have in the second part individuals engaged in the personal emotions almost to the exclusion of anything else.

Explanation on these lines was persuasively reformulated by J. Griffin (1979). The bees' totalitarian kingdom, so admirable in its way, involves nevertheless tragic conflict in terms of human individuality, represented by juxtaposition in the story of Orpheus. This conflict was to permeate Virgil's treatment of the story of Rome and Aeneas.

Such interpretations are hard to summarize, let alone summarize fairly. Their diversity suggests that others will be produced. For a short summary of views on the Aristaeus epyllion down to 1969 see Wilkinson, 111–20 and Appendix IV of that publication.

5. OTHER POETIC FEATURES

A synopsis such as that given in the previous section may convey what the poem is *about*, but it can only begin to convey why it is *good*. Its merits are as multifarious as its subject matter. As to verse, the individual hexameter is that of the *Eclogues*, but much less often self-contained. Although, after the preliminary invocations (two headlong Lucretian periods of nineteen lines each), the sentences are rarely long, they have acquired impetus because the breaks within the line occur at such a variety of positions. The balanced 'Golden Line', overworked by Catullus, is reserved almost exclusively for rounding off a sentence, sometimes to great effect, as in

> impiaque aeternam timuerunt saecula noctem. (1.468)

and an impious age feared that eternal night had come.

The rhetorical figures too are effectively but not obtrusively employed. Virgil's ear is faultless. In general he keeps his sound harmonious, with assonance and alliteration used discreetly; but he is still more distinguished for the expressiveness of sound and rhythm accommodated to sense, as can be observed particularly in the storm and the weather-signs in Book 1.[1] This greatly enhances the pictorial

[1] For expressiveness in *Georgics* 1.43–293 see Wilkinson (1963) 74–83.

quality so important in the poem. So does his habit of describing in terms of action. Thus where Varro says that a cow's tail should reach to her heels, Virgil says, 'and as she walks she sweeps her tracks with the tip of her tail' (3.59). Everything is seen in human terms. The plane-tree planted is 'destined to provide shade for drinkers'. The general tendency to anthropomorphize nature, especially animals, imparts vitality; and where men are concerned he shows that *humanitas*, sympathetic understanding, which is one of his chief characteristics.

6. TRANSITION TO THE AENEID

In the eight-line epilogue (4.559–66), as in the proem to Book 3, Virgil boldly presents himself alongside Caesar, this time by way of playfully ironical contrast: while Caesar has been thundering on the Euphrates, dealing laws to willing peoples and qualifying for immortality, he himself has been composing this kind of poetry at Naples, 'flourishing in the pursuits of inactive obscurity'. At the end of the proem to 3 he undertakes that, when he has finished the *Georgics*, he will sing of Caesar's battles. Though Rome's Trojan origins are emphasized by the statues of *Tros parens* and the line of Assaracus that are to stand in his imaginary temple, the idea of the *Aeneid* has not yet taken shape. He only knows that what he composes next will be epic of some kind inspired by the Caesarian revival of Rome's greatness.

18

THE *AENEID*

I. THE 'AENEID' AND ITS AUGUSTAN BACKGROUND

Virgil's *Aeneid* was conceived and shaped as a national and patriotic epic for the Romans of his day. Certainly the Romans hailed it as such, and it rapidly became both a set text in education and the natural successor to the *Annales* of Ennius as the great poetic exposition of Roman ideals and achievements. As will be seen later on, there are discordant elements in the patriotic theme, but it is essential to recognize that Virgil's primary intention was to sing of his country's glories past and present, and of the greatness yet to come. For all his universality he is a true Augustan.

For many years Virgil had been preparing himself for this crowning achievement of poetic ambition. The Romans regarded the epic poem as the highest form of literature, a form constantly refused by Horace and Propertius as too heavy for their frail shoulders. There is a passage in the *Eclogues* where Virgil himself says that his thoughts were beginning to turn towards epic, but he was rebuked by Apollo, god of poetry:

> cum canerem reges et proelia, Cynthius aurem
> uellit et admonuit: 'pastorem, Tityre, pinguis
> pascere oportet ouis, deductum dicere carmen.' (*Ecl.* 6.3–5)

When I was going to sing of kings and battles, the god of Cynthus plucked my ear and chided me: 'Tityrus, a shepherd should feed his sheep to grow fat but sing a song that is slender.'

In his comment on the passage Servius tells us that this refers either to the *Aeneid*, or to the deeds of the kings of Alba Longa, which Virgil had begun to write about, but had abandoned the project because the names were unmanageable. Donatus (*Vita* 19) has the statement that Virgil began a Roman theme, but finding the material uncongenial went over to pastoral instead. We cannot be sure that these interpretations are correct, as the Virgilian passage may be a conventional 'refusal' (*recusatio*) of the Alexandrian type,[1] but it is quite certain that a few years later Virgil was indeed planning and preparing himself for the

[1] See Clausen (1964) 181ff. and above, p. 317.

heroic poem that would celebrate Rome's greatness. At the beginning of *Georgics* 3 he speaks of his future poetic ambitions – he will not write on the well-worn themes of Greek mythology, but will dedicate a special temple of song in Mantua, his birthplace. In the midst of his temple will be Caesar Augustus, with triumphal processions from all parts of the world offering their tributes: Trojan ancestors of the race of Assaracus along with Apollo the patron god of Troy will be present in the great concourse of Roman majesty. This is a clear prolepsis of the *Aeneid*, with the Trojan connexion of the Romans in general and the Julian *gens* in particular well to the fore. Evidently at this time Virgil's ideas were already focused on the two extremes of the time-scale of the *Aeneid* – the dramatic date which is the period immediately after the Trojan war, and the symbolic date which is the Augustan age, of which so much in the *Aeneid* is prototype and anticipation.

The eventual choice of Virgil's epic subject was becoming clearer in his mind while he was writing the *Georgics*. He rejects the mythology of Greece; the reason he gives is that it has become trite, but a deeper reason can clearly be seen, namely that to satisfy him his subject had to be Roman. He did not wish to write about the Argonauts (the theme of his later imitator Valerius Flaccus), nor about the Seven against Thebes (on which Statius wrote a century later), because his deepest poetic inclinations were rooted in Rome and Italy, the country of which his own Cisalpine Gaul had only recently become a part, which he already loved for the natural beauty of its farmlands and mountains and was soon to love also for its imperial message of peace and civilization for the world. But he decided too that direct historical writing or contemporary panegyric would confine his sensitivity for the universal application, would clip the wings of poetic symbolism; and so he left the panegyrics of Augustus to the prose-writers, and the historical theme to the Silver Age poets Lucan and Silius Italicus. He chose instead a subject which was national, yet shrouded in the mists of legend; a subject capable of readjustment to suit his poetical purpose; a theme which was well known but flexible, not unlike our King Arthur story before it received its more definitive shape from Malory. The theme was the foundation by the Trojan prince Aeneas of Lavinium in Latium: from here Aeneas' son Ascanius (also called Iulus, as founder of the Julian *gens*) would move to Alba Longa, and three hundred years later Romulus would transfer the settlement to Rome. The voyage of Aeneas to Hesperia, the western land, was destined by the gods so that a new city should replace the ruins of Troy; the theme of destiny, the theme of the responsibility of Aeneas to fulfil the will of the gods, is dominant throughout the whole poem, and is perhaps the major point in which the *Aeneid* differs from its Homeric models. References to the legend can be traced as far back as the sixth century B.C., but it was evidently in the third century B.C. (as Rome began to expand into the Greek world) that the story became well known and more fully developed (as for example in Lycophron's *Alexandra*); by the time of Naevius and Ennius it had become a special part of Rome's prehistory.[1]

The methods which Virgil used to connect this ancient legend with his modern world were diverse and subtle: the double time-scale gave him many opportunities both to universalize the particular, and to describe the past as an essential ingredient in the present and the future. His love for the old Italian virtues, prototypes of what he admired in his own times, is expressed very fully in the catalogue of the warriors in 7.647f., prefixed as it is by an appeal to the Muse to tell of the glories of the distant past:

> ...quibus Itala iam tum
> floruerit terra alma uiris, quibus arserit armis;
> et meministis enim, diuae, et memorare potestis;
> ad nos uix tenuis famae perlabitur aura. (7.643–6)

tell of the heroes by whose qualities the mother-land of Italy even then was glorious, tell of the martial ardour she had; for, goddesses, you remember and can tell, but to us barely does a faint breath of the story come through.

Aetiological allusions, so much a part of Alexandrian literature, are frequent: sometimes these are based directly on place-names (Segesta, 5.718; Misenus, 6.234; Palinurus, 6.381; Caieta, 7.3); sometimes on family names (Iulus, 1.288; Mnestheus, 5.117; Atys, 5.568); sometimes on contemporary buildings (6.69; 8.338) or contemporary institutions (3.278ff., 3.443ff., 5.59ff., 5.602). By means of dreams and prophecies, and devices such as the description of Aeneas' shield, later historical events enter the narrative (1.267ff., 6.756ff., 8.626ff.). Above all the values of the Augustan world are foreshadowed as Aeneas learns to leave the Trojan world of heroic and impetuous daring and inaugurate the Roman world of forethought, duty, responsibility (*pietas*).

Another method of allusion which links the past with the present is that of allegory and symbolism. Virgil's allegory is beneath the surface, suggestive rather than precise; the story of Dido is coloured by our thoughts of Cleopatra; we may think of Augustus and Antony when Aeneas and Turnus come to their final confrontation; but the method is always oblique and unexplicit. Similarly symbolism is often present beneath the actual narrative: Hercules acts as an *exemplum* of that endurance which must be shown by Aeneas and by Augustus as they face their labours; the description of Atlas in 4.246ff. offers a symbol of *duritia*; the contests in the funeral games in Book 5 illustrate some of the characteristics which can prevail in the sterner context of real life. Again and again the story of the events of long ago carries undertones, presents a kind of

[1] For further discussion and references see R. D. Williams (1962) Intro. 7ff.

penumbra of allusion which enriches and adds to the density and universality of the legend, so that Virgil could extend its significance from the heroic days of Troy to his own contemporary world.

What were the reasons which led Virgil to wish to extol Augustan Rome by symbolizing its trials and achievements in the person of its first founder? The ancient commentators were clear that this was his purpose, and, although it will be argued later that other purposes came more and more to the fore as the composition of the poem proceeded, their view was basically right. Servius says (at the beginning of his commentary on the *Aeneid*): 'Virgil's intention is to imitate Homer and to praise Augustus by means of his ancestors'; in Donatus (*Vita* 21) we are told that Virgil's special interest in the subject of the *Aeneid* was that it would contain the origin of the city of Rome and of Augustus; finally Tiberius Claudius Donatus (*Prooem. Aen.* 1) says 'his task was to depict Aeneas as a worthy first ancestor of Augustus, in whose honour the poem was written'. What reasons would Virgil have for regarding Rome under Augustus as the proper subject for his *magnum opus*?

First and foremost he had lived his life in a period of disastrous and appalling civil war, a period in which all that Rome had achieved through the long centuries of her history appeared likely to vanish in carnage and confusion. The wars of Marius and Sulla were succeeded by the struggle for power between Pompey and Caesar, culminating in the invasion of Italy by Caesar and his Gallic veterans. Pitched battles followed in which Roman fought Roman: the victory of Caesar was annulled by his assassination, and the power struggle broke out again, first with Antony and Octavian against Brutus and Cassius, and then with Antony and Octavian jockeying for power against each other, with the remnants of the Republican party of Pompey still threatening both of them. The sense of guilt felt by the Romans is powerfully expressed by Virgil himself at the end of the first *Georgic*:

di patrii, Indigetes, et Romule Vestaque mater,
quae Tuscum Tiberim et Romana Palatia seruas,
hunc saltem euerso iuuenem succurrere saeclo
ne prohibete. satis iam pridem sanguine nostro
Laomedonteae luimus periuria Troiae;
iam pridem nobis caeli te regia, Caesar,
inuidet atque hominum queritur curare triumphos,
quippe ubi fas uersum atque nefas; tot bella per orbem,
tam multae scelerum facies, non ullus aratro
dignus honos, squalent abductis arua colonis,
et curuae rigidum falces conflantur in ensem.
hinc mouet Euphrates, illinc Germania bellum;
uicinae ruptis inter se legibus urbes
arma ferunt; saeuit toto Mars impius orbe;

ut cum carceribus sese effudere quadrigae,
addunt in spatia, et frustra retinacula tendens
fertur equis auriga neque audit currus habenas. (*Geo.* 1.498–514)

Gods of our father-land, our native gods, and Romulus and mother Vesta, you who keep safe our Etruscan river Tiber and the Roman Palatine, do not forbid this young man at least from rescuing our ruined generation. Long ago now we have sufficiently atoned with our blood for the perjury of Laomedon's Troy; long ago now the palace of heaven has begrudged you to us on earth, Caesar, complaining that you are intent on mortal triumphs. For here right and wrong are interchanged: all these wars in the world, all these shapes of crime, no proper regard for the plough, the fields overgrown with their farmers taken away from them, the curved sickles beaten into steely swords. On one side Euphrates moves to war, on another Germany; neighbouring cities break their bonds of loyalty and bear weapons against each other: wicked Mars rages all over the world, just as when chariots stream forth from the starting-posts and speed on, lap after lap, while the charioteer vainly tugs at the reins but is carried on headlong by the horses and the chariot does not obey his control.

Two of Horace's *Epodes*, written at about the same time, convey the same sense of horror and guilt: *Epode* 7 and *Epode* 16.

Quo, quo scelesti ruitis? aut cur dexteris
 aptantur enses conditi?
parumne campis atque Neptuno super
 fusum est Latini sanguinis?

. . .

furorne caecus, an rapit uis acrior?
 an culpa? responsum date!
tacent et albus ora pallor inficit
 mentesque perculsae stupent.
sic est: acerba fata Romanos agunt
 scelusque fraternae necis,
ut immerentis fluxit in terram Remi
 sacer nepotibus cruor. (*Epode* 7.1–4, 13–20)

Where are you rushing, where indeed are you rushing, men of crime? Or why are hidden swords ready in your hands? Has not enough Latin blood been shed on the land and the seas . . ? Is it blind madness or some wilder impulse that whirls you onwards, or is it sin? Answer! They give no answer, and a white pallor tinges their cheeks, and their hearts are smitten and astounded. Thus it is: bitter fate harasses the Romans, and the crime of a brother's murder, ever since the blood of guiltless Remus flowed on the ground, a curse on generations to come.

Altera iam teritur bellis ciuilibus aetas,
 suis et ipsa Roma uiribus ruit,
quam neque finitimi ualuerunt perdere Marsi,
 minacis aut Etrusca Porsenae manus,
aemula nec uirtus Capuae nec Spartacus acer
 nouisque rebus infidelis Allobrox,

nec fera caerulea domuit Germania pube
  parentibusque abominatus Hannibal,
impia perdemus deuoti sanguinis aetas,
  ferisque rursus occupabitur solum. (*Epode* 16.1–10)

Another generation is now being worn down by civil war, and Rome rushes to destruction by her own might. Her neighbours, the Marsians, could not destroy her, nor the Etruscan forces of the threatening Porsena, nor the jealous power of Capua nor the fierce Spartacus, nor the Allobrogians, disloyal and rebellious, nor fierce Germany with her blue-eyed youths, nor Hannibal, a curse to our ancestors. But we, a wicked generation of accursed blood, shall destroy her, and the ground will once again become the habitation of wild beasts.

It is essential that these outcries should be properly understood in all their sincerity and poignancy in order for us to appreciate properly the sense of relief and hope which Augustus brought to a war-torn world. The outcries come from poets who had no love for the military way of life, who wished only to gain from war the hope that it would end war: the gentle Virgil played no part in military activities, and Horace's role in the civil wars was undistinguished and a subject for the poet's own mild depreciation (*Odes* 2.7). There is every reason to suppose that many Romans felt as Virgil and Horace did, and that when they express their gratitude to Augustus for what seemed to be a final end to this madness they were themselves sincere and were expressing the sincere thoughts of many of their compatriots.

For there was not only the negative achievement (the removal of violence and bloodshed) to be greeted with joy, but also the positive prospect of a return to what was seen as Rome's true self, a return to the *mos maiorum*, the way of life of their ancestors. This concept was coloured by romance (as we see very clearly from the stories in the early books of Livy) and idealized into an idyllic vision of the simple virtues, virtues of *fides*, *pietas*, *religio*, *disciplina*, *constantia*, *grauitas*. These virtues were not only embodied in the folk-lore and early legends of Rome, but were considered to have been exemplified in the lives of their historical heroes, men like Fabricius, Regulus, Fabius Maximus, Cato the Censor and countless others. In addition to this they were the kind of virtues valued most highly by contemporary Stoics,[1] and no doubt many Romans who (like Horace) were not ardent adherents of Stoicism would have echoed the admiration for Stoic qualities which he expresses in his Roman odes.

Upon this resurgence of hope and national pride Augustus set about building his social and moral policy, and indeed his political stance of restoring the Republic fitted into the scheme. He had been able to lead the Romans out of a period of political confusion and instability into a new security, and all his endeavours were directed to convincing the Romans that the new order was

[1] On Stoicism in the *Aeneid* see Bowra (1933–4) 8ff., Edwards (1960) 151ff.

nothing other than a restatement of the old order, nothing other than a restoration of the Roman state to what it had been and was by nature. He was removing alien elements which had been introduced and enabling the Romans to be their true selves again. How far this was true is another question – what seems very likely is that Augustus commanded the support of the majority of the Romans in this view of their contemporary situation, and it was to explore and to clarify these hopes that Virgil wrote the *Aeneid*. In it he presents his anticipations of history (the pageant at the end of Book 6, the description of the shield at the end of Book 8) in a fashion which accords with the Augustan view of the Roman achievement; and in his hero he exemplifies those virtues of *pietas*, *constantia*, *religio* which seemed so desirable in Romans of his day. In the last analysis Virgil found that these qualities fail, or seem to fail, to make complete order out of the world's chaos; but they were the qualities which his epic was designed to illustrate and exemplify, and the *Aeneid* in exploring what the Roman way of life had achieved and could achieve leaves the reader free to ponder on what it seemed in the last resort unable to achieve. And this surely is a primary virtue in a national epic.

2. THE 'AENEID' AND ITS LITERARY BACKGROUND

One of the fountains of the *Aeneid*'s inspiration was, as has been shown, the national aspiration of Rome in Virgil's time; another, of equal if not greater importance, was the epic poetry of Homer. The *Iliad* and the *Odyssey* represented in the classical world the highest achievement of Greek poetry, and the admiration universally felt by the Romans for Homer was for the great national poet of the Greek world whose literature they revered. His poetry was considered in Virgil's time to embody the perfect form of epic in its construction and organization, and to offer the reader moral lessons about life and how to live it as well as the excitement and intensity of dramatic action at its highest pitch and the aesthetic satisfaction of description and story-telling in a distant world which was half real and half supernatural. There can be no doubt that the poetry of Homer cast its spell over Virgil, and the idea of adapting and indeed continuing the Greek stories fascinated his poetic imagination. The comparison was immediately made by Propertius (2.34.65–6):

cedite, Romani scriptores, cedite Grai;
nescioquid maius nascitur Iliade.

Yield, you writers of Rome, yield, you Greeks; something is being born that is greater than the Iliad.

The idea was expressed in the Donatus life (21), where the *Aeneid* is described as a kind of equivalent of both Homer's poems – *quasi amborum Homeri carminum instar*; and much later one of the characters in Macrobius' *Saturnalia* (5.2.13) speaks of the *Aeneid* as a 'mirrored reflection of Homer'.

All of this is true: the *Aeneid* is indeed a full-scale *aemulatio* of Homer, and in it Virgil uses again for his own purposes many aspects of the structure of the Homeric poems, their conventions (such as the similes, or the double action in Olympus and on earth), their episodes (like the catalogue, the visit to the underworld, the funeral games, the single combat), their characters (Aeneas and Turnus have strong relationship with Hector and Achilles, Pallas is like Patroclus, Palinurus like Elpenor), their very phraseology.[1] It has often been remarked that the first half of the *Aeneid* is Virgil's *Odyssey*, describing the wanderings of the hero, and the second half his *Iliad*, describing the battles; it is astonishing to find from a close investigation how very similar in structure and episode the first book of the *Aeneid* is to *Odyssey* 5–8; or how densely the last scenes of *Aeneid* 12 echo the events of *Iliad* 22.

But it is not only these similarities of epic structure and phraseology which constantly challenge comparison with Homer; the story itself is contemporary with, or a continuation of, the stories of Homer. Aeneas is an important character in the *Iliad*, the most important Trojan warrior after Hector, a man renowned for his religious observances as well as for his prowess in war. When he leaves Troy his voyage is contemporary (within a few months) with that of Odysseus, and several times in the *Aeneid* (for example with Achaemenides in Book 3, the Sirens in Book 5, Circe in Book 7) Aeneas is following in the footsteps of Odysseus very shortly afterwards. Virgil uses this Homeric time-scale to point the differences between Homer's heroes and his: Odysseus is one of the last heroes of the heroic world, attempting to re-establish his way of life in Ithaca as he knew it before the Trojan war; but Aeneas is the first hero of a new world, a proto-Roman world.

Similarly Aeneas' attitude towards battle can be contrasted with the Homeric attitude. In many ways his opponent Turnus has been built up as a new Achilles, and Aeneas – the new Hector – must confront his opponent as Hector had to confront Achilles. Yet he must confront him differently: he must show the valour and vigour of a Homeric warrior, but also the mercy and justice of a Roman ruler of empire. He does not wholly succeed, as all readers of the *Aeneid* know well; but it is by means of the Homeric comparison that Virgil tries to define the position and behaviour of the new hero, destined for an age no longer 'heroic'. More will be said later on this subject.

Virgil was deeply versed in post-Homeric classical Greek literature, and was especially influenced by Greek tragedy (see Macrobius, *Sat.* 5.18f.). There are individual echoes of the plays of Aeschylus, Sophocles and Euripides, and in particular *Aeneid* 2 shows marked signs of the influence of Euripides' *Troades*

[1] For a very full discussion of Virgil's use of Homer see Knauer (1964).

and *Hecuba*; elements that recall dramatic structure can be observed especially in this book and in *Aeneid* 4. But the real debt is one of concept rather than form: the concept of the whole development of Dido's love, leading to her ultimate self-destruction, is tragic in the fullest and most technical sense; similarly the events leading to the death of Turnus have the closest possible similarity to those in a Greek tragedy as the hero moves along his self-chosen path to destruction. And in a broader sense Virgil's whole attitude towards the human scene which he explores in his poem is similar to that often found in Greek tragedy: an intense sensitivity towards the suffering which human people bring upon themselves or have brought upon them by the pressure of hostile circumstances, coupled with a profound conviction that somehow in spite of all the catastrophes the world is not a senseless one, and that in some way hardly comprehensible to men these sufferings may form a necessary part in the ultimate fulfilment of the divine purpose for mankind.

Like the other literary figures of his time Virgil knew well the post-classical Greek literature of the Hellenistic age: the *Eclogues* with their fundamental debt to Theocritus, and the *Georgics* with their imitation and paraphrases of the didactic writers like Aratus and Nicander bear full witness to this. In the *Aeneid* it is Apollonius Rhodius whose story of Jason and Medea captured Virgil's imagination and contributed towards the construction of the story of Aeneas and Dido. Elsewhere in the *Aeneid* Apollonius is rarely recalled, and other parts of Apollonius' *Argonautica* than those about Medea hardly ever are used; but the second half of Book 1, which introduces the story of Dido, the whole of Book 4 which continues and finishes it, and the meeting of Aeneas with Dido's ghost in Book 6 use ideas and phraseology from Apollonius. Servius introduces his commentary on *Aeneid* 4 with the words: 'Apollonius wrote the *Argonautica* and in his third book brought in the love-story of Medea, from which all this book is taken.' This is a wild exaggeration, but it contains some seeds of truth: the marriage in the cave, the frivolous and selfish behaviour of the goddesses, the sleeplessness of Dido, her recourse to magic – these all find their origins in Apollonius. And in more general terms it is fair to say that the concept of using epic poetry to reveal the inner and intense emotions of the heroine (a feature far more normally associated with elegy) came from Apollonius. It is not to be found in Homer, nor in Ennius. But when this has been said, it needs to be said also that for all the material which Virgil took from Apollonius he did not make his Dido in the least like Apollonius' Medea. The queenly dignity, the resolution, the high tragic stature are Virgil's own, and quite alien from the gentle and confused young girl of Apollonius.

Of Roman poets Virgil knew and used especially Naevius, Ennius, some of the tragedians, Catullus and Lucretius. His debt to Lucretius was very great in the *Georgics*, and is considerable in phraseology and metrical movement in the

Aeneid (for example in the minstrel's song in *Aeneid* 1 and in Anchises' speech about the nature of life after death in *Aeneid* 6); but it is Ennius and Catullus who call for particular mention here. No two poets could be more unlike (Catullus' dislike for poetry of Ennius' type is well known), and it is one of the clearest indications of Virgil's many-sidedness that he deeply appreciated both, and used both in his epic.

Ennius stood in a special relationship to Virgil as being the father of Roman patriotic poetry, whom it was Virgil's aim to emulate. From the fragments of Ennius which survive a wide-ranging impression of Virgil's verbal debts can be gained.[1] Ennius is constantly quoted in Servius' commentary as a source of Virgil's phrases, and a substantial passage of Macrobius' *Saturnalia* (6.1–3) is taken up with citation and discussion of parallel passages. Virgil's debt to Ennius in structure and characterization is far less than to Homer, because Ennius' treatment of his theme was annalistic rather than dramatic, but in addition to verbal reminiscences there are two major ways in which Ennius influenced Virgil. One is that Ennius was the first Roman to adapt the Greek hexameter to the Latin language, so that all subsequent hexameter writers owed a debt to him as they set about modifying and smoothing the movement of the metre in Latin. By the time of Virgil such developments had taken place through the writings of poets like Lucretius, Catullus, Cicero that it was possible to recall the distinctive style of Ennius by deliberate metrical archaizing, and this Virgil quite often does in order to achieve an effect of antiquity. The second, and perhaps the most important aspect of Ennian influence, is in the national tone and spirit; the toughness and simplicity of the Romans of old is powerfully portrayed by Ennius, and this must have strengthened and enlarged Virgil's own sympathy for the ancestors of his race and his love of antiquity, especially that of his own country. It also helped him in the robust style of narrative in which much of the second half of the *Aeneid* is written. Consider for example the second half of Book 9. The first part has been taken up with the emotional story of Nisus and Euryalus, written in a style calling for the reader's personal involvement with the fate of these two young warriors. At the end of it the theme changes to the stern vigour of the narrative of the *aristeia*[2] of Turnus; this is more sinewy writing, more matter-of-fact in its presentation of events. It is introduced with a sentence immediately reminiscent of Ennius (*Aen.* 9.503–4 *at tuba terribilem sonitum procul aere canoro | increpuit* 'But the trumpet with ringing bronze uttered its dreadful sound in the distance', cf. Enn. *Ann.* 140), a reminiscence reinforced in the invocation (*Aen.* 9.528 *et mecum ingentes oras euoluite belli* 'and unroll with me the vast scroll of war', cf. Enn. *Ann.* 174) and immediately afterwards in the narrative (*Aen.* 9.532–3 *expugnare Itali summaque*

[1] See Bowra (1929) 65ff. and Norden (1915).

[2] *Aristeia*: an episode in which an individual warrior displays great prowess.

euertere opum ui | *certabant* 'The Italians strove to storm and overturn it with all their power and might', cf. Enn. *Ann.* 161). The mood of the narrative is active, vigorous, often reminiscent of Homer's *Iliad*, often of Ennius' *Annals*: the speech of Numanus (9.598ff.) expresses the values and ideals of archaic Rome; and the final scene of Turnus' exploits (*Aen.* 9.806ff.), when Turnus could at last hold out no longer, is very closely based on a passage of Ennius (*Ann.* 401–8), itself adapted from Homer (*Il.* 16.102ff.).

Virgil's debt to Catullus[1] is of a very different kind, virtually the opposite kind. Reminiscences of Catullan phrases are much rarer than reminiscences of Ennius, but where they do occur they are always memorable, always in passages of emotional sensitivity. There are the two flower similes, one for the death of Euryalus (9.435ff.) and one at the funeral of Pallas (11.68ff.), both reminiscent of flower similes in Catullus (11.22ff., 62.39ff.); there are Aeneas' last words to Pallas (11.97–8 *salue aeternum mihi, maxime Palla,* | *aeternumque uale* 'Hail and farewell for ever, great Pallas'; cf. Cat. 101.10 *atque in perpetuum, frater, aue atque uale* 'and for ever hail and farewell, my brother'); but above all there are the reminiscences in the story of the desertion of Dido, recalling the pathos of Ariadne's desertion in Catullus 64. Dido's pleading speech to Aeneas (4.305f.) begins as Ariadne's had with the reproach of broken faith (*perfide*) and she speaks of her hopes in Ariadne's phrases (4.316 *per conubia nostra, per inceptos hymenaeos* 'by our marriage and by the wedding on which we have begun'; Cat. 64.141 *sed conubia laeta, sed optatos hymenaeos* 'but (you promised me) a happy marriage and a longed-for wedding'); she uses a diminutive adjective in the style of Catullus – nowhere else in the *Aeneid* does Virgil use a diminutive adjective (4.328–9 *si quis mihi paruulus aula* | *luderet Aeneas* 'if a tiny Aeneas were playing in the palace'). At the end, just before she kills herself, she – like Ariadne – bitterly wishes that the ships that brought her lover had never touched her shores (4.657–8 *felix heu nimium felix si litora tantum* | *numquam Dardaniae tetigissent nostra carinae* 'blessed, o too much blessed, if only the Trojan keels had never touched our shores'; cf. Cat. 64.171–2 *Iuppiter omnipotens, utinam ne tempore primo* | *Cnosia Cecropiae tetigissent litora puppes* 'Almighty Jupiter, if only that first time the Athenian ships had never touched Cretan shores'). Of course Virgil's Dido is at most times very different from Catullus' Ariadne – but in her moments of pathos and desolation the impact of Virgil's description is increased by recollections of Catullus' tender heroine.

To survey the surviving literary sources of Virgil's *Aeneid* (and there were many other sources which have not come down to us) makes it very plain that as well as being moved by a commitment to contemporary Roman problems and aspirations he aimed at univeralizing his exploration of human behaviour by relating the contemporary with the past through the medium of literature. In

[1] See Westendorp Boerma (1958) 55ff.

some sense the *Aeneid* is a synthesis of certain aspects of human experience as presented by writers of the past. Like Dante and Milton Virgil aims at including those things which had moved him in past literature as well as those which moved him in the contemporary scene. And what is especially remarkable in the *Aeneid*, and indeed perhaps unique, is the extent to which Virgil could sympathize with, and seek to incorporate, the attitudes and outlook of such totally different epochs as the Homeric and the Alexandrian and of such totally different poets as Ennius, sonorous and severe exponent of the national theme, and Catullus, the emotional and sensitive poet not concerned with the state at all but with the private world of the lonely individual.

3. THE COMPOSITION AND STRUCTURE OF THE 'AENEID'

The *Aeneid* as we have it is unrevised. We know on the authority of Servius and Donatus that at the time of his death in 19 B.C. Virgil planned to spend three more years revising the poem, and because he had not finished work on it he gave instructions on his deathbed that it should be burnt. These instructions were countermanded by Augustus, who ordered that it should be published by Varius and Tucca with the removal of unnecessary material (*superflua*) but without additions. There are a number of features in the poem, as we shall see, that testify to its lack of the poet's final revision, but there is no evidence whatever for thinking that any major alterations would have been made, and the poem as a whole should not be regarded in any important sense as unfinished. We can guess if we like that it might have been rewritten (to make it more Augustan or less Augustan) but if so it would have been another poem; our poem is finished in all but minor details of revision.

We have a good deal of ancient evidence about Virgil's method of composition,[1] and it agrees well with what we might deduce from the poem itself. Donatus tells us that Virgil first sketched the poem in prose and divided it into twelve books; then he composed the different sections as the mood took him, and so that the flow of his inspiration should not be checked he left some parts unfinished and in other parts he put in 'props' (*tibicines*) to hold up the structure till the permanent columns were ready. Instances of these *tibicines* have been collected and discussed by Mackail,[2] and the half-lines attest the method, as Servius saw: they indicate small gaps awaiting completion. Many of the fifty-odd instances of incomplete lines[3] are very effective as they stand, and give a haunting effect of pathos (e.g. 2.346, 623, 640): they would have been very difficult for Virgil to fill up to his satisfaction, but it should be regarded as certain that they are an indication of lack of revision and not a deliberate poetic

[1] See Mackail (1930) Intro. xlviiff.

[2] Ibid. liiff.

[3] There is a full treatment in Sparrow (1931).

technique. None of his predecessors had used the technique, and – more significant – none of his imitators used it; there is a story in Donatus that Virgil completed certain half-lines *ex tempore* when giving a *recitatio*; it is also the case that quite a few of the half-lines (like *tum sic effatur*, 9.295) are clearly incomplete stop-gaps.

Servius has preserved for us what seems to be another instance of incomplete revision in the passage about Helen (2.567–88) – though there are still dissenting views about whether the passage is Virgilian or not.[1] This passage is not in any of the major MSS, but is quoted in Servius' introduction as an indication of lack of final revision. It reads like Virgil, but it contains certain awkwardnesses, and it is not completely dovetailed into the structure of the section. Evidently the last part of *Aeneid* 2 was undergoing revision, as the presence of six incomplete lines in the last two hundred suggests; and it is interesting to notice that here we have one of the finest parts of all the *Aeneid*, but still Virgil was not yet satisfied.

Other indications of the lack of final revision may be found in certain inconsistencies within the plot of the poem.[2] Too much should not be made of these – they are all minor, and a detailed scrutiny of any long work is likely to uncover a number of small inconsistencies or contradictions. Some of these are easily explicable: for example in 3.255 the Harpy Celaeno prophesies that Aeneas will not found his city until hunger has forced him to eat his tables, and when in 7.112f. the Trojans do in fact eat their tables, Aeneas joyfully recalls that this was the prophecy given to him by Anchises. He is wrong, but his error (or Virgil's) serves to remind us of the enormously important part played by Anchises in helping and advising his son during the voyage. Again, the chronology of the seven-years' voyage is difficult to fit into the events of Book 3, and the term '*septima aestas*' is used by Dido at the end of Book 1 and by Beroe, a year later, in 5.626. Certain shifts of emphasis centre on Book 3: Apollo is the guide there, not Venus as in the rest of the poem; there are difficulties about the progressive revelation of the Trojan goal; Helenus says that the Sibyl will tell of the wars to come, whereas in fact Anchises does. Book 3 is at a lower level of poetic intensity than the rest of the *Aeneid*, and there is only one simile. There was a tradition that originally Book 3 was written in third-person narrative (not in direct speech), and began the poem. This may suggest that when Virgil set out for Greece in 19 B.C. his intention was to gain local colour for the revision of Book 3, which is set in Greek waters; but it does not suggest any need for radical alteration.

The structure[3] of the poem is carefully and elaborately composed. This is to be expected from literary epic: the poet who undertakes this most ambitious and

[1] See for example Austin (1961) 185ff. and (1964) 217ff., and Goold (1970) 101ff.

[2] See Crump (1920).

[3] See Mackail (1930) Intro. xxxvii ff., Otis (1963) 217ff., Duckworth (1954) 1ff. and (1957) 1ff., Camps (1954) 214ff. and (1959) 53ff.

massive of genres proclaims his intention to be a builder, to undertake the architecture of symmetries and contrasts on a large scale. The most obvious way of looking at the *Aeneid*'s structure is to see two halves corresponding to Homer's two poems, the first six books being Virgil's *Odyssey* and the last six his *Iliad*. But an equally valid and significant division is into three parts, the tragedy of Turnus in 9–12 corresponding with that of Dido in 1–4, with the middle section taken up with material often closely related to Roman history and origins. There is also a balance round Book 7 so that 6 and 8 correspond as the great Roman books, 5 and 9 as episodic, 4 and 10 as the tragedies of Dido and Pallas, 11 and 3 as episodic, 12 and 2 as the triumph of Rome and the destruction of Troy. An alternative symmetry is seen by balancing 1 with 7, 2 with 8 (Troy and Rome), 3 with 9, 4 with 10, 5 with 11, 6 with 12. A particular kind of symmetry has been generally accepted since Conway elaborated it: the alternation of the Odyssean, more expansive books with the grave and Iliadic books, so that the even-numbered books which are intense are varied and relieved by the odd-numbered books. The function of Books 3 and 5, separating 2, 4, and 6, is very obvious in this connexion.

More elaborate schemes of structure have been proposed in recent times, including the large-scale use by Virgil of the mathematical ratio known as the Golden Section,[1] a ratio of 0.628 to 1. This ratio has played a most important part in the visual arts, but it seems impossible as well as inappropriate to apply it to a poem of the scale of the *Aeneid*. However important structural considerations are to an epic poet, we must remember that they constitute the supports to what he wants to say. In a cathedral the structure *is* what the architect wants to express, but in a poet it is the means to his end.

4. THE CHIEF CHARACTERS

Aeneas

The hero of the *Aeneid* has very often been a target for adverse criticism, even (somewhat paradoxically) from those who have regarded the *Aeneid* as among the greatest poems ever written. Charles James Fox's phrase is famous: 'always either insipid or odious'. Page, in often quoted words, says 'Virgil is unhappy in his hero. Compared with Achilles, Aeneas is but the shadow of a man', and Wight Duff conveys what has until recently been the general view: 'Aeneas is too often a puppet.' The key to a proper understanding of Aeneas is Leopardi's description of him as the opposite of a hero: in some senses this is exactly what he is. Virgil is trying to define the nature and behaviour of a hero in an age no longer heroic: not to produce a second-hand Achilles or Odysseus, but to investigate the qualities required in a complex civilization in which the straight-

[1] Duckworth (1962).

forward and simple individualism of an Achilles would be useless. Aeneas cannot cut a figure like Achilles because he must subordinate his individual wishes and desires to the requirements of others; he must be the group hero, and this is the quality which Virgil constantly stresses in him, his quality of *pietas*. This involves Aeneas in situation after situation where he must weigh up conflicting claims upon him, where he must ponder in anxious thought the proper course of action. He does not stride magnificently through life: on the contrary he is under constant emotional and intellectual pressure and only with extreme difficulty and often against all the odds does he succeed in keeping on going.

The most obvious and important way in which Aeneas differs from a Homeric hero is that he has devoted himself to a divine mission, he has accepted the will of heaven that he should be the agent of Jupiter's plan for the future happiness and prosperity of the human race under the civilizing rule of the Romans. This is abundantly clear through the *Aeneid*: in line 2 Aeneas is 'an exile because of fate' (*fato profugus*) and the poem is heavily laden with the concept of destiny throughout. The contrast between Aeneas' personal wishes and his divine duty is brought out especially clearly in his desertion of Dido (4.361 *Italiam non sponte sequor* 'it is not of my own free will that I go to seek Italy', 6.460 *inuitus, regina, tuo de litore cessi* 'unwillingly, o queen, did I leave your land'), but it is a perpetual theme throughout the whole action (e.g. 11.112 *nec ueni, nisi fata locum sedemque dedissent* 'and I should not be here, had not the fates allotted me an abiding-place').

Two principal criticisms have been levelled at Aeneas as man of destiny, two branches of the same objection: neither of them is true. One is that as man of destiny he is possessed of such supernatural strength and resolution that interest in him as an ordinary human being cannot be sustained: on the contrary, as we shall see, he is often frail and uncertain and barely able to continue. The other is that by accepting the divine destiny he sacrifices his free will. It would indeed be possible to present a man in Aeneas' situation in that way, but Virgil has certainly not done so. At each and every moment of the poem Aeneas is free to reject his mission – to say 'Thus far and no further.' When Mercury appears to him in Book 4 to tell him to leave Dido, he could refuse: he has to take the decision what to do, and he decides to return to his mission and sacrifice Dido. In one place the process of decision is presented to us in the most explicit terms – after the Trojan women have set fire to their own ships and Jupiter, in response to Aeneas' prayers, has quenched the fire Aeneas is so shaken by this turn of events that he wonders whether to give up the whole mission (5.700ff.):

at pater Aeneas casu concussus acerbo
nunc huc ingentis, nunc illuc pectore curas
mutabat uersans, Siculisne resideret aruis
oblitus fatorum, Italasne capesseret oras.

But father Aeneas, shattered by this bitter blow, turned and revolved his heavy anxieties one way and another in his heart: should he settle in the fields of Sicily and forget the fates, or press on to the shores of Italy.

Nothing could be more precise than this: he has two options, to give up his mission and forget the fates or to continue, and it is a long time before he decides. The Stoic platitudes of Nautes do not convince him, and it takes a vision of his father Anchises to make him realize that he must follow his duty and continue on to Italy.

The essential human frailty and fallibility of Aeneas, the courage with which he continues on a mission almost too much for his shoulders to bear, is revealed again and again in the poem. The hostility of Juno and the undeserved suffering she causes is presented in powerful terms at the beginning of Book 1, and the prelude to the poem ends with the famous and unforgettable line *tantae molis erat Romanam condere gentem* 'so great a task it was to found the Roman race' (1.33). Indeed it was, and one in which Aeneas succeeded by the narrowest of margins.

On Aeneas' first appearance in the poem, as he and his men are battered by the storm sent by Juno, we see him frightened and in despair –

extemplo Aeneae soluuntur frigore membra;
ingemit et duplicis tendens ad sidera palmas
talia uoce refert... (1.92–4)

Straightway Aeneas' limbs were loosened in cold fear; he groaned, and holding out his two hands to the sky thus he spoke...

And the burden of his speech is that he wishes he had died along with his comrades at Troy.

After the storm has been calmed by Neptune Aeneas speaks to his men in heartening terms (1.198ff.), but immediately after the speech Virgil tells us that his confidence was feigned:

talia uoce refert curisque ingentibus aeger
spem uultu simulat, premit altum corde dolorem. (1.208–9)

So he spoke, and sick at heart with his terrible anxieties he feigned hope in his expression and suppressed his agony deep in his heart.

The scene of the poem shifts to Olympus where Venus indignantly complains to Jupiter of her son's apparently unending suffering, and Jupiter replies to her in the serene and glowing tones of his promise for Rome's future greatness. The reader is inspired with optimism, feeling that with such a reward the task must be and will be fulfilled. But the mortal Aeneas has not heard the speech in heaven, and must continue on darkly, helped only by vague knowledge of his destiny. His divine mother, in disguise, meets him as he explores the coast where his Trojans have been shipwrecked, and to her he complains bitterly (1.372ff., especially 385 *querentem*); as she leaves him she manifests her divinity, and again Aeneas complains of his hard fortune, deprived of normal maternal affection as he is (*crudelis tu quoque*, 407).

The hard and apparently almost hopeless quest continues. Aeneas gazes in envy at the walls of Carthage, already rising:

> 'o fortunati, quorum iam moenia surgunt!' (1.437)
>
> '*Lucky those whose city already is being built.*'

How far away seems his own city.

Throughout the first book the episodes and incidents have been closely modelled on *Odyssey* 5–8: the shipwreck, the landing on an unknown shore, the meeting with a disguised goddess, the friendly reception in a strange city, the banquet, the minstrel's song, the request for the story of the past.[1] We are invited to see Aeneas as a new Odysseus, and at the same time challenged to observe and ponder the difference. The difference is the decree of destiny, the requirement of future history as outlined in Jupiter's speech; and this means that Aeneas is not like Odysseus, a man seeking, if only he can, to return to the old way of life in his own home, but a man stepping out into the unknown future, leaving the ashes of Troy to found not merely a new city in a distant western land, but also a new way of life. From being the last Trojan he must become the first Roman. He is therefore involved, as Odysseus was not, in the needs of his followers; he must be the group hero, the social hero, bringing a new nation safely to a new country. Odysseus, the splendid individual, survived and reached home when his comrades, lesser men in resources and endurance, did not – but Aeneas must lead his Trojans safely to their Roman destiny. The pressure upon him is greater, a pressure only to be resolved by devotion to his divine mission, by what the Romans called *pietas*; and because this pressure is so much greater we see in him a figure who often seems frail and unequal to the task. And yet through toil and danger, through despair and agony, he keeps on going. This is the nature of the new heroism.

The remainder of the first half of the poem is filled with the trials, physical and psychological, which Aeneas must encounter. His account of his agonized sorrow at the fall of Troy (Book 2) reveals the human and impetuous side of him, not yet capable of accepting his divine destiny. The story of the long weary wanderings in the third book shows a gradual acceptance of fate, aided by the counsels of his father Anchises. In the fourth book, as will be seen later, the temptation of personal happiness comes near, very near, to causing Aeneas to abandon his mission altogether. The key to an understanding of this book is

[1] For details see R. D. Williams (1963) 266ff.

that Aeneas could have given up the whole thing, personally wished to do so, and yet – because of conscience, duty, *pietas* – did not.

The fifth book is a particularly poignant depiction of how Aeneas bears a burden almost too heavy for him. It begins with a last backward look at the events at Carthage, and the tragic outcome; it moves to a happier tone as the games are celebrated in honour of Anchises. Now for the first time the weight is for a few brief days off Aeneas. As he acts as president of the games he relaxes – but immediately comes another blow from Juno as she intervenes to cause the Trojan women to set fire to the fleet. Jupiter, in response to Aeneas' prayer, quenches the fire; but Aeneas is in deep distress, ponders whether to give up his mission, and is only persuaded to continue by the vision of his father's ghost, sent by Jupiter to urge him on with the divine task. Aeneas obeys, makes the necessary arrangements, and sails on the last lap to the western coast of Italy. One further disaster befalls him before arrival: the loss of his faithful helmsman Palinurus, who had guided the fleet thus far, through seven years of wanderings, but was fated not to survive until the final arrival to which he himself contributed so much.

Aeneas' visit to the underworld is for the most part full of gloom and sorrow: the ghosts of his past haunt him and he feels guilt and remorse at having failed to save them, or, worse, having caused their deaths. He meets the shade of Palinurus, so recently dead, of Dido – to whom he speaks in tones of deep remorse – , of Deiphobus, who died at Troy when Aeneas survived. These are traumatic personal experiences of events all brought upon Aeneas solely because of his acceptance of his mission: these are the prices he must pay for the Roman achievement.[1]

But at this moment when it seems that Aeneas' grief is unbearable (especially because of his personal responsibility for these tragedies) the light begins to shine in the underworld. He reaches Elysium, hears from his father of the nature of life after death, the rewards for the virtuous and the purification of sin, and then is shown a pageant of Roman heroes[2] waiting to be born if – and only if – he succeeds in his mission. They pass before his astonished eyes – the Alban kings, Romulus, and then (with the chronology broken) Augustus himself, a second Romulus who will re-found the city and bring back the golden age to Latium. The chronology is resumed with the kings of Rome, Brutus and the great heroes of the Republic, and the final summary by Anchises contrasts the artistic and intellectual achievements of the Greeks with the practical and political destiny of the Romans, namely to bring peace and civilization to the peoples of the world.

This is one of the great patriotic pieces in the poem, but it should not be regarded as a detachable purple passage: it is most closely integrated with the

[1] See Otis (1963) 290ff. and (1959) 165ff.

[2] See R. D. Williams (1972) 207ff.

development of Aeneas' character, and Virgil points this with emphasis. After the description of Augustus Anchises breaks off to ask his son

> et dubitamus adhuc uirtutem extendere factis,
> aut metus Ausonia prohibet consistere terra? (6.806–7)

And do we still hesitate to enlarge our prowess by deeds, or does fear prevent us from founding a settlement in the Ausonian land?

Aeneas does not answer – but we can answer for him; there can be no more hesitation now. And finally as Anchises escorts Aeneas along the way back to the upper world he has fired his heart with passion for the glory awaiting him: *incenditque animum famae uenientis amore* (6.889). This passion must overcome all other passions which Aeneas as an individual has felt and will feel again. His passive acceptance of duty now turns into a positive and dynamic urge.

In the second half of the poem the interest shifts from the question of whether Aeneas is strong enough and devoted enough to achieve his mission (his experiences in the underworld have ensured that he will be) to the question of how he is to achieve it. What does the man of *pietas*, the man of deep human sympathies, do when he is confronted by violent opposition? Virgil was too much a realist, and too much a child of his violent times, to pretend that opposition promptly melts away before righteousness; yet he was himself a gentle person with nothing of the soldier in him, and could take little pleasure in the ruthless triumph of power, however justly based it might seem to be. The second half of the poem explores this question, and this is one of the things which Virgil meant when he said in his new invocation (7.44–5):

> maior rerum mihi nascitur ordo,
> maius opus moueo

A greater series of events arises before me; I undertake a greater task.

For most of the time during the war in Latium Aeneas presents a picture of a just and merciful general, caring for his own men, and generous to the enemy. When Lausus intervenes in the battle to try to save his father Mezentius, and Aeneas is forced to kill him, he is filled with remorse and sorrow and himself lifts up the dead body with words of compassion (10.821ff.). When the Latin envoys ask for a truce to bury the dead, Aeneas willingly grants it and wishes there could have been a truce for the living too (11.106ff.). When the arrangements for a single combat between himself and Turnus are violated and general fighting breaks out again, Aeneas rushes into the midst, unarmed and unhelmeted, urging his men to control their anger (12.311ff.). It is on the whole true to say that Aeneas hates war and fights because it is his bitter duty, in contrast with Turnus who is most himself on the battlefield.

But there are very strong qualifications which must immediately be made. Quite apart from the fact that Turnus for all his violence is often presented sympathetically there are three places in particular in this part of the poem where Virgil goes out of his way to emphasize Aeneas' own lapses into the violence which is a characteristic of his opponent. The first of these is after the death of Pallas (10.510ff.), where Aeneas' behaviour is wild and savage in the extreme, including the capture of eight of the enemy for human sacrifice at Pallas' tomb (a horrible piece of barbarism which is fulfilled at 11.81ff.). The second is when Aeneas is wounded (12.441ff.), and his fierce deeds in battle are in every way similar to those of Turnus. The third, and perhaps the most significant of all, is at the very end of the poem. This is a passage on which we must pause.

During the single combat between Aeneas and Turnus (12.697ff.) we have been constantly reminded of the duel between Achilles and Hector in *Iliad* 22. Many of the famous passages have been recalled (*Il.* 22.304–5 ~ *Aen.* 12.645–9; *Il.* 22.209ff. ~ *Aen.* 12.725ff.; *Il.* 22.158ff. ~ *Aen.* 12.763ff.; *Il.* 22.199ff. ~ *Aen.* 12.908ff.) and we are aware that the second Achilles (Turnus, cf. 6.89) is fighting now against the second Hector (Aeneas), but that the outcome will be the opposite from Homer's story. We recall that Aeneas is fighting to avenge Pallas as Achilles was fighting to avenge Patroclus, but we know that the character of Aeneas is different, more civilized, more just than that of Achilles. Consequently we are confident that in the moment of victory he will show mercy; he will not display the arrogant joy of Achilles (*Il.* 22.344ff.); he will surely spare the conquered.

This parallelism with Homer makes it all the more shattering when Aeneas does not in fact spare his victim, but rejects his pleas precisely as Achilles had rejected Hector's. After a thousand years it is exactly the same in the end; the victor, in his wild anger (is it 'righteous' anger?), takes vengeance by killing his victim. Much has been written on these final scenes, sometimes in defence of Aeneas (he can do no other than remove from the scene a barbarous opponent whose way of life cannot be accepted in the new order of things), sometimes against him (he yields to wild fury, he gives in to the very kind of behaviour which throughout the poem he has been combating in himself and others). But two things are evident from Virgil's text: the first is that there is no other motive for Aeneas' action than the desire to exact vengeance (940–1, 945, 948–9) even although Turnus has been brought low and is no longer one of the proud (930). We are perhaps invited to think of Augustus' temple to *Mars Vltor* and of his vengeance on the assassins of Julius Caesar. The second is that this action is taken by the hero of the poem with whose behaviour and destiny all Romans are closely identified: it is certainly not the case that the hero has turned villain at the last (as some recent writers[1] have argued), but rather that in an imperfect

[1] For example Putnam (1965) chapter 4.

world the best of us (like the worst) take actions which in a perfect world would be unacceptable. The poem ends with confusion, with paradox; the poet would have us ponder. This is the measure of the greatness of the poem – it shirks no issues, it aims at no specious falsifications. Nothing could have been easier than to avoid this dilemma: Aeneas' spear-cast could have killed Turnus instead of wounding him, and the final situation would not have arisen. But it was Virgil's intention, here as elsewhere in the poem, to involve his readers in a dilemma concerned with real human issues as he saw them in the Roman world.

Dido

From the *Aeneid*'s publication up to the present day the story of Dido has always been the most popular part of Virgil's epic (Ov. *Trist.* 2.535–6) in spite of, or sometimes because of, the fact that we are here further away than elsewhere in the poem from the Roman theme. Here we have the strongest possible protest against the apparently senseless suffering of the world, and many readers who have been unmoved by the Roman ideals and values of the poem have, like St Augustine, shed tears for Dido. Here Virgil shows how the private world of the individual is violated by the march of Roman destiny, and he leaves his readers profoundly unhappy that it should be so. There are of course many undertones in the story – the defeat of Carthage by Rome, the triumph of Stoic ideals over Epicurean (4.379–80), the threat of Cleopatra in Virgil's own times – but basically and essentially the presentation is concerned with the personal suffering and tragedy of its heroine. It is Catullan in its deep sympathy and sensitivity, and there are many echoes of the phraseology and episodes of Catullus' poem about Theseus' desertion of Ariadne. No poet was more interested in people and less in affairs of state than Catullus, and here in the midst of his state poem Virgil speaks with a voice often reminiscent of the pathos of Catullus' desertion poems.

The whole of the second half of *Aeneid* 1 is about Dido, and in it Virgil builds up a picture of a totally admirable and enviable queen. Dido is beautiful, like Diana; she is kind and hospitable to the Trojans; she is highly efficient as a ruler and beloved by her people; she has been through hardship and exile and is now triumphantly achieving what Aeneas seeks to achieve in the future – the foundation of a new city for her people. In the joyful scenes of the banquet which she gives in honour of the Trojans the notes of disaster to come are not absent, yet it is hard to imagine that a person of such qualities could destroy herself as Dido does.

The first half of the fourth book depicts how she yields completely to a love which she must have known was impossible; she allows it to annihilate all her other qualities and Carthage comes to a halt (4.86–9). Her situation is presented with strong pathos, culminating in her plea to Aeneas (305–30) not to leave her when she has given her whole self to her love for him. Aeneas replies that he is not free to stay, and at this Dido changes from a pathetically deserted woman to a personification of hatred and vengeance. In a highly rhetorical speech (365–87) she distances herself from her lover, ceases to be a human individual with whom communication is possible, and becomes instead a kind of avenging Fury, an archetypal and terrifying symbol of slighted pride and bitter anger. In her long curse against her lover (590–629) she revolves thoughts of the horrors she could have inflicted (600–2) and ends by invoking the long years of history to achieve her vengeance, calling on every Carthaginian to hate and destroy the Romans at every possible opportunity. In her last speech of all, just before she kills herself, she unites both aspects of her tragic character, first re-invoking (651–8) the pathos which was the dominant feature of the first part of the book, and finally returning to her passionate hatred for the lover who has scorned her, upon whom she must have vengeance (661–2).

As so often with a Greek tragedy the reader is astonished and horrified not merely at the actual events of the disaster, but at the total disintegration of what had once been a strong, noble and virtuous character.[1] He seeks explanations, he seeks to apportion blame. There are clearly contributory causes, things that might have been done otherwise: Aeneas should have perceived that he was allowing a situation to develop from which he might escape but Dido would not; Dido should not have broken her vow of chastity to her dead husband Sychaeus, and she should have fought against a passion which she must have known could lead her nowhere. But in essence what we have is a tragic and moving study of a wholly sympathetic character broken and destroyed by the pressure of circumstances which she could not in fact resist. She might have done, it was not impossible to try, but they were in the event too strong for her. To a large extent this is symbolized in the scheming of the goddesses Venus and Juno – they enmeshed Dido in a net from which she was not in the end able to break out. She had to measure her own character and her own will against the force of hostile circumstances. The tragedy of her story is that she allowed herself to be defeated.

The last word should be on the significance of the tragedy of Dido within the structure of the poem (far too often it has been treated as if it were detachable). Above all it introduces a note alien to the serene prophecy of Jupiter in Book 1: it becomes apparent that the Roman mission is not to be achieved without tragic events which cast doubts on the whole concept (it has indeed been a common view that Book 4 'breaks the back of the whole poem'). Nothing could have been easier than for Virgil to depict Dido as an obstacle to the Roman destiny whose removal we could all applaud, a sort of Circe, a Calypso, a Siren.

[1] See Quinn (1963) 29ff., and (1965) 16ff.

But that was exactly what Virgil was not prepared to do, whatever the cost to the credibility of Rome's heaven-sent mission. We are left deeply unhappy at the close of the book, but it is important to end with the thought that while Dido rejected all her obligations to her people and destroyed herself for reasons entirely personal to her, Aeneas was able to dismiss the promptings of self and return to the duty which he owed to others.

Turnus

The role of Turnus[1] in the *Aeneid* is in broad ways very like that of Dido: in brief he is an obstacle to the Roman mission, yet often arouses our sympathy. He does this in two ways: like Dido (but much less poignantly) he is an individual who does not belong to the cosmic plan – he must suffer because his hopes and aspirations are contrary to those of destiny. But unlike Dido he also wins sympathy because he represents a people even more important to the greatness of Rome than Aeneas' Trojans, namely the ancestors of the Italians.

But for all this there are aspects of Turnus which alienate us. He represents personal prowess, irresponsible individuality, barbaric energy in contrast with the public and social virtues which Aeneas shows or tries to show. He is fierce and violent (the word *uiolentia* is used of him only in the *Aeneid*) in contrast with Aeneas' attempts to show control; he represents, in Horace's phrase (*Odes* 3.4.65–6) *uis consili expers* in contrast with *uis temperata*. Words applied to Turnus and not to Aeneas are *uiolentia*, *fiducia*, *audax*, *superbus*, *turbidus*, *insania*; words applied to Turnus more often than to Aeneas include *amens*, *ardere*, *furor*, *ira*. Turnus fights for his own glory and reputation: Aeneas fights because he must, in order to establish peace and bring civilization. Aeneas fights a *bellum iustum*, Turnus does not. Examples of Turnus' violence and arrogance may be found at 7.413ff.; 7.461–2 *saeuit amor ferri et scelerata insania belli*, | *ira super* 'passion for steel rages in him, and the accursed madness of war, and anger above all'; 7.785ff.; 9.126 (= 10.276); 9.760–1 *sed furor ardentem caedisque insana cupido* | *egit in aduersos* 'but his frenzy and his mad lust for slaughter drove him all ablaze against the enemy'; 10.443; 10.492; 12.9–11; 12.101ff. (a description of his delight as he arms for battle). No less than fifteen similes are used to describe him, almost all conveying energy and ferocity: he is compared three times with a lion, twice with a bull, twice with a wolf, once each with an eagle, a tiger, a war horse, Mars, the north wind, fire and torrent, a land-slide, and finally, when all is lost, with the helplessness of the dream world.

The treatment of Turnus' story is deepened and made more intense (like that of Dido) by similarities with the progression of a hero of the Greek tragic stage towards a disaster which he himself makes more and more inevitable. His proud

[1] On Turnus see Otis (1963) 345ff., Small (1959) 243ff.

self-confidence leads him to arrogant behaviour such as the gods do not love. The outstanding instance of this is when he kills Pallas in circumstances of cruelty and brutality (reminiscent of Pyrrhus killing Polites before Priam's eyes), wishing that Pallas' father were there to see (*aspere et amare dictum*, comments Servius), and after his victory in the unequal fight returning Pallas as Evander 'deserved to have him' (*qualem meruit Pallanta remitto*). Virgil intervenes here into his narrative to reflect on the tragic outcome that must await these deeds:

nescia mens hominum fati sortisque futurae
et seruare modum rebus sublata secundis!
Turno tempus erit... (10.501–3)

How ignorant are men's hearts of fate and destiny to come, and of how to keep within bounds when exalted by success! A time will come for Turnus...

At the moment when defeat and disaster surround him he is seen reduced to total perplexity – the tragic hero, under the too heavy pressure of adverse forces, no longer is master of himself:

obstipuit uaria confusus imagine rerum
Turnus et obtutu tacito stetit: aestuat ingens
uno in corde pudor mixtoque insania luctu
et furiis agitatus amor et conscia uirtus. (12.665–8)

Turnus stood amazed, confounded by the shifting picture of events, and he halted, gazing and not speaking: in one human heart there seethed deep shame, madness mingled with grief, love driven on by frenzy, and the knowledge of his prowess.

Just before the final scene, Jupiter sends a Fury in the shape of an owl to beat its wings in Turnus' face, and we are reminded of the lonely and terrified Dido whose nightmare visions and torments of conscience were accompanied by the long-drawn hooting of an owl (4.462ff.). This reminiscence of the events of Book 4 is immediately reinforced as Juturna bids farewell to her doomed brother in phrases and terms reminiscent of Anna's farewell to her sister (12.871 ~ 4.673; 12.880–1 ~ 4.677–8). The last scenes of the tragedy of Turnus are thus linked with the tragedy of Dido.

These aspects of Turnus' bravery in battle (cf. also 12.894–5, 931–2), coupled with his native Italian qualities, have led Voltaire and some since to take his side against Aeneas: Scaliger had said of him 'dignus profecto qui aut vinceret aut divinis tantum armis neque aliis vinceretur' 'Turnus indeed deserved to conquer or at least to be conquered only by heavenly arms and no other'. We think of Blake's statement that in *Paradise Lost* Milton was 'of the Devil's party without knowing it', and it is interesting that a number of Milton's descriptions of Satan are based on Turnus.[1] But in the end it is the Homeric

[1] See Harding (1962).

aspects of Turnus' behaviour which mean that he cannot survive in the proto-Roman world which Aeneas is founding. In the Sibyl's prophecy (*Aen.* 6.89) Turnus is said to be another Achilles; he is equated, or equates himself, with the Greeks in 7.371–2, 9.136–9, 9.742; in the final scenes he is the Achilles figure placed now in the loser's position. We have already seen that Aeneas has by no means succeeded fully in replacing Homeric violence by a new and more civilized attitude towards the defeated – by no means; but he has made a start in that direction, he wishes to find a new way however imperfect his efforts to find it. Turnus on the other hand is wholly devoted to the old Homeric way, and however much our sympathies may sometimes be with him, our judgement must be in favour of the new way.

5. DESTINY AND RELIGION IN THE 'AENEID'

Above everything else, the *Aeneid* is a religious poem. It is based on the unquestioned assumption that there exist powers outside the world of men, and that these powers direct and influence mortal actions in accordance with a far-reaching plan of their own, extending over the centuries as far as history can reach, and concerned with the long destiny of nations.

The nature of this divine plan and the part which Rome is to play in it is outlined in Jupiter's speech to his daughter Venus in 1.257ff. In it he reveals to her the fates of the future as he will bring them to pass, especially with regard to the Roman mission. He has given the Romans rule without end (*imperium sine fine dedi*) and he stresses two aspects of their destiny. The first is by means of conquest to establish universal peace:

aspera tum positis mitescent saecula bellis...
dirae ferro et compagibus artis
claudentur Belli portae... (1.291–4)

Then the harsh generations will be softened with wars laid aside...the gates of War, terrifying with their tight bands of steel, will be closed...

The second is to establish law (*iura dabunt*, 293; cf. 4.231 *totum sub leges mitteret orbem*). This concept of the mission is broadened in the famous words of Anchises at the end of the pageant of the ghosts of Roman heroes (6.851–3):

tu regere imperio populos, Romane, memento
(hae tibi erunt artes), pacique imponere morem,
parcere subiectis et debellare superbos.

But you, Roman, must remember to rule the peoples with your government – this will be your art – to add to peace a civilized way of life, to spare the conquered and crush the proud.

Here again we see both aspects of the mission: first peace after crushing the proud, and mercy to the conquered; then government, i.e. settled laws, administrative order (*regere imperio*). This last concept is enlarged by the use of the word *mos* in its sense of a moral way of life, a civilized way of behaving (the word is more common in the plural in this sense, but cf. 8.316 *quis neque mos neque cultus erat* 'who had no code of morals and no civilization').

Another passage in which the destined history of Rome is given full and vivid expression is the description of Aeneas' shield (8.626.). Amidst the famous scenes around the outside the most striking is the one at the top, a picture of the delivery of Rome from the Gauls by the sacred geese, with religious orders such as the Salii and the Luperci included in the description; the gods have saved the righteous Romans from destruction. In the centre is the Battle of Actium with Augustus leading his Italians to battle 'with the Senate and the people, the gods of the hearth and the great gods'. And at the end Aeneas picks up the shield, lifting on to his shoulder the fame and destiny of his descendants – *attollens umero famamque et fata nepotum*.

Thus the part played in the poem by fate, and by Jupiter as its agent, is clear and unequivocal: the Romans, as a god-fearing people, will rule the world (cf. Cic. *Nat. D.* 3.5, Prop. 3.22.21ff.) and guide all the nations in the way that providence decrees; in the words of Horace, addressed to the Roman people (*Odes* 3.6.5) *dis te minorem quod geris imperas* 'because you are servants of the gods, you rule on earth'. But the situation in heaven is more complex than this: the Olympian deities, major and minor, constantly influence the human action, and are crucial to the poetic concept of the poem. This was a feature of epic technique which Virgil took from Homer and adapted in various ways. In Homer the anthropomorphic aspect of the Olympian deities was real in religious thought; the Homeric warrior might indeed believe that Apollo or Athene in person could intervene to save him from death. In Virgil's time a more sophisticated concept of deity prevented this belief except in a very symbolic sense. Yet Virgil decided to accept the Homeric convention in a poem written in a different religious environment – Why?

First and foremost Virgil uses the Olympian deities so as to enlarge the range of his poetic imagination. The visualization of shapes not seen by mortal eyes fascinated him, and he could paint pictures of the world beyond the clouds as if with brush on canvas. Consider the majestic figure of Juno moving with regal majesty in the halls of Olympus (1.46); the radiant brilliance of Iris descending by her rainbow (4.700–2); the strange splendour of Neptune and his sea-deities (1.144–7); the swooping figure of Mercury (4.252–8); the supernatural beauty of Venus as she re-assumes her divinity (1.402–5). These were magical shapes which captured Virgil's visual imagination, imbued as he was with the Greek art and literature which had so constantly portrayed them. With them he could transport his readers into another world of fancy and beauty, and achieve for them what Venus achieved for her son when she showed him what the gods could see, but mortals not:

> aspice (namque omnem, quae nunc obducta tuenti
> mortalis hebetat uisus tibi, et umida circum
> caligat, nubem eripiam...) (2.604–6)

Look, for I will remove from you all the cloud which now veils and dims your mortal sight, and casts a damp shadow around you...

The Olympian deities enabled Virgil to enter in description the mythological world which delighted Ovid in his *Metamorphoses*.

But the Olympian deities do more than provide another world of visual imagination: they also symbolize the relationship between man and the divine. We have seen how Jupiter (interpreting fate) is a symbol of the benevolence of providence towards the righteous: the lesser Olympians symbolize different aspects of man's total environment and experience. Juno represents the hostility of fortune towards the Trojans, and more will be said about her shortly; Venus is a strange mixture of the protecting mother-goddess (*alma Venus*) caring for her children, for Aeneas and for all his Romans, and the reckless Greek goddess Aphrodite, rejoicing in her power over mortals (cf. 1.657–94, 4.105–28); Apollo is the guardian god of Troy and also the god who helps those who set out on difficult and dangerous expeditions (this aspect of him is especially seen in Book 3) – he is also the special patron of Augustus (8.704–6); Neptune is the saviour by sea (1.124–56, 5.779–826). In some cases the deities may be seen as symbolizing an aspect of personality of the human actors: the torch which Allecto at Juno's instigation hurls at Turnus (7.456–66) easily fires an already inflammable character; the intervention of Mercury on Jupiter's orders to instruct Aeneas to leave Carthage (4.265–78) may well be seen as a manifestation of Aeneas' guilty conscience: he has allowed himself to become out of touch with the divine, but now he listens to Jupiter's instructions, being the kind of man who can and does respond to a message from heaven.

But it is of course Juno of all the Olympians who plays the major part in the poem. Visually she is strikingly portrayed, and as a character in her own right she is formidable, relentless, brilliantly rhetorical in expressing her anger or her guile (1.37–49, 4.93–104, 7.293–322); but above all she is symbolic of opposition to the Trojans. Some reasons for her opposition are given by Virgil in mythological and personal terms, reminiscent of the motivation of Homeric divinities; she was angry because of her support for the Greeks whom the Trojans had opposed for ten years, because of the judgement of Paris, because of Ganymede (1.23–32). But other reasons also are given, with strong emphasis, in historical terms: Juno is the guardian deity of Carthage

(1.12–22) and therefore opposes the Trojans by whose descendants her favourite city would be destroyed. This historical opposition is an undertone throughout the story of Dido, as Juno schemes to divert the kingdom of Italy to the shores of Libya (4.106). And in addition to both these aspects of her, Juno symbolizes in the broadest possible way the hostile environment, the apparently senseless disasters that befall the virtuous, the 'slings and arrows of outrageous fortune'. Everywhere and implacably she attempts to bring disaster upon the Trojans (1.36ff., 5.606ff., 7.286ff., 9.2 ff., 12.134ff.), and she is directly responsible for much of the suffering in the poem. Her relationship with the fates is a paradox which Virgil sensitively explores; she cannot change the immutable purposes of destiny, but in all kinds of ways she can delay its fulfilment, cause such difficulty that the fulfilment may be less glorious, less complete. She does not in fact seriously impair the purpose of the fates, but she does – again paradoxically – modify it to the great benefit of the Romans.

In the final reconciliation scene between Jupiter and Juno (12.791–842) Juno makes specific requests which are fully granted. She asks that the Latins should keep their name, their language, and their habit of dress; Jupiter accepts all these conditions for the Roman people who are to spring from Trojan–Italian stock, with the significant enlargement of 'habits of dress' into 'way of life' (*mores*). He continues by saying that he himself will give them religious rites and customs (thus superseding the Trojan deities which Aeneas had brought with him), and promising that the Roman race will in its *pietas* surpass all other mortals and indeed the gods themselves. Thus Juno is wholly successful in her pleas against the Trojans, and we see that her hostility has in fact achieved for the Romans what was essential to their greatness – that a large Italian element should combine with the exiles from Troy. Under these conditions (*sit Romana potens Itala uirtute propago* 'let the Roman stock be mighty because of Italian qualities' 12.827) Juno is prepared to be accepted as a Roman deity, to be one of the Capitoline Triad, to defend the Romans and Italians with her help (as she certainly would not have defended the Trojans, cf. Hor. *Odes* 3.3). Ironically and paradoxically her opposition to Aeneas turns out to be beneficial for the Romans, not only because they had been hardened through suffering (*tantae molis erat Romanam condere gentem* 'so great a task it was to found the Roman race' 1.33; cf. Donatus' comment *magna enim sine magno labore condi non possunt* 'great things cannot be achieved without great toil'), but also because it was Juno who secured for the Italians, the enemies of Aeneas, their dominance in the Roman race whose achievements Virgil anticipates in his poem.

The Olympians, then, apart from forming part of the machinery of the poem and offering Virgil opportunity for pictorial imagery in a supernatural world, also enabled the poet to symbolize his thoughts and feelings about the relationship of human beings to the powers above them, about the nature of their individual free will within the framework of a divine purpose, about the problems of evil and suffering in a world guided by benevolent providence. His preoccupations are those to which Christianity was so shortly to give its answers; his own answers are very halting and uncertain. In his invocation to the Muse (1.8–11) he asks to be told the causes for Juno's hostility towards a man outstanding for his devotion to his gods and his fellow men (*insignem pietate uirum*), and he concludes with the question *tantaene animis caelestibus irae?* 'Can there be such anger in the minds of the gods?' For all the final success of Jupiter's purpose, for all the final reconciliation of Juno, the note of suffering and pathos is very often dominant in the poem. Unlike Milton, Virgil does not profess to be able to 'justify the ways of God to men', but this is the theme which he explores in countless situations in the poem, as he sets different aspects of human experience, human aspiration, human suffering in the context of a story laden with destiny.

The religious content of the poem is (naturally enough) largely concentrated in the narrative as the Olympian deities scheme and counter-scheme and Jupiter guides events towards the way which destiny demands, and as the human actors pay their worship, make their prayers and fulfil their religious ceremonies (the *Aeneid* is remarkably full of religious ritual, partly because of Virgil's love of ceremony and antique customs, and partly because of the essentially religious nature of Aeneas' destiny). But there is one place in the poem where an exposition of theological doctrine is set forth in a didactic fashion; this is where the ghost of Anchises explains to his son when they meet in Elysium the nature of the life after death (6.724–51). The exposition does indeed serve the plot, because it is needed to explain the presence of the ghosts at the river of Lethe, but it is primarily a religious message to the Roman reader, several times reminiscent in style of the didactic method of Lucretius and strongly coloured with the Stoic ideas which Virgil had come to find more acceptable than the Epicureanism which he followed in his youth. The message is the more striking because of its total contrast with the afterlife in Homer, whose *Nekyia* in *Odyssey* 11 had suggested some of the structure of *Aeneid* 6. The essence of the speech[1] is based on Orphic and Pythagorean ideas as purified by Plato: this life is merely a preparation for a richer life to come, and in proportion as we concentrate on the spirit and not on the body during this life our soul will be the more easily purified of its stains and made fit to dwell for ever with the divine essence from which it came. Upon death we all undergo purification – only a few can be purified sufficiently to stay in Elysium, while the rest must be reborn for a new life on earth. But the gates of Elysium are open wide (6.660–4), not only for those who died for their country, or were priests and poets, or enriched life by their discoveries, but also for those who

[1] See Bailey (1935) 275ff.

made people remember them by their service. Thus in some way only dimly seen virtue in this world is rewarded in the next; the confusion and suffering and sorrow of our life will be compensated for after death. It is a vague picture, and not presented with any kind of certainty – the whole of *Aeneid* 6 is really a vision personal to Aeneas rather than a confident statement about the hereafter. It is presented in groping hope, not in the sureness of faith; but it prevents a poem which is not always serenely confident about the potential perfection of Rome's Golden Age and which is so deeply preoccupied with suffering from becoming a poem of pessimism.

6. STYLE AND METRE

It is only possible here to make a few brief remarks about Virgil's style and metre. His narrative method can be contrasted with that of Homer in a number of ways: it has less directness and immediacy, but rather aims at density and elaborate balance[1] in a way appropriate for literary epic, and it is more concerned with foreshadowing and interweaving: it looks backwards and forwards. It is essentially a subjective style of narrative[2] in which the author involves himself and the reader empathetically in the action. This is done in many different ways: e.g. by elaborating the state of mind or the viewpoint of the character concerned rather than of the observer (e.g. 4.465ff., 12.665ff.); by the use of apostrophe in moments of particular intensity (e.g. 4.408ff., 10.507ff.); by 'editorial' intrusion into the narrative (4.412, 10.501ff.). The use of imagery[3] is highly sophisticated, containing correspondences with other parts of the narrative of such a kind as to illuminate the particular situation or character involved; this can be seen especially in a study of the similes,[4] where the imagery often serves not merely to illustrate and strengthen the immediate narrative but also to make thematic links with the mood and tone of the wider context (e.g. *Aen.* 1.498ff., 4.69ff., 4.441ff., 12.4ff., 12.908ff.).

The movement of Virgil's narrative is indeed much less rapid than that of Homer (Ovid is much nearer to Homer in speed and directness), and a slow, descriptive and reflective mood is generally thought of as especially characteristic of Virgil (e.g. 2.624ff., 5.833ff., 6.450ff., 11.816ff.). This is basically true, but what is really remarkable about Virgil's style is its extraordinary variety; this is what maintains the impetus throughout the length of the poem. He can be ornate and baroque (1.81ff., 3.570ff., 5.426ff.) or plain and matter-of-fact (as often in Book 3 or in the ship-race, 5.151ff.); he can be sonorous and sublime (1.257ff., 6.756ff.) or exuberantly mock-heroic (6.385–416). And he

[1] See the analysis of Virgil's adaptation of Homer's games in R. D. Williams (1960) Intro. xiii ff.
[2] See Otis (1963) *passim*.
[3] See Pöschl (1950) *passim*, Putnam (1965) *passim*.
[4] See Hornsby (1970).

can on occasion use the crisp and rapid narrative of Homer (e.g. the disguised Trojans in 2.370ff., the hunt in 4.129ff., the Rutulian attack in 9.33–46, the episode of Nisus and Euryalus in 9.314–445 and much of the second half of Book 9). But generally Virgil aims at and achieves a denser style by extending and enlarging the conventional vocabulary of epic, not perhaps so much by neologisms (though there are some) as by unusual combinations of words, by the *callida iunctura* of Horace (*A.P.* 47–8). Epithets are transferred, the constructions of verbs altered, the attention arrested by unusual phrases which seem to hover around several meanings rather than pinpoint one in the Ovidian manner. This penumbra, this evocative indistinctness may be what Agrippa meant when he accused Virgil of a new kind of stylistic affectation (*cacozelia*: *Vita Don.* 44). Some outstanding examples of this dense and evocatively pictorial style may be studied at 1.159ff., 2.230ff., 7.177ff., 11.59ff., 12.587ff.

The arrangement of the words, while nothing like as intricate as that of Horace's *Odes*, nevertheless differs greatly from that of normal Latin prose. Nouns and their adjectives are often separated so as to make a patterned line, though extreme patterning such as that in a Golden Line is rarer than in the *Eclogues*. With this expectation of style set up in his readers Virgil can make a great impact by abandoning it in favour of the simple order of noun and adjective placed adjacently, as for example the famous lines beginning *ibant obscuri* (6.268–70) or the description of Elysium (6.638–9).

Words and constructions with a prosaic ring are avoided (for example *cum* with the pluperfect subjunctive is never found), and the normal Latin method of subordinating clauses within a long period is much rarer than in Virgil's predecessors (Lucretius was fond of clauses with subordinating conjunctions and Catullus of participial clauses). The effect of this is to produce what is perhaps the most striking of all the stylistic features of the *Aeneid* – its very high proportion of main verbs, that is to say its paratactic style. Examples of this directness may be found easily and frequently, e.g. 1.208–13, 2.407–12, 3.561–9, 4.579–83, 5.673–9. All this is not to say that Virgil does not use the slower, more conventional Latin sentence where he needs it, e.g. the description of Iris at 4.693–702, the speech of old Neptune at 5.804–11, the picture of the Tiber at 8.86–9, the description of Pallas' funeral at 11.39–41.

A large proportion of the *Aeneid* is taken up with speeches,[1] and here Virgil commands a vivid rhetorical and oratorical skill, as is attested by the speakers in Macrobius' *Saturnalia* (5.1) where they discuss whether a student of oratory would learn more from Cicero or Virgil, and Eusebius suggests that Virgil has more variety of oratory than Cicero – *facundia Mantuani multiplex et multiformis est et dicendi genus omne complectitur* 'His eloquence is manifold and diverse, embracing every style of speaking'. Examples of particularly

[1] See Highet (1972).

powerful rhetoric are found especially in the speeches of Juno and Venus (1.37–49, 1.229–53, especially 10.18–62, 63–95), and of Sinon (2.108–44), Dido (4.365–87, 590–629) and Drances and Turnus (11.342–75, 378–444). Often the nature of the situation requires that the rhetoric should be less overpowering, e.g. 1.257–96, 1.562–78, 2.776–89, 3.154–71, and here Virgil demonstrates that he can use his art to conceal art as well as to flaunt it.

A final word must be said about epic dignity. It was conventional to use heightened phrases to describe ordinary events (as Virgil does everywhere in the *Georgics*, a form of convention which the English eighteenth century fully accepted); examples are the servants and kitchenmaids in 1.701–6, the pigs of Circe in 7.15–20, the simile of the top in 7.378–84, the sow and its piglets in 8.81–5. Virgil does not attempt to imitate the 'low' style (*humilis*) which Homer achieved so outstandingly when describing ordinary or homely situations: Quintilian recognized this when he said that no one could possibly surpass Homer's propriety in small things (*proprietas in paruis rebus*). Virgil's sublimity and grandeur, never or very rarely broken by un-epic situations or phraseology, is sustained and strengthened by a fondness for poetic Grecisms and for archaisms in appropriate places to match the antiquity of his subject (Quintilian called him *amantissimus uetustatis* 'deeply enamoured of what was old'); echoes of the phraseology of Ennius and of archaic forms used by Ennius and Lucretius often occur, enhancing the dignity and conventional remoteness of the epic form by means of which Virgil was able to express concepts and ideas which are intimately connected with the real life of real people.

Metre

Virgil's command of the rhythm of the hexameter has always been acclaimed: Dryden spoke of 'the sweetness of the sound' and Tennyson's line is well known: 'Wielder of the stateliest measure ever moulded by the lips of man'. Virgil was fortunate in receiving from Ennius the heritage of a metre of extraordinary flexibility, both in regard to the speed of the line as regulated by the interchange of dactyls and spondees, and especially because the system of quantity taken over from the Greek hexameter could be used as a metrical base (ictus) against which the word-accent of Latin with its stressed syllables could be used as a second rhythm in the line. This potentiality had been barely explored by Virgil's predecessors, Ennius, Lucretius, Catullus, Cicero; in Virgil's hands it became a highly sophisticated method for conveying conflict and struggle (when the two rhythms are opposed) or serenity and peace (when they coincide). This aspect of Virgil's hexameter has been studied widely in recent times[1] and figures largely in modern commentaries on the *Aeneid*, and

[1] See Knight (1939) and (1966) 292ff., Wilkinson (1963) 90ff.

more cannot be said here than to indicate that this is one of the most fruitful methods of appreciating the infinite variety of Virgil's verse.

A second area in which Virgil greatly developed the work of his predecessors was in the relationship of sentence structure to verse pattern. Ennius, Lucretius and Catullus had for the most part (with exceptions, of course) preferred a metrical movement where the sentence structure corresponded with the verse ending: for example in Catullus 64 the proportion of run-on verses (or mid-line stops) is very small. Virgil, like Milton, experimented with an enjambment involving a frequent tension between verse structure and sentence structure. The variety of the position of his sense-pauses is very great, and the effect achieved by (for example) the verb run on to the end of the first foot of the following line (e.g. 2.327, 467) or by a series of lines where the clauses stop in different places in the line (e.g. 5.670–3, 9.390–401) can be very great indeed. As there is a tension between ictus and accent, so there is a tension between verse and sentence.

Virgil's employment of unusual metrical features (hiatus, spondaic fifth foot, monosyllabic ending, absence of caesura and so on) is highly selective and used generally for special effect. In Ennius, Lucretius and Catullus these features often indicate either an insufficient mastery of technique, or a special idiosyncrasy (like Catullus' fifth-foot spondees); in Ovid and his successors they are used much more rarely. Virgil succeeds in departing from the expected norm sufficiently often, but only sufficiently often, to arrest the reader's attention.

Finally Virgil used the devices of alliteration and assonance, of lightness or heaviness in metre, in such a way as not to cloy. It was traditional in Latin poetry to use these effects, and Virgil follows in the tradition, but in a fashion sufficiently sophisticated almost to escape notice until detailed analysis is made. In poetry these effects are generally significant potentially rather than in themselves: that is to say that if other methods are being employed to raise the reader's interest in particular directions the use of alliteration and assonance can reinforce the impact. This is the essence of Virgil's ability to suit the sound to the sense; we are aroused by the context to expect and respond to a particular effect before the effect is presented to us. Consider for example the angry speech of Iarbas to Jupiter (4.206–18) where he complains of how Aeneas the intruder is preferred in Dido's eyes to himself; we are involved in his indignation and when he ends:

nos munera templis
quippe tuis ferimus famamque fouemus inanem (217–18)

we are reinforced in our feeling by the unusual and violent alliteration of *f*.

Consider as an example some of the stylistic and metrical effects in Dido's last long speech:

'pro Iuppiter! ibit
hic,' ait 'et nostris inluserit aduena regnis?
non arma expedient totaque ex urbe sequentur,
deripientque rates alii naualibus? ite,
ferte citi flammas, date tela, impellite remos!
quid loquor? aut ubi sum? quae mentem insania mutat?
infelix Dido, nunc te facta impia tangunt?
tum decuit, cum sceptra dabas. en dextra fidesque,
quem secum patrios aiunt portare penatis,
quem subiisse umeris confectum aetate parentem!
non potui abreptum diuellere corpus et undis
spargere? non socios, non ipsum absumere ferro
Ascanium patriisque epulandum ponere mensis?
uerum anceps pugnae fuerat fortuna. – fuisset:
quem metui moritura? faces in castra tulissem
implessemque foros flammis natumque patremque
cum genere exstinxem, memet super ipsa dedissem.
Sol, qui terrarum flammis opera omnia lustras,
tuque harum interpres curarum et conscia Iuno,
nocturnisque Hecate triviis ululata per urbes
et Dirae ultrices et di morientis Elissae,
accipite haec, meritumque malis aduertite numen
et nostras audite preces. si tangere portus
infandum caput ac terris adnare necesse est,
et sic fata Iouis poscunt, hic terminus haeret,
at bello audacis populi uexatus et armis,
finibus extorris, complexu auulsus Iuli
auxilium imploret uideatque indigna suorum
funera; nec, cum se sub leges pacis iniquae
tradiderit, regno aut optata luce fruatur,
sed cadat ante diem mediaque inhumatus harena.
haec precor, hanc uocem extremam cum sanguine fundo.
tum uos, o Tyrii, stirpem et genus omne futurum
exercete odiis, cinerique haec mittite nostro
munera. nullus amor populis nec foedera sunto.
exoriare aliquis nostris ex ossibus ultor
qui face Dardanios ferroque sequare colonos,
nunc, olim, quocumque dabunt se tempore uires.
litora litoribus contraria, fluctibus undas
imprecor, arma armis: pugnent ipsique nepotesque.' (4.590–629)

The speech begins in mid-line with staccato phrases, with unusual sense pauses after the fifth foot of 590 and after the first syllable of 591: emphasis is given to the bitter words *inluserit aduena* enclosed within the rhyme from caesura to line ending (*nostris...regnis*). The staccato impression is continued with a very strong sense pause after *naualibus* (echoing that in 590) and the series of short clauses in 594 with violent alliteration of *t*. Then as Dido realizes that there is no one to hear her agitated commands the metre slows totally and the simple words of 596 produce an entirely spondaic rhythm; the question she asks herself is answered in equally simple words, in an even shorter sentence of absolute finality (*tum...dabas*).

Now Dido's anger rises again as she passes from self-blame to emotional resentment of her lover's actions: alliteration of *p* in 598–9 reinforces her disbelief in the traditional stories of Aeneas' virtues and the impersonal *aiunt* is strongly contemptuous. Had she not heard it all from his own lips? The gruesome imagery of 600 is allowed to run on to the next line; and again emphasis is put on the intervening words *epulandum ponere* by the rhyme from caesura to line ending (602). As she reflects on the doubtful issue of the horrifying deeds she has suggested to herself her words are given impetus by two very rare trochaic sense pauses (603, 604); and the certainty that all the actions she might have taken are now for ever unfulfilled is reflected by the remarkable rhyming effect of the pluperfect subjunctives (*tulissem*, *implessem*, *exstinxem*, *dedissem*).

Now the trend of her thoughts changes direction entirely from the agony of the unfulfilled past to her passion for vengeance in the future. The rhythm slows entirely, with a high proportion of spondees and two monosyllables to commence her invocation (607), with rhyme of *harum...curarum* (echoing *terrarum*), with lines that are complete in themselves with pauses at the end of each, and with the strange sound-repetition of *et Dirae...et di*. After the solemnity of the invocation the prayer itself is given in three short clauses involving sense pauses in the second foot, at the line ending, and in the fourth foot (611–12). Thus the invocation itself has a sonorous majesty as each verse, complete in itself, reinforces the previous one; while the actual prayer reflects metrically the urgent call for action.

The subject matter of the prayer begins with a long sweeping sentence with end-stopped lines, given vehemence by places of marked conflict of accent and ictus (613, 615) and coming to a pause abruptly and powerfully on the word *funera*: death is her desire for others as well as for herself and there is no more emphatic way of stressing the word than by placing it last in its sentence and first in the line. The next phrase begins very slowly with monosyllables (618) and comes to its violent climax with the conflict of accent against ictus on the word *cadat*.

In the resumption of her curse, as she extends it from Aeneas personally to the long vista of the years to come she uses the same technique as in 618 to give emphasis to the intense irony of *munera* (624). Her invocation of the unknown avenger has hissing *s*'s to reinforce the syntactical strangeness of the third person *aliquis* with the second person verb *exoriare*, and rhyme of *Dardanios*...*colonos* as well as of *exoriare*...*sequare*. After the three self-contained lines (625–7) the speech concludes with lines containing mid-line stops (after the fourth foot in 628, after the first and in the third of 629), and ends with the very rare device of hypermetric elision, a device which is in fact impossible here because the speech is over and Dido's last word *nepotesque* cannot be elided. She is unable at the end to fit the torrent of her words to the metrical scheme.

A brief and very selective analysis of this kind gives perhaps some idea of the complexity and variety of Virgil's rhythm, a variety sufficient to sustain the interest over many thousands of lines. More than any other Roman poet Virgil was able to make the movement of his words and the sound of his verse match and therefore reinforce the content and mood of the subject matter.

7. CONCLUSION

The *Aeneid* is above all a poem of the exploration of conflicting attitudes, an attempt to harmonize the different and often discordant facets of human experience. Its relationship with the poems of Homer sets up a double time-scale in which the qualities and ideals of Homeric life can be compared and contrasted with the needs of a new type of civilization. Its parallel narrative on two planes, divine in Olympus and human in the mortal world, perpetually compels our attention to the interrelationship of the everlasting divine laws and transient human action. But above all the poem explores the relationship between the strong vigorous national world of Roman organization and empire and the quiet private world of the lonely individual who is not interested in, or is excluded from, or is destroyed by the cosmic march of Roman destiny.

We may distinguish these two elements by speaking of Virgil's public voice (patriotic, national, concerned with the march of a people) and his private voice (sorrowful, sensitive, personal). There need be no doubt that the *Aeneid* is intended primarily to celebrate the public aspect of optimism, of power, of organized government. But side by side with this, and perhaps increasingly as the poem progressed, Virgil was preoccupied with the suffering of those who fall by the way, or are trampled underfoot as the march of destiny proceeds forward. The outstanding examples of this are of course Dido and Turnus, but instances of tragic and unhappy death occur throughout the poem: Orontes drowned by Juno's storm (1.113ff.), Priam and Laocoon and many others in Book 2, like Coroebus, Rhipeus, Polites; there is the pathos of Andromache and Achaemenides in Book 3; the sudden and inexplicable loss of Palinurus in Book 5; the plight of the ghosts in Book 6, especially Palinurus, Dido and

Deiphobus; the deaths of Galaesus in 7, of Nisus and Euryalus in 9, of Pallas and Lausus in 10, of Camilla in 11, of Aeolus in 12:

> hic tibi mortis erant metae, domus alta sub Ida,
> Lyrnesi domus alta, solo Laurente sepulcrum. (12.546–7)

Here was your end of death; your lofty house was beneath Mt Ida, at Lyrnesus your lofty house, but your tomb is in Laurentian soil.

All of these and many more mark Virgil out as the poet of *lacrimae rerum* (1.462), of sympathy for the world's suffering; this has been the aspect of his poetry which has been most strongly stressed and most widely appreciated during the last hundred years. Sainte-Beuve spoke of *tendresse profonde*, Matthew Arnold of 'the haunting, the irresistible self-dissatisfaction of his heart', Myers of 'that accent of brooding sorrow'.

We may move this conflict between Virgil's public voice and his private voice into a literary setting. His public voice is set firmly in the tradition of Ennius, national poet of Rome's history and the greatness of her people; it would have been approved by Cicero, and it is echoed in Livy's history and Horace's Roman odes (3.1–6). It is stern, severe, detached, epic in the full sense in that it deals with the large-scale movement of great events. His private voice is in the tradition of Catullus, the poet of the individual's hopes and fears and joys and sorrows. There is a lyric quality, even an elegiac quality in many passages in the *Aeneid*, as for example the funeral of Pallas with its reminiscences of Catullus (11.59–99). Virgil has combined two modes, the hard and the soft, because he could sympathize with both. He has a foot in both camps; no other Roman poet was less dogmatic, more able to appreciate the viewpoint of contrasting personalities. It is because of his many-sidedness that in every generation since his own Virgil has been the most widely read of the Roman poets.

19

HORACE

I. A CRITIQUE OF THE TRADITIONAL STEREOTYPE

Horace is commonly thought of as a comfortable cheerful figure, well adjusted to society and loyally supporting the Augustan regime; a man without any strong beliefs or emotions, who smiled gently at human foibles, wrote and behaved with unfailing tact and good taste, and was in all respects the personification of *mediocritas*. As this picture has been remarkably consistent over the years and has not varied with the poet's popularity (but rather explains such variations) one would expect it to contain a good deal of truth. And so indeed it does; but on closer inspection we find that the colours have faded, contrasts of light and texture have disappeared, much of the detail has been lost, and the result is like a fresco damaged by time and neglect.

To recover a more vivid sense of the original we have to remind ourselves of a few fundamental points. First, it is misleading to classify Horace as an Augustan poet *tout court*. His life was more than half over when the Augustan age began, and the Emperor survived him by more than twenty years. Most of the satires and epodes belong to the period before Actium (31 B.C.). Few of these touch on politics, and those that do convey attitudes of disgust (*Epod.* 4), disillusion (*Sat.* 1.6), or despair (*Epod.* 7 and 16). Only five poems mention Octavian. They were all written at the time of Actium or shortly after, and except in the case of *Epod.* 9 the lines in question are of minor importance.

Secondly, although his imagination normally operated in the central areas of human experience, Horace was far from being average or typical. Even in an age of social ferment it was extraordinary for a freedman's son to go to school with the aristocracy, to study at the Academy in Athens, to serve as a military tribune under Brutus, and later to become accepted and esteemed by the imperial court. Success of this kind was not achieved without cost. In an early satire (written about 36 B.C.) Horace complains that everyone runs him down for being a freedman's son – *libertino patre natum* (*Sat.* 1.6.45–6). Elsewhere, especially in the first book of *Epistles* (about 20 B.C.), he shows a keen, almost anxious, awareness of social nuances, and even at the height of his fame he speaks as if he can still detect traces of resentment (*Odes* 4.3.16, about 13 B.C.).

Thirdly, in the late fifties, when Horace was in his teens, life in Rome was disrupted by riots and gang warfare. The political atmosphere grew steadily more oppressive until the storm of civil war broke in 49 B.C. After Caesar's assassination Horace joined Brutus and saw the carnage at Philippi 'when bravery was smashed' (*Odes* 2.7.11). He returned to Italy under a general amnesty to find that his father had died and the family home had been confiscated. Peace was still dreadfully precarious. In 37 B.C., as described in *Sat.* 1.5, Horace accompanied Maecenas to the conference at Tarentum, where Octavian met Antony. Later he was on the point of going to Actium (*Epod.* 1), though it is doubtful if he was actually present at the battle. We do know, however, that on another occasion (perhaps earlier, in 36 B.C.) he narrowly escaped drowning (*Odes* 3.4.28). If in middle age he opted for a quiet life, most people would feel he had earned it. In any case we must beware of the notion fostered by the older source criticism that Horace absorbed all his experience at second hand by reading Greek texts.

Again, when the doctrine of the mean is applied too rigidly to Horace's work, we get the impression of a rather dull and insipid personality. It is true, of course, that he often affirms the traditional belief (most fully developed by Aristotle) that virtue lies between two extremes. But in many cases he is primarily concerned to ridicule the extremes. Thus in *Epist.* 1.18 he states the doctrine succinctly in l. 9 – *uirtus est medium uitiorum* – and then immediately goes on to describe the sycophant and the boor. When he does speak of the mean itself he usually brings out its elusive nature – it varies according to a man's character, circumstances, and situation. Above all, it involves movement; for however stable the right condition may be in theory, we do not live in a stable world. We are always adjusting our position in order to maintain equilibrium:

rebus angustis animosus atque
fortis appare: sapienter idem
contrahes uento nimium secundo
  turgida uela. (*Odes* 2.10.21–4)

When in the straits of fortune show yourself spirited and brave. You will also do well to reef your sails when they are swollen by too strong a following wind.

The mean, then, is not easy to achieve; and it is certainly not attained, or even sought, in all Horace's poetry. Granted, he did not write about his sexual emotions with the intensity of Catullus, or goad himself into long rhetorical tirades in the manner of Juvenal; yet there were times when he deliberately flouted the accepted standards of good taste:

rogare longo putidam te saeculo
  uiris quid eneruet meas,
cum sit tibi dens ater et rugis uetus
  frontem senectus exaret

hietque turpis inter aridas natis
podex uelut crudae bouis. (*Epod.* 8.1–6)

To think that you, who are rotten with decrepitude, should ask what is unstringing my virility, when your one tooth is black, and extreme old age ploughs furrows across your forehead, and your disgusting anus gapes between your shrivelled buttocks like that of a cow with diarrhoea.

Whether the victim of this foul attack existed or not we cannot say. If she did, Horace was not concerned to tell us who she was. On the other hand, we have no right to assume that because the poem contains no name and clearly belongs to the abusive tradition of Archilochus the woman must therefore be fictitious. Better to admit ignorance and pass on to a more important question, viz. what effect had the poet in mind? When we discover that the woman is aristocratic (the masks of her ancestors will attend her funeral), wealthy (she is weighed down with big round jewels), pseudo-intellectual (volumes of Stoicism lie on her silk cushions), and adulterous (she is eager for extra-marital thrills), the only plausible interpretation is that the whole thing is a horrible kind of joke, based on deliberate outrage. The poem is exceptional but not unique – *Epod.* 12 shows the same scabrous ingenuity, and two later odes, though less offensive, exploit a similar theme (1.25 and 4.13). Needless to say, the unpleasant epodes, and also most of *Sat.* 1.2 (which is bawdy, but clean in comparison) were omitted by the Victorian commentators; and as those admirable scholars have not yet been superseded it still has to be pointed out that Horace was not invariably polite.

Nor was he always happy. The struggle for tranquillity is well illustrated in *Odes* 2.3, which begins by affirming the importance of keeping a level head when things are steep (*aequam memento rebus in arduis | seruare mentem*). The next two stanzas speak of enjoying a bottle of Falernian in a secluded field with trees overhead and a stream running by. 'Bring wine, perfume, and roses', says the poet; but already there are darker overtones, for the lovely rose-blossoms are 'all too brief' and we can only enjoy ourselves 'while circumstances and youth and the black threads of the three sisters allow us'. The prince will have to leave his castle (17–20); like the poor man he is a victim of pitiless Orcus (21–4). Continuing the image of the victim (i.e. a sheep or a goat), the final stanza begins *omnes eodem cogimur* 'we are all being herded to the same place'; then the picture changes:

omnium
uersatur urna serius ocius
sors exitura et nos in aeternum
exilium impositura cumbae. (25–8)

Everyone's pebble is being shaken in the jar. Sooner or later it will come out and put us on the boat for unending exile.

The choice of image whereby the shaken pebble conveys both the randomness and the inevitability of death, the compression of thought in which a lot-pebble puts someone on board a boat, and the sonorities of the whole stanza with its sequence of *-er-*, *ur-*, *-er-*, *-or-*, *-ur-*, *-er-*, *-ur-* and its two final elisions – these features produce a powerful effect; but it is hardly one of cheerful serenity.

On other occasions we find Horace in a state of high excitement. *Odes* 3.19 begins in a tone of good-humoured exasperation, saying in effect 'You keep talking about the dates and genealogies of the early Greek kings, but you say nothing about the cost of a party and who will act as host' (one notes the balance of dates/how much, genealogies/who). We then move forward in time; the party is under way, and Horace, now in exalted mood, calls for a series of toasts in honour of Murena the new Augur. As a thunderstruck (i.e. inspired) bard he can demand an especially potent mixture. 'Let's go mad!' he cries; 'Why is there no music? Start it at once! Throw roses! Let old Lycus and the girl who lives next door hear the wild uproar.' Wine, poetry, music, roses, and finally love: Rhode wants the romantically good-looking Telephus; Horace longs for his Glycera.

There Bacchic inspiration is loosely, and humorously, connected with a symposium. In *Odes* 3.25 it is directly related to the praises of Augustus. This is a more ambitious poem in that it attempts to convey the actual nature of a mystical experience:

quo me, Bacche, rapis tui
   plenum? quae nemora aut quos agor in specus
uelox mente noua? (1–4)

Where are you rushing me, Bacchus, after filling me with yourself? To what woods and caves am I being hurried away in this strange condition?

It is not surprising that this dithyramb, with its exciting rhythm and fluid structure, should also contain one of the most striking pictures in Horace:

non secus in iugis
exsomnis stupet Euhias
   Hebrum prospiciens et niue candidam
Thracen ac pede barbaro
   lustratam Rhodopen, ut mihi deuio
ripas et uacuum nemus
   mirari libet. (8–14)

On the mountain ridge the sleepless Bacchanal gazes out in astonishment at the river Hebrus and Thrace white with snow and at Mt Rhodope traversed by barbarian feet; so too, away from the paths of men, I love to marvel at the lonely riverbanks and woods.

Such passages must be given full weight if we are to appreciate the poet's richness and diversity.

A similar point can be made about Horace's ideas. If we compare what he says in different places on any particular subject we find that his opinions are usually reconcilable; but there are exceptions, and these sometimes occur in quite important odes. As an illustration let us consider what he says about the course of history. Some passages speak of man as having emerged from barbarism guided by rational self-interest (*Sat.* 1.3.99ff.) or a divine bard (Orpheus in *A.P.* 391f.) or a god (Mercury in *Odes* 1.10). But this process is never regarded as steady or assured, and at times, within the narrower context of Roman history, we are faced with a decline. In *Odes* 3.6, written about 28 B.C. before the Augustan recovery had got under way, the decline is supposed to date from the early part of the second century; and it will continue, says the poet, until the old religion is revived. In *Epod.* 7, where a curse is said to have pursued the Roman people ever since Romulus murdered his brother, we have a different kind of assertion. The vague chronological reference, located at a point before history emerged from legend, provides rhetorical force, but we are not meant to examine the statement's literal accuracy. After all, the Rome which became mistress of Italy and then went on to conquer Hannibal and Antiochus could hardly be thought of as accursed. So too, when Horace calls on his fellow-citizens to sail away to the isles of the blest where the golden age still survives (*Epod.* 16), he is not appealing to anything historically verifiable, but is using a myth (which is exploited for rather different ends by Virgil in the fourth *Eclogue*) to condemn the mad world in which he is living. Allowing for differences of perspective and idiom, there is no basic contradiction between these passages.

In *Odes* 1.3, however, there *is* a contradiction. The hardiness of the first sailor is seen as an arrogant defiance of god's will; and that sailor was typical of mankind as a whole which 'has the audacity to endure all, and goes hurtling through what is wrong and forbidden'. Examples follow: Prometheus stole fire and gave it to men – all kinds of sickness ensued; Daedalus invaded the air, Hercules the underworld. 'Nothing is too steep for mortals. We make for heaven itself in our folly, and by our wickedness we do not allow Jove to lay aside his angry thunderbolts.' This is not a manifesto of heroic humanism. Admittedly by using the word *audacia* Horace may acknowledge the other tradition in which Prometheus, Daedalus, and Hercules were admired for their courageous services to mankind, but he explicitly repudiates that tradition by giving *audacia* an unfavourable sense. Human inventiveness has led only to disaster. Such a view is, of course, naive and one-sided (though no more so than the belief in progress which has recently withered). And the uncompromising statement which it receives in *Odes* 1.3 is indeed untypical. But Horace was not always typically Horatian, and *Odes* 1.3 is a very good poem.

Finally, perhaps the most serious point forgotten in the popular conception of Horace is the fact that he was a great innovator. In the rest of the present section this will be illustrated by observations on his poetic career.

The seventeen epodes, which Horace referred to as *iambi*, were something quite new in Roman literature. One could amplify this by saying that no one had yet written a collection of Latin poems modelled on the work of Archilochus. Yet that would be misleading, not only because Horace differed in many ways from the seventh-century Greek, but because the whole vocabulary of modelling, copying, and imitating is apt to suggest something external and even mechanical. It is better to suppose that Horace found in Archilochus a poet with whom he had an instinctive affinity, and then used him as an aid to realizing and expressing what was in himself.

Keeping that in mind, we may turn to *Epist.* 1.19.23ff. where Horace says that he followed the *numeri* (metres) and *animi* (vehemence or spirit) of Archilochus, but not his *res* (subject matter) or *uerba* (words). Of the epodes nos. 1–10 consist of iambic couplets in which trimeters are followed by dimeters, nos. 11–16 contain various combinations of iambic and dactylic rhythms, and no. 17 is in trimeters throughout. Here there is a direct debt to Archilochus, for most of the schemes are found in his fragments; yet the technical achievement of producing these rhythms in Latin should not be underrated.

By *res* and *uerba* Horace means the subject matter of Archilochus' personal life and the language in which it was presented. Such features could only have been reproduced in a translation. In a more general sense, of course, Horace does use the same material as Archilochus (love, wine, war etc.), and his diction ranges from noble to foul as the situation requires. But the setting and characters are in most cases unmistakably Roman, and there are several poems, e.g. the melodramatic mimes about the witch Canidia (5 and 17) and the two poems addressed to Maecenas at the time of Actium (1 and 9), where the contribution of Archilochus is negligible.

As for the *animi*, if Horace means 'vehemence' then nos. 4, 6, 8, and 12 would be the most obvious examples, though the force of the attack is weakened by the victims' anonymity and by the lack of any explicit account of their relation to Horace. If *animi* has the vaguer meaning of 'spirit' then more pieces could be included, but we should not press this comparison too far, for the epodes were also influenced by more recent literature, such as Hellenistic mimes (as in 5 and 17) and perhaps even Latin elegies (as in 11 and 15). And in one case at least Archilochus' spirit is taken over only to be transformed into something utterly different. This is in no. 10, where Horace prays that the voyage of

Mevius may end in disaster. Similar imprecations are found in the so-called Strasbourg epode, usually attributed to Archilochus,[1] which Horace almost certainly knew. The difference between the two poems is not between the real and the imaginary (for Mevius was a real person, whether or not he was making a journey), but between the deadly seriousness of Archilochus and Horace's playful malice. *Epod.* 10, in fact, is a literary joke, in which the kindly form of the *propemptikon* (or send-off poem) is filled with grandiloquent invective so as to annihilate a fellow poet.

In satire Horace's role was rather different. Here the pioneer work had been done by a Latin poet, Gaius Lucilius, a hundred years earlier. That ebullient and wide-ranging man had taken over the idea of verse miscellanies (*saturae*) from Ennius. Then, by settling on the hexameter and using it to project a lively critical spirit, he had succeeded in creating a new and specifically Roman genre. It was, however, undeniably rough and sprawling, and Horace's contribution was to reduce and refine it so as to meet his own, more purely classical, standards. This meant concentrating mainly on a few central topics – in particular man's enslavement to money, glory, gluttony, and sex; narrowing the linguistic range by restricting the use of vulgarisms, archaisms, Greek importations, and comic coinages; cutting down on elisions and end-stopped lines so as to ease the rhythmic flow; and modifying Lucilius' buffoonery, coarseness, and abuse. Yet Horace greatly admired the older satirist, and he carried on the Lucilian tradition not just by ridiculing vice and folly but by writing in an informal and amusing way about himself.

The main differences between the two books of satires are as follows: Book 1 (published in 35 B.C. or soon after) includes a few pieces where the ethical element is small (as in 8 and 9) or negligible (as in 5 and 7) and the main purpose is to entertain; the attacks on moral and literary faults are conducted by the poet himself (sometimes with the aid of an anonymous opponent), and they are made specific and interesting by the frequent use of proper names. In Book 2 (30 B.C.) fewer figures are attacked, and new techniques are employed for communicating the ideas. Thus Horace sometimes delivers the homily himself, sometimes reports it, sometimes listens to it, sometimes appears as a person being warned or rebuked, and sometimes withdraws completely. Dramatic presentations are more frequent, and there is an extensive use of parody.

Perhaps the most notable feature of the *Satires* as a whole is their pervasive reasonableness. Horace assumes at the outset that we are living in a civilized society where there is no need to handle such monstrous aberrations as sadism, cannibalism, and incest. He also assumes that within our social and moral

[1] See Kirkwood (1961) 267–82, van Sickle (1975).

framework we have the power to discriminate between different degrees of wickedness, that we have a sense of proportion to which he can appeal, and that in however faltering a way we can bring thought to bear upon our attitudes and conduct. He therefore pays us the compliment of addressing our intellect. In most pieces the satirical attack is carried out through an argument or disquisition which moves in an orderly though subtle way from one point to another. The poet's tone is rarely abusive. He does not seek to establish too much; he hears objections; makes concessions. And so at the end of the poem the reader feels not only that he has been listening to a sensible man but also that the ethical point has been made progressively clearer and more precise. Such an impression would, of course, be ruined if Horace appeared self-righteous or superior. He avoids this danger by laughing at himself and adopting a manner which, though basically serious, never asks for a heavily emotional response. Horace is not, in fact, primarily concerned to influence the reader's morals. He invites him, rather, to contemplate human folly as a subject of perennial interest. The contemplation is made enjoyable by the satirist's art. And then, as Persius observes (1.116–18), the moral insights emerge from the enjoyment.

After the publication of the *Epodes* and *Satires* 2 in 30 B.C. Horace confined himself to lyric, and in the next seven years produced what is normally regarded as his greatest work – viz. the first three books of *Odes*. Thirty years earlier Catullus had written two poems in sapphics, four in combinations of glyconics and pherecrateans, and one in asclepiads, but there was as yet no body of verse that could be called Roman lyric, and in fact the idea of a *Latinus fidicen* ('Latin minstrel') would have sounded paradoxical. In *Odes* 3.30 Horace claims to be 'the first to have adapted Aeolian verse to Italian tunes' – i.e. to have written Latin poetry in Greek verse-forms.[1] To have taken over these metres, modified them, and employed them for larger poetic ends was a significant part of Horace's originality. But only a part. Horace was a different kind of poet from any of his Greek predecessors. He was closest to Alcaeus and worked with many of the same lyric types, such as hymns, love-poems, and drinking songs. But Alcaeus was an aristocrat, an important figure in the political struggles of a small city state, a poet who sang to the accompaniment of a lyre poems which were often immediately related to the occasion of their performance. None of this was true of Horace. Moreover, the Roman poet also drew on such different writers as Pindar (fifth century), Callimachus (third century), and Meleager (first century); on Greek sermons and panegy-

[1] The main systems which he employed – viz. the four-line alcaic and sapphic stanzas and various combinations of asclepiads, glyconics, and pherecrateans – are set out in every edition and are analysed in detail by Nisbet–Hubbard.

rics; and on Latin literature from Ennius to Virgil. He was therefore a sophisticated writer, availing himself of a long cultural tradition. To a lesser poet such a position could have been stifling, but Horace was able to assimilate these influences and use them to create something of his own.

In interpreting the *Odes* it is hard to maintain the conventional distinction between Greek and Roman. The two are blended in various proportions. We might, for instance, want to say that for Horace national affairs meant the traditions, values, and welfare of Rome; but for over a century Rome had been the capital of an empire which included Greece, and the city itself had a sizeable Greek population. Again, love in the *Odes* is love as Horace observed and knew it; but his attitude and treatment must have been coloured by his reading of Anacreon and poets of the Greek Anthology. His friends were (of course) living contemporaries, but they were also bilingual, and when one of them died, like Quintilius, it was natural to cast the Latin lament in the form of an epicedion (1.24). Conversely an ode like the hymn to Mercury (1.10), which had no Roman features except the god's name, would not have seemed foreign to Horace's readers, because from childhood they were as familiar with Greek mythology as with the stories of early Roman history. So too, in the prophecy of Nereus (1.15) they would all have picked up the allusions to the *Iliad* and some would have caught the flavour of Bacchylides. In the symposium odes the mixture is especially hard to analyse. Undoubtedly Horace had read many Greek poems set in the context of a party with its wine, music, and girls. But as a Hellenistic city Rome had absorbed countless Greek customs, including that of the symposium, and parties were a regular feature of Horace's life. So it is best to assume that he drew on both kinds of experience. How many elements of a given party were historically authentic is another question, and one which is usually unanswerable. In such matters we must follow logic and common sense as far as they take us and then stop. The same applies in other areas too. Thus we disbelieve the story that doves covered Horace with leaves (3.4), accept that he was narrowly missed by a falling tree (2.13), and keep an open mind about what he did with his shield at Philippi (2.7).

All this is a rather crude summary of a complex question, but it may serve to show that the *Odes* were a new phenomenon in ancient literature. One should add that as well as marking the beginning of Roman lyric they also represent its highest point. Here the closest parallel comes from pastoral, in which Virgil's *Eclogues* hold a similar position.

On finishing *Odes* 1–3 Horace returned to *sermones* (conversational hexameters) using them as a vehicle for moral comment of a more general and less satirical kind. The epistles of Book 1 (published in 19 B.C. or slightly earlier) had no direct antecedents in Greek literature, though scholars have suggested various sources of influence, including Epicurus, Theocritus, and Menippus. In Latin, leaving aside the correspondence of Cicero, which is only marginally relevant, one can point to a verse-epistle of Lucilius in which he complained that a friend had failed to visit him when sick,[1] and to certain 'humorous letters in verse' written by Lucilius' contemporary Sp. Mummius in 146 B.C.[2] But the idea of composing a whole book of verse-epistles was something quite novel.

The nature of the epistles was also distinctively Horatian. They were addressed to real people; they contained real information about the poet's opinions and way of life; and although not inspired by anything like reforming zeal they were surely meant, like the *Satires*, to have *some* effect on the reader's moral outlook. (It is an aberration of our own century to believe that Horace made ethical assertions without any ethical purpose.) At the same time the *Epistles* should not be thought of as just ordinary letters versified. They are primarily poems, and they vary considerably in their relation to actuality. In *Epist.* 1.3 the relation is very close – Horace asks Julius Florus various questions about himself and his friends and looks forward to receiving an answer. In *Epist.* 1.9 we are at one remove from a real letter; presumably Horace had in some way recommended Septimius to Tiberius, but the epistle itself does not constitute the original recommendation. At the other end of the scale *Epist.* 1.6 is a set of reflections on peace of mind (*nil admirari*); its epistolary status is purely nominal.

Epist. 2.2 (19 or 18 B.C.) takes the form of an excuse for not writing lyrics: 'I was always lazy and never pretended to be anything else; Rome is impossible – the noise is appalling and I've no patience with the literary set; poetry is hard work, and anyhow at my age one has more serious concerns – like philosophy.' Within this framework there are passages of great vividness and diversity, including autobiography, complaints about urban life, a fine statement of classical poetic theory, and amusing stories like those about Lucullus' soldier and the lunatic of Argos.

Epist. 2.3, referred to by Quintilian (8.3.60) as the *Ars poetica*, may also belong to the period 23–17 B.C.; if not, it must have been written after *Odes* 4, near the end of the poet's life; for in l. 306 he implies that he has given up lyric. Unfortunately the addressees – Piso and his two sons – cannot be identified with any confidence. In the case of the *Ars poetica* the problem of originality passes into one of structure; for while the individual precepts are easily apprehended, difficulties begin when we try to group them under larger headings and to discern some overall plan in the work. Is there, as many have thought, a division between *ars* (1–294) and *artifex* (295–476)? Should we go further

[1] Lucilius, ed. Warmington (1967) frs. 186–93. Lucilius may well have written some other epistles too. He refers to the epistle as a form in fr. 404.

[2] Cicero, *Ad Atticum* 13.6*a*.

and subdivide *ars* into style (*poema*) and content (*poesis*)? Advocates of this view point out that the same three terms were used by Neoptolemus of Parium (a scholar-poet of the third century B.C.) and that according to Porphyrio (a commentator of the third century A.D.) Horace 'gathered together the precepts of Neoptolemus of Parium on the art of poetry, admittedly not all, but the most significant'. But can we be sure that *poema* and *poesis* had these functions in Neoptolemus, and what degree of precision can be attributed to the statement of Porphyrio? These and other problems surrounding the *A.P.* 'have resulted in a neurotic confusion unexcelled even in classical studies'.[1] We need not add to that confusion here, but it is fair to observe that if Horace took over this tripartite scheme (as he may have done) he put such varied material into each section, and so blurred the lines of demarcation, that the separate parts would not have been readily apprehended by his readers. From which one infers that the scheme as such was not meant to be of central importance.

The question of the *A.P.*'s relevance is also disputed, and it may well be that no neat answer can be given for the poem as a whole. Some of the precepts – e.g. those on how to revivify the language (46–72) and on the need for disinterested criticism (419–51) – are applicable to all Roman poetry; others – e.g. those regarding structural unity (1–22 and 136–52) – are equally general in principle, though Horace is mainly concerned with epic and tragedy; others again – e.g. those about characterization (99–127, 153–78) – apply almost entirely to tragedy and comedy. This last point raises the question: 'How vital was new dramatic writing in the age of Augustus?' As none has survived and the evidence is very meagre, we may infer that tragedy and comedy were almost extinct; or that performances still went on, though we don't happen to know about them. As for Horace's intentions, we may believe that he was hoping to revive the old theatrical traditions in opposition to the increasingly popular mimes and pantomimes; or that he was not really addressing himself directly to the contemporary situation at all.

The same question arises in a more acute form in connexion with the passage on satyr-plays (220–50); for this was a genre which no Roman had attempted. The same range of answers is available. If we maintain that here too Horace was trying to encourage young playwrights, we cannot be refuted and the poem remains homogeneous in its relevance. But many would find it uncomfortable to hold a view for which there was so little evidence. If we take the other line, we can suggest that the long section on drama was included partly for its intrinsic interest, partly because drama held a dominant position in the most important Greek criticism, viz. that of Aristotle and his successors, and partly because it offered various topics which could be exploited for satire, moral affirmation, or simply general reflections on life. This may be the right

[1] D. A. Russell in Costa (ed.) (1973) 116.

approach, but if so it fails to preserve the poem's unity of intent, for, as we have seen, a good deal of the *A.P.* refers directly to the Roman literary situation. But whatever view we adopt, there can be no doubt that the *A.P.* covers an immense historical scope; it handles a variety of topics with lightness, humour and good sense; and as no one had ever previously written a poem on poetics it remains a work of impressive originality.

Epist. 2.1, addressed to Augustus about 15 B.C., deals with the role of poetry in society, and again there is quite a lot of general discussion about drama. But the spirited defence of contemporary poetry and the complaints about conservative taste (1–92) are certainly coloured by Horace's own experience:

> indignor quicquam reprehendi, non quia crasse
> compositum illepideue putetur, sed quia nuper;
> nec ueniam antiquis, sed honorem et praemia posci. (76–8)

I find it deplorable that a thing should be criticized not because it's considered coarse or clumsy in style but because it's modern, *and that instead of excusing the poets of the past* [e.g. Plautus, Naevius, and Ennius] *we should be expected to honour and reward them.*

Those words *crasse* and *illepide* (cf. *tenui* in l. 225) recall how Catullus and the moderns of an earlier generation used to talk about poetry. Horace had never been totally opposed to them. He accepted the ideals of neatness and craftsmanship which they had derived from Callimachus, and like them he avoided the larger genres. But his more extrovert temperament, and perhaps his social background, led him to choose forms which had less room for affectionate diminutives, mellifluous Greek words, 'aesthetic' effects of sound and metre, and the romantic and sentimental use of mythology. More important, Horace always enjoyed making poetry out of human behaviour and the ideas which were meant to regulate it. This interest eventually enabled him to respond to the achievement of Augustus by writing on political themes. Finally, although he felt incapable of undertaking epic and tragedy himself, he never regarded these genres as outmoded or impossible; the work of Varius and Virgil proved the contrary. When all due respect had been paid to Callimachus' dictum (*Hymn to Apollo* 108ff.), a large river was not *invariably* dirty (*Epist.* 2.2.120f.)

Before *Epist.* 2.1 Horace had already written the *Carmen saeculare* to be sung at the celebrations of 17 B.C., which, as they were supposed to mark the end of an epoch, were called the *Ludi Saeculares.* This choral hymn (the only ode composed for musical performance) was specially commissioned by Augustus. As a result of its success and of further encouragement from the Emperor, Horace went back to lyric and eventually in 13 B.C., or perhaps later, published a fourth book of odes. Three or four of the pieces (2, 3, 7, and perhaps 5) show him at his very best; all the others contain memorable stanzas; and even the smallest (10) makes a positive impression. If we take the book as a whole it is interesting to see how the magnificence of the laureate, addressing the Emperor and his family in lofty Pindaric style and confident of his ability to confer lasting fame, is tempered by personal feelings of melancholy and nostalgia. The poet is close on fifty (1); Cinara is dead (13); Ligurinus is young and heartless (10); Lyce is a sad reminder of the past (13); Phyllis will surely be his last love (11). If Virgil in no. 12 is the dead poet and not some unknown contemporary, then that ode too evokes memories of earlier days. Like the other collections, *Odes* 4 shows signs of deliberate arrangement; 4 and 5 (on Augustus' step-sons and Augustus himself) correspond to 14 and 15, and the opening poem includes several themes which occur later, viz. love, ageing, poetry, and the praise of a distinguished contemporary. For the rest, it is hard to observe anything sufficiently bold and regular to be called an architectural pattern, but this view is disputed.[1]

Adapting and promoting new poetic forms naturally entailed the development of an individual style, or range of styles. No modern critic would dare to describe such an achievement in a few words, but Quintilian made a brave attempt. Writing of the lyric Horace in the first century A.D. he said: *insurgit aliquando et plenus est iucunditatis et gratiae et uarius figuris et uerbis felicissime audax* 'He rises every now and then to grandeur; he is full of delight and charm; he shows variety in his figures of speech, and in his language he is triumphantly adventurous' (10.1.96). Here are a few examples of the sort of thing that Quintilian had in mind:

1.

parcus deorum cultor et infrequens,
insanientis dum sapientiae
consultus erro nunc retrorsum
uela dare atque iterare cursus
cogor relictos. (1.34.1–5)

I was a niggardly and infrequent devotee of the gods; expert in a senseless philosophy I strayed from the truth. Now I am forced to sail back and resume the course I had abandoned.

The whole poem is made up of antitheses, some so sharp as to be paradoxical, and they dramatize the central paradox of thunder from a clear sky – an event which brought two philosophies into collision. It is unusual for the meaning of an ode to be enacted so fully by the form (another example is the teasing repartee of 3.9); but the ingenious placing of semantic blocks so as to build a

[1] See Ludwig (1961) 1–10.

poetic structure is entirely typical. One should perhaps add that Horace was not really an Epicurean before this ode or a Stoic after it.

2. eheu fugaces, Postume, Postume,
labuntur anni, nec pietas moram
rugis et instanti senectae
adferet indomitaeque morti (2.14.1–4)

Alas, Postumus, Postumus, the years are slipping swiftly by, nor will devotion succeed in checking wrinkles, the onset of old age, and invincible death.

The repetition of a proper name is without parallel in Horace (and how apt a name it is!). By putting it here he delays the completion of the sentence, thus linking the key word *fugaces* to the emotional *eheu*. The beginning almost certainly suggests a river (cf. *lympha fugax* in 2.3.12), but the second sentence brings a change of metaphor – viz. the hopeless fight against age and death. One notes the climax *rugis*, *senectae*, *morti*, and the Homeric phrase *indomitae morti* (Ἀΐδης ἀδάμαστος) which contributes to the stanza's sombre dignity.

3. gelidos inficiet tibi
rubro sanguine riuos
lasciui suboles gregis. (3.13.5–8)

The offspring of the frisky herd will stain your cool streams with his red blood.

Here we have a chiastic pattern of adjective...adjective noun noun – 'cool... red blood streams'. At the same time two other adjectives are implied, for the red blood is warm and the cool streams are clear. The result is a strong sensuous effect. The ode offers a subtle blend of realism and pathos. To call it callous is unnecessarily squeamish, unless one happens to be a vegetarian.

4. urit me Glycerae nitor. (1.19.5)

I am burned by Sweetie's brilliance

– a triple assault on the senses.

5. post equitem sedet atra Cura. (3.1.40)

Behind the horseman sits Angst dressed in black

– a picture worthy of Dürer.

6. nauis, quae tibi creditum
debes Vergilium finibus Atticis
reddas incolumem, precor,
et serues animae dimidium meae. (1.3.5–8)

O ship, you to whom Virgil has been entrusted and who owe him to the soil of Attica, discharge him there intact, I pray you, and save fifty per cent of my soul.

I have overtranslated to bring out the extended commercial metaphor.

7. pallida Mors aequo pulsat pede pauperum tabernas
regumque turris. o beate Sesti,
uitae summa breuis spem nos uetat incohare longam.
iam te premet nox fabulaeque Manes
et domus exilis Plutonia. (1.4.13–17)

Pale Death kicks with impartial foot the poor man's cottage and the prince's castle. My well-off Sestius, the short span of life forbids us to initiate long hopes. Soon night and the storied spirits and the meagre Rich house will hem you in. [Pluto, like Dis, means 'rich'.]

Note the plosives and dentals in the first sentence, the contrast of *summa breuis* with *spem longam*, and the juxtaposition of *exilis* and *Plutonia*, which gives an added reminder to the *beatus Sestius*. (The meaning of *exilis* is guaranteed by *Epist.* 1.6.45f.)

8. 'o sol
pulcher! o laudande!' canam, recepto
Caesare felix. (4.2.46–8)

I shall sing 'Day of beauty, day of glory!' in my happiness at having Caesar back.

Here the trochaic rhythm of a popular song of triumph has been cleverly incorporated in a sapphic stanza.

9. illic omne malum uino cantuque leuato,
deformis aegrimoniae dulcibus alloquiis. (*Epod.* 13.17–18)

There lighten every misfortune with wine and song, those sweet assuagers of ugly depression.

Chiron is advising the young Achilles on how to face the miseries of the Trojan war, from which he will never return. This is the first recorded instance of *alloquium*; and it is used in the extended sense of 'assuager'. Bentley, who noticed the peculiarity, took it to indicate textual corruption instead of poetic originality; but he was probably right in thinking that Horace had in mind the Greek παραμύθιον. The expression *deformis aegrimoniae* looks back to 'scowling moroseness' (5) and to the glowering storm of l. 1.[1]

10. parcius iunctas quatiunt fenestras
iactibus crebris iuuenes proterui,
nec tibi somnos adimunt, amatque
ianua limen. (1.25.1–4)

Not so relentlessly do wild young men shake your closed shutters with volleys of stones; they do not rob you of your sleep, and the door hugs the threshold.

The sarcasm derives its force from the implication that to any respectable woman the cessation of these disturbances would be a welcome relief; whereas

[1] See Rudd (1960*b*) 383–6.

for Lydia it marks the beginning of the end. Later in the ode, women past their prime are spoken of as *aridae frondes* 'dry leaves'. In another place (4.13.12) Horace talks of *capitis niues* 'head snow', when he means 'white hair'. This may not strike us as very daring, but no parallel is recorded and Quintilian (8.6.17) thought it a harsh metaphor (*dura translatio*). What, one wonders, did he think of 2.11.6–8 where sexual pleasure is driven away by 'dry whiteness' – *arida canitie* – an expression combining the two ideas of dry leaves and white hair?

T. S. Eliot once spoke of 'that perpetual slight alteration of language, words perpetually juxtaposed in new and sudden combinations'. He can hardly have been thinking of Horace's dictum in *A.P.* 46ff., yet the resemblance is remarkably close:

in uerbis etiam tenuis cautusque serendis
dixeris egregie notum si callida uerbum
reddiderit iunctura nouum.

You should also be subtle and careful in weaving words together. If a clever combination makes a familiar word new, that is distinguished writing.

2. A CRITIQUE OF THE ACADEMIC DICHOTOMY

Whereas the traditional stereotype is popular and superficial, the two divergent views which we shall shortly consider are represented (in various degrees) by several important works of scholarship. Before coming to them, however, let us grant that Horace's poetry offers a number of contrasting features, e.g. public/private, urban/rural, Stoic/Epicurean, grand/plain. How should these be interpreted? Certain answers may be set aside at once. One might say, for instance, that consistency was not to be expected – Horace wrote as the mood took him. There is something in this, for the poet refuses to be tidied up. Yet to distinguish two sides of his poetic character and then to leave the matter there is not satisfactory. (A similar procedure has failed with Catullus and Juvenal.[1]) Or we could say that the whole question was irrelevant – Horace simply dons different masks, which must, presumably, be taken at their face value. But this only moves the question one step back, for we still want to know whether the *personae* are themselves related. Or we might try to see a chronological development in which Horace gradually moved from one side to the other. But this doesn't work, because both sets of concerns are visible at every period.

Of the two serious approaches which we have to discuss, one maintains that most of what is lasting and important in Horace is to be found in the public column, whereas the private column contains engaging but essentially ephemeral *nugae*. According to the other view the true Horace only reveals himself

[1] See Frank (1928) and Ribbeck (1865).

in the private column; the public compositions show signs of strain and artificiality; and the natural explanation is that they were written to order. Instead of adopting either of these approaches it seems better to ask how clear the dichotomy really is. Are there not ways in which the two sets of characteristics may be related?

First of all, form. Let us take a poem which belongs very clearly to the right-hand column, viz. the little ode to Pyrrha (1.5). Boy and girl are together in a grotto; the boy will weep when he discovers Pyrrha's fickle nature; now unsuspectingly he enjoys her charms; Horace has discovered what she is like. Within this scheme of present, future, present, past, the characters and their relationships are presented. The boy – slim, perfumed, trusting – is in for a shock. The girl is bright and alluring; her appearance smart yet uncontrived (*simplex munditiis*); but her simplicity will prove deceptive. Now comes a metaphorical substitution: the boy will gaze at 'the rough sea with its black winds', i.e. the new, hostile, Pyrrha (not 'the sea of love' or 'the couple's relationship'). Another substitution follows: the boy is 'unaware of the treacherous breeze'. Then the two terms of the metaphor (Pyrrha and the sea) are brought explicitly together: *miseri, quibus intemptata nites* 'poor devils who, not having embarked on you, are fascinated by your shimmer'. Finally another substitution: Horace has hung up his wet clothes as a thank-offering to Neptune for his escape.

The grotto-scene is part of a wistful reverie and represents a single imagined occasion. The second vignette – that of Pyrrha binding back her hair – is probably of the same kind; for the two pictures appear to be companion pieces (boy embracing girl, girl setting out to attract boy). No background is supplied for the second; so we can, if we wish, imagine Pyrrha finishing off her hair-do in her bedroom – but not in the grotto, where she is otherwise engaged. The pictures are cleverly brought together in l. 9 where *qui nunc te fruitur* 'who now enjoys you' recalls the grotto-scene and *aurea* 'golden' glances back to Pyrrha's hair.

For the movement of the poem across the stanzas, the enfolding word-order of l. 1, the novelty of *emirabitur insolens* 'he will gaze in astonishment', the verbal play of *aurea/aurae*, and various other features, reference must be made to Nisbet–Hubbard.[1] But perhaps enough has been said to show that what looks like a piece of dainty porcelain is as strongly made as many of the large Alcaic odes. Its feeling is correspondingly complex: for the boy an amused, slightly patronizing pity, mixed with envy; and on Horace's own part relief, with a touch of nostalgia. It is all conveyed very lightly (much more lightly than in *Epod.* 15), but it is still there.

Odes 1.5 revolves around Pyrrha, and the tone and style remain fairly constant. In many other cases, however, there is a discernible movement. *Odes* 2.13,

[1] Nisbet and Hubbard (1970) 72–80.

for instance, opens with a series of imprecations directed at a rotten tree which had nearly killed the poet. The tone is one of mock horror, rather as in the epode on garlic (no. 3). Then, in stanzas four and five, Horace goes on to reflect in a calmer mood on the unpredictability of fate – death comes from the most unexpected quarter. This leads into the second half of the poem – a vision of the underworld in which Sappho and Alcaeus give joy and comfort by singing to the dead. So the lyric poet's narrow escape from death, which is treated comically, paves the way for a profoundly serious affirmation: even death cannot prevail against the powers of lyric poetry.

Before leaving this ode it is perhaps worth noting that of the two Greek poets Alcaeus has the keener audience, and *his* story is of battles and the expulsion of tyrants – i.e. political events. If Horace's chief model could write of politics as well as of love and wine (cf. *Odes* 1.32) we may be sure that Horace saw nothing anomalous in doing the same.

The kind of tonal variety described above is also claimed for satire:

> et sermone opus est modo tristi, saepe iocoso,
> defendente uicem modo rhetoris atque poetae,
> interdum urbani... (*Sat.* 1.10.11–13)

You also need a style that is sometimes severe, sometimes gay, now suiting the role of an orator or poet now that of a sophisticated talker...

Often an elevated tone is used for comic contrast, as in *Sat.* 1.5.9ff. where the beautiful description of night is a prelude to the backchat of bargees, or for purposes of burlesque, as in *Sat.* 1.7 where a vulgar altercation is reported in Homeric style. But there are passages in both the *Satires* and the *Epistles* where the level rises because the theme is noble. One thinks of the prayer to Mercury (*Sat.* 2.6.1ff.), the portrait of the Stoic sage (*Sat.* 2.7.83ff.), the encomium of Augustus (*Epist.* 2.1.1ff.) and the lines on the mortality of man and his words (*A.P.* 60ff.).

In the *Odes* the spectrum is wider, for they include adaptations of various types of Greek lyric ranging from the stately choruses of Pindar to Anacreon's little songs about love and wine. Again, the divisions are not always clear-cut. In the opening of *Odes* 3.11 the invocation of Mercury, the explanatory *nam* clause, the myth of Amphion, and the reference to the seven-stringed lyre and its welcome presence at banquets and religious ceremonies – all this prepares the reader for a dignified Pindaric ode. It then transpires that the god is being asked to provide a song which will sway the affections of Lyde – a skittish young filly who is refusing to think of marriage. The filly comes from Anacreon. The serious style is resumed as we hear of the marvellous achievements of the lyre in the hands of Orpheus. But Lyde is still in the background, for if song can charm tigers and the savage Cerberus surely it can tame a filly. As the poet's imagination moves through Hades it comes to rest on the daughters of Danaus. These girls had rejected marriage in the most violent way by murdering their bridegrooms, and are now paying the penalty by filling a leaky barrel. Here is a story Lyde ought to hear; so Horace tells it, very economically, ending with the words of the noble Hypermnestra who alone deceived her father (*splendide mendax*) and allowed her husband to escape. Although the ode may be in some way related to an actual situation, Lyde should not on that account receive too much attention. It is equally wrong, however, to assert that she is there simply to introduce the story of Hypermnestra. The two girls come from different poetic neighbourhoods. It was Horace's clever idea to bring them together and let them interact.

Another hymn begins with a solemn address to a deity, recalling the circumstances of her birth and the various ways in which she controls the life of men. Horace then begs her to come down and join her devotees; he rehearses the numerous blessings she confers, and promises that she will be the centre of a joyful celebration. The diction is reverent and ceremonious, but it is also shot through with double meanings, because the deity in question is a wine-jar. The whole piece (3.21) is a delightful parody of a cletic hymn.[1]

High and low are brought together for a rather different purpose towards the end of *Epist.* 2.1. Horace is addressing the Emperor: poets, he says, like artists and sculptors, can commemorate a ruler by portraying his achievements; Virgil and Varius have performed this service for you. I too, instead of composing 'conversation-pieces that crawl on the ground' (*sermones...repentis per humum*), would prefer 'to tell of your exploits, of distant lands and rivers, of castles on mountain-tops, and barbaric kingdoms, of warfare concluded under your inspired leadership throughout the world, of the bars that enclose Janus the guardian of peace, and of the terror brought to the Parthians by your imperial Rome'. Hardly a specimen of the low style. Horace then continues: '...if only my desires were matched by my abilities. But a small poem is not appropriate to your exalted state, and I in my diffidence am not so rash as to attempt a task too heavy for my strength.' Thus, with a neat manoeuvre, the poet is back again on his usual level.

The most interesting example of *recusatio* (a refusal to write a more ambitious type of poem) is found in the first half of *Odes* 4.2. There Horace states in the sapphic metre that he cannot hope to write a Pindaric ode; he fashions his poems in the painstaking manner of a bee; not for him the swan's flight or the rushing torrent of Pindar's eloquence. But as that great periodic sentence sweeps through five stanzas displacing caesuras and submerging line-divisions, and as Pindar's lyric forms come past us one by one from dithyramb to dirge, celebrating gods, heroes, and men, we become aware that Horace has achieved some-

[1] I.e. a hymn in which the god is called on to appear: see Norden (1913) 143ff.

thing very like the effect which he has disclaimed. So here again, in the ironic structure of the *recusatio*, two contrasting styles co-exist. It only remains to add that the event which the poet was so superbly unfit to celebrate was the return of Augustus from Gaul.

Finally, the two styles may be related by placing two contrasting poems side by side. *Odes* 1.37 is an ode of triumph on the destruction of Cleopatra. Nearly six centuries earlier Alcaeus had cried exultantly νῦν χρῆ μεθύσθην 'Now's the time to get drunk...for Myrsilus is dead.' So when Horace begins with *nunc est bibendum* he is not only 'acknowledging a shared culture' (to use Nisbet–Hubbard's excellent phrase) but also asserting a kindred political experience: a tyrant is dead. Lines 5–21 present the dissolute, drunken, power-mad queen of Octavian's propaganda. As we read about her, however, we should not use our historical sources to censure Horace's inaccuracy; for he was not reporting the battle of Actium as it actually took place, but rather reflecting the general mood of triumph and delirious relief. Then, as in *Odes* 2.1, the poet's initial and spontaneous reaction gives way to something altogether deeper and more humane, and in ll. 21–32 we are shown the defeated Cleopatra, determined to avoid humiliation, calmly taking her own life like a Roman Stoic. Both moods are accommodated in the grand style with its glorious effects of sound and diction.

Some of Horace's most dignified 'public' compositions end on a quiet note, e.g. 3.5 and 4.2; once or twice he checks an ode apparently in mid flight and brings it back to the level on which he normally meets the reader, e.g. 2.1 and 3.3. An analogous effect is produced by placing the very short ode *Persicos odi* after 1.37 and using it to round off the book. Though not strictly a sympotic poem it is related to 1.37 by the theme of drinking and by the anti-oriental sentiment. Also, in its own way, it is artfully contrived. For example, the first stanza deprecates Persian elaborateness, garlands woven on *philyra* (a Greek word, meaning lime bast), and the search for late roses; but it contains no negative words. The second affirms the sufficiency of myrtle (*simplici myrto*) and the pleasure of sheltered relaxation, but it is couched entirely in negatives. Yet the contrasts with 1.37 are more obvious and important. Instead of complex periods we have two sapphic stanzas with short asyndetic sentences; the literary ancestry is found in Anacreon and Hellenistic epigram, not in Alcaeus or Pindar; and after the jubilant celebration of Cleopatra's defeat we are brought back to the Horatian norm by the picture of the poet enjoying a quiet drink in his summerhouse.

In this section we have noted how small light poems can be structurally complex, how within a given ode the style may shift from one level to another, how parodies use solemnity for comic effect, how in a *recusatio* the grand style can be disavowed and employed at the same time, and how a contrast can be exploited by juxtaposition.

After style, theme. One theme, recurrent at all periods, is that of simplicity. Here perhaps the best example of a public ode is 2.15 (*iam pauca aratro*). The abuse in question (viz. uncontrolled building) is a civic abuse affecting the country's economy. No one is addressed, except the community at large, and at no point does the poet speak in the first person. An appeal is made to the traditions of Romulus, Cato, and the Romans of an earlier day who spent their money on public rather than private buildings, and these old traditions were, we are told, enforced by law. Several of the same features are found in 3.24; there too the poet asserts that no change of heart can come about without the aid of laws.

When we turn to 3.1, however, the situation is less straightforward. For although *odi profanum* is the first of the so-called 'Roman odes', its argumentation comes from the world of private ethics. Acquisitiveness and extravagance are criticized not for their social or national effects but for what they do to the individual. The greedy man is reminded that money does not guarantee happiness and that it usually brings worry and resentment. Such reasoning is familiar from the *Satires* and *Epistles*. Again, though the poet appears initially as the Muses' priest (*Musarum sacerdos*), at the end of the ode we hear the familiar Horace talking about his Sabine farm. So apart from the first two stanzas the ode is essentially a lyrical diatribe.

Although the theme of simplicity connects both sides of Horace's work, his treatment of the matter is not simple. First, Horace had no objection to wealth in itself, as long as it was used in a generous and enlightened way (*Sat.* 2.2.101–5, 2.8; *Odes* 2.2). His main target was acquisitiveness; for the man who thought only of making money harmed both himself and society. Secondly, Horace was not so hypocritical as to maintain that extreme poverty was in some way beneficial. His *aurea mediocritas* ruled out 'the squalor of a tumbledown house' just as firmly as 'the mansion that excites envy' (*Odes* 2.10.5–8; cf. *Epist.* 2.2.199). He does, however, occasionally express the view that since life is precarious any man may find himself in poverty, and that he should be able to survive the experience without being shattered (*Odes* 3.29.53ff.; cf. 4.9.49). In particular, young men in military training should learn to rough it (*Odes* 3.2.1).

Thirdly, it is sometimes helpful to distinguish between what Horace admired and what he liked. We cannot doubt, for instance, that he admired the toughness of the early Romans, but he would hardly have chosen to sit beside Regulus at a dinner party. If pressed hard, this distinction could leave him open to the charge of insincerity, and he knew it. 'You praise the good fortune and character of the men of old', says Davus (*Sat.* 2.7.22ff.), 'but if a god urged you to go back you'd strenuously refuse.' But we must be careful here, for some of the warmest praise of the hardy peasant is uttered by characters other than Horace himself. The homily in *Sat.* 2.2 is delivered by Ofellus, Cervius tells the story of the two mice (*Sat.* 2.6) and the rustic idyll in *Epod.* 2 turns out to be a money-lender's day-dream. While Horace admired certain (idealized) features of country life, he never yearned to be a farmer. Anyone careless enough to identify him with the speaker in *Epod.* 2 deserves to fall into the trap at the end.

Certain inconsistencies remain. They are amusingly described in the letter to Numonius Vala (*Epist.* 1.15). There Horace compares himself to Maenius, a parasite, who if he failed to cadge a dinner used to inveigh against the luxury of the rich, but who when given the chance would devour every delicacy in sight. As far as Horace is concerned the picture is, of course, a caricature (cf. *Sat.* 2.7.29ff.); and when he says that 'the only people who know anything about the good life are those whose money is solidly and conspicuously based on splendid villas' he is obviously pulling his friend's leg. The nucleus of truth consists in the idea of alternation. For while Horace respected the monolithic type of character who was always predictable because always the same, and may indeed have acknowledged that ideal as a steadying influence, the pattern of his own life was less monotonous. He needed change, and occasionally this led to restlessness and depression (*Sat.* 2.7.28–9; *Epist.* 1.8.12); but normally the poet's sense and good taste enabled him to control his temperament, and so he was in a position to laugh at the wild oscillations of men like Priscus and Tigellius (*Sat.* 2.7 and 1.3). We need not doubt, for instance, that he enjoyed the hospitality of Maecenas and could look after himself very well when on holiday (*Epist.* 1.15), but his usual style of living was much simpler. And although with eight farmhands to run his estate he may seem well enough off to us, there was no comparison at all between him and the great men to whom he addressed his poetry.

This adaptability, which has an obvious analogy in the poet's style, cannot be confined within the doctrines of any philosophy (*Epist.* 1.1.14–19). And yet it does represent a kind of principle: to live a life of civilized hedonism as far as one's nature and circumstances allow, but to retain a tough core for withstanding hardship. Correspondingly, in national affairs, we find Horace rejoicing in Rome's prosperity (*Epist.* 1.12.28–9; *Carm. Saec.* 53–60) and sharing in her various celebrations (*Odes* 3.14, 4.2), but employing Stoic ideas of virtue when handling ideas more closely concerned with her well-being and survival (*Odes* 3.2, 3, 5).

We now come to a number of odes connected in one way or another with hospitality. At first sight they seem to show that Horace was a thoroughgoing escapist, too sensitive or too indolent to contemplate the world of affairs: 'Have the good sense to put an end to your sadness and the troubles of life with mellow wine', 'Fill the gleaming cups with Massic wine that brings forgetfulness', 'Why not lie at ease beneath this tall plane or pine and drink while we may?' 'Gladly accept the gifts of the present moment and forget all that's grim.' It is tempting to compare such advice with Omar's:

> Ah fill the cup; what boots it to repeat
> how time is slipping underneath our feet?
> Unborn tomorrow and dead yesterday –
> Why fret about them if today be sweet?

Tempting, but misleading; for the passages must be read in context. The first is from 1.7, addressed to the consular L. Munatius Plancus, who in 41 B.C. joined Antony but went over to Octavian in 32 and retained his influence in the years that followed. Velleius called him 'a pathological traitor' (*morbo proditor*), but no one with any historical sense will accept that as a final verdict on his character.[1] The point we are concerned with here is that, whether or not he held a military command at the time of the ode's composition, he was certainly engaged in public life. At the end of the poem the heroic Teucer concludes his speech with the words: *nunc uino pellite curas* | *cras ingens iterabimus aequor* 'now drive away your troubles with wine, tomorrow we renew our journey over the vast ocean'. So too, Plancus is being urged to relax when he can. The second passage is addressed to Horace's old comrade Pompeius, who has just returned to Italy after fighting for over twelve years on the side of Octavian's enemies (2.7). The third quotation is from the ode to Quinctius Hirpinus, who is worrying overmuch about foreign affairs (2.11). To judge from *Epist.* 1.16 he was a man of considerable wealth and importance. We may be sure that when Horace sent him this invitation he was not urging him to abandon his political career. The same is true *a fortiori* of 3.8, which is addressed to Maecenas. As a final illustration we may take 1.20 (*uile potabis*) – a very slight and informal piece. But the central stanza recalls the ovation given to Maecenas when he reappeared after a serious illness. That public dimension is entirely lacking in the epigram of Philodemus (*Anth. Pal.* 11.44) which Horace is thought to have used.

These hospitality poems are therefore set against a background of busy public life. What did Horace know about this kind of world? Perhaps more than one sometimes assumes. As schoolboy and student he must have mixed on reasonably free terms with upper-class people – see, e.g., the end of *Sat.* 1.10 and *Sat.* 2.1.75–6. He obtained a post in the treasury about 40 B.C. and ten years later he talks as if he still had to attend meetings (*Sat.* 2.6.36–7). On the strength of *Sat.* 1.6 some commentators believe he was encouraged to stand for the quaestorship. What we do know is that later Augustus tried to make him his private secretary. Horace managed to get out of it (his health was so

[1] See Tyrrell and Purser (1933) lxxvi–lxxxiv.

terribly unreliable...), but the offer shows that his competence and discretion were recognized in the highest quarters. It is amusing to reflect that Q. Horatius Flaccus might have been the first of those imperial secretaries who later acquired such immense power and dislike. As it was, he kept out of public affairs, but socially he was much in demand (see *Odes* 2.18.10–11; 3.11.5–6); great men, including Augustus, were eager to be mentioned in his poems; and we may be sure that at the dinner tables on the Esquiline he heard a good deal of political conversation.

Another unifying thread is the poet's love of the Italian countryside. An early example is the second epode, where the idealized picture is qualified but not cancelled by the final twist. A smaller, but not dissimilar, picture is painted at the end of the last Roman ode (3.6). Or again, the delightful hymn to Faunus (*Odes* 3.18) contains the stanza:

ludit herboso pecus omne campo,
cum tibi Nonae redeunt Decembres;
festus in pratis uacat otioso
  cum boue pagus.

The whole herd plays over the grassy fields when the Nones of December come round again to do you honour; the villagers keep the festival, taking it easy in the meadows with the oxen which are also on holiday.

A shorter scene occurs in *Odes* 4.5:

tutus bos etenim rura perambulat,
nutrit rura Ceres almaque Faustitas.

The ox safely wanders through the land. Ceres and benign Prosperity nourish the land.

The second picture, however, has a political frame: rural Italy is flourishing under the Augustan peace. To recall the importance of this idea in imperial ideology one has only to think of Virgil's *Georgics* and the figure of Tellus (or Venus) on the Ara Pacis.

In several odes the countryside is related to Horace's vocation as a writer. In 1.17 (a very private piece) Faunus is said to protect the Sabine farm because the poet and his muse are dear to the gods. 3.13 has a wider scope and shows a new awareness of power; for while the *fons Bandusiae* with its bright water and shady trees inspires a lyric poem, the poem in turn makes Bandusia as famous as the legendary springs of Greece. Later again, the streams and foliage of Tibur are said to have made Melpomene's favourite known for Aeolian song (*Odes* 4.3); this fame is then defined: Horace is 'the minstrel of the Roman lyre'. So there was no real boundary between the national and the local. Horace was aware of this when, at the end of his first collection of odes, he wrote: 'I shall grow for ever renewed by the praises of posterity, as long as the priest climbs the Capitol with the silent Vestal' – and then immediately added: 'I shall be spoken of where the wild Aufidus roars and where Daunus, poor in water, ruled over rustic folk' – i.e. in the remote country district where he was born.

On a personal level Horace's love of the countryside, like his love of simplicity, involved a tension between rural and urban values. At first sight this is not obvious because he spends so much time praising the country and grumbling about the city (e.g. *Sat.* 2.6; *Epist.* 1.10 and 14). Yet Rome was more than smoke and noise. It also represented vitality, excitement, and the pleasures of a cultivated society. In due course it became the centre of his national recognition (*Odes* 4.3.13–15), but even in earlier days the city had other, humbler, attractions: 'I wander off by myself wherever I wish, asking the price of greens and flour. In the evenings I often stroll around the Circus and Forum, those haunts of trickery; I loiter beside the fortune-tellers; then I make my way home to a plate of minestrone with leeks and peas' (*Sat.* 1.6.111–15). As a student of the human comedy Horace could never be wholly satisfied with rural seclusion. His personality had room for the town- as well as the country-mouse.

When one comes to talk about Horace's conception of nature it is useful to distinguish the area over which man has some control (e.g. fruit, crops, animals) from that which is beyond him (e.g. the weather and seasons). In the first case the poet assumes the presence of a natural power which has to be tended and trained and brought to full growth. That is the farmer's work. It demands skill and labour, and it is sometimes frustrated (*Odes* 3.1.29–32; *Epist.* 1.7.86–7); but when it succeeds, the result not only sustains the community but gives delight too (*Epist.* 1.16.1–16). The writer has a similar task, for his natural powers produce a crop of words which have to be disciplined by art:

luxuriantia compescet, nimis aspera sano
leuabit cultu, uirtute carentia tollet. (*Epist.* 2.2.122f.)

He will check excessive growth, smooth what is too rough by beneficial care and take out whatever lacks strength.

Similar metaphors are applied to human nature – temper is like a horse which has to be bridled (*Epist.* 1.2.63); a wild young girl is not yet broken in (*Odes* 2.5.1); sin has to be cut back (*Odes* 3.24.34). A particularly interesting example is *Odes* 4.4.29–34:

fortes creantur fortibus et bonis;
est in iuuencis, est in equis patrum
uirtus...
doctrina sed uim promouet insitam,
rectique cultus pectora roborant.

The valiant are born from the valiant and the good. Steers and steeds have their fathers' quality...but training develops inborn power and the right kind of care strengthens the heart.

Here the principle has a special application, because Horace is talking of the young princes Tiberius and Drusus. Education is related to imperial power by the fostering of authority.

Since we cannot control the weather and seasons, there is naturally no direct connexion between the official odes and poems like *Odes* 1.4, 9, 11, 4.7, and *Epod.* 13. But these poems command attention in their own right because they contain some of Horace's most memorable writing. *Odes* 1.11 (*tu ne quaesieris*) urges Leuconoe to stop trying to foretell her death and the poet's by means of astrology:

ut melius, quidquid erit, pati
seu pluris hiemes seu tribuit Iuppiter ultimam,
quae nunc oppositis debilitat pumicibus mare
Tyrrhenum.

How much better to endure whatever comes, whether Jupiter has allotted us more winters or this be our last which is now exhausting the Tuscan sea on cliffs of volcanic rock.

What is the function of the storm? Why is it at the centre of the poem? Wouldn't a bright summer day have done just as well? One has only to put these questions to realize that the sea must not be calm, because the girl herself is not calm. The tossing waves suit her thoughts. Furthermore, the most striking line is that which describes winter as wearing out the sea by pounding it against a barrier of rock. In those three choriambic words *oppositis debilitat pumicibus*, with the metrical ictus pulling against the accent, we hear 'the tired waves vainly breaking'; and this reminds us that Leuconoe's attempts at precognition are a futile waste of effort. The curtain between present and future is just as impenetrable as the rock.

Another winter scene is used in a rather similar way in *Odes* 1.9:

uides ut alta stet niue candidum
Soracte, nec iam sustineant onus
siluae laborantes, geluque
flumina constiterint acuto?

Do you see how Soracte stands white with deep snow, how the straining trees no longer bear their burden and the streams are halted by sharp ice?

Although dazzlingly vivid, it is a harsh scene, and Horace at once turns away from it, calling on his host to make merry indoors with wine and a good fire. The second part of the poem contains a similar set of ideas – don't worry about the future, enjoy life to the full while you're still young and 'while from you being green hoariness cantankerous is absent'. (That is a literal translation of *donec uirenti canities abest morosa*.) In other words, the lapse of time and the onset of old age are, like the snowy day, part of a natural process over which we have no control. But we do have some control over our friendships and our own state of mind. That is where happiness and serenity must be sought.

As one reads through the ode the initial image of Soracte acquires symbolic overtones. This does *not* mean that the snow-covered mountain is a poetic fiction or that the stanza really represents something else. In Hemingway's famous story 'The Snows of Kilimanjaro' the mountain is put into our minds at the outset; we then hear nothing more about it until the end, when the dying writer dreams that he is being taken there in an aeroplane. Hemingway provided an introductory note: 'Its western summit is called by the Masai "Ngàje Ngài", the House of God.' But we hardly need that information any more than we need Servius' note on Soracte: *dis manibus consecratus est* 'It is sacred to the gods of the dead.'[1]

The same simple yet profound ideas lie behind *Odes* 1.4 and 4.7. Here the warning is given by spring, not winter; but since the year is a circle one can start from any point on its circumference. From one aspect spring is a season of pure happiness. That is the view presented by a number of delightful poems in the Greek Anthology – notably 9.363 (Meleager) and the opening pieces in 10 (Leonidas, Antipater, and others). Yet there is also something poignant about it, for while the seasons return men do not. This perennial theme is capable of endless variations – 'When lilacs last in the dooryard bloomed', 'Loveliest of trees the cherry now', 'April is the cruellest month'; the two odes themselves present striking differences. 1.4 is more intricate. It has two panels: spring (1–12) and death (13–20), but in ll. 1–4 spring is seen as the departure of winter, and in 18ff. death is described as lacking certain joys of life. Antithetical images of warm/cold and liberation/confinement are found in both panels, and the ambivalence of certain phrases contributes to the poem's complex unity. For example, in the joyful panel the words *imminente luna* 'beneath the overhanging moon' have a faint undertone of uneasiness,[2] and the expression *caput impedire myrto* 'to bind one's head with myrtle' foreshadows the prisonhouse of death (16–17), because *impedire* nearly always implies *unwelcome* constraint. The poem is also less sombre. The joy of the first part is reflected in various occupations – shipping, pastoral farming, ploughing, and (on the mythological level) industry. This gives the section a solid vitality. Death, on the other hand, means farewell to wine-parties and rather fragile young men. So at the end of the ode the balance remains tilted towards life.

[1] Servius on Virgil, *Aen.* 11.785.

[2] The moon is associated with change in *Odes* 2.11.10–11; 2.18.16; 4.7.13.

In 4.7, however, death begins to intrude as early as l. 7 – *immortalia ne speres* – and in l. 15 he asserts his dominion over great figures of Roman legend and history – Aeneas, Tullus, and Ancus. As Manlius Torquatus, the addressee, is an important barrister (*Epist.* 1.5) and belongs to a noble family with traditions of loyalty (Livy 7.5), he embodies the old values of *genus* (birth), *facundia* (eloquence) and *pietas* (devotion); but even those qualities cannot prolong life. This Roman *grauitas* helps to give the poem a deeper and more impersonal despair. In the opening scene there are no human figures; and (apart from Gratia) all the mythological names are found in Hades, where they testify to the power of death. The opposite is the case in *Odes* 1.4. Finally the language of 4.7 is simple and forceful, with few of the ambiguities which we noticed in the earlier piece.

In these odes the pattern of nature is used as the basis for recommending some kind of behaviour. The propriety of this behaviour is sometimes stated (e.g. *nunc decet* in *Odes* 1.4.9 and 11, *decet* in *Epod.* 13.5), elsewhere implied (e.g. *Odes* 2.9, 10, 11). In other places the standard of decorum is supplied by the human cycle of youth, maturity, and decay. This is sometimes linked with the cycle of plants and animals – e.g. Lalage is like a young heifer or an unripe grape, so Horace advises his friend to be patient (*Odes* 2.5); Chloe behaves like a young fawn, though she is really old enough for a man – *tempestiua uiro* (*Odes* 1.23). At other times the human cycle functions by itself: Ibycus' wife is too old to frolic with teenagers; her behaviour is not becoming – *non decet* (*Odes* 3.15.8 and 14; cf. 4.13.2–3). Frivolous amusements, like lyric poetry, are suitable for youngsters; the same is true of riotous parties (*Epist.* 2.2.142 and 216). Here, as elsewhere, Horace at times ruefully admits that he has failed by his own standards. His interest in love-poetry at the age of fifty is hardly proper (*Odes* 4.1.9 and 35).

In a famous passage of the *A.P.* words, like men, are said to have a life-cycle (60–72). At one point it looks as if usage (*usus*) is what determines the vitality of any given word (71–2); but there is more to it than that, for a good poet will *modify* usage, by reviving old words, producing novel combinations, and admitting new words. All these procedures are governed by propriety. This concept, which was elaborated by the Peripatetics, is also important in other passages of the *A.P.* Thus theme should be appropriate to ability (38ff.) and style to subject matter (73ff.). A speaker's language ought to suit his emotion (99ff.) and also his rank, age, occupation, and nationality (114ff. and 156ff.). An understanding of these matters is obtainable from moral philosophy (309ff.). From here we can move across to *Epist.* 1, where one of the main philosophical strands is the question of 'what is right and proper' – *quid uerum atque decens* (*Epist.* 1.1.11). The emphasis lies on individual behaviour; when the context is supplied it is that of social relations, whether with friend, patron, or slave. A further dimension is added in some of the official odes, which present a picture of benign protection and supervision descending from Jupiter to Augustus, and from him to the Senate and people of Rome. Rising upwards in return are feelings of gratitude and devotion which find expression in religious observances and acts of patriotism. Hence in times of danger 'it is sweet and fitting to die for one's country' – *dulce et decorum est pro patria mori* (*Odes* 3.2.13). Now there are, of course, obvious differences between these situations – differences which could be used to draw a more detailed map of the poet's ideas. The common factor, however, is the belief that it is prudent to acknowledge and adapt oneself to some given pattern whether of nature, language, or morals.

With the theme of *pax* we can be more specific. I use the Latin term because it admits the two ideas of 'peacefulness' and 'pacification' and so enables us to take account of Horace's attitude to imperialism. In the decade after Philippi there was no stability in the country at large. As firm government had broken down, happiness and peace of mind could only be attained within the circle of one's friends; and so comradeship, contentment, and inner serenity were all-important. The various kinds of folly that interfered with these private values were ridiculed in the *Satires*. In *Epod.* 13 wine, music, and good fellowship were seen as the only answer to the *horrida tempestas* in the world outside, while nos. 7 and 16 cried out in despair against the madness and chaos of civil war. These last two poems, however, contained another significant idea in that they deplored civil war not only as crime and impiety but also as a betrayal of Rome's imperial tradition (7.5–10, 16.3–10). In this respect they foreshadowed certain odes in the first collection. Pondering on the guilt of civil war in 1.2, Horace thinks how much better it would have been for the Romans to turn their weapons against the Parthians (l. 22; cf. 51–2); similar sentiments are found in 1.21.13ff. and, at greater length, in the Fortuna ode (1.35). In 3.6 Rome's civil wars, which are seen as a symptom of moral corruption, are said to have left her open to foreign attack:

> paene occupatam seditionibus
> deleuit urbem Dacus et Aethiops. (13–14)

The Dacian and Egyptian almost destroyed the city, occupied as it was with internal strife.

(The Egyptian menace was, of course, the combined strength of Antony and Cleopatra.) But the most elaborate treatment of this dual theme is presented in 3.3, where Juno promises world dominion, provided there is no revival of the corruption and discord of the late Republic.

Juno's speech is also interesting for another reason. It is one of the very few references to territorial expansion. The other passages are 2.9.18–24 and 3.5.1–4, neither of which is comparable in rhetorical grandeur. But this rhetoric draws attention to a further point, viz. that the emphasis falls heavily on the proviso noted above: 'You may conquer every corner of the globe *provided* you check internal disunity and decay.' Those might be the words of a man who was passionately keen on the spread of Roman power, but they might not. If we turn to 3.5 we see that there Horace is less interested in the conquest of Britain and Parthia than in the character of Regulus; the first stanza is a kind of starting mechanism to get the poem under way. Instead of dwelling on the acquisition of new territory Horace more often speaks in terms of defence: the Medes must not be allowed to raid unpunished (1.2.51), the kings defeated by Caesar were once a menace (2.12.12), the Parthians are a threat to Latium (1.12.53). This does not mean that Augustus' foreign wars were always defensive; in fact there is a good case for believing that the Emperor's policy was one of continuous, though deliberate, expansion until the disaster of the Teutoburg forest in A.D. 9.[1] I am only pointing out that in the passages cited above Horace chose to present the campaigns in that light.

Other passages again present quite a different view. Because he is in love (1.19) or inspired (1.26) Horace professes an airy indifference to frontier battles; and he urges Quinctius Hirpinus (2.11) and Maecenas (3.29) not to be obsessed with foreign affairs. But (at the risk of stressing the obvious) this does not mean that in the poet's total scheme of things such issues were unimportant. There is only one ode which is ostensibly anti-imperialist, and that is 1.29 which jokingly remonstrates with Iccius for joining in the campaign against Arabia.

In *Odes* 4, where the laureate is more in evidence, two ideas are developed from the earlier collection. The first is that the Romans have already *achieved* world domination. The germ of this is found in 3.8.17–24, but it becomes a feature of the later lyrics in *Carm. Saec.* 53–6, 4.14.41–52 and 4.15.21–4. The second, which is closely related, is that since Augustus is in charge of the empire, the men and women of Italy can go about their business in safety. This is foreshadowed in 3.14.14–16 and recurs with greater emphasis in 4.5.17–20 and 25–8 and in 4.15.17–20.

To sum up: with the victory at Actium chaos was pushed back to the borders of the empire, and this allowed Horace's private ethic (seen in the *Satires* and *Epodes* and in many of the informal odes) to expand into a Roman ethic. The state now assumed a position analogous to that held by the individual. Happiness still depended on inner peace, but this could now be seen to include peace within the empire. As the individual's well-being demanded a careful discipline of the emotions, so Rome's health depended on the control of destructive

[1] See Brunt (1963) 170–6.

social forces like extravagance, lawlessness, and domestic immorality. And, as in times of trouble the individual had to build spiritual defences against the outside world, so Rome's security required a strong policy against the hostile and unruly peoples beyond her frontiers. It is a commonplace of history that the heirs of an imperial tradition are usually in favour of maintaining it, as long as they can assert their superiority without an unacceptably heavy cost. Horace was no exception. He was proud to be a Roman and could on occasion rise to the imperial theme. But his work as a whole suggests that he valued the empire not so much for its power and prestige but rather because it enabled him and others to enjoy in peace the pleasures of friendship and poetry and the amenities of civilized life:

quis Parthum paueat, quis gelidum Scythen
quis Germania quos horrida parturit
fetus, incolumi Caesare? quis ferae
bellum curet Hiberiae? (*Odes* 4.5.25–8)

Who would fear the Parthian or the icy Scythian or the young brought forth in the forests of Germany as long as Caesar is unharmed? Who would care about the war in wild Spain?

The poet's private *otium* is guaranteed by the *pax Augusta*.

Another approach, which will take us closer to Augustus, is through religion. In an early ode, written in the form of a Pindaric paean, Horace reflects on the disasters which have shaken Rome. Only divine intervention can save her; Apollo, Venus, and Mars are invoked in turn; but perhaps there is already a god on earth; is the young Octavian really Mercury in human form (*Odes* 1.2.41ff.)? To explain why Octavian is associated with Mercury scholars have referred to the Emperor's youthfulness, beauty, and eloquence. But surely the main clue is supplied by *Odes* 1.10: 'Mercury, eloquent grandson of Atlas, who didst shape the savage ways of new-born men.' Was it not the god's benign, civilizing, spirit that made him a possible model for the young ruler? As the inventor of the lyre, Mercury had also a special significance for Horace. It was Mercury who rescued him at Philippi (*Odes* 2.7.13), and because the poet was one of Mercury's men he escaped being killed by a falling tree (*Odes* 2.17.27ff.).

Naturally Horace also owes allegiance to the Muses, who preside over both his formal and his informal poetry (*Musarum sacerdos* in *Odes* 3.1.3 and *imbellisque lyrae Musa potens* in 1.6.10). In *Odes* 3.4 he tells how as a small child he strayed from his nurse and fell asleep, and how he escaped harm thanks to the protection of heaven. Then addressing the Muses, he says: 'As long as you are with me I will gladly sail into the raging Bosphorus or walk into the scorching desert of Syria.' Half the poem is taken up with this intimate spiritual relationship, then suddenly we come upon this surprising stanza:

uos Caesarem altum, militia simul
fessas cohortes abdidit oppidis,
finire quaerentem labores
Pierio recreatis antro. (37–40)

You refresh great Caesar in a Pierian cave as he longs to bring his labours to an end after settling his battle-weary troops quietly in the towns.

So the Emperor too is under the Muses' care. They refresh his spirit (i.e. he takes pleasure in poetry), but more important they advise him to act with gentleness and good sense:

uos lene consilium et datis et dato
gaudetis almae. (41–2)

It is significant that Horace should have given a central position among the Roman odes to a poem which expressly connects his own activity with that of Augustus and ascribes both poetic and political power to the same divine source.

A similar point can be made with reference to Bacchus. On the one hand we have passages like *Epist.* 2.2.77–8, where Horace protests that as a servant of Bacchus (i.e. a poet) his proper milieu is the countryside, or *Odes* 3.8 where he offers a goat to Bacchus to celebrate his escape from death. On the other hand Bacchus is also associated with Augustus. As a hero who has benefited mankind, Bacchus achieved divinity; the same will be true of Augustus (*Odes* 3.3.11–15). Only after becoming a god did Bacchus receive due praise from men; Augustus receives it already (*Epist.* 2.1.5ff.). The triangular relationship becomes closer in *Odes* 2.19, a hymn to Bacchus which testifies to Horace's inspiration and then goes on to record some of the god's achievements. One of these was his defence of Jupiter against the Giants. That same battle, which symbolized the triumph of civilization over barbarism and was known to Horace's readers from Pindar and Greek sculpture, is used again in *Odes* 3.4.49ff. as a means of glorifying Augustus. Finally, in *Odes* 3.25 Bacchus' inspiration is specifically connected with Horace's new political lyrics in honour of the Emperor.

The deity most closely associated with Augustus, however, was Apollo. In the Republican period Vediovis, the god of the Julian gens, became assimilated to Apollo; Apollo was the son of Jupiter, and Augustus was the (adopted) son of Julius, who in his lifetime had assumed the attributes of the king of the gods; Apollo had helped Rome's Trojan ancestors against the Greeks, and as the god of sanity and order he had been a powerful psychological ally in the struggle against Antony/Dionysus. These and other affinities were attested in the magnificent temple of Apollo on the Palatine, dedicated in 28 B.C. It is interesting to hear that within the temple a prominent place was occupied by a statue of Apollo the lyre-player, which is said to have borne the features of Augustus himself.[1]

At the end of an amusing satire (1.9) Apollo intervenes to rescue Horace from the clutches of a pest who has been trying to wangle an introduction to Maecenas. In *Odes* 1.32 Horace addresses the lyre as the 'glory of Phoebus' (*o decus Phoebi*) and asks it to inspire his alcaic verse. On the official side we have the *Carmen saeculare*, which was written to be sung by a choir of boys and girls at the celebrations of 17 B.C. The performance took place before the temple of Apollo, and several stanzas are addressed to him. Augustus also figures in the hymn as 'the illustrious descendant of Anchises and Venus'. Elsewhere public and private coalesce. The occasion envisaged in *Odes* 1.31 is the vintage festival of the Meditrinalia, which in 28 B.C. took place just after the dedication of Apollo's temple. In the opening stanza the *uates* wonders what he should pray for; the answer is given in the last stanza by Horace the private individual: it is health of body and mind, and continued inspiration. *Odes* 4.6 is a hymn to Apollo, prompted by the success of the *Carmen saeculare*. It recalls how the god slew Achilles and preserved Aeneas to found Rome. Apollo the minstrel is asked to protect 'the glory of the Daunian Muse' – which could mean either Italian or Horatian poetry. Then in the remaining stanzas Horace speaks of his personal debt to the god:

> spiritum Phoebus mihi, Phoebus artem
> carminis nomenque dedit poetae. (29–30)

Phoebus granted me inspiration, the art of song, and the name of poet.

Apollo's dual aspect was represented by the lyre and the bow (see *Odes* 1.21.11–12; 2.10.18–20). Another Apolline symbol which linked poet and Emperor was the laurel. In *Odes* 3.4.19 the infant Horace is said to have been covered with laurel leaves; later, at the end of his first collection of odes Horace asks Melpomene to place a crown of Delphic laurel on his hair (3.30.15–16). In other passages the laurel is that worn by a triumphant general – viz. *Odes* 2.1.15 and 4.3.6–7. As early as 36 B.C., following his victory over Sextus Pompeius, Octavian was voted a laurel crown. Later, in 27 B.C., the doors of his house were decorated with laurel, and the same symbol appeared on coins and reliefs.

Last of all, we should bear in mind certain words which describe the processes and powers of lyric composition. Orpheus 'led' forests and checked rivers (*ducere* and *morari* in *Odes* 1.12.12 and 9, cf. 3.11.14); Cerberus 'surrendered' to the lyre (*cedere* in 3.11.15); Amphion 'led' the stones of Thebes (*ducere* in *A.P.* 396). The word for tune or rhythm is *modus*, and the verbs *moderari* and

[1] Servius on Virgil, *Ecl.* 4.10; ps.-Acro on Horace, *Epist.* 1.3.17.

modulari are both used of playing the lyre (1.24.14; 1.32.5; *Epist.* 2.2.143). But as the central idea in *modus* is that of limit or proportion, the management of the lyre is seen as a kind of organization. The same idea lies behind *temperare*. In *Odes* 1.12.16 and 3.4.45 the earth, sea, and sky, and the affairs of men, are said to be 'tempered' or 'controlled' by Jupiter. In *Odes* 4.3.18 the Muse 'tempers' the sweet din of the golden lyre. Or again, in *Odes* 2.12.4 themes are 'adjusted' (*aptare*) to the strains of the lyre (cf. *Epist.* 1.3.13); in *Odes* 3.30.14 aeolian verse is 'set to' or 'settled amongst' Italian tunes (*deducere*); and in *Odes* 4.9.4 an 'alliance' has to be made between strings and words (*sociare*). Like the creator in the old myths the poet imposes order and harmony on already existing material. This material, which is shapeless, discordant, and meaningless, is sometimes seen as the lyre, sometimes as language, and sometimes as theme; but whatever it may be, it must eventually yield to the poet's authority.

Horace's attitude to Augustus was complex, and it is hard to see it in perspective. One can appreciate the poet's independent spirit by recalling that he did not speak about Octavian until the time of Actium; that he remained loyal to old Republican friends; that only a small proportion of *Odes* 1–3 was written in praise of Augustus and those odes were notably restrained in comparison with the usual type of Hellenistic panegyric;[1] and that although the Emperor took a more direct interest in Horace and his work after 17 B.C. no very close friendship ever existed between the two men. Nevertheless, Horace acknowledged and admired the colossal achievements of Augustus; he saw that the Princeps had a power and status which set him apart from ordinary men, and that this power had on the whole been used to promote harmony throughout the empire. Finally, he recognized that after a century of civil war Rome stood in desperate need of regeneration, and that this involved *religious* regeneration too. Such feelings, which were shared by the vast majority of his countrymen, allowed Horace at certain times to adopt the role of *uates* ('priest' or 'bard') and to speak about Roman affairs in traditional religious language. It is quite true that all this did not add up to theological conviction and that Horace's normal attitude to the state religion was one of indifference. Yet this area of expression is notoriously imprecise. A patriotic feeling for the past, the sense of a great occasion, a close familiarity with the age-old symbols of one's culture – such factors combine to blur definitions and blunt charges of hypocrisy. Housman's '1887' (commemorating Victoria's golden jubilee) concludes thus:

Oh, God will save her, fear you not:
  Be you the men you've always been,
Get you the sons your fathers got,
  And God will save the Queen.

[1] See Doblhofer (1966).

Housman, of course, was an unbeliever; but he fiercely repudiated the suggestion that '1887' was not seriously intended.[1]

If this account is in any way correct it means that, when allowance has been made for untypical passages and for a range of inconsistency to which anyone is entitled, there remains a large central area in Horace's work where the main strands criss-cross. The dichotomy outlined above is therefore artificial and gives little help towards a just appreciation of his work. When we take the lyrics as a whole we can point to a memorable ode about Horace's poetic achievement (3.30) and a poor one (2.20), a great Roman ode (3.4) and an inferior one (3.2), a strong attack on an ageing beauty (1.25) and a weaker one (4.13), an impressive tribute to Augustus' step-sons (4.4) and a less attractive one (4.14), a substantial invitation-poem to Maecenas (3.8) and a slight one (1.20). Horace would have cheerfully accepted this attitude, for he did not look for indiscriminate adulation either as a poet or as a man (*Epist.* 1.4.1; *Sat.* 1.3.69–72). He might, however, have added that if we wanted to study one ode which more than any other contained the essence of his spirit we should turn to *Tyrrhena regum* (3.29). In that magnificent poem we find the Greek past alive in the Roman present, an inimitable blend of grandeur and intimacy, solemnity and humour; and a sad awareness of transience and insecurity combined with a tough-minded intention to survive. No translation can hope to do it justice, but two stanzas in Dryden's paraphrase give a measure of its quality:

Happy the Man, and happy he alone,
He who can call to day his own:
He, who secure within, can say
To morrow do thy worst, for I have liv'd to day.
Be fair, or foul, or rain, or shine,
The joys I have possest, in spight of fate are mine,
Not Heav'n it self upon the past has pow'r;
But what has been, has been, and I have had my hour.

[1] See C. Brooks in Ricks (ed.) (1968) 76.

20

LOVE ELEGY

I. GENERAL INTRODUCTION

The elegiac distich appears as a fully developed poetic form in Greece in the seventh century B.C. It is used, as far as we know, for inscriptions, but also in long poems which were sung or chanted to the music of the *aulos* (Latin *tibia*), a pipe with a reedy tone something like the modern oboe. There seems to be a linguistic connexion between the Armenian word *elegn* 'reed' and the Greek term ἐλεγεῖον (*sc.* μέτρον). The derivation from ἒ ἒ λέγειν 'to say woe! woe!' offered as an etymology by Alexandrian scholars is fanciful, to say the least. For Propertius (2.30B.13–16; 3.10.23) the sound of the *tibia* is somehow associated with drinking wine, making love and, possibly, reciting love poetry. On the other hand, both Horace (*A.P.* 75–8) and Ovid (*Amores* 3.9.1ff.) seem to think that the elegiac metre is ideally suited for laments. This probably means that they knew Greek funeral elegies of the archaic or classical period which we no longer have. Horace limits the elegiac distich to votive inscriptions (*uoti sententia compos*) and laments (*querimonia*), i.e. epigrams of the kind which we have in Books 6 and 7 of the Greek Anthology. He ignores the erotic epigrams of Meleager's Garland which now form Books 5 and 12 of the Greek Anthology, though he must have known some of them. Incidentally, the satiric epigram was not yet a popular genre in the Augustan age.

In the earliest period, Greek poets of such different temperaments and tastes as Callinus, Tyrtaeus and Mimnermus (all seventh century B.C.) wrote elegiac poems on a variety of themes, but of the three only Mimnermus seems to have dealt with love. *Nanno*, the title traditionally given to Mimnermus' collection of elegies (of which we have only fragments), might be the name of a woman he loved (a flute-player, it is sometimes said). Propertius 1.9.11 *plus in amore ualet Mimnermi uersus Homero* 'In love Mimnermus' verse is more powerful than Homer' contrasts light erotic poetry in the elegiac manner with the heroic epic; for him Mimnermus is the poet of love, just as Homer is the great epic poet.

We hear about late classical and Hellenistic collections of elegies which had a woman's name as a title, perhaps following Mimnermus' example: Antimachus'

Lyde, Philitas' *Bittis* (or *Battis*), Hermesianax' *Leontion*. They may have dealt with love-tales of mythological heroes and heroines, and yet they were related, it seems, to a real woman. Antimachus is said to have comforted his grief by putting mythological tales (tragic love-stories, no doubt) into elegiac verse when his wife or mistress, Lyde, had died. Hermesianax gave a long catalogue of poets in love, presumably because he was a poet in love himself; but then he must have said so in at least one poem of the collection. Similarly, Antimachus must have said that he loved Lyde, Philitas that he loved Bittis (cf. Ovid, *Tristia* 1.6.1–4). Still this does not tell us anything about the character of a whole elegiac *Gedichtbuch* in the Hellenistic period.

Among the many papyrus fragments which have contributed so much to our knowledge of Callimachus not one elegy has been found that might be compared to, e.g., one by Propertius. But perhaps such texts will be discovered. Recently two elegiac fragments have been published in the series of the *Oxyrhynchus Papyri* (vol. 39, 1972): nos. 2884 and 2885. The first one is the lament of a woman who confesses her 'passionate love', θαλυκρὸς ἔρως, to the goddess Artemis and complains about the cruelty of the man she loves. The other one lists some mythological heroines who hurt close relatives because they were in love with a man; this is addressed to all women in love as a warning. We also have the Sorbonne Papyrus 2254, a curious curse-poem not unlike Ovid's *Ibis*, but not related to anything we read in the *Amores*.[1] Perhaps the Hellenistic poets did prefer the format of the epigram when they talked about their own love experiences. It is true that some Latin elegies could be interpreted as expanded Greek epigrams (cf. Prop. 2.12 and *Anth. Pal.* 5.176 and 177 or Ovid, *Amores* 1.13 and *Anth. Pal.* 5.172). Or a fairly close translation of a Greek epigram may be woven into the context of a Latin elegy (e.g. Leonidas, *Anth. Pal.* 9.337 (= XXIX Gow–Page) in Prop. 3.13.43–6). But it would be wrong to derive one genre from the other; both seem to have co-existed from the earliest times.

In a broader sense all Roman elegiac poets were influenced by the great Hellenistic poets, for instance Callimachus, because they mention him frequently as a model, but probably more as a model of style. Others, such as Euphorion, may have furnished obscure myths to serve as *exempla*. When Virgil, *Ecl.* 10.50f. makes Gallus say *ibo et Chalcidico quae sunt mihi condita uersu | carmina, pastoris Siculi modulabor auena* this simply means that Gallus will now write pastoral poems in the style of Theocritus (like Virgil himself) rather than epic or elegiac poems in the style of Euphorion.[2] In the Ἐρωτικὰ παθήματα, 'Stories of passionate love', Gallus' friend and literary adviser Parthenius gives, among other things, prose versions of Euphorion's *Thrax* and his *Apollodorus*. The Roman poets probably did not find it too difficult to

[1] Barnes and Lloyd-Jones (1963) 205–27.

[2] Schöpsdau (1974) 268ff.

transform Greek narrative elegies into their own preferred 'subjective' form: Propertius 1.18 is a good example.[1] But the Romans did not commit the elegy to one specific theme or genre: they wrote elegiac *epicedia* (Prop. 3.18; Ovid, *Amores* 3.9) which differ in metre only from such lyric epicedia as Horace, *Odes* 1.24.

This chapter will concentrate on the four famous Augustan love-poets. For our purposes the love elegy or the book of love elegies may be considered a creation of the Augustan age, though Catullus is sometimes included. His poem 68 would seem to represent the prototype of the Augustan love elegy though love is only one theme among many; it is interwoven most skilfully with the themes of friendship, the loss of his brother, the Trojan War. Their interrelationship is the following: Catullus' friend Allius offered him a house for secret meetings with Lesbia; hence the poem is a token of gratitude. The death of Catullus' brother had a serious impact on his life: it ended abruptly the happy, playful period of his life (*multa satis lusi*, l. 17). Now that his brother is dead, it would be time for Catullus to marry and settle down. Catullus, as his curious wedding poems prove, understands the middle-class morality of Verona.[2] But marriage is out of the question, for in the meantime he has met Lesbia and fallen in love with her. Brief, superficial love affairs are no longer possible, but neither is a conventional marriage. Finally, his brother's death in the Troad reminds him of the Trojan War; the place has been cursed ever since then. These are the themes, and this is the way in which they are interwoven; no later elegist has achieved such a degree of complexity.

2. CHARACTERISTICS OF THE AUGUSTAN LOVE ELEGY

(*a*) The elegy does not claim to be one of the elevated genres of literature; it places itself below epic and tragedy though, it would seem, above the mime and the satire. The elegists (Tibullus excepted) like to call their verse *nugae* 'trifles' or *lusus* 'playthings'. All the same they are proud of their work; they look down on the *profanum uulgus* just like the greatest lyric poet of the age (cf. Propertius 2.23.1ff.; Lygd. 3.20) and they count on immortality. This is the attitude of the Alexandrian literary coterie: enough to be admired by a small group of connoisseurs which hardly included the typical Roman businessmen and politicians, Catullus' 'rather rigid old men' (*senes seueriores* 5.2; cf. Prop. 2.30.13ff.; Ovid, *Amores* 1.15.1ff.).

(*b*) The elegiac poets of the Augustan age, beginning with Gallus, write whole books of elegies. The collection sometimes bears the name of a woman, following the Greek tradition mentioned above. Propertius probably published Book 1, the *Monobiblos*, under the title *Cynthia*. Tibullus' two books of elegies

[1] Cairns (1969) 131–4.

[2] Luck (1974) 23ff.

may have been known as *Delia* and *Nemesis* respectively, for Ovid (*Amores* 3.9.31ff.) in his vision of the two women at the poet's funeral seems to be speaking of the two books as well: *altera cura recens, altera primus amor* 'one a recent interest, the other his first love', where *cura recens* can mean 'a new book' as well as 'a new love'. *Neaera* was almost certainly the title of Lygdamus' small book of six poems (*Corp. Tib.* 3.1–6), and the first (lost) edition of Ovid's *Amores* may have been published under the title *Corinna*.[1]

(*c*) We still know too little about the status of women in Rome during the first century B.C., and we ought to be careful not to interpret love poetry as if it were historical evidence. But roughly speaking we can distinguish three types of 'elegiac women':[2]

(i) the *matrona*, the married woman who enjoys a certain independence. She may have many affairs, like Clodia (Catullus' Lesbia), or she may be faithful to her husband like Cornelia (Prop. 4.11).

(ii) the *femme entretenue* who may be married but is more likely to be single or divorced and who has firm attachments that last for months or years.[3]

(iii) the *meretrix*, the prostitute with whom men have brief, casual encounters.

It is essential to keep these three classes apart; Cynthia, for instance, is not a *meretrix*. Propertius (2.23) and Ovid (*Amores* 1.10.21ff.) make the distinction quite plain, though, of course, there are transitions from one class to the other. Contrary to general opinion today,[4] affairs with married ladies were not the rule. Propertius, in theory at least (loc. cit.), is against such involvements; he uses the arguments of the Hellenistic diatribe which are best known from Horace, *Sat.* 1.2. Such affairs were risky, for anyone caught *in flagranti delicto* could be whipped or even killed by the angry husband. Sex was a natural and necessary activity, and marriage was not always conducive to intellectual and artistic pursuits; hence some philosophers recommended using prostitutes, and even snobs like Propertius (loc. cit.) did not always despise the cheap and simple pleasures found on the Via Sacra. The women of the second class, as well as those of the first, may belong to the high aristocracy; this could be true for Cynthia, if Prop. 1.16 refers to her (the lady of 3.20 is certainly not Cynthia). Tibullus' Delia seems to belong to the lower middle class, a pretty girl who becomes for a while the mistress of a rich and well-bred gentleman before marrying someone of her own class, a phenomenon not entirely unknown today. To complete the picture, Gallus' Lycoris was an ex-slave, a music-hall artist of great fame and beauty, and a formidable courtesan who attracted not only the poet but such political figures as Mark Antony and Brutus.

[1] Luck (1959) 174ff.

[2] Luck (1974) 15ff.

[3] Maurois (1957) 188–9 amusingly describes the *demi-monde* in nineteenth-century Paris, and what he says about the *aristocratie de la galanterie* and the fact that even the *hautes coquines*, under the influence of romantic literature, dreamt of pure love may serve as an illustration.

[4] G. W. Williams (1968) 542.

(*d*) Homosexual love no longer plays the important role it played in Hellenistic poetry. All of Callimachus' love poems were addressed to boys: *Anth. Pal.* 12.43 (= II Gow–Page) and 12.73 (= IV Gow–Page) may be considered classics of the genre; the latter was translated into Latin by the consul of 102 B.C., Q. Lutatius Catulus. This shows, perhaps, a taste not only for this kind of poetry but also for this kind of love, among the Roman aristocracy of the late second century B.C. In Catullus' book, four love poems (24; 48; 81; 99), the last two in elegiac distichs, are addressed to a young man whom Catullus calls 'dear flower of the Juventii', *flosculus Iuuentiorum* (24.1). In their intensity they are comparable to the Lesbia poems; if the wish to give Lesbia thousands of kisses is sincere in poem 5, the same wish in a Iuventius poem (poem 48) is probably not mere rhetoric. These are highly emotional affairs, and it should surprise no one that we find here exactly the same *topoi* (e.g. the cruelty of the beloved, 99.6) as in the other poems.

The Marathus elegies in Tibullus' Book 1 seem to form a cycle within a cycle. The god Priapus, in his role as 'love counsellor', *praeceptor amoris*, lectures in 1.4 about the technique of seducing handsome boys, and Priapus' reputation would suggest that physical love, not just a romantic attachment, is meant. Another poem of the cycle, 1.8, presents a curious set of relationships: Tibullus, in love with the boy Marathus, urges the girl Pholoe whom Marathus happens to desire, to be kind to the boy; but Pholoe is apparently in love with a third man who, in turn, longs for another woman. Tibullus pleads on the boy's behalf (1.8.17ff.) and even arranges secret meetings with Pholoe for him (1.9.41ff.). Because of this rather unusual constellation the poems have never been clearly understood; but that seems to be the rather complicated relationship they imply, and if anything could stimulate the jaded tastes of the Augustan gilded set, this is it.

Homosexual love is practically absent in Propertius and Ovid, though Ovid's friend Proculus (*Pont.* 4.16.32) still writes in the Callimachean manner. Propertius' comparison (2.4.17ff.; cf. 9.31–6; 3.19.1–10) is more theoretical and mainly designed to show that woman is the more emotional, irrational, intractable creature. Ovid (*Ars Am.* 2.683f.) makes another point: 'I dislike any kind of sex that does not relax both partners; this is why making love to a boy appeals to me less' *odi concubitus qui non utrumque resoluunt: | hoc est cur pueri tangar amore minus.*

(*e*) Much of elegiac poetry is persuasive, directed towards a very practical, very simple aim: to conquer the woman. Some poems are written to please her, some promise to make her immortal. This is especially true in the case of Propertius, less so for Catullus.[1]

(*f*) The elegiac poets vary in their attitude towards politics. Catullus attacks

[1] Stroh (1971) *passim.*

several political figures of his time, Caesar among them, but this type of polemic disappears from the Augustan love elegy, and the poets, with the exception of Tibullus, are paying lip service to Augustus. Tibullus never even mentions him, but his silence may not mean anything. Propertius' family seems to have been on the wrong side in the civil war (cf. 1.21; 4.1), but his friendship with Maecenas opens to him the house of the Emperor, and he dutifully celebrates Roman victories (4.6), echoes the themes of official propaganda (3.11.29ff.), and inclines himself before the ruler (3.3.1; 11.66; 4.6.14; 11.60).[1] But he refuses to write an epic in honour of Augustus (2.1.17) and, like Tibullus, is more impressed by Rome's past (see the Roman Elegies of Book 4) than by its present. Ovid's poetry expresses his loyalty to the Emperor, and the tragic incident which brought about his exile was clearly not a political crime.

(*g*) Cornelius Gallus, like Virgil and Horace, was born of humble parents but given a first-rate education. He worked his way up as a protégé of his former class-mate Octavian. Tibullus was a Roman knight from a wealthy family (the complaints about his poverty seem to be a literary *topos*) and served on Messalla's staff in several military campaigns. When in Italy he preferred country-life to life in the city. Propertius was born in Umbria, the son of impoverished land-owners. After the publication of Book 1 Maecenas became his patron, and in later years he lived in a fashionable neighbourhood in Rome, as a man-about-town. Ovid, also a Roman knight, had an excellent education in Rome and later travelled in Greece and Asia Minor. For a short time he was, like Tibullus, a member of Messalla's circle. He held minor political offices but preferred a writer's independence and lived comfortably at the foot of the Capitol, keeping the old family estate in Sulmo in the Abruzzi and cultivating his gardens outside of Rome. To sum up: most of these poets belong to fairly prosperous (or just recently impoverished) families. Two are known to have been Roman knights. All seem to have enjoyed the best education that was to be had at the time. All of them had, at least for a time, a powerful patron. At least Propertius and Ovid seem to have been celebrated writers in their lifetime; whether they had any income from the sale of their works we do not know.[2] The careers of Gallus and Ovid were cut short by disgrace which led the one to suicide, the other to permanent exile.

3. CORNELIUS GALLUS

Since Virgil's *Ecl.* 10 in which Gallus is made to speak of his unhappy love was probably not written before 40 B.C. we may assume that the elegies which made him famous appeared between 50 and 40 B.C. when Gallus was in his

[1] With Prop. 2.16.41f. cf. Virg. *Aen.* 6.847ff.; Livy 30.42.17; Aug. *Res Gest.* 2.42.

[2] Luck (1959) 173ff.

twenties. Of the four books only one line is preserved. He calls his mistress Lycoris; her real name was Volumnia, her stage name Cytheris.

We have only a few clues as to the character of Gallus' poetry, but since he was Virgil's friend he may have influenced the *Eclogues*, and *Ecl.* 10.31ff. especially is said to be an imitation of Gallus' elegiac themes. Gallus himself was influenced by Callimachus and Euphorion; he also used a collection of thirty-six love stories in prose compiled for him by a late Hellenistic poet, Parthenius of Nicaea: they were to be inserted as *exempla* in Gallus' epyllia and elegies. Gallus is called *durior* 'harsher' than both Tibullus and Propertius by Quintilian, *Inst.* 10.1.93; according to the same critic, Ovid is *lasciuior* 'more frivolous' than the others. Horace's *Epod.* 11 may be a parody of Gallus' themes and manner. He was certainly an important link between the Neoterics and the later Augustans.

4. ALBIUS TIBULLUS AND THE 'CORPUS TIBULLIANUM'

Tibullus' friendship with the great statesman M. Valerius Messalla Corvinus is one of the main themes of his poetry. He accompanied Messalla, probably between 31 and 27 B.C., on various campaigns, notably in Gaul and in the Near East. Messalla may have known Horace, either as a student in Athens or as an officer in Brutus' army. He fought in the battle of Philippi (42 B.C.) with distinction, later served under Antony and finally made his peace with Augustus without ever forsaking his Republican ideals. He became a patron of the arts and encouraged young poets. Messalla's 'circle' seems to have included, at one time or another, his niece Sulpicia, the young Ovid (cf. *Tristia* 4.4.27f.; *Pont.* 1.7.27f.) and others. The *Corpus Tibullianum*, as we have it today, may be considered an anthology of poems written by members of that circle, probably published after Messalla's death. It is reasonable to assume that all these authors had some connexion with Messalla, even if we did not know this in the case of Tibullus and Sulpicia. We do not have to discuss the *Panegyricus Messallae* here, since it is not an elegy. It is not great poetry, but it is more than an exercise in rhetoric, and given the character of ancient *encomia* and the difference between the genres it may well be a work of the young Tibullus.

'Lygdamus' is perhaps the most professional or at least the most ambitious of these other poets. He describes the year of his birth (3.5.17f.) in the same words Ovid uses (*Tristia* 4.10.5f.): it is the year 43 B.C. when both consuls, Hirtius and Pansa, died of wounds received in the War of Mutina. There are many other striking parallels between the six relatively short elegies of 'Lygdamus' and Ovid's works from all periods of his life. One short passage, Lygd. 5.15–20, shows similarities to Ovid's *Amores* 2.14.23f.; *Ars Am.* 2.670 and *Tristia* 4.10.6. One tends to assume that Lygdamus imitates Ovid (just as he imitates Tibullus, especially in his second and fifth elegies), but there is a difficulty: he calls himself *iuuenis* (in 3.2.2) which seems impossible considering that this contemporary of Ovid's is old enough to read Ovid's exile poetry. Could he be the young Ovid who imitates himself later on? No satisfactory solution has been found.[1] The poetry itself is competent and not without a certain grace, but definitely sentimental.

The poems dealing with the love of Sulpicia and Cerinthus (here the man has a pseudonym, just like the women in Catullus, Propertius and Tibullus) are probably identical with the *epistulae amatoriae* mentioned in the ancient *Vita*. The first group (3.8–12 = 4.2–6) consists of poems ostensibly not written by Sulpicia herself, but by a sympathetic observer of her love affair, perhaps Tibullus. They form a poetic commentary on the affair by a third person, which is rather unusual (but cf. Prop. 1.10). The second group (3.13–18 = 4.7–12) consists of poems written by Sulpicia herself. Messalla's niece is an independent young woman who insists on her right to love; she is educated (she must have read at least some of the authors prescribed by Ovid, *Ars Am.* 3.329ff.) and handles language and metre well.

Tibullus' favourite themes are romantic love and the pleasures of country life. His pastoral passages show the influence of Virgil's *Eclogues* and *Georgics*. Though he is the only elegiac poet known to have spent years of his life in military service, he hates war and denounces the greed for power and wealth which leads to it. Money also corrupts love; this is something Tibullus claims to have experienced in all the affairs he tells about. A woman he calls Delia dominates Book 1 (above, p. 408); her real name was Plania; she seems to have lived with her old mother, and apparently she was a devotee of Isis. Nemesis, the mistress of Book 2, looks more like an experienced courtesan who may have been under the control of a 'go-between' (*lena*). Marathus, also mentioned in Book 2 (above, p. 409) is a handsome boy who attracted, at least for a short time, Tibullus as well as other men.

As a poet, Tibullus is, perhaps, more self-centred than the other elegists. He seems to live in a dream-world of his own. His nostalgia for a distant Golden Age may have obscured, for him, the grandeur of the Roman Empire and the blessings of the *Pax Augusta*. The only poem with 'national' themes (2.5) shows, perhaps, the influence of the *Aeneid*; it is important as a forerunner of Propertius' Roman Elegies (Book 4) and Ovid's *Fasti*.

From his poetry Tibullus appears to have been a great Roman gentleman. There is a delicacy of feeling in his elegies that is, perhaps, only found in Virgil, but Mackail was perhaps less than fair when he called Tibullus a 'Virgil without the genius'. There is genius as well as good breeding and good taste. Though he never mentions other poets and avoids any ostentation of learning,

[1] On the efforts to make him a contemporary of Statius and Martial see Luck (1959) 207ff.

mythological or otherwise, he is very well read, especially in Alexandrian authors.[1] Of course he knows Virgil and Horace, and his Book 2 may already reflect Propertius' Books 1 and 2. He has a charming sense of humour (not the biting kind which is Propertius' speciality), and the glimpses of real life which he gives us are welcome: the farmer's tipsy return, on his cart, with wife and children, after a country festival (1.10.51–2); the old grandfather playing with the baby (2.6.93–4); the invitation to the god Apollo to attend Messallinus' inauguration in his best attire (2.5.7–10).

Often, it seems as though he lets his mind, his imagination, wander from theme to theme; thus 1.1 begins with the praise of the simple but secure life of a poor farmer (ll. 1–44), continues with the theme of happy love (45–58), followed by a vision of the poet's death and funeral (59–68), recalls the enjoyment of life and love (69–74) and ends with the contrast of war and peace, wealth and poverty (75–8). There is a unity of mood and feeling; and the last two sections clearly echo the first two, but in a more concentrated form. Scholars have attempted to transpose couplets and whole passages, especially at the beginning of Book 1, to establish a more 'logical' order; but none of these transpositions is convincing, and careful interpretation usually reveals the poet's intention and his art.

5. SEXTUS PROPERTIUS

Propertius is, perhaps, the most difficult of the Roman elegiac poets, but also the one who appeals most to the modern taste. His tempestuous love affair with a woman he calls Cynthia (her real name was Hostia) fills most of the four books of elegies he wrote. The affair itself seems to have lasted five years (3.25.30) but whether a period of separation (3.16.9) was counted or not, is unknown. We may assume that the earliest poems of Book 1 were written in 29 B.C., and Book 3 with its emphatic farewell to Cynthia (3.24 and 25) was probably published in or shortly after 23 B.C. This would allow us to fit the five (or six) years conveniently between 29 and 23, but fact and fiction are so closely intertwined that no straight answer can be given. It should be said, however, that 3.20 tells of a new liaison with an unknown woman whom Propertius may have married; this elegy gives us no further information about Cynthia.

In Book 1 we meet some of the poet's friends in Rome: Tullus, a wealthy young man about to embark on a political career, the poets Ponticus and Bassus. He does not mention Ovid, though we know from *Tristia* 4.10.45–8 that they were all friends, *sodales*, and that Propertius used to read his love poems to Ovid. These might be some of the elegies now included in Book 2; Ovid was probably too young to have heard those of Book 1.

[1] Bulloch (1973) 85ff.

After a brief but not unhappy affair with a woman whom he calls Lycinna (3.15) Propertius fell in love with Cynthia. He speaks of her flaming eyes (2.13.14), her auburn hair (2.2.5–6), her long fingers and her striking figure (2.2.5–6). She was well read, musical, wrote verse herself and danced. Later, Propertius admits that he exaggerated her beauty (3.24 and 25), and after Cynthia's death her ghost gives a cruel assessment of Propertius, the lover, in a magnificent poem (4.7) which represents a supreme effort at self-criticism and self-irony by the poet; the result is a gentle but gripping evocation of the real Cynthia, nostalgic and without bitterness on his part.

His own image, as Propertius projects it, is that of a pale, intense young man (1.5.21), something of a dandy with perfumed hair and a slightly affected walk (2.4.5–6), who enjoys parties (3.5.19–22) and all the other pleasures of city life; the country does not attract him as much as it does Tibullus (but cf. 2.19). In later years, he seems to have become 'respectable' without losing his ability to view himself with irony (4.1).

The poems of Book 1 made him famous (a *succès de scandale*; cf. 2.24A.1ff.), and after Maecenas became his patron, the house of the Emperor was open to him. He wrote funeral elegies for two persons close to Augustus: 3.18 for his nephew Marcellus, and 4.11 for Cornelia. It speaks for Maecenas that he was capable of friendship with men as different as Virgil, Horace and Propertius (we know too little about the other members of his circle, such as L. Varius or Valgius Rufus). Propertius himself had the greatest admiration for Virgil, and around 25 B.C. he hails (2.34) the great new Roman epic in progress, though he probably knew little of the shape into which it grew. He never mentions Horace, though the influence of the *Odes* is fairly obvious, especially in the elegies of Book 3;[1] and Horace never mentions him by name, unless the slightly foppish elegist caricatured in *Epist.* 2.2.90ff. happens to be Propertius. Neither he nor Tibullus mention each other, but it is difficult to imagine that they ignored each other's work. Propertius 1 and Tibullus 1 may, in fact, be independent of each other, but Propertius 2 and 3 seem to show the influence of Tibullus 1, and his Roman Elegies (in Book 4) owe something to Tibullus 2.5.

Propertius sees himself as the great romantic lover. Like Byron, like D'Annunzio, he flies or wants to fly from woman to woman, always ready to offer, though not always giving, all of himself. To play this role (for it is a role) it is not enough to be passionate and tender: one needs a kind of contemptuous pride, an air of mystery; and behind the lover the reading public must feel the hero always engaged in fighting against the jealousy of the gods, the man who is greater than his destiny. Love, to him, is a transcendental power, and all accepted values – nobility, power, wealth – are revalued by love. Three lines,

[1] Cf., for example, 3.9.1 with Horace, *Odes* 1.1.1; 3.2.17 with *Odes* 3.30.2; 3.9.17 with *Odes* 1.1.2; 3.13.60 with *Epod.* 16.2 and on the whole question Wili (1947) 181ff.; Solmsen (1948) 105ff.

taken from his earlier poems, are characteristic: 1.5.24 *nescit amor priscis cedere imaginibus* 'love cannot yield to ancestral portrait busts'; 1.14.8 *nescit amor magnis cedere diuitiis* 'love cannot yield to great wealth'; 2.7.6 *deuictae gentes nil in amore ualent* 'conquered nations mean nothing if you are in love'. Here the three traditional Roman values are summed up and matched against the irrational force of love. But *amor* is also close to *pietas*; Propertius says to Cynthia (1.11.23–4) *tu mihi sola domus, tu, Cynthia, sola parentes: | omnia tu nostrae tempora laetitiae* 'you alone, Cynthia, are my house; you alone my parents; you are, for me, every moment of joy'. This love takes the place of all the emotional, religious attachments within the house, the family, and it becomes the ruling passion of one's life.

Propertius is not a philosophical poet. He wishes to keep more serious thoughts and studies for his old age, when he is no longer in love.[1] A clear line leads from the Alexandrian manner of Book 1 to the new realism of Book 4 with its awareness of Roman history. A great empire has come to be and is in danger of falling. Rome, too, will fall some day (*frangitur ipsa suis Roma superba bonis*, 3.13.60), just as the great kingdom of the Etruscans is a thing of the past: *heu Veii ueteres! et uos tum regna fuistis, | et uestro posita est aurea sella foro* 'alas, ancient Veii! once you were a kingdom, and the golden throne was placed on your market place' (4.10.27–8). The idea that Rome has become too powerful for her own good returns in Lucan and was perhaps a theme in Livy's preface to his famous account of the Civil War.

Invited by Maecenas to write an epic on Roman history Propertius refuses time and again (2.1; 3.3; 3.9) but finally offers a sort of compromise in the Roman Elegies of Book 4. Here he has found a congenial new theme and a fresh style. It is not true that he lost his poetic genius along with Cynthia – on the contrary: he continues to be creative in a different genre. The witty portrait of the astrologer in 4.1, the powerful caricature of the bawd in 4.5, the very funny description of the private orgy to which he treats himself in Cynthia's absence (4.8) reveal a gift of satire, a sardonic humour reminiscent of Horace in his best pieces. And 4.11, the 'queen of the elegies', is one of the most beautiful and moving poems written in Latin.

Propertius' early style is best described as *blandus* 'smooth and winning'. He is fond of this adjective,[2] and his friend Ovid applies it to him (*Tristia* 2.465; 5.1.17). It characterizes well the verbal melodies, the sometimes luxuriant use of lovely Greek names (1.3.1–4), the subtle technique of alliteration (1.1.1–2).

[1] 3.5.23–46 is a catalogue of philosophical (or scientific) themes. Cf. Lucr. 1.102ff.; 3.977ff.; Virg. *Geo.* 2.477ff.

[2] Propertius calls himself *blandus amator* (2.3.16); he speaks of the appeal of his verse as *blandi carminis obsequium*. The nameless lover in 1.16 who is suppliant (l. 14) and full of misery (l. 45) may be Propertius himself, because of the *arguta...blanditia*, the 'eloquent flattery' of his songs (l. 16).

6. PUBLIUS OVIDIUS NASO

Ovid is the last in the series of the Augustan elegists; and it seems the genre itself was dead long before Ovid's death in exile. His earliest elegies were collected in five books, the books probably coming out in chronological sequence, and then published as a whole, it would seem, under the title *Corinna.*[1] This edition is lost; Ovid replaced it by another in three books which is preserved under the title *Amores*. In the prefatory epigram the poet says that two books (i.e. a corresponding number of elegies) were suppressed to make the work more agreeable to read. Most scholars agree that he added some poems, and attempts have been made to identify them, but the whole problem of the revision may be more complicated. Thus 2.18 with its clear reference to the finished tragedy *Medea* (ll. 13–14), the *Ars amatoria* (ll. 19–20) and the *Epistulae Heroidum* (ll. 21–38) must belong to the second edition. Some of the elegies can be dated, e.g. 3.9 on the death of Tibullus (shortly after 19 B.C.), but a poem like this could have been written 'between editions' and then included in the second one.

Perhaps we can postulate that none of the poems that show the influence of Propertius' Book 4 (and *Amores* 3.9 is one of them) was part of the first edition. This hypothesis is based on two assumptions: (1) Propertius influenced Ovid, not vice versa; (2) his Book 4 represents a new style, a new artistic achievement, and therefore a challenge to his younger friend. It has often been observed that Ovid likes to treat the same theme in two poems, usually separated by other elegies. The most striking pair is 1.5 and 2.11, both describing the first time the poet made love to Corinna. This shows how futile any biographical interpretation of these poems would be. In such a case, one poem may very well have been kept from the first edition, while the other was written some years later. Ovid may want to show how he treats the same theme ten or fifteen years later, as a more experienced craftsman, possible under the influence of Propertius' late style. To determine which of the two belongs to the second edition we would have to search for passages that show the influence of Propertius' later poems. This is not so simple in this case, since neither poem has striking parallels to the elegies of Propertius' Book 4; only the imagery of 2.12 (the conquest of a beautiful woman is like a military victory) is close to Propertius 3.8.29–36, whereas no possible Propertian reminiscence in 1.5 seems to lead beyond Book 2. This would make 2.12 a poem of the second edition, treating the theme of the earlier 1.5 in Ovid's mature manner. But this is just a hypothesis which will have to be tested in other cases.

Rome with its streets, its colonnades, its temples and theatres, is the background of the *Amores*; only a few poems, e.g. 3.13, take us out of the city, to

[1] Luck (1959) 172ff.

the countryside (here, incidentally, the influence of Propertius Book 4 is strong). Rome is the capital of the world, a beautiful city full of life, but also the city of constant temptation; it is difficult not to fall in love or to have an affair: *illic Hippolytum pone: Priapus erit* 'put Hippolytus here, and he will be Priapus' (2.4.32). Ovid is the amused chronicler of a society for which pleasure was everything and which treated a love-affair as a work of art. Many poems are built around the stock characters of this society; some of them are familiar from New Comedy.

Ovid is skilful at developing a theme in the rhetorical manner, showing his early training. He argues, e.g., against abortion in 2.14, as a lawyer might in court. Or he describes scenes that might be taken from Comedy, e.g. the sequence 2.7 and 8. In the first poem he denies Corinna's accusation of having been unfaithful to her with her maid. Apparently she believes him, for in the next piece he boasts to the maid: 'See how cleverly I lied; haven't I earned a reward? You refuse? I shall tell her everything.'

Ovid's *Medicamina faciei femineae*, a fragmentary collection of cosmetic recipes for ladies in verse, is usually counted among his erotic poetry. It really celebrates beauty, love and the kind of sophistication which improves upon nature. The introduction is a lecture on the theme *culta placent* (ll. 3–50), the appeal of 'culture' in the broadest sense of the word, including bodily care. It is difficult to judge the effectiveness of the cosmetic preparations which Ovid lists; but he seems to have done a good deal of research. He himself calls this work *paruus, sed cura grande, libellus, opus* 'a book, small in size but great in care' (*Ars Am.* 3.206).

The *Ars amatoria* is more an 'Art of pleasing' or a 'Technique of seduction' than an 'Art of love'. It is not comparable to one of the sex manuals which are so popular today; it reads more (at least in parts) like one of the essays on women and love produced in such abundance, with infinite variations on the same few themes, by the French moralists of the seventeenth and eighteenth centuries. They studied the same kind of society for which Ovid wrote, and they considered love a fascinating game of enticement and temporary involvement. Love-making, to them, is a legitimate artistic pursuit; everything has to be done with a certain style. Though Ovid claims that his work is based on his own experience (*usus opus mouet hoc*, 1.29) he insists later on, in exile (*Tristia* 2.349–60), that 'a large part of my works are invented and fictitious and took more liberties than their author' (*magna...pars mendax operum est et ficta meorum: | plus sibi permisit compositore suo*); hence, it would be wrong to judge his morals on the basis of his works. He probably used some Greek sources, possibly Philaenis' 'Art of love' which is known to us now from papyrus fragments.[1] Some didactic themes he found in Tibullus 1.4 and Propertius 4.5.

[1] P. Oxy. 2891 (2nd century A.D.) contains parts of the 'Technique of seduction' and the section 'On kissing'.

The tone is debonair and occasionally borders on the frivolous, but the work as a whole can hardly be called immoral or corrupting. There are passages that must have annoyed Augustus; for example, Ovid's comment on religion (1.637–8): *expedit esse deos et, ut expedit, esse putemus: | dentur in antiquos tura merumque focos* 'it is useful that gods should exist, and since it is useful, let us believe that they exist, and let incense and wine be offered on ancient altars.' At least Ovid fully believed in equal opportunities for women, for Book 3 (perhaps added in a later edition) is addressed to them.

As a sequel to the *Ars* Ovid wrote a few years later the *Remedia amoris*, a guide for those who wish to fall out of love. The idea itself is amusing, but it has a serious background, and it almost looks as though Ovid had found a new role: that of helper and adviser to those who are troubled and unhappy. Stoics and Epicureans agreed that love was a form of madness, a mental disease; they only disagreed about the therapy. In this work, Ovid seems to have borrowed from both Stoic and Epicurean sources, and in a sense the *Remedia* represent a playful version of the ψυχαγωγία theme which was so popular in Hellenistic philosophy; it is a spiritual guidebook for the soul towards a better, saner, more rational life. Though many themes are taken from the elegiac tradition, Ovid's concern, his desire to help, are real, and his psychological insight and understanding are admirable.

7. OTHER ELEGISTS

There were other elegiac poets in Rome during this period but very little is known about them. Ovid (*Tristia* 2.423–66) gives a list of poets of the late Republic who dealt with the theme of love, some of them in elegies: Catullus, Calvus, Cinna, Valerius Cato, Anser, Cornificius, Ticida, etc. Another list (*Pont.* 5.16) contains mainly names of younger contemporaries; the only elegists identified as such are Montanus and Sabinus; the only love poets described as such are Tuscus and Proculus; of the latter Ovid says (ll. 31–2) *cum... Callimachi Proculus molle teneret iter* 'while Proculus kept to the soft path of Callimachus'; which must refer to homoerotic epigrams or elegies in Callimachus' style. Horace seems to have written elegies, too; but Suetonius (*Vita Horatii*) who claims to have seen them finds them 'trivial' (*uulgares*); perhaps they were never published.

In the *Appendix Vergiliana* several elegiac poems are preserved, but since this collection is dealt with elsewhere we shall only mention here the charming piece *De rosis nascentibus* which seems to show the influence of Ovid's exile poetry. Though this would exclude Virgil's authorship the poem cannot be dated with certainty; some scholars have placed it in the fourth or fifth century; others have attributed it to Ausonius.

The Latin love elegy thus appears to be the rather short-lived creation of the late Republic and the early Empire. Ovid's younger friends no doubt imitated him, as Passennus Paulus, a direct descendant of Propertius, imitated his ancestor (Pliny the Younger, *Epist.* 6.15; 9.22) in the second half of the first century A.D. But there is no evidence of a fresh creative impulse. The genre was revived by Maximian, in the middle of the sixth century A.D.; his five elegies seem to deal with erotic experiences of his distant youth and his advanced years; but idiom and imagery are still those of the Augustan elegists, especially Ovid.

21
OVID

I. 'FAME IS THE SPUR'

There had been nothing diffident or tentative about Ovid's literary début. In the very first of his surviving works, the *Amores* (Loves), he manifests astonishing confidence in himself and in his professional future. The three opening poems of Book 1, read as they are clearly intended to be read, that is as a connected sequence, sketch a poetic programme which is then carried through with masterful assurance until it achieves its ordained end in the double renunciation, of 'elegiac' love and of love-elegy, in the last poem of Book 3. The design and execution of the *Amores* can be properly understood only in relation to Ovid's predecessors. He had taken a genre already exploited, after Gallus, its inventor, by Tibullus and Propertius, and exploited it in his turn, originally but with a deadly efficiency that left no room for a successor. (The work of 'Lygdamus' shows how barren a mere recombination of the conventional motifs of love-elegy was bound to be.) As a demonstration of technical virtuosity the *Amores* verges on insolence; it was a remarkable, and tactically profitable, feat of literary originality, as originality was understood by the ancients, to impart to a well-established form with the inherent limitations of love elegy this new semblance of vitality. More than a semblance it cannot be accounted, but for Ovid's purpose that was enough. In the *Amores* he had put himself on the map; he had measured himself against his elegiac precursors, implicitly criticized them and some of the literary values accepted by them, and shown himself at the very least their technical equal. Having established his claim to consideration he began to look around for fresh worlds to conquer. In his farewell to Elegy (by which he means elegiac poetry of the Gallan-Tibullan-Propertian type) he speaks of the more important tasks awaiting him:

corniger increpuit thyrso maiore Lyaeus:
pulsanda est magnis area maior equis. (*Am.* 3.15.17–18)

Horned Bacchus has struck me with a weightier thyrsus: a greater plain is to be smitten by greater horses.

The symbols are old and conventional; the poet's passion for fame is vital and sincere. One genre has served its turn; in retrospect it will be seen chiefly as having been a stepping-stone to higher things.

The phrase *area maior* suggests the major genres of tragedy and epic. Of Ovid's only tragedy, *Medea*, nothing remains but a tiny handful of fragments, and the praises of Quintilian and Tacitus reveal nothing of its quality.[1] Some notion of his treatment of the heroine may perhaps be inferred from her other appearances in the surviving works, in *Heroides* 12 and *Metamorphoses* 7; and it seems hardly possible that Seneca's play on the same theme was not influenced by Ovid. Already in Book 3 of the *Amores* he had displayed an unusual – one might say, Euripidean – ability to see things from a woman's point of view. The new direction taken by his genius, which was to culminate in the *Metamorphoses*, allowed this ability full play. We meet the new Ovid for the first time in his extant works in the *Heroides*, which he himself went out of his way to claim as an original literary creation:

ignotum hoc aliis ille nouauit opus. (*Ars Am.* 3.345)

This kind of poetry was unknown until he invented it.

The chronology of Ovid's early poetry is perplexed and obscure, so that the composition of the *Heroides* cannot be exactly placed in a sequence with the two editions of the *Amores* and with the *Ars amatoria* (Art of love). It appears that Ovid had already embarked on the single letters, and probably the *Ars amatoria* as well, before completing the final revision of the *Amores*.[2] Thus, before the ink was dry on his initial *tour de force*, he was already carrying the congenial theme of love into one new literary field after another. Under the cool wit of 1.1–3 and the other programmatic poems of the *Amores* burned a flame of ambition and creative enterprise for which Ovid's limitless fertility of invention and technical resource was to provide abundant fuel.

In the proem to Book 3 of the *Georgics* Virgil had dismissed mythological subjects as too hackneyed for poetry; in later poets the idea became something of a cliché.[3] Ovid's whole poetic career constituted an implicit rejection of this position. From the beginning his imagination had nourished itself on mythology and legend. Even in the *Amores* an interest in mythological themes begins to make itself evident in Book 3, where it plays a part in the gradually developing and carefully stage-managed reaction against the inherited *leitmotiv* of devotion to a wilful mistress and the sort of poetry associated with such devotion.[4] In the *Ars amatoria* and *Remedia amoris* (Cure for love) a major part in the power of the poems to entertain is played by the narrative illustrations, in which Ovid

[1] Quint. *Inst.* 10.1.98, Tac. *Dial.* 12.

[2] *Am.* 2.18.19–34; cf. Appendix.

[3] Virg. *Geo.* 3.3–8; cf. Manil. 2.49–52, Nemes. *Cyn.* 15–47, *Aetna* 17–23, Juv. 1.7–13.

[4] Cf. *Am.* 3.6 (ll. 45–82), 10, 12, 13.

drew freely on myth and legend. In the *Heroides* the material is taken entirely from this sphere; and in this sense they may be seen, not only as important poetry in their own right, but also as foreshadowing Ovid's *chef d'œuvre*, the *Metamorphoses*.

2. THE 'HEROIDES'

The first series of *Heroides* consists of letters from famous women of Greek legend to absent husbands or lovers. For this new genre there was no single Greek or Roman model. Its originality, however, as with love-elegy itself, consisted in the blending of existing elements from the literary and rhetorical tradition. Catullus, Propertius and Ovid himself had already handled erotic themes from Greek mythology in the new 'subjective' style. Separation from the beloved, and attendant ideas of infidelity and betrayal, played a prominent role in love-elegy. Several of the *Amores* are essentially semi-dramatic monologues; and Ovid's early training in declamation was calculated to foster his predilection for this type of composition. Monologues by wronged or abandoned or suffering women were to be found in more than one existing genre, but the monologue as such was not a recognized literary form or *genus*; it required a setting such as that provided by a play or epyllion (e.g. Ariadne in Catullus' *Peleus and Thetis*). Ovid legitimated, so to say, his heroines' soliloquies by couching them in the form of letters. Strictly speaking the letter was not a genre in the full sense, but as a literary form it was as old as Plato, and it had been naturalized in Latin poetry by Lucilius and Horace. The convention could be, and by Ovid was, handled with considerable freedom. Unlike real letters the *Heroides* are self-contained works of art, neither needing nor indeed leaving room for an answer. The idea of the letter-form seems to have come to Ovid from Propertius' epistle of 'Arethusa' to 'Lycotas' (4.3); the scale on which he exploited this modest hint strikingly illustrates his powers of reception and re-creation.

The material of the *Heroides* comes principally from Greek epic and tragedy; the exceptions are the epistles of Dido (7), where his only source was the *Aeneid*, and Ariadne (10), where he drew extensively on Catullus. Given the fundamental identity of theme, monotony could be avoided only by the greatest possible variety of treatment and tone. About this undertaking there is an obvious whiff of the *tour de force*: to write no fewer than fourteen substantial poems of this sort in itself smacks of bravado. One limitation which at best could only be palliated was inherent in the letter-form itself, its basically static and undramatic character. Apart from the perhaps doubtful case of Deianira,[1] Ovid respects the rule that nothing affecting the course of events is allowed to happen during the writing of the letter. The heroine's situation is given; the

[1] *Her.* 9.143; see Appendix.

resultant action is entirely in her mind and heart. Relief is provided by brilliant rhetoric and by narrative retrospects, which include some very lively writing (e.g. Ariadne on her awakening, 10.7–50; Hypermnestra on her wedding night, 14.21–84), but it is on their merits as psychological drama that these poems must stand or fall.

To exemplify Ovid's treatment of his material two epistles which invite comparison with known originals may be briefly examined. Euripides had handled the story of Phaedra and Hippolytus in two plays, the first of which, now lost, had given offence by presenting Phaedra as totally shameless. It appears to have been this lost play on which Ovid principally drew for his Phaedra (*Her.* 4).[1] The implausibility (not to mention the anachronism, which is common to all the epistles) of her writing to Hippolytus is simply brazened out. Love-letters were part of the apparatus of contemporary intrigue (*Ars Am.* 1.455–86, 3.469–98, 619–30), and Ovid's Phaedra is envisaged very much as a contemporary elegiac figure. The hunting motif which in Euripides formed part of her delirium (*Hipp.* 215–22) is transmuted by Ovid into the typical *obsequium* (devotion to the wishes of the beloved) of elegy (37–50).[2] The logic of her pleading is elegiac and declamatory: Theseus' treacherous abandonment of her sister Ariadne (a cross-reference, as it were, to *Her.* 10) becomes the basis of her appeal to Hippolytus to betray his father with herself. The grim message of Euripides is trivialized and 'elegized' into a snippet of proverbial wisdom:

quid iuuat incinctae studia exercere Dianae
  et Veneri numeros eripuisse suos?
quod caret alterna requie, durabile non est;
  haec reparat uires fessaque membra nouat. (4.87–90)

How does it profit to cultivate the pursuits of the huntress Diana and rob Venus of her function? Nothing lasts if it is not allowed occasional rest; this is what restores strength and refreshes the weary body.

Without Venus the countryside is – countrified (102); the thought is straight from the world of the *Amores* and *Ars amatoria*. In the elegiac triangle Theseus is cast for the role of deceived husband, and it is elegiac logic that he deserves no better; he has his consolation in the arms of Pirithous (110–11). Equally elegiac is Phaedra's defence of her 'new' morality (129–46). Here too *rusticus* is used as a term of contempt for what is old and unfashionable; her remarks on family honour take the reader straight into the Rome of Augustus (131–2). In general in the *Heroides* Ovid can be seen reverting to a traditional pre-elegiac view of love as a passion felt in its full intensity only by women; but his

[1] In some places, however, he is clearly indebted to the extant *Hippolytus*. Whether these were passages retained by Euripides from the earlier version or whether Ovid laid both plays under contribution we cannot tell.

[2] Cf. Prop. 1.1.9–16, Tib. 1.4.49–50, [Tib.] 4.3.11–18, Ov. *Ars Am.* 2.185–96.

Phaedra expresses herself in the style of the bawd Dipsas (*Amores* 1.8). What she proposes is a clandestine affair in the palace itself, and she uses the very clichés of *furtiuus amor*:

non tibi per tenebras duri reseranda mariti
ianua, non custos decipiendus erit. (4.141–2)

There will be no stern husband's door to unbar at dead of night, no guard to trick.

Her final appeal crystallizes the matter in a single phrase: *quid deceat non uidet ullus amans* 'a lover does not know the meaning of shame' (154).

This epistle is the closest in spirit of the single *Heroides* to the *Ars amatoria*; in it Ovid seems to have deliberately modernized and degraded his heroic and tragic material. It was not part of his plan to reinterpet in this way all the stories that he took in hand: in the epistles of Canace (11) and Hypermnestra (14) equally bizarre situations are handled so as to bring out tragic or noble qualities in the protagonists. His treatment of Phaedra may have been intended to suggest that her love was indeed essentially squalid, if not actually comic; possibly he was simply showing off. The same light-hearted devaluation of mythical and heroic love recurs in his great apologia in *Tristia* Book 2, a line of defence from which prudence perhaps ought to have restrained him (*Trist.* 2.259–62, 289–300). Devaluation of a rather different kind is at work in his treatment of Dido (*Her.* 7); this makes sense only if it is read as a challenge to Virgil's justification of Aeneas' behaviour towards her.

The contrast with Virgil and a hint of Ovid's aim emerge in the first line of the epistle with the word *abiectus* 'cast away'. Dido is attempting what she already knows to be hopeless, but when all else is lost, what does the loss of a few words signify (5–6)? This is a different Dido from Virgil's stormy and imperious queen. From time to time a bitter epithet or reflection escapes her, but in the main her tone is one of gentle pleading or reproach, and her logic is woman's logic. Ovid's Dido has no conception of her lover's divine mission; to her his wanderings are merely a judgement on him (37–8). His orders from heaven are the special and specious pleading of the eternal predatory male, who gratifies his desire and passes on; she is equally the eternal female, whose instinct is to tame, to settle, to domesticate (15–22). She calls herself Aeneas' wife, using a word which belongs to elegy, *uxor*, rather than the epic *coniunx*. The famous disclaimer put by Virgil into the mouth of Aeneas (*Aen.* 4.172) and allowed by his Dido (4.431) is by Ovid implicitly treated as an evasion of the truth. His Dido's love for Aeneas is elegiac in its quality: her hope that he may at least suffer her to love him even if he cannot return her love is straight from the *Amores* (*Her.* 7.33–4 ~ *Am.* 1.3.3–4). As with his Phaedra, Ovid has transposed a theme from elegy, here the conventional subjection of the poet-lover, the *servitium amoris*, into his new feminine mode. Nowhere does his

Dido threaten; the destinies of Rome and Carthage are nothing to her. All she asks is that Aeneas should be a little kind to her.

In this portrait of a highly un-Virgilian Dido Ovid deliberately draws heavily on the *Aeneid*. By doing so he directs attention to what he is doing and challenges his readers to compare the two interpretations of the story. It was the essence of school declamation to devise *colores* 'colours', new and ingenious (often perversely so) interpretations of the given data; but there is more than declamatory ingenuity here. In presenting Dido as a woman pure and simple rather than a queen Ovid declares himself. He instinctively rejected the Augustan myth, whatever lip-service he might on occasion pay it, and with it much of the literature in which the myth found expression. He did not much believe in divine missions, excepting that of the poet; for a man to betray a woman was inhuman and wrong. Virgil had pleaded for the worse cause, even if he had shown some, perhaps involuntary, sympathy for the better. Compared with the subtle ambivalence of Virgil's treatment Ovid's is bound to appear simplistic, even crude; but the case that he argues is not an ignoble one. Faced with the choice of deserting his country or his beloved, is it beyond question which a man should choose? A critic should be very sure of his own position before he ventures to say that Ovid's was untenable.

The more carefully the *Heroides* are read, the more differences of intention and treatment between the different epistles will be found to emerge. Nevertheless the single letters cannot be altogether rescued from a charge of monotony. But Ovid had by no means finished with the genre. Some years later, stimulated we may guess by the action of his friend Sabinus in equipping some of the single letters with answers (*Am.* 2.18), he published three pairs of epistles in which a man wrote first and a woman answered him. These are considerably more ambitious compositions; the combined total of lines in each pair (646, 428, 490; average length of *Her.* 1–14 *c.* 150) amounts to that of a short *libellus*.[1] In each case the situation and the poetic treatment are carefully differentiated. The correspondence of Paris and Helen (16–17) is a highly entertaining *jeu d'esprit* in the spirit of the *Ars amatoria*. That of Acontius and Cydippe (20–1) is a study in obsession. For Paris and Helen he drew on several sources, the background to the Trojan War being common mythological property. For Acontius and Cydippe he used Callimachus' *Aetia*, but altogether transformed the story by endowing the protagonists, especially Cydippe, with new personalities and presenting the situation as a clash of wills, male against female, strong against weak.[2] The story of Hero and Leander (18–19) cannot have been long familiar when Ovid decided to use it. Its first appearance is in the *Georgics*, by way of passing allusion (3.257–63). Evidently the legend had come to notice

[1] See above, p. 18.

[2] Kenney (1970*b*). Callimachus' story had already inspired Propertius (1.18) and possibly Gallus (Ross (1975*a*) 89).

in the latter part of the first century B.C., probably in a lost Hellenistic poem.[1] It was Ovid who gave it the literary form which has proved definitive. Comparison with the *Hero and Leander* of the late fifth-century A.D. Greek poet Musaeus, who in certain respects followed the original source quite closely, shows the freedom with which Ovid treated it. An obscure story originally connected with a local landmark, the 'Tower of Hero', was immortalized in one of the most romantic poems in all ancient literature.

The epistle of Leander (*Her.* 18) begins *in mediis rebus*: a storm is brewing and he cannot cross the straits to Hero. This emphasis on separation and the emotions which it engenders in the two lovers dominates Ovid's handling of the story; with the mechanics of the plot he scarcely concerns himself. In Musaeus' poem the social status of Hero and the circumstances of their first meeting bulk large; Ovid does not mention them, and we are left to surmise why Leander's parents must be kept in the dark (13). As in a Savoy Opera, the situation is given, what interests the poet is the consequences. In Musaeus the crossing of the straits is dealt with briefly and drily, in Ovid the narrative of Leander's visits to Hero and their romantic concomitants form the centrepiece of his letter (53–124). The actual descriptive touches are not many, but they are sketched in surely and delicately; this is what Macaulay called 'sweet writing':

unda repercussae radiabat imagine lunae
  et nitor in tacita nocte diurnus erat;
nullaque uox usquam, nullum ueniebat ad aures
  praeter dimotae corpore murmur aquae.
Alcyones solae, memores Ceycis amati,
  nescioquid uisae sunt mihi dulce queri. (18.77–82)

The water shone with the reflected radiance of the moon, and the silent night was bright as day. No voice, no sound came to my ears but for the murmur of the water as I swam. Only it seemed to me that I heard the halcyons singing some sweet lament in memory of the beloved Ceyx.

Similarly the lovemaking of the pair is suggested rather than described (105–10). With a brief account of his departure and return Leander comes back to Abydos and the present (124), but the poem is not yet half over. There follows a long expostulation, liberally embellished with verbal and mythological conceits, against his situation. Like Narcissus in his celebrated soliloquy in the *Metamorphoses* (3.446–53), he dwells on the paradoxes of his position, and like Narcissus he resorts to elegiac cliché:

quo propior nunc es, flamma propiore calesco,
  et res non semper, spes mihi semper adest. (177–8)

As it is, the closer you are, the hotter I burn; but it is only the hope of you, not the reality, that is always with me.

[1] Cf. Page (1950) 512–13, Kost (1971) 20–1.

Finally his impatience breaks out into a vow that, come what may, he will try his luck again; if he is drowned he prays to be washed up dead at Hero's feet (193–200). This shallow and heartless posturing, like the manic persistence of Acontius, is essential to Ovid's portrayal of Leander's character. Though he immediately retracts and promises that he will not be rash (a promise not kept), his restless attitudinizing contrasts painfully with the passive and anxious role for which Hero is cast.

Her reply (*Her.* 19) begins with extraordinary address and delicacy. From her impatience to see Leander again, which equals his own, she passes to the disparity between their positions. Men can find distractions in manly pursuits (9–14); her only resource is her love (15–16). Here are epitomized the opposing roles of the protagonists – his to take risks, hers to endure and think of him:

quod superest, facio, teque, o mea sola uoluptas,
plus quoque quam reddi quod mihi possit amo. (19.17–18)

All there is for me to do, I do – I love you, my only joy, more even than you can ever love me.

It is the tragedy of a love such as Hero's that she should think more of her lover than he of her; her words are an implied reproach to the selfish boasting of his letter (18.195–200). Throughout the long day and the longer night that follows her thoughts are all of him. In the picture of Hero spinning with her nurse Ovid exploits a familiar image of a peculiarly Roman type of domesticity[1] to illustrate both the quality of her love and the contrast between the calm lamplit sanctuary which is his goal and the storm through which he must pass (and in which he will perish) to reach it. From conversation with the nurse Hero passes (55–6) to a soliloquy, occupying most of the letter, in which she reviews her doubts and fears and hopes. Whereas heroines such as Byblis (*Met.* 9.474–520) and Myrrha (10.320–55) argue with themselves about, and must in the end reach, a decision, Hero's part – and this, as has already been said, is the essence of her position – is purely passive. Thus her letter presented Ovid with a more demanding technical challenge than even that of Cydippe, who had in the end to say yes or no to her suitor. Hero's only resource is self-torment:

omnia sed uereor: quis enim securus amauit?
cogit et absentes plura timere locus. (19.109–10)

I fear everything – a lover knows no peace, and distance and separation increase one's fear.

[1] Virg. *Aen.* 8.407–15, Prop. 4.3.41–2 (Arethusa), Tib. 1.3.83–8 (Delia), Ov. *Fast.* 2.741–58, Livy 1.57.9 (Lucretia); cf. Ogilvie (1965) 222.

Eager as she is for him to come, she urges caution in words which reflect her conflicting feelings:

> me miseram, cupio non persuadere quod hortor,
> sisque precor monitis fortior ipse meis,
> dummodo peruenias excussaque saepe per undas
> inicias umeris bracchia lassa meis. (19.187–90)

Alas, I find myself wishing that my words shall not carry conviction and praying that your valour will outrun the discretion which I urge – just so long as you come safely across and throw about my neck those arms tired from long swimming.

With her account of an ominous dream (193–204) she returns to the long vigil that began at l. 33 and that has provided the setting for her soliloquy. Her vision of the dying dolphin, which even she can scarcely misread (203), held no mystery for Ovid's readers,[1] and her parting injunction reminds us again of the deep and unselfish quality of her love:

> si tibi non parcis, dilectae parce puellae,
> quae numquam nisi te sospite sospes ero. (19.205–6)

If you will not spare yourself, spare the girl you love, for without you I shall not be able to live.

In the double *Heroides* Ovid achieved a substantial technical advance. Viewing relationships from opposite sides in this way undoubtedly added depth and interest to the psychological portrayal. Yet the possibilities were still restricted by both the form and the verse medium. Even in the double letters very little in the way of real interaction occurs between the characters; the drama is still, as it were, frozen, though at two points rather than one. Moreover, for large-scale poetry the elegiac couplet, though handled in virtuoso fashion, has serious limitations. That these, in a particular genre, might be to some extent transcended, is shown by the *Fasti*; but the peculiar turn of Ovid's genius for exploring the vagaries of the human heart needed, for the full realization of its capabilities, the broader canvas of the epic.

3. THE 'FASTI'

At the end of the *Amores* Ovid had announced that a 'greater room' (*area maior*) awaited him. In his apologia for his life and work he listed as his three great voyages on the sea of poetry the lost tragedy *Medea*, the *Fasti*, and the *Metamorphoses* (*Trist.* 2.547–56). The two latter poems complement each other in more than one way. The obvious progenitors of the *Fasti* (Calendar) were Callimachus and Propertius. In Ovid's early work, apart from *Heroides* 20–1

[1] Cf. *Anth. Pal.* 7.215 (Anyte), 216 (Antipater of Thessalonica), 214 (Archias).

(Acontius and Cydippe), Callimachus figures only by way of sporadic allusion.[1] This is in contrast to Propertius, who had pledged formal allegiance to Callimachus (2.1.39–41, 3.1.1–2); who, indeed, in announcing the new kind of antiquarian elegy to which he had turned after the rupture with Cynthia (3.24, 25), had actually styled himself the Roman Callimachus (4.1.64). Now Ovid, as he had done with the *Heroides*, moved in to annex and consolidate the new genre. Whereas Propertius had experimented in a rather tentative fashion with a mixed collection of erotic and aetiological elegies, Ovid, as was his habit, went the whole hog and projected a single homogeneous poem of epic scale; the *Fasti* if completed would have been almost exactly the same length as the *Aeneid*. The break with love and love-elegy announced at the end of the *Amores* was now apparently complete.

Ovid's plan was to describe the Roman calendar and the various observances and festivals of the Roman year, and to explain their origins:

> tempora cum causis Latium digesta per annum
> lapsaque sub terras ortaque signa canam. (*Fast.* 1.1–2)

The seasons of the Roman calendar in due order, their origins, and the risings and settings of the constellations – these shall be my theme.

His chief models were Hellenistic, Callimachus' *Aetia* and Aratus' *Phaenomena*, and the ostensible impulse for the poem came from Propertius. However, the *Aeneid* must also be taken into account. The originality of Ovid's undertaking, as usual in Latin literature, consists in the combination of hitherto disparate elements: learning of a distinctively Hellenistic type is used to adorn themes from Roman history and antiquities, with a gloss of contemporary allusion which frequently shades into outright propaganda for the *Pax Augusta*. In crude terms this would also serve as a description of the *Aeneid*. That the two poems are in fact vastly different from each other is due in the first place to their different literary forms: the epic is impersonal, whereas Ovid's Callimachean model was didactic and anecdotal. More important still is the difference in temperament between the two poets, with their respective preference for the suggestive and the explicit. Most important of all, however, is the fact that the *Aeneid* represents a deeply meditated *credo*, whereas the *Fasti* is a purely literary exercise.

This was Ovid's first and only attempt at an Augustan poem, in the sense that, whatever derogations from high solemnity he might permit himself, his ostensible aim was to celebrate the idea of Rome, the *res Romana*. The original proem, displaced in revision, not only stresses the literary

[1] E.g. *Ars Am.* 1.619–20 ~ Callim. *Epigr.* 44.3–4. The same is generally true of Augustan poetry: Ross (1975*a*) 6–7.

importance of the work (2.3–8) but also claims it as a contribution to the public service:

haec mea militia est: ferimus quae possumus arma,
dextraque non omni munere nostra uacat. (2.9–10)

Here is my service: I bear such arms as I can, and my right hand is not totally exempt from duty.

In the light of the general tone of the poem and what has been called the 'eroticization' of his Roman material this must be regarded as window-dressing. It is precisely the discrepancy between matter and manner – the *res Romana* served up *à la grecque* – that constitutes the attraction of the *Fasti*. Much of the material is indeed Roman only by courtesy and contrivance, for Ovid introduced a good deal of Greek legend, including the occasional episode also incorporated in the *Metamorphoses* (e.g. Proserpine, *Fast.* 4.417–620 ~ *Met.* 5.341–661; Callisto, 2.155–92 ~ 2.401–530). The patriotic flourishes and the flattery of the Princeps and his family serve only to accentuate the fundamental frivolity of the work. But Ovid was not simply writing a comic history of Rome, Livy *travesti*; he was challenging Alexandrian *doctrina* on its own ground. Writing the *Fasti* necessitated much research, and Ovid drew on many sources, Greek and Roman. The astronomical, antiquarian and religious learning of the poem is an essential element in it, bulking almost as large as the illustrative narratives. As literature the result is not entirely satisfying. In the narratives Ovid was free to be himself, and they contain much brilliant and effective (though little affecting) writing. In the rest of the poem he was constrained to play the part of *Romanus uates*, and the sly wit with which he performs his role merely draws attention to its inappropriateness. Like nearly everything else he wrote the *Fasti* is a *tour de force*, but the fact is more obtrusive even than in the *Ibis*. Comparison with the contemporary *Metamorphoses* again emphasizes the inferiority of the elegiac couplet, however adroitly handled, to the hexameter as a medium for sustained narrative. Students of Roman religion must (perforce and with caution) use the *Fasti* as an important source of information, and generations of schoolboys have first met Ovid in its more (ostensibly) edifying pages. From the literary critic it tends to elicit admiration tempered with apology.

4. THE 'METAMORPHOSES'

In the *Ars amatoria* and *Remedia amoris* Ovid had illustrated and diversified his precepts by narrative excursuses. These vary in tone and elaboration, ranging from the mildly lubricious (Achilles on Scyros, *Ars Am.* 1.681–704; Mars and Venus, 2.561–92) through the marvellous-aetiological (Ariadne, 1.527–64; Daedalus and Icarus, 2.21–96) and the grotesque (Pasiphae, 1.289–326) to the tragic (Cephalus and Procris, 3.685–746; Phyllis, *Rem.* 591–606). Retrospective narratives also contribute to the effectiveness of *Heroides* 10–14, 16–21. The *Fasti* was the first of his works in which narrative played a quantitatively significant, if not a preponderant, part. However, the *Fasti* was more than an exercise in story-telling; in it Ovid applied to the creation of a specifically Roman poem a formula already used (with profoundly different results) by Virgil in the *Aeneid.* Considered as a bid for the highest poetic honours the *Fasti* suffered from the fundamental handicap of not being an epic. Ovid saw himself as the Virgil of Roman elegy:

tantum se nobis elegi debere fatentur,
quantum Vergilio nobile debet epos. (*Rem.* 395–6)

Elegy acknowledges that it owes as much to me as the epic owes to Virgil.

The claim bears examination, indeed what Ovid made of elegy is in some ways even more surprising than what Virgil had made of epic. The fact, however, remained that the epic, deriving from Homer, the source of all poetry and eloquence,[1] was the *genus nobile*, the genre of genres. If Ovid wished to assert a serious claim to a place in the muster-roll of the greatest Roman poets he had to write an epos. To this ambition the greatest single obstacle, given that Ovid suffered from no doubts about his talents, was the existence of the *Aeneid.*

Ovid was far too genuinely respectful of Virgil and far too shrewd to think of emulating him on his own ground. Neither Dido's epistle to Aeneas nor the later, 'Aenean', books of the *Metamorphoses* constitute such a challenge; and the form and character of the *Fasti* show Ovid to have been well aware of the imprudence of a direct confrontation. It was one thing to offer to displace Propertius as the Roman Callimachus; the position of the Roman Homer was secure. Virgil had revitalized the genre by a unique and unpredictable fusion of Greek and Roman elements, but by the same token he had killed traditional epic stone dead. After the *Aeneid* a reversion to historical epic *à la* Ennius or mythological epic *à la* Apollonius ought to have been unthinkable. Ovid and the best of the epic poets of the Silver Age understood and acted on this essential premiss. The problem was to find a formula for a poem that in scale and originality could stand alongside the *Aeneid.* Ovid's solution was an even more brilliant feat of creative adaptation than those which produced the *Ars amatoria*, the *Heroides*, and the *Fasti.* The *Metamorphoses* (Transformations) is a long poem of some 12,000 lines in 15 books which in effect presents an anthology of Greek and Roman, but predominantly Greek, myth and legend. The length and elaboration of the individual episodes vary enormously, from passing allusions in a single verse to almost-autonomous epyllia occupying

[1] Cf. Ov. *Am.* 3.9.25–6, Dion. Hal. *De comp. verb.* 24, Quint. *Inst.* 10.1.46.

several hundred lines. Formally a semblance of unity is given in several ways. Most obviously the theme of metamorphosis, change of shape, plays a part, though with marked variations of emphasis, in nearly every story. Since however Ovid's ingenuity was equal to inventing a connexion or even a metamorphosis whenever it suited him, whether the tradition offered one or not, this ostensible *leitmotiv* imposed very little restriction on his choice of material. The narrative follows a chronological pattern from the Creation to the murder and apotheosis of Julius Caesar. Here too, since mythical chronology has never been an exact science, he might permit himself considerable latitude in the ordering of his material. Continuity between episodes is provided by hugely ingenious transitional and framing devices which earned the poet a magisterial rebuke from the humourless Quintilian (*Inst.* 4.1.77).

No single model for such a poem as this existed in Greek or Latin. In its character as what some critics have called a 'collective' poem (*Kollektivgedicht*) it is Hesiodic; and to the extent that Ovid had enrolled himself under the banner of Hesiod it might be claimed that the *Metamorphoses* implicitly claimed different but equal status with the *Aeneid.* More than one Hellenistic poet had exploited the theme of transformation. Callimachus in the *Aetia* had used the format of discrete and disparate episodes strung on a thread of 'editorial' association.[1] In scale and scope, however, the *Metamorphoses* is unique. By drawing on the last syllable of recorded time (as known to his sources) Ovid allowed himself *carte blanche* to include whatever stories appealed to him and to develop them in what seemed to him the appropriate style. Thus the poem includes samples of all the important genres, though transposed, so to say, into the peculiar idiom of the *Metamorphoses*: comedy, elegy, pastoral, tragedy, oratory, didactic, hymn – not forgetting the epic itself.

The impression received from a continuous reading of the poem is thus one of incessant variety, of change (metamorphosis, in fact), and of pleasure springing from the unexpected. The surprises range all the way from the light play of linguistic wit, as when the length of the seasons is figured in the words and metre used to describe them –

∪ ∪ – – – – – –
et inaequales autumnos
– ∪ ∪ –
et breue uer (1.117–18)

unequal autumns and brief spring

– to the inclusion of a complete episode by way of a *tour de force*, as with the long monologue of Pythagoras (15.12–478). Ovid indeed begins the poem by playing a little trick on the reader. The opening words: *in noua fert animus* seem to be a self-contained sentence meaning 'my inspiration carries (me) on

[1] For his technique see fr. 178 Pf.

to new things' – a proclamation of the novelty of his literary undertaking. In what follows the reader is undeceived:

> in noua fert animus mutatas dicere formas
> corpora,

my inspiration carries me to tell of shapes changed into new bodies;

yet the ambiguity remains and must be deliberate. In a declaratory proem of only four verses every phrase and every word must have been carefully weighed; by allowing himself this verbal sleight of hand at the outset Ovid was showing his readers something of what was in store for them, as well as emphasizing two points: that nothing like the *Metamorphoses* had ever been attempted before and that he was coming before the public in a totally new guise. The very obliquity and allusiveness of the communication is an implicit act of homage to Callimachus.

In what follows the innuendo becomes more specifically Callimachean. Ovid continues

> di, coeptis (nam uos mutastis et illa)[1]
> adspirate meis primaque ab origine mundi
> ad mea perpetuum deducite tempora carmen.

Gods, favour my undertaking – for it was you who changed that too – and bring down from the beginning of the world to my own times a continuous song.

First, the conventional plea for divine assistance is manipulated so as to represent the poem itself, the *Metamorphoses*, as the product of a metamorphosis. As with the opening words this can be understood on two levels. The obvious sense is that Ovid has been metamorphosed from elegist into epicist. But if the original sense of *coepta* as 'beginnings' is pressed, the phrase reflects on the character of the poem as well. Just as Apollo had intervened to turn Callimachus and Virgil from epic (Virg. *Ecl.* 6.3–5, Callim. fr. 1.21–8 Pf.), so the gods have saved Ovid from setting his hand to some less auspicious plan.[2] Still with Callimachus in mind he asks the gods to further his intention of writing a *perpetuum carmen*, a 'continuous song'. This is precisely what Callimachus had disavowed and had been criticized for not producing.[3] So a wilful paradox is propounded. Though metamorphosis was a specifically Alexandrian subject (Nicander's *Heteroeumena*, 'Things changed', must have been quite well known), Ovid's treatment is not to be Callimachean but conventionally epic, for this is the obvious implication of *perpetuum*.[4] The paradox is underlined discreetly by the use of the word *deducite*. In the context this seems to mean no more than 'bring down', 'carry through'; but its use with the gods rather than

[1] *illa* P. Lejay: *illas* MSS. Cf. Kenney (1976) 47–9.
[2] Cf. Galinsky (1975) 103–7; *contra* Wilkinson (1955) 214–18.
[3] Callim. fr. 1.3 Pf. ἓν ἄεισμα διηνεκές 'one continuous song'.
[4] Cf. Hor. *Odes* 1.7.6 and Nisbet–Hubbard (1970) ad loc.

the poet as subject is unusual and may be intended to draw attention to a further implication. The result, if the gods cooperate, will in literal terms be a *deductum carmen*, the 'fine-spun song' enjoined by the Virgilian-Callimachean Apollo – a contradiction in terms. Ovid's language, however, implies that the *Metamorphoses* will manage to be both Callimachean and un-Callimachean at once.

This brief scenario, closely read, excites both attention and a measure of surprise. Its effect is to redirect the reader to the opening words of the poem: *in noua*...no question but that the *Metamorphoses* is to be something unexampled in the annals of poetry. The reader soon finds, however, if his previous acquaintance with Ovid has not already taught him, that it will not do to take all this quite literally. There is continuity, of a kind, in the poem, but it is very different from the continuity of the *Annales* or the *Aeneid*; and continuity, after all, is not the same thing as unity. What the *Metamorphoses* is supposed to be about, apart from metamorphosis, does not readily emerge. The *Aeneid* had a clear message, well summarized in Donatus' Life of Virgil, to present *Romanae simul urbis et Augusti origo*, the origins of Rome and of Augustus – in other words, to justify the present and the future in terms of the legendary past. It might indeed be held that in one way or another this had been the purpose of all the specifically 'Augustan' poetry of Virgil and Horace. What, if anything, was Ovid trying to prove in the *Metamorphoses*? The question is intimately bound up with that of the poem's unity. If it is simply a collection of good stories written to entertain, the quest for unity and a message is a wild-goose chase. The scale and the tone of the coda, at all events (15.871–9), suggest higher pretensions.

Attempts have been made to detect a unity and hence a message in such aspects of the poem as its structure or its symbolism – even (perhaps a counsel of despair) in its very diversity. As to structure, critics have generally agreed in identifying three main divisions of approximately equal length in which the protagonists of the stories are, respectively, the gods (1.452–6.420), heroes (6.421–11.193), and what (on the premiss that ancient history began with the Trojan War) may broadly speaking be termed historical figures (11.194–15.744). The main body of the poem is framed by what may be called a Prologue (1.5–450: Creation–Deluge–Repeopling of Earth) and an Epilogue (15.745–870: Apotheosis of Julius Caesar), the latter being introduced by what is perhaps the most blatantly contrived transition of all, bridging a chasm into which six centuries of Roman history disappear without trace. The fleshing of this simple skeleton is complex and has given rise to much disputable interpretation. Within the overall chronological scheme, which is not followed rigidly, the stories are arranged in groups of varying size and complexity, the stories within a particular group and the groups themselves being linked and related in varying ways – thematic, geographical, genealogical – now by association, now by contrast, now by ingenious and unscrupulous legerdemain. Though flexible the structure is far from anarchic; but it is not easy to reduce to system. Attempts have been made to show that under this informal, though not formless, arrangement of the material there may be detected a more strictly ordered architecture of proportion and symmetry. It seems *a priori* unlikely that Ovid, who is sometimes elusive but almost never obscure, should have expected readers of the *Metamorphoses* to detect structural subtleties on which modern critics disagree so sharply; and difficult to see what emphases he intended them, when detected, or subliminally apprehended, to convey. Moreover he has incorporated in the structure of the poem one hint which seems to point the other way. In the *Aeneid* the division into books, originally a matter of practical convenience,[1] is made to play an essential literary role in the economy of the poem. Ovid's narratives are deliberately contrived to overrun these divisions, which in consequence have a merely local effect, by way of surprise or creation of suspense; and the individual books have a unity only in so far as the poet takes care that the literary texture of each one should in its variety reflect the texture of the poem as a whole. This can be read as a tacit declaration that balance and symmetry of the Virgilian type, with such emphases as they may connote, are not to be looked for in this quite un-Virgilian epic.

Little or nothing, therefore, of the poet's intention appears to emerge from the structure of his poem except for an evident intention to surprise, divert and amuse. A clue to deeper meaning has been sought in the symbolism of, for instance, his descriptions of landscape. There can certainly be no question of the symbolic significance of the setting of some of the stories, notably the pool of Narcissus (3.407–12). These landscapes, it is suggested, are places where anything can happen; and that accords with the sense of otherness (so to call it) with which Ovid has invested this world of his own creation. This is an autonomous universe in which for the most part it is divine caprice that reigns unchecked. But such symbols as these seem to possess no more than a, so to say, local validity when compared with the pervasive symbolism of the *Aeneid* or the imagery on which Lucretius relies to enforce his argument, and they cannot be seen as a strongly unifying element in the *Metamorphoses*. At most they provide immediate but limited emphasis.

If the *Metamorphoses* is in some important sense significant – if, that is, it ought to be regarded as something better than a graceful florilegium of ancient mythology – it can only be on the strength of Ovid's treatment of his material, the myths themselves. Outside a purely factual handbook myth cannot be treated 'straight'. Literary treatment of myth inescapably entails interpretation, and it would have been impossible for Ovid to avoid imparting an individual colouring to the stories that he chose to tell, even had he wished to. Of course

[1] Cf. above, p. 18.

he had no such wish. *In noua fert animus*: the whole scope of his poem demanded that he reshape and reinterpret the myths. Critics differ as to whether the reshaping was purely in the interests of entertainment value, the imparting of a modern verve and piquancy to the traditional tales through the free play of Ovid's iconoclastic wit, or whether the treatment did in truth deepen their significance. This question has a bearing on that of unity, if it can be shown that Ovid's treatment of his mythical material was guided by some principle which in this sense informed the poem.

That these are not straightforward questions is shown by the difficulty experienced by critics when they try to define the *Metamorphoses*. Clearly it is a special kind of epic, an epos *sui generis*, but of what kind? What most interested Ovid and provided him with a limitless field for exploration (in the end, most tragically, in his own case) was human behaviour under stress. The *Metamorphoses* is above all an epic of the emotions. Given both Ovid's own predilections and the basic facts of human nature the predominant emotion is, predictably, love. By taking his plots from traditional mythology and creating a special world for his characters to inhabit Ovid released himself from the need to respect certain aspects of probability. The premisses of the situations in which his characters found themselves could, as in the *Heroides*, be taken for granted; what mattered was their reactions. Of these premisses the most fundamental is the almost absolute power of the gods and their lack of moral scruple in its use. Like the human actors in the drama the gods are the slaves, though less frequently the victims, of their passions. Granted all this, however improbable or even outrageous the particular circumstances, the interest lay in following out the consequences. As a literary formula this was not new: it had been brilliantly used by Aristophanes and it was of the essence of the declamatory exercises on which Ovid and his generation cut their literary teeth. But by contrast with this attitude to the given premisses, in Ovid's development of the story therefrom probability, or at all events conviction, was paramount; all the poet's art was applied to achieve credibility (*fides*) and to persuade the reader that in the circumstances described people must have behaved so. Callimachus had put the matter in a nutshell: 'let me so lie as to convince my hearer'.[1] In reading the story of Pygmalion (10.242–97) we forget that in the real world statues do not come to life; we know only that if they did this is how it would be. In principle no situation was too bizarre or morally reprehensible (incest is the subject of two episodes) to qualify for this poetical analysis.

The formula in itself carries no guarantee of the success which it achieves in Ovid's hands. Simply to ring rhetorical and emotional changes on traditional material was not enough. The *Metamorphoses* might have emerged as yet

[1] *Hymn* 1.65 ψευδοίμην ἀΐοντος ἅ κεν πεπίθοιεν ἀκουήν.

another catalogue of suffering heroines and star-crossed lovers; that it did not is due to Ovid's prodigious fertility of invention, his wit, and his masterful way with the Latin language. In treating the original stories freely he availed himself of a traditional licence, but being Ovid used the licence to the full. As he found it the story of Pygmalion was a smoking-room anecdote; its charming and innocently sensuous character as one of the great stories of wish-fulfilment is entirely his achievement. Just as he had transformed Acontius from a love-sick youth into a man with an obsession bordering on the psychopathic, so the credibly middle-class Erysichthon of Callimachus' Hymn to Demeter becomes in the *Metamorphoses* (8.738–878) a fairy-tale monster. Conversely the Iliadic Odysseus is downgraded in the wrangle over the arms of Achilles (13.1–398) into a contemporary committee-man, public relations expert, and smart-aleck lawyer. Ingenious combination brings familiar or less familiar figures into new and piquant situations. In the story of Cyclops and Galatea (13.735–897) the pastoral setting of the Alexandrian treatment (Theoc. 6, 11) is retained, but Theocritus' rustic booby is reinvested with the horrendous attributes of the original Homeric Cyclops; and the theme of Beauty and the Beast is accentuated by the introduction of Acis in the character of the successful rival. But the episode has something of a pantomime quality; Acis is crushed under a rock hurled, in Homeric fashion, by the monster, but all ends happily with a transformation scene and tableau in which he emerges as a river-god, equipped with the typical attributes of his new status, the whole being rounded off with an *aition* (13.887–97). By skilful assimilation of elements from several literary sources (including Virgil, who had also drawn on the story in the *Eclogues*) Ovid constructs a grotesque-idyllic episode of a unique kind, burlesque of a high poetic order, which was to bear its full fruit only after some seventeen centuries in the collaboration of Gay and Handel:

> Galatea, dry your tears!
> Acis now a god appears.

This example, which could be multiplied a hundredfold, of the reception and exploitation of the *Metamorphoses* by later European writers and artists, is the strongest possible testimony to Ovid's importance, already referred to apropos of the story of Hero and Leander, as mediator between the old world and the new.

Even in his moments of inspired nonsense Ovid's preoccupation with abnormal psychological states is not forgotten. In his version of the story Galatea hears the lament of the Cyclops with her lover lying in her arms. This is characteristically Ovidian, a touch of sexual cruelty to emphasize the unbridgeable gulf between Beauty and the Beast; and the passion of the Cyclops, like that of Acontius, is a type of the love that will destroy if it cannot possess. The fact that the Middle Ages found in the *Metamorphoses* an endless store of symbol and allegory shows that in reshaping the myths to provide varied and piquant entertainment Ovid certainly did not – to put it no higher – divest them of their inherent validity. A particularly striking case is that of Narcissus and Echo (3.339–510). The story as Ovid tells it can be made to yield more than one moral. It is a lesson against the desire and pursuit of the unattainable. More specifically it illustrates the destructive quality of self-love seen in its effects on both self (Narcissus) and others (Echo). But the length and elaboration of Ovid's treatment cannot be attributed to a wish to underscore any moral that the story may offer; still less (as a rule) does he draw attention overtly to such implications. His interest is in exploiting to the full the paradox, indeed the absurdity, of the situation. By emphasizing at the outset the oddity of Narcissus' passion and its outcome (3.350 *letique genus nouitasque furoris*) he shows what is in his mind. Echo, with the incidental comedy that her disability entails and the wistful ghost of her voice, is a foil to bring out the lengths to which Narcissus' own emotional disability ends by taking him. On the way to the dénouement the poet of the *Amores* diverts himself and us by standing all the elegiac clichés of the thwarted lover on their heads:

> uror amore mei, flammas moueoque feroque:
> quid faciam? roger anne rogem? quid deinde rogabo?
> quod cupio, mecum est; inopem me copia fecit.
> o utinam a nostro secedere corpore possem!
> uotum in amante nouum: uellem quod amamus abesset. (3.464–8)

It is myself for whom I burn, I both inflict and suffer this fire. What am I to do? Court or be courted? But what will courting effect? What I desire is mine already; it is riches that make me a pauper. If only I could quit my own body – a novel thing this for a lover to wish, that the beloved were elsewhere!

The mixture of sentiment and humour in such an episode is a challenge to the reader, who must react with a corresponding mixture of emotional participation and intellectually detached amusement. So in the story of Ceyx and Alcyone, one of the longest and most elaborately constructed episodes in the poem (11.410–748), the truly tragic treatment of Alcyone's selfless love for her husband and of the fate of the pair is offset by the extravagance of the two contrasting descriptive excursuses, the storm (which verges on a parody of a stock epic theme) and the Cave of Sleep. It is not always easy to know where to have Ovid or how to respond to these astonishing stories.

The culminating metamorphosis of the body of the dead Narcissus to the flower that bears his name sits very loosely to the story of his passion. Similarly the metamorphosis of Ajax into a hyacinth is a very slender excuse for the inclusion and extended treatment of the *Iudicium armorum*, the debate between Ajax and Ulysses as to who should inherit the arms of the dead Achilles

(13.1–398). This is a brilliant demonstration of how to argue on both sides of a question. That the Unjust Argument wins the day is not stated in so many words, but an attentive reader is left in no real doubt of it. However, the outcome might also be construed as demonstrating the superiority of intelligence (*consilium*) over brute force (*uis*). It is not surprising that the passage enjoyed an independent circulation in the Middle Ages and was esteemed by Macaulay. Here too Ovid shows great skill in transforming his sources. In the main he drew on the *Iliad*, but the gloss that he places on the exploits of the heroes is heavily influenced by the post-Homeric tradition in which Ulysses became a type of unscrupulous cunning. In general the choice of episodes and the scale of the treatment were suggested by the content of the stories and what might be made of them rather than by the metamorphoses with which they were (or might be) associated. It is unusual when, as with Pygmalion, a metamorphosis is integral to the story. Sometimes it provides a purely mechanical release from an intolerable situation: Daphne is changed into a laurel as an alternative to being raped (1.548–56). True 'happy endings' are not very common in the *Metamorphoses*; the story of Ceyx and Alcyone achieves its dénouement in a rare mood of tranquil beauty:

fatis obnoxius isdem
tum quoque mansit amor, nec coniugiale solutum est
foedus in alitibus: coeunt fiuntque parentes,
perque dies placidos hiberno tempore septem
incubat Alcyone pendentibus aequore nidis.
tum iacet unda maris; uentos custodit et arcet
Aeolus egressu praestatque nepotibus aequor. (11.742–8)

Their love survived in their new guise, and even after they became birds the marriage-bond was not severed. They mate and rear young, and through seven calm days each winter Alcyone hatches her brood in a nest floating on the water. Then the sea is smooth: Aeolus shuts up the winds in their prison and grants his grandchildren a level ocean.

Even this pretty conceit is an *aition* thinly disguised; and similarly Baucis and Philemon, though happy in the manner and occasion of their death, serve in the end chiefly to point a moral and launch an epigram:

cura deum di sunt et qui coluere coluntur. (8.724)

Those who guarded the gods have become gods and the worshippers are themselves worshipped.

In general Ovid is not concerned to find solutions to the predicaments of his characters. It is of course broadly true that all good poets avoid simplistic 'explanations' of the great myths, preferring to accept, even to compound, their uncertainties. That is not quite Ovid's position, which is one of calculated detachment. It is rare for him to involve himself (his narrative *persona*, that is), except for apostrophes of a conventionally pathetic kind, with the fates of his actors. Sometimes indeed this detachment rises to a degree that repels the modern reader, as in the gruesome details of the Battle of the Centaurs and Lapiths (12.245–458) or the flaying of Marsyas by Apollo, where the victim in the midst of his agonies is made to utter a punning comment on what is happening to him (6.385–91). In such passages detachment seems to pass over into open relish of suffering. They are not, however, so numerous as to dominate or fundamentally colour the poem as a whole, and no doubt represent an unfortunate concession to a certain kind of contemporary taste for the sado-masochistic. Essentially they represent an excess of a quality which continually pervades and informs the *Metamorphoses*: what the Romans called *ingenium* and the English Augustans wit. Ovid's approach to the stories he tells is intellectual rather than emotional; the subject is the passions, but the object is less to excite sympathy in the reader in any profoundly moving way (let alone attempt any sort of catharsis) than to stimulate and feed a well-informed interest in the illimitable variations of human experience. Life and people being what they are, experience mostly takes the form of inflicting or enduring suffering; a fact which one need not be hard-hearted in order to contemplate with amusement. 'Life is a comedy to those that think, a tragedy to those that feel.' The *Metamorphoses* is written for those that think. Moreover profound emotion is bound up with morality, and the world of the *Metamorphoses* is conspicuously amoral. Ovid's gods are beings emotionally human but invested with supernatural powers and free from all moral constraint because not subject to any sanctions from above – they are what most men and women, if absolutely free to choose, would be if they could. Ovid was certainly in the conventional sense an unbeliever, but his treatment of the Olympian pantheon is not a sneer at traditional religion so much as a sardonic comment on human nature. In spirit he is much nearer to Lucretius than to Virgil, though he did not believe in prophets either.

In certain respects it can be suggested that the *Metamorphoses*, which in spite of the great surface disparities persistently invites comparison with the *Aeneid*, is the more universal poem of the two. Certainly it is more difficult to evaluate its message or even to be sure if it has one. Ovid shows humanity to itself in a great distorting mirror of its own creation, the myths that formed the staple of both popular and literary culture. The great Virgilian commentator James Henry found Ovid 'a more natural, more genial, more cordial, more imaginative, more playful poet...than [Virgil], or any other Latin poet'[1] – in a word, more human; and the essential unity, or, better, harmony of the *Metamorphoses* is to be sought in its humanity. In spite of the intellectual distance

[1] Henry (1873–89) I 618.

maintained by the poet between himself and his creations, in spite of the excesses and lapses of taste into which his wit was apt to lead him, in spite of the relentless pursuit of point and paradox, in spite even of the apparent heartlessness of some episodes, this remains the distinctive quality of the poem. Its unclassical characteristics, which also emerge from the comparison with the *Aeneid*, should offer no obstacle to appreciation in an age which appears to have broken definitively with classicism in literature, art and music. Balance and proportion are not necessarily and self-evidently the most important of the artistic virtues. Ovid's vision of the world was not one of order and uniformity but of diversity and change. For him the Augustan settlement was not, as it had been for Virgil, the start of a new world, *nouus saeclorum ordo*, but another sandbank in the shifting stream of eternity. The *Aeneid* stops where it does because of the logic of a situation: there is a knot which can be cut only by the sacrifice of Turnus. Blood must be shed so that reconciliation may follow. The *Metamorphoses* stops where it does because this is where history has got to. In the coda to the poem Ovid foretells his own metamorphosis and apotheosis:

iamque opus exegi, quod nec Iouis ira nec ignis
nec poterit ferrum nec edax abolere uetustas.
cum uolet, illa dies, quae nil nisi corporis huius
ius habet, incerti spatium mihi finiat aeui;
parte tamen meliore mei super alta perennis
astra ferar, nomenque erit indelebile nostrum,
quaque patet domitis Romana potentia terris,
ore legar populi perque omnia saecula fama,
siquid habent ueri uatum praesagia, uiuam. (15.871–9)

And now I have finished a work which neither Jove's anger nor fire nor iron nor gnawing age shall have power to destroy. That day which has authority only over my body may when it pleases put an end to the uncertain span of my life; with the better part of me I shall soar immortal high above the stars and my name shall not be extinguished. Wherever the sway of Rome shall extend over the conquered lands, I shall be read by the tongues of men and for all time to come, if the prophecies of bards have any truth in them, by and in my fame shall I live.

In a perilous and uncertain universe the only created thing that can hope for survival is poetry, for it comes from and lives through the spirit. In the mind of a rationalist and a humanist this is the only kind of immortality that there is. Only so can man's unconquerable soul ensure its own survival.

5. THE POEMS OF EXILE

The *Metamorphoses* was, so far as can be seen, substantially complete, if not formally published, in the shape in which we now have it by A.D. 8. Ovid then stood on the pinnacle of success; none could challenge his position as Rome's most eminent living poet. That he was himself acutely conscious of this fact is an essential key to the understanding of much of his later poetry. The *Metamorphoses* had concluded with a group of transformations that might be seen as the climax of all those that had preceded: the apotheoses of Julius Caesar (accomplished) and of Augustus (awaited) and, linked with them, the last great metamorphosis of history, begun by Caesar and to be completed by his successor (Jupiter on earth: 15.858–60), of an age of war and confusion into one of peace and stability (15.832–9). It was therefore supremely ironical that Augustus should have chosen the moment when the *Metamorphoses* was about to appear before the world to visit its author with disgrace and ruin. It was also ironical that one of the reasons for his downfall was a poem, the *Ars amatoria*. The other reason remains unknown; Ovid calls it an indiscretion (*error*). On the evidence available it cannot be categorically said that Augustus' resentment was unjustified; Ovid indeed, for what that is worth, acknowledges that it was not. The form that it took, on the other hand, was severe to the point of calculated cruelty. Ovid was exiled, or rather relegated (for he was not deprived of citizenship or property), not to one of the usual Mediterranean islands customarily used for this purpose, but to a place on the very edge of the civilized world, where he was cut off from everything that for a man of his temperament made life worth living: friends, the society of the capital, books, the Latin language itself – and above all peace of mind. Spiritually it was a death sentence.

Ovid refused to die. More than once in the poems of exile he alludes to his peculiar gifts, his *ingenium*, as the cause of his destruction;[1] but by the same token they were his only resource in his hour of need:

indignata malis mens est succumbere seque
  praestitit inuictam uiribus usa suis...
ergo quod uiuo durisque laboribus obsto
  nec me sollicitae taedia lucis habent,
gratia, Musa, tibi: nam tu solacia praebes,
  tu curae requies, tu medicina uenis,
tu dux et comes es, tu nos abducis ab Histro
  in medioque mihi das Helicone locum,
tu mihi, quod rarum est, uiuo sublime dedisti
  nomen, ab exequiis quod dare fama solet.

(*Trist.* 4.10.103–4, 115–22)

My mind disdained to sink beneath misfortune and by its own strength showed itself unconquerable... And so the fact that I still live and hold out against affliction, the fact that for all its vexations I am not yet weary of life, this, o Muse, I owe to you. It is you who offer me consolation, you come as rest and medicine to my unhappiness; you are my guide and companion, you carry me away from the Danube and bring me to an honourable seat on Helicon. You have given me what is rarely given, a lofty name while I still live, something that fame is apt to confer only after death.

[1] *Trist.* 2.1–2, 3.3.73–7, *Pont.* 3.5.4.

Ovid was not a philosopher and he did not endure his fate philosophically. His reply to the good advice of his friend Rufinus is, for all its ostensible submission to the lesson of patience, perceptibly ironical (*Pont.* 1.3). So far as he could, he protested, using the one means open to him, his poetry. Augustus was an autocrat, accountable, whatever constitutional fictions might suggest, to none, and his later years were embittered by a series of misfortunes[1] which rendered him increasingly touchy and suspicious and therefore the more prone to arbitrary exercise of his enormous power. It behoved Ovid to be careful; but he had some room for manoeuvre. Augustus clearly wanted him out of the way, but had stopped short of putting him to death, which (as Ovid himself repeatedly insists) he might well have done. If Augustus baulked at the extreme measure, it can only have been through respect for public opinion; in Tomis he must have hoped that Ovid, out of sight, would also be out of mind. To the extent, however, that Ovid had access through his poetry to Roman public opinion, the Princeps might be amenable to pressure. If it was too much to hope for pardon, at least a more tolerable place of exile might be conceded.

Some such reasoning must underlie what may be called the grand strategy of the first and most important part of Ovid's production in exile, the five books of the *Tristia* ('Sorrows'). Form and style were a matter of tactics, but the elegiac form in a manner imposed itself. For Ovid's contemporaries the elegiac couplet was still the vehicle *par excellence* of love-poetry, but it had reputedly originated as a metre of lament. In terms of tone and situation an Ovidian model was to hand in the *Heroides*. But whereas the *Heroides*, like all Ovid's earlier work, dealt in impersonation, in the *Tristia* he was now writing *in propria persona* and with a strictly practical end in view: to keep his name before the public, to ensure that he was not (from Augustus' point of view) conveniently forgotten, and above all to indicate with all the emphasis possible short of outright statement that in consigning, on his own authority, the greatest poet of Rome to a living tomb[2] Augustus had gone too far; that he had indeed, in so far as it was merely temporal, exceeded his authority.

That this was from the first the main aim of the *Tristia* is evident from Book 1, composed on the voyage to Tomis and sent to Rome on arrival. The introductory poem sets the tone. Formally it is a valediction addressed to the book, a device used by Horace in the epilogue (20) to his first book of Epistles. A number of important motifs are broached. The book is an ambassador, sent where the writer may not venture (1–2, 57–8). It is to be discreet, and its appearance must be unkempt, as befits the representative of an exile (3–14). It must not force itself on people (21–6). Above all it must not intrude incontinently upon Augustus (69–86) but must be satisfied for the present to find readers in the public at large (87–8). Later a friend may introduce it at Court

[1] Plin. *N.H.* 7.149–50.

[2] *Trist.* 3.3.53–4, 1.3 *passim*, 1.7.38, 3.14.20, *al.*

(91–8), for there are still some who wish Ovid well (27–34). He has no illusions about the quality of his work, produced in physical and mental distress, but it is not fame that he now seeks (35–56). What he does seek is clear, reconsideration of his case; and the real addressee of the poem, and hence of the book, is Augustus. These are the opening shots in a campaign which Ovid waged with more of both finesse and courage than he has usually been given credit for. His attempt to work on Augustus' feelings relies less on his frequent invocation of the Princeps' famed clemency, celebrated by himself in his *Res gestae* (chh. 3, 34), than on the constantly reiterated implicit appeal over Augustus' head to contemporary public opinion and the verdict of posterity. The appeal harps on two ideas, both illustrated by *Tristia* 1.1: the irresponsible, indeed tyrannical, character of Augustus' authority; and its ultimate inferiority to the power of mind and spirit. This is the ground on which poet and Princeps meet in the *Tristia*, and the moral victory is with the poet.

In warning his book to steer clear of the Palatine Ovid introduces an image that is to become familiar. He dreads the spot because from it was launched the thunderbolt that destroyed him:

> ignoscant augusta mihi loca dique locorum:
> uenit in hoc illa fulmen ab arce caput.
> esse quidem memini mitissima sedibus illis
> numina, sed timui qui nocuere deos...
> uitaret caelum Phaethon, si uiueret, et quos
> optarat stulte, tangere nollet equos.
> me quoque, quae sensi, fateor Iouis arma timere,
> me reor infesto, cum tonat, igne peti. (*Trist.* 1.1.71–4, 79–82)

Without offence to that august place and its gods, it was from that citadel that there fell the bolt on my head. I remember that the Beings who live there are most merciful, but I fear the gods who have done me harm...If Phaethon had lived he would have stayed clear of heaven and would have shrunk from meddling with the team that he had foolishly asked to drive. I admit that I too fear the weapon of Jupiter, having felt it, and whenever it thunders I think that I am the target of the threatening flame.

A reader fresh from the *Metamorphoses* might recall that Phaethon had been in Ovid's version of the story an innocent victim of the thunderbolt, which is described as 'unjustly launched' (*Met.* 2.377–8).[1] The identification of Augustus with Jupiter, often in association with the thunderbolt image, occurs in over thirty of the fifty poems that make up *Tristia* Books 1 and 3–5. The cumulative effect of these allusions is unflattering. In his lifetime the *numen* and *genius* of Augustus received divine honours, but he was not yet officially a god; the

[1] It is possible that our text of the *Metamorphoses* goes back to a copy revised (like the *Fasti*) by Ovid in exile, and that one or two apparently 'prophetic' touches such as this were introduced by him during revision. They are certainly striking, but hardly numerous enough for coincidence to be ruled out.

distinction is carefully observed by the punctilious Horace (*Odes* 3.5.1–4, *Epist.* 2.1.15). In ascribing actual divinity to Augustus, as he had already done more than once in the *Fasti*, Ovid was no doubt voicing a common sentiment. In the *Tristia*, however, the reiteration of the idea, given the writer's situation, was bound to be tinged with bitterness, more especially when it is remembered how often in the *Metamorphoses* divine anger is the prelude to an act of cruelty or injustice. This repeated equation of Augustus with the traditional Jupiter and of his power with the thunderbolt is more critical than complimentary. Ovid's reflections on the character of 'divine' justice are indeed not always merely implicit: in his apologia he observes that the gods punish mistakes just as savagely as crimes:

scilicet in superis etiam fortuna luenda est,
  nec ueniam laeso numine casus habet. (*Trist.* 2.107–8)

Apparently when one is dealing with the gods even ill-luck must be expiated, and when a deity is offended misfortune is not accepted as an excuse.

Recurring variations on these ideas and catalogues of *exempla* illustrating them leave no room for doubt as to what Ovid thought of the way in which he had been treated. The message is clear: he was a victim of tyranny and injustice.

It is not, however, primarily as a citizen wronged before the law or at all events in equity that Ovid presents his case, but in his special quality of poet. This is clearly evident in the elaborate apologia that forms the whole of the second book of the *Tristia*; it is also implicit in the poetry itself, often unjustly belittled by critics, and in the very fact that it was through the public medium of poetry that he chose to appeal. The existence of the *Tristia* was a demonstration that Ovid still counted; that his hat, so to say, was still in the ring. Even a poem that begins by apologizing for the technical deficiencies of his work (*Trist.* 4.1.1–2) will modulate into a more positive strain:

utque suum Bacche non sentit saucia uulnus,
  dum stupet Idaeis exululata modis,
sic ubi mota calent uiridi mea pectora thyrso,
  altior humano spiritus ille malo est;
ille nec exilium Scythici nec litora ponti,
  ille nec iratos sentit habere deos. (*Trist.* 4.1.41–6)

And as a Bacchante though wounded does not know it, so rapt is she while she shrieks in orgiastic strains, so when my spirit has taken fire, struck with the burgeoning thyrsus, it rises above human ills; it does not feel exile or the Scythian shore or the anger of the gods.

A similar apology ushers in Book 5 (5.1.3–4); the promise that follows, to write in a better and happier vein if Augustus will relent (35–46), is another way of bringing moral pressure to bear. It is a fresh reminder that Ovid, as a poet, has been destroyed by what has been done to him. This emphasis on his status as poet is evident from the first: *Tristia* 1.1 ends with what amounts to a reminder of his achievement, in the shape of an enumeration of the books that stand on the shelf ready to welcome the newcomer (105–18). Even in deprecating the *Ars amatoria* he manages to convey a suggestion that there is really nothing to deprecate:

tres procul obscura latitantes parte uidebis:
  sic quoque, *quod nemo nescit*, amare docent.
hos tu uel fugias uel, *si satis oris habebis*,
  Oedipodas facito Telegonosque uoces. (*Trist.* 1.1.111–14)

Three volumes you will see skulking in a dark corner; even there they continue to teach – not that anyone needs the lesson – how to love. Them you should avoid or, if you have the face, make a point of calling them Oedipus or Telegonus [i.e. parricides].

The subsequent reference to the *Metamorphoses* is also glossed: the fate of its author may itself rank as a metamorphosis (119–22). The wit of the paradox – the creator of the poem now part of his own subject matter – reads like a bitter echo of the proem of the *Metamorphoses*; in the context it is sharp and, in the light of the previous characterization of Augustus' power, suggestive. Not only is Ovid's fate cruel, but the writer of such a poem might have expected some better recognition of his achievement than himself to be numbered among the victims of divine anger.

Thus the first poem of the first book of poetry sent home by Ovid after his sentence is, for the most part implicitly but still unambiguously, programmatic. If *Tristia* 1 consists of a series of sighting shots, Book 2 is a full-scale barrage. Ovid here comes as near as anywhere in the *Tristia* to defiance; when he turns from pleading to refutation the tone is almost overtly satirical.[1] He addresses himself to the sense of his cultivated readers, appealing over the head of the powers that be to enlightened public opinion. 'His reply...is a riotous *reductio ad absurdum*, and what is meant to seem absurd is the attitude of the Emperor.'[2] But though the manner of presenting his case may be flippant or sarcastic, his fundamental premiss is absolutely serious. He is saying that the world of poetry is autonomous, a spiritual domain where the writ of temporal rulers does not run. In Book 3 he was to restate this thesis in lines in which Macaulay hailed 'a Miltonic loftiness of sentiment':

singula ne referam, nil non mortale tenemus
  pectoris exceptis ingeniique bonis.
en ego cum caream patria uobisque domoque
  raptaque sint, adimi quae potuere mihi,

[1] Wilkinson (1955) 310; cf. Wiedemann (1975) 268–71. [2] Wilkinson, ibid. 310–11.

ingenio tamen ipse meo comitorque fruorque:
  Caesar in hoc potuit iuris habere nihil.
quilibet hanc saeuo uitam mihi finiat ense,
  me tamen extincto fama superstes erit,
dumque suis uictrix omnem de montibus orbem
  prospiciet domitum Martia Roma, legar. (*Trist.* 3.7.43–52)

In short, all that we possess is mortal except for what mind and spirit confer. Even to me, who have lost my country, my family and my home, from whom has been snatched all that there was to take, my mind is company and pleasure: over that Caesar could have no power. Anyone may put an end to my life by the edge of the sword, but my fame will survive my death, and so long as warlike Rome shall survey the whole world victorious from her hills, I shall be read.

And he was to conclude Book 4 with a pronouncement in the same vein:

siue fauore tuli, siue hanc ego carmine famam,
  iure tibi grates, candide lector, ago. (*Trist.* 4.10.131–2)

Whether it is partiality or merit that has earned me my fame, to you, kind reader, are rightly due the thanks.

To his readers *and to no one else* – so runs the implication – is he beholden. Supposing that Augustus read these poems and took the point, he is unlikely to have been much mollified. The *Tristia* have been criticized as abject; in some respects they show Ovid as bold to the point of foolhardiness.

The individual books of the *Tristia*, like those of the *Amores*, are constructed so as to throw their main themes into relief.[1] Books 3 and 4 begin and end with poems that in one way or another are about Ovid's poetry. *Trist.* 3.1 again uses the book-as-ambassador motif, this time with the book personified and speaking; 3.14 commends his poetry to a friend and apologizes for its quality. *Trist.* 4.1 begins on the same note of apology, to which, after the more positive development previously noted, it returns. A phrase in this concluding section looks forward to the last poem in the book: Ovid records his frustration at the contrast between what he now was and what he had been – *qui sim fuerimque recordor* (99); and what he had been is precisely the theme of 4.10: *qui fuerim... ut noris, accipe, posteritas* (1–2). This latter poem is usually referred to as an autobiography, but it is rather what would now be called a personal statement: what Ovid wished to go on record to allow posterity to judge between him and Augustus. It is therefore highly selective. Ovid attempts to show that, though he had done his duty as best he could by the state and by his family, his first loyalty was to poetry, and that this was not merely a matter of personal preference but an imperative vocation. In a famous (and frequently misinterpreted)[2]

[1] Martini (1933) 52, Froesch (1968) 61–2, Dickinson (1973) 160–1, 175, 180, 183–4.
[2] Stroh (1968).

passage he recalls that he had tried to repudiate the Muses but that their claims were too strong to be denied:

motus eram dictis totoque Helicone relicto
  scribere temptabam uerba soluta modis.
sponte sua carmen numeros ueniebat ad aptos,
  et quod temptabam scribere uersus erat. (*Trist.* 4.10.23–6)

In obedience to my father I abandoned Helicon completely and tried to write prose. Willy-nilly a poem would come in correct metre, and all my attempts to write were verse.

That was the faith by which he had lived and now must die: the word *ergo* ('therefore', 'and so') at l. 115 introduces a final apostrophe to the Muse which culminates in words clearly designed to recall the epilogue to the *Metamorphoses*:

siquid habent igitur uatum praesagia ueri,
  protinus ut moriar, non ero, terra, tuus. (129–30)

So if the prophecies of bards have any truth in them, though I die tomorrow, earth will not claim me as her own.

The traditional symbols and the repeated prediction of posthumous survival enshrine a real certainty that the poet is a channel between the rest of humanity and something greater than himself:

est deus in nobis et sunt commercia caeli;
  sedibus aetheriis spiritus ille uenit. (*Ars Am.* 3.549–50)

There is godhead in poets and we enjoy communion with heaven. Our inspiration comes from on high.

It is inspiration or genius or whatever it is to be called that entitles a poet to honour and consideration. In this he partakes of the immortality otherwise reserved for the gods. So Ovid proclaims his independence of temporal authority and his citizenship of a polity of letters in which it is the judgement of posterity and not the arbitrary sentence of a monarch that determines the fate of a writer.

Such affirmations, placed in commanding positions in their collections, are reinforced by the implications of the other poems. The technique is essentially that of the *Amores*, but now applied in deadly earnest. Ovid must have been deeply aware of the need to avoid monotony in poetry which was designed to keep the public well disposed towards him; now of all times he could not afford to bore his readers. Under the superficial sameness for which he apologizes there is in *Tristia* 1 and 3–5 a considerable diversity of subject matter. Critics have tended to single out the obvious anthology pieces, the poems in which he describes the incidents of his journey (1.2, 10), the place of his exile (3.10, 5.7,

10), or his personal sufferings (1.3, 3.3). These are indeed attractive because immediately appealing, but they do not give a complete or adequate idea of the purpose and nature of Ovid's poetry in exile. In particular the anthologizing approach disguises the extent to which Ovid was, as he himself says, identified with his poetry: *carmina maior imago | sunt mea* (*Trist.* 1.7.11–12). Everything he wrote was in some sense a declaration and made a point: thus the well-known poem on the fate of Absyrtus (*Trist.* 3.9) is a demonstration that something could be made poetically out of even dismal Tomis and a reminder, since in form it is an aetiology, of the literary heritage of Greece and of Ovid's role in its transmission. The storm described in *Trist.* 1.2 no doubt really occurred; but it is in its details the conventional epic storm as Ovid had previously described it in the *Metamorphoses* (11.490–569) and as Ulysses and Aeneas had experienced it in the *Odyssey* and *Aeneid.* Ovid compares himself in this poem (7–12) to these heroes and more than once reverts to the comparison: again the implied paradox that he is now at the mercy of forces which as a poet he had controlled.

To diversity of subject matter is allied diversity of literary artifice. A good example of the allusive and ingenious way in which Ovid manipulates his material, in particular through the exploitation of earlier poetry so as to awaken echoes in the reader's mind, is given by *Trist.* 4.8. It opens with an apparently innocent remark; Ovid is showing the first signs of age:

iam mea cycneas imitantur tempora plumas,
inficit et nigras alba senecta comas. (1–2)

Now my temples imitate the plumage of the swan and the whiteness of old age dyes my black hair.

The image in *cycneas* is especially appropriate to a poet. Swans were associated with Apollo and figure prominently in programmatic contexts.[1] There is here too the suggestion of the swan-song (cf. *Trist.* 5.1.11–14): the poetry Ovid is writing now may be his last. Our reader fresh from the *Metamorphoses* might also recollect that the first of the three persons called Cycnus who are there changed into swans met his fate as a consequence of Phaethon's death by the thunderbolt and that it was in fear of the fire described by Ovid as 'unjustly launched' that the newly-fledged bird flew low. Besides these possible associations, a contemporary reader could hardly fail to be reminded of Horace's symbolical metamorphosis into a swan (*Odes* 2.20). That Ode is a proud boast, Ovid's elegy is a gentle complaint. He too contemplates (perforce) a metamorphosis, but a less romantic one: not a whole suit of feathers but a touch of white plumage at the temples. The image is ironically devalued by the follow-

[1] Callim. *Hymn* 4.252, Theoc. 5.137, Lucret. 3.6–7, 4.180–2, Virg, *Ecl.* 8.56, 9.36.

ing paraphrase;[1] and so far from thinking of flying, Ovid has trouble in walking: *iamque parum firmo me mihi ferre graue est* (4).

There follows (5–12) a conventional description of the pleasures of a peaceful retirement, a generalized image of the settled contentment to which a man may aspire when his life's work is done. For this Ovid had hoped and believed he had earned: the equation of his deserts with his hopes is suggested by the parallel phrasing of the verses (13–14). But though he proposed, the gods disposed:

non ita dis uisum est, qui me terraque marique
actum Sarmaticis exposuere locis. (15–16)

The gods decided otherwise; they have driven me over land and sea and cast me away on the Sarmatian shore.

The reminiscence here is unmistakeable; but the famous half-line of Virgil which Ovid has adapted must be recalled in its context for the innuendo to be clear:

cadit et Rhipeus, iustissimus unus
qui fuit in Teucris et seruantissimus aequi
(dis aliter uisum)... (*Aen.* 2.426–8)

There fell too Rhipeus, who in justice and respect for the right was without peer among the Trojans – but the gods thought otherwise.

'The comment...may show resignation, it may be accusing...it is hard not to hear the accusing note.'[2] Ovid clearly intended to accuse. The adapted tag follows on the words *dignus eram* 'I was worthy' (14), exactly as the original in Virgil followed on the statement of Rhipeus' merits, and the allusion to Virgil deepens the bitterness. This was not the first time that the gods had oppressed a just man. So an English writer steeped in the Bible might allude to Job. The rest of the couplet also glances at Virgil: Ovid's fate is compared to that of Aeneas, who was 'harried by land and sea' (*Aen.* 1.3) – but whereas Aeneas in the end attained a peaceful haven, Ovid is a castaway (*exposuere*).

Next the reflection that to all things comes a time of superannuation, illustrated by a cluster of images (17–24) adapted from Ovid's own earlier treatment of the same commonplace at *Am.* 2.9.19–22:[3] ships, horses, soldiers, gladiators As often in the poems of exile Ovid turns to serious ends imagery that had previously embellished a *jeu d'esprit*. Here the earlier arrangement is changed so as to bring the gladiator into the apodosis of the comparison:

...sic igitur, tarda uires minuente senecta,
me quoque donari iam rude tempus erat. (23–4)

Just so, now that old age is slowing and diminishing my force, it is high time that I was presented with my wooden sword.

[1] The words of l. 2 are borrowed from Propertius (3.5.24).

[2] Austin (1964) 173–4.

[3] Cf. Prop. 2.25.5–8.

The language and the application of the idea to the case of a poet again recall Horace: at the beginning of his first book of *Epistles* he had written of having earned his congé: *spectatum satis et donatum iam rude* (*Epist.* 1.1.2), and had gone on to apply the image of the ageing gladiator quite explicitly to himself. Delicately Ovid is hinting that he, no less than (for instance) Horace, had done honour to poetry and had deserved the sort of retirement that Horace – whether in earnest or jest is no matter – had laid claim to for himself. He rounds off the argument by restating the two themes of retirement, now with specific reference to himself (25–8 ~ 5–12, 29–30 ~ 13–14), and of ruin (35–6 ~ 15–16). With mention of old age as the moment when he might reasonably have expected to be granted his *otium cum dignitate* (29–36) the poem returns to its point of departure.

An emphatic *ergo* ('so then') introduces the final section. These hopes were shattered because Ovid in his folly had offended the man who was the very personification of clemency (37–9). True, he was allowed to live – but at Tomis (40–2). If Delphi and Dodona had foretold his fate he would have disbelieved them, but the moral is clear:

> nil adeo ualidum est, adamas licet alliget illud,
> ut maneat rapido firmius igne Iouis;
> nil ita sublime est supraque pericula tendit,
> non sit ut inferius suppositumque deo.
> nam quamquam uitio pars est contracta malorum,
> plus tamen exitii numinis ira dedit.
> at uos admoniti nostris quoque casibus este
> aequantem superos emeruisse uirum. (45–52)

Nothing is so strong, though adamant bind it, that it can resist the swift fire of Jove; nothing is so high or reaches so far above danger that it is not lower than and subject to god. For although some part of our misfortunes are brought on us by wrong-doing, more destruction is caused by the anger of godhead. But do you be warned by my fate to deserve well of the man who is the equal of those above.

From Jupiter to Augustus the argument moves through a series of variations: from *Iouis* (46), the king of the conventional pantheon, through *deo* (48), 'god', and *numinis* (50), 'godhead', to (52) the man with all the attributes of divinity. Lines 45–8 are bound to recall yet once more the proud affirmation at the end of the *Metamorphoses*:

> iamque opus exegi quod nec Iouis ira nec ignis
> nec poterit ferrum nec edax abolere uetustas. (*Met.* 15.871–2)

In an earlier poem (*Trist.* 1.7) Ovid had implied that in condemning him Augustus had condemned his creation, the *Metamorphoses*, or tried to.[1] Now it seems to be suggested that the condemnation had been effective: that here is

[1] Grisart (1959).

a power before which nothing – not even the traditional immortality of the poet through his works – is secure. There is an especial bitterness in the wording of the final couplet: *emeruisse* connotes time-serving. It is not enough, Ovid is saying, to write good poetry; the poet who wishes himself and his work to survive must keep on the right side of the man who combines the power with the irresponsibility (for such, after the *Metamorphoses*, is the implication of *numinis ira*) of deity.

This is irony and not to be taken literally. The very next poem shows that Ovid had not given up. *Trist.* 4.9 breathes anger and defiance; in it he claims the power, through his poetry, of blasting his correspondent's name for all time to come. The man addressed is not identifiable, and may be a fiction; the message is in effect a retractation of 4.8.45–52, and the cap, were it not for the (detachable) parenthesis of ll. 11–14, fits Augustus better than anyone else. Only here does Ovid attribute to himself (3) the *clementia* which elsewhere in the *Tristia* (cf. especially 4.8.39) is the prerogative of the Emperor. This is not the only poem in which his words can be construed as a threat against Augustus. In his prayer to Bacchus at *Trist.* 5.3.35–46 the references to the mythical figures of Lycurgus and Pentheus are pointed. These were kings who offended the god who protects poets and were in consequence destroyed. What Ovid dwells on, however, is not their deaths but their posthumous infamy, which is contrasted with the eternal glory reserved for those who deserve well of Bacchus. The corollary is the unspoken question: is Augustus to figure in their company?

It has proved unfortunate for Ovid's reputation that his fight to rehabilitate himself and his poetry had on his side to be conducted with the gloves on. The stakes were enormous, indeed incalculable: not merely his own existence and poetical identity, but the freedom of the artist to express what the gods have given him to express. Such momentous ideas could only be suggested through the techniques of literary allusion[1] and the significant placing of poems intended to be read in contrast or complement to each other: *Trist.* 4.8–10 is a striking example of such a group. This is to demand a good deal of the reader, and even Ovid's more sympathetic critics have preferred to dwell on the human interest – great but essentially incidental – of the *Tristia* to the neglect of the qualities which are fundamental to their message. In writing these poems Ovid's aim was not to crystallize personal experience or communicate a sense of suffering, though it may on occasion suit him to represent his poetry as a mere reflex, a cry of pain. His will to write and the nature of what he chose to write are the index of a moral strength in him for which self-respect is too weak a term. It is bound up with his consciousness of identity as a poet. Seen in this

[1] A particularly poignant instance at *Trist.* 1.3: Ovid's description of his last night in Rome is presented in terms intended to recall Aeneas' last night in Troy as narrated by Virgil in *Aeneid* 2.

light the *Tristia* are as characteristic of him as anything he ever wrote, and do him as much credit.

The criticisms which have been directed against Ovid's exile poetry as 'abject' or the like[1] apply with much more force to the *Epistulae ex Ponto* ('Letters from the Black Sea') than to the *Tristia*. Formally they differ from the *Tristia* only in being called letters and in naming the addressees (*Pont.* 1.1.17–18); and they do not suggest that his poetical powers had completely deserted him. There is probably less artifice in the arrangement of the poems in their books,[2] but literary associations are still, as in the *Tristia*, exploited in new and ingenious ways to reinforce the continual appeal.[3] A poem such as *Pont.* 3.1 shows Ovid consciously using the poetical implications of his situation: his own case ranks as an *exemplum* in the canonical lists (49–56). Such passages, however, are rarer than they are in the *Tristia*, and in general the *Epistulae ex Ponto* are less forceful; indignation is succeeded by resignation, even apathy. The allusions lack the edge of irony and the tone is predominantly pathetic. At his best in these poems Ovid is moving because simple and dignified; a poem such as *Pont.* 3.7 depends for its effect on directness of acceptance and statement. He has nothing more to say, and will cease to pester his friends and his wife for help. He will bow to the inevitable and resign himself, if Augustus allows (here, however, a note of rather tired irony is allowed to intrude), to dying steadfastly as an exile:

dummodo non nobis hoc Caesaris ira negarit,
fortiter Euxinis immoriemur aquis. (*Pont.* 3.7.39–40)

In this poem Ovid has finally arrived, it would appear, at that philosophy of fortitude in adversity which some of his critics, such as Macaulay, would have had him robustly profess from the start. The lesson went against the grain and was in the end forced upon him by sickness, age, and despair. These are the accents of a broken man, as we hear them again at the end of the poem which the unknown redactor of the posthumous Book 4 chose to place last in that book:

omnia perdidimus: tantummodo uita relicta est,
praebeat ut sensum materiamque mali.
quid iuuat extinctos ferrum demittere in artus?
non habet in nobis iam noua plaga locum. (*Pont.* 4.16.49–52)

I have lost everything; only life itself remains to provide material for and consciousness of suffering. What is the use of plunging a sword into a body already dead? There is no longer any room in me for a fresh wound.

[1] Cf. Wilkinson (1955) 347, Otis (1966) 339. Before assenting to such judgements a critic would do well to ponder the words of Johnson: 'Those are no proper judges of his conduct who have slumbered away their time on the down of plenty, nor will any wise man presume to say, "Had I been in Savage's condition, I should have lived or written better than Savage."'

[2] But cf. Froesch (1968).

[3] E.g. *Pont.* 3.3; cf. Kenney (1965) 44–8.

The choice was apt in more ways than one, for the body of the poem consists of a catalogue of contemporary poets; and it is in this context that Ovid, for the last time, assesses his own achievements:

dicere si fas est, claro mea nomine Musa
atque inter tantos quae legeretur erat. (*Pont.* 4.16.45–6)

If it is allowable to say so, my poetry was of good repute and worthy to be read in this company.

It is these dignified and restrained lines, rather than the final despairing outburst which may best serve as epigraph for the *Tristia* and *Epistulae ex Ponto*. As a modern English poet has said: 'The only effective answer that a poet can make to barbarism is poetry, for the only answer to death is the life of the spirit.'[1]

During his first years at Tomis Ovid had written one poem in something like his old vein, though novelly motivated, the *Ibis*. This is a curse, imprecating on an unidentified enemy some scores of gruesome and mutually incompatible fates as suffered by various mythical and historical characters. His motives for writing the work were literary rather than personal. Callimachus had written an attack on Apollonius of Rhodes and called it *Ibis*; but Ovid probably took little from Callimachus except the original idea, the metre, and the riddling language. Invective was almost a minor genre in its own right, and Ovid's misfortunes must have given him the idea of showing what he could do in this department, if only – supposing, as seems most likely, that 'Ibis' was not a real person[2] – by way of notifying the world that with a pen in his hand he was still to be reckoned with. It is almost impossible to take the *Ibis* at its face value. The undertaking was in any case out of character for Ovid, as he begins by stressing: hitherto his poetry had harmed nobody but himself (1–8). For his catalogue of unenviable deaths, which occupies nearly 400 of a total of 642 verses, he had combed the highways and byways of the learned tradition, and the expression is often as obscure as the sources. Everything suggests that the *Ibis* is intended as a practical demonstration of the *doctus poeta* in action. Ovid had few books at Tomis; the material was probably for the most part in his head or his notebooks at the time of his exile. He must have read enormously in preparation for the *Metamorphoses* and the *Fasti*; here was an opportunity to turn to account a surplus that would otherwise have been wasted. As a technical *tour de force* the *Ibis* has a limited appeal to the modern reader, but for the contemporary public it was another reminder of Ovid's poetic status. Augustan literary history can be viewed (in part at all events) as a process of coming to terms with Callimachus and what he was thought to stand for. In comparison with Callimachus' *Ibis*, which Ovid calls a little book (*Ibis* 447),

[1] Sassoon (1945) 193.
[2] Housman (1972) 1040.

Ovid's was a much more ambitious undertaking. Here was exemplified in yet another genre the prodigious fertility, exuberance and versatility of his genius. In a sense the *Ibis* rather than the *Epistulae ex Ponto* should be reckoned as his swan-song.

6. ACHIEVEMENT AND CHARACTERISTICS

For an epitome of Ovid's poetical career one need look no further than to the opening words of the *Metamorphoses* previously discussed: *In noua fert animus*. Every one of his surviving works represents a new literary departure, an unpredictable and individual variation on inherited themes and techniques. Originality in this sense was of course what the Roman public expected of its poets, and it was not peculiar to Ovid; none exemplifies it with greater brilliance and versatility. In the technical sphere he left a mark on the Latin poetic tradition that still endures: for the modern composer of elegiac couplets is normally expected to abide by the Ovidian 'rules'. The Augustan rejection of the metrical freedoms enjoyed by Catullus was not arbitrarily motivated but dictated by the phonetic realities of the Latin language; however, Ovid seems almost to have gone out of his way to accentuate the inherent limitations of the couplet form. Thus he not only avoids enjambment between couplets,[1] but in securing the obligatory disyllable at the end of the pentameter[2] he often resorts to the use of colourless words in this position.[3] The effect, by throwing the verbal interest back into the body of the verse, is to make each couplet even more autonomous than its metrical nature already dictates: and Ovid further accentuates this tendency by his distinctively antiphonal treatment of hexameter and pentameter. For the crisp epigrammatic strokes of wit appropriate to the *Amores* and *Ars amatoria* this was an ideal medium; only Pope, using a broadly comparable type of verse, has excelled him in such writing. For the more ample effects aimed at in the *Heroides* elegiacs are less satisfactory; the double epistles especially, for all their undoubted merits, are often diffuse, and the fact has something to do with the verse medium. It was in the management of the hexameter that Ovid's dexterity in the manipulation of language enjoyed full play. Epic called for a kind of expressiveness inappropriate in elegy, and Ovid's ingenuity in coining words and varying diction and syntax, tempo and stylistic coloration to suit the demands of his narrative came into its own in the *Metamorphoses*.

The influence of his technical achievements may be clearly traced in subsequent Latin poetry. Of later composers in elegiacs one only is a major artist, Martial. If anything he is even more accomplished than Ovid, but that verdict

[1] True enjambment is very rare in Ovid's elegiacs: Platnauer (1951) 33 finds two examples in the entire corpus.

[2] Breaches of this 'rule', nearly all in the poems of exile, are few: Platnauer (1951) 15–17.

[3] Axelson (1958).

must be heavily qualified. The epigrammatist's square of ivory is a very small one, and technical perfection is correspondingly easier to compass; and after all the trail had already been blazed by Ovid. In epic the debt to Ovid's hexameter is less obvious but quite pervasive and extremely important. In the verse of the *Metamorphoses* he had perfected what may be called a poetic *koine*, an omnicompetent dialect of literary Latin. His verse, like Virgil's, was carefully tailored for the work in hand;[1] unlike Virgil's, however, his style is (to a degree) imitable. This is because his linguistic manipulations are of a kind that can be classified and even learned. He takes liberties with Latin, but they are, as Virgil's are not, the sort of liberties that any poet might take once he had thought of them for himself. He is very much a craftsman, *poeta* in the full sense of the original ποιητής, a maker. The technical differences between Ovid and Virgil are a function of both temperament and aims. Virgil is ambiguous and ambivalent where Ovid is definite; Ovid said only what he had the means of expressing, whereas for Virgil the resources of language – the prose of Henry James being as yet in the womb of time – were clearly insufficient to convey all that he felt of the conflicts and uncertainties of the human condition. The strain shows: Virgil's commentators inconclusively dispute the meaning of a word or phrase as Ovid's hardly ever need to do. Thus the only epic poet of the Silver Age who aspired to close stylistic imitation of Virgil, Valerius Flaccus, merely succeeded in being obscure. Into this trap Lucan and Statius, even (to some extent) Silius Italicus, were too prudent to fall. Statius professed to follow Virgil, but his style owes much more to Ovid.[2] Lucan and Silius are fundamentally more Virgilian than Statius: Silius simply and avowedly so, Lucan as the poet of an epic that is, so to say, programmatically anti-Virgilian and that must be read as in a sense an answer to the *Aeneid*. Both write hexameters that resemble Ovid's much more than Virgil's. Neither could possibly be mistaken for Ovid: but whereas Lucan's verse atones in weight and dignity for what it lacks in speed and variety, Silius' is at best drearily efficient. Outside the epic tradition Ovid also left his mark on Juvenal, the best poetic craftsman (at his best) of the Silver Age.

Both in spirit and execution the most Ovidian of later Latin poets is Claudian, whose native tongue was Greek. The fact invites remark, since so much of Ovid's best work, above all the *Metamorphoses*, is Greek in matter, in manner, and even in versification.[3] For the Romans the legacy of Greek culture was a persistent problem with which in the end they never really came to terms. Virgil and Horace took the process of assimilation begun (essentially) by Ennius a stage further; Ovid, if he did not actually deflect the current, struck out a course of his own. In the *Aeneid* Greek and Roman elements were blended

[1] Kenney (1973).
[2] Vessey (1973) 11.
[3] Duckworth (1969) 73.

in a new and timeless synthesis; in the *Metamorphoses* Greek myth is translated and transposed into a contemporary idiom. The two poems demand from the reader a fundamentally different response. Without firsthand knowledge of (at least) Homer innumerable and essential resonances and implications in the *Aeneid* will simply be missed. The reader of the *Metamorphoses*, though he may relish in passing the contrast between Ovid's sources (if he chance to recognize them) and what Ovid made of them, does not depend on such recognition for the understanding and enjoyment of the poem. In this sense the *Metamorphoses* is more autonomous and more universal than the *Aeneid*; Ovid has rendered his models (almost) expendable. It is here that Ovid stands in truth between two worlds: his response to the riches of the Greek poetic imagination bore fruit, paradoxically, in a self-sufficient work of art that could serve, and in the Middle Ages perforce did serve, as a substitute for direct access.

This is the most important respect in which Ovid is 'un-Augustan'. A man of his sceptical and rationalist disposition growing up in the generation after Actium was bound, it might be surmised, to react against the Augustan 'myth' which was developing at this time and which depended heavily on an implicit and of course highly selective appeal to the authority of the past. Overt resistance is hardly to be detected in his work on any significant scale before the *Tristia*; the pin-pricks administered to official pomposity in the *Ars amatoria*[1] are hardly sufficient to identify its author as a dissident. So far as his poetry is concerned his reaction took the form of simply going his own way, which was the way of a poet to whom what mattered were individual human beings. It is this confidence in his fellow creatures, expressed with an exuberance and gaiety to which extant Latin literature offers no counterpart, that has chiefly recommended Ovid to the posterity on the ultimate rightness of whose judgement he has told us that he relied.

[1] Rudd (1976) 13–29; but cf. Holleman (1971).

22

LIVY

Internal evidence suggests that Livy began to write his History of Rome in or shortly before 29 B.C. by which time Octavian, the later Augustus, had restored peace and a measure of stability to the Roman world. A note in the *periocha* of Book 121 records that that book (and presumably those which followed) was published (*editus*) after Augustus' death in A.D. 14. The implication is that the last twenty books dealing with the events from the Battle of Actium until 9 B.C. were an afterthought to the original plan and may also have been too politically controversial to be published in Augustus' lifetime.

The sheer scope of the undertaking is formidable, presupposing, as it does, the composition of three books a year on average. The introductions, especially to Books 6, 21 and 31, show that Livy began by composing and publishing in units of five books, the length of which was determined by the size of the ancient papyrus roll. As his material became more complex, this symmetrical pattern is less self-evident but it is likely that he maintained it. So far as can be reconstructed, the shape of the history was as follows (the lost books being in brackets).

1–5 From the foundation of the city until the sack of Rome by the Gauls (386 B.C.)
6–10 The Samnite Wars
[11–15 The conquest of Italy
16–20 The First Carthaginian War]
21–30 The Second Carthaginian War (until 201 B.C.)
31–45 Events until the end of the war with Perseus (167 B.C.)
[46–50 The final subjugation of Greece and Asia
51–60 Internal affairs from the fall of Carthage to the legislation of C. Gracchus
61–70 The thirty years between Gracchus and M. Livius Drusus
71–80 Civil Wars until the death of Marius (86 B.C.)
81–90 Civil Wars until the death of Sulla (78 B.C.)
91–100 The rise of Pompey to 66 B.C.
101–110 The dominance of Pompey
111–120 Civil War: from the death of Pompey to the death of Cicero (43 B.C.)

The final 22 books (perhaps unfinished on his death) comprised an appendix on contemporary events which was presumably not planned when he embarked on the main history.]

Historical activity had flourished at Rome for 200 years before Livy and the project of writing the complete history of the state was not a new one. But unlike his predecessors Livy was not a public figure. Whereas Q. Fabius Pictor, the elder Cato, L. Calpurnius Piso, C. Licinius Macer or Sallust himself had all been active in politics, Livy, so far as we know, held no office and took no part in affairs. This had certain consequences. His exclusion from the Senate and the magistracies meant that he had no personal experience of how the Roman government worked and this ignorance shows itself from time to time in his work (as at 1.32.12, or 3.40.5). It also deprived him of first-hand access to much material (minutes of Senate-meetings, texts of treaties, laws, the records of the priestly colleges, etc.) which was preserved in official quarters. But the chief effect is that Livy did not seek historical explanations in political terms. For others history was a political study, through which one might hope to explain or excuse the past and the present, but Livy saw history in personal and moral terms. The purpose is clearly set out in his Preface:

> I invite the reader's attention to the much more serious consideration of the kind of lives our ancestors lived, who were the men and what the means, both in politics and war, by which Rome's power was first acquired and subsequently expanded: I would then have him trace the process of our moral decline, to watch first the sinking of the foundations of mortality as the old teaching was allowed to lapse, then the final collapse of the whole edifice, and the dark dawning of our modern day when we can neither endure our vices nor face the remedies needed to cure them. The study of history is a fruitful medicine; for in history you have a record of the infinite variety of human experience plainly set out for all to see: and in that record you can find for yourself and your country both examples and warnings.

Livy was, indeed, acquainted with Augustus (Tacitus, *Annals* 4.34), who called him a Pompeian, which implied a conservative independence of outlook (Seneca, *Contr.* 10 *praef.* 5), and he acted as literary adviser to the future emperor Claudius (Suetonius, *Claudius* 41.1), but it is impossible to trace political motives in his writing. There is no sign of his attempting to justify, or to attack, the policies and aims of Augustus, although like any other creative writer, he does reflect to some extent contemporary preoccupations, such as the desire for peace, stability and liberty.

Although Sallust and earlier historians had also adopted the outlook that morality was in steady decline and had argued that people do the sort of things that they do because they are the sort of people that they are, that is, have the moral character that they have, for Livy these beliefs were a matter of passionate concern. He saw history in terms of human personalities and representative individuals rather than of partisan politics. And his own experience, going back perhaps to his youth in Padua, made him feel the moral evils of his time with peculiar intensity; for, like most Roman men of letters, he was a provincial and retained something of a provincial austerity in his attitude to life. He punctuates his history with such revealing comments as 'fortunately in those days authority, both religious and secular, was still a guide to conduct and there was as yet no sign of our modern scepticism which interprets solemn compacts to suit its own convenience' (3.20.5). Yet his attitude to religion is ambivalent. On the one hand he stresses, as in the history of Camillus, the importance of *pietas* and attributes disasters, such as the defeat of the Fabii at Cremera, to religious neglect. On the other, he frequently rationalizes miracles (e.g. the apotheosis of Romulus) and is sceptical about divine intervention in human affairs. Such a contradiction was not uncommon among educated Romans of his day: Caesar and Cicero showed it. But certainly, for Livy, human nature, not divinity, determines the course of human events.

In interpreting history in terms of individuals, Livy was following very much in the Hellenistic tradition. It goes back at least to Theopompus who, in his *Philippika*, organized his account of contemporary events round the person of Philip of Macedon. This was the approach even of Aristotle who defined history as being concerned with 'what Achilles did or suffered' (*Poet.* 1451b10), that is, with the particular doings of individuals, and we can presume that this was the character of the lost works by historians such as Ephorus and, later, Duris and Phylarchus. Interest in human character was predominant, as much in works such as Aristotle's *Nicomachean Ethics* or Theophrastus' *Characters* as in the biographies or biographical encomia which were a feature of the fourth and third centuries. But although Aristotle sharply differentiated drama from history, it was inevitable that some of his dramatic theory should be applicable to more general literary composition. There is no evidence that his successors developed a special Peripatetic or 'tragic' mode of writing history any more than they 'invented' biography, but Hellenistic historians do seem increasingly to have reworked their material in order to dramatize the individual.

Such an approach inevitably conditioned his historical technique. There was a wide range of source material at his disposal: the antiquarian researches of Atticus, Cicero's friend and correspondent, or M. Terentius Varro, whose *Human and divine antiquities* had been published perhaps in 46 B.C. And even if he did not have access to some documents, there were many manuscripts and inscriptions in Rome for all to see. Livy, by his own confession, did not explore such resources. His mission, as he saw it, was not to collect material – that was for the composer of *commentarii* – but to produce creative writing. So it should be no surprise that he shows no knowledge of Atticus or Varro, that he did not inspect the surviving inscriptions in the temples of Jupiter Feretrius (4.20) or Diana on the Aventine (1.45) or in the Comitium (4.17.2). Nor, if the careful analysis of scholars can be trusted, did he critically assess the historical accounts which were already at his disposal. He was content to have as a basis a narrative which he could elaborate and write up. What his practice was when dealing with contemporary history we are sadly unable to know, but with earlier history, certainly down to 100 B.C., he selected the more recent historians and simply reshaped and rewrote their material. For the very early period he seems to have relied on two main authors, Valerius Antias and C. Licinius Macer, who wrote in the aftermath of the Civil Wars of the 80s and interpreted earlier history in the light of their conflicting standpoints at the time. Antias was a political supporter of Sulla, Macer of Marius: both wrote history to justify and explain the present. Despite the fact that our knowledge derives only from fortuitous fragments, we can reconstruct the scale and character of their works. In the period of the mid-Republic he had Polybius to consult and, although for an educated Roman, who might be expected to be bilingual, he was demonstrably deficient in his knowledge of Greek, he made the fullest use of Polybius and we can in several passages make a detailed assessment of how he adapted and transformed him. This is of incalculable value in trying to view his own contribution to the composition of history. Polybius, as a Greek, was primarily interested in Graeco-Roman relations but Livy was able to turn to Antias and to two other Latin historians of the Sullan age, L. Coelius Antipater and Q. Claudius Quadrigarius, for the raw material of Italian and western events.

His method was to follow one historian for a section, largely working from memory, and to switch to another when a particular theme had been exhausted. As an intelligent man he was indeed aware of the conflicts between his sources, and also of their individual prejudices, but he did not regard it as necessary or possible to unravel such discrepancies. A typical comment is (4.23.3): 'When so much is veiled in antiquity this fact also may remain uncertain.'

Given, therefore, the assumption that the most important thing about history is that people have a certain inherited personality (*ingenium*, cf. 3.36.1; Ap. Claudius) which determines their actions and that a historian can, even when the specific evidence is lacking, infer how someone of a certain character would have behaved in any given set of circumstances, Livy's aim was to construct a meaningful series of scenes. To understand how he does this it is necessary to remember that he, like his contemporaries, had been educated along almost exclusively rhetorical lines. That education involved learning how to compose a speech (whether forensic or merely ceremonial) and a major stage in any such speech was the essential business of expounding in the simplest possible terms the basic facts that led up to the present situation. The *narratio*, as it was called, is analysed by all the leading exponents of rhetorical training (e.g. *De inventione* 1.28; Cicero, *Orator* 122) and is perfected in such speeches as Cicero's *Pro Archia* (4–7). The requirements were three. A *narratio* should be brief (*breuis*), that is, it should not go into unnecessary preliminaries or diversions. It should be lucid (*aperta*), that is, it should be factually and chronologically coherent, even if this entailed the suppression or revision of some of the evidence. Above all, it should be plausible (*probabilis*), that is in particular the facts should be adjusted to the natures of the actors involved (*ad naturam eorum qui agent accommodabitur*). The whole technique, as has been indicated above, stems from the observations which Aristotle made in the *Poetics* about the necessary and sufficient qualities of a good plot in tragedy. Indeed Aristotle even went so far as to say that 'one could praise someone for doing something, even if there were no evidence, if he were the kind of person who might have done it' (*Rhet.* 1367).

It was this rhetorical background which enabled Livy, both on a practical level, to cope with the great undifferentiated mass of Roman historical happenings and, philosophically speaking, to make sense of it. The genre required of him that he should preserve to a large extent the annalistic framework, according to which, as in a chronicle, the events of every year were recorded, even down to the trivialities of prodigies and minor elections, but from these he selected certain topics which were inherently significant. In early Republican history this was relatively easy. Events were of a sufficiently short compass to form self-contained units in themselves. But even here Livy displayed his art of creating coherent episodes that revealed the character of the participants. Coriolanus, for instance, conducted his campaign against Rome over a number of years and led at least two separate expeditions against the walls of the city. In Livy's account two complete consular years are simply omitted and the two distinct expeditions are combined with an arbitrariness that makes as much geographical nonsense of the whole resulting narrative (2.33–40) as the two quite different routes combined for Hannibal's crossing of the Alps (21.31–7). But that narrative is, for the reader, brief, lucid and plausible, and, therefore, as a work of art, carries its own conviction. When Livy came on to deal with more extended episodes, such as the Hannibalic and Macedonian wars, the problem was on a very much greater scale. Yet, even so, one can see his instinct at work in shaping the material into manageable units, such as the siege of Abydus in 200 B.C. (31.17–18). One unifying factor in this process was to single out the special quality of the protagonist. Thus his account of the reign of Tullus Hostilius centres on the king' *ferocia* (a word which, with its derivatives, occurs nine times in as many chapters) and the events are tailored to bring out that characteristic. So Camillus is built up as an example of *pietas*; an undistinguished soldier, Tempanius, as an example as much of moderation as of bravery (4.40–1); Hannibal, as a model of perfidy and impetuosity; or Flamininus, as Polybius' very different picture of him makes very clear, as a sympathetic and philhellene man of action. On a less personal scale, the siege of Abydus is told in terms of madness (*rabies*, a word which occurs three times in Livy's account and for which there is no prompting in his source, Polybius). History was, for Livy, a psychological record.

One extended example will illustrate the technique. Livy 3.1–8 deals with a series of minor wars against the Aequi and Volsci, spread over five years. In themselves they are of no great significance. They are typical of the aimless happenings (γενόμενα) which Aristotle scorned as the raw material of history: they do not comprise an action, they are not a plot, they have no coherence, no end. Dionysius of Halicarnassus (9.58–71) relates the same facts from the same, or very similar, sources and a comparison between the two authors shows how Livy has handled the problem. In the first place he has concentrated on two basic themes – Rome's external relations both with the Aequi and Volsci and with her allies, and Rome's internal difficulties (e.g. plague, unrest) which affect those relations. As a result he omits a number of irrelevant details to be found in Dionysius: Aemilius' abortive invasion of Sabine land, Servilius' activities in 466 B.C., the dedication of the temple of Semo Sancus Dius Fidius, the fighting on the ramparts, the description of the walls of Rome, the abortive proposals of Sex. Titius. Secondly he tries to secure a natural and logical flow in the narrative so that each event seems to be motivated by its predecessor. One way of achieving this was to make one individual, Q. Fabius, responsible for much of the initiative. In Dionysius it is the Senate, in Livy Fabius who proposes the colony at Antium: in Dionysius it is the Senate, in Livy Fabius who offers peace-negotiations to the Aequi. In Dionysius the unrest at Antium in 464 B.C. is quite unmotivated: Livy attributes it to the Aequi and Volsci stirring up feeling among the former inhabitants who have been dispossessed by the colony. Unlike Dionysius, Livy makes the plague the direct cause of the Roman inability to help their allies, and transfers the account of the combined attack by Aequi and Volsci on Tusculum from 462 to 463 B.C. in order to simplify and smooth the chain of events in 462 B.C. These are all small points: collectively they bring order out of chaos. But even in the details Livy is at pains to make the narrative coherent. Dionysius made the Romans retreat in 465 B.C. because their swords were blunt – a charming detail, but improbable, and omitted by Livy. Dionysius asserts that in 463 B.C., when the plague was at its height, the allies arrived to ask for help from the Senate on the very day that the consul died and the senators were carried into the senate-house on stretchers. That is too melodramatic for Livy's purpose. Finally Livy unites all the events of these five years by a common thread – the clemency (*clementia*) and good faith (*fides*) of the Romans (3.2.5, 6.5, 7.4, 7.5) against the treachery (*perfidia*) and vindictiveness (*odium*) of the Aequi and Volsci (3.2.4, 2.6, 2.12, 7.1). These moral overtones are not in Dionysius and they serve to give the whole section unity and significance. Livy pays the highest attention to the literary structure of each episode and this determines his selection and emphasis of the details.

But the enormous field of history which he had set himself to cover raised further problems. How was the interest of the reader to be sustained over all 142 books? Quintilian characterized his style as possessing a 'milky richness' (10.1.32, *lactea ubertas*) which might be thought to imply the measured pace of a Gibbon, but, in fact, Livy is remarkable for the extreme range of styles which he uses in his narrative in order to achieve variety. At one moment, when recounting essentially perfunctory details he will use a matter-of-fact style, with stock vocabulary and the minimum of syntactical subordination. A major episode, such as the battle of Cannae, Trasimene or Cynoscephalae, will have its own unity. There will be the indication of a temporal break (e.g. *sub idem forte tempus* 'about the same time') and a summary of the scene and thc actors (e.g. 2.31.5 *erat tum inter castra iuuenis Cn. Marcius nomine* 'there was in the camp at the time a young man called Cn. Marcius'). Then will follow a series of complicated sentences which set out the preliminary dispositions, often with participial clauses explaining the motives and thoughts of the chief figures. The action will be described in the stereotyped language of a military communiqué (especially the use of the impersonal passive) or short, staccato sentences, employing the historic infinitive or historic present. Finally, in describing the climax or its aftermath, Livy will allow his language to be coloured with words which (such was the particularity of the Latin stylistic tradition) could normally only have been used in heroic poetry. A terse comment – *haec eo anno acta* 'this happened that year' – will round off the episode. By this variation Livy was able to convey an impression not only of the military facts but also of the emotional experience of the participants.

Livy's language has been much studied and the publication of a complete *Concordance*[1] has opened new doors for the appreciation of his verbal sensitivity, such as, for example, the realization that he uses the exclamation '*o*' only once in the surviving books, in the solemn reply of the Delphic oracle to Brutus and the Tarquins (1.56.10). If Livy's concern was to see history as the literary embodiment of individuals, then his success depended to a very large extent on making those historical characters come alive and sound authentic. Earlier historians – Thucydides, Xenophon, Philistus – had been criticized for putting speeches into the mouths of their leading characters which did not truly bring out their individuality (Dionysius of Halicarnassus, *ad Pomp.* 3.20 *et al.*), but Livy, as he himself says, was able to enter into the spirit of his characters (43.13.2 *mihi uetustas res scribenti nescio quo pacto antiquus fit animus*). The climax of any episode is often a passage of direct or indirect speech, which characterizes the chief actor. In the passage analysed above (Livy 3.1–8) one of the high-

[1] Packard (1968).

lights occurs when the Aequi taunt the Romans with being cowards. The speaker uses *ne* with the imperative for a prohibition (*ne timete* 'be not a-feared'), an archaic and poetical usage. He also strengthens a common taunt (*ostendere bellum* 'to make a show of fighting') by substituting the much rarer and more forceful frequentative *ostentare*. The effect is subtle and suggestive. Sometimes the idiom will be coarse and colloquial if the speakers are lower-class. Again, a rough citizen from Aricia, Turnus Herdonius, who was described by Livy as a seditious criminal (1.50.7 *seditiosus facinerosusque homo*) inveighs against Tarquinius Superbus in a bitter repartee which includes the word *infortunium* 'hard luck', not found elsewhere in classical prose authors but common in the slave-talk of Plautus and Terence. Or some embittered tribunes of the people complain that the patricians thwart their ambitions at every turn (4.35.5–11) using several expressions found also only in colloquial context (e.g. *sugillari* 'to rebuff', *praebere os* 'to expose oneself to'). Sometimes when the occasion is one of high drama Livy will allow his speakers to use language more associated with poetry than prose. Thus the climax of the story of Coriolanus is the great scene with his mother at the gates of Rome. She speaks to him, as Jocasta to her sons in Greek tragedy, and her speech contains several unique features which stamp it as tragic (2.40.5–7): *sino* 'I allow' with the subjunctive rather than the accusative and infinitive, *quamuis* 'although' with the indicative (only here in Livy), the rare *senecta* for *senectus* 'old age', the phrase *ira cecidit* 'anger subsided' found elsewhere only in the poets.

As he moved on to history of more recent times, Livy, inevitably, did not characterize his speakers quite so graphically. In consequence there has been thought to be a development away from the highly coloured vocabulary of the speeches of Books 1–10. But this does not reflect any fundamental change of style. It is simply that the protagonists of the late third century were nearer in time to Livy and he made them speak more like orators of his own day. Indeed some of their actual speeches, such as Cato's *On the Rhodians*, survived and were on hand to be utilized. Nevertheless Livy, at least in the surviving books, maintained his practice of using speeches to bring out the character of the actors. A good example of this is the interchange between Philip and M. Aemilius over the siege of Abydus (31.18.2–3). Polybius preserves a version of their conversation but Livy rewrites it in more powerful language, which gives a grandeur to Philip that was lacking in the original, and makes it the turning-point of the episode. Philip's brief words contain a striking *tricolon*, two notable clausulae (*ferociorem facit*, *sentietis*), two effective alliterations (*ferociorem facit*, *nomen...nobile*) and a dramatic use of the present tense instead of the future in a future conditional clause. One can *hear* him speak. In fact detailed research into Livy's latinity in recent years makes it evident that, as far as we can tell from the surviving portions of his work, he continued both to pay special attention to the language of speeches and to employ more generally a vocabulary that was appropriate to the genre of historical writing, as Coelius Antipater and Sallust had sophisticated it. Such a vocabulary was bound, from the nature of the subject matter, to contain its fair share of archaic or unusual words.

Livy was criticized stylistically by a contemporary for his '*Patauinitas*' (Paduanness: Quint. *Inst.* 1.5.56, 8.1.3). The point of the criticism eludes us, but perhaps it did concern his use of such wide-ranging vocabulary in his speeches. Certainly no other Roman historian was so inventive.

23
MINOR FIGURES

I. POETRY

The poetic output of Augustan times was prolific. Sadly, however, we have lost the works of several important figures – Varius, Aemilius Macer, Valgius Rufus, Domitius Marsus. Our evidence for them is poor, their fragments scanty or lacking. Nonetheless we can see that the genres were well subscribed, and of some we have considerable remains. In didactic, we have the works of Grattius and Manilius; for the minor Alexandrian forms, we can point to the *Appendix Vergiliana.* Horace, especially in his hexameter works, tells us a certain amount about the literary scene – about Fundanius, Titius and Iullus Antonius for instance – and Virgil's *Eclogues* help to reconstruct the literary atmosphere of the triumviral period, when the work of Calvus and Cinna was still in vogue, and new poets like Varius and Pollio were emerging. For later times, when the flush of enthusiasm for experiment had died away, leaving openings for reversion, or else a pale and standardized reflection of the poetics of Callimachus, our evidence is the poetry of Ovid's exile, which often gives us little more than names, but at least serves to show that verse was not in short supply at Rome. Several writers attempted more than one literary form; but in what follows, the attempt has been made as far as possible to group authors according to genre. First of all, the *Appendix Vergiliana* and other minor forms are discussed, especially epigram and elegy; then didactic, mythological epic and tragedy, other drama, and finally historical epic.

First then, the minor poems attributed to Virgil, the so-called *Appendix Vergiliana.* Donatus, probably drawing on Suetonius, attributed a *Dirae*, Servius and Charisius, a *Copa*: but we have to wait until the ninth century before we hear of a *Moretum.* All three works (four in fact; the *Dirae*, a series of curses, is succeeded at line 103 by an independent love lament, the *Lydia*) look like productions of the Augustan age: none of them pretends to be by Virgil. A realistic vignette of country life, the *Moretum*, like most of the poems in the collection, is an example of later Roman Alexandrianism. Its subject allies it to compositions such as Callimachus' *Hecale*, where the poet recounted Theseus' humble entertainment in the house of an old woman; Ovid's Philemon and Baucis episode in *Metamorphoses* Book 8 is of the same type.[1] Its style is patchwork, but accomplished, sometimes self-consciously prosaic and circumstantial, sometimes mock-heroic and poetic: above all, it has movement. The main affinity is with pastoral, but not that of Virgil, even given his brief description of the preparation of a salad at *Ecl.* 2.10–11. Theocritus, with his realistic bucolics and mimes, provides a better parallel. In the earlier first century, probably the seventies, Sueius had written a *Moretum* too: Macrobius, who quotes eight lines, calls it an idyll, further proof of the Theocritean affiliations of the type.[2] A Greek source may have been used: a poem about a salad (μυττωτός) is linked, somewhat dubiously, with Gallus' client Parthenius.[3] But mannerism of the kind found in our *Moretum* – a mixture of mime and pastoral – could have been an indigenous creation, in Ovid's time, at any rate. Virgilian, or early Augustan authorship is ruled out by the poem's vocabulary, and metrical fluency: there are no fewer than sixty-nine non-Virgilian words in the piece, amongst them *excubitor* (2), and only five elisions in one hundred and twenty-four hexameters. Dating is more or less decided by an epigram of Martial, 13.13, where it is said that whereas our grandfathers ate lettuce at the end of a meal, now it is consumed at the beginning. Since *Moretum* 76, *grataque nobilium requies lactuca ciborum*, agrees with the earlier habit, the poem cannot be later than the reign of Nero – especially if, as has been argued, Columella used it – and, on a stricter interpretation of Martial's *auorum*, is probably closer to the turn of the century. In the *Copa*, an invitation to drink occasioned by thoughts of human mortality, Propertian elegy consorts with pastoral. It has been disputed whether the bucolic debt is to Virgil or Theocritus – the *Copa* echoes the second *Eclogue*, and beyond that, *Idylls* 7 and 11 – but our most likely candidate is Virgil.[4] Imitations of Propertius' fourth book date the piece after 16–15 B.C., and therefore after Virgil's death.[5] We need not look much later: polysyllabic pentameter endings indicate a poet unconcerned about Ovidian elegiac technique, a conscious archaist who wished to adapt pastoral formulae to the uneven Propertian couplet.

Callimachus and Euphorion, with their curse poems, Ἀραί and Ἀραὶ ἢ Ποτηριοκλέπτης – Ovid's *Ibis* is a later example of the type – are the formal antecedents of the Virgilian *Dirae*: not that the poem is by Virgil himself. But

[1] See Hollis (1970) ad loc.

[2] See *FPL* 53; Macrob. 3.18.11. For the poem's realism (e.g. its depiction of the old negress) cf. the epigrams of Leonidas of Tarentum, Gow–Page (1965) I 107–39 and II 307–98. For the element of parody, Ross (1975*b*) 254–63.

[3] By a fifteenth-century Ambrosian manuscript, which tells us *Parthenius moretum scripsit in Graeco quem Vergilius imitatus est.*

[4] See Drew (1923) 73–81, and (1925) 37–42.

[5] See Wilamowitz (1924) I 311–15. Note *Copa* 29 and Prop. 4.8.37, and especially 18–22, and 4.2.13–16; also 15–16, and 3.13.29–30. *Cineri ingrato*, 35, is from Virg. *Aen* 6.213. Drew (above), like Drabkin (1930), with their conviction of Virgilian authorship, are forced into making Propertius the imitator.

unlike the *Copa* and *Moretum*, this piece should be regarded as a conscious variation on a theme from Virgil: another mixed composition, this time pastoral and curse, the *Dirae* borrows its theme from *Eclogues* 1 and 9, recounting to its addressee, Battarus, the depredations of one Lycurgus, a veteran newcomer. Virgil had supplied the hint: *quod nec uertat bene* (*Ecl.* 9.6). Varius has been claimed as its author, as well as Valerius Cato: but difficulty of construction, even given the state of the tradition, unconvincing pastoral mannerism, and passages of inapposite inflation rule out an accomplished craftsman. Since the question of the confiscations was of particular interest to later generations we cannot argue from simple topicality towards an early date; but the fact that our poet is not expressly creating Virgilian juvenilia – for which there was a demand once the poet achieved celebrity – at least leaves room for that. Response to Virgil's *Eclogues*, whether immediate or not, has left us with a mediocre exercise, devoid of bearing on actual events.

Our manuscripts make no distinction between the *Dirae*, and the eighty hexameters of pastoral love lament which follow. It is not clear whether the *Lydia* was written as a sequel to the *Dirae*, where the poet's mistress had the same name, or was accidentally appended to the curse poem through a process of association. If it is a sequel, the *Lydia* need have no more relationship to the *Dirae* than the *Dirae* to the *Eclogues*; it is certainly unnecessary to postulate that its author accepted the *Dirae* as Virgilian and inserted references there to his own Lydia, then, thirsty for anonymous fame, appended his love poem simply in order that Virgil's name might ensure its preservation. But apart from the name, which was common enough, there is little reason to link the two poems: since there is no external support for a Virgilian *Lydia*, the confusion with the *Dirae*, accidental or not, probably took place in antiquity. Valerius Cato has again been favoured for authorship: but his *Lydia*, one of the most celebrated products of Republican literature, would surely have maintained a separate identity. Our poem, with its refrains, spondaic hexameter endings, and measured repetitions looks reasonably early: it could be Augustan. Its Alexandrianism and pastoral colour align it generically with the *Copa*, *Moretum*, and *Dirae*: smoother and more accomplished than the latter, it was probably written around the turn of the century, towards the end of the wave of enthusiasm for neoteric poetry.

Donatus and Servius assign Virgil a *Ciris*, presumably ours. Another Alexandrian composition, this time of decidedly non-Virgilian colour, the *Ciris* cannot be authentic, not only because of the circumstances of its author – a retired politician dedicated to philosophy[1] – but also because everything points to its having imitated, not inspired, all three canonical works: when

[1] See 1ff., 14ff. In his middle years, Virgil was employed on the *Georgics* and *Aeneid*. Why our author chooses to supply this biographical information is unclear.

paralleled by the *Ciris*, Virgil is generally better, that is – for poetry of this kind – earlier.[1] Furthermore, its clumsy imitations of Catullus and Lucretius are improbable a mere decade after publication: fifty years later, they might make sense.[2] Our author also seems to have imitated Ovid, and maybe Manilius: but once we pass A.D. 8, we run into problems over the identity of the poem's addressee – Messalla, the patron of Tibullus, who died in that year.[3] After that, we must find some descendant: Messalinus, born 42 B.C., has been canvassed, but it is not very likely that the *Ciris* was composed after Messalla's death. A date roughly contemporary with Ovid's *Metamorphoses* is probably our best choice. The poem's style is remarkably consistent with that of the Republican epyllion: spondaic line endings (e.g. *Amphitrites* 72, *latratus* 82, *ulciscendum* 158) are frequent, as are diminutives (*hortulus* 3, *paruulus* 138 and 479, *tabidulus* 182, *frigidulus* 251 and 348, *nutricula* 257 and 277, *lectulus* 440, *labella* 496: an especially non-Virgilian characteristic), excess in the use of colour terms (e.g. *purpureos...soles* 37), invocations, digressions (e.g. on the different versions of the myth, 54ff.: a very Alexandrian touch), exotic geographical and aetiological allusions, explanatory parentheses, long, ramshackle sentences – twice the average length of Virgil's – and congested speeches. Uneven and archaistic in his style, the author's morbid subject matter and quirky narrative technique are likewise throwbacks: Scylla's betrayal of her father, unrequited love for Minos, and final metamorphosis are indirectly and disjointedly recounted with the static pathos and histrionic gestures of Catullus in his sixty-fourth poem and presumably a dozen neoteric contemporaries.[4] Yet amidst these hallmarks of Republican Alexandrianism are embedded the tell-tale imitations of later work.[5] Our author does not impersonate Virgil; nor is he a *Vergilianus poeta*.[6] What we have in the *Ciris* is a genuine neoteric

[1] For example, cf. *Ciris* 59ff. and *Ecl.* 6.74ff., 538–41 and *Geo.* 1.406–9, 402–3 and *Aen.* 2.405–6, 474 and *Aen.* 3.74. *Ciris* 280 '*aut ferro hoc*': *aperit ferrum quod veste latebat*, is an interesting line, easier and more obvious than *Aen.* 6.406 '*at ramum hunc*': *aperit ramum qui ueste latebat*: perhaps a common source?

[2] Cf. *Ciris* 1ff., and Catull. 65.1ff.; 16ff., and Lucr. 2.9ff.

[3] Note that *Catalepton* 9 is likewise addressed to Messalla: though that is probably mere coincidence, despite the arguments of P. Jahn (1908), who wants a common author.

[4] In particular, note Ovid's version of the story of Io in *Met.* 1, probably in imitation of Calvus.

[5] After Virgil, the most frequent imitations are of Ovid: note, for instance, *Ciris* 285 *questus anilis* and *Met.* 9.276; also the frequency of Ovidian words absent from Virgil – though found in other writers – for example, *charta*, *libido*, *ocellus*, *releuo*, *tribuo*. In all, 142 non-Virgilian terms have been counted, many of them Ovidian: note for instance *alumna*, used a surprising twelve times. But the negative argument fails to convince. Manilius 5.569 *felix ille dies*, if it is the source and not the progeny of *Ciris* 27, begins to point to a later date, although the phrase looks formulaic. Obviously much depends on Stat. *Silv.* 1.4.120ff., if that is the source of *Ciris* 478–80; but there again Statius could be the imitator. Lyne (1971) has collected a great deal of first-century A.D. material, while arguing for a later date, but much of it could be common stock, or else inspired by our poem. An Augustan dating is not in principle necessary – after all epyllion was still being written in the time of Persius – but the identity of the addressee then poses real problems.

[6] For the term, see Lee *ap.* Herescu (1958) 457–71.

survival, written according to the principles of Catullus, probably before the death of Messalla, another chapter in the history of Alexandrianism, and archaism, at Rome.

We are left with the *Culex*, a humorous pseudo-narrative displaying some features of epyllion technique – unlike the *Ciris* it does pretend to be by Virgil – and the *Catalepton*, a collection of fifteen epigrams some of which may in fact be authentic. The only substantial forgery of the *Appendix*, the *Culex* was written to parallel the supposedly Homeric *Battle of frogs and mice*, a *praelusio* to greater work. Obvious echoes of the *Aeneid*, an unlikely prophecy of more important work to come, and a mock address to Octavian, the future Augustus, combine to indict this second-rate poem as the work of a *Vergilius personatus*, some schoolboy or grammarian who wished to align Virgil's early career with that of Homer. Yet Lucan, Statius, Martial, and Suetonius were all deceived: libraries must have been careless, critical examination scant. Not much happens during the course of the poem. A gnat warns a sleeping shepherd of the onslaught of a monstrous snake, is killed for its pains, appears, like the ghost of Patroclus, from the nether world, tells of its experiences there, in a long, inapposite νέκυια (the Roman heroes of the *Aeneid* have no bearing on the theme) and is awarded a tumulus for its merits. Catalogues abound; the narrative is static, the texture of the writing too smooth for the pretended date. Phrases occur which are otherwise first attested in the *Aeneid*, for example *hinc atque hinc*;[1] also, Ovid is imitated: *Culex* 133 *perfide Demophoon*, corresponds to *Rem. Am.* 597.[2] We cannot say much more than that our poet wrote before Lucan, and after Ovid – and, since time was needed for the acceptance of the impersonation, that a late Augustan date is more likely than early Imperial.

Virgilian authorship is claimed by external sources for the whole *Catalepton* – a title used, incidentally, by Aratus for a collection of short poems – and the testimony for the second piece – Quintilian, *Inst.* 8.3.27–9 – is relatively early. We can eliminate the final poem, which also makes that claim (*illius haec quoque sunt diuini elementa poetae*, 15.5), on the grounds that Virgil would hardly have produced such a poem so late in his career – after the unfinished *Aeneid* – as his last word on a body of material, some of which is demonstrably unauthentic, or else the kind of thing he would probably not have wished on posterity. The fifteenth poem is clearly the work of an editor, the man who brought the collection together, from whatever sources. Another forgery is 14, which purports to have been written while the *Aeneid* was still being composed, a vow of dedication to Venus if ever the epic is finished, suspect for the blandness of its style and unlikely psychology. Stylistic grounds also disqualify

[1] Twice in the *Culex*, eight times in the *Aeneid*, but we have lost much Latin poetry.

[2] Note also that *letare*, *Cul.* 325, is not used in Latin poetry until Ovid, and that *Cul.* 181 *sanguineae guttae* probably depends on *Met.* 2.358ff., although the phrase could be a formula.

the third poem, a wooden piece on the mutability of fortune, probably the thirteenth, an epode in the Horatian manner, and most certainly the ninth, a laborious, ill-structured panegyric of Messala. Of these, the last two are Augustan, but un-Virgilian: poem 3, on the other hand, is severe and prosaic in style, insufficiently ornate to be early, and rhetorical enough to belong to the first century. Alexander is not its subject: he was never exiled (line 8). Phraates and Mithridates were hardly world-conquerors (line 3): so perhaps we should opt for a Roman magnate – Pompey, preferably. Antony needs special pleading – he was not exactly exiled – even though he was more of a menace to Rome.

If the thirteenth poem had been included in Horace's *Epodes*, nobody would have been surprised. Its metre – alternating trimeter and dimeter – is Horatian, as much as its realistic vocabulary and scurrilous tone: its twenty-four non-Virgilian words are not the best argument against authenticity in view of its genre,[1] but if Virgil had ever written such an anomalous piece we would probably have heard so; and Virgil, unlike the author of the epigram, was never a soldier. No firm date can be assigned; even the name of its addressee is in doubt – Bücheler's suggestion, *Lucienus*, does not help in dating – and although the *collegia compitalia*, referred to in line 27, were disbanded in 46 B.C., they were restored by Augustus. All we can say is that since the poem must have been written after the *Epodes*, it must therefore follow the restoration of the *collegia*; also that its skilful author's relationship to Horace is similar to that of the writer of the *Dirae* to Virgil. A recently established form provides the impulse for an excursion into fashionable territory.

Messalla's triumph over the Aquitani, the event eulogized in *Catalepton* 9,[2] and known only too well from Tibullus, took place in 27 B.C.: since forgery and hence backdating are not in question, we may assign the piece to that year. Virgil is ruled out by the poem's extreme clumsiness,[3] his lack of connexion with the protagonist, and the fact that the author intends to turn some of Messalla's Greek pastorals into Latin:[4] now engaged on the *Aeneid*, Virgil would hardly have thought of being sidetracked into such a venture. The writer has learned something from Propertius – particularly noteworthy is the long, obscurely-phrased list of heroines beginning at line 25 – and besides the *Eclogues* and *Georgics* he knows Catullus, and the pseudo-Tibullan *Panegyricus*

[1] *inedia* and *turgidos*, l. 40, for example, have an iambic colour. Carcopino (1922) 164, notes that *Thybris*, l. 23, is a form which occurs 17 times in the *Aeneid*, but never in the *Eclogues* or *Georgics*: if it is a Virgilian epic innovation then we should begin our searches later on. But there is no reason to turn to Ovid, as do Hubaux (1930) and Radford (1928).

[2] The author knows the rules for Panegyric, as at, e.g. *Rhet. ad Her.* 3.11ff.

[3] Note the coincidence of the poem's opening with that of *Ecl.* 10 and the parallel between 17 and *Ecl.* 1.1.

[4] Strangely, Messalla seems to have written in Attic, not Doric; l. 14. He also translated Hyperides into Latin.

Messallae of 31 B.C.[1] A high proportion of his pentameters end in convenient polysyllables, and sometimes contain elisions; his structure is fluid and incoherent – the end of the poem is particularly loose – and his vocabulary is sparse, repetitive, and prosaic.[2] Our author is as inept as he is anonymous: better, then, not to insult Ovid, Propertius, or even Lygdamus, with claims for authorship.[3]

Next, a group of poems directly addressed to three of Virgil's associates: Octavius Musa, a historian who was involved in the land disputes around Mantua, and Varius and Tucca, Virgil's later editors. Given their themes, as well as their addressees, we can tentatively assume these poems to be genuine, part of Virgil's output in the forties. For none of them, apart from 4, is especially ambitious; none of them handles obvious or expected material.[4] The first, to Tucca, and the seventh, to Varius, are light, erotic pieces: the first is based on some local scandal, its point at first sight somewhat unclear: the seventh, in a context of homosexual love, raises the question whether Latin poetry should admit Greek words. Strict topicality is the key: a forger would hardly have bothered to invent so obscure an occasion for the epigram to Tucca, or so trivial and local a point for the poem to Varius. Octavius Musa, the little-known recipient of epigrams 4 and 11, was not the obvious choice: nothing is said about his *History*, nothing about his connexions with Mantua. A forger would have been more likely to choose Pollio or Varus. In all four poems, everything squares with authenticity: the metrical technique is early, the style mainly unassuming and akin to that of Catullus. And in particular, as we have said, no forger worth his salt would have dared provide an inquisitive audience with so little information about Virgil's youth. Our sole hesitation might be over the possibility that the verses were composed by a contemporary of Virgil with common associates, to be later reassigned by some well-meaning scholar or editor.

Epigrams 5, in scazons, and 8, in couplets, are more obviously autobiographical, therefore the more likely to have been forged. Siro, Virgil's teacher, figures in both. But this time, the contexts are expected, the style more elaborate and daring: in 5, 'Virgil' bids farewell to rhetoric and poetry in favour of philosophy; in 8, Siro's villa is hailed as a refuge from the evictions. Immediate suspicion is provoked by the subject matter of 8, and to a lesser degree by that of 5: the poems could all too easily be by a youthful Virgil – but there is no final court of appeal. The second epigram, on the other hand, can hardly be

[1] For the Tibullan parallel, see Sonner (1910).

[2] In particular, our author overworks *carmen*, *maximus*, and *uincere*; amongst his prosaisms, note 7 *nec minus idcirco*; 14 *cum...tum*; 24 *altera non...dixerit*; 56 *quin ausim hoc etiam dicere.*

[3] See Westendorp Boerma's commentary (1949) for details.

[4] A forger would hardly have resisted reference to the land confiscations in the epigrams to Musa, nor to their editorial activities in the poems to Varius and Tucca.

a forgery – though it need not be by Virgil – referring as it does to the archaizing fad of the forties, and in particular, to the taste for Thucydides which emerged at that time. We have no special reason to link Virgil with Annius Cimber, the poem's offending and criminal rhetorician: but at least we have a genuine, if obscure, product of the forties.

Catullus is the main influence on the sixth and twelfth epigrams, as on the tenth, a parody of the *phaselus* poem, number 4 in our collection. In the first two, fairly straightforward abusive exercises, a certain Noctuinus is assailed: once more obscurity of occasion perhaps rules out a forger – although it does not guarantee Virgilian authorship. And if Sabinus, the muleteer recipient of the parody *Catalepton* 10, is Ventidius Bassus, that poem too belongs to the forties: Bassus, friend of Caesar and *consul suffectus* in 43, was lampooned as an upstart by Cicero, Plancus, and the populace at large (Cic. *Fam.* 15.20 and Gell. 15.4). We are left with the insignificant 13, an epitaph on a literary man, of uncertain date, and three Priapic poems. Although Donatus and Servius may have thought Virgil wrote the whole of the *Priapea*, an entirely separate collection, probably compiled by one author in the late first century A.D.,[1] the three poems in question were chosen in antiquity for inclusion with the *Catalepton*. Their main distinguishing characteristic is their bucolic colour, taken from the *Eclogues*:[2] probably Augustan, they are unlikely to be the work of Virgil himself.

Tradition further ascribes a pair of elegies on the death of Maecenas, neither of them the work of any great talent: Scaliger is responsible for first noticing that the continuous elegy of the manuscripts should be divided into two. Whoever composed the first poem had also written an *epicedion* for some young man:

defleram iuuenis tristi modo carmine fata:
sunt etiam merito carmina danda seni. (*Eleg. Maec.* 1.12)

My saddened muse of late had mourned a young man's death: now to one ripe in years also let songs be duly offered. (Tr. J. Wight Duff)

An obvious, but not inevitable, candidate for the *iuuenis* is Drusus, whose death in 9 B.C. antedated that of Maecenas by a year. Virgil, who died in 19 B.C., has never been a serious contender for the poem – at least not since the Middle Ages. But what of Ovid? That question is, unfortunately, posed by the couplet just quoted, since under Ovid's name has been transmitted a *Consolatio ad Liviam*, a lament on the death of Drusus. Though tedious, the *Consolatio* is better than either of the *Elegiae*, and is most unlikely to be the *epicedion* of the first elegy's first couplet. It could be the work of an Ovid composing in more official vein – but we need posit no more than influence: in terms of its conceits, its rhetorical deployment of ideas, the poem prefigures Lucan.

[1] See Buchheit (1962) and Kenney's review (1963).

[2] See Galletier (1920) 25f.

The *elegiae*, on the other hand, are not especially Ovidian, and the patchwork mythology at the end of the first is clearly the work of a bungler.[1] In neither case can we really talk of deliberate imitation: there is no conscious attempt to produce a particular style or tone, no feeling for language or metre, no ability to control a conceit, or work from within the material chosen.

Were it not for the reference at 1.9–10 to Lollius, Consul in 20 B.C., dead in 1 B.C., there would be little reason for adhering to an Augustan date.[2] Indeed, the depiction of the *princeps* at 1.163–4 smacks more of early Imperial hindsight than of the times of Augustus himself:

> Caesar amicus erat: poterat uixisse solute,
> cum iam Caesar idem quod cupiebat erat.

The Emperor was Maecenas' friend: so he was free to live a life of ease when the Emperor was all he longed to be.

Moreover, the portrait of Maecenas is very much a stereotype, the kind of thing an aspiring poet might find in a textbook – so much so, that it has been argued that the poem is a rebuttal of Seneca's charges in the rhetorical picture of his one hundred and fourteenth letter.[3] But then again, myths were fast to grow in Rome, and the life style of Maecenas was notorious in his own day.

Another point needs making: whoever wrote the first elegy did not necessarily write the second. Indeed, the second poem – a monologue by the dying Maecenas which looks for all the world like a fragment of something longer[4] – is more rhetorical, somewhat more obscure, and altogether more sparse and prosaic in its style. There is nothing to link it to names or events. The fact that the phrase *Caesaris illud opus*, line 6, also occurs at line 39 of the *Consolatio* says nothing about authorship. As in the case of the cliché shared by *Eleg.* 1.7 and *Cons.* 372, *illa rapit iuuenes*, the parallel could be the result of imitation, or even a formula of common stock; there is certainly no point in pressing verbal similarity to yield a common author. It seems most likely that both the *Consolatio* and the first elegy are genuine products of occasion, no matter how far they differ in terms of literary quality, while the second elegy may be no more than an exercise of the schools, of uncertain date at that.

Another poem transmitted as being by Ovid is the *Nux*, a complaint by a nut tree of its ill-omened fertility. Our piece is quite well managed, an expansion

[1] Bickel (1950) goes so far as to conclude that the end of the first elegy, from 107ff., is a separate poem.

[2] Unless, of course, we are dealing with a different Lollius; in which case we could give more weight to 'parallels' with Ovid's poetry of exile.

[3] See, e.g., Haupt (1875) I 347, developed by Birt (1877) 66, and Steele (1933).

[4] *sic est Maecenas fato ueniente locutus* is a strangely abrupt way to begin a poem.

from an epigram in the *Greek Anthology* where a nut tree tells how it is perpetually bombarded by greedy passers-by. It is most unlikely that the lament in any way reflects on Ovid's fate – undeservingly suffering punishment in exile. But the question of allegory apart, the author of the *Nux* can on occasions sound very much like the genuine Ovid, as, for instance, at lines 107–8:

fructus obest, peperisse nocet, nocet esse feracem;
quaeque fuit multis, ei mihi, praeda mala est.

My fruit is my bane, it is harmful to bear, it is harmful to be fertile; gain, which has hurt many, has hurt me too. (Tr. J. H. Mozley)

But as Lee points out in his article on authenticity, the author is more likely to be an *Ovidianus poeta* – a conscious imitator of a distinctive style – than Ovid himself.[1] Criteria are unstable: Lee demonstrates that 'un-Ovidian' diction is to be found in the genuine Ovid, hence the thirteen 'singletons' of the *Nux* should not sway the argument; likewise, un-Ovidian phrasing is of little help – except in the case of the poem's 'high frequency of *at*, the prosaic use of *aliquando*...the use of *quilibet* in a series of distributive clauses, and of *sic*...*sic*...*sic ego* in a series of comparisons, possibly too *aliquis*...*hic*... *hic*...*est quoque*'.[2] We are on slightly firmer ground when it comes to imitation: as Lee shows, *Met.* 8.747 and 14.663–4 are more likely to be the origin than the progeny of *Nux* 35–6, which in turn is more likely to be the work of an anonymous imitator, since it uses two expressions in a non-Ovidian way, than the work of Ovid himself. Similar conclusions are to be drawn from the parallelism between *Tristia* 5.5.17–18 and *Nux* 165–6 – the latter a conceit about the beaver's self-castration – though less should be made of *Heroides* 1.55 and *Nux* 127–8. Finally, there is the parallel between Silius 15.484–7 and the passage about the beaver, where probabilities are loaded in favour of Silius' priority. In the *Nux*, then, we have an accomplished poem, the work of someone who had mastered Ovid's style, who most likely lived towards the end of the first century A.D.

In the field of erotic elegy, it is not only the work of Gallus that we have lost. C. Valgius Rufus, *consul suffectus* in 12 B.C., besides his treatises on herbs and grammar, wrote lachrymose elegies, only to be recommended the epic: Horace's invitation is backed up by the *Panegyricus Messallae*, which implies that Valgius actually tried the grand manner. Of his dirges on the boy Mystes we know no more than is implied by Hor. *Odes* 2.9 – that they were plaintive, and somewhat dreary. But that he was not simply a second Tibullus, intent solely on his love, is shown by the most important fragment, fr. 2, which praises the poetry of Codrus, the shadowy bard of the *Eclogues*:

[1] Lee, *ap.* Herescu (1958) 457–71.
[2] Ibid. 463–4.

Codrusque ille canit, quali tu uoce canebas
  atque solet numeros dicere, Cinna, tuos,
dulcior ut numquam Pylio profluxerit ore
  Nestoris aut docto pectore Demodoci
. . .
. . .
falleris insanus quantum si gurgite nauta
  Crisaeae quaerat flumina Castaliae.

Codrus sings with the strains that you once used, and the measures that Cinna favoured, the like of which never flowed more sweetly from the mouth of Pylian Nestor or the breast of learned Demodocus . . .

You are wrong and mad, as if a sailor were to seek the waters of Castalia in the depths of the sea.

Like Propertius, Valgius shows that he can handle afresh the water imagery of Callimachus, recreating the atmosphere of Alexandria in the midst of Augustan Rome. Our other two elegiac fragments deal with a journey down a river. We also have a snatch of abrasive hendecasyllables, and two apparently bucolic hexameters, which look later than the *Eclogues*, but earlier than Ovid. His connexion with Horace and Virgil shows that it was Propertius, rather than elegy as such, which was out of tune with the literary mainstream; and the prose works suggest a gentleman and a courtier, not an obsessed lover.[1]

Domitius Marsus may have written elegies, although *fusca Melaenis*, his mistress, might just as well have figured in his collection of epigrams, the *Cicuta*. In its most important fragment Virgil's enemy, Bavius, is arraigned in the Catullan fashion: Marsus does not worry about polysyllabic pentameter endings, and his language is prosaic. On several occasions Martial claims him as his master, also providing evidence for a connexion with Maecenas.[2] Ovid knew him, and Augustus' teacher, Apollodorus, corresponded with him. It looks as if he belonged to the group around Maecenas, a contemporary of Virgil and Horace, though living longer than they: yet the fragment to Epirota, another figure from that circle, could be sarcastic,[3] and if Haupt is right,[4] Horace pokes fun at his *Amazonis*, no doubt an unfortunate venture,[5] in the difficult passage at *Odes* 4.4.18. At any rate, Horace never refers to him by name, and this, as in the case of Propertius, is suspicious. He also wrote *Fabellae*, and a prose work, entitled *De urbanitate*, for which he receives the epithet *eruditissimus* from Quintilian. Another scholar like Valgius, he too

1 See Appendix.

2 See Mart. 7.29.5 *et Maecenati Maro cum cantaret Alexin | nota tamen Marsi fusca Melaenis erat.* On the basis of such evidence, Virgil might just as easily be claimed for elegy as Marsus.

3 See fr. 3, *Epirota tenellorum nutricula uatum*, with its somewhat ambiguous diminutives.

4 Haupt (1876) III 333.

5 Note Mart. 4.29.7 *leuis in tota Marsus Amazonide.*

shows how Romans had become more adventurous in letters, more resourceful and catholic than the previous generation.

Maecenas himself was a poet, writing occasional verse along the lines of Catullus, but taking his neoteric mannerisms to excess. We have fragments with contrived, affected diction, in hexameters, glyconics, hendecasyllables, galliambics, trimeters: but none of this was really *avant-garde*. Laevius had trifled in the same way fifty years before, and similar preciosities were to emerge in the second century A.D. Mannerism of this kind is germane to Roman literature, and though no doubt Alexandrian in origin, does not warrant the invocation of Greek models on its each and every occurrence. Augustus and Seneca were amused or appalled by his affectations: but such Asianism was probably common coinage. Maecenas also tried prose, writing *Dialogi*, one of which was a *Symposium* at which Horace, Virgil and Messalla were the guests.

Less needs to be said of Servius Sulpicius, a friend of Horace, who, according to Ovid, wrote *improba carmina*, and appears in a long list of erotic poets in Pliny. Other minor talents of a slightly later date are Proculus, who followed Callimachus, writing elegies; Alfius Flavus, a declaimer, and probably author of amatory trifles; Sabinus, who composed appropriate replies to Ovid's *Heroides* (Ov. *Am.* 2-18.27–34), an epic of uncertain name, and a *Fasti*; Fontanus, probably a bucolic poet; the elegist Capella; Tuscus, who wrote about Phyllis; M. Aurelius Cotta, perhaps an epigrammatist; Horace's addressee, Julius Florus; the brothers Visci; and Montanus, an elegist and, probably, writer of epyllia. Seneca preserves two hexameter fragments, descriptions of dawn and dusk, topics of which he was a devotee. Lyric is sadly represented: we only hear of Perilla, a pupil of Ovid, addressed in *Trist.* 3.7; and Titius and Rufus, imitators of Pindar, mentioned by Horace and Ovid – who may have been one and the same person.

Didactic remains the most neglected area of Latin literature. We still need a study of the formal characteristics of the genre; and general discussions tend too often to be limited to Lucretius and Virgil. Yet we have complete or fragmentary didactics by Cicero, Varro Atacinus, Columella, Nemesianus, Q. Serenus and Avienius – as well as three relatively extensive works from the early first century: the *Astronomica* of Manilius, the *Aratea* of Germanicus, and the *Cynegetica* of Grattius. Not only do these poems contribute to our knowledge of the contemporary world view; they also show how one of the favourite Alexandrian forms had become the property of Rome. Unfortunately we have lost the most important didactic poets of the age – after Virgil, that is. Aemilius Macer, who belonged to the older generation of Augustans, and is to be distinguished from the later epicist of the same name, was famed for his *Ornithogonia*, *Theriaca*, and *De herbis*. Ov. *Trist.* 4.10. 43:

saepe suas uolucres legit mihi grandior aeuo
quaeque nocet serpens, quae iuuat herba, Macer.

Often Macer, my elder, read to me his birds,
poisonous serpents, and medicinal herbs.[1]

It has been argued with some cogency that the *Theriaca* and *De herbis* belong to one and the same work – that Macer followed his model Nicander in writing one book on bites and a second on remedies.[2] His *Ornithogonia*, although inspired by the Greek poet Boios, contained Italian legends, for instance that of Picus, found also in Virgil and Ovid (fr. 1: cf. *Aen.* 7.189ff., *Met.* 15.320). But, as Bardon notes, there is a certain monotony in his verses:

tum sacrae ueniunt altis de nubibus Ibes

then from the high clouds come the sacred ibises;

auxilium sacrae ueniunt cultoribus Ibes (frs. 5 and 6 M)

to the help of the cultivators come the sacred ibises.

Too much of that would easily have palled. Varius, like Macer, is half Republican, slightly old-fashioned in tone, but with more movement. Older than Virgil, he too adopted the didactic genre, writing a *De morte*, of which Macrobius, with his eye on Virgilian parallels, gives us a few lines. Fragment 2, which shows the influence of diatribe, was imitated by Virgil in the *Georgics*:

incubet ut Tyriis atque ex solido bibat auro

to sleep on purple and drink from solid gold,

and

ut gemma bibat et Sarrano dormiat ostro (*Geo.* 2.506)

to drink from jewelled goblets and sleep on foreign purple.

Fragment 3 is Virgilian in movement, with a hint of Lucretius:

quem non ille sinit lentae moderator habenae
qua uelit ire, sed angusto prius ore coercens
insultare docet campis fingitque morando.

Pulling in the supple reins he does not let him go the way he wants, but checking him with the narrow bit he makes him gallop on the plain and wins the mastery by slowing him down.[3]

Hunting is Grattius' theme, the stars that of Manilius and Germanicus: their common aim is successful poetic arrangement of recalcitrant material, according to principles laid down in Hellenistic times, when interest in the

[1] As Hollis (1973) 11 points out, *grandior* seems to be in some sort of balance with *Macer*, the verbal play depending upon the idea of size.

[2] Bardon (1956) II 45–6, following Schulze (1898) 541–6.

[3] The *De morte* has been claimed for epic, but the title stands against that view.

form revived. Aratus, acclaimed by Callimachus for his polish and lightness of touch,[1] is the ancestor of a series of Roman imitations, some of them considerably altered: as Latin verse technique became standardized, interest gravitated towards adaptation and moral colouring, away from poetic finish – which, by the time of Germanicus (15 B.C.–A.D. 19) had become more or less a matter of course. Not that this is any detraction from his work, an accomplished composition, written slightly after Augustus' death. Like Manilius, he displays a certain Ovidian finesse, but is less pointed and rhetorical; he corrects Aratus' mistakes quite freely, and supplies his own insertions at will. One instance of his freedom of treatment is his depiction of Astraea's dereliction of the world: the passage relies on personification, moralistic comment, and concrete detail, where the original was colourless and abstract – a typically Roman expansion from source. Grattius, an acquaintance of Ovid (*Pont.* 4.16.34), is likewise not averse to the moralizing digression: but this time we have no Greek model against which to judge him – at least if, as has been argued, he did use a Greek source, none of it remains. Less accomplished than Germanicus, his main debt, though not as obvious as sometimes claimed, is to Virgil, and, to a much lesser degree, Lucretius:[2] it is unlikely that Manilius drew on him. Rare technical terms and *hapax legomena* – *plagium*, *metagon*, *praedexter*, *perpensare*, *offectus*, *cannabinus*, *nardifer*, *termiteus* – contribute to his reader's problems. But it is not in the technical sections, which maintain a certain degree of fluency, that he is most difficult. In the digressions – the double proem, the invective against luxury, the excursus on the Sicilian cave[3] – he is at his worst: misplaced grandiosity, vague prosaic phrasing, and unclear progressions of thought make him least attractive at precisely those points where a didactic poet might be expected to shine.

Of Manilius the man we know nothing: there is no external testimony; he gives us no personal information, and, apart from an invocation to Caesar at 1.7, has no addressee. A late Augustan date for Books 1 and 2 is indicated by a reference at 1.899 to the disaster of Varus which took place in A.D. 9, and by various passages which assume Augustus to be still alive. Housman has argued that the difficult passage at 4.764 implies that Augustus is dead: but that is not the only possible interpretation.[4] More than that we cannot say: Books 3 and 5 have no indication of date. The poem is something of a mystery. It is also probably unfinished: Book 5 breaks off abruptly, and there are places in the poem where Manilius promises material which does not appear.[5] Book 1

[1] Callim. *Epigr.* 29. See *CHCL* 1.

[2] See the introduction to Enk's commentary (1918), and Pierleoni (1906).

[3] It is tempting to ask if Grattius used Augustus' poem on Sicily.

[4] See Housman (1903–30) 1 lxixff., marshalling the various pieces of evidence. The problem at 4.764 is that Tiberius is called *recturus*, then *lumen magni sub Caesare mundi*; is he therefore still heir apparent, a secondary light to Augustus, or already on the throne, the only light of the world?

[5] For example, 2.965, promising an account of the planets: see Housman, ibid. lxxii.

concerns the origins of astrology and the appearance of the heavens – their various zones and circles – concluding with a Virgilian finale, on the ability of the planets to presage the future. Book 2, after a proem which pays homage to Homer, Hesiod and other didactic poets, is devoted to the signs of the zodiac; the proem to Book 3 again concerns poetry, this time the difficulty of his theme compared to those of earlier writers, the bulk of the book being occupied by a treatment of the twelve *athla* which correspond to the signs. Book 4 begins in Lucretian vein, inveighing against our mortal cares, then moves on to the power of fate in history, and thence to the character traits connected with the signs, the geographical regions which they govern, the ecliptic signs, and finally, a vindication of the view that the heavens foretell the future. Book 5, without more ado, launches into a discussion of the *paranatellonta*, the signs which appear at the same time as the constellations of the zodiac, but outside the zodiac itself: it finishes suddenly, after a comparison between the earthly order and the order of the heavens.

Manilius' stylistic masters are Lucretius,[1] Virgil and Ovid. The old prosaic connectives are fully in evidence – *ergo age*, *perspice nunc*, *quin etiam*, *accipe*, *nunc age*, but there is a new polish, a new fluency, and a love of point, antithesis and word play: in terms of the rhetorical qualities of his verse, Manilius stands half way between Ovid and Lucan. He knows the imagery of the Callimachean poetic, but when he writes of untrodden paths, trite epic themes, and the struggle to create,[2] he reflects not the master himself, but the mainstream Latin tradition: the Callimachean programme was now itself banal.[3] Virgil is most obviously laid under contribution at the end of Book 1, where Manilius imitates the close of the first Georgic, incorporating echoes of the *Furor* ἔκφρασις from *Aeneid* 1:

iam bella quiescant
atque adamanteis Discordia uincta catenis
aeternos habeat frenos in carcere clausa. (1.922ff.)

Now let wars end and Discord, tied with chains of adamant, be bound forever, coerced within a prison.

Yet even here there is a suspect facility, a non-Virgilian ease, which is the legacy of Ovid. Ovidian influence, visible throughout, is clearest in the Andromeda digression of Book 5. 549ff.:

[1] He worries less than Lucretius about using Greek terms, simply prefacing them with an apology, as at 2.693, 830, 897 and 3.41.

[2] Note *luctandum*, 2.34: cf. the Callimachean πόνος, Latin *labor*.

[3] See Wimmel (1960) 105–6, and Newman (1967) 196ff., 418ff. Manilius' claim to isolation (2.136ff.) may be no more than a variant on the Callimachean exclusiveness topic. He makes the conventional boast of originality at 1.4, 113, 2.57 and 3.1. The rejection of myth in favour of science, as at 3.5ff., is a commonplace of didactic.

at, simul infesti uentum est ad litora ponti,
mollia per duras panduntur bracchia cautes;
adstrinxere pedes scopulis, iniectaque uincla,
et cruce uirginea moritura puella pependit.
seruatur tamen in poena uultusque pudorque;
supplicia ipsa decent, niuea ceruice reclinis
molliter ipsa suae custos est uisa figurae,
defluxere sinus umeris fugitque lacertos
uestis et effusi scapulis haesere capilli.
te circum alcyones pinnis planxere uolantes
fleueruntque tuos miserando carmine casus
et tibi contextas umbram fecere per alas.
ad tua sustinuit fluctus spectacula pontus
adsuetasque sibi desit perfundere rupes,
extulit et liquido Nereis ab aequore uultus
et, casus miserata tuos, rorauit et undas.
ipsa leui flatu refouens pendentia membra
aura per extremas resonauit flebile rupes.

But when they came to the edge of the hostile sea, they stretched her soft arms across the harsh crag, bound her feet to the rock, and enchained her: the doomed maiden hung from her virgin cross. Despite the torture she kept her modest looks. The punishment became her: gently inclining her white neck she guarded her body. Her garments slipped from her shoulders, her robe slid down her arms and her hair, shaken out, spread close to her shoulders. Around her the sea birds flew and wailed, lamenting her fate in a song of misery, giving her shade from their intertwined wings. The sea stopped its waves to watch her, forsaking its usual rocky haunts; the Nereids raised their faces from the limpid waters, and pitying her plight, dropped tears on the waves. The breeze fondled her hanging limbs, and whistled sadly around the edges of the rocks.

This erotic sentimentalism, heavily reliant on the pathetic fallacy, with its coy rococo touches and rhetorical conceits, apart from occasional congestion, approaches the very essence of Ovid's *Metamorphoses*: never before had didactic so blatantly departed from its seriousness of intent.

But elsewhere, Manilius behaves with more dignity, his Stoicism precluding frivolity. Like Lucretius and Virgil before him, he goes to the diatribe in search of moral lessons, as in the proem to Book 4.[1] And like other didactic poets, he is concerned to set forth the *ratio* of this world,[2] and the place of his subject within it. There is an order within the universe, like the political order on earth – and both must be preserved if the machine is to function properly, 5.734ff.:

[1] Cf. 2.596ff., reminiscent also of Lucan's proem, especially 601ff., *et fas atque nefas mixtum, legesque per ipsas | saeuit nequities.*

[2] Note especially the expressions of his pantheistic beliefs at 1.247–54 and 2.60ff.: cf. Grattius on *ratio* in his proem.

utque per ingentis populus discribitur urbes,
principiumque patres retinent et proximum equester
ordo locum, populumque equiti populoque subire
uulgus iners uideas et iam sine nomine turbam,
sic etiam magno quaedam res publica mundo est
quam natura facit, quae caelo condidit urbem.
sunt stellae procerum similes, sunt proxima primis
sidera, suntque gradus atque omnia iusta priorum.
maximus est populus summo qui culmine fertur;
cui si pro numero uires natura dedisset,
ipse suas aether flammas sufferre nequiret
totus et accenso mundus flagraret Olympo.

And as a people is distributed through great cities – the senators hold the topmost position, the equestrian order the next; after the equites come the people, and after the people the lazy mob and then the nameless dregs – so in the cosmos at large there is a political order, the creation of nature, who has founded a city in the heavens. The constellations are the nobility, there are stars which are next in order, there are degrees and prerogatives: if nature had given sovereignty proportionate to their numbers to the greatest multitudes which revolve in the topmost zone, the aether would be unable to hold up the fiery stars which it supports, and the whole universe would go up in flames, setting light to the sky.

It would be hard to find a better example of Stoic Roman conservatism. Dorcatius remains, an uninteresting figure who wrote on ball games, mentioned by Ovid, and the author of two lines preserved by Isidore; also Plotius Crispinus, who, according to the scholia on Horace, versified the Stoic doctrine.

Names of authors and titles of works are more or less all that we have of Augustan mythological epic. We know of a Ponticus, who wrote a *Thebaid*, possibly in imitation of Antimachus; of a Homeric essay, the story of Nausicaa, by a friend of Ovid, Tuticanus; of an *Heracleid* by Carus, educator of Germanicus' children; of epics on Antenor's settlement in Gaul – like Aeneas' in Latium – by Largus, on Hercules' taking of Troy by Camerinus, on the *nostos* of Menelaus and Helen by Lupus, and of an anonymous *Perseid.* Iullus Antonius, son of Marcus, wrote a *Diomedēa* in twelve books, some time before 13 B.C., the date of Hor. *Odes* 4.2; the recipient of Propertius 2.24, Lynceus – perhaps a pseudonym – wrote a *Thebaid* and *Heracleid*; and Arbronius Silo was heard by Seneca the Elder reciting a poem on the Trojan war. We have two lines:

ite, agite, o Danai, magnum paeana canentes:
ite triumphantes: belli mora concidit Hector.

Come, come together, Greeks, singing a loud song of praise: come in triumph: Hector, their bulwark in war, has fallen.[1]

[1] Silo's phrase *belli mora* seems to have been the source of Sen. *Ag.* 211 *Danais Hector et bello mora*, and Lucan 1.100 *Crassus erat belli medius mora*, but cf. Virg. *Aen.* 10.428. Seneca discusses the phrase at *Suas.* 2.19.

Sabinus may have written an epic on the city of Troesmes: that depends on an emendation of Ov. *Pont.* 4.16.13. Numa and Priscus are mere names, perhaps epicists. This leaves us with Ovid's friend Macer, a poet of the Trojan cycle. At *Am.* 2.18, he is said to have dealt with material prior to the Trojan War; and *Pont.* 2.10.13 could perhaps be pressed to yield a *Posthomerica*. Sparse though the evidence may be, it is at least clear that the oldest form of poetry lost none of its attractions, despite the Roman adoption of Callimachean theory, with its many reservations about full scale epic.

Tragedy did not fare quite so well, but we do know of seven or eight writers who handled the genre – Varius, Gracchus, Pupius, Turranius and Ovid, as well as Pollio, and the *princeps* himself. Varius' *Thyestes*, produced in 29 B.C., survives in one alliterative, rather precious fragment:

iam fero infandissima
iam facere cogor.

Now my lot is unspeakable; now I must do unspeakable things.

Gracchus, mentioned at Ov. *Pont.* 4.16.31, seems to have treated the same myth. We have one line of his *Thyestes*:

mersit sequentis umidum plantis humum

the soft ground hid the tracks of the pursuer,

as well as a grandiose snatch from his *Atalanta*:

sonat impulsu regia cardo

the regal door sounded beneath the shock.

He also wrote a *Peliades*, of which a dimeter survives. Pupius and Turranius are just names, and Ovid's famous *Medea*, a work of his middle period, is only known in two lines, cited by Quintilian and Seneca. Pollio is a greater loss: we do not have much more than the tributes from Virgil and Horace, and the criticism of Tacitus. We cannot specify in what way his tragedies were 'modern' – as Virgil implies, perhaps with metre in mind[1] – but he was undeniably an important figure for the earlier group of Augustan poets, a survivor from the late Republic, who knew Catullus, Calvus, and Cinna. Suetonius informs us of an *Ajax* by Augustus; but again, we have no fragments.

[1] *Pollio et ipse facit noua carmina*, *Ecl.* 3.86. Virgil may have regarded Pollio's use of the trimeter (see Hor. *Sat.* 1.10.43, and cf. *A.P.* 251ff.) as an advance on senarii, but the epithet *nouus* still strikes one as strange: perhaps we are too accustomed to associating 'New Poetry' with the type of composition which Catullus and Calvus wrote. Certainly the grandiose image of the bull which prefaces the allusion to Pollio's *noua carmina* seems to designate tragedy. If there is a connexion between the present use of *nouus* and the literary pretensions of the previous generation, then what we have here is yet another instance of the increasingly loose interpretation of Callimachus' ideals; and perhaps it is significant that Pollio knew Calvus, was mentioned by Catullus, and was the recipient of a *propempticon* by Cinna.

Rome, it seems, never lost her taste for the grandiose, even at a time when many vaunted the ideals of Alexandria.

Surdinus and Statorius Victor were also dramatists, whether tragic or comic we cannot say; the son of Arbronius Silo wrote pantomimes; and Aristius Fuscus, the friend of Horace, wrote comedies. Fundanius and Melissus were more important, the first writing *palliatae* about Greek society, on which Horace complimented him, the second the author of *trabeatae*, a new form of comedy with the equestrian class as its subject – also of *Ineptiae* 'witty sayings', later retitled *Ioci*, maybe a work on grammar, and perhaps a natural history. We also hear of an Antonius Rufus, author of *praetextae* and *togatae*.

In the field of historical epic, one problem is that of finding precursors to Lucan: is he writing in a tradition, or is the *Bell. Civ.* an isolated phenomenon? Petronius' classicizing objections, albeit composed in a spirit of parody, might imply that he was an outrageous *Wunderkind*, a rebel against the absolute dominion of Virgil; but equally they could be taken as evidence for no more than a classicizing trend, which emerges in the preferences of Quintilian and the practice of the Flavians, Valerius, Statius and Silius. That the latter is the case is suggested by the nature of pre-Neronian epic: Cornelius Severus in particular, Albinovanus Pedo to some extent, and maybe Sextilius Ena and Rabirius, show that in terms of style at any rate, Lucan was not alone. Two parallel traditions existed in epic: first, the Virgilian, with its roots in Homer, and, to some degree, Ennius; second, the historical, a more sparse, abstract, and prosaic mode.

True, historical epic could have a Homeric slant, foreshadowing or reflecting Virgil's own conflation of Homer and history – in Callimachean terms, of heroes and kings. History was Homerized before Augustan times, Virgilianized afterwards: Ennius and Cicero employ *deorum ministeria*, and their style is a fusion of Greek and Roman; Petronius recasts Lucan in a Virgilian mould. But classicizing historical epic was not the same as that of Lucan, nor did it dominate the scene before him. Hellenistic *epos* was not all Homeric, and parts of Ennius' *Annales* – where the interest is contemporary and political – foreshadow the more prosaic methods of Severus and his like. Later Republican epic was presumably similar: for Homer could be too distant, or too elevated a model for contemporary themes. Varius Rufus, Rome's first epicist in 35 B.C. (Hor. *Sat.* 1.10.43), editor of the *Aeneid* in 19, and still a major force, along with Virgil, at the time of the *Ars Poetica* (541) has, in his lines on Antony, the familiar unpoetic ring of diatribe:

> uendidit hic Latium populis agrosque Quiritum
> eripuit, fixit leges pretio atque refixit.

This man sold Latium to the nations[1] *and took away the fields from the citizens, meddling with the laws for money.*

[1] See Hollis (1977) 188, interpreting the words as a reference to Antony's extension of Latin rights.

Epic or didactic, and presumably the latter, Varius' *De morte*, the origin of these lines, like the political sections of Lucretius' *De rerum natura*, shows the trend towards the abstract, undecorated manner of Lucan: Virgil's imitation at *Aen.* 6.621f. is an epic impulse to reincorporate its own – that is, if such material reached didactic via Ennius. But of Varian *forte epos* – epic as such – we have nothing.[1]

Rabirius and Sextilius Ena both chose civil war for their theme. Described by Ovid as *magni...oris* (*Pont.* 4.16.5), classed with Virgil by the soldier-critic Velleius (2.36.3), and relegated by Quintilian to the rank of Pedo (*Inst.* 10.1.90: before faint praise of Lucan), Rabirius shows, in three fragments of his anonymous epic on the war between Antony and Octavian, an unpolished affinity with the *Bellum civile*. Fragment 2:

hoc habeo quodcumque dedi

What I have is what I have given

a motto from Antony's suicide – which also foreshadows the early Imperial Herculaneum papyrus on the Egyptian war – is reminiscent of the Stoic sentiments of Lucan's Vulteius episode in the fourth book, or Cato's pre-suicide ruminations in the ninth. Scientific colour brings the fourth fragment

in tenerum est deducta serum pars intima lactis

the essence of the milk was reduced to a soft curd

into line with the didactic aspect of the *Bellum civile*; and Lucan rewrote fragment 3

ac ueluti Numidis elephans circumdatur altus

and as a massive elephant is surrounded by Numidians

during his account of Scaeva's single combat, 6.208,

sic Libycus densis elephans oppressus ab armis

so a Libyan elephant overwhelmed by many weapons,

a simile not so novel as sometimes claimed.[2] For the rest, Rabirius is Virgilian, or incomprehensible. Fr. 3,

portarumque fuit custos Erucius

Erucius was the guardian of the gates

directs us to *Aen.* 9. 176:

Nisus erat portae custos acerrimus armis

Nisus eager for war was the guardian of the gate

[1] All the fragments seem to be from the *De morte*, or the dubious *Panegyricus Augusti* (Porph. on Hor. *Epist.* 1.16.27–9, where Horace supposedly recasts Varius). See Norden (1926) 3 on *Aen.* 6.621 for fr. 1.

[2] Discussed by Aymard (1951).

while fr. 1,

Idaeos summa cum margine colles

Idean hills with their topmost verge

is conventional in word-order, as well as diction. Civil war reappears as an epic theme at Ov. *Pont.* 4.16.21 and 23, *ueliuolique maris uates*, and *quique acies Libycas Romanaque proelia dixit*, the latter, a poem on the campaigns in Africa, perhaps a source for Lucan Book 9, the former, probably an epic on Sicily or Actium. Next, more substantially, Cornelius Severus and Albinovanus Pedo.

One significant thing about their fragments is that they are embedded in the *Suasoriae* – and that Seneca adduces both as instances of a poet capping the *prosateurs*. The line between prose and verse has become blurred. If an epicist is comparable to a rhetorician or a historian, an epicist is discussable in terms appropriate to prose: and the terms appropriate to declamation and history are only occasionally appropriate to Virgil. We therefore have an alternative epic tradition: Lucan did not write in magnificent isolation. True, the Petronian parody, the debate reflected by Martial ('some say I'm not a poet'), and the criticisms of Quintilian ('the *Bellum civile* is stuff for orators, not for poets') show that Lucan caused a stir in his own day: and today he still has a reputation for extremism. But studied against the background of the fragments of Augustan historical epic his extremes are not only the extravagances of a youth in love with rebellion: and after all, when even younger, Lucan was a 'Neoteric'.

Severus' fragment on the death of Cicero is prosy, cold, logical – the work of a writer arranging words around ideas. Sextilius Ena's single line:

deflendus Cicero est Latiaeque silentia linguae

tears for Cicero and the silence of the Latin tongue,

hardly as ingenious as Seneca would have us believe, disappoints by contrast. One of Severus' phrases (8–9 *ille senatus* | *uindex*) crops up in Lucan: but common stock may explain the parallel as easily as imitation. His historical *exempla* reflect the trend which produced the handbook of Valerius Maximus; his declamatory negligence of historical detail shows that Lucan was not the first to be offhand with events: disregard for narrative – abridgement, curtailment, or total neglect – a factor common to both poets, leads to insistence on, and rationalistic hypertrophy of, the rhetorical moment. It cannot be said with certainty that Cornelius dispensed with the Olympians: but Jupiter would have looked decidedly unhappy in such surroundings.

Scope is uncertain: conflating the three ancient titles – *res Romanae, carmen regale, bellum Siculum* – we are left with an epic on Roman history, part of which may have consisted of an account of the regal period, and part, of the war with Sextus Pompeius around Sicily. Evidence for a regal section is tenuous: Ovid's phrase at *Pont.* 4.16.9, *carmen regale*, does not necessarily involve the kings of Rome; one need only compare Horace's allusion to Pollio's *regum facta* at *Sat* 1.10.42. But Quintilian's liking for the first book ('its style, if applied throughout the *Bellum Siculum*, would have won Severus second place to Virgil', 10.1.89) might, given his preferences, imply a consistently elevated, classicistic Virgilian colour, more suitable for the early kings than for the great men of the recent Republic. Certainly, a grandiose, archaizing manner is attested by fragments such as *stabat apud sacras antistita numinis aras*, and *pelagum pontumque moueri*[1] (frs. 4 and 1). As for the title *Bellum Siculum*, Quintilian probably had in mind the best part, or best known part, of a longer *res Romanae*: a book, or series of books, which, if written in one rather than two or several styles, would have earned Severus a higher place in epic. Conceivably, though not necessarily, a separate publication, this part of the epic fell short of the homogeneity of the first book, the postulated *carmen regale*. The fragments are, in fact, considerably uneven. In addition to the prosaic quality of the passage on the death of Cicero, and the archaizing colour of fragments 1 and 4, there is the average poetic manner of fragment 11 *stratique per herbam* | '*hic meus est*' *dixere* '*dies*...',[2] as also of fragment 3 *huc ades Aonia crinem circumdata serta*,[3] fragment 5 *ignea iam caelo ducebat sidera Phoebe* | *fraternis successor equis*, and fragments 7 *flauo protexerat ora galero*, and 8 †*therua purpureis gemmauit pampinus uuis*. In the same category we can place fragments 6 *et sua concordes dant sibila clara dracones*, 9 *pomosa lentos seruabat in arbore ramos*, and 10 *pinea frondosi coma murmurat Appennini*. But this time we can adduce Lucan himself, who likewise occasionally employed standard poetic language: with fragments 6 and 9 we can compare the ornamental Hesperides excursus, 9.348ff., and with fragment 10, the similar spondaic ending of 2.396 *umbrosis mediam qua collibus Appenninus*, another epic usage of an effeminate neoteric device.[4] Closer to the essential Lucan are the moralizing fragments 2 *ardua uirtuti longeque per aspera cliua* | *eluctanda uia est: labor obiacet omnis honori*,[5] and 12 *luxuriantur opes atque otia longa grauantur*, the first perhaps a comment on the destiny of Rome, the second, a description of the causes of civil war. Quintilian himself implies the connexion with Lucan: Severus, he writes, was a better versifier than poet.[6] Ovid, significantly, was rather more complimentary.

[1] Probus, *GLK* IV 208 notes that fr. 1 comes from the first book; the other fragments are not allocated.

[2] Cf. Lucr. 2.29; Virg. *Georg.* 2.527; *Aen.* 9. 104; Sen. *Med.* 1017. Sen. *Suas.* 2.12 criticizes the lines.

[3] From a proem: for *huc ades* cf. Virg. *Ecl.* 9.39, and Caesius Bassus fr. 2.1.

[4] Cf. Hor. *Epod.* 16.29; Ov. *Met.* 2.266; Pers. 1.95; Quint. *Inst.* 9.4.65 *est permolle*...*cum uersus clauditur* '*Appennino*' *et* '*armamentis*'.

[5] Cf. Lucan 9.402, where the schol. quotes the passage of Severus.

[6] Quint. *Inst.* 10.1.19. Grenade (1950) discusses the influence of Severus on Lucan.

Pedo is more Virgilian. Usually seen as a forerunner of Lucan, his fragment on the voyage of Germanicus is, ironically, full of small-scale parallels, well integrated on the whole, from the *Eclogues*, the *Georgics*, as well as the *Aeneid*:

iam pridem post terga diem solemque relictum
†iamque uident†,[1] notis extorres finibus orbis,
per non concessas audaces ire tenebras
ad rerum metas extremaque litora mundi.
nunc illum, pigris immania monstra sub undis
qui ferat, Oceanum, qui saeuas undique pristis
aequoreosque canes, ratibus consurgere prensis
(accumulat fragor ipse metus), iam sidere limo
nauigia et rapido desertam flamine classem,
seque feris credunt per inertia fata marinis
a ! non felici laniandos sorte relinqui.
atque aliquis prora caecum[2] sublimis ab alta
aera pugnaci luctatus rumpere uisu,
ut nihil erepto ualuit dinoscere mundo,
obstructa in talis effundit pectora uoces:
'quo ferimur? fugit ipse dies orbemque relictum
ultima perpetuis claudit natura tenebris.
anne alio positas ultra sub cardine gentes
atque alium nobis[3] intactum quaerimus orbem?
di reuocant rerumque uetant cognoscere finem
mortales oculos: aliena quid aequora remis
et sacras uiolamus aquas diuumque quietas
turbamus sedes?'

For some time now sun and daylight have been behind them, exiles from the earth they knew, who dare to travel through illicit darkness to the verge of existence and the final shores of the world. At one moment they think that Ocean – the home of monstrous beasts beneath its sluggish waves, of sea dogs and savage monsters in profusion – rises to overwhelm their boats, their fears increased by the crashing breakers; at another, they think their ships are foundering on mud, that their fleet is abandoned by the rapid winds, and that they are to suffer the awful plight, the impotent death of being left as prey to the ferocious animals of the deep. And now some sailor high on top of the prow tries to thrust his vision into the impenetrable fog, but fails to see anything in a world beyond his reach. 'What is our course?', he chokes from his tightened lungs, 'Day has fled and outermost nature encloses the world we have left in everlasting shadows. Do we travel in search of nations living far beneath another pole and another world as yet unknown to man? The gods recall us and forbid our mortal eyes to know the end of things. For what reason do our oars violate foreign seas, and forbidden waters, why do we disturb the silent seats of the gods?'[4]

[1] Possibly *respiciunt*. The text I print is my own. I am pleased to find it does not differ substantially from that of Winterbottom (1974) II 502–4.

[2] Possibly *densum*.

[3] Suggested by R. G. M. Nisbet in a private communication; better than Haupt's *flabris*.

[4] I revise Kent's translation (1912).

But echoes from Virgil apart,[1] Albinovanus is still a declaimer's poet (although less fussy than they), the general shape of the fragment being determined by the rhetorical scheme for descriptions of Ocean: the prose deliberations of Alexander, later used of Caesar crossing the Channel,[2] have here been more aptly transferred to Germanicus' voyage across the North Sea – and this in epic verse.

His sentences have an analogous movement to, although greater length than, those of Lucan, while his conceits and wording – the former are neither bizarre, nor especially pointed: the latter sees a considerable amount of reduplication and variation[3] – have some of Lucan's abstraction, but some of Virgil's congestion: in the speech of his frightened sailor, less fanciful, but still similar to that of Cato's men at *Bell. Civ.* 9.848f.,[4] he is closest to Neronian epic. Once more the gods would have looked uncomfortable. And again, Quintilian, unlike Ovid, was not enthusiastic (10.1.90). Tacitus may have known him,[5] but the schools might be all they have in common.

From the mixed quality of most of this material, considered against Lucan's later innovations, we might conclude that his place in historical epic was similar, if not in intention, at least in effect, to that of Ovid in the mythological:

[1] Since most of the points of contact with Virgil, definite or doubtful, have gone unnoticed, they are listed here: *Ecl.* 6.47 and 52 *a!...infelix*, and 6.77 *a! timidos nautas canibus lacerasse marinis* ~ Pedo, l. 11 *a! non felici* (supporting the exclamation supplied by Gertz); ibid. *canibus...marinis* ~ 7 *aequoreosque canes*, and 10 *feris marinis*; *lacerasse* ~ 11 *laniandos*; *timidos nautas*, and *Aen.* 7.587f. *ut pelagi rupes magno ueniente fragore | quae sese multis circum latrantibus undis | mole tenet* ~ 8 *accumulat fragor ipse metus* (on writing *canes*, Pedo makes an associative transition from the Scylla of the sixth *Eclogue* to the seventh *Aeneid* – in effect, from dogs to barking waves – and as a result remembers *fragor*, the word there taken up by *latrantibus*?); *Geo.* 2.122–3 *extremi sinus orbis* ~ 4 *extremaque litora*; 2.503 *sollicitant alii remis freta caeca* ~ 21–2 *aliena quid aequora remis | et sacras uiolamus aquas*; 2.512 *atque alio patriam quaerunt sub sole iacentem* ~ 18–19 *anne alio positas ultra sub cardine gentes | atque alium nobis intactum quaerimus orbem* (but cf. Hor. *Odes* 2.16.18f. *quid terras alio calentes | sole mutamus*); *Aen.* 1.88 *eripiunt subito nubes caelumque diemque* ~ 1 *diem solemque*, and 14 *erepto mundo*; 2.724 *ferimur per opaca locorum* ~ 16 *quo ferimur?*, and the ensuing description of darkness; 3.583 *immania monstra* ~ 5 *immania monstra*; 4.241 *rapido...flamine*, 5.832 *flamina classem*, and 5.612 *desertosque uidet portus classemque relictam* ~ 9 *rapido desertam flamine classem*; 4.616 *finibus extorris* ~ 2 *extorres finibus*; 5.482 *effundit pectore uoces* (cf. 5.723, 8.70, 11.377 and 840) ~ 15 *obstructa in tales effundit pectora uoces*; 6.729 *fert monstra sub aequore* ~ 5–6 *monstra sub undis | qui ferat*; 10.447 *truci...uisu* ~ 13 *pugnaci... uisu* (*uisu*, in mitigation of *erepto...mundo*, which is equivalent to *erepto oculis prospectu mundi*, not *nisu*: *Aen.* 1.88, above, continues *Teucrorum ex oculis*, and cf. 8.254 *prospectum eripiens oculis*). For some possible imitations of Ovid, see Bardon (1956) 72 n. 1.

[2] Quint. *Inst.* 7.4.2 *Caesar deliberat, an Britanniam impugnet*; the other world motif crops up in this context at Vell. 2.46.1.

[3] Witness *diem solemque* 1; *immania monstra, saeuas undique pristes, aequoreosque canes* 5–7; *nauigia et...classem* 9; *sublimis ab alta* 12; *anne alio...gentes | atque alium...orbem* 18–19. But also note nonchalance about repetition: *dies* and *relictum* occur at 1 and 16, *relinqui* at 11; *orbis* at 2, 16 and 19; *tenebrae* at 3 and 17; *mundus* at 4 and 14.

[4] Note *segnia fata* 849, and *inertia fata* 10; *claustra ferit mundi* 865, and *ad rerum metas extremaque litora mundi* 4; *euoluimur orbe* 876, and *notis extorres finibus orbis* 2. But against direct imitation here, cf., with *imus in aduersos acies*, 876, and *anne alio positas ultra sub cardine gentes* 18, *Bell. Civ.* 8.335–7 *quid transfuga mundi | terrarum totos tractus caelumque perosus, | auersosque polos alienaque sidera quaeris?*

[5] See Tac. *Ann.* 2.23, describing the same storm.

another area of Latin literature met its master, and refused future development. Retrogression was the only solution. For after Ovid, mythological epic reverted to the Virgilian mode in the works of Valerius and Statius; and after Lucan, whose innovations served, amongst other things, to diminish the Homeric and Virgilian affiliations of the genre, there is only Silius – the victim of a poetic which sought salvation in an unimaginative classicism from the generic changes threatened a generation ago.

2. PROSE

Apart from Justin's epitome of Pompeius Trogus' *Historiae Philippicae*, we have little Augustan historiography: Livy, of course, excepted. Pollio, Fenestella, and a considerable number of important memoirs and contemporary histories are known merely by name, or a few scrappy fragments. We do, however, possess Augustus' record of his own achievements, the *Res gestae Divi Augusti*, and some works of a technical nature: the medical part of Celsus' Encyclopaedia, the *De architectura* of Vitruvius, and an abridgement – albeit at two removes – of Verrius Flaccus' *De verborum significatu*. Of Augustan oratory we have almost nothing.

Trogus, a writer of Gallic origin with Sallustian affiliations, set out to rival Livy in scope, dealing with the history of the Near East in forty-four books: beginning with the legendary Ninus of Babylon, he takes us through Macedonian history – hence the title, used by Theopompus and Anaximenes of Lampsacus for their histories of Philip II – into Roman times, closing his account with the year 20 B.C. It is not clear which sources he used: Timagenes has been a favourite candidate, but scholars have also canvassed Herodotus, Ctesias, Dinon, Ephorus, Timaeus, Phylarchus, Polybius, Clitarchus, Posidonius and Livy, as well as Theopompus. Justin's abridgement, of uncertain date, does not give us much of the original. But we do have a speech of Mithridates, at 34.4–7, quoted *in extenso* to give an idea of Trogus' style: wordier and flatter than that of Sallust, but more antithetical and less bland than that of Livy. Like Caesar, he favoured *oratio obliqua* in his speeches, censuring the direct discourse of Livy and Sallust. He also wrote on botany and zoology, providing material for the elder Pliny.

Pollio's *Historiae* are a greater loss: not only for their scope – they covered the period from 60 B.C., perhaps down to Philippi – but also for their style. Pollio began to write his History around 35 B.C., the year of Sallust's death – he inherited Sallust's learned freedman, Ateius Philologus – after an important political career, first as a Caesarian, and then as a supporter of Antony. He had retired after his consulate of 40 B.C. and triumph of 39,[1] to devote himself to letters – oratory, poetry and criticism, as well as historiography. He made quite

[1] 38 B.C. is also a possible date.

an impact by his criticisms of other writers (Caesar wrote without due diligence and regard for truth; Sallust was too archaic, obscure, and figurative; Cicero was faulty, Livy provincial), also by his own peculiar manner of writing, characterized by later estimates as rugged, ascetic and dry. But in the one long fragment which we have, on the death of Cicero, there is no archaism, no perversity. His word order is difficult, and there is a certain starkness – a lack of *nitor* and *iucunditas*, as Quintilian noted. Pollio is certainly an Atticist: but he is no eccentric Thucydidean. Horace tantalizes with his description of the histories in *Odes* 2.1, whence we gain the impression of a pathetic, rhetorical manner, not far distant from the methods of the dramatic historiography of Hellenistic times. Such rhetorical colouring and emotionality, combined with the ideals of the Roman Atticists – an abrupt *Latinitas* and a dour propriety – would have produced a truly remarkable work. Since the last century, much labour has been expended on the question whether he provided a source for Plutarch and Appian in their accounts of the civil war: it seems that he did, but only at second hand, through a Greek intermediary.[1] Fenestella was quite different, an antiquarian in spirit, who wrote an annalistic history of Rome in over twenty-two books. He is quoted for the information he gives on customs and society, not political events. His style is bare and matter-of-fact, ideal for the material he chooses to convey. Not a competitor with Livy, Fenestella is closer to Varro than mainstream historiography.

L. Arruntius is a lesser figure, but of some interest for the history of the Sallustian manner in Rome. According to Seneca his history of the Punic wars brimmed with the more perverse of his predecessor's mannerisms: *bellum facere*, *hiemauit annus*, *ingentes esse famas de Regulo*. Clodius Licinus, a contemporary of Ovid and Iulius Hyginus, likewise went to the earlier Republic for his matter, composing a *Res Romanae*, from the third book of which Livy quotes an event for the year 194 B.C., and Nonius one from the twenty-first book, perhaps for the year 134 B.C.: but that is all we know of its scope, and nothing of its style.

Octavius Ruso may be an invention of Porphyrio, but L. Furnius, a friend of Horace, is real enough, although we know no details, as once again in the case of Octavius Musa, the recipient of two poems in the *Catalepton*. We reach contemporary history with Q. Dellius, who dealt with the Parthian wars of Antony, and a group of five historians who wrote about Augustus: Iulius Marathus, the secretary of the *princeps*, C. Drusus, Julius Saturninus, Aquilius Niger, and Baebius Macer. Suetonius mentions the first four: Servius the fifth. In addition, there were memoirs: Augustus himself wrote *Commentarii*, in thirteen books, dealing with his life up to the war in Spain, 27–24 B.C. Our sole original fragment deals with the star which heralded Caesar's

[1] See Gabba (1956), esp. 83–8, 230–49.

apotheosis in a stiff, rather official style, Atticist and laboured. Agrippa also wrote an autobiography – this, in addition to his cartographical enterprise: in letters, according to Pliny the Elder, he was rustic. Messalla published pamphlets, and, more likely than not, memoirs. Cicero praised his oratory: for Tacitus, he was *Cicerone mitior...et dulcior et in uerbis magis elaboratus*, a verdict substantiated by the fragment in Suetonius, which offers Augustus the title of *pater patriae*. A classicist through and through: Appian, as well as Suetonius, seems to have used his autobiography in Book 5 of the *Civil war*. Maecenas too may have written memoirs, but of this we cannot be certain.

According to Suetonius, Augustus had no time for affectation and archaism; he was equally dismissive of the very different styles of Maecenas, Tiberius and Antony; and Sallust's thefts from Cato were as objectionable to him as the volubility of the Asianists. His own style was

> chaste and elegant, avoiding the variety of attempts at epigram and an artificial order, and as he himself expresses it, the noisomeness of far-fetched words, making it his chief aim to express his thoughts as clearly as possible. With this end in view, to avoid confusion and checking his reader or hearer at any point, he did not hesitate to use prepositions with names of cities, nor to repeat conjunctions several times, the omission of which causes some obscurity, though it adds grace.

Not to say that Augustus had no quirks: Suetonius tells us that he was sometimes popularist in questions of orthography, and had an eccentric preference for *baceolus* over *stultus*, for *uacerrosus* over *cerritus*, for *betizare*, a facetious coinage, over *languere*, and for *uapide se habere* instead of *male se habere*. In his letters, too, he shows an individuality which is hardly a sign of the purist. But the *Res gestae*, a list of Augustus' exploits and achievements, was written to be set up as an inscription; and as we might expect, the manner is official, cold and formal. There is no doubt that in Augustus we have lost a stylist of some interest and accomplishment: but that judgement must be based upon the fragments and what we glean from the critics, not the inscription from Ancyra.

Augustan oratory, despite the impression given by the elder Seneca's collection of specimens, was not all puerile brilliance: the generation prior to the declaimers, and of it, notably Messalla, showed that the style of Cicero – or at least a version of it – was a viable alternative to the follies and extravagances of the schools. Renowned in antiquity for the purity of his manner, Messalla was a moderate, a classicist who translated Hyperides, and wrote on philology. A Republican of the civil war period, he attracted a circle of writers, including Tibullus, thus continuing the system of patronage which appertained in pre-Augustan times.

Vitruvius, the author of ten books on architecture, left style to the experts and schools. A practical fellow, he did not find it easy to write, and he tells us as much. Often obscure, his pages are full of Grecisms, most of them necessitated by his subject matter, but he maintains an admirable objectivity. Antiquity had no specialized scientific or technological idiom, and writers of textbooks and tracts were for the most part at the mercy of rhetoric. Celsus is more stylistically accomplished than Vitruvius but now of greater interest to historians of medicine than students of literature. The eight books we possess constitute the medical section of a larger encyclopaedia, which went by the title of *Artes*. Behind such productions we catch glimpses of an urge to match Greece in scholarship, to fill in cultural gaps – the concept of the complete man is now fully entrenched at Rome. Grammatical and literary studies also had their audience: Hyginus, friend of Ovid, and librarian of the Palatine; Q. Caecilius Epirota, commentator on Virgil; Cloatius Verus, who wrote on the debt of Latin to Greek; Sinnius Capito, grammarian and literary historian; Crassicius, commentator on Cinna, and a philosopher to boot; Scribonius Aphrodisius, writer on orthography; Verrius Flaccus, author of a *De verborum significatu*, a *De obscuris Catonis*, and an *Etruscan antiquities* – such men, too often slighted by literary history, helped Romans feel true rivals to Greece, continuing a trend that Varro had made respectable, after the earlier opposition offered by figures like the elder Cato.

V

EARLY PRINCIPATE

24

CHALLENGE AND RESPONSE

The first century of the Christian era has often been termed the 'age of rhetoric'. Such a designation, which has been used polemically, can be misleading. Nearly all human communication involves 'rhetoric' to some degree: for it is nothing other than the art of effective speaking and writing. It is only in relatively recent times that the hypothesis that such a skill can be schematized and taught has passed out of fashion. Among the Greeks and Romans it was the pivot of a whole educational system; they would have found it hard to understand a critical terminology that equates the rhetorical with the artificial and insincere. Just as they recognized medicine or astronomy as sciences (*artes*) with their own rules and expertise, so the ancients believed that a man could acquire specific techniques to aid him in public speaking and in literary composition. The techniques alone might not suffice, but they were nonetheless indispensable as prerequisites. A young Roman received the rudiments of his education from a *litterator*; thereafter he studied literature under a *grammaticus*; a *rhetor* finally instructed him in the practice of oratory itself. *Disertus*, *eloquens*, *facundus*: the epithets express the aim and object of the whole process. An educated Roman was expected to possess the power of speaking impressively and convincingly in the senate, in the courts and elsewhere. The technicalities of the law could be left to the jurisconsults: but eloquence was universally desirable. There was nothing new in such an outlook. Nor was it any more revolutionary for the precepts and principles of the schools to be adapted to creative writing. Poetry and prose in the Republic and during the Augustan principate were deeply affected by rhetoric. Yet there is a real and obvious disparity between the style of Virgil and Lucan, Cicero and Seneca, Livy and Tacitus. To attribute the change – frequently in tones of regret – solely or largely to the rise of a malign 'rhetoric' is fallacious. Other considerations too have to be given due weight.

The establishment of Augustus' restored Republic, however much a sham it has appeared to later historians, gave birth to a truly classical or 'golden' age of Roman letters. With hopes of the emergence of a peaceful and stable society after long years of civil turmoil arose also a miraculous flowering of literature. The pre-eminence of the early Augustan writers was quickly acknowledged.

Their immediate successors – of whom Ovid, harbinger of the 'silver' age, may be reckoned the first – sought for new ways to validate their own work within the tradition of which they were part. Classical periods are normally followed by a reaction: artists, while implicitly or explicitly conceding and profiting from the achievements of their forerunners, try to avoid sterile imitation. They explore fresh dimensions in style, thought and content, in quest of a justifiable claim to originality and to circumvent odious comparisons.

Tacitus' *Dialogus* is a valuable witness to the attitudes and aspirations of the first century. The arguments of Vipstanus Messalla (25–6, 28–32, 33–6) have been cited to prove the corrupting effects of rhetorical education. Messalla is an advocate of older values in oratory, a stern antagonist of contemporary developments. For him the late Republic was the zenith of oratorical splendour, with Cicero as indisputable master. But the discourse of his impetuous opponent, the modernist Marcus Aper, is equally revealing, for it typifies what must have been a not uncommon viewpoint. Aper sensibly prefaces his exposition with the opinion that the style and types of oratory change with the times (*mutari cum temporibus formas quoque et genera dicendi*, 18). In 19, he remarks that, whereas once a knowledge of rhetorical doctrines (*praecepta rhetorum*) and of philosophical aphorisms (*philosophorum placita*) was something of a rarity, the situation had now radically altered:

at hercule peruulgatis iam omnibus, cum uix in cortina quisquam adsistat quin elementis studiorum, etsi non instructus, at certe imbutus sit, nouis et exquisitis eloquentiae itineribus opus est, per quae orator fastidium aurium effugiat.

But now everything is common knowledge. There is scarcely anyone in the body of the court who, even if he has not been fully instructed, has not at least acquired some acquaintance with the basic tenets of the schools. There is, therefore, a need for new and subtle paths of eloquence, by which an orator may avoid boring his audience.

Changed conditions demanded novelty. Rhetoric and philosophy, at least at a superficial level, were more widely disseminated. Orators had to respond to the situation. Audiences were more critical, more prone to boredom (*fastidium*) if their attention was not firmly held. A little later, Aper comments further on the predilections of the day:

iam uero iuuenes et in ipsa studiorum incude positi, qui profectus sui causa oratores sectantur, non solum audire, sed etiam referre domum aliquid inlustre et dignum memoria uolunt; traduntque in uicem ac saepe in colonias ac prouincias suas scribunt, siue sensus aliquis arguta et breui sententia effulsit, siue locus exquisito et poetico cultu enituit. (20)

What is more, the young men, still at the formative stage of their training, who are seeking to make progress by attaching themselves to established orators, desire not merely to hear but to carry away with them some brilliant and memorable passage. They pass such things on to each other and often cite them in letters to their home towns among the colonies and provinces: perhaps some idea that glitters with a pointed and brief epigram or a paragraph that is illuminated by a subtle and poetic beauty.

His words present a vivid picture of Rome as an educational centre for the whole empire. (It is indeed notable that, in the early Imperial period, men from the provinces, and especially from Spain, played a leading role in oratory and literature.) Aper stresses the love of verbal brilliance, the eagerness to invent epigrams (*sententiae*) and the borrowing of poetic devices by orators. All three of these traits have been repeatedly traced as characteristic qualities of the post-Augustan style. These were the days when, according to H. E. Butler, we find above all 'a straining after effect, a love of startling colour, produced now by over-gorgeous or over-minute imagery, now by a surfeit of brilliant epigram'.[1] To him, the 'silver' writers lacked restraint and propriety.

Butler's tone is pejorative. Such trends have always been objectionable to critics directly or indirectly oriented towards Romanticism. They were equally repugnant to Quintilian, whose *Institutio oratoria* was aimed at revivifying classical ideals – in part an ethical programme, for Quintilian held that morality and stylistics were closely interrelated. Perverse, degenerate rhetoric was, for him, symptomatic of a malaise infecting society and individuals.

Leaving aside modern critical and ancient moral presuppositions, we may still plausibly link the rise of the 'new style' with one feature of rhetorical education: *declamatio*. *Declamationes* were set speeches on given themes, either deliberative (*suasoriae*) or forensic (*controversiae*). They were not merely scholastic exercises. Professors of rhetoric found in them a vehicle to display their own talents, to attract a clientele. The declamations became, therefore, a form of public entertainment. Seneca the Elder, who compiled a large collection of *declamationes* delivered by rhetors and others in his lifetime (with introductions and commentary), states that declamation first became a widespread activity in the reign of Augustus. Teachers, it appears, entered into what amounted to a contest with each other as purveyors of words and conceits. That these performances were conducive to the growth of exotic and extreme styles is not surprising. They doubtless imbued their audiences with a sophisticated appreciation of that dazzling 'brilliance' which, as we have seen, was much esteemed by Marcus Aper. Seneca's compilation reveals that the results were often hollow and strained, sometimes *outré*. Yet the fault did not lie in rhetoric itself; rather it was in the ends to which rhetoric was prostituted. *Declamatio* was attacked at the time as one of the causes of the 'decline of eloquence'. Messalla in the *Dialogus* (35) voices a standard criticism: the themes chosen for declamation were bizarre and unrelated to the real-life situations pupils would

[1] Butler (1909) 1.

eventually have to face in the courts. Such attacks should not be taken too literally: it is certainly erroneous to regard the declamations as valueless in preparing youths for practical advocacy.[1] On the other hand, the subject matter of the *suasoriae* was more prone to be fantastic (and hence susceptible to stylistic floridity) than that of the *controversiae*: and it was the former which often had direct points of contact with the material treated by poets, historians and philosophers. The commonplaces and 'purple patches' beloved by the declaimers are often recognizable in first-century literature – as also the forms, structures and methods of deliberative orations. But it may be said that if rhetoric affected poetry the reverse process was also true. Ovid's style was much admired by the declaimers. Quintilian, hardly with approval, said that Lucan was 'fit rather to be imitated by orators than by poets' (*Inst.* 10.1.90). Sententiousness and *panni purpurei* were, after all, more obviously a legacy of poetry than prose: and the adoption of a poetic style by prose writers (which is as true of Livy as of the 'silver' historians) inevitably led to the inclusion of poetic/declamatory *topoi* and attitudes in their work. Historiography had, in any case, traditionally been viewed as a genre akin to poetry, and especially to tragedy and epic.

So far as poetry was concerned the rising popularity of public readings (*recitationes*) at this time – in many ways parallel to the burgeoning of *declamatio* in the schools – may have provided an impetus for the assumption of more overtly declamatory techniques. Marcus Aper in the *Dialogus* (9) speaks slightingly of poets who, after all their labours, are constrained to plead with people to attend their recitations – and to pay for hiring a hall and chairs and for producing programmes (*libelli*) into the bargain. Satirists like Persius, Petronius and Juvenal are no less scathing in their allusions to *recitatio*. Nonetheless, it had a real function. It was a form of cultural recreation as well as a means by which poets could establish a reputation. Audiences might well have to face effusions of bad verse (as Juvenal grumbles at the beginning of his first satire), but they also had the chance of hearing more skilful writers. Pliny saw in *recitatio* a way for authors to subject their work to independent assessment (*Epist.* 7.17.13). For a professional poet in need of patronage the recitation must have been of some assistance. Statius, for instance, at one point refers to the fact that senators were in the habit of attending his readings (*Silv.* 5.2.160–3) – and Juvenal, in sarcastic vein, confirms their success, though denying that they brought Statius any financial benefit (*Sat.* 7.82ff.).[2] For poets like Statius and Martial, the problem of finding patrons was urgent and pressing. The days of such coteries as those presided over by Maecenas and Messalla Corvinus

[1] Cf., esp., Parks (1945) 61ff.

[2] On Juvenal's allusion to Statius, cf. Tandoi (1969) 103–22. The satirist's remarks on Statius' financial status should not be taken at face value.

under Augustus had passed.[1] Commissions had now to be canvassed among the denizens of a new aristocracy of wealth. For many of the poets of the first century known to us this difficulty did not arise: they were rich men themselves. For them *recitationes* were more a self-indulgence than a necessity. One thinks of the millionaire consular Silius Italicus who, according to Pliny, frequently submitted his *Punica* to criticism by recitations (*Epist.* 3.7.5): it is improbable that he encountered much candour. The contrast between two figures like Silius and Statius is instructive: in this period, we see side by side the dilettante and the professional. The climate of the times did not endow poets with the status once enjoyed by Virgil and Horace. Martial bewailed the altered scene (1.107).

If the 'silver' writers have been lambasted for their addiction to 'rhetoric', their supposed pedantry has been no less thoroughly vilified. It is true that the tradition of *doctrina* in poetry, deriving from the innovations of the republican *novi poetae* and hence from the Alexandrians, could be taken too far, that allusiveness and obscurity can be fatiguing for a modern reader. One sometimes gains the impression that a poet such as Statius deliberately set out *épater les savants*. This 'learning' too has been viewed as a façade: the outgrowth of an over-zealous culling of earlier authors and of handbooks. For the first century was a time of encyclopaedism. The gathering of information on diverse subjects into a convenient form was educationally helpful: for the rhetoricians liked to pose as polymaths, to have ready to hand those *exempla* and anecdotes which could easily be worked into their orations. To fill this need, digests and handbooks were produced, an extant example of which is Valerius Maximus' *Facta et dicta memorabilia*. This work, in nine books, was dedicated to the Emperor Tiberius some time after the disgrace of Sejanus in A.D. 31. It comprises a loosely-constructed collection of historical instances and quotable aphorisms. Valerius makes it clear in his preface that the purpose of his work is to save the reader from the arduous task of searching directly for such material in the many distinguished authors he claims to have consulted. For the sake of easy reference, each book is subdivided under various headings, with most sections presenting Roman and non-Roman instances. As well as anecdotal expositions on such topics as religion (Book 1), social, political and military institutions (Book 2) and well-known legal causes (Book 8), he cites illustrations of moral qualities both good (Books 3 to 6) and bad (Book 9), interlarded with disquisitions, at a generally superficial level, on well-worn philosophical themes. In such a work it would be wrong to expect deep insight or originality. Valerius' approach is declamatory, his style often pedantically sententious, his ideas

[1] C. Calpurnius Piso, forced to suicide by Nero in 65, may be seen, in his encouragement of a literary circle, as a pale reflection of his Augustan forerunners. On the background, cf. Cizek (1972) esp. 67–9.

threadbare and hackneyed. Yet, for orators and writers wishing to add a veneer of learning to their narratives, such a compendium would have been of considerable service. In later antiquity it was more than once abridged; in the Middle Ages and Renaissance it became a favourite educational text. Valerius has now lost both his usefulness and his appeal; but as a sidelight on first-century rhetoric he is worthy of examination.

In assessing other possible influences on changing stylistic fashions in this period, caution is always necessary. The autocratic rule of the emperors may have affected profoundly the outlook of such writers as Lucan and Tacitus: but it is dangerous to speak too glibly of forms of government engendering particular literary or oratorical styles. The creed of Stoicism – dominant at this time – impregnated a great deal of poetry and prose: but the Stoic theory of style, which emphasized the necessity of 'naturalness' and 'clarity' does not seem to have produced the results we might have predicted on such men as Seneca, Lucan, Persius or Statius. To see the literature of the first century in perspective, it seems best to bear in mind a number of disparate but possibly cumulative factors, educational, social, political and philosophical, all of which are, to a greater or lesser degree, relevant to the whole picture. The most satisfactory starting-point, however, is surely to be found in an analysis of literary developments in terms of a response to the challenge of the 'golden' age that had occurred so shortly before: for in coming to terms with himself, an artist has first to come to terms with his predecessors.

25

PERSIUS

The satires of Persius are preceded by fourteen choliambic lines, which say in effect: 'I have not undergone any of the usual rituals of consecration; I only half belong to the bards' fraternity. But, as we know, the prospect of cash makes all kinds of untalented people poetic.' By this disclaimer Persius hopes to win indulgence. The clichés of inspiration are presented with unmistakable irony: Persius has not drunk from the *fons caballinus* 'the nag's spring' (a deflationary translation of the Greek Hippocrene); 'as far as he remembers' he has not had any dreams on Mt Parnassus (a satirical reference to the dreams of Callimachus and Ennius); and he leaves the *Heliconides* 'the daughters of Helicon' to established writers. Nevertheless, although he is only 'a half clansman' (*semipaganus*), Persius does regard himself as in some sense a *poeta* with a *carmen* to contribute; and since his pose as a starving hack is clearly a comic device (because he was quite well off), we assume he has other reasons for writing.

The lines have caused much dispute, but while the choice of metre is odd (cf. Petronius, *Satyricon* 5), there is no good reason to doubt that they form a single piece and were intended to serve as a prologue, not as an epilogue.

Satire 1

In Ovid (*Met.* 11.180ff.) we read how King Midas' barber discovered that his master had asses' ears and whispered the secret into a hole in the ground. Persius' secret, however, is that everyone in Rome has asses' ears; and instead of trying to bury it he confides it to his book. In the myth Midas was given the ears as a punishment for his critical incompetence – he had judged Pan superior to Apollo in a musical contest. So in Persius the Romans' asininity is shown in their corrupt literary taste. Poets become fashionable without serving a proper apprenticeship, their recitals are occasions for affectation and self-advertisement, and their main purpose is to win applause. The works themselves are objectionable for various reasons. Some are grandiose (epic and tragedy), some are sentimental (pastoral and elegy), some are a mixture of both (epyllion and romantic epic), but all are artificial in the sense that they are not based on any profound experience and offer no serious interpretation of life. Poetry has become a social pastime.

Some of the best lines describe recitations:

scilicet haec populo pexusque togaque recenti
et natalicia tandem cum sardonyche albus
sede leges celsa, liquido cum plasmate guttur
mobile collueris, patranti fractus ocello.
tunc neque more probo uideas nec uoce serena
ingentis trepidare Titos, cum carmina lumbum
intrant et tremulo scalpuntur ubi intima uersu.

On your birthday you will finally read this stuff
from a public platform, carefully combed, in a new white toga,
flashing a gem on your finger, rinsing your supple throat
with a clear preparatory warble, your eyes swooning in ecstasy.
Then, what a sight! The mighty sons of Rome in a dither,
losing control of voice and movement as the quivering strains
steal under the spine and scratch the secret passage.

This and other examples show that although the satire is primarily about literature it also carries a wider condemnation; for a degenerate taste is the sign of a degenerate character. Romans have lost their virility. Later, after quoting lines from a wild Bacchic scene in which the vocabulary is markedly Greek and the musical effects overdone, Persius is warned about the dangers of writing satire – not unreasonably, for exotic subjects of that kind were employed by Nero and his acquaintances. But Persius evades the point by a clever manoeuvre: he won't tell anyone about Rome's stupidity, he will simply confide it to his book. That, he says, will be read only by the discerning few. The vulgar can find their entertainment elsewhere.

Satire 2

In describing wrong types of prayer Persius moves from hypocrisy to superstition and then to sheer stupidity (e.g. the man who prays for a long and healthy life while gorging himself on rich food); offerings of livestock and gold are really an insult, for they imply that the gods are as greedy as the people who worship them.

Images of grossness recur: e.g. *pulmone et lactibus unctis* 'offal and greasy guts', *grandes patinae tuccetaque crassa* 'huge platefuls of thick goulash', *extis et opimo ferto* 'innards and rich cakes'. Even the qualities mentioned at the end are presented in culinary terms: human and divine law are to be 'blended in the mind' (*compositum animo*) and the heart is to be 'cooked in high-quality honour' (*incoctum generoso honesto*). Such spiritual food-offerings, however, *are* acceptable to heaven.

Several people are addressed, but as Persius' presence is not acknowledged in return, no dialogue develops. Instead the poet assumes the worshippers' voices, quotes their prayers (often in a ridiculous form), and then comments satirically *in propria persona*. The liveliness of the style comes partly from the varied use of statement, question, and prayer, partly from the comic device whereby things are treated as living agents and vice versa (a prayer is acquisitive – *emax*, a coin sighs in despair, a dead man is a *bidental* – i.e. a piece of ground which has been fenced off after being struck by lightning), and partly from the shifts of tone produced by different levels of diction. Thus some prayers run as follows: 'If only my uncle would pop off (*ebulliat*)' and 'O that I might rub out (*expungam*) that ward of mine.' At the other end of the scale we have a line worthy of a Hebrew prophet:

o curuae in terris animae caelestium inanes

O souls bent on earth, devoid of the things of heaven!

And sometimes the two effects come together, when a sordid prayer is offered in the solemn language of supplication.

Although the second satire lacks the breadth and variety of Juvenal's tenth, it is more consistently noble in spirit. This quality gained esteem for Persius among the Church Fathers, the monks of the Middle Ages, and all who had been taught that 'to obey is better than sacrifice and to hearken than the fat of rams'.[1]

Satire 3

Late in the morning a lazy student, who is a comic representation of Persius himself, is wakened by a companion. He tries in a rather hectic and dishevelled way to start work, but fails to make any progress. The companion lectures him on indolence and complacency, and finally launches into a sermon on remorse:

magne pater diuum, saeuos punire tyrannos
haut alia ratione uelis, cum dira libido
mouerit ingenium feruenti tincta ueneno:
uirtutem uideant intabescantque relicta.

O mighty father of the gods, when sadistic lust with its point
dipped in fiery poison incites despots to savage
cruelty, may it please thee to inflict just one punishment on them:
let them behold Goodness and waste with remorse at having spurned her.

These lines have a grandeur which impressed even Milton.[2] We tend to forget that they are addressed to an audience of one student with a hangover.

[1] Samuel 1.15.22. Cf. Plato, *Alcibiades* 2 149ff.

[2] Milton, *P.L.* 4.846ff.

Soon after, the student disappears and the friend's voice merges with that of the poet as he goes on to stress the supreme importance of philosophy – knowing why we're here and what really matters. Objections are supposed to come from a centurion – 'one of that smelly breed' – who ridicules philosophers and their dreary rubbish in language well beyond the range of a simple soldier. And then comes the best passage of all. A glutton disobeys his doctor:

turgidus hic epulis atque albo uentre lauatur,
gutture sulpureas lente exhalante mefites.
sed tremor inter uina subit calidumque trientem
excutit e manibus, dentes crepuere retecti,
uncta cadunt laxis tunc pulmentaria labris.
hinc tuba, candelae, tandemque beatulus alto
compositus lecto crassisque lutatus amomis
in portam rigidas calces extendit. at illum
hesterni capite induto subiere Quirites.

Bloated with food and queasy in the stomach our friend goes off
to his bath, with long sulphurous belches issuing from his throat.
As he drinks his wine a fit of the shakes comes over him, knocking
the warm tumbler from his fingers; his bared teeth chatter;
suddenly greasy savouries come slithering from his loose lips.
The sequel is funeral-march and candles. And then the late lamented
plastered with heavy odours reclines on a high bed,
pointing his stiff heels to the door. He is raised on the shoulders
of pall bearers with freedmen's caps – citizens as of yesterday.

Though loose dramatically, the satire is held together by its theme, which might be summed up as 'health requires training.' Physical and spiritual interact; thus pallor, swelling, fever, and shivering are related to moral defects, while gluttony, rage, lust, and fear produce bodily symptoms. Medical language came naturally to the Stoics, who laid much stress on the therapy of the emotions.

Satire 4

In the opening section Socrates takes the young Alcibiades to task:[1] although clever at managing the mob, he doesn't know right from wrong and cares only for his own pleasures. No one tries to know himself; everyone criticizes the defects of others. A successful farmer is dismissed as a miser; one who lazes in the sun is accused of being a male prostitute. In this malicious world a man may try to hide his sores, even from himself. He gets used to depending on other people's admiration. But it's better to face the truth, however unflattering.

The poem begins well, and arresting phrases occur throughout. The two samples of abuse, directed at the farmer and the idler, have a Juvenalian force.

[1] The setting is taken from Plato, *Alcibiades 1*.

(In the second, one notes the figurative vulgarisms and the use of terminology from the *Georgics* to describe homosexual depilation.) The satire as a whole, however, is rather weak. The ridicule of the demagogue Alcibiades has little bearing on imperial Rome. The sequence of thought is sometimes confusing. For example, after comparing malicious talk to a battle (42f.), Persius mentions someone with a secret wound. We assume it has been inflicted by a fellow-citizen, but in fact it is a moral defect which the man is concealing from his neighbours. Finally, some apparent links between the Greek/political background of the first half and the Roman/social background of the second prove illusory – or rather they connect things which don't belong together. Thus the sunbather is abused by a stranger for showing his posterior to the public (36). Clearly we are meant to condemn this foul attack, yet the insulting words recall what Socrates has previously said to Alcibiades: 'Your highest aim is to pamper your skin with sunshine' (17f.) and 'stop wagging your tail at the admiring public' (15f.). These blemishes cannot be explained away.

Satire 5

After a discussion of style, in which tragedy (pompous, artificial, insincere) is contrasted with satire (plain, down-to-earth, genuine), Persius goes on to speak of his friendship with the Stoic Cornutus, who held that only the truly free man could live a virtuous life.[1] About sixty lines explore the distinction between legal and moral freedom, and then another sixty demonstrate that greed, sex, ambition, and superstition are all forms of slavery. In an ironical coda Pulfenius, a massive centurion, sweeps all this Greek nonsense away with a coarse guffaw.

In this, the longest and most elaborate of the satires, several forms are employed, including dialogue, autobiographical narrative, monologue, diatribe (with hypothetical protests), and a dramatic scene based on Menander's *Eunuch*. Of many excellent passages the following is perhaps the most lively:

> mane piger stertis. 'surge' inquit Auaritia, 'eia
> surge.' negas. instat. 'surge' inquit. 'non queo.' 'surge.'
> 'et quid agam?' 'rogat! en saperdas aduehe Ponto,
> castoreum, stuppas, hebenum, tus, lubrica Coa.
> tolle recens primus piper et sitiente camelo.
> uerte aliquid; iura.' 'sed Iuppiter audiet.' 'eheu,
> baro, regustatum digito terebrare salinum
> contentus perages, si uiuere cum Ioue tendis.'

It's daylight and you're lying snoring. 'Get up' says Lady Greed,
'Hey, get up!' You won't. She persists, 'Up!'

[1] For the idea that 'Only the wise man is free' see Cicero, *Paradoxa Stoicorum* 5 and Horace, *Sat.* 2.7.

'I can't.
'Up!'
'What for?'
'What a question! Go and fetch kippers from Pontus,
plus beaver-musk oakum ebony frankincense slippery silk.
Grab that fresh pepper before the camel's had a drink.
Get there first. Do a deal; swear an oath.'
'But God will hear.'
'Ha! Listen, you numbskull, if you want God on your side,
you'll spend your days happily scraping the bottom of the barrel.'

The fifth satire is particularly interesting for its ingenious transformations of Horace. The *Satires* and *Epistles* were always near the surface of Persius' mind, and he drew on them again and again in a spirit of admiring emulation. In 5.52ff. we hear of men's various pursuits:

hic satur irriguo mauult turgescere somno.

Another lies replete and bloated in well soaked sleep.

The source of *irriguo somno* is Horace, *Sat.* 2.1.8–9:

transnanto Tiberim, somno quibus est opus alto,
irriguumque mero sub noctem corpus habento.

For sound sleep: swim across the Tiber; before retiring
ensure that the system is thoroughly soaked in strong wine.

Persius has compressed 'sound sleep' and 'a body well soaked in wine' into 'well soaked sleep'. That is an example of a clever *iunctura*, i.e. a combination of ordinary words which produces a new and striking phrase.

Satire 6

This is a letter in which Persius develops an idea found in Horace, *Epist.* 2.2. 190ff., namely that one should live to the limit of one's income and not worry unduly about the claims of an heir. Other Horatian features are the procedure whereby objections are stated and overcome, the epistolary framework which implies a friendly interest in someone else's doings, the pleasant description of Luna and its climate,[1] and above all the advocacy of enjoyment as a principle of behaviour. This relaxed manner is no doubt partly due to the addressee, for Caesius Bassus was a lyric poet who carried on Horace's tradition by his interest in metres and his lighthearted approach to love; he even had a Sabine farm.

Yet the poem is not quite so genial as the opening suggests. While gluttony and parsimony are attacked with typical vigour, the *via media* has few positive features. Perhaps that is why, unlike Horace, Persius 'fails to convince us that

[1] The modern Luni, now inland from the bay of Spezia.

enlightened self-indulgence is a true facet of his character'.[1] Nevertheless, the satire succeeds in a number of respects. There is a splendid scene where a despatch arrives from Caesar reporting that the pride of Germany has crashed to defeat; plans are being eagerly made for a public celebration. Then the whole edifice begins to crumble as we learn that the occasion in question is Caligula's farcical triumph in which men in yellow wigs were passed off as German prisoners. There follows an argument between Persius and his heir, in which we don't actually hear the latter speak and yet we know what he's saying. The technique is like that of an actor talking on the telephone. The literary texture is also very rich. Several expressions recall the language of Propertius, a repulsive slave-dealer is satirized through a parody of Virgil, and Ennius is directly quoted.[2] This is learned satire for a sophisticated audience; there can be no question of general reform.

The poems outlined above were written by a well-to-do young man in his mid twenties. Aules Persius Flaccus was an *eques* from the Etruscan town of Volaterrae. He went to school in Rome, where he came under the influence of the Stoic Cornutus, a freedman of the Seneca household. He also knew other Stoics, like the senator Thrasea Paetus. Such men had little use for Nero, and the Emperor regarded them with suspicion. After an unsuccessful plot in A.D. 65 (three years after Persius' death) a number of them perished; others were exiled. Had Persius been alive he could hardly have escaped. The satires themselves were politically harmless, except for the first, which attacked the writings of wealthy dilettanti and *ipso facto* the poetry of Nero and his friends. Nothing, however, was published in Persius' lifetime, nor did he finish the book. According to the *Vita* (42–5) some lines were removed from *Sat.* 6 to give the impression of completeness; then the poems were handed over to Caesius Bassus, who produced the first edition.

The poet's interest in Stoicism had some bearing on his choice of themes, and it helps to explain his earnest tone and his rather intolerant attitude to human failings. Unlike Lucilius and Horace, he does not really care about places or people; he is primarily interested in behaviour and in ethical (which includes literary) ideas. These ideas are worked out within a very restricted social framework. The *plebs* exists only as an anonymous mass (*plebecula*, *popellus*); the mercantile class is insensitive and greedy; politicians have no constructive role – their only function is to placate the mob; soldiers are boors; women are largely ignored. Happiness appears to consist in having a comfortable income from land, which makes it possible to spend one's time studying and discussing philosophy.

[1] Nisbet (1963) 67.

[2] With *turdarum saliuas* (24), *surda uota* (28), *cinere ulterior* (41) cf. Propertius 4.8.28, 5.58; 3.1.36; with *nec sit praestantior alter* (76) cf. Virgil, *Aen.* 6.164; l. 9 is from the *Satires* of Ennius – see Skutsch (1968) 25–7.

These limitations disqualify Persius from greatness, but he never claimed to be a major poet, and it is the critic's business to appreciate him for what he was. The ideals implied in his work are sensible and honourable (1, 4, 6) and at times noble (2, 3, 5). If he doesn't always affirm them with dignity – well, dignity is not a satirist's prime concern. And if there is some flexibility of viewpoint between, say, 2.64ff. and 6.68ff., that may tell in his favour. He is certainly consistent enough not to raise doubts about his sincerity – doubts of a kind which will always hamper any interpretation of Juvenal as a serious moralist. Persius *can* laugh at himself (see the Prologue and the beginning of 1 and 3), and for all his loyalty to Stoicism his picture of the school is not oppressively reverent (3.53–5). It is mainly his verbal artistry, however, which claims permanent attention. Some of his words are rarely encountered elsewhere (e.g. *canthus*, *obba*, and *tucceta*); others are given extended meanings (e.g. *aqualiculus*, *aristae*, *pulpa*); others he made up himself (e.g. *Pegaseius*, *semipaganus*, and *poetrides*); grammatical forms have odd functions (e.g. infinitives are used as nouns, and nouns are used as adjectives); there are strong tonal contrasts and abrupt transitions of thought. But Persius' most interesting feature is his gift for compressed and unusual metaphors. Sometimes these can be understood in the light of their origins; thus in 5.92 'tearing old granny-weeds out of someone's lungs' – i.e. 'getting rid of his long-standing misconceptions' – is a variation of 'pulling thorns (i.e. vicious desires) from the heart' (Horace, *Epist.* 1.14.4–5). Sometimes the metaphor unfolds itself, as in 3.20ff. where it gradually becomes plain that the student is a badly made pot. But sometimes the strands are so tightly twisted that they cannot easily be unravelled. Thus when the untalented are tempted by cash (Prologue 14), *cantare credas Pegaseium nectar* 'you'd swear they were carolling nectar worthy of Pegasus' spring';[1] and philosophers walk about staring at the ground, *murmura cum secum et rabiosa silentia rodunt* (3.81) – literally 'gnawing mutterings and mad silences with themselves'.

When all these features are taken together they add up to an idiosyncratic but nonetheless impressive achievement. In recommending the poet today we can do no better than quote his own appeal (1.125):

aspice et haec, si forte aliquid decoctius audis

If you've an ear for a concentrated brew, then have a look at this –

which reminds us that for reading Persius one sense is not enough.

[1] This seems to be derived from a line of Honestos: Πηγασίδος κρήνης νεκταρέων λιβάδων '[You had your fill of] the nectar-flow of Pegasus' spring.' See Gow and Page (1968) I 270.

26

THE YOUNGER SENECA

I. INTRODUCTION: THE STYLISTIC REVOLUTIONARY

A generation after Seneca's suicide Quintilian composed his survey of Greek and Roman authors, classified by genres. Only in its very last paragraph (*Inst.* 10.1.125–31) does he mention Seneca:

In treating each genre of literature I have deliberately postponed discussion of Seneca. The reason is a belief which has falsely circulated concerning me: it has been supposed that I condemn him, and even that I detest him. This befell me in the course of my efforts to bring style back into conformity with stricter standards at a time when it was depraved, and paralysed by every kind of fault. Now at that period Seneca was practically the only author being read by the young. I protest that I was not trying to banish him entirely; but neither was I about to let him be preferred to his betters. These Seneca had attacked endlessly, realizing that his own style was utterly different from theirs...And the young did not so much imitate him as worship him; they dropped as far away below him as he himself had fallen from the heights of the ancient authors...Generally speaking, however, Seneca had many virtues as a writer. His mind was ready, and well stocked. He was capable of immense application. His factual knowledge was great (although in this he was sometimes misled by the people to whom he delegated some of his researches). He treated almost every subject of literary study: speeches of his, poems, letters, and dialogues are all before the public. In philosophy he was not thorough enough; and yet he was a superlative assailant of the vices. There are many brilliant *sententiae* [see below, p. 513] in him, as there is also much that is worth reading for moral improvement. In style, however, much of his writing is depraved; and its effect is all the deadlier because it is rich in attractive faults.

This passage has naturally exerted enormous influence on Seneca's literary reputation; but it has not always been read critically and in its historical context. On objective questions of style and ancient literary history, Quintilian's opinion may usually be accepted; and so here. He is to be believed when he represents Seneca's work as nothing less than a one-man revolution against the entire tradition of Rome, and indeed of Greece also. All the other authors in Quintilian's survey could be neatly slotted into a traditional genre; Seneca, alone, attempted almost all the genres. Other Romans might painfully acquire a style, like pupils in the eighteenth-century Royal Academy, by sedulous imitation of the Old Masters, and delicate variations on them; Seneca both neglected and despised the ancient models, substituting a manner of writing that was all his own. We may further believe Quintilian when he indicates that the Senecan revolution might well have succeeded, had not Quintilian himself laboured in the classrooms of Flavian Rome to recall Latin style to the norms of antiquity.

So much is literary history. The rest is a matter of sympathy and taste, and here Quintilian cannot be allowed the same absolute authority, any more than any other critic. Style is his primary interest. For all his openmindedness he cannot be expected to sympathize with the style which has dominated the preceding generation, which violates all his principles, and which he has spent a lifetime in eradicating. Still less can he be fairly expected to probe beneath that style's surface, and to attempt a balanced evaluation of Seneca's literary achievement in all its aspects. In fact, a very long time was to pass before anybody attempted such a thing. The life-work of Seneca resembles many other artistic and political phenomena of the later Julio-Claudian dynasty, in that it is innovative, contemptuous of earlier categories and conventions, hyperbolic – and shortlived, barely surviving the catastrophic collapse of the dynasty. In the reaction towards classicism which followed (and is nobly represented by Quintilian), it had little hope of sympathy. Almost the only later Roman authors who show a genuine admiration for Seneca as a writer are the Christians; and this is no accident, inasmuch as they themselves are anticlassicists and revolutionaries in their way.[1] The era of his greatest influence on European literature belongs, in fact, not to the classical period at all, but to the sixteenth and seventeenth centuries.[2] Thereafter it declined, approximately *pari passu* with the decline of Latin itself from the status of a major literary dialect to that of a scholastic pursuit. With the exception of T. S. Eliot,[3] no literary critic of the first rank has seriously occupied himself with any part of Seneca's work in the twentieth century. Professional classicists, on the other hand, have been paying ever-increasing attention to him; yet even among these there have been relatively few attempts at a general literary-critical estimate, and nothing approaching a *communis opinio* has yet emerged. There is, indeed, a general disposition to take Seneca more seriously than was customary at any time between the ideological upheavals of the seventeenth century and those of the twentieth; but he continues to resist conventional literary categorization as stoutly as he did in Quintilian's day. For these reasons the present survey,

[1] For the pagan and Christian *testimonia* to Seneca, see Trillitzsch (1971) II.

[2] See, e.g., Eliot (1927), for his effect on dramatic poetry; Williamson (1951), for his importance in the story of English prose style; and Regenbogen (1927/8) for a general summary of his influence on continental European literature.

[3] Eliot (1927).

while it endeavours to respect both the ancient texts and the enormous variety of modern opinions, must necessarily be tentative, and in some degree personal.

2. LIFE AND WORKS

Seneca was no more free of extremes in his life than in his writings, and his biography is as dramatic in its vicissitudes as any in the story of Rome. Here, however, we are to consider only the aspects of it that seem directly related to his education as a writer. Broadly speaking, these are three: his family connexion with the declamation-schools, his early-acquired enthusiasm for philosophical studies, and his prolonged, intimate experience of despotic power.

His father Seneca (usually distinguished as 'the Elder' or – inaccurately – 'the Rhetor') has recorded his vivid memories of the Augustan declamation-schools in the *Suasoriae* and *Controversiae*. The latter work was composed in about A.D. 37, at the express request of his three sons Novatus, our Seneca, and Mela. They were passionately interested, the father informs us, in the declamatory skills of the generation that had just passed, and above all in the *sententiae* uttered by the declaimers: that is, the concisely formulated generalities *tamquam quae de fortuna, de crudelitate, de saeculo, de diuitiis dicuntur* 'such as those which are pronounced about Fortune, cruelty, the times we live in, and riches' (*Controversiae* 1 *praef.* 23). Among those who were present at such exhibitions the elder Seneca records many of his most able contemporaries in all fields: statesmen, from Augustus himself downwards; historians such as Livy and Cremutius Cordus; poets, most notably Ovid; and the philosophers Papirius Fabianus and Attalus. With some of them he formed close personal ties. For example, L. Junius Gallio, a senator and a friend of Ovid's, later adopted his eldest son, Novatus. This inherited familiarity with the declaimers seems to have been decisive in the formation of the younger Seneca's prose style; all the major characteristics of that style can already be discerned in the elder's verbatim accounts of the extemporary debates.

To the same cause, no doubt, the younger Seneca owed his special interest in Ovid and his poetry (below, section 4); and also his abiding enthusiasm for philosophy. Two out of the three philosophers whom he mentions as having inspired him in his youth were in fact also declaimers – Fabianus and the Stoic Attalus.[1] Fabianus in particular was admired for his *dulces sententiae*, his attacks on the wickedness of the age, his copious descriptions of rural and urban landscapes and of national customs (Seneca the Elder, *Controversiae* 2 *praef.* 1–3). In these men's oral discourses on philosophy, therefore, Seneca may already have noted that application of school-rhetoric to moral instruction

[1] Motto (1970) 187 collects Seneca's references to his philosophical teachers; the most extensive is *Epist.* 108.

which is such an important characteristic of his own literary achievement. The third teacher whom he mentions, Sotion the Pythagorean, is not known to have declaimed; but as a lecturer he was eloquent enough to convert the youthful Seneca, temporarily, to vegetarianism – an instance of that quasi-religious zealotry which recurred sporadically during Seneca's life, and in his hour of death.

Yet for long periods this gifted and inconsistent man was at least equally attracted to the charms of power. The elder Seneca, even as he was composing the *Controversiae* to satisfy his sons' passion for rhetoric, noticed that to the two elder ones *ambitiosa curae sunt; foroque se et honoribus parant, in quibus ipsa quae sperantur timenda sunt* 'they are concerned with a political career, preparing for the law and for public office – in which our very hopes are what we have to fear' (*Controversiae* 2 *praef.* 4). That double-edged prediction justified itself for the rest of the younger Seneca's life. Before Caligula's reign was over, he was prominent enough as an orator to excite the Emperor's hatred. From then on his fortunes, good and ill, were tied directly to the imperial house. Exiled to Corsica by Claudius in A.D. 41; recalled by Agrippina in 49, and appointed tutor to Nero; joint adviser to the latter on the administration of the empire from 54 to 62; retired (in effect) by Nero in 62, and instructed by him to commit suicide in the spring of 65 – Seneca was to experience, as few major writers in the history of the world have ever experienced, the nature and effects of unlimited political power. He was to observe how those effects radiated from the psychology of the rulers themselves to the entire commonwealth; how an emperor's passion might work havoc among populations. *Principum saeuitia bellum est* 'the savagery of princes is war', he says in the *De clementia* (1.5.2); and in the *De beneficiis* (7.20.4) the extreme of wickedness in a tyrant is *portenti loco habita, sicut hiatus terrae et e cauernis maris ignium eruptio* 'equated with a portent, like the opening of a chasm in the earth, like fire flaring out of ocean-caves'.

School-rhetoric, the lectures of the philosophers, and the long practical experience of power: although innumerable nuances of Seneca's biography no doubt elude us, these are securely documented as major elements in his formation. Out of them above all, it seems, he wrought a new kind of literature, both in prose and in verse.

3. SENECAN PROSE

'Tu me' inquis 'uitare turbam iubes, secedere et conscientia esse contentum? Ubi illa praecepta uestra quae imperant in actu mori?' Quid? Ego tibi uideor inertiam suadere? In hoc me recondidi et fores clusi, ut prodesse pluribus possem. Nullus mihi per otium dies exit; partem noctium studiis uindico; non uaco somno sed succumbo, et oculos uigilia fatigatos in opere detineo. Secessi non tantum ab hominibus sed a rebus, et in primis a meis rebus; posterorum negotium ago.

You tell me (you say) to shun the crowd, to withdraw, to find my satisfaction in a good conscience? What happened to those famous [Stoic] doctrines of yours which tell us to die while doing? Really! Do you think that I am advising you just to be lazy? I have hidden myself away and barred the door for one reason only: to help more people. No day of mine expires in idleness; I claim possession of part of the nights for my studies. I leave no time for sleep; I only collapse under it. My eyes weary, they drop with sleeplessness, yet still I hold them to their work. I have withdrawn my presence not just from mankind but from business, my own business above all. My deals are done for our posterity.

The reader fresh from Cicero on the one hand, or from Quintilian on the other, will at once be struck by the *staccato* effect of this typical sample of Seneca's prose (*Epist.* 8.1–2). The sentences are short and grammatical subordination is avoided. The insistence of most earlier classical prose writers that a sentence should seem to glide logically out of its predecessor, the transition being smoothed by a connective particle or relative pronoun, is no longer to be felt (as it happens, this passage contains not a single instance). Senecan prose, although no less contrived than its predecessors, depends for its effect on a series of discrete shocks: paradox, antithesis, graphic physical detail, personification (here the nights, sleep, and Seneca's own eyes all become transient aggressors or victims), and metaphor or simile (most often drawn from military life, medicine, law, or – as in the final sentence here – commerce).[1] There is great insistence on metrical clause-endings, all the more evident to the ear because the clauses are so short, and Seneca's range of clausulae[2] is rather limited (his favourite, – ⏑ – – –, occurs half a dozen times in this passage). But perhaps the most significant single characteristic of Senecan prose style is *the relative infrequency of the third person* in it. The grammatical persons natural to Seneca are the first and second. In the Letters, of course, this phenomenon is to be expected (although even here one is struck by the heavy emphasis: *Tu me! Ego tibi!*). But the fact is that it is universal in Seneca's prose works, whatever their nominal genre or subject. Each of these works is addressed to an individual, and the direct 'I–thou' relationship thus established is maintained throughout the book.

To sum up: Senecan prose stands to the prose of Cicero or Livy much as pointillism stands to the style of the Old Masters. Instead of a clear-lined, integrated design, Seneca relies on the abrupt juxtaposition of glaring colours. For the real or apparent objectivity of the periodic style, depicting in the third person a situation that is *out there*, he substitutes the subjectivity – or the egocentricity – of the first person imposing himself on the second. Well might Quintilian disapprove! This is an intellectual as well as a stylistic revolution.

[1] Summers (1910), Introduction, offers an excellent characterization of Seneca's prose style. The metaphors and similes of Senecan prose are catalogued by Steyns (1906).

[2] Norden (1898) I 310–12; Bourgery (1922) 145–9.

It is a denial of the finest achievements of Graeco-Roman classical culture – the seeming detachment, the creative use of traditional modes, the imposition of coherent and harmonious form on the chaos of the phenomena.

Seneca's approach to composition on the grand scale is similar. Again one misses the architectonic faculty possessed by the earlier classical masters. His procedure – no doubt based on the practice of the impromptu orators in the schools – seems to have been to block out the main headings to be treated in a given book, sometimes announcing them in a formal *divisio* immediately after his proem (e.g. *Constant.* 5.1, *Helv.* 4.1), sometimes not. Within those headings it is often difficult to observe much order in the argument.[1] The effect is again that of an impromptu speaker, developing various aspects of his topic as they occur to him, often at inordinate length and with much repetition. Here may be formulated the most important criticism to which Seneca is liable, in his prose and – to a lesser extent – in his verse: his deficiency in a sense of proportion, his inability to stop. Like so much of the best and worst in Seneca, this is essentially the attribute of a *speaker* rather than a writer – of a supreme virtuoso among conversationalists, whose *métier* is to captivate his hearer from moment to moment.

In the school-declamations and in the diatribes of the philosophers the art of the *exemplum* and the description had long been cultivated: the hearer was to be convinced by an appeal to some exemplary precedent in myth or history, his imagination to be conducted wholly into those scenes or situations which would best illustrate the speaker's point. Seneca consummated that art. His talent perhaps appears at its finest in the paragraphs of *exemplum* or description that are so frequent in his prose works; some of which are scarcely equalled for majesty in all Latin prose. Examples are *Q. Nat.* 1 *praef.* (the greatness of the universe, the littleness of man); *Q. Nat.* 3.27–end (the vision of the Deluge); *Consolatio ad Marciam* 17 (the voyage that is the life of man); *De brevitate vitae* 14–15 (the wise man's converse with the wise of all ages); *De providentia* 2.8–11 (Cato's gladiatorial duel with Fortune); *Ben.* 4.5–6 (the vision of God's *beneficia* to man); *Helv.* 8.4–6 (the heavens circling above the exile, reminding him of his true home). In such passages above all we glimpse the Stoic world-vision, which is in a sense the only subject of Seneca's extant prose works. He never described it systematically or as a whole, for only a *sapiens*, a perfect Stoic sage, was capable of so comprehending it (*Epist.* 89.2); and Seneca repeatedly disclaimed this status (e.g. *Helv.* 5.2, *Ben.* 7.17.1, *Epist.* 57.3, *Epist.* 87.4–5). All his treatises either describe a facet of that majestic vision (e.g. in the *De ira* and *Q. Nat.*), or apply the principles deducible from it to a given human situation (e.g. in *Clem.*, *Helv.*, and the majority of the Dialogues and Epistles).

[1] A more favourable view of Seneca's compositional art, as it is seen in the *Dialogi*, will be found in Abel (1967).

In either case, however – even in the *Naturales quaestiones* – his prime concern is to explore its practical consequences for daily moral conduct, *omnia ad mores et ad sedandam rabiem adfectuum referens* 'applying all to morals, and to calming the fury of the passions' (*Epist.* 89.23). Seneca was by no means a slavish follower of the Stoics. He would readily accept a moral hint from a Cynic, or from Epicurus himself;[1] and in one important doctrinal matter, the ethics of suicide, he seems to have made his own original contribution.[2] But on the whole his mind dwells in the Stoic universe as naturally and securely as the mind of a medieval thinker dwelt in the universe pictured by the Church. Its splendours and terrors, its vastness, its periodic destruction by fire or water, were ever present in his thoughts and his visual imagination;[3] but present above all was the inseparable bond between it and the soul of any individual man. The painter's saying, 'There are no lines in Nature', well applies to the Senecan universe. Its unity is perhaps most simply grasped by a consideration of the relations which exist in it between man and God. *Quid est deus? Mens uniuersi. Quid est deus? Quod uides totum et quod non uides totum* 'What is God? Mind of the whole. What is God? All that you see and, of what you don't see, all' (*Q. Nat.* 1 *praef.* 13). He is also Nature, Fate, and Reason (*ratio*) as we learn from other passages.[4] Below the stars, visible reminders of his majesty and peace, however, the universe is alive with apparent terrors: not merely the physical terrors of thunderbolt, earthquake, and deluge, but also those which surge out of the soul of man, the *rabies adfectuum* ('fury of the passions') which may have an equally disastrous impact on the visible world. Passion set free in the soul will distort features and gestures first, and then lay waste the individual and his surroundings. It may destroy a vast region, above all if it captures the soul of a prince (*De ira* 1, 2, *Clem.* 1.5.2). The individual who seeks peace or freedom inside or outside himself has one hope only: all men's souls contain a particle of the *ratio* which is God, and to perfect that *ratio*, to purge it of all contact with the passions, is to become God's equal in all respects save personal immortality (e.g. *Constant.* 8.2). And this way, Seneca insists, is open to all human beings, whatever their external condition. To this tenet we owe his famous and moving protests against the maltreatment of slaves and the inhumanity of the gladiatorial games.[5] The noble mind, he says, is a god that sojourns in a human body, *deum in corpore humano hospitantem*. That body may be a Roman knight's, a freedman's, or a slave's (*Epist.* 31.11).

[1] Motto (1970) 149 collects his admiring references to his friend Demetrius the Cynic; for Epicurus, see ibid. 150–1.

[2] Rist (1969) 246–50.

[3] See below, p. 529 n. 1.

[4] Motto (1970) 92 item 2.

[5] On slaves, *Epist.* 47 is the *locus classicus*; the many further references are collected in Motto (1970) 195–6. For the games, see especially *Epist.* 7.3–5.

Such, in general terms, is the central doctrine which irradiates all his extant prose treatises. Seneca may, and does, discuss it from many angles and apply its consequences to many political and moral dilemmas; but in its essentials it is invariable. This invariability of theme is paralleled by a remarkable invariability of style. Although the prose works extend over a period of at least twenty-five years, it has so far proved impossible to establish objective criteria for dating any of them on purely stylistic grounds, where they lack allusion to any datable historical event. For example, the *De providentia* has been placed by modern scholars as early as A.D. 41/2 and as late as A.D. 64.[1] Seneca in fact seems to have formed his style while still relatively young, before the period of any of his extant works, and never to have substantially modified it. The most that may be said regarding his literary development – and that subjectively – is that in the works of his last phase (A.D. 62–5), the *Naturales quaestiones* and the *Epistulae morales*, one may perhaps sense a greater maturity, a greater urgency and conviction.

It remains to consider the nature of Seneca's achievement in prose, and the measure of his success. Technically, his major innovation consisted in taking over a personal, extempore, *speaking* style which had been developed by the declaimers and philosophical preachers, and implanting it in formal Latin literature. In that rhetorical technique he was a supreme master, far outranging his predecessors (if their quality is fairly to be judged by Seneca the Elder's reports of them). Yet it will not do to dismiss him as a mere rhetorician, as has been customary since the Romantic period. Obviously he was a rhetorician, as are all serious writers; the proper question is, what did he express through his rhetoric, and how effectively? He had indeed much to express: a profound imaginative grasp of this universe as the Stoics understood it, a keen and sensitive observation of the visible world, and a prolonged acquaintance with human nature and politics. If he is not consistently successful, the prime reasons are his diffuseness and his lack of a sense of proportion. From a compositional point of view, there is no masterpiece among the prose works of Seneca. Perhaps the least disconcerting in that respect are the *Consolatio ad Helviam*, which in many other respects also is the most carefully finished of his treatises, and the *Epistulae morales*. The *Epistulae* have always been the most popular of his works, and understandably so; for here Seneca finally discovered the literary medium that suited his genius. The formlessness, the spontaneity, the powerful exercise of the writer's personality upon the reader, are both natural to Seneca and natural to the letter.

The diffuseness is indeed a grave fault. It is quite possible that Seneca's reputation as thinker and stylist might today stand infinitely higher if his work, like that of Pascal, had never progressed beyond the stage of disconnected

[1] Münscher (1922) 75; Abel (1967) 158.

Pensées – a paragraph here, a sentence there, each projecting its separate shaft of light into the mystery of human existence. For in short, or momentary, effects he is at his finest. He is a world master in the art of crystallizing a notable thought in a few, lasting words; and the unexampled force of his great descriptive passages has already been noted. Nevertheless, there remains a half-forgotten way of appreciating the prose works even as they stand; which is to *hear* them. Possibly the best advice yet given in modern times on reading Seneca is to be found in the following paragraph:

> It is interminable. As we go round and round like a horse in a mill, we perceive that we are thus clogged with sound because we are reading what we should be hearing. The amplifications and the repetitions, the emphasis like that of a fist pounding the edge of a pulpit, are for the benefit of the slow and sensual ear which loves to dally over sense and luxuriate in sound – the ear which brings in, along with the spoken word, the look of the speaker and his gestures, which gives a dramatic value to what he says and adds to the crest of an extravagance some modulation which makes the word wing its way to the precise spot aimed at in the hearer's heart. (Virginia Woolf, *The second common reader*, pp. 9–10; she is actually referring here to the Elizabethan stylist, Gabriel Harvey.)

4. SENECAN TRAGEDY

The Appendix on the tragedies will show that the external evidence concerning Senecan tragedy is minimal – far less than exists for any other dramatic (or supposedly dramatic) corpus of comparable importance in the history of European literature. Above all, there is no indication, either in the manuscripts or in the relatively few ancient allusions to the tragedies,[1] as to when or how they were performed; or even whether they were performed at all. Until about 150 years ago the general assumption was that they were regular stage dramas. Only after A. W. Schlegel's onslaught on them[2] did the opinion begin to prevail that they were intended merely for recitation, either in the recitation-auditorium or by the solitary reader. The question is far more doubtful than it is sometimes made to seem. Yet certain fundamental points may be agreed on. First: in the later first century B.C. tragedies were certainly being performed *both* in the live theatre *and* by simple recitation, but we have almost no knowledge of the conventions obtaining in either category of performance. The most concise of much evidence for the co-existence of both kinds of tragedy is found in Quintilian, *Inst.* 11.3.73: *itaque in iis quae ad scaenam componuntur fabulis artifices pronuntiandi a personis quoque adfectus mutuantur, ut sit Aerope in tragoedia tristis, atrox Medea*... 'Thus *in those plays that are composed for*

[1] Collected in Peiper and Richter (1902) xxiv–xxx.

[2] In his *Vorlesungen über dramatische Kunst und Litteratur* of 1809; the relevant extract is reprinted in Lefèvre (1972) 13–14.

the stage the actors likewise borrow the emotional tones of their pronunciation from the masks, so that in tragedy Aerope is mournful, and Medea savage...'[1] Second: to decide on the category to which the Senecan tragedies may have belonged we have one recourse only, and that is to analysis of their texts. Third: such analysis has so far produced no passage that is physically impossible to stage. Zwierlein, in his valuable discussion of the texts from this point of view,[2] has indeed shown that many passages defy the conventions of the fifth-century B.C. Attic stage; but has taken no account of the possibility, or probability, that the Neronian live theatre may have been as different from that of classical Greece as the Golden House was from the Parthenon. There remains nothing in the Senecan tragedies that could not have been staged with, for example, the resources of English Restoration drama. The atrocious *Oedipus* of Dryden and Lee (1679) is, by Zwierlein's standards, far less stageable than any scene in Seneca (the stage-direction for Oedipus' death, for example, reads: 'Thunder. He flings himself from the window. The Thebans gather around his body'). Yet it was composed for the stage; all that was necessary was some miming, and some machinery – neither of them by any means unknown to Neronian public entertainment. It may finally be noted that the only actable English poetic translation of any of Seneca's plays, Ted Hughes's *Oedipus* (1969) has responded well to the production-methods and theatrical expectations of the later twentieth century.

In view of the extreme deficiency of relevant data, the question of the manner of performance of the tragedies should probably, in method, be left open. The following discussion of their literary character will aim rather at those aspects which would be equally significant whether Seneca intended performance on the stage, or in the salon, or in the mind's eye. The works primarily referred to will be the seven tragedies which are both complete and generally acknowledged as authentic. Much of what is said will apply also to the *Phoenissae*, which is incomplete (it lacks choruses, and is apparently an ill-coordinated series of draft scenes for a play covering the events in the Theban saga that followed the deposition of Oedipus),[3] and to the remaining mythological play in the corpus, the probably spurious *Hercules Oetaeus*. A Senecan tragedy takes for its subject a Greek mythical episode, and in presenting that episode follows, *in outline*, a play by one of the great Attic tragedians. As it happens, almost all the Greek prototypes have survived for comparison[4] – perhaps an indication

[1] For live theatre in Seneca's time see *Epist.* 80.7–8 and *De ira* 2.17.1. The evidence for 'recitation drama' is assembled by Zwierlein (1966) 127–66.

[2] Zwierlein (1966).

[3] Such is the school of thought to which the present writer inclines; it presents far less difficulty than the alternative view, that the *Phoenissae* was originally completed by Seneca, but has been mutilated in the course of transmission. There is a recent survey of the piece by Opelt (1969).

[4] A general survey of the probable prototypes of the Senecan tragedies is found in Herrmann (1924) 247–327. The subject in detail still presents much uncertainty. There are many cases where

that the literate public of Seneca's time was already beginning to narrow its reading in Greek tragedy towards the limits of the 'Selection' of the tragedians preserved in the medieval Greek manuscripts. The major exception to this rule is the *Thyestes*; its theme was enormously popular among both Greek and Roman playwrights. Nauck[1] indexes eight Greek authors of a *Thyestes*, and one of an *Atreus*; Ribbeck[2] indexes seven Roman plays (besides Seneca's) named *Thyestes*, and four named *Atreus*. Of the Roman plays, no less than ten are datable in the Roman Imperial period. But none of these other versions survives, and it is impossible to be sure which of them Seneca may have followed. Yet the Senecan tragedies cannot properly be called *translations* from the Greek, any more than Virgil's Eclogues can be called translations from Theocritean pastoral. There is hardly a line in which Seneca reproduces the Greek word for word; there are very many scenes (including all the Prologues)[3] which have no parallel at all in the Greek; and even those scenes that do follow the general shape of a Greek prototype are given new colours and different proportions. The critic can make no more disastrous initial error than to assume that Seneca is merely aping the Greeks, or that Attic tragedy can serve as a point of reference for the assessment of Senecan tragedy.

Nor does it seem satisfactory to dismiss the tragedies out of hand, as so many critics have done under the influence of Schlegel and above all of Leo, as empty displays of rhetoric and nothing more. Leo[4] offers, indeed, a superb statement of the observable facts; but the literary-critical principles there applied require careful scrutiny. Leo's judgement on the subject is summed up in a sentence on his p. 158, which may be translated: 'These are no tragedies! They are declamations, composed according to the norm of tragedy and spun into acts. An elegant or penetrating saying, a flowery description with the requisite tropes, an eloquent narration – in these compositions that was enough: the audience would clap, and Art's claims would have been satisfied.' Before anyone adopts so easy an exit from his critical responsibilities, he should perhaps take the following considerations into account. First: while Senecan dramatic poetry is admittedly rhetorical, and indeed declamatory, it is hardly more or less so than the great bulk of Imperial Roman poetry in other genres, from Ovid to Juvenal. Ovid indeed, the founding father of this poetic manner, a star of the late-Augustan declamation-halls, and a family acquaintance (above, p. 513; cf. Seneca the Elder, *Controversiae* 2.2.8–12), was of enormous importance to Seneca, as numerous quotations in his prose works testify.[5] In the

contamination of a surviving Greek prototype with one or more lost plays is reasonably posited; for example the *Phaedra*, where elements of both the Euripidean Hippolytus-plays and of Sophocles' *Phaedra* have been detected by some scholars.

[1] *TGF* 964–5. [2] *TRF* 364–5. [3] See Anliker (1960).

[4] Leo (1878) I 147–59 (the chapter 'De tragoedia rhetorica').

[5] Haase (1852) Index.

tragedies his influence is even more pervasive, being apparent in the diction, in the phrasing, in the rhetoric, in characters, and in situations. All these points may be compendiously verified by a comparison of two admired passages in Seneca's *Phaedra*, 110–28 and 646–66, with Ovid's *Heroides* 4 (*Phaedra Hippolyto*) 37–62 and 63–78 respectively. Many more instances could be cited.[1] If Ovid's one essay in tragedy, the *Medea*, had survived, there can be little doubt that the debt of Senecan tragedy to him would be seen to be even greater, in many aspects.[2] But where Ovid fails to supply a parallel to Senecan dramatic poetry, one can generally be found without long search in the Latin poetry of the following two generations – most notably in the *De bello civili* of Seneca's nephew Lucan. In short, the rhetoric and the poetic manner of Senecan tragedy belong squarely in the tradition of what is commonly called Silver Latin poetry; and it is against the standards of that tradition – not against the standards of Euripides or even of Virgil – that his work deserves to be judged in the first instance. Almost all those features in it which have so displeased critics who insist on reading the tragedies with one eye misdirected towards Attic drama, are in fact shared with post-Ovidian Roman poetry: its pointed *sententiae*, its generalizations from one or a few instances, its habit of attaining its effects by caricature-like exaggeration of the literal facts, its powerful and often horrific realism, its tendency to enforce a point by piling up mythological or geographical instances in long catalogues, its abandonment of narrative architecture and a smooth story-line in favour of a series of discrete, brilliantly-worked episodes. If these features are to be condemned in themselves, then so is the bulk of later Roman poetry. Perhaps a more fruitful procedure will be to accept them as given for a poet of Seneca's time, and to enquire how he applies them to the creation of a poetic drama. Are they there for themselves alone, mere showpieces of technical virtuosity? Or are they media for the artistic expression of a coherent statement?

In recent decades, especially since Regenbogen's essay,[3] there has been an increasing tendency to suppose that the latter alternative is the correct one; or in other words, that Senecan tragedy is somehow to be taken seriously as literature. In the details of interpretation there remains a vast diversity. The most that may be undertaken here is a general theory of Seneca's dramatic aims and methods, illustrated by a brief consideration of a single play, the *Thyestes*.

Each of the Senecan tragedies, viewed as a whole, will make coherent sense as a concentrated study in one or more of the elemental terrors which ever threaten to disrupt human existence: omnipresent death, the passions, guilt voluntary and involuntary, and political tyranny. Each is pervaded from end to end by an appalling aura of *evil*, as are perhaps no other works of ancient

[1] Cf. Canter (1925) 42–54.
[2] Leo (1878) I 148–9.
[3] Regenbogen (1927/8).

literature (modern parallels might be found in the fiction of Edgar Allan Poe). It is above all to communicate that aura that Seneca consistently applies the contemporary stylistic techniques which were surveyed above – techniques which happen to be excellently adapted to his purpose. Since the emphasis of his drama is on the evil and its workings, rather than on the activities of individuals for their own sake, a logically developing plot at the human level is not his main concern. At the same time the evil in itself, and the dread effects of its operation, may be most graphically expressed (as they are also in Lucan and Juvenal) through images that in other contexts would appear monstrous, grotesque, or revolting.

The evils which thus dominate the tragedies, and in a sense are their main actors, are none other than those which preoccupy Seneca the prose-writer. The tragedies too, although Dante did not mean as much when he uttered the phrase, are clear manifestations of *Seneca morale*.[1] Yet there is an important difference: whereas the Senecan prose corpus endeavours to combat these moral terrors, primarily with the weapon of Stoic doctrine, the tragedies scarcely go beyond presenting them. It seems misleading to characterize Seneca's plays as 'Stoic tragedy'. Indeed, one may doubt whether such a thing can exist, strictly speaking; as Plato long ago saw (*Laws* 7.817a–d), the absolute acceptance of any coherent and exclusive metaphysical system, and the composition of tragedy, are mutually exclusive. In Senecan tragedy the remedies against evil, with which a practising Stoic was most profoundly concerned, are hardly touched on; and uniquely Stoic doctrine of any kind is rare. The most important exceptions to this rule will be observed in the *Thyestes*. Other major exceptions are the analyses of the onset and progress of passion, notably in those in the *Medea* and the *Phaedra*;[2] and the idea, which surfaces in almost all the plays but is most pervasive in the *Troades*, of death (often by suicide) as the ultimate guarantor of human liberty.[3] A number of other evident allusions to Stoic doctrine will of course be found, but they are brief, and not firmly woven into the tragic fabric; for example: *H.F.* 463–4 and *Phoen.* 188–95 (evidently on the qualities of the *sapiens*, the Stoic sage); *Phaedra* 959–89 and *Oed.* 980–94 (thoughts on Providence and Fate, respectively, which are closely paralleled in the prose writings). Here and there a Senecan character seems to show some of the attitudes of a *sapiens* or *proficiens* ('progressor', the technical term for one who is still seeking to attain the state of a *sapiens*): Thyestes; Hippolytus;

[1] *Inferno* 4.141; cf. Eliot (1927) vi.

[2] The *locus classicus* for the onset of passion is Act II of the *Phaedra* (85–273); its physiological and psychological impact on the individual is described, e.g. in *Phaedra* 360–83, and *Med.* 380–430; its ultimate triumph is best seen in the Atreus of the *Thyestes*, to be discussed below. The doctrines on passion implied in these plays are overtly stated in the prose treatise *De ira*, especially 1.1–8, 2.1–5.

[3] *Tro.* 142–63, 418–20, 574–7, 791; cf. *H.F.* 511–13, *Phaedra* 139, the great choral meditation on death in *Ag.* 589–611, and *Thy.* 442.

Polyxena and Astyanax in the *Troades*. On the whole, however, although the tragedies are no doubt related to Seneca's philosophical mission, their function here must be considered as almost entirely protreptic. They rest not so much on a philosophy as on the universal human experience of evil, typified in certain familiar myths and conveyed primarily by the resources of contemporary verse-rhetoric. They are addressed, in short, to unenlightened, non-Stoic, man – to the common reader, whether of Seneca's time or of our own.

Yet if the positive side of Stoic doctrine is rare in the tragedies, Seneca's Stoic habit of mind indirectly influences their composition at almost all points. His imaginative vision of the universe as a moral–physical unity, and his almost morbid sensitivity to evil, seem in fact largely responsible for that aspect of his theatre which has most vexed his critics since the early nineteenth century: the grotesque and often (to moderns) physically impossible exaggerations and horrors. In these tragedies, when evil once takes control of a human being it does not manifest itself merely in his features and walk,[1] or in bestial outrage against other human beings. The surrounding landscape may feel and reflect it (e.g. *Oed.* 569–81, *Med.* 785–6); and so, often, do the clouds, the sun, the stars, the very universe itself (e.g. *Phoen.* 6–8, *Med.* 739, *Ag.* 53–6). *Fecimus caelum nocens* 'we have put guilt into the sky!', is the cry of Oedipus at *Oed.* 36; *omnia nostrum sensere malum* 'all things have felt our evil', echoes the Chorus in line 159 of the same play, as it catalogues the ever-spreading horrors of the Theban plague. All these things are consequences of the Stoic sense of the vast power of evil, and of the Stoic vision of the universe as a whole interrelated in all its parts, which are expressed equally clearly in the prose treatises and also in Lucan. In the tragedies they seem to serve the same end as does Seneca's use of the contemporary techniques of verse-rhetoric: the realization, in almost palpable form, of evil.

Some consideration of a single tragedy in action (as it were) may help to clarify and complete the above general account of Seneca's dramaturgy. It may also suggest that a Senecan play, while obviously lacking in the Aristotelian virtues of consistently drawn character and satisfying story-line, may yet achieve a kind of unity peculiar to itself. The *Thyestes* has been chosen for this purpose, as being a play that has been particularly coolly treated by most critics later than the eighteenth century. The most recent full commentary on the *Thyestes* is still that originally published by Gronovius (1661 and 1682). Even Eliot[2] describes it as 'the most unpleasantly sanguinary' of Seneca's plays.[3] The coolness was justifiable only on their literal-minded assumption that the play's subjects were butchery and cannibalism photographically

[1] See above, p. 523 n. 2., for examples from the *Medea* and *Phaedra*.

[2] Eliot (1927) xxiii.

[3] Sympathetic critics are much rarer; Gigon (1938) is a valuable representative.

reproduced for their own gory sake. Thus read, it indeed makes little sense – either in itself or in the context of the rest of Seneca's *œuvre*. Yet all that we otherwise know of Seneca's mental and artistic habits would suggest a very different reading. Seneca has here adapted the hideous ancient fable to the combined expression of three themes which ever preoccupied him both as a prose-writer and as a politician: the temptations of political power, the passion of anger, and the dire effects of that passion once it has occupied the soul of a despot. On such a reading, the *Thyestes* might even be considered the most concise and powerful expression of Seneca's life-experience among all his extant works.

The *Thyestes*, like most of the Senecan tragedies, is divided into five acts (the Prologue being reckoned as Act I), with four choric songs in the intervals.[1] It opens before the palace at Mycenae, in darkness, and appropriately so. The traditional Thyestes story already contained a moment of unnatural night, when the Sun reversed his course in horror; but Seneca, to whom 'darkness' elsewhere signifies 'evil' (*Epist.* 110.6–7, 115.3–4, 122.4), effectively exploits this symbolism throughout the play, bringing it to a crashing climax in the fourth Ode. As usual, the Prologue involves little action, being dominated by one sombre figure, who carries with him the miasma of evil which will pervade the play.[2] This is the Ghost of Tantalus, the founder of the family and the initiator of its grim propensity to cannibalism in the furtherance of ambition. One of the simple, dreadful truths that are to be embodied in this play is that *ambition eats people*, including above all its own kindred. Another is that *ambition will never be sated* – a point which is now elaborated, by mythological means, in the first choral Ode.

Senecan choruses are in most respects quite unlike those of Attic tragedy. The precise identity of a chorus, or even its sex, can rarely be deduced from its utterances;[3] it is not always present during the actor-episodes;[4] and even when present it does not actually intervene in the dialogue if more than one speaking actor is on stage.[5] Scholars are now less inclined than they were to

[1] Possible exceptions to this rule among the genuine and complete plays are the *Phaedra* and *Oedipus*; cf. Anliker (1960) 93–7. The *Hercules Oetaeus* is also a five-act play. The *Octavia* can be so divided, as it is in Gronovius (1682) and Sluiter (1949); but the division is highly artificial, and obscures the real articulation of the play (see below, p. 531).

[2] The Prologue of the *Thyestes* is slightly more diversified than most; it contains, besides Tantalus, the subsidiary figure of a Fury, and some stage business (real, or to be imagined) is implied at lines 23–5, 67, 83–4, 100–5. The Prologue of the *Oedipus* also introduces two figures, Oedipus and Jocasta. The prologues of all the other complete plays contain one character alone.

[3] The exceptions in the genuine plays are the chorus of the *Troades*, and the second chorus of the *Agamemnon*; which both consist of captive Trojan women, and speak and act as such.

[4] The clearest, but not the only, evidence for this is found at *H.F.* 827–9 and *Ag.* 586–8. In each case the entrance of the singers of the ensuing choral ode is announced by an actor, in mid-play.

[5] This convention was observed by Leo (1897*b*) 513. There is an apparent exception to it at *Phaedra* 404–5, which would be removed by Friedrich's convincing reassignment of the speakers, (1933) 24–38; and a probable exception at *Oed.* 1004–9.

attribute these technical peculiarities merely to Seneca's impudent contempt for the best Greek models; a certain amount of recent evidence suggests that Hellenistic conventions offered him some precedents, at least.[1] The metrical character of his choral odes, again, differs widely from that of Athenian dramatic lyric. The great majority consist simply of stretches of one or two verse-forms, repeated stichically. His favourite verse-form is the anapaestic dimeter, which occurs in all the complete plays, and which he handles, perhaps, as ably as any extant Latin poet. Next in his preference are a number of Horatian metres (notably lesser asclepiads, glyconics, and sapphic hendecasyllables). His solitary approach to a strophic arrangement is found in *Med.* 579–669 (sapphic hendecasyllables, punctuated as regular strophes by adonii). Only four of his odes exhibit anything near the metrical complexity and virtuosity of the Greek choral lyric.[2] The first Ode of the *Thyestes* is metrically of Seneca's simplest type – lesser asclepiads from one end to the other – and is in other respects also a fair specimen of his lyric manner. The thought-structure is not complex: a prayer to the gods of Peloponnese (catalogued) to end the series of crimes in the Tantalid house (catalogued); and in conclusion a description of Tantalus' torment in Hades by insatiable hunger and thirst. The style is influenced by Horace,[3] but at no point approaches Horace's mastery; if nothing else, Seneca's besetting sin of diffuseness, and the narrow range of his poetic vocabulary, would exclude him from that class. Yet it also often shows that peculiar vividness of description which has also been noted in Seneca's prose works; as here, in the final presentation (152–75) of the sinner's swivelling eyes, his desperately clenched teeth, the tempting apple-cluster looming ever nearer until he yields, and it tosses aloft into the sky; and, at the last, the deep, thirsty, swig from the swirling river of... dust.

Act I and Ode I have developed the moral atmosphere of the play – a prodigal expenditure of versification indeed, if (but only if) Senecan dramaturgy aimed primarily at the sadistic representation of physical horrors for their own sake. With Act II (176–335) the play's movement – it can hardly yet be termed *action* – begins. King Atreus enters, lashing himself into a rage against his exiled brother Thyestes. This rage is almost all we shall learn about Atreus in the course of the play. If it could, it would embroil the world in war, set fields and cities aglow with flames,[4] and annihilate Atreus himself, provided that in so doing it might destroy his brother.[5] Atreus is now encountered by a *satelles*,

[1] Herington (1966) 445, with note 57.

[2] These 'polymetric odes' are restricted to the *Oedipus* (403–508, 709–37) and the *Agamemnon* (589–637 and 808–66). Technically, they are unparalleled in extant Latin verse before the Renaissance. On their metrical character see, e.g., Leo (1878) I 110–34, and Pighi (1963).

[3] Keseling (1941).

[4] *Thy.* 180–3, closely paralleled in *De ira* 1.2.1, *fin.*

[5] *Thy.* 190–1. The self-destructive effect of anger is likewise emphasized in *De ira* 1.1.1–2, and in the great allegorical portrait of Anger, ibid. 2.35.5 (which might serve almost equally effectively as a portrait of Seneca's Atreus, Medea, or Phaedra).

an Attendant; and the rest of the act is a debate between them on issues connected with Atreus' revenge-plot. The Attendant at first opposes the plot as contrary to the principles of right government, religion, and morality, but finally submits to becoming the passive instrument of Atreus' rage. Such scenes, often called 'dissuasion scenes', are a characteristic feature of Senecan tragedy; in most cases they are placed, as here, in Act II. Fine shades of characterization will be found neither in them nor elsewhere in the tragedies, with very few exceptions. There are perhaps only two extensive scenes in which the modern reader may feel something of that sympathetic interest in the characters as human individuals which he feels throughout a Shakespearean play: *Troades* 524–813 (the confrontation between Andromacha and Ulysses) and *Phaedra* 589–718 (Phaedra's revelation of her passion to Hippolytus). The reasons behind these two exceptions present a critical problem too great to be entered into here; it need hardly be said that the customary response is to assume that these superb scenes must be 'translations' from lost Greek 'originals'. But in general Seneca's speakers are accorded no personal background, very few modulations of tone, and no distinctive syntax or diction. They 'all seem to speak with the same voice, and at the top of it', as T. S. Eliot justly remarked.[1] Atreus here presents himself bluntly as *iratus Atreus* (180), while his Attendant is quite without fixed characteristics, being a conduit now for words of justice and piety, now for words of tame assent.

The second Ode is the most overtly Stoic of all Senecan tragic passages, setting up as it does the antithesis between the true kingship of the soul and the false kingship of political power; even as an adolescent, Seneca had thrilled to the discourse of Attalus the Stoic on this fundamental doctrine (*Epist.* 108.13, *Ben.* 7.2.5–3.3). It also coheres perfectly with the dramatic context, for that is precisely the choice which Thyestes is to make before our eyes in the ensuing act. The ode used to be one of the most admired poems of Seneca; [*chorus*] *ille divinus* 'that divine chorus', the scholar Daniel Heinsius called it.[2] The closing period (391–403) has become part of English poetry in translations by Wyatt, Heywood, and Cowley,[3] and by Marvell. Simply composed in lightly-running glyconics, the ode can be reproached only for the usual diffuseness, the tendency to catalogue. Even that fault is absent from the noble period at its close.

In Act III Thyestes arrives before the palace with his three sons. He has been invited by Atreus, in accordance with the plans laid in the preceding act, to share the throne of Mycenae. Yet exile and privation have taught Thyestes the nature of true kingship: *immane regnum est posse sine regno pati* 'it is a vast kingdom to be able to bear a kingdom's absence' (407). He would rather live

[1] Eliot (1927) ix.
[2] *Ap.* Scriverius (1621) II 297.
[3] Mason (1959) 181–5.

the natural life, in the woods, without fear; only under pressure from his son, significantly named Tantalus, does he sadly resign himself to advancing and greeting Atreus. The act closes with what may be one of the finest symbolic spectacles in ancient drama, next to Aeschylus' tapestry-scene in the *Agamemnon*. The exile, dirty, unkempt, and ragged (505–7, 524), stands grasping the sceptre (532–3) and crowned with the royal diadem (531, 544), pressed on him by his smiling brother. In full understanding of the true kingship, he has accepted the false. This rich act is, further, the only one in the play that requires as many as three speaking actors. Like the Attic tragedians, Seneca is economical with speaking parts, and follows the Attic precedent in limiting their number to three, with rare exceptions.[1]

The third Ode (546–622) consists almost entirely of a series of general reflections on fraternal piety, the terrors of imminent war, and the vicissitudes of Fortune. Odes of this character occur at some point in most of the plays. While their sentiments are blameless, and while they may often include impressive descriptions by way of example,[2] one feels that they would be almost equally appropriate anywhere – even outside a play altogether. Yet in this case some such pause for the hearer's emotions may be justified, for he is nearing the climax of horror. By a pattern that is discernible in most of Senecan tragedy, the climate of evil has been established in the first, static, movement of the play (here in Act I and Ode I); in the second, deliberative, movement (here Acts II–III), choices have been made through which the evil has taken root in the souls of the human actors; in the third and last, it will burst over the people and the landscape like a firestorm. In Act IV a messenger describes to the Chorus the things that Atreus has done within the palace – a palace which he first describes at length, from its pompous and glittering front to its inmost courtyard, where eternal darkness reigns and hellish beings walk. That description is no mere verbal ornament; for the scene is both a just emblem of false kingship, and an appropriately dark setting for Atreus' maniacal sacrifice of Thyestes' sons, which is next described. Then follows the butchery of the bodies, then the cookery, in atrocious detail. The Sun has meanwhile recoiled in his course, and darkness has covered all – or is to be so imagined – throughout the act (*Thy.* 637–8, cf. 776–8, 784–8. Whether or not the *Thyestes* was staged in antiquity, a modern director might brilliantly exploit the opportunities which the darkness presents – and the contrasting glare of torchlight in the banqueting-hall at 908). This darkness is taken up in the fourth Ode (789–884); and is enlarged to the scale of the universe. The singers wonder whether it is a mere

[1] The exceptions are *Oed.* 291–402 and *Ag.* 981–1012, each of which episodes will be found to require the presence of four speaking actors. A recent discussion of the Senecan 'three-actor rule' is that of Zwierlein (1966) 46–7.

[2] Noteworthy in the present ode are the contrasting tableaux of the Storm and the Calm (577–95), emblems respectively of the threat of war and of *détente*.

eclipse, or is the prelude to a cosmic destruction, perhaps (880–1) as the consequence of human wickedness. The major movement of the song is occupied by a surrealist vision of the collapse of the flaming constellations into chaos – its effects marred only by the fact that every sign of the Zodiac is catalogued in detail.[1]

In Act V Seneca returns from the impact of evil on the skies, to describe its effects on the two chief human actors. Atreus enters, transfigured by passion. He has reached the ultimate delirium, in which he feels himself beyond common mortality, the king of kings (*Thy.* 911–12, *regum atque regem*, cf. 885–9); this final and irremediable degree of anger is further described in *De ira* 1.20.2 and 2.5.5. The themes of anger and false kingship are here consummated. Only one pain afflicts Atreus through this act. *He has not had revenge enough* (890–5, 1052–68); nor will he ever, if the figure of Tantalus at the play's beginning had any significance. The palace door is now swung open, displaying Thyestes at his torchlit banquet. He is singing a drunken song – a song with no close parallel in ancient tragedy – in which joy battles with uncanny fears. There follows a swift crescendo of horrors. Atreus serves Thyestes a cup of wine mixed with his children's blood; then (1004–5) reveals their remains; and lastly (1034) discloses that Thyestes himself has feasted on their flesh. As the play closes Thyestes is lamenting, Atreus responding with triumphant sarcasms. The rancorous interchange, one feels, will go on into eternity.

All Seneca's writings, the verse as well as the prose, are imperfect in some degree. In the tragedies the familar faults recur: the tendency to run on and on to the ruin of all proportion, the lapses from taste and humour,[2] the occasional inconsistencies, the general air of work produced in too great haste and with too great facility. There persists also that egocentricity which was already observed in the prose works. Here also, whoever the nominal speakers may be, the dominating moral ideas are Seneca's ideas, and the many voices are, in the end, the lone voice of Seneca. It might be said of him, as it might be said of most of the great moralists, that all his work is in a sense a dialogue with *himself.* Writing of this kind, as Quintilian saw, resists classification within any particular genre, whether ancient or modern. Accordingly the Senecan tragedies can only be in part reconciled with the genre of tragedy, as the Greeks or Elizabethans practised it. Like the prose works, they are best approached in the

[1] The destruction of the universe by fire or water is a Stoic theme that particularly fascinated Seneca: *Cons. ad Marciam* 26.6, *Cons. ad Polybium* 1.2, *Ben.* 6.22, *Epist.* 71. 12–13, *Q. Nat.* 3.27–30 and 6.2.9; cf. *Octavia* 377–437 (in the mouth of the stage-character Seneca), where again the catastrophe is ascribed to the sins of men.

[2] These are relatively not so frequent as might be supposed from a perusal of the nineteenth- and early twentieth-century critics; but they certainly occur. Two striking examples will suffice: *Helv.* 16.3–4, where our author gravely commends his own mother for not wearing maternity-gowns to conceal her pregnancies, not resorting to abortions, and not wearing makeup; and *Thy.* 999–1004, where the noisy symptoms of Thyestes' indigestion after his banquet are described.

first instance as the unique expressions of an extraordinary mind – a mind sensitive as few others have been to the spiritual and political problems of the human condition. Unlike the prose works, however, the tragedies are controlled by the external limitations of metre, of dramatic form, and of mythic subject; and to that extent are perhaps Seneca's greater works of art.

5. EXCURSUS: THE OCTAVIA

As is explained in the Appendix, the *E*-recension of the Senecan tragic corpus contains nine plays only, whereas the *A*-manuscripts preserve a tenth, the *Octavia*, unanimously ascribing this little historical drama to Seneca. The arguments against that attribution, however, seem very strong. They are best studied in Helm's exhaustive article (1934). His historical arguments against Senecan authorship (notably the accurate knowledge of the exact manner of Nero's death displayed in the prophecy of *Oct.* 629–31) are impressive, but not totally convincing; overwhelming are his arguments from style. Some further considerations will be found in Coffey (1957) 174–84, and in Herington (1961). The majority of editors, in fact, from Gronovius (1661)[1] to Giardina (1966), have treated the *Octavia* as non-Senecan. Attempts to identify its author by name have failed for want of evidence, but certain of his characteristics can reasonably be inferred from the contents and style of the play. He was an opponent of Nero and all that Nero stood for; an admirer, possibly an acquaintance, of Claudius' ill-fated children, Britannicus and Octavia; and an impassioned believer in Seneca's moral and political ideals. He was completely familiar with the Senecan tragedies and prose works; indeed, one strong indication of the non-authenticity of the *Octavia* is its persistent and rather clumsy borrowings from them (notably 381–90, borrowed from *Helv.* 8.4–6, and 440–532, borrowed from *Clem.* I *passim*; many examples will be found in Hosius (1922)). Finally, although a man of some learning and of deep feeling, he was a mere amateur in the craft of verse-drama (Herington (1961)). The date of his play's composition cannot be earlier than A.D. 64, since it contains apparent allusions to the great fire of Rome (831–3) and to Nero's construction of the Golden House (624–5). How much later it may be than that is hard to determine. The view of most investigators, however, that it belongs to the early Flavian period (after the death of the tyrant in 68, before the strong reaction against Senecanism visible in Quintilian's work), seems reasonable. Tentatively one might set it in the decade A.D. 70–80.

If the individual who wrote the *Octavia* has here been correctly reconstructed, he is clearly of some interest as a minor witness both to imperial Roman politics and to the career and influence of Seneca (cf. Trillitzsch (1971) I 44–8). Even more significant, perhaps, is the contribution of his play to our understanding of the potentialities of ancient classical drama. It is one of the only two ancient plays on historical themes that have survived complete (the other, of course, being Aeschylus' *Persians*). Moreover, it is the sole extant survivor of an entire Roman dramatic genre, the *fabula praetexta* (on the genre as a whole see Helm (1954)). The title of our play often found

[1] Gronovius follows the practice of his age in reproducing the vulgate text, complete with the attribution to Seneca; but his own opinion is made quite clear in the notes (esp. *ad* 185 and 516).

in modern discussions, *Octavia praetexta*, is not in fact justified by the manuscripts or earlier editions, which entitle it simply *Octavia*. Yet there are reasons to suppose that it is a fair representative of the genre *praetexta* in the second, Imperial, phase of its development (*c*. A.D. 40–80). Possibly to the conventions of the genre the *Octavia* owes a singular structural feature: the three major movements into which its action falls are each set in one of three successive days.[1] The second of these days, the wedding-day of Nero and Poppaea,[2] is represented only by a brief *kommos* (646–89). The first and third days (1–592 and 690–983, respectively) approximately balance each other both in theme and in structure; the notable difference in length between them may well be due to the author's progressively failing powers of invention. Another unique feature is the apparition (593–645) of Agrippina's ghost, on a stage temporarily cleared of all human actors. In character this interlude is extremely like a Senecan prologue (especially those of the *Agamemnon* and *Thyestes*), but there is no parallel in the genuine Seneca, nor indeed in ancient tragedy, for the intrusion of such a totally detached episode into the middle of a play. The tragic function of Agrippina's apparition, in drawing together the historical and moral causes of the catastrophe, is paralleled to some extent by that of Darius' ghost in Aeschylus' *Persians*. But the Darius episode is no 'postponed prologue'; the only structural parallels to such a feature (and remote parallels, at that) are to be found in ancient comedy, e.g. Menander, *Aspis* 97–148. The final major difference to be noted between the *Octavia* and other ancient dramas is that its non-iambic portions – the choral odes, the two monodies, and the three *kommoi* – are all restricted to a single metre, the anapaestic dimeter; another sign, perhaps, of the composer's inexperience at his craft. In most other purely stylistic respects the *Octavia* closely resembles the genuine Senecan plays. One misses only the inimitable essence of Seneca: the wit, the descriptive power, the gift of apt comparison, the occasional concise and ever-memorable phrase.

Yet the author also shows certain qualities that Seneca lacks. Although the *Octavia* is not a great play, it can yet be read with pleasure, and even with profound sympathy – once one has ploughed through the rambling and repetitive opening sections (1–272), in which the writer seems still to be trying his hand at an unfamiliar task. His chosen theme is moving in itself. It is a story of the early summer of A.D. 62, when a young and orphaned princess is repudiated by the husband whom she was forced to marry; sees the Roman *plebs* rise up in vain to protest against that husband's remarriage to the radiant Poppaea; and finally, on the pretext of her responsibility for the uprising, is dragged off the stage to her exile on a lonely island and inevitable death. The characters in this story are hardly less moving. Here one becomes aware of what may be the most profound difference between the *Octavia* and Senecan tragedy. Whereas in the genuine plays (as has been seen above) the human figures are almost colourless in comparison with the evil which informs and dominates the action, the *Octavia*'s principal characters, and even its Choruses,[3] live and act independently, in their own right.

[1] Sluiter (1949) 9–10, and Herington (1961), esp. 24–5, on the indications that the 'unity of time' may also have been flouted in some *praetextae* of the Republican period.

[2] This is established by *Oct*. 646–7 and 669–73. The evidence that the play's first movement is set on the preceding day is provided by *Oct*. 592; the evidence that the third movement takes place on the day after the wedding is found in lines 712–17.

[3] There are evidently two Choruses in the *Octavia*, as there are in the genuine *Agamemnon* and in the probably spurious *Hercules Oetaeus*. The first Chorus consists of Roman citizens who are fervent

Evils enough, indeed, are involved in the events here; but none of them is represented as the central, controlling force in the shaping of the plot. Thus it comes about – possibly through the author's very incompetence in the creation of a truly Senecan-type drama – that his Nero, Poppaea, Seneca, and (above all) Octavia, however imperfectly rendered, are the most vivid and credible human figures in the entire Senecan tragic corpus.

The student of Seneca's works will perhaps be most interested by the representation of Seneca himself in *Oct.* 377–592. Both in ancient and modern times Seneca's personal character has been vilified by some critics,[1] although it needs to be said that the peculiar practice of using his supposed morals as a criterion for the literary criticism of his writings is comparatively recent.[2] At least the author of the *Octavia*, who may well have known him, offers us a believable portrait of the man. This stage-Seneca is strangely like the Senecan Thyestes in that he has learned from exile the true delights of philosophy, but has adopted the fatal choice of returning to power when power was offered him (*Oct.* 377–90; cf. *Thy.* 404–90). Yet, having fallen once more to the temptations of ambition, he still applies his philosophical insight as best he may, under the foul circumstances, to the betterment of humanity. Seneca is seen desperately attempting to convince a rabid Nero that the true model for imperial behaviour is the mature, benevolent Augustus, that clemency and respect for the opinion of his subjects are the only right way to rule,[3] that morality and piety forbid the divorce of Octavia. All this is in vain; *liceat facere quae Seneca improbat* (*Oct.* 589: 'Be it my right to do what Seneca condemns!') cries Nero; and the tragedy marches on to its terrible close. This stage-character does not, after all, seem too remote from the Seneca whom one reconstructs from his writings and the scattered testimonies to his life. Here is a man tragic in his inconsistency: an eloquent moralist fascinated, even to his own destruction, by power.

partisans of Octavia, and appears in the first and second of the play's three movements. The Chorus of the final movement is of a very different fibre: it adores Poppaea's beauty (762–77) and condemns (785, 806) the folly of the uprising perpetrated by the First Chorus (683–9, cf. 786–803).

[1] The earliest recorded is Suillius, in Tacitus, *Ann.* 13.42 (year A.D. 58). Some of Dio Cassius' sources were equally critical or more so (60.8.5, 61.10.1–6, 61.12.1, 62.2.1). Yet they must be balanced against another source, according to which Seneca 'excelled the Romans of his time, and many others too, in wisdom' (59.19.7); Dio himself, unfortunately, did not trouble to do this.

[2] An example: 'Of [Seneca's] works the writer finds it hard to judge fairly, owing to the loathing which his personality excites' – H. J. Rose *ap.* Motto (1973) 45.

[3] Just so the prose-writer Seneca had argued in the *De clementia*.

27

LUCAN

Petronius' classicistic reaction to Lucan's Stoic epic, the *Bellum civile*, foreshadows the later response: why the neglect of convention, the disregard for precedent, the carelessness about poetry? He prefaces his *Civil war* (*Satyricon* 119–24), a Virgilian pastiche on Lucan's theme, its style a mixture of the old and the new, with a prescription for the correct approach:

> ecce belli ciuilis ingens opus quisquis attigerit nisi plenus litteris sub onere labetur. non enim res gestae uersibus comprehendendae sunt, quod longe melius historici faciunt, sed per ambages deorumque ministeria et fabulosum sententiarum torrentem praecipitandus est liber spiritus, ut potius furentis animi uaticinatio appareat quam religiosae orationis sub testibus fides. (*Satyricon* 118.6)
>
> *Look at the immense theme of the civil wars. Whoever takes on that without being immersed in literature must falter beneath the load. Historical events are not the stuff of verses – that's much better dealt with by historians. Instead, the free spirit must be plunged in complexities of plot, divine machinery, and a torrent of mythological material. The result should be the prophecies of an inspired soul, not the exact testimony of a man on oath.* (Tr. M. Winterbottom)

Quintilian had no doubts: Lucan is a model for orators, not poets. Martial shows that prose and verse had become polarized – that sense was now distinct from sensibility – when he records that Lucan, for many, had forfeited the name of poet: there were rules, and the rules were there to be followed.[1] Fronto's judgement we might question, but he too helped in the devaluation of Neronian baroque.[2] What strikes the reader of the ancient *testimonia* is their conservatism about the proper limits of poetry and prose, their lack of sympathy for experiment and innovation, and their distrust of wit and intelligence in verse: poetry was to be rich, ornamental and mellifluous, not sparse, economical and cerebral. Lucan, of course, is both rhetorician and poet: the two are

[1] Quint. *Inst.* 10.90 *Lucanus ardens et concitatus et sententiis clarissimus, et ut dicam quod sentio, magis oratoribus quam poetis imitandus*; Mart. 14.194 *sunt quidam qui me dicant non esse poetam: | sed qui me uendit bibliopola putat.*

[2] Front. 2.105f. '... in the first seven verses at the beginning of his poem he has done nothing but paraphrase the words *wars worse than civil.* Count up the phrases in which he rings the changes on this ... wilt never be done, Annaeus!' (tr. Haines, Loeb). An unfavourable contrast with Apollonius follows.

quite compatible. Yet modern estimates usually see fit to follow the ancients and undervalue a way of writing which, albeit extreme in Lucan's case, is quite in agreement with the trends of Roman poetry, if not of Roman criticism: Ennius on occasions and Lucretius, as well as Propertius, Manilius and Ovid, had prepared the way for his intellectualized conceits, and their rhetorical, often prosaic formulations. And his infrequent admirers have been more concerned with aesthetic vindication of his verbal and intellectual extravaganzas than with discovering a rationale for his rejection of tradition.[1]

Anything but unoriginal in the *Bellum civile*, Lucan began with tired neoteric essays, stylistically akin to those of the *princeps*, quite mainstream, and accomplished. One might compare his clever *Thebais Alcmene, qua dum frueretur Olympi | rector, luciferum ter iusserat Hesperon esse* 'while the lord of Olympus enjoyed Alcmene of Thebes he ordered three nights in succession', fr. 8 M, from the *Catachthonion*, with Nero's *colla Cytheriacae splendent agitata columbae* 'the necks of Venus' doves are ruffled then shine', fr. 2 M: except for a certain Ovidian flavour, both fragments could have been written in the late Republic, during the heyday of the epyllion – supporting evidence for Persius' demonstration that neoteric poetry continued to thrive at Rome.[2] Perhaps there was agreement then, between the Emperor and Lucan, but soon we hear of discord – of enmity arising after the publication of part of the epic. But there is little point in clinging to the *Vita* in pursuit of three books composed before the supposed quarrel: anti-Caesarian comment is rife in the *Bellum civile*, and consistently so; nor is there any reason to assume that Nero would have identified with Julius.[3] Domitius Ahenobarbus, the ancestor of Nero that mattered, is awarded an unrepresentatively heroic end in Book 7; and Nero is praised at the opening of Book 1 in terms which may be overly fulsome, but are hardly ironic.[4] Poetic rivalry there might have been: but there is nothing in the poem

[1] For the ancient response see Ahl (1976) 74–5, and Sandford (1931) 233–57.

[2] It is tempting to speculate as to the identity of the *noui poetae* in Seneca's *Apocolocyntosis* (12.29), but *nouus* there probably means no more than 'modern'. Nero's second fragment is more reminiscent of Lucan's epic style: *quique pererratam subductus Persida Tigris | deserit et longo terrarum tractus hiatu | reddit quaesitas iam non quaerentibus undas* 'the Tigris, which meanders through Persia then disappears and leaves it, drawn underground in a passage through many lands, then finally surrenders its lost waters to a people which does not expect them' (I owe the interpretation to Dr R. Mayer). This could be from one of Lucan's many geographical excursuses: but it still has a preciosity which we associate with the term 'neoteric'.

[3] *Vita Vaccae*, p. 335 Hosius: *cum inter amicos enim Caesaris tam conspicuus fieret profectus eius in poetica, frequenter offendebat; quippe et certamine pentaeterico acto in Pompei theatro laudibus recitatis in Neronem fuerat coronatus et ex tempore Orphea scriptum in experimentum aduersum complures ediderat poetas et tres libros, quales uidemus, quare inimicum sibi fecit imperatorem.* It used to be assumed that the first three books were the *tres libri, quales uidemus*, but there is nothing to distinguish them from the rest in terms of antipathy to Caesar; nor do other proposals convince. For Lucan's politics, see Brisset (1964); for the quarrel, Gresseth (1957).

[4] Lucan imitates the proem of Virgil's first *Georgic* in the latter passage: for the issues, see P. Grimal (1960).

to warrant the hypothesis of a growing discontent with Caesarism – a dubious concept anyway – culminating in the conspiracy and suicide of A.D. 65.[1]

As the epic unfolds, we find a greater sympathy for the Republican party: but that is inevitable, as Pompey moves towards his death, and Cato emerges as Stoic saint. Rhetoric may demand an increasing amount of anti-Caesarian invective, but that has no necessary bearing on Lucan's relations with the *princeps*. It has been argued that the completed epic's structure was to be tetradic, the first four books concerned with Caesar, and culminating in the death of the Caesarian Curio, the second four with Pompey, whose death occupies the last half of Book 8, while the projected final tetrad – the epic breaks off part way through Book 10 – was to end with the death and apotheosis of Cato.[2] If Lucan's aim was a vindication of the Republican cause through Cato's suicide – and Book 9, an allegory of the testing of the Stoic sage, gives every indication that it was – then structural requirements are sufficient explanation of any increase in his antipathy towards Caesar, the tyrannical egotist, and Stoic villain.

But we should not press the tetradic structure too closely: in the first two sets of four books, focus alternates between the Pompeians and Caesarians without overdue regard for a principle of organization, and Book 10 is as dedicated to Caesar as 9 is to Cato. Moreover there is some indication, tenuous though it may be, that Lucan thought in terms of two hexads: lists of sympathetic omens are common to Books 1 and 7, and 6, with its closing inferno, reminds us of the *Aeneid* and its twelve books.[3] But Lucan's method of composition, by the self-contained episode, paratactically arranged, as well as the unfinished state of the poem, should warn us against imposing schemata and eliciting interior correspondences: for instance, we cannot make much of the fact that Books 5 and 9 both have storms in common, while geographical excursuses – scientific, not pseudo-scientific – occupy a great deal of Books 2, 6 and 10.[4] Unlike the *Aeneid*, the *Bellum civile* shows few traces of organic design. And, again unlike the *Aeneid*, it has no single hero: tetradic structure, or, more plausibly, the exigencies of his theme, occasion the choice of three main characters, Pompey, Caesar, and Cato, along with various ancillary figures, like Julia and Curio.[5] Pompey, the least impressive of the three, comes across most forcefully in the oak tree and lightning simile of Book 1, but is a rather shadowy figure after that.[6] His stoical death in Book 8 is a literary failure,

[1] See Tac. *Ann.* 15.70, with its story of Lucan's narcissistic death-bed recitation of his own poetry.

[2] For structure see the summaries in Due (1962), Rutz (1965) 262–6, and Marti (1968).

[3] In general, see Guillemin (1951), and for particular Virgilian debts, Thompson and Bruère (1968).

[4] See Eckhardt (1936).

[5] For the characters, see Ahl (1976) 116–274. Julia, who could be a figure from Ovid's *Heroides*, needs a closer study.

[6] 1.136–43, contrasting with the lightning simile used of Caesar, 151–7.

Lucan devoting too much space to moralization, and little, if any, to narrative; and his apotheosis at the beginning of Book 9 is too abstract to reflect on him as an individual. As one of the initiators of civil war he must die in order that the Republican cause be satisfied; but whether he has reached any personal moral goal at the moment of his death – as Marti puts it, whether he is a προκόπτων, a Stoic acolyte progressing to salvation – is a doubtful proposition.[1] Cato is more obviously a product of the philosophy textbook, a negatively characterized moral archaist in Book 2,[2] yielding to the impersonal saint of Book 9, who prepares himself, and his men, for a death which will be the ultimate vindication of the Liberty destroyed by Caesar. Cato had long since been an *exemplum* for poets and moralizing historians: in Book 9 he is more fully drawn than ever before, an imaginative, at times incomprehensible counterpart to the rigid hero of Seneca's *De constantia sapientis* – the tract which helps explain the more extreme of Lucan's metaphysical Stoic conceits.[3] Where, in the case of Cato, Stoic abstractions called for a rarefied, almost mathematical manner of writing, with Caesar we find an unphilosophically passionate conception, a nervous enthusiasm, learnt from the rhetoricians in their declamations on Alexander. Caesar, like the *felix praedo* of Macedon at the opening of Book 10, is a predecessor of Christopher Marlowe's heroes – an overreacher, an evil genius who pits himself against nature and mankind in an attempt to subjugate their order to his individual will. Sallust, who likewise went to the rhetorical portrait of Alexander for his depiction of young Catiline, would have applauded the idea: the evil self-will of one person is responsible for chaos in the state, and beyond that, chaos in the universe.[4] But it would be romantic, and false, to give pride of place to the anti-hero: Book 9, abstract and difficult though it is, begins to redress any imbalance caused by the flagging of our spirits during Pompey's last hours, and Book 12 would surely have set Cato over Caesar. If the two Republican heroes are less convincing to us, that is a result of a failure of execution on Lucan's part, or a failure of understanding on ours: there is clearly no intention that Caesar should steal the epic.

No single hero, then: but what of theme? Civil war, as the title states, not the loss of Liberty, or any other ancillary topic implied in that title.[5] Rome had seen a good deal of civil war, and a literature had been adapted to the theme. No single genre claimed it as its own, but a series of stock motifs and conventional sentiments became the vehicle for its presentation: epic, history,

[1] Marti (1945).

[2] See especially 2.354–64, on Cato's unconventional marriage, with its remarkable number of negatives.

[3] For the figure of Cato in Roman literature, see Pecchiura (1965).

[4] See Levin (1952), and for Alexander, Sen. *Suas.* 1.

[5] See, for example, the rather inconsequential discussion in Marti (1945), and Due's summary (1962).

declamation, epode – all strike a common note when lamenting civil strife.[1] Fabianus' declamatory piece is typical, showing the contribution of Cynic–Stoic diatribe:

See! Armies of fellow-citizens and relatives often face each other in battle-order, determined to engage in close combat. The hills are filled with horses and soldiers, and shortly afterwards the whole region is covered with mutilated corpses. Among that mass of corpses and of enemies robbing them one might wonder, What cause brings man to such a crime against his fellow man? There are no wars among animals, and even if there were, they would not be becoming to man...What pestilence is it, what fury that drove you to mutual bloodshed, though you are of one origin and of one blood? Is it worth murdering your kinsmen that banquets may be served by hordes of people and that your roofs may be flashing with gold? Truly it is a great and splendid aim, for which men have preferred to gaze upon their dinner-tables and their gilded ceilings as murderers, rather than see the light of the sun as guiltless people!

(Sen. *Contr.* 2.1.10–11)[2]

and so on, in a similar associative vein, for another two pages or so. Not a far cry from the proems of Lucan and Petronius, this way of looking at human corruption finds its way into Sallust's monographs, Virgil's *Georgics*, Horatian lyric, and even the elegy of Propertius. Behind it lie the history of Thucydides, and, more generally, the sermons of the Hellenistic philosophers, and the moralistic iambography of writers like Cercidas and Phoenix of Colophon. A basic assumption of writing of this kind is that the cosmos is an ordered, balanced entity, and that the ideal society is one which obeys the laws of nature, each living thing observing its station within the grand design.[3] Any individual who oversteps the limits of the natural order is preparing his fellows for internecine strife. By laying claim to a portion which is not his own, he unlooses the forces of greed and ambition: nature becomes man's victim, ransacked for what she will yield, and conflicting appetites lead to civil war.[4] Natural confusion, as much as human confusion, is the result of the primal rebellion. Lucan's assumptions are the same: man and nature suffer as human values are reversed, *fas* being replaced by *nefas*, while at the level of cosmic interdependence, the breakdown of earthly order leads to the distressed protestations of a nature whose laws have been defied. He states the theme of the reversal of values in the second line of his proem:

iusque datum sceleri canimus

I sing of legality conferred on crime

[1] See Jal's impressive study (1963).

[2] Leeman's translation (1963) II 470.

[3] See Manil. 5.734ff. (above, p. 483). Ulysses' speech in Shakespeare's *Troilus and Cressida* is derived from the ancient view, and expresses it admirably: see Tillyard (1943).

[4] See also, e.g., 1.226, 666–7; 9.190–1; contrast 2.381–2, of Cato. At Virg. *Geo.* 1.510–11, the infringement of law and order is a prelude to civil strife. The translations of Lucan which follow are those of J. D. Duff (Loeb), sometimes adapted.

and redeploys it in various forms throughout his epic, as at 1.667–8:

> scelerique nefando
> nomen erit uirtus

atrocious crime shall be called heroism

or again, at 6.147–8, as a preface to the inverted ἀριστεία of Scaeva:

> pronus ad omne nefas et qui nesciret in armis
> quam magnum uirtus crimen ciuilibus esset.

Ready for any wickedness, he knew not that valour in civil war is a heinous crime.

In the fourth line of the proem – *rupto foedere regni* – the bond which previously contained the ambitions of self-seeking individuals is broken; and the laws of Rome are rescinded by the onslaught of war at 1.176–7:

> hinc leges et plebis scita coactae
> et cum consulibus turbantes iura tribuni.

Hence came laws and decrees of the people passed by violence; and consuls and tribunes alike threw justice into confusion.

This confusion and transgression of law and proportion has its counterpart in nature. Cicero sees civil war as involving a violent and universal upheaval (*uis et mutatio omnium rerum et temporum*, *Fam.* 4.13.2), while Sallust connects political discord with lawlessness in nature: *considerate quam conuorsa rerum natura sit* (*Hist.* 1.77.13 M). And Petronius, like Lucan, connects cosmic disturbance with the onset of civil strife:

> aedificant auro sedesque ad sidera mittunt,
> expelluntur aquae saxis, mare nascitur aruis;
> et permutata rerum statione rebellant. (*Bell. Civ.* 87–9)

They build in gold and raise their homes to the stars, expelling water from the seabed and introducing sea to the fields, rebels from an order they have changed.

Lucan's version is more general:

> iamque irae patuere deum, manifestaque belli
> signa dedit mundus, legesque et foedera rerum
> praescia monstrifero uertit natura tumultu
> indixitque nefas. (2.1ff.)

And now Heaven's wrath was revealed; the universe gave clear signs of battle; and Nature, conscious of the future, reversed the laws and ordinances of life, and, while the hurly-burly bred monsters, proclaimed civil war.

Another sign of nature's confusion prefaces the climactic battle:

> segnior Oceano, quam lex aeterna uocabat
> luctificus Titan numquam magis aethera contra
> egit equos. (7.1ff.)

Unpunctual to the summons of eternal law, the sorrowing sun rose from Ocean, driving his steeds harder than ever against the revolution of the sky.

The imminent rupture of all *lex* and *ius*, of all Roman values, on the field of Pharsalus, is foreshadowed by a parallel unwillingness in nature to perform her proper functions. Lucan then develops the theme through the omens which, like those of the first book, image Nature's involvement in Roman *furor*.[1]

No single source supplied the basic concepts, nor indeed the method of treatment. Livy is pointlessly, but necessarily invoked:[2] Augustan epic had attempted the civil war, but again, fragments yield as little as epitomes. The early-first-century *Bellum Actiacum*, partially preserved on a Herculaneum papyrus, proves that the epic continued to show interest, and that the style remained prosaic.[3] Lucan's ideas are those of the mass of civil war literature, his style an extension from the sparse, realistic idiom of Augustan civil war epic,[4] while the elements of his theme could have been derived from moral tradition, declamation, or any Republican-biased digest of the events.[5] Only one thing was anathema, mainstream epic, with its poetic embellishments and superannuated gods: the *deorum ministeria* of previous epic are replaced by the sympathetic reactions of an outraged cosmos, additional colour being supplied by frequent recourse to witchcraft, omens and magic, while the concepts of *fatum* and *fortuna* – with occasional invocations of generalized *dei* – supply the theological basis.[6] In the realms of diction, convention and narrative technique Lucan consistently adapts the resources of tradition to an unpoetic subject whose demands went quite counter to those of other epic themes. Homer and Virgil could not provide a model for the topic of civil war: their methods would have elevated where Lucan wants despair.

Moralization, cynical and pessimistic, takes the place of organized narrative: the rhetorical moment, seen whole, and interpreted for its moral implications, becomes the unit of composition, replacing sequential action. Lucan's plan is too large, his mood too negative, to dwell on the details of any individual event. Homer, in describing the act of shooting an arrow, maintains a complete step-by-step objectivity, *Il.* 4.122ff.:

...and now, gripping the notched end of the bow and the ox-gut string, he drew them back together till the string was near his breast and the iron point was by the bow. When he had bent the great bow to a circle, it gave a twang, the string sang out, and the sharp arrow leapt into the air, eager to wing its way into the enemy ranks.[7]

1 There has been no full study of this theme, nor of the related topics of disease in the body politic and the decay of agriculture; nor of Lucan's images of collapse and cataclysm: all of which help create a picture of a world on the edge of dissolution.

2 See especially Pichon (1912), who has influenced most later discussion.

3 Text in *Anth. Lat.* 1.1–6 B; see Bardon (1956) II 73–4.

4 See above, pp. 486–8.

5 For instance, Valerius Maximus' handbook of *exempla* could have supplied material.

6 For divine machinery, see Petron. 118.6, above, p. 533. In Lucan, fate and fortune are indistinct: but they do *not* take the place of the mythological interventions of previous epic, despite the impression conveyed by the secondary literature.

7 Rieu's translation (1950).

The poet is not present in his own person: the only concern is with the exact, literal presentation of every single stage in a succession of events. Lucan, on the other hand, refuses to narrate: Virgil, admittedly, had introduced emotional and moral language into his narratives of such actions, but narratives they remained. But now sequence is minimal, ousted by static moral comment: when Crastinus launches the first javelin of the climactic battle of Book 7, the action itself is relegated to a subordinate clause:

di tibi non mortem, quae cunctis poena paratur,
sed sensum post fata tuae dent, Crastine, morti,
cuius torta manu commisit lancea bellum
primaque Thessaliam Romano sanguine tinxit.
o praeceps rabies! cum Caesar tela teneret,
inuenta est prior ulla manus? (7.470–5)

Heaven punish Crastinus! and not with death alone, for that is a punishment in store for all mankind alike; but may his body after death keep the power to feel, because a lance that his hand brandished began the battle and first stained Pharsalia with Roman blood. O reckless madness! When Caesar held a weapon, was any other hand found to precede his?

And even within the subordinate clause emphasis on action as such is minimal: the participle, *torta*, is the only word concerned with the actual throwing of the spear. It is the moral aspect of the deed, not the deed itself, which occupies the poet. *Nefas* – the *nefas* of civil war – here occasions the substitution of an indignant, moralistic rhetoric for Homeric-style narrative. In the historical accounts, the javelin cast of Crastinus occurred after the signal for battle, being thereby absolved of its guilt by the priority of the trumpet-sound.[1] In Lucan's account, the javelin is launched before the signal, immediately joining those other deeds of civil war which violate accepted values. Hence the acrimonious apostrophe, in lieu of epic treatment: for that would have glorified, where Lucan wants to denigrate. He begins to write his poem at a point where narrative has ceased to matter: his audience, with its knowledge of Livy, and of the paradigmatic history conveyed by the rhetoricians, is expected to supply the background, and the links. Pompey's death is not mentioned at the end of Book 8, although four hundred lines are devoted to his final hours; nor does Lucan record the outcome of the lengthy sea battle in front of Massilia at the end of Book 3. His interest is in interpretation, in throwing light on aspects of a story which we would not have noticed for ourselves.[2]

[1] See Dilke (1960) 24, 28.

[2] For Homer's narrative technique, see Auerbach (1953) ch. I; for Virgil's, Otis (1963) ch. III: some interesting comments are to be found in Brower (1959), chh. IV and V. I am indebted to Seitz (1965) for his analysis of this episode: also for his treatment of the flight from Rome, below, pp. 545–8.

Likewise, in the sphere of diction and metre Lucan avoids the precedent of mainstream epic. He abandons the versatility of the Virgilian hexameter, opting for a rhythm which is unmusical and prosaic. *Logopoeia* – 'poetry that is akin to nothing but language, which is a dance of intelligence among words and ideas, and modifications of ideas and words'[1] – is his chosen mode, a more suitable vehicle for the abstractions and difficulties of his theme than the musicality of Virgil.[2] In diction he is less concerned to embellish his material than present it in a dry sardonic light. For instance, *cadauer*, a real and uncompromising word used only twice in the *Aeneid* and once in the *Metamorphoses*, occurs thirty-six times in the *Bellum civile*,[3] while *mors*, the everyday term, is preferred to the poetic *letum*[4] – for in civil war, death is not romantic. By the same token he prefers the realistic *pilum* to *iaculum*, the heroic word.[5] His prosaic tendency is seen again in the precedence of *terra* over *tellus*, *caelum* over *polus*, *uentus* over *aura*, *aqua* over *lympha* or *latex*;[6] and, once more, the modernity and realism of his subject matter dictate a predilection for *gladius*, with its forty incidences, against five in Virgil, two in Valerius, and one in Statius. Unpoetic verbs are rife, many of them compounds. Constantly at odds with conventional epic, Lucan is not averse to coinages, or taking words from other areas of Latin literature: but most of the innovations have a cold, metallic ring. There is nothing especially ornamental about his coinage *quassabilis* or his four otherwise unattested verbs, *circumlabi*, *dimadescere*, *intermanere*, *supereuolare*, or again, his cumbersome three new compounds, *illatrare*, *iniectare*, *superenatare*; *peritus*, *formonsus*, and *deliciae* have no place in the higher genres;[7] nor should *lassus* have been so frequent, when *fessus* was available. Nouns like *auctus*, *ductus* and *mixtura* are more reminiscent of Lucretius and Manilius than the vocabulary of epic,[8] and *uxor*, like *alloquium*, *arca*, *armamentum*, *bucetum*, *columen*, *constantia*, *excrementum*, *opera* and *sexus* would not have pleased the critics. Of his verbal nouns in *-tor*, which are many, seven of them new, several are unnecessarily prosaic, or even bizarre. Technical terms are frequent, for instance *bardus*, *biblus*, *bracae*, *cataracta*, *coccus* and *couinnus*: sparingly used by most poets, Lucan likes them for their scientific edge, which is especially

[1] Pound (1918).

[2] For details on Lucan's metre, see Ollfors (1967).

[3] *corpus* is the more usual word in poetry: see Norden on Virg. *Aen.* 6.149. In what follows, I am indebted to Axelson (1945).

[4] *mors* 126 times; *letum* 36; note *interficere* at 4.547, absent from Virg., Ov. *Met.*, Val., Sil.; also *obire* at 9.190, allowed in Senecan tragedy, but with only two occurrences in the Augustans.

[5] *pilum* 19; *iaculum* 8.

[6] Respectively 183:99; 84:32; 61:0:3. Cf. *pater* 20 (5 times it means senator), against *genitor* 5; and *mater* 17, *genetrix* 8; yet *equus* 12, against *sonipes* 11, and *cornipes* 2.

[7] Before Lucan, *peritus* only occurs once each in Virgil (*Eclogues*) and Ovid, twice in Propertius, and three times in Horace (twice in the more prosaic hexameter works); *formonsus* is a lyric and elegiac word, like *deliciae*.

[8] For Manilius' influence on Lucan – which was considerable – see Hosius (1893).

apt for digressions.[1] He has also read his Virgil with an eye for such terms: from the *Georgics* he takes *ardea*, *defectus*, *dilectus*, *donarium* and *monstrator*; from the *Aeneid*, *asylum* and *caetra*. Virgil's 'poetic' vocabulary, on the other hand, is consistently avoided. Ovid too supplied him with several prosaic or technical words, and there is a relatively high frequency of Ovidian adjectives – usually more poetic.

We find the same suspicion of poeticism and ornament when it comes to groups of terms: for example, in those relating to fear, joy and colour, where other epicists deploy a large and varied range, Lucan limits himself to the more neutral and more obvious words. He uses the conventional *dirus* as frequently as the other epicists, but has a marked distaste for the Virgilian *horreo* and compounds, along with related adjectives such as *horridus*; nor is he as fond of *terreo* as his predecessors. Conversely, he likes the less colourful *metuo*, the prosaic *timeo* and *uereor*, and the un-Virgilian *paueo*, as well as its adjective, *pauidus*.[2] He also reacts against Virgil in his use of the vocabulary of joy: ignoring the stronger words – *alacer*, *laetitia*, *ouans* – as also the Homeric *subrideo*, he prefers the more ordinary *laetus*, *laetor*, *gaudeo* and *iuuat*.[3]

Similarly, his colour vocabulary[4] is less rich than that of mainstream epic; roughly half as many terms, used rather less then half as frequently. From a total of 34 terms, white, grey and black are the dominant tones, accounting for 15 terms with 64 occurrences. Black is preferred to white, but Lucan draws no distinction between the epic *ater*, Virgil's option, and the more ordinary *niger*:[5] likewise, he rejects the Virgilian *albus* and the evocative *niueus*, in favour of the neutral *pallidus* and *palleo*.[6] Red is Lucan's next favourite colour – we remember the frequency of deaths in his epic – but the conventional *purpureus* which accounts for 15 of Virgil's 38 reds, and the decorative *roseus* are entirely absent, replaced by *rubere* and cognates, which claim 14 out of the 25 incidences in the *Bellum civile*. Blues, yellows, and greens are sparse: *caeruleus* and *caerulus* only appear once each, ousted by the duller *liuens* and *liuor*; the epic *fuluus* has only three incidences, *flauus* five, and *croceus* one; while *uirens*, at 9.523, is the only green in this predominantly monochrome epic. A dark and negative theme, and the spirit of revolt: these explain the style. Traditional epic was too wordy, too august.

[1] Lucan's serpent catalogue at 9.700–33 is rich in technical terms: cf. the sole poetic incidence of *musculus* at 9.771, during the serpent-bite episode.

[2] See MacKay (1961) for full statistics.

[3] See Miniconi (1962).

[4] I rely on André (1949) for what follows.

[5] Lucan has 13 incidences of *ater*, 14 of *niger*. Val. and Stat. likewise do not discriminate; Sil. has a liking for *nigrans*.

[6] *albus* accounts for 22 of Virgil's 48 whites; Sil. and Stat. like *niueus*, 19 out of 44, and 19 out of 33. Lucan has only 5 conventional whites, *albus* 2.720, *candidus* 2.355, 5.144, 10.141, and *niveus* 10.144.

As with poetic diction, so with epic convention. The stock ingredients are either missing, or accommodated to the themes of the reversal of values and the breakdown of order. Where, for example, in Virgil's underworld scene we have the founder of Rome, a venerable Sibyl, and a parade of future heroes, in Lucan's νέκυια we find a coward, a witch, and the triumph of Rome's villains. The cycle is at an end: decay replaces birth, discord follows greatness.[1] Likewise, single combat – the ἀριστεία of Homeric and Virgilian epic – is not at home in its usual form in a poem on civil war. It occurs but once – the Scaeva episode of Book 6 – and even then Lucan takes pains to modify its meaning, 6.189–92:

illum tota premit moles, illum omnia tela,
nulla fuit non certa manus, non lancea felix
parque nouum Fortuna uidet concurrere, bellum
atque uirum.

All the host and all the weapons made him their sole object; no hand missed its aim, no lance failed of its mark; and Fortune sees a new pair meet in combat – a man against an army.

Because this is a time of civil strife, *uirtus* is now a crime:[2] hence the extravagance of the episode, the claim to novelty – *par nouum*, one man against an army – and the absence of the convention elsewhere in the epic. True, the Homeric colour crops up in the sea fight at the end of Book 3: but the ναυμαχία itself is devoid of epic precedent.[3] His only other concession to the ἀριστεία is to nod at the related motif of the dying hero's words, during the death of Ahenobarbus in Book 7, a book singularly lacking in Homeric or Virgilian narrative action: but there the heroic send-off is more ignobly motivated – by Nero's ancestry, not the nature of his theme.

Lucan is at his best when he has some pattern to follow, adapting, reversing, or negating it. Declamation alone does not stand him in good stead during his account of the battle of Pharsalus, despite his feeling that the event was too big to warrant mere narrative:[4] apart from the death of Domitius, his only conventional gesture is his variation on the motif of the signal for battle.[5] In Virgil, women and children tremble at Allecto's trumpet blast:

et trepidae matres pressere ad pectora natos (*Aen.* 7.518)

and trembling mothers pressed their children to their breasts.

[1] As Lucan says at 6.780–1, *effera Romanos agitat discordia manes* | *impiaque infernam ruperunt arma quietem*; civil war affects the underworld as well.

[2] See 6.147–8, quoted above, p. 538.

[3] For details, see Miniconi (1951), and Opelt (1957).

[4] See 7.633–4 *illic per fata uirorum,* | *per populos hic Roma perit.* Lucan has just refused to write of *singula fata* – a rejection of the Homeric tradition – giving instead a précis which catalogues the elements of a battle, 7.617ff.

[5] In my analysis I follow Seitz (1965).

The legacy of Apollonius Rhodius 4.129ff., these women and children reappear in Virgil's imitators, Valerius and Statius: in Lucan, the stereotype is changed. Gone is the pathetic terror of the innocent: it is the belligerents themselves who fear their own actions:

uocesque furoris
expauere sui tota tellure relatas. (*Bell. Civ.* 7.483–4)

The armies were terrified of their own madness repeated from all the earth.

One of the keynotes of the proem was the self-destruction of a powerful people:

populumque potentem
in sua uictrici conuersum uiscera dextra. (*Bell. Civ.* 1.2–3)

I tell how a powerful people turned their victorious hands against their own vitals.

Like the hand which turns in on its own entrails, the signal for battle rebounds on the impious armies, their guilt increased by their shouts. A simple adjustment to convention continues the notion that in civil war, the normal laws no longer hold. Earlier in the book, another reversal had done the same work: Cicero, the traditional champion of liberty, martyred for peace by Antony, had been shown counselling war. Historical accuracy – Cicero was not in fact at Pharsalus – is subordinated to the theme of the triumph of *nefas*. But apart from these touches, and the general anti-Virgilian tenor of the book, there is insufficient connexion with epic, and insufficient action. Originality needs some basis: Lucan's private rhetoric cannot support the battle. We find a new direction in the last few pages, where Caesar gloats over the dead: but although the gory innovation caught on with Silius, it is no real substitute for the adaptation of tradition.[1]

When faced with tired or unsuitable conventions, Lucan has constant recourse to one particular mannerism: the negation antithesis, *non* followed by *sed*. Sometimes it merely indicates formal divergence, like *nouus* or *insolitus*; at others it enacts the themes of discord and disorder.[2] During the *descriptio luci* (3.399ff.), we find several examples of the negation antithesis, partly formal in intention, partly thematic: at one and the same time, Lucan claims literary originality, and mirrors his theme. Nature's laws cease to operate, and the grove becomes original, and forbidding, as Lucan denies Virgilian associations, replacing conventions with personal fancy:

hunc *non* ruricolae Panes nemorumque potentes
Siluani Nymphaeque tenent; *sed* barbara ritu
sacra deum; structae diris altaribus arae,
omnisque humanis lustrata cruoribus arbor. (3.402–5)

[1] See Miniconi (1962) for details.

[2] Nowak's thesis (1955), part III, 'Negationsantithesen', discusses the interior mechanics of the device. For Lucan's grove, see Phillips (1968).

No rural Pan dwelt there, no Silvanus, ruler of the woods, no Nymphs; but gods were worshipped there with savage rites, the altars were heaped with hideous offerings, and every tree was sprinkled with human gore.

Virgil's pastoral ideal is deliberately revoked:

est ingens gelidum lucus prope Caeritis amnem,
religione patrum late sacer; undique colles
inclusere caui et nigra nemus abiete cingunt.
Siluano fama est ueteres sacrasse Pelasgos,
aruorum pecorisque deo, lucumque diemque,
qui primi finis aliquando habuere Latinos. (*Aen.* 8.597ff.)

There's an extensive woodland near the cool stream of Caere
Reverenced by all around in the faith of their fathers; encircled
By hills, that wood of dark green fir-trees lay in a hollow.
The legend is that the ancient Pelasgians, the first settlers
Of Latium in the old days, had dedicated the wood
And a festival day to Silvanus, the god of fields and cattle.
(Tr. C. Day Lewis)

Not only that: Lucan's variation strips Nature of her functions, suggesting an uncanny automatism:

nec uentus in illas
incubuit siluas excussaque nubibus atris
fulgura; *non* ulli frondem praebentibus aurae
arboribus suus horror inest. (3.408–11)

No wind ever bore down upon that wood, nor thunderbolt hurled from black clouds; the trees, even when they spread their leaves to no breeze, rustled of themselves.

The reader's response to the norm, exploited by the negatives, provides the basis for the paradox: order and disorder, comprehended in sequence, present a vision of a world that is awry.

In the first book's account of the abandonment of Rome the same techniques recur: civil war transforms a rhetorical prescription accepted by history and epic alike. Reminded of what ought to happen, we deplore the breach of the code. Quintilian gives the ingredients:

sic et urbium captarum crescit miseratio...apparebunt effusae per domus ac templa flammae et ruentium tectorum fragor et ex diuersis clamoribus unus quidam sonus, aliorum fuga incerta, alii extremo complexu suorum cohaerentes et infantium feminarumque ploratus et male usque in illum diem seruati fato senes. (8.3.67)

So, too, we may move our hearers to tears by the picture of a captured town...we shall see the flames pouring from house and temple, and hear the crash of falling roofs and one confused clamour blended of many cries; we shall behold some in doubt whither to fly, others clinging to their nearest and dearest in one last embrace, while the wailing of women and children and the laments of old men that the cruelty of fate should have spared them to see that day will strike our ears. (Tr. H. E. Butler)

Fire, crashing buildings, shouts, uncertain flight, final embraces, wailing women and children, old men: the possibilities are exploited by Petronius, Virgil and Silius, as well as Dio and Livy.[1]

Lucan begins his treatment with a version of the negation antithesis, reproving the flight of the Senate:

> *nec* solum uolgus inani
> percussum terrore pauet, *sed* curia et ipsi
> sedibus exiluere patres inuisaque belli
> consulibus fugiens mandat decreta senatus. (1.486–8)

Nor was the populace alone stricken with groundless fear. The Senate House was moved; the Fathers themselves sprang up from their seats and the Senate fled, deputing to the consuls the dreaded declaration of war.

We might excuse the flight of the *uolgus*: but that of the Senate is not to be pardoned. Two similes follow, neatly adapted again to the irregular state of affairs. In the first, Lucan recalls the rhetorical formula, then implicitly denies its application:

> credas aut tecta nefandas
> corripuisse faces aut iam quatiente ruina
> nutantes pendere domos: sic turba per urbem
> praecipiti lymphata gradu, uelut unica rebus
> spes foret adflictis patrios excedere muros,
> inconsulta ruit. (1.493–8)

One might think that impious firebrands had seized hold of the houses, or that the buildings were swaying and tottering in an earthquake shock. For the frenzied crowd rushed headlong through the city with no fixed purpose, and as if the one chance of relief from ruin were to get outside their native walls.

'One might have thought...but one would be wrong': that is the upshot. Lucan's *faces* and *ruina*, the equivalent of the *effusae per domus ac templa flammae* and *ruentium tectorum fragor* prescribed by Quintilian, would normally be just reason for deserting a city. But on this occasion, the absence of the usual causes is an indictment of Rome's unnatural susceptibility to rumour and panic. By abrogating the rule, Lucan highlights the guilt. His nautical simile has a like effect. Plutarch uses it straightforwardly: οἰκτρότατον δὲ τὸ θέαμα τῆς πόλεως ἦν, ἐπιφερομένου τοσούτου χειμῶνος ὥσπερ νεὼς ὑπὸ κυβερνητῶν ἀπαγορευόντων πρὸς τὸ συντυχὸν ἐμπεσεῖν κομιζομένης. 'But most pitiful was the sight of the city, now that so great a tempest was bearing down upon her, carried along like a ship abandoned of her helmsman to dash against whatever lay in her path' (*Vit. Caes.* 34.3). Lucan, on the other hand, shows that the

[1] See Nowak (1955) 8ff., and Seitz (1965); also Caplan on *Rhet. ad Her.* 4.39.51.

desertion is premature; worse than that, it is a flight into war. After an orthodox start and central section, a final accommodation to the motif of reversal:

nondum sparsa compage carinae
naufragium sibi quisque facit (1.502–3)

and each man makes shipwreck for himself before the planks of the hull are broken asunder.

If the timbers really had broken up, the ship might reasonably have been abandoned: as it is, the crew is too hasty. And as Lucan adds, desertion makes things worse:

sic urbe relicta
in bellum fugitur. (1.503–4)

Thus Rome is abandoned, and flight is the preparation for war. Corresponding to *nondum*...*carinae* and *naufragium*...*facit*, the two parts of the epigram bring the perversity to a head. Panic in the face of civil war causes men to forsake the natural patterns of behaviour, breaking the natural bonds of family and home: the idea is developed at lines 504–9, where the individual points of the rhetorical scheme are prefixed by negatives:

nullum iam languidus aeuo
eualuit reuocare parens coniunxue maritum
fletibus, aut patrii, dubiae dum uota salutis
conciperent, tenuere lares; *nec* limine quisquam
haesit, et extremo tunc forsitan urbis amatae
plenus abit uisu; *ruit inreuocabile uolgus.*

No aged father had the power to keep back his son, nor weeping wife her husband; none was detained by the ancestral gods of his household, till he could frame a prayer for preservation from danger; none lingered on his threshold ere he departed, to satiate his eye with the sight of the city he loved and might never see again. Nothing could keep back the wild rush of the people.

That this was novel, and noticed, is borne out by Petronius, who sets the record straight by omitting the negatives:

hos inter motus populus, miserabile uisu,
quo mens icta iubet, deserta ducitur urbe.
gaudet Roma fuga, debellatique Quirites
rumoris sonitu maerentia tecta relinquunt.
ille manu pauida natos tenet, ille penates
occultat gremio deploratumque reliquit
limen et absentem uotis interficit hostem.
sunt qui coniugibus maerentia pectora iungunt
grandaeuosque patres umeris uehit aegra iuuentus.
(*Bell. Civ.* 221–30)

In the turmoil the people themselves, a woeful sight, are led out of the deserted city, whither their stricken heart drives them. Rome is glad to flee, her true sons are cowed by war, and at a rumour's breath leave their houses to mourn. One holds his children with a shaking hand, one hides his household gods in his bosom, and weeping, leaves his door and calls down death on the unseen enemy. Some clasp their wives to them in tears, weary youths carry their aged sires on their shoulders.

(Tr. M. Heseltine)

Despite the occasional bow to the theme of civil war – note the impious behaviour of 224–5, and the unexpected *absentem* at 228 – the account is the antithesis of Lucan's, a classicistic refusal to violate convention. Behind this orthodoxy, and Lucan's nonconformism, is the sad but responsible exodus from Troy, treated correctly, and with dignity, at the end of *Aeneid* 2. Father, *penates*, son and wife: Aeneas' retinue summarizes the piety so signally lacking in Lucan.[1] But what Petronius forgets is the disparity of theme: the Rome of Aeneas is falling to Caesar. No reason, then, for the conventional antics of rhetorical prescription. Instead, unruly headlong flight.

Traditional patterns are likewise adapted at the end of Book 4, in the account of Curio's defeat. Epic had its formulae for treating the pitched battle: and, once again, the negation antithesis is prominent in Lucan's redeployment. Encouraged by Hercules' victory over Antaeus, Curio decides to give battle to King Juba, heedless of the fact that the mission must be pious for the *fortuna locorum* to work.[2] The struggle of Hercules and Antaeus – of good against evil – is developed along orthodox lines. For Curio, on the other hand, Lucan invents a battle which breaks the literary rules, but coheres with the over-all theme: when civil war claims its instigator, the ordinary cannot be excepted. Lucan sets the tone with:

bellumque trahebat
auctorem ciuile suum (4.738–9)

and civil war was claiming the man who made it.

Curio is out of step with fortune. At line 747, the Romans are surrounded and a standstill ensues; at 750–64 the Roman cavalry attempts an ineffectual charge, answered by a counter-charge at 765–8. The focus now switches to the beleagured infantry, and its inability to move, leading up to the climactic paradoxes of 781–7. Negatives are rife – 749 (*bis*), 750, 759, 760, 761, 762, 770, 775, 781, 784, 785: Curio's defeat is not like other battles. It is only in the treatment of the African attack that traditional motifs are employed without demur – the noise of the galloping horse, and the cloud of dust, complete with Homeric simile:

[1] See Virg. *Aen.* 2.657f., 710f., 717, 723f., 728f., and 3.10–12: Silius adopts the orthodox Virgilian scheme at 4.27ff.

[2] There is some discussion in Longi (1955), Grimal (1949), and now Ahl (1976) ch. III.

at uagus Afer equos ut primum emisit in agmen
tum campi tremuere sono, terraque soluta,
quantus Bistonio torquetur turbine puluis
aera nube sua texit traxitque tenebras. (4.765–8)

But as soon as the African skirmishers launched their steeds at the host, the plains shook with their trampling, the earth was loosened, and a pillar of dust, vast as is whirled by Thracian stormwinds, veiled the sky with its cloud and brought on darkness.[1]

Elsewhere, the battle is unheroic and abnormal: for the Romans, unlike the Africans, are at war with one another.

At 749 the brave man and the coward are refused their usual actions, the negatives creating an air of paralysis:

non timidi petiere fugam, *non* proelia fortes

the coward did not flee, nor the brave man fight.

And then, in contrast to the ensuing African charge, follow the feeble, listless movements of the Roman war horses, all epic associations denied, and replaced by reminiscence of the plague of *Georgic* 3. Firstly, the negations:

quippe ubi *non* sonipes motus clangore tubarum
saxa quatit pulsu rigidos uexantia frenos
ora terens spargitque iubas et subrigit aures
incertoque pedum pugnat non stare tumultu. (4.750–3)

For there the war-horse was not roused by the trumpet's blare, nor did he scatter the stones with stamping hoof, or champ the hard bit that chafes his mouth, with flying mane and ears erect, or refuse to stand still, and shift his clattering feet.

The Roman horse is not roused by the trumpet; nor does it strike the ground with its hoof; nor champ at the bit; nor shake its mane; nor prick up its ears; nor refuse to stand its ground – a far cry from Virgil's noble animal:

tum, si qua sonum procul arma dedere
stare loco nescit, micat auribus et tremit artus (*Geo.* 3.83–4)

If he hears armour clang in the distance,
He can't keep still, the ears prick up, the limbs quiver

or the fiery creature of Statius:

qui dominis, idem ardor equis; face lumina surgunt,
ora sonant morsu, spumisque et sanguine ferrum
uritur, impulsi nequeunt obsistere postes

[1] The motif of the galloping horse begins with Hom. *Il.* 10.535, passes into Ennius, *Ann.* 439 V, and thence to Lucr. 2.329–30, Virg. *Aen.* 8.596, 9.599–600, and 975, Stat. *Theb.* 12.651, and Sil. 4.95–6. The dust cloud was equipped with a wind simile at Hom. *Il.* 3.10ff: Virgil drops it at *Aen.* 11.876–7, 908–9, 12.407–8, and 444–5. See Miniconi (1951).

claustraque, compressae transfumat anhelitus irae.
stare adeo miserum est, pereunt uestigia mille
ante fugam, absentemque ferit grauis ungula campum.
(*Theb.* 6.396–401)

The steeds are as ardent as their masters: their eyes dart flame, they loudly champ the bits, and blood and foam corrode the iron; scarce do the confining posts resist their pressure, they smoke and pant in stifled rage. Such misery it is to stand still, a thousand steps are lost ere they start, and, on the absent plain, their hooves ring loud. (Tr. J. H. Mozley)

Bereft of heroic features, Lucan's horse looks sick and weary, 754ff.:

fessa iacet ceruix, fumant sudoribus artus,
oraque proiecta squalent arentia lingua,
pectora rauca gemunt, quae creber anhelitus urguet,
et defecta grauis longe trahit ilia pulsus,
siccaque sanguineis durescit spuma lupatis.

The weary neck sinks down; the limbs reek with sweat, the tongue protrudes and the mouth is rough and dry; the lungs, driven by quick pants, give a hoarse murmur; the labouring breath works the spent flanks hard; and the froth dries and cakes on the blood-stained bit.

Here we have an amalgam of Virgil's plague symptoms: *fessa iacet ceruix* corresponds to *Geo.* 3.500 *demissae aures* and 524 *ad terramque fluit deuexo pondere ceruix*; *fumant sudoribus artus* to 500–1 *incertus ibidem* | *sudor* and 515 *duro fumans sub uomere taurus*; *oraque proiecta squalent arentia lingua* to 501–2 *aret* | *pellis* and 508 *obsessas fauces premit aspera lingua*; *pectora rauca gemunt*, *quae creber anhelitus urguet* to 497 *tussis anhela* and 505–6 *attractus ab alto* | *spiritus*; *et defecta grauis longe trahit ilia pulsus* to 506–7 *interdum gemitu grauis*, *imaque longo* | *ilia singultu tendunt*; and *siccaque sanguineis durescit spuma lupatis* to 507–8 *it naribus ater* | *sanguis* and 516 *mixtum spumis uomit ore cruorem*. Static as ever in his narrative technique, Lucan remodels tradition to reflect his ignoble theme. Even the purported narrative of 759–64 – the actual Roman charge – is subordinate to a pair of antitheses which increase our awareness that the rules no longer hold:

iamque gradum, *neque* uerberibus stimulisque coacti
nec quamuis crebris iussi calcaribus, addunt:
uolneribus coguntur equi; *nec* profuit ulli
cornipedis rupisse moras, *neque* enim impetus ille
incursusque fuit; *tantum perfertur ad hostes*
et spatium iaculis oblato uolnere donat.

Neither blows nor goads, nor constant spurring can make the horses increase their pace: they are stabbed to make them move; yet no man profited by overcoming the resistance of his horse; for no charge and onset happened there: the rider was merely carried close to the foe, and by offering a mark, saved the javelin a long flight.

The horses are stabbed, not spurred; yet even when this is effective, the increased speed merely brings the rider nearer to the spears of the enemy. Lucan has begun to make the battle into a non-battle: there was no *impetus* or *incursus*, as would have been natural from a charging horse. For what follows at 769ff., the epigram *pugna perit* might have been a suitable motto.

Death takes the place of fighting, the paradox explained by two flanking negations:

ut uero in pedites fatum miserabile belli
incubuit, *nullo* dubii discrimine Martis
ancipites steterunt casus, *sed tempora pugnae*
mors tenuit; *neque* enim licuit procurrere contra
et miscere manus. (4.769–73)

And when the piteous doom of battle bore down upon the Roman infantry, the issue never hung uncertain through any chance of war's lottery, but all the time of fighting was filled by death: it was impossible to rush forward in attack and close with the enemy.

There were none of the usual hazards of a two-sided battle; nor could anyone advance and join in the conflict. We find a similar one-sidedness in the seventh book's culminating battle:

perdidit inde modum caedes, ac *nulla* secuta est
pugna, *sed* hinc iugulis, hinc ferro bella geruntur. (7.532–3)

Unlimited slaughter followed: there was no battle, but only steel on one side and throats to pierce on the other

where the abnormality once again displays the special nature of the war. Lucan continues to innovate with the motif of the cloud of weapons – found in Homer, Ennius and Virgil[1] – which not only transfixes its victims, but also crushes them under its weight:

sic undique saepta iuuentus
comminus obliquis et rectis eminus hastis
obruitur, *non* uolneribus *nec* sanguine solum,
telorum nimbo peritura et pondere ferri. (4.773–6)

So the soldiers, surrounded on all sides, were crushed by slanting thrusts from close quarters and spears hurled straight forward from a distance – doomed to destruction not merely by wounds and blood but by the hail of weapons and the sheer weight of steel.

A new type of destruction joins the old, as yet another convention is altered.

[1] See Hom. *Il.* 17.243, Enn. *Ann.* 284 V, Virg. *Aen.* 10.801–9, 12.284: also Lucan 7.519–20 – an orthodox usage of the motif: cf. 2.501–2 – and *Il. Lat.* 359, 743–4. See Miniconi (1951).

Death from the swords of their companions awaits those who step out of line: so densely packed are the Romans:[1]

uix impune suos inter conuertitur enses (4.779)

he could scarce move about unhurt amongst the swords of his comrades.

Here we are back in the civil war ambience, where the harm and violence is done to oneself. Prefiguring his treatment of the trumpet signal in Book 7, Lucan lets self-destruction take over from the normal pattern of conflict:

non arma mouendi
iam locus est pressis, *stipataque membra teruntur,*
frangitur armatum conliso pectore pectus (4.781–3)

The crowded soldiers have no longer space to ply their weapons; their bodies are squeezed and ground together; and the armoured breast is broken by pressure against another breast.

After the prefatory negative – never before was there a battle in which one side could not move – a bold inversion: dispensing with one set of combatants, Lucan sets Roman against Roman with a verbal scheme more appropriate to two opposing forces. Homer, admittedly, had used it of one army; but Virgil, and Lucan himself, had established a more natural usage.[2] On reading *stipataque membra teruntur; | frangitur armatum conliso pectore pectus*, we think of Virgil's equivalent of *Iliad* 16.215:

haud aliter Troianae acies aciesque Latinae
concurrunt; haeret *pede pes* densusque *uiro uir* (*Aen.* 10.360–1)

Just so did the ranks of Troy and Latium clash
Together, foot to foot, man to man locked in the mêlée,

or again, of the pattern Virgil uses for two opposing chargers:

perfractaque quadrupedantum
pectora pectoribus rumpunt. (*Aen.* 11.614–15)

their horses collided, head on, so that breast
Was broken and shattered on breast.

Expecting the Roman context of a clash between two armies – Lucan himself employs the schema thus, at 7.573, *confractique ensibus enses* – the reader is asked to remember Lucan's introduction to the battle – *bellumque trahebat | auctorem ciuile suum* – and, beyond that, the proem's motif of the hand that turns on itself. The destruction has become internal, confined to Curio's army: the instigator of civil strife will die according to its laws.

[1] Note the progression, from *spissantur* 77 to *densaturque globus* 780, *constrinxit gyros acies* 781, *pressis* and *stipata* 782, and finally *compressum* 787.

[2] It would help to know the contexts of Enn. *Ann.* 572 V, and Bibac. fr. 10 M.

Lucan now completes his demolition of the recognized battle scene by telling us that the victors could not see the vanquished – unusual in itself – and that there were none of the customary streams of blood, or falling bodies, 784ff.:

> *non* tam laeta tulit uictor spectacula Maurus
> quam fortuna dabat; fluuios *non* ille cruoris
> membrorumque uidet lapsum et ferientia terram
> corpora: compressum turba stetit omne cadauer. (4.784–7)

The victorious Moors did not enjoy to the full the spectacle that Fortune granted them: they did not see rivers of blood or bodies striking the ground; for each dead man was held bolt-upright by the dense array.

Homer established the first motif and Apollonius and the Romans took it over; Lucan himself employs it elsewhere:

> sanguis ibi *fluxit* Achaeus,
> Ponticus, Assyrius; cunctos haerere cruores
> Romanus campisque uetat consistere *torrens.* (7.635–7)

Here the blood of Achaea, Pontus and Assyria was poured out, and all that bloodshed the torrent of Roman gore forbids to linger and stagnate on the field.

Ovid had made a great deal of it, for instance:

> cruor est *effusus* in auras (*Met.* 6.253)

blood streamed into the air

or again:

> plenoque e gutture *fluxit*
> inque toros inque ipsa niger carchesia sanguis (*Met.* 12.325–6)

from the open wound in his neck the blood flowed over the couches and into the cups.

Later, Valerius varies it with

> thorax egerit imbres
> sanguineos (*Arg.* 6.186–7)

a bloody rain was driven through their armour.

Statius has his version too:

> eruptusque sinus uicit cruor. (*Theb.* 7.683)

blood spurted out and stained his chest.[1]

An unaccustomed direction is likewise given to the motif of the falling body. Virgil had taken it over from Homer with, for instance:

> at ille
> fronte *ferit terram* et crassum uomit ore cruorem (*Aen.* 10.348–9)

> *so Dryops*
> *Struck the ground with his forehead and vomited up thick gore.*

[1] Cf. Hom. *Il.* 4.140, Ap. Rh. 3.1391–2, Ov. *Met.* 6.259–60; also Lucan 3.572–3, 589, 6.224, 7.625–6.

and again:

sternitur infelix Acron et calcibus atram
tundit humum (*Aen.* 10.730–1)

and felled poor Acron, who dying drummed with his heels
On the darkening ground.

Later, in the probably Neronian Latin *Iliad* – a useful compendium of epic devices – we find for example:

concidit et *terram* moribundo uertice *pulsat* (*Il. Lat.* 376)

he fell and dying struck the earth with his forehead.[1]

No streams of blood then, and no falling bodies: instead, a standing mass of corpses. There has been no battle in the usual sense of the word, not even an ordinary one-sided massacre: for Juba has been in the background, the Romans subjected in isolation to the relentless mechanics of internecine strife, a plight delineated through Lucan's alterations of the epic format. He wavers momentarily over Curio's death:

non tulit adflictis animam producere rebus
aut sperare fugam, ceciditque in strage suorum
impiger ad letum (4.796–8)

he would not stoop to survive defeat or hope for escape, but fell amid the corpses of his men, prompt to face death.

As direct narrative takes over from the obliquities of the battle scene, one heroic deed is on the verge of rescue – but Lucan's negativity wins the day: *et fortis uirtute coacta* 'brave in forced courage' (4.798). In the cynical *coacta* we return from normal epic to the world of civil war.

In Book 5, during his account of Caesar's storm, Lucan's policy of negation recurs. Through the negation-antithesis, and a few slight changes in tradition, he enlivens the prodigies of the *poetica tempestas*,[2] converting them into images of nature's internal dissension – at the same time reversing the role of the hero. Nature no longer assails a helpless human victim: Caesar rides superior, as nature fears her own violence. The parallel with the war is clear: Caesar the superman, cause of civil strife, measures his stature against the fury of the storm, and laughs at a world at variance with itself.

Lucan's rehabilitation of disorder begins at line 597 with a *concursus uentorum*. If he had simply followed precedent, all four winds would have blown at once – and probably gone unnoticed. As it is, scientific theory is invoked to make us more aware of the breach in natural law.

[1] Cf. Virg. *Aen.* 9.708, 488–9, 12.926, *Il. Lat.* 370–1, 382; Miniconi (1957).

[2] For background, parallels, and bibliography, see Morford's extensive treatment (1967), chapters III and IV.

non Euri cessasse minas, *non* imbribus atrum
Aeolii iacuisse Notum sub carcere saxi
crediderim; *cunctos* solita de parte ruentes... (5.608–10)

I cannot believe that the threats of the East wind were still then, and that the South wind black with storm was idle in the prison of Aeolus' cave: all the winds rushed forth from their usual quarters.

This time, cleverly, the negations help to reinstate the norm of previous epic: but in Virgil and Homer physical laws were not the thing at issue. Reminding us of science Lucan causes apprehension about a world we thought we knew. All four winds now blow with a vengeance. What is more, the military imagery previously used for the assault of nature on man is now redeployed to show a world at odds with itself: the winds fight one another, the seas migrate, and mountains are submerged. And the threat to nature continues, when the waters that surround the earth begin to send in their waves:

non ullo litore surgunt
tam ualidi fluctus, alio*que* ex orbe uoluti
a magno uenere mari, mundumque coercens
monstriferos agit unda sinus (5.617–20)

No shore gave birth to these mighty waves: they came rolling from another region and from the outer sea, and the waters which encircle the world drove on these teeming billows.

Lines 620–4, with their comparison of the cataclysm, confirm our fear that the boundaries of the world are on the verge of dissolution: and still no battle of hero and the elements. Soon, a summary of the menace to the universe; but first a variation on the traditional ideas of darkness and upward-surging waves:

non caeli nox illa fuit: latet obsitus aer
infernae pallore domus nimbisque grauatus
deprimitur, fluctusque in nubibus accipit imbrem. (5.627–9)

The darkness was not a darkness of the sky: the heavens were hidden and veiled with the dimness of the infernal regions, and weighed down by clouds; and in the midst of the clouds the rain poured into the sea.

In previous epic the waves reached the sky, but this is now impossible since there is no sky – no intervening space between cloud and sea. Lucan replaces the usual upward movement with a movement downwards, causing the upper world to vanish from sight: hence the only darkness can be that of the lower. Scientific observation – of the depression of cloud in a storm – helps once more to resuscitate convention, and further our fears on nature's behalf. For another department of the world has now disappeared.

Having disposed of the sky, Lucan discards lightning, again enlisting science:

lux etiam metuenda *perit*, *nec* fulgura currunt
clara, *sed* obscurum nimbosus dissilit aer. (5.630–1)

Light, albeit fearful, disappeared as well: no bright lightnings darted, but the stormy sky gave dim flashes.

In a state of total cloud there cannot be collisions: hence lightning is replaced with a dark internal dissolution of the atmosphere.[1] Nature continues to suffer, and another element is lost – *lux* as well as *caelum*: for the prefatory negation ending in *perit* has larger designs than the simple *fulgura clara*.

Having infringed the literary order for the description of confusion, replacing the old conceits with scientifically based prodigies, Lucan now presents us with a picture of universal chaos:

tum superum conuexa fremunt, atque arduus axis
intonuit, motaque poli compage laborant.
extimuit natura chaos; rupisse uidentur
concordes elementa moras, rursusque redire
nox manes mixtura deis: spes una salutis,
quod tanta mundi nondum periere ruina. (5.632–7)

Next, the dome of the gods quaked, the lofty sky thundered, and the heavens, with all their structure jarred, were troubled. Nature dreaded chaos: it seemed that the elements had burst their harmonious bonds, and that Night was returning to blend the shades below with the gods above; the one hope of safety for the gods is this – that in the universal catastrophe they have not yet been destroyed.

Thunder provides the starting point, but then the simple allied notion of the falling sky – Virgil's *caeli ruina* – receives eschatological development into the idea of *mundi ruina*: Lucan's vocabulary – *mota*. . .*compage*, *concordes*. . . *moras* – becomes reminiscent of those places in his epic where war involves the demise of earthly order, while *extimuit natura chaos* leaves no doubt that the victim of this storm is nature herself. In other storms it is the *compages* of the boat which is threatened, not the structure of the universe: and it is the hero, not the gods, who fears for his safety. Lucan's Caesar, who had exclaimed:

caeli iste fretique
non puppis nostrae labor est (5.584–5)

yonder trouble concerns the sky and sea, but not our barque,

[1] See Morford (1967) 43.

proves right: he remains outside it, unscathed.[1] Nature's role and that of the hero have been interchanged: so much so, that the turmoil is no menace to Caesar, rather a measure of his demonic genius:

credit iam digna pericula Caesar
fatis esse suis (5.653–4)

he considers at last that the danger is on a scale to match his destiny.

No deity began the storm. It was Caesar who wanted to sail, despite the protests of the humble Amyclas. And it is almost as if it has been he who has directed the storm, not the gods or nature, when the tenth wave, which normally brings destruction, places him and his boat on dry land:

haec fatum decimus, dictu mirabile, fluctus
inualida cum puppe leuat, *nec* rursus ab alto
aggere deiecit pelagi *sed* protulit unda,
scruposisque angusta uacant ubi litora saxis,
imposuit terrae. (5.672–6)

As he spoke thus, a tenth wave – marvellous to tell – upbore him and his battered craft; nor did the billow hurl him back again from the high watery crest but bore him onwards till it laid him on the land, where a narrow strip of shore was clear of jagged rocks.[2]

What Lucan forgets to tell us is that the mission was a failure: for Caesar, who thrives on disorder, has risen superior to a world he has ruined.

[1] Lucan defers to tradition at 639 and 652–3, where sailors experience fear: but these *nautae* are generalized. The *magister* of 645 whose *ars* is defeated by *metus* is probably Amyclas, Caesar's humble companion. But he is an ordinary mortal, not a superman. Lucan continues the notion of a storm which cannot harm the usually helpless hero at 646, with *discordia ponti | succurrit miseris*: the last word is out of place, but Lucan nods on occasion, even given his own terms of reference.

[2] For the tenth wave, see Ov. *Met.* 11.530, *Trist.* 1.2.49–50. Lucan is thinking of *Odyssey* 5, where the hero was finally washed ashore by a 'great wave': but he had first been wrecked by a μέγα κῦμα . . . δεινὸν ἐπεσσύμενον (ll. 313–14): cf. *ingens . . . pontus* at Virg. *Aen.* 1.114. Caesar has just reversed another convention of the *poetica tempestas*, in his contempt for the thought of death, 656–71 (especially 668–9 *mihi funere nullo | est opus, o superi*): other epic heroes had trembled at the idea of lacking a proper burial. See Morford (1967) 44.

28

FLAVIAN EPIC

I. INTRODUCTORY

Each of the three epic writers of the Flavian era – Valerius Flaccus, Papinius Statius, Silius Italicus – sought to be Virgil's successor: a laudable but daring aspiration. Method and result differed widely. What is common to the epics is less important than what is distinct. This divergence is plainly revealed in their choice of subjects. Valerius selected the Argonautic myth, transmuting elements taken from Apollonius Rhodius in a Virgilian crucible: an audacious process for even the most skilful alchemist. Statius chose the war of the Seven against Thebes, a horrific saga of fraternal discord and moral dissolution but congenial to a poet steeped in the gloomy portentousness of Senecan tragedy and the spiritual nihilism of Lucan's *Bellum civile*. Silius rejected mythology, assuming the patriotic mantle of Ennius and Virgil: his was a national theme, the war waged by Hannibal and perfidious Carthage against the manifest destiny of the Roman people. The idea of composing a *carmen togatum* no doubt had a special appeal to one who had himself been a consul, provincial governor and statesman.

Within the context of European literature, only one of the three gained enduring eminence: Statius, whose *Thebaid* and inchoate *Achilleid* were highly valued and widely studied in late antiquity, in the Middle Ages and after. Dante, Boccaccio, Chaucer, Tasso, Spenser, Milton and Pope all bear witness to his stature. Valerius and Silius, by contrast, fell rapidly into neglect and oblivion; the *Argonautica* and *Punica* were not rediscovered until the Italian Renaissance and subsequently they provided pabulum for the nourishment of philologists rather than imitators. It would be quixotic to negate the verdict of history. Statius' achievement surpassed that of both his contemporaries. Valerius has, in recent times, found admirers, who have discovered in his unfinished epic the seeds of genius and the harvest of artistry. Silus' *Punica* has been rarely read but commonly disparaged: somewhat unjustly, for, despite its many and obtrusive blemishes, there is in it much that is not despicable. It is, however, too optimistic to expect that many readers should feel impelled to sift the seventeen books of the *Punica* in quest of its better passages.

It was only at the Renaissance too that Statius' shorter poems, the *Silvae*, were brought again to light. Four books of *vers d'occasion*, and the semblance of a fifth, prove that his literary skills were not confined to the grandeur of epic but were equally adapted to lesser genres. The *Silvae* rapidly acquired a high reputation among neo-Latin and vernacular writers. Today there are those who set a greater price upon them than upon the *Thebaid*, which Statius, adhering to the hierarchical view of poetic kinds, regarded as his masterpiece and his guarantee of immortality. Death prevented him from writing more than a fraction of the *Achilleid*. It breaks off at line 167 of the second book and what was composed is best regarded rather as a provisional draft than as a definitive version. How Statius intended to fulfil his ambitious project of narrating Achilles' life from birth to death must remain a matter of vain speculation.

Valerius, Statius and Silius had to come to terms with an array of predecessors whose claims to homage were coercive and dominant. Virgil, Ovid, Seneca and Lucan had established canons which could be neither ignored nor spurned. It is true that there was in the late first century a movement – Quintilian is its chief theoretical exponent – that saw much to condemn in the stylistic innovations that Seneca and his nephew Lucan, in the wake of Ovid, had developed and fostered. Virgilian purity, however, could not be reproduced in the Flavian era. None of the three epics is a replica, in manner or ethos, of the *Aeneid*. It is permissible to speak of degrees of proximity to Virgil.

At the end of the *Thebaid*, Statius proclaims his acquiescence in the inevitable. His *chef d'œuvre* would for ever remain in a place second to the 'divine' *Aeneid* (12.816–17). In the *Silvae*, he mentions visits to the tomb of Virgil, his 'great teacher', in the hope of inspiration (4.4.53–5). This quasi-religious devotion was shared by Silius. Pliny, in his famous necrological notice, remarks that the author of the *Punica* was in the habit of celebrating Virgil's birthday with more pomp than his own and of reverencing his tomb like a temple (*Epist.* 3.7.8). Indeed, Martial informs us that Silius – already the proud possessor of a villa that had once housed Cicero – went so far as to purchase the site of, and to embellish, Virgil's *monimentum* (11.48, 49). In the *Punica*, an explicit tribute occurs at 7.592–4, where Silius, conventionally, asserts the equality of Homer and Virgil.

So much for claims. Despite his veneration, Statius stands farthest from Virgil, closest to Seneca and Lucan. *Silvae* 2.7 is a commemorative poem on Lucan: Statius' hyperbolic praises indicate a genuine admiration. Silius, saturated in the *Aeneid*, was too much of an eclectic to be fully or even predominantly Virgilian. He owed much to Ovid, much, by imitation or purposeful contrast, to Lucan – who had, after all, also based his epic on Roman history. Silius saw himself, too, as an heir of Ennius, providing him with a generous eulogy in the *Punica* (12.393–414). That Silius should revere Ennius at all is a portent, showing him to be a harbinger of second-century archaism. Statius, including Ennius in a catalogue of Roman poets, designated him 'unpolished' and 'harsh' (2.7.75). The precise contribution of Ennius' *Annales* to Silius' *Punica* is indeterminable: but even lip service testifies to an attitude of mind. Valerius Flaccus was nearest in spirit to Virgil, but the assessment of proximity depends on an observer's location. Ovid necessarily exercised a considerable effect on Valerius' formal techniques. It seems certain that in the *Argonautica* he aimed at a restraint in language and thought which he considered to be Virgilian. Quintilian, the apostle of classicism, noted with regret the passing of Valerius (*Inst.* 10.1.90) – doubtless recognizing in him a kindred spirit.

No less than the Augustans, the Flavians drank deep at the fountain of Greek poetry. Valerius' principal narrative source was Apollonius Rhodius, though there was little of the servile in the relationship. From Homer, the 'wellspring of all poesie', both Statius and Silius adapted much, introducing not only episodes already reshaped by Virgil but fresh ones as well. Both poets, for example, have incidents based on Achilles' fight with the River Scamander (*Iliad* 21.234ff.): Statius describes Hippomedon's battle with Ismenus (*Theb.* 9.404ff.), Silius Scipio's conflict with Trebia (*Pun.* 4.638ff.). The riches of Homer were inexhaustible, and Statius quarried freely. Silius saw no difficulty in welding Homeric motifs on to the framework of Roman history.[1] Homer's primacy in the genre and Virgilian precedent were, therefore, simultaneously recognized.

For Statius, it was natural to study the Greeks. He was of Hellenic descent, born in Naples, where, as he says in a poem addressed to his wife Claudia, *Graia licentia* and *Romanus honos* were happily conjoined (*Silv.* 3.5.94). His father was a poetaster and schoolmaster specializing in the explication of Greek texts (*Silv.* 5.3.146ff.). Statius' Hellenism is not, however, obtrusive. He utilized Euripidean tragedy – the *Phoenissae* and *Suppliant women* had obvious relevance to the *Thebaid* and the *Hypsipyle* may have added something to Books 4–6 – but never without radical transformation. From Callimachus he derived, among other things, some details for the myth of Linus and Coroebus (1.557–672). Apollonius Rhodius played a subsidiary role in the evolution of Hypsipyle's narrative in Book 5. Old theories that he drew material from the Cyclic *Thebaid* or from Antimachus of Colophon may be dismissed as unproven and improbable.[2]

For a long time the Flavian writers were regarded as little better than plagiarists. Recent investigations have revealed the inadequacy and injustice of this approach. This is especially true in Statius' case. His originality has been

[1] See the full investigations of Juhnke (1972).

[2] Cf. Vessey (1970) 118–43.

thoroughly vindicated. All ancient poets were bound by the principle of *imitatio*. This implied not merely respect for the past but a desire to reach new and individual standards of excellence. Statius was rarely, if ever, subservient to those whom he would have named with pride as his models. Valerius also took pains to create his own interpretation of the Argonautic myth, reassigning to Jason a heroic status which the cynical Apollonius had eroded. Even Silius, the most patently dependent of the three, did not hesitate to modify the events of the Punic War to illuminate a wider philosophical perspective.

2. STATIUS

Family, friends and patrons; the Silvae

Statius may, then, be acquitted of plagiarism. He was a professional poet not a wealthy dilettante. He records, in a long epicedium (formal lament) for his father, that his family was financially straitened, stressing that his ancestors were freeborn and not without some distinction (*Silv.* 5.3.109–10, 115–17). The schoolmaster's son had, all the same, to make his way in the world by his own ingenuity. Prominent Neapolitans sent their sons to the elder Papinius for instruction in literature and other arts (*Silv.* 5.3.146ff., 176ff.). Such local connexions were, we may surmise, of assistance to Statius when he was establishing his reputation in Rome and seeking commissions for his work. He owed a profound debt to his father's guidance and precept in poetry (5.3.209ff.); the son was encouraged to follow in his father's footsteps by entering poetic contests, first in his home town, later in Rome.[1] Such laurels were valuable: they impressed potential patrons. Heredity and environment aided Statius in his chosen career. Inborn genius and artistic sensitivity crowned it.

The *Thebaid* was the offspring of twelve years of unremitting toil (12.811). It was published in its entirety in A.D. 90 or 91. Soon afterwards Statius began to issue the *Silvae*. Four books, each with an apologetic preface in prose, appeared between 91 and 95. The poems in them were obviously a selection from the large number of occasional pieces Statius must have written in previous years. The fifth book, so called, was put together, almost certainly, by an unknown literary executor – who may also have been responsible for the preservation of the *Achilleid*; it has no true preface, only a dedicatory epistle to the epicedium for Priscilla, wife of Flavius Abascantus.

The satirists' cynicism on the subject of patronage finds no confirmatory reflection in the *Silvae*. Statius does not present himself as a *cliens*. The recipients of his poems are not termed *patroni*. Friendship, deferential perhaps but sincere, is the bond that he claims. The *Silvae* are documents of great social

[1] *Silvae* 5.3.111–12, 141ff., 3.5.28ff.; 4.5.22ff. Statius failed to win the prize – to his chagrin – at the Capitoline contest, probably in 94: 3.5.31–3.

value; they reveal much about the outlook and pursuits of those who commissioned them. Taken as a group, they emerge as 'men of influence and wealth, either actively engaged in the imperial service or in a life of comfortable and affluent leisure. Cultured and critical dilettantes, many of them toyed with the art of poetry, dabbled in philosophy and spent their wealth in creating or acquiring objects of beauty.'[1] It was, in many ways, an unreal, exotic world. On these privileged denizens of Roman society Statius relied for support and encouragement. Nothing improper, vulgar or proletarian was permitted to intrude into the gilded and glittering *Silvae*.

Of the Neapolitans, the most prominent was the millionaire Epicurean Pollius Felix, owner of extensive estates in Campania. To him the second book of *Silvae* was dedicated. 2.2 and 3.1 immortalize the architectural and visual splendours of his property at Surrentum. 4.8 is a congratulatory poem addressed to his son-in-law Julius Menecrates on the birth of a third child. Menecrates had been granted the *ius trium liberorum* by Domitian (4.8.20–2) and his brother had held a military tribunate in Africa (4.8.12). Even if Pollius Felix, for dogmatic reasons, abstained from political activity, his kin had no such scruples: Statius predicts a senatorial career for Menecrates' sons (4.8.59–62).

Some of Statius' patrons were men of power and standing in public life. The first book of *Silvae* was dedicated to L. Arruntius Stella. This moneyed patrician was progressing rapidly through the *cursus honorum* under Domitian; a suffect consulship awaited him in Trajan's principate. He was also an elegiac poet. He extended his patronage to Martial as well as to Statius. His marriage to the rich and beautiful Violentilla – of Neapolitan ancestry – is celebrated in 1.2. C. Rutilius Gallicus (1.4) had been *praefectus urbi* and twice consul. Vitorius Marcellus had political aspirations – as well as a fondness for literature. Statius dedicated Book 4 to him and he was the recipient of an epistle in it (4.4); the same Vitorius was dedicatee of Quintilian's *Institutio oratoria*. C. Vibius Maximus (4.7), already in Domitian's day a man of consequence, eventually attained the prefecture of Egypt. M. Maecius Celer (3.2) was to end a career successfully inaugurated under the last Flavian with a suffect consulship in 101. The youth Vettius Crispinus, panegyrized on the occasion of his appointment to a military tribunate (5.2), was son of the patrician Vettius Bolanus, consular, sometime propraetorial legate in Britain and proconsul of Asia. Though nothing further is know of Crispinus, his twin brother was consul in 111.

Other patrons eschewed the pursuit of power in favour of more tranquil occupations: philosophy, literature, connoisseurship. Statius offered Book 2 of his *Silvae* to the elegant and generous Atedius Melior. Within it, the death of Melior's slaveboy Glaucias is fittingly lamented (2.1). In more humorous vein, the passing of his parrot is bewailed (2.4). Also included is an aetiological

[1] Vessey (1973) 27.

fantasia on a curious plane-tree on Melior's estate (2.3). Flavius Ursus, urbane, rich and eloquent, received consolatory verses when he too was deprived by fate of a beloved *puer* (2.6). Septimius Severus, from Lepcis Magna and probably an ancestor of the homonymous emperor, followed an Epicurean style of life on his country properties. For him, Statius penned a Horatian ode, praising the virtues of carefree *otium* but not overlooking his patron's forensic skills (4.5). Lighthearted hendecasyllables were addressed to Plotius Grypus (4.9), another budding orator and minor *littérateur*, son of the consul of 88. Novius Vindex was a fanatical collector of art treasures – but not unappreciative of well-turned verses. Statius lovingly describes a statue of Hercules in Novius' possession, attributed to Lysippus himself (4.6).

There was, too, Claudius Etruscus: a freedman's son, it had to be admitted. But at the time of his death at an advanced age the elder Claudius could have looked back on a long period of power in the imperial household (3.3.59ff.). Furthermore, he had married into the nobility (111ff.). The fruit of that unequal union was a cultivated man, his intellectual gifts balancing his financial resources. His sumptuous bath-house is commemorated in 1.5. Flavius Earinus, Domitian's Ganymede from Pergamum, dispatched his shorn locks in a jewelled casket to the shrine of Asclepius in his birthplace: the Emperor commanded Statius to enshrine the auspicious event in verses (3.4). The resulting poem, if bizarre to modern ears, is nonetheless a valuable revelation of Domitian's claims to godhead. Also close to the earthly Jupiter was Flavius Abascantus, his private secretary: the consolation written by Statius on his wife's demise opens the fifth book, and the epistle dedicatory voices the poet's unshakeable loyalty to the divine house.

Domitian showed marks of favour to one who so deftly expressed official propaganda under a dazzling veil of verbal conceits. 1.1 records, in an ecphrasis, the consecration of a vast equestrian statue to honour the Emperor's Dacian victories in 89. Imperial largesse during a Saturnalian festival is wittily applauded in 1.6. 4.1 is a formal panegyric for Domitian's seventeenth consulship in 95, composed not long before the death of both *Princeps* and poet. 4.2 crystallizes the poet's gratitude for an invitation to dine with senators and knights within the palace itself: a visit to Olympus, a vision of deity never to be forgotten. The Via Domitiana, stretching from Sinuessa to Naples, was completed in 95. Statius summed up the thanks of travellers in hendecasyllables (4.3). It may not be accidental that three laudations of the Emperor and his acts appear in Book 4, which was published in 95 or 96. Domitian, nervously conscious of mounting hatred and barely latent opposition, would have welcomed vociferous plaudits at this time. Statius' prayer, put in the mouth of Janus, that his lord might be granted a long life (4.1.35ff.; cf. 46–7) did not deflect the course of destiny. Whether the poet survived to witness the extinction of the Flavian house in 96 is unknown. He had been its faithful spokesman and servant. Unlike Martial, he did not live long enough to revile his former master – even if he had wished to do so. For that reason, he has, ever since, been accused of degrading servility. But he had no opportunity for that recantation which, it seems, posterity demands of those who write under a despotism.

Artists respond to the society in which they live: by alienation or conformity. Statius conformed. The galaxy of patrons, in orbit around the imperial sun or following more idiosyncratic courses, could not have been easy to satisfy. Lesser poets than Statius, in the face of such creative asphyxiation, would have descended to the banal and the repetitious. His talent was such that he could metamorphose even the most intractable material into a new and memorable form. His patrons were educated men, not to be content with mere hackwork. To titillate their passion for *doctrina*, Statius made full use of allusion and recondite learning. In literature and in the visual arts, 'the taste of the Flavian period favoured brilliance and splendour above all';[1] Statius sought to make his verse jewelled, gleaming and ornate to reflect the spirit of the times. Simplicity was not a virtue that he esteemed, whether in language, imagery, structure or thought. Swift movement and startling colour characterize his work. Critics have remarked on his ability to evoke visual responses in a reader's mind. It is, in consequence, no simple task to appreciate his poetry. For those nurtured on Virgil and Horace, first acquaintance with the *Silvae* and *Thebaid* is aesthetically disorienting. It is a contrast between sobriety and inebriation. Justus Lipsius appositely remarked that Statius possessed a 'luxuria ingenii non indecora' and that he was 'sublimis et celsus poeta, non hercle tumidus'. Unfitting exuberance and grotesque tumidity were hazards that threatened him: but he, unlike many of his imitators, generally avoided the pitfalls.

Artistic surfeit had to be measured against formal austerities. Rhetoricians had by Statius' day established rules and patterns for the subdivisions of the epideictic genre. Prescriptions devised for prose orations had been transferred to poetry. Most of the *Silvae* can be allocated to recognizable *genera*.[2] There is one epithalamium (1.2). Epicedia account for a substantial group (2.1, 2.4, 2.6, 3.3, 5.1, 5.3, 5.5). Add two eulogies (4.1, 5.2), two *gratulationes* written to celebrate the birth of children (4.7, 4.8), two propemptica (3.2, 3.4). There are single instances of the soterion (1.4), the genethliacon (2.7) and the eucharisticon (4.2). A favourite form was the ecphrasis (*descriptio*), the detailed description of a building, an object of virtù or other static object. Eight of the *Silvae* may be assigned to this category and they include some of Statius' finest work (1.1, 1.3, 1.5, 2.2, 2.3, 3.1, 4.3, 4.6). It is not fanciful to trace a rapport between his taste for architecture and the visual arts and the vivid, picture-making

[1] Gossage (1972) 186.

[2] For the theory and characteristics of the rhetorical genres, see Cairns (1972).

quality of his verse. To the ancients, all the arts were in sympathy. In an ecphrasis, dumb stones were given the power of speech, the ability to explain themselves – just as sculptors and painters represented for the human eye incidents from poetry. Whether specific or secondary (as in formalized descriptions of gods, heroes, buildings, landscapes and the like in his epic), ecphrasis was for Statius a natural part of composition. Few poets have more successfully exploited the mode.

Panegyric was an element unavoidable in any epideictic kind. Statius was adept at telling his patrons what they wished to hear, cunningly interweaving *laudatio* with his central themes. In the hands of a skilled poet, generic patterns and the commonplaces (*topoi*) associated with them were a valuable asset. It was part of the decorum of eulogy not to stint one's praise. Not least in addressing the emperor: to expect moderation there, would be to have honey sour. Many of the themes in the *Silvae* had long been conventionalized. The problem for the conscientious artist was not to escape the dictates of tradition and maxim, but to remould inherited material in a fresh, but still recognizable, manner. If *ars* implied a knowledge of and respect for *regulae*, *ingenium* had to provide the original approach which tempered rigidity and triteness.

Genres could be used in an unusual way. The genethliacon for Lucan (2.7) has some of the characteristics of a funeral laudation: for Lucan was dead. 3.4 embodies elements from the propempticon: it is not a human being who is setting out on a voyage, but the locks of Earinus. 2.4, on the death of Melior's parrot, is a parody of the epicedium. Of the two *gratulationes*, one, for Vibius Maximus, is written in sapphic stanzas under the patronage of Pindar (4.7.5–9) and is therefore allowed to stray over diverse themes; the other, for Julius Menecrates, is more solemn and formal, in Statius' customary hexameters (4.8). A few of the *Silvae* cannot be assigned to fixed *genera*. 1.6, the *Kalendae Decembres*, is cast in lively hendecasyllables, as befits its purpose. The poem on Melior's tree (2.3), though a kind of ecphrasis, is, like the lament for his parrot, termed by Statius in the preface a light-hearted work, akin to epigram. 3.5 is a *suasoria* addressed by Statius to his wife, urging retirement from Rome to Naples. We find too an epistle for Vitorius Marcellus (4.4), some jesting verses for Plotius Grypus (4.9) and an alcaic ode for Septimius Severus (4.5). Standing on their own for brevity are 2.5, on Domitian's tame lion, and 5.4, an exquisite nineteen-line call to Sleep.

The principle of variety (*poikilia*) is observed generically and thematically in Books 1–4. It may be added that there is order in diversity. Just as Statius expended great effort on the inner structure of all his work, so the disposition of the poems in each book of *Silvae* is elaborately organized.

In Book 1, the first and last poems (1, 6) are both laudations of Domitian.

The epithalamium for Stella (to whom the book was dedicated) predictably stands in second place. It is balanced by 4, the soterion for Rutilius Gallicus: both are highly personal poems of felicitation, though widely different in occasion. 1, 3 and 5 are all ecphraseis. 2, 4 and 6 are united by the motif of rejoicing and festivity. We arrive, therefore, at the following simple schema:

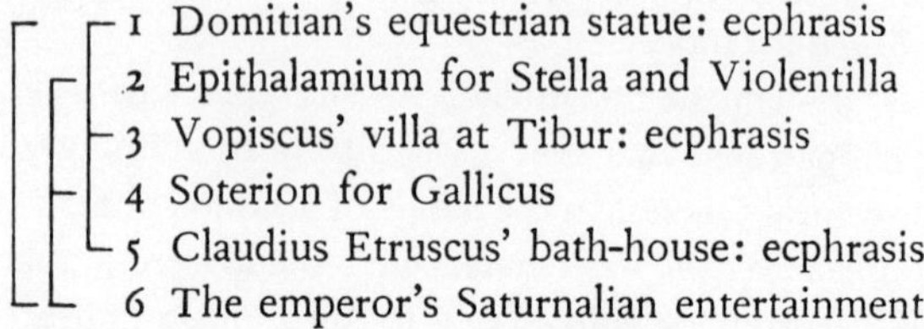

1 Domitian's equestrian statue: ecphrasis
2 Epithalamium for Stella and Violentilla
3 Vopiscus' villa at Tibur: ecphrasis
4 Soterion for Gallicus
5 Claudius Etruscus' bath-house: ecphrasis
6 The emperor's Saturnalian entertainments

In Book 2, the first poem, written for the dedicatee Atedius Melior, is an epicedium on the death of the slave-boy Glaucias: identical in kind and purpose is 6, for Flavius Ursus. 2 and 3, respectively for Pollius and Melior, are ecphraseis. 4 (on Melior's dead parrot) and 5 (Domitian's lion) are both devoted to remarkable animals. The genethliacon for Lucan (7), with its necrological aspects binding it to 2, 4 and 6, attains a climactic status as the last poem in the book. Again the plan is obvious:

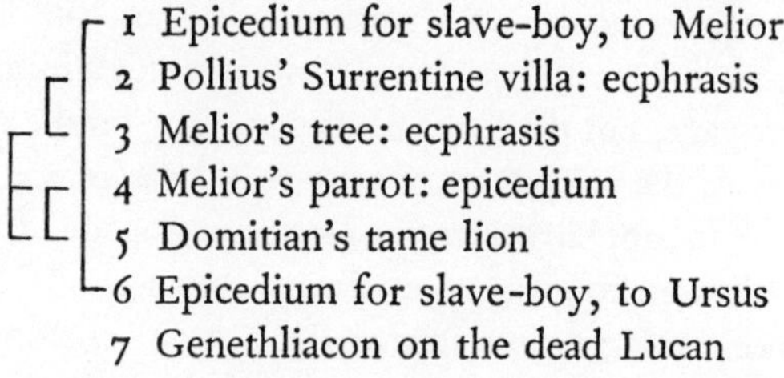

1 Epicedium for slave-boy, to Melior
2 Pollius' Surrentine villa: ecphrasis
3 Melior's tree: ecphrasis
4 Melior's parrot: epicedium
5 Domitian's tame lion
6 Epicedium for slave-boy, to Ursus
7 Genethliacon on the dead Lucan

The arrangement here is slightly more complex than that of Book 1, for the group 3, 4 and 5 are notable for their facetious tone and form a central block within the whole. In Book 2, even more than in 1, we see, as an aspect of *variatio*, the mingling of tragic and comic in the bounds of a single collection.

The third book comprises only five poems. 1 is a *descriptio* of the temple of Hercules erected at Surrentum by the recipient of the dedication, Pollius Felix. 2 is a propempticon for Maecius Celer; 3 a long *consolatio* for Claudius Etruscus on his father's death; 4 the poem on Earinus' *capilli* and 5 the *suasoria* to the poet's wife. The solemn *consolatio* aptly occupies the central place.

Statius' enthusiastic *descriptio* of the Surrentine Herculeum, linked as it is with a laudation of Pollius and his wife, forms a natural complement to his eulogy of Naples in poem 5. Poems 2 and 4 are counterbalanced, for the *capilli*-poem is in part a propempticon, since it wishes the tresses a safe voyage over the sea to Pergamum, just as in 4 Maecius is the recipient of greetings for his journey to the orient. The book, therefore, is neatly disposed round the central pivot of the *consolatio*.[1]

The scheme requires no summary.

In the longest book (4), the first three poems are all concerned with honouring the Emperor. It has also a high proportion of non-hexameter poems: 3, 5, 7 and 9. 4 and 5, addressed to Vitorius Marcellus and Septimius Severus, make up a fitting pair, for the preface informs us that the two men were friends. 7 and 8 are joined by the fact that both were occasioned by the birth of a child. The schema may be presented in this way:

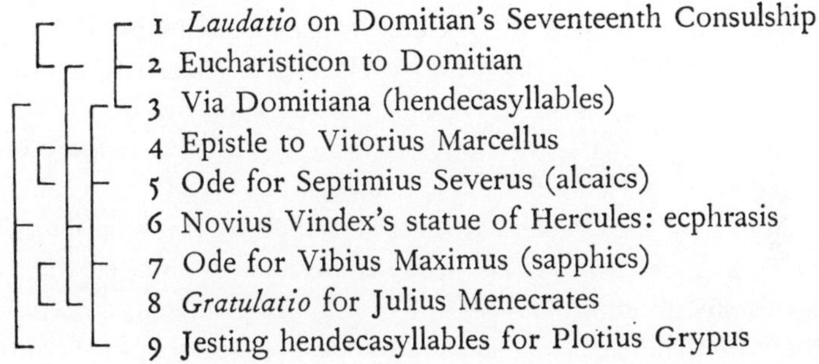

1 *Laudatio* on Domitian's Seventeenth Consulship
2 Eucharisticon to Domitian
3 Via Domitiana (hendecasyllables)
4 Epistle to Vitorius Marcellus
5 Ode for Septimius Severus (alcaics)
6 Novius Vindex's statue of Hercules: ecphrasis
7 Ode for Vibius Maximus (sapphics)
8 *Gratulatio* for Julius Menecrates
9 Jesting hendecasyllables for Plotius Grypus

This is the most complex structure of all. 1 and 2 occupy a special position as tributes to Domitian. Thereafter, hexameter poems alternate with those in other metres.

More might be said. These schemata are only outlines. The total structure of each book is enhanced by numerous and complex responsions within the poems: in theme and imagery, in mood, tone and tempo. Such analyses are evidence of the diligence with which Statius approached each detail of his literary work. But bad poems even well arranged would remain bad: what virtues stand out in the *Silvae* to commend them to us?

Statius has been arraigned for frigidity and obscurity, for an excessive use of mythology, for inventive aridity. Subjective criticisms cannot always be answered objectively. Romantic preconceptions about art in part account for Statius' fall from esteem. Insights must be sought from a different vantage point. An appreciation of craftsmanship may provide the foundation for a broader awareness of the beauty and subtlety of his best work.

There is no better proof of technical expertise than the epithalamium (1.2). The genre had been long established. A glance at Catullus' epithalamia (61, 62) is instructive. The neoteric poet, while making broad concessions to Roman rite and custom, in form and structure followed Hellenic precedents. Not so

[1] Vessey (1973) 29.

Statius. There are, as one would expect, parallels between his poem and the precepts laid down for hymenaeal orations by later Greek rhetors. In a wedding poem or speech, however, many features prescribed by theorists were but conventionalized commonsense: encomia of the bride and groom, a wish for marital harmony, a catalogue of the benefits of connubiality, a prayer for procreation. Even if Statius profited from contemporary rhetorical discussions of the genre, he permitted himself latitude for innovation. In his hands, the hymenaeal was personalized and reconstituted. Its smooth hexameters move sinuously between panegyric and aetiology, truth and fantasy, reality and myth, finding a resolution in a pithy final section which is a traditional epithalamium truncated (247–57).

Stella was bound to Statius by a common enthusiasm for the poetic art (247–8). The excellence of his amatory elegiacs is several times signalized (33, 96ff., 167ff., 197ff.). Tribute is paid to his constancy in love (32ff., 99ff.), his patrician ancestry (73–4), his physical charm (172), his military and civil achievements (174ff.). His bride, Violentilla, well-born (108) and wealthy (121), is a visible image of the Goddess of Love herself (236). It is a flawless diptych, displayed in a gilded frame. To demonstrate and to enhance the portrait, Statius, as commonly in the *Silvae*, turns to myth. He invents an aetiology, in the tradition of Callimachus, to explain the past and present love from which the blessed union has sprung.

His mythopoeia is grand and imaginative, epic in quality, lyrical in language. The wedding of Stella and Violentilla was forged in heaven to be a paradigm on earth. The tale of their love cannot be confined within the boundaries of mundane fact: the epithalamium is dominated by its mythic core. In 51–64, the scene is set on Olympus. Venus is in repose on her couch, circled by the Cupids, one of whom has inflamed Stella with an unequalled passion (83–4). He pleads with Venus to take pity on his victim, to grant fruition to his hopes (65–102). Venus accedes to his appeal in a speech which embodies a superb encomium of Violentilla's mental and physical attributes (106–40). The goddess descends to Violentilla's house in her chariot of swans; there she voices a persuasive plea for Stella. Violentilla should yield to love (162–93); old age will one day come and it is only through the power of love that the future can be created (184ff.). Her words are accepted by Violentilla, who recalls her suitor's 'gifts, prayers and tears' (195–6), his elegies written in her honour (197ff.). Two of the speeches introduced by Statius are *suasoriae*, one a *laudatio*. Rhetoric and fantasia are entwined to show that Stella's present bliss was divinely motivated.

There is no fixed calibration to determine frigidity in literature. To some, the aetiology invented by Statius will seem cold and artificial. The omnipresence of mythology in the *Silvae* requires explanation. It provided Statius, like other ancient poets, with a universal symbolic language, an instantly recognizable frame of reference. In the epithalamium, for example,

he utilises the myth to bring the marriage of Stella and Violentilla out of the particular moment of time into a reality that transcends time, into the world of the divine and the heroic, into a world where love, constancy, marriage, beauty are hypostatised. Through the mythic tale created by the poet, the marriage itself becomes as if a part of mythology, a universal *exemplum* rather than a specific event.[1]

In short, mythology was a valuable method of universalizing the particular, of giving a transcendental meaning to the transient events and situations that Statius was called upon to celebrate. It was a means, too, by which language could be dignified and the range of imagery expanded.

To demonstrate this, it is relevant to cite the passage in which Statius tells of Venus' descent to Rome and describes the house of Violentilla:

sic fata leuauit
sidereos artus thalamique egressa superbum
limen Amyclaeos ad frena citauit olores.
iungit Amor laetamque uehens per nubila matrem
gemmato temone sedet. iam Thybridis arces
Iliacae: pandit nitidos domus alta penates
claraque gaudentes plauserunt limina cycni.
digna deae sedes, nitidis nec sordet ab astris.
hic Libycus Phrygiusque silex, hic dura Laconum
saxa uirent, hic flexus onyx et concolor alto
uena mari, rupesque nitent, quis purpura saepe
Oebalis et Tyrii moderator liuet aeni.
pendent innumeris fastigia nixa columnis,
robora Dalmatico lucent satiata metallo.
excludunt radios siluis demissa uetustis
frigora, perspicui uiuunt in marmore fontes.
nec seruat natura uices: hic Sirius alget,
bruma tepet, uersumque domus sibi temperat annum.
exsultat uisu tectisque potentis alumnae
non secus alma Venus, quam si Paphon aequore ab alto
Idaliasque domos Erycinaque templa subiret. (140–60)

So speaking, Venus rose, her limbs bright as the stars. She crossed the exalted threshold of her bower and summoned her Amyclaean swans to rein. Cupid yokes them and, seated on the gem-encrusted pole, he drives his joyful mother through the clouds. Soon they see the Trojan towers of Tiber. There stands a soaring palace, broad with gleaming halls. The swans in rapture beat their wings against its brilliant portals. It was a dwelling well worthy of divine visitation: even after the gleaming stars of heaven it was no shame for Venus to enter there. On this side, it was fashioned of

[1] Vessey (1972) 183–4.

Libyan and Phrygian marble; on that, of tough Laconian stone, green-glowing; there was serpentine agate and masonry veined blue as the ocean deeps; porphyry, too, bright sparkling – a source of envy to Oebalian purple and to the Tyrian dyemaker with his brazen vat. The ceilings float above, supported by columns beyond counting; the wooden beams glitter, glutted with Dalmatian gold. Cool shadows, streaming from ancient trees, offer protection from the sun's rays; and fountains play, living-clear, in conduits of marble. Nature does not preserve her natural courses: for here Sirius is cool and winter warm. The palace changes and governs the year as it wills. Beneficent Venus was overjoyed to see her mighty fosterchild's abode, no less than if she were drawing near to Paphos from the deep sea, or to her Idalian halls or to her fane at Eryx.

Light and colour predominate in these lines: stars, jewels, marble of varying hues, gold, sunlight, running water, the sea. Vocabulary expressive of brightness is heaped up, clothing the whole passage in iridescent garb. As usual in Statius, words are used boldly (e.g. *pandit*, 145; *virent*, *flexus*, 149; *pendent*, 152; *satiata*, 153; *vivunt*, 155). Allusiveness and *doctrina* presuppose an informed receptiveness (*Amyclaeos...olores*, 142, *Thybridis arces | Iliacae*, 144–5; *Libycus Phrygiusque silex*, 148; *dura Laconum | saxa*, 148–9; *purpura | Oebalis*, 150–1; *Tyrii moderator...aeni*, 151; *Dalmatico...metallo*, 153; *Paphon...Idaliasque domos Erycinaque templa*, 159–60). On one occasion at least, the 'learning' reaches a point verging on grotesquerie (150–1). Hyperbole suffuses the description of Violentilla's palace, where even the columns are 'beyond counting' (152) and where, by a strained flight of rhetorical fantasy, neither summer nor winter can hold sway (156–7). Sound and metre reflect sense: *gaudentes plauserunt* (146) echoes the beating of the swans' wings at Violentilla's door; 155 evokes the movement of the fountains it mentions; the dactyls in 159–60 summon up the idea of speed in Venus' aerial flight over the ocean. Words are repeated to suggest significant comparisons: *superbum limen*, *clara limina*, 141–2, 146; *nitidos penates*, *nitidis astris*, 145, 147; *domus alta*, *alto mari*, *aequore alto*, 145, 149–50, 159. In 156–7, trope and paradox are combined to hammer home an exaggeration typical of Statius (*Sirius alget*, *bruma tepet*). The juxtaposition of contrasting images occurs several times: cloud and gems (143–4); stone and ocean (149–50); masonry, cloth and metal (150–1); masonry, wood and metal (152–3); heat and cold (154–5, 156–7); trees, water and marble (154–5); on a slightly different level, there is a pointed contrast between the toughness of the *saxa* in 148–9 and the verb implying growth in the same phrase (*virent*, 149), as also between *pendent* and *nixa* in 152. All these features, however, are cohesively integrated: so swiftly do the verses move, so densely packed is the interplay of idea and image, so complex and agglutinative the poet's mode, that an intense and vivid picture is imprinted on the reader's mind. The developed Statian style is one of linguistic impressionism, demanding empathy and vicarious participation. This applies not only to the formal elements in the poems, but equally to subtler problems of symbolism, structure, imitation and philosophy.

In *Silvae* 1.2, Stella and Violentilla are subjected to a virtual deification, assuming static and timeless roles in a cosmos peopled by gods and heroes. Elsewhere Statius had to deal with a ruler who proclaimed himself a *deus praesens*. The poems on Domitian are hymns of praise to an incarnate deity; rich and curious incense is burnt before his altar. In the panegyric on the Emperor's seventeenth consulship (4.1), for example, it is Janus who, in almost hysterical vein, pours out the breathless paean (17–43). Janus has power over Time (*immensi reparator maximus aevi*, 11), and it is natural that he should sing of Domitian's relationship with Eternity and with a New Age which his consulship is to inaugurate (17–20). Domitian is the 'mighty father of the whole earth' (*magne parens mundi*, 17); miracles attended his assumption of the consular office (23–7). The whole history of Rome has reached its pinnacle in this blessed year; even Augustus has been excelled in glory:

dic age, Roma potens, et mecum longa Vetustas,
dinumera fastos nec parua exempla recense,
sed quae sola meus dignetur uincere Caesar.
ter Latio deciesque tulit labentibus annis
Augustus fasces, sed coepit sero mereri:
tu iuuenis praegressus auos. et quanta recusas,
quanta uetas! flectere tamen precibusque senatus
promittes hunc saepe diem. manet insuper ordo
longior, et totidem felix tibi Roma curules
terque quaterque dabit. (28–37)

Come, give voice, almighty Rome, and with me reckon out, far-stretching Antiquity, each detail of our annals. Cite no trivial instances, but those alone fit to be surpassed by my Caesar. Thirteen times, as the years slipped by, did Augustus enjoy the consular power in Latium: but true merit came late to him. You, while still young, have outdone your forefathers. How often you have refused the honour! How often have you debarred it! But you will yield. You will vow, in answer to the Senate's prayers, time and again to repeat this day. A still longer course remains ahead. As often again – no, three and four times as often, will Rome prove her good fortune by offering you the curule chair.

The prediction of sixty-eight further consulships to a *Princeps* in his mid-forties is, even when attributed to a celestial mouth, a daring feat of adulation. But gods are immortal: Domitian and Janus are establishing a new aeon in the universe (36), in which the Emperor will conquer all nations and extend his sway over the entire globe (39–43). Mystical and religious notions vie with a more traditional aspiration of Roman leaders: to succeed and to outstrip Alexander the Great, prototype of the divine world-ruler. Janus' prophecy is endorsed by heaven; Jupiter promises to Domitian, his earthly counterpart, unending youth and life eternal as his own (45–7).

As a guide to Domitian's attitude to the imperial cult, the lines contain much of value. What can be said of their poetic quality? To conceive and to execute such extremities of propaganda brought vices in its train. Distortion and absurdity, repellent to a modern ear; shallowness veiled by a specious profundity; an insincerity born of too great a yearning to seem sincere: these and other faults have been, and are, listed in the indictment. It is hard, however, not to feel some compassion for a poet of talent constrained, whether willingly or not, so to prostitute his art. It was no mean achievement in such circumstances to instil in his verses a certain grace and grandeur which in part compensate for the distasteful theme. Statius' private life was controlled by the demands of his *patroni* and by the imprisoning rigours of despotism: hence the *Silvae*. Only in the *Thebaid* could Statius find a degree of independence from the insistent pressures of society.

The construction of a twelve-book epic is a daunting task. Statius lavished infinite care on the *magnum opus* which would render his name famous in future ages. Parts of the *Thebaid* were made public by recitations: at which, so Statius tells us, senators were present on the benches (*Silv.* 5.2.161–3). The sarcastic Juvenal bears testimony to the popularity of these readings: but sneeringly implies that Statius pandered to his audience like a whore to her lovers (*Sat.* 7.82ff.). Statius was, admittedly, never indifferent to the judgement of others; to borrow Tacitus' remark on Seneca (*Ann.* 13.3), his *ingenium* was 'admirably suited to contemporary ears'.

Statius was the authentic voice of Domitian's Rome. He evolved a style as unique in Latin verse as that of Tacitus in prose: and as inimitable. The finest and most individual features traceable in the *Silvae* were perfected and finalized within the grand design of the Theban epic. In language, theme and thought, the Statian manner is that of deliberate extremism. The explorations of Ovid, Seneca and Lucan had mapped out the terrain. Statius fixed the boundaries beyond which, as his imitators proved, a writer journeyed at his peril.

The Thebaid

The *Aeneid* may have presented a challenge to Statius. He abstained from direct response to it. The *Thebaid* is not a Roman epic; it has no national or patriotic motive. The story of Oedipus and his sons was used to illustrate the broadest moral and philosophical dilemmas: appropriate enough in the Flavian age, no doubt, but divorced from too intimate a connexion with it.

The allegorical and spiritual facets of the *Aeneid* beggar definitive analysis:

no less many-sided are its artistic splendours: yet it is Augustan in the same sense as Spenser's *The Faerie Queene* is Elizabethan. The *Thebaid* is Flavian more in the fashion that *Paradise Lost* is linked to the England of Cromwell. Lucan, writing under Nero, could hardly have shared Virgilian values or have revivified the defunct ideals of the Restored Republic. His mind was at once more dogmatic and more superficial than Virgil's: doctrines and words were not so much his tools as his shackles. The suave urbanity of Ovid and the sententious brevity of Seneca had an instantaneous appeal for Lucan. His uncle reinforced style with Stoicism; the nexus was irresistible. Virgil's serene and flawless majesty must dim Lucan's pyrotechnics, however scintillating. Statius' verses glitter and coruscate – but they are still sharp and sudden like Lucan's, not constant and diffused like Virgil's.

The obsession with logodaedaly was initiated by Ovid. His successors in the first generation were Seneca and Lucan; the next heir was Statius. From Senecan tragedy and the *Bellum civile* he also borrowed a world-view for his epic. The *Thebaid* is a panorama in which cosmos and destiny, god and man, piety and sin, corruption and redemption are displayed within the compass of a single history. Seneca had written dramas – including an *Oedipus* and a *Phoenissae* – in which plots passed to him from the tragedians of Athens were reinterpreted to reveal – and to debate – the tenets of his own brand of Stoicism. Lucan narrated the war between Caesar and Pompey; the historical confrontation is universalized and defined in terms of philosophical absolutes. Though Statius eschewed the Stoic evangelism of the *Bellum civile*, he adopted its cosmic outlook and its psychological approach. Lucan's theme had led him into rash polemic: the Theban legend was safer, but no less amenable to setting forth the horrors of passion, ambition and tyranny.

The destruction, in successive generations, of an accursed house (*deuota domus*) was a favoured topic of Senecan tragedy. In the descendants of Tantalus and of Laius, madness – in Stoic view the ineluctable concomitant of passion (*ira*) – continually broke out afresh. Violence follows violence, crimes worsen and multiply. It is a bleak and anguished world, its savagery scarcely leavened by hope or goodness. The same dark miasma enwraps Lucan's epic. Caesar's tyrannical frenzy causes the dissolution of Roman liberty, of ordered society. Even Cato, the Stoic saint, is presented as a grim and forbidding figure. In the *Thebaid*, Statius recounts the horrendous chronicle of a doomed dynasty. Before him were Seneca's Theban dramas, his *Thyestes* and *Agamemnon*. Statius' Thebes is a diseased realm, ruled by a corrupt and insane tyrant. The prologue epitomizes the grimness of his theme:

fraternas acies alternaque regna profanis
decertata odiis sontesque euoluere Thebas
Pierius menti calor incidit. (1.1–3)

The Muses' fire pervades my mind, bidding it to expound war between brothers, a kingdom apportioned to their alternate rule and fought for with sacrilegious hate, Thebes the guilty.

Family strife, war, hatred, depravity, guilt: the respondence with Seneca and Lucan is immediate and revealing. The opening words of the *Thebaid* echo *Bellum civile* 1.4 (*cognatasque acies*). Like the conflict between Caesar and Pompey, the war between Eteocles and Polynices is worse than civil (*bella... plus quam ciuilia, Bell. Civ.* 1.1). Fraternal discord had been exposed in all its horror in Seneca's *Thyestes* and *Phoenissae*. In the subsequent lines of his proem, Statius summarizes the long catalogue of madness and disaster that had afflicted the royal line of Thebes (5–16). He fixes the limits of his epic in the 'disturbed house of Oedipus' (*Oedipodae confusa domus*, 17): the last and worst act in a seemingly unending chain of doom and devastation.

Commentators have often written of Statius' pessimism. Its roots are palpable. Disillusion with the principate and the Stoic *Weltanschauung* had provided a double impetus to Seneca and Lucan in the days of Nero. Statius, admiring their style, took over profounder aspects of their work. No more tonally and symbolically fitting an introduction to the narrative could have been devised by Statius than 46ff. Oedipus, blind and vengeful, calls down a fearful curse upon his sons; his imprecation raises from hell the Fury Tisiphone who is afterwards a controlling force in the epic. Verbal echoes, as well as psychological similarities, link Statius' Oedipus with Seneca's. Tisiphone in the *Thebaid*, though related to Virgil's Allecto (*Aeneid* 7.323ff.), stands closer to the Fury who appears at the beginning of Seneca's *Thyestes*. Statius creates an infernal being who is a *figura* of hatred and madness. She owes her dominance in the rest of the epic principally to the irreversible effects of Oedipus' curse once it has been uttered – and confirmed by Jupiter, the executor of Fate (1.212ff.). Tisiphone is, in fact, nothing other than an objectified personification of the congenital evil that afflicts, and so destroys, the descendants of Laius: for it is Statius' custom to treat divine beings as allegories of abstract forces and ideas, in accordance with Stoic preconceptions. It follows that Tisiphone experiences no difficulty in inflaming Polynices and Eteocles with a legion of ruinous passions (1.125–30). They are members of a *deuota domus*, a *gens profana*, and so, by reason of their birth, predisposed to demonic possession. Seneca had examined the theme in depth; Statius made it a logical dynamic. And yet he tempered and moderated the harsh philosophy that he had assumed. Rays of light are allowed to illumine the gloom. Though the fatal results of *furor* occupy much of the *Thebaid* and though bestiality, insensate and uncontrolled, is almost omnipresent, piety and virtue are also given an exemplary role. Coroebus, Maeon, Amphiaraus, Menoeceus, Hypsipyle, Jocasta, Argia and Antigone all, in varying ways, figure forth a nobler vision of mankind.

The epic ends on a note of uplifting optimism. Theseus, king of Athens, a 'divine man' who embodies the highest ideals of justice and clemency, at last brings peace to Thebes and salvation to its people, cancelling the burden of punishment that had been imposed by Oedipus in Book 1. This purifying intervention is rightly kept until the final section of the *Thebaid* (12.464–813). Presentiments of it, foreshadowings of the Athenian king had indeed appeared earlier: only with the extinction of the whole House of Cadmus could equilibrium be fully restored and the plague be healed. By concluding his narrative with the dawning of a new age, Statius separated himself from the agonized, inflexible rigorism of Senecan tragedy. He pointed a contrast, too, with the ambiguous scene with which Virgil had closed the *Aeneid.* But the inner significance of this motif of renewal and redemption runs deeper. The Stoics believed in recurrence, that a new universe would arise after the destruction of the old. The advent of the saviour Theseus symbolizes this rebirth of the *mundus*. The Stoics argued that the cosmos would be overthrown by conflagration: Theseus' arrival is preceded by the cremation of Eteocles and Polynices (12.429ff.) and followed by the funeral rites of the Argive dead (12.797ff.). An *ecpyrosis* accompanies the refashioning of heaven and earth within the poetic universe of the *Thebaid.*

Predestination was a central dogma and problem in Stoicism. Free-will and the power of choice were excluded from a structured and interdependent *mundus*. What Fatum had fixed at the beginning of time was inescapable and had to be endured. The concept of *sympatheia* bound microcosm to macrocosm, man to nature. To modify any detail or particular in the working of destiny was not only impossible: it would bring about that primal chaos which ever hems in and threatens balance and order. Throughout the *Thebaid*, Statius adheres to the twin doctrines of inevitability and cosmic harmony. Events on earth are mirrored in heaven and in the physical world. The sins of men infect everything that exists, spreading the taint far and wide. The symptoms of this contagion may be ominous immensity. In Seneca's *Thyestes*, the blotting-out of the sun (a well-known part of the myth) attains a forceful dimension as a measure of the celestial and terrestrial disruption that has sprung from Atreus' ghastly vengeance (777ff., 789ff.). Thyestes himself invokes the universe, praying, in his torment of soul, that the darkness will be perpetual if condign punishment is not inflicted by the gods on his brother, guilty of 'boundless crimes' (1068–96). For Seneca, the *scelera* of one man are metamorphosed into an emblem of the inherent tension of the *mundus*, of the eternal conflict between moral polarities, threatening the stability of the whole system. It is a near-Manichaean standpoint: and one which Statius shares and to which he grants an informing validity in the *Thebaid.*

The reciprocal sympathy of animate and inanimate nature controls much of the imagery in Statius' epic – as well as some of its most impressive incidents. In Book 1, Polynices flees from Boeotia to Argos. He travels at night, through a storm of preternatural ferocity (1.336ff.). The elaboration of storm-scenes was a well-tried ingredient of epic: *Aeneid* 1 and Lucan, *Bellum civile* 5.504ff. provided Statius with a spur to emulation. Though both these predecessors may be justly said to have exploited the symbolic aspect of the storm-motif, Statius pressed still further in his integration of cosmos and psyche. The turmoil in the House of Cadmus, the madness of Polynices himself are mirrored in the troubled fury of the heavens. Nocturnal shadow is the setting for a journey which is to bring the corruption of Thebes to the still tranquil city of Argos. Indeed the ancient contrast between light and darkness, equated with life and death, good and evil, heaven and hell is to be cunningly developed throughout the *Thebaid.* In Book 2, Tydeus, after the failure of his embassy at Thebes, is ambushed at night by fifty Theban warriors sent by Eteocles to intercept him (2.496ff.). Though he defeats them single-handed, Tydeus is stimulated by this act of treachery to disseminate a gospel of war during the remainder of his journey and at Argos itself (3.1–164). It is just before dawn that King Adrastus of Argos, a man of peace enmeshed in the net of doom, finally agrees to launch a military expedition against Thebes in support of his son-in-law Polynices (3.684ff.). Shortly before the duel between the sons of Oedipus, Jupiter plunges the earth in gloom (11.130–3): for, at that moment, evil is triumphant. The fight, in which both brothers are killed, is watched by souls risen from the Underworld (11.422–3). The antithesis of light and darkness is a major facet in the symbolic pattern, repeated frequently but gaining, by its simplicity, an increasing vigour and imaginative strength. Other recurrent complexes may be viewed in similar terms: for example, the similes and metaphors identifying men with wild beasts, nautical imagery, allusions to storms and other violent natural phenomena, or – on a slightly different plane – the parallels drawn between Hercules, a popular subject for Stoic allegoresis, and the characters of the Theban story.

Dualism does not, however, underlie only the moral scheme of the *Thebaid*; it has also a structural importance. It explains, in part, the tendency which critics have traced for episodes to be doubled: such as the Council of the Gods in Books 1 and 7, or Tiresias' two magical operations in 4 and 10. The twin cities of Argos and Thebes, under their monarchs Adrastus and Eteocles, are themselves spiritual antitheses and the counterbalancing of them is thoroughly and pointedly specified. It may be seen expressed with especial clarity in the equivalent episodes in Books 3 and 4: whereas Adrastus seeks guidance from augury, bidding the pious priest Amphiaraus scan the supernal regions, Eteocles compels the blind prophet Tiresias to summon the ghost of Laius from the nether world by necromantic ritual. Thebes is truly a hell on earth. Its perverting mania spreads to Argos through Polynices' marriage to Argia; what was once a happy and blessed land becomes wretched and abased. Jupiter, in Book 1, decrees that both cities should suffer retribution for past misdeeds (224–7) and from that harsh mandate there can be no escape. It is notable that when Polynices and Tydeus – both agents of violence – arrive at Argos, the people have been celebrating a festival of Apollo, sun-god and lord of oracles; Book 1 ends with a sublime hymn to him by Adrastus. In direct contrast, Book 2 opens with the ascent of Laius from the Underworld at Jupiter's behest. He appears to Eteocles in a dream, redoubling the tyrant's loathing for his brother (94ff.). At the time of this grim visitation, the Thebans are in the midst of Bacchic *orgia* (83–8), rites redolent of blood and barbarism. In the end, it is only through the intervention of a third city, Athens, that peace is regained. At Athens stands the Altar of Mercy (12.481ff.): *clementia* is the only antidote to *ira*. Athens is the polar opposite to Thebes, but it is also Argos perfected. In the same way, its king, Theseus, is not only the diametric analogue of Eteocles (and his despotic successor Creon); he is also Adrastus shorn of weakness and failure.

The three cities have, therefore, the force of archetypes. In his characterization, Statius uses a figural technique. Its origin may again be traced to Seneca and Lucan, and to the Stoic psychology that they espoused. In Senecan drama, the principal characters are *figurae*, monochromatically represented. Caesar, Pompey, Cato are, for Lucan, largely exemplifications of specific types: tyrant, victim, sage. Though there are opportunities within this approach for a certain latitude, it can also be inhibiting. Statius defines in his proem the essential nature of several participants (1.33ff.). Eteocles and Polynices are *tyranni*. Tydeus is 'unrestrained in *ira*'. Amphiaraus is the pious minister of Apollo. Hippomedon is the turbulent warrior. Parthenopaeus is a pathetically gallant youth, Capaneus a blasphemer. These fundamental traits are sustained. They predicate the behaviour of *personae* in different situations. Sometimes this ploy is pressed too far. Neither Hippomedon nor Capaneus is sufficiently individualized: brute strength and sacrilege are their respective properties with almost nothing added. Eteocles is type-cast as a tyrant. Less prominent characters are similarly treated. In the House of Cadmus, we find Menoeceus, a sublime figuration of *uirtus* and *pietas*, Creon, indistinguishable from Eteocles in exhibiting the unlovely vices of absolutism. A degree of ambiguity may be detected in one or two portraits. Tydeus is a martial hero who, despite his better attributes, finally succumbs to the most bestial manifestation of *furor* at the moment of his death in Book 8; he is deprived of the apotheosis which Pallas wishes to grant him. Polynices is a potential but unfledged despot; though he cannot shed genetic predispositions, he is not completely devoid of moral sensibility. Adrastus is a wise and benevolent sovereign but he lacks fibre and foresight. More satisfying are Statius' womenfolk: the noble Hypsipyle, the majestically sorrowful Jocasta, the loyal Argia, the fearless Antigone, the modest Ismene. In general, however, Statius strictly observed the figural mode. Virgil's Aeneas is much more than a prototypical *exemplum* of piety. Statius' characters are statuesque rather than vital. The *Thebaid* was given an additional level of universality. It was also a surrender to dogma.

In his delineation of the gods, Statius likewise manifested a trend to full allegorization. Lucan denuded epic of divine machinery. Statius restored it – in consonance with his Stoic programme. Jupiter is omnipotent because he is responsible for effecting the designs of *Fatum*. The other deities have no power to thwart him, though they may modify attendant details. Often, as C. S. Lewis argued in *The allegory of love*, they are externalized depictions of internal processes in human minds.[1] Sometimes a little more: Bacchus is permitted to delay the Argive army at Nemea in Books 4 to 7, providing Thebes with a temporary respite. Apollo ensures that his protégé Amphiaraus descends, still living, from the battlefield to Elysian rewards (7.771ff.): in consequence of which Dis, enraged at an infringement of his prerogatives, ordains grim exits for the other Argive princes as well as Creon's folly in forbidding funeral rites to their corpses (8.65ff.). Diana aids Parthenopaeus in his boyish quest for glory in Book 9. In 10, Juno calls upon the assistance of Sleep, enabling the Argives to carry through a treacherous and brutal massacre of Thebans (49–346): she it is too who guides the Argive widows to Athens (12.134–6). Such celestial interpositions were sanctioned by Homer and Virgil, were part of the heritage of epic. Statius, however, does not allow the gods to disrupt his philosophical groundplan. *Fatum* is always paramount, *ira* always brings retribution. It is comprehensible that Statius presented, in company with familiar deities, other beings who are manifestly abstractions: no strangers to Roman religion but enhanced in stature. Virtus addresses Menoeceus before he resolves to sacrifice himself for Thebes in an uplifting act of patriotic *deuotio* (10.632ff.). Tisiphone is, as has been remarked, an overtly symbolic figure She is set in dramatic conflict with the personification Pietas shortly before the duel of Polynices and Eteocles (11.457ff.). Clementia, in Book 12 (481ff.), is a fructifying concept, suggestive of the highest impulses that can govern man and universe. At such points allegory and psychologization are united in the guise of *deorum ministeria*.

It has been commonly alleged that Statius was perverse in his inclusion of otiose material, that the *Thebaid* is incoherent. The falsity of such accusations can be demonstrated only by minute analysis. A story without a single hero has to rely on multiform cohesiveness. Statius clearly felt obliged to incorporate stock themes from received tradition: the mustering of armies (4.1–344, 7.243–373), nekyomanteia (4.419–645), funeral games (6.249–946), aristeiae with

[1] Lewis (1936) 49–56.

lengthy battle scenes (Books 7 to 11). These need not impair unity provided that, as in the *Thebaid*, they are assimilated and made to serve broader themes. Statius created in 4 a military catalogue formally correspondent with prototypes in *Iliad* 2 and *Aeneid* 7. The other is cast as a teichoscopy loosely inspired by Euripides, *Phoenissae* 88ff. The *athla* in 6 are, in detail, a propædeutic anticipation of the impending war (Books 7 to 11). The *aristeiae* are distinctive and scrupulously balanced. Even more reprehensible, so it is said, are features such as the myth of Linus and Coroebus (1.557ff.), the long narrative of Hypsipyle (5.49ff.). Not so: these subsidiary elements are germinal and instructive. They encapsulate much that is crucial for understanding the *Thebaid*. The myth contains a summary of the leitmotifs of the whole epic; the experiences of Hypsipyle at Lemnos are a parabolic résumé of truths fully enunciated elsewhere. The devices of foreshadowing, parallelism, antithesis are widely utilized to bind episode to episode. The *Thebaid* is dynamic, associative and interwoven. It is, like Ovid's *Metamorphoses*, a *carmen perpetuum*, serpentine and polymorphic in its construction. Its parts are endowed with a self-sufficient but ultimately dependent cohesion. They form part of an integrated chain, each link discrete but devoid of significance outside its context. In the end, the *Thebaid* ought to be perceived as structurally related to the Stoic doctrine of the *series causarum*, that indissoluble pattern of cause and effect in which no particular can be divorced from the whole.[1]

Alert perceptiveness is required to appreciate the nuances of Statius' artistry. As in the *Silvae*, so in the *Thebaid* the finest passages impress themselves indelibly on a reader's mind. It is invidious to make a choice. Some incidents may, however, receive special mention for their imaginative vigour: Polynices' journey to Argos and his fight with Tydeus on arrival (1.312–481), Tydeus' monomachy (2.496–743), the two appearances of Laius' ghost, first in a dream (2.1–133), then through sorcery (4.419–645), the massacre at Lemnos as recounted by Hypsipyle (5.85–334), the chariot-race at Nemea (6.296–549), Hippomedon's fight with Ismenus (9.315–539), the tale of Hopleus and Dymas (10.347–448), Menoeceus' *deuotio* (10.628–782), the duel with its preliminaries and aftermath in Book 11, the meeting between Argia and Antigone outside Thebes in 12, which culminates in the divided flames on the funeral-pyre of Oedipus' sons: their hatred has passed beyond death itself (204–446). The colours are bold, the rhetoric taut and demanding; in such scenes, Statius validated his claim on eternity, as formulated in the epilogue (12.812–13).

[1] See further Vessey (1973) 317–28.

The Achilleid

More debatable are the merits of the *Achilleid*. Judgements have shown profound disparity. Commenced at the end of the poet's life, it is a canvas on which only a few tentative brush-strokes have been laid. Its style is less ornate, less incisive than that of the *Thebaid*. It is probably best to see the fragment that remains as a cartoon, from which, by reworking and labour, a definitive version would at length have been evolved. In describing Achilles' youth, Statius is often poignant and deft: a lightness pervades the *Achilleid* that is found rarely in the Theban epic. And yet, his powers were waning, the fires were growing dim. Death brought the project to a premature end: but the *Achilleid*, despite its imperfections, has its own peculiar charm, arising from a directness of approach and a simplicity of tone lacking in Statius' other works.

3. VALERIUS

It is generally held that the grave claimed Valerius Flaccus before he had concluded the eighth book of the *Argonautica*. Of the man himself little can be said. Quintilian's brief notice (*Inst.* 10.1.90) is a solitary witness. A remark in Valerius' prologue may indicate that he was a *quindecemvir sacris faciundis* (1.5–7): if so, we may surmise that he was not without money and social standing. The epic was commenced before Statius' *Thebaid*, and it seems that work continued over a long period. An invocation of Vespasian, an allusion to Titus' destruction of Jerusalem, an obeisance towards the versifying of Domitian fix the proem to the early seventies (1.7–21). In Book 3, there is an apparent reference to the eruption of Vesuvius in 79 (207–8); elsewhere, it has been suggested, indirect mention is made of Domitian's campaigns against the Sarmatians in 89, even in 92 (6.162, 231ff.). Valerius, like Statius, presumably did not esteem rapidity of composition as a virtue. If he contemplated that the *Argonautica* should comprise twelve books, his progress during two decades was unusually slow. It may be that our chronological speculations are faulty; or, as C. W. Mendell has maintained, 'that the problem of how to finish the epic proved too much for the poet'.[1] The loss to the world, whatever the cause, may not be as great as Quintilian estimated.

Statius labelled the legend of the Argonauts among stale and hackneyed themes (*Silv.* 2.7.50–1). He also honoured the memory of Varro of Atax, who had, in the first century B.C., produced a version or adaptation of Apollonius (2.7.77). Varro had contributed something to the *Aeneid*; Quintilian damned his poem with faint praise (*Inst.* 10.1.87). Whether Valerius found guidance or inspiration in Varro is unknown. Apollonius was his prime source: in a

[1] Mendell (1967) 136.

sense to Valerius' detriment, for few would be prepared to dispute the innate superiority of the Greek poet. To have to contend for laurels not only with Virgil but also with Apollonius is Valerius' misfortune: add further the epic's incompletion and the total of disadvantages is formidable.

Apologists have nonetheless existed. One of Valerius' earliest champions, H. E. Butler, though admitting faults, held that he 'offends less than any of the silver Latin writers of epic', for 'he rants less and exaggerates less; above all he has much genuine poetic merit'. Butler saw that, in his choice of subject, Valerius faced difficulties: 'The Argonaut saga', he wrote, 'has its weaknesses as a theme for epic. It is too episodic, it lacks unity and proportion. Save for the struggle in Colchis and the loves of Jason and Medea, there is little deep human interest.' Compensation could, however, be found in 'variety and brilliance of colour', in 'romance' and 'picturesqueness'.[1] For some, the *Argonautica* has emerged primarily as a romantic epic, an adventure story, threading its way from incident to incident – a form predicated by its kinship with the *periplus*, the narrative of a coastal or circumnavigatory voyage. The first four lines perhaps bear out such an interpretation:

> Prima deum magnis canimus freta peruia nautis,
> fatidicamque ratem, Scythici quae Phasidis oras
> ausa sequi mediosque inter iuga concita cursus
> rumpere, flammifero tandem consedit Olympo. (1.1–4)

I sing of straits crossed first by the heroic offspring of gods, of the vessel with power to prophesy that dared the quest to the shores of Scythian Phasis and plunged headlong through the midst of the clashing rocks, at length finding its seat in the fiery heaven.

At first sight, the words seem almost naively functional: but there may be hidden depths in them. The idea of a voyage through hazards to a celestial reward suggests both the metaphor of human life as a journey and of the earth as a ship with mankind as its crew: it is worth remembering that in antiquity the myth of the Argonauts was used in an 'Orphic', allegorical context. The crew of the *Argo* are denominated in 1 as heroes of divine ancestry; man and god are brought into juxtaposition. Valerius, compared to Apollonius, augmented the role of deities in his epic, stressing their influence over terrestrial events. The first word, *prima*, may well imply that the Voyage of the Argonauts is to be regarded as archetypal and revelatory. In such terms, the supposedly ornamental epithet *fatidica* applied to the *Argo* – although it alludes to a famous feature of the ship – gains an added significance. Scythian Phasis and the Cyanean Rocks are determinate synonyms for barbarism and violence, for obstacles in the path of life, only to be overcome by struggle and

[1] Butler (1909) 190–1.

audacity: they are contrasted with the bright, unchanging tranquillity of Olympus, which is the *telos* attained through endurance.

In general, Valerius followed the outlines of Apollonius' narrative. There are expansions and excisions, variations and changes. Among Valerian innovations, we may cite the suicide of Jason's parents Aeson and Alcimede (1.730–851) and the rescue of Hesione by Hercules and Telamon (2.451–578). The story of the Stymphalian birds, found in Apollonius' second book, is omitted by Valerius. Of what he had in common with his Greek exemplar, the Latin poet always made far-reaching realignments in tone, tempo and motivation: in the Lemnian episode (Book 2), in the tragedy of Cyzicus (Books 2–3), in the disappearance of Hylas (Books 3–4), in the encounter of Pollux and Amycus (Book 4), in the salvation of Phineus from the Harpies (Book 4). After negotiating the Clashing Rocks, the Argonauts reach Colchis: the details of Jason's dealings with King Aeetes and of his relationship with Medea (Books 5–7), though in many ways similar to the Apollonian version, are reshaped and altered. The unfinished eighth book tells of the theft of the Golden Fleece and of the departure of the Argonauts, with Medea, from Colchis.

Apollonius' epic is objective and urbane, exuding Hellenistic cynicism. It is brittle, often amoral, impersonal. In it, Homeric values are consciously, even maliciously, subverted. None of these traits was copied by Valerius. It was from the *Aeneid* that he sought his outlook and philosophy. The *Argonautica* bristles with Virgilian echoes, not only verbally but in incident and in characterization. Apollonius' Jason, as Gilbert Lawall has rightly said, is an anti-hero.[1] He lives in a harsh world where conventional virtue is irrelevant and inadequate; his success springs from a ruthless opportunism. Valerius recast Jason on the pattern of Aeneas. This reinstatement of Jason to full heroic stature is aptly signalized by Valerius' invocation of the Muse at 5.217–19:

> Incipe nunc cantus alios, dea, uisaque uobis
> Thessalici da bella ducis; non mens mihi, non haec
> ora satis.

Now begin new songs, goddess; tell me of the wars waged by the Thessalian prince which you Muses saw; for my mind, my words cannot suffice.

Jason has now reached Colchis. He is to be tested and tried as a warrior, just as Aeneas was after his arrival in Italy. These *bella* waged by Jason on Aeetes' behalf occupy Book 6. They have no counterpart in Apollonius. They serve to magnify Jason's heroism and also to unmask Aeetes' treachery. The Colchian king promises Jason the fleece if he defeats the Scythian army of his insurgent brother Perses: but reneges on his vow after Jason's triumph. Only when so perfidiously handled does Jason turn to Medea's goetic skills to achieve his

[1] Lawall (1966).

object. By such a metamorphosis of the plot, Valerius purifies Jason. It also gave him the opportunity of trying his hand at battle scenes in emulation of the *Aeneid*. His Aeetes is depicted in familiar form: a stock *tyrannus*, with a dash of Virgil's Mezentius. His son Absyrtus consequently becomes another Lausus.

The cleansing and refining of characters, with concomitant denigration of others, at times leads Valerius into a sentimentality alien to Apollonius. Hypsipyle acquires a moral dignity, in part derived from Virgil's Dido but also indebted to Ovid, *Heroides* 6. The story of King Cyzicus is, as R. W. Garson has demonstrated, elaborated as a tragic drama.[1] A Virgilian motif is borrowed to provide a cause for its dénouement. Whereas Apollonius merely attributed the disaster to fate (1.1030), Valerius, in imitation of *Aeneid* 7.475ff., establishes its origin in the fact that Cyzicus had angered the goddess Cybele by killing one of her sacred lions (3.19ff.). This involuntary hybris brings about the peripateia, so that, in Book 3, Cyzicus is himself slain, in ignorance, by Jason. In his treatment of Hercules' loss of the boy Hylas in Book 3 (neatly complemented by the rescue of Hesione in 2), Valerius injects a wealth of amatory and pathetic colour lacking in Apollonius. He also invents a divine intrigue as the root of Hercules' misfortune. Theocritus 13 and Virgil were quarried. Apollonius depicts Hercules unflatteringly; Valerius consistently glorifies him. His Medea is perhaps more closely dependent on Apollonius. Torn between her filial duty (*pietas*) towards Aeetes and her passion for Jason, Medea, according to some, emerges not as a cunning and resolute sorceress but as a diffident and inexperienced girl. The view can be overstated. In Apollonius Medea is more robust and full-blooded. Valerius exhibits grace and charm, as well as sound psychological insight: but the resemblances to Apollonius are at all times substantial. Valerius rejects, however, the melodramatic Medea of Ovid, *Metamorphoses* 7 and Seneca's *Medea*.

When set beside Statius, Valerius is restrained and economical. Occasionally his terseness becomes jejune and effete. He sought Virgilian gravity as an antidote to the excesses of Seneca and Lucan; but, lacking his master's genius, he ran a perpetual risk of anaemia. The scenes of war in Book 6 are particularly tedious; they have none of the verve and panache of Books 7–11 of the *Thebaid*. His metre is often repetitive and unenterprising. An Ovidian smoothness prevails, but Valerius does not share Ovid's superb control over his medium – nor Lucan's fiery legerdemain which helped to offset his metrical sterility.

In Book 2, Hercules and Telamon, wandering on the coast of Phrygia, come upon Hesione, manacled to a rock. Hercules asks her identity, the reason for her predicament.

[1] Garson (1964) 269–70.

Hesione replies:

non ego digna malis, inquit; suprema parentum
dona uides, ostro scopulos auroque frequentes.
nos Ili felix quondam genus, inuida donec
Laomedonteos fugeret Fortuna penates.
principio morbi caeloque exacta sereno
temperies, arsere rogis certantibus agri,
tum subitus fragor et fluctus Idaea mouentes
cum stabulis nemora. ecce repens consurgere ponto
belua, monstrum ingens; hanc tu nec montibus ullis
nec nostro metire mari. primaeua furenti
huic manus amplexus inter planctusque parentum
deditur. hoc sortes, hoc corniger imperat Hammon,
uirgineam damnare animam sortitaque Lethen
corpora; crudelis scopulis me destinat urna.
uerum o iam redeunt Phrygibus si numina, tuque
ille ades auguriis promisse et sorte deorum,
iam cui candentes uotiuo in gramine pascit
cornipedes genitor, nostrae stata dona salutis,
adnue meque, precor, defectaque Pergama monstris
eripe, namque potes: neque enim tam lata uidebam
pectora Neptunus muros cum iungeret astris
nec tales umeros pharetramque gerebat Apollo. (471–92)

I am undeserving of such misfortunes, she said. You are looking at my parents' final gifts to me – rocks laden with purple and gold. We are scions of Ilus: once our race was blessed, till envious Fortune abandoned the halls of Laomedon. At first came plague; fair weather departed from the peaceful heaven. The fields were ablaze with a riot of funeral pyres. Then, suddenly, there was a thundering; waves shook the groves of Ida where beasts have their lairs. Straightway a vast and hideous monster emerged from the sea: you could not tell its size by comparison with any rocky pile, nor by our ocean. A youthful band was sacrificed to its frenzy, torn from the embraces, the lamentations of their parents. This was the command of the lot, this of horned Hammon: that a girl's life and body chosen by lot should be condemned to death. I it was that the savage urn doomed to the rocks. And yet, oh, if heaven's favour has returned to the Phrygians, if you have come as augury and divine lot foretold, if you are he for whom my father is at this moment pasturing white horses in the promised field, the fixed reward for my salvation, consent – save me, save Troy ravaged by monsters, for yours is the power to do so: for I have never beheld so broad a breast, not even while Neptune bound our walls to the stars – no, not even Apollo had such shoulders, such a quiver.

For a maiden in dire distress, Hesione's speech is surprisingly bathetic. It is plain enough that Valerius has eschewed rhetorical exaggeration, favouring brevity and reticence. The yearning for classical purity has, however, led him to stale aridity. The generally short sentences are not clear and concise but feeble and attenuated: obscurity in Valerius usually arises from over-compression. When he ventures into hyperbole, as in 479–80 and 490–2, the effect is jarring and incongruous: indeed, Hesione's outburst on Hercules' massive physique verges on the absurd. Hardly less banal is the strained remark about her parents' *suprema dona* in 471–2. The adjective *Laomedonteos* in 474 is portentous without purpose. The conceit in *certantibus* (476) is inapt; the phrase *cum stabulis* (478) is pointless. The words *amplexus inter planctusque parentum* (481) are stilted and trivial. The repetition *sortes* (482), *sortita* (483), *sorte* (486), in conjunction with the elegant variation *urna* (484) produce drabness where excitement and tension are needed. *Monstrum ingens* in 479 is extracted from *Aeneid* 3.658, but the echo is frigid and unimpressive. Other objections might be made: all in all, Valerius presents himself as a Virgil without *ingenium*, an Ovid without *ars*.

It would be wrong to suggest that Valerius did not often rise to greater heights than this. He is at his weakest in speeches. There are times when his avoidance of 'rant' and 'bombast' – so often praised by his admirers – was stylistically beneficial. An instance of this is the absence of grotesquerie from the magical rites that precede the suicide of Aeson and Alcimede in Book 1 (730ff.). There Valerius, unlike Statius in Book 4 of the *Thebaid*, repudiated the extravagances of Seneca and Lucan (*Oedipus* 530ff., *Bell. Civ.* 6.419ff.). The resulting simplicity is refreshing and original. In the Lemnian episode Valerius shows imaginative power and technical ingenuity; the parting of Hypsipyle and Jason (2.400–24) gains in emotive strength from its succinctness. There are elegant and moving lines in his account of the abduction of Hylas. Often quoted for their musical poignancy are 3.596–7 – derived from Virgil, *Ecl.* 6.43–4:

rursus Hylan et rursus Hylan per longa reclamat
auia; responsant siluae et uaga certat imago.

Again and again he cries 'Hylas, Hylas' through the endless wastes; the woods reply and straying echo vies with him.

The verses find a responsive parallel at 724–5, when the Argonauts are sailing away from Phrygia without Hercules:

omnis adhuc uocat Alciden fugiente carina,
omnis Hylan, medio pereuntia nomina ponto.

Still each of them calls 'Alcides' as the vessel flies away, each 'Hylas', but the names fade away in mid-sea.

At the beginning of Book 4, Hercules, exhausted by searching, sees a vision of Hylas by the pool; the boy's words are harmonious and pathetic (25–37). The conclusion contrasts Hercules' triumphant destiny with the tender love that he felt for Hylas:

surge age et in duris haud unquam defice; caelo
mox aderis teque astra ferent; tu semper amoris
sis memor et cari comitis ne abscedat imago. (35–7)

Now rise: even in the midst of troubles do not succumb to weakness. Soon heaven will be yours and your place will be with the stars. Never forget your love; never let the vision of your beloved comrade slip from your mind.

Godhead was approaching, but Hercules should not forget the passion that had revealed his humanity.

The seventh book of the *Argonautica* is usually reckoned the best, despite signs that it did not receive its author's final polishing. At 407ff. there occurs a dialogue between Jason and Medea in the grove of Hecate. The hero makes it plain that he is willing to die rather than return to Iolcos without the Golden Fleece. This determination fills Medea with fear and hardens her in her resolve to betray her father by using magical arts on Jason's behalf:

haec ait. illa tremens, ut supplicis aspicit ora
conticuisse uiri iamque et sua uerba reposci,
nec quibus incipiat demens uidet ordine nec quo
quoue tenus, prima cupiens effundere uoce
omnia, sed nec prima pudor dat uerba timenti.
haeret et attollens uix tandem lumina fatur.
'quid, precor, in nostras uenisti, Thessale, terras?
unde mei spes ulla tibi, tantosque petisti
cur non ipse tua fretus uirtute labores?
nempe ego si patriis timuissem excedere tectis
occideras, nempe hanc animam cras saeua manebant
funera. Iuno ubi nunc, ubi nunc Tritonia uirgo,
sola tibi quoniam tantis in casibus adsum
externae regina domus? miraris et ipse,
credo, nec agnoscunt haec nunc Aeetida silvae.
sed fatis sum uicta tuis; cape munera supplex
nunc mea; teque iterum Pelias si perdere quaeret
inque alios casus, alias si mittet ad urbes,
heu formae ne crede tuae.' (7.431–49)

Such were his words. She trembled, now that the suppliant hero's tongue was silenced and she must make reply. In her frenzy she can devise for her words no beginning, no logic, no conclusion: her desire is to tell everything at once: yet shame and fear restrain her from utterance. She hesitates and then, at length, with a struggle, raises her eyes towards him and says: 'Why, why, Thessalian stranger, have you come to our country? Why have you any confidence in my help? The trials are great: but why do you not face them relying on your own valour? If I had been afraid to leave my father's halls, you would assuredly have fallen – and as assuredly grim destruction would have awaited my soul on the morrow. Where now is Juno, where now is Pallas, since you have no other supporter in such adversity but me, a princess of an alien dynasty? Even you are astounded, I know it; not even these groves recognize me as Aeetes' daughter. But your destiny has conquered mine. Suppliant that you are, take now my gifts. And if Pelias again attempts to destroy you, if he sends you to meet other trials in other cities, do not, oh do not trust too much in your beauty.'

Valerius' exposition has considerable refinement. Though Jason is the suppliant (431), it is Medea who is in the position of weakness, as she ironically divulges in 446–7. She is neither physically nor mentally in control of herself (*tremens*, 431, *demens*, 433). Her seething emotions cause temporary aphasia, a breakdown of reason (433–4); her response is too swift, too confused to permit orderly discourse (434–5). It is only by compelling herself to look at Jason that Medea overcomes her diffidence and replies to him (436). The psychological perceptiveness of the lines is intensified by the loose, oblique structure of 431–5, measured against the transparent clarity of 436. The speech is founded on an adroit *gradatio*. First, Medea enunciates a specious wish that Jason had never come to Colchis, while tacitly recognizing that his hope resides in her because the *labores* are too great even for his *uirtus* (438–9). She admits that she has betrayed her father; she sees now that her life and Jason's are interdependent (440–2). In the face of apparent divine indifference, Medea, although a princess and a foreigner, must assume a protective function; yet, by doing so, she alienates herself from her past, from her homeland and family (442–5). She acquiesces and submits, offering Jason all that she has (446–7). Then, at the end, she shows her awareness, almost wistfully, that it is physical love that has reduced her to her predicament (447–9). Medea is, therefore, at one and the same time saviour and victim. By giving Jason succour, she denudes herself of everything. Through his victory, she is conquered. Ignorant that she has been a plaything in a divine conspiracy (155ff.), she equates herself with the goddesses Juno and Pallas at a time when her human frailty is most clearly revealed.

Valerius deserves commendation for delicacy and insight in many parts of his epic. The problem, however, remains: what aim and purpose prompted him to compose the *Argonautica*? To hazard an answer is greatly complicated by its unfinished state. To view the work simply as a romance, as an exercise in storytelling, seems an over-simplification. Recent scholarship has shown that Apollonius' *Argonautica* uses myth to unveil and actualize a deep assessment of the human condition. The profundities of Virgilian metaphysics can never be fully or finally plumbed. It is hard to believe that Valerius had no more abstruse intent than to revamp the Argonautic saga according to his own aesthetic predilections.

As Apollonius realized, the *periplus* of the Argonauts is a useful framework for a commentary on moral and philosophical truths. That Valerius shared this view may, as has been suggested, be divined from his proem. The 'series of incidents' which make up the story is a golden opportunity to crystallize a whole range of contrasting situations and events. Some structural features are immediately detectable. In Book 2, the Argonauts disembark at Lemnos, a community that has suffered a devastating social trauma. Their visit, after some initial resistance (2.311ff.), brings about regeneration and renewal. Later, however, they reach the kingdom of Cyzicus. They are received with generous hospitality (2.634ff.); but their return, in a mental blindness imposed by Cybele's *ira*, spins the wheel of fortune; prosperity and happines are replaced by grief and ruin. The realms of Hypsipyle and Cyzicus are set out as a diptych. Jason's abandonment of the queen can be seen as a prefiguration of his killing of the king. Similarly, the rescue of Hesione by Hercules (in Book 2) corresponds with his loss of Hylas (in 3). The fight between Pollux and King Amycus (4.49ff.) has a symbolic equivalence with the scattering of the Harpies by Calais and Zetes (4.423ff.). Mopsus' homily on cathartic rites (3.377ff.) is dexterously connected with Orpheus' exposition of the myth of Io (4.351ff.); in both, sacral and religious concepts are set forth which illumine wider aspects of the Voyage. The prophecies of Cretheus (1.741ff.), Helle (2.587ff.) and Phineus (4.553ff.) form an ordered sequence. The passage of the Cyanean rocks (4.636ff.) signifies the completion of the first stage of the quest. After that, the scene shifts to Colchis and to Jason's attempts to gain possession of the Fleece. He tries negotiation (Book 5) and displays his martial valour (Book 6). It is finally through the power of love, leading to the use of thaumaturgy and theft (Book 7–8), that he achieves his end and departs from Colchis.

In Book 1, Jupiter provides a commentary on the Voyage in reply to complaints from Sol, Mars, Pallas and Juno. His speech is momentous within the fabric of the *Argonautica*. He begins by enunciating a stern doctrine of necessity, of the inflexible dominion that he has imposed on the universe:

tum genitor: 'uetera haec nobis et condita pergunt
ordine cuncta suo rerumque a principe cursu
fixa manent; neque enim terris tum sanguis in ullis
noster erat cum fata darem; iustique facultas
hinc mihi cum uarios struerem per saecula reges.
atque ego curarum repetam decreta mearum.' (1.531–6)

Then the Father replied: 'All these events were laid down by me long ago. They are proceeding in due order and remain unchangeable from the primal inauguration of the universe. When I ordained the course of Fate, no descendants of ours existed in any quarter of the earth. For that reason, I had the opportunity for strict impartiality in establishing divers sovereigns for ages still to come. Now I shall reveal to you what I have decreed in my providential care.'

The words have a Stoic flavour, but the tenor of Jupiter's 'decrees' (*decreta*, 536) is unexpected. They disclose not a personal or a particular design but instead a historic *Weltbild*. The Argonautic voyage is to precede the transference of wealth and empire from Asia to Greece (543ff.). The art of navigation, now invented, will make international conflicts easier: hence the Trojan War, for which the Voyage is a preliminary (546ff.). Greece too will decline and fall. Her primacy will pass to another race. Jupiter does not specify the legatee, but it is Rome that is to have the *imperium sine fine*:

arbiter ipse locos terrenaque summa mouendo
experiar, quaenam populis longissima cunctis
regna uelim linquamque datas ubi certus habenas. (558–60)

By moving the centre of earthly governance I, as lord, shall prove what dominion I desire to be longest-enduring and universal, to whom I can, in safe assurance, entrust the reins of power.

Finally Jupiter looks down at Hercules, at Castor and Pollux aboard the *Argo*, remarking:

tendite in astra, uiri: me primum regia mundo
Iapeti post bella trucis Phlegraeque labores
imposuit: durum uobis iter et graue caeli
institui. sic ecce meus, sic, orbe peracto
Liber et expertus terras remeauit Apollo. (563–7)

Make your way to heaven, heroes! Only after war with savage Iapetus and struggles at Phlegra did I become ruler of the universe in my kingly palace. I have fixed for you a tough and onerous path to heaven. Only so did my own Liber, after traversing the globe, only so did my own Apollo, after dwelling on earth, return to Olympus.

There is an obvious parallelism between the *cursus* of the universe (531), the path of history, the voyage of the Argonauts and the *iter* of the heroes to Olympus. Valerius had already stated that Jupiter's sway had abolished the peace (*otia*) of Saturn's reign (1.500). Henceforth it is to be through hardship and suffering that godhead will be won. The journey of the Argonauts initiated a new epoch (as Catullus had seen in his *Peleus and Thetis*), an epoch that gave birth, purposefully and inevitably, to the Roman empire. Power shifted from Asia to Greece: and then from Greece to Rome, where dwelt the scions of Asian Troy. The Argonauts became emblematic figures, not merely of the new men of a new *saeculum* but of the providential and cyclic movement of history, predetermined by divine will. If Hercules and the sons of Boreas are precursors of the Roman emperors, then Jason is ultimately representative of the qualities of outmoded Hellenism. The Golden Fleece is a token of Fate – a veiled symbol of that glittering, but perhaps illusory, ambition that man, whether as an individual or as a part of a larger community, seeks in the long pilgrimage of life, an *arcanum* which he cherishes but which can be only temporarily or fraudulently possessed.

Overt and covert glances towards the Roman *imperium* occur elsewhere in the epic. They are not simply antiquarian curiosities or meaningless Virgilian accretions. They are a crucial element in the interpretation Valerius imposed on the Argonautic myth. The full realization of his plan was foiled. The general trend may be divined. Statius was concerned with spiritual dilemmas, with the interconnexion of cosmos and psyche, of passion and virtue. Valerius wished to show humanity in a broad historical perspective. He envisaged the whole process of reality as divine, whether manifested in individual, in nation or in the *mundus*. In this sense, the philosophical structure of the *Argonautica* is Virgilian. The Voyage of the Argonauts seemed to Valerius a perfect instrument for such a comprehensive aim. Yet, in the end, the epic proves a failure. The scintilla of poetic greatness was not there. Even more important, by pitting himself so directly against Virgil, Valerius laid himself open to inhibiting constraints. He gave the fanatical assent of a convert to a credo; he attempted to live up to its demands. Dispassionate appraisal concludes that he had not grasped the implications of his faith or, at least, he was incapable of living up to it – an apprentice saint whose relics have produced no miracles.

4. SILIUS

If the *Argonautica* is thematically a prelude to the *Aeneid*, then the *Punica* is its fugue – but a fugue made monotonous by unsubtle variations. Jason's expedition was presented by Valerius as an anticipation of, or a rehearsal for, the settlement of the Trojans in Italy. The Punic Wars were for Silius a fated consequence of it. The author of the *Punica* enjoyed a long and remarkable career. His biography is pithily summarized by Pliny (*Epist.* 3.7). Sidelights are cast on it in Martial's epigrams: from them, we may deduce that Silius was a man of inordinate pretensions and vanity – a supposititious Cicero, a reborn Virgil, the founder of a consular dynasty (Martial 7.63, 8.66, 9.86). Pliny's obituary is more candid. Silius was alleged to have sullied his reputation under Nero by voluntarily acting as an informer. Appointed consul in the year of the tyrant's fall, he switched his allegiance to the party of Vitellius. Vespasian had rewarded his fluctuating loyalty with the proconsulship of Asia. Covered with glory, Silius retired to Campania and a life of *laudabile otium*. His days were divided between working on the *Punica* and conversing with friends and clients on topics of literary interest. His enormous wealth enabled him to acquire an abundance of villas, books, *objets d'art*. When he shortened a terminal illness by starvation in the reign of Trajan, he was still acknowledged as a *princeps ciuitatis*: but he had made no improper use of his prestige. As for his epic, despite Silius' habit of seeking criticism at public readings, it was written, so Pliny believed, *maiore cura quam ingenio*, with painstaking diligence rather than native aptitude.

Pliny's words have survived with the *Punica*, an equivocal motto but one that contains a studied appropriateness. In modern times, it has been twinned with H. E. Butler's aphorism that Silius is 'best known to us as the author of the longest and worst of surviving Roman epics.'[1] Readers have been more willing to forgive the inferiority than the prolixity. If the death of the man Silius prompted Pliny to reflect on human frailty (3.7.10–11), a perusal of his epic is likely to persuade a man to recall the value of such time as he may have. Life is brief, but Silius is not. In his poetry, he is a leviathan, wallowing in shallow waters that have been made turbid by his own frantic efforts to reach the open sea. Martial found it expedient to label Silius as Virgil's heir. The patrimony was ill-used.

The *Punica* is a hymn to the goddess Rome. It chronicles that heroic period of tribulation followed by triumph, when the Romans, abased by defeat, arose from it to dominion of the world. A stirring theme: Livy had recounted it in prose of memorable grandeur. Silius absorbed his *History*, and others, for the outlines of his national epic. His annalistic method harked back to the primitive but venerable Ennius. But it was Virgil who had fixed the boundaries of his *œuvre*. In the thirteenth line of the *Aeneid*, Carthage and Italy were set in eternal confrontation, spiritually more than historically. In *Aeneid* 4, Virgil had displayed the seeds of this long enmity. Dido herself had predicted the advent of an avenger, of wars that would be kindled from the tragic flames of her pyre (*Aen.* 4.625–9). There Silius picks up the tale. Hannibal is Dido's *ultor*. Typically, he also informs us, at length, of the adventures of Dido's sister Anna (*Pun.* 8.25–231).

Such a flashback into legend is but one feature of Silius' diligence (*cura*). The Punic War provided him with rich scope for discursiveness and for pedantic disquisition. His excessive zeal embellished historical narrative with all the conventional *topoi* of his chosen genre: the *nekyia* in Book 13 and the funeral-games in 16 suffice to show the grotesque inappropriateness of his syncretistic method. The combination of mythopoeic scenes with actual events soon becomes insufferable: patience and credulity are stretched to rupture. So too with the *deorum ministeria* which throng the *Punica*. Lucan's excision of such machinery was poetically wise as well as Stoically orthodox. Juno, Venus and the Sibyl find an acceptable habitation in the world of Aeneas. In the era of Hannibal and Scipio their presence is obtrusive. The disciple of Virgil was compelled to site the Punic War in heaven as well as on earth, to mingle gods and men in a bizarre setting. Such a *bêtise* was perhaps less offensive to Roman ears than to our own; it adds nothing to the *Punica* as a *laudatio rerum Romanarum*. It is hardly less than absurd to discover that Venus persuades Vulcan to evaporate the River Trebia as a boon to the defeated Romans

[1] Butler (1909) 236.

(4.467ff.) or to learn that Juno preserved Hannibal from death at Scipio's hands (17.523ff.), just as she had saved Turnus in *Aeneid* 10. No less tedious than such contrivances is Silius' penchant for obscure information, for catalogues and for encyclopaedic *doctrina*.

His chief errors, however, were inherent in the extent and nature of his theme. In the first book, Hannibal commences the war by his treacherous attack on Saguntum; in the seventeenth we reach Scipio's victorious return to Rome after Zama. Seventeen years of military campaigning would have taxed the acumen of a greater poet than Silius. Of the six great battles of the war, four – Ticinus, Trebia, Trasimene and Cannae – occurred in close chronological proximity. Silius has the first three in Books 4 and 5 – a surfeit of carnage. Cannae is delayed until Book 9; it is not until Book 12 that Hannibal reaches the walls of Rome. The battle of the Metaurus is described in 15, Zama in 17. Needless to say, all six engagements are set-pieces treated in accordance with Homeric and Virgilian norms. Between them, Silius had perforce to intersperse details of strategic manoeuvring with highly-elaborated digressions.

Typical of these is the story of Bacchus and Falernus (7.162–211). The pretext for introducing it is that the triumphant Hannibal, faced by Fabius' delaying tactics, was ravaging Campania and burning the vines growing in the Falernian region round Mount Massicus. Silius invents an aetiology to show the reason for the proverbial excellence of Falernian wine. The story is uncomplicated. In primeval times the aged Falernus farmed this area. One day, Bacchus – his divinity for a time hidden – came to Falernus' house and was entertained by him with a simple repast. Overjoyed by the hospitality he received, the god revealed himself, miraculously bestowing on his host the gift of wine and ordaining that for evermore the region should bear the name of Falernus and be renowned for its vineyards.

In inserting such a myth, Silius recalled the story of Hercules and Cacus in *Aeneid* 8.185–275. In form it is reminiscent of the tales to be found in Hesiodic poetry, in Callimachus' *Aetia*, in Propertius' fourth book and in Ovid's *Fasti*. It owed much, in word and idea, to the myth of Philemon and Baucis in Ovid's *Metamorphoses* (8.619ff.) and that of Hyrieus in the *Fasti* (5.495ff.). Under the influence of his Ovidian exemplars, Silius turns aside from the solemnity of epic to a lighter vein. His purpose in doing so, as he states it (161–2), is to pay pious honour to the god of wine.

The lightness of the episode contrasts vividly with the gloom that surrounds it. The tale of Falernus sets in relief the impenetrable darkness and impious horror of Hannibal's recent victories at Ticinus, at Trebia and at Lake Trasimene. Bacchus' beneficent action is in symbolic antithesis to the havoc wreaked by the Carthaginians. Falernus himself is an embodiment of Italian *pietas*, who fulfils ungrudgingly his obligations towards a stranger. For that reason, he is the recipient of a divine benison. Silius portrays him with warmth and humour: he bustles about in his eagerness to please his guest (176–8); the drunkenness which follows his introduction to wine is described with a mischievous realism (199–205).

This *aition* exhibits a deftness and dexterity of touch not generally attributed to Silius. For a moment he introduces into the sombre atmosphere of the *Punica* a shaft of Ovidian brightness. Nor is it totally without relevance to the wider content of the epic. Hannibal's devastation of Campania, the land blessed by Bacchus, presages his eventual defeat. In Book 11, Silius tells how the Carthaginian army and its leader are enervated and corrupted (through the scheming of Venus) by the luxury of Capua – not least by the gifts of Bacchus put to the service of vice and excess (11.285–6, 299–302, 307–8, 406–7, 414). This demoralization of Hannibal's forces was the turning-point in the Punic War. Furthermore, the younger Scipio, the 'divine man' and figure of *pietas*, who is ultimately to humble Carthaginian might at Zama, is depicted as a new Hercules, Bacchus and Quirinus. In Book 15, when Scipio, like Hercules at the crossroads, is confronted by a choice between Virtue and Pleasure (18–128), he is reminded by the personification Virtue of those celestial beings who had passed through the portal of heaven (77–8) and whom Scipio should emulate. Bacchus appears in his role as global *triumphator* at 79–81. Because Scipio chose the path of *uirtus* (spurning the blandishments of *uoluptas* to which Hannibal and his army had fallen victim at Capua), he too achieves apotheosis. The epic ends with his triumphant procession to the Capitol, where Silius compares him first to Bacchus and then to Hercules (17.646–50). Hannibal had paid the full price of his impiety. His destruction of the vineyards, miraculously established by Bacchus himself, did not go unpunished. In the myth told by Silius in Book 7, occurring at a time when Hannibal was at the height of his power, we can see a prefiguration of his final fall from glory into wretchedness, overcome by the superior might and virtue of Scipio, a Bacchus reborn to bring salvation to Rome.

Nor was it beyond Silius' reach to attain flashes of true poetic grace. In Book 13, the god Pan intervenes to preclude the burning of Capua. The poet gives the following account of his appearance and character:

Pan Ioue missus erat, seruari tecta uolente
Troia, pendenti similis Pan semper et imo
uix ulla inscribens terrae uestigia cornu.
dextera lasciuit caesa Tegeatide capra
uerbera laeta mouens festo per compita coetu.
cingit acuta comas et opacat tempora pinus,
ac parua erumpunt rubicunda cornua fronte;
stant aures, imoque cadit barba hispida mento.
pastorale deo baculum, pellisque sinistrum

uelat grata latus tenerae de corpore dammae.
nulla in praeruptum tam prona et inhospita cautes,
in qua non, librans corpus similisque uolanti,
cornipedem tulerit praecisa per auia plantam.
interdum inflexus medio nascentia tergo
respicit arridens hirtae ludibria caudae.
obtendensque manum solem inferuerscere fronti
arcet et umbrato perlustrat pascua uisu.
hic, postquam mandata dei perfecta malamque
sedauit rabiem et permulsit corda furentum,
Arcadiae uolucris saltus et amata reuisit
Maenala; ubi, argutis longe de uertice sacro
dulce sonans calamis, ducit stabula omnia cantu. (326–47)

Pan had been sent by Jupiter, who wished that the Trojan dwellings be preserved – Pan who seems to float in the air, who scarcely imprints a track upon the ground with his horned hoof. His right hand wantons with a thong of Tegean goatskin as he joyfully rains blows on the festal throng at the crossroads [at the Lupercalia]. *Sharp pine wreathes his tresses and casts shadow on his temples and small horns break forth from his red-glowing forehead. Up-pointed are his ears and a bristly beard juts from the point of his chin. The god carries a shepherd's crook; the skin of a young roe pleasingly hides his left side. There is no rock so steep, precipitous and inhospitable where he cannot, balancing his body like a winged bird, pass over the headlong crags with horned stride. Sometimes he looks behind him to laugh at the merry antics of his hairy tail that sprouts from the middle of his back. He protects his forehead with his hand to ward off the scorching sun, and looks here and there over the pastures with shaded eyes. When he had fulfilled the commands of Jupiter, calming the malignant frenzy and soothing the hearts of the raging troops, he hastened back to the glens of Arcady and to his beloved Maenalus, on whose holy peak he makes enchanting music far and wide with harmonious reeds, drawing all the flocks after him with his melody.*

Silius' Pan owes a debt to Ovid (cf. *Metamorphoses* 1.699ff., 11.153ff.), but the passage has an overriding originality. The style is pictorial, but not narrowly descriptive. Silius reminds his readers of shared impressions of the sylvan god, so that they can build for themselves a composite image: it is not static, but lively and ebullient, consonant with the merriment, wild strangeness, half-human, half-animal nature of Pan. Verbal and metrical finesse is shown. The positioning of *parua* and *cornua* in 332 neatly suggests the sprouting horns. The heavy spondees of 336–7 are cunningly resolved in the swift-moving dactyls that follow, as we imagine fleet-footed Pan leaping down the precipitous crags. The echo of his pipes on Mount Maenalus is evoked by the framing words *argutis...calamis*. Alliteration is placed in effective service, especially at 329–30, 336–8 and 346–7: sound follows sense but, even more important, depths of sense are added by sound. The whole ecphrasis is a finely-wrought miniature. Silius' *cura* has for once produced a bounty, but to find such 'occasional gems, one must endure the dross'.[1]

One merit of Silius, even in his less inspired episodes, is linguistic perspicuity – a facet of his work that separates him from the tortuous complexities of Statius as well as from the sterile insipidity that afflicted parts of Valerius' *Argonautica*. This clarity of diction sprang, no doubt, both from Silius' reverence for Virgil and from his adoption of the annalistic tradition in epic. But even this merit has its limitations: it induces torpor. One spark of ardent animation – a quality that Lucan and Statius perhaps possessed in excess – would often have saved Silius from the chilling decorum, the fibreless and numbing dullness that pervades the *Punica*. In Pliny's terms, there was an absence of sustained *ingenium*.

It has sometimes been remarked that the *Punica* is an epic without a hero. It is in fact Hannibal, the consummate *exemplum* of Carthaginian perfidy, that dominates and controls the narrative. He is, like Turnus in the *Aeneid* (6.89), a rebirth of Achilles, the archetypal enemy of Troy–Rome; but he is also a Punic Aeneas, leading an invading force from North Africa to Italy in fulfilment of Dido's prophecy, but, because Punic, an impious Aeneas, foredoomed to defeat. In Book 2, the people of Spain present Hannibal with an engraved shield (395–496).[2] It is a heroic attribute, bringing him into relation with both Achilles and Aeneas. Hannibal's heroism is, however, superficial, for he lacks those virtues which enabled the progeny of Aeneas ultimately to overcome Carthage. Hannibal is a hero defeated by Fate, by the fact of his Punic origin as much as by his own innate depravity. It may not have been Silius' intention, but his portrait of Hannibal has a tragic nobility; the general with an inordinate lust for blood (cf. 1.40, 59–60, etc.) can nonetheless utter an exalted tribute to Aemilius Paullus when he comes upon his corpse after Cannae (10.572–8). The younger Scipio in the *Punica* is elevated to a semi-divine status, as we have seen. Yet, like Fabius Maximus Cunctator, Paullus and even Regulus, whose sufferings are described in retrospect in Book 6 (62ff.), Scipio, when measured against Hannibal, pales into the moral wanness of Stoic impeccability. The villain of the *Punica* is its fulcrum. For Silius the Stoic Hannibal may well have been the epitome of turpitude, just as was Scipio of rectitude. The war between Carthage and Rome may well have been an illustration for him of eternal verities in a similar fashion to Statius' treatment of the Argo-Theban conflict. But fact has, at the last, vanquished philosophy. Of all the characters that throng the *Punica*, Hannibal alone has a semblance of life, is more than a puppet. Silius' laudation of Roman majesty, of Roman *fides*, *pietas* and *uirtus* could not wholly expunge the glory of its mightiest foe, however *perfidus*,

[1] Vessey (1973) 2.
[2] On the significance of the shield, see Vessey (1975) 391–405.

impius and *saeuus*: or totally erase his greatness from record. Lucan had faced a similar problem with Caesar. In both the *Bellum civile* and the *Punica*, the axial polarization of good and evil, virtue and vice, painstakingly affirmed, has failed to persuade because the poets protested too much, too often and too stridently: perilous is the path of those who mythicize in verse the documents of history.

Statius, Valerius, Silius. Three poets with three distinct styles, purposes, attainments. Only the *Silvae* and, even more positively, the *Thebaid* can be accounted successful: within their limitations. Dante placed Statius in purgatory, where he freely acknowledges the supremacy of Virgil (*Purgatorio*, Canto 21); he names his cardinal sin on earth as prodigality (Canto 22). A not unfitting fancy: Statius was lavish in all his works of the *ars* and *ingenium* with which he was unquestionably dowered. Critically, the modern world has lodged him in a more straitened confinement than did Dante: with small hope of heaven. Silius is more justly damned. As Pliny saw, he had little else than *cura*: a literary Attis, who emasculated himself before the shrine of his gods. Valerius remains an enigma. Lacking the virtues of Statius and the vices of Silius, he reveals a mediocrity that, if not golden, has appeared to some at least well-burnished silver. A tribute from Quintilian: reward enough, perhaps, for the *Argonautica*.

29

MARTIAL AND JUVENAL

On the usual dating,[1] the beginning of Juvenal's literary career coincided with Martial's later years: the composition of the first satire, which contains a reference to the trial of Marius Priscus in A.D. 100, was probably contemporaneous with the epigrammatist's retirement to Spain. Martial praised three emperors, and when it was safe to do so, condemned the memory of the first: but it is essentially the age of Domitian in which he moves. His work spans the last quarter century, a medley of adulation, obscenity, and off-hand observation on a tired, neurotic world. Perhaps gloating, he writes to Juvenal from Spain, comparing town and country: he is at ease, while Juvenal is harassed in the city (12.18). Juvenal, strangely impersonal despite his spleen and violence, has nothing in reply. For one obsessed with the world of the dead, friendship could have had few attractions. Tradition has it that he mellows with time: in fact he simply writes less well after the vitriolic ninth satire, and the paradigmatic, rhetorical tenth.[2] In Satire 15 the venom returns, but it is for his first two books, Satires 1–6, that he is chiefly celebrated. With time, his manner becomes less taut and less intense, more leisurely and reflective; the later Juvenal is a declaimer's poet, preoccupied with theses. In his earlier work he castigated vice and poured scorn on the insufficiencies of virtue, rejecting the ironic manner of Horace and the sermons of Persius, to adopt a deeply pessimistic, hysterically tragic stance.[3] Martial provided him with material and characters, but the mood is all his own. Nor must we overemphasize a direct connexion between the two writers, since epigram and satire deal in common currency. Both forms are traditionally unambitious, both take life as their province – presenting sometimes, occasionally transforming; the higher flights, of epic and tragedy, are

[1] For Juvenal, see Coffey (1976) 119–23; and for Martial, Friedländer (1886) pref.

[2] Highet (1954), with his insistence that Juvenal is growing old, illustrates the tendency to explain away the change of tone by simplistic appeal to the passing of time: for example 'Book IV is the work of an ageing man' (122); 'signs of age were visible in Juvenal's Third and Fourth Books. Book III was weaker. Book IV was mellower' (138). But this is perhaps not so tiresome as the theory that Juvenal could not have been the author of the later satires, as Ribbeck (1859) thought, even though his conclusions are supported by stylistic criteria. Writers modify their manner, and without biographical evidence, we cannot say why.

[3] See, e.g., Scott (1927), and Bramble (1974) 164–73.

by strict convention avoided. But nonetheless, when that is said, literary propriety could inhibit – and on that Juvenal is emphatic. A Roman Medea in his satire on women elicits the confession that the limits of form can no longer restrain him:

fingimus haec altum satura sumente cothurnum
scilicet, et finem egressi legemque priorum
grande Sophocleo carmen bacchamur hiatu,
montibus ignotum Rutulis caeloque Latino?
nos utinam uani. sed clamat Pontia 'feci,
confiteor, puerisque meis aconita paraui,
quae deprensa patent; facinus tamen ipsa peregi.' (6.634–40)

Am I making the whole thing up, careless of precedents, mouthing
Long-winded bombast in the old Sophoclean manner
That's quite out of place here under Italian skies?
How I wish that it was *all nonsense! But listen to Pontia's*
Too-willing confession: 'I did it, I admit I gave aconite
To my children. Yes, they were poisoned, that's obvious.
But I *was the one who killed them.'* (Tr. Green)[1]

Earlier, in his fourth satire, an account of Domitian's council about 'a fish of wondrous size', he had recharged the resources of satire with devices taken from epic – and parody of Statius.[2] Likewise, in his second, the *Aeneid* had been used to vilify and condemn the profligacies of Otho.[3] Martial, on the other hand, will not disobey convention:

a nostris procul est omnis uesica libellis,
Musa nec insano syrmate nostra tumet. (4.49.7–8)

Any form of turgidity is alien to my works,
Nor does my Muse swell with unhealthy bombast.

Life is his theme: epic and tragedy are unreal and divorced from the world that we know, offering nothing to the simple observer of *mores* and fashion. True, Martial will sometimes stray from his course, to attempt the *genus medium* in his non-satiric poems, but without a great deal of success. A fifty line set-piece like 3.58, with its expansive, well-wrought opening:

Baiana nostri uilla, Basse, Faustini
non otiosis ordinata myrtetis
uiduaque platano tonsilique buxeto
ingrata lati spatia detinet campi,
sed rure uero barbaroque laetatur...

[1] Green's Penguin Translation of Juvenal (© P. Green 1970) is used throughout. Some of the translations of Martial are my own, some loose adaptations from Ker's version (1919).

[2] See Valla on 4.94, quoting four lines of Statius' *De bello Germanico* (*FPL*, 134); also Highet (1954) 258–9, and Griffith (1969) 134–50.

[3] See, for instance, Lelièvre (1958) 22–5.

Faustinus' villa at Baiae, Bassus, has no fruitless spaces of open land, laid out with idle myrtles, sterile planes or boxwood hedges, but is happy with real country and uncultivated land...

inspires as little enthusiasm as Statius' occasional poems, with which it has obvious affinities.[1] Another example of such dalliance with the Muse, well-written but unconvincing, is the thirtieth epigram of Book 10:

o temperatae dulce Formiae litus,
uos, cum seueri fugit oppidum Martis
et inquietas fessus exuit curas
Apollinaris omnibus locis praefert.
non ille sanctae dulce Tibur uxoris
nec Tusculanos Algidosue secessus
Praeneste nec sic Antiumque miratur;
non blanda Circe Dardanisue Caieta
desiderantur, nec Marica nec Liris
nec in Lucrina lota Salmacis uena.

O well-climed Formiae, pleasant shore, you, when he escapes austere Mars' town and weary sheds unquiet cares, Apollinaris prefers to every spot. Not so highly does he prize his chaste wife's dearest Tibur, the retreats of Tusculum or Algidus, Praeneste or Antium; not so deeply does he miss the charming headland of Circe and Trojan Caieta, or Marica or Liris, or Salmacis bathed in the Lucrine stream.

Anyone could have written that: and twenty lines follow in the same tedious vein. But, for the most part, he adheres to epigram's prevalent ethos, of rhetorical point and cynical comment, couched in everyday speech.

Juvenal, as we have seen, is less obedient to the rules of his genre and sometimes even anarchic, his language a medley of high and low, his tone contemptuous, and, in any normal sense of the words, unconstructive, negative. Tragedy no longer capped life in its horrors: hence his self-granted permission to depart from the canons of Horace and Persius – his deliberate resort from the pedestrian muse to upper reaches trodden as yet only by schoolboys and bards. He tells us in the preface to his programmatic satire that so far he has only listened – to bombastic recitations, to the nonsense of the schools. Yet he too has the training: so why spare the paper any longer? And since life is now so ghastly, why not be immodest and depart from prior tradition?[2] Irony, too urbane and content a device, is replaced by malevolent verbal extravagance, and an arch and vengeful stance. His arena is that of Lucilius, depicted as a charioteer, then later as a warrior: the *inventor* of the genre would hardly have agreed to the pretensions of the portrait. And in tone as in style the sweeping

[1] For Statius' *Silvae*, see above, pp. 561–72.

[2] See in particular 1.1ff., 15ff., and the comments of Bramble (1974) 164–73, on the first satire's implications that the style should now be high.

gestures are evident. His audience is passive and lacking in opinion, seeking amusement from vice, and corrupted by the ease with which the schools disgorged their poets. So Juvenal is despotic, and refuses to be virtuous: he treacherously takes part with his reader, then bullies him to admit that his tastes are sick and weak, that the world he has seduced him with is more vile than he suspected. Like the Stoic or the Cynic, for whom nothing was obscene, nothing so forthright as never to be said, Juvenal mockingly entertains us with the vice we all demand, but takes it much too far, disturbing us with half-voiced questions about the basis of our values. His ancestor is the Thersites of the *Iliad*'s second book, unwilling to acquiesce in accepted beliefs, and the butt of our distaste when our sensibilities pretend offence.[1]

Martial, by way of contrast, never plays the fool, and never makes us think. He is succinct, at the expense of others, with never a moral reflection; he is always uninvolved, protected by his reader's tastes. He is poetic – on occasions – and the rules remain intact: even Quintilian, perhaps against his will, receives an epigram (2.90). With no doubts and no anxieties about his position in society, he acts the courtier, no doubt receiving rewards, and from beneath the cover of the unobjectionably trivial or else the safely obscene, he delivers the jokes that he leads us to expect. A tradition stands behind him – venerable writers whose page was lascivious[2] – and so he stays unruffled, no victim to emotion, and without claim to be a poet. His Muse is his reader – *dictauit auditor*, as he puts it in the preface to Book 12 – and life is his theme, his justification for asking no questions: *hominem pagina nostra sapit* (10.4.10). Juvenal the misanthrope will not comply. His reader is assaulted, assumptions set at nought. His verse makes jokes in earnest, but is full of tragic colour. An emperor is invoked but once, and that without flattery.[3] Perverts are greeted with obscenities in Satires 2 and 9, but without that element of complicity which we come to expect from Martial. And as for tradition, Lucilius is brought back to life, while the Horatian mode is forgotten:[4] Persius is closer to him, but he does not use his methods.[5] Above all, he knows the dangers, and the insult, of standing as listener: *semper ego auditor tantum?* No audience could

[1] For Thersites ('The Railer'), see Elliott (1960) 130ff., and in general, the excellent study of the figure of the fool by Welsford (1935), although she overlooks Thersites.

[2] See below, p. 612 n.1.

[3] At 7.1ff. See Townend (1973) 149ff., and Rudd (1976) 84ff.

[4] For Juvenal's portrait of Lucilius – a portrait which the founder of satire would not have recognized, painted as it is in military and epic colours – see Anderson (1961) 12 n.25, and Bramble (1974) 169ff. For the essentially humble nature of satiric *sermo* see Fiske (1920): in fact Horace followed Lucilius in keeping his Muse pedestrian. It is Juvenal who enters new territory. Apart from 1.51 where the reference stands for satire in general, Juvenal only mentions Horace in the seventh satire, as an example of a text for the schools, and a poet who composed on a full belly: 7.62 *satur est cum dicit Horatius 'euhoe'*.

[5] Significantly, though only once, Persius is cynical at the expense of his professions, in the picture of Stoicism at 3.52ff.: an instance of amoral rhetorical obfuscation, of the kind we expect from Juvenal.

dictate to him: he sees the hypocrisy and collusion of the poet and his victim. Martial's reader is not for him: self-expression, pretended or real, replaces the urge to pander.[1] Like Persius, he knows that poetry cannot simply cater for hackneyed, senseless tastes.[2] Martial, an accepted poet, a figure from the ranks, would have recognized the content, but hardly the spirit, of Juvenal's dread questions; for patrician rage was out of date, or at least an unsatiric gesture, conservative though the form might be. Irony was the usual tool, but an unsuitable vehicle for Juvenal's *indignatio*. Epigram admittedly had never been the form for matters of much moment – Catullus, too, was trivial, though more sincere than Martial: enmity, love, the social *faux pas*, and sometimes poetry – those were his themes, but he entered them and lived them. His moods were uncommissioned, his technique more random and honest. But satire until Juvenal's day had answers as well as questions: steady, sane and sober, the form avoided the emotions in favour of normative morals. In Horace it was individuals, accepted individuals, and not society that sinned. For Persius, the norm was Stoic, and though the writing was brilliant, the answers were systematic. Neither faltered in their assumptions, and neither questioned virtue. It was not usual, even amongst the older Cynics, for negativity and anger to extend beyond human transgression to the basis of our morals: nature, or the golden age, were always there as a salve. Hence Juvenal's question – given that the world is wrong, our world, the world of Nero or Domitian, no matter with names and dates, can we play the Cato now, or are our values dying? – could not have fallen on sympathetic ears, at least amongst conservatives; could not have broken down reserves, except with some discomfiture.

Martial, indeed, would have found Juvenal too powerful. Yet even though he is a minor figure, he sets the precedent for later epigram: his cynicism, his invective, his obscenity – these were the qualities his imitators strove for. He never wearies of the credentials of tradition, and hence he never stumbles. He owes little to the Greeks, if we follow his own version. In the preface to the first book, he only mentions Romans: *sic scribit Catullus, sic Marsus, sic Pedo, sic Gaetulicus, sic quicumque perlegitur* 'So writes Catullus, Marsus, Pedo, Gaetulicus, anyone who is popular.' A popular form: these authors are read through and through. Pliny likewise omits the Greeks (5.3.5–6). Yet in the first century A.D., Argentarius, the second Nicarchus and Lucillius are composing epigrams in Greek in the pointed rhetorical vein. Meleager's *Garland*, collected around 80 B.C., and covering two centuries, does not offer parallels: except, perhaps, for Leonidas, who could be cynical and scabrous.[3] Nor does Latin display the mordant note until the time of Catullus: Ennius merely set

[1] The first satire is full of insistences that he must and will write satire: see Bramble (1974) 164f.

[2] In his first satire, Persius is at pains to show that few are left with discernment. Juvenal's audience was probably rather wider, but he maintains a similar stance.

[3] See Gow and Page (1965) I 107–39 and II 307–98.

the style for inscriptions, while Catulus, Aedituus, and Licinus were mannered poets of love, contemporaries of Meleager.[1] Catullus had no fixed metre; but elegiacs and hendecasyllables predominate. Nor, in this like Meleager, does he call his poems *epigrammata*; instead, they are *uersiculi*, *ineptiae*, or *nugae*. As much an iambist as an epigrammatist, Catullus looks forward at times to the abrasive side of Martial. In the ancient world 'iambic' is a tone of voice – biting, angry, aloof – and epigram has its iambic side. Archilochus and Hipponax, the impassioned iambists of Greece, were matched in Rome by figures as disparate as Lucilius, Catullus, Horace and Bibaculus: so runs the list of the grammarian Diomedes (*GLK* I 485). Of Marsus, Pedo and Gaetulicus we cannot really speak. But in Greek the trend is clear: the second of the two great anthologies, the *Crown* of Philip, published under Caligula, is witty and pointed, whereas the *Garland* of Meleager was polished and sentimental; and the satiric epigram, the form we associate with Martial, has arrived on the scene with the work of Nicarchus and Lucillius. But, as we have noted, on Greek epigram Martial is silent, and Pliny is too: so rather than a direct debt, perhaps better to assume that developments in Rome had been the same – that the successors of Catullus had written like the Greeks, in the declamatory pointed fashion, abandoning the seductive tone of Alexandria to pursue the affiliation with iambic.

Martial is Juvenal's senior, and, as we have said, his work covers the twenty years which provided the satirist with the matter for much of his first two books – the twenty-year period during which the satirist still listened. Born somewhere between A.D. 38 and 41 at Bilbilis in Spain, Martial came to Rome in A.D. 64, to be received by Seneca and Lucan, the important writers of the day. Although he appears to have composed juvenilia (1.113), we have nothing to show for his first sixteen years; then, in A.D. 80, he produced the *Liber spectaculorum*, on the occasion of the opening of the Flavian Amphitheatre by Titus. Books 13 and 14 of our present collection – the *Xenia* and *Apophoreta*, brief, sometimes ingenious mottos for presents – followed in A.D. 84, or thereabouts, and then, in A.D. 86, appeared Books 1 and 2 of his epigrams, more substantial, but still very much to the popular taste. A new book was published roughly each year from A.D. 87 to 96; in A.D. 97, a shorter edition of Books 10 and 11 was produced for the Princeps (12.8), then, in A.D. 98, he returned to his homeland.[2] Finally, in the winter of A.D. 101, after a three-year gap, Book 12 was published from Spain. Martial's death is recorded by Pliny in a letter of A.D. 104 (*Epist.* 3.21.1). His first nine books appeared under Domitian, and contain the expected adulation. He changed his tune in the remaining three, now damning the tyrant,

[1] See above, p. 175.

[2] 10.103.7ff. He had already spent some time abroad, in Cisalpine Gaul, whence he published the third book: see 3.1.

to laud the new masters, Nerva and Trajan. There are 1,561 epigrams in all: 1,235 written in elegiacs; 238 in hendecasyllables; 77 in scazons, and a few in hexameters and iambics. He knew, or at least addressed, the important figures of the Flavian literary establishment – Silius, Valerius, Pliny, Quintilian – and Juvenal as well.

Of Juvenal's career we know much less. Birth dates of A.D. 67, 60 and 55 have been suggested, but arguments are not conclusive.[1] Of his name, it has been argued that the gentile name Junius suggests possibly Spanish origin, while Juvenalis, his cognomen, is perhaps a sign of lowly birth.[2] Much has been made of an inscription from Aquinum – a place seemingly close to the satirist (3.318ff.); but it is unlikely that we shall ever know for certain if the Junius Juvenalis there mentioned, *duumvir quinquennalis*, *flamen* of Vespasian, and tribune of the soldiers, is the poet of the satires.[3] Juvenal claims autopsy of Egypt (15.45), but that need not have been as a soldier; nor is there strong reason for linking the reference to Ceres at the end of the third satire with the Ceres honoured in the inscription. We have several ancient lives, but they represent a single tradition.[4] According to the common source,[5] Juvenal, son of a wealthy freedman, declaimed into middle age – a story which may be based on extrapolation from the satires themselves (1.15ff.), and perhaps, to some extent, on conflation with Horace, *libertino patre natus* (*Sat.* 1.6.6). Then follows the tale of exile: Juvenal, now an old man, is sent to hold command on the furthest borders of Egypt, in disgrace for his comments about Paris the actor. The story is a part of Domitian's bad press, a concoction of later antiquity, intended to supply the wanted evidence for a writer about whom hardly anything was known – yet in recent times the tale has been revived: bitter and poor from his exile, Juvenal starts to write to voice the hatreds of his youth.[6] In fact, we know no more than that his output is a product of the first quarter of the second century. If he was active in the nineties, our only evidence would be Martial's seventh book, composed in A.D. 91–2, where the epithet *facunde*, addressed to Juvenal in the ninety-first epigram, perhaps suggests poetry: but declamation could explain it too, and Juvenal, it seems, had been a rhetorician. In A.D. 102, he might have been engaged on Book 1 of his satires – if that is what Martial has in mind when, in that year, he describes Juvenal as leading the life of a *cliens*. The clues are slight, but enough to make one think of the wretched existence portrayed in the early satires:

[1] As Coffey (1976) 120 points out, A.D. 55, the date offered by the *Vita*, is too early. Syme (1958) 774f. argues for A.D. 67, Highet (1954) 5 and 11–12, unconvincingly, for A.D. 60.

[2] See Coffey ibid.

[3] For details, see Highet (1954) 32ff.

[4] See Highet (1954) 21ff. and 238 with bibliography.

[5] Text in Clausen (1959) 179. For the other *Vitae* see Jahn (1851*a*) 386–90.

[6] Highet's book in particular is vitiated by this biographical mode of approach, but most studies show traces of it.

dum tu forsitan inquietus erras
clamosa, Iuuenalis, in Subura
aut collem dominae teris Dianae;
dum per limina te potentiorum
sudatrix toga uentilat uagumque
maior Caelius et minor fatigat... (12.18)

while no doubt you restlessly wander in the noisy Subura, Juvenal, or tread the hill of lady Diana; or while you fan yourself by the movement of your sweaty toga, as you visit the porches of the great, wearied by climbing the two Caelian hills...

The comparison which follows with Martial's easy life in Spain would hardly be charitable, unless Juvenal's life in Rome were a figment taken from his poetry. Ancient writers were often characterized in terms of the contents of their work,[1] so if Martial is following suit, Book 1 of the satires is already under way. But perhaps after all there is an element of *Schadenfreude*: at least, in Martial 7.24, animosity is denied, which perhaps makes one suspect that the friendship was not a smooth or simple matter. Beyond this – and Martial is the only contemporary who even mentions Juvenal – we glean a few dates from the satires themselves, some of them perhaps indicating time of composition, though usually not yielding more than a *terminus post quem*, some of them dramatic. Marius Priscus, tried in A.D. 100, is mentioned twice (1.47–50 and 8.120), perhaps because Pliny invested the case with some notoriety (*Epist.* 2.11.12 and 6.29.9). In the fourth satire there is an allusion to Domitian's death in A.D. 96, although the *mise en scène* belongs to A.D. 82 (4.153–4). Tacitus has been invoked to explain the second satire when it refers to Otho's antics as worthy of annals or history: the dates in question would be A.D. 105, when the *Histories* were under way, or A.D. 109, when published, or again, A.D. 115 in the case of the *Annals*. But the passage has a general ring, and no names are mentioned (2.102–3). We must wait till Satire 10 for Tacitean influence, in the portrait of Sejanus. Our other dates belong to the second and third decades of the second century: Trajan's harbour at Ostia, finished in A.D. 113, is mentioned at 12.75–81; a comet and earthquake of A.D. 115 occur at 6.407–12; the address to Hadrian[2] at 7.1ff. probably antedates his departure from Rome in A.D. 121; and finally, at 15.27, there is a reference to an event of A.D. 127.[3]

In the first, third, and fifth satires, it is Martial's Rome of which he writes; and elsewhere in the first two books the scenery and the characters are unmistakably those of epigram.[4] But the scope is more extensive, the colours more garish, the mood more fantastic. Juvenal's world is a mixture of memory,

[1] For instance, Gallus in the tenth *Eclogue*, and Tibullus in Hor. *Odes* 1.33 are depicted after the manner of their elegies.

[2] Some argue that the emperor is Trajan, or even Domitian – without much likelihood: see Rudd (1976) 85ff.

[3] For further details, see Highet (1954) 11ff.

[4] See Townend (1973) 148f.

imagination, and literary reminiscence, peopled by monsters and caricatures. Twenty years had passed, allowing the times of Domitian to become a paradise of crime, corruption, luxury and injustice. Juvenal's *cena*, the inequitable dinner of Satire 5, is based on Martial 3.60, a flatter, more objective account of the gap between client and patron:

cum uocer ad cenam non iam uenalis ut ante,
   cur mihi non eadem quae tibi cena datur?
ostrea tu sumis stagno saturata Lucrino,
   sugitur inciso mitulus ore mihi:
sunt tibi boleti, fungos ego sumo suillos:
   res tibi cum rhombo est, at mihi cum sparulo.
aureus inmodicis turtur te clunibus implet,
   ponitur in cauea mortua pica mihi.
cur sine te ceno cum tecum, Pontice, cenem?
   sportula quod non est prosit. edamus idem.

When I am asked to dinner, not, as before, a dependant on the dole, why is the same food not served to me as you? You enjoy oysters fattened in the Lucrine lake, I suck a mussel, and cut my lips on the shell; you have mushrooms, I get some dubious fungus – you tackle turbot, I tackle brill; you take your fill of a golden turtle-dove, its rump all bloated with fat, while I am served a magpie that died in its cage. Why do I dine without you, Ponticus, although I dine with you? Let us make something of the abolition of the dole: let us eat the same.

But here, apart from the black humour about the magpie dead in its cage, and the point of the penultimate line, there is little to remind us of Juvenal's scathing manner. Likewise, the third satire owes something to Martial 3.30:

sportula nulla datur; gratis conuiua recumbis:
   dic mihi quid Romae, Gargiliane, facis?
unde tibi togula est et fuscae pensio cellae?
   unde datur quadrans? unde uir es Chiones?
cum ratione licet dicas te uiuere summa,
   quod uiuis, nulla cum ratione facis.

The dole exists no longer; your reward is now a free dinner. Tell me, Gargilianus, what can you do in Rome? Where do you get your threadbare toga, where the rent for your dark garret? How do you get the money for a bath, how do you afford Chione? You might say that you've rationalized your life to the last farthing, but your living at all is not a rational act.

Chione, the garret, the penury – all reappear in Juvenal, and the third satire actually contains the words *quid Romae faciam?* (3.41). But Martial lacks bitterness and hyperbole, simply supplying the idea, 'a joker', as Townend calls him,[1] 'never shocked or distressed by the most horrific details that he

1 Ibid.

relates from everyday life'. Likewise, the first satire recreates the world of Martial. To quote from Townend again:

> when Juvenal opens his first sketch of Roman life in i.23, he leaves no doubt that this is Martial's scene, already several years, probably as much as twenty, in the past. Mevia, Crispinus, Matho are all Flavian figures from Martial, as Massa and Carus are informers from Domitian's last years, and the *magni delator amici* in line 33 can hardly be other then the great Regulus. Marius Priscus, the one apparent exception because his prosecution falls in the year 100 under Trajan, is nonetheless a creature of Domitian's reign, already in line for the proconsulate of Africa for 97/8, and perhaps actually appointed before Domitian was murdered in September 96. What Juvenal is doing in this section, and throughout the rest of the first satire, is to announce that his material belongs to a previous generation but is still first-rate scandal, to be reproduced with mock horror, and enjoyed with gusto.

True, as far as concerns Martial, and Juvenal's immersion in the past. But given Juvenal's fascination with bygone corruption, is he simply amoral, is his horror merely false?

There has been much debate. Critics have differed, some claiming Juvenal for a rhetorician, some for a social realist, others for a moralist – but not that many for a satirist.[1] Some appear worried that his characters are dead: but that hardly affects the issue. Given that his Rome is a recreation from the past, do his writings simply amuse, or imply that life might be different? Do we require a moral solution? Must his writings always be faithful? Ulrich Knoche, in his book on Roman satire, goes some way – further than most critics – towards answering these questions. Warning against the verisimilitude of Juvenal's Rome, he remarks on his subjectivity yet his apparent lack of philosophic commitment:

> The individual case is usually raised to the level of the norm and for this reason the individual picture itself is in turn raised to the monumental. The picture is meant to be the direct expression of the poet's thought and opinion with all their emotion and fervour. In Juvenal there is, generally speaking, no overlapping of pictures and thought as is perhaps characteristic of Persius. But there is an intensification of thought through an extremely concentrated build-up of successive pictures in a step-by-step process. Judgment as a rule results automatically from this without further deliberation and then it almost seems as if Juvenal just records it.[2]

Which, I think, is to say that there is no direct moral intervention, no evangelistic design: the images are not informed by any obvious idea, the process of

[1] H. A. Mason in Sullivan (1963) 93–167, for instance, stresses the quality of rhetorical entertainment in Juvenal, denying him moral concern, while Wiesen (1963) attempts to exculpate him from the charge of moral anarchy by appeal to individual maxims; Green (1967), on the other hand, in the preface to his translation, emphasizes the social aspect. An important study of rhetoric in Juvenal is that by De Decker (1913).

[2] Knoche tr. Ramage (1975) 152.

selection is apparently random and objective, but at root intensely personal. Emotion is lavished on the object, not on its significance. Juvenal is possessive with his material, but will not arrange it into easy patterns or expected sermons; and so he abandons the precedent of Horace, with all his disguising irony, and the methods of Persius, for whom reality was a web of Stoic prohibitions and ideals. To quote from Knoche again:

He confronts monstrous depravity, which he identifies everywhere, bravely and boldly as an individual. He is not the man to take refuge in the realms of mythology as so many other poets of the time did. He identifies anger and indignation as the driving forces of his satiric poetry, and these are genuine and strong. It is not fair either to Juvenal's attitude or to his poetic achievement to brush him off as a declaimer, for as such he would not be part of his subject, and what he had to say would have only a virtuoso value. Juvenal's poetry aims at being a personal creed, and the poet is always directly concerned with his subject. Actually, he could be criticised for an excess of inner commitment rather than the opposite. The subject matter, as a matter of fact, takes him prisoner, and he hardly ever has the power to separate himself from it and to raise himself above it. This is the powerful source of his descriptive strength, but it is also probably the main reason that Horace's joy in understanding, especially understanding the weaknesses of his fellow man, is missing in him, as is the ironic laughter which finds its high point in the amiable self-irony of the earlier satirist.

From this outlook of his Juvenal gathers the power to praise and condemn without compromise, the right to make everything either black or white. Attempts have been made to deny him this right also, since it has been asserted that he lacked any ideal that had to be based on philosophical principles. Certainly, while the influence of popular moral philosophy, especially that with a Stoic direction, on Juvenal's satires may be indisputable, a philosopher the poet most certainly was not, and he himself rejected a commitment to philosophy. But a guiding principle is by no means missing from his judgments on this account.

His opinion is firmly and clearly determined by his wide practical experience and his respect for the old Roman traditions; he clings firmly to these. And since the life of his time ran directly contrary to these ideals, because he also recognised the impossibility of bringing the old values into play again generally, and because, moreover, all of this appeared to him to be natural necessity arising from the human plan, he had to pass unilateral judgment, and frequently with a sharpness and accentuation which from the modern point of view does not always completely suit the subject. This, however, is no *declamatio* (declamation), but in spite of all the strangeness in the individual instance, the indignation is always genuine and sincere. Here is where the essential point of this brittle poetic personality with its fundamental pessimism lies. Of course, personal disillusionment and bitterness may have had a part to play in shaping his conception of life, but this determines the degree of his censure, not its subject matter and direction.[1]

Knoche's position is possibly too simple: Juvenal can be more distanced and less positive than he suggests; nor does he take into account the less abrasive

[1] Ibid. 150–1.

output of the later books. But his analysis is intelligent and approaches more closely to Juvenal's general ethos than many more recent discussions: more closely, for instance, than H. A. Mason's assessment, which finds no moral centre, and unfairly condemns him through comparison with the confidence of Johnson's unquestioned moral standards; or D. Wiesen's apologia, which attempts vindication by appeal to moral apophthegms taken out of context.[1] Juvenal, it must be repeated, is a satirist, not a moralist. He does not record, or pass immediate, obvious judgement: he creates, and closes in on chimaeras, pretending uncertainty, to make us uncertain too. We are assaulted by the attractions of vice, attractions that he has fabricated, but then we are refused the prerogative of coming to a verdict. Seduced by the glamour of a world he forces on us, we find our morals failing when we try to interpose objections: for Juvenal will allow no absolutes, no self-satisfied ideals. Black honesty is his only retort to our feeble cries for justice, yet somehow it unnerves us more. Myths which nourished ancestors are exposed for what they are – easy and insubstantial, the progeny of false rhetoric and poetic nostalgia. Vice and corruption had shocked, or titillated before – but puritan answers were present, in the shape of golden age myths and pastoral idylls. Utopianism had been the keynote of much popular philosophy,[2] and the Romans with their sense of original sin and collective guilt – their feeling that Romulus and Laomedon had somehow mortgaged their innocence[3] – were inordinately disposed to excuse their unwillingness, or inability, to reform by self-righteous identification with caricatures of virtue, with honour now lost. Juvenal, by way of answer, is negative, or at least assumes a negative posture, in order to question the values that we vaunt, but sometimes more than that: for negativity on occasions can redeem outworn ideals. Pretending to worthlessness, through the *persona* of the perverted Naevolus, the querulous male prostitute of the ninth satire, or through the indignant but ineffectual client of the first book, Juvenal's way is to intimate that our golden age yearnings are literary, self-conscious and futile, that his are being poisoned too, by the insufferable communal worldliness, but that, because at least he has some insight, his own corruption is less. Not an innocent, and perhaps, except for intimations, never one, Juvenal takes hell as a given fact, as something banal; he is insistent but resigned, sometimes persecuted, and yet he never grovels: there is no overt self-pity, little pity for others except occasionally glimpsed – but then maybe that is because it is he himself that suffers, with his regretful laughter and censorious anger, far more than his unfeeling crowd. Yet although he will entertain no solutions, he is not the monumental despairer, he never dabbles in *ennui*, he is

[1] See above, p. 606 n. 1.
[2] See Ferguson (1975) and the important collection of texts in Lovejoy and Boas (1935).
[3] See Jal (1963) 406–11.

never seen directly commanding his creatures, is never so unkind as to rise superior to his figments – in this, so different from Petronius, the detestable ring-master, a figure that could have occurred in his satires, albeit dead and maybe harmless. His bitterness alone, undeprived of energy and sometimes illumination, acts as a salve in the world which Rome has ruined, a world where worthless vices have tantalized moralists and despoiled their credibility, because they could not laugh. No doubt in some of his readers the moral sense was too trite for discomfiture; but some, at least, must have squirmed, not so much because they recognized themselves amongst his monsters, but because they saw their values indicted, as archaic and inadequate.

Martial is no match for his successor in seriousness of tone, but he tells us of the times that Juvenal had lived through before he began to write, of the bygone society that provided him with material for satire. Juvenal openly admits that his characters are dead:

experiar quid concedatur in illos
quorum Flaminia tegitur cinis atque Latina. (1.170–1)

For myself, I shall try my hand on the famous dead, whose ashes
Rest beside the Latin and the Flaminian Ways.

And the dangers he envisages as attending the writing of satire are just as artificial, survivals from the past:

pone Tigellinum: taeda lucebis in illa
qua stantes ardent qui fixo gutture fumant,
et latum media sulcum deducis harena. (1.115–17)

But name an Imperial favourite, and you will soon enough
Blaze like these human torches, half-choked, half-grilled to death,
Those calcined corpses they drag with hooks from the arena
And leave a broad black trail behind them in the sand.

Nero's favourite, Tigellinus, is selected to illustrate the risks of the satirist's profession: but Tigellinus is dead, chosen like the other figures to make us recall a stereotype, a past where colours are stronger, but a past that has infected the present, and a past which might recur. Horace had declined to attack any living person when told of the dangers of satire:

sed hic stilus haud petet ultro
quemquam animantem et me ueluti custodiet ensis
uagina tectus. (*Sat.* 2.1.39–41)

But this pen of mine will not gratuitously assail any living person but will protect me, like a sword laid up in its sheath.

That seems to have influenced Juvenal when he professed to restrain his freedom of speech. But at a more general level all three extant satirists appear to have paid court to the rhetorical theory of humour: jests must be constructive, not aimed in any spirit of vindictiveness at accidental defects, directed instead at culpable faults. It would have been illiberal, according to theory, to deliver indiscriminate broadsides at individuals; hence epigram, iambic, and satire – although in the last case there was the related tradition about the legal and personal perils of mentioning names – made the equitable insistence that their verse contained no malice, no *animus* against persons. Instead, although sometimes with irony, and sometimes self-contradiction, they adopted the liberal posture, presuming to defend the individual and his right to anonymous contemplation of vice other than his own. Martial, like the other practitioners of the lower genres, claims to take the general and the typical as his province, disregarding individuals: hence no offence to reputation or privacy. He sums up the doctrine at 7.12.9: *parcere personis, dicere de uitiis* 'to spare the individual, and talk about the vice'. Persons will be spared, in favour of generalities. The policy is stated elsewhere: at the very start, in the preface to Book 1, where he expresses the intention to avoid personal attacks – contrary to the practice of the older authors, meaning Catullus, and probably Lucilius – also in random epigrams scattered throughout the collection, for instance 2.23, 7.12, and 9.95. So when at the end of his first satire, Juvenal talks of the dangers of mentioning names, and says that his intention is to satirize the dead, he not only has in mind the conventional fear of the law relating to libel, but is also sending up the equally conventional theory appertaining to charity in humour. In attacking the dead he pretends to avoid the opprobrium attached to invective against the living – to be devoid of malice, a gentleman acquainted with the polite theories of rhetoric. But his conflation of the dangers of libel with the theory of the liberal jest turns out to be negative and sardonic: by exchanging malice towards the living for malice towards the dead, he incurs the wrath of his reader. For through this deliberately tasteless gesture he implies that his audience is smug and respectable, far too content to view a generalized spectacle of vice from a position of comfort. We do not wish to be reminded of the way we might react to his criticism, of the way that our self-righteouness has necessitated flight from the present and refuge in safe stereotypes taken from the past. True, the exemplary status of names now dead and gone allows satire and epigram a general dimension: rhetorical education ensured a wide publicity for the anecdotes and associations surrounding the names of famous men. *Exempla* literature – typical stories with self-contained morals, like the tale of Cato's Stoic death, or Sulla's cruel proscriptions – provided a storehouse of symbols, a short-hand for satire. But Juvenal, the reader wishes, might have been more tactful in telling us what we want, in reminding us of the rhetorical techniques at his disposal: his fault is that of honesty, of being too explicit about the conventions of his genre – and, it must be said, of wishing to wound through pointed bad taste.[1]

Martial, too, has his share of bad taste, but in theory all is defined and correct. There is no wish to outrage the reader, merely the desire to produce an acceptable shock. As at the feast of the Saturnalia, so in epigram there is the opportunity for a reversal of the normal code of behaviour. But the reversal is institutionalized, as much a part of the Roman way of life as the stern morality of Cato which on occasions it replaces:

triste supercilium durique seuera Catonis
  frons et aratoris filia Fabricii
et personati fastus et regula morum,
  quidquid et in tenebris non sumus, ite foras.
clamant ecce mei 'Io Saturnalia' uersus:
  et licet et sub te praeside, Nerua, libet.
lectores tetrici salebrosum ediscite Santram:
  nil mihi uobiscum est: iste liber meus est. (11.2)

Begone sad frowns and rigid Cato's pursed brow, daughters of Fabricius from the plough, masks of disdain and moral rules – all the things we are not when private in darkened rooms. See, my verse proclaims the Saturnalia: with Nerva as my emperor there is no interdiction: reversal is my pleasure. Go learn by rote the arid pedant Santra,[2] all prudish readers: my business is not with you. This book is mine alone.

Martial is the court jester, his role so well defined that nobody can take offence. Respectable men, orators and statesmen, had written epigrams before him: Pliny cites grave precedents and Martial does as well. Domitian, like Nerva, had been instructed in the topsy-turvy rationale of the form – epigram is not the place for traditional Roman morals:

contigeris nostros, Caesar, si forte libellos,
  terrarum dominum pone supercilium.
consueuere iocos uestri quoque ferre triumphi:
  materiam dictis nec pudet esse ducem.
qua Thymelen spectas derisoremque Latinum,
  illa fronte precor carmina nostra legas.
innocuos censura potest permittere lusus:
  lasciua est nobis pagina, uita proba. (1.4)

If by any chance, Caesar, you come across my books, do not wear the look that sternly rules the world. Your triumphs are accustomed to jests and frivolities, nor is there disrespect when wit sends up a general. I beg you to read my poems with the expression that you have when you watch disreputable mimes. Innocuous verse has no need of a censor: my page is lascivious, my life without rebuke.

[1] On the theory of humour and disclaimer of malice, see further Bramble (1974) 190ff.
[2] A grammarian of Republican times.

Catullus, Ovid, and Pliny had made similar protestations: literature is one thing, life is quite another.[1] Martial has a lot to say about his chosen genre: there are prose prefaces to Books 1, 2, 8, 9 and 12, and in addition many poems which belong to the area of literary apologetics. Epigram is thin – *tenuis*, whereas tragedy and epic are fat – *pinguis*.[2] Martial's poems are *nugae*, or *ioci*, slight occasional pieces, with few literary pretensions. The parallel with mime is frequently adduced. In the preface to Book 1, he mentions the games of Flora:

epigrammata illis scribuntur qui solent spectare Florales

epigram is written for those whose pleasure is in watching the plays at the Floralia.

Similarly, at 9.28 he likens himself to the mimic actor Latinus, calling himself a member of the guild of *mimi*, careful nonetheless to justify his private ways and remain the servant of the emperor:

sed nihil a nostro sumpsit mea uita theatro
  et sola tantum scaenicus arte feror:
nec poteram gratus domino sine moribus esse:
  interius mentes inspicit ille deus.
uos me laurigeri parasitum dicite Phoebi,
  Roma sui famulum dum sciat esse Iouis. (9.28.5–10)

But my own life has not been influenced in any way by the theatre I present, and it is only through my art that I have affinities with mime. Nor could I have pleased the emperor my master if my morals were deficient: that god on earth sees into the recesses of our minds. You may call me a mimic, an inferior member of laurelled Phoebus' guild, as long as Rome is certain that I am a servant of her lord.

Cautious and respectful, Martial has no doubts about his position in society. His mode is *sal Romanus*, Roman wit, more crude and abusive than its Greek counterpart, *sal Atticus*: he has licence, *lasciuia*, *petulantia*, the freedom to say whatever he wants, in a forthright brutal way – this he calls *simplicitas*, the deliberate employment of words which elsewhere would have been shocking and abrupt. But unlike Juvenal the satirist he never intends offence. He will titillate, he will shock: but that is merely part of a game whose rules are known. He is so hedged around with defences, with excuses and apologies, that no exception can be taken.

Finally, before a survey of some elements in Juvenal's satires, a word on Martial's humour, and the structure of his poems. Kruuse[3] makes the distinction between emotional, metaphoric humour, and intellectual, logical humour –

[1] Catull. 16.5–6, Ov. *Trist.* 2.353–60, Plin. *Epist.* 7.9; cf. Apul. *Apol.* 11, Auson. *Idyll.* 360f., *Anth. Pal.* 12.258.

[2] Catullus, his predecessor, is variously called *tenuis*, *argutus*, *lepidus*, *tener*, and *doctus*. Epic is criticized at, for instance, 3.45.1–2; 4.29.8; 4.49.3–6; 5.53.1–2; 9.50; 10.35.5–7; 14.1.11. See above, p. 598, for the realism of epigram, as against epic and tragic bombast; and, e.g., 8.3.19–20 *at tu Romanos lepido sale tingue libellos: | adgnoscat mores uita legatque suos.*

[3] Kruuse (1941) 248f.

the first of which relies upon the single image as the comic vehicle, the second, upon a logical or paradoxical argument, comprehended in entirety. The humour of the single image is obviously self-contained, whilst that of the intellectual, argumentative poem is a function of all its parts. Martial's humour belongs in the main to this second kind, where what matters is the whole, together with the qualities of point and paradox that are dependent on the whole. The preparation for the point, or the paradox, is sometimes amusing in itself, but more often than not, the poem relies upon a witty, intellectual conclusion, without which it would be almost meaningless. Concision and brevity are the distinguishing feature of Martial's final apophthegms. Sometimes it is a single word that concludes the poem, more often, a pair of words, or else a shortish phrase: the tendency is to compress, and jolt the reader's expectations. In terms of organization, there are, according to Kruuse, two main types of structure, the bipartite and the tripartite. In the first, the reader's curiosity is aroused by some statement or proposition, then satisfied by a final commentary or question. In the second, to this basic pattern of proposition and commentary, or proposition and question, a third element is added, usually one of reply: hence we find schemes of proposition–question–reply; question–reply–commentary; and occasionally proposition followed by two questions. Not all of Kruuse's instances are equally convincing, but it is fair to say that the majority of the epigrams fall into the categories he describes; and it is, perhaps, here, in the intellectual organization of his pieces, that Martial's merits most truly reside. His wit is ordered, on occasions too much so, but there is little feeling for language: the words he uses are normally secondary to a governing conceit or an intellectualized scheme.

Juvenal too will build up to a climax, or paradox – but he has more feeling for words, for their epic, or vernacular qualities, and often the force of his wit derives from a single word or phrase, strategically placed at the beginning or end of a line. Sometimes it is the trivial which his rhetorical development sets in relief. Of the many horrors of city life the culmination is – bad poetry under a blazing sun:

ego uel Prochytam praepono Suburae:
nam quid tam miserum, tam solum uidimus, ut non
deterius credas horrere incendia, lapsus
tectorum adsiduos ac mille pericula saeuae
urbis et Augusto recitantes mense poetas? (3.5–9)

Myself, I would value
A barren offshore island more than Rome's urban heart:
Squalor and isolation are minor evils compared
To this endless nightmare of fires and collapsing houses,
The cruel city's myriad perils – and poets reciting
Their work in August*!*

Likewise, in the eighth satire, the technique is to pinpoint the unimportant and the laughable in order to increase our sense of a need for real values. Nero's crimes are comparable to those of Orestes; but the Roman comes out as the worse – because he wrote an epic:

par Agamemnonidae crimen, sed causa facit rem
dissimilem: quippe ille deis auctoribus ultor
patris erat caesi media inter pocula. sed nec
Electrae iugulo se polluit aut Spartani
sanguine coniugii, nullis aconita propinquis
miscuit, in scaena numquam cantauit Orestes,
Troica non scripsit. (8.215–21)

Orestes' crime was the same, but circumstances made it
A very dissimilar case – he *killed with divine sanction*
To avenge a father slain in his cups. Orestes never
Had Electra's blood on his head, he never murdered
His Spartan wife, or mixed up a dose of belladonna
For any close relative. He *never sang on the stage*
Or composed a Trojan epic.

In both of these cases Juvenal reserves his paradox till the end of a progression, but the development is less highly organized than the type we find in epigram. There is nothing especially intellectual about either of these passages – and perhaps that is one reason why we sense a kind of nihilism. Nor is there an obvious structure in the way he arrives at his point. Instinctive and emotional – albeit with reserve – Juvenal lies in wait with his apparent moral anarchy to shock us into judgement. His procedure is accumulative and verbal, the opposite of Martial's.

Juvenal is preoccupied with realities – trivial, sordid, and irksome – yet there is little *simplicitas*, little of Martial's candid speaking. He values words too highly, and cannot resist hyperbole: his verse is loud, though brittle, its texture rich, concerned for much of the time with setting the past against the present, the noble against the real, or simply with the glorification of horrors and vices that go beyond all precedent. As Quintilian says: *tum est hyperbole uirtus, cum res ipsa, de qua loquendum est, naturalem modum excessit* 'hyperbole is permissible, when the subject matter to be discussed is something which has exceeded all natural limits' (*Inst.* 8.6.76). Hence, because of Juvenal's conception that vice is at its peak, the exaggerations, the grandiloquence – the struggle to create a grotesque yet epic pageant out of the Rome that inhabits his mind. At the outset of this study, we referred to Satire 6, and Juvenal's departure from the tradition of Persius and Horace: because the Medeas and Clytemnestras of myth are now once more alive, active and horrific in contemporary Rome, the *lex priorum* no longer holds, and stronger language is needed. He will rifle the resources of the tragedians and epicists, since life is larger than myth. We have seen from Satire 8 that Nero's crimes were worse than those of Agamemnon's son. And we find a similar lesson in his account of cannibalism in Egypt:

nos miranda quidem, sed nuper consule Iunco
gesta super calidae referemus moenia Copti,
nos uolgi scelus et cunctis grauiora cothurnis,
nam scelus, a Pyrrha quamquam omnia syrmata uoluas,
nullus apud tragicos populus facit. accipe, nostro
dira quod exemplum feritas produxerit aeuo. (15.27–32)

The incident I *shall relate,*
Though fantastic enough, took place within recent memory,
Up-country from sunbathed Coptos, an act of mob violence
Worse than anything in the tragedians. Search through the mythical
Canon from Pyrrha onwards, you won't find an instance of a
Collective crime. Now attend, and learn what kind of novel
Atrocity our *day and age has added to history.*

Juvenal, typically, has just written a review of Ulysses' after-dinner tales, casting doubt on their credibility. Reality, as he says, exceeds the proportions of myth: hence why should he submit to a set of stylistic laws which were evolved for the description of follies and minor offences? Horace's bland disquisitions and Persius' self-assured sermons are therefore replaced by parodistic flights of sublimity and a wryly anarchic *terribilità*.

Yet the effect is not always unconstructive. True, his mock heroics occasionally do little more than exaggerate vice to epic proportions – without a reminder that life could be noble. But sometimes through the parody we glimpse a nostalgia for lost ideals, and a more honest, worthwhile world: although even then there is often a pessimism that curbs simplistic faith in the past. When he calls his compatriots '*Troiugenae*', as he is fond of doing, he invokes grand associations: but if he writes about the past, he will often undercut that too.[1] Pathic Otho with his mirror occasions evocation of Turnus' spoils in war:

ille tenet speculum, pathici gestamen Othonis,
Actoris Aurunci spolium, quo se ille uidebat
armatum, cum iam tolli uexilla iuberet. (2.99–101)

Here's another clutching a mirror – just like that fag of an
Emperor Otho, who peeked at himself to see how his armour looked
Before riding into battle.

This time the upshot is positive: the Virgilian quotation works, like the catalogue of heroes in the poem's finale, as a touchstone for judgement:

[1] For the place of allusions to the heroic past in Roman satire see Bramble (1974) 29ff., and Lelièvre (1958) 22–5.

Curius quid sentit et ambo
Scipiadae, quid Fabricius manesque Camilli,
quid Cremerae legio et Cannis consumpta iuuentus,
tot bellorum animae, quotiens hinc talis ad illos
umbra uenit? (2.153–7)

how would our great dead captains
Greet such a new arrival? And what about the flower
Of our youth who died in battle, our slaughtered legionaries,
Those myriad shades of war?

Here, the indignation is pure, unsullied by comedy – even though Juvenal has only recently made a farce out of the infernal geography inhabited by the great ghosts. Likewise, *pace* Mason, the *divina tomacula porci* at the end of the tenth satire are merely a humorous, indignant finale to a solid and stoical comment on life: yes, by all means pray, for something that matters, but please avoid nonsensical ritual. But elsewhere epic allusion has no obvious moral function – as, for example, in the reference to Meleager during the fifth satire's lavish menu:

anseris ante ipsum magni iecur, anseribus par
altilis, et flaui dignus ferro Meleagri
spumat aper. post hunc tradentur tubera, si uer
tunc erit et facient optata tonitrua cenas
maiores. 'tibi habe frumentum,' Alledius inquit,
'O Libye, disiunge boues, dum tubera mittas.' (5.114–19)

Himself is served with a force-fed goose's liver,
A capon as big as the goose itself, and a spit-roast
Boar, all piping hot, well worthy of fair-haired
Meleager's steel. Afterwards, if it's spring time,
And there's been sufficient thunder to bring them on,
Truffles appear. 'Ah Africa!' cries the gourmet,
'You can keep your grain supply, unyoke your oxen,
So long as you send us truffles!'

In this passage, the mythological reference is cynical, serving to do little more than amaze us with the host Virro's propensity for show: the moral sting is reserved for Alledius' words, with their insistence on gourmandise to the detriment of nature, and ordinary people. As in the case of the black image of the pike fed on sewage at line 105, the idea is one of a natural order perverted by civilized whim – a notion found slightly earlier in this satire, at lines 92ff., where greed is described as having despoiled all the seas.

Epic and tragic allusions are rife, often positive, as reminders of bygone ideals, sometimes negative, as reinforcements of Juvenal's caricatures of evil, but sometimes merely neutral, yet another aspect of his fondness for epideixis. A favourite device is the intrusion of vernacular elements: obscenities, diminutives, Grecisms, words from the lower literary strata – these have the function of insisting on reality, and when they are placed next to grandiloquent language, what often greets us is a sense of dislocation, a feeling that there is a gap between life as it might be and life as it is.[1] Satire 4 is a case in point, where, with admirable control, Juvenal manipulates the associations of epic, and the silly business about the catching of the fish, in order to impress us with the notion that Rome is sick, unworthy of the pompous assumptions with which she hides her weakness. Epicisms here are at one and the same time cynical and positive: cynical because the trappings are vain, mere cloaks for deformity, but positive in that the language employed to describe them looks back to earlier days when Rome could take pride in an empire. Juvenal constantly belabours us with military and imperial allusion, contrasting it with diction which pinpoints cold realities. He begins with a preamble about Crispinus and a mullet: if an upstart Egyptian can spend so much on a fish, what should we expect when it comes to the tastes of the master of the world? The high style first appears when Crispinus buys his fish:

mullum sex milibus emit,
aequantem sane paribus sestertia libris,
ut perhibent qui de magnis maiora loquuntur. (4.15–17)

He bought a red
Mullet for sixty gold pieces – ten for each pound weight,
To make it sound more impressive.

Soon, Crispinus and the fish are put into perspective by the use of ordinary language:

hoc tu,
succinctus patria quondam, Crispine, papyro?
hoc pretio squamas?

Did you *pay so much for a fish, Crispinus, you who once*
Went around in a loin-cloth of your native papyrus?

Through the delayed and unexpected gibe in *papyro*, and the bald realism of *squamas*, the pretence is undermined. But better is to come, in the passage of transition from Crispinus to Domitian, where low and high language meet, to remind us of what Rome should be, and thereby indict the sordid actualities that are hidden by mere names:

qualis tunc epulas ipsum gluttisse putamus
induperatorem, cum tot sesertia, partem
exiguam et modicae sumptam de margine cenae,
purpureus magni ructauit scurra Palati;
iam princeps equitum, magna qui uoce solebat
uendere municipes fracta de merce siluros? (4.28–33)

[1] For Juvenal's diction, see in particular Anderson (1961) 51–87; also id. (1957) 33–90.

what kind of menu was it
That the Emperor guzzled himself, I wonder, when all that gold –
Just a fraction of the whole, the merest modest side-dish –
Was belched up by this purple-clad Palace nark, this
Senior knight who once went bawling his wares
(Job-lots of catfish from some wholesaler's auction)
Through the Alexandrian back-streets?

In the tension between the vernacular *gluttisse* and the epic archaism *induperatorem*, Juvenal summarizes his amusement and despair: Rome has sunk from her one-time magnificence into greed and self-abasement. His moral is the same in line 31, where *purpureus* and *magni* promise great things, only to be belied by the vulgarity of the two words which follow, *ructauit* and *scurra.* Finally, through the juxtaposition of the line about catfish and the official elevation of the title *princeps equitum*, the initial invective is completed; the old order is dead, replaced by a travesty. Now, after an ironic invocation of the muse, and an insistence that his story is true, Juvenal launches into the main part of his satire with full-blown epic parody:

cum iam semianimum laceraret Flauius orbem
ultimus et caluo seruiret Roma Neroni,
incidit Hadriaci spatium admirabile rhombi;
ante domum Veneris, quam Dorica sustinet Ancon,
impleuitque sinus... (4.37–41)

In the days when the last Flavian was flaying a half-dead world,
And Rome was in thrall to a bald Nero, there swam
Into a net in the Adriatic, hard by Ancona,
Where the shrine of Venus stands on her headland, a monstrous
Turbot, a regular whopper...

Once more, the idea is that life is a hyperbole, hence warrants epic diction: foreign enemies and threats to the state have now given way to turbots. High-sounding words are used, but the whole thing is a mockery:

iam letifero cedente pruinis
autumno, iam quartanam sperantibus aegris,
stridebat deformis hiems praedamque recentem
seruabat; tamen hic properat, uelut urgueat auster.
utque lacus suberant, ubi quamquam diruta seruat
ignem Troianum et Vestam colit Alba minorem,
obstitit intranti miratrix turba parumper.
ut cessit, facili patuerunt cardine ualuae;
exclusi spectant admissa obsonia patres.
itur ad Atriden. (4.56–65)

Now autumn
With its pestilential winds was yielding to winter's frosts;
Now patients were hopeful for milder, third-day fevers,
And icy blasts helped keep the turbot refrigerated.
On sped the fisherman, as though blown by a south wind,
Till below him lay the lakes where Alba, though in ruins,
Still guards the flame of Troy and the lesser Vestal shrine.
A wondering crowd thronged around him, blocking his way for a little
Till the doors on their smooth hinges swung inward, the crowd gave way,
And the Senators – still shut out – saw the fish admitted to
The Imperial Presence.

Domitian is anyone but *Atrides*, a second Agamenmon. He is as unworthy of that title as the Senate are of theirs – and that idea is paralleled by the epic paraphernalia about the time of year: another context might deserve it, but certainly not the present, where nature does her utmost, in the highest of all diction, to keep the turbot fresh. Similarly, the palace doors swing open with too much drama. But Juvenal is not just mocking the apotheosis of the trivial: the Trojan fire and Vesta remind us of Rome's heritage, saving the epic parody from its potentially negative status. For we remember that such language has a more appropriate, noble use, and that memory once stirred gives direction to the satire.

Not that Juvenal's cynicism normally falls into abeyance when he has past ideals in mind. One of his favourite formulae is the contrast *olim...nunc*:[1] the present is quite ghastly, but the past is seldom entirely spared. Sometimes his anarchic instinct will not leave well alone, and then all values seem to crumble. But more often than not, there is a saving humour which leaves the principle intact, even though the myth might be inadequate in some ways. We catch him on the verge of dissolving our convictions – but usually he stops short of the seemingly inevitable iconoclasm, by converting his disillusionment into a joke, or importing the insinuation that salvation might be possible, if only we were more subtle, less dedicated to the search for facile panaceas, and more prone to acquiesce in a recognized second best. His third satire is full of this – a realistic spirit which refuses to regard a rustic moral archaism as a simple or obvious cure. Where Horace had no doubts about the ethical value of his farm – the medicinal properties of his stream, the simplicity of his diet, above all, the mental hygiene of a life in accordance with nature – Juvenal's moral pastoral, like the 'frugal' dinner of Satire 11, has no mildness or composure, no pretence to self-assurance. In his account of the country festival at lines 171ff., he comes nearest to commitment, but even here there is something which fails to convince us entirely – a brittleness of tone, and something ridiculous in the

[1] See Bramble (1974) 30 n. 1.

image of the *rusticus infans*. Likewise his recommendation of a house out in the provinces turns into a miniature satire of the values supposedly espoused:

hortulus hic puteusque breuis nec reste mouendus
in tenues plantas facili diffunditur haustu.
uiue bidentis amans et culti uilicus horti.
unde epulum possis centum dare Pythagoreis. (3.226–9)

A garden-plot is thrown in
With the house itself, and a well with a shallow basin –
No rope-and-bucket work when your seedlings need some water.
Learn to enjoy hoeing, work and plant your allotment
Till a hundred vegetarians could feast off its produce.

Horace, too, had his joke about the vegetarian Pythagoreans. But Juvenal is more abrasive, and there is worse to come:

est aliquid, quocumque loco, quocumque recessu
unius sese dominum fecisse lacertae. (3.230–1)

It's quite an achievement, even out in the backwoods,
To have made yourself master of, well, say one lizard, even.

The joke about the lizard is rather weak, but the procedure is quite typical: a Parthian shot let loose, at the very end of a section, at a set of ideas which have hitherto been promoted. Towards the close of the satire we find the same technique, but employed with less bad taste:

qua fornace graues, qua non incude catenae?
maximus in uinclis ferri modus, ut timeas ne
uomer deficiat, ne marrae et sarcula desint.
felices proauorum atauos, felicia dicas
saecula, quae quondam sub regibus atque tribunis
uiderunt uno contentam carcere Romam. (3.309–14)

Our furnaces glow, our anvils
Groan everywhere under their output of chains and fetters.
That's where most of our iron goes nowadays: one wonders
Whether ploughshares, hoes and mattocks may not soon be obsolete.
How fortunate they were (you may well think), those early
Forbears of ours, how happy the good old days
Of kings and tribunes, when Rome made do with one prison only.

Deliberate scurrility is absent from the passage: but even though the echoes of Virgil in the lines about the farm implements produce a moral insistence on the virtues of agriculture – albeit that in Virgil it was epic swords, not mean, ignoble fetters, that were forged from the innocent ploughshare[1] – there is treachery afoot in Juvenal's parting gesture, in the cynical suggestion that even Rome's heroic days harboured a few criminals.

[1] Virg. *Geo.* 1.506f. and *Aen.* 7.635f.

Likewise Juvenal has his fun at the expense of the golden age proper. At the opening of the sixth satire, the times traditionally extolled by idealizing poets are amusingly transformed into an uncomfortable prelude to corruption and decay. But amidst the sardonic humour there is the thought that at least in those backward days women looked like women:

credo Pudicitiam Saturno rege moratam
in terris uisamque diu, cum frigida paruas
praeberet spelunca domos ignemque Laremque
et pecus et dominos communi clauderet umbra,
siluestrem montana torum cum sterneret uxor
frondibus et culmo uicinarumque ferarum
pellibus, haut similis tibi, Cynthia, nec tibi, cuius
turbauit nitidos extinctus passer ocellos,
sed potanda ferens infantibus ubera magnis
et saepe horridior glandem ructante marito. (6.1–10)

During Saturn's reign I believe that Chastity still
Lingered on earth, and was seen for a while, when draughty
Caves were the only homes men had, hearth fire and household
Goods, family and cattle all shut in darkness together.
Wives were different then – a far cry from Cynthia,
Or the girl who wept, red-eyed, for that sparrow's death.
Bred to the woods and mountains, they made their beds from
Dry leaves and straw, from the pelts of savage beasts
Caught prowling the neighbourhood. Their breasts gave suck
To big strong babies; often, indeed, they were shaggier
Than their acorn-belching husbands.

Juvenal concedes a point with his comparison to the poetic mistresses, Cynthia and Lesbia – but then, typically, he half retracts it, in his unattractive portrait of the caveman's full-blown wife. But half the point remains: cavewomen were closer to nature than the corseted specimens of today. Irreverence is similarly the keynote of the golden age picture drawn in the thirteenth satire. Here Juvenal writes of the gods, and their forfeited innocence, perhaps developing a point from the preamble to Satire 6, where, a few lines later than the passage just quoted, Jupiter's age is an index of honesty:

multa Pudicitiae ueteris uestigia forsan
aut aliqua exstiterint et sub Ioue, sed Ioue nondum
barbato, nondum Graecis iurare paratis
per caput alterius... (6.14–17)

Some few traces, perhaps, of Chastity's ancient presence
Survived under Jove – but only while Jove remained
A beardless stripling, long before Greeks had learnt
To swear by the other man's head, or capital...

But in Satire 13, the message is clearer, written up in a more leisurely manner. A broader humour, even signs of humanity, replace the accustomed malevolent posture – the old anger and indignation have gone:

quondam hoc indigenae uiuebant more, priusquam
sumeret agrestem posito diademate falcem
Saturnus fugiens, tunc cum uirguncula Iuno
et priuatus adhuc Idaeis Iuppiter antris;
nulla super nubes conuiuia caelicolarum,
nec puer Iliacus formosa nec Herculis uxor
ad cyathos, et iam siccato nectare tergens
bracchia Vulcanus Liparaea nigra taberna;
prandebat sibi quisque deus, nec turba deorum
talis ut est hodie, contentaque sidera paucis
numinibus miserum urguebant Atlanta minori
pondere; nondum imi sortitus triste profundi
imperium Sicula toruos cum coniuge Pluton,
nec rota nec Furiae nec saxum aut uolturis atri
poena, sed infernis hilares sine regibus umbrae. (13.38–52)

That was how primitive man lived long ago, before
King Saturn was ousted, before he exchanged his diadem
For a country sickle, when Juno was only a schoolgirl,
And Jupiter – then without title – still dwelt in Ida's caves.
No banquets above the clouds yet for Heaven's inhabitants,
With Hebe and Ganymede there to hand round drinks, and Vulcan,
Still black from the smithy, scrubbing the soot off his arms
With spirits of – nectar. Each God would breakfast in private;
There wasn't our modern rabble of divinities, the stars
Ran to far fewer deifications, the firmament rested lighter
On poor old Atlas' back. The throne of the nether regions
Stood vacant still – grim Pluto and his Sicilian consort,
The Furies, Ixion's wheel, the boulder of Sisyphus,
The black and murderous vulture, all these were yet to come:
While they'd got no monarch, the shades could enjoy a high old time.

Charm is hardly a quality one would usually associate with Juvenal – but here, at last, the wryness is fetching, not acid; the tone comic, not abrasive. Not that we really believe in the one-time innocence of the gods: but at least our satirist looks closer now to laughter than to bitterness or tears.[1] We admit his parody this time because it does not threaten us.

But, as we began by saying, it is for his earlier work that Juvenal is remembered: and there the world was out of joint, in almost all its aspects. Even our positives, our favourite opinions were subject to his scrutiny, and often his

[1] On the transition from the indignation of Satires 1–6 to the laughter of Satires 10–16 (arguing that the third book is transitional) see Anderson (1964) 174ff.

derision. Juvenal – the Juvenal, predominantly, of Satires 1 to 6 – allows us no moral respite, no refuge from his questions. Yet despite his treachery and deceptions – and one of them is pretending that the experience is literary, that all is words and rhetoric, a commodity made to please – despite his peevish aggression, towards the reader and his values, his uncharitable arrogance, something emerges which is tenuously hopeful, potentially constructive – the plain idea that honesty, though nasty, even vile, can direct us past appearances to see truths that live within. Contact may be sickening, when façades are stripped away: but interior truths once recognized, amendment can begin.

30

MINOR POETRY

I. PHAEDRUS

Phaedrus holds no exalted rank amongst Latin poets, but he claims serious attention by his choice of subject matter and his individualistic treatment of it. He was, as far as we know, the first poet, Greek or Roman, to put together a collection of fables and present them as literature in their own right, not merely as material on which others might draw. And on this collection he firmly imprinted his own personality, complacent, querulous, cantankerous. In prologues, epilogues, and occasionally elsewhere he reveals his grievances and aspirations. His fables contain elements of satire and 'social comment', not at all gentle: if he had chosen to write satire proper, he might have vied with Juvenal in trenchancy and bitterness.

Animal fables, usually purveying a simple moral, have a long prehistory in folklore. Thereafter they provided speakers and writers with a ready store of homely illustrations and precepts. The Greeks of the fourth century B.C. ascribed a mass of these fables to the wise and witty slave Aesop: how many of those which survive in fact go back to this shadowy figure we do not know, but we approach firmer ground with the collection of fables, attributed to Aesop or in the Aesopian tradition, compiled in prose by Demetrius of Phalerum (*c.* 300 B.C.). This book itself is lost (unless some parts have come to light on a papyrus)[1], but very probably it was Phaedrus' main source, perhaps his only source. We know of no other collections available to him. Certain recurrent features in Phaedrus may well derive from Demetrius, in particular *promythia*, initial statements of theme or moral, intended originally for the convenience of orators or others in search of illustrations. By couching his fables in verse Phaedrus gave them literary pretensions: they could no longer be regarded as rough material, to be shaped by others, for now the poet himself has done the polishing (1 *prol.* 1–2). Brevity is the virtue on which he most prides himself or which he feels conscious he must attain (2 *prol.* 12, 3 *epil.* 8, 4 *epil.* 7), but he is also aware of the need for variety (2 *prol.* 10) and strives to achieve it. He had virtually no precedents to guide him, since hitherto

[1] See Perry (1965) xiv–xv.

fables had appeared only incidentally in poetry, as in Horace amongst others, sometimes elaborated, sometimes brief. Horace's carefully developed story of the town and country mouse (*Sat.* 2.6.79–117) possesses a delicate humour worlds removed from the crude psychology which Phaedrus regularly offers. We have something nearer to Phaedrus' manner in the story of the fox and the corn-bin (*Epist.* 1.7.29–33). No doubt Horace had some influence on him, but it was not very deep. Phaedrus stands apart from the main stream of Augustan and post-Augustan poetry.

Demetrius' single book of fables could not supply Phaedrus with sufficient number or variety of themes. And so, particularly in Books 3–5, he adds much new material of his own (see 4 *prol.* 11–13), in part of contemporary interest, Roman rather than Greek. Hence such poems as 2.5 (the emperor Tiberius and the officious footman), 3.10 (the woman falsely suspected of adultery), and 5.7 (the inordinate conceit of the musician Princeps). In thus using the fable as a vehicle for very diverse themes Phaedrus is not uniformly successful, nor can he sustain overall the qualities of simplicity and artlessness which he affects. 3.10 and 5.7 are long-winded and tedious, as is 4.11 (the thief and the lamp), a fable more in the Aesopian vein, but apparently Phaedrus' own creation (see ll. 14–15). He is more interesting when he writes of his own poetry, as in 4.7, a derisive riposte to a detractor, reminiscent in some respects both of Persius and Martial. But even here, by clumsily appending an *epimythium* quite out of place in a personal poem, he reveals that he is ill at ease with his medium.

At the outset Phaedrus affirms that his purpose is to amuse and instruct, and he discharges this intention as best he can, baldly obtruding instruction in *promythia* or *epimythia*. He may, intermittently at least, have another, ulterior purpose, covertly to allude to circumstances and personalities of his day. We learn from 3 *prol.* 38ff. that he fell foul of Sejanus. What poems in Books 1–2 excited Sejanus' anger we cannot tell: they may, of course, be amongst those now lost. Phaedrus says (3 *prol.* 49–50) that he does not seek to brand individuals, but to display the manners of society generally. Whether that be true or not, it is not surprising that he caused offence, for the Romans of this period were alert to *double-entendre* and quick to sense an affront. And he does not always veil his thoughts: thus 1.1 is explicitly directed against those who 'use trumped-up charges to crush the innocent' and 1.15 is devised to illustrate that 'on a change in government the poor merely get a master with a different name'. For one of his humble status Phaedrus is singularly outspoken. And he is no *detrectator sui*: 3 *prol.* ought to have been a modest apologia, but it proves to be an impudent self-justification. Housman said that Phaedrus' 'spiritual home was the stable and the farmyard'. He might, one may feel, have been even more at home in the Subura: he would certainly not have denied that 'the proper study of mankind is man'.

Phaedrus' language is generally plain and commonplace, occasionally coarse. He admits colloquial and prosaic terms avoided by most of the poets. He does not try to create a distinct style for his fables: at the most we may discern a few mannerisms and favourite expressions. He chose to employ senarii like those of the early dramatists rather than the more restrictive trimeters used by Catullus and Horace amongst others: the looser verse-form was indeed better suited to his motley subject matter and unselective vocabulary. Linguistically he shows much similarity to satire and epigram, and a marked affinity to mime, as represented by the excerpted *sententiae* of Publilius Syrus.

Phaedrus has certain merits. Like Publilius, he can point a memorable phrase. His stories can be charmingly lucid and simple. But they would have been much improved by excision of *promythia*: here was a *damnosa hereditas* from Demetrius which, for all his independence, Phaedrus lacked the good sense to abandon. Again, his brevity is not always commendable: many of the fables seem flat and jejune, devoid of the detail and colour which their subjects invited. In antiquity Phaedrus won little recognition. He is ignored by all first-century writers, with the possible exception of Martial.[1] And when at a later day Phaedrus' poems were recast into prose, his name was removed from them. Avianus knew of his work, but scarcely used it, preferring to follow Babrius. Nowadays he seems wholly to have lost the appeal which he exercised in the seventeenth and eighteenth centuries. Yet animal stories are more popular now than ever before, although (or because) our society as a whole is remote from countryside and farmyard. Phaedrus' fall from favour may be explained variously. Only limited time is now available in schools for Latin reading and we tend to concentrate from the start on a few major authors. Again, moralizing has long been out of fashion, and Phaedrus' moralizing is trite and wearisome. Seneca has suffered a similar neglect for similar reasons, though we have recently seen a revival of interest in his works. Perhaps Phaedrus too will obtain some rehabilitation, but one may doubt it. His poems possess neither the substance nor the vigour nor the imagination necessary to secure them against the test of time.

2. CALPURNIUS SICULUS

That the seven eclogues of Calpurnius, the two Einsiedeln eclogues, and the panegyric on Piso all date from Nero's principate has long been accepted doctrine. They originate perhaps from a single literary coterie, centred upon the

[1] Mart. 3.20.5 *aemulatur improbi locos Phaedri* 'he imitates the passages [*sic*] of naughty Phaedrus', is doubly problematic. The paradosis *locos* is untenable and may reasonably be corrected to *iocos* 'jests' or *logos* 'fables'. The latter correction, if right, would strongly suggest that the fabulist is meant. But we cannot be sure that it is right. Again, it is debatable whether *improbus* fits the Phaedrus we know.

patron represented as Meliboeus in Calp. 1 and 4. Enthusiasm about a new golden age, evinced both by Calpurnius and the Einsiedeln poet, links these writers together and accords with other evidence for the optimism and sense of revival which seem to have marked Nero's accession to power. The period was prolific in literature, major and minor, and some modern critics attempt to determine the relationships which obtained between various writers or groups. Not enough evidence exists to support such reconstructions. And recently the conventional dating of Calpurnius' poems has itself been called in question.

Calpurnius is overshadowed by Theocritus and Virgil, who provided his main inspiration. But he kept bucolic poetry alive by somewhat extending its scope: though he acknowledges Virgil as a supreme model (4.64ff.), he does not entirely restrict himself to the paths which Virgil has trodden. Three of Calpurnius' eclogues (1, 4, 7) are more fully and obviously concerned with contemporary affairs than any of Virgil's, except (arguably) his fourth. In that poem (1–3) Virgil would fain excuse his unusual theme, but Calpurnius adopts such themes unhesitatingly, though he is careful to frame them still within a background of fantasy. Again, he draws readily upon other genres, particularly love elegy (3.45–91), didactic (5), and descriptive epigram (7.23–72). That is not wholly surprising, for bucolic had always been flexible: witness Theocritus' versatility, and Virg. *Ecl.* 6 and 10, which include material from 'miniature epic' and elegy. Certainly, by Calpurnius' time, variation on exclusively pastoral themes, limited in range, would have been uninteresting and arid. He had to offer something of a mixture: purism was not then in fashion in Latin poetry, if it ever had been.

Calpurnius' book of eclogues has an intentionally patterned structure: the first, central, and concluding poems (1, 4, 7) relate to the real world around him, while the others (2, 3, 5, 6) stand, ostensibly at least, apart from present circumstances. Again, the poems which have dialogue throughout (2, 4, 6) are interwoven with those which contain long monologues (1, 3, 5, 7). These patterns are plain enough, but what they signify, if anything of importance, is not easy to grasp. Further, while *Ecl.* 1 might well date from the beginning of Nero's rule (A.D. 54 or 55) and *Ecl.* 7 from some years later (not before A.D. 57), the order of the poems does not necessarily reflect sequence of composition. Some scholars argue that *Ecl.* 3, to their taste the crudest of the collection, is the earliest, and perhaps pre-Neronian. It may be so, but such arguments bring us on to perilously subjective ground.

Calpurnius' language is neither colourless nor wholly derivative. He had powers of observation and could deftly describe details or scenes. And he is generally quite lucid and unaffected. Though no ancient writer mentions

Calpurnius, he had a competent imitator in Nemesianus, who might have bypassed him and reverted directly to Virgil, and he is known to a few even later poets.

3. 'BUCOLICA EINSIDLENSIA'

These two incomplete and enigmatic eclogues may be dated to Nero's principate, but not to an exact time within it. 1.38ff. alludes to Nero's *Troica* as contemporary, but in what year that work first stunned the world is uncertain. The second poem is concerned with a new golden age, introduced by a ruler who assimilates himself to Apollo. This fits Nero, and best perhaps his early years. We cannot be sure that the poems are by the same author, but a few minor metrical differences do not preclude common authorship. It is notable, however, that *Buc.* 2, unlike *Buc.* 1, diverges from tradition in sometimes changing speakers within lines.

In the first eclogue two shepherds compete in singing the praises of the poet-emperor. The flattery which they effuse is exceptionally extravagant, and when, at 48–9, Mantua is represented as so conscious of Virgil's inferiority to Nero that it seeks to obliterate his works, we may well wonder whether the intention is not comic and derisive. The second eclogue is not a little perplexing. One of the speakers says that his joy is disturbed by care, and, pressed for explanation, that satiety is his trouble. Then he describes the blissful security which all may now enjoy. Perhaps he is playing with the old idea that peace is morally enervating, and, if so, offering a back-handed compliment to Nero's regime. There is thus a *prima facie* case for taking neither poem at face-value: sometimes, after all, impotent malice obtains refuge in riddles. The alternative is to dismiss both of them as vacuous and incoherent. The obscurity and clumsiness of their expression encourage the latter view, but the mutilation of the text enjoins hesitance.

4. 'LAUS PISONIS'

The 'Panegyric on Piso' is a distinctly odd composition and, if the poet expected Piso to approve of what he says, addressed to a distinctly odd person. He says first that Piso's personal qualities outshine his distinguished ancestry, then that he has won no military glory, but earned fame as a speaker in the courts and Senate (yet only a ceremonial speech is mentioned), and next, in 81–208 (about half of the poem), that he is affable, generous, and devoted to laudable recreations, cultural and physical, including a certain board game (190–208), at which he conspicuously excels. Having said this, he affirms (210) that Piso's merits defy adequate record, then importunes this up-to-date nobleman to become his patron, pointing out that the writers whom Maecenas favoured never feared an impoverished old age, and concludes by stating that he is not yet twenty. On first reading one might suppose the poem's aim to be other than it purports, even indeed that it is a burlesque. But its absurdities are not blatant enough to bear out this view. Much may be imputed to mere incompetence. Again, if the poem was indeed written under Nero, the writer had a delicate task: he could hardly extol military talents, proven or latent. It might have been better to abandon a hopeless enterprise: certainly the recurrent apologia seems very jarring in a eulogy. We may recall the inept *Elegies on Maecenas*. They, however, were posthumous and their subject retained general interest. Piso was no such subject, though perhaps he seemed to be to a circle of dependants. Altogether much in the *Laus Pisonis* remains unexplained.

The poem's style is commonplace and usually unexceptionable, sometimes bathetic or long-winded (e.g. 140ff.). In language and metre we find some affinities with Calpurnius and, to a lesser extent, with Lucan. Exact dating is unattainable.

5. 'AETNA'

Mt Etna, the most spectacular volcano known to antiquity, had challenged the descriptive skill of several poets, Pindar and Virgil amongst them. But no one, it seems, before the anonymous author of the didactic poem *Aetna* had in prose or verse attempted a separate and detailed treatment of volcanic activity. Those authorities, such as Posidonius, upon whom the *Aetna* depends treated volcanoes along with earthquakes, not separately. The conception of the poem is thus original, if its execution is not.

The *Aetna* is only 645 verses long, but it has a protracted introduction, in which the poet rejects mythological lore and poetic fancy, then emphasizes his own concern with truth. He proceeds to describe the earth's crust, which permits the activity of volcanoes. Then he begins to explain the cause of this activity, subterranean winds under high pressure, but breaks off into a lengthy digression on the value of natural science. Having at last dealt with the cause, he turns to discuss the fuel, lava-stone, on which volcanoes feed. Then, scientific discussion concluded, he adds an epilogue, first comparing natural spectacles with those of artistic or historical interest, and finally relating the story of the brothers of Catania. Various arguments converge to place the poem in the mid first century A.D. Clear debts to Ovid and Manilius show that it is post-Augustan. The brief, allusive references to mythological themes at 17ff. recall the impatience of Persius, amongst others, with such material. And very striking similarities in thought and expression to Seneca's *Natural questions* indicate a closer connexion with that work than merely a common source. The absence of any mention of Vesuvius gives A.D. 79 as a *terminus ante quem*.

A profound obligation to Lucretius (especially Book 6) is evident in thought and structure. The main scientific part of the poem is carefully divided into sections and subsections. Fallacious views are diligently refuted. And the poet repeatedly insists on a need for concrete evidence from the senses or appeals to graphic analogies. If his argumentation has one great fault, it is that he drives home his points too laboriously and unremittingly. In rejecting mythology (yet in the end using it), in asserting the virtues of his own approach, and in moralizing about worthwhile pursuits, he adopts attitudes conventional in didactic poetry and familiar elsewhere. Nevertheless, one detects in his writing a genuine enthusiasm for his task. Textual corruption makes it hard to assess the literary quality of the poem, but plainly its vocabulary is limited and its phraseology repetitious. Sometimes ideas and phrases flow easily, sometimes they seem halting and uneasy. The poet draws heavily on Lucretius, Virgil and Ovid, yet he is no slavish imitator. We find here nothing like the fumbling patchwork which disfigures the *Culex* and *Ciris*. We also find little distinctive or specially interesting, except a liking for personification and skilful use of various imagery, particularly that of warfare. The *Aetna* is not devoid of merit. One may applaud its firm structure, its earnest tone, its controlled and occasionally effective rhetoric. But it lacks freshness, warmth and imagination. Few Latin poems so completely fail to involve the reader.

6. EPIGRAMS ASCRIBED TO SENECA AND PETRONIUS

Amongst the Latin epigrams transmitted from antiquity are about a hundred, mainly in elegiacs, a few in other metres, which have, with varying degrees of plausibility, been ascribed to Seneca and Petronius. In nine cases out of ten the ascription is modern, and susceptible neither of proof nor disproof: the most we can usually do is to record the presence or absence of similarities in thought and expression between these poems and the authentic works of the two authors. Language and metre show scarcely any clear indications of composition later than the first century A.D., but, given the limited extent of the material and the conservatism of epigrammatic style, this negative consideration is not very weighty. Again, caution is enjoined both by the well known tendency for pieces originally anonymous to be fathered on a famous writer (witness the *Appendix Vergiliana*) and by the equally well known proneness of anonymous items in anthologies to be taken as belonging to the named authors of preceding items.

One or two of the poems ascribed to Seneca relate explicitly or very probably to his exile (*Anth. Lat.* 409, 236–7), while others treat of matters which interested him (though not him alone), such as mortality (*Anth. Lat.* 232), Cato (*Anth. Lat.* 397–9), and contempt for fortune (*Anth. Lat.* 444). One group of verses, on Claudius' British triumph (*Anth. Lat.* 419–26), seems to be fixed at Seneca's time by its subject matter, but other pieces look like variations on standard themes, such as Xerxes' expedition (*Anth. Lat.* 442, 461) and the fate of Pompey (*Anth. Lat.* 400–4), or school exercises (*Anth. Lat.* 462–3). Competence, and nothing higher, is the level attained. If a single writer is involved, he was one who did not always know when to stop. The treatment of the conquest of Britain is tediously repetitive and the indictment of the deceptions of hope (*Anth. Lat.* 415) labours under an excess of examples (contrast Tib. 2.6.19–28). These faults are perhaps not alien from Seneca. But where are his habitual merits? Pungency, for instance, is often lacking where it is most required, as at the conclusion of *Anth. Lat.* 412. Here, as elsewhere, one might have expected from a Seneca more novelty and ingenuity, as well as livelier expression.

Of the poems ascribed to Petronius several accord well with themes and attitudes to be found in the *Satyrica*, and may be fragments of that work, such as *Anth. Lat.* 466 (scepticism about the gods), *Anth. Lat.* 690 (oddities of nature), *Anth. Lat.* 469 (encouragement to a hero or mock-hero, who could be Encolpius), and *Anth. Lat.* 475 (an amusing parody of epic simile). The last two pieces, amongst others, are clearly taken from a narrative context, and not in fact epigrams at all. This favours attribution to the *Satyrica*, and incidentally makes the verses hard to judge in their own right. A few of the self-contained poems are of high quality, such as *Anth. Lat.* 706 (a pretty conceit about a snowball, but rather tender in tone for the Petronius we otherwise know) and *Anth. Lat.* 698 (a fine poem on a restless slave of love, after the manner of Tibullus and Ovid, but again hardly reminiscent of Petronius). We cannot, of course, tell how various were the moods which Petronius' fertile genius could compass. He might have written *Anth. Lat.* 698, 706 and several others which no internal evidence suggests that we should impute to him. To doubt it is not so much to question his versatility as simply to insist that attributions, if they are to be considered seriously, require some positive support.

7. 'PRIAPEA'

The book of epigrams concerned with Priapus (*Priapea*) is uninhibitedly obscene. Clearly the poet[1] revelled in the jokes which sexual activities so readily encourage, and would probably have been surprised to find that he had shocked, rather than diverted his readers. But the diversion which mere impropriety affords is ephemeral. Such stuff may catch a reader's attention, but will not long retain it unless presented with considerable artistic skill. Happily

[1] That these epigrams belong to one poet has been established beyond reasonable doubt by V. Buchheit (see Appendix).

the author of the *Priapea* possesses this skill in abundance. He is original, elegant, and witty, in command of different metres, adept at varying and conflating motifs, and subtle in the planning of his book as a whole. These qualities secure him a high rank amongst Latin epigrammatists.

Priapus figures somewhat tenuously in Greek poetry, and on occasion as an object of genuine cult. In Roman poetry he is almost exclusively associated with custodianship of gardens and with sexual matters, and easily lends himself to become an object of banter and ribaldry. He is treated light-heartedly or at best semi-seriously: so Hor. *Sat.* 1.8, Tib. 1.4, [Virg.] *Priap.* 1–3, *Copa* 23–5. From Martial he obtains a number of pieces (in particular 6.16, 49, 72, 73, 8.40), but they are very limited in thematic range and development. In contrast the book of *Priapea* offers a remarkable diversity of themes, which includes curses (e.g. 78), mockery (e.g. 12), riddles (e.g. 54), dedications to Priapus (e.g. 27), comparison of Priapus with other gods (e.g. 9), Priapus turning a blind eye (64), Priapus in despair (26), and Priapean interpretation of Homer (68). Amongst the characters the author sketches or derides we find prostitutes, pathics, the amorous but unamiable, poets, and respectable matrons. He can maintain suspense, even though we anticipate some obscene conclusion, he can deftly move into parody (e.g. 52. 11–12), and he can produce a neat pun (e.g. 55.6) or delightfully unexpected turn of phrase (e.g. 37. 13–14). And he enlivens hackneyed material, such as dedication of offerings, by ingenious novelty of treatment: conspicuously so in 37. The book is a *tour de force* and intended to be such: it shows the multiplicity of variations admitted by a subject at first sight extremely restricted.

Skilful though the author is in presenting Priapus from new aspects, items very similar in conception naturally occur in a corpus of eighty poems. Hence, to avoid tedium, he varies length, changes metre, and disperses, collocates, and interweaves his themes as they correspond or contrast. This is all so adroitly done that the overall planning appears only on close analysis. And it is not overdone: there is no obsession with patterns here. His artistry has enabled the poet to explore all the possibilities of his subject without wearying his reader. Perhaps his success deterred Martial from making much of Priapus, but, if that seems contrary to what we know of Martial, who might have been expected to take up the challenge, our author could well be the later.

31

PROSE SATIRE

I. 'APOCOLOCYNTOSIS DIVI CLAUDII'

For sparkle and malicious wit few works of Latin literature can match the only complete Menippean satire which has survived,[1] a skit upon the life and death of Claudius Caesar ascribed in manuscripts which transmit it to Seneca. It is commonly identified with a piece about Claudius which Cassius Dio tells us Seneca wrote under the title *apocolocyntosis*. This word, though hardly translatable,[2] clearly involves allusion to a pumpkin, *colocynta*, perhaps as a symbol of stupidity, and may well involve, as Dio supposed, parody of the idea of deification. But how does it relate to the actual work, in which Claudius becomes neither a pumpkin nor a god? No one has yet explained. We have either to contend that the joke is limited to the title itself or, if we feel that a work and its title ought to have some discernible connexion, admit that a very real problem remains with us. As to authorship, Seneca could certainly have written the satire. There is nothing surprising in the contradiction here of all the earlier adulation of the *Ad Polybium* (even if that had been sincere, his protracted exile gave Seneca reason enough to detest Claudius) or in the satire's liveliness and scurrility (Seneca was versatile and not lacking in wit). Nero himself derided the dead Claudius and presumably allowed his courtiers to do the same. If Seneca wrote his skit shortly after Nero's accession he would have found an appreciative audience. But, though Seneca possessed the talent, motive, and opportunity to produce the work, so too did others, and famous names attract attributions. It is not absurd to retain some doubts.

After protestations of truthfulness (1–2), sure token of a tall story, the satirist narrates the death of Claudius (3–4), his ascent to Olympus and vain attempt to be enrolled as a god (5–11), and his descent via Rome, where he witnesses his own obsequies, to Hades and final damnation (12–15). The narrative varies in tempo, but is usually brisk and not overburdened with detail. Transition from prose to verse, a distinctive feature of the Menippean

[1] A passage of some size is lost in a lacuna at 7.5.

[2] There are two difficulties. Apparently close translation, such as 'pumpkinification', will not be English. And, more seriously, since many theories are current about the word's meaning, some plausible, none cogent, we cannot with assurance settle for any one.

genre, is aptly and amusingly contrived. In general frivolity prevails, but the praise of Nero (4.1) can be taken seriously and, of course, many of the charges against Claudius, made by Augustus (10) and elsewhere, are in themselves grave enough. One must hesitate, however, to impute any of the views expressed to the author. For instance, the sneer at Claudius' extension of the citizenship (3.3) tells us nothing about the real opinions of Seneca or any other individual. The satirist adopts a stance, that of the plain and forthright man in the street, much as Aristophanes had done long before. His satire is political in that it is concerned with a political figure, but not because he says anything of political moment.

The work's prosimetric form links it most obviously with Varro's *Menippeans*, and, though nothing closely comparable in theme appears amongst Varro's fragments, a considerable debt is likely. Something too may be owed directly to Menippus: similarities to Lucian, notably his *Icaromenippus* and *Deorum concilium*, could indicate Menippus as a common source. And one need hardly doubt that Lucilius' council of the gods hovered somewhere in our author's mind. In Lucilius the gods pass judgement on the deceased Cornelius Lentulus Lupus, as they do here on the deceased Claudius. To these literary influences, readily absorbed and exploited by a fertile imagination, we may add the effects of a long Roman tradition of political abuse and invective. The special circumstances of the time of composition allowed that tradition, having long run underground, to surface again. Modern critics may take exception to the treatment of Claudius' personal deformities as being in bad taste. It would not have seemed objectionable to Catullus or Cicero.

The greatest of the many delights which this minor masterpiece affords lies in the way hits are scored in every quarter. Historians, for instance, are mocked for their claims to impartiality (1.1) and avoidance of quotations (9.2). Augustus is made to talk like an animated inscription (10.2). The formalities of senatorial debate are playfully caricatured (9.5, 11.5). So too are poetic conventions and poetic language, not excluding that of Seneca's tragedies. Irony, bathos, and all sorts of comic incongruity abound. The Latin is light and racy when necessary, and witticisms flow with effortless ease. Proverbs and colloquialisms lend the work almost a plebeian air, and issue rather charmingly from the mouths of the gods. Olympus indeed seems as motley and clamorous as the streets of Rome. The satire is utterly disrespectful (save, of course, towards Nero), a fitting entertainment for the Saturnalia. Its unsparing derision of Claudius and uproarious laughter do not, as some suspect, betoken hysteria, but rather the healthy exuberance of a man at last pleased with himself and the world around him.

2. PETRONIUS

Petronius' *Satyrica*, commonly but incorrectly known as *Satyricon*,[1] raise abundant problems for literary historians and critics alike. Some of these problems, concerning scale, structure, and plot, are due solely to the mutilation of the text: if it were complete, they would vanish. Others, concerning genre, style, and intention, are more deeply rooted, and could only be resolved if several earlier works, now lost or fragmentary, were rediscovered. No Latin writer excites more lively interest. Unfortunately it is not always accompanied by due recognition of our ignorance.

The old dispute about date and authorship remains tenuously alive. As to date, the social and economic situation presupposed, the cultural interests revealed, and a few plausibly datable references[2] argue for composition during Nero's reign, and a dramatic setting somewhat earlier. And, if Petronius echoes Lucan, composition in the sixties, not the fifties, is indicated. Further, no valid evidence supports a later dating. As to authorship, the work's character accords well with what Tacitus records (*Ann.* 16. 18–19) about Nero's 'arbiter of elegance' Petronius Niger, connoisseur and voluptuary extraordinary. Again, the rare name *Arbiter*, attached to the author in certain manuscripts and elsewhere, may well have derived (exactly how is unclear) from the denomination *arbiter elegantiae*. Such arguments fall short of proving identity, and a strict historian may still suspend judgement.

The title *Satyrica*, 'satyr histories' or, more freely, 'tales of wantonness', recalling, for example, *Milesiaca*, 'Milesian tales', and *poemenica*, 'Shepherd stories', suggests affinity to the Greek romantic novel, a genre which was establishing itself and probably already popular by Petronius' time. But some scholars maintain that *satyrica* is ambivalent: it would also, they think, have recalled the superficially similar word *satura*, and thus suggested a satirical purpose. Petronius' contemporaries could perhaps have confused these basically different words, but they hardly needed to be told of a connexion with satire evident throughout his work. His debt to the satirists is seen in subject matter, for instance the dinner party (cf. Hor. *Sat.* 2.8), in characterization, particularly of minor figures, and in employment of parody and burlesque. And he may have taken the prosimetric form of his novel from Varro's *Saturae Menippeae*: the genre was still alive, as the nearly contemporary *Apocolocyntosis divi Claudii* shows. In spite of difference in scale, we might regard the *Satyrica* as a natural development of Varro's satire, but a prosimetric fragment, recently published, of what seems to be a Greek picaresque novel argues that he had closer antecedents.[3] And Varro wrote a number of separate pieces (one ad-

[1] See Appendix.

[2] Rose (1971) 20ff.

[3] Parsons (1971) 63–6.

mittedly of some length), Petronius a coherent, if often discursive, narrative. That difference is decisive: emulation of Varro cannot alone account for Petronius' enterprise.

Petronius presents the adventures of a hero, or anti-hero, Encolpius, a conventionally educated young man, without money or morals, and his catamite, Giton, handsome and unscrupulous. Other characters come and go and reappear, amongst them Quartilla, priestess of Priapus, and Eumolpus, poet, teacher, and reprobate. How importantly any of these subsidiary characters figured in the whole work it is impossible to tell. Encolpius, as narrator and observer, holds the story together. He is a ludicrous victim of fortune's whims, raised up and thrown down, living for the day; he is a voyeur plagued with impotence, a swashbuckling coward, querulous, aimless, and neurotic. In the Greek romances hero and heroine are wont to be buffeted by fortune; their perils and escapes are dire and astonishing; but in the end true love obtains its reward. Petronius burlesques this kind of plot. His homosexual lovers are faithless and unfortunate. Virtue tested and triumphant is replaced by vice rampant and frustrated. But no moral is intended: Petronius seeks only to subvert or mock or suggest comic resemblances. He finds ample material, in epic as in romance. Encolpius, an unheroic wanderer, is pursued by Priapus' wrath, as Odysseus was by Poseidon's and Aeneas by Juno's. Like Odysseus he meets a Circe (127ff.), like Aeneas he sallies forth to wreak vengeance (82. 1–2). Petronius writes for a highly literate audience, able to recognize widely scattered allusions. Thus, for example, Habinnas' entrance at Trimalchio's party (65.3ff.) is based on Alcibiades' in Plato's *Symposium*. His exploitation of many poets and prose-writers has encouraged the opinion that Petronius of set purpose blended diverse genres, romance, satire, epic, elegy, mime, diatribe, and declamation, to produce an amalgam both original and anti-classical. But a less revolutionary explanation will account for the evidence: for his theme, Petronius' obligation is principally to romance, sentimental or picaresque, and his own inventiveness, for the form adopted, partially perhaps to Varro, while all debts to other genres are incidental. These other genres inform his treatment of episodes or individuals, but not his whole work. Ovid's variation of treatment in his *Metamorphoses* is somewhat analogous.[1]

Two longer poems included in the *Satyrica* (89 and 119–24), *Troiae halosis*, 'The capture of Troy', consisting of 65 iambic verses, and *De bello civili*, 'On the civil war', consisting of 295 hexameters, pose teasing difficulties of interpretation, the latter particularly. What is Petronius here attempting: to show how epic should be written, to parody Lucan, or something more subtle? Parody may be discountenanced: Lucan's thoughts and expressions are not

[1] I owe this point to Professor Kenney.

arrestingly adapted, the gods, whom Lucan discarded, fulfil their accustomed role, and, for a parody, the poem is inordinately long. It could, one must admit, have been intended to be exemplary, though few have seen any merits in it. We had best seek guidance from its context. Eumolpus (who is presented elsewhere as a scoundrel, if not a charlatan) offers it as a specimen of the elevated treatment which the subject demands of a poet, as against the mundane treatment which should properly be left to historians. And Lucan, we remember, was commonly abused for writing like a historian, not a poet. Petronius, it may be, had as little regard for traditional epic, purveyed by Eumolpus and his like, as for current innovations. His shrewd contemporary, Persius, was certainly disillusioned about all such effusions. And, since the *De bello civili* contains enough phrases and rhythms similar to Lucan's to argue, though not to prove, that Petronius knew something of Lucan's work, he may wish to point the irony of a conservative like Eumolpus being infected by modern vices. If so, Lucan is indirectly criticized. Much the same implicit criticism may be found in the iambic piece. Though not a parody of Seneca, it illustrates how easily vapid iambics, not unlike Seneca's, can be strung together.

Both in incident and character Petronius' novel is highly realistic, indeed startlingly so, if compared with sentimental romances. Violence, vulgarity, and decadence disfigure the society which he depicts. His erotic scenes are sometimes titillating, sometimes callously comic, sometimes both: but sympathetic humour is almost as hard to find here as sentiment. However, in his description of Trimalchio's party (26.7–79.7) we are feasted with humour, of a hilariously rumbustious brand. Petronius' presentation of the freedman millionaire and his cronies is as adept as it is original. No one had hitherto so fully portrayed the thoughts, attitudes, and mode of speech of a specific social class, and at that a low one, though something at least comparable had been effected in comedy and mime. And Petronius is not content with caricature. Beneath a brash and ridiculous façade he discloses unrealizable aspirations and chronic insecurity. His Trimalchio is a complex character: he now wallows in luxury and self-deception, but was once resilient and faced a hard world on its own terms. For all his coarseness and ostentation he is not utterly unlikable.

After every allowance for the fragmentation of our text, the novel still seems very episodic, and the episodes seem to vary considerably in scale. Occasionally topics of general interest (education, for instance) are handled at length, and the narrative slows down. Such fluctuation of tempo and the generous treatment of many details may reinforce the manuscript evidence (sometimes questioned) for sixteen or more books. References to several episodes now lost add confirmation. And the scene must have changed more than once. The parts of the story we have are centred somewhere in Campania, after escapades at Massilia. Doubtless Encolpius moved on, as those who live on their wits (and on the fringes of the law) commonly do. We have then no organic, inevitably developed plot. It is uncertain even whether the theme of Priapus' hostility ran from beginning to end or merely through a portion of the novel.

Two distinct styles stand out in our fragments, that of the narrative and the 'educated' characters and that given to Trimalchio and the other freedmen. For unaffected ease and raciness many passages where the former style is used are quite unsurpassed. It is also an extremely flexible medium, admitting endless changes of nuance. And the opportunity Petronius enjoys to switch into verse, without syntactical break if necessary, is a useful resource: sometimes he can in verse better convey emotion or indicate amusing parallels. He is particularly skilful in reproducing the absurdities and pomposity of the superficially educated. Encolpius and Giton, when in extremity, discourse as if in a school of rhetoric (114.8–12); other characters rant, gush, or pontificate whenever they get the chance. There is no less verisimilitude in the freedmen's conversation, fruity, solecistic, and irrepressible. They are characterized by what they say (e.g. 61.6–62.14), as well as by the way they speak. Admittedly Petronius exaggerates somewhat. That so many homely saws, so much slang, and so much gutter wit were ever in real life accumulated in such short compass is hard to believe. Sam Weller at his best could not compete. But the language used is not far removed from reality, as independent evidence for colloquial Latin attests. Of course some questions arise, for instance over the appreciable number of Grecisms. Are they representative of colloquial speech in this milieu only, or generally? And one other question is especially tantalizing. Did Petronius in the books now lost attempt to copy the language of clearly identifiable social groups? He may have done so, for we must remember that Trimalchio's party is only an extended episode, and not to be accorded unique importance.

Evidence for substantial use of Petronius in later Latin literature is hard to find. Apuleius, in his novel's conception and style, pursued a different course, though similarities too may be detected. In modern times we encounter numerous works which bear a passing resemblance to Petronius', but few traces of direct imitation. Fragments are not perhaps very tempting to imitators. The Spanish picaresque novels seem to owe more to Apuleius. Again, though Petronius should have been congenial to some of our eighteenth-century novelists, Fielding, Smollett, and Sterne, reminiscences there are tenuous indeed. But a deep and subtle influence has been discerned in certain classics of the present century, including Joyce's *Ulysses* and Eliot's *Waste Land*. The latter acknowledges a connexion in his epigraph.

32

HISTORY AND BIOGRAPHY

I. VELLEIUS PATERCULUS

Several major historians, including Aufidius, Servilius, and Pliny, flourished in the century between Livy and Tacitus, but change of fashion or ill chance has robbed us of their works. Of the historical writing of this period only two representatives survive, Curtius (whose subject matter separates him from the main stream) and Velleius. Such is the dearth of other evidence that, if the criticisms directed against Velleius, for bias and incompetence, were trebly deserved, he could still not be neglected.

Velleius' history is neither epitome nor rudimentary summary, but a highly personal and selective outline, marked by special interests and very much overloaded. He vastly expands his scale of treatment as he approaches his own times, and some have supposed that everything which precedes Augustus and Tiberius is mere introduction: Velleius hurries on to talk about contemporary history, desiring to present in Tiberius the consummation of Roman virtues. If that were entirely true, his earlier exposition would have been derivative and perfunctory. In fact it is often studied and independent, albeit patchy. The same attitudes and techniques are indeed evident throughout: in particular he constantly seeks to evaluate the worth and achievements of individuals, rather than to describe the political circumstances of past ages. For him character and personality form history's very essence, and, though this recurrent obsession prompts some memorable sketches (e.g. 2.29, 2.35, 2.127), it also weakens and distorts the whole picture.

Modern discussion of Velleius centres on Tiberius' principate: Velleius is commonly condemned for flattery of Tiberius and Sejanus. Something may be said on the other side. Most importantly, much of his account of Tiberius is true. As Velleius, one of his officers, well knew, Tiberius was an extremely competent general; he cared about his men; he did not, like Augustus, lose his nerve in the crisis of A.D. 6–9; he inspired and rewarded loyalty. Velleius is a valuable source for Tiberius' campaigns in Illyricum and Germany, though he deceives or at least misleads his readers at 2.106.2. Further, he is fair to Gaius Caesar (2.101–2) and rightly critical of Varus (2.117–18). His evasion of delicate issues concerning Tiberius' 'exile' at Rhodes is venial enough, and his panegyric of the emperor at 2.126 was an unavoidable obligation for a contemporary, though he may genuinely have believed what he says. Again, his treatment of Sejanus at 2.127–8, ostensibly very favourable, does not prove him one of Sejanus' adherents. Velleius completed his work at a time of tension and uncertainty, as his impassioned concluding prayer (2.131) reveals. Though staunchly loyal to Tiberius and perhaps the more inclined to praise him as his general popularity waned, he still foresees grave dangers. In the political situation of A.D. 30 he could be no more explicit. Such is a case for the defence, not devoid of force. But bias, however plausibly accounted for, prevents Velleius from judging recent history objectively. And, while panegyric as such at 2.126 is understandable, the blessings which Tiberius allegedly effected pass all credence, the more so because much the same has been said about Augustus at 2.89.3–4. Augustus' last years were indeed troubled, but honesty, authority, and discipline had not vanished, only to be resuscitated instantaneously by Tiberius' accession. Revival of lost virtues was or was to become a commonplace: that is no excuse for a historian. Is Velleius then just a propagandist for Tiberius? In the strictest sense (if Tiberius' prior approval is implied), no. Like other retired officers, he probably had the itch to write and could guess what would be acceptable. Thus he provides good evidence for various concepts and conventions nowadays comprehended under the unduly formal rubric 'ideology of the Principate'.

Velleius is much indebted to Livy and Sallust, more to the former, though he sets great store by brevity (see, e.g., 1.16.1, 2.29.2, 2.124.1). But he achieves brevity by his handling of material rather than contracted expression or Sallustian abruptness. He elaborates certain topics, while omitting or summarily dismissing others, even matters of undeniable importance (e.g. 2.52.3). And, for all his anxiety about speed, he not only lingers but also digresses: at the end of Book 1 he actually conjoins two digressions, on colonies and literature. The latter digression (cf. 2.9), in a work so circumscribed, is rather remarkable. He says that he is irresistibly fascinated by the brief flowering of great talents, in Greece and Rome. No doubt he is, and, in finding space for such material, he displays a refreshingly catholic approach to the study of history. Indeed one may debate whether this is history at all as the ancients understood it.

Velleius' writing is predictably artificial. He likes verbal point; he employs many patterns of word and phrase; he partially anticipates Seneca's ingenious antitheses and Tacitus' unfailing novelty. But he is often pleonastic and sometimes constructs long periods, after Livy's manner. Emotional and high-flown passages (e.g. 2.66.3–5) stand near to sections of colourless and skimpy narration. Velleius' style is not homogeneous.

In writing outline history Velleius had respectable predecessors, such as

Atticus (Cic. *Brut.* 14–15) and Nepos (Cat. 1.5–7). We cannot tell whether he found in them precedent for reference to his family and personal experiences, or for giving his dedicatee, M. Vinicius, an unwarranted historical prominence. Plainly Velleius was self-centred and prejudiced, a wilful amateur: he neither enquired nor reflected enough. But, if he merits scant esteem, he still claims much attention. No one would hesitate to exchange him for Cremutius Cordus, let alone Aufidius or Pliny, but he somehow survived when his betters were lost. Hence he is indispensable for students of history. For students of literature he represents a transitional phase in Roman historiography, permitting some appraisal of gradual change and blending of style.[1]

2. Q. CURTIUS RUFUS

Curtius' *History of Alexander* is enthralling and exasperating. He enthrals if we want to read of drama and high adventure. He exasperates if we want essential facts and a consistent assessment of them. And he has greatly perplexed modern scholars. Some find in him a rhetorician pure and simple, concerned only to entertain and excite his readers, comparable with our historical novelists rather than our historians. Others claim that, however many blemishes may mar his work, he seriously endeavoured to write history and must be treated seriously.

Much may be said on both sides. Curtius' irresponsibility and nonchalance are demonstrated repeatedly by inaccuracies, contradictions, implausible fabrication of detail, in speeches and elsewhere, and above all freely confessed willingness to mislead. He admits (9.1.34) that he has copied down more than he believes to be true. In selecting material for elaboration Curtius prefers whatever is pathetic, romantic, extraordinary; his geography is deplorable, but he adeptly describes scenic beauty or curiosities of nature (e.g. 5.4.6–9); his reports of battles are often unclear, indeed unintelligible, but he very carefully depicts oriental pageantry (e.g. 3.3.8–28). He neither grasps the major historical issues which Alexander's career raises, nor does he present Alexander credibly and coherently. His final remarks about the king (10.5.26–36) are at variance with the picture of progressive corruption, derived from Peripatetic teaching, which largely colours the preceding narrative (see e.g. 6.2.1–4). In a word, he is unreliable and, if he had priorities, got them badly wrong. On the other side, it is clear that Curtius independently employed several sources, including one or two good sources not otherwise now accessible: he did not merely reproduce an inferior tradition, embodied in Clitarchus. Hence he preserves precious items of information, hidden

[1] I am greatly indebted to Dr A. J. Woodman, who has kindly shown me two of his papers before publication and taught me much about Velleius.

sometimes under the rhetoric of his speeches, and explains various matters (particularly Persian actions and motives) nowhere else explained. He can be as shrewd as he is impish[1] and perverse, and, though not in Arrian's class, remains indispensable. Again in a word, he intermittently troubled himself about content as well as form.

Curtius writes volubly, almost precipitately, as if embarrassed by a surplus of material, but he is never in real difficulties. Trite reflections and incisive comments are invariably at his command; he can expand, abbreviate, vary tone and mood, even discard his usual rhetoric, all with consummate ease; if he is at times clumsy and repetitious in expression and inept in thought, it is probably through negligence, not incompetence. Apart from his historical sources, certain literary influences may be detected, notably epic poetry and Livy, perhaps Herodotus, but no single writer known to us exercised a dominant effect on him. His style is not so derivative or distinctly marked as to give firm evidence of date, but his frequent *sententiae*, his sentence structure (he readily uses short, abrupt sentences), some features of his syntax (e.g. very free use of future participles), light poetic colouring, and absence of extravagant archaizing all point to the beginning or middle of the first century A.D., and this dating is confirmed by similarities in thought and expression to Seneca and Calpurnius Siculus.

Why this accomplished dilettante chose to write about Alexander we cannot know: perhaps he explained in his preface, if he condescended to write one. But Alexander was a standard theme in the schools of rhetoric and it was not difficult to see the rich opportunities which a full-scale treatment of his life and deeds offered. If our tentative dating is right, the more general revival of interest in Alexander prompted by Trajan is irrelevant. Curtius is typical of much historiography of the first century A.D.: it was stuff such as his, showy and untrustworthy, but not devoid of substance, which Tacitus used and superseded.

3. TACITUS

Tacitus never became a classic or school-book in antiquity, for he arrived too late to enter a limited repertoire.[2] As a traditionalist in an age of declining standards he was averse from outline history and scandalous biography, and his brevity defied the tribe of excerptors and abbreviators. If he courted popularity, he failed to win it. A few Christians know of him and in Ammian he has a distinguished follower. Thereafter followed long neglect, precarious and truncated survival, and late rediscovery. But, once rediscovered, Tacitus

[1] 'There are things in Curtius which look like pure impishness, designed to annoy serious readers', Tarn (1948) II 103.

[2] Though, admittedly, a few comparatively late poets, such as Lucan and Juvenal, became classics of a sort.

compelled the attention of many of the best scholars and thinkers of the fifteenth and sixteenth centuries. He interested them not only because of his style and theme, but also because his views (real or supposed) seemed applicable to contemporary politics and statecraft. This latter interest faded long ago, but a basic dilemma remains in studying Tacitus, a consummate stylist and rhetorician who is also a major historian. To what extent is his content separable from his style?

In the *Agricola*, his earliest work, Tacitus amalgamates biography and historical monograph. But the success of the combination is questionable. He gives roughly two thirds of the work to Agricola's governorship of Britain, and treats the climax of Agricola's campaigns at length, providing direct speeches for the two leaders, almost as if he were experimenting with full-scale history. Such extensive development of a part, albeit an important part, unbalances the whole. Again, most of what he tells us about Agricola's personality is conventional and unrevealing. Characterization in more depth was reasonably to be expected, though not, in an avowedly laudatory composition (3.3), any critical assessment. Some contend that Tacitus exaggerated Agricola's achievements and wilfully misconstrued his relations with Domitian. We cannot be sure, but certainly many matters in the *Agricola* are unclear or, like the insinuation of poisoning against Domitian (43.2), ill substantiated. There is, however, a case for the defence. Tacitus probably found little else worth relating about Agricola except the governorship, and hence made the most of it. In thus concentrating on military and administrative achievements, he followed a hallowed Republican tradition, attested in surviving epitaphs and eulogies (cf. Nep. *Epam.* 1.4). A Roman aristocrat should possess and display *uirtus*, above all in warfare: to this pattern Agricola conformed. Thus one old-fashioned attitude underlies a work somewhat novel in conception.

Concern with *uirtus*[1] was to reappear in the *Germania* and recur often in the major works. Agricola, a colourless individual, is instructive as a type: indeed he probably influenced Tacitus' judgement of more important historical figures. Even under a ruler hostile to the Senate *uirtus* may still, Tacitus thinks, be exercised to good purpose, though very liable to be frustrated by envy and spite. Thus Agricola prefigures Germanicus and Corbulo in the *Annals*. He also represents dignified moderation, a theme to which Tacitus reverts at *Ann.* 4.20.2–3, where he debates whether a viable middle course exists between contumacy and subservience. The problem affected prominent senators acutely. Hence this thread of thought runs through Tacitus' writings, just as the bitter sense of guilt and humiliation, disclosed at *Agricola* 45.1–2, infects

[1] *Virtus* has no precise English equivalent. Neither 'manhood' nor 'excellence' nor 'virtue' hits it exactly.

his view of the first century A.D. generally. To understand Tacitus we must pay special attention to the *Agricola*. Later he effectively conceals what he would not have us know. Here his protective mask is still uncemented.

For the speeches at 30–4 Tacitus is much beholden to Sallust and Livy, for his powerful and moving conclusion to Cicero. As yet he had not formed his historical style, controlled, incisive, only intentionally ambiguous. In the *Agricola* we find infelicities and obscurities, not all imputable to textual corruption, and some padding. One may contrast the *Dialogus*. Here an appropriate style was already available and Tacitus employed it with complete mastery. For the *Agricola* no such guidance offered itself, and in style, as in structure, this first essay is imperfect.

The *Germania* has been subjected to microscopic study, and, where content is concerned, survived the test tolerably well. Independent evidence tends to confirm the information which Tacitus provides. He probably obtained it from Book 104 of Livy, Pliny's lost *Bella Germaniae*, and (through them or directly) certain Greek authorities, but seems to use considerable judgement in selection. He may call on first-hand experience, his own or others', to supplement and control his sources.

In 1–27 Tacitus deals with country and people generally, in 28–46 with the individual tribes. The title *De origine et situ Germanorum*, 'On the origins and homeland of the Germans', is well attested and probably genuine, but he is just as interested in their character and way of life, *mores* and *instituta* (27.2). No model for his work survives, unless we consider Herodotus as such, but Livy's approach in Book 104 may have been similar, as may Seneca's in his lost writings on Egypt and India. Tacitus may also have been influenced by Sallust's excursus on the Black Sea in *Histories* 3, and by geographical digressions in other historians. This affiliation to history helps to explain why the *Germania* is not purely descriptive, but full of comment and evaluation. Tacitus wants to explain an alien people in terms which Romans can readily understand. He shows that the Germans retain virtues which Rome once possessed, but does not idealize them or hide their weaknesses. There is no sustained contrast here, no consistent sermonizing. But Tacitus saw, as Seneca had seen (*De ira* 1.11.4), that the Germans posed a real, perhaps imminent, threat to the empire, and plainly indicates as much (33.2 and 37.3–5). Insofar as it embodies this message, the *Germania* is a 'tract for the times', though not intended to prompt or justify a specific policy. It is best described as an ethnographical treatise written from a historical viewpoint.

Stylistically this is Tacitus' least happy work. A starkly scientific approach was for such a writer inconceivable, but simple subject matter deserved simple treatment. Instead we find an excess of crude rhetoric and verbal dexterity. By repeated self-obtrusion Tacitus gives the unpleasant impression of seeking to demonstrate his talents rather than to instruct his readers. Sometimes, one may admit, point and epigram arise quite naturally, as at 19.1 *nemo illic uitia ridet, nec corrumpere et corrumpi saeculum uocatur* 'no one there makes a joke of vice, nor is seducing and being seduced called the way of the world'. But, most irritatingly, he cannot even state plainly the plain fact that the Germans have no precious metals (5.2): *argentum et aurum propitiine an irati di negauerint dubito* 'I know not whether divine grace or anger has denied them silver and gold'. Such meretricious adornments, only too conventional, disfigure an ostensibly serious treatise. The style of the *Germania* has justly been likened to Seneca's: there is much balance and antithesis here, all rather cloying. Fortunately Tacitus never again pandered thus to a decadent fashion.

The *Dialogus*, a book rich in ideas if tantalizingly elusive in purport, is separated from everything else Tacitus wrote by its Ciceronianism. In his classic works on oratory Cicero found a highly apposite style for literary treatment of the subject. And Tacitus, using (as Cicero often used) a dialogue form, was *ipso facto* further committed to emulating Cicero: his own historical manner would have been utterly unsuitable. Since the *Dialogus*' style was so much conditioned by genre, this style scarcely helps us in dating the work relatively to Tacitus' other writings. Dating depends here principally on obligations to Quintilian's *Institutio* and similarities, in expression or thought, to Pliny's *Panegyricus*. This evidence points to the early years of the second century, and accords with the subjective impression that the *Dialogus* is a mature, not a juvenile work.

Tacitus' theme, the decline of oratory, was familiar. It had been tackled by Quintilian, touched upon by Petronius and 'Longinus'.[1] Indeed, from the late Republic onwards, Roman critics, not all conservatives, battled over the merits of old and new styles. Tacitus treats the subject alertly and many-sidedly, conscious of the complex factors involved, particularly educational theory, literary fashion, and political change. The *Dialogus* has three protagonists, Maternus (a poet), Aper (an advocate), and Messalla (a connoisseur of oratory). Its argument runs thus: Aper questions Maternus' preference for poetry, extolling the advantages and satisfaction which oratory affords, while Maternus asserts that poetry, more delightful in itself, brings enduring fame; discussion now shifts to the dispute between 'ancients' and 'moderns', and Aper argues that contemporary orators should concede nothing to their predecessors, pioneers in their day, but by present standards inadequate, while Messalla replies that Cicero and his contemporaries are unsurpassed, and attributes decline to bad training and limited education; then a lacuna in the

[1] The Περὶ ὕψους was probably written in the first century A.D., but the interesting similarities in thought between Tacitus and 'Longinus' are not such as to prove a direct connexion.

text engulfs the end of Messalla's speech;[1] when the text resumes Maternus is explaining that oratory is nurtured by suitable political conditions, that Republican dissensions encouraged it, but the blissful stability of the Principate renders it largely superfluous. This bald sketch naturally gives no impression of the dialogue's manifold subtleties.

Critics are much concerned with the work's structure and intention, asking whether it is an organic whole and whether Tacitus endorses any of the opinions expressed. But, let us remember, there are writers who do not invariably press their own views, and dialogue form, realistically employed, hardly permits unbroken development of a single argument. All the views conveyed in the *Dialogus* obtain eloquent and persuasive presentation, just as they would from Cicero: none of the speeches wholly cancels out or annuls another. Those who find Tacitus' verdict embodied in Maternus' final contribution must explain how Maternus can not only accept the Principate but regard it as far superior to what preceded. If he speaks for Tacitus, he speaks with heavy irony. More probably Tacitus' thoughts and personality find partial and unclear reflection in Aper's modernism no less than Messalla's nostalgia and Maternus' detachment. No simple conclusion emerges, but his theme itself shows that he admits a decline in standards. The *Dialogus* holds together intelligibly, if loosely, in three stages: oratory is examined in the contexts of literature, education, and politics. The discussion is broad and discursive, but not random or undisciplined.

In vocabulary, phrasal structure, figures of speech, and expansive geniality the *Dialogus* is markedly after Cicero's manner, though not purely Ciceronian. Tacitus' language here is livelier and more polished than Quintilian's and richer and more virile than Pliny's. Cicero never had a better imitator.

In A.D. 98 (*Agr.* 3.3) Tacitus planned to write 'a record of former servitude and acknowledgement of present blessings', but the scheme partly aborted. He deferred Nerva and Trajan (*Hist.* 1.1.4), a rich but delicate theme, limiting his *Histories* to A.D. 69–96. This task occupied him for several years, as Pliny attests. Perhaps, after the common fashion, the *Histories* became known initially by private circulation and recitation. When he completed this first part of his major work is uncertain. And we cannot tell whether he proceeded immediately to the second, the Julio-Claudian period, the subject of our *Annals*. One thing is clear, that Tacitus' interests were drawn back inexorably into the past: at *Ann.* 3.24.3 he states that, if he embarks on another theme, it will be Augustus' era, thus, it seems, finally abandoning contemporary history. The more he pondered upon the events he records, the more he looked for explanation in earlier developments.

[1] If the lacuna contained only Messalla's conclusion and the beginning of Maternus' speech, we may usefully discuss the whole plan of the work. If it contained another speech, structural analysis is insecure.

Tacitus begins his *Histories* in annalistic manner, with the consular year 69, but compensates somewhat for thus starting *in mediis rebus* by his memorable survey of the state of the empire (*Hist.* 1.4–11). He begins the *Annals*, originally titled or subtitled *ab excessu divi Augusti*, non-annalistically, but then, in *Ann.* 1–6 at least, adheres quite strictly to an annalistic layout. How, we may wonder, did he conclude the work? If with Nero's death, not the end of A.D. 68, then he nowhere recorded about six months of that year, a curious gap in an otherwise complete narration. Some scholars have criticized his decision to commence with Tiberius' accession. Other starting-points, they say, would have been better historically. Perhaps so, but none would have been perfect.

Several structural questions remain unanswerable: how, for instance, did Tacitus dispose his material in the missing portions of the *Histories* and *Annals*, and did he attach special importance to grouping in sections comprising six books? Again, having virtually no firm evidence for date, we cannot say much about stages of composition. We may detect some considerable linguistic differences between *Hist.* 1–5, *Ann.* 1–6, and *Ann.* 11–16, but they prove only that Tacitus was incessantly experimenting. Again, in these three sections, we observe changes in historiographical technique: in *Hist.* 1–5 the material is tightly packed, the narrative rapid, the centre of interest often shifting, in *Ann.* 1–6 Tacitus proceeds in more leisurely manner, diverging little from a simple framework, and centring attention on one dominant figure, while in *Ann.* 11–16 the structure is looser, the presentation of material varied and episodic. But these changes are largely imputable to the subject matter; the momentous events of A.D. 69 required a wide scale and sustained intensity of treatment, Tiberius, as an individual, was more interesting than his three successors, and under Claudius and Nero there were distinct phases, historical and dramatic, for which soberly annalistic narration, focused on Princeps and Senate, was not altogether ideal. But we still face the disquieting possibility that the *Annals* were never completed and that Books 13–16 are unrevised. The occasional laxity in structure, certain inconsistencies, some imprecision in nomenclature, and arguable lack of polish in expression may so suggest. Much of this can, however, be explained by carelessness over detail (such as we sometimes find elsewhere in his work) or mere exhaustion or increasing self-assurance.

Tacitus claims (*Hist.* 1.1.3 and *Ann.* 1.1.3) to write dispassionately, untouched by malice or partisanship. That conventional assertion appears in many writers, Greek and Roman. Historians were expected to tell the truth and the whole truth (cf. Cic. *De or.* 2.62), but, of course, not all of them did. In his prefaces and at *Hist.* 2.101.1 Tacitus scathingly castigates certain predecessors, some of whom he must have employed as sources: they falsified history through ignorance (not knowing what went on) or flattery (to please those in power) or spite (once free to abuse the dead). To judge from Velleius and what source-investigation can recover about such writers as Cluvius Rufus, this damning verdict is justified. Tacitus' own sincerity and good intentions need not be doubted, but we may ask whether he lived up to his ideals. Though he had no reasons for personal bias in much of what he wrote, he could still be affected by other, more insidious causes of misconception and inaccuracy. Again (a point rarely noted), he blandly assumes and implies that he at least is well informed and qualified to pass valid judgements. Perhaps so, but egotism and consular rank are no safeguards against credulity or error.

A historian's first task is to collect and evaluate evidence. Some nineteenth-century scholars believed that ancient writers of history shirked this labour, content to follow a single source, altering only the style. Their views have rightly been abandoned or tempered. The obligation to compare and assess earlier writings was commonly recognized (cf. Plin. *Epist.* 5.8.12), and Tacitus, amongst others, tried to discharge it. Thus at *Hist.* 3.28 he admits uncertainty, faced with equally possible opinions from Pliny and Messalla, at *Ann.* 4.57.1 questions a conventional theory, and at *Ann.* 13.20.2 notes Rusticus' prejudice in favour of Seneca. He seems to adumbrate his own approach at *Ann.* 4.10.1: he will report what the majority of reliable sources say, but may append divergent views or comments of his own. Tacitus drew his material from general and special histories (cf. *Ann.* 1.69.2), memoirs (cf. *Ann.* 4.53.2), personal enquiry (cf. Plin. *Epist.* 6.16.1), and the official report of senatorial proceedings, *acta senatus*.[1] It is debatable whether he made the fullest use of these diverse sources. Perhaps he might have used the *acta* as some partial control upon the historians, but in fact he seems to use them only intermittently, for variety or to preserve a semblance of traditional subject matter: thus minor senatorial business tends to appear at the end of each year's record. We cannot well judge how conscientiously Tacitus handled primary evidence, since he mainly depends on secondary sources. If we had the later books of the *Histories*, we might better appraise his quality: here, for much of the Flavian period, there were no secondary sources to reshape and supersede, and here, if anywhere, he was liable to personal bias.

Tacitus may often, as he says, follow the consensus of witnesses or the more trustworthy. But analysis of his work and comparison with Cassius Dio, Suetonius, and Plutarch, who partly depend on the same sources, sometimes suggest another picture: Tacitus may indeed utilize several predecessors, yet, at any particular place, he is, like Livy, prone to follow one mainly, inter-

[1] This is no complete list. Much miscellaneous material was available, such as published speeches, eulogistic biography, and collections of memorable deeds and sayings. And there was unpublished material, for instance in the imperial archives, to which he might have had access, though probably he never bothered.

weaving details or opinions from subsidiary authorities. Sometimes favourable and unfavourable views of the same individual are mixed or juxtaposed, as with Antonius Primus in the *Histories* and Annaeus Seneca in the *Annals*. Such discrepancies may well be due to imperfect assimilation of two or more traditions. While absolutely unswerving use of any single source may be discounted, the presence of dominant or, at least, specially influential sources may not. Thus the picture of Tiberius as a hypocritical and rancorous tyrant, shared with Dio and Suetonius, was probably sketched in essentials by a first-century historian. Again, we learn much by comparing *Hist.* 1–2 with Plutarch's lives of Galba and Otho, since Plutarch largely reproduces a writer whom Tacitus follows in substance, but with many variations. Here, via Plutarch, we may virtually test Tacitus against one of his major sources, and observe how he can come near to plagiarism (even epigrams are taken over), while diverging radically in approach. The source (probably the elder Pliny) was very full and detailed, readily intelligible, and apparently a little superficial. Tacitus omits much detail, highlighting only carefully chosen aspects or scenes, rearranges and trajects material, for greater effect or other reason, and ignores or subverts facile interpretation, preferring complexity and indecision. He was no bringer of order into chaos: when he found order he was indeed only too ready to disrupt it. The wilful selection and manipulation of detail, along with independence of attitude, which comparison with Plutarch attests, may further be established by comparison with those parts of Suetonius where the same common source again is evident. Plutarch and Suetonius copy: Tacitus chooses and blends, not always judiciously.

Like many predecessors, Tacitus conceives that history should be moralistic and instructive (*Ann.* 3.65.1). Therefore he looks for examples of good or bad conduct, regularly praises and censures, and quite seriously attempts to probe the psychology of historical characters and discover their motives. Unfortunately, the thoughts of persons long since dead are rarely recoverable, and Tacitus imputes motives for which no evidence can exist, often very discreditable ones. Though he professes instruction as his principal aim, he is no less anxious to captivate and entertain his readers. Hence he does not always give most space to matters most important historically, but frequently chooses to elaborate such material as readily invites colourful and exciting treatment. Hence too he ever pursues variety, in subject matter and presentation. He can be simple or complex, detached or committed, solemn or (witness *Ann.* 12.5.3) ironical. Such are the proper skills of a first-class rhetorician. Tacitus was more than that because he also attempted to explain and interpret the events he narrates, and did not invariably accept easy and plausible explanations.

Did Tacitus adhere to his professed ideals? Not altogether. In particular he took over and developed a presentation of Tiberius which is ill-founded and psychologically unconvincing. No doubt he was influenced in so doing by later events and his own experience of Domitian, but this is no adequate excuse. Struggling to reconcile his preconceived view of Tiberius with the facts available to him, he had to resort to many illegitimate and reprehensible devices to make those facts seem other than they were or to explain them away. Thus, to suggest that Tiberius' conduct is not to be explained straightforwardly, he constantly reiterates the ideas of hypocrisy, dissimulation, and hidden malice. And he presents the Tiberian treason-trials in an unjustifiably horrific and lurid way. But he does not suppress or pervert evidence, and indeed he supplies us with the means to refute his own contentions. *Ann.* 1–6 show a sad lack of judgement and historical perspective, but not dishonesty. And, we may fairly add, the world's literature would be much poorer without Tacitus' Tiberius, a haunting and tragic figure.

Tacitus' historical style is a masterful and strange creation, difficult to characterize. It appears abnormal, but was any general norm recognized at this period? If there was a standard prose, we may find it in Quintilian, and, for history, Curtius may be typical. But, in spite of the strong influence of tradition, fashion was very fluid and individuality acceptable. Tacitus tried, as others did, to be colourful, original, and arresting. He also cultivated a hauteur in expression and attitude unlike anything else in Latin literature. Some adjudge him tortuous and artificial, and certainly his writing is anything but facile. Close analysis reveals innumerable changes of preference: for a time Tacitus favours particular words and phrases, then suddenly drops and supersedes them. No constant development is evident, but he is ever striving to be different, reacting against his own earlier experiments as well as against other styles. He is also, however, acutely conscious of a need for overall consistency of texture.

Tacitus adopted many prominent features of Sallust's style: choice and unusual vocabulary, asyndeton, avoidance of balanced phrases and rounded periods, and, above all, brevity. But in almost every respect in which he imitates Sallust he also diverges, usually showing more taste and restraint than his model. Thus he does not accept all Sallust's vocabulary: some of it was too outlandish and archaic. Again he does not employ asyndeton as frequently or as extravagantly. And, though he surpasses Sallust in brevity, he does not affect the same abruptness. Rejecting the Ciceronian period, Sallust devised a broken, staccato sentence-structure. Tacitus can write like this occasionally, but elsewhere, to replace the period, he uses a lop-sided and overloaded form of sentence, in which important thoughts are appended one to another, often by the use of ablatives absolute, and where what is formally the main clause may in fact be of little weight. In one way only does he go further than Sallust, in his inordinate love of variation, a feature which pervades his historical writing. Tacitus' style is in general more smooth and homogeneous than Sallust's, for Sallust, though his conciseness deserved and won applause, can sometimes be hispid and verbose. Such insouciance was not for Tacitus, and, when he adapted the famous sketch of Catiline to Sejanus (*Ann.* 4.1), he pared away the unevenness and superfluities of the original.

The stylistic influences on Tacitus, apart from Sallust, are many and various, and some too deeply interlocked to be separated out. Cicero and Seneca are important here, not only because he rebelled against them. Livy's influence is underestimated: we may trace it in vocabulary and in treatment of minor scenes and, occasionally, larger episodes. Then there are the poets, above all Virgil, and here we encounter some misunderstanding. Tacitus, like any educated Roman of his day, was steeped in Virgil's poetry: it coloured his language and from time to time, perhaps, his thought. But it was no major formative influence. He does not often, as some suppose, use allusions to Virgil to enrich and enhance his narrative, nor does he find in Virgil inspiration for his handling of incident and character. Doubtless a few of his Virgilian echoes are intentional, but most of them lack special significance. Following a tradition of historical writing in which Sallust and Livy were conjoined,[1] Tacitus worked day by day with the historians of the first century A.D., his main sources: they cannot have failed to affect his style. We may form some impression, from Velleius and Curtius, of what the historiography of this period was like. It was probably marked by keen interest in personality, elaboration of parts of the story, abbreviation of others, a good deal of moralizing comment, and a great deal of pointed, epigrammatic expression. The characterization may have been crude or schematic, the moralizing trite, and the expression inadequate, but there lay an opportunity which Tacitus could seize. He consummated what several predecessors had attempted.

Tacitus was certainly an innovator: he coined words, strained usage, and once or twice, as in the 'impressionistic' writing of *Ann.* 1.40.4–41.2, almost abandoned syntax. But he was not such a radical as he seems at first glance. The loss of his sources, as of Sallust's *Histories* and much of Livy, enjoins cautious appraisal of apparent Tacitean novelties. Many words first attested in Tacitus must have existed earlier. Again, some of our first-century evidence, drawn from poets or other genres of prose, suggests strongly that Tacitus was wont to extend and vary established modes of expression, not to make wholly new departures. He shied away from affectation and preciosity, and we may well imagine the distaste he must have felt for the pedantic, archaizing fancies of Hadrian's era, if he survived to contemplate them.

[1] Perhaps separate traditions, Sallustian and Livian, continued through the first century. But the surviving texts scarcely confirm this opinion. Is Velleius, for instance, Sallustian or Livian? It looks as if the two streams converged quite early.

It is often useful to consider the sort of expressions which particular Latin writers seem to avoid. And in Tacitus this approach has been very rewarding, although some of his preferences and dislikes are inexplicable, except by whim and idiosyncrasy. In general he avoids flat, lifeless, and over-used words, and abstracts (especially when vivid and concrete synonyms are available), also technical terms and official parlance, such as we find on coins and public inscriptions. Conversely he likes words which, without being extraordinary, are yet fresh, graphic, and memorable. His discontent with much normal and seemingly innocuous vocabulary may be attributed partly to a conscious desire for dignity, partly to pathological aversion from the half-truths and clichés of his society. But there is also a more mundane explanation: Tacitus, who after all often perforce uses standard terms, sometimes replaces them simply to escape the tedium of repetition. Like most stylists, he is anxious not to bore his readers.

'Although the style of Tacitus cannot match that of Livy for variety, it nevertheless changes perceptibly according to the nature of the subject matter.'[1] Perhaps, out of a concern for stylistic unity, Tacitus deliberately restricted his room for manoeuvre. But he still found opportunity enough to be flexible and varied. Some scenes obtain rich coloration, for instance *Ann.* 1.65, where poeticisms cluster, and *Ann.* 4.46–51, where asyndeton is strikingly used. When emotionally involved, as at *Ann.* 14.64, he can be stridently rhetorical. When relating routine business, he can write quite simply. In speeches he diverges somewhat from his narrative style: we find here more balanced clauses, various devices of style infrequent elsewhere, and generally a comparatively flowing and expansive manner. Some suppose that, though tradition and propriety excluded reproduction of the exact words of authentic speeches (see *Ann.* 15.63.3), Tacitus attempted to recall or recreate styles appropriate to his characters. It is doubtful whether this interesting theory can be sustained, but he apparently paid some regard to what was actually said, when the information was accessible. The original of Claudius' speech at *Ann.* 11.24 partly survives on an inscription (*CIL* 13.1.1668). Tacitus preserves something of its gist and a little of its phraseology, hardly enough, however, to resurrect Claudius' singular ineptitude. Again, the speech given to Seneca at *Ann.* 14.53–4, certainly a free composition by Tacitus, is perhaps intended to satirize the speaker, but, if so, it is the banality of thought which effects this object, not the expression, which is far from being Senecan. And again, while Tiberius' letters and speeches show a few distinct features, notably in vocabulary, we cannot prove that these features derive from Tiberius himself. We may assert that some of Tacitus' speeches have a more individual character than others, for instance *Hist.* 4.42, which is remarkably Ciceronian. Beyond this we embark on speculation.

[1] Adams (1973) 124.

Verbal sharpness, concomitant with brevity, is of the essence of Tacitus' style. He extracts the maximum force from individual words and their collocations, sometimes unexpected and paradoxical. This continual seeking for effect is most obviously apparent in *sententiae*, the craze and curse of his generation as of several generations preceding.[1] By common consent Tacitus' *sententiae* rank as the best in Latin prose, probably because he troubled himself about content as well as form. Some convey ideas not found before. Others have a long history: Tacitus added the final polish. Here are some examples: *Agr.* 30.4 *ubi solitudinem faciunt, pacem appellant* 'where they make a desert, they call it peace', *Hist.* 2.77.3 *qui deliberant, desciuerunt* 'discussion of rebellion is rebellion', *Hist.* 3.25.3 *factum esse scelus loquuntur faciuntque* 'they tell of crime done and do the same', *Ann.* 3.27.3 *corruptissima re publica plurimae leges* 'the more corrupt a state, the more numerous its laws'. Tacitus, more successfully than most writers, blends point and epigram into his narrative, as a longer excerpt, Arminius' obituary (*Ann.* 2.88.2–3), will show:

...liberator haud dubie Germaniae et qui non primordia populi Romani, sicut alii reges ducesque, sed florentissimum imperium lacessierit, proeliis ambiguus, bello non uictus. septem et triginta annos uitae, duodecim potentiae expleuit, caniturque adhuc barbaras apud gentes, Graecorum annalibus ignotus, qui sua tantum mirantur, Romanis haud perinde celebris, dum uetera extollimus recentium incuriosi.

...beyond doubt Germany's deliverer and one who, unlike other kings and generals, challenged not an infant Rome, but Rome's empire at its height, with various fortune in battles, unconquered in war. He lived thirty-seven years and had power for twelve, and he is sung of still by barbarian tribes, albeit unknown to Greek histories (the Greeks only admire their own achievements), nor properly noticed in ours, for we celebrate the remote past, uninterested in things recent.

Volumes have been devoted to Tacitus' opinions, thought, and outlook on the world. But there is little to show for all this effort. A few ideas, attitudes, and special interests may securely be attributed to Tacitus. Beyond that uncertainty reigns, largely because we cannot often tell whether views which Tacitus reports, above all in speeches, are views which he himself shares. Again, views presented in one place are sometimes contradicted in another. To put it harshly, he can be confused and inconsistent, or, to put it mildly, complex and elusive. But fault, if fault there be, lies rather with those who want a historian also to be a philosopher.

Tacitus' attitudes are coloured by his class and rank. He has often to relate the degradation and servility of the Senate, but to do so pains and embarrasses him (*Ann.* 14.14.3), and he continues to regard the Senate as centrally important (see perhaps *Hist.* 1.84.4). For the urban *plebs* he displays much contempt

[1] A *sententia* is a thought briefly and pointedly expressed, self-contained and therefore, if originally linked to a context, separable from it.

(*Hist.* 1.32.1 and 3.85), though he is interested in their behaviour and psychology, as indeed he is in the behaviour of mobs generally (witness his elaborate treatment of the mutinies in *Ann.* 1.16–49). He recognized the existence of public opinion, but usually treats it as negligible and sometimes sets against it the judgement of informed observers, *prudentes*. He assumes an air of superiority which becomes quite absurd at *Ann.* 11.21.1, where he refuses to discuss Curtius' low birth, and *Ann.* 4.3.4, where he implies that Livia's crime would have been less heinous had her seducer been a nobleman. Whether Tacitus was himself a *novus homo* is uncertain, but it is very possible. He certainly shows interest in the influx of newcomers into the Senate, and considers that older and better standards were preserved in provincial Italy and beyond (*Ann.* 3.55.3 and 16.5.1). However this may be, he writes like a descendant of a dozen consuls, with an added censoriousness which the elder Cato would have relished.

When Tacitus touches on major moral or religious questions, he is either quite at a loss or sceptical of solutions offered. He gives no convincing appearance of belief in the gods. Indeed his occasional references to them, like his reports of prodigies, may merely be part of the tradition he inherited, a part he was loath to discard, since these references could be useful stylistically, by adding weight and colour to his narrative. Thus at *Hist.* 1.3.2 he very effectively concludes an outline of his theme by asserting that events demonstrated *non esse curae deis securitatem nostram, esse ultionem* 'that the gods are concerned to chastise, not protect us'. Here he may seem to admit divine intervention, and yet, at *Hist.* 1.10.3, as at *Ann.* 14.12.2, he is utterly cynical about any kind of providence. Again, at *Ann.* 6.22, discussing astrology, he confesses complete uncertainty whether the life of man is guided by destiny or just the plaything of chance, and neither here nor elsewhere does he adopt the tenets of any philosophical school. If he tends to any view, it is that *fortuna*[1] directs the black comedy of life (*Ann.* 3.18.4): *mihi, quanto plura recentium seu ueterum reuoluo, tanto magis ludibria rerum mortalium cunctis in negotiis obuersantur* 'the more I think upon recent or earlier history, the more the universal farcicality of human affairs is apparent to me'. Tacitus was a pessimist through and through: not for him easy consolation and popular anodynes.

Tacitus' outlook on politics and political history is generally realistic and detached, sometimes distorted by his own unhappy experiences or tinged with nostalgia. The struggles and achievements of Rome's past excite his enthusiasm (*Ann.* 4.32.1), and he believes that liberty once flourished, though destined to a lingering death under the Principate (*Ann.* 1.74.5). But the old regime was not wholly admirable, least of all in its last years (*Ann.* 3.28.1). Internal dis-

[1] What Tacitus means by *fortuna* in such places as *Ann.* 3.18.4 and 4.1.1 (an important passage) is hard to determine. It is probably something more than chance, though far short of providence.

sension and lust for power brought tribulation, to the provinces as well as Rome (*Ann.* 1.2.2). Then the Principate established peace, at a price and without much honour. Tacitus is disillusioned with ideals and outdated causes, though he pays indirect homage to the Republican heroes Brutus and Cassius (*Ann.* 3.76.2). But about a few matters he cares deeply, perhaps above all freedom of speech. We see how much he cares about this in the *Agricola*, the prefaces to his historical works, and his treatment of the trial of Cremutius Cordus at *Ann.* 4.34–5, where, after Cremutius' speech and condemnation, he directly expresses his own feelings. Here we need have no doubt of what he thinks. In many other cases, where there is no express endorsement, it is perilous to assume that arguments given to others obtain his approval. He is, after all, adept, as any rhetorician should be, at finding the words suitable to the occasion. Thus at *Hist.* 1.15–16 Galba is made eloquently and forcefully to commend adoptive succession to the Principate. That was appropriate in the circumstances (disastrous though this particular adoption proved), but it does not follow that Tacitus, enamoured of Trajan, supposed adoptive succession to be the panacea for all Rome's troubles. He probably thought them past cure.

It is wiser to take Tacitus as he is than, as so many critics have done, require that he should be what he is not. He has grave weaknesses as a historian, if he is judged, as he often has been, by the most exacting modern standards. But he never consciously betrayed his own standards, such as they were: he sought to discover the truth, probing, questioning, rejecting mere plausibility. And he is a supremely gifted writer. In his mature works he commanded with ease the rhetoric which enslaved most of his contemporaries: such difficulties as he had were self-imposed. Yet he laboured long and hard not to write for his own day alone. Hence the magic of his style survives.

4. PLINY THE YOUNGER

Among Latin letters those of Pliny stand second only to Cicero's in interest and importance, though they are very different in character. In recent times they have attracted much attention, particularly, one suspects, because they provide such an excellent starting-point for study of the social history of the early Empire. But the fascinations of Pliny's subject matter should not divert us altogether from the more specifically literary questions, of form, style, and intention, which the letters raise. In what follows we shall look mainly at Books 1–9, the private correspondence published by the author. The letters to Trajan in Book 10 are not without literary interest, either in style (they are framed more simply than those in 1–9) or in content (they tell us much of Pliny's merits and limitations), but, since apparently he did not himself collect and publish them, they cannot be judged in the same terms as the others.

The primary questions are easy to pose and hard to answer. What kind of letters have we here and how were they chosen for publication? More particularly, were they sent to the addressees, then published in their original form, are they revised versions of authentic originals, are they literary exercises which never passed through the post at all, or do some belong to one of these categories, some to another? In his prefatory epistle (1.1) Pliny says: 'you have often urged me to collect and publish such letters as I had written with some special care. I have collected them, disregarding sequence in time (I was not writing a history), but as each one came to hand.' He adds that, if he finds or writes any more, he will not suppress them. At first sight this all seems helpful: it seems less so on further examination. To begin with, writing a letter is not for Pliny necessarily dependent on a call to send one: he explicitly testifies in 7.9 that epistolography was a commendable literary pursuit, an aid to versatility in style. Again, a rough chronological sequence has been established between the nine books, and some sequence may be found even within books. Thus 'disregarding sequence in time' is hard to credit. And the choice of letters for each book cannot be so random as 'as each one came to hand' suggests, for Pliny has plainly effected a balanced variety of themes within each of Books 1–7 (in 8–9 he begins to run short of sufficiently diverse material) and, to some extent, from book to book. There is then a conflict between what Pliny professes and what he has in fact done.

With few exceptions, each letter treats of a single subject: this is usually proposed or sketched at the outset, then developed, discussed, and illustrated. That the letters are planned as organic wholes is further attested by recurrent structural patterns, such as statement followed by three examples. Pliny clearly recognizes certain rules of epistolography, and he senses a need for apology if he breaks them: unity and brevity are especially important. He rarely hurries, or rambles, or adds a postscript. This control and conscious planning divorce Pliny's letters from real life and set them in marked contrast to Cicero's. If we consider the relationship between many of the letters and their addressees, we get a similar impression of unreality. Often, to be sure, subject matter and addressee are related (e.g. family affairs and Fabatus, history or rhetoric and Tacitus), but numerous letters might, as far as we can tell, have been addressed to anyone whom Pliny chose to flatter by his notice. And not infrequently, when he initially links theme and addressee, he proceeds as if oblivious of the addressee's continued existence. Compliment and courtesy are evident here, but it is a far cry from the lively dialogue of genuine correspondence. One may wonder how many of Pliny's letters would have elicited replies. When he has, as so often, not merely proposed a topic but handled it at length, what was a correspondent to add? For instance, is not 4.30 more a courteous acknowledgement of Sura's interest in natural science than a serious request for information and decision? Again, the number of separate addressees is noteworthy: 105 for 247 letters. Thus, while some get a fair number of letters, most get very few. Why is there such a multiplicity of names? After all most letter-writers have intimate friends, to whom they write frankly and often. The exclusion of revealing and embarrassing letters from a correspondence published by the writer is readily intelligible, but it remains surprising that no really close friends emerge, if these are real letters or even edited versions of real letters. A sceptic might say that, for variety or some other reason, Pliny decided to introduce as many addressees as possible: if there were no appropriate letters in his files, he could soon create them. The frequency of standardized openings perhaps supports this scepticism. But mere name-dropping was not Pliny's purpose: many influential contemporaries are not addressed. We need not doubt that the addressees were personally known to him. Having the critical reader much in mind, Pliny was concerned with verisimilitude as well as diversity. He selected or composed the letters accordingly.

Most of the letters fall easily into regular types, according to subject matter: public affairs, personalities, anecdotes, literature, personal business, descriptions, advice, recommendation, and so on. Some of these types correspond with recognized topics for epistolography. Nevertheless the letters probably give a fairly accurate reflection of Pliny's range of interests, which are various but unremarkable. Some subjects, familiar in other writers of the period, scarcely appear at all: antiquarian lore, language and grammar, religion, and, most surprisingly, philosophy. Pliny was not a learned man nor a thinker: it is hard to discover any recondite information in his letters and vain to look for profound or original thoughts. Again, he generally eschews or has erased adverse comment upon contemporaries, except for his *bête noire* Regulus (1.5, 2.20, 4.2, 4.7). And he is singularly delicate about literary matters. Though he talks much of the practice of detailed reciprocal criticism, he presents nothing of the kind in the published correspondence: instead mere appreciations, often vague or flattering. Similarly, in some correspondence about matters of business (such as 3.6), various mundane details, which must have been in the 'real' letters, have been edited out. Pliny was, it seems, guided in his revision not only by discretion but also by a sense of literary propriety and a fear of tedium. He clearly thought that his readers had tender stomachs, and sometimes, by weakening or indeed emasculating his original letters, he has lost the immediacy and realism which elsewhere he successfully retains.

There are numerous echoes of other writers in Pliny's letters, both in thought and in expression. Predictably Cicero and Virgil head the list, followed by Horace, Martial, and Statius amongst others. The Roman poets bulked large in Pliny's reading, as Quintilian would have enjoined: he seems not so well versed in Greek literature. Many of Pliny's reminiscences are such as mark the occasional writing of any educated man, but some may best be explained by conscious imitation and, if so, support the view that certain letters are literary exercises. We have a good 'test-case' in his account of the harbour at Centum Cellae (6.31.15–17: cf. Virg. *Aen.* 1.159–65 and Luc. 2.616–21). The place probably was much as Pliny presents it and as Virgil presented his imaginary harbour, but does that sufficiently explain Pliny's extensive obligation to Virgil for the terms of his own description here? In cases like this it is difficult to distinguish between subconscious association of ideas and deliberate intention to imitate. Elsewhere Pliny obviously wants to show that, in his new genre of prose writing, he can rival writers in more established genres. Thus in 1.15, a 'prose epigram' whimsical and teasing in tone, neat and elegant in style, he vies directly with Martial (5.78), more remotely with Catullus and Horace (13 and *Epist.* 1.5 respectively). Again, in 6.16 and 20, where he relates the eruption of Vesuvius, Pliny does not merely fulfil his ostensible purpose, to supply Tacitus with material. Though he will not write history himself (5.8), he will prove his ability to handle it even in letters, and at 6.20.14–15 he comes very near to Tacitus' most pathetic vein (cf. *Ann.* 4.62.3). But Pliny does not always succeed in carrying off other styles: his attempt at lofty and impassioned indignation in 8.6 proves a diaster. The grand manner ill suits him in the *Panegyricus*, and in his letters it is absurd. Happily such errors of taste are in the correspondence extremely rare.

Pliny's writing is flexible, graceful, and polished. Like Tacitus, he achieves variety without abandoning self-consistency. He is meticulously careful in his vocabulary and phraseology, indeed rather unadventurous. All the internal evidence confirms what he reports about the painstaking composition and revision of his works. Pliny's most characteristic (and classical) quality is restraint. He likes antithesis, but does not, as Seneca does, overplay it; he enjoys sound-effects, but does not, as Nepos does, pursue them until they become an idiosyncrasy; he shares the current craze for epigrams, but does not, as Tacitus does in his *Histories*, obtrude them on every possible occasion. If there is a virtue in being without vices, Pliny in his letters may lay fair claim to it. But he has some mannerisms and predilections which he has not completely restrained, above all delight in two-fold and three-fold asyndeta and, matched against love of anaphora and emphatic repetition, strenuous avoidance of repetition generally (see e.g. 7.27). Cicero is Pliny's ultimate model and inspiration: smooth and limpid phrases, well balanced architecture of clause and sentence, and recurrent rhythmic patterns all attest that predominant influence. But it was the Cicero of the speeches and treatises, rather than the letters, who fired Pliny to emulation. And so, not unaccountably, Pliny's style is much akin to Quintilian's, albeit in comparison somewhat thin and affected. By blending Ciceronian and modern ingredients Pliny created an apt medium for urbane and inhibited epistolography. In his letters we have the last flowering of classicism, before individual whim or the extravagances of the archaizers fatally infected prose style.

Pliny's view of his times is tinged with complacency and humbug: only a few letters reveal that this is not the best of all possible worlds. He readily and unquestioningly adopts the attitudes and conventions of the affluent and leisured class which he adorned. Social and cultural trivialities occupy him inordinately, and indeed his worst anxiety is lest public duties should distract him from the pleasures of friendship and study. For Pliny and his contemporaries, unlike Cicero and Sallust, literary activity needs no excuse. He is, of course, duly modest about his own compositions, as he might well be, if he were judged by the execrable verses he cites at 7.4.6 and 7.9.11, but, like so many Romans, he aspires to immortality. It is fortunate for his readers that his purview is not limited by the walls of his salon: he is a sharp and attentive observer of the world at large and he shows an intermittent regard for the beauties and complexities of nature (see e.g. 8.8). Perhaps his uncle's influence was at work here, though Pliny is as much a romantic *manqué* as a dilettante scientist. His best quality is a genuine kindness towards the less privileged: the sentiments expressed in 8.16 and elsewhere are not mere lip-service to the humanitarian fashion of the age. But Pliny's advertisement of his public and private benefactions remains highly distasteful. And he is not always honest with himself. He would like to believe, and have us believe, that he challenged dangers under Domitian: in truth he was a time-server, like most senators, and he would earn more respect if he admitted the fact. Perhaps Pliny intended his self-revelation to serve a didactic purpose: by displaying the satisfaction which a virtuous and cultured life brings, he could commend such a life to others.[1]

We do not come to know Pliny, as we know Cicero, from his correspondence. That is one inevitable result of selection and revision. Pliny's letters exhibit charm and variety in abundance, but they lack sinews. Pliny never grapples with hard problems, emotional or intellectual. He has neither trenchancy nor passion, and consequently he cannot move his readers. Yet, though he falls short of greatness, his achievement is substantial: he widened the scope of prose writing by demonstrating that a collection of personal letters, designed or reshaped for publication, could offer almost every opportunity for description, narration, and comment which a stylist and observer of life might conceivably desire. Pliny had no worthy imitator in antiquity nor much influence. Fronto possessed neither the ability nor the will to imitate him. Again, the arid Symmachus and the tortuous Sidonius are not successors he would have cherished. He finds them at last in Mme de Sévigné and Horace Walpole.

[1] I owe this interesting idea to Professor Kenney.

The *Panegyricus* ('Panegyric')[1] is the only complete Latin oration which survives from the first two centuries of our era. For that reason, if no other, it possesses considerable literary interest. Again, it throws some light upon a period otherwise poorly documented (A.D. 96–100), as upon several wider areas of social and political history. Nevertheless it has fallen, not undeservedly, into almost universal contempt. Pliny would have been wiser if he had not expanded and developed the more simple version actually delivered in the Senate (*Epist.* 3.18.1).

There is no earlier speech with which the *Panegyricus* is closely comparable, but it owes a good deal, particularly in style, to Cicero's *Pro Marcello*. Pliny describes and extols Trajan's virtues, denigrates Domitian, and, like Seneca in his *De clementia*, sets forth certain ideals of princely conduct (cf. *Epist.* 3.18.3). He had a delicate task, and on some topics, military and dynastic, he has to be extremely circumspect. When he affects outspoken independence or blends banter with praise (e.g. 59.3–6), one recalls Tacitus' sour words *ea sola species adulandi supererat* 'that was the only brand of adulation as yet untried'. No doubt Trajan merited acclaim as the best of emperors, but Pliny spoils his case by enthusing interminably over trivialities and by his obsession with Domitian, with whom Trajan is repeatedly contrasted. It is after all an odd form of eulogy to reiterate that a man is not a profligate, not a sadist, not a megalomaniac, and indeed Pliny apologizes for these comparisons at 53.1–3, not altogether convincingly. At first sight the *Panegyricus* may seem exuberantly optimistic, but occasionally a thread of deep gloom shows through. Bad emperors may return (see e.g. 88.9), and what the Senate has suffered in the past it may suffer again. Pliny's outlook is not utterly different from Tacitus', whom he sometimes imitated or prompted to imitation. But a ceremonial occasion imposed restrictions over and above those which inhibited freedom of speech generally: the most interesting matters in the *Panegyricus* are to be read between the lines.

The speech is couched in the grand style, being elaborately expansive, patterned in phrase and clause, and full of florid conceits and rhetorical artifice of every kind. The lucidity which distinguishes the letters is here liable to eclipse. And, while the antitheses and epigrams which Pliny readily excogitated are often as wearisome as they are vacuous (see e.g. 61.4, 62.9, 67.3, 84.5), it is probably his woolly repetitiveness, rather than misplaced ingenuity, which in the end reduces most readers to despair. He himself wonders (*Epist.* 3.18.10) whether more sober treatment might have been preferable, but plainly he remained in love with his own vices.

[1] This title may not be original. At *Epist.* 3.13.1 and 18.1 Pliny talks of *gratiarum actio*, 'expression of thanks', but that is not necessarily his title either.

5. SUETONIUS

Suetonius published many works, scholarly rather than literary, though this distinction was no more clear-cut in his time than it is now. For some years at least he was a member of the emperor's secretariat. And, while closely acquainted with the schools of grammar and rhetoric, he was probably never a professional teacher. We have here a talented and versatile man of letters, comparable with Varro, though hardly his equal. Doubtless Suetonius' writings required much anxious parturition (cf. Plin. *Epist.* 5.10): the two which survive, *De vita Caesarum*, 'On the life of the Caesars' and (fragmentarily) *De viris illustribus*, 'On eminent men', are evidently based on diverse and extensive reading.

Following an approach to biography used by some of the Alexandrian scholars, Suetonius treats his subjects very schematically, according to divisions and categories such as antecedents, birth, career, achievements, morals, appearance, and death, but with some variations according to the particular subject matter. This form of biography was perhaps originally employed for literary figures, and thence transferred, not by Suetonius alone (cf. Nep. *Epam.* 1.4), to persons distinguished in public life. He could, however, have chosen another form, well represented in Greek by his near contemporary Plutarch, and going back at least to the early Peripatetic school. Plutarch views and assesses his subjects' lives coherently and chronologically: he prefers narration, with occasional moralizing, to analysis and tabulation. And plainly Plutarch's approach is, unlike Suetonius', closely akin to that of the historians. But there is more in Suetonius' method than misguided application of Alexandrian pedantry. Roman funeral speeches and epitaphs were traditionally centred on the deceased's honours, deeds, and prowess: they did not characterize him in the round. The *Res gestae* of Augustus helps to explain Suetonius' attitudes and choice of material. He, for instance, like Augustus, records offices held, donatives, and buildings. The Alexandrians gave him a framework: he easily brought within it matters of established Roman interest. He was perhaps the first to recognize that the Caesars should be treated as a special class. Supreme power and the way of life it engendered set them apart. Here lies his best claim to originality.[1]

Some critics assert that, for all his categorizing, Suetonius pays serious regard to chronology. That, to an extent, is true. In passages where he outlines parts of a man's career he naturally tends to follow temporal sequence. And, when his material is specially curious and inviting, he may set it out consecutively and with abundant detail, as in his account of the last days of Nero (*Nero* 40.4–49.4), perhaps the best thing he ever wrote. In general, however,

[1] I owe this view of Suetonius' originality to Professor Kenney.

he has his plan, and adheres to it. Though his schematism was inimical alike to wide historical survey and gradual delineation of character, it suited him well enough, for he has but a fumbling grasp of history and psychology. He perceives, for example, that Tiberius' principate somehow changed for the worse, but offers no convincing explanation of this change. Indeed his picture of Tiberius is glaringly self-contradictory, unless we can stomach metamorphosis of a moderate, old-fashioned aristocrat into a perverted and sadistic tyrant. Here, as elsewhere, Suetonius' characterization anticipates the story of Jekyll and Hyde. Witness the monumental crudity of his division of Caligula's actions (*Cal.* 22.1) into those attributable (*a*) to a prince, and (*b*) to a monster. But he is not always beside the mark. In his *Julius* he conveys something of Caesar's extraordinary magnetism, and in his *Augustus* illustrates the complexities of Augustus' personality. And he is adept at finding the revealing anecdotes which are so essential to biography. Yet rarely, if ever, does he complete his picture, and, by rigorous exclusion of material, however important, not immediately relevant to the individual with whom he is concerned, he usually leaves the background blank. Thus his approach was not properly adjusted to treatment of major historical characters, who must be set in a full context, though arguably adequate for minor celebrities, such as poets and orators. In what remains of the *De viris illustribus* we have some admirable miniatures, and here, on a tiny scale, he provides the necessary background, by sketching the development of grammar and rhetoric at Rome.

Suetonius drew on many sources for his *Vitae Caesarum*, and had little compunction about copying them word for word. That he is generally uncritical is the more to be regretted since, when he chooses to investigate a problem, he can be sharp and judicious, as in his discussion of Caligula's birthplace (*Cal.* 8). In the first three lives he uses and cites much primary evidence, notably letters of Augustus. He had carefully scrutinized many of the original documents (see *Aug.* 87–8), presumably housed in the imperial archives and accessible to him while he held high rank in the secretariat. But, from his *Tiberius* onwards, the number of citations of such material decreases markedly, and, furthermore, the later lives are generally less detailed and precise, in nomenclature and in reference to sources. The reason for this change is still debated. Probably, after his dismissal from public service in (perhaps) 122, he could no longer freely consult the records he had previously exploited. It is harder to explain why he began to take fewer pains himself in the use of evidence available to anyone.

Suetonius writes simply and straightforwardly. He is brief, but not pregnant or epigrammatic. He neither rounds his sentences into periods nor overloads them with appended clauses. Indeed, apart from some liking for variation, he seems largely indifferent to niceties of style. Yet his vocabulary is interesting, not so much because of its occasional idiosyncrasies as because it is generally indiscriminate. Suetonius recognizes no obligation to select and exclude, though he may consciously avoid high-flown expressions. He is largely content with current usage, and not averse even from mongrelized words and official terminology. Being unconcerned about unity of texture, he can dispense with the art of paraphrase and admit, without embarrassment, any quotations large or small, including Greek. He also takes over some oddities from his sources: at least a considerable minority of the rare or unique words found in his writings may be attributed to pillage rather than innovation, and much resemble the riches of the magpie's nest. He might be contrasted with Gellius, who necessarily quoted often and at length, but who is much more fussy about his own style and altogether more self-conscious.

Except in the comparatively few places where he exercises his critical powers, Suetonius' value is that of his sources, and hence very mixed. He accommodates insubstantial rumour as generously as hard attested fact. He is inconsistent, as well as gullible. And he loves scandal, particularizing very meticulously on sexual vices, whether of emperors, poets, or grammarians (for example *Tib.* 43–5, *Nero* 28–9, *Gramm.* 23.5–6). Yet he tries, with some success, to give an impression of honest, impartial reporting, unemotional and not intentionally humorous, or, to borrow an apt term from a recent critic, dead-pan. Suetonius does not, like the historians, win effect by dramatizing his material. He leaves it to speak for itself, which it does well enough when it is intrinsically interesting and he troubles to present it fully. So, for example, some may prefer his description of Vitellius' ignominious death (*Vit.* 16–17) to Tacitus' selective and dramatized version (*Hist.* 3.84.4–85), precisely because he retails every sordid detail, without the pathos and comment which the theme invited. Though he never attempted to vie with writers of major history, he provides a wealth of information indispensable for any understanding of the first century A.D. But it requires careful sifting and redeployment.

We learn little about Suetonius from his writings. But it is clear enough that he possesses no original mind and that his attitudes, as far as he reveals them, are unsophisticated. Pliny attests (*Epist.* 1.18.1) that he was superstitious, and he certainly appears to take omens and prodigies very seriously. Some have found in the lives traces of hostility towards Hadrian. On inspection, they seem extremely tenuous. Others detect criticism of Tacitus, and perhaps Suetonius' discussion of Nero's poems (*Nero* 52) is directed against *Ann.* 14.16.1. But we have no unshakeable evidence that he was familiar with the *Annals*.

Suetonius has enjoyed lasting popularity. In the *Historia Augusta* (*Firm.* 1.1, *Prob.* 2.7), a mendacious compilation partly modelled on his *De vita Caesarum*, he is praised for honesty and candour. And of late his unpretentiousness has seemed an asset, now that airs and graces are at a discount. But, in the final assessment of his work, we must ask whether, to the best of his ability, he consistently tried to discover the truth and report it. The answer to that question cannot be favourable.

6. FLORUS

The historian

Florus' outline of Roman history, ending with Augustus, was in late antiquity inaccurately described as an epitome of Livy. Doubtless Livy was his main source, directly or at second hand. But we may detect debts to Sallust and Caesar, amongst others, and poetic influence, particularly Virgil's and Lucan's. And Florus records events later than the conclusion of Livy's history. Again, his attitudes differ from Livy's: he seems, for instance, largely uninterested in religion. Some contend that he is attempting to create a new genre, a sort of historical panegyric, midway between prose and poetry. This view is rather fanciful, but Florus' panegyrical tone is unmistakable. He personifies the *populus Romanus* and makes it the hero of his whole narrative. So central indeed is the position he accords it that sometimes it is simply understood as the subject of sentences. Conversely the Senate's role is obscured, one of several ways in which he over-simplifies history. While he commonly regards Roman leaders as merely the people's agents, he still, like Velleius, shows intense interest in individuals. Perhaps he meant his work for school use: he arranges his material simply, provides occasional summaries, and is generally more of a story-teller than an enquirer. One may compare Dickens's *A child's history of England*: Dickens too preferred to omit recent history.

Florus has little to say which is new or remarkable. Thus he claims, reasonably but not originally, that both *uirtus* and *fortuna* contributed to Rome's greatness (*praef.* 2), and emphasizes, perhaps with Hadrian in mind, that it is harder to retain than acquire provinces (1.33.8 and 2.30.29). Tending to see the past in contemporary terms he falls into anachronism, for instance by misapplying the concept of *imperium Romanum* to comparatively early periods. He adopts, perhaps *via* one of the Senecas and ultimately from Varro,[1] an interesting but unsatisfactory comparison of the Roman people's history with four stages of human life, infancy, adolescence, maturity, and old age (*praef.* 4–8). This scheme is nowhere properly justified, and the last period (from Augustus to Florus' own times), which he does not handle, evidently caused him difficulty and embarrassment. The *populus* could no longer credibly figure

[1] Though we cannot be sure how Varro used his scheme of four ages.

as hero (see 2.14.4–6), though he has perforce to talk of its rejuvenation under Trajan. Otherwise he would be obliged to admit that the Empire's demise is imminent. And plainly he is an optimist: Rome always triumphs in the end, and fortune, though apt to waver momentarily, is never long unfaithful. There is a striking contrast here with Tacitus' profound gloom. Florus purveyed such intellectually undemanding diet as his contemporaries and later generations could easily digest: hence he was much used and occasionally much praised. Being principally concerned to present matter for admiration and eulogy, he makes few trenchant or perceptive observations. Most of his numerous comments are fatuous, or express child-like wonder and astonishment. It is hard to find another Latin writer so utterly empty-headed.

Florus' style, though often precious and florid, is virtually untouched by the archaisms familiar in Fronto and Gellius. And all the endeavours to discover in his work a distinct African Latinity have come to nothing. In fact he has very little individuality. His embellishments cannot conceal extreme poverty in vocabulary; his use of prose-rhythm is conventional; his imagery seems equally commonplace, and his epigrams, while sometimes effective, are usually forced. But he can write clearly and fluently and tell a good story. If he had heeded the maxim *rem tene, uerba sequentur* 'look after the facts and the words will look after themselves', he might have been no disgrace to Latin literature. Sadly such effort was beyond him.

The rhetorician

We can only guess how Florus tackled the theme of his dialogue *Vergilius orator an poeta*, for we have merely part of its introduction, contrived, after Cicero's manner, to set the scene and introduce the participants. But the theme itself is of interest, recalling the first section of Tacitus' *Dialogus*, and comparable not only with a dispute mentioned by another near contemporary, Granius Licinianus (p. 33.9–10 Flemisch), whether Sallust is an orator rather than a historian, but also with arguments whether Lucan was a historian rather than a poet (see Serv. on *Aen.* 1.382). It looks as if such topics were frequently debated in schools of rhetoric: that did not preclude independent treatment. Perhaps Florus wanted to vie with Tacitus (a daunting enterprise), if, as is very possible, Tacitus' work was the earlier. His few surviving pages make lively and pleasant reading, though they are extremely self-centred. This is typical of the second century, when, as Fronto and Marcus Aurelius show, the anxieties and aspirations of individuals enjoy obsessive attention.

The poet

No poem ascribed to Florus possesses any substantial merit, though *ego nolo Caesar esse*, 'I don't want to be a Caesar', is superlatively cheeky. The poem about roses (no. 2 Jal) might seem charming if later poetasters had not worried the idea to death. Some attribute to Florus that celebrated and lovable composition, the *Pervigilium Veneris*. Their opinion has no firm basis, and others believe that language and metre alike indicate the fourth century, if not the fifth.

33

TECHNICAL WRITING

I. POMPONIUS MELA

The earliest surviving Latin work on geography, Pomponius Mela's *De chorographia*, 'Of description of countries',[1] has not won the approval of geographers, though Pliny the Elder, hardly a discriminating critic, seems to have taken it seriously. The work is no systematic and professional treatise, but an outline for general readers, and it offers little new material, being largely based on written sources, including, though not necessarily at first hand, Nepos and Varro. Mela states (1.2) that he aims to describe the world's main divisions, then its coastal areas in more detail (cf. 1.24), and to add memorable particulars of individual regions and their inhabitants. His worst fault is that he supplies no measurements. And he was sadly misguided in basing his detailed survey on a sort of circumnavigation, after the manner of the Greek writings ascribed to Scylax and Scymnus, for as a result important inland areas, such as Bactria and Dacia, are wholly omitted. Again, in his choice of ethnographical matter he is quite uncritical. Judged even on its own terms, as a piece of popularization, the *De chorographia* cannot be applauded: the exposition might have been clearer and the expression more relaxed.

For all his errors (e.g. 2.57), obscurities, and omissions, Mela still possesses some interest. Occasionally (e.g. 3.31 on the Baltic and 3.38 on the Caspian) traces of unusually accurate information have somehow got through to him. And, while he will readily swallow fables or travellers' tales (e.g. 1.47 on the Blemyes and 3.81 on the Pygmies) or take over unacknowledged from Herodotus much of his account of the Scythians, he also preserves information not found elsewhere about places and beliefs (e.g. 3.19 on the Druids and 3.48 on the island of Sena). Again, some may detect merit in his elaborate descriptions, like that of the Corycian cave (1.72–6), even if they are rather out of proportion in a work of three short books.

The deprecation of Mela's preface is part of a conventional pose: having

[1] *Chorographia* differs from geography, which is more general, and topography, which is more restricted. But the differences cannot be pressed very far. In so far as they are valid, *chorographia* fits what Mela produces well enough.

asserted that his subject does not admit stylistic embellishment, he sets about providing it. Intricate word-order, anaphora, occasional asyndeta and ellipses, and variation in the shape of sentences, from expansive to starkly abrupt, are calculated to earn the reader's attention and regard. The influence of Sallust may be seen in words and phrases, but there is no sustained imitation. In some ways Mela resembles Florus: he shares, in particular, a fondness for expressing admiration and wonderment (e.g. 1.38, 2.57), and lacks any real intellectual curiosity. The passage on tides at 3.1–2 may well represent his work as a whole. It is most carefully written and intended to impress, but to instruct with evidence or convince by argument is not Mela's business.

2. COLUMELLA

Columella's *Res rustica*, 'Agriculture',[1] the fullest treatment of the subject in Latin literature, is a product of wide reading and long personal experience. Columella is appalled by the decline he sees in Italian agriculture (1 *praef.* 13ff.), and aims to show what knowledge and determination can do to put matters right. He sets a high value upon rural life, as opposed to urban, and indeed he shares most of the sentiments expressed by Virgil in his *Georgics*. But he is no starry-eyed idealist. If the perfection of farming, as of oratory, is remote and hard to attain (1 *praef.* 28ff.), that gives him no motive for despair: second-best is better than nothing. He demands discipline, efficiency, and profit, but does not therefore lack humanity, for he wants his farm to be happy and thriving as a whole. In his *Res rustica* we learn much of what life in the country was like in ancient Italy, hard indeed, but not invariably wretched.

Columella treats first of the site, layout, and staff of a farm (1), then cereals and vegetables (2), fruit-trees, in particular the vine and olive (3–5), larger mammals (6), smaller mammals (7), poultry and fish (8), bees (9), the garden (10), then (11) the duties of the *uilicus* 'overseer' and (12) the duties of the overseer's wife. Book 10 is in hexameter verse, so written, Columella tells us, at the behest of his dedicatee, Silvinus, and the encouragement of Virgil (*Georg.* 4.147–8), who left horticulture for posterity to handle.

Plainly Columella is much indebted to earlier agricultural writers, including his most recent predecessors Atticus, Celsus, and Graecinus. The length of his work is partly at least due to his desire to consider and, where necessary, controvert their views. Comparison with the older treatises of Cato and Varro would suggest that Columella filled out what they were content to sketch, adopting from them (and in particular Varro) many basic ideas and certain divisions in subject matter. He appears to have scrutinized established opinions very closely, but, when he disagrees, he is normally as courteous in his dis-

[1] For the *De arboribus*, 'On trees', which requires no separate discussion here, see Appendix.

sension as he is independent in his judgements. He is well read and not averse occasionally from general philosophical reflections (e.g. 3.10.9ff.).

Columella writes clearly, neatly, even elegantly. That he cares about style is evident from various comments made on his predecessors (e.g. 1.1.12, 2.1.2). Though he does not always avoid repetition, he has at his command a rich variety of vocabulary in dealing with matters, such as planting, which often recur. Contemporary fashions in literary prose leave him virtually untouched (one may contrast Pliny the Elder), for he does not seek to impress his readers by ingenuities of antithesis or epigrammatic point. He lacks also, and more regrettably, that pungency and bite which not infrequently enlivens the writing of Varro. And, in view of the size of his treatise, he makes comparatively little use of digressions and 'purple passages'. A few there are indeed (e.g. 7.12.1, 8.8.10), but they are not extravagantly developed. Columella is ever anxious to get on with his business, for which his unaffected and resourceful style is singularly well fitted.

One can hardly doubt that Columella was an infinitely painstaking and very successful farmer (see, e.g., 3.3.13–14). His enthusiasm for his theme is evident in many ways, not least when argument, which he enjoys, is happily interwoven with exposition: sometimes he seems to be conducting a dialogue with himself, as well as other authorities. And he takes a modest pride in appealing to the results of his own experiments. Today he might be a professor of agriculture. Or perhaps that is what he was, if, as has been conjectured, he and Silvinus ran some sort of agricultural school. Still, his treatise has flaws, in substance and in structure. Some are venial, such as the instances of superstitious lore (e.g. 2.10.10ff.), of which more and worse may be found in other writers. But there are errors too (as in astronomical matters in Book 11) and some confusion or self-contradiction (e.g. 2.20.2, compared with 12.52.18). Again, Book 10 was a gallant, but ill-fated enterprise. If ever there was a case of versified prose, we have it here. Columella seems to have assembled the main material of Book 10 in his usual way, then forced it into hexameters and added some purely ornamental passages. Not that the poem is inept or faulty technically: it is such as a well educated man of the period might be expected to contrive. But comparison with Virgil, which Columella invites, works heavily to his disadvantage. Again, the treatise was not planned as a whole in its present form. Columella composed and published in stages, taking account in what followed of opinions expressed on earlier books (see 4.1.1). This, added to his habit of leaving matters to be resumed later, makes for some complexity, if not muddle. And Books 11 and 12 are an addition to his original scheme, which might have been concluded with Book 10 (see 11.1.1–2). It is, however, instructive to see here, with unusual certainty, how a work of ancient literature changed and developed in the course of its composition.

The neglect of Columella in recent times is readily explicable. Much of what he has to say can interest only specialists, and his language, unlike Cato's and Varro's, can hardly claim exceptionally close attention. One may regret this neglect nevertheless, for in the *Res rustica* we encounter not only Columella's warm and engaging personality, but also a sane and business-like Latin style against which the achievements or aberrations of some more spectacular writers might not unprofitably be judged.

3. PLINY THE ELDER

Pliny is one of the prodigies of Latin literature, boundlessly energetic and catastrophically indiscriminate, wide-ranging and narrow-minded, a pedant who wanted to be a popularizer, a sceptic infected by traditional sentiment, and an aspirant to style who could hardly frame a coherent sentence. That is the impression given by his only surviving work, and no other evidence gainsays it. In a busy life, much of it in public service, Pliny found time for many intellectual activities, but not often for second thoughts.

The *Natural history*,[1] dedicated (A.D. 77 or 78) in an unwieldy and effusive preface to the heir apparent Titus, comprises list of contents (Book 1), cosmology (2), geography (3–6), anthropology (7), zoology (8–11), botany (12–19), botany (20–7) and zoology (28–32) in relation to medicine, and mineralogy (33–7). Digressions, historical references, and elaborate descriptions vary and enliven the work. Frequently Pliny is carried away into bombast by enthusiasm for his theme, indignation, or a maudlin brand of moralizing (e.g. 7.2–5 and 142–6). He drew no clear line between report and comment, and offered not a cold appraisal of fact but a panegyric upon the wonders of nature, in which man, her most marvellous creation, gets more than his due. Yet he genuinely sought to instruct, to set down information possibly useful to somebody sometime. Many passages look like conglutination of notes made during reading (Plin. *Epist.* 3.5.17): certainly disparate matters are unhappily conjoined. Pliny catered for diverse interests, but not for experts: the *Natural history* was written by a learned amateur for the benefit of unlearned amateurs. An abundant repertory of miscellaneous knowledge, it survived in entirety, though eagerly pillaged and excerpted. No Roman possessed the will and enterprise to supersede it.

Since Pliny lists the sources of each book (an unusual and noteworthy procedure), and often cites them for details, we escape one familiar difficulty. Numerous residual problems, about the authorities principally used in particular sections, are beyond our scope. One or two general points claim notice. Pliny

[1] *Naturalis historia* is the title now conventional, but Plin. *Epist.* 3.5.6 suggests that the work was originally called *naturae historiae*.

was both patriotic and gullible. His patriotism sometimes led him into exaggeration (e.g. 37.201–2) and encouraged him to take second hand from Roman sources what he could have had first hand from the Greeks. His gullibility led him into many absurdities (e.g. 7.64–5), but incidentally benefited us: along with marvels and anecdotes, apparently the staple diet of Roman readers (cf. Valerius Maximus), he records much abstruse wisdom and mumbo-jumbo, and thus illuminates obscure areas of folklore, quackery, and superstitition. Yet elsewhere he is aggressively rationalistic and a sour commentator on human ineptitude (e.g. 30.1–2). A more singular mixture is hard to imagine.

Norden[1] justly remarked that stylistically Pliny is amongst the worst of Latin writers, and not to be excused by his subject matter, since Columella and Celsus, faced with fairly comparable material, wrote well enough. In truth Pliny had neither literary skill nor sense of propriety, and he failed to discipline his thoughts. Instead of adopting the plain and sober style appropriate to his theme, he succumbs to lust for embellishment. The ornaments he parades differ somewhat from those employed by his contemporaries, mainly because they are more crude. But in his concern for instantaneous effect Pliny is wholly typical. He can be florid in the extreme, accumulating vacuous and picturesque phrases (e.g. 9.102–3), much as Apuleius was to do; he strings together tedious patterns of balanced clauses (e.g. 10.81–2); and he turns out epigrams of exceptional extravagance and insipidity. Predictably he eschewed Ciceronian periods, but, unlike Seneca and Tacitus, devised no original sentence-structure with which to replace them, unless casual parataxis, regular outside the 'purple passages', should be termed structure. He may be compared with Varro, who also wrote rapidly and voluminously, and had no gift for elegant expression. Equally he may be contrasted, since Varro probably cared little about expression anyway.[2]

In an assessment of Pliny the lost works cannot be disregarded. The 'Uncertainties of expression' had considerable influence on grammatical writings down to Priscian's time. 'The student',[3] which dealt in part at least with rhetorical artifices (see Gell. 9.16), accords with and confirms Pliny's evident addiction to transient scholastic fashion. 'The German wars' and 'Aufidius Bassus continued' amply justified Suetonius' inclusion of Pliny amongst notable historians. The latter work is probably the basic common source for the period from Claudius until and perhaps beyond A.D. 69 which we can recognize, but not for certain identify, behind Tacitus, Plutarch, Dio, and (sometimes) Suetonius.[4] Full and detailed, but simplistic in approach, this source presented ideal material for exploitation and recasting: Tacitus recast,

[1] I 314.
[2] Laughton (1960) 1–3.
[3] Whether the title was *studiosus* or *studiosi*, and what exactly it meant, is debatable.
[4] Townend (1961 and 1964) *passim*.

others exploited. If it was Pliny, his stylistic weaknesses, as seen in the *Natural history*, would further have tempted his successors to do better themselves.

The size and technicality of the *Natural history* condemn it to few readers. And, after all, the information provided is now mainly of antiquarian interest. Yet students of Latin language and style neglect Pliny at their peril. Here, better than in most other places, we may see the contortions and obscurities, the odd combinations of preciosity and baldness, and the pure vacuity to which rhetorical prose, handled by any but the most talented, could precipitously descend and would indeed often descend again.

4. FRONTINUS

Frontinus' two surviving works, *De aquis* and *Strategemata*, have somewhat limited pretensions to be literature. He calls them *commentarii*, a description comprising or overlapping with our 'notes', 'memoranda', 'records', and 'treatises'. A *commentarius* could be a polished composition in the plain style, or lack polish altogether: there was no firm tradition, as for the major genres of prose. The subject matter and the author's personality, rather than rules of genre, determined the character and quality of the writing.

The *De aquis* is exactly what it claims to be, a systematic account of the water-supply of Rome. This practical, business-like and perhaps original treatise (we know of no antecedents, though, of course, hydraulic engineering was not a new field) is mainly of historical interest, and otherwise concerns the linguist more than the literary critic. Its language seems in general unaffected, though one finds occasional embellishments and may fairly suppose that Frontinus wrote for a wider public than experts like himself. The *Strategemata* pose considerably more questions. Frontinus asserts that this work too is practical: the information he has arranged and classified will be of use to generals. Yet the book is strangely divorced from reality. Frontinus scarcely calls at all upon recent experience, such as his own, but purveys a mass of hackneyed material, Greek and Roman, compiled from literary sources, some of them, like Livy, painfully familiar. Restriction on freedom of speech under Domitian provides no complete explanation. Frontinus probably conformed with fashion. The Romans of the Empire had no little liking for the collection and retailing of snippets of information, historical, legendary, and anecdotal. One cannot fail to note the similarity, in type and mixed provenance of material (Roman and foreign), between Frontinus' work and the wider ranging *Facta et dicta memorabilia* of Valerius Maximus. The language of the *Strategemata*, while sometimes diverging from the commonplace (perhaps under the influence of history), is on the whole impoverished and repetitive. Of course a long series of brief items gave scant opportunity for elaboration, and Frontinus may well have sought a very plain style as befitting his theme and appropriate to a military man and administrator. But possibly he could produce nothing better. The numerous errors of fact in the *Strategemata*, when tested against other and better sources, enjoin a rather sceptical view of his abilities as a writer generally.

The authenticity of the fourth book of the *Strategemata* has been debated at length. Many, perhaps most, scholars today would accept it as genuine. The linguistic differences from Books 1–3 can be accounted for by an intervening lapse of time and a partial change of topic. And there are, as well as differences, some telling similarities. Apart from the main problem concerning Book 4, we have reason to suspect serious interpolation in various places and so some caution is needed in use of the work as any kind of authority.

34

RHETORIC AND SCHOLARSHIP

I. QUINTILIAN

Quintilian, the leading *rhetor*, 'teacher of rhetoric', of the Flavian period, fostered and, in his own writing, represented a reaction in literary taste against the innovations of Seneca, Lucan, and their contemporaries. There was no major revision of rhetorical theory: the difference lay rather in practice, in preference for older and, as Quintilian believed, better models, notably Cicero. This shift of attitude can be associated with a wider social change, recorded by Tacitus (*Ann.* 3.55), who says that the extravagances of Nero's times gave way on Vespasian's accession to more sober fashions, partly because new men, from Italy and the provinces, rose to prominence and reintroduced stricter codes of conduct. Quintilian, who had his origins in Spain, belongs amongst them. He was a man of wealth and influence, favoured by the ruling dynasty, and probably the first to obtain a state chair of Latin rhetoric (Suet. *Vesp.* 18). That he flatters Domitian (10.1.91–2) or talks of him in courtly terms (4 *praef.* 2–5) is neither blameworthy nor remarkable, but his bitter hostility towards contemporary philosophers (1 *praef.* 15, 12.3.12) raises interesting questions. Perhaps he honestly considers them depraved and pernicious (cf. Juvenal *passim*), but he may also be paying politic deference to the emperor's prejudices, as arguably he does in his conventionally scathing remark about the Jews (3.7.21). No doubt he saw himself as the latter-day champion of rhetoric in its ancient quarrel with philosophy. He concedes that the orator requires a knowledge of ethics, and therefore wants moral philosophy to be absorbed in (indeed subordinated to) the study of rhetoric (12.2.6ff.). He finds some support for this idea in the *De oratore*, but the intolerance which he here displays is utterly alien to Cicero.

The *Institutio oratoria* 'The training of an orator' is a happy amalgamation of an *ars rhetorica*, 'handbook of rhetoric', with a treatise on the functions and ideals of oratory, into which much discussion of education and literature is additionally blended. Quintilian is determined to put lots of flesh on dry bones (1 *praef.* 23–4). For a *rhetor* he ranges extraordinarily widely, concerning himself with the whole shaping of his ideal pupil, from early infancy to full maturity.

In the long technical sections of Books 3–9 Quintilian attempts mainly to evaluate existing theories rather than to propound new ones: he is flexible and undogmatic. More originality is seen when he deals with the education of young children (Book 1), the proper duties of a teacher (Book 2), and the merits or utility of individual writers (10.1). And several shorter sections possess both special interest and novelty, for instance 12.10.27–37, where he compares the potentialities of Greek and Latin for a stylist. While his technical disquisitions are largely (and avowedly) derivative, he draws on his own rich experience in discussing the actual business of teaching. And he is not averse from polemic, particularly against faulty method and debased standards. He consistently adopts a high moral tone, both in his conception of the orator as necessarily also a good man (1 *praef.* 9), elaborated in Book 12, and in the absolute rectitude which he enjoins upon the teacher (2.2.4ff.). It is therefore curious that he retains no little regard for Domitius Afer (Tac. *Ann.* 4.52.4, 66.1). He is also uncompromising in his demand that even the most eminent *rhetor* should undertake routine teaching (2.3.1ff.): only the best, in his opinion, is good enough. He tried to provide it, and also ventured on some modest reforms, not apparently with much success, since the whole system of rhetorical training was firmly entrenched and parents and pupils alike were intransigent in their desire to retain it unchanged. More than once he appears to be fighting for lost causes, mildly liberal.

Quintilian compels admiration, for his seriousness and dedication and for the sanity and perception of the judgements which he passes on methods of teaching and (sometimes) on literature. And we may warm to his genial humanity, even though it does not embrace philosophers. But he has grave deficiencies. One of them is astonishing: he seems to know little directly of the major Greek writers. Again, his vision is narrow. If it were not, he would have perceived that more was required to repair the inadequacies of current education than tinkering with details and occasional lip-service to wider culture. And he shows scant historical sense: how, we may ask, could the paragon who satisfied all Quintilian's requirements and emerged a perfect orator ever fully benefit from his training in (say) A.D. 90? Tacitus and 'Longinus' grasped the importance of that question.

Quintilian's style exemplifies many of the virtues which he commends. He diligently pursues perspicuity, and he avoids archaizing or modernistic affectations (cf. 8.3.24ff., 12.10.73). Cicero is his principal model, but he is no thoughtless imitator. He prefers discourse to harangue, and controls his rhetoric in places which others would have empurpled. For colour, relief, and variety he resorts above all to metaphor and simile: he was clearly endowed with sharp powers of observation. His epigrams are usually neat and unlaboured and arise naturally from their contexts. Altogether this is a mellow and easy style, neither wearisome like that of Seneca nor brittle like that of the younger Pliny. Occasionally, however, when he has a lot to say and wants to say it all at once, he involves himself in inextricable complexities of thought and sentence structure (e.g. 2.4.28ff.).

Quintilian exercised vast influence on critics and teachers of the fifteenth to seventeenth centuries: he seemed to offer precepts they could accept and ideals they could try to realize. Thus he contributed to the establishment of certain canons of taste and bounds of acceptability, chronological or moral, which have constricted the study of Latin literature over the last five hundred years. But the *Institutio* has been beneficent as well as stultifying: those who would understand the vocation of teaching may still learn the essentials here. And for students of Latin literature Quintilian remains one of the essential starting-points, however much we may question his opinions.

2. FRONTO

Amongst his contemporaries of the mid second century Fronto stood high, as Gellius, an admirer, attests. Acknowledged the leading Latin orator of the day, he was chosen as tutor to the princes Marcus and Lucius. For three centuries his fame survived: we find him placed not second to, but equal with Cicero. Thereafter he virtually disappeared from view, until in the early nineteenth century part of a collection of letters and miscellanea was rediscovered. The letters proved flaccid, trivial, and uninformative, the other pieces flimsy, and they provoked a chorus of derision. But exculpation, of a sort, is possible. First, these letters were probably never meant for publication or published by Fronto. Again, since they are mostly to or from members of the ruling dynasty, we cannot here expect the confidentiality and freedom of expression of friends who are also equals. This correspondence could not have resembled Cicero's with Atticus or Brutus: to lament the difference is absurd. Finally, Fronto was celebrated for eloquence and learning, not letter-writing. The letters scarcely justify surmise, let alone judgement, about his oratory.

Fronto's letters, and numerous letters to him (mainly from Marcus), contain little to interest anyone except the correspondents, and they were sometimes merely exchanging elaborate courtesies. Amongst the most recurrent topics we find protestation of affection (e.g. 1–5),[1] enquiry about or description of illness (e.g. 64), comment, complimentary or pedantic, upon compositions attempted (e.g. 90–2), and discussion, often superficial, of literary and rhetorical questions (e.g. 40–2). Fronto's intellectual range, compared with Pliny's, itself not wide, seems pathetically circumscribed. His repetitions and variations

[1] References are to pages of Van Den Hout.

on threadbare themes exude tedium: he would not have written thus for publication (cf. his criticism of Lucan, 151). Of business, in Senate, courts, and administration, we hear only rarely. Language, literature, and rhetoric absorbed Fronto's attention. If he had discussed affairs of state with his sovereign, he could hardly have contributed much. Again, important personal matters, which might have been tackled forthrightly, such as Marcus' preference for philosophy over rhetoric, though not unmentioned (e.g. 149), are often evaded. This weak and limited teacher had no enduring influence on his unstable, self-tormenting pupil: witness the perfunctory acknowledgement accorded Fronto at *Meditations* 1.11. The words which the emperor there addressed to himself jar against the cordiality of his letters. Marcus, though greatly changed, had kept up appearances. Fronto played the old tricks faithfully. This was not one of the unshakeable friendships of all time.

Fronto is a rhetorician through and through. That is confirmed by an introduction to his projected history of Lucius' Parthian campaigns (191–200): he apparently intended to work up Lucius' own notes. The specimen, flattery included, is dismally predictable: imitation of Sallust, generalizing reflections pointedly expressed, commonplace description of a general's proper behaviour when faced by hardship and demoralized troops. Fronto did not explore the truth. Given suitable material, he procured embellishment. Such is 'rhetorical' history, as regularly practised. Some scholars fancy that Fronto invented it.

The principal interest of the correspondence lies in language and style. Fronto, some say, sought to revive and reinforce Latin prose against the challenge of Greek, then vigorously renascent. Whether he clearly discerned any such rivalry is arguable, but he certainly tried to exploit anew the latent resources of Latin literature, by going back beyond the stylists of the early Empire, and beyond Cicero and his contemporaries, to extract from the archaic writers whatever he might effectively use. He greatly esteems Ennius (57) and Cato (192), and loathes Seneca (150). His appraisal of Cicero (57) is curiously anachronistic and biased: Cicero, he opines, never troubled to enrich his vocabulary with choice, unlooked-for words. Yet Fronto's own writing is not garishly coloured by archaisms, though occasional oddities leap to the eye. Concern for propriety tempers his pursuit of the unusual (92). We should not, however, consider him a purist and reactionary, or equate Latin archaizing with Greek Atticism. Fronto owes more than he readily admits to the new and mixed styles of the preceding hundred years; he is not averse from verbal artifice and epigrammatic point, and he is extremely partial to similes and extensively developed imagery; he wants to be both arresting and dignified. If we judge by the letters, his endeavour failed. His style is alternately lifeless and falsely inflated, unredeemed by imagination and flamboyance such as Apuleius', who continued more boldly with experiments which Fronto, amongst others, had begun.

The correspondence reflects, albeit incompletely, a society humane and refined, brittle and decadent. The Romans were forever looking back to their past, but in the second century A.D. this retrospection became obsessive. Fronto was accounted the prime ornament of his age because he embodied its ideal of culture and learning, and, Janus-like, sponsored both tradition and novelty. Since his speeches are lost, we had best refrain from further assessment.

3. AULUS GELLIUS

In his miscellany *Noctes Atticae*, 'Attic nights',[1] so called since it originated from his lucubrations in Attica (*praef.* 4), Gellius ranges haphazardly in many fields, including language, literature, history, law, and philosophy, looking out for topics of antiquarian interest and problems subtle and recondite in flavour. He explains in his preface that he has based his work on notes taken from reading and lectures, that the arrangement of this material is fortuitous, that he makes no pretence to laboured elegance, and that he aims to improve his readers' leisure rather than to instruct serious enquirers. We are not obliged to accept what he says, and may smile at his feigned modesty where style is concerned, but his prefatory statements are largely borne out by examination of his writing.

Miscellanies were much in favour in antiquity, amongst Greeks and Romans. They naturally differed considerably in size, range, and intention. Athenaeus' *Deipnosophistae* 'Connoisseurs at dinner' affords a fair analogy with the *Noctes Atticae*, and we may also recall Pliny's *Natural history*, though that is as much encyclopaedia as miscellany, and Valerius Maximus' collection of memorable deeds and sayings, though Valerius' scope is appreciably different. And perhaps Suetonius attempted a comparable mixture in his *Pratum*. There were also more remote Roman precedents, in works of Cato and Varro. Gellius is particularly notable because of his kaleidoscopic variety: the average space he accords to any single topic can hardly exceed two standard pages. Being both abundantly diverse and unpredictable, he well serves the needs of those who desire only an occasional dip into culture.

A 'perpetual student', not a professional teacher, Gellius venerated learning and retained an adolescent's awe for scholarly *tours de force*. In this we see the child of an age when few thought it strange that a rhetorician should become consul. He specially loved linguistic minutiae, and here too, perhaps, he reflects current fashion. But his modest deference to learned authorities

[1] Ancient anthologists and miscellanists commonly affected fanciful titles, as Gellius attests (*praef.* 5–10). He followed the fashion which he there elegantly deprecated.

has benefited us greatly, since he habitually names his sources, sometimes giving precise references. Hence we learn much about the activities of numerous scholars and critics. And we are above all indebted to Gellius for the preservation of many fragments of early Latin literature, not all of them meagre. Were it not for him (and Cicero), we could scarcely venture to appraise several important poets and prose-writers of the archaic period, for we should depend mainly on the scrappy and unrepresentative citations found in the grammarians. By citing at length, Gellius, like Cicero, enables us to judge for ourselves. His work is indeed 'a veritable monument of the second century's enthusiasm for all things archaic',[1] but he has no exclusive predilection for the antique, such as Hadrian allegedly showed. The fascinations of Ennius, Cato, and Gracchus never prevented him from enjoying Virgil and Cicero: his sober judgement and catholic taste deserve praise in warm terms such as he applies at 1.4.1 to Antonius Julianus. But another merit specially distinguishes him, his accuracy. Where we can test his reports against independent evidence, he seems nearly impeccable. He therefore claims a measure of trust elsewhere.

Some doubt whether Gellius ever read all the works he cited. To be sure many of his discussions involved study of extensive passages, not mere snippets, and he was eager to find old texts, long neglected (see 9.4.1–5). But perhaps, once he had taken pen in hand, he did not always go to the originals, if he could conveniently reproduce passages selected by others. He was certainly prepared to proceed thus with legal authorities (see e.g. 4.2.3 and 15.27.1). And on occasion he may have reported at second hand the opinions of older scholars, such as Varro, Hyginus, Verrius, and Probus. He has been suspected of playing down his debts to contemporaries. Perhaps he did sometimes, yet elsewhere he seems to attribute more credit to them than they deserve (see particularly 18.5.12). It is plain that his use of his sources admits of no simple explanation.

Gellius was not the kind of archaizer who would import artificial and obsolete terms wherever and whenever he could. Very occasionally they cluster, as at 2.29, where he may be paraphrasing Ennius, but for the main part he sprinkles his adornments lightly. And he generally prefers archaisms of a mild variety. Attentive reading discloses the immense pains he took to avoid repetitions and to find words both choice and apt. Lucid and uncomplicated in phraseology, Gellius writes Latin not vastly different from Quintilian's.

The *Noctes Atticae* was much used by later writers, not always with due acknowledgement. We may easily perceive why. Gellius retails numerous fascinating details of Greek and Roman life, language, and thought, suitably predigested. And he transmits some very good stories, amongst which

[1] Jocelyn (1964) 284.

'Androclus and the lion' (5.14) is justly celebrated. Again, his opinions are always worth hearing: witness his balanced discussion of Cato's speech 'In defence of the Rhodians' (6.3) and his comparisons of passages in Caecilius and Menander (2.23) and in Cato, Gracchus, and Cicero (10.3). He compels our attention, not only as a source of information, but in his own right. We should, for instance, before we presume to judge Latin literature, try to discover how the Romans themselves judged it. Here, as elsewhere, we have in Gellius a helpful and congenial guide.

VI

LATER PRINCIPATE

35

INTRODUCTORY

The period to be studied in this chapter extends roughly from the middle of the third century to the middle of the fifth century A.D. Looked at from the point of view of the history of the Roman Empire it can be divided into several stages. The first extends from the death of Alexander Severus in 235 to the proclamation of Diocletian as emperor in 284. This was a half-century of chaos and disorder throughout the empire. The delicate balance of political power broke down, and legitimacy was no longer conferred upon emperors by a consensus, however formal, of Senate, people and army, and sustained by the general consent of the ruling classes of the cities in both east and west. Local interest groups began to proclaim their own candidates for imperial power. The most effective of these were the provincial armies and to a lesser degree the Praetorian Guard at Rome. The half-century of disorder was begun by the assassination of Alexander Severus at Moguntiacum (Mainz) and the proclamation by the army there of Maximinus, a Thracian officer who had risen from the ranks. Soon the influential land-owning class of Africa proclaimed their candidate, Gordian. The powerless Senate vacillated between the two claimants and for a time put forward its own candidates, Balbinus and Pupienus. And so it went on. The situation was one of almost permanent civil war, marked not only by several pitched battles between Roman armies, but also by a break-down of civil administration and legality and the growth of arbitrary rule by military commanders, who could maintain their armies in being only by letting them live directly on the produce of the citizens they were supposed to defend. Rarely throughout the half-century were there not several claimants to imperial power in the field at once, each striving to exercise the civil and military authority of a *princeps* without enjoying the support upon which that authority was based. More and more effective, even if short-lived, power passed into the hands of a class which had enjoyed little esteem or influence in the heyday of the Empire, namely the military men from the frontier provinces. This does not mean, as some of our sources suggest and as some modern scholars have believed, that power passed into the hands of peasant soldiers. The officers who aspired to imperial authority and their entourages were rather men from the small towns which had grown up near legionary headquarters along the Rhine and Danube, and often persons of some substance. But they had not hitherto enjoyed the direct or indirect influence upon decisions which belonged to the senatorial order and to the urban upper classes of the Mediterranean provinces. What they gained in power the older ruling classes lost.

At the same time as this breakdown of the old power structure, the ring of military defences which surrounded the empire began to be more frequently and more seriously breached. It would be hard to say which was cause and which effect. The Alemanni and Franks invaded Gaul and Raetia again and again. Goths, Carpi, Vandals, Taifali and other east Germanic peoples swept southwards through Moesia and Thrace year after year. In 267 they captured and pillaged Corinth, Argos and Athens. Dacia was submerged under a barbarian tide and lost for ever to the empire. On the eastern frontier a renascent Persia under a new dynasty challenged Rome. In 256 Antioch fell to the Persians, who installed a puppet emperor there. In 260 the emperor Valerian was taken prisoner by a Persian army, which went on to invade Cilicia and Cappadocia. Further south the client kingdom of Palmyra profited by Roman weakness to extend its sway as far as Egypt in the south and Antioch and Cilicia in the north. Not unnaturally this succession of calamities was accompanied by rapid debasement of the currency and raging inflation. This was a half-century during which those social groups which had provided both patronage and readership for literature were in disarray, and the occasions for public display of literary skill were few. Little remains of Latin writing from the period, and little seems to have been written of any value. But one must not exaggerate the sharpness of the break. Urban life and culture were much less threatened in the Greek east than in the Latin west, in spite of the aggressive policies of Persia and Palmyra. And in the more disturbed west Plotinus continued giving lectures on philosophy to his distinguished and influential audience in Rome from 244 to 269 without apparently suffering any interruption. But Rome was no longer at the centre of power.

The next period, that of Diocletian (284–305) and Constantine (307–37) saw the re-establishment of firm central power in the empire on a new basis. Diocletian inaugurated a system of collegiate imperial power, with two senior and two junior emperors, who derived their legitimacy from a supposed divine selection and protection. A radical restructuring of imperial administration was undertaken, in which the number of provinces was increased, the senatorial order was excluded from holding military command, and a new concentration of power appeared in the much enlarged imperial court, which no longer resided at Rome but moved from province to province in the frontier regions as the military situation demanded. This arrangement institutionalized the accession to power of a new class from the frontier provinces which did not entirely share Italian traditions and ideals.

Constantine, after a series of confrontations with co-emperors and rivals, abandoned the system of collegiate power and ruled from 324 to 337 as sole emperor. He completed the work of reorganization of Diocletian, re-established the currency on a firm basis, founded a new second capital city at Byzantium on the Bosphorus, and began to draw into the circle of power once again, although only to a limited degree, the Italian senatorial class. He also sought support from a group in Roman society which hitherto had been unconcerned with or actually excluded from power. The Christian religion was first tolerated and later preferred and patronized by Constantine, who sought in it a source of legitimation of his own authority. The church, though still comprising only a minority of the subjects of the empire, gained rapidly in prestige, influence and wealth. Bishops formed a part of Constantine's court entourage. The urban upper classes began to embrace the new religion in greater numbers and to bring with them into the Christian milieu many of the attitudes and values of traditional classical culture.

By Constantine's death stability had been restored in the military, administrative and economic spheres. Literature and art began to find patrons once again, and the pen began to replace the sword as an instrument of persuasion. The last two thirds of the fourth century were not without civil wars and disturbances. But on the whole they were an age of steady government and of relative prosperity. Literature flourished more fruitfully than it had since the days of the Antonines. But it was a literature changed both in form and in content. Some genres were no longer practised. There was no epic poetry, no drama, no forensic or political oratory. Others, as will be seen, extended their range. As the Christians increased in numbers and influence, overtly Christian writing formed an ever larger part of Latin literature. This falls into several categories. Writing by Christians on classical or at any rate not specifically Christian themes will be treated in the following pages in exactly the same way as pagan writings. Works written by Christians on Christian topics for Christian readers will generally not be discussed. This category comprises dogmatic and homiletic writing, works dealing with ecclesiastical organization and discipline, sectarian polemic, pastoral treatises, and the like. There remains a considerable body of literature on Christian topics addressed expressly to non-Christians and of Christian works couched in more or less strictly classical form, and hence likely to be read and appreciated by the classically educated. This literature will be discussed briefly in the light of its place in classical literary tradition, but there will be no systematic treatment of its place in the development of Christian thought in the Latin west. Needless to say, none of these categories is demarcated with unequivocal clarity. There are grey areas around all of them.

The final period, in the first half of the fifth century, saw the political separation between the eastern and western parts of the empire, which had been a temporary expedient in the past, become permanent. From being temporary invaders or mercenary forces, Germanic peoples from beyond the frontier became permanent settlers in the empire, and often set up their own governments in the territories which they occupied. In 410 the Visigoths captured Rome, an event whose effect upon the imagination of contemporaries it would be impossible to exaggerate. Visigoths and Burgundians established themselves permanently in southern Gaul, setting up there what were in effect independent kingdoms. Parts of the Iberian peninsula were similarly occupied by Visigoths and Suebi. Towards the middle of the century the Vandals, after sweeping through Spain, crossed the straits of Gibraltar and by 439 were in control of the rich and populous province of Africa and its capital city Carthage. Their power soon extended to Sardinia and Corsica, and by 455 a Vandal force captured and pillaged Rome itself, causing far greater damage to life and property than the Visigoths had done. During this period Christianity became not merely the predominant but virtually the sole religion of the empire. A synthesis of classical and Christian culture began to be formed in the west, which was distinct from that of the Greek east. The church and its hierarchy took over some of the functions and the prestige which had hitherto belonged to officials of the state, and cultural leadership began to pass to bishops, who themselves were often the sons or grandsons of pagan men of literary distinction. The whole social framework within which classical literature had been written, read and criticized was unmistakably changed. It is symptomatic that a great landed proprietor and senator who had written panegyrics upon emperors replete with classical allusions and motives ended his days as a Christian bishop in a Germanic kingdom.

Certain general features of the life and literature of late antiquity call for brief discussion at this point as part of the background to the study of particular writers and their works. They will all find illustration and exemplification in the pages which follow this general introduction. The first is the loosening of the cultural unity of the upper classes of the empire, and in particular of the bonds between the Greek east and the Latin west. They had always been conscious, and indeed proud, of the differences which separated them. Yet the Greek sophists of the second century had moved easily between Ephesus or Pergamum and Rome. Aelius Aristides had given eloquent expression to his consciousness of belonging to a Roman society which embraced and transcended the world of Greek culture. Greeks like Appian, Cassius Dio and Herodian wrote on Roman history. A Roman emperor wrote his diary not only in the Greek language but in terms of Greek philosophical concepts. During the fifty years of anarchy the Greek east suffered much less than the Latin west. The Latin world was to some extent left to its own resources, and knowledge of the Greek language, Greek literature and Greek thought became much rarer in the west than it had been in the previous three centuries. This break in contact did not begin to be healed until the late fourth century. Even a man like Augustine – Manichaean, Neoplatonist, rhetorician and Christian philosopher – was not at his ease in Greek, and the intellectual leaders of the Roman aristocracy often had only a school-room knowledge of the language. Towards the end of the century a new strengthening of contact began. Several leading Latin writers were actually Greeks by birth and culture. The Gaulish aristocracy of the early fifth century were often familiar with Greek literature and thought, their Italian counterparts on the whole less so. But the old sense of unity was never restored. Greek and Latin remained separate, their relations often having a diplomatic or missionary character. Latin literature ceased to draw continuously upon Greek sources and Greek models, as it had done since the days of Ennius, and became more self-contained. The sharpness of the cultural break must not be exaggerated. There were always men in the west who knew and read Greek. But they were fewer in number and in influence than in the great days of the Roman Empire. This is as true of Christians as of pagans, perhaps even truer, in spite of the ecumenical nature of the Christian church. In the fourth and fifth centuries Christian thought and expression struck a different tone in Latin and in Greek. The Cappadocian Fathers Gregory of Nyssa, Basil and Gregory of Nazianzus, and their younger contemporary John Chrysostom were little known to western Christians, Ambrose and Augustine were totally unknown in the east. Men like Jerome and Rufinus tried to build a bridge between the two halves of the Christian world by their translations and adaptations, but met with only limited success.

A second feature of the period which has significant effects on Latin literature is the 'depoliticization' – if such a word is permissible – of the Roman senatorial class. Excluded in the half-century of anarchy from participation in the exercise of state power, and only partially and grudgingly re-admitted to a limited group of public offices in the fourth century, the senatorial order retained its immense landed wealth and much of its social prestige. As patrons, writers and readers of literature the senatorial class tended to adopt a backward-looking, antiquarian stance, reflecting its disengagement from contemporary affairs. Idealization of an imagined past and obsessive concentration upon traditional forms became almost the symbols of status. The grammarian, the lexicographer, the antiquarian and the commentator took the place of the original and creative writer. Instead of writing the history of their own times, in which they often had little interest, senators of literary inclination would prepare – or have prepared for them by others – luxurious manuscripts of Livy or Virgil or Sallust. The distinction between school and real life became blurred. There is often a curiously juvenile quality in the literature of late antiquity. A similar development can be seen in the Greek east too. But it was much less marked and its social basis was less clear. For in the east there was no class corresponding to the senatorial order of the west, rich, long-established, sure of its local authority and accustomed to participate in the affairs of the empire. This 'disengagement' of the senatorial class is a peculiarly western phenomenon.

A further feature, connected in part with the changed position of the Roman senatorial order, is the development of centres of literature outside Rome itself. The removal of the court from Rome to Milan, Trier, Sirmium, Constantinople, Nicomedia or Antioch meant that a new centre of imperial patronage existed. The provincialization of the senatorial order, and the citizenship of all free men, contributed to creating the conditions for a Latin literature less exclusively Rome-centred than in the past. Africa had already established a more locally based Latin literature, though many African writers, like Fronto, lived and wrote in Rome. Christian writers, from Tertullian onwards, were often closely concerned with the problems of the provincial society of which they were members. For all these, and no doubt other less readily identifiable reasons the Latin literature, both pagan and Christian, of late antiquity has to some extent broken with Rome. Ausonius writes in Bordeaux and at Trier, Claudian's poems are recited in Milan. Sidonius Apollinaris' life and work are centred on his native Auvergne. Augustine writes largely in Africa and often for an African readership, Juvencus composes his poem in Spain, Rufinus writes most of his works in Aquileia, Jerome in Bethlehem. Latin literature is no longer necessarily Roman literature.

The growth of a 'committed' literature within the expanding Christian community is a topic which largely falls outside the scope of the present study. But the entanglement of Christian–pagan polemic with the antiquarian frondism of the Roman senatorial order in the second half of the fourth century lent a sharp edge to controversy and made the confrontation between Christianity and paganism take a somewhat different course, in literary terms, in the Latin west from that which it followed in the Greek east. For a time the conflict of religions threatened to become a conflict of cultures, in which the whole classical Roman tradition was set against a new Christian culture which expressly rejected much of the pagan past. Jerome's famous dream, in which he saw himself accused of being a Ciceronian rather than a Christian (*Epist.* 22.20) has no parallel in the east, nor has the bitter but dignified polemic between Ambrose and Symmachus over the altar of Victory in the senate-house. Roman society and Latin literature surmounted this conflict, and a viable synthesis of classical and Christian tradition was in the end attained. But it never had the easy and unstrained character of Christian classicism in the Greek east. There was no Latin equivalent of Basil's address to the young on how to read profane literature.

There is another general characteristic of literature and art, and indeed of all aspects of public life, in late antiquity which is hard to define, but whose reality is clear enough to all students of the period. Public deportment acquires a theatrical character, public utterance a tone of declamatory exaggeration. At the imperial court an elaborate ceremonial serves to isolate an emperor whose public appearances, carefully stage-managed, have something of the character of a theophany. Men admired Constantius II on his visit to Rome, recounts a contemporary historian, because he held himself immobile in his carriage, his eyes raised to heaven, looking neither to left nor to right. The same emperor is depicted on a silver dish from Kerch, now in the Hermitage at Leningrad, seated on his horse, larger than the other human figures, a nimbus round his head, gazing through the spectator with huge, wide-open eyes. The sculptured head of Constantine in the Palazzo dei Conservatori at Rome and the colossal statue of an unknown emperor at Barletta show this same hieratic remoteness from ordinary people and everyday life. In the missorium of Theodosius, now in the Academía de la Historia, Madrid, the emperor, nimbate and of superhuman stature, wearing a jewelled diadem and a large jewelled clasp, stares into space with the same unnaturally large eyes. Examples could be multiplied indefinitely. Court officials and provincial governors affected the same style, no longer walking through the streets but travelling in ornate carriages accompanied by guards of honour. Modes of address became more complex and honorific. An emperor spoke of himself as *serenitas nostra* and addressed a Prefect of the City as *tua celsitudo*. Even Symmachus, the champion of ancient senatorial usage, addresses his friend Ausonius in a letter as *unanimitas tua*. Laws, proclamations, and official correspondence of all kinds are couched in an inflated, circumlocutory, repetitious style with a plethora of abstract expressions. This is as true of Greek as of Latin, and applies with equal force to the decrees of an emperor and the letters of a minor tax official in Egypt. Often the tone of such a document, with its repeated – and vague – protestations and threats, suggests to the modern reader that the writer was on the verge of hysteria. Naturally not all literature is equally affected by this tendency to overstatement. But even those who swim against the tide are carried with it. Everywhere the restraint and reserve which marked much of classical culture give way to a more strident and declamatory tone.

All these factors, and no doubt many others which we cannot so clearly discern, led in late antiquity to an effacement of the traditional distinctions between literary genres. Panegyric – and its opposite, invective – are composed in the metre and language of epic poetry. Didactic poems are written in elegiac couplets. The tale of the Trojan war is retold in flat, uniform prose. The letter is used for public polemic. The principles of Christian dogma are set forth in Horatian lyrics. Satire as such is no longer written. But the satirical manner colours many other kinds of writing, such as Arnobius' refutations of pagan doctrines, Claudian's political lampoons, many of Jerome's letters on moral and theological themes. New genres begin to emerge, as writers seek an appropriate literary form for new kinds of content. An example is the kind of autobiography in which the writer reveals something of his inner life. Augustine writes his in highly rhetorical prose. Paulinus of Nola chooses traditional hexameter verse, but without all the apparatus of classical allusion which traditionally belonged to it. In a period in which traditional rules no longer held there was naturally much formless, rambling writing, both in prose and in verse. But it would be a mistake to suppose that the chief characteristic of late Latin literature is decadence. The period saw the development of new literary forms and new techniques. Among the most important of these, judged by its consequences, is the sustained allegory, first developed by Prudentius in verse and by Martianus Capella in prose. Augustine was in many respects a most unclassical writer. But that he wrote powerfully and compellingly cannot be denied. Claudian uses the metre and language of epic poetry for strange purposes. But he uses them strikingly and effectively. The literature of late antiquity combined tradition and innovation, and often in a truly creative fashion.

Finally, the gradual, non-revolutionary character of the changes in life and literature must be emphasized. Two hundred years is a long time. It would be a great mistake to suppose that late antique man was as aware that he was living in an epoch of radical and irreversible change as we are today. Nothing was sudden. The old persisted along with the new. Much continued apparently unchanged. Among the literate the sense of continuity was sustained by a highly traditional system of education based on the detailed study of a small number of classical texts. No one, not even the most innovatory of new men in power, thought for a moment of changing this system. Constantine confirmed the privileges of professors. More than two centuries later, after Italy had been devastated by twenty years of war, Justinian restored the emoluments and privileges of teachers of rhetoric. Everything conspired to create the illusion of immutability, and innovators could only conceive of their own measures as acts of restoration. From none of the epitomizing historians of late antiquity would the casual reader gain the impression that the fourth century was in any significant way different from the centuries that preceded. Only Ammianus Marcellinus had the insight to perceive that he was living and writing in an age of crisis, though he never attempts to define the nature of the crisis. Christian writers, with their essentially historical view of the world, were sometimes more sensitive to the signs of change than their pagan contemporaries. Augustine's *City of God* in its way marks the end of the ancient world in the west as clearly as do the great barbarian invasions.

36

POETRY

The Latin epic had come to an end with the generation of Statius, Valerius Flaccus and Silius Italicus at the end of the first century A.D. Personal elegy, that peculiarly Roman creation, had ended with Ovid. There is no trace of significant dramatic writing, whether intended for the genuine stage or for 'concert performances', after Seneca. Juvenal was the last of the Roman satirists. Many of the principal genres of classical Latin poetry had thus virtually ceased to be practised before the great break in the middle of the third century. The great works of the past had become school-books, embedded in a mass of linguistic commentary and factual exegesis. The younger Pliny might dabble in lyric poetry in the Horatian manner, which his third wife set to music, but it is his letters that survive. The age of Hadrian, the Antonines and Septimius Serenus was one of prose. What little poetry was written is known to us only by fragments preserved by grammarians and metricians. Annianus and Septimius Serenus wrote on pastoral themes. Alfius Avitus composed a poem, apparently of some length, on Roman history. Marianus was author of a *Lupercalia*. These poets are called '*Poetae nouelli*' by the metrician Terentianus Maurus. Occasional poems by the historian Florus, by L. Aelius Verus and others survive, as well as Hadrian's famous address to his soul:

Animula uagula blandula
hospes comesque corporis,
quae nunc abibis in loca
pallidula, rigida, nudula,
nec ut soles dabis iocos?

O blithe little soul, thou, flitting away,
guest and comrade of this my clay,
whither now goest thou, to what place
bare and ghostly and without grace?
nor, as thy wont was, joke and play.

(Tr. A. O'Brien-Moore in Magie (1921–32))

It is perhaps rash to base general judgements on so tiny a sample. But the work of all the writers mentioned appears to be marked by three striking characteristics. The first is the loosening of the link between form and content which has already been mentioned. Annianus' and Serenus' poems on the joys of country life follow neither the pattern of Virgil's *Eclogues* nor that of Tibullus' elegiac poems, but are written in a variety of metres. Avitus' poem on Roman history rejects the epic hexameter for the iambic dimeter, a metre found in the *Epodes* of Horace, and in choral passages in the tragedies of Seneca. The second trait common to these poets is metrical innovation, i.e. the creation of new metres by modification or combination of established patterns. Their third common feature is the abandonment of the traditional vocabulary of the various poetic genres and the use of vulgar, archaic, rustic, diminutive and other forms. Whether these poets formed a School or not is a matter of debate. But they all in various degrees appear to have rejected much of the classical tradition of Latin poetry and attempted to strike out in new directions. The few fragments surviving suggest an antiquarian taste, a baroque embellishment of the trivial and a rather self-conscious avoidance of the grand manner and the solemn tone of voice. None of them appears to have been more than a gifted minor versifier.

In the period which is the subject of these chapters many of the trends marking the previous period continue to prevail. Minor subjects, a light, sometimes idyllic and sometimes frivolous tone, a taste for realism, are the order of the day at first. There are no long poems. The classical genres no longer impose themselves. But the elaborate metrical experiments of the later second century were abandoned, and most of what was written was in the well-tried hexameter or elegiac couplet. Most of the productions of the third century and the early fourth century cannot be securely dated; and sometimes the uncertainty extends even over more than a century. So there can be no question of reconstructing the history of poetry until we reach the second half of the fourth century. From the earlier part of the period we have a number of works, most of which can at best be dated somewhere between A.D. 250 and 350.

Marcus Aurelius Olympius Nemesianus of Carthage was the author of a didactic poem in hexameters on hunting, the *Cynegetica*, of which only the first 325 lines survive, and of four bucolic poems modelled on those of Calpurnius Siculus. Poems on fishing (*Halieutica*) and on sailing (*Nautica*) are also attributed to him, but do not survive. The *Cynegetica* can be dated to *c.* A.D. 284, and appears to draw on the Greek poem on the same theme by Oppian of Apamea in Syria, written in the first half of the third century. In spite of his avoidance of legendary material and his claim to originality, Nemesianus' inspiration is purely literary. The Eclogues embody traditional pastoral themes: lament for the death of an old shepherd-poet, rival shepherds singing the praises of their respective loves, Pan appearing to shepherds, a singing match between two shepherds. Both the *Cynegetica* and the *Eclogues* are full of Virgilian and Ovidian echoes. Some have seen in Nemesianus' poems some reference to the programme of political restoration attributed to the emperor Carus and his sons, but this is highly doubtful. Nemesianus is a competent and uninspired imitator of classical models, whose poetic persona is entirely traditional.

The mythological epyllion of Reposianus, *De concubitu Veneris et Martis*, in 182 hexameters, cannot be dated with certainty. It recounts the story of the amorous dalliance of Venus and Mars, first told in the Odyssey (8.266–360; developed by Ovid, *Ars Am.* 2.573–600, *Met.* 4.169–89) with an abundance of picturesque and on occasion slightly lubricious description. The tone is graceful and sentimental, but the poet is unable to convey any depth of feeling or to make his characters come to life. It has been suggested, but can be neither proved nor disproved, that the poem is an adaptation of a Greek original.

Six short elegiac poems by Pentadius are of equally uncertain date. The first, *De fortuna*, in 36 lines, proclaims with a series of illustrations from Greek mythology, each contained in a single couplet, the fickleness of fortune. The second, *De adventu veris*, in 22 lines, is an example of *versus echoici*; the first half of each hexameter is repeated in the second half of the following pentameter, e.g.

Laeta uireta tument, foliis sese induit arbor,
uallibus apricis laeta uireta tument.

The joyous greensward swells, the trees put on their leaves,
in the sunny valleys the joyous greensward swells.

The remaining four poems are short epigrams. Pentadius' sole virtue is neatness.

A letter from Dido to Aeneas in 150 hexameters is a frigid piece of rhetoric stuffed with classical reminiscences. In the *Iudicium coci et pistoris iudice Vulcano*, in 99 hexameters, by an otherwise unknown Vespa the speeches of the two contendants are decked out with much rather obvious mythological learning. An anonymous poem in 89 hexameters sets out the speech of Achilles, hiding in the women's quarters, when he hears the trumpet of Diomedes. These and similar productions owe more to the schoolmaster than to the Muse. Their value, if they have any, is as indicators of the continuation of elements of the classical tradition of poetry in education. But everything in them is small in scale, mean in conception, and trite in expression.

The *Pervigilium Veneris* purports to be a processional song for a festival of Venus at Hybla in Sicily, in 93 trochaic tetrameters catalectic, with the recurring refrain

Cras amet qui numquam amauit quique amauit cras amet.

Tomorrow he will love who never loved and he who loved will love tomorrow.

It has been dated at various times from the second to the fifth century. Editors have argued that it is a work of the historian Florus, a contemporary of Hadrian, but without winning general assent. Unique in Latin literature, the poem recalls by its metre the acclamations of soldiers and populace at a triumph. There are also possible popular features in the syntax, though the vocabulary is largely classical. The simplicity of the style and the clarity of the descriptions confer an unusual freshness and charm on the poem. Typical are such passages as:

Ecce iam subter genestas explicant tauri latus,
quisque tutus quo tenetur coniugali foedere.
subter umbras cum maritis ecce balantum greges.
et canoras non tacere diua iussit alites.
iam loquaces ore rauco stagna cygni perstrepunt.
adsonat Terei puella subter umbram populi,
ut putes motus amoris ore dici musico
et neges queri sororem de marito barbaro.

Deeply bedded, look, the bulls in broom with massive flanks now lie.
Every safety threading life must surely hail the marriage-tie.
Bleating through the shadows, look, among the hes the bitches throng.
Venus comes to tell the birds to be no niggards of their song.
Raucous-crying swans go winging by and crash across the pool,
and the nightingale is singing out where poplar-shades are cool.
Surely it's a lover singing – one who sings a lover's joy –
not a wandering sufferer who laments her sister and her boy.
(Tr. J. Lindsay, *Song of a Falling World* (London, 1948) 67–8)

Yet it is clearly a work of literary art and not an actual ritual song. There are many reminiscences of classical poetry. And there is no real religious ceremony at which it is likely to have been sung. It echoes the style and interests of the *Poetae nouelli* Annianus and Septimius Serenus (p. 692) though it may well have been written much later by an imitator or follower of their school.

To the same period of the late third or early fourth century belong the *Disticha Catonis*, a collection of about 130 (the number varies in different recensions) hexameter couplets each embodying a practical rule of conduct, e.g.

Iratus de re incerta contendere noli,
impedit ira animum, ne possis cernere uerum. (2)

Do not dispute in anger on a contentious matter;
anger prevents your mind discerning the truth.

The general tone is that of popular Stoicism, and there is no trace in the *Disticha* themselves of Christian attitudes, though a series of brief maxims in prose prefixed to the collection in many recensions shows Christian features. The author of the *Disticha* is unknown; the 'Cato' to whom they are attributed is Cato Uticensis rather than Cato the Censor. The collection is interesting as an echo of how the silent majority thought they ought to behave, and recalls the *Sententiae* of Publilius Syrus (p. 293). What makes it worth mention in a history of literature is the enormous success which it enjoyed in the Middle Ages, when a number of different recensions, some interpolated, others abbreviated, circulated in hundreds of manuscripts, excerpts were embodied by many authors in their works, and translations and adaptations were made in the vernacular languages.

Publilius Optatianus Porfyrius, most probably an African, and to be identified with the *Praefectus urbi* in 329 and 333, addressed to the emperor Constantine in 325 or 326 a collection of twenty short panegyric poems, to which he later added seven others. Several poems in the Latin Anthology attributed to 'Porfyrius' are probably also by his hand. Porfyrius' poems, which appeal to the eye rather than to the ear, let alone to the mind, of the reader all involve complicated double or triple acrostics, lines which can be read backwards or forwards, words arranged according to the number of syllables they contain, and the like. His *tours de force* are his figurate poems, in the shape of a palm tree (9), a water organ (20), an altar (26) and a shepherd's flute (27). Such word games had been played by men of letters in their less serious moments since Hellenistic times. What confers on the poems of Porfyrius some importance in the history of Latin literature is that these trifles won the approval and patronage of Constantine, who deigned to address a letter of commendation to the ingenious versifier. Roman poets needed a patron but the level of taste at the imperial court in the early fourth century offered little hope of recognition to serious poetry.

Tiberianus, who may be identified with C. Annius Tiberianus, *comes Africae* in 325–7, *comes Hispaniarum* in 332–5, and Praetorian Prefect of Gaul in 336–7, is known as the author of four short poems – or fragments of longer poems. The first is a description in 20 trochaic tetrameters catalectic of an idyllic country scene, which recalls in metre and tone the *Pervigilium Veneris*. The others are an attack on the power of money in 28 hexameters, which draws its examples exclusively from Greek legend, a description in 12 hendecasyllables of the death of a bird, from which an edifying moral is drawn, and a hymn in 32 hexameters which is monotheistic but not specifically Christian. Tiberianus is an elegant and graceful poet, whose works were still read and quoted with approval by Servius in the fifth century. But it is difficult from the few fragments to form an idea of the scope and quality of his writing.

A poem in 85 elegiac couplets on the Phoenix is attributed to Lactantius in some manuscripts and by Gregory of Tours and may well be by his hand. It is in a rather inflated, rhetorical style, crammed with mythological references. In the Middle Ages it was taken to be an allegory of the Fall and Redemption of Man, but it is very doubtful if it was so intended by its author. There are no overt Christian references, though many passages are susceptible of a Christian interpretation, especially when separated from their context, such as the concluding line

aeternam uitam mortis adepta bono

Winning eternal life at the cost of death

The earliest major poem surviving from the fourth century is the *Evangeliorum libri* in four books by Gaius Vettius Aquilinus Juvencus, a Spanish priest of '*nobilissimum genus*', according to Jerome, written *c.* 330. It is also the earliest Latin poetry on a Christian theme, if we except the enigmatic poems of Commodian, which are variously dated by scholars. Unlike Commodian, who owes little to classical tradition and whose hexameters are half quantitative and half accentual, Juvencus remains firmly within the usage of classical epic. He writes for a readership which is mainly Christian, but which has studied Virgil, Horace, Ovid and Lucan and learnt to love them. His theme is the gospel story. His main source is Matthew, though he also draws on the other gospels, which he read both in the original Greek and in one of the pre-Hieronyman Latin versions. He concentrates on the main narrative and passes over the genealogy of Christ and the references to fulfilment of Old Testament prophecies. His language is the traditional epic *Kunstsprache*, enriched by occasional archaisms like *plebes*, *fuat*, *redimibit*, which are probably owed to a study of the grammarians of the Antonine age rather than to a direct familiarity with pre-classical Latin. Like the Greek historians of late antiquity he avoids the technical language of the church – *nuntius*, not *angelus* is his term for angel – and his neologisms are formed within the rules of epic language – words like *auricolor*, *glaucicomans*, *flammiuomus*, *altithronus*. His poem is full of echoes and flosculi of classical poetry, some of which are used for their deliberate effect. Thus in recounting the resurrection of Christ he uses the evocative phrase *in luminis oras*, which Lucretius borrowed from Ennius, Virgil from Lucretius and Valerius Flaccus from Virgil (Enn. *Ann.* 114, 131 V^2, Lucr. 1.22, Virg. *Geo.* 2.48, *Aen.* 7.660, Val. Flacc. 4.702). In his *praefatio* he takes up the traditional topic of the poet conferring immortality on those whose exploits he describes, and cites Homer and Virgil as examples. But he goes on to make the point that in his case it is the subject that will confer upon the poet such immortality as is possible in a transient world, and to call for inspiration not to Apollo and the Muses, but to the *sanctificus...spiritus*.[1] Juvencus is a conservative purist in matters of language and style, and the way in which he uses a highly traditional medium to treat a new theme is interesting. In particular his

[1] *sanctificus* appears for the first time in Juvencus, though *sanctificare* and *sanctificatio* had been used by Tertullian and clearly belonged to the technical language of the church (cf. Mohrmann (1961) 238). This use by Juvencus of a specifically Christian word in his invocation is not fortuitous.

personal involvement in the matters which he recounts leads to a change in the traditional persona of the narrative poet. It is no longer a mask concealing the man.

Juvencus sought to adapt the traditional form of didactic poetry to new purposes. Others continued to follow age-old models in form and content. Postumius Rufius Festus Avienius was a member of an ancient Italian family of Volsinii in Etruria, who numbered among his ancestors Musonius Rufus, the Stoic philosopher of the age of Nero and the Flavian emperors, teacher of Epictetus and the younger Pliny, and author of a manual of pagan theology in Greek. He was related to Valentinian's Praetorian Prefect Petronius Probus and held the proconsulships of Achaea and Africa probably a little after the middle of the fourth century, and his tombstone survives with a verse inscription celebrating his fame as a poet. Three didactic poems by Avienius survive: an adaptation in hexameters of the Greek astronomical poem of Aratus (*Phaenomena*), a similar adaptation of the geographical poem of Dionysius Periegetes (*Descriptio orbis terrarum*) and the beginning of a poem on the sea-coast in iambic senarii, which describes the coast of Europe from Britain to Massilia (*Ora maritima*). The last is of particular interest since Avienius chose to adapt a Greek original of the fourth century B.C., and his poem therefore represents the earliest account we possess of western Europe. He was not a mere translator, but supplemented his sources with material from commentators, encyclopaedias and other sources. His style is smooth, classical and somewhat flat. His antiquarian interest is characteristic of the senatorial class of the fourth century, as is the maintenance of a poetic persona wholly detached from the age and circumstances in which the writer lived. The correct form of his name is given by an inscription. Until its publication he was generally known as Avienus. An epitome of Livy and a poem on the legends used by Virgil, both lost, and attributed by Servius to Avienus, are possibly the work of the fabulist 'Avianus', whose real name has recently been shown to have been Avienus and who wrote in the first half of the fifth century.

After this discouraging catalogue of poetasters and minor versifiers we at last reach in Ausonius a poet who can claim some stature, if only on account of the quantity and range of his writings. Decimus Magnus Ausonius was born in Bordeaux in 310. His father was a doctor, probably of Greek descent. His mother was descended on both sides from long-established aristocratic families of southwestern Gaul. Educated first at Toulouse by his uncle Arborius, who held a chair of rhetoric at Constantine's new capital city on the Bosphorus, and later at Bordeaux, the young Ausonius was appointed about 334 to an official teaching post in his native city, first as a grammarian and soon afterwards as a rhetorician. Thirty years later, when he had acquired a reputation as a teacher throughout Gaul, he was suddenly summoned to the imperial residence at

Trier to become tutor to Gratian, the six-year-old son of Valentinian. He remained attached to the court for some twenty years, accompanied Valentinian on his campaign against the Alemanni in 368–9, became a *comes* in 370, and *Quaestor sacri palatii* from 375 to 378. In the latter year he was appointed Praetorian Prefect of Gaul, while his son Hesperius was Praetorian Prefect of Italy, Illyricum and Africa. In fact, though Ausonius no doubt enjoyed considerable influence, the real power in Gaul was exercised by his son. In 379 he held the consulate along with Quintus Clodius Hermogenianus Olybrius, a member of a very distinguished Italian senatorial family who had had a long public career (and whose mother had some claim to literary fame as author of a Virgilian cento *De laudibus Christi*). After the murder of his pupil Gratian in 383 Ausonius returned to Bordeaux and lived there or on his estates in southern Gaul until his death in 393 or 394.

Ausonius provides an interesting example of the social mobility which literary distinction could bring in the fourth century. The son of a provincial doctor and of the daughter of a local notable, he not only became an influential member of the imperial court, but was accepted as an equal by the long-established senatorial aristocracy of Italy. His near contemporaries Libanius (*c.* 314–93) and Themistius (*c.* 317–88) provide similar evidence from the eastern half of the empire.

Ausonius wrote a great number of poems in many genres. Some are catalogue-poems, redolent of the school-room, such as the *Caesares*, the *Ordo urbium nobilium* 'List of notable cities', the *De nominibus septem dierum* 'The names of the days of the week' and the mnemonic poems on days of the week and months. Others are pieces of trivial virtuosity, like the macaronic poems in Greek and Latin ('Ελλαδικῆς μέτοχον Μούσης *Latiaeque Camenae* | ἄξιον Αὐσόνιος *sermone adludo bilingui*, etc.), the *Cento nuptialis*, the poems in which every line ends in a monosyllable, and so on. But there remains a considerable body of serious poetry on which Ausonius' fame rests. This includes: the *Parentalia*, in which he gives a brief account of the life and character of thirty deceased kinsmen or kinswomen, and the other poems connected with his family, in particular the funeral poem on his father and the poems addressed to his grandson Ausonius; the *Commemoratio professorum Burdigalensium* 'In memory of the professors of Bordeaux', in which he describes the person and career of twenty-six colleagues: the *Ephemeris*, describing the course of his daily round (incomplete); the short epyllion *Cupido cruciatus*; the seven poems on the German slave-girl Bissula, who had been given to him out of the booty of Valentinian's Alemannic war; the verse letters to his protégé and friend Paulinus of Nola; and the *Mosella*, a panegyric in 483 hexameters of the river, with many descriptive set pieces, composed in connexion with a journey which the poet made from Vingo (Bingen) to Augusta Trevirorum (Trier). Of his innumerable epigrams the great majority are displays of virtuosity or erudition, though a few show a sharp eye for the world around him. There also survive a number of prose works by him, mostly prefaces and letters, but including a long address of thanks to Gratian on the occasion of his consulship.

The chronology of Ausonius' writings presents many problems which are unlikely ever to be satisfactorily solved. The vast majority of the epigrams and technical *tours de force* from their nature contain no indication of date. Of the other poems some are dated by occasion or by reference to events, others by reference in a separate preface. But the date of publication of a poem is not necessarily the date of its writing. And Ausonius evidently reissued some of his poems in a revised edition. He seems to have published an edition of his opuscula about 383, and to have addressed a collection of poems to the emperor Theodosius in 390. But it is not clear what poems these collections included. The manuscript tradition does not point to a single, authoritative corpus of Ausonius' poetry. It is striking that we appear to have virtually nothing by Ausonius until he was in his later 50s. His extraordinary facility for extempore composition scarcely suggests a late vocation to poetry. Probably he did not deem some of his earlier works worthy of preservation (though one wonders when one reflects on what he did preserve). And much of his minor light verse was probably written, if not circulated, during his long years as a teacher in Bordeaux. Nevertheless it remains true that much of his poetry can be firmly dated in the seventh or eighth decade of his life, a period when the poetic vein in most men is wearing thin.

Ausonius was a Christian throughout most if not all of his life, and a few of his poems treat specifically Christian themes, e.g. the prayer in his *Ephemeris* 'Diary' and *Versus Paschales* 'Easter verses'. But he is not a Christian poet; his Christianity did not affect his poetic persona. When he composes a prayer in verse on the theme of his consulship it is addressed to Janus and to Sol. And the ideas and images which fill his poetry are entirely owed to traditional classical paganism. In his many poems on dead kinsmen and friends he makes no allusion to Christian hopes of an after-life. Only in the last poem (26) of the *Commemoratio professorum Burdigalensium* do we find a phrase capable of a Christian, as well as a pagan interpretation:

sedem sepulcri seruet immotus cinis,
memoria uiuat nominum,
dum remeat illud iudicis dono dei
commune cum dis[1] saeculum. (11–14)

May your ashes rest undisturbed in the tomb, but may the memory of your names live until there returns, through the gift of God who is judge, the age to be shared with the gods.

[1] *cunctis* Baehrens; in which case the sense is 'the age which all will share alike'.

In the words of a perceptive French scholar, 'C'est un Chrétien, païen d'imagination et épicuréen de tempérament.'[1] Ausonius' changing relations with his young friend and protégé Paulinus of Nola will be discussed below (p. 717). Whatever lessons Ausonius the man may have learnt in the long and varied course of his life, Ausonius the poet shows no signs of intellectual, moral or aesthetic development. A prodigious memory, a facile talent for versification, a cheerful and kindly optimism, and an avoidance of all that was serious or profound or disquieting mark him throughout his literary life. In a century which saw the frontiers of the empire breached by barbarians, its ruling classes converted to a new religion which made urgent personal demands on its adherents, its ancient capital replicated in the middle of the Greek world, Ausonius appears to have retained at 80 the outlook and values of his youth. He is a man who, in the words of Dürrenmatt, passes through life without actually experiencing it. But within his rather narrow limits his excellence is striking. He can express everyday thoughts and emotions clearly, elegantly and with infinite variety. Completely at home in the classical tradition, he is never overwhelmed by it. Though his poetry is filled with conscious or unconscious reminiscences of Virgil, Horace, Ovid, Lucan, Statius, it is his own poetic voice that we hear. In a few poems, particularly those on Bissula and the *Mosella*, he displays a talent for sympathetic observation and strikingly vivid description which suggest that had he looked less at his books and more at the world about him he might have been a better poet. An example of his occasional capacity to see and describe something new is the scene of boys fishing in the river (*Mosella* 240–82) where the classical allusions and the traditionally structured simile are not mere external ornamentation, but serve to give sharper focus to the poet's vision.

Iam uero, accessus faciles qua ripa ministrat,
scrutatur toto populatrix turba profundo
heu male defensos penetrali flumine pisces.
hic medio procul amne trahens umentia lina
nodosis decepta plagis examina uerrit;
ast hic, tranquillo qua labitur agmine flumen,
ducit corticeis fluitantia retia signis;
ille autem scopulis deiectas pronus in undas
inclinat lentae conuexa cacumina uirgae,
inductos escis iaciens letalibus hamos.
quos ignara doli postquam uaga turba natantum
rictibus inuasit patulaeque per intima fauces
sera occultati senserunt uulnera ferri,
dum trepidant, subit indicium crispoque tremori
uibrantis saetae mutans consentit harundo;

[1] Pichon (1906) 214.

nec mora, et excussam stridenti uerbere praedam
dexter in obliquum raptat puer; excipit ictum
spiritus, ut fractis quondam per inane flagellis
aura crepat motoque adsibilat aere uentus.
exultant udae super arida saxa rapinae
luciferique pauent letalia tela diei.
cuique sub amne suo mansit uigor, aere nostro
segnis anhelatis uitam consumit in auris.
iam piger inualido uibratur corpore plausus,
torpida supremos patitur iam cauda tremores
nec coeunt rictus, haustas sed hiatibus auras
reddit mortiferos expirans branchia flatus.
sic, ubi fabriles exercet spiritus ignes,
accipit alterno cohibetque foramine uentos
lanea fagineis alludens parma cauernis.
uidi egomet quosdam leti sub fine trementes
collegisse animas, mox in sublime citatos
cernua subiectum praeceps dare corpora in amnem,
desperatarum potientes rursus aquarum.
quos impos damni puer inconsultus ab alto
impetit et stolido captat prensare natatu.
sic Anthedonius Boeotia per freta Glaucus,
gramina gustatu postquam exitialia Circes
expertus carptas moribundis piscibus herbas
sumpsit, Carpathium subiit nouus accola pontum.
ille, hamis et rete potens, scrutator operti
Nereos, aequoream solitus conuerrere Tethyn,
inter captiuas fluitauit praedo cateruas.

Here where the bank an easy access yields
A throng of spoilers through the river-depths
Are busy, probing everywhere (poor fish,
Alack, ill guarded by the inmost stream!);
One in mid water, trailing his moist lines
Far from the bank, sweeps off the finny droves
Caught in his knotted seine; another, where
The river floats along in tranquil course,
Spreads wide his drag-net buoyed on floats of cork.
A third, bent o'er the waters slumbering far
Beneath the boulders, dips the arching top
Of his lithe rod, casting upon the stream
Hooks sheathed with deadly baits. The wandering tribes,
Unwary, rush thereon with gaping jaws:
Too late their open mouths feel, deep within,
Stings of the hidden barb; they writhe; down drops
The float; the rod jerks to the quivering twitch
Of vibrant line. Enough! with one sharp stroke

The prey is hooked, and slantwise from the flood
The lad has flicked his prey. A hissing wind
Follows the blow, as when a lash is plied
And a wind whistles through the stricken air.
The dripping victims flounder on the rocks;
In terror of the sunlight's deadly rays
They quake; the fire that moved them while they lived
Down in their native element, expires
Beneath our sky; gasping, they yield up life.
Dull throbs go shuddering through their weakened frame;
The sluggish tail flaps in one final throe;
Mouths gape; the breath they drew returns again
In pantings linked with death. As when some breeze
Fans a forge-fire, the valve, that works within
The beechen bellows, first admits the wind
Then holds it, now by this vent, now by that.
Some fish have I beheld which, in their last
Death-struggle, have put forth their powers, to plunge
Head downward to the river; and so reached
The once despaired-of waters. Quick the lad,
Impatient of his loss, dives from above
And seeks to grasp them in his wild pursuit, –
A bootless quest! Ev'n so fared Glaucus once
(That old man of the sea); soon as his lips
Touched Circe's deadly herbs, he ate the grass
Sucked by the dying fish: then headlong leapt –
Strange denizen! – into Carpathia's main.
He that was wont, furnished with hooks and net,
To plunder Nereus in his watery realm,
Floats – the once pirate of those helpless tribes. (Tr. Blakeney (1933))

This passage displays Ausonius' sympathetic observation of everyday features of country life, and his ability to transform his observations by firm control and adaptation to a sophisticated literary tradition. Of the three fishermen two are described statically in neat couplets (243–6), the third is depicted at length in the process of catching and landing his fish (247–69). Ausonius is always skilful at varying the pace of his exposition. The poet goes on to comment in his own person on the difficulties attendant on rod-and-line fishing (270–5). There are two extended similes in the epic manner. The first (267–9) is entirely original, depending on the poet's own perception of the similarity between the movements of gills and mouth of a stranded fish and those of the valves of a blacksmith's double bellows. It is, incidentally, probably the first description in European literature of the double bellows, a technological development of late antiquity which made possible the casting of iron. The second (276–82) is an elaborate allusion to a Greek myth which had been recounted by Ovid, *Metamorphoses* 13.904–68. The whole passage is permeated by reminiscences of classical Latin poetry, varying from overt quotation to fleeting echo. Thus the picture of the various fishermen owes something to Virgil, *Georgics* 1.141–2 *atque alius latum funda iam uerberat amnem* | *alta petens, pelagoque alius trahit umida lina*; *letalia tela diei* (260) is a quaintly inverted echo of Lucretius' famous *lucida tela diei* (1.147); line 241 contains a purely verbal reminiscence of Statius, *Silvae* 3.2.86 *Siculi populatrix uirgo profundi* (of Scylla); in line 272 the rare word *cernuus* 'downward turned', 'head-over-heels', occurs in the same sedes in the verse as in Silius Italicus 10.255 *cernuus inflexo sonipes effuderat armo.* The whole passage is marked by an Ovidian neatness of expression, particularly in the numerous 'golden' lines (in which two nouns and their attendant adjectives are grouped in various arrangements round a verb), e.g. 241, 244, 246, 248, 249, 252, 254, 258, 263, 264, 266, 268, 278. Indeed the very frequency of these tightly-structured lines leads to a certain monotony. By way of more general critique of the *Mosella* and of some of his other poems, it may be observed that Ausonius is sympathetically responsive to man-made, 'tame' landscape, but blind to 'wild' landscape and to many aspects of nature. Thus birds and their song are not mentioned in the poem. There is nothing romantic in Ausonius' response to his surroundings.

Most of Ausonius' poems are in hexameters or elegiac couplets. But he also writes in a number of other metres, including some of those 'invented' by the writers of the Antonine age. Thus the brief epitaph on his aunt Veneria is in the resolved anapaests previously used by Septimius Serenus:

◡ ◡ ◡◡ ◡◡◡◡ ◡ ◡◡◡ ◡ ◡⏓
Et amita Veneria properiter obiit.

And aunt Veneria suddenly died.

His prosody shows occasional departures from classical usage which mark the changing language of his age, such as *pālatia, parrīcida, tertiūs horum, omnium.* His vocabulary is firmly classical, with relatively few neologisms, all following classical patterns. His syntax shows only occasional late Latin features, such as *ad* + accusative for dative, *de* + ablative for genitive, comparatives formed with *magis.*

A collection of 72 poems, the *Epigrammata Bobiensia*, mostly in elegiac couplets, ranging from two to seventy lines, was discovered in 1950 in a manuscript in the Vatican Library. Some of these are attributed to Julius (or Junius) Naucellius, a friend and correspondent of Symmachus, probably born *c.* 305–10. A few others are by named authors and had been already published. The majority of the poems are without attribution. The first editor of the corpus believed that they were all the work of Naucellius, but this view has been challenged. They are brief occasional poems – descriptions of places and buildings, prayers, developments of popular ethical themes and the like. Dull and imitative, often clumsy in expression, they are a specimen of the trivial classicizing versification which passed for literature in some Italian senatorial circles in the later fourth century. Their dreary mediocrity brings out the relative brilliance of Ausonius, Naucellius' contemporary.

Ausonius, as we have seen, owed his career largely to his literary distinction. But his relation to Valentinian and Gratian was not that of client to patron, and few of his poems arose out of his dependence on his imperial protectors. With Claudian we move into the very different world of the professional poet who lives by his pen and most of whose poems were occasioned by events in the life of his patron. Claudius Claudianus, a native of Alexandria, was born about 370. We know nothing of his early career, but he had clearly studied rhetoric, and had probably found his vocation as a poet by the time he was twenty. About 394 he came to Rome to seek a patron and further his career. His earliest surviving work is a panegyric poem addressed to the consuls Anicius Probinus and Anicius Hermogenianus Olybrius, sons of the rich and influential senator Petronius Probus and his wife Anicia Faltonia Proba, and delivered at Rome in January 395. Claudian was no doubt adequately rewarded by his senatorial patrons and could have counted on other commissions from members of their extensive family in due course. But his panegyric – and perhaps other poems which we no longer possess – attracted the attention of a more powerful patron, the Vandal general Stilicho, husband of Serena, niece and adoptive daughter of the emperor Theodosius, and regent after his death on 18 January 395 for his ten-year-old son Honorius. The poet moved from Rome to the imperial capital at Milan, where he was appointed to the sinecure post of *tribunus et notarius*, thereby obtaining senatorial rank.

In early January 396 he recited his *Panegyric on the Third Consulate of Honorius*. From then until his death in 404 he was a kind of official poet laureate and propagandist for Stilicho, delivering panegyrics on official occasions, invectives upon Stilicho's enemies, and tendentious accounts of such public affairs as the war against Gildo in Africa. He may have travelled with Stilicho on his not very successful campaigns. But he did not return to Rome until early in 400, when he delivered before the Senate the third book of his panegyric on the consulate of Stilicho. On that occasion he received the singular honour of a bronze statue in the Forum of Trajan, set up by the emperor at the request of the Senate. The plinth still survives, in which Claudian is described in Latin as *praegloriosissimus poetarum* and is said in Greek to combine the mind of Virgil and the Muse of Homer (*CIL* VI 1710). Later in the same year he married the daughter of a wealthy African senator, thanks to the influence exerted by his patroness Serena. He apparently remained in Africa for some time on an extended honeymoon, but returned to Rome in time to recite a panegyric on the sixth consulate of Honorius in January 404. This is his last datable poem, and the probability is that he died in the course of 404. Otherwise he would scarcely have failed to celebrate Stilicho's second consulate in January 405.

This is virtually all we know of Claudian's life. Before going on to examine his poetry, there is one general consideration which springs to the mind. Claudian, who has often, and not unreasonably, been described as the last classical poet of Rome, was a Greek. Intellectual contact between the Greek east and the Latin west had been one of the casualties of the half-century of anarchy in the mid third century. The political unification of the empire under Constantine and his successors had done little to bridge the gap. It had been subject to interruption in the reign of Valens and Valentinian, and with the death of Theodosius in 395 the division of the empire became permanent. The Italian senatorial class and those who aped its life-style had more and more withdrawn from an imperial role – which involved some acquaintance with the Greek half of the empire – and knowledge of the Greek language and Greek thought had become rarer and more superficial in the west. By the time Claudian came to Rome the two halves of the empire had to some extent been going their separate ways in cultural matters for a century and a half. The occasional migrant from east to west like Claudian or his older contemporary the historian Ammianus Marcellinus brought to the Latin world a breath of the very different, and often more invigorating, air of the Greek east. Their problem was how to make an effective synthesis between the two cultural traditions, and not to remain outsiders in the west. We know how Ammianus acquired his knowledge of Latin and his understanding of Roman tradition; it was by long years of service in the army, often in western provinces and under western commanders, followed by private study in Rome. Claudian is more of an enigma. The evidence of papyri suggests an upsurge in the study of Latin language and literature in Egypt, as in other eastern provinces, in response to the foundation of a new imperial capital in the middle of the Greek world and the new career prospects which a knowledge of Latin offered. But it is a long way from word-for-word cribs to Sallust and Virgil to the superb command of literary Latin and the sympathy with traditional Roman ways of thought shown by Claudian. Perhaps he belonged to a bilingual family descended from a Roman official. Perhaps he had close associations with a Latin-speaking milieu in Alexandria. Be that as it may, he seems to have arrived in Rome already a more than ordinarily competent Latin poet.

But he brought more from Egypt in his baggage than a knowledge of Latin. If the Muses had long been silent in the west they had been unusually vocal in the Greek world, and in particular in Egypt, where the fourth and fifth centuries saw the flourishing of a school of poets. These poets travelled widely throughout the Greek cities of the empire, and took over many of the public functions which in earlier generations had belonged to rhetoricians. They were the spokesmen of their communities, reciting odes on official occasions, serving as propagandists for those in power, and both reflecting and creating public opinion. Two genres which they developed to a high pitch of technical perfection were the descriptive set-piece or ἔκφρασις and the panegyric, both of which had been treated in the third-century treatises of Menander as falling within the domain of rhetoric. Both of these genres normally made use of the language and style of post-Homeric epic. Claudian, who wrote poetry in Greek as well as in Latin – a Greek *Gigantomachia*, probably a youthful production, survives – brought with him to the west familiarity with the public role of the Greek poets of his time and a command of their technique of composition. Now the western world had been familiar with the prose panegyrical address since the days of Pliny the Younger, and a collection of twelve such prose panegyrics from the end of the third and the first two thirds of the fourth century survives (pp. 757–8). What Claudian did was to introduce to the Senate at Rome and the court at Milan the Greek practice of the poetic panegyric, first under the patronage of the Anicii, then under that of Stilicho. His success in fusing together the Greek genre and Roman habits of thought and allusion was such that the old prose panegyric – whose roots went back through classical rhetorical theory to the ancient Roman tradition of the *laudatio funebris* – died out completely. More than that, Claudian gave to Roman poetry a new vigour as well as new genres.

His surviving works, which run to close on 10,000 lines, fall into three main categories: panegyrics and other occasional poems, historical epics, and mythological epics. The first class includes the panegyric on Probinus and Olybrius of 395, those on the third, fourth and sixth consulates of Honorius, dated 396, 398 and 404 respectively, the panegyric on Stilicho of 400, the *laus Serenae* of 404, the epithalamium for the marriage of Honorius and Maria of 398, and that for the marriage of Palladius and Celerina, and the great invectives on the ministers of the eastern court Rufinus (397) and Eutropius (399). The second category comprises the *Bellum Gildonicum* of 398 and the *Bellum Geticum* of 402. To the third category belong the *De raptu Proserpinae* in three books, whose date is uncertain, and the unfinished Latin *Gigantomachia*, which was probably interrupted by the poet's death in 404. In addition there are a number of very short poems and epigrams on a variety of topics. The major poems are all written in hexameters, often preceded by a preface in elegiac couplets, a combination often found in Greek poetry of the period.

Though the distinction between the three categories of poems is clear enough, Claudian uses the same type of structure in all his longer poems. They are composed almost entirely of speeches and descriptive set-pieces, linked by the most slender line of narrative. The same structure is to be observed in much of the Greek poetry of late antiquity. Men had lost interest in sustained narrative on the grand scale, despite – or perhaps because of – the role played in education by Homer and Virgil. Personified abstractions play some role both in the epics and in the panegyrics and invectives. The figure of Roma in particular regularly appears. But there is no tendency towards sustained allegory. Indeed the episodic structure of Claudian's poems, in which successive speeches and ἐκφράσεις would each elicit a round of applause in public recitation, would make sustained allegory difficult. Claudian's strength – and what distinguishes his poetry from the rather loose and verbose compositions of contemporary Greek panegyrists – is his superb exploitation of all the tricks of rhetoric, his masterly use of the traditional language of Latin epic, with all its possibilities of allusion, and his unfailingly inventive imagination. And Claudian knows when to stop. His sentences and his paragraphs are tightly organized, and he scarcely ever yields, as Ausonius did, to the temptation to launch into a catalogue. In Claudian few words are wasted, yet every line contains a surprise.

What he has to say is largely drawn from Roman tradition. He was no original political or historical thinker, nor was he expected by his patrons to be one. Yet he knew how to select from the traditional amalgam just those commonplaces and those *exempla* which would put his patron's case in the best light, and how to vary his choice among traditional arguments to suit his audience, whether Senate at Rome or court in Milan. He was not just a technician of versification. Though much of his writing may seem bombastic to modern readers, it is bombast of a very high order – as a glance at the writings of his imitator Sidonius Apollinaris (q.v.) will show – and it clearly suited the taste of the times. He has many passages which are moving and impressive – reflecting feeling that was more than superficial – and a few which can stand comparison with the work of the giants of Latin literature. Examples are his eulogy of Rome in *Laudes Stilichonis* 3.130–60, the speeches of Rome and Africa at the opening of the *Bellum Gildonicum* (28–200), the description of the tapestry woven by Proserpine in *De raptu Proserpinae* (1.244–75). While he makes no attempt at suiting words or descriptions to character, he has at his fingertips the rhetorician's full range of 'stances' (*status*, στάσις). Thus the two invectives on eastern ministers adopt quite different tones. Rufinus is depicted as the embodiment of evil, malignant, threatening and powerful; Eutropius is treated as a buffoon and showered with ridicule and contempt. Strangely enough for a poet who devoted so much effort and skill to descriptions, Claudian has no visual sense. We do not know what Rufinus or Gildo looked like; and of Stilicho we know only that his hair was white (*Bellum Geticum* 459–60 *emicuit Stilichonis apex et cognita fulsit* | *canities*, probably the last passage of Claudian ever to be quoted in the House of Commons). Claudian's descriptive passages are based upon rhetoric and reminiscence, not upon observation. His poetry is shot through with echoes not only of Lucretius and Virgil and Ovid, but of Lucan and Statius and Silius Italicus. But he rarely quotes directly and he often fuses together reminiscences of two or more classical poets. Sometimes the classical echo was meant to add depth to his own expression. But it would be unwise to suppose that the Roman Senate or the imperial court could pick up and appreciate in the course of a recitation every fleeting allusion to earlier literature, as some scholars have tended to suggest. Rather he was himself so steeped in classical poetry that the quotations and allusions came unbidden to his pen. His deep familiarity with classical Latin poetry is reflected in his vocabulary, which has few neologisms, in his syntax, which is scarcely affected by the spoken language of his time, and in his prosody, which scarcely ever departs from classical rules, in spite of the tendency of living speech to neglect phonological distinctions of vowel length.

Claudian is described by Augustine as *a Christi nomine alienus* and by Orosius as *paganus peruicacissimus* (*Civ. Dei* 5.26, *Hist. adv. pag.* 7.35.21). Both men were his contemporaries, though neither can have known him personally. But it is by no means certain that they were right. He wrote an Easter hymn, *De Salvatore*, which is really rather a poem offering Easter wishes to Honorius. Otherwise his poetry has no trace of Christian expressions or allusions, and is filled with traditional references to the Olympians. But this is a matter of literature, not of life. It is striking that when Claudian first came to Rome he enjoyed the patronage of a senatorial family that had long been Christian, and that he then became court poet at the intensely Christian court of Honorius. He may well have been a nominal Christian. And if he was a pagan, his attachment would not be to the official cult of the Roman pantheon, which still had a powerful appeal to senatorial aristocrats like Symmachus, but to the Isis and Sarapis cults of his native Alexandria. In any case Christianity did not affect his poetic persona.

His 'official' poems appear to have been issued in a collected edition at the instigation of Stilicho between 404 and 408. The *Raptus Proserpinae* and the various minor poems survived separately.

The virtues and the shortcomings of Claudian's style may be exemplified by two passages, one of encomium, the other of invective.

Proxime dis consul, tantae qui prospicis urbi,
qua nihil in terris complectitur altius aether,

cuius nec spatium uisus nec corda decorem
nec laudem uox ulla capit; quae luce metalli
aemula uicinis fastigia conserit astris;
quae septem scopulis zonas imitatur Olympi;
armorum legumque parens quae fundit in omnes
imperium primique dedit cunabula iuris.
haec est exiguis quae finibus orta tetendit
in geminos axes paruaque a sede profecta
dispersit cum sole manus. haec obuia fatis
innumeras uno gereret cum tempore pugnas,
Hispanas caperet, Siculas obsideret urbes
et Gallum terris prosterneret, aequore Poenum,
numquam succubuit damnis et territa nullo
uulnere post Cannas maior Trebiamque fremebat
et, cum iam premerent flammae murumque feriret
hostis, in extremos aciem mittebat Hiberos
nec stetit Oceano remisque ingressa profundum
uincendos alio quaesiuit in orbe Britannos.
haec est in gremium uictos quae sola recepit
humanumque genus communi nomine fouit
matris, non dominae ritu, ciuesque uocauit
quos domuit nexuque pio longinqua reuinxit.

(*Cons. Stilichonis* 3.130–53)

Consul, all but peer of the gods, protector of a city greater than any that upon earth the air encompasseth, whose amplitude no eye can measure, whose beauty no imagination can picture, whose praise no voice can sound, who raises a golden head amid the neighbouring stars and with her seven hills imitates the seven regions of heaven, mother of arms and of law, who extends her sway o'er all the earth and was the earliest cradle of justice, this is the city which, sprung from humble beginnings, has stretched to either pole, and from one small place extended its power so as to be co-terminous with the sun's light. Open to the blows of fate while at one and the same time she fought a thousand battles, conquered Spain, laid siege to the cities of Sicily, subdued Gaul by land and Carthage by sea, never did she yield to her losses nor show fear at any blow, but rose to greater heights of courage after the disasters of Cannae and Trebia, and, while the enemy's fire threatened her, and her foe smote upon her walls, sent an army against the furthest Iberians. Nor did Ocean bar her way; launching upon the deep, she sought in another world for Britons to be vanquished. 'Tis she alone who has received the conquered into her bosom and like a mother, not an empress, protected the human race with a common name, summoning those whom she has defeated to share her citizenship and drawing together distant races with bonds of affection. (Tr. M. Platnauer)

Posteritas, admitte fidem: monumenta petuntur
dedecoris multisque gemunt incudibus aera
formatura nefas. haec iudicis, illa togati,
haec nitet armati species; numerosus ubique
fulget eques: praefert eunuchi curia uultus.
ac ueluti caueant ne quo consistere uirtus
possit pura loco, cunctas hoc ore laborant
incestare uias. maneant inmota precamur
certaque perpetui sint argumenta pudoris.
subter adulantes tituli nimiaeque leguntur
uel maribus laudes: claro quod nobilis ortu
(cum uiuant domini!), quod maxima proelia solus
impleat (et patitur miles!), quod tertius urbis
conditor (hoc Byzas Constantinusque uidebant!).
inter quae tumidus leno producere cenas
in lucem, foetere mero, dispergere plausum
empturas in uulgus opes, totosque theatris
indulgere dies, alieni prodigus auri. (*In Eutropium* 2.70–87)

Ye who come after, acknowledge that it is true! Men must needs erect monuments to celebrate this infamy; on many an anvil groans the bronze that is to take upon it the form of this monster. Here gleams his statue as a judge, there as a consul, there as a warrior. On every side one sees that figure of his mounted on his horse; before the very doors of the senate-house behold a eunuch's countenance. As though to rob virtue of any place where she might sojourn undefiled, men labour to befoul every street with this vile image. May they rest for ever undisturbed, indisputable proofs of our eternal shame; such is my prayer. Beneath the statues one reads flattering titles and praises too great even for men. *Do they tell of his noble race and lineage while his owners are still alive? What soldier brooks to read that single-handed he, Eutropius, won great battles? Are Byzas and Constantine to be told that this is the third founder of Rome? Meanwhile the arrogant pander prolongs his revels till the dawn, stinking of wine and scattering money amid the crowd to buy their applause. He spends whole days of amusement in the theatres, prodigal of another's money.*

(Tr. Platnauer (1922))

The first passage develops in majestic style some of the traditional topics of the *laudes Romae*, the poetic origins of which are to be sought in Horace's Roman odes and in Virgil's *Aeneid* (6.781–853), while for some of the matter Claudian is probably indebted to Aelius Aristides' Roman oration (*Or.* 26). A slightly later treatment of the same theme is to be found in Rutilius Namatianus, *De reditu suo* 47–164. The emphasis which both poets of late antiquity, the one writing before the capture of the city by Alaric, the other after that event, give to Rome's resilience after disaster underlines a preoccupation of the age. For Virgil there had been no such problem. Claudian carefully avoids verbal echoes of his Virgilian model. The varying rhythm of his hexameters, with their absence of end-stopping, the play with evocative words like *Cannae* and *Trebia* (at both of which Roman armies suffered a shattering defeat at the hands of Hannibal), the tight structure of the passage and the absence of ornamental words or padding, and the striking figure of Rome as a mother rather than a mistress (what Aelius Aristides calls the φιλανθρωπία of Rome (*Or.* 26.66)) combine to give to this tissue of commonplaces a seriousness of tone and a certain impressive grandeur.[1]

The second passage owes more to Juvenal than to Virgil. The apostrophes, the exaggerations, the unexpected turn which phrases take (*nimiae...uel maribus laudes* when the reader expects the much less effective point 'too much for a eunuch'), the dramatic rhetorical questions answered by the poet himself, are all part of the satirical manner. What is Claudian's own contribution is the tenseness of the structure, without a superfluous word, the careful arrangement, according to which the three rhetorical questions and answers are in order of increasing length, and the classical purity of the language, which recalls Virgil rather than Juvenal.

While Claudian brought new vigour and distinction to Latin poetry through his own brilliance and through the new attitudes and techniques which he imported from the Greek world, his older contemporary Prudentius pursued a very different course of innovation. The two poets are very likely to have known one another, and Prudentius had certainly read some of Claudian's works. Whether Claudian shows any acquaintance with Prudentius' poetry is still an open question.

Aurelius Prudentius Clemens, born in 348 in Hispania Tarraconensis – perhaps at Calahorra or Zaragoza – studied rhetoric and practised at the bar. Following a common career pattern in late antiquity he held two provincial governorships and a high office at the court of Honorius – perhaps that of *comes primi ordinis*. He spent some time in Rome. In 405 at the age of 57 he retired from public life to devote himself to writing devotional poetry. He may have become a member of an ascetic Christian community like the *servi Dei* to whom Augustine belonged. He left a corpus of poetry preceded by a preface and followed by an epilogue, and consisting of two cycles of poems in lyric metres: one of hymns for various times of the day, the other of hymns in praise of martyrs, all western and largely Spanish, two didactic poems in hexameters respectively on the doctrine of the Trinity and on the origin of evil, an allegorical poem in hexameters on the struggle between virtues and vices to possess the soul, a hexameter poem in two books replying to the *Relatio* of Symmachus, and a series of some fifty hexameter quatrains describing biblical scenes. The chronology of the poems is uncertain. His *Preface* suggests that Prudentius wrote them all after his retirement. But in fact some are likely to be of earlier date. In any case he must have written earlier poetry

[1] Cf. Cameron (1970) 352–61.

which he did not wish to survive, for his technical mastery points to long practice of the art.

Not since Horace had any Latin poet written such a substantial body of lyric verse, and Prudentius has been called the Christian Horace. He certainly knew Horace. But his use of lyric metres, often written κατὰ στίχον (that is, with every line repeating the same metrical pattern), owes more to the lyric passages of Seneca's tragedies and to the Antonine *Poetae novelli*. His long didactic poems (1,084 and 966 lines) have led some to see in him a Christian Lucretius. But though he has Lucretius' fervour, he lacks his powerful visual imagination and his pathos. His *Psychomachia* breaks new ground in being the first wholly allegorical poem in Latin. In it the virtues and vices fight it out in pairs like epic heroes. It was immensely popular in the Middle Ages and soon acquired a cycle of illustrations.

Prudentius takes over classical forms in language, metre and figures of speech without the body of classical allusion which traditionally accompanied them. His biblical characters and his martyrs do not appear in classical dress, his God is never *rector Olympi* or the like. He has few long descriptive passages. He dispenses with such conventions as the invocation, except in his *Preface*, where he gives it a Christian turn. And he introduces into Latin poetry an allegorizing pattern of thought derived ultimately from Christian interpretation of the Old Testament. At his best Prudentius writes with an economy and force equal to those of the classical models he so often imitates. But his prevailing vice is long-windedness and repetition. He is, accordingly, better in his lyric than in his hexameter poems.

His poetry, while not of first quality – how little was in late antiquity – is important as marking a new departure in Latin literature and a creative synthesis for his own purposes by a Christian poet from the amalgam of tradition, in which old forms are infused with new content, and in which the distinction between the poet as poet and as man is largely effaced. It is also indicative of the existence of a highly educated and refined reading public for poetry on Christian themes. In essence his audience probably coincided largely with that of Claudian. None of his poetry was intended for liturgical use, unlike, say, the hymns of Ambrose. (Though excerpts from the *Peristephanon* were later adopted by the Mozarabic liturgy.) And just as Prudentius' hymns are a literary reflection of those actually used in liturgy, so his poems on martyrs are a literary reflection of the artless accounts in the *Acta martyrum*, or of the short epigrams written by Pope Damasus to adorn the interior of churches. As a theologian he is insignificant: indeed he probably did not fully understand the heretical views which he sought to refute in his dogmatic poems. Prudentius' reply to Symmachus has sometimes been taken as evidence of a fresh struggle between Church and Senate over the famous altar of Victory in the

Senate House in Rome, after those of 381–4 and 392. It is better interpreted as a final refutation, based on the writings of Symmachus and Ambrose, of the whole ideology of the now dwindling group of pagan senators. Fervent Christian though he was, Prudentius treated those whom he attacked with respect and on occasion with magnanimity. Even the emperor Julian gets a word of praise from him. His reply to Symmachus – perhaps dead when the poem was written – displays a sense of measure and generosity not always present in religious polemic. It is entirely fitting that an edition of his poems should have been prepared in the sixth century for a descendant of Symmachus.[1]

Claudian and Prudentius each tried to do something new with a very old and by now rigid literary tradition. Others were content to work within that tradition. All were writing for the same audience, all adopted in some degree the same declamatory tone. Poetry in the late fourth and early fifth century was for public reading. At the same time others, who belonged to the same social class and shared the same culture, were making a conscious and deliberate break with the whole tradition in which they had been brought up. The two attitudes are embodied in two men whose lives must have spanned the same period, and who both belonged to that society of western magnates whose interests had gradually fused with those of the Italian senators, Rutilius Namatianus and Paulinus of Nola.

Rutilius Claudius Namatianus belonged to an aristocratic Gaulish family, possibly from Toulouse. The closing decades of the fourth century see the Gaulish landed families more and more drawn into the orbit of the Italian senatorial class.[2] Rutilius' father Lachanius had held a series of high offices, culminating in a prefecture. He himself became *magister officiorum c.* 412 and *praefectus urbi* in 414. In 417 he returned from Italy to his native Gaul where his estates had suffered in the invasion, and vanished from history.

His only recorded work is his poem in elegiac couplets describing his journey from Italy to Gaul. All that survives is the first book, of which the beginning is lost (644 lines) and the first 68 lines of the second book. In 1973 a further fragment of the second book, consisting of 39 half lines, was published from a piece of parchment which had been used to repair a Turin manuscript. The title of the poem was lost with the opening of Book 1. It has conventionally received the provisional title *De reditu suo*. The loosely structured poem describing a journey is a genre well established in Latin literature, from Lucilius' *Iter Siculum* (fr. 96–147 M) through Horace's *Iter Brundisinum* (*Sat.* 1.5), Ovid's journey to Tomis (*Trist.* 1.10), Statius' *Propempticon* (*Silv.* 3.2) to Ausonius' *Mosella*. The metrical form of Rutilius' poem suggests that Ovid was his particular model, and this is confirmed by the large number of Ovidian echoes. But Rutilius imports into the traditional genre much that

[1] Momigliano (1962) 216.

[2] Cf. Matthews (1975) 349–51.

is characteristic of the classicizing poetry of late antiquity, and in particular its declamatory tone. The digressions, which were traditional in the genre, are mainly in the form of speeches and descriptions, and the descriptions often turn into rhetorical soliloquies.

The poem in the form in which we possess it begins with an address to the reader on the greatness of Rome (1.1–46) and a long speech of farewell by the poet to the city, in which most of the traditional topics of the *laudes Romae* are rehearsed (1.47–164), and goes on to recount day by day the stages of the journey by sea from Portus Augusti (Porto) via Centumcellae (Civitavecchia), Portus Herculis (Porto Ercole), Faleria, Populonia, Vada Volaterrana, Portus Pisanus, to Luna, at which point the text breaks off. The description of each stage is accompanied by references to friends of the poet connected with the places passed or visited, and to their historical associations, as well as by personal reflections of the poet. The most noteworthy of these are his attack on the Jews (1.383–98), his invective against the monks of Capraria (1.439–52), his account of the life and virtues of his father (1.575–96), and his attack on Stilicho for 'betraying the secret of empire' and allowing Alaric and his Visigoths into Italy (240–60). These varied disgressions are designed to break the monotony of a necessarily repetitive narrative.

Rutilius has been generally held to have been a pagan, though a few scholars have argued that he must have been a nominal Christian. Be that as it may, his poetic persona stands firmly in the classical literary tradition and shows no sign of Christian ideas or expressions. Rutilius combines a sometimes moving reverence for ancient Roman tradition with an optimism concerning the future which takes in its stride Alaric's recent sack of Rome and the devastations of the Visigoths and the Bagaudae in his native Gaul.

Rutilius' predominating stylistic feature is parallelism and antithesis, often emphasized by patterns of alliteration or assonance. There is little enjambment between couplet and couplet, and few long periods. He has a gift – which recalls Juvenal – for expressing traditional and conventional ideas in striking phrases. Some of his verses are among the most memorable in Latin literature, e.g.

Fecisti patriam diuersis gentibus unam;
  profuit iniustis te dominante capi,
dumque offers uictis proprii consortia iuris
  urbem fecisti quod prius orbis erat. (1.63–6)

You made one fatherland for scattered nations; it profited the uncivilized to fall under your overlordship. In offering to those you conquer a share in your own rights you have made a city of what was formerly the world

or

Vere tuo numquam mulceri desinit annus
  deliciasque tuas uicta tuetur hiems. (1.113–14)

The year is unendingly caressed by your spring, and winter yields before your charms or

Illud te reparat quod cetera regna resoluit:
ordo renascendi est crescere posse malis. (1.139–40)

That which destroys other realms renews you: the secret of rebirth is to be able to grow by your own adversities

or

Munera fortunae metuunt, dum damna uerentur:
quisquam sponte miser, ne miser esse queat? (1.443–4)

They are afraid of the gifts of fortune because they fear its penalties: does any man choose to be wretched in order not to be wretched?

Rutilius' poem is studded with echoes and half-quotations – conscious or unconscious – not only of Virgil, Horace, Ovid and Juvenal, but also of his own contemporaries Ausonius and Claudian. His language and metre are classical, and show few concessions to the living tongue of his age.

Rutilius is a pleasing poet, elegant and often original in expression, capable of expressing depth of feeling on occasion, particularly when he dwells on the memory of Rome's greatness. His poetic persona moves in a limited world, but one within which he is entirely in control of his medium. The loss of at least half of his poem is regrettable. The new fragments are too brief and broken to add anything to our understanding of the poem, and are still the subject of controversy and discussion.

Meropius Pontius Paulinus, born *c.* 355 of a wealthy and noble family of Bordeaux, was a pupil and protégé of Ausonius, and began the languid career of intermittent public office typical of his class. After a mysterious personal crisis he and his wife took up the religious life, sold their vast estates, and ultimately settled at Nola in Campania, of which he became bishop *c.* 410 and where he died in 431.

Paulinus left a corpus of fifty-one letters and thirty-six poems, mainly in hexameters, but also in the lyric metres of Horace. Several of the poems are polymetric. Three, which date from before his conversion, are trivial personal or mnemonic poems in the manner of Ausonius (1–3). The rest are Christian in content. They comprise a panegyric on John the Baptist (6), paraphrases, with exegetical additions, of three of the psalms (7–9), verse epistles (10, 11, 24), three prayers to St Felix of Nola (12–14), a propempticon for bishop Nicetas (17), a marriage poem or epithalamium (25), a consolatory poem on the death of a child (31), two protreptic poems (*Epist.* 8, poem 22), and thirteen poems written annually in celebration of the festival of St Felix between 395 and 407. A few fragments of other poems survive.

Paulinus distinguishes more clearly than any other poet of late antiquity between classical content and classical form, rejecting completely the former while adopting the latter. The whole universe of mythological allusion, which had supplied so much of the imagery of classical poetry, is excluded from his verse, its place being taken by biblical or hagiographic matter. Conventions like the invocation of the Muse are firmly rejected – *negant Camenis nec patent Apollini | dicata Christo pectora* 'Hearts dedicated to Christ reject the Muses and are closed to Apollo' (10.22–3) – and replaced by invocation of Christ (6.1ff., 21.672). His marriage poem banishes Juno, Cupid and Venus, condemns dancing, merriment and finery, holds up the example of Eve, Sarah, Rebecca and the Virgin Mary, and ends with a prayer that the marriage be not consummated or that if it is the children may adopt the religious life. Yet his verse follows classical models closely in metre and diction and is filled with echoes of classical poetry, which stand side by side with elements of specifically Christian language. Thus God is called both *tonans* and *creator*; *caro* is used of the incarnation; *Tartara* vies with *Gehenna*; technical terms like *euangelium*, *apostolus*, *mysterium*, *sacramentum*, *martyr* occur cheek by jowl with Virgilian flosculi like *nec inania murmura miscet* (10.121 ~ *Aen.* 4.201), *inlusas auro uestes* (25.43 ~ *Geo.* 2.464) or *odoratum nemus* (31.587, of Heaven ~ *Aen.* 6.685, of Elysium). Moreover Paulinus sets out clearly his poetic principle of taking over old forms with a new content in *Epist.* 16 and poem 22. His exchange of letters in prose and verse with his old teacher and friend Ausonius, who was shocked by his abandonment of his life-style and career, is a revealing and sometimes moving example of total lack of comprehension between two men apparently inhabiting the same intellectual world. (Aus. *Epist.* 19–25; Paulin. *Poems* 10, 11; the dossier is not complete.) Ausonius uses all the traditional arguments of the schools to re-establish contact while Paulinus replies in an anguished poem expressing the unbridgeable gap between them.

Though he displays the taste of his age for the declamation and the descriptive set-piece, Paulinus lacks the brilliance of Claudian and the neatness of Prudentius. His poems are inordinately long, and punctuated by digressions and personal reflections. He conveys the impression of one who does not know when to stop. The structural principle of his sentences is not antithesis and balance, but subordination. He composes in enormous clumsy sentences full of qualifications expressed in subordinate clauses of first, second and third degree, sentences which sometimes get out of control, which are never easy for the reader, and which must have been peculiarly difficult for those to whom they were recited aloud. His is no longer the confident, declamatory voice of the traditional poetic persona, but the slow, hesitant, private tone of one who thinks aloud, and who thinks about matters of supreme importance to himself. The poet and the man are no longer distinct. His attempt to preserve the classical forms while throwing overboard the whole of classical content had only limited success. His long-windedness, his didacticism, and his inability to vary his tone of voice put first-class poetry beyond his reach. His literary culture and his spiritual enthusiasm never fully fused together.

His letters are mainly on religious matters. Those to Ausonius, and the long 16th letter to Jovius on the relation between Christianity and classical culture are of more general interest.

Though in the eyes of Augustine Paulinus was an authority on Plato, he had, like most of his generation, only a superficial acquaintance with Greek culture, acquired during his schooldays.

One of the participants in Macrobius' *Saturnalia*, whose sole contribution to the dialogue is a series of amusing anecdotes, is a young man called Avienus. He is probably to be identified with the Avianus or Avienus (the orthography in the manuscripts varies) who about 430 dedicated a collection of forty-two fables in elegiac verse to a certain Theodosius, the name by which Macrobius was known to his contemporaries. Most of the fables were taken over from Babrius via the lost Latin prose translation by Julius Titianus, a third-century rhetorician, and a few come from another now lost Latin Aesopic source; there is no evidence that Avianus knew Greek. Elegiac verse, organized in discrete couplets, is ill suited to the narrative structure of fables. And Avianus has little poetic talent. His style is pompous and often obscure, and loaded with reminiscences of Virgil and Ovid. His Latinity, in spite of his efforts at classicisms, displays many features of the spoken tongue of his time, e.g. indirect statement with *quod* + subjunctive, *necdum* in the sense 'no longer', *diurnus* = *quotidianus*, and much inept anacoluthon. In spite of his shortcomings, Avianus enjoyed immense success as a moralist in the Middle Ages. He is probably the author of a lost epitome of Livy and a poem on legends in Virgil attributed by Servius (*Aen.* 10.272, 388) to 'Avienus'. His work is an example of the trivial versification in imitation of classical models which was valued as an accomplishment in senatorial circles in the fifth century.

Yet even in the turbulent fifth century literary talent could open the way to high office. Flavius Merobaudes, a Spanish rhetorician, made his way to the court of Valentinian III at Ravenna and tried to do for Valentinian and Aetius what Claudian had done for Honorius and Stilicho. He was rewarded with the dignity of *comes sacri consistorii* and a statue set up in 435 in the forum of Trajan at Rome, the base of which, with its laudatory inscription, still survives (*ILS* I 2950). In an age of war and invasion he had to wield the sword no less than the pen – *inter arma litteris militabat et in Alpibus acuebat eloquium* 'In the midst of arms he served letters and sharpened his eloquence in the Alps' – and reached the rank of *magister utriusque militiae*, commanding an army in Spain in operations against the Bagaudae. All that survives of his work is a series of purple passages excerpted by a later connoisseur. These include two ἐκφράσεις (descriptive set-pieces) of mosaics in an imperial palace or villa, in which Valentinian and his family were depicted, a short poem in hendecasyllables on the birthday of Aetius' infant son Gaudentius, part of a prose panegyric on Aetius' second consulate in 437, and a verse panegyric on his third in 446 (of which about 200 hexameters are readable), and a short poem on Christ. Merobaudes models himself on Claudian and Statius. He handles classical Latin and classical allusion with neatness and even elegance, but he lacks the force of Claudian and his inventive verbal imagination. The torch of classical tradition was clearly burning rather low in fifth-century Ravenna. The main interest of his poems today is as historical sources for a period in which the historian is ill served.

Yet in neighbouring Gaul, despite the establishment of Visigothic and Burgundian kingdoms in a large part of the province, a society of rich senatorial landowners not only maintained Roman culture in the fifth century but even re-established some intellectual contact with the Greek east. Knowledge of Greek was not uncommon, and could be more than merely superficial or school-based. Men read Plotinus and Porphyry and the Greek Fathers. They were interested in Greek astronomical and astrological learning. They translated Philostratus' *Life of Apollonius of Tyana*, with its clear message that the moral virtues are independent of the Christian faith. It is against the background of this short-lived Greek renaissance that we must view the life and work of Sidonius Apollinaris.

Gaius Sollius Apollinaris Sidonius was born in Lyons about 431 of a very wealthy senatorial family of Auvergne. Both his father and his grandfather had been Praetorian Prefects of Gaul. Educated in grammar and rhetoric at Lyons and probably at Arles, where public schools seem to have continued to exist, he was married in 451 to the daughter of another aristocrat from Auvergne, Flavius Eparchius Avitus, who had close connexions with the Gothic court at Toulouse. In 455, after the Vandal sack of Rome and the lynching of the ineffectual emperor Petronius Maximus, Avitus was proclaimed western Roman emperor at Arles. Sidonius accompanied his father-in-law to Rome and delivered a verse panegyric upon him, for which he was rewarded by the now customary statue in the forum of Trajan. The Italian aristocracy, the eastern court, and the Frankish general Ricimer made common cause against Avitus, and in October 456 he was obliged to abdicate and accept a bishopric. Sidonius was in danger for a time but soon made his peace with the new emperor Majorian, on whom he pronounced a panegyric in 458 when the emperor came to Lyons. Appointed *comes*, he accompanied Majorian on his campaigns until his assassination in 461. Sidonius then returned to Gaul and spent some years in private study, the management of his estates, and the *dolce vita* of the late Roman aristocrat. When in 467 the eastern emperor Leo appointed Anthemius, a Greek and a Neoplatonist, to the imperial throne of the west, Sidonius was sent on a mission to the new ruler by the Gaulish aristocracy. In 468 he delivered a panegyric upon Anthemius and was appointed by him *Praefectus urbi*. The hostile demonstrations of the hungry inhabitants of the Eternal City were not to the taste of a Gaulish magnate, and as soon as he could Sidonius escaped to the peace of his estates in Auvergne, dignified by the rank of *patricius*. Things were not going well in Gaul. The Visigothic king Theodoric had been succeeded by his son Euric, who was eager to extend his territory at the expense of the Romans. The great landowners governed their own territories in virtual independence of the central government. Peasant revolts were brewing. Sidonius now seems to have spent more and more of his time in the company of bishops and other clerics, who offered the hope of a kind of stability and continuity.

In 471 he was elected bishop of the Arverni, with his seat at Clermont-Ferrand, perhaps after a few months in lower ecclesiastical orders. Several of his kinsmen and friends entered the church at about the same time. In 472 King Euric attacked Auvergne. Although many of the Gaulish aristocracy sided with the Visigoths in the hope of retaining their estates Sidonius headed the resistance to the invaders. It was in vain. In 475 Auvergne was ceded to the Goths, and Sidonius became the subject of a barbarian king. Imprisoned for a time, he purchased his freedom at the price of a short panegyric on Euric. In 476 he returned to Clermont, where he devoted himself to administering and leading his diocese until his death in 486. He was later canonized.

His surviving works consist of twenty-four poems, in an edition prepared by the author in 469, and *c.* 150 letters in nine books. The poems are divided into *Panegyrici* (poems 1–8) and *Nugae* (poems 9–24). The *Panegyrici* begin with the panegyric on Anthemius in 548 hexameters (1) preceded by a preface in elegiac metre. There follow the panegyric on Majorian in 603 hexameters (5) preceded by two short prefatory poems, that on Avitus in 602 hexameters (7) with its preface, and a short elegiac poem addressed to Priscus Valerius, a kinsman of Avitus and former Praetorian Prefect of Gaul. The *Nugae*, in hexameters, elegiac couplets or hendecasyllables, comprise addresses to friends, two epithalamia, descriptions of buildings and works of art and the like. They vary in length from 512 lines to 4. A number of further short poems – including that in honour of King Euric – are contained in the letters. The letters are not real items of correspondence, but rhetorical set-pieces. In his preface he says that he imitates Pliny and Symmachus rather than Cicero, and describes his epistles as *litterae paulo politiores*. They are thus full of the commonplaces of ancient epistolography. The earliest of the letters, the description of King Theodoric (*Epist.* 1.2) dates from 455–60; the remaining letters of Book 1 are connected with Sidonius' mission to Rome in 467. The book was probably published in the following year. Thereafter there are few sure indications of date, and it is clear that the letters are not arranged in chronological order. Books 2–7 were probably published in 477, Book 8 in 479, Book 9 in 482. Apart from these indications each letter has to be dated by internal evidence.

Sidonius' style, both in verse and in prose, is inflated and precious, full of word-plays, complex figures of speech, mythological and historical allusions, to which is added biblical imagery in the letters written after his assumption of the bishopric. He is a man of considerable learning, though he not infrequently gets things wrong. For him, as for the other aristocrats who compose his world, literary culture is the outward and living sign of his Romanity, which he sees threatened by a tidal wave of barbarism. Yet like other members of his class he is ready to come to terms with the new rulers in the hope of retaining something of his economic and social position. He praises one of his friends for his perfect knowledge of Gothic. His entry into the church was the only way out of his dilemma. As a bishop he was the defender of a culture in which the Goths too, Arians though they were, could share. And he was able to continue the role of paternalistic leadership which his family had exercised in his province for generations. His prestige and influence in Romania and Gothia alike were immense. Today he is of interest primarily as a priceless historical source. Few would read Sidonius for his literary merit. Yet behind his often absurd preciosity lies a real talent for description and narrative. His descriptions of the Visigoths (*Epist.* 1.2, poem 23, *Epist.* 5.12, 6.6, 33, 8.9), the Burgundians (poem 12), the Franks (poem 5.237ff., *Epist.* 4.20), the Saxons (*Epist.* 86) and the Huns (poem 2.243ff.) show sharp observation which goes beyond the commonplaces of the genre. His account of the 'satire' of Arles (*Epist.*1.11), of the trial of Arvandus (*Epist.*1.7), of the adventures of the reader Amantius (*Epist.*7.2) show him a superb raconteur.

For all his limitations – and he scarcely seems to have noticed Romans who did not belong to his own class – Sidonius is an attractive character and on occasion an attractive writer. We know that he lived through the decline and fall of the western Roman empire. This was knowledge denied to him. But he tried to keep his head in difficult circumstances, and in a large measure succeeded.

Ausonius' grandson Paulinus of Pella had to face the same problems as Sidonius, but with inferior resources both personal and material. Born at Pella in Macedonia during the praetorian prefecture of his father Hesperius, he was soon brought to Bordeaux where his education, in both Greek and Latin, was supervised by Ausonius. For a number of years he lived the idle life of a selfish aristocrat, a Sidonius without Sidonius' cultural interests. In 396 he married, without much enthusiasm, a rich heiress. This life of ease was interrupted by the Gothic invasion of 406, when Bordeaux was sacked and Paulinus lost much property. He left Bordeaux for the more defensible Bazas, which in its turn was besieged by the Goths. Paulinus raised the siege by coming to terms with the Goths' allies the Alans, a compromise which many Romans regarded as treasonable. His position was not improved by his accepting office under the puppet emperor Attalus in 410. For a time he thought of returning to the tranquillity of the east, or becoming a monk, but both projects were resisted by his wife. For many years he lived in relative poverty on a farm near Marseilles, and later returned to Bordeaux to a similar small estate. More and more alone as his family died one by one and prevented by age from running his farm, he was saved from destitution by a Goth who gave him a good price for it, paid in cash.

In his eighty-fourth year he wrote a curious autobiographical poem, the *Eucharisticon Deo sub ephemeridis meae textu* 'Thanksgiving to God in the form of my diary'. The memories of his long life come tumbling out in his clumsy tortuous Latin. Paulinus was no scholar or man of letters, but was driven by an urge to examine his own life. His message is to thank God that things might have been worse. Virgilian tags from his schooldays spring to his pen, but there is very little else of classical tradition in matter or manner, and his striving for self-revelation is the antithesis of the classical poetic persona. He has no animus against the Germans. Paulinus' poem provides a fascinating picture from an upper-class point of view of the disintegration of a traditional society.

37

BIOGRAPHY

The form of imperial biography established in the second century by Suetonius continued to be followed during late antiquity, and was later adopted as a model by Einhard for his *Life of Charlemagne*. Of other classical forms of biography, such as the life of the philosopher, there is no trace in the Latin west, though the Greek east provided excellent examples in the *Life of Plotinus* by Porphyry (*c*. 234–*c*. 305) and the *Lives of the Sophists* by Eunapius of Sardis (*c*. 345–*c*. 414). The *vie romancée*, whether its aim was to instruct or to amuse, is represented by a single translation from a Greek original, the *Res Gestae Alexandri Magni* of Julius Valerius.

The expansion of Christianity in the fourth century transformed or revivified many classical literary genres to fulfil its own purposes. Thus Eusebius originated a new type of history, in which the methods and skills of the antiquarian were united with those of the rhetorician, which had dominated historiography since Hellenistic times. So too in biography Athanasius struck out in a new direction with his *Life of Anthony*, which provided the model for lives of holy men and bishops for centuries. Latin writers soon took up the new genre, as for example in Jerome's *Life of Paul*, an entirely fictitious biography of an alleged predecessor of Anthony (*MPG* 23.17–28). The *Life of Cyprian* which survives under the name of Pontius is, at any rate in its present form, not the third-century text which it purports to be.

Marius Maximus, who is probably to be identified with Lucius Marius Maximus Perpetuus Aurelianus, consul for the second time in 223, wrote twelve biographies of the emperors from Nerva to Elagabalus (†222). His work, along with that of Juvenal, was avidly read by those late fourth-century Roman aristocrats whose libraries were usually kept closed like tombs (Amm. Marcell. 28.4.14). The biographies have not survived, and it is sometimes hard to know how much credit to attach to statements about them in the *Historia Augusta*. They seem to have followed in style and treatment, as in number, the *Lives* of Suetonius, i.e. the activities of an emperor after he attained power, which inevitably form the bulk of an imperial biography, were treated not chronologically, but by categories arranged in an elaborate system of dichotomies. What we cannot be sure of is whether Marius Maximus really wrote at much greater length than Suetonius – he is called *homo omnium uerbosissimus* by *S.H.A. Firm.* 1.2 – or whether he included more documentary material. He seems to have had, in an even higher degree than Suetonius, a taste for trivial and occasionally scabrous details. But he was clearly a thoughtful writer who used his own judgement, and, within the limits imposed by the genre, a reliable source. There is no reason to believe, however, that he had the access to material in the imperial archives which confers particular historical value on Suetonius' *Lives*. His popularity seems to have been shortlived. He is not quoted by later writers except in the *Historia Augusta*.

The *Historia Augusta* is a collection of lives of emperors from Hadrian to Numerian, dealing not only with reigning emperors, but with co-emperors and pretenders as well. It is likely that Lives of Nerva and Trajan have been lost from the beginning. The title was given by Isaac Casaubon, who published the *editio princeps* in 1603. The manuscripts have variations on the theme 'Vitae diuersorum principum et tyrannorum a diuo Hadriano usque ad Numerianum a diuersis scriptae' 'Lives of the various Princes and Usurpers from Hadrian to Numerian written by divers hands'. There are thirty biographies in all, some dealing with groups of emperors or pretenders. They are addressed to Diocletian, Constantine and various personages of their period, and purport to have been written at various dates from before 305 till after 324. They are attributed to six authors, of whom nothing else is known: Aelius Spartianus (7 lives), Julius Capitolinus (9), Vulcatius Gallicanus (1), Aelius Lampridius (4), Trebellius Pollio (4) and Flavius Vopiscus (5). The lives range in length from 49 printed pages (Severus Alexander) to 6 (Antoninus Geta), though in the composite biography entitled *Tyranni Triginta*, 'The Thirty Tyrants', 'Trebellius Pollio' polishes off thirty-two alleged pretenders in exactly as many pages. The arrangement of the lives is Suetonian, in that each author recounts his subject's life chronologically until he becomes emperor, and thereafter by categories – public life and private life, war and peace, at home and abroad, and so on – until with the approach of his death the chronological method takes over again. The lives contain more documents, letters, speeches, laws and the like, than those of Suetonius, and at least as much curious anecdotal information on the personal lives of their subjects – Firmus ate an ostrich a day (*Firm.* 4), Maximus consumed a 'Capitolina amfora' of wine and 40 pounds – or as some say 60 – of meat per day (*Maximini duo* 4), Tacitus on the other hand entertained a convivium with a single chicken eked out with eggs, and rarely took a bath (*Tac.* 11), Elagabalus had tame lions and leopards which were trained to take their places at the dinner-table, to the discomfiture of the guests (*Heliog.* 21). Many otherwise unknown authorities are quoted, some for their writings, others for information supplied orally.

Since its first publication the *Historia Augusta* has been recognized to be a particularly unreliable source. The majority of the numerous documents which it contains were soon shown to be false. No differences in language and style could be detected between the six authors. The distribution of the various Lives between them was found capricious. And there were inconsistencies – Spartianus in his Life of Niger (8.3) claims to be about to write the Life of Clodius Albinus, but that Life is actually attributed to Julius Capitolinus. Readers saw more and more apparent allusions to persons and events of the later fourth century in these Lives allegedly composed at the beginning of the century. And verbal echoes of the *Caesares* of Aurelius Victor, published in 360, and of the *Breviarium* of Eutropius, published in 370, suggest dependence on these works, since neither Aurelius Victor nor Eutropius was in the habit of copying out his sources verbatim. But no systematic explanation of the cause or nature of the unreliability was offered by scholarship until the late nineteenth century, when it was argued that the whole work was a forgery, written by a single hand towards the end of the fourth century, and reflecting the views and events of that period. Attempts to defend the authenticity of the *Historia Augusta* by postulating a later edition or a series of editors have in general foundered, as has the suggestion that it was a work of propaganda on behalf of the emperor Julian. Today most scholars accept that the work is a piece of deliberate mystification, written much later than its purported date, though the fundamentalist position still has distinguished support. Those who believe the *Historia Augusta* to be a forgery are not in agreement on its purpose. Some argue that the work is a piece of propaganda, probably connected with the pagan senatorial reaction at the end of the fourth century. Others point out that the political views expressed in the lives are trivial and that it is better seen as a hoax, the product of the eccentric imagination of some maverick *grammaticus*, to be compared with the roughly contemporary correspondence of Seneca and St Paul (cf. Appendix) or the later historical fantasies of Geoffrey of Monmouth. No solution to the problems presented by the *Historia Augusta* is ever likely to satisfy all critics. Too much depends on subjective valuation. And it is never easy to determine whether an error or absurdity is better explained as the result of misunderstanding or imposture. Knaves and fools cannot always be distinguished a millennium and a half later.[1]

Be that as it may, the value of the collection for the historian depends largely on the sources used. As has been observed, a great many authorities are quoted whose existence can be neither proved nor disproved, since they are

[1] Cf. Appendix, for a brief history of the controversy on the nature and date of the *Historia Augusta*.

otherwise unknown. Marius Maximus is often quoted in the earlier lives, the longer of which on the whole contain more verifiable material and fewer absurdities and improbabilities than the later lives, or the shorter lives of Caesars, short-lived emperors and usurpers. Marius' imperial biographies were certainly an important source, perhaps the principal source, for the main lives from Hadrian to Elagabalus. The shorter lives in this section are largely composed out of bits and pieces from the longer lives, supplemented by invention – in Mommsen's words 'nicht etwa eine getrübte Quelle, sonder eine Kloake' 'not so much a troubled spring, rather a sewer'. There may well have been a second biographical source available for the early lives; the hypothesis that they also drew on a lost annalistic historian of the Severan age has by now been generally abandoned. For the later lives the postulate of a lost narrative history, dating perhaps from the time of Constantine, still stands though shakily. The same source may also have been used by Eutropius and Aurelius Victor. But its authorship, structure and tendency remain unclear. Much of the rest of the material in the later lives, including the many fictitious pretenders, must be put down to imagination and inventiveness, backed up by wide reading and a retentive memory. Occasionally one sees, or fancies one sees, how the author's mind worked: *Memmia, Sulpicii consularis uiri filia, Catuli neptis*, the unconfirmed and probably fictitious second wife of Alexander Severus (*Alex.* 20.3), is almost certainly derived from the description of Sulpicius Galba's wife in Suetonius, *Mummiam Achaicam, neptem Catuli* (*Galba* 3.4).

It is hard to attribute an ideology to the *Historia Augusta*. Its good emperors are those who govern along with the Senate. But this is traditional political wisdom rather than a practical programme for the fourth century. The work in its present state has no general preface. There are secondary prefaces to the Lives of Macrinus (in which the probably fictitious biographer Junius Cordus, who had already appeared in the Life of Clodius Albinus under the guise of Aelius Cordus, is formally introduced), of the two Maximini, of the three Gordians, of the Thirty Tyrants, of Claudius, of Aurelian (in which the author recounts how Iunius Tiberianus promised to obtain for him from the Bibliotheca Ulpia the *libri lintei* in which Aurelian had kept his diary), Tacitus, Probus (in which he sets out in impressive detail a list of fictitious sources), of Firmus, Saturninus, Proculus and Bonosus, and of Carus and Carinus (in which he gives a bird's-eye view of Roman history from the foundation of the city). But only in the preface to the Life of Claudius does the author expressly discuss the qualities of the ideal emperor. They are hardly the result of profound political thought or intense partisan feeling. He must combine the *uirtus* of Trajan, the *pietas* of Antoninus, the *moderatio* of Augustus, and so on. While the *Historia Augusta* is written from a pagan point of view, it is not concerned with anti-Christian polemic. Indeed it is probably too frivolous a work to have any serious political or religious message.

The style is in general simple and unrhetorical, recalling that of Suetonius. It lacks the strident, declamatory tone of much fourth-century Latin prose, to which the author(s) rise(s) only in some of the prefaces.

Probably written by a practical joker for entertainment rather than information and aiming to titillate and satisfy the interest of readers preoccupied with details of the private life of the great and powerful, the *Historia Augusta* is also, unfortunately, the principal Latin source for a century of Roman history. The historian must make use of it, but only with extreme circumspection and caution. Other readers are drawn to this extraordinary work by curiosity rather than by a taste for literary excellence. Those whose taste inclines towards speculation on the psychology of the impostor will find in the *Historia Augusta* much food for thought.

To the category of *vie romancée* belongs the Alexander-Romance of pseudo-Callisthenes, a strange amalgam of history, fantasy and dead political pamphleteering. First put together in Greek, perhaps in the third century A.D., the original text has been translated, modified and supplemented many times through the centuries, and versions in the vernacular are known from places as far apart as Iceland and Java. The earliest Latin version was written in the closing decades of the third or the opening decades of the fourth century by one Julius Valerius (Alexander Polemius). He has been tentatively identified with Flavius Polemius, one of the consuls of 338; but it would be safer to admit that we really know nothing of his person. His text is a translation of a Greek version akin to but not identical with Version A.[1] He writes with some pretension to elegance of style. But his Latin is full of strange words like *anguina* (= *anguis*), *equitium* (= *equites*), *extuberasco*, *furatrina* (elsewhere only in Apuleius), *inconspectus*, *intranatabilis*, *lubentia*, *supplicialis*, and of unclassical constructions like the genitive of comparison (*tui sollertiorem*), *habere* + infin., *impendere* + accus., *laudare aliquem alicuius rei*, *prae* + accus. This suggests the work of a provincial rhetorician, perhaps more at home in Greek than in Latin, rather than of a scholar or a member of a learned senatorial circle.

Julius Valerius' text was used by the unknown author of an *Itinerarium Alexandri* dedicated to Constantine. This is a very rough summary of Alexander's campaigns, based partly on Arrian and partly on Julius Valerius, and without any pretension to literary merit.

The Metz Alexander Epitome represents the *disiecta membra* of another Latin version of the Alexander-story. In its present form it tells the story of Alexander's life from just after the death of Darius to the Indian campaign, and then goes on to recount the plot to poison the king, his death, and the

[1] Ed. Kroll (1926).

terms of his testament. The first portion is based directly or indirectly on Diodorus and Quintus Curtius, i.e. it represents historical rather than legendary tradition. The second portion corresponds closely to that of the early versions of pseudo-Callisthenes. The work cannot be dated with certainty, but belongs to late antiquity rather than to the Middle Ages. All these works testify to the attraction which the personality and exploits of Alexander – real or imagined – had for the men of late antiquity. It is no wonder that John Chrysostom (*Ad illum. catech.* 2.5 (2.243E)) upbraided the Christians of Antioch for using coins of Alexander as amulets.

It should be noted that none of these early Latin versions provided the starting-point for the rich and varied Alexander-tradition in western European literature. That honour belongs rather to the *Historia de preliis*, translated from the Greek in the middle of the tenth century in Naples by the Archipresbyter Leo at the behest of Duke John of Campania. The Greek version used by Leo was akin to that which, via Middle Persian and Syriac translations, gave rise to the extensive Alexander tradition of the Moslem world.

An example of romantic biography even more remote from reality and aiming at entertainment rather than instruction, is the *Ephemeris Belli Troiani*, 'Diary of the Trojan War', attributed to Dictys the Cretan, a companion on the Trojan campaign of Idomeneus and Meriones. Allegedly written in Phoenician characters, the work was said to have been discovered by Cretan shepherds in the age of Nero and transcribed into Greek. The Latin adaptation is the work of a certain L. Septimius and is dedicated to Q. Aradius Rufinus, who is probably to be identified with the consul of 311. The book recounts the story of the Trojan War from the Greek point of view from the seduction of Helen to the death of Odysseus, with much imaginative detail on the personal appearance of the heroes and such matters. A papyrus of A.D. 206 contains a portion of the original Greek Dictys, which Septimius appears to have translated fairly faithfully. The style is clear and simple, though monotonous. Occasional poetic or archaic expressions are designed to lend a patina of antiquity to the work. The ultimate source of Dictys and Dares Phrygius is to be sought in Hellenistic treatises in which the post-Homeric treatment of Homeric themes, particularly by the Attic tragedians, was discussed. It was from Dictys and Dares that the western world in the Middle Ages learned what it knew of the Tale of Troy. The Greek east, although it had access to Homer, made much use of the lost Greek originals of Dictys and Dares, which are reflected in the *Antehomerica* and *Posthomerica* of John Tzetzes, the *Chronicle* of Constantine Manasses (both twelfth century) and the *Trojan War* of Constantine Hermoniakos (fourteenth century).

A similar account of the Trojan war from the Trojan point of view is attributed to Dares the Phrygian. It covers the period from the death of

Laomedon to the capture of Troy by the Greeks. A preface attributes the Latin translation to Cornelius Nepos, who is said to have dedicated it to Sallust. This is mere mystification. A date in the fifth or sixth century is suggested by the language, which is less classical than that of Dictys. Like the *Ephemeris* of Dictys, Dares' work is doubtless based on a Greek original, but no trace of this has so far been found.

The history of Latin hagiography falls outside the scope of the present volume, and the Lives of Saints written in the period under review can be dealt with very briefly, with one important exception. Three main classical literary genres contributed to the formation of the model followed by the typical saint's life. These are the report of the trial and execution of the martyr, often comprising authentic or spurious documents, the biography of the philosopher or man of letters, and the account of the revelation of the superhuman powers of the god in human guise or the man in a special relationship to the gods. All three are found in various proportions in pagan texts such as the *Life of Apollonius of Tyana* by Philostratus II and in certain of the *Lives of the Sophists* by Eunapius. The Latin *Life of Cyprian* by his disciple Pontius, which survives in a much interpolated form, still concentrates on the martyrdom of its subject, and deals only with the last few years of his life. The *Life of Ambrose* by pseudo-Paulinus and the *Life of Augustine* by Possidius remain much more within classical patterns of biography. The three Lives of eastern monks written by Jerome, those of Paul, Malchus and Hilarion, contain more elements of aretalogy, as the miraculous ascetic feats of their subjects form the main subject of the narration. The fascinating *Life of Martin of Tours* by Sulpicius Severus combines a narrative of the exploits of its hero with the revelation of his superhuman powers, culminating in his raising of a dead man to life.

There is little trace of Christian autobiography until the end of the fourth century, though Jerome records a certain Aquilius Severus from Spain who died in the reign of Valentinian and who wrote a work containing '*totius suae uitae statum*' in prose and verse under the title Καταστροφή or Πεῖρα. This work, which does not survive, may have been the first example of the specifically Christian genre of 'inner' autobiography, in which a man recalls and examines his own spiritual development. The first undoubted example of inner autobiography, a work which opens new paths in terms of ancient literary traditions and which exercised immense influence on western European literature, is the *Confessions* of Augustine. Augustine's role in the history of Christian thought is a topic which does not fall within the scope of the present study. But it would be impossible to discuss Latin literature in late antiquity without dwelling on two of his principal works, the *Confessions*, which will be examined here, and the *City of God*, which will be discussed in the context of the historiography of the late Empire.

The *Confessions*, in thirteen books, were written about 397, in the early years of Augustine's episcopate of Hippo. In form they are a dialogue between the author and God, or more strictly a monologue addressed by the author to God. The ancient reader on opening the work might well feel that what he had before him was a philosophical treatise written in the form of a prayer, for which Plotinus himself, and even more his successors, provided a model. In content the first nine books recapitulate in chronological order the development of Augustine's spiritual understanding from his first infancy to the death of his mother Monnica in 387, dwelling in anxious detail on those episodes, often trivial in themselves, which marked an advance in the author's insight into his own nature and his place in the created universe. The last four books are a philosophical and theological anaylsis of the state of Augustine in particular and of man in general with reference to God and to the Christian church. The *Confessions*, however, are not a series of reminiscences. Though Augustine can project himself back into early manhood, youth and childhood with marvellous empathy, he is not interested in recreating a past which might otherwise be lost, or in telling a good story. What concerns him is how he, Augustine, came to be chosen by God for the gift of grace and what it implies. Yet is it not a story with a happy ending, as, in a sense, were the lives of the martyrs. At the end of it all Augustine recognizes that he has made progress. But his new state brings with it even more problems than his original innocence. Understanding brings a bleak and discouraging view of mankind, and little by way of comfort.

Augustine has a talent for narrative, and there are many brilliant narrative passages in the *Confessions*, such as the story of the boys stealing the pears in Carthage (2.4.9) or of Alypius, future lawyer and bishop, being arrested as a burglar (6.9.14). But a story is never told for its own sake. The brooding presence of the Bishop of Hippo is always there to comment, interpret, draw the lesson. In the numerous passages of direct address to God all the devices of ancient rhetoric are brought into play, as might be expected of the former holder of a chair in that subject. Augustine varies the pace and style of his long soliloquy with the skill expected of a successful professional. And he adds a new quality to his Latin prose by the continuous references, sometimes by verbatim quotation, sometimes by the most indirect allusion, to the Bible and in particular to the Psalms (naturally in a pre-Hieronyman version). This resulted not merely in adding a certain depth of meaning to what Augustine had to say, but also in the incorporation into artistic Latin prose of a whole exotic vocabulary and a strange universe of reference which had been hitherto spurned by men of classical learning, even if they were Christians.

This long account of the spiritual journey of a man brought up in the purest of classical tradition through Manichaeanism and Neoplatonism to a wholehearted commitment to a somewhat daunting Christianity is unique in Latin literature. Probably intended in the first place for the author's fellow-clerics and *serui Dei*, the book has enjoyed immense influence throughout a millennium and a half. To the reader sensitive to such matters it is a work which still touches the heart and mind with astonishing power. Others find the pervasive rhetoric cloying and dissuasive. To the student of the psychology of religion it is a document of deepest interest. Augustine himself, rereading his *Confessions* at the age of seventy-four, as the restless Berbers pressed even harder on the great Roman landlords of Africa, and as Gaiseric and his Vandals stood poised by the Straits of Gibraltar, observed 'they still move me when I read them now, as they moved me when I first wrote them' (*Retractationes* 2.32).

38

HISTORY

After the death of Tacitus the Muse of history maintained virtual silence in the Latin west for two and a half centuries. This is partly to be explained by the role of history in Roman culture. Traditionally, the writing of history—the history of one's own times or of the immediately preceding age—had been an occupation for retired or failed statesmen, an aspect of their *otium* which corresponded to their political *negotium*. This meant that it was essentially an activity of senators. From Cato the Censor through Calpurnius Piso, Caesar, Sallust, Asinius Pollio, Cluvius Rufus to Tacitus the succession of senatorial historians stretches across the centuries. But by Tacitus' time there was no longer an independent political role for senators to play. They needed neither to proclaim their successes nor to justify their failures. The making of decisions had passed into other hands than theirs. They could only look back nostalgically and recount the successive stages by which they had lost their *libertas* (in the special sense which the word bore in senatorial thinking[1]). After Tacitus' time it was too late to do even that. The memory of *libertas* had perished. At the same time the composition of the senatorial class itself had changed. From being a small, close-knit, relatively exclusive group of central Italian landowning families, traditionally concentrating in their hands the exercise of the power of the Roman *res publica*, in spite of, or sometimes thanks to, the occasional maverick who appealed over the heads of his colleagues to the people of Rome, it had become a wide-open group of upper-class families from Italy and the western provinces, with little of the old solidarity or sense of destiny. As men from the eastern provinces, whose native tongue was Greek and who were heirs to a very different political tradition, began to enter the Senate in increasing numbers in the late second century, the complexion of the senatorial class became even more unlike what it had been in the later Republic or under the Julio-Claudian emperors. Thus the peculiarly Roman phenomenon of the senatorial historian, for whom history was an extension of politics, vanished with the social system which had given him birth.

[1] Cf. Wirszubski (1950) 124–71.

Not all Republican or early Imperial historians had been senators, of course. Some were probably clients of great senatorial houses, like Claudius Quadrigarius or Valerius Antias. Others were independent men of letters, pursuing no public career and owing allegiance to no patron. The greatest of these was Livy. Livy wrote at a time when men were sharply conscious of change. A historical epoch was coming to an end within his own lifetime. As his later books have perished we scarcely know with what thoughts and feelings he greeted the end of the Republic and the institution of autocratic rule – however much tempered by formal concessions to the authority of the Senate. But we can hardly suppose that the sense of radical change was absent from his mind as he wrote his rich, slow-moving nostalgic panorama of the history of the Roman people from Romulus to Augustus. That sense of change, of movement from one epoch to another, was no longer present in Roman society after the Julio-Claudians. However much things did in fact change, the changes were slow and almost imperceptible. They did not awaken in men's minds a sense of crisis and a need to re-examine the whole of their historic past. So Livy had no successors, only epitomators.

In the Greek world Clio was not silent. There the writing of history had different roots, going back to Polybius, Isocrates, Thucydides. Some of it was merely *belles-lettres*, designed to give pleasure or to move the emotions harmlessly. Much was concerned with understanding and edification. Much of it, such as the history of Polybius, had a political side to it – Polybius strove for pragmatic understanding of what had made Roman power, at a particular conjuncture in the history of the Mediterranean world, irresistible; what he was not concerned with, overtly at any rate, was the justification of his own conduct or that of a faction to which he belonged. This was a stance very different, and much more 'intellectual' than that of the Roman senatorial historian. So Greek historiography was less dependent on the survival of a particular political and social structure than was that of the Roman world. In fact all the many strands of the rich Greek historical tradition continued to run through the 230 years after Tacitus, and there was a continuous and varied succession of historians writing in Greek on a variety of topics throughout the period.

In the second century Arrian of Nicomedia wrote not only a history of Alexander based on reliable contemporary sources, but also a whole series of local or provincial histories – *Bithynica*, *Parthica* etc. – and a history of the Greek world under the successors of Alexander; none of these last has survived. His contemporary Appian of Alexandria wrote twenty-four books of Roman history. Lucian's satirical *How to write history* reveals a dozen or more historians writing in a variety of styles – largely archaizing – on the Parthian war of Lucius Verus. In the first half of the third century Cassius Dio Cocceianus of Nicaea, consul in 223/4 and again in 229, devoted his retirement to writing a vast history of Rome from Aeneas to Severus Alexander in eighty books, much of which now survives only in excerpts or in an eleventh-century epitome. Derivative for the most part and displaying all the shortcomings of the rhetorical culture of the age, it is nevertheless a major work of synthesis, upon which the author has imposed the impress of his own personality and the political outlook of the senatorial class of his time. It is the first major history of Rome since Livy, and significantly it is written in Greek. In the same period Herodian, possibly a Syrian, wrote his history of the Roman world from the death of Marcus Aurelius in 180 to the accession of Gordian III in 238, a work much inferior in insight to that of Cassius Dio. Later in the century P. Herennius Dexippus of Athens wrote four books on Greece under the successors of Alexander, largely dependent on the work of Arrian, a universal chronicle from mythical times to the reign of Claudius Gothicus, and a history of Gothic wars up to at least 270. At the beginning of the fifth century Eunapius of Sardis wrote a continuation of the chronicle of Dexippus up to 404. As well as these major figures we hear of many other historians writing in Greek, some dealing with local or regional history, others with larger themes, like the apparently Roman Asinius Quadratus, who wrote a history of Rome from the foundation of the city to the reign of Severus Alexander in Ionic dialect in imitation of Herodotus.

In the same period Christians were beginning to write in Greek either on the history of the church or on universal history seen from the Christian point of view. Sextus Julius Africanus, an African philosopher turned Christian, wrote a history of the world from the creation to the reign of Macrinus (217–18) as well as a treatise on chronology in which Old Testament and Greek history were brought together. This in itself was a departure from the rhetorical tradition of classical historiography, which concerned itself only spasmodically and unsystematically with such matters. But the man who set a new stamp on Christian history-writing was Eusebius of Caesarea. Like Julius Africanus he was interested in tying together biblical history and the political history of the Graeco-Roman world, and to this end engaged in chronological researches, and published a world chronicle accompanied by comparative tables of dates, which does not survive in the Greek original. When he came to write the history of the Christian church from its beginnings to his own times in ten books he faced a new problem. The point of view which he expressed would be disputed not only by traditional pagans, but also by sectarian fellow-Christians. Neither would be likely to be convinced by rhetorical set-pieces, fictitious speeches, descriptive passages, general arguments, and the like, of which so much use had been made by the historians of the Roman empire, themselves the products of a rhetorical education and addressing themselves to a readership which shared their culture. What was needed was evidence, above all documentary evidence. So Eusebius turned his back on the literary approach of traditional historians and quoted his sources, together with the arguments for their authenticity, in his text. In so doing he was taking over for history the techniques and methods hitherto used exclusively by the antiquarian and the philologist, and restoring to it that concern for truth to which it had always laid claim but often forgotten in its preoccupation with matters of form.

This development began in the more lively world of Greek historiography and found for a time no echo in the Latin west, which produced scarcely any historical writing between the early second and the late fourth century.

Florus (pp. 664–5) wrote his summary of Roman history from the foundation of the city to Augustus in two books in the reign of Hadrian. Granius Licinianus' brief history of Rome, of which only a few fragments survive in a palimpsest manuscript, is probably to be dated in the same period, though some have argued for a date towards the end of the second century. When the surviving epitome of Livy was written – *T. Livi periochae omnium librorum ab urbe condita* – itself based on an earlier and longer résumé of Livy's immense history, is uncertain. It was used by Julius Obsequens for his collection of *prodigia* in the third or fourth century. We possess an epitome of the universal history – *Historiae Philippicae* – of Augustus' Gaulish contemporary Pompeius Trogus by M. Junianus Justinus. Nothing is known with certainty regarding his date. But it has been plausibly conjectured that he wrote some time in the third century. The relation of Justin's epitome to the lost work of Trogus is far from clear. It seems to consist of a mixture of excerpts and summaries, to have concentrated on what had exemplary value, and to have been written with students of rhetoric in mind. Thus most of the richness of Trogus' work, which depended largely on lost Greek sources, has been lost in the flat, sententious and awkward narrative of his epitomator. The best that can be said for Justin is that in a barbarous age he provided Latin readers with some insight, however distorted, into the wider world of Hellenistic historiography.

The political and economic stabilization of the empire begun under Diocletian and completed in the long reign of Constantine provided the foundation for a revival of culture in general and of literature in particular in the west in the fourth century. In the field of history the recovery was slow. There was no writing of history on the grand scale until the end of the century. And this renaissance of Latin historiography, like the rebirth of Latin poetry in the hands of Claudian, owed much to the Greek world, as will be seen. In the meantime the 60s and 70s saw the production of a series of epitomes or potted histories of Rome. Two of these – the *Breviaria* of Eutropius and of Festus – were written under imperial patronage; we know virtually nothing of the origins of the others. However they all seem to have answered the needs of a new ruling group, who had to be reminded of the past of the empire which they now administered, and at the same time to have served as vehicles for the political outlook of those who still remembered the Roman past, the Italian senatorial class and its dependants, now partly excluded from the key decision-making positions in the empire. One must beware of exaggerating the gulf which separated the two groups. Illiterate soldiers may briefly have held supreme power in the dark days of the third century. But the military establishment that surrounded Valentinian and Valens and which monopolized so many high offices of state did not consist of ignorant barbarians. Its members came in the main from the towns of the Danubian provinces, from Rhaetia to the Black Sea. Sons of middling landowners and members of small town councils, they had been to school, though few of them had gone on to study rhetoric. But their whole outlook was provincial and local and in particular non-Mediterranean, their experience military rather than political. What they lacked was a sense of the greatness of the Roman empire, of the stages through which it had passed, of the problems which its rulers had solved, of the dangers of regionalism and division. Similarly, the civilians who filled posts in the vast new bureaucracy created – or tolerated – by Diocletian and Constantine were not ignoramuses. They too were the sons of local worthies from the cities of Gaul, Spain, and Africa, men who had learned their Virgil at school as well as studying the shorthand which was now often the key to promotion. But they were provincials, their horizon limited by the boundaries of their city or their province. The ecumenical outlook of the old Roman Senate was strange to them. They had to be indoctrinated with it. They had to learn to surmount the narrow limits of space and time within which their political thinking had been confined, and draw long-term lessons from the contemplation of the more than millenary history of the Roman state. So, in broad outline, thought the authors of these fourth-century compendia of Roman history and their patrons. And each sought to meet the need in his own way.

Before coming to the surviving compendia, however, a word must be said about a fourth-century historical work which does not survive and which, in the view of some scholars, never existed. In 1884 E. Enmann argued at length that the numerous agreements between Aurelius Victor, Eutropius, and the *Historia Augusta* pointed to a common source, a narrative history of the Roman empire from the second to the end of the third century, which he dated in the reign of Diocletian. Subsequent studies suggest that a date shortly after the death of Constantine in 337 provides a better working hypothesis. This anonymous – and hypothetical – work of history is generally referred to as Enmann's *Kaisergeschichte*. Opinions vary as to its scale, but it is generally thought to have been a fairly brief chronicle in the style of Florus rather than a long and discursive history. Many scholars have denied its very existence, and they may well be right. But in general it is today accepted, but with caution. It appears to have contained detailed information on places and events on the Danubian frontier. The *Kaisergeschichte* maintains a ghostly existence just beyond our field of vision. There are however many historical compendia which still survive.

The earliest in date is that of Sextus Aurelius Victor. Born in Africa probably about 330 he was, he declares, of humble country stock. Perhaps he was the son of a small-town *curialis*, or of a *colonus* under the lex Manciana, who acquired quasi-ownership of waste land which he brought under cultivation. At any rate, like many men in the fourth century, he found literary skill a means of upward social mobility. He probably practised at the bar or entered the ranks of the civil service. He was in Sirmium when it surrendered to Julian in 361. He attracted the favourable notice of the emperor, who appointed him governor (*consularis*) of the province of Pannonia Secunda, corresponding roughly to present-day Serbia. He presumably fell from office, like most of Julian's appointees, after the emperor's death in 363. But he must have commended himself to subsequent emperors, as we find him holding the office of *iudex sacrarum cognitionum* under Theodosius, who in 389 appointed him to the prestigious dignity of Prefect of the City of Rome, an office usually held by senior members of the Senate. Thereafter he disappears from view. Ammianus Marcellinus, who was writing his history in Rome in 389 and who may well have known Victor personally, speaks with approval of his *sobrietas* (soundness, steadiness: 21.10.6). One would like to know more about a man who rose so high from such unpromising beginnings. Our only source of information is his résumé of the history of the Roman empire from Augustus to Constantine II in about fifty printed pages written, on internal evidence, in 360. It is generally known as the *Caesares*, though it bears other titles in some manuscripts. Though Julian probably knew of its existence, it was not composed at his behest or dedicated to him.

It is biographical in its approach, in the sense that Victor treats Roman history reign by reign and concentrates on the character and activities of each emperor. But he does make some attempt to surmount the limits of biography and to write history both by the inclusion of narrative passages and by the frequent moral and political judgements which he expresses, often in rather sententious fashion. His work is an example of that fusion of the methods of history and biography which was characteristic of the age.[1] Victor's method is not to give a balanced summary of the political and military events of each reign, but rather to pick on one or two episodes to the neglect of the rest. He tries not to present his characters in black and white, but to see both their

[1] Cf. Momigliano (1969) 286–303.

good and their bad points. His point of view is senatorial, as was that of almost all Roman historians, and he condemns strongly the exercise of state power by military men with military methods. For him the anarchy of the third century was a nightmare, the stabilization under Diocletian and above all under Constantine and his sons a restoration of proper government. But he blames the senatorial class for having let power slip from its hands through selfishness—*Dum oblectantur otio simulque diuitiis pauent, quarum usum affluentiamque aeternitate maius putant, muniuere militaribus et paene barbaris uiam in se ac posteros dominandi* 'Taking their pleasure in idleness and trembling for their riches, the enjoyment and abundance of which they looked on as more important than immortality, they [i.e. the senators] paved the way for soldiers and near barbarians to tyrannize over themselves and their descendants' (37.7). He attaches the highest value to literary culture, which can confer some dignity on even the meanest of rulers (43.8), and the lack of which abases even the noblest natural endownments (40.13). He is clearly a pagan, but avoids anti-Christian pronouncements. His style is jumpy and uneven, moving from well-structured and occasionally pompous rhetoric to loose anecdotal narrative. He mingles echoes of Sallustian terseness with the inflated verbosity of the administrative language of his age. His sources certainly included Suetonius and Marius Maximus. He probably also had before him lists of emperors with brief accounts of their reigns, like those put into verse by Ausonius. Whether he also consulted the hypothetical *Kaisergeschichte* is best regarded as an open question. The same holds good of recent suggestions that he knew the work of Tacitus. Whatever his sources, he made many stupid mistakes in using them. But his aim was a lofty one; he wanted to write a history of the Roman empire which combined interest in the character of individual emperors with an overall moral view of the empire. That he was not a Tacitus is scarcely to be held against him.

Aurelius Victor's compendium dealt only with the history of Rome since Augustus. At some time – probably in the fourth century or the beginning of the fifth, but some have conjectured a much later date – it was combined by an unknown editor with two other historical summaries to give a continuous history of Rome from the earliest times to the fourth century. The first of these, the *Origo gentis Romanae*, dealt with the legendary period from Saturn to Romulus. The second, *De viris illustribus urbis Romae*, covered the period of the monarchy and the Republic. Both works are of unknown authorship; they are manifestly not by the same hand. The *Origo gentis Romanae* was thought by Niebuhr to be a forgery by some Renaissance antiquarian. This it cannot be, as it is quoted by an early twelfth-century writer. It is now generally recognized to be a work of late antiquity, probably of the fourth century. In consequence of its subject matter it draws largely on Virgil and on his commentators. But it also contains many references to authorities of the Republican period and to others of whom nothing whatever is known. Its author has often been accused of falsification, but the charge must remain not proven. It cannot be excluded that this fourth-century scholar had access to a handbook of the Augustan age also used by Dionysius of Halicarnassus. The general tone of his exposition is rationalizing and euhemeristic, treating mythology as misunderstood history. The language and style are those of the fourth century, without the usually declamatory tone of voice, a language and style which suggest the grammarian rather than the rhetorician. The *Origo* is still something of an enigma, in spite of the vindication of its authenticity.

The *De viris illustribus* is a series of eighty-six biographies of leading men, beginning with Proca, king of Alba Longa, and Romulus, going on through the kings of Rome and the founding fathers of the Republic to the heroes of the early Republic like Camillus, P. Decius Mus and T. Manlius Torquatus, historical figures like Appius Claudius Caecus, Quintus Fabius Maximus Cunctator, Cato the Censor and Scipio Africanus, and concluding with the men of the last century of the Republic, the Gracchi, Marius, Saturninus, Sulla, Caesar, Cicero, Antony and Octavian. It includes biographies of a few enemies of Rome, such as King Pyrrhus of Epirus, King Antiochus of Syria, Mithridates, and Cleopatra, whose brief biography concludes the series. In its present form the work contains no preface and no narrative links between the biographies. The style at its best is crisp and epigrammatic, with a tendency to forced antitheses – Cleopatra *tantae libidinis fuit, ut saepe prostiterit, tantae pulchritudinis, ut multi noctem illius morte emerint* 'So great was her lust that she often prostituted herself, so great her beauty that many gave their lives for a night with her'. At its worst it is awkward and pretentious. The language is post-classical. The editor who compiled the corpus of Roman history believed that the *De viris illustribus* was an epitome of Livy. In fact the sources are, as might be expected in the case of a compendium of generally accessible information, not easy to identify. They may include Hyginus and Florus as well as some kind of Livian epitome. The *De viris illustribus* is useful in that it covers two gaps in the surviving epitome of Livy. None of the three works included in the corpus has any systematic chronological framework.

Of Eutropius all that is known with certainty is that he accompanied the emperor Julian on his Persian campaign and that he was private secretary (*magister memoriae*) to Valens, at whose behest he wrote his historical compendium in 369 or 370. He may well have been private secretary to all emperors from Constantius II to Valens. He is very probably to be identified with the Eutropius who was proconsul of Asia in 371–2, was accused of treason by his successor in office but acquitted, was Praetorian Prefect of Illyricum in 380–1, and consul along with Valentinian in 387. Thus he would be a senator who held a series of high offices over a long period of years. Whether he is to be identified with a Eutropius from Bordeaux who was interested in medicine is more than doubtful, as is also the statement in a tenth-century encyclopaedia that he was a teacher of rhetoric. His *Breviarium ab urbe condita* in ten books provides a survey of Roman history from the foundation of the city to the accession of Valens in 364. It is a conscientious, careful work, which seeks to provide information on the main events, particularly in the field of military and foreign affairs, without the capricious selectivity characteristic of Victor. Eutropius is precise, though not always correct, in matters of chronology, dating events not only by consulates, but by years from the foundation of the city, for which he accepts Varro's date of 753 B.C., and by the period which had elapsed since other important events. He gives countless names and figures. The scale of the *Breviarium*, and the author's limitations as a historian, preclude any serious analysis of historical causes. There are few, and very brief, descriptive passages, and fewer anecdotes than in the *De viris illustribus* or Aurelius Victor. Eutropius has no time for frivolity. His narrative is carefully structured, avoiding sudden jumps. The view of Roman history which he presents is conventional in his age. Collaboration between emperor and Senate, essential for the wellbeing of the state, was abruptly interrupted in 235 with the accession of the rude soldier Maximinus, and restored only under the family of Constantine. It is interesting, however, to note that Julius Caesar, a hero for Aurelius Victor, is a tyrant for Eutropius. He makes no mention of Christianity and was presumably a pagan. His style is smooth and lucid, if a trifle dry, without either far-fetched figures or lapses into formlessness. His sources are difficult to identify. They probably included an epitome of Livy, Florus, and the lost history of the empire written in the age of Constantine, if indeed it existed. While all the fourth-century epitomators are mediocre writers and poor historians, Eutropius is decidedly the best of them. His work enjoyed great popularity and was only partially replaced by the Christian compendium of Orosius in the fifth century. It was translated into Greek before the end of the fourth century by Paeanius or Paeonius, a pupil of Libanius, and again in the sixth century by the Lycian Capito, perhaps in connexion with Justinian's programme to bring the Latin west back under Roman rule. The former translation survives entire, the latter only in fragments.

Festus (his full name is unknown) was another self-made man, from Tridentum in Raetia, who rose to high rank through literary talent, practice at the bar, and marriage to a rich wife. In the later 60s he was governor (*consularis*) of Syria, where he tried to trap Libanius by accusing a friend of his of magical practices. Before the end of the decade he had become private secretary (*magister memoriae*) to Valens, probably in succession to Eutropius, and about 372 was appointed Proconsul of Asia. In this post he had the philosopher Maximus,

Julian's teacher and friend, executed. He was dismissed after the death of Valens in 378 and died of a stroke in the temple of Nemesis at Ephesus in 380. He is almost certainly the Festus who wrote the *Breviarium rerum gestarum populi Romani*, a very brief compendium of Roman history from the foundation of the city to the reign of Valens, written in 369 at the request of that emperor. It is much shorter than the *Breviarium* of Eutropius – about fifteen printed pages against about sixty – and somewhat differently arranged. There is no real chronological narrative of Republican history. The three Punic wars, which get fairly full treatment in three separate passages in Eutropius, are dismissed with the words *ter Africa rebellauit* 'thrice Africa revolted'. What Festus offers instead is a region by region account of the growth of the Roman empire. Similarly, the history of the empire is represented by a description of the wars on the eastern frontier waged by Pompey, Crassus, Augustus, Nero, Lucius Verus, Severus Alexander, Valerian, Aurelian, Diocletian, Constantine, Constantius II, Julian and Jovian. This concentration on Persian wars explains the genesis of the work. It is a piece of propaganda in connexion with Valens' planned campaign in the east, to which reference is made in the concluding words *etiam Babyloniae tibi palma pacis accedat* 'may the prize of pacifying Babylon too be granted to you'. Festus' text is so compressed that it can scarcely be said to have a style at all. His sources, as in all such cases, are hard to determine. Florus, an epitome of Livy fuller than that now surviving, Suetonius, Eutropius, and the putative history of the empire written under Constantine have been suggested. For the historian what is valuable in this jejune compendium is the list of dioceses and provinces in the reign of Valens and some of the details on the eastern wars of Aurelian and Diocletian.

The last of the fourth-century historical compendia has been handed down anonymously. The *Epitome de Caesaribus* is described in the two manuscripts in which it survives as being a résumé of the work of Aurelius Victor. It does indeed draw on Victor for material on the earlier emperors, but it is an independent work. It occupies about forty printed pages. In form it is a succession of brief imperial biographies, from Augustus to Theodosius, usually beginning with each emperor's birthplace, the length of his reign, and the principal events in it, and going on to a description of his personal appearance and character. The author is particularly interested in the details of his subjects' private life and above all in their sexual habits. The style is pompous, forced, and cliché-ridden, e.g. *stabant acerui montium similes, fluebat cruor fluminum modo* 'Piles of corpses stood high as mountains, blood flowed in rivers' (42.14). The author frequently draws on Eutropius. Many of the personal details come from Suetonius and doubtless from Marius Maximus. He may have used the supposed imperial history written in the age of Constantine, and it has been plausibly suggested that he also used the lost *Annales* of Nicomachus Flavianus.

His identity is likely to remain a mystery. He can hardly be an official of Theodosius' court, as he makes too many mistakes about the reign of that emperor. Perhaps he was a Roman senator or a member of his entourage. He could be the mysterious historian to whom Symmachus addressses *Epist.* 9.110, but this can be neither proved nor disproved. At any rate he was a pagan – he never mentions Christianity – and he identifies himself with pro-senatorial points of view. The *Epitome* must have been written shortly after Theodosius' death in 395. But to see in it a defence of the stance adopted by the pagan senators during the usurpation of Eugenius, as some scholars have done, is to force the evidence. The *Epitome* is riddled with errors, and any information for which it is the sole authority must be treated by the historian with circumspection.

There is no doubt of the anti-Christian sympathies of Virius Nicomachus Flavianus, one of the leaders of the Roman Senate in the closing decades of the fourth century. Governor (*consularis*) of Sicily, where his family owned estates near Henna in 364, he became successively *uicarius* of Africa (in 377), *quaestor sacri palatii* (in 389) and twice Praetorian Prefect (in 390 and 393). A militant pagan, who looked forward to the collapse of Christianity, he took the side of the pro-pagan usurper Eugenius in 393 and held the consulate under him in 394. After the defeat of Eugenius by Theodosius in that year he committed suicide. He translated from Greek Philostratus' *Life of Apollonius of Tyana*, which was seen in the fourth century as a pagan counterpart to the Christian gospels, and wrote a history of Rome, entitled *Annales*, which he dedicated to Theodosius. Neither work survives, and it is difficult to form a clear idea of the scope, scale and style of the *Annales*. Nicomachus Flavianus is treated by Symmachus with something like idolatry and is represented in the *Saturnalia* of Macrobius as a man of immense erudition, and is described in the inscription set up in the Forum during his consulship in 394 as '*historicus disertissimus*'. It would be rash to argue from this that his history must have been lengthy, penetrating and discursive. The circle of vastly rich senators to which he belonged were far too preoccupied with their own affairs to have deep insight into the political problems of the empire. As Nicomachus Flavianus himself writes in a letter to Symmachus (*Epist.* 2.34.2), *nihil hac aetate tractandum pensius domesticis rebus* 'these days nothing calls for greater attention than our private affairs'. His work is shown by its title to have been arranged annalistically, and in this point it is distinguished from the surviving compendia. It has sometimes been thought to have been used by Ammianus Marcellinus in his later books; the hypothesis is possible but undemonstrable. We have no reliable evidence on the period covered by the *Annales* of Nicomachus. The work may not have dealt with the author's own times.

There survives in a medieval florilegium a short history of the Roman empire under Constantine, which appears to be an excerpt from a longer work.[1] Crisp, clear and accurate, the extract makes no mention of Christianity – except in a few passages where verbatim excerpts from Orosius have been interpolated into the text – and the author may be taken to have been a pagan. Some have seen in this fragment a portion of the *Kaisergeschichte* of Enmann. At any rate it reminds us how much of the literature of late antiquity has perished and how provisional any judgements must be that are based on what chance and prejudice have preserved.

Roman historiography appeared to be degenerating into a series of jejune, derivative and superficial compendia, designed to remind a new ruling group of a tradition which they had forgotten or never learned, when suddenly towards the end of the fourth century a major historian, comparable with Sallust or Tacitus, appeared. Ammianus Marcellinus, though writing in Latin, was a Greek, familiar with the living tradition and practice of Greek historiography and welding it together with Roman gravity and sense of tradition to form a new whole. His situation can be compared to that of Claudian, who brought to the Latin west the skill and flexibility of contemporary Greek poetry, and successfully united it to Roman tradition to form a new, vigorous and viable poetic manner.

Ammianus Marcellinus was born in Antioch in Syria *c.* A.D. 325–30. He probably belonged to a family of *curiales* – wealthy city landowners whose members served on the city council. He would have the usual literary education of the upper-class youth in a great Greek city, studying classical literature and rhetoric. There is no reason to believe that he was ever a pupil of Libanius, though they knew one another in later life. His education completed, he took the unusual step of entering the army, perhaps as a means of escape from the increasing burdens falling on members of the curial class. He was enrolled in the *protectores domestici*, a corps recruited partly from experienced men from the ranks, partly from young men of good family, whose members acted as liaison officers and staff officers at the headquarters of commanders. From 353 or 354 he was attached to the staff of Ursicinus, the *magister equitum*, who was then in command of the Roman army on the Persian frontier, and remained with him for some seven years, travelling back from Mesopotamia through Antioch to Milan and on to Gaul and Cologne, then back via Sirmium to the east, again to Thrace, and back to Nisibis for Constantius II's campaign of 359. He took an active part in the fighting, was in Amida throughout its siege and capture by the Persians, and had several hair's-breadth escapes,

[1] Formerly attributed, along with an excerpt on Italy under Odovacar, to an Anonymus Valesianus (from Valesius, the Latin form of the name of the first editor Henri Valois), the work is now usually referred to as *Excerptum Valesianum* I. The other excerpt belongs to the work of a much later writer.

not all of which were to his credit. After the dismissal of Ursicinus in 360 we lose sight of Ammianus for several years, during which he presumably continued to perform his military duties. He is next found joining Julian's army at Cercusium for his ill-fated Persian campaign. After Julian's death and the disastrous failure of the campaign, Ammianus seems to have retired from the army – he had by now gained immunity from service in the *curia* – and to have devoted some years to study and travel. He certainly visited Egypt, ascending the Nile as far as the Thebaid, and was in Greece shortly after 366. He was in Antioch during the trials for magic and treason in 371, and may have been in some personal danger. It was during this period, probably quite soon after Julian's death, that he decided to write his history, and much of his study and travel was devoted to the collection of material for it. Some time after 378 he settled in Rome in order to complete his work. As a senior army officer, a man of letters and a wealthy man he would enjoy wide contacts there. But it is probably a mistake to suppose that he belonged to the circle of Symmachus, Nicomachus Flavianus and Praetextatus. These proud and self-centred aristocrats would probably have treated him as a kind of superior client, if they had deigned to notice him at all. On the other hand he is likely to have known the historian Eutropius, who had been with him in Julian's army in Persia, and he may well have known Aurelius Victor. He apparently gave readings of parts of his history as they were completed, and the news of the success of these reached distant Antioch, evoking a rather formal letter of congratulation from Libanius. Book 14 was written shortly after 383, Book 21 not earlier than 388–9, Book 22 by 391, and Book 31 possibly not until the death of Theodosius in 395. These dates give us a rough time-scale for the completion of the work. But Ammianus had clearly been occupied with it since the 60s of the fourth century. The date and manner of his death are unknown.

His history – *Res gestae* – in thirty-one books covered the period from the principate of Nerva to the death of Valens (96–378). Though Ammianus does not mention Tacitus, his choice of a starting point shows that he regarded himself as the continuator of Tacitus and implicitly dismisses all Latin histories since Tacitus as second-rate and unworthy. What survives are Books 14 to 31, dealing with the period 353 to 378. This leaves thirteen books to cover 257 years in the lost portion. Struck by the evident discrepancy in scale some scholars have suggested that Ammianus wrote two separate historical works, one in thirty-one books dealing with his own time, and one of unknown length recounting the previous two and a half centuries. But there is no trace of the alleged second work. And Ammianus' own references to his history of the early Principate are couched in exactly the same terms as those to earlier portions of the surviving text. It is likely that he dealt with the earlier period in more summary fashion, either by epitomizing, like the writers of compendia, or by selecting what he regarded as the most significant events, much as Procopius later prefaced to his history of the Persian wars of Justinian a survey of the military situation on the eastern frontier during the preceding century. Ammianus' method of work, as will be seen, was unsuitable for writing the history of the more distant past, for which he would have to depend on secondary sources. The question arises at what point detailed treatment began. The beginning of the surviving books, in the middle of the caesarship of Gallus, is an unlikely point. Most probably Ammianus began his large-scale treatment with the death of Constantine in 337, but other hypotheses are possible.

Ammianus' subject is the history of the Roman empire, which for him comprised the greater part of the known world. He sees it against a larger but less distinct background, in which the ominous movements of peoples beyond the frontier can be discerned with greater or lesser clarity, while his curious eye on occasion ranges throughout the barbarian world, from the Attacotti, Scotti and Picti of northern Scotland (26.4.5, 20.1.1, 27.8.5) through the Goths (26.4.5, 27.4.1 etc.), the Sarmatians (26.10.20, 31.4.13), the Huns (31.2.1–2), the Sogdians (23.6.14) and the Indians (14.3.3, 23.6.12, 23.6.72–3, 31.2.16) to the distant Seres of China (14.3.3, 23.6.60–8, 31.2.15). His arrangement is chronological, but not strictly annalistic. His interest is no longer centred on court and Senate at Rome, with occasional glances at the activities of the frontier armies, as was that of Tacitus. The imperial court now moved from Trier to Milan, to Sirmium, to Constantinople, to Antioch. And sometimes the moment of decision was with the army rather than with the emperor. So Ammianus' scene shifts from Mesopotamia to Constantinople or Milan or Gaul, or even on occasion to Rome, as momentous events and decisions require. His canvas is far wider than that of Tacitus and the technical problems which he faces more complex. Indeed in Books 26 to 31, dealing with the period of Valentinian and Valens, the chronological sequence is virtually abandoned in favour of a geographical arrangement, as events in east and west follow their largely independent course.

The history of events is also the history of people. Ammianus' narrative is crowded with individuals, many of whom are introduced with a brief characterization: Orfitus is 'a man of prudence and a thoroughly experienced lawyer, but with a background in the liberal arts inadequate for a nobleman' (14.6.1), Viventius is 'a Pannonian, yet honest and prudent' (27.3.11). It is noteworthy that this treatment is reserved for civilians and that military men are never thus characterized. Some of the major figures receive somewhat longer and more formal descriptions, dealing with their physical appearance as well as their character, e.g. Gallus (14, 11, 27–78) or Procopius (26.6.1ff., 26.9.11). Petronius Probus, Praetorian Prefect in 368, head of the powerful Anician family, and clearly a man whom Ammianus detested, is honoured by a long and malicious character study (27.11.1–7). But it is above all the emperors whose appearance and character are described at length, often in formal set-pieces composed in accordance with the precepts of the rhetoricians: Julian (25.4.1–22), Jovian (21.6.4), Valentinian (30.7.1–30.9.6), Valens (31.14.1–9), Gratian (31.10.18–19), the usurper Silvanus (15.5.32–3). This interest in the personalities of rulers reflects the confusion of history and biography in late antiquity. There are only seventeen speeches in the surviving eighteen books, and most of these are addresses by emperors to their troops. Speeches in the Senate were no longer of significance. That the existing speeches are in general constructed in accordance with the handbooks does not mean that they are not true to life. Generals haranguing their soldiers rarely express original ideas.

The descriptions of military operations, of which there are many, are usually clear when Ammianus speaks as an eye-witness, but often obscure when he relies on the evidence of others. His unwillingness, in accordance with the precepts of rhetoric, to use technical terms often contributes to the obscurity of such passages. He owes little to the emotion-charged style of the traditional 'battle-piece', the roots of which go back to the pupils of Isocrates.

There are many digressions, usually formally marked as such, dealing with geography and ethnology, with physical matters such as earthquakes, eclipses, comets or the origin of pearls, with philosophical or religious topics like fate, prophecy or tutelary deities, and with aspects of the society of his time, such as life in Rome, the moral corruption of Roman society, or the shortcomings of lawyers. Many of those excursuses are explicitly intended to provide background to Ammianus' narrative: examples are those on the city of Amida (18.9.1–4), on Thrace and the regions bordering the Black Sea (22.8.1–48), on the history, geography and demography of the Persian empire (23.6.1–88), and on the Huns (31.2.1–12). Other digressions of the same type were evidently intended to provide similar background information. Others, like the long moralizing note on the decadence of Roman society (14.6.2–26) were connected with the author's overall view of the process of Roman history. Many of the scientific digressions were from the point of view of the ancient reader legitimate comment on the events narrated. They were also a display of the author's wide knowledge. Ammianus had read a great deal, was in his rather disorganized way a learned man, and had a deep respect for erudition in others. The next group of digressions, such as those on Egyptian hieroglyphic writing (17.4.1–23), on foreknowledge and augury (21.1.8–14), on the tragedian Phrynichus (28.1.3–4), are best understood as gratuitous displays of erudition which would give pleasure to like-minded readers. Finally there are those which are expressions of the author's own experience and judgement, such as that on the Roman nobility (28.4.6) or that on the legal profession (30.4.3–22). Occasionally we can hazard a guess at the sources used by Ammianus in his excursuses; in most cases they are unknown to us, but bear witness to the omnivorous character of his reading during the long years of gestation of the *Res gestae*.

Ammianus knew much more than he put down in his history. Again and again he dismisses certain topics as too trivial to record – anecdotes about emperors, the tittle-tattle of Roman aristocracy, minor details of campaigns, matters on which there is no agreement among authorities, and *quae per squalidas transiere personas* 'the exploits of humble individuals' (28.1.15). The reader is constantly reminded of the presence of the historian, selecting, rejecting and ordering his information in accordance with his conception of the dignity of history.

Ammianus was evidently a pagan. But he viewed with detachment verging on contempt the traditional Roman state religion. He is well informed on the organization and doctrine of the Christian church and freely uses some of its technical language. His attitude towards Christianity is on the whole detached and objective. But he can be scathing on the sectarian rivalries of the Christians and on the widening gap between profession and practice as Christianity spread among the upper classes of the empire (27.3.12–15). His own religious and philosophical views are never set out clearly. Perhaps they were not very clear. He was a monotheist, but in his explanation of human affairs he oscillates between providentialism and determinism, and at the same time leaves room for the *uirtus* of great men to determine the outcome of events. The background of his thought is probably the kind of second-hand Neoplatonism current in intellectual circles in the Greek east, its vagueness and confusion typical of the uncommitted and unphilosophical.

Ammianus was a patriot. For him the Roman empire was a universal and permanent state. Barbarians, though individually sometimes winning his respect, were in general objects of his contempt. Rome itself is *urbs aeterna*, 'the eternal city', *urbs sacratissima* 'the most sacred city', *templum mundi totius* 'the temple of the whole world', *imperii uirtutumque omnium lar* 'the domicile of empire and of every virtue', *caput mundi* 'the head of the world'. These terms refer to Rome as a political concept. The city itself still filled him with admiration, but its inhabitants – the fickle and greedy mob and haughty, idle and ignorant aristocrats – inspired his deepest misgivings. This discrepancy between the ideal and the real was a symptom of the crisis through which the empire was passing. That it was in crisis was not a matter of doubt. He comments sadly, if a little inaccurately, that Jovian was the first man in history to diminish the territory of the empire (25.9.9). Corruption and civil strife spread within the empire, as the rulers and their friends preferred personal advantage to honour (30.4.1). The ominous gathering of barbarian forces on the frontier led to the terrible climax of Adrianople, when a Roman army was destroyed and an emperor slain in battle. On every hand the clouds were gathering. What the nature of the crisis was remained vague. The quantifying methods of the economic or social historian were not available to Ammianus, or to any other historian of antiquity. Their approach was a moral one. The decadence and corruption of individuals and institutions was for them a sufficient explanation. Ammianus could not conceive of the fall of the Roman empire. But he was agonizingly aware of its decline, and this is the grand theme of his history.

His hero is Julian, whom he must have known personally. Julian's reign is recounted in detail in Books 16–25, his wisdom and the soundness of his policy are emphasized – though not without reserve – and the long obituary notice of him (25.4) makes it clear that for Ammianus his qualities far outshone those of any other ruler of his age – *uir heroicis paene connumerandus ingeniis*, 'a man to be numbered almost among the characters of legend'. Those passages were written a quarter of a century after Julian's death, the fruit of long study and reflection. Even in his old age Ammianus was haunted by the thought that had Julian lived, the squalor and disaster of succeeding years might have been avoided. In this sense there is a tragic colouring to Ammianus' view of Roman history. It was a tragedy of lost opportunity

Discussion of Ammianus' sources was a favourite occupation of nineteenth-century scholars. Today the matter can be dealt with briefly. There was no continuous narrative source on any scale available to Ammianus for the period covered by the surviving books. He made extensive use of documents – diplomatic and official correspondence, laws and edicts, speeches of emperors, and the like – to which his position must have given him easy access. Such sources he evidently sought out in public archives. He read Aurelius Victor, and probably Eutropius, and he may well have had other compendia at his disposal. But apart from documents his main sources were his own observation and the critical examination of witnesses – *ea quae uidere licuit per aetatem, uel perplexe interrogando uersatos in medio scire* 'what I could see myself because of my age, or what I could learn by careful interrogation of "participants"' (15.1.1). This is the method of Thucydides rather than that of Tacitus. That Ammianus can sometimes be shown to have got things wrong is no argument against the validity of his method.

Ammianus' native language was Greek. He probably learned Latin in his native Antioch – Libanius inveighs against the growing interest in the language of court, army and law – and he certainly used it daily throughout his army service. In his retirement, if not before, he read much classical Latin literature. His Latin has a Greek tinge to it, particularly in the frequency of participial phrases, and perhaps also in his sometimes odd word-order. But it is not, as some scholars used to suggest, a kind of translationese. He combines the freedom to form new words and the verbose style of official Latin of his own day with an eagerness to stud his text with archaic and poetic words and classical flosculi, in particular from Virgil. His training in rhetoric is responsible for his frequent and startling metaphors, such as *orientis fortuna periculorum terribilis tubas inflabat* 'the destiny of the East sounded the fearsome trumpet-blast of danger' (18.4.1) or *tempore quo primis auspiciis in mundanum fulgorem surgeret uictura dum erunt homines Roma* 'at the time when Rome, destined to live as long as mankind exists, was first beginning to rise to world-wide splendour' (14.6.3). He takes great pains to vary his expression in accordance with the precepts of rhetoric; his description of oil-wells in Assyria (23.6.17–18), too long to quote, is a palmary example, verging almost on caricature. Yet at the same time he makes use of a number of recurring clichés, like *supra modum*. He observes stress accent as well as quantitative metre in his clausulae. His style, though clearly belonging to the age in which he wrote, is highly personal and idiosyncratic. It is not compressed and suggestive, like that of Tacitus, and there are few well-constructed periods. Ammianus' sentences are long and rambling, and over-filled with qualifications, some of which in their turn form the nucleus of a string of subordinate clauses.

At the conclusion of his *Res gestae* Ammianus reminds his readers that he writes *ut miles quondam et Graecus* 'as a former soldier and a Greek' (31.16.9) the history of the Roman empire. The phrase is chosen for its paradoxical suggestions – a man of Greek culture writing Roman history, a member of the military profession – from which senators were excluded – engaging in a traditionally senatorial activity, a man from the Greek world of cities and peace practising the martial arts of Rome. All these points serve to underline the uniqueness of Ammianus and the grandeur of his achievement. A Greek soldier, he was the last of the great Roman historians.

History henceforth belonged to the Christians. Their purposes were in general different from those which had inspired Roman historians from Fabius Pictor to Ammianus Marcellinus. Christian Latin literature as such falls outside the scope of the present study. But a brief glance at some of the Christian works of history written in Latin in the two generations after the death of Theodosius will help to make clear the interplay of tradition and innovation in historical thinking as the western Roman empire crumbled away.

Jerome (340/50–419/20) was a writer of wide-ranging interests and activities, and his historical writings are not among his most important works. But they deserve mention in the present context. As Christianity made headway among the educated upper classes of the Latin world, they found themselves faced with the fact that Greek Christian literature was so much richer and more varied than their own. In particular thanks to Eusebius of Caesarea, who built on the foundations laid by Julius Africanus, the Greeks possessed an authoritative survey of world history from the Christian point of view, based on a firm chronology, and uniting Graeco-Roman history, biblical history, and the miscellaneous information on oriental history which the Greek world had acquired since the days of Alexander the Great. During his stay in Constantinople Jerome decided to translate and adapt the second book of Eusebius' *Chronicle*, consisting largely of tables of chronological concordance. To make this more attractive to the Latin reader of his own day he added material from Roman history, largely taken from Eutropius, from Suetonius' *De viris illustribus*, and from Roman lists of magistrates, and added a final section carrying on the *Chronicle* from 325 till 378. The adaptation was made, as Jerome himself tells us, in great haste. And though he displays his usual care for elegant writing, including the observation of metrical clausulae, there are many errors and signs of carelessness. The section which Jerome himself added is full of factual information, but its judgements are marked by his usual violent prejudices and his tendency to exaggerate the importance of his own circle of friends. Yet the *Chronicle* answered a need and enjoyed immense popularity during the author's lifetime and for many centuries afterwards.

Twelve years later, in 392, when he was established in his monastery at Bethlehem Jerome wrote his second historical work, which answered a similar need. Though Christianity was now firmly established as the state religion it was still open to the charge that its literature was poor in quality and quantity in comparison with that of paganism. As the devil has all the best tunes, so then he had all the best books. At the prompting of Nummius Aemilius Dexter, son of a bishop of Barcelona, who had already been proconsul of Asia and *comes rerum priuatarum*, and who was to be Praetorian Prefect of Italy in the last year of Theodosius' reign, Jerome compiled his *De viris illustribus*, a collection of 135 notes on Christian writers, both Greek and Latin, beginning with Peter and ending with Jerome himself. Most of the information came from Eusebius' *Ecclesiastical history*. But Jerome added much contemporary and Latin material from his own reading. To make up his number he includes not only Jews and heretics – a point for which Augustine censured him – but also Seneca, on the basis of his spurious correspondence with St Paul. This first manual of patrology is written in a simple and unadorned style. Like the *Chronicle* it betrays by its errors and confusion the haste with which it was written. Yet it remains a precious source of information. And, as with so much that Jerome wrote, it was a pioneering work, breaking new ground. It was translated into Greek in the early Middle Ages.

The richness of Greek Christian literature prompted the many translations made by Tyrannius Rufinus of Concordia near Aquileia, friend and later enemy of Jerome. He went to the east in the company of the elder Melania in 371, founded a monastery in Jerusalem and remained there until his return to Aquileia in 397. From then until his death in 410 he was mainly engaged in translating works of the Greek Fathers, particularly Origen, Basil and Gregory of Nazianzus. Most of these, as well as the polemical works which he wrote during his sojourn in Palestine, fall outside the scope of the present study. His *Ecclesiastical history*, however, calls for some notice. Rufinus was induced some time in the first decade of the fifth century by Chromatius bishop of Aquileia to translate the *Ecclesiastical history* of Eusebius, as nothing comparable existed in Latin. He abbreviated his original text, omitted many of the documents which it cited, and added two books of his own covering the period from 324 to 395. The translation is very free, and the style simple and unrhetorical, as befitted what was in essence a technical work. The two final books are based on Rufinus' own recollections and on the writings of the fourth-century church Fathers. In careful scrutiny of sources and critical acumen Rufinus falls short of Eusebius. He did however introduce a new genre into Latin literature.

About the same time or shortly afterwards Sulpicius Severus, a member of the cultivated Gaulish aristocracy, educated at Bordeaux and a friend of Paulinus of Nola, wrote a briefer but in some ways more original Christian history. His *Chronicle*, in two books, covers the period from the creation to A.D. 400, and is mainly devoted to biblical and church history. Sulpicius was a man of scholarly habits, with a feeling for the importance to the historian of documents. Inevitably he turned to Eusebius for much of his material. But he also drew on pagan historians and on his own very wide general reading. As befits the fellow-countryman, and perhaps even the pupil, of Ausonius, he writes clear, classical Latin. But his style is rather flat and undistinguished, without the panache which Jerome succeeded in displaying even in writing dry catalogues. He furnishes much useful information on events of his own lifetime.

On 24 August 410 the troops of Alaric the Visigoth captured and pillaged Rome. The Goths remained in the city only three days. The damage and loss of life were by ancient standards fairly light. Many of the better-off citizens had long ago left the city and taken refuge in Sicily, Africa or the east. Yet the reaction to the sack of Rome was out of all proportion to its real importance. The impossible had happened, and men could no longer be sure of anything. In far-off Bethlehem Jerome could no longer work on his Commentary on Ezekiel. *Quis crederet*, he exclaims, *ut totius orbis exstructa uictoriis Roma corrueret?* 'Who could believe that Rome, built upon victories over the whole world, could collapse?' (*In Ezech.* prol. in lib. 3, *PL* 25.75D). In a letter written at the same time he asks *Quid saluum est, si Roma perit?* 'What is safe, if Rome perishes?' (*Epist.* 123.16). Augustine's changing reaction to the catastrophic event can be traced in the sermons which he preached in 410 to 412 to his congregation in Hippo, which included many émigrés from Italy. He began by counselling asceticism, a *passe-partout* response to any difficult situation. But soon he turned to examining the grounds for the belief in the universality and eternity of the Roman empire. 'Heaven and earth will pass away, according to the Gospel, and if Virgil claims the contrary, it is purely from flattery. The poet well knew that all empires are perishable' (*Serm.* 105.7.10). His definitive response to the sack of Rome was his *magnum opus et arduum* the *De civitate Dei*, of which Books 1–5 were published in 413, Books 6–10 in 415, Books 11–13 in 417, Books 14–16 in 418, Book 17 in 420, and Books 18–22 not until 425. Full discussion of this remarkable work is inappropriate to the present context. But a brief treatment of Augustine's attitude to and use of Roman history is called for.

Alaric's capture of Rome provoked attacks on the position of the Christian church both by pagans and by Christians or former Christians. The pagans claimed that the recent disasters were due to the cessation of the worship of the old gods, and alleged by way of proof that things had been much better in the old days. The Christians complained that the fall of the city cast doubt upon the providential role of the Roman empire, in which men had come to believe more and more since the days of Constantine. Events also put in trenchant form the old problems of why the innocent suffered and the guilty were spared. Both these lines of attack were pursued at two levels. The man in the street thoughtlessly blamed the Christians for everything: *Pluuia defit, causa Christiani* 'There is not enough rain, the Christians are to blame' (Aug. *Civ. Dei* 2.3). *Multi, praeteritarum rerum ignari ... si temporibus Christianis aliquod bellum paulo diutius trahi uident, ilico in nostram religionem proteruissime insiliunt* 'Many who are ignorant of history ... if they see some war drag on rather too long in the Christian age, at once impudently attack our religion' (Aug. *Civ. Dei* 5.22). *Si reciperet circum, nihil esse sibi factum* 'If the circus reopened, nothing would have happened to us' (Oros. 1.6.4). At another level the Neoplatonizing pagan scholars, the men for whom Macrobius wrote his *Saturnalia*, opposed to the historicism of Christianity an unchanging and eternal universe and a sophisticated and subtle theory of the position in it of man in general, and Roman man in particular. It was above all to the pagan cultivated upper classes that Augustine addressed himself in the *De civitate Dei*. His object was to provide an intellectual foundation for Christianity which would withstand their criticism and win their assent. At the same time he also sought to make some kind of reply to the more popular complaints. In the course of both these endeavours he sought to demythologize the idealized Roman past which both groups believed in, and into which the pagan intellectuals were wont to retreat as an escape from the harsh reality of their own times. This he did by demonstrating: (1) that Roman history is not full of moral *exempla*, (2) that disaster was as frequent and grave in the past as in the present, (3) that it was a symptom of human sinfulness, and had nothing to do with the virtues or vices of the Romans, who were no better or no worse than any other people, (4) that the Roman empire, while like all else the object of divine providence, was not essential for the salvation of mankind, but that it was a historical phenomenon which would some time pass away.

All these points demanded constant historical illustration and historical discussion. And the readership to which Augustine addressed himself, so different from his down-to-earth congregation at Hippo, was accustomed to thinking in terms of Roman history. So the *De civitate Dei*, and especially the earlier books, is full of long polemical treatments of topics from the history of Rome and particularly of the Roman Republic, in which Augustine gave proof of his wide reading in the classical historians as well as in the recent epitomators. He examines the whole tradition of Roman history in a new light and subjects it to a new critique. Virgil had defined Rome's imperial mission as *parcere subiectis et debellare superbos* 'spare the submissive and conquer the proud' (*Aen.* 6.853). Augustine observes *Inferre autem bella finitimis et in cetera inde procedere ac populos sibi non molestos sola regni cupiditate conterere et subdere, quid aliud quam grande latrocinium nominandum est?* 'But to make war on one's neighbours, to go on then to others, to crush and subject nations who do us no harm out of mere greed for power, what else can we call that but brigandage on the grand scale?' (*Civ. Dei* 4–6).

At the same time his purpose went far beyond refuting erroneous ideas about the Roman past, and he began to resent the time spent in seeking out, analysing and refuting historical exempla. *Si narrare uel commemorare conemur*, he complains, *nihil aliud quam scriptores etiam nos erimus historiae* 'If I try to recount or mention [all those events] I too will be nothing but a historian' (*Civ. Dei* 3.18), *Si haec atque huiusmodi*, he asks *quae habet historia, unde possem colligere uoluissem, quando finissem?* 'If I had wanted to gather together from where I could these and suchlike historical matters, when would I have finished my work?' (*Civ. Dei* 4.2). He was therefore glad to be able to entrust to a young Spanish priest called Orosius, who had come to visit him in Africa, the task of compiling a historical dossier as a kind of appendix to the early books of the *De civitate Dei*.

Orosius (the name Paulus is first attested by Jordanes in the sixth century and is of doubtful authenticity) was born in the Spanish provinces, probably at Bracara (now Braga in northern Portugal) about 375–80. About 410–12 he came to Hippo, either on a personal visit or as the delegate of the Spanish clergy. Augustine was impressed with his ability and willingness, and invited him to write a study of Roman history which would refute the criticisms both of pagans and of Christians. In 415 he sent him to Jerome in Bethlehem with a warm letter of introduction. In the same year Orosius took part in a local synod at Jerusalem, where he was the spokesman of the anti-Pelagians. By 416 he was back in Africa, where he remained until later 417 or 418. Thereafter all trace of him is lost. During this second stay in Africa he put the finishing touches to his *Historiarum adversus paganos libri VII*. This was committed history, written to prove a point. In it Orosius surveys the history of the world from the creation until his own time using as a framework the concept of four successive empires – Babylonian, Macedonian, Carthaginian and Roman. His praiseworthy attempt to write universal rather than Roman history soon peters out, and the bulk of the work is concerned exclusively with the history of Rome. The treatment is highly selective, as Orosius' aim was to emphasize the grimness and unpleasantness of life in pagan times. So bloody battles, earthquakes, famines and plagues are described at length, while Rome's civilizing and pacifying mission is constantly minimized. Orosius continually interrupts his narrative to make personal comments, moral or ironical, on the matter which he narrates, and to suggest to his reader the appropriate reaction. His apologetic purpose leaves no room for the detached objectivity – real or feigned – of the classical historian. So too his style owes little to traditional aesthetic theory. He writes a Latin which is usually clear, vigorous and vivid, though sometimes clumsy, with little use of rhetorical figures and of such traditional features of historical narrative as the historic infinitive or the set speech. It is the language of natural eloquence rather than that of the schools. He names many sources, such as Plato, Polybius and Fabius Pictor, whom he cannot have read since he knew no Greek. And many of the Latin sources which he mentions, like Pompeius Trogus, Valerius Antias, or the emperor Claudius, he is unlikely to have read. His true sources he mentions rarely or not at all. They are Justin, from whom he gets most of his non-Roman history, Florus, Eutropius, Jerome's *Chronicle*, perhaps the first five books of Augustine's *De civitate Dei*, Arnobius, Sulpicius Severus. He may well have read Tacitus, and he had probably read Sallust, who was a school author. Among poets he quotes Virgil and Lucan whom he will have studied at school, and surprisingly enough Claudian (*De III Cons. Honorii* 96–8, quoted at 7.35.21).

Orosius' highly partial survey of Roman history corresponds only to a part of Augustine's purpose in the *De civitate Dei*, that of replying to popular claims that everything had been better in the good old days and of undermining belief in an idealized Roman past. He does not attempt to meet the philosophical objections of the cultivated Neoplatonizing intellectuals, which is the principal task that Augustine sets himself. His survey is hasty and not infrequently muddled. But its simple style, its apologetic purpose and its clear message made its fortune. It became the handbook of history *par excellence* in the Middle Ages, used and excerpted by writers from Jordanes and Gregory of Tours to the eve of the Renaissance. A translation into Old English was made on the orders of King Alfred in the ninth century. In 1059 the Byzantine emperor Romanus II sent a copy to the Caliph of Cordoba 'Abd ul-Rahmân III, who had it translated into Arabic. It was one of the first classical texts to be printed (Augsburg 1471).

39

ORATORY AND EPISTOLOGRAPHY

The study of rhetoric and the practice of declamation went on throughout the half-century of military anarchy in the third century. And though the occasions for great speeches in the Senate on matters of high policy were doubtless fewer than in the days of Pliny and Tacitus, debates continued. Some of them are recorded, however unreliably, in the *Historia Augusta*. It may be that one type of oratory even became more frequent. Roman emperors had always spent a surprising proportion of their time listening to speeches made by representatives of the Senate and delegates of provinces and cities. The only weapon which the senatorial class and the provincial upper classes could use to defend their position against their unpredictable and usually short-lived overlords was eloquence. We may be sure that they used it, even though none of their loyal addresses has been preserved. The stabilization effected by Diocletian and Constantine, with its concentration of the power of decision in the imperial court, resulted in the address to a ruler becoming almost the sole form of genuine public oratory, as opposed to mere declamation. From the fourth century we have a number of surviving speeches, all of which take the form of addresses to emperors. Whatever their ultimate purposes, such addresses inevitably struck a panegyric note.

But before going on to examine these surviving speeches, it would be well to glance at the material for the teaching of rhetoric produced during the period. It is in no sense literature, yet it must have exercised some influence on the oratory of its time. A number of such works survive, not so much because of their own qualities as because nothing better was ever written to replace them. Some deal with particular branches of rhetoric. An example is the *De figuris sententiarum et elocutionis* 'On figures of thought and speech' of Aquila Romanus, probably written in the third century, and completed by Julius Rufinianus in a work of the same title dating probably from the fourth century. Two short works, *De schematis lexeos* 'On figures of speech' and *De schematis dianoeas* 'On figures of thought' are also attributed in the manuscripts to Rufinianus. Aquila Romanus takes most of his illustrations of figures of rhetoric from Cicero, Rufinianus draws largely on Virgil. An undatable work of late antiquity, the *Carmen de figuris* 'Poem on figures of speech', treats the same subject matter in verse as an aid to memory. Three hexameters are given to each figure, generally one for definition and two for illustration. Many of the examples are drawn from classical Greek and Latin writers, adapted in form to the needs of metre.

Other works on rhetoric are text-books covering the whole subject. They are impossible to date with certainty, as they never refer to contemporary events. Among such manuals are the *Ars rhetorica* of C. Julius Victor, which is based almost entirely on Quintilian, the *Institutiones oratoriae* 'Principles of oratory' of Sulpicius Victor, who claims to follow a certain Zeno (probably Zeno of Athens, whose manual of rhetoric in ten books does not survive), and the *Artis rhetoricae libri III* of C. Chirius Fortunatianus, arranged in the form of question and answer and drawing its doctrine from Quintilian and its illustrations from Cicero. The *Praecepta artis rhetoricae* 'Precepts of the art of rhetoric' of Julius Severianus, which claims to meet the needs of the practising advocate and which draws all its examples from Cicero, has been variously dated from the second to the fifth century. A fragment is preserved of Augustine's *De rhetorica*, which formed part of his handbook of the liberal arts (Halm 137–51). Augustine himself had lost most of this handbook by the time he came to write his *Retractationes* about 427.

What is striking about all these works, apart from their lack of originality, is the almost total absence of any Greek influence. The theory of rhetoric had not stood still in the Greek world. Hermogenes, the erstwhile infant prodigy turned teacher, wrote at the end of the second century a series of text-books of rhetoric which because of their orderly arrangement and their clarity of expression became standard works, commented upon endlessly by Greek schoolmasters up to the fifteenth century. Following in the wake of Hermogenes, Menander of Laodicea in Phrygia wrote in the third century a treatise on epideictic oratory, clear in exposition, copiously illustrated, and answering the needs of the age. (It survives in two versions, one of which may not be the work of Menander himself.) In the fourth century Aphthonius of Antioch wrote a manual of graded preliminary exercises (*Progymnasmata*) which partly replaced those of Hermogenes. And early in the fifth century Nicolaus of Myra in Lycia wrote a similar manual of *Progymnasmata*, which, like that of Aphthonius, was used and commented on by teachers in the Greek world throughout the Middle Ages. Of all this pedagogical literature, which introduced new distinctions and new methods of study, there is virtually no trace in the surviving Latin manuals of the fourth and fifth centuries. Quintilian is still their model, whether at first or second hand, and Cicero provides most of their illustrative material. They concentrate on deliberative and forensic oratory, for which there was little room in late antiquity, and have little to say about the panegyric and other forms of epideictic eloquence. Even in the humble sphere of the rhetorical school the division between Greek east and Latin west is clearly visible. It is worth recalling that Augustine, who taught rhetoric at Carthage and Milan, had little knowledge of Greek and depended on translations. The rhetoric of the fourth-century west owed nothing to the world of Libanius, Themistius and Himerius.

Some time towards the end of the fourth century a collection of twelve addresses to emperors dating mainly from the end of the third century and the first two thirds of the fourth was compiled, probably by a teacher of rhetoric and perhaps in Gaul. The collection is conventionally known as the *Panegyrici Latini*; there is no general title in the manuscripts. It begins with the Panegyric addressed to Trajan by the younger Pliny on the occasion of his consulship in A.D. 100, which is evidently regarded as a model for such compositions. The rest comprises eleven panegyrics delivered by persons having some connexion with Gaul. Mamertinus, a Gallic teacher of rhetoric, possibly from Trier, addresses two speeches to Maximian, one in 289 and the other probably in 291 (Nos. 2 and 3). Both were delivered in Trier. Eumenius, a rhetor from Autun and later – perhaps as a result of his speech – *magister memoriae* to Constantius Caesar in Gaul, delivered in 298 a speech of thanks for his appointment by Constantius as professor of rhetoric and organizer of the city schools in his native town, after it had been sacked by the Bagaudae (No. 4). Nazarius, a rhetor from Bordeaux, pronounced a panegyric on Constantine – in his absence – in 321 (No. 10). It was probably delivered somewhere in Gaul. Claudius Mamertinus, a man of probably Gaulish origin who rose to high office under Julian and held the consulship in 362, delivered an address of thanks to the emperor in Constantinople at the beginning of the year (No. 11). Latinius Pacatus Drepanius, a Gaul from near Bordeaux who was also something of a poet, delivered a panegyric on Theodosius in 389 in celebration of his defeat of Maximus (No. 12). It is no accident that he was appointed proconsul of Africa in 390 and *comes rerum priuatarum* in 393. The remaining speeches are transmitted anonymously. One, probably delivered in Trier in 297, is an address on behalf of the *ciuitas Aeduorum* (Autun) to Constantius Caesar, which dwells in particular on his recovery of Britain from the usurper Allectus (No. 5). A second was delivered in 307 on the occasion of the marriage of Constantine and Fausta, the daughter of Maximian (No. 6). It treats with coy reserve the abdication of Maximian, which everyone knew was forced upon him by Diocletian. The third was delivered in Trier in 310 by an orator from Autun in the presence of Constantine, who is congratulated on his victory over his father-in-law Maximian (No. 7). The fourth, a speech of thanks on behalf of the citizens of Autun, was delivered in 312 in Trier in the presence of Constantine (No. 8). The fifth was delivered in a Gaulish city, probably Trier, in 313 to congratulate Constantine on his victory over Maxentius (No. 9). Some of these anonymous speeches are probably by Eumenius, the author of No. 4, but proof is impossible. There is great similarity in style and arrangement between all the speeches. All of them strike a note of almost absurd adulation. Everything their hero does is superhuman, his very faults are turned into virtues. The splendour of the emperor's outward appearance is vividly described. His meanest achievements are compared with the greatest exploits in myth or history, to the detriment of the latter. All the devices of the trained rhetorician are made use of to enhance the speaker's message, the content of which is as much emotional as factual. The language is in general classical and Ciceronian, without any of the archaism of Apuleius or the swollen verdosity of contemporary legal enactments. The speakers had evidently learnt the art of rhetoric from such classicizing manuals as those listed on pp. 755–6. Only Claudius Mamertinus, in his speech to Julian, makes frequent use of poetic words. The speeches are a mine of information for the historian of the period, but of information which must be critically examined; the speakers were not on oath. The collection is also an interesting document of the classicizing culture of the Gaulish upper classes, parallel to that provided for a somewhat later period by Ausonius. Both are marked by a curious unwillingness to look long and seriously at the real world. This very remoteness from everyday circumstances was itself one of the factors which enabled Claudian to replace the prose panegyric by the verse panegyric, which offered greater scope for imagery, adornment and suggestiveness (cf. p. 707).

Quintus Aurelius Symmachus, known also as Eusebius, belonged to one of the most distinguished senatorial families of Rome. His father L. Aurelius Avianius Symmachus, his father-in-law Memmius Vitrasius Orfitus Honorius, and probably his maternal grandfather, had all held the office of Prefect of the City, the normal culmination of a senatorial career at this period. The family owned vast estates in Africa, Numidia, Sicily and southern Italy. Symmachus was born *c.* 345, studied rhetoric at Rome under a teacher from Bordeaux, perhaps Tiberius Victor Minervius who is mentioned in Ausonius' poem on the professors of Bordeaux. We do not know when he held the quaestorship and praetorship, the duties of which were by now limited to giving lavish games. In 365 he was probably *corrector* (governor) of Bruttium, then spent a short time at Valentinian's court in Gaul. In 373–4 he was Proconsul of Africa for eight months. In 384–5 he was Prefect of the City. In 391, as a result of special circumstances, he was appointed one of the consuls of the year, a dignity at this time more often held by generals or court officials than by senators. Twice he took the side of a usurping emperor, first of Maximus in 383 then of Eugenius in 392–4. On both occasions he succeeded in ingratiating himself with Theodosius after the defeat and death of the usurper. His position as one of the recognized leaders of the senatorial class, whose support Theodosius needed, saved him. He died after 402.

Such was the career of Symmachus. It should be noted that in fact he held only three offices which involved any serious duties, and each for only about a year. *Otium* was the way of life of the senatorial class, devoted to managing their estates – whether energetically or languidly – and pursuing their *dolce vita* of exquisite good taste, backed by a sure sense of social equalities and distinctions. Political activity was an interruption of their life, not its main content. This does not mean that when office interrupted their leisure they did not take the duties of their posts seriously. As will be seen, Symmachus got through a great deal of awkward paperwork in his year as Prefect of the City.

He is appreciated today principally for his letters. But during his lifetime he enjoyed the reputation of being one of the greatest orators of his age. His erudition was much admired, as was his care for the classics of Roman literature. There are traces in later manuscripts of recensions of Virgil and Livy prepared for him. Like many members of the senatorial class, whose spokesman he often was, Symmachus was a pagan. He combined a Neoplatonizing monotheism with an antiquarian regard for the traditional religion of the Roman state, though he could not claim the deep and wide knowledge of sacred lore possessed by his colleague and friend Vettius Agorius Praetextatus. It is one of the curious ironies of history that it was the pagan Symmachus who recommended Augustine for the chair of rhetoric in Milan.

Eight speeches by Symmachus survive in a palimpsest manuscript unfortunately in a fragmentary state.[1] They include two panegyric addresses to Valentinian delivered in 369 and 370, one to his young son and co-emperor Gratian delivered in 369, two speeches delivered in the senate in 376 and voicing the relief of the senators at the new political rapprochement between Senate and emperor, the *Pro Trygetio* and the *Pro patre*, and three further speeches in the senate on behalf of individuals. We know from his correspondence and elsewhere of many other speeches delivered by Symmachus, and possibly gathered together in a collected edition, which do not survive. Their style and manner recall those of the *Panegyrici Latini*. The first three display the forced expressions and occasional lapses of taste characteristic of the panegyric genre.

The letters, though intended by their author for publication, were not in fact published until after his death, when his son brought out an edition in ten books comprising some 900 letters written between 364 and 402. Book 10 consists of the *Relationes*, the official reports sent by Symmachus as Prefect of the City to the emperor Valentinian II. The model of Pliny's letters evidently prompted the arrangement of those of Symmachus. The letters are not arranged chronologically, but by addressee, and many of them are impossible to date. They have

[1] Now divided into two parts, cod. Ambrosianus E 147 inf. and cod. Vaticanus latinus 5750.

been described as verbose but empty of content. This is a little harsh. Symmachus well knew that the epistolary genre calls for brevity and compression. And their content was not meant to consist of factual information, but of the affirmation and cultivation of *amicitia*, naturally within a very limited section of late Roman society. The editorial activity of the younger Symmachus may be responsible for some of the bland emptiness of the letters. His father had made many political misjudgements in a long life, which called for excisions and covering of tracks. But the editor cannot have changed the basic tone of the correspondence, which was concerned with social relations and not with information. If information had to be conveyed, it would be conveyed verbally or in a separate enclosure. The letter itself was primarily a work of art. Within the limitations imposed by the rules of the art Symmachus skilfully varies his tone to suit the addressee, striking a philosophical note with Praetextatus, with others affecting archaism, with others a racy informality, with others an irony which sometimes approaches self-parody. But the letters are always studied, never spontaneous. They provide an interesting picture of the intellectual and social interests of a cultivated and idle aristocracy. They contain scarcely any references to the momentous events of the age, in some of which Symmachus was himself involved, though never in a decisive role. The tenth book, the *Relationes*, is a different matter. It contains forty-nine official dispatches sent by Symmachus to the emperor. Some are formal greetings. Many are on complex legal questions involving conflict of laws, which came before the Senate and which were referred to the supreme legislator. Many were in their original state accompanied by dossiers of documents, summaries of evidence and the like, which have not survived. They give an insight into the obsessionally conscientious mode of operation of late Roman government in certain fields. But it must be borne in mind that Symmachus himself was not a bureaucrat. For him office and its responsibilities were fleeting and in some ways regrettable interruptions in a life of *otium* and *amicitia*.

The most striking of the *Relationes* is the plea for the restoration of the altar of Victory in the senate-house. Ever since the days of Augustus senators had offered a pinch of incense on this altar at the outset of the proceedings of the Senate. When Constantius II visited Rome in 357, he had the altar removed, as an offence to Christianity, but it was soon restored to its place, presumably under Julian. In 381 the young emperor Gratian, a devout and even bigoted Christian, the first emperor to drop the title of *Pontifex Maximus*, had the altar removed once more and the revenues of the Vestal Virgins and other Roman priesthoods confiscated. The next year the Senate petitioned for the reversal of these decisions, but Pope Damasus and Ambrose, bishop of Milan, succeeded in persuading Gratian to stick to his decision. After Gratian's death in 383 another petition was organized, and it is this which Symmachus reports to Valentinian II in his famous *Relatio*. It is a balanced and noble plea for religious tolerance, for the avoidance of imposed uniformity, and for respect for the traditions of the past. Naturally, it is the kind of declaration which only threatened minorities make. It did not succeed in its purpose. But it was a sufficiently serious and effective plea to provoke a response from Ambrose (*Epist.* 17) setting out with unequivocal clarity the principle of Christian intolerance. The Christian poet Prudentius also composed a refutation of its arguments (cf. pp. 713–14).

Symmachus was the last great Roman orator in the classical tradition and the last senator whose correspondence was collected and published. But both oratory and epistolography found a new place in the life of the Christian church. The detailed study of this Christian literature falls outside the domain of the present volume. But it may be noted that Ambrose left a collection of 91 letters, Jerome one of 154, and Augustine one of 270. Like the letters of Symmachus, these epistles are works of art, written by men trained in the discipline of literature. But they are unlike those of Symmachus in almost every other respect. They are full of biblical quotation and allusion, which imports a new element into their language. They are often very long. And they are not mere tokens of friendship, but are full of information and argument. The needs of Christian communication broke the narrow bounds within which classical epistolography flourished.

In the same way the Christian sermon was a new form of oratory. We do not possess any sermons of Jerome or Ambrose, at any rate not in their raw form. But an extensive collection of Augustine's *Sermones*, delivered before his congregation at Hippo, survives. The former professor of rhetoric displays a confident command of all the artifices of the discipline. But at the same time he realizes that these artifices may in fact impede communication with an average audience. So he deliberately uses a popular or on occasion vulgar register, quite distinct from that of the *De civitate Dei*: *melius in barbarismo nostro*, he observes, *uos intellegitis quam in nostra disertitudine uos deserti estis* 'It is better for you to understand through my solecism than for you to be left behind by my eloquence' (*Enarr. in psalm.* 36, serm. 3.6); and in another passage he remarks, *melius est reprehendant nos grammatici quam non intellegant populi* 'It is better that grammarians should censure me than that the people should not understand me' (*Enarr. in psalm.* 138.20). It is hard to imagine a more radical break with the tradition of late classical rhetoric.

40

LEARNING AND THE PAST

I. SCHOLARS

Macrobius Ambrosius Theodosius, apparently an African, is probably to be identified with the Theodosius who was Praetorian Prefect of Italy in 430. He seems to have been related to the family of the Symmachi. Nothing more is known of his life. But he was evidently an aristocrat rather than a professional scholar. Three works of his survive: the *Commentary on the Dream of Scipio*, the *Saturnalia*, and a treatise *De differentiis et societatibus graeci latinique uerbi*, which is preserved only in excerpts from excerpts made in the Middle Ages. The two former works are dedicated to the writer's son Eustachius.

The *Commentary* is a loose and discursive discussion of the famous dream recounted in Cicero's *De re publica*, in which Scipio Africanus the Elder appears to his grandson, reveals to him his own future destiny and that of his country, expounds the rewards awaiting virtue in the after-life, and describes with impressive majesty the universe and the place of the earth and of man in it. Macrobius does not provide an exhaustive commentary on his text, but launches into a series of expositions in Neoplatonic vein on dreams, on the mystic properties of numbers, on the nature of the soul, on astronomy, on music. He quotes many authorities but it is unlikely that he had read all or even most of them. Plotinus and Porphyry are probably his principal proximate sources, and Virgil is quoted frequently by way of adornment. However the work does embody Neoplatonic thinking which is not directly preserved elsewhere. The style is rather uneven, as Macrobius copies or translates his sources without reducing them to stylistic uniformity.

The *Saturnalia*, in seven books, of which the end of the second and the beginning of the third, the beginning and second half of the fourth, and the ends of the sixth and seventh are missing, purports to be a report at third hand of the discussions of a group of senators and scholars on the three successive days of the Saturnalia in 384. The host on the first day is Vettius Agorius Praetextatus. On the second day the guests assemble in the house of Nicomachus Flavianus, and on the third in that of Q. Aurelius Symmachus. The parallelism in form to some of Cicero's philosophical dialogues – and to such works as Varro's *Res rusticae* – is evident. It may be that Athenaeus' account of an imaginary conversation of scholars at a banquet – the *Deipnosophists* – also contributed to Macrobius' inspiration. The participants in the discussion include, besides the three hosts, the senators Caecina Albinus, Furius Albinus, the grammarian Servius, a young man called Avienus, a Greek rhetorician named Eusebius, a philosopher Eustathius, a doctor Disarius, and an 'uninvited guest' Evangelus. The conversation ranges over a variety of topics, from the terms for various times of day to the history of the *toga praetexta*, from Saturn and Janus to the care shown by the gods for slaves, from jokes to pontifical law. But the central theme, which occupies most of Books 3 to 6, is the poet Virgil. His command of rhetoric, his knowledge of philosophy and astrology, his dependence on Greek sources, his knowledge of Roman religious law and augural practice, his language and metre are all discussed discursively, and interpretations are offered – by Servius – of a number of obscure passages. It is clear that for Macrobius as for Dante Virgil is 'quel Savio gentil, che tutto seppe' (*Inf.* 7.3). The existence of Christianity is completely ignored. The learning displayed by Macrobius is stupendous, if often trifling, and it is backed up by the names of an impressive list of authorities. But Macrobius takes care not to quote the immediate sources from which he gained his information, the principal of which are Aulus Gellius, various commentators on Virgil, and Plutarch's *Quaestiones convivales* in a fuller form than that which we now possess. He did, however, consult other sources from time to time, many of which cannot readily be identified. As in his *Commentary*, so too in his *Saturnalia* he tends to quote his material nearly verbatim. Only the narrative and dramatic framework is really his own.

Macrobius observes that several of the participants were too young to have been present at such a gathering on the dramatic date of December 384 (1.1.5). Recent research has identified the anachronistic participants as Servius and Avienus – who is probably to be identified with the fabulist Avianus or Avienus (p. 718). These and other considerations – such as the posthumous rehabilitation of Nicomachus Flavianus in 430 from the disgrace of espousing the cause of the usurper Eugenius – have led recently to the suggestion of a new date for the composition of the *Saturnalia*, which used to be dated at the beginning of the fifth century. It now seems likely to have been written shortly after 430. This means that it is not a picture of cultivated pagan senatorial society by a man who knew it from personal observation. It is rather a sentimental re-evocation of a lost world which was rapidly becoming idealized. In the harsh environment of 430, when Rome had been sacked by Alaric, when barbarian invasions were tearing whole provinces out of the fabric of the empire, there were still men who liked to look back on the civilized elegance of life in *la belle époque*. That they probably did not understand all its nuances did not diminish their nostalgia, but it no doubt resulted in a certain rigidity and formalism in its depiction. The picture painted by Macrobius of late fourth-century senatorial society is the very antithesis of that provided by Ammianus Marcellinus. But it is probably going too far to suggest that the desire to rebut Ammianus was high among Macrobius' motives. Wooden and mechanical as much of it is, the *Saturnalia* is a touching picture of the nostalgia of a class which had been overtaken by events, not the least among which was the conversion to Christianity of the great bulk of the Roman aristocracy. But there is no controversial intent behind the dialogue; classical culture and pagan religion are simply assumed without question to be identical.

About the same time as Macrobius was completing his *Saturnalia* in Rome, Martianus Capella published in Carthage his *Marriage of Mercury and Philology*, one of the most extraordinary works in all Latin literature, and in some ways more indicative of the spirit of the age than the sober and dignified exchanges of Macrobius' bookish grandees. Of Martianus Min(n)e(i)us Felix Capella little is known save that he lived in Carthage and wrote his book in his old age. He may have been a teacher of rhetoric. The short autobiographical poem which concludes his work has been transmitted in so corrupt a form as to be virtually useless; but one passage in it may indicate that he practised as an advocate in the proconsular court at Carthage. The date of the work is equally unclear; probably after 410, because of an allusion to the sack of Rome, certainly before 439, when Carthage passed into the hands of the Vandals. Earlier dates have been proposed, but the arguments in their favour carry little conviction.

The *De Nuptiis Mercurii et Philologiae*, in nine books, is an encyclopaedia of the liberal arts set in an allegorical narrative framework. Short poems are interspersed through the prose text in the manner of the *Satura Menippea*. The first two books describe, with a wealth of elaborate fancy, the selection of a bride for Mercury (the god of eloquence) in the person of Philology, her preparation and purification for the marriage, her ascent to the astral heaven, the diverse guests, human and divine, there assembled, and finally the marriage ceremony itself. Philology is accompanied in her ascent to the higher world by seven *feminae dotales* – not bridesmaids, but slave women forming part of the bride's dowry – each representing one of the seven liberal arts. In Books 3 to 9 they give each in turn a systematic account of the art which they represent, in the order Grammar, Dialectic, Rhetoric, Geometry, Arithmetic, Astronomy and Music. The account of the marriage in Books 1 and 2 is certainly inspired by the marriage of Cupid and Psyche in Apuleius' *Metamorphoses*. But there is much more to it than that. The description of the stages through which Philology passes on the way to her apotheosis reflects the actual liturgy of the Neoplatonist mystic worship of Hecate, into which Julian had been initiated by Maximus of Ephesus, with its syncretism of Orphic, Neopythagorean and Chaldean elements. Whether Martianus owed his acquaintance with this liturgy to a literary tradition now lost or to a ritual tradition of clandestine paganism is an open question. A third element pervading the whole of Books 1 and 2 is the elaborate allegorical interpretation given of all the events recounted. If Prudentius was the father of Christian allegory, Martianus is at the origin of profane allegory in the European tradition.

The succeeding books vary in scope and systematic treatment. Grammar (Book 3) starts with exhaustive discussion of letters and syllables, goes on to the parts of speech, declension and conjugation, then to a long discussion of analogy and finally a short section on anomaly. The proximate sources cannot be identified. But Martianus' doctrine does not differ significantly from that of other grammarians of the fourth and fifth centuries. Dialectic (Book 4) is an account of Aristotelian formal logic interspersed in a rather muddled way with precepts on practical rhetoric, and with some remarkable omissions. The sources probably include Varro – whether directly or indirectly – Porphyry's *Isagoge* and Aristotle's *Categories* via a Latin adaptation, and Apuleius' Περὶ ἑρμηνείας. The section on Rhetoric (Book 5) uses Cicero's *De inventione* as a prime source but also draws on Cicero's other rhetorical works and the commentaries on them by Marius Victorinus, as well as on the manuals of rhetoric of the late Empire. Martianus seems indeed to have used a greater variety of sources here than in any other section, which lends support to the conjecture that he was a teacher of rhetoric. The section on Geometry (Book 6) does not consist, like the preceding sections, of definitions, axioms and propositions, but is mainly made up by a geographical survey of the known world in the form of long lists of place-names with occasional comments. Only at the end of this does the allegorical lady admit that she has been digressing, and gives a very brief and inadequate introduction to Euclidean geometry, with the excuse that the lateness of the hour precludes a systematic treatment. The main source is Solinus' *Collectanea rerum memorabilium* and Pliny's geographical books (3–6). Martianus either could not handle Euclidean geometry – he makes a complete hash of Eratosthenes' method of measuring the circumference of the earth – or believed that his readers would not understand it. And indeed it would be difficult to provide a satisfactory exposition without the use of diagrams. For this reason he filled out the space allocated to geometry with this curious geographical farrago. The section on Arithmetic (Book 7) – by which is meant not computation but the theory of numbers – is mainly a digest of the *Introduction to arithmetic* of Nicomachus of Gerasa and of Books 7 to 9 of Euclid's *Elements*. Martianus is unlikely to have used either in the original, and one can only speculate on his proximate sources. The whole exposition is overlaid by a stratum of numerology and mysticism not to be found in Nicomachus or Euclid. This section is one of the most systematically arranged in the whole work. Astronomy makes her entry in a kind of space-ship before expounding her art. Her discourse (Book 8) is perhaps the best exposition of classical geocentric astronomy available in Latin until the twelfth century and enjoyed immense influence. It may stem originally from a handbook by Varro derived from Posidonius, but we can only guess at Martianus' immediate source. Finally Harmony or Music (Book 9) enters, and after reciting a long list of instances of the emotional or therapeutic effects of music gives a digest of classical musical and metrical theory drawn entirely from Aristides Quintilianus' Περὶ μουσικῆς 'On music' (1.1–19). At the conclusion of her discourse the gods lead the bride and bridegroom to the marriage chamber. There follows an autobiographical poem of 27 lines, so flamboyant in expression and so corruptly transmitted as to be practically unintelligible.

Martianus writes a baroque and convoluted Latin often of extreme obscurity. His vocabulary comprises many neologisms, either new compounds or derivatives such as *hiatimembris*, *astriloquus*, *dulcineruis*, *uernicomus*, *latrocinaliter*, *perendinatio*, *interriuatio*, or technical words, often of Greek origin, such as *acronychus*, *egersimon*, *helicoeides*. When he is setting out stock handbook material, his style is fairly prosaic, though usually long-winded. But in his narrative and above all in his descriptive passages, and thus particularly in Books 1 and 2, he uses a florid style, overloaded with abstract nouns, with imagery and word-play, which has no parallel in classical Latin. His desire for self-expression evidently exceeded his capacity, and the result is often a torrent of words which obscure rather than reveal his meaning. In his verse passages the language, style and metre are more classical, so far as the often defective transmission enables us to judge. There was evidently a strong strain of exhibitionism about Martianus, visual as well as verbal. His descriptions, particularly of the remarkable allegorical ladies, are vivid in detail and not without lasciviousness. These features of content and language, together with the allegorical narrative framework, ensured his book conspicuous success from the Carolingian age to the Renaissance, in spite of the mediocrity of the information which it contained. What we should like to know, but cannot, is what kind of reader Martianus had in mind in his own day. He is too difficult for schoolboys and too inadequate for scholars.

2. GRAMMARIANS

Throughout the period under review grammar, in its Hellenistic sense of the systematic study of language and literature, continued to form the main content of the education of those who proceeded beyond mere practical ability to read and write. In every city of the Latin-speaking world *grammatici* – sometimes holding public appointments – drilled their pupils in letters, syllables and words, instilled the doctrine of the parts of speech, their distinctions and inflections, taught the principles of metre, and illustrated their precepts by reading and commenting on classical Latin poets, above all Terence and Virgil. Prose writers were mainly left to the teachers of rhetoric.

Of the many text-books and manuals written – and in a sense each teacher produced his own text-book – only a few survive, and they have few original features. The pattern of the *Ars grammatica* had been set long ago by such men as Remmius Palaemon, who in their turn built upon the work of their Greek predecessors. The grammarians of late antiquity drew on their classical forerunners through the grammarians and scholars of the Antonine and Severan age. A brief survey will therefore suffice. Towards the end of the third century, probably in the reign of Diocletian, Marius Plotius Sacerdos wrote his *Artes grammaticae* in three books, the third of which treated metre. He still quotes many Greek examples in the course of explaining Latin grammar and metre. From the early part of the second half of the fourth century we have three surviving manuals of grammar. The *Ars grammatica* in five books of Flavius Sosipater Charisius, probably to be identified with an African appointed to a public chair of grammar in Constantinople in 358, deals with the traditional topics of grammar in the first three books, and with metre and stylistics in the last two. The fifth book is incomplete. Charisius' grammar is a rather mechanical compilation from earlier works. About the same time Diomedes published his *Ars grammatica* in three books. In the first he deals with the parts of speech, goes on to treat the elementary principles of grammar and to discuss questions of style in the second, and expounds the principles of metre in the third. This unusual order of treatment is probably determined by practical considerations of teaching, and offers an interesting example of the ability of these tradition-bound scholars to innovate. The relation between Diomedes and Charisius cannot be determined with certainty. They draw on too many common sources.

Aelius Donatus, Jerome's teacher, is recorded as flourishing in 353. His *Ars grammatica* in two versions, elementary and advanced (*Ars minor* and *Ars maior*) is a shorter work than those of Charisius and Diomedes, with whom he shared common sources. In clarity of exposition and judicious selection of material it far surpasses them. The longer work covers in more detail the same ground as the shorter, but omits the more elementary topics such as verb paradigms. It was evidently meant to be studied after the *Ars minor*. Donatus was clearly an unusually gifted teacher. Jerome enjoyed every minute of his schooldays, and remembered his old master with warmth in his old age in distant Bethlehem. Donatus' grammar soon became a standard work, in so far as such a thing existed before the invention of printing. A dense thicket of commentaries grew up around it, the earliest surviving those by Servius in the early fifth century and by Cledonius and Pompeius a little later, later commentaries being composed by Julian of Toledo in the late seventh century and Remigius of Auxerre about 900. Donatus' Latin grammar became a classic just as had the Greek grammar of Dionysius the Thracian, and each dominated the study of its respective language in the Middle Ages. Donatus also wrote commentaries on Virgil and Terence. That on Virgil is lost but for the introduction. That on Terence survives, though probably in somewhat modified form. It is a work of notable scholarship, dealing not only with language but also with problems of staging and the relation of Terence to his Greek models. What it does not provide, and from its form as a line by line commentary cannot, is adequate discussion of structure, dramatic form and character.

Jerome's teacher of rhetoric, C. Marius Victorinus Afer, was a man of immense learning and deep philosophical interests. Indeed he was the intellectual leader of the Roman Neoplatonists in the middle of the fourth century. His works include an *Ars grammatica* in four books which deals almost exclusively with metre. It was meant for advanced students. But his main influence was exercised through his series of translations of Greek philosophical works, from Plato through Aristotle to Plotinus and Porphyry. He also wrote commentaries on Aristotle's logical works and on Cicero's *De inventione*. His conversion to Christianity in his old age was a scandal to his pagan admirers and followers. As a Christian he wrote polemical anti-Arian treatises, a commentary on the Pauline epistles, a poem, with many Virgilian echoes, on the Maccabaean brothers, and possibly hymns in hexameters. Victorinus provides an interesting example of the adaptation of the traditional skills of the pagan scholar to new Christian ends. His works survive only in part.

Among the interlocutors in Macrobius' *Saturnalia* there is a young man named Servius, who elucidates Virgil. It has been convincingly argued that his presence at such a gathering in 384 is an anachronism, and that his active literary activity falls within the fifth century. His long commentary on Virgil probably belongs to the 20s of that century. It illumines for us as no other work can the way in which men of culture in late antiquity studied the masterpieces of their literary heritage. Servius' careful and sometimes almost reverent observations cover the whole range of Virgilian scholarship, from elementary points of language to Virgil's creative use of his Greek and Latin models. His commentary is particularly rich in antiquarian information – not all of equal reliability – on early Italy. The presentation is not dogmatic; often he sets out two interpretations and leaves the choice to the reader. His material is largely drawn from the older commentators on Virgil – Probus, Asper, and others – but Servius is no mere mechanical compiler. His own judgement, often expressed, is sound rather than original. A devoted and gifted pedagogue as well as a scholar, he succeeds in conveying much of the richness of classical Roman study of Virgil, firmly based on the text and eschewing the flights of allegorizing imagination of many later interpreters. His shortcomings are those of any literary critic who restricts himself, in the classical manner, to line by line and word by word explication. Yet without Servius, our understanding of Virgil today would be both narrower and shallower. The text survives in two recensions. In the longer of these – the so-called Servius Danielis – Servius' original commentary has been supplemented, probably in the seventh or eighth century, by material from other commentators, including Aelius Donatus. Much of this supplementary material is of the utmost value. A good critical text of the whole of Servius is still lacking. Servius also wrote a commentary on the two versions of the *Ars grammatica* of Donatus and several minor grammatical and metrical treatises.

Finally, there survives under the name of Claudius Donatus a rhetorical and stylistic commentary on Virgil. This mediocre work, which takes for granted the linguistic and material explication which forms the bulk of Servius' commentary, reminds us that Virgil was studied not only by grammarians but also by rhetoricians, who sought in his works illustrations of the concepts of their science. This interest of the rhetorician in Virgil is part of a larger phenomenon characteristic of late antiquity, the blurring of the boundaries between prose and poetry and the loss of feeling for the appropriateness of literary genres.

A rather different kind of grammatical activity is represented by the *De compendiosa doctrina* of Nonius Marcellus, an African who was probably active in the first half of the fourth century. His vast compilation is a lexicon of Republican Latin. The first twelve books are arranged grammatically, i.e. the entries are based on words or forms, the remaining eight are organized by subject matter, e.g. articles of clothing, weapons. The entries in each case are substantially of the same character, and consist of brief definitions supported by a series of citations from Republican authors. Nonius Marcellus was evidently reaching across the gap of the third century to the antiquarian scholarship of the age of Fronto, Aulus Gellius and Apuleius. His lexicon with its copious quotations is the product of the habit of making excerpts which Fronto tried to instil into his students. Nonius Marcellus works largely at second hand, from earlier collections of excerpts rather than from the original texts. His ignorance and inattention diminish but cannot destroy the value of his compilation. Without him our knowledge of such major Republican writers as Lucilius, Pacuvius and Accius would be sadly reduced.

41

MINOR FIGURES

Astrology was believed in and practised by all classes in the Late Empire. The Neoplatonist doctrine of a hierarchical universe provided an intellectual foundation for astrology which made it acceptable as a science and conferred on its practitioners new respectability and dignity. Only the Christians condemned astrology out of hand. And the frequency with which the Church Fathers repeat their denunciations of the art suggests that it had many adherents even in Christian communities. Shortly before the middle of the fourth century Julius Firmicus Maternus, a Sicilian of senatorial rank who had practised as an advocate, completed his handbook of astrology – *Matheseos libri VIII*. It is dedicated to Q. Flavius Maesius Egnatius Lollianus, otherwise Mavortius, *comes Orientis* 330–6, proconsul of Africa 334–7, Prefect of the City of Rome 342, consul 355, Praetorian Prefect 355–6, who had encouraged Maternus to write his manual.[1]

In his first book Maternus defends astrology against sceptical criticism and alleges that he was the first to introduce the science to Rome. By this he means that he was the first to write a treatise on the subject in Latin. His claim is in fact unfounded, as Manilius had written on the subject in verse three centuries earlier. But Maternus may not have known of Manilius' poem, and the many resemblances between the two are likely to be due to the use of common sources in Greek. The remaining seven books set out in great detail, with many examples, the principles of the alleged science. Maternus' treatise is the longest and most systematic exposition of astrology surviving from antiquity. He has a lofty concept of his calling and demands of the astrologer the highest moral standards and the most circumspect behaviour, including refraining from attending the Circus lest he be thought to influence the results of the races. Maternus never squarely faces the inconsistency between the strict determinism which he postulates in human affairs – only the emperor is exempt – and the moral responsibility of the individual.

His style is uneven. Much of his treatise is in the simple, no-nonsense style appropriate to scientific writing. But from time to time he launches into elabo-

[1] On Mavortius' possible family connexions cf. Arnheim (1972) 136–7.

rate rhetorical purple passages. In these he tends to run his metaphors on to the point of absurdity. His vocabulary includes many late Latin words such as *concordialis*, *mansuetarius*, *quiescentia*, and he is particularly fond of *intimare*. He mentions a number of other astrological works which he has written, but these do not survive.

There also exists a work of Christian anti-pagan polemic, *De errore profanarum religionum* 'On the error of profane religions', attributed to Julius Firmicus Maternus *vir clarissimus* and written, on internal evidence, about the middle of the fourth century. It is a savage attack on pagan cults and mysteries, which it sees as the work of the devil. It provides valuable information on pagan religious practices in late antiquity. It has generally been believed that its author is the Firmicus Maternus who wrote on astrology, and that the second work is the fruit of his conversion to Christianity. But the matter cannot be proved, and the two writers could well be brothers or cousins or totally unrelated. There is certainly a difference of tone between the two works. The astrologer is solemn and composed, the Christian fiery and combative. But the zeal of the convert may be the explanation. No significant differences in linguistic usage have been noted. If both works are by the same author they provide an interesting document in the intellectual history of the fourth century.

Some time in the late fourth or early fifth century Palladius Rutilius Taurus Aemilianus, *vir illustris*, wrote a handbook of agriculture, the precise title of which is uncertain. After an introductory book dealing with agriculture in general, Books 2 to 13 set out the tasks of the farmer month by month. Book 14, which was not discovered until the present century, deals with the care of farm animals and the rudiments of veterinary science. The work is completed by a poem in 85 elegiac couplets on the grafting of fruit-trees. Palladius evidently models his book on that of Columella, whom he frequently draws on, sometimes copying him almost word for word. But the tone and style of the work are quite different from those of Columella. The rhetorical veneer of Columella is absent, and Palladius writes very simple, clear Latin, without any attempt at producing a work of *belles lettres*. And the scientific treatment of agriculture, which Columella inherited from his Greek forbears, is abandoned in favour of a series of short recipes or instructions for dealing with particular practical problems.

Palladius' main source is Gargilius Martialis (first half of the third century), of whose handbook of agriculture only a few fragments survive. But he also makes extensive use of Columella – particularly Books 2, 6–9, and 11, of the epitome of Vitruvius by Faventinus, and occasionally of the lost Greek Συναγωγὴ γεωργικῶν ἐπιτηδευμάτων of Anatolius of Beirut (written *c.* 361). He occasionally adds observations based on his own experience as a landowner. Some of these throw a revealing light on the agrarian world of late antiquity, e.g. the remark that a broken column was handy for levelling a threshing-floor (7.1). The strictly practical orientation of Palladius' handbook made it a favourite in the Middle Ages. A Middle English translation exists. There were also translations into Italian and Catalan in the fourteenth century.

Flavius Vegetius Renatus, who held the rank of *comes*, published his *Epitoma rei militaris* 'All the soldier needs to know' in four books after 383 and before 450. The emperor to whom it is dedicated is probably Theodosius I, but could be Valentinian III or even Theodosius II. The author is a Christian, but not a *dévot*. Book 1 deals with the selection and training of recruits, Book 2 with military organization, Book 3 with tactics and strategy, Book 4 with engines of war and – briefly – with naval warfare. There is much lamentation about the decline of the Roman army and the need to return to ancient models and practices. There is a curious patina of antiquity over the whole work, even when the author is writing about the army of his own day. In fact he draws much of his information from earlier sources, such as Cato, Celsus and Frontinus, and fails to distinguish clearly between what happened in the past – and ought to happen now – and the military realities of the present. Each book is preceded by a rhetorical preface and followed by a rhetorical conclusion. The bulk of the work is written in a plain, businesslike style, appropriate for technical writing, and open to neologisms. The same Vegetius is almost certainly the author of a veterinary handbook – *Mulomedicina* – based largely on Celsus, Pelagonius and on the so-called *Mulomedicina Chironis*, a manual of veterinary medicine written in rather unclassical Latin. Indeed much of Vegetius is a rewriting at a somewhat higher stylistic level of the *Mulomedicina Chironis*.

Another work, this time anonymous, also deals with the military problems of the Late Empire. Entitled *De rebus bellicis*, the little treatise of about fifteen printed pages was written between 337 and 378, and probably in the period 366 to 375. It puts forward proposals for the reduction of public expenditure, spread of tax liability, reform of the mint, and introduction of a number of new articles of military equipment. These include a kind of armoured chariot with movable scythe blades, a felt undershirt to wear beneath armour, a portable bridge supported by bladders, a warship driven by paddles worked by oxen, a super-ballista and the like. It is hard to say whether the author is a serious military reformer or a member of the lunatic fringe. His work is probably a fortuitous survivor from many proposals for reform in the Late Empire duly submitted, docketed and forgotten. Few reformers, however, can have had such a touching faith in gadgetry.

Arnobius, a pagan teacher of rhetoric and advocate from Sicca Veneria (Le Kef) in Africa, born *c.* 240, was impressed by the bearing of Christians haled before the courts during Diocletian's persecution (302–4). Eventually he experienced a sudden conversion to Christianity. The local bishop was at first suspicious of his good faith, and asked for evidence of the sincerity of his conversion. Arnobius thereupon wrote his apologetic treatise *Adversus nationes* 'Against the Gentiles' and was as a result accepted into the Christian community. The treatise is in seven books. The first two defend the Christian religion against the popular charge that it is responsible for the present misfortunes of the Roman world, as well as against more philosophical objections. The remaining five are devoted to an onslaught on the paganism of his time; Books 3 and 4 deal with pagan mythology, Books 5 to 7 with cult practices.

Arnobius knew little about Christianity when he composed his work; he does not understand the divinity of Christ, supposes human souls to be by their nature mortal and to acquire immortality through merit, and shows little acquaintance with the Christian scriptures. On the other hand he knew a great deal about the theory and practice of pagan belief and ritual. His book is a mine of information on myths and cults and in general on the religious concepts and practices of the educated but unphilosophical Roman citizen of his time. Though he shows scarcely any signs of Neoplatonist influence, he was familiar with the vaguely philosophical syncretism of much late Roman religion.

His method is to score debating points. Wit, ridicule and the discovery of apparent contradictions are his instruments. As befits a professional rhetorician he handles them with aplomb. Apostrophe, exclamation, rhetorical question, syllogism, and enthymeme follow one another with dizzy rapidity. All the contradictions of his opponent's position are revealed with merciless thoroughness but little real profundity. Antithesis, alliteration, homoeoteleuton and other figures of speech abound. Arnobius uses a wide-ranging vocabulary, including many archaisms and poetic words, and often piles synonym upon synonym for the same idea. As a display of rhetorical pyrotechnics his treatise has few rivals. As a serious contribution to its declared subject its value is negligible. It is noteworthy that his style is very different from the sober, rather dull Ciceronianism of the contemporary Gaulish orators whose speeches survive in the *Panegyrici Latini*. Perhaps the influence of Apuleius and Tertullian was still strong in their native land.

42

APULEIUS

Apuleius (no *praenomen* is attested) was born at Madauros (Mdaurusch in Algeria) in the middle 120s A.D., the son of a wealthy duumvir. His *Apology* sketches the main lines of his earlier career. Having studied locally at Carthage under the *grammaticus* and *rhetor* and having developed philosophical interests there, he continued his researches for some years at Athens and spent a period in Rome. By the time of his chance arrival at Oea (Tripoli) in 155–6, he was a literary celebrity. His marriage there to Pudentilla, a wealthy widow, led to indictment on a charge of magic. After acquittal he resided in Carthage, his life as sophist and leading dignitary being documented in his *Florida*. Nothing is known of any activities after about A.D. 170.

In the history of Latin literature Apuleius has two main claims to attention. As a philosopher without original genius he is important for his transmission of the ideas of Middle Platonism, and as a writer of fiction he is the author of the *Metamorphoses* ('Transformations'), the one Latin romance to have survived complete from the classical period. These contributions have traditionally been studied in isolation from each other, to the impoverishment of criticism of the *Metamorphoses*. The student of the novel cannot adequately assess its nature and purpose without prior investigation of its author's leading attitudes and preoccupations.

Everything that the man touches reflects the curiosity of the scientist or the enthusiasm of the philosophical littérateur. Practical treatises on trees, agriculture, medicines; a long compilation in Greek on natural history (*Quaestiones naturales*); educational works on astronomy, music, arithmetic, as well as a disquisition on proverbs; light verses after the manner of Catullus of both a risqué and a satirical kind; symposium-literature in the manner of Gellius or Athenaeus; in the sphere of fiction, in addition to the *Metamorphoses* a second romance *Hermagoras*, an anthology of love-anecdotes, not to mention a mysterious *Epitome historiarum* – no one seriously regrets the loss of much of this, but the catalogue indicates the author's phenomenal intellectual energy. Yet his main concerns lay beyond these enthusiasms. Philosophy was his major love; in addition to his surviving volumes he composed a *De re publica*,

('On the commonwealth') and a translation of Plato's *Phaedo*. He had also a reputation as a public speaker, and the *Apology* and *Florida* allow us to gauge his effectiveness as advocate and sophist.

I

The *Apologia* (more correctly *Apulei Platonici pro se de magia*) was a speech of self-defence delivered before the proconsul Claudius Maximus at Sabrata in 158–9. After his marriage to Pudentilla, widowed mother of his undergraduate friend Pontianus, an envious indictment on a charge of magic had been laid by Sicinius Aemilius, brother of Pudentilla's first husband, on behalf of Pontianus' brother Sicinius Pudens. An additional charge of the murder of Pontianus was hastily dropped. Conviction for magic under the *lex Cornelia de sicariis et veneficiis* of Sulla could have been punishable by death, but Apuleius' characteristically witty, learned, long-winded oration demolished the flimsy fabric of charges like a sledgehammer cracking a nut.

Within the conventional frame of exordium and peroration, Apuleius structures the content idiosyncratically but firmly under three separate issues. In the first section he rebuts attacks on the manner of his private life with the techniques of the public lecturer, regaling the court-president with disquisitions on 'The private innocence of the lascivious versifier', 'The proper deployment of the mirror', 'The enlightened master', 'The true nature of poverty', and interlarding these with a host of quotations from Greek and Latin poetry. Having comfortably established his cultural and moral superiority over his opponents, he proceeds to his second section, in which he demonstrates that the 'magical malpractices' were the zoological studies befitting a second Aristotle, the medical researches of an aspiring Hippocrates, and the religious devotions befitting a Roman Platonist. (The distinction drawn here between the devotee of magic and the true philosopher should be weighed by students of the *Metamorphoses*.) The third section crisply delineates events at Oea since the defendant's arrival, and in shattering the arguments of the prosecution Apuleius attains an urgency of argumentation worthy of Cicero himself.

The gulf which divides this proficient litigant from the forensic achievements of a Republican advocate is manifest in the more professorial style of address, in the occasionally outlandish diction, in the sudden bursts of luxuriant antithesis. But the effective technique in the later speech indicates how much Apuleius has learnt from the best orators. Cicero would have been proud to own him as a disciple.

The *Florida* (lit. 'Flowery things'), a collection of twenty-three extracts from published speeches and lectures, contains little of intrinsic interest but offers useful documentation on the activities and status of Apuleius after his return to Carthage. The few evidences of dating are confined to the 160s, and the snatches of civic addresses to Roman officials, references to tenure of the chief priesthood and to honorific statues, and the pungent odour of complacent self-satisfaction reveal him as the province's social lion of that decade. The passages have a homogeneity in that each is part of a personal exordium prefacing a speech or lecture, the content being polite philosophy for everyman. Apuleius makes his public appearances as the African Plutarch, discoursing now on the life-style of Hippias or Crates, now on the voyages of Pythagoras or the gymnosophists of India.

II

The extant philosophical works traditionally attributed to Apuleius are *De deo Socratis*, *De Platone et eius dogmate*, *De mundo*, Περὶ ἑρμηνείας, and *Asclepius*. The authenticity of the first is generally accepted, though the *praefatio* is now assigned to the *Florida*. Scholars have been divided about the second and third because of their less exuberant style, but this may be explicable not only by an earlier date but also by the likelihood that the *De deo Socratis* was *declaimed* whereas the other two were written with no epideictic intent for a reading public. The content and attitudes revealed in the works encourage attribution of them to Apuleius, as does identification of the author by the manuscripts and by Augustine. The Περὶ ἑρμηνείας ('On interpretation') has less well authenticated claims, for it appears in a separate manuscript-tradition, and is more jejune in content; it cannot however be dismissed out of hand as non-Apuleian. The *Asclepius* is a Latin translation by an unknown hand of a lost Greek hermetic work. This brief survey of Apuleius' importance as philosopher concentrates on the first three of the five treatises.

De deo Socratis ('On Socrates' god') is a thoroughly misleading title, for Apuleius' primary concern is to preach the existence of demons in general; the treatise has immense importance in the history of ideas as the most systematic exposition of the subject from the ancient world. With admirable clarity of structure the first section surveys the separated worlds of gods (visible stars and invisible members of the Pantheon) and of men; the second part describes the place of demons in the hierarchy of rational beings as intermediaries between the two. After outlining their role and nature, Apuleius assigns them into three classes. The first are souls within human bodies. The second have quitted human shape to become Lemures, Lares, Larvae, Manes. The third are wholly free of bodily connexions, being endowed with special powers and allotted specific duties. Somnus and Amor are offered as examples, the second being of particular interest to the student of the *Metamorphoses*. The nature of Socrates' demon forms the final section; Apuleius labels it *deus* because this is the word familiar to his readers from Cicero and Ovid. The protreptic conclusion exhorting those readers to embrace wisdom incorporates numerous motifs of the Roman diatribe from Horace and Seneca.

Though the treatise reflects familiarity with Plato, the subject of the hierarchy of intelligent creatures and their demarcated regions owes more to Plato's successors from Xenocrates onwards. The work is a contribution to a lively debate within Middle Platonism, perhaps a counterblast to the more rationalistic approach of an Albinus; for Apuleius is heir to Plutarch in his exploitation of the Platonist philosophy to justify popular piety and confidence in the beneficence of a transcendent god. The texture of the work, with its evocation of Latin poetry (Lucretius and Virgil are pervasive) and baroque Latinity, categorizes it as the *conférence brillante* of the literary salon. The author's fervid evangelism is overlaid with the bland veneer of the man of letters.

By contrast *De Platone et eius dogmate* ('On Plato and his doctrines') is written in the more restrained style appropriate to a summary of philosophical teaching composed for a reading public. The work is an outline in two books of Plato's physics and ethics. Such a synthesis if original would have been an impressive achievement. But the similar organization of topics in Albinus' teaching-manual of Plato's doctrines may indicate that both are reproducing with different emphases the schematic annotations of an earlier philosopher of the Middle Porch. Albinus, more professional, prefaces his discussion of Plato's physics and ethics with a section on logic; though Apuleius promises such a threefold analysis, Plato's logic is never treated. (It may have appeared in the lacuna at the end of Book 1, but more probably Apuleius found the subject too dry and abstruse. The gap between promise and performance has encouraged commentators from Cassiodorus onwards to regard Περὶ ἑρμηνείας as Apuleian.)

The discussion of Plato's physics is preceded by a hagiographical life, important as preceding the not dissimilar account of Diogenes Laertius. The treatment of physics is faithful to the *Timaeus* and *Republic*, but the explanation of ethical tenets owes more to the post-Platonist tradition. Middle Platonism, beginning with the eclectic Antiochus of Ascalon, had incorporated Peripatetic and Stoic elements into its developed system, and this later systematization Apuleius misleadingly attributes to Plato himself. The brief appendix on politics draws more faithfully on *Republic* and *Laws*. The importance of this treatise is twofold; it offers precious evidence of the intellectual history of Middle Platonism, and its bold simplifications provide leading indications of the author's intellectual and religious preoccupations, not to be ignored in analysis of the *Metamorphoses*.

De mundo ('On the world') likewise addressed to Faustinus, is a close adaptation (unacknowledged) of ps.-Aristotle's Περὶ κόσμου, which was composed about the time of the birth of Christ. The treatise is divided into two sections. The longer part is devoted to cosmology, beginning with an account of the aether and descending thereafter to various aspects of earth. After a bridging discussion on the harmony between constituent parts of the earth, the second section is devoted to theology; God, known to men under different names (compare the Isiac aretalogy in the final book of the *Metamorphoses*), animates and preserves all things. Systematic comparison with the original reveals how Apuleius has lent his translation a Roman flavour for his Roman audience. There is citation of Roman as well as Greek poetry. Various concordant aspects of city-life at Rome are adduced to exemplify the harmony in the larger world. Beyond these cultural changes, minor divergences reveal the translator's philosophical predilections. He stresses the higher significance of the theological facet, claiming that God can be known only through meditation. There is more emphasis than in the original on the concord in the world, and less on its eternity. The distinction in the Greek between God's transcendent *ousia* and his immanent *dunamis* is adapted to accommodate the demons of *De deo Socratis*. Style and latinity occupy a position intermediate between that of *De deo Socratis* and that of *De Platone*; occasional evocations and rhythmical riots reveal the characteristics of the first, but the general presentation is more akin to the sobriety of the second, perhaps lending substance to the notion that *De mundo* and *De Platone* were composed at Rome in the 150s.

III

It is right to treat Apuleius' novel as the climax of his work not because a late date is indisputable (though the probabilities support composition in Africa after 160) but because it is the most original and the most justifiably celebrated of his writings. Augustine remarks that Apuleius called it *Asinus aureus*, 'The golden ass', but the manuscript-evidence favours the title *Metamorphoses*. The plural would appear inapposite if the hero-narrator Lucius did not make it clear in the proem that the theme is transformation and restoration of 'men's shapes and fortunes'. So the title embraces not only Lucius' changes of shape but also his changes of fortune, above all his spiritual conversion; and it makes ancillary reference to the changes wrought in other characters like Thelyphron, experiencing a change of countenance, and Psyche, who achieves apotheosis.

In spite of its unusual aggregate of eleven books, the romance is carefully structured. In 1–3 Lucius describes how he visited Thessalian Hypata, embroiled himself in a casual affair with a slave-girl, persuaded her to assist his metamorphosis into a bird, and was accidentally changed into an ass; this initial section includes also Aristomenes' account of how his friend Socrates lost his life at the hands of a witch, Thelyphron's testimony of how his rash offer to guard a corpse led to his facial mutilation, and the episode of Lucius' 'trial' at the Festival of Laughter. The second section (4–7.14) describes how robbers drive the human donkey off to their mountain-lair, and how after an abortive attempt at escape with the kidnapped maiden Charite he is freed with her by her lover Tlepolemus; the lawless society of the brigands is depicted in three anecdotes, but the central feature is the tale of Psyche extending over two books, told to Charite by an old woman who tends the robbers. The third section (7.15–10) strings together the grisly, cruel and comic experiences of the ass as he works successively on a farm, with mendicant priests, in a bakery, in a market garden, and in the retinue of a landowner Thiasus; these experiences, prefaced with the pathetic tale of Charite's death, are interspersed with patterned episodes of conjugal infidelity and destructive magic. In the fourth and climactic section Lucius escapes the prospect of public copulation with a female criminal at Corinth by bolting to the nearby shore at Cenchreae. His prayer for deliverance is answered by Isis' promise that the morrow will bring deliverance. A priest in an Isiac procession duly proffers him roses; in gratitude for his restoration to human shape, Lucius becomes successively an initiate of Isis at Corinth and of Osiris at Rome.

Lucius in the prologue calls this a story adapted from the Greek (*fabula Graecanica*). The original Greek story, whose author the ninth-century patriarch Photius calls 'Lucius of Patrae', is now lost, but an abridged version of it appears in the works of Lucian, the most probable candidate for the authorship of the original. This short story, the *Onos* ('Ass'), reveals that Apuleius has followed the original narrative closely, but with two important enlargements. First, he has transformed the climax. In the Greek version the ass was taken not to Corinth but to Thessalonika, and he escaped public copulation with the female criminal by devouring rose-petals carried by a visitor in the amphitheatre; after restoration to human shape he eventually sailed home. So the entirely different climax in the Latin novel has been grafted on by Apuleius himself. Secondly, various anecdotes and episodes have been sewn into the original to fulfil Lucius' initial promise, *uarias fabulas conseram* 'I shall string together sundry tales'.

The extent to which Apuleius is responsible for this anecdotal material is controverted. Scholars' opinions range from the 'minimalist' position, in which little more than *Cupid and Psyche* and the more sentimental stories are conceded to him, to the more popular thesis, assumed in this discussion, that our novelist has transformed a Greek short story into a full-length romance by incorporation of all the episodes not contained in the *Onos*. It is relevant to remember here both that Apuleius was a professional collector of stories and that the works of Lucian offer astonishingly close indications of the kind of material available to Apuleius.

More important than speculation on the provenance of the individual stories is appreciation of the extraordinary transformation in purpose and tone achieved by Apuleius. The *Onos* reveals that Photius was wrong to regard the original Greek version as a serious story; though its plot hinges on the follies of curiosity and dabbling in magic, there is no moral censure. It is intended purely as entertainment, and the author concentrates on the erotic, sadistic, humorous and scabrous elements. Apuleius at the outset gives the impression that his treatment will be little different. Lucius promises stories told in the language of Miletus, which suggests a volume of risqué escapades after the manner of Aristides; and he offers to soothe the reader's friendly ear with 'elegant whispering'. 'Reader, please concentrate; you'll be delighted.' This programmatic promise, introduced to beguile and deceive, has lulled scholars innocent of Apuleius' evangelical enthusiasms into a false security. Below the sweetness of the fictions lies the usefulness of the message; the parallel with Rabelais' *Gargantua and Pantagruel* is striking. The *Metamorphoses* does not merely expand the original by incorporating a novel medley of spooky, bawdy and sentimental stories; it is also subtly articulated to become a fable with a religious moral.

The hero Lucius, who boasts Plutarch among his forbears, is a youth of good family and liberal education who is impelled by uncontrolled curiosity to seek knowledge of the world of magic through a casual sexual relationship. The anecdotes and additional episodes are artfully aligned to underline his culpability. *En route* to Hypata Aristomenes tells Lucius of the history of Socrates, who forgetful of his family bound himself sexually to Meroe the witch; this is the first warning against the combination of sorcery and sex. At Hypata, a meeting with Lucius' kinswoman Byrrhaena (who again recalls the connexion with Plutarch) reinforces the warning; the statuary in her house depicts the metamorphosis of Actaeon as punishment for curiosity, and Byrrhaena's warning against the witch Pamphile significantly echoes Aristomenes' description of Meroe. In spite of these cautions, Lucius rushes 'like a madman' to satisfy his curiosity by way of Photis the slave-girl's bed, 'however unsafe it proves to be'. Photis adds her ambivalent warning, and at Milo's dinner-table the flickering lamp and (ironically) Lucius' own story of the seer Diophanes should also have given him pause. At the dinner given by Byrrhaena Thelyphron appends his witness; he was a brash visitor to Hypata, like Lucius, and he suffered through underrating the malevolent powers of witches. Finally Lucius undergoes the humiliation of the mock-trial; he thinks he has killed three footpads on his drunken return to Milo's house, whereas he had merely perforated the inflated wineskins exemplifying Pamphile's powers as magician. None of these experiences deters the wilful curiosity of Lucius, with the resultant punishment that he changes himself into an ass.

The two main anecdotes in this section, told by Aristomenes and Thelyphron, are each an ingenious patchwork of different tales stitched together by the professional collector. In themselves they can be criticized for minor inconsistencies, but in their function as indicators of Lucius' weaknesses and as creators of the Hypatan atmosphere of malevolent magic they are most felicitous. But what was the precise nature of Lucius' fault indicated by these warnings? Critics are agreed that the *unhealthy* curiosity for knowledge through magic is central; the proper way to attain knowledge of God and the cosmos, to bridge the chasm between the human and the divine, is not by magic but by the healthy curiosity of study and meditation, a lesson which Plutarch's descendant should not have had to learn. But was the preliminary sexual romp also culpable? The exchanges with Photis are told with such verve that some critics discount sexual culpability. Yet Socrates, the primary *exemplum*, is reprehended for this fault, and in the final book the priest of Isis tells Lucius that his sufferings have been the 'unhappy price for unpropitious curiosity after your descent to slavish pleasures'. Lucius himself confesses the evil errors (*malis erroribus*) of his entanglement with Photis. We should be concerned here not with ancient attitudes in general to such sexual relationships but with the Platonist preoccupations of our author, who in a key passage of the *Apology* (12.1–5) distinguishes the true love of the few from the enslaved passions of beasts and mankind at large. Lucius' sin was chiefly curiosity but also lasciviousness.

The sufferings consequent upon this sinning follow the general pattern of the *Onos*. Of the two sections the first, played against the backcloth of the robbers' hideout, demonstrates the essential ambivalence of the novel. On the one hand the trinity of bandits' stories is recounted in a mock-serious tone undercutting the savagery of Lucius' experiences and encouraging the reader to interpret the romance as light-hearted escapism; on the other, the *conte* of Cupid and Psyche adds a mythological dimension to the serious theme of the romance. Artistically inserted at the heart of the book by Apuleius himself, it presents the experiences of Psyche in parallel with those of Lucius.

Versions of the folk-tale of the bride forbidden to gaze on her husband, who departs in anger when she breaks the taboo and whom she then seeks forlornly through the world, becoming reunited with him only after surmounting apparently impossible tasks imposed by a witch, were already widespread in Apuleius' day; a known North African variant is of particular interest. But no written version incorporating Cupid and Psyche as protagonists predates Apuleius. The likelihood is that our Platonist philosopher has created the story of the marriage, separation and reunification of the god of love and the maiden symbolizing the soul by fusing a version of the folk-tale with a developing motif of literature and art; for the poetry and sculpture of the Alexandrian age exploit that love of Eros and Psyche rooted in the *Phaedrus* and *Symposium*, the dialogues in which Plato depicts the attraction of the soul to the divine by the power of love.

Apuleius shapes the story round the naive curiosity of the ingenuous Psyche, whose jealous sisters plot her downfall. Though urgently warned by Cupid against such 'sacrilegious curiosity', she is persuaded to gaze on the sleeping form of her husband. The oil which in her agitation she spills from the lamp wakes him, and he flies away. Already pregnant, she sunders herself from earthly attachments by contriving the deaths of her sisters, and surrenders herself to the trials of Venus. The last of these is a journey to Proserpina in Hades, from whom she brings a box not to be opened; her 'rash curiosity' in disobeying this injunction renders her insensible, but Cupid rescues her. The child of their marriage in heaven is Voluptas. As Lucius listens to this story told to Charite, he hears without understanding his own history and his future deliverance. He too had been seduced by curiosity, and he too endures the weary pilgrimage, but Isis is to rescue him as Cupid rescues Psyche. He too will undertake a visit to Hades within the symbolism of the Egyptian mysteries, and the fruit of his mystical union with Isis will be *inexplicabilis uoluptas*, a pleasure which cannot be unfolded. Book 11 contains repeated echoes of the story of Psyche to underline that Lucius' relationship with Isis after his wanderings symbolically re-enacts the apotheosis of Psyche.

In the second section of Lucius' sufferings, in which the sequence of peripatetic experiences described in the *Onos* is retained, each adventure is presented as a facet of the degenerate world into which Lucius is plunged. For example, Apuleius enlarges the account of the ass's sufferings at the hands of the cruel boy to superimpose the final laceration of the boy by a bear, thus intensifying the sense of meaningless violence in the world. The radical change introduced to the story of Charite's death (accidental drowning in the original) illustrates the destructive madness induced by Thrasyllus' lust. When Lucius is sold to the eunuch-priests, the hazards experienced in their company from the hostility of both natural and supernatural forces are explored in a trinity of weird stories, and the debased religion of his masters is a further aspect of the corrupt world. The donkey's experiences with later owners repeatedly incorporate anecdotes of sexual promiscuity and destructive magic, themes of particular significance in Lucius' own history; the malevolence of Fortune is a recurring motif throughout, for those whose vision is bounded by the material world are subject to her arbitrary cruelties. But the tone is not one of unrelieved gloom. The artful ambivalence of comedy alternating with the sense of eery, irrational cruelty in the world continues.

Lucius finds his deliverance at the harbour of Cenchreae, a suburb of Corinth. Apuleius may have chosen this locale to achieve an effective contrast between a traditionally dissolute city and the purity of the Isiac regimen; more probably, however, his motive was a desire to describe a centre of Isiac worship with which he was personally acquainted. The existence of a temple to Isis at Cenchreae (and two others at Corinth) is attested by Pausanias and confirmed by archaeological discoveries. The novel now assumes an increasingly autobiographical flavour. In its final scene at Rome the hero, hitherto a Corinthian, refers to himself as a native of Madauros, the provenance of Apuleius himself. Though attempts have been made to explain away this embarrassing change of *patria*, scholars have usually concluded that the device is adopted to allow Apuleius to present a personal testament. In this final book there is no action beyond Lucius' reversion to human shape and his subsequent initiations; there is little dialogue or interplay with other characters. The exalted narrative is punctuated only by the occasional prayer or sermon. Thus the romance which initially masquerades as titillating entertainment and which unfolds as fable ends on an unabashed note of resounding apologetics, wholly contrasting in tone with the lighter touch of all that precedes.

So the initial prayer of Lucius proclaims Isis as the universal principle of female deity. The description of her appearance in the ensuing vision closely approximates to the iconography of the goddess, and her words exploit an aretalogy to indicate the range of her power and concern and her claim on Lucius' future life. This didactic presentation continues with the detailed description of the ritual and participants in the *Navigium Isidis*, in the course of which Lucius' resumption of human shape provides an occasion for hymning Isis' power afresh. The priest's review of Lucius' sinning and suffering carefully explains the role of Isis as 'the Fortune with eyes', service to whom is true liberty. The description of the temple-ritual incorporates protestations of loyalty to the Roman imperial system. There is an outline of the initiation-ceremony, followed by Lucius' prayer of thanksgiving and praise. The mere catalogue of the content of the final book disposes of the simplistic view that it is nothing more than a final marvel to round off the sequence of weird adventures. The explicit account of the Isiac theology, ritual and observance, recounted with none of the puckish exuberance marking the earlier adventures, is a teaching exercise, a recommendation of the Egyptian religion to a Roman audience. It is legitimate to speculate that it is occasioned by the meteoric growth of contemporary Christianity in North Africa as attested in the writings of Tertullian.

Such a judgement of the nature and purpose of the romance is supported by most modern critics through visualizing the author in the round. The *Apology* delineates the distinction between pursuit of the occult and genuine religious meditation, a distinction which is a central concern of the novel; but the essential key to its psychology resides in the attempt by Middle Platonists to reconcile their philosophy with the religious ideas of the Egyptians, and Plutarch's *De Iside et Osiride* is the most valuable testimony of this.

This treatise explains how and why the cult of Isis and Osiris is worthy of the Platonist's adhesion, and Apuleius' acceptance of the thesis is manifest in both *Apology* and *Florida*. It also offers a clue to the Platonist–Isiac interpretation of the ass-story, which probably originated in Egypt. Plutarch explains that in the dualistic system of Egyptian belief the ass resembles and is controlled by the Satanic principle of evil, Typhon. When Lucius is turned into an ass through magical practices he passes into the dominion of Typhon; and the completely new climax introduced to the novel, by which Apuleius following the example of Xenophon of Ephesus introduces the saving hand of Isis, provides an appropriate deliverance for an asinine Lucius enslaved by Typhon.

How far should this Platonist–Isiac interpretation be pressed? The romance begins with the request of Lucius to the reader 'not to disdain to inspect the Egyptian papyrus inscribed with the subtlety of the Nile reed', and this statement certainly invites symbolic interpretation. But two controlling factors counsel against excesses. The first is the fact that Apuleius follows closely the *Graecanica fabula*, which militates against detailed allegory; secondly, he writes for a lay readership immune from arcane allusion. The main lines of the story could be profitably exploited by the Middle Platonist. In addition to Isiac interpretation of the donkey's career, there is the condemnation of magical practices which becomes more comprehensible in the light of the theory of demonology outlined in *De deo Socratis*, and the animadversions on lust and greed which reflect a central preoccupation of Plato. Moreover, details and motifs introduced into the romance indicate Platonist–Isiac connexions, as when the Egyptian priest Zatchlas appears in the Thelyphron story, or again when Lucius' horse Candidus, implicitly contrasted with the tawny ass of Typhon and evoking the white steed of the tripartite soul in the *Phaedrus*, turns up quite superfluously in the final book. But to interpret the whole romance as a coded aretalogy strains all credibility. Photis is a most improbable 'mystagogic-allegorical figure' antithetic to the true light of Isis; and again the aedile Pythias' command to the vendor to jump on Lucius' fish in the market seems impossibly recondite as an indication of a religious attitude. Similarly the story of Psyche can be generally accepted as Platonist allegory of the progress of the soul, with allusions to the Isiac initiation in the final book, but the suggestion that every detail is invested with mystological significance fails to persuade because the folk-tale cannot sustain such a close-knit interpretation, and even if it could Apuleius' intended readers would have failed to comprehend it.

The characterization in the novel firmly subserves its purpose. Lucius inevitably has a static role. As a man he learns nothing, and becomes an ass; as an ass he evinces no moral progress (how could he?), and his rescue is attributable to an impulsive prayer. Photis (her name is derived from the Greek for 'light', so she is contrapuntal to Lucius, derived from *lux*) is more romantically and sentimentally depicted than is Palaestra ('Wrestling-arena'), the slave-girl of the original. Milo is more miserly, Pamphile ('Love-all') more horrific than their counterparts in the Greek romance. The characters in the inserted anecdotes (their names usually by etymology or historical association indicate their role, sometimes ironically) are frequently inconsistently drawn, partly because Apuleius takes pleasure in welding together different tales, partly because his main effort goes into the alignment of the anecdote with the main plot. So, for example, the widow in the story of Thelyphron, the stepmother in the 'Phaedra' tale (10.2ff.), the female criminal (10.23ff.) all undergo implausible changes of character.

The audience envisaged by Apuleius was one of highly educated Romans. As in Petronius the texture of the story can be highly literary, evoking a wide range of Greek and Latin authors for the pleasure of sophisticated readers. Psyche, for example, not only recalls by her appearance the heroines of the Greek love-romances but also by the nature of her wanderings reincarnates the Io of Aeschylus' dramas, and in her progress through Hades evokes the similar journey of Aeneas. The literary model for Charite's psychological anguish as she prepares suicide is Virgil's Dido. There are scenes in which the more histrionic aspects of forensic speeches are parodied for comic effect, as in the 'trial' at the Festival of Laughter, and again in the speech by the cruel boy's mother after his death (7.27). The novel abounds also in legal quips and jocose references to the activities and interests of the senatorial class at Rome.

The style of the *Metamorphoses*, paralleled in parts of the *Florida* and *De deo Socratis*, is profitably analysed in the company of Fronto and Gellius. The studied artificiality and verbal extravagance which mark all three are not attributable to a peculiar African tradition (though Apuleius' trilingualism in Punic, Greek, and Latin may have fostered a tendency towards exotic diction) but rather to the epideictic tendencies of the Second Sophistic. The *elocutio nouella* associated with the three writers consists of the artistic collocation of words of arresting novelty – a combination of archaisms and Graecisms, vulgarisms and neologisms. The language of comedy is frequently exploited in dialogue, especially where the homely, old-fashioned flavour is apposite to the characters. Occasionally the etymological sense of a word is restored with bizarre effect; Cupid, for example, is not only *inuisus* ('unseen') but also *inhumanus* ('divine'). The influence of Asianic oratory, so marked in the Greek novels of Achilles Tatius and Longus, is even stronger in Apuleius, inspiring the rhythmical, rhyming riots of double, triple and quadruple phrases and clauses, consummately balanced by isocolon, homoioteleuton, alliteration, and assonance.

The influence of Apuleius' novel on European literature since the Italian Renaissance has been profound. Boccaccio helped to popularize it by transcribing the Monte Cassino manuscript with his own hand. Within fifty years of the invention of printing, editions had appeared in several Italian cities and at Paris, and the sixteenth century introduced influential translations in Italian, Spanish, French, German and English. Apuleius was the most powerful single influence at the birth of the picaresque novel in Spain; *Lazarillo de Tormes*, Alemán's *Guzmán*, Úbeda's *La pícara Justina* and other early works of fiction appropriate incidents from the *Metamorphoses* which are told by the peripatetic servant in the I-narrative with frequent allusions to the asinine forbear. *Cupid and Psyche* has its own distinguished history at the hands of Boccaccio, Calderón, La Fontaine, Heywood, Beaumont, Marmion, to name only a few. Many of Apuleius' ironical anecdotes are incorporated in Italian and French collections of such tales. Finally, the florid, ornamental texture of Apuleius' language had its imitators in the Euphuistic romances of Lyly and his successors.

VII

EPILOGUE

The primary aim of any literary history is to foster a deeper appreciation of the creative writing which it describes; to define the qualities of the works themselves must be its main concern. Roman literature, however, demands the reader's attention for a second reason, because more than any other national literature it has dictated the forms and modes of thought of subsequent European letters. For more than fifteen centuries after Virgil and Livy, Latin remained the learned language of Europe, constantly evoking the great *auctores* of the classical period. Then, side by side with the Latin writings of the High Middle Ages and the Renaissance, the vernacular literatures of the twelfth to the sixteenth centuries likewise boast their proud descent from the antique Romans, who continue to breathe inspiration into Western letters after the Renaissance. This epilogue concerns itself chiefly with the medieval period and the more important classical influences within it.

The ways in which the Latin classics impinged on the imaginative experience of later generations were shaped by a complex of political, economic and social factors but above all by the emergence of dominant Christian thinkers in the fourth-century West. These Christian leaders, emerging shortly after the establishment of Christianity as the favoured religion of the state, exploited their education in classical eloquence to proclaim the superiority of Christian beliefs over traditional Roman values. As Christians they inherited attitudes towards classical literature in which the denunciation of a Tertullian rang louder than the approval of a Lactantius; as educated Romans they found their modes of thought and powers of expression moulded by the authors they sought to reject. Thus in Africa, Italy, Gaul, Spain an ambivalence towards classical literature is evinced not only in the same milieux but even in the same individuals. The Ambrose who proclaimed that the scriptures contained all necessary instruction was the Ambrose who exploited Cicero's *De officiis* for his *De officiis ministrorum*. The Jerome who asks *quid facit cum Apostolo Cicero?* 'What has Cicero to do with Paul?', is the Jerome whose justification of classical studies elsewhere encourages later churchmen in their pursuit of them. The Paulinus who bids Ausonius reject the pagan Muses and spurns the voices of

Terence and Virgil is the Paulinus who adapts the genres of classical poetry to the proclamation of the Christian message. The Augustine whose *De doctrina Christiana* sponsors the teaching of the liberal arts is the Augustine who later argues against their relevance for the Christian life.

This ambivalence remains characteristic of much Christian thinking throughout the Middle Ages, for clerics are susceptible to the 'humanist' enthusiasm of men like Prudentius and Cassiodorus on the one side, and to the condemnations of those like Gregory the Great ('The same lips cannot sound the praises of both Jupiter and Christ') on the other. Even Alcuin, whose verses so often evoke Virgil and who is known by the soubriquet Flaccus at Charlemagne's court, can reprimand his monks for enjoying Virgil in private. But by the ninth century the value of classical literature, initially as ancillary to biblical study but increasingly as inculcating higher cultural standards in both state and church, is almost universally recognized.

Utilitarian functions rather than literary qualities dictate the pattern of survival and study of texts up to the Renaissance, as the contents of libraries at York, Corbie and Lorsch demonstrate. Lyric and love-elegy lie below ground; Catullus, Tibullus, Propertius appear only occasionally in a catalogue or isolated quotation, though Horace's *Odes* become popular from the eleventh century, and Ovid's fame is even more widespread subsequently. The fiction of Petronius and Apuleius, irrelevant to Christian education, is ignored till the Renaissance, when Apuleius aids the creation of the Spanish picaresque novel. The letters of Cicero and Pliny remain virtually unread until the fourteenth century. The didactic epic of Lucretius, closely studied by Christian savants like Lactantius and Prudentius, vanishes subsequently till rediscovered by Poggio.

The most pervasive classical genre throughout the medieval period was epic, and the epic poet dominating the millennium was Virgil. Evoked or echoed on almost every page by Prudentius and Paulinus, exploited by practitioners of biblical and courtly epic in the late Empire, allegorized by Fulgentius in the sixth century as by Bernard Silvester in the twelfth, Augustine's *poeta nobilissimus* reaches the summit of his glory in the Carolingian age, the *aetas Vergiliana*. Subsequently, he continues to be the model of epic poets, both Latin and vernacular. Dante signals his supremacy by greeting Virgil as 'lo mio maestro e il mio autore', and the *Aeneid* likewise inspires the epics of Camoens, Tasso and Milton. But if Virgil is the sun, lesser stars of Roman epic twinkle round him. Lucan's colourful style won him regular imitators from Lactantius to the Renaissance, and Dante places him with Homer, Horace and Ovid in the reception-party for Virgil in Hades. Statius' *Thebaid* is another perennial favourite for its flavour of mythological romance and its allegorical mode. Claudian is not continually popular, but his poetry is familiar especially to twelfth-century *literati*.

Of the epic composed between the ninth and thirteenth centuries, five works stand out proclaiming their debt to classical Roman poetry. *Waltharius*, composed in the late ninth century by the Geraldus cited in the prologue, is a romantic epic which in structure recalls Statius' *Thebaid* and in texture reveals (on occasion with ironical humour) close acquaintance with Virgil. *Ruodlieb*, the German epic of romantic chivalry composed in the eleventh century, incorporates imitations of Virgil and of Virgil's Christian imitator Prudentius. The three other poems signal the range of twelfth-century epic. Alan of Lille's *Anticlaudianus* is a philosophical epic which proclaims a connexion with Claudian's *In Rufinum*, but which in texture effortlessly evokes the whole sweep of Roman epic poets. As mythological epic Joseph of Exeter's *Frigii Daretis Yliados libri sex* likewise contains ubiquitous echoes of Virgil, Lucan, Statius and Claudian. Walter of Châtillon's *Alexandreis* exemplifies historical epic, the versification of Curtius Rufus by a learned poet with echoes of Roman epic at his mind's command.

In this survey of the epic tradition the *Metamorphoses* must not be forgotten, but Ovid merits separate discussion. His virtuosity with the elegiac couplet is widely imitated by Christian versifiers from the fourth to the sixth centuries; Venantius Fortunatus, for example, adapts Ovidian techniques for both polite verse-epistles and religious verses, presenting the great Pauline paradoxes (death to the world as spiritual life, the dead wood of the Cross as a living tree) in the Ovidian manner. Though little read in Ireland and England from the sixth to the eighth centuries, Ovid was a model for composition for learned Carolingians, and during the eleventh to the thirteenth centuries (the *aetas Ovidiana*) became the most influential representative of Roman letters. His role as *magister amoris curialis* 'master of courtly love' begins with the churchmen Marbod, Baudry, and Hildebert, who in verse-epistles and epigrams deploy Ovidian rhythms and tricks of style in essaying chaster themes. Subsequently, in the less inhibited, more secularized twelfth-century France, Ovid is echoed constantly in the classicizing poems and in the rhythmical rhyming verses of medieval lyric – in Hugo of Orléans, in the Archpoet, in Walter of Châtillon, in the numerous collections of anonymous versifiers preserved in such collections as the *Carmina Burana*.

But turn the coin, and the love-practitioner of the *Ars amatoria* and the *Heroides* assumes a more sober demeanour. The myth of creation in the *Metamorphoses* is deployed by Bernard Silvester and his fellow-Chartrians to launch the figure of *Ovidius physicus*. A stream of commentators – Manegold of Lautenbach in the eleventh century, Arnoul of Orléans in the twelfth, John of Garland's *Integumenta Ovidii* in the thirteenth, the vernacular poem *Ovide moralisé* in the fourteenth – allegorizes the *Metamorphoses* to unveil the *Ovidius mythographus*. The *florilegia* which assemble his moral tags are the basis of

Ovidius ethicus. Not surprisingly therefore this teacher of physics, ethics, and allegory is depicted as a Christian in the pseudo-Ovidian *De vetula* (*c*. 1260), and the popular derivation of his name (*Ouidius quasi ouum diuidens, id est occultum reserans* 'Ovid, because he splits the egg, in other words uncovers what is hidden') alludes to him as the fountainhead of knowledge.

Third in importance in medieval influence come the satirists Horace, Persius and Juvenal, perennially popular from the later Empire to the Renaissance both as models for classroom-composition and as critics of human folly. When satire as a genre emerges in the self-critical society of twelfth-century France, this trinity constantly hovers near.

Flaccus Horatius et Cato, Persius et Iuuenalis
Quid facerent, rogo, si foret his modo uita sodalis?

Horatius Flaccus, Cato, Persius, Juvenal – what would they do, I ask, if they shared the life of today?

asks Bernard of Cluny in *De contemptu mundi*. The targets of satire are those pilloried by Juvenal and his Christian imitator Jerome – sexual vice, the monstrous regiment of women, gluttony in food and drink, the avarice and meanness of the powerful – but within the changed framework of the Christian ecclesiastical establishment. When Nigel Longchamps in his *Speculum stultorum* and other satirists berate the vices of monks and clerics, Juvenal naturally comes through more loudly than Horace and Persius. But the greatest medieval satirist, Walter of Châtillon, using rhythmical rhyming measures, constantly underpins pungent attacks on his society with evocations of all three. The technique is particularly impressive in poems like *Missus sum in uineam*, where Walter ends each stanza with a line from Horace, Persius, Juvenal, Ovid, or other *auctor*. Martial is another popular model for the satirical epigram of this period.

Pastoral poetry in classical Rome had been dominated by Virgil; flanked by Calpurnius Siculus and Nemesianus (whose work was much studied in the Carolingian age), his *Eclogues* have a curious after-history in which the Arcadian *pastor* and his sheep merge with the ecclesiastical *pastor gregis*. In the Carolingian age, Alcuin's 'cuckoo'-poems are Virgilian pastiche spoken by Virgilian shepherds in description of the life of the palace-school. Sedulius Scottus likewise uses the eclogue-form to describe the circle of bishop Hartgar at Liège. But the most influential ninth-century adaptation of Virgilian pastoral was the *Ecloga Theoduli*, in which the shepherd Pseustis and shepherdess Alithia ('Deceit' and 'Truth') recommend respectively pagan mythology and biblical truth in bucolic contest. In the twelfth century the eclogues of 'M. Valerius', usually regarded merely as literary exercises, are better interpreted as facets of clerical experience in a courtly milieu. The classical formulation of pastoral now exists side by side with the Latin pastourelle which emerges from imitation of Provençal poetry.

The absence of secular drama from the medieval stage spelt neglect of Roman dramatists. Seneca's tragedies had considerable literary influence in the late Roman period, conspicuously in Boethius' *Consolation of philosophy*, in which the verses constantly echo Senecan odes. But subsequently the plays are known only to widely-read scholars, to an Aldhelm in Anglo-Saxon England, to a Eugenius Vulgarius in ninth-century Italy, and later to a Liutprand, a Papias, a Richard de Fourneval. The fame of Seneca comes later with the Italian humanists, the Elizabethan dramatists and with Corneille. Of the comic playwrights, Plautus throughout the Middle Ages remained less known even than Seneca, but by contrast Terence was a favourite author, because of his philosophic reflections on the human condition. Terence inspires the dramas of the tenth-century nun Hrotsvitha, whose six plays on Christian themes reflect in structure and dialogue the influence of the *Andria* and to a lesser degree the *Eunuch* and *Adelphoe*. In the twelfth century Ovidian narrative-comedies become popular, deriving their themes from Plautus and Terence through prose-summaries of the plays. Vitalis of Blois wrote an *Amphitruo* and an *Aulularia*, Matthew of Vendôme a *Miles gloriosus*; an unknown author's *Pamphilus et Gliscerium* derives from the *Andria*. The Renaissance established a vogue for the Roman comic playwrights as for Seneca; translations of their plays, and original Latin plays based on them, were performed in Venice and other Italian cities.

Cicero dominates the study of rhetoric. He was a special favourite of the Christian apologists Lactantius and Jerome, whose seven polemical treatises echo Ciceronian phraseology and techniques. Gradually, however, Cicero's speeches fell out of general currency, though in the Carolingian period the best-read scholars like Sedulius Scottus and Lupus of Ferrières knew one or another of them; Christian eloquence had different objectives. Augustine initiated Christian theory on the art of preaching; epistolary style, extending more generally into rules for artistic prose, became important from the eleventh century: and the theory of poetic composition was also extensively discussed. The bases of instruction for all three were the *De inventione* of Cicero and the *ad Herennium*, known familiarly as *Rhetorica prima* and *Rhetorica secunda*; Horace's *Ars poetica* is also important for poetic theory. The *De inventione* fathers innumerable manuals between the fourth and thirteenth centuries. Of other classical treatises, Cicero's *Brutus* remained unread, but his *De oratore* and Quintilian's *Institutio* were known to the best scholars from Lupus of Ferrières to John of Salisbury, whose contemporary Ulrich of Bamberg remarks: *In rethorica educandus legat primam Tullii rethoricam, et librum ad Herennium, et Tullium de oratore, et causas Quintiliani* [the ps.-Quintilian] *et Quintilianum de oratoris institutione* 'So far as rhetoric goes, the person to be instructed should read the first rhetorical treatise of Cicero, the volume to Herennius, Tully's *On the orator*, the cases of Quintilian and Quintilian's *On the education of the orator*.'

The fate of the classical historians has little relevance to their quality. Tacitus, largely unread in the third century when the emperor of the same name had copies made *ne lectorum incuria deperiret* 'so that the historian should not be lost through the indifference of readers', might have vanished for ever through neglect but for the vigilance of Renaissance humanists. Livy's massive history was epitomized within a century of his death, and the summaries ousted all but the earlier romantic sections of political and martial glory. These early books were studied by scholars of the Carolingian and Ottonian periods, and from the eleventh century appear increasingly in library-catalogues; it is difficult to affirm positively that in the golden age of medieval historiography historians like William of Malmesbury had read Livy, but the general presentation and especially the prominence of the speeches strongly suggest it. But Livy becomes a giant only with the new dawn of Petrarch and Boccaccio, Bruni and Machiavelli. Before the Renaissance only Sallust of the major historians was widely known, being studied for his simpler style and heavier moralizing. He is an important model for historians from the tenth to the twelfth century, such as Richer, William of Poitiers, and the author of *Vita Heinrici IV Imperatoris*. The close imitation of Suetonius' *Vitae* by Einhard's *Life of Charlemagne* was exceptional; the Roman biographer was not widely studied. Caesar too was a neglected author, though known to Bede, Einhard, William of Poitiers and William of Malmesbury. The fact is that Christian historiography has other models for histories of church and people, especially Eusebius, Orosius, and (for biography) Sulpicius Severus.

Popular philosophy as represented by Cicero and Seneca forms a pervasive strand of medieval thought, the vocabulary of which owes much to Ciceronian innovation. Cicero is influential chiefly as transmitter of Hellenistic philosophical ideas to the increasingly Greekless Christians of the west. Augustine's celebrated tribute to the *Hortensius* (now lost) as the work which converted him to philosophy, Macrobius' commentary on the *Somnium Scipionis*, Boethius' interest in Ciceronian logic exemplify different facets of his influence in late antiquity, but the chief importance of Cicero as of Seneca lies in the formulation of Stoic ethical ideas, much of which graduated into Christian moral theology. At the apogee of medieval philosophy, thinkers from Abélard to Aquinas repeatedly signal their respect for the two pagan *auctores*. For Abélard, Cicero is *maximus philosophorum latinorum* 'the greatest of the Latin philosophers', and Seneca *summus inter uniuersos philosophos morum praedicator* 'the greatest of all philosophers as a preacher of manners'. The psychological and ethical sections of Aquinas' *Summa theologiae*, which attempt to reconcile the re-emergent Aristotle with the traditional Stoic–Christian position, repeatedly quote from the *Tusculans* and from the *De officiis*, which was the main source for ancient ethical theory till Aristotle was rediscovered. The *De amicitia* is another seminal work of Cicero, repeatedly quoted in treatises on human and divine love. Though no scholar before William of Malmesbury knew the entire corpus of Seneca's *Moral epistles*, his work was studied in more restricted compass in the schools and the monasteries, and the *Quaestiones naturales* inspired a treatise of the same title by Adelard of Bath.

This brief sketch reveals how vital the study of the classical authors is for a thorough understanding of the central intellectual concerns of the Middle Ages. The scholar who carries forward his knowledge of the Roman authors, and complements this secular learning with a knowledge of the Latin Bible and the Fathers, will have the indispensable tools for an understanding of medieval literature.

APPENDICES

The authors in the following Appendix are listed in the order in which they occur in the main text, with the exception of Seneca the Elder who is to be found on p. 935.

INDEX TO GENERAL BIBLIOGRAPHIES

APPENDIX OF AUTHORS AND WORKS

ANDRONICUS, LUCIUS LIVIUS

LIFE

(1) Name. Livius, L. Livius, or Livius Andronicus in extant sources. The name T. Livius (twice in Nonius, once in Jerome) is presumed to be an error due to confusion with the Augustan historian. That he was called L. Livius Andronicus is strictly an inference.

(2) Status and origin. Apparent implication of these *tria nomina* is that the poet was a Greek by birth, named Andronikos, that somehow he became a slave in the household of a Roman Livius, and that he was manumitted and became a *ciuis libertinus* with the *praenomen* Lucius; he might, however, be the son of such a person. Accius in his *Didascalica* (reported by Cic. *Brut.* 72 and Jerome, *Chron.* 187 B.C.) said that he was a native of Tarentum and came to Rome in 209 B.C. when the city was taken by the Romans (Livy 27.15–16; for problems in the Cicero passage see A. E. Douglas, *M. Tulli Ciceronis Brutus* (Oxford 1966) 62–4); further, that he was granted his freedom by M. Livius Salinator (he has in mind the victor of the battle at the Metaurus in 207 B.C., *RE* 33), as a reward for teaching his children (cf. Suet. *De gramm. et rhet.* 1 for A. as teacher).

(3) Career according to Accius. Most circumstantially documented fact in A.'s life is that in 207 B.C. he composed or re-used a ritual hymn to be sung by thrice nine girls in procession; during a rehearsal the temple of Juno Regina on the Aventine was struck by lightning; as an important part of the especially elaborate rite of expiation which the curule aediles ordered, the girls performed A.'s hymn in procession to Juno's temple (Livy 27.37, cf. 31.12). This happened shortly before Salinator's important victory at the Metaurus, and retrospectively this was seen as the time at which Juno had given up her hostility to the Trojans and their descendants (cf. Ennius, *Ann.* (8) 291 V = *ROL* 293). As a result the *scribae* and *histriones* were given the right to hold official meetings in the Temple of Minerva on the Aventine and make offerings (Festus p. 448 L; see p. 84). On Accius' view this would have been the beginning, not the end of A.'s public life; and Cicero (loc. cit.) makes it clear that Accius thought A.'s first play was not produced until the votive games of his patron Salinator at the *ludi Iuventutis* in 197 B.C. (so Cicero; Livy dates the games to 191 B.C.,

36.36.5). Jerome unreliably puts A.'s *floruit* in 187 B.C. Other traces of this Accian account of A.'s career in Porcius Licinus fr. 1 *FPL* p. 44 (arrival of the Muse at Rome during Second Punic War), Hor. *Epist.* 2.1.162 (tragedy developed after Punic Wars), Valerius Antias *ap.* Livy 36.36.5 (first *ludi scaenici* those of 191 B.C.; untrue), and in failure of Volcacius Sedigitus to mention A. at all in his list of the best comic poets, not even *antiquitatis causa* (fr. 3 *FPL* pp. 46f.).

(4) View of Varro, Atticus and Cicero. Cicero (*Brut.* 72) refutes Accius' view on A.'s chronology by alleging that A. was the first to produce a play and did so in 240 B.C. the year before Ennius' birth (cf. *Tusc.* 1.1.3). For this he cites the authority of Atticus (in his *Liber annalis*), who was in turn following Varro in his *De poetis* (cf. Gell. 17.21.42), and 'old *commentarii*' which Cicero himself had seen, presumably documents like those which gave 204 B.C. as date of Naevius' death (*Brut.* 60). Status of these documents is important but indeterminable: it would be sanguine to suppose they were official contemporary records, but they must have been older than the Gracchan era, because Cicero commends them as old in order to imply that their authority was better than that of Accius. Other reflections of Varro's opinion in Cassiodorus *Chron.* who speaks of a tragedy and comedy put on at the Roman Games in 239, not 240 B.C., and the *Glossae Salomonis* (9–10th c., St Gall) 7 (*CGF* I Kaibel p. 72; H. Usener, 'Vergessenes', *Rh.M.* 28 (1973) 418 = *Kleine Schriften* III (Berlin 1914) 37), *tragoedias comoediasque primus egit idemque etiam composuit Liuius Andronicus duplici toga infulatus*, as well as in Gellius (loc. cit.: *primus omnium L. Liuius fabulas docere Romae coepit*), and in the unreliable source used by Livy in his account of the growth of Roman drama (7.2.4ff., see p. 78), who in passing also mentions A. as he *qui ab saturis ausus est primus argumento fabulam serere.* On Varro's fondness for *primi inuentores* see H. Dahlmann, *Abh. Akad. Mainz* 1970, 94f. Under this label it is easy to confuse 'earliest known' and 'ultimate originator', and it is not clear what Varro meant, for if it was his claim that A. was the first to adapt Greek plays for the Latin stage, or the earliest known, it is rather odd that none of the citations make this explicit by using some such expression as *uertit ex graeco*. Evidently it was not being claimed that he invented the iambo-trochaic metres of dialogue and recitative or the quantitative polymetry of *cantica* (to the performance of which, however, Livy (loc. cit.) would have it that he made changes of presentation, see p. 79).

(5) Modern interpretation of chronology. Accius alone is our authority for the Tarentine origin of A. and for his connexion with the Livii Salinatores in particular; for Cicero *Brut.* 72 does not attribute belief in either of these points to Atticus, and they appear nowhere in the remains of the Varronian account. As Cicero's sole concern was to demonstrate what he believed to be a gross error on Accius' part as regards chronology, his silence on these two points cannot be interpreted either as affirming or denying the claims that A. was a Tarentine and a slave of the Salinatores. Nevertheless scholars generally accept that A. did come from Tarentum and that Accius has confused the assault on Tarentum in 272 B.C. with its capture in 209 B.C. In this case A. would have been a slave of the grandfather of the Salinator whom Accius

had in mind. The superficial attraction of this would be that it allows one to reconcile and partly account for the widely discrepant sources; a difficulty which arises, however, is that in this case we must suppose that A. can hardly have been born later than 290 B.C., for otherwise he could not have acquired the education which he exploited at Rome, and therefore that he must have been a very old man in 207 B.C. when he composed his *carmen*. H. B. Mattingly (*C.Q.* n.s.7 (1957) 159–63) would see Livy 27.37 and 31.12 as confused, Festus p. 448 L as wrong, and Cic. *Sen.* 50 as implying that A. died *c.* 215 B.C., so that the *carmen* of 207 B.C. would be a revival of a work composed for an earlier occasion. However, even if A. had been born *c.* 300 B.C. (so Mattingly), it is not beyond belief that he should have still been alive and active (like Sophocles) in his nineties; nor is Mattingly's treatment of Livy and Festus satisfactory. G. Marconi (*M.A.L.* 8.12.2 (1966) 125–213) asserts the authenticity of Accius' account: A.'s arrival as a slave at Rome from Tarentum 209 B.C.; hymn, 207 B.C.; stage-début, 197 B.C.; *floruit* 187 B.C. See review by H. B. Mattingly, *Gnomon* 43 (1971) 680–7. If Accius is to be saved at all costs from a gross blunder in his dating – and Mattingly and Marconi overestimate his quality as a scholar – it would seem better to raise the question whether perhaps there were not two Livii Andronici, father and son, whose activity stretched from the middle of the third century into the second decade of the second and whom history has confused.

WORKS

(1) *Odusia* (*Odyssey*), an adaptation in saturnians of Homer; undated; *c.* forty-five fragmentary lines. (2) *Fabulae palliatae* (comedies). *Gladiolus* (from an *Enchiridion* 'The dagger'; Menander's was famous, cf. S. Charitonides, L. Kahil, R. Ginouvès, *Les mosaïques de la maison du Ménandre*, *Antike Kunst* VI (Bern 1970) pl. 4, though there were others by Philemon and Sophilus); *Ludius* ('The player'?); *Livius in* †*Virgo*. Half a dozen citations. (3) *Fabulae crepidatae* (tragedies). *Achilles*, *Aegisthus* (*TRF* 38 = *ROL* 38 ~ Aesch. *Choeph.* 897f.), *Aiax mastigophorus* (*TRF* 16f. = *ROL* 16f. ~ Soph. *Aj.* 1266f.), *Andromeda*, *Danae*, *Equos Troianus* (both also titles of plays by Naevius), *Hermiona*, *Tereus*. About 140 fragmentary lines. (4) Apotropaic hymn (sung in honour of Juno 207 B.C.). (5) *Ino* falsely attributed to A. by Terentianus Maurus, *GLK* VI 383 (line 1931); the four extant lines are by Laevius. (6) [Evanthius], *De comoedia* 5.1.4 (Donatus vol. I p. 23 Wessner) states that A. not only invented comedy and tragedy but also the *togata*. (7) *Carmen Nelei* 'Poem about Neleus', five fragmentary citations all in Festus except one from Charisius (*GLK* I 84) who quotes as if from A.; the work was regarded as ancient and anonymous in antiquity and it is not clear whether it was a play or a narrative poem.

BIBLIOGRAPHY

TEXTS: (1) COMPREHENSIVE: *ROL* II 2–43; M. Lenchantin de Gubernatis (Turin 1937). (2) 'ODUSIA': *FPL* 7–17; S. Mariotti (Milan 1952: with essay; text 93ff.), cf. O. Skutsch, *C.R.* n.s.4 (1954) 252–4. (3) TRAGEDIES: *TRF* 1–7. COMEDIES: *CRF* 3–5.

STUDIES: COMPREHENSIVE: Leo, *Gesch.* 55–75; E. Fraenkel, *RE* suppl. v (1931) 598–607 (valuable remarks on style). LIFE AND CHRONOLOGY: Mattingly and Marconi cited under *Life* (5) above; W. Beare, 'When did Livius Andronicus come to Rome?', *C.Q.* 34 (1940) 11–19, cf. *The Roman stage*, 3rd ed. (London 1964) 25–32; W. Suerbaum, *Untersuchungen zur Selbstdarstellung älterer römischen Dichter* (Hildesheim 1968) 1–12, 297–300 (full doxography); J.-H. Waszink, 'Zum Anfangsstadium der römischen Literatur', *ANRW* 1.2 869–902 (important survey). 'ODYSSEY': S. Mariotti, under *Texts* above; G. Broccia, *Ricerche su Livio Andronico epico* (Padua 1974); A. Traina, 'Sulla Odyssia di Livio Andronico', *Paideia* 8 (1953) 185–92, rev. ed. in *Vortit barbare* (Rome 1970) 10–28. TRAGEDIES: H.-J. Mette, *Lustrum* 9 (1964) 41–50. COMEDIES: J. Wright, *Dancing in chains: the stylistic unity of the comoedia palliata* (Rome 1974) 15–32.

NAEVIUS, GNAEUS

LIFE

Served in First Punic War (Gell. 17.21.45, quoting N. himself) and was therefore born *c.* 285–260 B.C. Either a Capuan with Roman *ciuitas sine suffragio* by birth until city's disgrace in 211 B.C. (connexion severed because of Capua's having sided with Hannibal), or from area of Capua and belonging to a community *nominis Latini*, 'of the Latin name', allied to Rome (inference from Gell. 1.24). Varro had evidence of some sort that N. produced *fabulas* (for the first time) in 235 B.C. (Gell. 17.21.45). N. had a reputation for outspokenness, and in 1st c. B.C. there was an evidently widespread story that he had crossed verbal swords with the Metelli and had suffered punishment. Story apparently referred to the consulship of Q. Caecilius Metellus (*RE* 81) in 206 B.C., but its details are too ill-preserved for it to be reconstructed or evaluated; see Cic. *Verr.* 1.29 with ps.-Ascon. *ad loc.*; [Caesius Bassus], *GLK* VI 265; Gell. 3.3; Jerome, *Chron.* 201 B.C.; Plaut. *M.G.* 209–12 with Festus p. 32 L s.v. 'barbari'. Varro found it written in 'old *commentarii*' (see also under Andronicus) that N. died in 204 B.C., but regarded this as erroneous (perhaps because he saw that really this date was only the latest record of a new Naevius-play) and extended his life 'longius' (Cic. *Brut.* 60); Jerome (*Chron.* 201 B.C., of dubious value) put his death in that year at Utica, where he had gone into 'exile'.

WORKS

(1) *Bellum Poenicum* (*Punicum*) in saturnians represented by *c.* sixty fragments. Originally undivided, the work was presented in seven *libri* by Octavius Lampadio, a scholar of the mid-2nd c. B.C. (Suet. *De gramm. et rhet.* 2), and it is from this version

that the citations (almost all due to grammarians) come; third of total come from bk 1.

(2) *Fabulae palliatae* (*c.* 130 fragmentary verses, almost all in iambo-trochaic metres). Thirty-four titles known: *Tarentilla*, 'The girl from Tarentum', is easily the best represented (more than twenty fragmentary verses). Others: *Acontizomenos* 'Struck by a spear' (from Dionysius' play of that name?); *Agitatoria* 'The driver-play'; *Agrypnuntes* 'Sleepless nights'; *Apella* 'The Jew' (?); *Ariolus* 'The soothsayer' (not to be taken as an Italian *togata*); †*Assitogiola* (*CRF* 25 = Naevius *com. ROL* 103); *Asteiologia* 'The art of wit' (?): this citation is the only lyric fragment of a Naevian comedy, cf. E. Fraenkel, *Elementi plautini in Plauto* (Florence 1960) 327); *Carbonaria* 'The charcoal comedy' (Menander's *Epitrepontes*? Plautus is credited with this play too); *Clamidaria* 'The greatcoat comedy'; *Colax* 'The toadie' (Menander; attributed to 'Plautus and Naevius' by Ter. *Eun.* 23–6); *Commotria* 'The beautician'; *Corollaria* 'The garland comedy'; *Dementes* 'The lunatics'; *Demetrius* (Alexis; also turned by Caecilius Statius); *Dolus* 'The trick'; *Figulus* 'The potter'; *Glaucoma* 'The cataract'; *Gymnasticus* 'The trainer'; *Lampadio*; *Leo(n)*; *Ludus* (?); *Nautae* (?) 'The sailors'; *Nervolaria* 'The prison play' (?), also attributed to Plautus; *Pellex* 'The temptress'; *Personata* 'The girl in the mask' (?), cf. Festus p. 268 L; *Proiectus* 'The outcast'; *Quadrigemini* 'The quadruplets'; *Stalagmus*; *Stigmatias* 'Black and blue'; *Technicus* 'The artful dodger'; *Testicularia* 'Balls'; *Tribacelus* 'Superqueer'; *Triphallus* 'His chopper's a whopper'; *Tunicularia* 'The underwear play'.

(3) *Fabulae crepidatae.* Six or seven titles known among which *Lycurgus* (thirty-five verses) is by far the best represented (only *c.* seventy verses altogether). Others: *Andromacha* (?); *Danae* (also title of play by Andronicus); *Danae TRF* 5 = *ROL* 10f. is in cretico-bacchiac metre, from a *canticum*; *Equos Troianus* (also title of play by Andronicus); *Hector proficiscens*; *Hesione*; *Iphigenia* (*in Tauris*?) (possibly from Euripides).

(4) *Fabulae praetextae. Clastidium*; *Romulus* or *Lupus* (?). Three lines.

(5) 'Naevius in Satyra', Festus p. 306 L; cf. Gell. 7.8.5 and see p. 162.

(6) Epitaph, Gell. 1.24; cf. H. Dahlmann, *Abh. Akad. Mainz* 1962, 65ff.

(7) There is no evidence that N. invented the *fabula togata*; *Ariolus* was a *palliata*. See p. 94.

BIBLIOGRAPHY

TEXTS AND COMMENTARIES: (1) 'BELLUM POENICUM': *FPL* 17–29; S. Mariotti (Rome 1955: with essay); Ł. Strzelecki (Warsaw 1959: two chapters of prolegomena); M. Barchiesi (Padua 1962: full examination of fortunes of N. through the ages); Ł. Strzelecki (BT, 1964: abbreviated version of 1959 ed. with minor changes to text; on both edd. see S. Mariotti, *Gnomon* 39 (1967) 242–8); A. Mazzarino (Messina 1966: 2nd ed. 1969). (2) 'BELLUM POENICUM' AND PLAYS: E. V. Marmorale, 3rd ed. (Florence 1953: with useful *introduzione biobibliografica* and commentary); *ROL* II 45–156. (3) PLAYS ONLY: *TRF* 7–16; *CRF* 6–35.

STUDIES: Leo, *Gesch.* 76–92; E. Fraenkel, *RE* suppl. VI (1935) 622–40, with important correction in *Elementi plautini in Plauto* (Florence 1960) 436; W. Beare, *The Roman stage*, 3rd ed. (London 1964) 33–44; H.-J. Mette, *Lustrum* 9 (1964) 50–4 (*Forschungsbericht* 1945–64); B. Snell, 'Ezechiels Moses-Drama', *A. & A.* 13 (1967) 150–64; W. Suerbaum, *Untersuchungen zur Selbstdarstellung älterer römischer Dichter* (Hildesheim 1968) 13–42 and *passim*; H. D. Jocelyn, 'The poet Cn. Naevius, P. Cornelius Scipio, and Q. Caecilius Metellus', *Antichthon* 3 (1969) 32–47; J.-H. Waszink, *ANRW* I.2 902–27 (critical *Forschungsbericht* 1953 and earlier to 1968); U. Hübner, 'Zu Naevius' Bellum Poenicum', *Philologus* 116 (1972) 261–76; J. F. Killeen, 'Plautus, Miles gloriosus 211', *C.Ph.* 88 (1973) 53–4; J. Wright, *Dancing in chains: the stylistic unity of the comoedia palliata* (Rome 1974) 33–59; G. Morelli, 'Il modello greco della Danae di Nevio', *Poesia latina in frammenti* (Genoa 1974) 85–101; M. von Albrecht, 'Zur Tarentilla des Naevius', *M.H.* 32 (1975) 230–9.

ENNIUS, QUINTUS

LIFE

b. 239 B.C. (Cic. *Brut.* 72, Varro *ap.* Gell. 17.21.43) at Rudiae (*Ann.* 377 V; Cic. *Arch.* 22, Strabo 6.281 *ad fin.*) in Calabria (hence *Calabrae Pierides* at Hor. *Odes* 4.8.20), a Messapian area; he claimed descent from King Messapus (Serv. *ad* Virg. *Aen.* 7.691, cf. Suda s.n. Ἔννιος) and said that he had *tria corda*, three personalities, because he spoke Greek, Latin and Oscan (Gell. 17.17). Suetonius (*De gramm. et rhet.* 1) calls him *semigraecus* (cf. Festus p. 374 L) and he evidently received a full Greek education, perhaps at Tarentum (Jerome, *Chron.* 240 B.C., wrongly dating his birth). Came to Rome in 204 B.C. having met the quaestor Cato in Sardinia (Nepos, *Cato* 1.4); what he was doing there is unclear (soldiering? Sil. Ital. 12.390ff. is fiction). At Rome he taught (Suet. loc. cit.); when he began writing for the stage is unclear, but he made his reputation in the tragic theatre in the 190s (he was less successful in comedy) and it will have been this which induced M. Fulvius Nobilior to take E. with him on campaign to celebrate his *gesta* (189–187 B.C.) in Ambracia (Cic. *Tusc.* 1.2, Livy 39.4); Choerilus of Iasos had accompanied Alexander (Curt. 8.5.8, Hor. *Epist.* 2.1. 233) as propagandist-poet, and more recently Simonides of Magnesia (Suda s.n.) and Leschides (Suda s.n.) had respectively celebrated the deeds of Antiochus III of Syria and one of the kings of Pergamum named Eumenes. The capture of Ambracia was celebrated in a work, probably a *fabula praetexta* rather than a narrative poem, which might appropriately have been staged at the votive games put on by Nobilior in 186 B.C. (Livy 39.22). Nobilior had celebrated his triumph a year earlier (August 187 B.C., Julian) and was severely criticized both for the liberality of his donatives to his soldiers (Livy 39.5 *ad fin.*, Gell. 5.6.24–6) and (by Cato) for taking *poetas* (i.e. Ennius; Cic. loc. cit.) on campaign. E. liked to put it about (in his *Satires*) that he lived in genteel but contented poverty (cf. Jerome, loc. cit., Cic. *Sen.* 14). A late source (Symm. *Epist.* 1.20.2), usually discounted, states that Nobilior merely awarded E. an old cloak after returning home; this is not beyond belief, because in the face of Cato's and others' criticisms in 188/187 B.C. it would have been impolitic to be seen to award a non-combatant with more than the least of the citizen soldiery. The real reward for the propaganda represented by the *Ambracia* was E.'s enrolment as a *ciuis Romanus* and *colonus* by Nobilior's son Quintus (*RE* Fulvius 93) when as *triumuir coloniae deducendae* in 184/183 B.C. he was in part-charge of the establishment of the settlements at Potentia and Pisaurum (Livy 39.44 with Cic. *Brut.* 79). Cato (now censor, and exercising a very strict review of the census-roll) must have given his tacit approval. Cicero (*Arch.* 22) is wrong in implying that the grant of citizenship was a reward for the (completed) *Annales*; it was only now that E. got seriously down to work on this his *magnum opus*. Besides Cato and the Fulvii Nobiliores, E. is associated in our sources with Scipio Africanus (Cic. *Arch.* 22), Scipio Nasica (Cic. *De or.* 2.276) and Ser. Sulpicius Galba (Cic. *Acad.* 2.51), his eminent neighbour on the Aventine where he lived modestly with only one servant-girl to 'do' for him. For a time he shared with Caecilius (q.v.) (Jerome, *Chron.* 240 and 179 B.C.). See E. Badian, 'Ennius and his friends', *Entretiens XVII* (Fondation Hardt 1972). He died in 169 B.C. (Cic. *Brut.* 78) during the *ludi Apollinares* at which his (new) *Thyestes* was being performed. He never married and his heir (legal as well as literary) appears to have been his nephew Pacuvius, who seems to have been a Roman citizen by birth, implying that E. had long been related by the marriage of some sister to a Roman of the *gens Pacuvia*.

WORKS

(1) DRAMATIC: (*a*) Tragedies. More than forty extant verses: *Alexander*, *Medea exul* (both from Euripides), *Hectoris lytra*. More than twenty: *Andromacha aechmalotis*, *Hecuba*, *Iphigenia* (*in Aulis*) (all from Euripides), *Telamo*. Other plays: *Achilles* (from Aristarchus; alluded to at Plaut. *Poen.* 1, produced 188/187 B.C., though the authenticity of the beginning of the prologue is problematic), *Aiax*, *Alcmeo* (possibly from Euripides), *Andromeda* (from Euripides), *Athamas*, *Cresphontes* (possibly from Euripides), *Erechtheus* (from Euripides), *Eumenides* (from Aeschylus), *Melanippa* (from Euripides), *Nemea*, *Phoenix*, *Telephus*, *Thyestes* (169 B.C.). *c.* 425 lines in all. (*b*) Comedies. A *Caupuncula*, *Pancratiastes* and *Telestis* are meagrely attested (five citations). Volcacius Sedigitus lists Ennius tenth and last in his list of the best comic poets (*ap.* Gell. 15.24) *antiquitatis causa* 'out of respect for his venerable age', which is faint praise indeed. (*c*) *Fabulae praetextae. Ambracia* (see above), *Sabinae* 'The Sabine Women' (seven citations).

(2) 'ANNALES' (*Romais*, Diomedes, *GLK* 1 484, not inaptly) in eighteen books. Over 500 citations/allusions.

(3) MINOR WORKS: (*a*) *Hedyphagetica* 'Tit-bits', in mock-heroic hexameters, experimental in technique, based on the *Hedypatheia* ('Luxury') or *Gastronomia* ('Belly-rule') of Archestratus of Gela (*fl.* 350 B.C.). Apul. *Apol.* 39 cites eleven lines which may be compared with their model, cited by Ath. 3.92D. Composed after E.'s

return from Ambracia, i.e. 187 B.C. or later (O. Skutsch, *Studia Enniana* (London 1968) 38); texts and discussion, W. M. Lindsay, *Early Latin verse* (Oxford 1922) 1f. Possibly the earliest extant Latin hexameters. (*b*) *Sota*, i.e. Σωτᾶς, a hypocoristic form of Sotades, who wrote *c*. 280 B.C. and invented the Sotadean verse (E. uses this). Bawdy in character (fr. 1 σκατοφαγία; fr. 5 *natem*, a coarse synonym for *lumbum*). (*c*) *libri saturarum* IV (Porph. *ad* Hor. *Sat*. 1.10.46; VI, Donat. *ad* Ter. *Ph*. 339). (*d*) *Scipio*: a non-dramatic *laus* of Scipio Africanus, perhaps partly in trochaic septenarii (Gell. 4.7.3, Macr. *Sat*. 6.2.26) and hexameters (Lucil. 1190 M, cf. Suda s.n. Ἔννιος); relation to the preceding problematic. (*e*) *Epicharmus* in trochaic septenarii (Cic. *Acad*. 2.51, Prisc. *GLK* II 341.20, Varro, *Ling. Lat*. 5.59 and 68); fourteen surviving verses. (*f*) *Praecepta*, Priscian, *GLK* II 532.17, perhaps identical with *Protrepticum* (*-us*?), Charisius, *GLK* I 54.19; cf. Leo, *Gesch*. 204. (*g*) *Euhemerus* or *historia sacra*, a version of the philosophical 'novel' of Euhemerus (b. *c*. 340 B.C.). Lactantius (*Inst*. 1.11.33ff., cf. 1.14.1) quotes several paragraphs of what he took to be E.'s actual words, in decidedly jejune prose; it is, however, more probable (*pace* E. Laughton, 'The prose of Ennius', *Eranos* 49 (1951) 35f. and E. Fraenkel, 'Additional notes on the prose of Ennius', ibid. 50ff.) that this, like E.'s other didactic works, was written in iambo-trochaic verse, and that Lactantius is quoting a school paraphrase for children; see R. M. Ogilvie, *The library of Lactantius* (Oxford 1978) 56. (*h*) Epigrams. Three distichs on Scipio Africanus; one in the form of an epitaph (Cic. *Leg*. 2.57, Sen. *Epist*. 108.32), though in Livy's time it was uncertain where Scipio was buried, another (Lact. *Inst*. 1.18.10) makes Scipio claim the right to enter heaven (like Hercules or a Hellenistic king); a third comments that from West to East none could equal his *gesta*. Two other epigrams are on E. himself as public poet and private artist; cf. W. Suerbaum, *Untersuchungen zur Selbstdarstellung älterer römischer Dichter: Livius Andronicus, Naevius, Ennius* (Hildesheim 1968) 208–15, 332–6, who also presents literary evidence for iconography of Ennius (210–11); see G. Hafner, *Das Bildnis des Q. Ennius* (Baden Baden 1968), cf. D. E. Strong, *C.R.* n.s.20 (1970) 254. An acrostic 'signature' *Q. Ennius fecit* is mentioned by Cicero (*Div*. 2.111) as occurring in *quibusdam Ennianis*; Diog. Laert. 8.78 says that 'Epicharmus' similarly signed most of his ὑπομνήματα with an acrostic (see Suerbaum above 11, 135f., 261f.). (i) Orthographical precepts attributed to E.: regular gemination of consonants (Festus p. 374 L s.v. 'solitaurilia') (though it appears sporadically in earlier inscriptions); the change of the spelling of some words to suit etymological fancies (Varro, *Ling. Lat*. 5.86, Charisius, *GLK* I 98.12); two books *de litteris syllabisque* and *de metris* attributed by some to E. the poet are mentioned by Suetonius (*De gramm. et rhet*. 1), who, however, agreed with the view of one L. Cotta that these and some *libri de augurandi disciplina* were the work of another Ennius. Tenuous evidence for a S. Ennius the inventor of scholarly symbols and shorthand signs is offered by the *anecdotum parisinum* (*GLK* VII 534.4), *in adnotationibus Ennii Lucilii et historicorum usi sunt Varros* (with *u* written above) *hennius* (sic) *haelius* . . . , and by the quotation of Isid. *Orig*. 1.22.1 in the *tractatus grammaticus de V nominum declinationum* of *codex Bernensis* 611 fol. 72 verso (s.VIII) (W. Arndt, *Schrifttafeln zur Erlernung der lateinischen Palaeographie* 1, 4th ed.

M. Tangl (Berlin 1904) 26 (transcription), Tafel 35 (reproduction); H. Hagen, *Catalogus codicum Bernensium* (*Bibliotheca Bongarsiana*) (Bern 1875) 479–83), *de uulgaribus notis: uulgares notas sennius primus mille et centum inuenit*...

BIBLIOGRAPHY

TEXTS: (1) COMPREHENSIVE: J. Vahlen (Leipzig 1903; repr. Leipzig 1928, Amsterdan 1963), cf. O. Seyffert, *B.Ph.W.* 1904, 1322–6, C. Bailey, *C.R.* 18 (1904) 169–72, J. Paulson, *Eranos* 6 (1905) 55–65; *ROL* I 2–465, cf. C. J. Fordyce, *C.R.* 49 (1935) 188, A. Klotz, *Ph.W.* (1938) 645–9. Vahlen's numeration (*Ann.* 356 V, *Sat.* 15 V) is standard for all E.'s works except the plays (cited from *TRF* pp. 17ff., pp. 323f. and *CRF* pp. 5f.); in this book we follow this convention, with cross-references to numeration in *ROL*, adding in brackets the book-number where appropriate, e.g. *Ann.* (17) 443–5 V = *ROL* 430–2; *Medea exul TRF* 231f. = *ROL* 284f. (2) TRAGEDIES: H. D. Jocelyn (Cambridge 1967: with commentary), cf. S. Timpanaro, *Gnomon* 40 (1968) 666–71. (3) 'ANNALES': E. M. Steuart (Cambridge 1925: with commentary); L. Valmaggi (Turin 1900, repr. 1947, 1962: with commentary). (4) MINOR WORKS: E. Bolisani (Padua 1935: with commentary and tr.). (5) SELECTIONS: J. Heurgon, *Ennius I: Les Annales; II: Fragments tragiques* (Paris 1960) has a running commentary on the Ennius-fragments in A. Ernout, *Recueil de textes latins archaïques*, 2nd ed. (Paris 1957).

STUDIES: FUNDAMENTAL: F. Skutsch, *RE* v (1905) 2589–2628 and introductions to edd. of Vahlen and Jocelyn; Leo, *Gesch.* 150–211; E. Norden, *Ennius und Vergilius: Kriegsbilder aus Roms grosser Zeit* (Leipzig 1915); for *c.* 1940–52 see S. Timpanaro, *A.A.O.H.G.* 5 (1952) 195–212; H.-J. Mette, *Lustrum* 9 (1964) 14–16, 55–78 (tragedies); papers on various topics by O. Skutsch, collected in his *Studia Enniana* (London 1968); J.-H. Waszink, 'The proem of the Annales of Ennius', *Mnemosyne* 4.3 (1950) 215–40, revised version 'Il proemio degli Annales di Ennio', *Maia* 16 (1964) 327–40; idem, 'Retractatio Enniana', *Mnemosyne* 4.15 (1962) 113–32; S. Mariotti, *Lezioni su Ennio* (Pesaro 1951; repr. Turin 1963), cf. O. Skutsch, *C.R.* n.s.4 (1954) 254–5; K. Ziegler, *Das hellenistische Epos*, 2nd ed. (Leipzig 1966) 53–77 (E. as a Hellenistic poet); W. Suerbaum, *Untersuchungen zur Selbstdarstellung älterer römischer Dichter* (Hildesheim 1968) 43–295 (mainly on *Annales*; exhaustive bibliography, supplementing Timpanaro up to *c.* 1967); Williams, *TORP* 359ff., 691ff., *passim*; (ed.) O. Skutsch, *Ennius. Sept exposés suivis de discussion*, *Entretiens XVII* (Fondation Hardt 1972); H. D. Jocelyn, 'The poems of Quintus Ennius', *ANRW* I.2 987–1026; J. Wright, *Dancing in chains: the stylistic unity of the comoedia palliata* (Rome 1974) 61–7 (comic fragments).

PLAUTUS, TITUS MACCIUS

LIFE

(1) Fragments of speciously biographical information deriving ultimately from Varro, *De poetis* and *De comoediis plautinis libri* (?) *tres*: the comic playwright Maccius, an Umbrian from Sarsina, acquired the *cognomen* Plotus, later Plautus (urban form) because he had flat feet (Pauli Festus s.v. 'ploti'; Jerome, *Chron.* 200 B.C.); there was, according to Varro, another playwright Plautius, which added to the confusion after P.'s death as to which were his plays, for both names have genitive *Plauti* (Gell. 3.3.10). On coming to Rome P. worked *in operis artificum scaenicorum*, 'in the service of the stage-artists (i.e. actors)' (for the expression cf. Cic. *Fam.* 13.9.3), which should mean 'as a stage-hand' (Gell. 3.3.14, quoting Varro from memory). Varro *may* also have said that P. later became an *histrio*, actor; cf. Livy 7.2, in the old days all poets *agebant*, produced and acted in their own plays. P. was supposed to have made money through this employment (cf. Hor. *Epist.* 2.1.170) and left Rome on an abortive business venture; returning to Rome he hired his services (*addicere*) to a miller. During this time he allegedly wrote three comedies, *Saturio*, *Addictus*, and a third whose name Gellius (loc. cit.) could not remember. Jerome (*Chron.*) wrongly states that P. died in 200 B.C.; Gellius rightly implies that his *floruit* agreed with that of Cato in politics, i.e. *c.* 195–184 B.C. (17.21.47). Cicero, indirectly following Varro on this, implies that P. was an old man when he produced the *Truculentus* (*c.* 188 B.C.) and the *Pseudolus* (Megalensian Games and inauguration of the Great Mother's temple, Nov. 192 B.C. (Julian); not April 191 B.C. as usually stated (the Roman calendar was four months adrift at the time)), and he does not merely mean *senex* in the technical sense that so defined anyone over 40½ years of age. Elsewhere (*Brut.* 60) he says that P. died in the censorship of Cato (184/183 B.C.). Gellius quotes an epigram in rough hexameters from Varro's *De poetis* (1.24) praising P. retrospectively as the irreplaceable master of *risus ludus iocusque et numeri innumeri* (referring to his metrical virtuosity), and is rightly sceptical of Varro's apparently unqualified assertion that P. actually wrote this himself and intended it to be incised on his tomb. No tradition as to his resting-place, nor even the pretence of an iconographical tradition.

(2) Evaluation of Varronian account. Varro himself was drawing on the 'researches' of scholars of the Gracchan era such as Accius and Aelius Stilo (*c.* 154–90 B.C.). Neither they nor he had access to documentary evidence about P. other than the scripts which passed under his name or combinations of his names (*Plautus* and various cases but not the genitive, *Maccus*, *Macci Titi* are attested in prologues; *T. Macci Plauti Casina explicit* only in Ambrosian palimpsest); some at least of these scripts included production-notices giving details of the first performance. Only two of these survive (*Stichus*, Plebeian Games 200 B.C.; *Pseudolus*, see above) and it is hypercritical to entertain suspicions about these particular notices. The critical standards set by the example of Pergamene scholarship were low (see R. Pfeiffer, *History of classical*

scholarship (Oxford 1968) I 241f.) and Accius and others were guilty of passing off dubious inferences and combinations as fact within the limits of what seemed *a priori* likely, for example, that P. should have been an alien of low standing whose livelihood was precarious and depended on the theatre. The romantic tale of his vicissitudes in business and of his working and writing in a mill has no authority and is probably fabricated from well-known themes of P.'s *oeuvre* – changes in material fortune, slaves' remarks such as *Per.* 21f. and fathers' complaints such as *Trin.* 820ff. The statement that P. came from Sarsina looks like an inept construction on the joke at *Most.* 770, and the dogmatic allegation that he died in 184 B.C. probably represents an inference from the absence of later production-notices; maybe P. simply retired, or was invited to retire by the censor Cato. Although Cicero (*Sen.* 50) certainly implies that he and Varro thought that P. was born earlier than 250 B.C., there is no antique authority for the frequently repeated statement that P. was born either in 254 or 259/258 B.C. The first date is arrived at by counting back three score years and ten from 184 B.C., while the second depends upon an absurd combination: at *M.G.* 629 Periplectomenus mentions that he is fifty-four years of age; since antiquity it has been supposed (not necessarily rightly) that *M.G.* 211f. contains an allusion to the imprisonment of Naevius in 205/204 B.C.; *ergo*, P. was born in 259/258 B.C. Either or both of these arguments is worthy of Accius, but seem to have been worked out in post-Renaissance times by scholars as yet unidentified (P. Crinitus, *De poetis latinis* (Florence 1505) is exonerated). On the available evidence, P. could have been ten years younger than Cato (b. 234 B.C.). We do not even know his real name: Varro apparently assumed that Maccius was the real *nomen gentile* and took Plautus to be a *cognomen* which had nothing to do with the writer's profession. T. Maccius Plautus, however, appears to be a jocose pseudonym connoting 'Phallus the son of Clown (Maccus of Atellane Farce), the Entertainer (*plautus* 'flatfoot' = *planipes* 'mime')', i.e., as it were, 'Dick Dopeson Prancer'; see A. S. Gratwick, *C.Q.* n.s.23 (1973) 78–84, W. Beare, *The Roman stage*, 3rd ed. (London 1964) 47f., F. Leo, *Plautinische Forschungen*, 2nd ed. (Berlin 1912) 81ff. On the positive side: all the surviving plays are essentially the work of one hand, and date, in so far as they can be dated, from between the last years of the Second Punic War and the mid-180s; the author was associated over a long period with T. Publilius Pellio (an important actor-impressario); he may have acted in his own productions, though the only possible direct evidence for this depends upon the interpretation of the joke at *Bacch.* 211ff., which is wittiest if Pellio is playing Pistoclerus and P. himself Chrysalus; the occasion at which the *Pseudolus* was produced was a particularly special celebration for which greater funds than usual were available, and the play calls for unusually though not uniquely extravagant resources, which implies that P.'s reputation already stood very high as a successful dramatist; and he was the first to specialize in a single genre of drama, as had been the standard practice of Greek dramatists.

WORKS

(1) DUBIOUS AND SPURIOUS WORKS: No authentic canon of P.'s plays existed in or near his own time (contrast the case of Caecilius), and his scripts were the property of such as Publilius Pellio, stage-managers who contracted for plays individually. In the Gracchan era some 130 scripts passed under P.'s name(s), not as reading-editions, but as actors' copies. Not only were there several species of authentic 'signatures' (see above) – Varro's Plautius may be one of these – but also a large number of patently spurious works had been staged as 'rediscovered' comedies. Aelius Stilo thought only twenty-five genuine (Gell. 3.3.11), which should mean our surviving plays and four others; someone else, probably Varro, counted forty as genuine (Serv. *praef. Aen.* p. 4 15 Th). We know that Varro listed twenty-one plays as genuine *consensu omnium*, meaning that none of his predecessors had impugned the authenticity of any of these, and that he acquiesced in that view. These twenty-one are rather inappropriately named the *fabulae Varronianae* by Gellius (3.3.3), and it is virtually certain that it is they that survive to us. The name *fabulae Varronianae* would more properly be applied to the second group of plays segregated by Varro, namely those which he himself regarded as genuine on stylistic grounds against the doubts or denials of one or more scholars; if Varro thought forty in all genuine, there were nineteen of these, and he recognized a third group of ninety forgeries. It seems certain that at least several genuine works have been lost. Accius denied the authenticity of a *Commorientes* 'Partners in death', which Terence in 160 B.C. had thought genuine (Ter. *Ad.* prol.); Gellius may well have been right in asserting with Varro the authenticity of a *Boeotia* also attributed by some to one Aquilius and again damned by Accius (see A. S. Gratwick, *C.Q.* n.s.29 (1979) 308–23). The issue was further complicated by the possibility of revision and joint authorship, as in the case of a *Colax* which Terence assigns to 'Plautus and Naevius' (*Eun.* prol.). Citations amounting to about 110 fragmentary lines from thirty-two named plays not among the canon of twenty-one and about sixty non-canonical citations simply of 'Plautus' are preserved, almost all made by grammarians.

(2) THE FABULAE VARRONIANAE: *Amphitruo*, the only mythological comedy. *Asinaria* 'Horse-play', from the *Onagos* 'Muleteer' of one Demophilus. Later than *Menaechmi* (*Asin.* 879–930 repeats ideas from *Men.* 563ff. and 621ff.). *Aulularia* 'The pot of gold', possibly from Menander. *Bacchides* 'Bacchis and Bacchis', from Menander's *Dis exapaton* 'The double deceiver', of which important fragments exist. One of P.'s latest surviving works; beginning lost. *Captivi* 'The prisoners'. *Casina* 'Miss Godot', from the *Kleroumenoi* 'The lot-takers' of Diphilus. After 186 B.C. *Cistellaria* 'The little casket', from Menander's *Synaristosai* 'The ladies at elevenses'. Shortly before 201 B.C.; badly damaged. *Curculio* 'Weevil'. Seriously cut. *Epidicus* 'Mr Legally Liable'. Before *Bacchides*, cf. *Bacch.* 211ff. *Menaechmi* 'Standspeare and twin'. Not necessarily an early work. *Mercator* 'The merchant', from Philemon's *Emporos* 'The merchant'. *Miles gloriosus* 'The braggart warrior', from an *Alazon* 'Braggart'.

Mostellaria 'Whigmaleerie', possibly from a *Phasma* 'Apparition'. *Persa* 'The man from Persia' (not 'woman', as often translated). *Poenulus* 'The wretch from Carthage', from Alexis' *Karchedonios* 'The Carthaginian'. 188/187 B.C. Heavily interpolated. *Pseudolus* 'What, me lie?'. *Rudens* 'The rope', from Diphilus. *Stichus* 'Sketch', from Menander's first *Adelphoi* 'The brothers'. 200 B.C. *Trinummus* 'Threepence', from Philemon's *Thesauros* 'The treasure'. Later than *Curculio*, cf. *Trin.* 1016, where read *Curculiost*. *Truculentus* 'The grumpy fellow'. *c.* 188 B.C. *Vidularia* 'The wallet', from a *Schedia* 'The raft', possibly of Diphilus; all but lost.

BIBLIOGRAPHY

TEXTS AND COMMENTARIES: TEXTS: F. Leo (Berlin 1895–6); W. M. Lindsay (OCT, 1903). TEXTS WITH TRANSLATIONS: P. Nixon (Loeb, 1916–38, rev. ed. 1952–62: with Leo's text); A. Ernout (Budé, 1932: best *apparatus criticus*). COMMENTARIES: (1) Complete. A. Turnebus (Paris 1587); F. Taubmann (Wittenberg 1605); M. Z. Boxhorn (Leiden 1645); J. F. Gronovius (Amsterdam 1684); J. L. Ussing, 5 vols. in 7 parts (Copenhagen 1875–86). (2) Individual plays. *Amphitruo*: A. Palmer (London 1890); W. B. Sedgwick (Manchester 1950). *Asinaria*: F. Bertini, 2 vols. (Genoa 1968). *Aulularia*: C. Questa (Milan 1972). *Bacchides*: C. Questa, 2nd ed. (Florence 1975: with fragments of Menander's *Dis exapaton*). *Captivi*: W. M. Lindsay, 2nd ed. (Oxford 1930); J. Brix, O. Niemeyer, O. Köhler, 7th ed. (Leipzig–Berlin 1930). *Casina*: W. T. MacCary and M. M. Willcock (Cambridge 1976). *Cistellaria*: none; cf. G. Thamm, *Zur Cistellaria des Plautus* (diss. Freiburg 1971). *Curculio*: J. Collart (Paris 1962); G. Monaco (Palermo 1969). *Epidicus*: G. E. Duckworth (Princeton 1940). *Menaechmi*: J. Brix, O. Niemeyer, F. Conrad, 6th ed. (Leipzig–Berlin 1929). *Mercator*: P. J. Enk, 2 vols., 2nd ed. (Leiden 1966). *Miles gloriosus*: A. O. F. Lorenz, 2nd ed. (Berlin 1886). *Mostellaria*: A. O. F. Lorenz, 2nd ed. (Berlin 1883); E. A. Sonnenschein, 2nd ed. (Oxford 1927); J. Collart (Paris 1970). *Persa*: none; cf. G. L. Müller, *Das Original des plautinischen Persa* (diss. Frankfurt 1957). *Poenulus*: G. Maurach (Heidelberg 1975), cf. A. S. Gratwick, *The Poenulus of Plautus and its Attic original* (diss. Oxford 1968). *Pseudolus*: A. O. F. Lorenz (Berlin 1876). *Rudens*: E. A. Sonnenschein (Oxford 1891); F. Marx (Leipzig 1928); A. Thierfelder, 2nd ed. (Heidelberg 1962); H. C. Fay (London 1969). *Stichus*: H. Petersmann (Heidelberg 1973). *Trinummus*: J. Brix, O. Niemeyer, 5th ed. (Leipzig–Berlin 1907). *Truculentus*: P. J. Enk, 2 vols. (Leiden 1953), cf. K.-H. Kruse, *Kommentar zu Plautus' Truculentus* (diss. Heidelberg 1974). Fragments: F. Winter (diss. Bonn 1885).

TRANSLATIONS: W. Warner (London 1595: *Menaechmi*); H. T. Riley (London 1852); B. B. Rogers (Oxford 1907: *Menaechmi*); (ed.) G. Duckworth, *The complete Roman drama*, 2 vols. (New York 1942); A. Thierfelder (Stuttgart 1962–5: *Miles gloriosus, Curculio, Captivi*); L. Casson (New York 1963: *Amphitruo, Aulularia, Casina, Menaechmi, Pseudolus, Rudens*); E. F. Watling (Penguin, 1964–5: *Rudens,*

Mostellaria, *Trinummus*, *Amphitruo*, *Aulularia*, *Captivi*, *Menaechmi*, *Miles gloriosus*, *Pseudolus*); E. Segal (New York 1965: *Miles gloriosus*); S. Allot (London 1967: adapted from *Mostellaria*, *Miles gloriosus*, *Rudens*); A. G. Gillingham (Andover, Mass. 1968: *Captivi*, *Curculio*, *Mostellaria*, five scenes from other plays); P. Grimal (Paris 1971: with Terence).

SURVEYS: A. O. F. Lorenz, *J.A.W.* 1 (1873) 341–428; 3 (1877) 606–71; 18 (1880) 1–90; 22 (1880) 1–89; O. Seyffert, *J.A.W.* 31 (1882) 33–111; 47 (1886) 1–138; 63 (1890) 1–94; 80 (1894) 227–351; 84 (1895) 1–60; W. M. Lindsay, *J.A.W.* 130 (1906) 116–282; 167 (1912) 1–58; O. Köhler, *J.A.W.* 192 (1922) 1–45; 217 (1928) 57–81; F. Conrad, *J.A.W.* 247 (1935) 63–90; J. A. Hanson, *C.W.* 59 (1966) 103–7, 141–8 (for 1950–66); J. D. Hughes, *A bibliography of scholarship on Plautus* (Amsterdam 1975); D. Fogazza, *Lustrum* 19 (1976) 79–284 (for 1935–75).

STUDIES: (1) GENERAL: E. Fraenkel, *Plautinisches im Plautus* (Berlin 1922), Italian tr. with additional notes *Elementi plautini in Plauto* (Florence 1960); P. Lejay, *Plaute* (Paris 1925); G. E. Duckworth, *The nature of Roman comedy* (Princeton 1952); E. Paratore, *Plauto* (Florence 1961); W. Beare, *The Roman stage*, 3rd ed. (London 1964); E. Segal, *Roman laughter* (Harvard 1968); W. G. Arnott, *Menander, Plautus, and Terence* (Oxford 1968); F. H. Sandbach, *The comic theatre of Greece and Rome* (London 1977) 118–34; J. Blänsdorf, 'Plautus', in (ed.) E. Lefèvre, *Das römische Drama* (Darmstadt 1978) 135–222. (2) PARTICULAR TOPICS: Transmission: F. Leo, *Plautinische Forschungen*, 2nd ed. (Berlin 1912) ch. 1 *passim*. Usage: W. M. Lindsay, *The syntax of Plautus* (Oxford 1907). Metre: W. M. Lindsay, *Early Latin verse* (Oxford 1922); L. Braun, *Die Cantica des Plautus* (Göttingen 1970); H. Drexler, *Die Iambenkürzung* (Hildesheim 1969); C. Questa, *Introduzione alla metrica di Plauto* (Bologna 1967). Dating: K. H. E. Schutter, *Quibus annis comoediae plautinae primum actae sint quaeritur* (Groningen 1952). Interpolations: A. Thierfelder, *De rationibus interpolationum plautinarum* (Leipzig 1929). Lexicons: G. Lodge (Leipzig 1914–33); A. Maniet (Hildesheim 1969). Dramaturgy: H. Marti, *Untersuchungen zur dramatischen Technik bei Plautus und Terenz* (Zurich 1959). Law: U. E. Paoli, *Comici latini e diritto attico* (Milan 1962); A. Watson, *Roman private law around* 200 B.C. (Edinburgh 1971). Prologues: K.-H. Abel, *Die Plautusprologe* (Mülheim-Ruhr 1955). Relation to Greek originals: E. W. Handley, *Menander and Plautus: a study in comparison* (*London* 1968); K. Gaiser, 'Zur Eigenart der römischen Komödie: Plautus und Terenz gegenüber ihre griechische Vorbildern', *ANRW* 1.2 1027–1113; V. Pöschl, *Die neuen Menanderpapyri und die Originalität des Plautus* (Heidelberg 1973), French version in *Association Guillaume Budé, Actes du IXe Congrès, Rome* 13–18 *avril* 1973 vol. 1 (Paris 1975) 306–21. See further under Terence.

CAECILIUS STATIUS

LIFE

Jerome (*Chron.*) makes 179 B.C. his *floruit* as a comic dramatist, adding that he was by birth an Insubrian Gaul, and that some said he came from Milan. It is inferred from this that he was captured and brought to Rome as a slave *c.* 223/222 B.C. after the battle of Clastidium. Statius appears to be the Latinized form of his Celtic name, which became his *cognomen* on manumission by the Caecilii; his Roman *praenomen* is unknown (Gell. 4.20.13 is confused). Thus he was an alien freedman like Andronicus and Terence. Jerome says that he was 'at first a close associate' (*primum contubernalis*) of Ennius and that he died the year after Ennius, i.e. 168 B.C., and was buried next to the *mons Janiculus*. This information derives at several removes from Varro's *De poetis* and sounds more circumstantial than his account of the life of Plautus. The story that the young Terence met C. and read him some of his *Andria* is hard to reconcile with this (Suet. *Vita Ter.* 3, Jerome, *Chron.* 159 B.C.); the *Andria* was put on in 166 B.C. The size of C.'s oeuvre and the date of his *floruit* imply that he had begun writing in Plautus' heyday. At first he had difficulty in gaining a name, but succeeded thanks to the persistence of the actor-impressario Ambivius Turpio (Ter. *Hec.* 9–27). Volcacius Sedigitus (*ap.* Gell. 15.24) judged C. the best of all the comic poets (above Naevius and Plautus), and it is evident from the way that Cicero cites him and expects others to know his text that he was, like Terence but unlike Plautus, a school-author in the 1st c. B.C. There is no explicit reference to revival-productions, but this is no doubt an accident. Ancient judgements: Varro, *Sat. Men.* 399 Buecheler; idem, *ap.* Charisius, *GLK* I 241.28; Cic. *De opt. gen. orat.* 1.2; Hor. *Epist.* 2.1.59; Vell. Pat. 1.17.1; Quint. 10.1.99; Gell. 2.23 *passim* (Gellius' adverse judgement, together with Cic. *Att.* 7.3.10, may in part account for C.'s failure to survive).

WORKS

Forty-two titles known, represented by *c.* 280 fragmentary verses. The *Plocium* is by far the best represented (forty-five verses) (next best *Synephebi*, seventeen verses). It is of importance as Gellius cites the Menandrian original for comparison; passages of Plautus' *Bacchides* corresponding to papyrus fragments of Menander's *Dis exapaton* provide the only other opportunity for direct, extensive examination of the techniques of adaptation used by Roman comedians.

(1) Probably or certainly from Menander. *Andria* 'The girl from Andros', *Androgynos* 'Epicene', *Chalcia* 'The coppersmiths' holiday', *Dardanus*, *Ephesio* (?), *Epiclerus* 'The heiress', *Hymnis*, *Hypobolimaeus* (*subditivos*, *Chaerestratus*, *rastraria*) 'The changeling' (probably only two and possibly one play), *Imbrii* 'The Imbrians', *Karine* 'The wailing-woman', *Nauclerus* 'The captain', *Plocium* 'The necklace', *Polumenoe* 'The men for sale', *Progamos* (?), *Synaristosai* 'The ladies at elevenses'

(also the original of Plautus' *Cistellaria*), *Synephebi* 'The likely lads', *Titthe* 'The nurse'.

(2) From other Greek authors. *Aethrio*, *Chrysion*, *Davos* (corrupt title), *Demandati* 'The boys in care', *Epistathmos* 'The quartermaster' (?), *Epistula* 'The letter', *Ex hautou hestos* 'Standing on his own two feet', *Exul* 'The exile', *Fallacia* 'The trick', *Gamos* 'The wedding', *Harpazomene* 'The girl who gets seized', *Hypobolimaeus Aeschinus* 'Aeschinus the changeling' (relation to other *Hypobolimaei* problematic), *Meretrix* 'The courtesan', *Nothus Nicasio* 'The bastard [or 'fake'?] Nicasio', *Obolostates/Faenerator* 'The moneylender', *Pausimachus*, *Philumena*, *Portitor* 'The janitor', *Pugil* 'The boxer', *Symbolum* 'The token', *Syracusii* 'The Syracusans', *Triumphus* 'The triumph'.

BIBLIOGRAPHY

TEXTS: *CRF* 2.40–94; *ROL* III 468–561; T. Guardi (Palermo 1974).

STUDIES: P. Faider, 'Le poète comique Caecilius: sa vie et son oeuvre', *Mus. Belge* 12 (1908) 269–341, 13 (1909) 5–35; Leo, *Gesch.* 217–26; H. Haffter, *M.H.* 10 (1953) 5ff.; W. Beare, *The Roman stage*, 3rd ed. (London 1964) 76–80; Williams, *TORP* 363–6; A. Traina, *Vortit barbare* (Rome 1970) 41–53; J. Wright, *Dancing in chains: the stylistic unity of the comoedia palliata* (Rome 1974) 86–126.

TERENTIUS AFER, PUBLIUS

LIFE

Main source is Suetonius' *Vita Terenti*, written *c.* A.D. 100 and preserved in preface of Donatus' commentary. Although Suetonius quotes Volcacius Sedigitus and Porcius Licinus (writing later-2nd c. B.C.), and probably (though without acknowledgement) used Varro's *De poetis* (mid-1st c. B.C.), it is evident that they knew very little for certain.

Suetonius reports (*Vita* 5) that T. died in 159 B.C. (Jerome, *Chron.* says 158 B.C.) when he had not yet completed his twenty-fifth, or thirty-fifth year (MSS divide evenly). The younger age would make T. a contemporary of Scipio Aemilianus and Laelius, and, with suspicious neatness, would put his birth in 184 B.C., supposed year of Plautus' death. Cornelius Nepos claimed that Scipio, Laelius and Terence were 'of an age' (Suet. *Vita* 2), and this seems to have been assumed also by those who alleged that Scipio's real interest in Terence was sexual (Suet. *Vita* 1, 2) and who told the story of his meeting with Caecilius (see below). On the other hand Fenestella (late-1st c. B.C.) argued that T. was older than Scipio and Laelius, but not so old as to have been captured in the Hannibalic War 'as some think' (Suet. *Vita* 1–2), and this fits well with the alternative birth-date in 194 B.C. Suetonius says that T. was born at Carthage and was a slave at Rome of the senator Terentius Lucanus (otherwise unknown) (Oros. 4.19.6 mentions a Terentius Culleo (*RE* Terentius 43), an expert in

Carthaginian affairs); he was educated and manumitted early 'because of his brains and good looks' (Suet. *Vita* 1). This may merely be based on inference from the form of T.'s name, but is not conclusive; he could be the descendant, for example, of someone captured and manumitted after the First Punic War. On offering his first play, the *Andria*, to the aediles he was told to read it to the doyen of the comic stage Caecilius Statius, who was filled with admiration for it. The story (Suet. *Vita* 3) has added point if Caecilius' own *Andria* had also been a version of Menander's play, but is suspicious as a 'succession-tale', and also on chronological grounds: Caecilius died in 168 B.C., and the *Andria* was put on first in 166 B.C. (production-notice).

Suetonius (*Vita* 4 and 6) reports anecdotes and rumours that T. was helped in composition by his noble friends Scipio Aemilianus, C. Laelius and L. Furius Philus; not so much friends as sexually motivated exploiters, according to the pathetic and hostile imagination of Porcius Licinus (Suet. *Vita* 2 = *FPL* fr. 3). These speculations have their origin in the allusions which T. makes at *H.T.* 23–6 and at *Ad.* 15ff. to charges that he received aid from *amici* and *homines nobiles*, charges which T. does not refute, but mentions with some pride; cf. Cic. *Att.* 7.3.10, Quint. 10.1.99. A C. Memmius, more probably the Gracchan orator and *inimicus* of Scipio Aemilianus (*ORF* pp. 214–17) than the orator and poet of mid-1st c. B.C. (so *ORF* p. 404), mentioned in a speech *pro se* that 'Aemilianus, borrowing the mask from Terence, presented on stage what he had scribbled himself at home' (cf. Volcacius Sedigitus *ap.* Suet. *Vita* 9 = *FPL* fr. 3). Cornelius Nepos had what he thought was unimpeachable evidence for a story that Laelius, on being told by his wife to hurry up and come to dinner, asked not to be disturbed; at last, coming in late, he remarked that his writing had gone particularly well that day and read out the passage of *H.T.* beginning *satis pol proterue me Syri promissa huc induxerunt* . . . (723ff.); the point of this story is that it took place on the first of March, the feast of the Matronalia, the Roman 'Mothers' Day', and, apart from the fact that *mutatis mutandis* the passage was wittily appropriate to the occasion, the speaker is the formidable and mercenary courtesan Bacchis (Suet. *Vita* 4). T.'s relationship to Scipio Aemilianus, if any, remains entirely obscure.

T. travelled to Greece 'on holiday, or to avoid the charge of publishing others' work as his own, or to acquire a better grasp of Greek life and manners, which he had not perfectly expressed in his writings' (Suet. *Vita* 5). If true, this would be the earliest recorded example of the 'cultural tour' which became common among the wealthy in the next generation. Volcacius Sedigitus said that he was going to Asia, i.e. Pergamum, and was never seen again (Suet. *Vita* 5 = *FPL* fr. 2); Q. Cosconius said that he perished on the return journey at sea with 108 plays turned from Menander's Greek; others, that he died at Stymphalus in Arcadia or at Leucas (cf. Auson. *Epist.* 13.16; Ambracia, schol. *ad* Luc. 5.652), having fallen ill, or through grief at the loss at sea of his baggage, which had been sent on ahead and included a number of fresh plays (Suet. *Vita* 5). In assessing the credibility of this it should be remembered that Menander was supposed to have drowned in the Piraeus (schol. *ad* Ovid, *Ibis* 591f., Pfeiffer on Call. fr. 396), and that according to one count Menander wrote 108 plays

(Gell. 17.4.4). Fenestella wisely left the matter open, stating merely that T. lived and died between the Second and Third Punic Wars (Suet. *Vita* 1).

T. supposedly left a daughter, who later married a man of equestrian rank, and a small but comfortable estate of twenty iugera. His description (Suet. *Vita* 6) is merely the stock appearance of any Carthaginian (cf. Plaut. *Poen.* 112). For the iconographical tradition (spurious) see: Schanz–Hosius I 104; S. Charitonides, L. Kahil, R. Ginouvès, *Les mosaïques de la maison du Ménandre* (Bern 1970) 28–31, 103, and pl. 2 (relationship to iconography of Menander).

WORKS

(1) *Andria* 'The girl from Andros', from Menander with ideas or elements also from his *Perinthia* 'The girl from Perinthos' according to T. (9ff.), though this is a quite inadequate account of all the changes he made. Criticized by Luscius Lanuvinus (contemporary writer of *fabulae palliatae*) on the ground that *contaminari non decere fabulas* (16). Produced at Megalensian Games 166 B.C. with moderate success (Donat. *praef. An.* 7). Curule aediles M'. Acilius Glabrio (*RE* 36) and M. Fulvius Nobilior (*RE* 93); principal players L. Ambivius Turpio and L. Atilius Praenestinus (see C. Garton, *Personal aspects of the Roman theater* (Toronto 1972) 245).

(2) *Hecyra* 'The mother-in-law', from Apollodorus of Carystus without substantial changes. A failure at its first trial, Megalensian Games (so the production notice in the *codex Bembinus* and Donat. *praef. Hec.* 6; Roman Games, Calliopian MSS) 165 B.C. Curule aediles Cn. Cornelius Dolabella (*RE* 132) and Sex. Iulius Caesar (*RE* 148/9). Principal player L. Ambivius Turpio (prol. *passim*, Donat. loc. cit.).

(3) *Heauton timorumenos* 'The self-tormentor', from Menander. T. says it is a fresh (i.e. previously untried Latin) version of a fresh (i.e. previously unexploited) Greek model, and that it is a play *duplex quae ex argumento factast simplici* – whatever that may mean (4–6). He alludes to Luscius' charge *multas (se) contaminasse graecas dum facit paucas latinas* (17f., cf. *An.* 16) and to the accusation that he depended on his friends' brains, not his own talent (24). Performed successfully at the Megalensian Games 163 B.C.; curule aediles L. Cornelius Lentulus Lupus (*RE* 224, later *princeps senatus* and *bête noire* of Lucilius) and L. Valerius Flaccus (*RE* 174). Principal players as in *Andria.*

(4) *Eunuchus* 'The eunuch', from Menander with two characters taken from his *Colax* 'The flatterer' (20ff.), though that is in no way an adequate explanation of the manifold alterations T. has made to his model. He was accused in this case of plagiarism by Luscius, for there had been a previous version of *Colax* 'by Plautus and Menander' about which T. says he had known nothing. Performed with great success at the Megalensian Games 161 B.C., it was sold a second time, as if a new play, for 8,000 sesterces, a record price (Donat. *praef. Eun.* 6, Suet, *Vita Ter.* 10). Curule aediles L. Cornelius Merula (*RE* 271) and L. Postumius Albinus (*RE* 42). Principal players as in *Andria* (so the production-notice; Ambivius and L. Minucius Prothymus, Donat. *praef. Eun.* 6, on which see Garton, under *Andria* above, 257).

(5) *Phormio*, from Apollodorus of Carystus' 'The rival suitor', with little substantial alteration. Performed successfully at the *ludi Romani* (so the production-notices in Calliopian MSS; Megalensian Games, *codex Bembinus* and Donat. *praef. Ph.* 6) 161 B.C. with same presiding magistrates as for *Eunuchus*; actors as in *Andria* (*L. Cassio Atilio* (sic) *et L. Ambivio*, Donat. loc. cit.). The charge laid here by Luscius was that T.'s previous plays *tenui esse oratione et scriptura leui* (5).

(6) *Adelphoe* 'The brothers', Menander's second play of that name, with a scene (154–96) taken from the *Synapothnescontes* 'Partners in death' of Diphilus; Plautus had turned this play, but omitted the material in question, so that no charge of plagiarism from a Latin source could arise. Again this is not an adequate account of all the substantial changes T. has made (6ff.). T. here returns to the charge that he received more than encouragement from *homines nobiles* (15ff., cf. *H.T.* 24). Performed at funeral games of L. Aemilius Paullus (*RE* 114) 160 B.C., financed and put on by his sons by blood Q. Fabius Maxumus Aemilianus (*RE* 109) and P. Cornelius Scipio Aemilianus. Principal actors uncertain: L. Ambivius Turpio and L. Atilius Praenestinus (production-notice in *codex Bembinus*); L. Atilius Praenestinus and Q. Minucius Prothynus (production-notice in Calliopian MSS); L. Ambivio et L. [vac.] (Donat. *praef. Ad.* 6).

A second attempt to produce the *Hecyra* failed at this festival (*Hec.* prol. 1). It was finally produced successfully at one of the regular festivals run by curule aediles of 160 B.C. (Donat. *praef. Hec.* 6 is confused) Q. Fulvius Nobilior (*RE* 95; in honour of whom Ennius had taken his *praenomen* Quintus) and L. Marcius Censorinus (*RE* 46, dedicatee of a work by the philosopher Clitomachus, Cic. *Acad.* 2.102). These philhellenes must have been sympathetic to Terence's ideas to have backed such a loser.

BIBLIOGRAPHY

TEXTS AND COMMENTARIES: TEXTS: F. Umpfenbach (Berlin 1870: still fullest source of information as to MSS); K. Dziatzko (Leipzig 1884); R. Y. Tyrrell (Oxford 1902); R. Kauer, W. M. Lindsay (OCT, 1926; slightly revised O. Skutsch 1958); S. Prete (Heidelberg 1954), but cf. O. Skutsch, *C.R.* n.s.6 (1956) 129–33. TEXTS WITH TRANSLATION: Sir J. Sargeaunt (Loeb, 1912); J. Marouzeau (Budé, 1942–9; vol. 1 rev. 1963); R. Ranzato, R. Cantarella, vol. 1: *Andria, Heauton timorumenos* (Milan 1971: in progress). COMMENTARIES: (1) Complete. M. Antonius Muretus, 2 vols. (Venice 1555); G. Faernus, 2 vols. (Florence 1565); F. Lindenbruchius (Paris 1602: with Donatus' comm.); N. Camus (Paris 1675); R. Bentley (Cambridge 1726, Amsterdam 1727: includes Bentley's *De metris terentianis* σχεδίασμα, fundamental work on relation of ictus and word-accent in iambo-trochaic verse, i–xix); W. Wagner (Cambridge 1869); S. G. Ashmore (New York 1908). (2) Individual plays. *Andria*: G. P. Shipp, 2nd ed. (Oxford 1960). *Hecyra*: T. F. Carney (Pretoria 1968). *Heauton timorumenos*: K. I. Lietzmann, 2 vols. (Münster 1974). *Eunuchus*: P. Fabia (Paris

1895); ed. by P. McG. Brown (Oxford) in preparation. *Phormio*: R. H. Martin (London 1959). *Adelphoe*: idem (Cambridge 1976). K. Dziatzko's edition of *Phormio* rev. E. Hauler (Berlin 1913), of *Adelphoe* rev. R. Kauer (Berlin 1921).

TRANSLATIONS: H. T. Riley (London 1853); (ed.) G. Duckworth, *The complete Roman drama* II (New York 1942) 141–452 (anonymous except *Phormio*, tr. B. H. Clark); L. Echard (1689), ed. R. Graves (London 1963); F. O. Copley (Indianapolis 1967); B. Radice, 2nd ed. (Penguin, 1976).

BIBLIOGRAPHICAL AIDS AND SURVEYS: W. Wagner, *J.A.W.* 1 (1873) 443; 4 (1874–5) 798; A. Spengel, *J.A.W.* 6 (1876) 356–94; 27 (1881) 177–200; 39 (1884) 74–90; 68 (1891) 171–209; F. Schlee, *J.A.W.* 84 (1897) 116–64; R. Kauer, *J.A.W.* 143 (1909) 176–270; H. Marti, *Lustrum* 6 (1961) 114–238 (for 1909–59), 8 (1963) 5–101 and 244–64 (exceptionally useful); S. Prete, *C.W.* 54 (1961) 112–22. See also: P. W. Harsh, 'Early Latin metre and prosody 1904–55', *Lustrum* 3 (1958) 215ff.; H.-J. Mette, 'Der heutige Menander', *Lustrum* 10 (1965) 5ff.; G. Duckworth, *The nature of Roman comedy* (Princeton 1952) 447–64.

STUDIES. (1) COMPREHENSIVE: P. E. Legrand, *Daos, Tableau de la comédie grecque ... dite nouvelle* (Paris 1910: English tr. by J. Loeb, *The Greek New Comedy* (London 1917)); Leo, *Gesch.* 232–58; G. Norwood, *Plautus and Terence* (New York 1932: good on T., bad on Plautus); G. Jachmann, *RE* VA.1 (1934) 598–650; B. Croce, 'Intorno alle commedie di Terenzio', *La Critica* 34 (1936) 401–23 (illuminates certain traits of much subsequent Italian scholarship); E. Reitzenstein, *Terenz als Dichter* (Amsterdam-Leipzig 1940); G. Duckworth, *The nature of Roman comedy* (Princeton 1952); W. Beare, *The Roman stage*, 3rd ed. (London 1964: good on *contaminatio*); H. Marti, *Untersuchungen zur dramatischen Technik bei Plautus und Terenz* (Zurich 1959); M. R. Posani, 'Aspetti del comico in Terenzio', *A. & R.* 7 (1962) 65–76; O. Bianco, *Terenzio: problemi e aspetti dell'originalità* (Rome 1962), cf. W. Ludwig, *Gnomon* 36 (1964) 152ff.; D. Klose, *Die Didaskalien und Prologe des Terenz* (Freiburg 1966); H.-J. Gluecklich, *Aussparung und Antithese: Studien zur terenzischen Komödie* (Frankfurt 1966), cf. H. Marti, *Gnomon* 43 (1971) 354–9; H. Haffter, *Terenz und seine künstlerische Eigenart* (Darmstadt 1967) = *M.H.* 10 (1953) 1–20, 73–102, Italian tr. by D. Nardo, *Terenzio e la sua personalità artistica* (Rome 1969); B. Denzler, *Der Monolog bei Terenz* (Zurich 1968), cf. E. Fantham, *Phoenix* 23 (1969) 406–8; P. Flury, *Liebe und Liebessprache bei Menander, Plautus, und Terenz* (Heidelberg 1968); W. Ludwig, 'The originality of Terence and his Greek models', *G.R.B.S.* 9 (1968) 169–92; Williams, *TORP* 289–94, al.; E. Lefèvre, *Die Expositionstechnik in den Komödien des Terenz* (Darmstadt 1969); K. Gaiser, 'Plautus und Terenz gegenüber ihre griechischen Vorbildern', *ANRW* I.2 1027–1113; W. Goerler, 'Doppelhandlung, Intrige, und Anagnorismos bei Terenz', *Poetica* 5 (1972) 241–55; H. Gelhaus, *Die Prologe des Terenz: eine Erklärung nach den Lehren von der inventio et dispositio* (Heidelberg 1972);

B. Taladoire, *Térence, un théâtre de la jeunesse* (Paris 1972), cf. E. Segal, *A.J.Ph.* 96 (1975) 203–5, E. Lefèvre, *Gnomon* 48 (1976) 78–80; *Association Guillaume Budé, Actes du IXe Congrès, Rome* 13–18 *avril* 1973 vol. 1 (Paris 1975: papers on Plautus and T.); (ed.) E. Lefèvre, *Die römische Komödie: Plautus und Terenz*, Wege der Forschung 236 (Darmstadt 1973), cf. P. McG. Brown, *Gnomon* 48 (1976) 244–9; L. Perelli, *Il teatro rivoluzionario di Terenzio* (Florence 1973); K. Büchner, *Das Theater des Terenz* (Heidelberg 1974); W. G. Arnott, *Menander, Plautus, and Terence* (Oxford 1965); F. H. Sandbach, *The comic theatre of Greece and Rome* (Oxford 1977); H. Juhnke, 'Terenz', in (ed.) E. Lefèvre, *Das römische Drama* (Darmstadt 1978) 223–307.

(2) LEXICON: P. McGlynn, 2 vols. (Glasgow–London 1963–7), cf. J.-H. Waszink, *Mnemosyne* 20 (1967) 88–98, 23 (1970) 214.

(3) INDIVIDUAL PLAYS (since Marti's *Lustrum*-survey): *Heauton timorumenos*: A Primmer, 'Zum Prolog des Heautontimorumenos', *W.S.* 77 (1964) 61–75; idem, 'Die homo-sum-Szene im Heautontimorumenos', *W.S.* 79 (1966) 293–8; E. Fantham, 'Hautontimorumenos and Adelphoe. A study of fatherhood in Terence and Menander', *Latomus* 30 (1971) 970–98; H. D. Jocelyn, 'Homo sum: humani nil a me alienum puto', *Antichthon* 7 (1973) 14–46; E. Lefèvre, 'Der "Heautontimorumenos" des Terenz', *Die römische Komödie: Plautus und Terenz*, Wege der Forschung 236 (Darmstadt 1973) 443–62. *Eunuchus*: B. Bader, 'Terenz, Eunuchus 46–57', *Rh.M.* 116 (1973) 54–9; K. Gilmartin, 'The Thraso-subplot in Terence's Eunuchus', *C.W.* 69 (1975) 263–7; C. F. Saylor, 'The theme of planlessness in Terence's Eunuchus', *T.A.Ph.A.* 105 (1975) 297–311. *Phormio*: W. G. Arnott, 'Phormio Parasitus', *G.&R.* 17 (1970) 32–57. *Adelphoe*: W. G. Arnott, 'The end of Terence's Adelphoe: a postscript', *G.&R.* 10 (1963) 140–4; O. Rieth, *Die Kunst Menanders in den 'Adelphen' des Terenz* (Hildesheim 1964: ed. with Appendix by K. Gaiser); W. R. Johnston, 'Micio and the perils of perfection', *C.S.C.A.* 1 (1968) 171–86; E. Fantham, 'Terence, Adelphoe Act II', *Philologus* 112 (1968) 196–216; H. Tränkle, 'Micio und Demea in den terenzischen Adelphen' *M.H.* 29 (1972) 241–55; H. Lloyd-Jones, 'Terentian technique in the Adelphi and the Eunuchus', *C.Q.* n.s.23 (1973) 279–84; J. N. Grant, 'The ending of Terence's Adelphoe and the Menandrian original', *A.J.Ph.* 96 (1975) 42–60; V. Pöschl, 'Das Problem der Adelphen des Terenz', *S.H.A.W.* 1975, 4, cf. C. Garton, *C.W.* 70 (1976) 203–7.

(4) STYLE: J. B. Hoffman, *Die lateinische Umgangssprache* (Heidelberg 1926: 3rd ed. 1951); J. T. Allardice, *The syntax of Terence* (Oxford 1929); H. Haffter, *Untersuchungen zur altlateinischen Dichtersprache* (Berlin 1934); J. Straus, *Terenz und Menander: Beitrag zu einer Stilvergleichung* (diss. Bern 1955); G. Luck, *Rh. M.* 108 (1965) 269–77.

(5) TRANSMISSION: G. Jachmann, *Die Geschichte des Terenztextes im Altertum* (Basel 1924); L. W. Jones, C. R. Morey, *The miniatures of the MSS of Terence prior to the thirteenth century*, 2 vols. (Princeton 1932); S. Prete, *Il codice di Terenzio Vaticano 3226: saggio critico e riproduzione del manoscritto*, Studi e testi 262 (Vatican City 1970: full photographic reproduction of *codex Bembinus*); J. N. Grant, 'Contamination in the mixed MSS of Terence: a partial solution?', *T.A.Ph.A.* 105 (1975) 123–53.

(6) DONATUS' COMMENTARY: Text: P. Wessner (BT, 1902–8; repr. Stuttgart 1963); H. T. Karsten (Leiden 1912–13). Cf. J. N. Grant, 'Notes on Donatus' commentary on Adelphoe', *G.R.B.S.* 12 (1971) 197ff.

AFRANIUS, LUCIUS

LIFE

Active *c.* 160–120 B.C. as a writer of *fabulae togatae* (Vell. Pat. 1.17.1, 2.9.3) and possibly also as an orator in the lawcourts (Cic. *Brut.* 167 *homo perargutus*; Leo, *Gesch.* 375 n.4).

WORKS

Forty-two titles represented by *c.* 430 fragmentary verses, almost all cited by grammarians, are known. More than fifty verses: *Vopiscus* 'The surviving twin'. More than twenty verses: *Divortium* 'The divorce'; *Emancipatus* 'Free from father' (?); *Epistula* 'The letter'; *Exceptus* 'Rescued from shipwreck' (?); *Fratriae* 'Sisters-in-law'; *Privignus* 'The stepson'. Others: *Abducta* 'The kidnapped girl'; *Aequales* 'The friends'; *Auctio* 'The auction'; *Augur* 'The augur'; *Brundisinae* 'The ladies from Brindisi'; *Cinerarius* 'The hairdresser'; *Compitalia* 'The Crossroads Festival'; *Consobrini* 'The cousins'; *Crimen* 'Calumny'; *Deditio* 'Capitulation'; *Depositum* 'The sum set aside'; *Ida* (corrupt title); *Incendium* 'The fire'; *Inimici* 'The rivals'; *Libertas* 'Freedom'; *Mariti* 'The husbands'; *Materterae* 'Mother's sisters'; *Megalesia* 'The Feast of the Great Mother'; *Omen* 'The sign'; *Pantaleo* (personal name, or corrupt); *Pompa* 'The procession'; *Prodigus* 'The wastrel'; *Proditus* 'Betrayed'; *Promus* 'The steward'; *Purgamentum* 'The expiation'; *Repudiati* 'The rejected lovers' (?); *Sella* 'The seat'; *Simulans* 'The feigner'; *Sorores* 'The sisters'; *Suspecta* 'The girl under suspicion'; *Talio* 'Tit for tat'; *Temerarius* 'Jumping to conclusions'; *Thais*; *Titulus* 'The notice'; *Virgo* 'The girl'.

The character and categories of these titles closely match those of New Comedy playwrights such as Menander as opposed to those of the older *palliata*-writers. Afranius was evidently a self-conscious and well-educated artist, borrowing a good deal in technique and themes from Menander (Cic. *Fin.* 1.3.7, Hor. *Epist.* 2.1.57) and 'even from the Latins' (Macr. *Sat.* 6.1.4. (25–30 Ribbeck, *Compitalia*), cf. Suet. *Vita Terenti* p. 8) – Terence, whom he greatly admired (for his Menandrian aspirations?) (Macr. loc. cit.), the tragedian C. Titius (Cic. *Brut.* 167), and Pacuvius (a quotation, fr. 7 Ribbeck). The prologue of the *Compitalia* included or consisted of a defence of his eclectic approach in the same argumentative manner as in a Terentian prologue; elsewhere (277, 298f., 403f.) there are fragments of prologues spoken by divinities and abstractions, which implies that Menandrian ironies arising from the superior knowledge of the audience were a feature of his plays. Quintilian qualifies his praise of Afranius as an excellent all-round author for school-use like Menander because of the explicitly homosexual themes of some of the plays (Quint. 10.1.100). This boldness must be set against what appears to have been a relatively pusillanimous if realistic treatment of slave-roles, if Donatus' comment at Ter. *Eun.* 57, that clever slaves were not permissible in the explicitly Italian ambience of the *fabula togata*, is to be taken literally. It is important to note that although he wrote after Terence's time the musical and metrical presentation and the diction of Afranius' plays is essentially a direct continuation of the manner of the older *fabula palliata*: anapaests, bacchiacs, other lyric metres, and the jaunty iambic septenarius are well represented among the fragments. His verbal inventiveness and use of alliteration is like that of Caecilius and Plautus.

Afranius was well known in later times: Cicero refers to a performance of *Simulans* (*Sest.* 118); there was an extravagantly realistic performance of *Incendium* in Nero's reign (Suet. *Nero* 11); Quintilian thought highly of him except in one respect; and one Paulus wrote a commentary on some of his plays in the Hadrianic period (Charis. *GLK* I 241.1f.). The suggestion, however, that *P. Hamb.* 167, a fragment of prose mime, is from an Afranius-play must be rejected (J. Dingel, 'Bruchstück einer römischen Komödie auf einem Hamburger Papyrus (Afranius?)', *Z.P.E.* 10 (1973) 29–44; B. Bader, 'Ein Afraniuspapyrus?', ibid. 12 (1973) 270–6; J. Dingel, 'Zum Komödienfragment *P. Hamb.* 167 (Afranius?)', ibid. 14 (1974) 168).

BIBLIOGRAPHY

TEXTS: *CRF* 193ff. (not in *ROL*). A selection of the fragments is given by E. Diehl, *Poetarum Romanorum veterum reliquiae*, 6th ed. (Berlin 1967) 95–102.

STUDIES: Leo, *Gesch.* 374ff.; W. Beare, 'The fabula togata', *Hermathena* 55 (1940) 35–55; idem, *The Roman stage*, 3rd ed. (London 1964) 128ff.; M. Cacciaglia, 'Ricerche sulla fabula togata', *R.C.C.M.* 14 (1972) 207–45.

PACUVIUS, MARCUS

LIFE

b. 220 B.C. (Cic. *Brut.* 229 with Jerome, *Chron.* 139 B.C.); nephew of Ennius (Pliny, *N.H.* 35.19; Jerome wrongly says grandson). Jerome puts his *floruit* in 154 B.C. and says he came from Brundisium (Pacuvius an Oscan name). Varro quotes an epigram by one Pompilius who claims to have been a 'pupil' of P. as he was in turn of Ennius and Ennius of the Muses (*Sat. Men.* 356); cf. traditions that Menander was nephew and pupil of Alexis (Suda s.n. Ἄλεξις Θούριος κωμικός, anon. *De comoedia* (*CGF* ed. Kaibel I p. 9) 17). This implies that P. was a *ciuis ingenuus* and not necessarily *libertino patre natus* like, say, Horace: Ennius' family claimed descent from king Messapus. P. was, after Ennius, the first unequivocally 'respectable' poet. It is evident from the facts that he was the first to specialize exclusively in serious drama, and that his output was relatively small for one who lived so long, that he did not depend upon the pen for his livelihood. Pliny (loc. cit.) says he was the painter of a picture still to be seen in the Temple of Hercules in the *forum Boarium* and was the first to lend prestige (through his theatrical fame) to the art of painting in Rome; cf. Jerome, *Chron.* 154 B.C. Cicero makes Laelius mention P. as his *hospes et amicus* (*Amic.* 24), implying that he was one of the 'Scipionic circle'. Both P. and Accius staged plays at festival of 140 B.C. (Cic. *Brut.* 229). Gellius (13.2.2; cf. Jerome, loc. cit.) says that P. retired to Tarentum owing to illness and tells a *traditio*-story according to which Accius, on his way to Asia, stopped at Pacuvius' and read him his *Atreus c.* 135 B.C. d. *c.* 131 B.C. (Gell. loc. cit.). Varro quoted his epitaph in *De poetis* (*ap.* Gell. 1.24.4); this, unlike the epitaphs which he quotes for Naevius and Plautus, is probably genuine in the sense that it appeared on his tombstone, but it is far from certain that he wrote it himself as Varro claims: essentially the same epitaph is attested for two others of this period (*CIL* I^2 1209–10; *CLE* 848, 53), and though the poet's name is accommodated to the metre better than in these other cases, it is still awkwardly fitted in (. . . *Pacuui Marci sita* | *ossa. hoc uolebam* . . .); there is no difficulty in the inversion of *nomen* and *praenomen*, but the enjambment with hiatus followed by elision across a strong breath-pause is suspiciously artificial. It is probable that in all three cases we have a standard epitaph from the copy-book of a mason of the Gracchan era. Reputation: Favourable comment: Cic. *Opt. gen. orat.* 1.2; Hor. *Epist.* 2.1.55; Vell. Pat. 2.9.3; Quint. 10.1.97; Gell. 6.14.6. Adverse: Lucilius bks 26–9 *passim* (early 120s, not long after P.'s death: word-formation, gloom, pretentiousness, contorted diction); Cic. *Brut.* 258 (his and Caecilius' *latinitas* unfavourably contrasted with that of Laelius and Aemilianus), cf. *Or.* 152; Quint. 1.5.67 (word-formation); Pers. 1.77 (cf. Lucilius).

WORKS

(1) TRAGEDIES: Twelve or thirteen titles, of which *c.* 380 assigned and *c.* 55 unassigned verses survive. More than thirty-five extant lines: *Chryses* (from Sophocles), *Dulorestes*, *Medus*, *Periboea*, *Teucer*. More than twenty: *Antiopa* (from Euripides), *Atalanta*, *Hermiona*, *Iliona*, *Niptra* (from Sophocles: the earliest known Odysseus-drama on the Roman stage). Others: *Armorum iudicium* (Aeschylus), *Pentheus*, perhaps *Protesilaus* (but see R. Helm, *RE* XVIII (1942) 2172; the only evidence is in Antonius Volscus' introduction to Ovid, *Her.* 13 (*Epistulae Heroidum*, Venice 1497)). (2) FABULA PRAETEXTA: *Paullus*, after 168 B.C.; in honour of L. Aemilius Paullus, the victor at Pydna (four citations). (3) SATURA mentioned by Diomedes, *GLK* I 485.32, Porph. *ad* Hor. *Sat.* 1.10.46. No fragments.

BIBLIOGRAPHY

TEXTS: *TRF* 86–157; *ROL* II 158–322; (ed.) A. Klotz, with O. Seel, L. Voit, *Scaenicorum Romanorum fragmenta* vol. I: *Tragicorum fragmenta* (Oldenbourg 1953), cf. O. Skutsch, *Gnomon* 26 (1954) 465–70 (review more important textually than the edition, which had been intended to replace *TRF*; both examined with special reference to P.); R. Argenio (Turin 1959); G. d'Anna (Rome 1967), cf. C. Garton, *A.J.Ph.* 91 (1970) 228–33.

STUDIES: FUNDAMENTAL: Leo, *Gesch.* 226–32; R. Helm, *RE* XVIII (1942) 2156–74 (excellent survey of post-Leo scholarship and accounts of individual plays); I. Mariotti, *Introduzione a Pacuvio* (Urbino 1960: complementary to Helm), cf. H. Haffter, *Gnomon* 40 (1968) 206; M. Valsa, *Marcus Pacuvius, Poète tragique* (Paris 1957). SEE ALSO: H.-J. Mette, *Lustrum* 9 (1964) 78–107, al. (Roman tragic poets 1945–64); B. Bilinski, *Contrastanti ideali di cultura sulla scena di Pacuvio* (Warsaw 1962), cf. J.-H. Waszink, *Mnemosyne* 19 (1966) 82–4; W. Beare, *The Roman stage*, 3rd ed. (London 1964) 79–84.

ACCIUS, LUCIUS

LIFE

b. 170 B.C. at Pisaurum; his family freedmen *coloni*. Put on a tragedy at same festival as the aged Pacuvius in 140 or 139 B.C. (Jerome, *Chron.* 139 B.C., given as his *floruit*). Wrote his *Brutus* and a triumphal saturnian inscription (*Works* 2 and 5) for D. Junius Brutus Callaicus (*RE* Iunius 57, cos. 138 B.C.); cf. Cic. *Arch.* 27, schol. Bob. *ad loc.*, Val. Max. 8.14.2, Cic. *Leg.* 2.54, Plut. *Q. Rom.* 34, Cic. *Brut.* 107 and 229. *c.* 135 B.C. travelled to 'Asia' (Gell. 13.2), i.e. Pergamum; before embarking is supposed to have met and stayed with Pacuvius at Tarentum and read him his *Atreus* (Gell. loc. cit.). In 120s was object of repeated attacks by Lucilius and became official head of the College of Poets, on which he had erected a gigantic statue of himself (Pliny, *N.H.* 34.19, cf. Lucilius (28) 794 M = *ROL* 844: he himself was very short); cf. Serv. *ad Aen.* 1.8, B. Tamm, *Opusc. Rom.* III (1961) 157–67, H. Cancik, *M.D.A.I.(R)* 76 (1969) 323, E. Badian, 'Ennius and his friends', *Entretiens XVII* (Fondation Hardt 1971) 151–95. It was noted that A. would not rise in honour of the senatorial poet Julius Caesar Strabo *in collegium poetarum uenienti*, an anecdote referring to *c.* 95–87 B.C. (Val. Max. 3.7.11); Cicero heard him lecturing in early 80s B.C. His latest known tragedy was *Tereus* (104 B.C., Cic. *Phil.* 1.15.36). The freedman scholar Lutatius Daphnis was educated as a slave by A. and he sold him for a record price to the *princeps senatus* M. Aemilius Scaurus (Pliny, *N.H.* 7.128). He successfully prosecuted an actor who named him on the stage (auct. *Ad Her.* 1.24, cf. 2.19). Reputation: Cic. *Planc.* 24, *Sest.* 56; Ovid, *Am.* 1.15.19; Vitr. 9 *praef.* 16; Vell. Pat. 1.17.1. Comparisons with Pacuvius: Hor. *Epist.* 2.1.55; Vell. Pat. 2.9.3; Quint. 10.1.97.

WORKS

(1) FABULAE CREPIDATAE (*c.* 700 verses): (*a*) more than forty verses: *Epigoni*, *Eurysaces*, *Philocteta Lemnius*; (*b*) more than twenty verses: *Armorum iudicium*, *Astyanax*,

Atreus (*c.* 135 B.C.), *Bacchae*, *Epinausimache*, *Medea* or *Argonautae*, *Phoenissae*, *Telephus*; (*c*) fewer than twenty verses: *Achilles*, *Aegisthus*, *Agamemnonidae*, *Alcestis*, *Alcmeo*, *Alphesiboea*, *Amphitryo*, *Andromeda*, *Antenoridae*, *Antigona*, *Athamas*, *Chrysippus*, *Clytaemestra*, *Deiphobus*, *Diomedes*, *Hecuba*, *Hellenes*, *Io*, *Melanippus*, *Meleager*, *Minos* or *Minotaurus*, *Myrmidones* (= *Achilles*?), *Neoptolemus*, *Nyctegresia*, *Oenomaus*, *Pelopidae*, *Persidae*, *Phinidae*, *Prometheus*, *Stasiastae* or *Tropaeum liberi*, *Tereus* (104 B.C.), *Thebais*, *Troades*.

(2) FABULAE PRAETEXTAE: *Aeneadae* or *Decius*, *Brutus*.

(3) SCHOLARLY WORKS: (*a*) *Didascalicon libri ix*, partly in Sotadic metre and partly in prose (so Leo, *Gesch.* 389, n.3, rightly; Warmington, *ROL* II 578 is wrong), on the history of the Greek and Roman theatre and other literary questions (e.g. the priority of Homer and Hesiod, lib. i *ap.* Gell. 3.11.4, contradicting Eratosthenes (R. Pfeiffer, *History of classical scholarship* I (Oxford 1968) 164)). (*b*) *Pragmatica*, two or more books in trochaic verse on literary themes. (*c*) *Annales* in hexameters: the only long fragment (Macr. *Sat.* 1.7.36) is aetiological, explaining the Roman Saturnalia as an imitation of the Athenian Kronia. (*d*) *Parerga*, two or more books: the one citation (senarii) is about ploughing. (*e*) *Praxidica* twice mentioned as by 'Attius' (Pliny, *N.H. praef.* 18 and 18.200). (*f*) *Sotadicon libri* assumed to be identical with *Didascalica* (Gell. 6.9.16), but perhaps erotic in theme and to be identified with

(4) AMATORY VERSE (Pliny, *Epist.* 5.3): but this might be elegiac epigrams like those of Q. Catulus and Valerius Aedituus (Gell. 19.9.11, Apul. *Apol.* 9).

(5) SATURNIANS on the temple of Mars dedicated in later 130s by A.'s patron D. Junius Brutus Callaicus (Cic. *Arch.* 27, schol. Bob. *ad loc.*).

(6) ORTHOGRAPHICAL PRECEPTS: write *-gg-* for *-ng-*; use *u* and *s* not *y* and *z*; distinguish long vowels by writing, e.g., *-aa-* not *-a-*; but in the case of long *-i-* write *-ei-*; use *-i-* for the short vowel; do not Latinize the oblique cases of Greek names (*Hectora* not *Hectorem*). See Mar. Vict. *GLK* VI 8.11, Prisc. *GLK* II 30.12, Vel. gramm. *GLK* VII 55.25, Scaur. gramm. *GLK* VII 18.12, Varro, *Ling. Lat.* 7.96, 10.70; cf. Lucilius (9) 351ff. M = *ROL* 368ff.

BIBLIOGRAPHY

TEXTS: (1) COMPLETE: *ROL* pp. 326–606; A. Resta Barrile (Bologna 1969). (2) PLAYS ONLY: *TRF* pp. 157–263; O. Seel, L. Voit (ed. A. Klotz), *Scaenicorum Romanorum fragmenta* vol. 1: *Tragicorum fragmenta* (Oldenbourg 1953); Q. Franchella (Bologna 1968). (3) OTHER WORKS: *GrRF* I. (4) SELECTIONS: *Poetarum Romanorum veterum reliquiae* selegit Ernestus Diehl, 6th ed. (Berlin 1967) 73–92; R. Argenio, *Frammenti tragici scelte* (Rome 1962) with 'Tragedie acciane', *R.S.C.* 14 (1966) 5–53.

STUDIES: Leo, *Gesch.* 384–405; J. Glaser, 'Bericht über Accius 1926–1930', *J.A.W.* 224 (1934) 70f.; H.-J. Mette, 'Die römische Tragödie und die Neufunde zur griechischen Tragödie für die Jahre 1945–64', *Lustrum* 9 (1964) 17f., 107–60;

I. Mariotti, 'Tragédie romaine et tragédie grecque: Accius et Euripide', *M.H.* 22 (1965) 206–16; E. Dobroiou, 'A propos des oeuvres d'érudition d'Accius', *Analele Univ. Bucureşti*, St. Soc. fil. 15 (1966) 13–35; R. Argenio, 'Tragedie acciane', *R.S.C.* 14 (1966) 5–53; H. D. Jocelyn, 'The quotations of Republican dramatists in Priscian's treatise De metris fabularum Terenti', *Antichthon* 1 (1967) 60–9 (appendix on the *Medea* or *Argonautae*); E. Gabba, 'Il Brutus di Accio', *Dioniso* 43 (1969) 377–83; H. Cancik, 'Die Statue des L. Accius im Tempel der Camenen', *Silvae: Festschrift für E. Zinn zum 60. Geburtstag*, ed. M. von Albrecht, E. Heck (Tübingen 1970) 7–17; idem, *M.D.A.I.(R)* 76 (1969) 323; A. Traina, *Vortit barbare* (Rome 1970) 181–203; A. de Rosalia, 'L'alliterazione in L. Accio', *A.L.G.P.* 7–8 (1970–1) 139–215; V. d'Anto, 'L'Athamas di Ennio e di Accio', *B. Stud. Lat.* 1 (1971) 371–8; D. Ferrin Sutton, 'Aeschylus' Edonians' (and the *Stasiastae* of Accius), *Saggi in onore di V. d'Agostino* (Turin 1971) 387–411; S. Sconocchie, 'L'Antigona di Accio e l'Antigone di Sofocle', *R.F.I.C.* 100 (1972) 273–82; A. di Benedetto-Zimbone, 'L'Atreus di Accio', *Sic. Gymn.* 26 (1973) 266–85; G. Paduano, 'Sul prologo delle Fenicie di Accio', *A.S.N.P.* 3 (1973) 827–35; G. B. Pighi, 'Gli annali di Accio', *Scritti in onore di C. Vassalani raccolta da L. Barbesi* (Verona 1974) 373–80; M. R. Ruiz de Elvira y Serra, 'Los Pelópidas en la literatura clásica', *C.F.C.* 7 (1974) 249–302.

CATO, MARCUS PORCIUS

LIFE

b. at Tusculum 234 B.C. of peasant stock; served in Hannibalic War (217/216 B.C., Campania; 214 B.C., military tribune in Sicily; 207 B.C., distinguished conduct at battle of Sena). Impressed the aristocratic L. Valerius Flaccus with whose help he embarked on a political career. Quaestor in Sicily 204 B.C., C. is supposed to have been responsible for bringing Ennius to Rome in 203/202 B.C. from Sardinia. Plebeian aedile 199 B.C., praetor 198 B.C. in charge of Sardinia; reputation as a just and strict governor, expelling usurers and cutting the 'perks' which as praetor he could have exploited (*leges Porciae de prouocatione* and *de sumptu prouinciali* may be dated to this year). Consul 195 B.C. (with Valerius Flaccus) he opposed the repeal of the *Lex Oppia* which limited the public display by women of family wealth, and took charge of Spain, where he behaved with severity towards the Spanish tribes and cultivated his reputation for frugality and efficiency. In 191 B.C. as military tribune with Valerius Flaccus under Acilius Glabrio the consul he fought at Thermopylae and conducted an important diplomatic mission to Athens and other Greek cities. In 190 B.C. prosecuted Q. Minucius Thermus, the first known in a long succession of prosecutions aimed at the then dominant Scipionic faction, and supported charges of peculation against Acilius Glabrio who, as C. himself, was a candidate for the censorship of 189 B.C. This time he failed, but in the sequel he was a central figure in the now obscure manoeuvres which led to the downfall of the Scipios in politics (188 B.C.). Exploiting this and other shocks to public confidence, he became censor (again with L. Valerius Flaccus) in 184 B.C. presenting himself as the champion of the good old Roman virtues at a time of unprecedented social, economic and moral upheaval; see Plut. *Cato maj.* 17–19. Most of C.'s writings date from this time or later, and for the rest of his life he continued to advocate the *mores maiorum*, presenting himself as a bluff and canny peasant, with the self-made man's contempt for those born to wealth and power. He made many enemies and was constantly involved in prosecutions both as prosecutor and defendant, though he himself was never convicted. He was the enemy and mocker not of Hellenism as such, but of pretentiousness, as he saw it, humbug, and vice in philhellenes of noble houses (e.g. the Quinctii Flaminini, the Fulvii Nobiliores) who paid scant attention to the 'ways of their ancestors' – as C. defined them: for what was *noua res* to one generation was *mos maiorum* to the next. He was himself, paradoxically, an outstanding example of the versatility and individualism of the Hellenistic period. He opposed the repeal of a sumptuary law, the *Lex Orchia* (181 B.C.), supported the *Lex Voconia* which limited women's rights of inheritance (169 B.C.), opposed war with Rhodes (167 B.C.) and favoured independence for Macedonia; in 155 B.C. he spoke against the Athenian ambassadors, all three of them philosophers, who caused a stir at Rome, especially the sceptic Carneades. In 153 B.C. he visited Carthage and became convinced then if not earlier that Rome to survive must destroy her old enemy. His overriding political concern was to restore and preserve social cohesion in Rome and Italy, which he saw as a question of morals and moral education; Greece and the East could be left to themselves. On the other hand the government of Spain, still at the end of his life far from settled, concerned him closely from the time of his consulship; in 171 B.C. he prosecuted P. Furius Philus for extortion and in the last year of his life (149 B.C.) Sulpicius Galba on behalf of the Lusitanians. He was survived by two sons, Cato Licinianus by his first wife and Cato Salonianus (grandfather to Cato Uticensis) by a second. Sources: Plut. *Cat. maj.*; Livy 29.25, 32.27, 34, 36, 38–9 *passim*, 43.2, 45.25; Cic. *Sen. passim*; Nepos, *Cato*; and C.'s fragments, see below.

WORKS

(1) Speeches. Cicero found and read more than 150 (*Brut.* 65) and seems to have been responsible for a revival of interest. Today the titles or occasions of some eighty are known (list, *ORF* pp. 553–6), among which twenty belong to the year of his censorship. Best represented or most notable are the following: (*a*) From his consulship (195 B.C.) to his censorship (184 B.C.). (i) Against repeal of *Lex Oppia* (195 B.C.), arguing against relaxation of sumptuary regulations relating to women's expenditure and ornament. Only known from Livy's extensive paraphrase (34.2–4); not in *ORF* (but see *ORF* p. 14). (ii) To cavalry at Numantia (195 B.C.), *ORF* fr. 17–18 (iii) In defence of his actions as consul (191/190 B.C.?), *ORF* fr. 21–55. (iv) To Athenians (191 B.C.), *ORF* fr. 20; important as the earliest known assertion of Latin as a language of international diplomacy on a par with Greek. (v) Against Q. Minucius Thermus *De falsis pugnis*

(190 B.C.), *ORF* fr. 58. (*b*) From his censorship (184/183 B.C.). (vi) Against L. Quinctius Flamininus, *ORF* fr. 69–71. (vii) Against L. Veturius, *ORF* fr. 72–82. (viii) Anticipating a prosecution threatened by tribune of plebs M. Caelius, *ORF* fr. 111–20. (*c*) From his censorship to his death (149 B.C.). (ix) On his Own Fine Qualities, against L. Minucius Thermus after his censorship (183 B.C.), *ORF* fr. 128–35. (x) Against repeal of *Lex Orchia* (181 B.C. or later), *ORF* fr. 139–46; the *Lex Orchia* (182 B.C.) had fixed sumptuary regulations relating to banqueting. As in the case of the *Lex Oppia* C.'s opposition was unsuccessful. (xi) On behalf of the Rhodians (167 B.C.), *ORF* fr. 163–71; the best represented speech, together with (xii) *De sumptu suo* (164 B.C.), *ORF* fr. 173–5. (xiii) Against Ser. Sulpicius Galba on behalf of the plundered Lusitanians (149 B.C.), *ORF* fr. 196–9, delivered by C. aged 85.

(2) *Origines*, a title which properly applies only to the first three of seven books of historical, geographical and political studies, didactic in character, composed during 160s and 150s B.C. in C.'s old age. Bk 1: the Kings of Rome; thirty citations or allusions. Bk 2 (thirty-seven citations) and bk 3 (nine): *origines* of towns, cities and peoples of Italy other than the Roman. Bk 4: First Punic War (fifteen citations). Bk 5: Second Punic War (thirteen citations, including a lengthy passage of the speech *For the Rhodians* (*ORF* fr. 163). Bk 6 (one citation) and bk 7 (twelve): recent and contemporary history, right up to year of C.'s death (149 B.C.), including citation of his speech against Ser. Sulpicius Galba (*ORF* fr. 198). A further twenty-eight citations or allusions of uncertain or ambiguous attribution are preserved.

(3) *De agri cultura*, one book lacking formal structure, the only 'complete' surviving work of C. Extent of interpolation indeterminable.

(4) A book *De disciplina militari* (fifteen citations, pp. 80–2 Jordan) probably not to be distinguished from

(5) A series of pamphlets or letters addressed to his son Marcus (Porcius Cato Licinianus, b. *c.* 192 B.C.): a story-book 'written in big letters' (Plut. *Cato maj.* 20.7); *libri ad filium de agri cultura* (Serv. *ad* Virg. *G.* 2.412), eight citations; *De medicina* (five citations); on rhetoric (three citations including the famous *rem tene, uerba sequentur*, Julius Victor in K. Halm, *Rhetores Latini minores* I (Leipzig 1863) 374.17). Also allusions to a letter of C. to his son (notably Cic. *Off.* 1.10, Plut. *Cat. maj.* 20) written during his service in the army in Macedonia 168 B.C. Relation of these works to each other and manner in which they came to be 'published' is problematic. It goes beyond the evidence and probability to suppose that C. himself published them as a collection which constituted a kind of encyclopaedia.

(6) *Carmen de moribus*, a book of saws attributed to C., only known from Gell. 11.2: no reason to suppose that *carmen* here implies a verse-form, and the three fragments are all prose; cf. *OLD* s.v. *carmen* 'sacred utterance'.

(7) A collection of C.'s 'sayings' and witty remarks was already current in Cicero's day (cf., e.g., *De or.* 2.256, Hor. *Sat.* 1.2.31), the source of some ten anecdotes or examples in Cicero and more in Plutarch's *Life of Cato*. While some of these may be traced to speeches of C., much of this material will have been adventitious. The

versified *Dicta Catonis* which enjoyed a wide circulation in the middle ages derives from a source hardly earlier than the 3rd c. A.D.

(8) The popular belief that C. ended all his speeches by saying *Carthago delenda est* or *ceterum censeo Carthaginem esse delendam* is an overinterpretation of Plut. *Cat. maj.* 27 (cf. Diod. Sic. 34/35.33.3): in the first place, this would only apply to speeches by C. delivered in the senate, and in the second there is no Latin source for the quoted formulations which have been current since only the early 19th c. See S. Thürlemann, *Gymnasium* 81 (1974) 465–75.

BIBLIOGRAPHY

TEXTS AND COMMENTARIES: Speeches: *ORF* 12–97, cf. E. Badian, *J.R.S.* 46 (1956) 218–21, 58 (1968) 256. *Origines*: *HRR* cxxvii–clxiv, 55–97; W. A. Schroeder (Meisenheim 1971: bk 1, with commentary). *De agri cultura*: H. Keil (Leipzig 1882–1902); G. Goetz (Leipzig 1922); E. Bréhaut (New York 1933, repr. 1966: tr. and notes); W. D. Hooper and H. B. Ash (Loeb, 1934); A. Mazzarino (BT, 1962); P. Thielscher (Berlin 1963: with tr.); R. Goujard (Budé, 1975). Remaining works are conventionally cited from H. Jordan, *M. Catonis praeter librum De re rustica quae extant* (Leipzig 1860).

STUDIES: (1) COMPREHENSIVE: M. Gelzer, *RE* XXII (1953) 108–45; Leo, *Gesch.* 265–300; P. Fraccaro, *Opuscula* vol. 1: *Scritti di carattere generale*, *Studi Catoniani* (Pavia 1956) 43–386; E. V. Marmorale, *Cato maior* (Bari 1949); F. della Corte, *Catone censore: la vita e la fortuna* (Florence 1949; 2nd ed. 1969); H. H. Scullard, *Roman politics* 220–150 B.C. (Oxford 1951; 2nd ed. 1973); D. Kienast, *Cato der Zensor: seine Persönlichkeit und seine Zeit mit einem durchgesehen Neuabdruck der Redenfragmente Catos* (Heidelberg 1954). (2) STYLE: R. Till, *Die Sprache Catos*, *Philologus* suppl. 28.2 (1936), Italian tr. by C. de Meo, *La lingua di Catone* (Rome 1968: with supplementary observations); Leo under (1) above; E. Fraenkel, *Leseproben aus den Reden Ciceros und Catos* (Rome 1968). (3) HISTORICAL WORK: B. Janzer, *Historische Untersuchungen zu den Redenfragmenten des M. Porcius Cato. Beiträge zur Lebensgeschichte und Politik Catos* (diss. Würzburg 1936); D. Timpe, 'Le origine di Catone e la storiografia latina', *Atti e Mem. dell'Accademia Patavina* (Classe di Sc. mor., Lett., ed Arti) 83 (1970) 1–33. (4) MINOR WORKS: P. L. Schmidt, 'Catos Epistula ad M. filium und die Anfänge der römischen Briefliteratur', *Hermes* 100 (1972) 568–76.

LUCILIUS, GAIUS

LIFE

(1) DATES: Jerome (*Chron.* 102 B.C.) says L. was honoured with a public funeral at Naples when he died there that year aged 46. This implies he was born in 148 B.C. (coss. Sp. Postumius Albinus and L. Calpurnius Piso), that he was on Aemilianus' staff

at Numantia (Vell. Pat. 2.9.3) at the age of only fifteen, and began writing his Satires before he was twenty. This is not intrinsically impossible but is ruled out by Horace's allusion to L.'s oeuvre as a whole as giving a comprehensive *uita senis* (Hor. *Sat.* 2.1.34); it is generally accepted that Jerome confused the consuls of 148 B.C. with those of 180 B.C. (A. Postumius Albinus and C. Calpurnius Piso); for a compromise (168/167 B.C.), see I. Mariotti, F. della Corte, W. Krenkel, *Maia* 20 (1968) 254–70; W. Krenkel, *ANRW* I.2 1240–59. (2) FAMILY: Came from distinguished family of the Latin aristocracy whose seat was at Suessa Aurunca on the borders of Campania (Juv. 1.20, schol. *ad loc.*). Horace calls him *auus* (ps.-Acron *ad* Hor. *Sat.* 2.1.29) and *auunculus* (Porph. *ad* Hor. *Sat.* 2.1.75) to Pompey the Great through his sister; Pompey's mother was herself another Lucilia. This makes L. great-uncle of Pompey. His precise relationship to Lucilius Hirrus, pr. 134 B.C. and to M'. Lucilius M.f. Pomptina, a senator who visited Pergamum as ambassador in 129 B.C., is obscure (C. Cichorius, *Untersuchungen zu Lucilius* (Berlin 1908) 2f.; *RE* XIII (1927) 1638–40, 1642–3, 1647; M. Coffey, *Roman satire* (London 1968) 35f., and nn. 6 and 8). L. owned estates in Campania and Sicily (*Sat.* 3 *passim*, Cic. *Fin.* 1.3.7) and the house at Rome which had been built to accommodate Demetrius, son of Antiochus III, while he was a hostage at Rome (Asconius, *Pis.* p. 12.9 K.–S.), and L. or a relative was among those accused of ranching illegally on *ager publicus c.* 114–111 B.C. (Cic. *De or.* 284). It is not clear whether he ever became a *ciuis Romanus* himself or whether he married.

WORKS

Thirty books of Satires: some 1,300 citations, all but a handful very brief. On order of composition, arrangement, 'publication', and character of these books, the earliest of which are those numbered 26–30 (iambo-trochaic metres with a small element of hexameter-writing), see pp. 168–70.

BIBLIOGRAPHY

TEXTS: F. Marx, vol. I (Leipzig 1904), vol. II, commentary (Leipzig 1905), cf. A. E. Housman, *C.Q.* I (1907) 53–74, 148–59, F. Leo, *G.G.A.* 168 (1906) 837–61; E. Bolisani (Padua 1932); N. Terzaghi (Florence 1934, 1944: rev. I. Mariotti, 1964); *ROL* III (with brief notes); J. Heurgon (*Les cours de Sorbonne*: Paris 1959); W. Krenkel, 2 vols. (Leiden 1970: with German tr. and commentary), cf. A. S. Gratwick, *J.R.S.* 63 (1973) 302–4; F. Charpin (Budé, 1978–9).

SURVEYS: E. Lommatzsch, *J.A.W.* 139 (1908) 213–16; 175 (1919) 91–8; 204 (1925) 211–15; 235 (1932) 139–42; 260 (1938) 89–94; R. Helm, *J.A.W.* 282 (1943) 1–37; K. Büchner, *Gymnasium* 62 (1955) 220–5; W. S. Anderson, *C.W.* 50 (1956) 33–40; 57 (1964) 293–301; 63 (1970) 181–99; J. Christes, *ANRW* I.2 1182–1239, and W. Krenkel, ibid. 1240–59.

STUDIES: C. Cichorius, *Untersuchungen zu Lucilius* (Berlin 1908) and *Römische Studien* (Berlin 1922); Leo, *Gesch.* 405–29; G. C. Fiske, *Lucilius and Horace: a study in the classical art of imitation* (Madison 1920); A. Kappelmacher, *RE* XIII (1927) 1617–37 (Lucilius 4); U. Knoche, *Die römische Satire* (Berlin 1949); M. Puelma-Piwonka, *Lucilius und Kallimachos. Zur Geschichte einer Gattung der hellenistisch-römischen Poesie* (Frankfurt 1949); H. Bardon, 'Catulle et ses modèles poétiques de langue latine', *Latomus* 16 (1957) 614–27; I. Mariotti, *Studi Luciliani* (Florence 1960: helpful as to style); M. Coffey, *Roman satire* (London–New York 1976); J. Christes, *Der frühe Lucilius. Rekonstruktion und Interpretation des XXVI. Buches sowie von Teilen des XXX. Buches* (Heidelberg 1971).

VALERIUS AEDITUUS, PORCIUS LICINUS, QUINTUS LUTATIUS CATULUS

LIVES

Listed in this order by Gellius (19.9.10) and Apuleius (*Apol.* 9). Aedituus called 'old' (*ueteris poetae*) by Gellius; Licinus wrote after the death of Terence (*c.* 159 B.C.; *FPL* 45); Catulus was consul 102 B.C. and wrote on Roscius (b. 134 B.C.). On dating see Ross (below) 141.

WORKS

Four short erotic elegiac epigrams preserved by Gellius: two by Aedituus, one each by Licinus and Catulus; one epigram by Catulus preserved by Cicero (*Nat. D.* 1.79). Licinus also wrote in trochaics on the early history of Rome.

BIBLIOGRAPHY

TEXT: *FPL* 42–6.

STUDIES: R. Büttner, *Porcius Licinus und der litterarische Kreis des Q. Lutatius Catulus* (Leipzig 1893); Bardon I 123–32; D. O. Ross, *Style and tradition in Catullus* (Cambridge, Mass. 1969) 139–47.

LAEVIUS, ?MELISSUS

LIFE

Conventionally dated to early 1st c. B.C., but the ancient sources offer little firm evidence. See Leo (below) 180 n.1 = 268 n.1.

WORKS

Erotopaegnia (Love-plays) on erotic and mythological themes in (at least) six books: Charisius 2, p. 265. 12 B (*GLK* I 204.16). Other titles are probably those of works in the collection: cf. Charisius 4, p. 376. 1–2 B (*GLK* I 288.6). Nearly thirty fragments survive in a variety of metres.

BIBLIOGRAPHY

TEXT: *FPL* 55–63.

STUDIES: F. Leo, *Hermes* 49 (1914) 180–8 = *Ausgew. kl. Schriften*, ed. E. Fraenkel (Rome 1960) I 268–75; D. O. Ross, *Style and tradition in Catullus* (Cambridge, Mass. 1969) 155–60; J. Granarolo, *D'Ennius à Catulle. Recherches sur les antécédents romains de la 'poésie nouvelle'* (Paris 1971).

CATULLUS, GAIUS VALERIUS

LIFE

Dates probably 84–54 B.C.; b. in Verona. Jerome (*Chron.*) gives dates as 87–57, but C. was certainly alive in 55 (Pompey's consulship, 113.2; *porticus Pompeii*, 55.6; invasions of Britain, 11.12, 29.4, cf. 45.22). At Rome had affair with a Clodia (called Lesbia in his poems), possibly the elder sister of P. Clodius and wife of Q. Metellus Celer. Visited Asia Minor 57/56 as member of entourage of C. Memmius, governor of Bithynia. Sources: own poems; Apul. *Apol.* 10 (Lesbia's real name); Suet. *Iul.* 73 (Caesar entertained by C.'s father). On identity of Clodia see T. P. Wiseman, *Catullan Questions* (Leicester 1969) 50ff.

WORKS

Collection of 116 poems, in various lyric metres (1–61, 63; mainly phalaecian hendecasyllables), hexameters (62, 64), and elegiac couplets (65–116). On arrangement and publication see pp. 194–7.

BIBLIOGRAPHY

(for 1934–59 see H. J. Leon, *C.W.* 65 (1959–60) 104–13, 141–8, 174–80, 281–2; for 1960–9, D. F. Thomson, *C.W.* 65 (1971–2) 116–26; also (1929–57) J. Kroymann in Kroll, under *Texts* below)

TEXTS AND COMMENTARIES: TEXTS: L. Schwabe (Berlin 1886); R. A. B. Mynors (OCT, 1958); D. F. Thomson (Chapel Hill 1978). COMMENTARIES: R. Ellis, 2nd ed. (Oxford 1889); W. Kroll, 3rd ed. (Stuttgart 1959); C. J. Fordyce (Oxford

1961; corrected ed. 1973), reviewed by E. Fraenkel, *Gnomon* 34 (1962) 253–63; K. Quinn, 2nd ed. (London 1973).

TRANSLATIONS: E. S. Duckett, *Catullus in English poetry* (Northampton, Mass. 1925); F. W. Cornish (Loeb, 1913).

STUDIES: (1) HELLENISTIC AND NEW POETRY: F. Leo, 'Die römische Poesie in der sullanischen Zeit', *Hermes* 49 (1914) 161–95; S. Gaselee, *The love romances of Parthenius* (Loeb, 1916); R. Pfeiffer, 'A fragment of Parthenios' Arete', *C.Q.* 37 (1943) 23–32; W. Clausen, 'Callimachus and Latin poetry', *G.R.B.S.* 5 (1964) 181–96; G. W. Bowersock, *Augustus and the Greek world* (Oxford 1965) 122–39 (Greek teachers in Rome); H. Tränkle, 'Neoterische Kleinigkeiten', *M.H.* 24 (1967) 87–103; D. O. Ross, 'Nine epigrams from Pompeii (*CIL* 4.4966–73)', *Y.Cl.S.* 21 (1969) 127–42; N. B. Crowther, 'οἱ νεώτεροι, Poetae Novi and Cantores Euphorionis', *C.Q.* n.s.20 (1970) 322–7; idem, 'Valerius Cato, Furius Bibaculus, and Ticidas', *C.Ph.* 66 (1971) 108–9; idem, 'Parthenius and Roman poetry', *Mnemosyne* 29 (1976) 65–71; J. Soubiran, *Cicéron: Aratea, fragments poétiques* (Budé, 1972); T. P. Wiseman, *Cinna the poet* (Leicester 1974); R. O. A. M. Lyne, 'The neoteric poets', *C.Q.* n.s.28 (1978) 167–87.

(2) CATULLUS – GENERAL: R. Reitzenstein, 'Zur Sprache der lateinischen Erotik', *S.H.A.W.* 12 (1912) 9–36; A. L. Wheeler, *Catullus and the traditions of ancient poetry* (Berkeley 1934); E. A. Havelock, *The lyric genius of Catullus* (Oxford 1939; 2nd ed. New York 1967); J. P. Elder, 'Notes on some conscious and subconscious elements in Catullus' poetry', *H.S.Ph.* 60 (1951) 101–36; K. Quinn, *The Catullan revolution* (Melbourne 1959); D. O. Ross, *Style and tradition in Catullus* (Cambridge, Mass. 1969); T. P. Wiseman, *Catullan questions* (Leicester 1969); J. W. Loomis, *Studies in Catullan verse*, *Mnemosyne* suppl. 24 (1972).

(3) INDIVIDUAL POEMS: 1: J. P. Elder, *H.S.Ph.* 71 (1966) 143–9; P. Levine, *C.S.C.A.* 2 (1969) 209–16; F. Cairns, *Mnemosyne* 22 (1969) 153–8. 4: E. Fraenkel, *Iktus und Akzent im lateinischen Sprechvers* (Berlin 1928) 322–6 (rhythms of ordinary speech in 4, 8, 25); J. Svennung, *Opuscula Romana* I (Lund 1954) 109–24; M. C. J. Putnam, *C.Ph.* 57 (1962) 10–19 (also 31, 46, 101). 5: F. Cairns, *Mnemosyne* 26 (1973) 11–21; E. A. Fredericksmeyer, *A.J.Ph.* 91 (1970) 431–45. 8: E. Fraenkel, *J.R.S.* 51 (1961) 46–53 (also 42). 27: F. Cairns, *Mnemosyne* 28 (1975) 24–9. 31: F. Cairns, in (edd.) A. J. Woodman and D. West, *Quality and pleasure in Latin poetry* (Cambridge 1975) 1–17. 36: V. Buchheit, *Hermes* 87 (1959) 309–27; D. O. Ross, *Mnemosyne* 26 (1973) 60–2. 44: C. P. Jones, *Hermes* 96 (1968) 379–83. 45: D. O. Ross, *C.Ph.* 60 (1965) 256–9. 51: W. Ferrari, *A.S.N.P.* 7 (1938) 59–72; R. Lattimore, *C.Ph.* 39 (1944) 184–7; E. Fraenkel, *Horace* (Oxford 1957) 211–14 (vv. 13–16). 56.5–7: A. E. Housman, *Hermes* 66 (1931) 402. 58.5: R. J. Penella, *Hermes* 104 (1976) 118–20. 61: P. Fedeli, *Seges* 16 (Freiburg 1972; repr. in *London Studies in Classical Philology*, vol. VI, 1980). 62: U. von Wilamowitz-Moellendorff, *Hellenistische Dichtung* II (1924) 277–310 (also 61, 34, 4, 64–5); E. Fraenkel, *J.R.S.* 45 (1955) 1–8. 64: R. Reitzenstein, *Hermes* 35 (1900)

73–105; F. Klingner, *S.B.A.W.* 6 (1956); M. C. J. Putnam, *H.S.Ph.* 65 (1961) 165–201; L. C. Curran, *Y.Cl.S.* 21 (1969) 171–92; J. C. Bramble, *P.C.Ph.S.* 16 (1970) 22–41; W. Clausen, *I.C.S.* 2 (1976) 219–23 (vv. 116–20). 66: R. Pfeiffer, *Philologus* 87 (1932) 179–228; B. Axelson, *Studi in onore di Luigi Castiglioni* 1 (Florence 1960) 15–21; M. C. J. Putnam, *C.Ph.* 55 (1960) 223–8 (vv. 75–88); W. Clausen, *H.S.Ph.* 74 (1968) 85–94 (65 and 66). 68: H. W. Prescott, *T.A.Ph.A.* 71 (1940) 473–500; G. Luck, *The Latin love elegy*, 2nd ed. (London 1969) 58–69; T. P. Wiseman, *Cinna the poet* (Leicester 1974) 77–103. 96: E. Fraenkel, *W.S.* 69 (1956) 279–88 (also 53, 14, 50). 106, 112, 93, 94, 105, 85: O. Weinreich, *Die Distichen des Catull* (Tübingen 1926).

INDEX: M. N. Wetmore (New Haven 1912; repr. Hildesheim 1961).

LUCRETIUS CARUS, TITUS

LIFE

Dates *c.* 98–55 B.C., but certainty impossible. Jerome (*Chron.*) gives year of birth as 94 or 93, the *Codex Monacensis* (ed. H. Usener, *Rh.M.* 22 (1867) 442) as 97. According to Jerome L. died 'in his forty-fourth year'; Donatus (*Vit. Verg.* 6) makes his death coincide with Virgil's assumption of the *toga virilis* and improbably dates this event to the consulship of Pompey and Crassus (55). Cicero's letter (*Q.Fr.* 2.9.3) suggests, but does not prove, that L. was dead by Feb. 54. Tradition of his madness and suicide is attested only by Jerome and the 'Borgia life' (printed by J. Masson, *J.Ph.* 23 (1895) 220–37; probably a Renaissance forgery); for criticism of the story see K. Ziegler, *Hermes* 71 (1936) 420–40. Refs. to L. in contemporary and Augustan writers: Cic. (cited above); Nepos, *Att.* 12.4; Vitr. 9 *praef.* 17; Ovid, *Am.* 1.15.23 and *Trist.* 2.425; cf. Virg. *Geo.* 2.490–2.

WORKS

De rerum natura (6 bks): L.'s only known work, unfinished at his death (unfulfilled promise at 5.155 to write about abodes of the gods). Internal evidence for date of composition is thin: the dedicatee Memmius is probably the praetor of 58; 2.40–1 cannot refer to troop movements in 58, as is often supposed (see T. P. Wiseman, *Cinna the poet* (Leicester 1974) 11–12); 4.75–86 need not have been written after the opening of Rome's first permanent theatre in 55 (but see L. R. Taylor, in (ed.) M. E. White, *Studies in honour of Gilbert Norwood* (Toronto 1952) 149–50).

BIBLIOGRAPHY

(see A. Dalzell, *C.W.* 66 (1972–3) 389–427, and 67 (1973–4) 65–112; Boyancé (1963) under *Studies* below; E. J. Kenney, *G. & R. New surveys in the classics* 11 (1977))

TEXTS AND COMMENTARIES: TEXTS: A. Ernout, 10th ed. (Budé, 1966); J. Martin, 6th ed. (BT, 1969); C. Müller (Zurich 1975); W. H. D. Rouse, rev. M. F. Smith (Loeb, 1975). COMMENTARIES: C. Lachmann (Berlin 1850); H. A. J. Munro, 4th ed. (Cambridge 1886); C. Guissani, 4 vols. (Turin 1896–8); A. Ernout and L. Robin, 3 vols. (Paris 1925–8); W. E. Leonard and S. B. Smith (Madison 1942); C. Bailey, 3 vols. (Oxford 1947; repr. with corrections 1950: with prolegomena and tr.). Bk 3: R. Heinze (Leipzig 1897); E. J. Kenney (Cambridge 1971). Bk 6: A. Barigazzi (Turin 1946).

TRANSLATIONS: Prose: H. A. J. Munro (Cambridge 1864); R. E. Latham (Penguin, 1951); M. F. Smith (London 1969). Verse: R. Humphries (Bloomington 1968.)

STUDIES: C. Martha, *Le poème de Lucrèce* (Paris 1867); W. Y. Sellar, *The Roman poets of the republic*, 3rd ed. (Oxford 1889) chs. 10–14; J. Masson, *Lucretius: Epicurean and poet* (London 1907–9); G. Santayana, *Three philosophical poets: Lucretius, Dante and Goethe* (Cambridge, Mass. 1910); O. Regenbogen, *Lukrez, seine Gestalt in seinem Gedicht, Neue Wege zur Antike* 2.1 (Leipzig 1932) = *Kl. Schr.* (Munich 1961) 296–386; E. E. Sikes, *Lucretius: poet and philosopher* (Cambridge 1936); M. Roselaar, *Lukrez: Versuch einer Deutung* (Amsterdam 1943); E. Bignone, *Storia della letteratura latina* II (Florence 1945) chs. 6–8; J. B. Logre, *L'anxiété de Lucrèce* (Paris 1946); A. Ernout, *Lucrèce* (Brussels 1947); A. Traglia, *Sulla formazione spirituale di Lucrezio* (Rome 1948); F. Klingner, 'Philosophie und Dichtkunst am Ende des zweiten Buches des Lukrez', *Hermes* 80 (1952) 3–31; J.-H. Waszink, 'Lucretius and poetry', *Mededelingen Nederl. Akad. van Wetensch., Afd. Letterkunde* 17 (1954) no. 8, 243–57; F. Giancotti, *Il preludio di Lucrezio* (Messina 1959); U. Pizzani, *Il problema del testo e della composizione del De rerum natura di Lucrezio* (Rome 1959); P. Boyance, *Lucrèce et l'Épicurisme* (Paris 1963); (ed.) D. R. Dudley, *Lucretius* (London 1965); C. J. Classen, 'Poetry and rhetoric in Lucretius', *T.A.Ph.A.* 99 (1968) 77–118; A. Amory, '*Obscura de re lucida carmina*: science and poetry in *De rerum natura*', *Y.Cl.S.* 21 (1969) 145–68; D. West, *The imagery and poetry of Lucretius* (Edinburgh 1969); E. J. Kenney, 'Doctus Lucretius', *Mnemosyne* 23 (1970) 366–92; P. H. Schrijvers, *Horror ac divina voluptas: études sur la poétique et la poésie de Lucrèce* (Amsterdam 1970). *Concordance.* L. Roberts, ΑΓΩΝ suppl. (1968).

CICERO: THE RELATIONSHIP OF ORATORY TO LITERATURE

GENERAL WORKS

(1) Background

Boissier, G., *Cicéron et ses amis* (Paris 1865), tr. Jones, A. D., *Cicero and his friends* (London 1897).

Heinemann, I., 'Humanitas' in *RE* suppl. v (1931) 282–310.
Kroll, W., *Die Kultur der ciceronischen Zeit*, 2 vols. (Leipzig 1933).
Warde Fowler, W., *Social life at Rome in the age of Cicero* (London 1908; repr. 1963).

(2) Rhetoric and dialogue

Clarke, M. L., *Rhetoric at Rome: a historical survey* (London 1953).
Hirzel, R., *Der Dialog* (Leipzig 1895).
Kennedy, G., *The art of rhetoric in the Roman world* (Princeton 1972).
Kroll, W., 'Rhetorik', in *RE* suppl. VII (1940) 1039–1138.
Lansberg, H., *Handbuch der lateinischen Rhetorik* (Munich 1940: elucidation of technical terms).
Leeman, A. D., *Orationis ratio*, 2 vols. (Amsterdam 1963).
Norden, E., *Die antike Kunstprosa*, 2 vols. (Leipzig 1898; repr. Stuttgart 1973).

CICERO, MARCUS TULLIUS

LIFE

b. 106 B.C. Arpinum; equestrian family. Educ. at Rome with younger brother Quintus; mentors L. Crassus and two Scaevolas. Friendship with Atticus begun. 89: served in Social War under Pompeius Strabo; got to know his famous son. 81: debut as advocate. 79–77: peregrination; Athens (joined Academy), Asia Minor, Rhodes. On return married Terentia (d. Tullia b. 76, s. Marcus b. 65). 75: quaestor, W. Sicily. 70: triumphantly prosecuted Verres, governor, for Sicilians; recognized as leader of Bar. 69: curule aedile. 66: praetor, supported Pompey. 60: pubd *Catilinarians*; refused invitation to join First Triumvirate (Caesar, Pompey, Crassus). 58: exiled, nominally for having put Catilinarians to death without trial; his house wrecked. 57: triumphant recall. 56–51: having attempted independence, was brought to heel and used by Triumvirs; active as advocate and as writer (*De oratore; De republica*; began *De legibus*). 51–50: unwilling but upright governor of Cilicia. 49: on outbreak of civil war attempted neutrality, but eventually joined Pompeians as the more republican side. Crossed to Epirus, but not present at Pharsalus. Returned after the defeat and submitted to Caesar's clemency. 46: resumed writing (*Brutus* and *Orator*). Divorced Terentia; briefly married to his young ward Publilia. 45: Tullia died; series of philosophical works begun, lasting sixteen months. 44: after Caesar's murder, resumed political activity in September, to combat Antony (*Philippics*). Coordinated activity of senatorial majority till 43, when his young protégé Octavian discarded him, seized Rome and the consulship, and joined the Second Triumvirate, which outlawed him. Killed in consequence, 7 December 43 B.C. Main sources his own works, esp. correspondence, *Brutus*, prologues in dialogues and treatises, some speeches. Also Plutarch's Life.

WORKS (dates B.C. in brackets)

TEXTS AND COMMENTARIES: (1) IN SERIES: Mondadori (for *Collegium Ciceronianis Studiis Provehendis*; in progress); BT (under revision); OCT (except philosophical works and fragments); Budé; Loeb.

(2) SPEECHES (some with comm.): All: G. Long, 4 vols. (London 1851–8); C. Halm, rev. Laubmann–Sternkopf (1886–93); M. Fuhrmann, 7 vols. (Zurich–Stuttgart 1970–: with German tr.). *Pro Quinctio* (81): T. E. Kinsey (Sydney 1971). *Pro Roscio Amerino* (80): G. Landgraf, 2nd ed. (Leipzig 1914). *Pro Roscio comoedo* (?77). *Divinatio in Caecilium* and *Verrines* (70): E. Thomas (Paris 1894); *Verr.*, W. Peterson (London 1907). *Pro Tullio* (69). *Pro Fonteio* (69). *Pro Caecina* (69). *Pro Cluentio* (66): W. Y. Fausset (London 1887); W. Peterson (London 1899). *De imperio Cn. Pompeii = Pro lege Manilia* (66): F. P. Donnelly (New York 1939); C. Macdonald (London–Harvard 1966). *Contra Rullum* I–III (63). *Pro Rabirio perduellionis reo* (63): W. E. Heitland (Cambridge 1882). *Pro Murena* (63): W. E. Heitland (Cambridge 1874). *In Catilinam* I–IV (63): A. Haury (Paris 1969). *Pro Sulla* (62): J. S. Reid (Cambridge 1902). *Pro Archia* (62): J. S. Reid (Cambridge 1877; repr. 1938). *Pro Flacco* (59): T. B. L. Webster (Oxford 1931). *Post reditum in senatu* (57). *De domo sua* (57): R. G. Nisbet (Oxford 1939). *De haruspicum responso* (56). *Pro Sestio* (56): H. A. Holden, 9th ed. (1933). *In Vatinium* (56): L. Pocock (London 1926: comm. only). *Pro Caelio* (56): R. G. Austin, 3rd ed. (Oxford 1960). *De provinciis consularibus* (56): H. E. Butler and M. Cary (Oxford 1924). *Pro Balbo* (56): J. S. Reid (Cambridge 1878). *In Pisonem* (55): R. G. M. Nisbet (Oxford 1961). *Pro Plancio* (54): H. A. Holden, 3rd ed. (Cambridge 1891). *Pro Scauro* (54). *Pro Rabirio Postumo* (54). *Pro Milone* (52): A. G. Poynton, 3rd ed. (Oxford 1902); J. Quémener (Paris 1972). *Pro Marcello* (46): M. Ruch (Paris 1965). *Pro Ligario* (46). *Pro rege Deiotaro* (45). *Philippics* (44–3): J. R King, 2nd ed. (Oxford 1878); I and II, J. D. Denniston (Oxford 1926).

(3) RHETORICA: *De inventione* (*c.* 84). *De oratore* (55–4): K. W. Piderit and O. Harnecker, 6th ed. (Leipzig 1886–90; repr. Amsterdam 1962). *Partitiones oratoriae* (*c.* 54). *De optimo genere oratorum* (52). *Brutus* (46): O. Jahn and W. Kroll, 7th ed. rev. B. Kytzler (Berlin 1964); A. E. Douglas (Oxford 1966). *Orator* (46): J. E. Sandys (Cambridge 1885); O. Jahn and W. Kroll, 8th ed. (Berlin 1913; repr. 1961); O. Seel (Heidelberg 1962). *Topica* (44): A. S. Wilkins (Oxford 1901).

(4) POLITICA: *De republica* (54–1): G. H. Sabine and S. B. Smith, *Cicero on the commonwealth* (Columbus, Ohio 1929: intr. and tr.); K. Ziegler, 5th ed. (Leipzig 1960). *De legibus* (51–?): W. D. Pearman (Cambridge 1881); K. Ziegler (Heidelberg 1950; 2nd ed. 1963).

(5) PHILOSOPHICA: *Paradoxa Stoicorum* (46): A. G. Lee (London 1953). *Academica* (45): J. S. Reid (Cambridge 1885). *De finibus* (45): W. M. L. Hutchinson (London 1909); I and II, J. S. Reid (Cambridge 1925). *Tusculans* (45): J. W. Dougan (vol. I Cambridge 1905; vol. II ed. R. M. Henry 1934); M. Pohlenz and O. Heine, 4th ed. (Leipzig 1929; repr. 1957); O. Gigon, 2nd ed. (Munich 1970). *De natura deorum* (45):

A. S. Pease, 2 vols. (Cambridge, Mass. 1955–8). *De fato* (44): A. Yon, 3rd ed. (Paris 1950). *Cato maior de senectute* (44): L. Huxley (Oxford 1887; repr. 1951); F. G. Moore (New York 1903); M. Ruch (Paris 1972). *Laelius de amicitia* (44): J. S. Reid (Cambridge 1887; 2nd ed. 1893). *De officiis* (44): H. A. Holden, 3rd ed. (Cambridge 1899; repr. Amsterdam 1966); J. Higginbotham (London 1967; intr., tr. and notes).

(6) CORRESPONDENCE: *Ad familiares* (16 bks), *Ad Atticum* (16 bks), and *Ad Quintum fratrem* (27 letters). Complete: R. Y. Tyrrell and L. C. Purser, 2nd ed. (Dublin 1885–1933); D. R. Shackleton Bailey, 10 vols. (Cambridge 1965–81). (Translation by D. R. Shackleton Bailey, Penguin 1978 (*Ad Att.*), 1979 (remainder).)

(7) TRANSLATIONS: Plato's *Timaeus*. See R. Poncelet, *Cicéron traducteur de Platon* (Paris 1957).

(8) VERSE (fragments): *Juvenilia*: *Aratea* (tr.); *De consulatu suo*; *De temporibus suis*; *Marius*; *Limon* (a miscellany). W. W. Ewbank, *The poems of Cicero* (London 1933); A. Traglia, *Ciceronis poetica fragmenta* (Rome 1952); J. Soubiran, *Cicéron: Aratea, fragments poétiques* (Budé, 1972). *Studies*. E. Malcovati, *Cicerone e la poesia* (Pavia 1943); A. Traglia, *La lingua di Cicerone poeta* (Bari 1950).

(9) LOST PROSE WORKS: *Consolatio* (45). *Hortensius* (45): M. Ruch (Paris 1958). *Laus Catonis* (45). *De gloria* (44). *De consiliis suis* (? = *Anecdota*). *Geographica* (? = *Admiranda*). Translations: Plato's *Protagoras*; Xenophon's *Oeconomica*.

(10) SCHOLIA: T. Stengl (Vienna–Leipzig 1912). Asconius on five speeches: A. C. Clark (Oxford 1907).

STUDIES: (1) CRITICAL SURVEYS OF LITERATURE: W. Allen, *C.W.* 47 (1954) 129–39 (for 1935–53); R. J. Rowland, *C.W.* 60 (1966) 51–65, 101–15 (for 1953–65); P. Boyancé, in *Actes Congr. Budé* (1960) 254–91 (for 1933–58), repr. in *Études sur l'humanisme Cicéronien*, *Coll. Latomus* 121 (Brussels 1970); A. E. Douglas, *G.&R.*, *New surveys in the classics* 2 (1968). *Rhetorica*: *FYAT* 416–64; A. E. Douglas, *ANRW* I.3 (1973) 95–138. *Philosophica*: S. E. Smethurst, *C.W.* 51 (1957) 1–4, 32–41; *C.W.* 58 (1964–5) 36–44; *C.W.* 61 (1967) 125–33.

(2) GENERAL ACCOUNTS OF CICERO: J. W. Duff, *A literary history of Rome from the origins to the close of the golden age* (London 1909; rev. A. M. Duff 1953); T. Petersson, *Cicero: a biography* (Berkeley 1920); O. Plasberg, in (ed.) W. Ax, *Cicero in seinen Werken und Briefen* (1926; repr. Darmstadt 1962); M. Gelzer et al., *RE* VIIA.1 (1939) 827–1274, separately printed for 'Studierende' only (Stuttgart 1961); E. Bignone, *Storia della letteratura latina* (Florence 1950) III 442–685; F. Klingner, *Römische Geisteswelt*, 4th ed. (Munich 1961) 110–59; Schanz–Hosius I 400–550, in I. von Müller's *Handbuch der Altertumsw.*, 4th ed. (Munich 1966).

(3) STUDIES OF CICERONIAN TOPICS: E. Becker, *Technik und Szenerie des ciceronischen Dialogs* (Osnabrück 1938); M. Rambaud, *Cicéron et l'histoire romaine* (Paris 1953); A. Haury, *Ironie et humour chez Cicéron* (Leiden 1955); M. Ruch, *Le prooemium philosophique chez Cicéron* (Paris 1958); A. Michel, *Rhétorique et philosophie chez Cicéron* (Paris 1960); (ed.) E. Paratore, *Collana di studi ciceroniani*, 2 vols. (Rome 1961–2);

K. Büchner, *Cicero: Studien zur römischen Literatur* II (Wiesbaden 1962); (ed.) T. A. Dorey, *Cicero* (London 1965); (ed.) G. Radke, *Cicero, ein Mensch seiner Zeit* (Berlin 1968); P. Boyancé, *Études sur l'humanisme cicéronien* (Paris 1970); K. Büchner, *Das neue Cicerobild*, *Wege der Forschung* 27 (Darmstadt 1971).

(4) SPEECHES: T. Zieliński, 'Das Clauselgesetz in Ciceros Reden: Grundzüge einer oratorischen Rhythmik', *Philologus* suppl. 9 (1904) 589–875; L. Laurand, *Études sur le style des discours de Cicéron*, 3 vols. (Paris 1907; 4th ed. 1936–8); J. Humbert, *Les plaidoyers écrits et les plaidoiries réelles de Cicéron* (Paris 1925); F. Klingner, 'Ciceros Rede für den Schauspieler Roscius: eine Episode in der Entwicklung seiner Kunstprosa' *S.B.A.W.* 1953, 4; C. Neumeister, *Grundsätze der forensischen Rhetorik gezeigt in Gerichtsreden Ciceros* (Munich 1964); R.G.M. Nisbet, in (ed.) T. A. Dorey, *Cicero* (London 1965) 48–80.

(5) RHETORICA (see also under *General works* (2) above): H. C. Hubbell, *The influence of Isocrates on Cicero, Dionysius and Aristides* (New Haven 1913); H. K. Schulte, *Orator: Untersuchungen über das ciceronische Bildungsideal* (Frankfurt 1935); K. Barwick, 'Das Rednerische Bildungsideal Ciceros', *Abh. der Sächs. Akad. der Wiss. in Leipzig* 54 (1963) 3; A. Weische, *Ciceros Nachahmung der attischen Redner* (Heidelberg 1972).

(6) POLITICA: R. Harder, 'Über Ciceros "Somnium Scipionis"', *Abh. Königsb., Geistesw. Kl.* 1929, *Heft* 3, 115–50 = *Kleine Schriften*, ed. W. Marg (Munich 1960) 354–95; V. Pöschl, *Römischer Staat und griechisches Staatsdenken bei Cicero* (Berlin 1936); K. Büchner, 'Die beste Verfassung', *S.I.F.C.* 26 (1952) 37–140 = *Cicero: Studien zur römischen Literatur* II (Wiesbaden 1962) 25–115.

(7) PHILOSOPHICA: M. Pohlenz, *Antikes Führertum: Cicero 'De officiis' und das Lebensideal des Panaitios* (Leipzig 1934); L. Labowsky, *Der Begriff des 'prepon' in der Ethik des Panaitios* (Leipzig 1934); M. van den Bruwaene, *La théologie de Cicéron* (Louvain 1937); M. O. Lișcu, *L'expression des idées philosophiques chez Cicéron* (Paris 1937); H. A. K. Hunt, *The humanism of Cicero* (Melbourne 1954); W. Süss, 'Cicero: eine Einführung in seine philosophische Schriften', *A.A.W.M.* 1965, 5, 210–385.

(8) INFLUENCE: T. Zieliński, *Cicero im Wandel der Jahrhunderte*, 4th ed. (Leipzig 1929); C. Becker, s.v. 'Cicero' in *RAC* III 86–127; M. L. Clarke and A. E. Douglas, in (ed.) T. A. Dorey, *Cicero* (London 1965) 81–103, 135–70.

(9) LEXICA: Speeches: H. Merguet, 4 vols. (Jena 1873–84). *Philosophica*: H. Merguet, 3 vols. (Jena 1887–94). Letters: W. A. Oldfather et al. (Urbana 1938). Verse: M. J. W. Speath (Urbana 1955). *Rhetorica*: K. M. Abbott et al. (Urbana 1964).

SALLUSTIUS CRISPUS, GAIUS

LIFE

b. *c.* 86 B.C. at Amiternum. Tribune of the plebs 52; opposed T. Annius Milo. Expelled from senate 50, but reinstated as quaestor a year or two later. Served under Caesar during civil war 49–45. Elected praetor 46 and appointed first governor of *Africa Nova* Retired to write after Caesar's death and d. in Rome 35 or 34 B.C. Main sources: Jerome, *Chron.* (birth); Ascon. *ad* Cic. *Milo* p. 34 Stangl (tribunate); *Invect. in Sall. passim* (esp. 15 for evidence of a previous quaestorship); Dio 40.63.2ff. (expulsion from Senate); idem 42.52.1ff., 43.9.2; *Bell. Afr.* 8.3, 34.1–3, 97.1; App. 2.92, 100 (praetorship and African career); Sall. *Cat.* 3.3–4.2 (retirement); Gell. 17.18; ps.-Acron *ad* Hor. *Sat.* 1.2.41, 49. See Syme (1964, under *Studies* below) 1–59; G. Perl, 'Sallusts Todesjahr', *Klio* 48 (1967) 97–105. Further testimonia in preface to Kurfess's ed.

WORKS

(1) *Bellum Catilinae*, pubd *c.* 42, and *Bellum Iugurthinum*, pubd *c.* 40: historical monographs, each in a single book. *Historiae*: preserved by over 500 fragments covering the years 78–67, including four complete speeches and two complete letters; begun *c.* 39 and left incomplete in bk 5 at S.'s death.

(2) Spurious. Two *Epistulae ad Caesarem senem de re publica*, and *In M. Tullium Ciceronem invectiva*: probably emanate from the rhetorical schools.

BIBLIOGRAPHY

(for 1879–1964, see A. D. Leeman (Leiden 1965))

TEXTS AND COMMENTARIES: TEXTS: *Cat.* and *Iug.*: H. Jordan (Berlin 1866); A. W. Ahlberg (BT, 1919); A. Kurfess (BT, 1951); A. Ernout (Budé, 1946). *Invect.* and *Epist.*: A. Kurfess (BT, 1914); A. Ernout (Budé, 1962). COMMENTARIES: *Cat.* and *Iug.*: R. Dietsch (Leipzig 1846); F. Kritz (Leipzig 1853). *Cat.*: R. Jacobs, H. Wirz, A. Kurfess (Berlin 1922); J. Hellegouarc'h (Paris 1972); K. Vretska (Heidelberg 1976); P. McGushin (Leiden 1977). *Iug.*: R. Jacobs and H. Wirz (Berlin 1922); E. Koestermann (Heidelberg 1971). *Hist.*: B. Maurenbrecher (Leipzig 1891–3). *Invect.* and *Epist.*: K. Vretska (Heidelberg 1961).

STUDIES: H. Schnorr von Carolsfeld, *Über die Reden und Briefe bei Sallust* (Leipzig 1888); A. Kunze, *Sallustiana* (Leipzig 1892–8); E. Schwartz, 'Die Berichte über die catilinarische Verschwörung', *Hermes* 32 (1897) 554–608 = *Gesamm. Schr.* (Berlin 1956) II 275–336; G. Boissier, 'Les prologues de Salluste', *J.S.* n.s.1 (1903) 59–66; idem, *La conjuration de Catilina* (Paris 1905); A. W. Ahlberg, *Prolegomena in Sallustium* (Göteborg 1911); R. Ullmann, 'Essai sur le Catilina de Salluste', *R.Ph.* 42 (1918) 5–27; G. Funaioli, in *RE* IA (1920) 1913–55; W. Kroll, 'Die Sprache des Sallust', *Glotta* 15 (1927) 280–305; R. Ullmann, *La technique des discours dans Salluste, Tite-Live et Tacite* (Oslo 1927); F. Klingner, 'Über die Einleitung der Historien Sallusts', *Hermes* 63 (1928) 165–92 = *Studien* (Zurich 1964) 571–93; O. Seel, *Sallust von den Briefen ad Caesarem zur Coniuratio Catilinae* (Leipzig 1930); F. Egermann, *Die*

Prooemien zu den Werken des Sallust, *S.B.A.W.* 214.3 (1932); E. Skard, *Ennius und Sallustius* (Oslo 1933); W. Schur, *Sallust als Historiker* (Stuttgart 1934); K. Bauhofer, *Die Komposition der Historien Sallusts* (diss. Munich 1935); K. Latte, *Sallust*, *Neue Wege zur Antike* 2.4 (1935); S. Pantzerhielm-Thomas, 'The prologues of Sallust', *S.O.* 15–16 (1936) 140–62; K. Vretska, 'Der Aufbau des Bellum Catilinae', *Hermes* 72 (1937) 202–22; V. Pöschl, *Grundwerte römischer Staatsgesinnung in den Geschichtswerken des Sallust* (Berlin 1940); P. Zancan, 'Prolegomeni alla Giugurtina I', *A.I.V.* 102 (1942–3) 637–65; K. von Fritz, 'Sallust and the attitude of the Roman nobility at the time of the wars against Jugurtha', *T.A.Ph.A.* 74 (1943) 134–68; E. Skard, 'Die Bildersprache des Sallust', *S.O.* suppl. 11 (1943) 141–64; H. Last, 'Sallust and Caesar in the Bellum Catilinae', *Mélanges Marouzeau* (Paris 1948) 355–69; P. Perrochat, *Les modèles grecs de Salluste* (Paris 1949); K. Büchner, *Der Aufbau von Sallusts Bellum Iugurthinum*, *Hermes Einzelschriften* 9 (1953); A. D. Leeman, 'Sallusts Prologe und seine Auffassung von der Historiographie', *Mnemosyne* 7 (1954) 323–39, and 8 (1955) 38–48; K. Vretska, *Studien zu Sallusts Bellum Iugurthinum*, *S.B.A.W.* 229.4 (1955); E. Skard, *Sallust und seine Vorgänger* (Oslo 1956); W. Avenarius, 'Die griechischen Vorbilder des Sallust', *S.O.* 33 (1957) 48–86; A. D. Leeman, *Aufbau und Absicht von Sallusts Bellum Iugurthinum* (Amsterdam 1957); W. Steidle, *Sallusts historisch Monographien*, *Historia Einzelschriften* 3 (1958); K. Büchner, *Sallust* (Heidelberg 1960); D. C. Earl, *The political thought of Sallust* (Cambridge 1961); R. Syme, *Sallust* (California 1964); A. la Penna, *Sallustio e la 'rivoluzione' romana* (Milan 1968); H. Gugel, 'Bemerkungen zur Darstellung von Catilinas Ende bei Sallust', *Festschrift Vretska* (Heidelberg 1970) 361–81; V. Pöschl, 'Die Reden Caesars und Catos in Sallusts Catilina', in *Sallust*, *Wege der Forschung* 94 (Darmstadt 1970) 368–97; A. la Penna, 'Congetture sulla fortuna di Sallustio nell' antichità', *Studia Florentina A. Ronconi oblata* (Rome 1971) 195–206; K. Bringmann, 'Sallusts Umgang mit der historischen Wahrheit in seiner Darstellung der catilinarischen Verschwörung', *Philologus* 116 (1972) 98–113; L. Canfora, 'Il programma di Sallustio', *Belfagor* 27 (1972) 137–48; D. Flach, 'Die Vorrede zu Sallusts Historien in neuer Rekonstruktion', *Philologus* 117 (1973) 76–86; C. Questa, 'Sallustio, Tacito e l'imperialismo Romano', *Atti e memorie dell' Arcadia* 3.6 (1975–6) 1–43.

INDEXES: O. Eichert, 4th ed. (Hannover 1890); A. D. Bennett (Hildesheim 1970).

APPENDIX (mainly concerning the spurious pieces). H. Last, 'On the Sallustian Suasoriae', *C.Q.* 17 (1923) 87–100, 151–62; W. Kroll, 'Sallusts Staatsschriften', *Hermes* 62 (1927) 373–92; B. Edmar, *Studien zu den Epistulae ad Caesarem senem de re publica* (Lund 1931); E. Skard, 'Studien zur Sprache der Epistulae ad Caesarem', *S.O.* 10 (1931) 61–98; G. Carlsson, *Eine Denkschrift an Cäsar über den Staat, historisch-philologisch untersucht* (Lund 1936); O. Seel, *Die Invektive gegen Cicero*, *Klio Beiheft* 47 (1943); M. Chouet, *Les lettres de Salluste à César* (Paris 1950), reviewed by E. Fraenkel, *J.R.S.* 41 (1951) 192–4; A. Dihle, 'Zu den Epistolae ad Caesarem senem',

M.H. 11 (1954) 126–30; R. G. M. Nisbet, 'The *Invectiva in Ciceronem* and *Epistula Secunda* of Pseudo-Sallust', *J.R.S.* 48 (1958) 30–2; O. Seel, *Sallusts Briefe und die pseudo-sallustische Invektive*, *Erlanger Beiträge* 25 (Nuremberg 1967); E. Pasoli, *Problemi delle Epistulae ad Caesarem sallustiane* (Bologna 1970).

CAESAR, GAIUS IULIUS

LIFE

b. 13 July 100 B.C. Consul 59, proconsul of Cisalpine and Transalpine Gaul 58–50, dictator 49, campaigns against Pompey and his sons 48–45. Assassinated 15 March 44 B.C. Main sources: his own writings and the spurious works mentioned below; Suetonius, *Divus Iulius*; Cicero's speeches and letters; Plutarch, *Caesar* and other lives; Appian, *Bellum civile*; Dio Cassius 36–44. Evidence fully treated by M. Gelzer, *Caesar: politician and statesman*, tr. P. Needham (Oxford 1968).

WORKS

(1) EXTANT: *Commentarii de bello Gallico* (7 bks; bk 8 composed by his subordinate A. Hirtius to complete account of campaign), and *Commentarii de bello civili* (3 bks); verse epigram to Terence (*FPL* 91). (2) LOST (Suet. *Iul.* 56.5–7): Speeches (several collected and pubd; out of fashion by end of 1st c. A.D., Tac. *Dial.* 21); two books on style, *De analogia*, written early summer 54; poem *Iter* on his journey to Spain 45; pamphlet in two books attacking memory of Cato (Plut. *Cato min.* 36.4–5, 52.5–7). (3) SPURIOUS: *Bellum Alexandrinum*, *Bellum Africum*, *Bellum Hispaniense*, dealing with later episodes of the civil wars; subsequently attached to C.'s name but written by unknown officers.

BIBLIOGRAPHY

(see H. Gesche, *Caesar*, *Erträge der Forschung* (Darmstadt 1976))

TEXTS AND COMMENTARIES: TEXTS: A. Klotz and W. Trillitzsch (BT, 1927–64). COMMENTARIES: *Bell. Gall.*: F. Kraner, W. Dittenberger, H. Meusel, H. Oppermann (Zurich–Berlin 1964–6). *Bell. Civ.*: F. Kraner, F. Hofmann, H. Meusel, H. Oppermann (Berlin 1959). TEXTUAL PROBLEMS: F. Beckmann, *Geographie und Ethnographie in Caesars Bellum Gallicum* (Dortmund 1930); G. Jachmann, 'Caesartext und Caesarinterpolation', *Rh.M.* 89 (1940) 161–88; K. Barwick, 'Ist der Caesartext heillos interpoliert?', *Rh.M.* 91 (1942) 28–51.

STUDIES: H. Drexler, 'Zum Begriff Commentarii', *Hermes* 70 (1935) 227–34; K. Barwick, *Caesars Bellum Civile: Tendenz, Abfassungszeit und Stil* (Leipzig 1951); U. Knoche, 'Caesars Commentarii, ihr Gegenstand und ihre Absicht', *Gymnasium* 58

(1951) 139–60; F. Bömer, 'Der Commentarius', *Hermes* 81 (1953) 210–50; M. Rambaud, *L'art de la déformation historique dans les Commentaires de César*, 2nd ed. (Paris 1966); J. P. V. D. Balsdon, *J.R.S.* 45 (1955) 161–4 (review of Barwick and Rambaud); G. Walser, 'Caesar und die Germanen', *Historia Einzelschriften* 1 (1956); F. E. Adcock, *Caesar as man of letters* (Cambridge 1956); D. Rasmussen, *Caesars Commentarii: Stil und Stilwandel* (Göttingen 1963); S. Weinstock, *Divus Julius* (Oxford 1971); J. H. Collins, 'Caesar as political propagandist', *ANRW* I.1 (1972) 922–66; F.-M. Mutschler, *Erzählstil und Propaganda in Caesars Kommentarien* (Heidelberg 1975); H. A. Gärtner, *Beobachtungen zu Bauelementen in der antiken Historiographie, Historia Einzelschriften* 25 (1975).

LEXICON: H. Merguet (Jena 1886; repr. Hildesheim 1963).

VARRO, MARCUS TERENTIUS

LIFE

b. 116 B.C., possibly at Reate (mod. Rieti). Pupil of antiquarian L. Aelius Stilo and philosopher Antiochus of Ascalon. *IIIvir capitalis* in 90s, quaestor 85 (?), tribune of the plebs and praetor at uncertain dates. Served in Dalmatian campaign 78–7; proquaestor under Pompey against Sertorius 76–1 and legate in pirate war 67–? (awarded *corona rostrata*). *XXvir agris dandis assignandis* 59. Legate under Pompey in Spain ?–49. Joined Pompeians at Dyrrhachium; returned to Italy after Pharsalus and regained his property which was then threatened by Antony and rescued by Caesar. Commissioned by Caesar to collect a great library 46; lost some property 44; proscribed 43 to his own library's detriment, but saved by Fufius Calenus. d. pen in hand 27 B.C. Sources: Jerome, *Chron. ann. Abr.* 1901 and 1989, Symm. *Epist.* 1.2, Val. Max. 7.3 (birth, death); Varro, *Ling. Lat.* 7.2, Cic. *Brut.* 205 and *Acad. post.* 1.7.12 (teachers); Gell. 13.12.6 (*IIIvir*, tribune); Varro, *Sat. Men.* 478 (quaestor); App. 4.47 (praetor); Varro, *Res Rust.* 2.10.8, 3.12.7, 2. *proem.* 6 (Dalmatia, proquaestor, pirate war); Pliny, *N.H.* 7.115 and 176 (*corona*, *XXvir*); Caes. *Bell. Civ.* 2.17 (in Spain); Cic. *Fam.* 9.6.3 (Dyrrhachium); Suet. *Iul.* 44.2 (library); Cic. *Phil.* 2.103, App. 4.47, Gell. 3.10.17 (property threatened, proscription etc.).

WORKS

Had written 490 books (as distinct from whole works) by age of 77 (Gell. 3.10.17) and over 600 by time of his death (Auson. *Prof. Burd.* 20.10; 620 according to F. Ritschl, *Opuscula philologica* III (Leipzig 1877) 488). Jerome's incomplete catalogue, of uncertain origin, has been accidentally preserved (see G. L. Hendrickson, *C.Ph.* 6 (1911) 334–43); numerous titles attested elsewhere (Ritschl 472–4). A representative selection follows.

(1) EXTANT: *De lingua Latina*: six mutilated books survive out of twenty-five. Completed after July 45 and before Cicero's death (Cic. *Att.* 13.12.3). Bks 2–4 dedicated to his quaestor P. Septimius, 5–7 (and possibly rest of work) to Cicero (*Ling. Lat.* 7.109). *De re rustica*: completed 37 B.C. (1.1.1), but perhaps written in sections over previous twenty years (see Martin and White, under *Studies* (4) below). Bk 1 dedicated to his wife Fundania, who has just bought a farm, 2 to his landowner friend Turranius Niger, 3 to his neighbour Pinnius.

(2) LOST OR FRAGMENTARY (no. of bks in Roman numerals): Verse. *Saturarum Menippearum* CL: about ninety titles and 600 fragments preserved; of early date (Cic. *Acad. post.* 1.8). Also ten books of 'poems', four of satires, six of tragedies. Prose. (*a*) History, geography, antiquities. *Antiquitates*: *Rerum humanarum* XXV written first; *Rerum divinarum* XVI probably completed and dedicated to Caesar as pontifex maximus 46. *De vita populi Romani* IV (dedicated to Atticus); *De gente populi Romani* IV, 43–2; *De familiis Troianis* (cf. Virg. *Aen.* 5.117ff., etc.); *De vita sua* III and *Legationum* III (both autobiographical); *Annales* (see p. 291); Εἰσαγωγικὸς *ad Pompeium* (70: instructions to P. on how to behave in the senate; Gell. 14.7); *Ephemeris navalis ad Pompeium* (probably 77: cf. *De ora maritima*, *De litoralibus*, *De aestuariis*). (*b*) Language and literary history. *De antiquitate litterarum ad L. Accium*; *De origine linguae Latinae*; *De similitudine verborum*; *De sermone Latino* V (after 46); *Quaestionum Plautinarum* V; *De scaenicis originibus* III; *De actionibus scaenicis* III; *De poematis* III (cf. Aristotle's *Poetics*, Neoptolemus of Parium, Philodemus); *De poetis* (fundamental literary chronology); *Hebdomades vel De imaginibus* XV (probably completed 39: see p. 291). (*c*) Rhetoric and law. *Orationum* XII; *Laudationes* (Cic. *Acad. post.* 1.8, *Att.* 13.48.2); *De iure civili* XV. (*d*) Philosophy and science. *De philosophia*; *De forma philosophiae*; *Logistoricon* LXXVI, dialogues on philosophical and historical themes whose double titles (eleven extant plus eight fragmentary titles) signify the chief participant in the dialogue and the subject matter on which he is an expert; of late date; *Disciplinarum* IX (written 34–3?).

BIBLIOGRAPHY

(see B. Cardauns in *Entretiens IX: Varron* (Fondation Hardt, Geneva 1963) 209–12 (for 1950–62); H. Dahlmann, *ANRW* 1.3 (1973) 3–18; J. Collart, *Lustrum* 9 (1964) 213–41 (grammatical works); K. D. White, *ANRW* 1.4 (1973) 495–7 (*Res Rust.*))

TEXTS AND COMMENTARIES: (1) EXTANT: TEXTS: Complete: F. Semi (Venice 1965–Padua 1966: reprints many earlier texts). *Ling. Lat.*, *Res Rust.* and grammatical fragments: A. Traglia (Turin 1974). *Ling. Lat.*: G. Goetz and F. Schoell (Leipzig 1910: with gramm. fragments); R. G. Kent, rev. ed. (Loeb, 1951). *Res Rust.*: G. Goetz, 2nd ed. (BT, 1929); W. D. Hooper and H. B. Ash, rev. ed. (Loeb, 1935: with Cato); J. Heurgon (Budé, 1978: bk 1 only, with brief notes). COMMENTARIES: *Ling. Lat.* Bk 5: J. Collart (Paris 1954: with French tr.). Bk 8: H. Dahlmann, *Hermes*

Einzelschriften 7 (1940: with German tr.). Bk 10: A. Traglia (Bari 1956). *Res. Rust.* J. G. Schneider, *Scriptorum rei rusticae*, vol. 1 (Leipzig 1794: only full comm. on agricultural matters); H. Keil, 3 vols. (Leipzig 1891–1902: with Cato).

(2) FRAGMENTS: Verse. *Sat. Men.*: A. Riese (Leipzig 1865); F. Buecheler and W. Heraeus, *Petronii Saturae* (Berlin 1922) 177–250; E. Bolisani (Padua 1936); J.-P. Cèbe, 3 vols. so far (Rome 1972–5). Prose. (*a*) Historical etc. *Antiquitates*: P. Mirsch, *Leipzig Studien* 5 (1882). *Res divinae*: R. Merkel, *Ovidi Fasti* (Berlin 1841) 106–247; R. Agahd, *N.J.Kl.P.* suppl. 24 (1895: bks 1, 14–16); B. Cardauns, *Abh. Akad. Mainz* 1976. *De vita pop. Rom.*: B. Riposati (Padua 1907). *De gente pop. Rom.*: P. Fraccaro (Milan 1939); see also *HRR* II 9–25. (*b*) Language etc. G. Funaioli, *Grammaticae Romanae fragmenta* (BT, 1907). (*c*) Law. F. P. Bremer, *Iurisprudentiae antehadrianae quae supersunt* (BT, 1896) I 122–7. (*d*) Philosophy etc. *De philosophia*: G. Langenberg (diss. Köln 1959). *Logistorici*: Riese, with *Sat. Men.* above; C. Chappuis (Paris 1868: with *De forma philosophiae* and *Imagines*); E. Bolisani (Padua 1937). *Catus de liberis educandis*: R. Müller (diss. Bonn 1938). *Curio de cultu*: B. Cardauns (diss. Köln 1960). *Tubero de origine humana*: R. Heisterhagen, *Abh. Akad. Mainz* 4, 1957, 20–37. *Disciplinae*: see F. Ritschl, *Opuscula philologica* III (Leipzig 1877) 352–402, and M. Simon, *Philologus* 110 (1966) 88–101. (*e*) Others. *Epistulae*: Riese, with *Sat. Men.* above; D. Wolff (diss. Marburg 1960); see too *R.C.C.M.* 9 (1967) 78–85. *Sententiae*: C. Chappuis (Paris 1856); P. Germann (Paderborn 1910).

TRANSLATIONS: *Res Rust.*: L. Storr-Best (London 1912); B. Tilly, *Varro the farmer* (London 1973: selections).

STUDIES: (1) GENERAL: G. Boissier, *Étude sur la vie et les ouvrages de Varron* (Paris 1861); Ritschl, under (*d*) above, III 419–505 and *passim*; H. Dahlmann, *RE* suppl. VI (1935) 1172ff.; *Entretiens IX: Varron* (Fondation Hardt, Geneva 1963). (2) BIOGRAPHICAL: C. Cichorius, *Römische Studien* (Leipzig 1922) 189–241; K. Kumianecki *Athenaeum* 40 (1962) 221–43; R. Astbury, *C.Q.* n.s.17 (1967) 403–7; N. M. Horsfall, *B.I.C.S.* 19 (1972) 120–8. (3) 'LING. LAT.' etc.: H. Dahlmann, *Varro und die hellenistische Sprachtheorie* (Berlin 1935); F. della Corte, *La filologia latina delle origini a Varrone* (Turin 1937) 101–46, 149–60; H. Dahlmann, 'Varros schrift "De poematis"' *Abh. Akad. Mainz* 3, 1953; idem, 'Studien zu Varros "De poetis,"' *Abh. Akad. Mainz* 10, 1962; J. Collart, *Varron, grammarien latin* (Paris 1954); D. J. Taylor, *Declinatio* (Amsterdam 1973). (4) 'RES RUST.': J. Heurgon, 'L'effort de style de Varron dans les Res rusticae', *R.Ph.* 76 (1950) 57–71; H. Dohr, *Die italischen Gutshöfe* (diss. Köln 1965); J. E. Skydsgaard, *Varro the scholar* (Copenhagen 1967); R. Martin, *Recherches sur les agronomes latins* (Paris 1971) 213–35, 257–86; K. D. White, *ANRW* I.3 (1973) 463–94. (5) 'SAT. MEN.': F. della Corte, *La poesia di Varrone reatino ricostituita*, *Mem. Acad. Torino* n.s.69.2 (1937–8); E. Norden, *Kleine Schriften* (Berlin 1966) 1–87; E. Woytek, *Sprachliche Studien zur Satura Menippea Varros*, *W.S.* suppl. 2 (1970) (6) HISTORY etc.: P. Boyancé, 'Sur la théologie de Varron', *R.E.A.* 52 (1955) 57–84; H.

Hagendahl, *Augustine and the Latin classics* (Göteborg 1967) 589–630; K. G. Sallmann, *Die Geographie des älteren Plinius in ihrem Verhältnis zu Varro* (Berlin 1971); G. Lieberg, 'Die Theologia tripartita', *ANRW* I.4 (1973) 63–115. (7) 'LOGISTORICI': H. Dahlmann, 'Varronische Studien' I (with R. Heisterhagen), *Abh. Akad. Mainz* 4, 1957, and II, ibid. 11, 1959, 5–25. (8) 'IMAGINES': E. Bethe, *Buch und Bild im Altertum* (Leipzig 1945) *passim*; A. von Salis, 'Imagines illustrium', in *Eumusia, Festgabe E. Howald* (Zurich 1947) 11–29. (9) OTHERS. E. Laughton, 'Observations on the style of Varro', *C.Q.* n.s.10 (1960) 1–28.

NEPOS, CORNELIUS

LIFE

b. in Po valley possibly *c.* 109 B.C.; probably a native of Ticinum. Associated with Catullus (Cat. 1), Atticus and Cicero. d. after 27 B.C. Praenomen unknown. Sources: Nepos 25.19.1 (birth); 25.13.7 (Atticus); Pliny, *N.H.* 3.127, 10.60; Pliny, *Epist.* 3.28.1 (birthplace and death); Macr. *Sat.* 2.1.14 (Cic.'s letters to him); Fronto p. 20N (N.'s role as editor of Cic.).

WORKS

(1) *De viris illustribus* (at least sixteen books, *GLK* I 141.13). Extant: *De excellentibus ducibus exterarum gentium* (title not quite certain); *Cato* and *Atticus* from *De historicis Latinis*. Books *De Romanorum imperatoribus* (23.13.2), *De historicis Graecis* (10.3.2), and *De regibus* (21.1.1) are certain; categories *De poetis*, *De oratoribus* and *De grammaticis* are likely. First pubd probably 35/34 B.C. (25.12.1f., 19.2); 2nd ed. before 27. Was there a 2nd ed. of the whole work? See H. Rahn, *Hermes* 85 (1957) 205–15. (2) Lost. Separate lives of Cato (24.3.5) and Cicero (Gell. 15.28.1); *Chronica*, 3 bks (Cat. 1.6; cf. Gell. 17.21.3); *Exempla*, at least 5 bks (Gell. 6.18.11); a geographical work (?), see K. G. Sallmann, *Die Geographie des älteren Plinius in ihrem Verhältnis zu Varro* (Berlin 1971) 119ff.; *versiculi severi parum* (Pliny, *Epist.* 5.3.6); letters to Cicero (Lact. *Inst.* 3.15.10).

BIBLIOGRAPHY

TEXTS AND COMMENTARIES: TEXTS: E. O. Winstedt (OCT, 1904); J. C. Rolfe (Loeb, 1929: with Florus); E. Malcovati (Paravia, 1945); P. K. Marshall (BT, 1977: bibliography xiii-xvi). COMMENTARIES: K. Nipperdey and K. Witte, 12th ed. (Berlin 1962). *Hannibal*, *Cato*, *Atticus*: M. Ruch (Paris 1968).

STUDIES: E. Jenkinson, 'Nepos. An introduction to Latin biography', in (ed.) T. A. Dorey, *Latin biography* (London 1967) 1–15; idem, 'Cornelius Nepos and biography at Rome', *ANRW* I.3 (1973) 703–19 (718–19 provide bibliography for 1939–72); A. D. Momigliano, *The development of Greek biography* (Harvard 1971) 96–9.

THE LITERARY MIME

LIVES

DECIMUS LABERIUS: b. *c.* 106 B.C. (Macr. *Sat.* 2.7.5(12) = Laber. *Mim.* 109). Acted in own mime at celebrations following Caesar's triumphs 46. d. 43 B.C. (Jerome, *Chron. ann. Abr.* 1974). PUBLILIUS SYRUS: probably an Antiochene (Pliny, *N.H.* 35.199.) Brought to Rome as a slave and manumitted. Surpassed Laberius in competition commissioned by Caesar (Macr. *Sat.* 2.7.6f.). *fl.* 43 B.C. (Jerome, loc. cit.).

WORKS

Laberius: titles of forty-three mimes and 183 lines survive in part or complete, including twenty-seven lines (Macr. *Sat.* 2.7.3) of his prologue before Caesar; perhaps this was the only part of the mime regularly committed to writing in advance. Publilius: titles of two mimes only (one hopelessly corrupt) and less than five lines survive, outside the *Sententiae* (700 lines), an incomplete reproduction made under Nero or earlier (Sen. *Epist.* 8.9, 94.43, 108.8ff. etc., O. Skutsch, *RE* XXIII.2 (1959) 1924) and used in Roman schools (Jerome, *Epist.* 104.8; cf. Sen. *Epist.* 33.6); not all the *Sententiae* (like those attributed to Epicharmus, Menander, Cato, Varro and Seneca) need be authentic: see Gratwick and Jory under *Studies* below.

BIBLIOGRAPHY

(see P. Hamblenne, *ANRW* I.3 (1973) 698–70)

TEXTS AND COMMENTARIES: *CRF* 337–85; M. Bonaria, *Mimorum Romanorum fragmenta* (Genoa 1956); idem, *I mimi romani* (Rome 1965). *Sententiae*: J. W. and A. M. Duff, *Minor Latin poets* (Loeb, 1934) 1–111; O. Friedrich (1880: repr. Hildesheim 1964: with comm.); H. Beckby (Munich 1969).

STUDIES: G. Boissier, in Daremberg–Saglio, s.v. 'Mimus'; J.-P. Cèbe, *La caricature et la parodie* (Paris 1966) *passim*; F. Giancotti, *Mimo e gnome* (Messina 1967), reviewed by A. S. Gratwick, *C.R.* n.s.19 (1969) 185–7 and E. J. Jory, *Gnomon* 42 (1970) 125–9; W. Beare, *The Roman stage* 3rd ed. (London 1964) 149–58.

VERGILIUS MARO, PUBLIUS

LIFE

b. 15 October 70 B.C. at Andes near Mantua. If (which is doubtful) the ancient sources may be trusted, father was a prosperous self-made man of modest origins, mother possibly well-connected. Educ. Cremona, Milan and Rome. Chronology of early life uncertain; renunciation of rhetoric for philosophy and adherence to Epicurean circle under Siro at Naples rests on dubious authority (*Catal.* 5). Story (current early in antiquity) that family estate was involved in confiscations after Philippi and restored by Octavian is ostensibly supported both by poems (*Catal.* 8, *Ecl.* 9, 1) and by Servius *auctus* (*Ecl.* 9, 10; cf. L. P. Wilkinson, *Hermes* 94 (1966) 320–4), but this too may be plausible fiction. With pub. of *Ecl.* passed from ambit of C. Asinius Pollio to that of Maecenas (to whom he introd. Horace) and Octavian. Rest of life uneventful; d. 20 September 19 B.C. at Brundisium (Brindisi) on way back from Greece. Buried at Naples. Main sources: poems, esp. *Catal.* 5, 8; *Ecl. passim*; *Geo.* 3.1–48; Horace, esp. *Sat.* 1.5; ancient *Vitae* (ed. J. Brummer, BT, 1912; C. Hardie, OCT 2nd ed., 1957) and commentators (Servius ed. G. Thilo–H. Hagen, 3 vols., Leipzig 1881–7; E. K. Rand et al., Harvard–Oxford 1946–); cf. Büchner, under *Studies* below, 1–41 (pagination of independently printed ed. of *RE* article).

WORKS

Juvenilia: of the poems in the so-called *Appendix Vergiliana* (q.v., pp. 859–61) one or two of the short pieces in various metres entitled *Catalepton* (= κατὰ λεπτόν 'miniatures', 'trifles') have been identified as V.'s. See (ed.) R. E. H. Westendorp Boerma, 2 vols. (Assen 1949–63). *Eclogues* (*Bucolica*): book of ten pastorals generally accepted as having been written and pubd *c.* 42–37, but precise order and dating still controversial. See G. W. Bowersock, *H.S.C.Ph.* 75 (1971) 73–80; W. Clausen, ibid. 76 (1972) 201–6; R. J. Tarrant, ibid. 82 (1978) 197–9; Bowersock, ibid. 201–2. *Georgics*: didactic poem in four books, seven years in the writing, completed by 29 B.C. (*Vit. Don.* 85). *Aeneid*: epic in twelve books begun immediately after *Geo.* (*Vit. Don.* 85), incomplete at V.'s death; pubd on Octavian's orders by his literary executors Varius and Tucca 'lightly corrected' (*summatim emendata*: see *Vit. Don.* 140–65, raising controversial problems).

BIBLIOGRAPHY

(see Williams (1967) under *Studies* (1) below; *ANRW* II 31.1, 2 (1981))

TEXTS AND COMMENTARIES: TEXTS: O. Ribbeck (Leipzig 1859–68; 2nd ed. 1894–5); E. de Saint-Denis, H. Goelzer, R. Durand, A. Bellessort (Budé, 1925–56); H. R. Fairclough, 2nd ed. (Loeb, 1934–5); R. Sabbadini (Rome 1930), repr. with minor alterations L. Castiglioni (Paravia, 1945–52); M. Geymonat (Paravia, 1973); R. A. B. Mynors (OCT, 1969; 2nd ed. 1972), replacing F. A. Hirtzel (OCT, 1900). For Servius' commentary see under *Life*. COMMENTARIES: (1) Complete. J. L. de la Cerda (repr. Cologne 1642); C. G. Heyne, G. P. E. Wagner, 4th ed. (Leipzig 1830–41); J. Conington, H. Nettleship, F. Haverfield (London 1858–98); T. E. Page (London 1894–1900); F. Plessis, P. Lejay (Paris 1919); R. D. Williams (London 1972–9).

(2) Individual works. *Aeneid*: J. Henry (London, Edinburgh and Dublin 1873–89); J. W. Mackail (Oxford 1930). *Aen.* 1: R. G. Austin (Oxford 1971). *Aen.* 2: idem (Oxford 1964). *Aen.* 3: R. D. Williams (Oxford 1962). *Aen.* 4: A. S. Pease (Cambridge, Mass. 1935); R. G. Austin (Oxford 1955). *Aen.* 5: R. D. Williams (Oxford 1960). *Aen.* 6: E. Norden, 3rd ed. (Stuttgart 1926); F. Fletcher (Oxford 1941); R. G. Austin (Oxford 1977). *Aen.* 7–8: C. J. Fordyce (Oxford 1977). *Aen.* 8: P. T. Eden (Leiden 1975); K. W. Gransden (Cambridge 1976). *Aen.* 12: W. S. Maguinness (London 1953). *Georgics*: W. Richter (Munich 1957). *Georg.* 1 and 4: H. H. Huxley (London 1963). *Eclogues*: R. Coleman (Cambridge 1977).

TRANSLATIONS: J. Dryden (1697); C. Day Lewis (1940–63). *Eclogues*: P. Valéry, *Oeuvres* I (1962) 207–22; G. Lee, *Virgil's Eclogues* (Liverpool 1980).

STUDIES. (1) GENERAL, and dealing particularly with *Aeneid*. C. A. Sainte-Beuve, *Étude sur Virgile* (Paris 1857); W. Y. Sellar, *The Roman poets of the Augustan age: Virgil* (Oxford 1877; 3rd ed. 1897); D. Comparetti, *Vergil in the middle ages*, tr. E. F. M. Benecke (London 1885); R. Heinze, *Virgils epische Technik* (Leipzig 1903; 3rd ed. 1915); T. R. Glover, *Virgil* (London 1904; 7th ed. 1942); H. W. Prescott, *The development of Virgil's art* (Chicago 1927); R. S. Conway, *The Vergilian age* (Harvard U.P. 1928); R. M. Henry, 'Medea and Dido', *C.R.* 44 (1930) 97–108; C. S. Lewis, *A preface to Paradise Lost*, ch. 6 (Oxford 1942); W. F. J. Knight, *Roman Vergil* (London 1944; 2nd ed. 1966); E. Paratore, *Virgilio* (Rome 1945; 2nd ed. 1954); C. M. Bowra, *From Virgil to Milton* (London 1945); T. S. Eliot, *What is a classic?* (London 1945); V. Pöschl, *Die Dichtkunst Virgils: Bild und Symbol in der Aeneis* (Innsbruck 1950; tr. Seligson, Michigan 1962); B. M. W. Knox, 'The serpent and the flame: the imagery of the second book of the Aeneid', *A.J.Ph.* 71 (1950) 379–400; A. M. Guillemin, *Virgile* (Paris 1951); J. Perret, *Virgile, l'homme et l'oeuvre* (Paris 1952; 2nd ed. 1965); R. A. Brooks, 'Discolor aura: reflections on the Golden Bough', *A.J.Ph.* 74 (1953) 260–80; E. M. W. Tillyard, *The English epic and its background* (London 1954); K. Büchner, *RE* VIIIA (1955–8) 1021–1486, separately pubd Stuttgart 1961; G. B. Townend, 'Changing views of Vergil's greatness' *C.J.* 56 (1960–1) 67–77; M. Coffey, 'The subject matter of Virgil's similes', *B.I.C.S.* 8 (1961) 63–75; J. Lockwood, 'Virgil and his critics', *P.V.S.* 2 (1962–3) 1–8; A. Parry, 'The two voices of Virgil's Aeneid', *Arion* 2 (4), (1963) 66f.; V. Buchheit, *Vergil über die Sendung Roms* (Heidelberg 1963); Brooks Otis, *Virgil: a study in civilised poetry* (Oxford 1963); W. V. Clausen, 'An interpretation of the Aeneid', *H.S.C.Ph.* 68 (1964) 139–47; M. C. J. Putnam, *The poetry of the Aeneid* (Harvard 1965); (ed.) Steele Commager, *Virgil, Twentieth-Century Views* (New Jersey 1966); R. D. Williams, *Virgil*, *G.&R.*, *New surveys in the classics* 1 (1967; repr. with Addenda 1978); F. Klingner, *Virgil* (Zurich 1967); K. Quinn, *Virgil's Aeneid, a critical description* (London 1968); R. G. Austin, '*Virgil*, Aeneid 6.384–476' *P.V.S.* 8 (1968–9) 51–60; (ed.) D. R. Dudley, *Virgil* (Studies in Latin literature and its influence, London 1969); G. K. Galinsky,

Aeneas, Sicily and Rome (Princeton 1969); W. A. Camps, *An introduction to Virgil's Aeneid* (Oxford 1969); A. G. McKay, *Virgil's Italy* (Bath 1970); G. Highet, *The speeches in Vergil's Aeneid* (Princeton 1972); W. R. Johnson, *Darkness visible* (Berkeley 1976).

(2) 'ECLOGUES': (*a*) GENERAL: G. Jachmann, 'Die dichterische Technik in Vergils Bukolika', *N.J.A.* 49 (1922) 101–20; H. J. Rose, *The eclogues of Vergil* (Berkeley 1942); K. Büchner, *P. Vergilius Maro* (Stuttgart 1960) 160–243 = *RE* VIIIA.1 (1955) 1180–1264; V. Pöschl, *Die Hirtendichtung Virgils* (Heidelberg 1964); F. Klingner, *Virgil* (Zurich 1967) 9–174; G. Williams, *Tradition and originality in Roman poetry* (Oxford 1968: for *index locorum* see p. 801); T. G. Rosenmeyer, *The green cabinet* (Berkeley 1969); M. C. J. Putnam, *Virgil's pastoral art* (Princeton 1970); R. Kettemann, *Bukolik und Georgik* (Heidelberg 1977). (*b*) INDIVIDUAL ECLOGUES: 1 (or 1 and 9): F. Leo, *Hermes* 38 (1903) 1–18; R. Coleman, *G.&R.* 13 (1966) 79–97; P. Fedeli, *G.I.F.* n.s.3 (1972) 273–300; W. Clausen, *H.S.C.Ph.* 76 (1972) 201–5. 2: E. Pfeiffer, in *Virgils Bukolika* (Stuttgart 1933) 1–34; O. Skutsch. *H.S.C.Ph.* 74 (1968) 95–9. 4: E. Norden, *Die Geburt des Kindes* (Leipzig 1924); W. W. Tarn, *J.R.S.* 22 (1932) 135–60; G. Jachmann, *A.S.N.P.* 21 (1952) 13–62; H. C. Gotoff, *Philologus* 111 (1967) 66–79; G. Williams, in (edd.) A. J. Woodman and D. West, *Quality and pleasure in Latin poetry* (Cambridge 1974) 31–46. 5: A. G. Lee, *P.C.Ph.S.* n.s.23 (1977) 62–70. 6: G. Jachmann, *Hermes* 58 (1923) 288–304; O. Skutsch, *Rh.M.* 99 (1956) 193–201; Z. Stewart, *H.S.Ph.* 64 (1959) 179–205; J. P. Elder, *H.S.Ph.* 65 (1961) 109–25; D. O. Ross, in *Backgrounds to Augustan poetry* (Cambridge 1975) 18–37; W. Clausen, *A.J.Ph.* 97 (1976) 245–7. 8: G. W. Bowersock, *H.S.C.Ph.* 75 (1971) 73–80. 10: F. Skutsch, in *Aus Vergils Frühzeit* (Leipzig 1901) 2–27; idem, in *Gallus und Vergil* (Leipzig 1906) 155–92; D. O. Ross, in *Backgrounds to Augustan poetry* (Cambridge 1975) 85–106. (*c*) STRUCTURE: C. Becker, *Hermes* 83 (1955) 314–28; J. van Sickle, *T.A.Ph.A.* 98 (1967) 491–508; O. Skutsch, *H.S.C.Ph.* 73 (1968) 153–69; idem, *B.I.C.S.* 18 (1971) 26–9; N. Rudd, in *Lines of enquiry* (Cambridge 1976) 119–44; J. van Sickle, *The design of Virgil's Bucolics* (Rome 1978). (*d*) THEOCRITUS: A. S. F. Gow, *Theocritus* (Cambridge 1952: with tr.); K. J. Dover, *Theocritus* (London 1971); S. Posch, *Beobachtungen zur Theokritnachwirkung bei Vergil, Commentationes Aenipontanae* 19 (Innsbruck 1969); L. E. Ross, *S.I.F.C.* n.s.43 (1971) 5–25. (*e*) PASTORAL LANDSCAPE: B. Snell, in *The discovery of the mind*, tr. T. G. Rosenmeyer (Cambridge, Mass. 1953) 281–303; G. Jachmann, *Maia* 5 (1952) 161–74; A. M. Parry, *Y.Cl.S.* 15 (1957) 3–29.

(3) 'GEORGICS'. T. Keightley, *Notes on the Bucolics and Georgics of Virgil* (London 1846); T. F. Royds, *The beasts, birds and bees of Virgil* (Oxford 1914); G. Wissowa, 'Das Prooemium von Vergils Georgica', *Hermes* 52 (1917) 92–104; J. Sargeaunt, *The trees, shrubs and plants of Virgil* (Oxford 1920); W. E. Heitland, *Agricola* (Cambridge 1921: in English); R. Billiard, *L'agriculture dans l'antiquité d'après les Géorgiques de Virgile* (Paris 1928); E. Burck, 'Die Komposition von Vergils Georgica', *Hermes* 64 (1929) 279–321; H. M. Fraser, *Beekeeping in antiquity* (London 1931); L. A. S. Jermyn, 'Weather-signs in Virgil', *G.&R.* 20 (1951) 26–37, 49–59; H. Altevogt,

Labor improbus (Münster, Westfalen 1952: in German): H. Dahlmann, *Der Bienenstaat in Vergils Georgica* (Wiesbaden 1955); F. Klingner, *Vergils Georgica* (Zurich 1963); E. Abbe, *The plants of Virgil's Georgics* (Ithaca, New York 1965); L. P. Wilkinson, *The Georgics of Virgil* (Cambridge 1969); M. C. J. Putnam, *Vergil's poem of the earth* (Princeton 1979); G. B. Miles, *Virgil's Georgics: a new interpretation* (California 1980).

(4) CONCORDANCE: H. H. Warwick (Minnesota 1975).

HORATIUS FLACCUS, QUINTUS

LIFE

b. 8 Dec. 65 B.C. at Venusia in Apulia, son of a freedman. Educ. at Rome by Orbilius, and later at Athens. Appointed *tribunus militum* by Brutus 43 B.C.; after defeat at Philippi received pardon and purchased position of *scriba quaestorius*. Acquainted with Virgil, Maecenas, and Augustus, whose offer of a secretaryship he refused. d. 27 Nov. 8 B.C. Buried on Esquiline. Main sources: ancient *Vita* (printed in Klingner (BT), under *Texts* below; tr. by J. C. Rolfe, *Suetonius* (Loeb, 1914) vol. II); Hor. *Epist.* 2.1.71 (Orbilius), 2.2.41ff. (education), 1.20.20ff., *Sat.* 1.6.45ff. (introduction to Maecenas and father's supervision of education). See J. F. d'Alton, *Horace and his age* (London 1917), E. Fraenkel, *Horace* (Oxford 1957) 1–23.

WORKS

Satires 1, 35–34 B.C.; *Satires* 2, 30–29 B.C.; *Epodes*, 30–29 B.C.; *Odes* 1–3, 23 B.C.; *Epistles* 1, 20–19 B.C.; *Epistles* 2.2, 19–18 B.C.; *Carmen saeculare*, 17 B.C.; *Epistles* 2.1, *c.* 15 B.C.; *Odes* 4, 13 B.C. or later; *Ars poetica*, either between 23 and 17 B.C. or after *Odes* 4. See C. O. Brink, *Horace on poetry* I (Cambridge 1963) 239–43, G. Williams, *Horace*, *G.&R.*, *New surveys in the classics* 6 (1972) 38–48.

BIBLIOGRAPHY

(see W. S. Anderson, *C.W.* 50 (1956) 33–40 and 57 (1964) 293–301; R. J. Getty, *C.W.* 52 (1959) 167–88 and 246–7; *ANRW* II 31.3 (1981))

TEXTS AND COMMENTARIES: TEXTS: E. C. Wickham, 2nd ed. rev. H. W. Garrod (OCT, 1912); F. Klingner, 3rd ed. (BT, 1959); M. Lenchantin de Gubernatis and D. Bo, 1st–2nd edd. (Paravia, 1958–60: with indexes, metrical and linguistic data). COMMENTARIES: Pomponius Porphyrio (3rd c. A.D.) ed. A. Holder (Innsbruck 1894); pseudo-Acro (5th c. A.D.) ed. O. Keller (BT, 1902–4); R. Bentley (Cambridge 1711); J. G. Orelli and J. G. Baiter, 4th ed. rev. W. Hirschfelder and W. Mewes (Berlin 1886–92); E. C. Wickham (Oxford 1891–6); A. Kiessling, rev. R. Heinze, 5th–10th edd. (Berlin 1957–61: all with bibliographies by E. Burck). *Odes* and *Epodes*: T. E.

Page (London 1895); J. Gow (Cambridge 1895). *Odes*: P. Shorey and G. J. Laing (Chicago 1910); H. P. Syndikus (Darmstadt 1972–3). *Odes* 1–2: R. G. M. Nisbet and M. Hubbard (Oxford 1970–8). *Odes* 3: G. Williams (Oxford 1969). *Satires* and *Epistles*: E. P. Morris (New York 1909–11). *Satires*: A. Palmer (London 1891); J. Gow (Cambridge 1901–9); P. Lejay (Paris 1911). *Epistles*: A. S. Wilkins (London 1896). *Epistles* 1: O. A. W. Dilke, 3rd ed. (London 1966). *Ars poetica*: C. O. Brink (Cambridge 1971).

TRANSLATIONS: E. C. Wickham (Oxford 1903); C. E. Bennett and H. R. Fairclough (Loeb, 1927–9). *Odes*: J. Michie (Penguin, 1967). *Satires* and *Epistles*: N. Rudd (Penguin, 1979).

STUDIES: (1) GENERAL: W. Wili, *Horaz und die augusteische Kultur* (Basel 1948); E. Fraenkel, *Horace* (Oxford 1957); C. Becker, *Das Spätwerk des Horaz* (Göttingen 1963); C. O. Brink, *Horace on poetry* (Cambridge 1963); A. la Penna, *Orazio e l'ideologia del principato* (Turin 1963); J. Perret, *Horace l'homme et l'oeuvre*, Eng. tr. B. Humez (New York 1964); K. J. Reckford, *Horace* (New York 1969); (ed.) H. Oppermann, *Wege zu Horaz* (Darmstadt 1972); (ed.) C. D. N. Costa, *Horace* (London 1973). (2) 'ODES': L. P. Wilkinson, *Horace and his lyric poetry*, 2nd ed. (Cambridge 1951); S. Commager, *The odes of Horace* (London 1962); G. Pasquali, *Orazio lirico*, ed. A. la Penna (Florence 1964); E. Doblhofer, *Die Augustuspanegyrik des Horaz* (Heidelberg 1966); D. A. West, *Reading Horace* (Edinburgh 1967); V. Pöschl, *Horazische Lyrik* (Heidelberg 1970); K. E. Bohnenkamp, *Die horazische Strophe* (Hildesheim 1972). (3) 'EPODES': V. Grassman, *Die erotischen Epoden des Horaz* (Munich 1966); R. W. Carruba, *The Epodes of Horace* (The Hague 1969). (4) 'SATIRES': N. O. Nilsson, *Metrische Stildifferenzen in den Satiren des Horaz* (Uppsala 1952); N. Rudd, *The Satires of Horace* (Cambridge 1966); C. A. van Rooy, 'Arrangement and structure of satires in Horace, Sermones Book I', *Acta Classica* 11 (1968), 13 (1970), 14 (1971), 15 (1972). (5) 'EPISTLES': E. Courbaud, *Horace, sa vie et sa pensée à l'époque des Épîtres* (Paris 1914); M. J. McGann, *Studies in Horace's first book of Epistles* (Brussels 1969). (6) 'ARS POETICA': W. Steidle, *Studien zur Ars Poetica des Horaz* (Hildesheim 1967).

CONCORDANCES: L. Cooper (Washington 1916); D. Bo (Hildesheim 1965).

LOVE-ELEGY

GENERAL WORKS

Day, A. A., *The origins of Latin love-elegy* (Oxford 1938).
Luck, G., *The Latin love elegy*, 2nd ed. (London 1969).
idem, *ANRW* 1.3 (1973) 361–8.

Platnauer, M., *Latin elegiac verse. A study of the metrical uses of Tibullus, Propertius and Ovid* (Cambridge 1951).
Ross, D. O., *Backgrounds to Augustan poetry: Gallus, elegy and Rome* (Cambridge 1975).
Sellar, W. Y., *Horace and the elegiac poets*, 2nd ed. (London 1899).
Stroh, W., *Die römische Liebeselegie als werbende Dichtung* (Amsterdam 1971).
Sullivan, J. P. (ed.), *Elegy and lyric* (London 1962).
Wilkinson, L. P., *Golden Latin artistry* (Cambridge 1963).
Williams, G., *Tradition and originality in Roman poetry* (Oxford 1968).

GALLUS, GAIUS CORNELIUS

LIFE

b. 70/69 B.C. at Forum Iulii (mod. Fréjus) in Gaul, of humble birth; later rose to equestrian rank. Educ. at Rome by same teachers as Virgil, thenceforth a close friend. Fought in Civil War on Octavian's side from 43 B.C. to Actium; appointed first prefect of Egypt 30 B.C. Vaunted his achievements in an inscription (*ILS* 8995), fell into disgrace and committed suicide 26 B.C. Sources: Jerome, *Chron.* (birth); Probus, Thilo–Hagen III. 2.328 (education); Suet. *Aug.* 66, Dio Cass. 53.23.5ff. (military career and death). See also Ovid, *Am.* 3.9.63f., *Trist.* 2.445f. On his birthplace and background see R. Syme, *C.Q.* 32 (1938) 39ff.; on the inscription E. Hartman, *Gymnasium* 72 (1965) 1–8, and H. Volkmann, ibid. 328–30.

WORKS

Four books of elegies, of which one pentameter (*FPL* 99) and some ten other lines survive, the latter first pubd by R. D. Anderson, P. J. Parsons, R. G. M. Nisbet, 'Elegiacs by Gallus from Qaṣr Ibrîm', *J.R.S.* 69 (1979) 125–55. Cf. Prop. 2.34.91f., Ovid, *Am.* 1.15.30, *Ars Am.* 3.537, Mart. 8.73.6. Some lines echoed in Virg. *Ecl.* 10 (Serv. *ad loc.*); on G.'s relation to Virgil see F. Skutsch, *Aus Vergils Frühzeit* (Leipzig 1901); idem, *Gallus und Vergil* (Leipzig 1906); R. Coleman, 'Gallus, the Bucolics, and the ending of the fourth Georgic', *A.J.Ph.* 83 (1962) 55–71.

BIBLIOGRAPHY

STUDIES: E. Bréguet, 'Les élégies de Gallus', *R.E.L.* 26 (1948) 204–14; Bardon II 34–44; J.-P. Boucher, *Caius Cornélius Gallus* (Paris 1966); indexes to Ross and Stroh under *General works* above.

TIBULLUS, ALBIUS

LIFE

b. *c.* 55 B.C. of equestrian rank, possibly in Gabii (cf. *v.l.* in *Vita Tib.*). Lived between Praeneste and Rome in the *regio Pedana*. Closely connected with circle of M. Valerius Messalla Corvinus, with whom he campaigned in Aquitania in 27 B.C. d. as *iuuenis* (i.e. before age 46) either in same year as Virgil (19 B.C.) or shortly after (2.5 shows influence of *Aeneid*, pubd soon after V.'s death). Sources: anonymous *Vita* (birth); Ovid, *Trist.* 4.10.45ff. (chronological list of Roman poets); Tib. 1.7.9ff (campaign); epigram by Domitius Marsus, *FPL* 111 (death; cf. M. J. McGann, *Latomus* 29 (1970) 774ff.); Hor. *Epist.* 1.4, *Odes* 1.33.

WORKS

(1) GENUINE: First two books of *Corpus Tibullianum* (sixteen elegies). Bk 1 pubd *c.* 27 B.C. (1.7 describes Messalla's triumph), 2 at unknown later date. (2) DUBIOUS OR SPURIOUS: Remainder of the Corpus, comprising: six elegies written by a 'Lygdamus'; a *Panegyricus* of Messalla in hexameters; five anonymous elegies on the love of Sulpicia for Cerinthus; six short elegies by Sulpicia herself; one elegy whose author calls himself Tibullus; one four-line epigram. Majority of these probably written by minor poets of Messalla's circle. On Lygdamus see B. Axelson, 'Lygdamus und Ovid', *Eranos* 58 (1960) 92–111.

BIBLIOGRAPHY

(see H. Harrauer, *A bibliography to the Corpus Tibullianum* (Hildesheim 1971))

TEXTS AND COMMENTARIES: TEXTS: E. Hiller, in *Corpus poetarum Latinorum* (London 1894); J. P. Postgate (Loeb, 1913); idem, 2nd ed. (OCT, 1915); F. W. Lenz (BT, 1937); M. Ponchont, 6th ed. (Budé, 1967); F. W. Lenz, 3rd ed. rev. G. K. Galinsky (Leiden 1971); A. G. Lee, bks 1–2 (Cambridge 1975: with tr.). COMMENTARIES: K. F. Smith, complete except for Lygdamus and *Panegyricus* (New York 1913; repr. Darmstadt 1964). Bk 1: J. André (Paris 1965); P. Murgatroyd (Pietermaritzburg 1980). Bks 1–2: M. C. J. Putnam (Norman, Oklahoma 1973).

STUDIES: (1) GENERAL: A. Cartault, *A propos du Corpus Tibullianum* (Paris 1906); M. Schuster, *Tibull-Studien* (Vienna 1930); J. P. Elder, 'Tibullus: tersus atque elegans', in (ed.) Sullivan, under *General works* above; F. Solmsen, 'Tibullus as an Augustan poet', *Hermes* 90 (1962) 295–325; A. W. Bulloch, 'Tibullus and the Alexandrians', *P.C.Ph.S.* n.s.19 (1973) 71–89; F. Cairns, *Tibullus: a Hellenistic poet at Rome* (Cambridge 1979). (2) INDIVIDUAL POEMS: See Harrauer above and the following: J. H. Gaisser, *A.J.Ph.* 92 (1971) 202–16 (1.6); eadem, *C.Ph.* 66 (1971) 221–39 (1.7);

A. G. Lee, in (edd.) A. J. Woodman and D. West, *Quality and pleasure in Roman poetry* (Cambridge 1974) 94–114 (1.1).

CONCORDANCE: E. N. O'Neil (Ithaca, N.Y. 1963).

PROPERTIUS, SEXTUS

LIFE

b. *c.* 50 B.C. of equestrian family in Umbria, probably (cf. correction at 4.1.125) in Assisi; part of his family estate confiscated 41/40 B.C. When still young rejected rhetoric in favour of poetry; closely associated with Ovid. d. not much later than A.D. 2. Of the names ascribed to him by MSS – Propertius Aurelius Nauta – the second is impossible and the third based on a corruption in 2.24b. 38; the *praenomen* Sextus has ancient testimony (Donat. *Vita Verg.*). Sources: own works, esp. 1.21–2 (discussed by Williams, *TORP* 172ff.) and 4.1.127–34. Other testimonia in Butler and Barber, under *Commentaries* below.

WORKS

Four books of elegies: bk 1 pubd in or before 29 B.C. (2.31, datable to 28 B.C., not included); 2 *c.* 26 B.C. (Gallus recently dead at 2.34.91); 3 between 23 and 20 B.C.; 4 *c.* 16 B.C. (death of Cornelia described in 4.11).

BIBLIOGRAPHY

(see H. Harrauer, *A bibliography to Propertius* (Hildesheim 1973))

TEXTS AND COMMENTARIES: TEXTS: J. P. Postgate, in *Corpus poetarum Latinorum* (London 1894); H. E. Butler (Loeb, 1912); M. Schuster and F. Dornseiff, 2nd ed. (BT, 1958); E. A. Barber, 2nd ed. (1960). COMMENTARIES: Complete: H. E. Butler and E. A. Barber (Oxford 1933); W. A. Camps (Cambridge 1961–7). Bks 1–2: P. J. Enk (Leiden 1946–62). Bk 1: P. Fedeli (Florence 1980). Bk 4: idem (Bari 1965).

STUDIES: (1) GENERAL: A. W. Allen, 'Sunt qui Propertium malint', in (ed.) Sullivan, under *General works* above; J.-P. Boucher, *Études sur Properce* (Paris 1965); E. Lefèvre, *Propertius ludibundus* (Heidelberg 1966); M. E. Hubbard, *Propertius* (London 1974); J. P. Sullivan, *Propertius: a critical introduction* (Cambridge 1976). (2) ON BK 4: C. Becker, *Hermes* 99 (1971) 449–80. (3) INDIVIDUAL POEMS. See Harrauer above and the following: R. O. A. M. Lyne, *P.C.Ph.S.* n.s.16 (1970) 60–78 (1.3); F. Cairns, *C.Q.* n.s.21 (1971) 455–60 (2.29a); idem, *C.Q.* n.s.24 (1974) 94–110 (1.1); J. Bramble, in (edd.) A. J. Woodman and D. West, *Quality and pleasure in Roman poetry* (Cambridge 1974) 81–93 (1.20). (4) TEXT AND INTERPRETATION: D. R. Shackleton

Bailey, *Propertiana* (Cambridge 1956); G. Luck, *A.J.Ph.* 100 (1979) 73–93. (5) MANUSCRIPTS: A. E. Housman, *J.Ph.* 21 (1893) 101–97, and 22 (1894) 84–128 = *Classical papers* 232–304, 315–47.

CONCORDANCE: B. Schmeisser (Hildesheim 1972).

OVIDIUS NASO, PUBLIUS

LIFE

b. 20 March 43 B.C. at Sulmona (Abruzzi), of equestrian family. Sent to Rome as a boy to study rhetoric under Arellius Fuscus and Porcius Latro. Visited Athens and travelled in Greek lands. Held minor judicial posts, but abandoned official career for literature; cultivated society of poets, esp. those in circle of M. Valerius Messalla Corvinus. Thrice married. In A.D. 8 banished by Augustus on account of the *Ars Amatoria* and another cause, never specified, to Tomis (mod. Constanţa, Romania), where he d. A.D. 17. Main source for life his own works, esp. *Trist.* 4.10; also Sen. *Contr.* 2.2.8–12, 9.5.17 (rhetorical studies); Jerome, *Chron.* (death; cf. Ovid, *Fast.* 1.223–4 and Bömer, under *Commentaries* below, *ad loc.*); R. Syme, *History in Ovid* (Oxford 1978). On his official career see E. J. Kenney, *Y. Cl. S.* 21 (1969) 244–9; on his exile J. C. Thibault, *The mystery of Ovid's exile* (Berkeley 1964).

WORKS

(1) EXTANT: (All in elegiac couplets except *Met.*) *Amores*: three books totalling fifty elegies (15+20+15); in this form pubd shortly before *Ars Am.* (q.v.). *Heroides* or *Epistulae Heroidum* (G. Luck, *Die römische Liebeselegie* (Heidelberg 1961) 223–4): single letters (1–14) pubd between the two edd. of the *Amores* (*Am.* 2.18); double (16–21) written before A.D. 8 but possibly not pubd until after O.'s death. For *Ep. Sapph.* (15) see under (3) below. *Medicamina Faciei Femineae*: fragment of 100 vv. on cosmetics, pubd. before *Ars Am.* 3 (ibid. 205–6). *Ars Amatoria* (see Sen. *Contr.* 3.7, *GLK* v 473.5): bks 1–2 pubd not before 1 B.C. (*Ars Am.* 1.171ff.), bk 3 added later (*Ars Am.* 2.745–6). *Remedia Amoris*: mock recantation in one book; no indication of date. (On the chronology of the early works see discussion and previous literature cited by H. Jacobson, *Ovid's Heroides* (Princeton 1974) 300–18; Syme, under *Life* above, 1–20.) *Metamorphoses*: epic in fifteen books of hexameters; substantially complete by A.D. 8. *Fasti*: calendar poem planned in twelve books, one per month; only bks 1–6 (Jan.–June) completed by A.D. 8, but some revision at Tomis (*Fast.* 1.3, 2.15). *Tristia*: bks 1, 3–5 are made up of short poems to various addressees (unnamed except for his wife and Augustus); bk 2 is a single continuous poem, an apologia for his poetry addressed to Augustus. Individual books sent to Rome at intervals during A.D. 9–12. *Epistulae ex Ponto*: as *Trist.* 1, 3–5, but to named addressees. Bks 1–3

compiled from poems of various dates (*Pont.* 3.9.53) and pubd A.D. 13; bk 4 probably posthumous. *Ibis*: pubd *c.* A.D. 11.

(2) LOST: *Amores* (version in five books): his first attested work, pubd in his early twenties (*Trist.* 4.10.55–60). Relationship with three-book ed. obscure: see Jacobson under (1) above. *Medea*: his only tragedy: *Am.* 2.18, 3.1, *Trist.* 2.553–4, Quint. 10.1.98, Tac. *Dial.* 12.6. Other lost works included epigrams and an abbreviated tr. of Aratus' *Phaenomena*. Fragments and testimonia: Owen, *Tristia* (OCT), Lenz, *Halieutica* etc. (Paravia), Postgate (*Corpus*), under *Texts* below.

(3) DUBIOUS OR SPURIOUS: *Heroides*: 9 (Deianira): D. W. T. C. Vessey, *C.Q.* n.s.19 (1969) 349–61. 15 (*Epistula Sapphus*): Jacobson (see *Works* (1) above) 277–99; H. Dörrie, *P. Ovidius Naso. Der Brief der Sappho an Phaon* (Munich 1975); R. J. Tarrant, *H.S.C.Ph.* (forthcoming). 16–21: B. Latta, *Die Stellung der Doppelbriefe* (*Heroides* 16–21) *im Gesamtwerk Ovids* (diss. Marburg 1963); E. Courtney, *B.I.C.S.* 12 (1965) 63–6; (on 16.39–144, 21.145–248) U. Fischer, *Ignotum hoc aliis novavit opus* (Augsburg 1969); E. J. Kenney, *C.Q.* n.s.29 (1979) 394–431. *Priapeum* 3: ascribed to O. on the strength of Seneca (*Contr.* 1.2.22), but see V. Buchheit, *Studien zum Corpus Priapeorum* (Munich 1962) 15–18. Certainly not by O. *Somnium* (*Am.* 3.5): E. J. Kenney, ΑΓΩΝ 3 (1969) 1–14. *Halieutica*, on sea-fishing: A. E. Housman, *Classical papers* 698–701; B. Axelson, *Eranos* 43 (1945) 23–35. *Nux*: A. G. Lee, in *Ovidiana*, under *Studies* below, 457–71. *Consolatio ad Liviam* (see pp. 474–5).

BIBLIOGRAPHY

(see R. J. Gariepy, *C.W.* 64 (1970) 37–56; Barsby, *Studies* below; *ANRW* II 31.4 (1981))

TEXTS AND COMMENTARIES: TEXTS: (1) Complete works: R. Ehwald, F. Lenz, F. Levy, W. S. Anderson, E. H. Alton, D. E. W. Wormell, E. Courtney (BT, 1916–78); E. J. Kenney, S. G. Owen (OCT, 1915–); J. H. Mozley, G. Showerman, F. J. Miller, A. J. Wheeler, (Sir) J. G. Frazer (Loeb, 1916–29: *Am.* and *Her.* rev. G. P. Goold 1977); A. Palmer, G. M. Edwards, G. A. Davies, S. G. Owen, A. E. Housman, J. P. Postgate, in *Corpus poetarum Latinorum* (ed. Postgate), vol. 1 (London 1905). (2) Individual works: *Amores*: A. G. Lee (London 1968: with tr.); F. Munari, 5th ed. (Florence 1970: with Italian tr.). *Heroides*: H. Sedlmayer (Vienna 1886); H. Dörrie (Berlin 1971). *Metamorphoses*: H. Magnus (Berlin 1914); cf. D. A. Slater, *Towards a text of the Metamorphosis of Ovid* (Oxford 1927). *Tristia*: S. G. Owen (Oxford 1889). COMMENTARIES. *Amores*: P. Brandt (Leipzig 1911); F. W. Lenz, 3rd ed. (Berlin 1976: with German tr.). Bk 1: J. A. Barsby (Oxford 1973: with tr.). *Heroides*: A. Palmer, 2nd ed. by L. C. Purser (Oxford 1898: with Greek prose tr. of M. Planudes). *Ep. Sapph.*: H. Dörrie (Munich 1975). *Med. Fac.*: A. Kunz (Vienna 1881). *Ars Amatoria*: P. Brandt (Leipzig 1902); F. W. Lenz (Berlin 1969: with German tr.). Bk 1: A. S. Hollis (Oxford 1977). *Remedia Amoris*: (with *Med. Fac.*) F. W. Lenz, 2nd ed. (Berlin 1968: with German tr.); A. A. R. Henderson (Edinburgh 1979). *Metamorphoses*:

M. Haupt, O. Korn, R. Ehwald, 10th ed. rev. M. von Albrecht, 2 vols. (Zurich 1966); F. Bömer (Heidelberg 1969–). Bk 1: A. G. Lee (Cambridge 1953). Bks 6–10: W. S. Anderson (Norman, Oklahoma 1972). Bk 8: A. S. Hollis (Oxford 1970). *Fasti*: (Sir) J. G. Frazer, 5 vols. (London 1929: with tr.); F. Bömer, 2 vols. (Heidelberg 1957–8: with German tr.). *Tristia*: G. Luck, 2 vols. (Heidelberg 1967–77: with German tr.). Bk 2: S. G. Owen (Oxford 1924: with tr.). Bk 4: T. J. de Jonge (Groningen 1951). *Epistulae ex Ponto*: Bk 1: A. Scholte (Amersfurt 1933). *Ibis*: R. Ellis (Oxford 1881); A. la Penna (Florence 1957). [*Halieutica*: J. A. Richmond (London 1962); F. Capponi, 2 vols. (Leiden 1972). *Nux*: S. Wartena (Groningen 1928). *Cons. ad Liviam*: A. Witlox (Groningen 1935).]

TRANSLATIONS: H. T. Riley, 3 vols. (Bohn, 1852–9); Loeb, under *Texts* (1) above). M. Planudes: (*Heroides*) A. Palmer (under *Commentaries* above); M. Papathomopoulos, 2nd ed. (Joannina 1976); (*Ars Am.*, *Am.*, *Rem.*) P. E. Easterling and E. J. Kenney, *Ovidiana Graeca*, *P.C.Ph.S.* suppl. 1 (Cambridge 1965); (*Metamorphoses*) J. F. Boissonade (Paris 1822).

STUDIES: (1) GENERAL: E. Martini, *Einleitung zu Ovid* (Prague 1933); W. Kraus, 'Ovidius Naso', in von Albrecht and Zinn, *Ovid* (see below) 67–166 = rev. version of *RE* XVIII (1942) 1910–86; H. Fränkel, *Ovid: a poet between two worlds* (Berkeley 1945); L. P. Wilkinson, *Ovid recalled* (Cambridge 1955); J.-M. Frécaut, *L'esprit et l'humour chez Ovide* (Grenoble 1972); J. Barsby, *Ovid*, *G.&R.*, *New surveys in the classics* 12 (Oxford 1978). (2) MISCELLANIES: (ed.) N. I. Herescu, *Ovidiana: recherches sur Ovide* (Paris 1958); *Atti del Convegno internazionale Ovidiano*, 2 vols. (Rome 1959); (edd.) M. von Albrecht and E. Zinn, *Ovid* (Darmstadt 1968); (ed.) J. W. Binns, *Ovid* (London 1973). (3) INDIVIDUAL WORKS: *Heroides*: H. Jacobson, *Ovid's Heroides* (Princeton 1974). *Metamorphoses*: B. Otis, *Ovid as an epic poet*, 2nd ed. (Cambridge 1970); G. K. Galinsky, *Ovid's Metamorphoses: an introduction to the basic aspects* (Berkeley 1975). (4) SURVIVAL: W. Stroh, *Ovid im Urteil der Nachwelt* (Darmstadt 1969); (*Heroides*) H. Dörrie, *Der heroische Brief* (Berlin 1968). (5) CONCORDANCE: R. J. Deferrari, M. Inviolata Barry, M. R. P. McGuire (Washington 1939).

LIVIUS, TITUS

LIFE

b. 54 B.C. in Patavium, d. A.D. 17 (Jerome, *Chron. ann. Abr.* 1958). A case has been made by R. Syme (*H.S.Ph.* 64 (1959) 27ff.) for a life-span five years earlier. For his activities in Rome see Pliny, *Epist.* 2.3.8; Suda s.v. 'Κορνοῦτος'; Quint. 1.5.56, 8.1.3; Tac. *Ann.* 4.34; Suet. *Claud.* 41.1.

WORKS

Ab urbe condita libri: history of Rome from foundation to 9 B.C., originally in 142 books (perhaps 150 were planned), of which 1–10 and 21–45 survive. Of the lost books there are fragments preserved by grammarians and others (including a passage from bk 120 on Cicero's death) and summaries (*Periochae* of whole work preserved in MSS and a 3rd c. papyrus from Oxyrhynchus containing epitomes of bks 37–40 and 48–55); see Mart. 14.190.1; Suet. *Dom.* 10.3. There is no trace of the philosophical dialogues which he wrote in his youth (Sen. *Epist.* 100.9), but the excursus on Alexander (9.17–18) possibly betrays the style of his youthful declamations.

BIBLIOGRAPHY

TEXTS AND COMMENTARIES: TEXTS: W. Weissenborn, M. Müller and W. Heraeus (BT, 1887–1908: bks 21–2 rev. T. A. Dorey 1971); R. S. Conway, C. F. Walters, S. K. Johnson, A. H. McDonald and R. M. Ogilvie (OCT, 1919–74: bks 1–35 so far pubd); J. Bayet and P. Jal (Budé, 1940–79: bks 1–7, 41–2, 45 and frs. so far pubd). COMMENTARIES: W. Weissenborn and H. J. Müller, 4th ed. (Berlin 1910). Bks 1–5: R. M. Ogilvie, 2nd ed. (Oxford 1969). Bks 31–7: J. Briscoe (Oxford 1973–81).

STUDIES: (1) GENERAL: P. G. Walsh, *Livy, his historical aims and methods* (Cambridge 1961); (ed.) E. Burck, *Wege zu Livius* (Darmstadt 1967); (ed.) T. A. Dorey, *Livy* (London 1971); P. G. Walsh, *G.&R., New surveys in the classics* 8 (1974); T. J. Luce, *Livy: the composition of his history* (Princeton 1977). (2) LIFE AND CONNEXIONS: R. Syme, 'Livy and Augustus', *H.S.Ph.* 64 (1959) 27–76; H. Petersen, 'Livy and Augustus', *T.A.Ph.A.* 92 (1961) 440ff.; H. J. Mette, 'Livius und Augustus', *Gymnasium* 68 (1961) 278ff.; T. J. Luce, *T.A.Ph.A.* 71 (1965) 209ff.; E. Mensching, *M.H.* 24 (1967) 12ff. (3) ATTITUDE: E. Burck, 'Livius als augusteischer Historiker', *Die Welt als Geschichte* 1 (1935) 448ff.; I. Kajanto, *God and fate in Livy* (Turku 1957); M. Mazza, *Storia e ideologia in Livio* (Catania 1966); W. Liebeschütz, 'The religious position of Livy's history', *J.R.S.* 57 (1967) 45ff. (4) SOURCES: H. Nissen, *Kritische Untersuchungen über die Quellen der vierten und fünften Dekade des Livius* (Berlin 1868); A. Klotz, *Livius und seine Vorgänger* (Leipzig–Berlin 1940–1); R. M. Ogilvie, 'Livy, Licinius Macer and the Libri Lintei', *J.R.S.* 48 (1958) 40ff. (5) COMPOSITION AND STYLE: K. Witte, 'Über die Form der Darstellung', *Rh.M.* 65 (1910) 270ff., 359ff.; E. Burck, *Die Erzählungskunst des T. Livius* (Berlin 1934; 2nd ed. 1964); idem, *Einführung in die dritte Dekade des Livius* (Heidelberg 1950); A. H. McDonald, 'The style of Livy', *J.R.S.* 47 (1957) 155ff.; J.-P. Chausserie-Laprée, *L'expression narrative chez les historiens latins* (Paris 1969). (6) LANGUAGE: E. Wölfflin, *Livianische Kritik und livianischer Sprachgebrauch* (prog. Winterthur 1864); S. G. Stacey, 'Die Entwicklung des livianischen Stiles', *Arch. Lat. Lex.* 10 (1896) 17ff.; K. Gries, *Constancy in Livy's Latinity* (New York 1947); H. Tränkle,

'Beobachtungen und Erwägungen zum Wandel der livianischen Sprache', *W.S.* n.s.2 (1968) 103ff.

CONCORDANCE: D. Packard (Cambridge, Mass. 1968).

APPENDIX VERGILIANA

Collection of poems in various metres; so called, since Scaliger, from being printed as an appendix to the three canonical works of Virgil. At the most, a few epigrams in the *Catalepton* are genuine. In the case of the *Culex* and some of the *Catalepton*, demand for juvenilia created forgeries; elsewhere, ascription of extant works supplied the need. In the following list, D, S, and M denote ascriptions to Virgil by Donatus' *Vita Vergilii*, by the *Vita Servii*, or by the 9th- c. Murbach catalogue alone. For the *Vitae* see H. Nettleship, *Ancient lives of Vergil, with an essay on the poems of Vergil* (Oxford 1879); E. Norden, 'De Vitis Vergilianis', *Rh.M.* 61 (1906) 166–77; E. Diehl, *Die Vitae Vergilianae und ihre antiken Quellen* (Bonn 1911: Kleine Texte 72); A. Rostagni, *Suetonio: De poetis e biografi minori* (Turin 1944); OCT by C. Hardie, 2nd ed. (1957).

Moretum (M): description of country life; pre-Neronian (Mart. 13.13). *Copa* (S; cf. Charisius, *GLK* I 63.11): an invitation to drink, written after pub. of Prop. bk 4. *Dirae* (D, S), a farmer's curse, and *Lydia*, a love lament: not distinguished as two poems until discovery by F. Jacobs in 1729 that *Dirae* 104 marked beginning of a new poem in a Vatican MS. *Ciris* (D, S): Epyllion relating story of Scylla. *Culex* (D, S): mock-epic on death of a gnat; see Suet. *Vita Luc. ad init.* (cf. Stat. *Silv.* 2.7.73); Stat. *Silv.* I *praef.*; Mart. 8.56.20, 14.185; Nonius 211. *Catalepton* (D, S, mentioned along with *Epigrammata*): fifteen poems in various metres, the second accepted as V.'s by Quint. 8.3.27–9. *Priapea* (D, S): three poems, perhaps alluded to by Pliny, *Ep.* 5.3.6. *Elegiae in Maecenatem* (M): distinguished as two poems by Scaliger. *Aetna* (D, expressing doubt, S): see pp. 629–30 and 886.

BIBLIOGRAPHY

(1) General

TEXTS: R. Ellis (OCT, 1907); H. R. Fairclough, *Virgil* (Loeb, 1954) vol. II; R. Giomini (Florence 1962: with tr. and bibliography); W. V. Clausen, F. R. D. Goodyear, E. J. Kenney, J. A. Richmond (OCT, 1966).

SURVEYS: R. Pichon, *Journal des Savants* n.s.9 (1911) 113–25; G. D. Hadzsits, *C.W.* 15 (1922) 106–21; H. W. Prescott, *C.J.* 26 (1930) 49–62; R. Henry, *A.C.* 6 (1937) 357–95; G. E. Duckworth, *Vergilius* 1 (1938) 44–6, 3 (1939) 33–4, 6 (1940) 49–50; idem, *C.W.* 51 (1958) 92, 116–7; N. I. Herescu, *Bibliographie de la littérature latine* (Paris 1943) 159–65.

STUDIES: F. Skutsch, *Aus Vergils Frühzeit* (Leipzig 1901); idem, *Gallus und Vergil* (Leipzig 1906); H. R. Fairclough, 'The poems of the Appendix Vergiliana', *T.A.Ph.A.* 53 (1922) 5–34; A. Rostagni. *Virgilio minore, saggio sullo svolgimento della poesia virgiliana* (Turin 1933); E. H. Clift, *Latin pseudepigrapha* (Baltimore 1945); K. Büchner, *RE* VIIIA.1 (1955) 1061–1180; R. E. H. Westendorp Boerma, 'L'énigme de l'appendix Vergiliana', in (edd.) H. Bardon and R. Verdière, *Vergiliana* (Leiden 1971).

(2) Individual works

'MORETUM': F. L. Douglas, *A study of the Moretum* (New York 1929); R. B. Steele, 'The authorship of the Moretum', *T.A.Ph.A.* 61 (1930) 195ff.; W. Kroll, *RE* XVI (1933) 298–9; D. A. Ross, 'The Culex and Moretum as post-Augustan literary parodies', *H.S.C.Ph.* 79 (1975) 235ff. For Parthenius' doubtful *Moretum*, see R. Sabbadini, *R.F.* 31 (1903) 472. 'COPA': Commentary: E. H. Blakeney (Winchester 1933: with *Moretum*). Studies: M. Haupt, *Opuscula* I (Berlin 1875) 143ff.; F. Vollmer, *Rh.M.* 55 (1900) 527ff.; D. L. Drew, *C.Q.* 17 (1923) 73–81 and 19 (1925) 37–42; U. von Wilamowitz-Moellendorff, *Hellenistische Dichtung* II (Berlin 1924) 311–15; I. E. Drabkin, *The Copa* (Geneva–New York 1930); R. E. H. Westendorp Boerma, *Mnemosyne* 11 (1958) 331ff.; idem, *Hermeneus* 29 (1958) 114ff. 'DIRAE' AND 'LYDIA': Commentary: C. van der Graaf (Leiden 1945). Studies: W. M. Lindsay, *C.R.* 32 (1918) 62f. (ascribed to Cato), answered by R. P. Robinson, *T.A.Ph.A.* 54 (1923) 98–116; P. J. Enk, *Mnemosyne* n.s.47 (1919) 382–409 (ascribed to Varius); R. B. Steele, *The authorship of the Dirae and Lydia* (Nashville 1930); E. Fraenkel, *J.R.S.* 56 (1966) 142–55, answered and modified by F. R. D. Goodyear, *P.C.Ph.S.* n.s.17 (1971) 30–43. 'CIRIS': Commentaries: M. Lenchantin de Gubernatis (Turin 1930); R. Helm (Heidelberg 1937); H. Hielkema (diss. Utrecht 1941); D. Knecht (Bruge 1970); R. O. A. M. Lyne (Cambridge 1978). Studies: F. Leo, 'Vergil und die Ciris', *Hermes* 37 (1902) 14–55; R. F. Thomason, 'The Ciris and Ovid', *C.Ph.* 18 (1923) 239–62 (survey of earlier views), also ibid. 334–44, and 19 (1924) 147–56; F. Munari, 'Studi sulla Ciris', *Atti Accad. d. Italia, sci. mor. e stor.* 7.4 (1944) 273–314; F. Ehlers, 'Die Ciris und ihre Original', *M.H.* 11 (1954) 65–88; R. O. A. M. Lyne, 'The dating of the Ciris', *C.Q.* 65 (1971) 233–53. 'CULEX': Commentaries: F. Leo (Berlin 1891); C. Plésent (Paris 1910); C. Curcio (Turin 1928: with *Ciris*). Studies: D. L. Drew, *Culex* (Oxford 1925); R. S. Radford, 'The Culex and Ovid', *Philologus* 86 (1930) 18–66; E. Fraenkel, 'The Culex', *J.R.S.* 42 (1952) 1–9; R. Helm, 'Beiträge zum Culex', *Hermes* 81 (1953) 49ff.; D. Güntzschel, *Beiträge zur Datierung des Culex* (Münster–Aschendorff 1972); D. A. Ross (see above on *Moretum*). 'CATALEPTON' AND 'PRIAPEIA': Commentary: R. E. H. Westendorp Boerma, 2 vols. (Assen 1949–63). Studies: E. Galletier, *Epigrammata et Priapea* (Paris 1920); idem, *R.Ph.* 50 (1926) 153–72; J. Carcopino, *R.Ph.* 46 (1922) 156–84; R. S. Radford, 'Ovid's carmina furtiva', *Ph.Q.* 7 (1928) 45–59; R. B. Steele, *The Catalepta of the Virgilian Appendix* (Nashville 1936). *Catalepton* 9: P. John, *Rh.M.* 63 (1908) 100; P. Sonner, *De P. Virgili Maronis Catalepton carminibus quaestionum capita tria* (diss. Halle 1910).

Catalepton 13: G. Némethy, *De epodo Horatii Cataleptis Virgilii inserto* (Budapest 1908); J. Hubaux, 'Une épode d'Ovide', in *Serta Leodiensia* (Liège 1930) 187–245; idem, *A.C.* 7 (1938) 77–80.

VALGIUS RUFUS, GAIUS

LIFE

Consul *suffectus* 12 B.C. (Prosop. 3.382.N.169); mentioned at Hor. *Sat.* 1.10.82, and the recipient of *Odes* 2.9. Refs. in the fragments to Codrus and Cinna imply an early Augustan dating: no reason to suppose he was younger than Horace.

WORKS

Elegiac laments (Hor. *Odes* 2.9); hendecasyllables (preserved by Charisius, *GLK* I 108.7); bucolic hexameters (quoted by Philargyrius *ad* Virg. *Geo* 3.177); book on herbs (Pliny, *N.H.* 25.4); translation of Apollodorus' *Rhetoric* (Quint. 3.1.18, 5.17, 5.104); etymological work (Gell. 12.3.1, Charisius, *GLK* I 108.28). Fragments in *FPL* 105–6. See Schanz–Hosius II 172–4; Bardon II 19–22.

DOMITIUS MARSUS

LIFE

Dead at time of Ovid, *Pont.* 4.16.5, but still alive in 19 B.C. (date of lines on deaths of Virgil and Tibullus). For his connexion with Maecenas see Mart. 5.29.5, 8.56.23. Also mentioned at Mart. *praef.* 1, 2.71.3, 2.77.5, 5.5.5, 7.99.7.

WORKS

Epigrams: probably represented by frs. 3 (Epirota), 4 (Horace's schoolmaster Orbilius), 5 (*hircum et alumen olens*), and 7 (Virgil and Tibullus). Philargyrius (*ad* Virg. *Ecl.* 3.90) attests the title *Cicuta*: since, however, it implies something rustic, it might have been a collection within a collection; cf. Martial's *Liber spectaculorum*. Elegies (?): *fusca Melaenis* mentioned at Mart. 7.29.5, although she could have figured in the epigrams. Also an epic, *Amazonis* (4.29.7), *Fabellae* (Charisius, *GLK* I 72.4), and a prose work *De urbanitate* (Quint. 6.3.102, 104ff.). Fragments in *FPL* 110–11. See Schanz–Hosius II 174–6, Bardon II 52–7.

AEMILIUS MACER

LIFE

b. in Verona (Serv. *ad Ecl.* 5.1, identifying him with Mopsus), d. in Asia 16 B.C. (Jerome, *Chron. ann. Abr.* 2001). An acquaintance of Tibullus (Tib. 2.6.1).

WORKS

Didactic poems on birds, serpents and herbs (Ovid, *Trist.* 4.10.43), the last two possibly belonging to one work. Diomedes (*GLK* I 374.21) and Nonius (220.18 and 518.32) attest the title *Ornithogonia*; Charisius (*GLK* I 81.18) attests a *Theriaka*, in two books, as shown by *Comm. Bern. ad* Lucan 9.701. *Dist. Cat.* 2, *praef.* 2 is of dubious value for the *De herbis*. Boios has been claimed as source for *Ornithogonia* by G. Knaack, *Analecta Alexandrino-Romana* (Greifswald 1880) 11, and G. Lafaye, *Les métamorphoses d'Ovide* (Paris 1904) 43: ref. to *pictas uolucres* at Manil. 2.43 is probably to Boios, not Macer. Quint. 10.1.56 notes M.'s unsuccessful imitation of Nicander (in his *Theriaka*), for which see also R. Unger, *De Aemilio Macro Nicandris imitatore* (Friedland 1845), Schneider's edition of Nicander (Leipzig 1856) 74, Knaack (above), and K. P. Schulze, *Rh.M.* 53 (1898) 543. Quintilian calls his style *humilis* at 10.1.87.

BIBLIOGRAPHY

Fragments in *FPL* 107–10. Discussions in Teuffel II 22–3, Schanz–Hosius II 164–5, Bardon II 44–7.

VARIUS RUFUS

LIFE

A contemporary of Virgil and Horace (Jerome, *Chron. ann. Abr.* 2000), but older than they (Virg. *Ecl.* 9.35, bracketing him with Republican poet Cinna), he introduced Horace to Maecenas (Hor. *Sat.* 1.6.55), and is mentioned several times in the *Satires* (1.5.41 and 93, 1.9.23, 1.10.81, 2.8.21 and 63). Editor with Tucca of Virgil's *Aeneid*, on the author's death (Quint. 10.3.8, Donat. *Vita Verg.* 39, Jerome, *Chron.* above, Serv. *praef.*).

WORKS

De morte (title attested by Macr. *Sat.* 2.19.20, 6.1.39–40): most probably a didactic with Epicurean flavour (on V.'s philosophy see Quint. 6.3.78); appears to have attacked Antony. Some critics identify it with the *forte epos* of Hor. *Sat.* 1.10.81, changing its title to *De morte Caesaris*: but the preposition *de* implies didactic, and no ancient epic has a similar title. Fr. 1 imitated at Virg. *Aen.* 6.621, 2 at *Geo.* 2.506, 3 at *Geo.* 3. 115 and 4 at *Ecl.* 8.88. Of Varian epic we have nothing: *recusatio* at Hor. *Odes* 1.6 implies that V. is a suitable author for Agrippa's exploits, also that he contemplated a *Diomedea*, but no more. A tragedy, *Thyestes*: produced at games for Actium 29 B.C. (Parisinus 7530); see Quint. 10.1.18, 3.8.45. Valgius Rufus and the Varus of the *Eclogues* have been claimed for authorship, but Tac. *Dial.* 12 and Quint. 3.8.45 and 11.3.73 are quite clear on the name. Bardon (II 82) claims other tragedies for V., perhaps correctly. *Panegyricus Augusti*: attested by Porph. and ps.-Acron *ad* Hor. *Epist.* 1.16.27–9, which has been claimed as a recasting of the original; the rhythm, at any rate, is clearly that of Horace. Elegies mentioned at Porph. *ad Odes.* 1.6.1 have no other ancient testimony and are therefore suspect. Fragments in *FPL* 100–1.

BIBLIOGRAPHY

R. Unger, *Varii de Morte eclog. reliqu.* (Halle 1870); A. E. Housman, 'The Thyestes of Varius', *C.Q.* 11 (1917) 42–8; Schanz–Hosius II 162–4; A. Momigliano, 'Epicureans in revolt', *J.R.S.* 31 (1941) 151–7; E. Bickel, *S.O.* 28 (1950) 100ff.; Bardon II 28–34; Nisbet and Hubbard (1970) on Hor. *Odes* 1.6; H. D. Jocelyn, *C.Q.* n.s. 30 (1980) 387–400.

GRATTIUS

LIFE

Wrote before A.D. 8 (Ovid, *Pont.* 4.16.34) and is often assumed to have come from Falerii (see v.40). *Bella ferarum* at Manil. 2.43 is an allusion to a Greek *Cynegetica*, not to G.

WORKS

An incomplete *Cynegetica*, in 536 lines, with five fragments. For his improbable bucolics (on the basis of Ovid, *Pont.* 4.16.33) see Bardon II 58.

BIBLIOGRAPHY

TEXTS AND COMMENTARIES: TEXTS: *PLM* I 29–53; J. W. and A. M. Duff, *Minor Latin poets*, 2nd ed. (Loeb, 1935). COMMENTARIES: P. J. Enk (Zutphen 1918); R. Verdière, 2 vols. (Wetteren 1964).

STUDIES: M. Fiegl, *Des Grattius Faliscus Cynegetica, seine Vorgänger und seine Nachfolger* (Görz 1890); G. Pierleoni, 'Fu poeta Grattius?', *R.F.* 34 (1906) 580ff.; P. H. Damsté, 'Ad Grattium notulae'. *Mnemosyne* 53 (1925) 299ff., J. Tolkiehn, Bursian 153 (1911) 95, and 171 (1915) 5; M. Schuster, ibid. 212 (1927) 82.

GERMANICUS IULIUS CAESAR

LIFE

b. 15 B.C., adopted by his uncle Tiberius A.D. 4; served under him in Pannonia and Germany (7–11), consul 12, proconsul in Gaul and Germany from 13. d. A.D. 19.

WORKS

Aratea: 686 lines (in MSS, *Claudi Caesaris Arati Phaenomena*), an adapted translation of Aratus' *Phaenomena*. Apostrophe to Augustus at 558 implies he is dead: *genitor* at 2 is Tiberius. Domitian, who also took title Germanicus, has been unnecessarily canvassed for authorship. Epigrams: *Anth. Lat.* 708, which has a Greek version (*Anth. Pal.* 9.387), *Anth. Lat.* 709 (= *Anth. Pal.* 7.542), *Anth. Pal.* 9.17–18 (see also Pliny, *N.H.* 8.55). Greek comedies (Suet. *Cal.* 3.2, *Claud.* 11.2). Ovid addresses him at *Fast.* 1.19, *Pont.* 2.5.55 and 4.8.67ff.

BIBLIOGRAPHY

TEXTS AND COMMENTARY: TEXTS: A. Breysig (Berlin 1867: with scholia); idem (BT, 1899); *PLM* 1; A. le Boeuffle (Budé, 1975). COMMENTARY: D. B. Gain (London 1976).

STUDIES: J. Frey, *De Germanico Arati interprete* (Culm 1861); G. Sieg, *De Cicerone Germanico, Avieno Arati interpretibus* (Halle 1886); J. Maybaum, *De Cicerone et Germanico Arati interpretibus* (Rostock 1889); A. E. Housman, 'The Aratea of Germanicus', *C.R.* 14 (1900) 26ff.; J. Tolkiehn, Bursian 153 (1911) 102, and 171 (1915) 14; M. Gelzer and W. Kroll, *RE* x (1919) 435–64.

MANILIUS, MARCUS

LIFE

No external testimonia, though he was imitated by, e.g., Lucan. Wrote his poem under Augustus (and Tiberius?): internal evidence for dating discussed by Housman (under *Texts* below: 1903, lxix ff. and 1930, 111ff.). 5.513 (so Housman, *ad loc.*) is not an allusion to the burning of Pompey's theatre in A.D. 22. For his name see Housman (1930, 108ff.).

WORKS

Astronomica in five books, probably unfinished: Housman asks if there originally may have been eight books (1903, lxxii).

BIBLIOGRAPHY

TEXT AND COMMENTARIES: TEXT: A. E. Housman (Cambridge 1932); G. P. Goold (Loeb, 1977). COMMENTARIES: A. E. Housman, 5 vols. (London 1903–30; repr. in two vols. Hildesheim 1972). Bk 2: H. W. Garrod (Oxford 1911: with tr.).

STUDIES: G. Lanson, *De Manilio poeta eiusque ingenio* (Paris 1887); A. Kraemer, *De Manilii qui feruntur astronomicis* (Marburg 1890); R. Ellis, *Noctes Manilianae* (Oxford 1891); C. Hosius, 'Lucan und seine Quellen', *Rh.M.* 48 (1893) 393ff.; F. Cumont, *Astrology and religion among the Greeks and Romans* (New York 1912); F. Schwemmler, *De Lucano Manilii imitatore* (Giessen 1916); R. B. Steele, 'The Astronomica of Manilius', *A.J.Ph.* 53 (1932) 320.

RABIRIUS, GAIUS

LIFE AND WORKS

Author of an epic on the civil war between Antony and Octavian. Most important notices are Ovid, *Pont.* 4.16.5, Vell. Pat. 2.36.3, Sen. *Ben.* 6.3.1 (ascribing fr. 2 to the dying Antony) and Quint. 10.1.90. Rightly, Bardon (II 69) sees him as a precursor of Lucan, and denies (73–4) that he is the author of the Herculaneum Papyrus on the Egyptian war: community of subject matter has encouraged the ascription; see Bardon loc. cit. and 136–7, Schanz-Hosius II 267–8. M. Alfonsi, 'Nota a Rabirio', *Aegyptus* (1944) 196ff., has credited him with the supposedly Virgilian lines on the Egyptian war mentioned by the humanist Decembrius, *armatum cane, Musa, ducem belloque cruentam Aegyptum*: see R. Sabbadini, *Le scoperte dei codici latini e greci ne' secoli XIV e XV* (Florence 1905) 138–9. For the elephant simile see J. Aymard, *Quelques séries de comparaisons chez Lucain* (Montpellier 1951). Fragments in *FPL* 120–1.

CORNELIUS SEVERUS

WORKS

Epic on Roman history, scope uncertain: Ovid attests the '*carmen regale*' (*Pont.* 4.16.9, cf. 4.2.1 and 11), Quintilian the '*bellum Siculum*' (10.1.89), Probus the *res Romanae* (*GLK* IV 208.16). Sen. *Suas.* 6.26 preserves fragment on death of Cicero; Sen. *Epist.* 79.5 mentions a description of Etna. See Schanz–Hosius II 268–9; Bardon II 61–4; P. Grenade, 'Le mythe de Pompée et les Pompéiens sous les Césars', *R.E.A.* 52 (1950) 28–67 (influence on Lucan).

ALBINOVANUS PEDO

LIFE

Contemporary of Ovid (*Pont.* 4.16.6), who calls him *sidereus* (an adulatory epithet, cf. Colum. 10.434 of Virgil; not implying a *De sideribus*); probably the *praefectus equitum* of Tac. *Ann.* 1.60; coupled by Quint. (10.1.90) with Rabirius. Called *fabulator elegantissimus* at Sen. *Epist.* 122.15 (cf. Sen. *Contr.* 2.10.12).

WORKS

Poem on Germanicus' expedition in North Sea A.D. 16 (fr. preserved by Sen. *Suas.* 1.15); an epic, *Theseis* (Ovid, *Pont.* 4.10.71); epigrams (Mart. *praef.* 1, 2.77.5, 5.5.5, 10.19.10). See R. G. Kent, *C.R.* 17 (1903) 311ff.; Bardon II 69–73.

POMPEIUS TROGUS

LIFE AND WORKS

For his Gallic ancestry, see Justin 43.5.11; his cursory treatment of early Italian history, 43.1.2.; his censure of direct discourse, 38.3.11. *Historiae Philippicae* (44 bks): history of Near East down to 20 B.C., extant only in fragments and in Justin's epitome. Scientific works attested by Charisius, *GLK* I 102.10 and 137.9, Pliny, *N.H.* 17.58.

BIBLIOGRAPHY

TEXTS: Fragments: O. Seel (BT, 1956). Justin's epitome: idem (BT, 1972).

STUDIES: H. Peter, *Die geschichtliche Literatur über die römische Kaiserzeit bis Theodosius I und ihre Quellen* (Leipzig 1897); Schanz–Hosius II 319–77; W. Kroll, *RE* X (1919) 956; E. Norden, *Die antike Kunstprosa*, 4th ed. (Leipzig–Berlin 1923) 300; A. Momigliano, 'Livio, Plutarco e Giustino su virtu e fortuna dei Romani', *Athenaeum* (1934) 45–56; M. Rambaud, 'Salluste et Trogue-Pompée', *R.E.L.* 26 (1948) 171ff.; O. Seel, *Die Praefatio des Pompeius Trogus* (Erlangen 1955); A. D. Leeman, *Orationis ratio* (Amsterdam 1963) 244–7 (T. a *Sallustianus*, his predilection for *oratio obliqua* perhaps deriving from Caesar); O. Seel, *Eine römische Weltgeschichte, Studien zum Text der Epitome des Justinus und zur Historik des Pompeius Trogus* (Nuremberg 1972).

VITRUVIUS POLLIO

LIFE

A late Republican, early Augustan date is usually given: he addresses Augustus in his proem, but does not mention any of the important buildings of the reign.

WORKS

De architectura in ten books. See Schanz–Hosius II 386–95.

BIBLIOGRAPHY

TEXTS: V. Rose, 2nd ed. (Leipzig 1899); F. Krohn (BT, 1912); F. Granger (Loeb, 1931); C. Fensterbusch (Darmstadt 1964).

CELSUS, AULUS CORNELIUS

WORKS

Artes: encyclopaedia, possibly composed under Tiberius, dealing with agriculture, medicine, the military arts, rhetoric, philosophy and jurisprudence (see Quint. 12.11.24); medical section alone survives, in eight books. Alternative title suggested by schol. Plaut. *Bacch.* 69, *Celsus libros suos a uarietate rerum 'cestos' uocauit*. Sources include the Hippocratic Corpus, Asclepiades, Heraclides of Tarentum, Erasistratus, Philoxenus and Meges of Sidon.

BIBLIOGRAPHY

TEXTS: E. Milligan, 2nd ed. (Edinburgh 1831: with index); S. de Renzi (Naples 1851: with lexicon); C. Daremberg (BT, 1859), rev. F. Marx, *Corp. Med. Lat.* 17 (Leipzig 1915); W. G. Spenser (Loeb, 1935). Bks 1–4: F. Serra (Pisa 1976).

STUDIES: Schanz–Hosius II 722–9; J. Scarborough, *Roman medicine* (Ithaca, N.Y. 1969); *OCD* s.v. 'Medicine'; J. Ilberg, in (ed.) H. Flashar, *Antike Medizin, Wege der Forschung* 221 (Darmstadt 1971); E. D. Phillips, *Greek medicine* (London 1973).

PERSIUS FLACCUS, AULES

LIFE

b. 4 Dec. A.D. 34, a wealthy Etruscan knight. Knew Lucan and Thrasea Paetus (addressee of *Sat.* 5), and was influenced by the Stoic Cornutus. d. 24 Nov. A.D.

62. Sources: ancient *Vita*, based on material collected *c.* end of 1st c. A.D., printed by Clausen in his larger ed. (Oxford 1956) 35–9; tr. by J. C. Rolfe, *Suetonius* II (Loeb, 1914) 495–9.

WORKS

Six Satires (650 hexameters), with a preface in scazons, pubd by Cornutus and Caesius Bassus after P.'s death.

BIBLIOGRAPHY

TEXTS AND COMMENTARIES: TEXTS: W. V. Clausen (Oxford 1956); idem (OCT, 1966: with Juvenal); D. Bo (Paravia, 1969: with bibliography). COMMENTARIES: O. Jahn (Leipzig 1843; repr. 1967); J. Conington, 3rd ed. rev. H. Nettleship (Oxford 1893); F. Villeneuve (Paris 1918).

TRANSLATIONS: G. G. Ramsay (Loeb, 1918); N. Rudd (Penguin, 1979).

STUDIES: F. Villeneuve, *Essai sur Perse* (Paris 1918); T. Ciresola, *La formazione del linguaggio poetico di Persio* (Rovereto 1953); G. Faranda, 'Caratteristiche dello stile e del linguaggio poetico di Persio', *R.I.L.* 88 (1955) 512–38; D. Henss, 'Die Imitations-technik des Persius', *Philologus* 99 (1955) 277–94; R. G. M. Nisbet, 'Persius', in (ed.) J. P. Sullivan, *Satire* (London 1963); J. H. Waszink, 'Das Einleitungsgedicht des Persius', *W.S.* 76 (1963) 79–91; W. S. Anderson, 'Persius and the rejection of society', *Wiss. Zs. Univ. Rostock* 15 (1966) 409–16; O. Skutsch, *Studia Enniana* (London 1968) 25ff. and 126ff.; J. Bramble, *Persius and the programmatic satire* (Cambridge 1974); N. Rudd, 'Association of ideas in Persius', *Lines of enquiry* (Cambridge 1976) 54–83.

LEXICON: D. Bo (Hildesheim 1967).

SENECA, LUCIUS ANNAEUS

LIFE

Date of birth undetermined, but generally placed *c.* 4 B.C. (see M. Préchac, *R.E.L.* 11 (1934) 360–75; N. Scivoletto, *G.I.F.* 19 (1966) 21–31). b. Corduba, educ. Rome; already well known as writer and speaker by *c.* A.D. 39. Exiled to Corsica 41; recalled at the instance of Agrippina, made tutor to Nero, and designated praetor 49; joint chief adviser (with Burrus) in administration of empire from Nero's accession in 54 until 62; consul *suffectus* 55 or 56. Fell from favour 62, and virtually retired from public affairs. Shortly after discovery of Pisonian conspiracy (April 65) was charged with complicity, and committed suicide on Nero's orders. Ancient sources printed by W. Trillitzsch, *Seneca im literarischen Urteil der Antike. Darstellung und Sammlung der Zeugnisse*

(Amsterdam 1971). Most important are Tac. *Ann.* 12–15; Dio Cassius 59–61; Suet. *Cal.*, *Claud.*, *Nero*; allusions in S.'s own works, esp. *Helv.* and *Ep.* See also *PIR*² I 103–4 for a compendious statement of the sources for each of the main events in S.'s career.

WORKS

Seneca's extant works descended through the middle ages in seven groups, each with its own more or less separate manuscript tradition; modern editors retain this grouping, as follows: (1) *Dialogorum libri XII*: collection of tracts datable to various periods from end to end of S.'s career. Apart from opening section of bk 9, there is no attempt at 'dialogue' in the Platonic or modern sense. 'Talks', or even 'chats' might be a more accurate rendering of the title. All treat of ethical or psychological topics, and, with the exception of the three books *De ira* (*Dial.* 3–5), are relatively short. Three are entitled Consolations: the *Consolationes ad Marciam* (*Dial.* 6, on the death of Marcia's son), *ad Polybium* (*Dial.* 11, ostensibly to console the famous freedman of Claudius on his brother's death, but evidently a plea for the remission of S.'s exile-sentence), and *ad Helviam* (*Dial.* 12, to his mother, consoling her for his absence in exile). Topics of remaining treatises sufficiently indicated by their transmitted titles.

(2) *De beneficiis* and *De clementia.* Neither title can be exactly rendered into English. The seven books of *De beneficiis* are concerned not so much with 'benefits' or 'favours' as with mutual kindness between man and man, and man and god – the very foundations of civilized and religious living. *De clementia*: originally in three books, only bk 1 and opening part of bk 2 survive. The only treatise in the corpus that is formally addressed to Nero, it is a statement of the right attitude of a monarch towards his responsibilities and his people. In this *clementia* plays an essential part; but it is a rational and humane quality, lacking the element of condescension implied in its English derivative.

(3) *Naturales quaestiones*: seems originally to have consisted of eight books, two of which (4A and 4B in modern edd.) are mutilated. Half the books are concerned nominally with meteorological phenomena; the remainder with terrestrial waters (bk 3), the river Nile (4A), earthquakes (6) and comets (7).

(4) *Epistulae morales ad Lucilium*: originally in at least twenty-two books, of which twenty (124 letters) have survived. For the specially complex history of this group's transmission, see L. D. Reynolds, *The medieval tradition of Seneca's letters* (Oxford 1965); strictly speaking it forms not one group, but two.

(5) Ten *tragoediae*, enumerated and discussed below.

(6) *Apocolocyntosis*: see p. 888.

(7) *Epigrams*: see pp. 886–7.

DATING: On dates of prose works see Münscher, under *Studies* (1) below, and K Abel, *Bauformen in Senecas Dialogen* (Heidelberg 1967: with bibliography). Following list shows those datings, or approximate datings, on which there is more or less general agreement. *Cons. ad Marciam*: within reign of Caligula (37–41). *De ira* 1–2: 41, between accession of Claudius and banishment of S. How much later bk 3 may be is still disputable. *Cons. ad Helviam*: early in S.'s exile-period; probably not later than summer 43. *Cons. ad Polybium*: in exile-period, before Polybius' death in 47; probably in summer 43. *De brevitate vitae* (*Dial.* 10): not later than 49; probably in exile-period. *De beneficiis*: between Nero's succession (September 54) and 64. *De clementia*: 56. *Naturales quaestiones*: between S.'s retirement from public affairs in 62, and his death in 65. Some reasons to put completion of work no later than 64. *Epistulae morales*: between S.'s retirement and death.

LOST WORKS: Titles and fragments last printed in full by Haase, under *Texts* below. Discussed by Münscher, under *Studies* (1) below. Four of them investigated by M. Lausberg, *Untersuchungen zu Senecas Fragmenten* (Berlin 1970). Representative selection follows: biography of Seneca the Elder, *De vita patris*; two geographical and ethnographical treatises, *De situ et sacris Aegyptiorum* and *De situ Indiae*; four physical treatises, *De motu terrarum volumen* (written by S. as a *iuuenis*, *Q. Nat.* 6.4.2), *De lapidum natura*, *De piscium natura*, and *De forma mundi*; published speeches (cf. Quint. 10.2.129 and Haase III 437–40); moral or philosophical works, *De amicitia*, *Exhortationes*, *De immatura morte liber*, *De matrimonio*, *Moralis philosophiae libri* (general systematization of his moral doctrines, in progress *c.* 62–5; cf. *Epist.* 106.2, 108.1, 109.17), *De officiis*, *De remediis fortuitorum*, *De superstitione dialogus*; treatise of unknown title which S. dictated on his deathbed, subsequently pubd (Tac. *Ann.* 15.63.7). For conjectures as to dates of lost works see Münscher, under *Studies* (1) below (results summarized 142–3).

DUBIOUS OR SPURIOUS: *Epistulae ad Novatum* (Haase fr. 109; cf. Münscher 44 n.2) and *ad Caesonium* (Haase fr. 109, Münscher 63), and a tract on shorthand symbols (Haase fr. 128). A number of spurious works circulating in the middle ages are extracts from, or rehashes of, extant Senecan treatises; such is the *De paupertate* (Haase III 459–61). Most notorious of the certainly spurious compositions is the *Epistulae Senecae ad Paulum Apostolum et Pauli Apostoli ad Senecam* (ibid. 476–81); ed. C. W. Barlow (Rome 1938); see also K. M. Abbott, 'Seneca and St. Paul', in (ed.) D. C. Richel, *Wege der Wörter. Festschrift für Wolfgang Fleischhauer* (Cologne–Vienna 1978) 119–31, bibliography 119 n. 1.

TRAGEDIES: Transmitted as a group of almost bare texts: the MSS contain no arguments to the plays, no lists of dramatis personae, and no commentaries. The two recensions into which they divide do not agree on the order or number of the plays in the canon, or even on some of their titles. These two recensions are conventionally known as 'E' (after the recension's main representative, the *Codex Etruscus*, *c.* A.D. 1100) and 'A' (some 300 MSS; most dating from Italian renaissance; none earlier than

13th c. A.D.). Problems presented by the MSS discussed by Giardina,[1] Axelson,[2] and Philp.[3] Following table shows order and titles given by the two recensions:

E:	A:
Hercules	*Hercules Furens*
Troades	*Thyestes*
Phoenissae	*Thebais* (= E.'s *Phoenissae*)
Medea	*Hippolytus* (= E.'s *Phaedra*)
Phaedra	*Oedipus*
Oedipus	*Troas* (= E.'s *Troades*)
Agamemnon	*Medea*
Thyestes	*Agamemnon*
Hercules	*Octavia*
	Hercules Oetaeus

Since E.'s existence was first made public by Gronovius,[4] most editors have adopted E.'s order and titles, except that they continue to distinguish the two Hercules plays, following A, as Furens and Oetaeus. Because the MSS further disagree as to the praenomen of the tragedian, and because neither Quintilian nor Seneca the Philosopher mentions expressly that the latter composed any tragedies, scholars long debated their authorship. Daniel Heinsius[5] distinguished no less than five dramatists in the Senecan corpus, and Milton was still among the doubters as to Senecan authoship (pref. to *Samson Agonistes*); general account of the controversy by Herrmann.[6] Question still not conclusively settled, but in recent times the general – and reasonable – consensus has been that the bulk of the corpus is by S. The present survey assumes that only two plays are spurious: the little *Octavia* (discussed in the Epilogue), and the elephantine *Hercules Oetaeus*, apparently a semi-skilled imitation of the Senecan manner by a near contemporary; see Friedrich[7] and Axelson.[8] Dates of the eight plays here taken as genuine are uncertain. S. had probably written some of them, including *Hercules Furens*, by the end of 54 (evidence in Coffey[9]); possibly his dramatic activity was renewed in the years just before 62 (Tac. *Ann.* 14.52.3, *carmina crebrius factitare*, if here *carmina* means 'tragedies', as it does in *Ann.* 11.13.1). More precise datings based on supposed historical or political allusions (surveyed by Herrmann[10]) are not generally accepted.

[1] I. C. Giardina, *L. Annaei Senecae tragoediae*, 2 vols. (Bologna 1966: with bibliography).

[2] B. Axelson, *Korruptelenkult: Studien zur Textkritik der unechten Seneca-Tragödie Hercules Oetaeus* (Lund 1967).

[3] R. H. Philp, 'The manuscript tradition of Seneca's tragedies', *C.Q.* n.s.18 (1968) 150–79.

[4] J. F. Gronovius, *L. Annaei Senecae tragoediae* (Leiden 1661).

[5] D. Heinsius, 'De tragoediarum auctoribus dissertatio', in (ed.) P. Scriverius, *L. Annaeus Seneca Tragicus*, 2 vols. (Leiden 1621).

[6] L. Herrmann, *Le théâtre de Sénèque* (Paris 1924) 31–77, 85–99.

[7] W. H. Friedrich, 'Sprache und Stil des Hercules Oetaeus', *Hermes* 82 (1954) 51–84.

[8] Axelson, op. cit.

[9] M. Coffey, *Lustrum* 2 (1957) 150.

[10] Herrmann, op. cit.

BIBLIOGRAPHY

TEXTS AND COMMENTARIES: TEXTS: (1) Prose works. Haase (Leipzig 1852: with fragments, *index rerum memorabilium*); J. W. Basore, T. H. Corcoran, R. M. Gummere (Loeb, 1917–72). *Dialogi*: L. D. Reynolds (OCT, 1977). *De beneficiis* and *De clementia*: C. Hosius, 2nd ed. (BT, 1914). *Naturales quaestiones*: P. Oltramare (Budé, 1929). (2) Tragedies. I. C. Giardina (Bologna 1966). COMMENTARIES. *Medea*: C. D. N. Costa (Oxford 1973); *Agamemnon*: R. J. Tarrant (Cambridge 1976).

TRANSLATIONS: F. J. Miller (Loeb, 1917); E. F. Watling, *Seneca: four tragedies and Octavia* (Penguin, 1966).

STUDIES: (1) S.'S BIOGRAPHY AND GENERAL STUDIES: K. Münscher, *Senecas Werke: Untersuchungen zur Abfassungszeit und Echtheit*, *Philologus* suppl. 16, Heft 1 (1922); Schanz–Hosius II 456–75; V. d'Agostino, 'Seneca Filosofo e Tragico negli anni 1953–1965: Saggio Bibliografico', *R.S.C.* 14 (1966) 61–81; W. Trillitzsch, *Seneca im literarischen Urteil der Antike. Darstellung und Sammlung der Zeugnisse*, 2 vols. (Amsterdam 1971); A. L. Motto, *Seneca sourcebook: guide to the thought of Lucius Annaeus Seneca* (Amsterdam 1970); G. Cupaiuolo, 'Gli studi su Seneca nel triennio 1967–1971', *Boll. di Studi Latini* 2 (1972) 278–317; A. L. Motto, *Seneca* (New York 1973); M. Griffin, *Seneca: a philosopher in politics* (Oxford 1976); M. Rozelaar, *Seneca: eine Gesamtdarstellung* (Amsterdam 1976). (2) PROSE WORKS AND FRAGMENTS: Bibliographies by A. L. Motto, *C.W.* 54 (1960–1) 13–18, 37–48, 70–1, 111–12 (for 1940–58); idem, *C.W.* 64 (1970–1) 141–58, 177–86, 191 (for 1958–68). Also A. Bourgery, *Sénèque prosateur* (Paris 1922); M. Lausberg, *Untersuchungen zu Senecas Fragmenten* (Berlin 1970). (3) TRAGEDIES AND OCTAVIA: Bibliographies by M. Coffey, *Lustrum* 2 (1957) 113–86 (for 1922–55), and in E. Lefèvre, *Senecas Tragödien* (Darmstadt 1972) 583–92 (for 1956–*c.* 1971). Also F. Leo, *L. Annaei Senecae tragoediae* I (Berlin 1878); M. Coffey, *FYAT* 316–23. (4) CONCORDANCE: R. Busa and A. Zampolli (Hildesheim 1975).

LUCANUS, MARCUS ANNAEUS

LIFE

b. A.D. 39 at Cordoba, grandson of elder Seneca, nephew of younger (Vacca, *Vita Luc.*). Met Persius, and admired his poetry, at lectures of Stoic Cornutus (Probus, *Vita Pers.*). Involved in Pisonian conspiracy, forced to commit suicide A.D. 65, aged 26 (Tac. *Ann.* 15.56 and 70). Epigrams on his birthday to his widow Polla at Mart. 7.21–3 (cf. 10.64), also Stat. *Genethliacon Lucani*, *Silv.* 2.7; possible ref. to the young L. at Sen. *Helv.* 43.4.5; boast of excelling Virgil, Suet. *Vita Luc.*; stories of rivalry with Nero in both *Vitae*.

WORKS

(1) EXTANT: *De bello civili* (so the MSS; Housman (under *Texts* below, 296), explains *Pharsalia nostra* at 9.985 as a ref. to the battle fought by Caesar, and described by L.): unfinished epic, breaking off at 10.546; several passages might have been excised on revision. In the *Vita Codicis Vossiani*, Seneca is wrongly accredited with first four lines of bk 1, probably as a result of a misinterpretation of *Annaeus* at Fronto 2.105ff., above p. 533 n. 2. Jerome mentions a commentary at *Apol. c. Rufin.* 1.16: cf. Lyd. *De mag.* 3.46. Two ancient commentaries survive, the *Commenta Bernensia*, ed. H. Usener (BT, 1869), and the *Adnotationes super Lucanum*, ed. J. Endt (BT, 1909). (2) LOST: A long list of works in Vacca, five of which are attested by Stat. *Silv.* 2.7.54–63, who also mentions an *Adlocutio ad Pollam.* We have fragments of the *Catachthonion*, *Iliacon*, *Orpheus* and *Epigrammata*, but the *Laudes Neronis*, *Silvae*, *Saturnalia*, *Medea*, *Salticae fabulae*, *De incendio urbis*, *Epistulae ex Campania* and *Prosa oratio in Octavium Sagittam* are only titles.

BIBLIOGRAPHY

(for 1925–42, see R. Helm, *Lustrum* 1 (1956) 163–228; for 1943–63, W. Rutz, ibid. 9 (1964) 243ff.; also Morford (1967, under *Studies* below) 89–90, and Ahl (1976) 355–64)

TEXTS AND COMMENTARIES: TEXTS: C. Hosius, 3rd ed. (BT, 1919); A. Bourgery and M. Ponchont (Budé, 1926–9); J. D. Duff (Loeb, 1928); A. E. Housman, 2nd ed. (Oxford 1950), with review of 1st ed. by E. Fraenkel, *Gnomon* 2 (1926) 497. COMMENTARIES: C. E. Haskins, with intr. by W. E. Heitland (London 1887). Bk 1: P. Lejay (Paris 1894); R. J. Getty (Cambridge 1955); P. Wuilleumier and H. le Bonniec (Paris 1962). Bk 7: J. P. Postgate, rev. O. A. W. Dilke (Cambridge 1960). Bk 8: J. P. Postgate (Cambridge 1917).

STUDIES: C. Hosius, 'Lucan und seine Quellen', *Rh.M.* 48 (1893) 380ff.; R. Pichon, *Les sources de Lucain* (Paris 1912); W. Kroll, 'Das historische Epos', *Sokrates* 4 (1916) 2ff.; E. Fraenkel, 'Lucan als Mittler des Antiken Pathos', *Vorträge der Bibliothek Warburg* (1924) 229ff.; E. M. Sandford, 'Lucan and his Roman critics', *C.Ph.* 26 (1931) 233–57; L. Eckhardt, *Exkurse und Ekphraseis bei Lucan* (Heidelberg 1936); E. Malcovati, *Lucano* (Milan 1940); B. Marti, 'The meaning of the Pharsalia', *A.J.Ph.* 66 (1945) 352–76; idem, 'La structure de la Pharsale', in *Entretiens* (1968 below) 1–50; J. André, *Étude sur les termes de couleur dans la langue latine* (Paris 1949); P. J. Miniconi, *Étude des thèmes guerriers de la poésie gréco-romaine*, *Publ. Fac. Lettr. Alger.* 2.19 (Paris 1951); idem, 'La joie dans l'Éneide', *Latomus* 21 (1962) 503–11; A. Guillemin, 'L'inspiration Virgilienne dans la Pharsale', *R.E.L.* 29 (1951) 214–27; I. Cazzaniga, *Problemi intorno alla Farsaglia* (Milan 1955); E. Longi, 'Tre episodi del poema di Lucano', *Stud. in on. di G. Funaioli* (Rome 1955) 181–8; H. Nowak, *Lukanstudien* (diss. Vienna 1955); G. K. Gresseth, 'The quarrel between Lucan and Nero',

C.Ph. 52 (1957) 24–7; I. Opelt, 'Die Seeschlacht vor Massilia bei Lucan', *Hermes* 85 (1957) 435–45; H. P. Syndikus, *Lucans Gedicht vom Bürgerkrieg* (Munich 1958); L. Thompson and R. T. Bruère, 'Lucan's use of Virgilian reminiscence', *C.Ph.* 63 (1968) 1–21; P. Grimal, 'L'éloge de Néron au début de la Pharsale', *R.E.L.* 38 (1960) 296–305; idem, 'L'épisode d'Antée dans la Pharsale', *Latomus* 8 (1949) 55–61; L. A. Mackay, 'The vocabulary of fear in Latin epic poetry', *T.A.Ph.A.* 92 (1961) 308–16; O. S. Due, 'An essay on Lucan', *C.&M.* 22 (1962) 68–132; P. Jal, *La guerre civile à Rome* (Paris 1963); J. Brisset, *Les idées politiques de Lucain* (Paris 1964); P. Pecchiura, *La figura di Catone Uticense nella letteratura latina* (Turin 1965); K. Seitz, 'Der pathetische Erzählstil Lucans', *Hermes* 93 (1965) 204ff.; M. P. O. Morford, *The poet Lucan* (Oxford 1967); A. Ollfors, *Studien zum Aufbau des Hexameters Lucans* (Gothenburg 1967); *Entretiens XV: Lucain* (Fondation Hardt, Geneva 1968); O. C. Philips, 'Lucan's grove', *C.Ph.* 63 (1968) 296–300; A. W. Lintott, 'Lucan and the history of the civil war', *C.Q.* 21 (1971) 488–505; F. M. Ahl, *Lucan, an introduction* (New York 1976).

CONCORDANCE: R. J. Deferrari et al. (Washington 1940).

FLAVIAN EPIC

GENERAL WORKS

Bardon, H., 'Le goût à l'époque des Flaviens', *Latomus* 21 (1962) 732–48.

Bolaffi, E., 'L'epica del I secolo dell' impero', *G.I.F.* 12 (1959) 218–30.

Butler, H. E., *Post-Augustan poetry from Seneca to Juvenal* (Oxford 1909).

Gossage, A. J., 'Virgil and the Flavian epic', in (ed.) D. R. Dudley, *Virgil* (London 1969) 67–93.

Hadas, M., 'Later Latin epic and Lucan', *C.W.* 29 (1936) 153–7.

Mendell, C. W., *Latin poetry: the age of rhetoric and satire* (Hamden 1967).

Schönberger, O. 'Zum Weltbild der drei Epiker nach Lukan', *Helikon* 5 (1965) 123–45.

Steele, R. B., 'The interrelation of the Latin poets under Domitian', *C.Ph.* 25 (1930) 328–42.

Summers, W. C., *The silver age of Latin literature* (London 1920).

Williams, G., *Change and decline: Roman literature in the early Empire*, Sather Classical Lectures 45 (Berkeley–London 1978).

STATIUS, PUBLIUS PAPINIUS

LIFE

b. at Naples *c.* A.D. 45; his father a poet and schoolmaster. At Rome established himself as a poet (recitals, Juv. 7.82–7; see V. Tandoi, *Maia* 21 (1969) 103–22), and was favoured by Domitian (cf. *Silv.* 3.1.61ff.). d. at Naples *c.* 96. For a dubious allusion to S. by Martial, see H. Heuvel, *Mnemosyne* 3.4 (1937) 299–330; see also F. Delarue, 'Stace et ses contemporains', *Latomus* 33 (1974) 536–48. For his father, see *Silv.* 5.3, with G. Curcio, *Studio su P. Papinio Stazio* (Catania 1893) 3–18; A. Traglia, *R.C.C.M.* 7 (1965) 1128–34; D. Vessey, *Statius and the Thebaid* (Cambridge 1973) 49–54; K. Clinton, 'Publius Papinius ST[---] at Eleusis'; *T.A.Ph.A.* 103 (1972) 79–82.

WORKS

Silvae: five books of poems, mostly in hexameters, pubd in stages from 92. *Thebaid*: epic in twelve books, pubd *c.* 91. *Achilleid*: epic, unfinished in bk 2 at S.'s death. Also (lost), *De bello Germanico* (schol. *ad* Juv. 4.94) and a pantomime, *Agave* (Juv. 7.87).

BIBLIOGRAPHY

(for 1925–42, see R. Helm, *Lustrum* 1 (1956) 272–99)

TEXTS AND COMMENTARIES: TEXTS: Complete works: A. Traglia and G. Aricò (Turin 1980: with bibliography 55–72 and tr.). *Silvae*: A. Baehrens (BT, 1876); A. Klotz, 2nd ed. (BT, 1911); J. S. Phillimore, 2nd ed. (OCT, 1918; repr. 1962); H. Frère and H. J. Isaac (Budé, 1944); J. H. Mozley, rev. ed. (Loeb, 1955). *Thebaid*: H. W. Garrod (OCT, 1906; repr. 1965; with *Achilleid*); J. H. Mozley, rev. ed. (Loeb, 1955); A. Klotz, rev. T. C. Klinnert (BT, 1973). *Achilleid*: A. Klotz (BT, 1902); J. H. Mozley, rev. ed. (Loeb, 1955); J. Méheust (Budé, 1971); A. Marastoni (BT, 1974). COMMENTARIES: *Silvae*: F. Vollmer (Leipzig 1898; repr. 1968). *Thebaid*: Bk 1: H. Heuvel (diss. Groningen, Zutphen 1932); F. Caviglia (Rome 1973). Bk 2: H. M. Mulder (diss. Groningen 1954). Bk 3: H. Snijder (Amsterdam 1968), cf. P. Venini, in *Studi Staziani* (Pavia 1971) 110–24 = *Athenaeum* 58 (1970) 132–8. Bk 6.1–295: H. W. Fortgens (diss. Utrecht, Zutphen 1934). Bk 10: R. D. Williams, *Mnemosyne* suppl. 22 (Leiden 1972). Bk 11: P. Venini (Florence 1970). *Achilleid*: S. Jannoccone (Florence 1950); O. A. W. Dilke (Cambridge 1954). See also P. M. Clogan, *The medieval Achilleid of Statius* (Leiden 1968).

TRANSLATIONS: *Silvae*: D. A. Slater (Oxford 1908: with notes). *Thebaid*: J. B. Poynton, 3 vols. (Oxford 1971–5).

STUDIES: (1) GENERAL INTRODUCTION: R. Helm, *RE* XVIII.3 (1949) 984–1000; A. J. Gossage, in (ed.) D. R. Dudley, *Neronians and Flavians: Silver Latin* 1 (London 1972) 184–235.

(2) STATIUS AND DOMITIAN: K. Scott, *A.J.Ph.* 54 (1933) 247–59; idem, *The imperial cult under the Flavians* (Stuttgart–Berlin 1936); F. Sauter, *Der römischer Kaiserkult bei Martial und Statius* (Stuttgart 1934); D. Vessey, *Statius and the Thebaid* (Cambridge 1973) 28–36.

(3) PATRONS: R. Syme, 'Vibius Maximus, Prefect of Egypt', *Historia* 6 (1957) 480–7; G. Aricò, 'Stazio e Arrunzio Stella', *Aevum* 39 (1965) 345–7; P. R. C. Weaver, 'The father of Claudius Etruscus, Statius, Silvae III.3', *C.Q.* n.s.15 (1965) 145–54; D. Vessey, *Statius and the Thebaid* (Cambridge 1973) 15–28; P. White, 'Notes on two Statian ΠΡΟΣΩΠΑ', *C.Ph.* 68 (1973) 279–84 (Marcellus, Crispinus); idem, 'Vibius Maximus, the friend of Statius', *Historia* 22 (1973) 295–301; idem, 'The presentation and dedication of the Silvae and Epigrams', *J.R.S.* 64 (1974) 40–61; idem, 'The friends of Martial, Statius and Pliny and the dispersal of patronage', *H.S.C.Ph.* 79 (1975) 265–300 (Arruntius Stella, Atedius Melior, Claudius Etruscus, Argentaria Polla, Novius Vindex, Earinus).

(4) 'SILVAE': J. Danglard, *De Stace et surtout sur les Silves* (Lyon 1864); G. Luehr, *De P. Papinio Statio in Silvis priorum poetarum imitatore* (diss. Königsberg 1880); A. Herzog, *Statii Epithalamium, Silvae I.ii* (diss. Leipzig 1882: text and comm.); O. Lottisch, *Trostgedicht an den Claudius Etruscus* (*Silv. III.*3) *mit sachlichen und kritischen Erklärungen* (prog. Hamburg 1893: text and comm.); H. Lohrisch, *De Papinii Statii Silvarum poetae studiis rhetoricis* (diss. Halle 1905); J. F. Lockwood, in *Ut pictura poesis: studia Latina P. J. Enk septuagenario oblata* (Leiden 1955) 107–11 (*Silv.* 4.4); A. Marastoni, 'Per una nuova interpretazione di Stazio poeta delle Selve', *Aevum* 31 (1957) 393–414 and 32 (1958) 1–37; V. Buchheit, *Hermes* 88 (1960) 231–49 (*Silv.* 2.7); R. Argenio, *R.S.C.* 34 (1962) 128–32 (*Silv.* 5.3); idem, *R.S.C.* 37 (1965) 160–73 (*Silv.* 4.3); idem, *R.S.C.* 20 (1973) 221–62 (*Silv.* 2.1, 5.5); A. Traglia, 'De P. Papinio Statio Silvarum poeta', *Latinitas* 12 (1964) 7–12; H. Cancik, *Untersuchungen zur lyrischen Kunst des P. Papinius Statius* (diss. Tübingen 1965) = *Spudasmata* 13 (Hildesheim 1965); idem, *A.U.* 11 (1968) 62–75 (*Silv.* 2.2); Z. Pavlovskis, 'Statius and the late Latin epithalamia', *C.Ph.* 60 (1965) 164–77; idem; 'From Statius to Ennodius: a brief history of prose prefaces to poems', *R.I.L.* 101 (1967) 535–67; J. H. Bishop, in (ed.) M. Kelly, *For service to classical studies: essays in honour of Francis Letters* (Melbourne 1966) 15–30; H. Szelest, 'Die Originalität der sog. beschreibenden Silvae des Statius', *Eos* 56 (1966) 186–97; idem, *Meander* 22 (1967) 261–8 (*Silv.* 4.7 and 8); idem, *Meander* 23 (1968) 298–305 (*Silv.* 1.4); idem, 'Mythologie und ihre Rolle in den Silvae des Statius', *Eos* 60 (1972) 309–17; E. Mensching, *Hermes* 97 (1969) 252–5 (*Silv.* 2.7); D. Vessey, *A.C.* 39 (1970) 507–18 (*Silv.* 4.5); idem, 'Varia Statiana', *C.B.* 46 (1970) 49–64; idem, *Mnemosyne* 4.25 (1972) 172–87 (*Silv.* 1.2); idem, *A.C.* 43 (1974) 257–66 (Silv. 4.8); idem, *C.J.* 72 (1976–7) 134–40 (*Silv.* 3.5); G. Aricò, 'Sulle trace di una poetica staziana', *Ricerche Staziane* (Palermo 1972) 37–71 = *B.S.L.* 1 (1971) 217–39; E. B. Holtsmark, *C.J.* (1972–3) 216–20 (*Silv.* 1.5); R. Häussler, *Živa Antika* 25 (1975) 106–13 (*Silv.* 5.4); S. T. Newmyer, *The Silvae of Statius: structure and theme*, *Mnemosyne* suppl. 53 (Leiden 1979).

(5) 'THEBAID' AND 'ACHILLEID': see the works cited by D. Vessey, *Statius and the Thebaid* (Cambridge 1973) 329–41, and the following: G. Aricò, 'Adrasto e la guerra Tebana (Mondo spirituale staziano e caratterizazione psicologia)', *Ricerche Staziane* (Palermo 1972) 109–31 = *Annali del liceo classico 'G. Garibaldi' di Palermo* 7–8

(1970–1) 208–23; M. Goetting, *Hypsipyle in der Thebais des Statius* (diss. Tübingen 1966, Wiesbaden 1969); P. Venini, 'Ancora su Stazio e Lucano', *Studi Staziani* (Pavia 1971) 81–3; S. von Moisy, *Untersuchungen zur Erzählweise in Statius' Thebais, Habelts Dissertationsdrucke, Reihe Klass. Phil.* 11 (Bonn 1971); J. F. Burgess, 'Pietas in Virgil and Statius', *P.V.S.* 11 (1971–2) 48–61; idem, 'Statius' altar of mercy', *C.Q.* n.s.22 (1972) 339–49; E. Burck, 'Die Thebais des Statius, Die Achilleis des Statius', in (ed.) E. Burck, *Das römische Epos, Grundriss der Literaturgeschichte nach Gattungen* (Darmstadt 1979) 300–58.

(6) TEXT: L. Håkanson, *Statius' Silvae: critical and exegetical remarks with some notes on the Thebaid* (Lund 1969: select bibliography 7–11), reviewed by D. Vessey, *C.Ph.* 66 (1971) 273–6, and G. Aricò, *Maia* 25 (1973) 180–2; J. A. Willis, 'The Silvae of Statius and their editors', *Phoenix* 20 (1966) 305–24; L. Håkanson, *Statius' Thebaid: critical and exegetical remarks* (Lund 1973: select bibliography 89–91); G. Lotito, 'In margine alla nuova edizione teubneriana della Silvae di Stazio', *A.&R.* 19 (1974) 26–48.

CONCORDANCE: R. J. Deferrari and M. C. Eagan (Brookland 1943).

VALERIUS FLACCUS, GAIUS

LIFE

Unknown, except that he was *XVvir sacris faciundis* (1.5, 8.239–41). Only contemporary ref. is Quint. 10.1.90.

WORKS

Argonautica: epic, unfinished in bk 8 at V.'s death A.D. 92/93.

BIBLIOGRAPHY

(see L. Ieep, Bursian 23 (1896) 72–93; for 1925–42, R. Helm, *Lustrum* 1 (1956) 236–55; for 1940–71, W.-W. Ehlers, *Lustrum* 16 (1971–2) 105–42)

TEXTS AND COMMENTARY: TEXTS: A. Baehrens (BT, 1875); P. Langen, *Berl. Stud. f. class. Phil. u. Archäol.*, n.s.1.1–2 (Berlin 1896; repr. Hildesheim 1964); O. Kramer (BT, 1913; repr. Stuttgart 1967); J. H. Mozley (Loeb, 1934; rev. ed. 1936, 1958, 1963); E. Courtney (BT, 1970). COMMENTARY: Bk 1: H. G. Blomfield (Oxford 1916: with tr.).

STUDIES: H. Gebbing, *De C. Valerii Flacci tropis et figuris* (diss. Marburg 1878); J. Peters, *De C. Valerii Flacci vita et carmine* (Königsberg 1980); A. Grueneberg, *De*

Valerio Flacco imitatore (diss. Berlin 1893); W. C. Summers, *A study of the Argonautica of Valerius Flaccus* (Cambridge 1894); R. Harmand, *De Valerio Flacco Apollonii Rhodii imitatore* (Nancy 1898); R. Stroh, *Studien zu Valerius Flaccus, besonders über dessen Verhältnis zu Vergil* (diss. Munich 1902 (1905)); R. Syme, 'The Argonautica of Valerius Flaccus', *C.Q.* 23 (1929) 129–37; K. Scott, 'The date of the composition of the Argonautica of Valerius Flaccus', resumé of diss., *T.A.Ph.A.* 64 (1933) lxvi; idem, 'La data di composizione della Argonautica di Valerio Flacco', *R.F.* 62 (1934) 474–81; F. Mehmel, *Valerius Flaccus* (diss. Hamburg 1934); J. Stroux, 'Valerius Flaccus and Horaz', *Philologus* 90 (1935) 305–50; R. J. Getty, 'The date of the composition of the Argonautica of Valerius Flaccus', *C.Ph.* 31 (1936) 53–61; idem, 'The introduction of the Argonautica of Valerius Flaccus', *C.Ph.* 35 (1940) 259–73; J. M. K. Martin, 'Valerius Flaccus, poet of romance', *G.&R.* 7 (1937–8) 137–48; W. Morel, 'Zu den Argonautica des Valerius Flaccus', *Rh.M.* 87 (1938) 60–74; A. Kurfess, *RE* VIII.1 (1955) 9–15; V. Ussani, *Studio su Valerio Flacco, Studi e Saggi* 6 (Rome 1955); E. Merone, *Sulla lingua di Valerio Flacco, Bibl. del Giorn. It. Fil.* 8 (Naples 1957); H. MacL. Currie, 'Virgil and Valerius Flaccus', *V.S.L.S.* 48 (1959); W. Schetter, 'Die Buchzahl der Argonautica des Valerius Flaccus', *Philologus* 103 (1959) 297–308; R. W. Garson, 'The Hylas episode in Valerius Flaccus' Argonautica', *C.Q.* n.s.13 (1963) 260–7; idem, 'Some critical observations on Valerius Flaccus' Argonautica', *C.Q.* n.s.14 (1964) 267–79 and 15 (1965) 104–20; idem, 'Metrical statistics of Valerius Flaccus' Argonautica', *C.Q.* n.s.18 (1968) 376–9; idem, 'Homeric echoes in Valerius Flaccus' Argonautica', *C.Q.* n.s.19 (1969) 362–6; idem, 'Valerius Flaccus the poet', *C.Q.* n.s.20 (1970) 181–7; H. O. Kröner, 'Zu den künstlerischen Absichten des Valerius Flaccus', *Hermes* 96 (1968) 733–54; G. Cambier, 'Recherches chronologiques sur l'oeuvre et la vie de Valerius Flaccus', *Hommages à M. Renard, Coll. Latomus* 101–3 (Brussels 1969) I 191–228; R. Nordera, 'I virgilianismi in Valerio Flacco', *Contributi a tre poeti latini* (Bologna 1969) 1–92; J. Adamietz, 'Jason und Hercules in den Epen des Apollonios Rhodios und Valerius Flaccus', *A.&A.* 16 (1970) 29–38; idem, *Zur Komposition der Argonautica des Valerius Flaccus* (Munich 1976); E. Burck, 'Kampf und Tod des Cyzicus bei Valerius Flaccus', *R.E.L.* 47.2 (1970) 173–98; idem, 'Die Argonautica des Valerius Flaccus', in (ed.) E. Burck, *Das römische Epos, Grundriss der Literaturgeschichte nach Gattungen* (Darmstadt 1979) 208–53; W.-W. Ehlers, *Untersuchungen zur handschriftlichen Überlieferung der Argonautica des C. Valerius Flaccus, Zetemata* 52 (Munich 1970: bibliography 126–33); E. Lefèvre, 'Das Prooemium der Argonautica des Valerius Flaccus: Ein Beitrag zur Typik epischer Prooemien der römischen Kaiserzeit', *Abh. Akad. Mainz* 1971, 6; P. Venini, 'Valerio Flacco e l'erudizione Apolloniana: note stilistiche', *R.I.L* 105 (1971) 582–96; idem, 'Sulla struttura della Argonautiche di Valerio Flacco', ibid. 597–620; idem, 'Su alcuni motivi della Argonautiche di Valerio Flacco', *B. Stud. Lat.* 2 (1972) 10–19; J. Strand, *Notes on Valerius Flaccus' Argonautica, Stud. Graec. et Lat. Gothoburg* 31 (Göteborg 1972); S. Contino, *Lingua e stile in Valerio Flacco* (Bologna 1973); J. P. Perkins, 'An aspect of style of Valerius Flaccus' Argonauticon', *Phoenix* 28 (1974)

290–313; J. G. Fitch, 'Aspects of Valerius Flaccus' use of similes', *T.A.Ph.A.* 106 (1976) 113–24.

CONCORDANCE: W. H. Schulte (Scottdale 1934; repr. Hildesheim 1965).

SILIUS ITALICUS, TIBERIUS CATIUS ASCONIUS

LIFE

Dates *c.* A.D. 26–101. Advocate in Rome, consul 68, supporter of Vitellius, governor of Asia *c.* 77. Starved himself to death after contracting an incurable disease. Sources: Pliny, *Epist.* 3.7 (obituary); Mart. 7.63, 8.66, 9.86, 11.48, 49 (all addressed to S.); Tac. *Hist.* 3.65 (S. and Vitellius). For inscription relating to his governorship of Asia, see W. M. Calder, *C.R.* 49 (1935) 216–17. Cf. also D. Vessey, 'Pliny, Martial and Silius Italicus', *Hermes* 102 (1974) 109–16; W. C. McDermott and A. E. Orentzel, 'Silius Italicus and Domitian', *A.J.Ph.* 98 (1977) 24–34.

WORKS

Punica: epic in seventeen books on second Punic war, written from 88 onwards.

BIBLIOGRAPHY

(for 1929–42, see R. Helm, *Lustrum* 1 (1956) 255–72)

TEXTS: L. Bauer (BT, 1890–2); J. D. Duff (Loeb, 1934); A. Petrucci (Milan 1947: with tr.).

STUDIES: L. Legras, 'Les "Puniques" et la "Thébaïde"', *R.E.A.* 7 (1905) 131–46, 357–71; L. B. Woodruff, *Reminiscences of Ennius in Silius Italicus, Univ. of Michigan Studies* 4 (New York 1910) 355–424; R. Rebischke, *De Silii Italici orationibus* (diss. Königsberg–Danzig 1913); R. B. Steele, 'The method of Silius Italicus', *C.Ph.* 17 (1922) 319–33; C. W. Mendell, 'Silius the reactionary', *Ph.Q.* 3 (1924) 92–106; A. Klotz, *RE* IIIA. 1 (1927) 79–91; D. J. Campbell, 'The birthplace of Silius Italicus', *C.R.* 50 (1936) 56–8; J. Nicol, *The historical and geographical sources used by Silius Italicus* (Oxford 1936); S. Blomgren, *Siliana: De Silii Italici Punicis quaestiones criticae et interpretariae, Årsskrift Upps. Univ.* 1938.7 (Uppsala–Leipzig 1938); M. Sechi, 'Silio Italico e Livio', *Maia* 4 (1951) 280–97; L. Ramaglia, 'La figura di Giunone nelle Puniche di Silio Italico', *R.S.C.* 1 (1952–3) 35–43; R. T. Bruère, 'Silius Italicus, Punica 3.62–162 and 4.763–822', *C.Ph.* 47 (1952) 219–27; idem, 'Color Ovidianus in Silius' Punica I–VII', in (ed.) N. I. Herescu, *Ovidiana* (Paris 1958) 475–99; idem,

'Color Ovidianus in Silius' Punica VIII–XVII', *C.Ph.* 54 (1959) 228–45; idem, 'Some recollections of Virgil's Drances in later epic', *C.Ph.* 66 (1971) 30–4; E. Wistrand, *Die Chronologie der Punica des Silius Italicus: Beiträge zur Interpretation der flavischen Literatur, Göteborgs Univ. Årsskrift* 62 = *Studia Graeca et Latina Gothoburgensia* 4 (Göteborg 1956); E. L. Bassett, 'Silius Italicus in England', *C.Ph.* 48 (1953) 155–68; idem, 'Regulus and the serpent in the Punica', *C.Ph.* 50 (1955) 1–20; idem, 'Silius, Punica 6.1–53', *C.Ph.* 54 (1959) 10–34; idem; 'Scipio and the ghost of Appius', *C.Ph.* 58 (1963) 73–92; idem, 'Hercules and the hero of the Punica', in (ed.) L. Wallach, *The classical tradition: literary and historical studies in honor of Harry Caplan* (New York 1966) 258–73; M. V. T. Wallace, 'The architecture of the Punica: a hypothesis', *C.Ph.* 53 (1958) 99–103; idem, 'Some aspects of time in the Punica of Silius Italicus', *C.W.* 62 (1968) 83–93; M. von Albrecht, 'Gleichnis und Innenwelt in Silius' Punica', *Hermes* 91 (1963) 352–74; idem, *Silius Italicus, Freiheit und Gebundenheit römischer Epik* (Amsterdam 1964: bibliography 215–37); idem, 'Silius Italicus: Ein vergessenes Kapitel Literaturgeschichte', in *Argentea Aetas: In Memoriam E. V. Marmorale, Univ. di Genova Ist. di Fil. Class. e Mediev. Pubbl.* 37 (Genoa 1973) 181–8; J. Delz, 'Die erste Junoszene in den Punica des Silius Italicus', *M.H.* 26 (1969) 88–100; P. Venini, 'Silio Italico e il mito Tebano', *R.I.L.* 103 (1969) 778–83; idem, 'Cronologia e composizione nei Punica di Silio Italico', *R.I.L.* 106 (1972) 518–31; idem, 'Tecnica allusiva di Silio Italico', ibid. 532–42; H. Juhnke, *Homerisches in römischer Epik flavischer Zeit: Untersuchungen zu Szenennachbildungen und Structurentsprechungen in Statius' Thebais und Achilleis und in Silius' Punica*, *Zetemata* 53 (Munich 1972); D. Vessey, 'Silius Italicus on the fall of Saguntum', *C.Ph.* 69 (1974) 28–36; idem, 'The myth of Falernus in Silius Italicus, Punica 7', *C. J.* 68 (1972–3) 240–6; idem, 'Silius Italicus: the shield of Hannibal', *A.J.Ph.* 96 (1975) 391–405; K. H. Niemann, *Die Darstellung der römischen Niederlagen in den Punica des Silius Italicus* (diss. Bonn 1975); E. Burck, 'Die Punica des Silius Italicus', in (ed.) E. Burck, *Das römische Epos, Grundriss der Literaturgeschichte nach Gattungen* (Darmstadt 1979) 254–99.

CONCORDANCE: N. D. Young, *Iowa Stud. in Class. Phil.* 8 (Iowa City 1939).

MARTIAL AND JUVENAL

GENERAL WORKS

(1) Juvenal in conjunction with Martial, literary life of the times.

Bardon, H., *Les empereurs et les lettres latines* (Paris 1940).

Colton, R. E., *Juvenal and Martial* (diss. Columbia 1951).

idem, 'Juvenal and Martial on literary and professional men', *C.B.* 39 (1963) 49–52.

idem, 'Juvenal's second satire and Martial', *C.J.* 61 (1965–6) 68–71.

idem, 'Juvenal on recitations', *C.B.* 42 (1966) 81–5.

Guillemin, A.-M., *Pline et la vie littéraire de son temps* (Paris 1929).
Marache, R., 'La poésie romaine et le problème social à la fin du Ier siècle chez Martial et Juvénal', *L'Information Littéraire* 13 (1961) 12–19.
Scivoletto, N., 'Plinio il Giovane e Giovenale', *G.I.F.* 10 (1957) 133–46.
Steele, R. B., 'Interrelation of the Latin poets under Domitian', *C.Ph.* 25 (1930) 328–42.
Townend, G., 'The literary substrata to Juvenal's satires', *J.R.S.* 63 (1973) 148–60.
White, P., 'The friends of Martial, Statius, and Pliny, and the dispersal of patronage', *H.S.C.Ph.* 79 (1975) 265–300.

(2) Roman satire

Coffey, M., *Roman satire* (London–New York 1976).
Duff, J. W., *Roman satire* (Cambridge 1937).
Knoche, U., *Die römische Satire*, 3rd ed. (Göttingen 1971).
Terzaghi, N., *Per la storia della satira*, 2nd ed. (Turin 1944).
Weinreich, O., *Römische Satiren*, 2nd ed. (Zurich–Stuttgart 1962).

MARTIALIS, MARCUS VALERIUS

LIFE

b. *c.* A.D. 38–41 at Bilbilis in Spain. At Rome knew Silius, Valerius, Pliny, Quintilian and Juvenal. Pliny subsidized his return to Spain, where he died *c.* 104 (Pliny, *Epist.* 3.21.1). See above, p. 602, and U. Scamuzzi, *R.S.C.* 14 (1966) 149–207.

WORKS

Twelve books of epigrams, pubd 86–101; *Liber spectaculorum*, 80; *Xenia* and *Apophoreta* (now bks 13–14), *c.* 84. See above, pp. 602–3; H. F. Stobbe, *Philologus* 26 (1867) 44–80; E. T. Sage, *T.A.Ph.A.* 50 (1919) 168–76.

BIBLIOGRAPHY

(for 1915–25, see M. Schuster, *J.A.W.* 211 (1927) 144–67; for 1925–42, R. Helm, *Lustrum* 1 (1956) 299–318, and 2 (1957) 187–206; for 1901–70, G. W. M. Harrison, *Lustrum* 18 (1975) 301–37)

TEXTS AND COMMENTARIES: TEXTS: W. M. Lindsay (OCT, 1903); W. C. A. Ker (Loeb, 1919); H. J. Izaac (Budé, 1930); W. Heraeus, rev. J. Borovskij (BT, 1976). COMMENTARIES: L. Friedländer (Leipzig 1886). Bk 1: M. Citroni (Florence 1975); P. Howell (London 1980).

STUDIES: A. Zingerle, *Martial's Ovid-Studien* (Innsbruck 1877); W. M. Lindsay, *The ancient editions of Martial* (Oxford 1903); K. Preston, 'Martial and formal literary criticism', *C.Ph.* 15 (1920) 340–52; K. F. Smith, *Martial the epigrammatist and other essays* (Baltimore 1920); C. W. Mendell, 'Martial and the satiric epigram', *C.Ph.* 17 (1922) 1–20; O. Weinreich, *Studien zu Martial* (Stuttgart 1928); J. W. Spaeth, 'Martial and Virgil', *T.A.Ph.A.* 61 (1930) 19–28; K. Barwick, 'Zur Kompositionstechnik und Erklärung Martials', *Philologus* 87 (1932) 63–79; F. Sauter, *Der römische Kaiserkult bei Martial und Statius* (Stuttgart–Berlin 1934); J. Kruuse, 'L'originalité artistique de Martial', *C.&M.* 4 (1941) 248–300; A. Nordh, 'Historical exempla in Martial', *Eranos* 52 (1954) 224–38; R. Helm, in *RE* VIIIA.1 (1955) 55–85; K. Barwick, *Martial und die zeitgenössische Rhetorik* (Berlin 1959); H. Szelest, 'Martials satirische Epigramme und Horaz', *Altertum* 9 (1963) 27–37; J. Ferguson, 'Catullus and Martial', *P.A.C.A.* 6 (1963) 3–15; P. Laurens, 'Martial et l'épigramme grecque du Ier siècle après J-C', *R.E.L.* 43 (1965) 315–41; E. Siedschlag, *Zur Form von Martials Epigrammen* (Berlin 1977).

CONCORDANCE: E. Siedschlag (Hildesheim–New York 1979).

IUVENALIS, DECIMUS IUNIUS

LIFE

b. A.D. 67 (?), d. sometime after 127 (last datable refs. *Sat.* 13.17, 15.27). Not mentioned by any contemporary except Martial (Mart. 7.24 and 91, 12.18). Did not achieve popularity until 4th c. A.D.; see Highet (1956, under *Studies* below), and Coffey (under *General works* (2) above) 144–6 with notes. See above, pp. 603–4, for the problems, and authors and evidence cited there in notes; also G. Highet, *T.A.Ph.A.* 68 (1937) 480–506; W. S. Anderson, *C.Ph.* 50 (1955) 255–7; G. Brugnoli, *Studi Urbinati* 37 (1963) 5–14; Coffey (1963, under *Bibliography* below) 165–70.

WORKS

Fifteen complete satires, and a fragment of a sixteenth, divided into five books. *Sat.* 1 composed after 100, *Sat.* 15 after 127. Additional thirty-six lines, generally agreed to be genuine and belonging to *Sat.* 6, were discovered in 1899; see Housman (under *Texts* below) xxix–xxx and xxxix–xl; Coffey (1963, under *Bibliography* below) 179–84; J. G. Griffith, *Hermes* 91 (1963) 104–14; G. Luck, *H.S.Ph.* 76 (1972) 217–32. The contention of O. Ribbeck, *Der echte und der unechte Juvenal* (Berlin 1865) that the later satires are not authentic is now discounted. For author-variants, see J. G. Griffith, *Festschrift B. Snell* (Munich 1956) 101–11; for interpolations, E. Courtney, *B.I.C.S.* 22 (1975) 147–62.

BIBLIOGRAPHY

(for 1918–40, see E. Lommatzsch, *J.A.W.* 204 (1925) 221ff., 235 (1932) 149–51, 260 (1938) 102–5; for 1941–61, R. Helm, *J.A.W.* 282 (1943) 15–37, and M. Coffey,

Lustrum 8 (1963) 161–217); for 1937–68, W. S. Anderson, *C.W.* 50 (1956) 38ff., 57 (1964) 346–8, 63 (1970) 217–22. See also bibliographies in Adamietz (1972) and Gérard (1976), under *Studies* below)

TEXTS AND COMMENTARIES: TEXTS: A. E. Housman, 2nd ed. (Cambridge 1931); U. Knoche (Munich 1950); W. V. Clausen (OCT, 1959). COMMENTARIES: G. A. Ruperti (Glasgow 1825); L. Friedländer (Leipzig 1895), intr. tr. J. R. C. Martyn, *Friedländer's essays on Juvenal* (Amsterdam 1969); J. E. B. Mayor (London 1901); J. D. Duff and M. Coffey (Cambridge 1970); E. Courtney (London 1980). SCHOLIA: D. Wessner (BT, 1931). See G. B. Townend, *C.Q.* 22 (1972) 376–87. MANUSCRIPTS: U. Knoche, *Die Überlieferung Juvenals* (Berlin 1926); idem, *Handschriftliche Grundlagen des Juvenal-Textes, Philologus* suppl. 33 (1940); Coffey (1963, under *Studies* below) 170ff.; J. G. Griffith, *M.H.* 15 (1968) 101–38.

STUDIES: J. de Decker, *Juvenalis declamans* (Ghent 1913); I. G. Scott, *The grand style in the satires of Juvenal* (Northampton, Mass. 1927); P. de Labriolle, *Les satires de Juvénal: étude et analyse* (Paris 1932); F. Gauger, *Zeitschilderung und Topik bei Juvenal* (diss. Greifswald 1937); E. Smemo, 'Zur Technik der Personenzeichnung bei Juvenal', *S.O.* 16 (1937) 77–102; G. Highet, 'The philosophy of Juvenal', *T.A.Ph.A.* 80 (1949) 254–70; idem, 'Juvenal's bookcase', *A.J.Ph.* 72 (1951) 369–94; idem, *Juvenal the satirist* (Oxford 1954); W. C. Helmbold, 'Juvenal's twelfth satire', *C.Ph.* 51 (1956) 14–23; W. S. Anderson, 'Studies in book 1 of Juvenal', *Y.Cl.S.* 15 (1957) 31–90; idem, 'Juvenal and Quintilian', *Y.Cl.S.* 17 (1961) 3–93; idem, 'The programs of Juvenal's later books', *C.Ph.* 57 (1962) 145–60; idem, 'Anger in Juvenal and Seneca', *Univ. Calif. Publ. Class. Phil.* 19.3 (1964); A. Serafini, *Studio sulle satire di Giovenale* (Florence 1957); E. Thomas, 'Ovidian echoes in Juvenal', in (ed.) N. Herescu, *Ovidiana* (Paris 1958) 505–25; G. Lawall, 'Exempla and theme in Juvenal's tenth satire', *T.A.Ph.A.* 89 (1958) 25–31; E. J. Kenney, 'The first satire of Juvenal', *P.C.Ph.S* 8 (1962) 29–40; J. G. Griffith, 'Juvenal and the stage-struck patricians', *Mnemosyne* 4.15 (1962) 256–61; idem, 'The ending of Juvenal's first satire and Lucilius xxx', *Hermes* 98 (1970) 56–72; E. J. Kenney, 'Juvenal, satirist or rhetorician?', *Latomus* 22 (1963) 704–20; H. A. Mason, 'Is Juvenal a classic?', in (ed.) J. P. Sullivan, *Satire* (London 1963) 93–167; N. Scivoletto, 'Presenze di Persio in Giovenale', *G.I.F.* 16 (1963) 60–72; J. J. Bodoh, *An analysis of the ideas of Juvenal* (diss. Wisconsin 1966); idem, 'Artistic control in the satires of Juvenal', *Aevum* 44 (1970) 475–82; A. S. McDevitt, 'The structure of Juvenal's eleventh satire', *G.&R.* 15 (1968) 173–9; J. P. Stein, 'The unity and scope of Juvenal's fourteenth satire', *C.Ph.* 65 (1970) 34–6; S. C. Fredericks, 'Rhetoric and morality in Juvenal's 8th satire', *T.A.Ph.A.* 102 (1971) 111–32; L. Edmunds, 'Juvenal's thirteenth satire', *Rh.M.* 115 (1972) 59–73; J. Adamietz, *Untersuchungen zu Juvenal, Hermes Einzelschriften* 26 (1972: on satires 3, 5 and 11); J. Gérard, *Juvénal et la réalité contemporaire* (Paris 1976).

INDEXES: L. Kelling and A. Suskin (Chapel Hill 1951); M. Dubrocard (New York 1976).

PHAEDRUS (Augusti libertus)

LIFE

Dates *c.* 18 B.C.–A.D. 50 (not universally accepted). Thracian slave, manumitted by Augustus. Offended Sejanus through allusions in his fables and received some unknown punishment. Sources: Phaedr. 3 *prol.*, 3 *epil.*, 4 *prol.*; Mart. 3.20.5; Avian. *Epist. ad Theod.* See A. de Lorenzi, *Fedro* (Florence 1955: speculative).

WORKS

Remnants of five books of Aesopian fables in iambic senarii, pubd at intervals between *c.* A.D. 20–50. Order of books seems to correspond with sequence of composition, and bk 3 is definitely later than A.D. 31. The codex Pithoeanus transmits ninety-four fables and some seven other pieces, and some thirty other items are added by the *appendix Perottina* (a 15th-c. transcription by N. Perotti from a MS apparently less truncated than P). But the collection is still far from complete: paraphrases of prose translations give substance of fables not extant in metrical form. P. probably wrote at least 150 fables.

BIBLIOGRAPHY

TEXTS: L. Müller (BT, 1877); L. Havet (Paris 1895); J. P. Postgate (OCT 1919); B. E. Perry, *Babrius and Phaedrus* (Loeb, 1965). See also L. Hervieux, *Les fabulistes latins depuis le siècle d'Auguste jusqu'à la fin du moyen âge*, vols. I–II, 2nd ed. (Paris 1893–4); B. E. Perry, *Aesopica* I (Urbana 1952).

STUDIES: A. Hausrath, in *RE* XIX (1938) 1475–1505; B. E. Perry, 'The origin of the epimythium', *T.A.Ph.A.* 71 (1940) 391–419; idem, 'Demetrius of Phalerum and the Aesopic fables', *T.A.Ph.A.* 93 (1962) 287–346, and in intr. to his edition, lxxiii–xcvi.

INDEX: A. Cinquini (Milan 1905).

CALPURNIUS SICULUS, TITUS

LIFE

Dates of birth and death unknown, but almost certainly wrote his poems under Nero (see particularly 1.44–5, 77–83, 7.23–4). Contra: E. Champlin, *J.R.S.* 68 (1978) 95–110. If his name is rightly transmitted, *Calpurnius* might indicate some unknown connexion with the Calpurnii Pisones, *Siculus* place of origin or association with Theocritean bucolic. Claims to be of humble rank.

APPENDIX OF AUTHORS AND WORKS

WORKS

Seven eclogues after the manner of Virgil: long conjoined with four others, shown by Haupt (1854, under *Studies* below) to belong to Nemesianus, *pace* A. E. Radke, *Hermes* 100 (1972) 615–23.

BIBLIOGRAPHY

TEXTS AND COMMENTARIES: Calpurnius. TEXTS: *PLM*, vol III; H. Schenkl, in (ed.) J. P. Postgate, *Corpus poetarum Latinorum*, vol. II (London 1905); C. Giarratano (Turin 1924); J. W. and A. M. Duff, in *Minor Latin poets* (Loeb, 1934). COMMENTARIES: C. H. Keene (London 1887); R. Verdière (Brussels–Berchem 1954); D. Korzeniewski (Darmstadt 1971).

Bucolica Einsidlensia. TEXTS: *Anth. Lat.* 725–6; *PLM*, Giarratano, Duff (above). COMMENTARIES: Verdière and Korzeniewski (above).

Laus Pisonis. TEXTS: *PLM*, vol. I; Duff (above). COMMENTARIES: Verdière (above); A. Seel (Erlangen 1969).

STUDIES: M. Haupt, *De carminibus bucolicis Calpurnii et Nemesiani* (Berlin 1854) = *Opuscula* I (Leipzig 1875) 358–406; F. Chytil, *Der Eklogendichter T. Calpurnius Siculus und seine Vorbilder* (Znaim 1894); E. Groag, in *RE* III (1899) 1378–9; F. Skutsch, ibid. 1401–6, and V (1905) 2115–16; S. Lösch, *Die Einsiedler Gedichte* (diss. Tübingen 1909); B. L. Ullmann, 'The text tradition and authorship of the Laus Pisonis', *C.Ph.* 24 (1929) 109–32; J. Hubaux, *Les thèmes bucoliques dans la poésie latine* (Brussels 1930); A. Momigliano, 'Literary chronology of the Neronian age', *C.Q.* 38 (1944) 96–100 = *Secondo contributo* (Rome 1960) 454–61; W. Schmid, 'Panegyrik und Bukolik in der neronischen Epoche', *B.J.* 153 (1953) 63–96; idem, 'Nochmals über das zweite Einsiedler Gedicht', *Hermes* 83 (1955) 124–8; M. L. Paladini, 'Osservazioni a Calpurnio Siculo', *Latomus* 15 (1956) 330–46, 521–31; W. Theiler, 'Zu den Einsiedlern Hirtengedichten', *S.I.F.C.* 27–8 (1956) 565–77 = *Untersuchungen zur antiken Literatur* (Berlin 1970) 430–41; H. Fuchs, 'Der Friede als Gefahr: zum zweiten Einsiedler Hirtengedichte', *H.S.C.Ph.* 63 (1958) 363–85; D. Korzeniewski, 'Die "panegyrische Tendenz" in den Carmina Einsidlensia', *Hermes* 94 (1966) 344–60; G. Scheda, *Studien zur bukolischen Dichtung der neronischen Epoche* (diss. Bonn 1969); D. Korzeniewski, 'Die Eklogen des Calpurnius Siculus als Gedichtbuch', *M.H.* 29 (1972) 214–16; R. W. Garson, 'The Eclogues of Calpurnius. A partial apology', *Latomus* 33 (1974) 668–72; G. B. Townend, 'Calpurnius Siculus and the *Munus Neronis*', *J.R.S.* 70 (1980) 166–74; R. G. Mayer, 'Calpurnius Siculus: technique and date', ibid. 175–6.

BUCOLICA EINSIDLENSIA

Two eclogues, discovered in a manuscript at Einsiedeln and first published by W. Hagen (*Philologus* 28 (1869) 338–41); text seriously mutilated. Generally dated, on internal evidence, to time of Nero. Authorship utterly uncertain, but differences in thought and attitude suggest that they were not written by Calpurnius Siculus, to whose work they are nevertheless somewhat akin. For bibliography, see under Calpurnius Siculus.

LAUS PISONIS

A panegyric (261 hexameters) on a certain Calpurnius Piso, perhaps the conspirator (Tac. *Ann.* 15.48) or the consul of A.D. 57. Its language and metre may indicate, and certainly do not preclude, a Neronian date. Much speculation about the author: Calpurnius Siculus remains a possibility, but no more. For bibliography, see under Calpurnius Siculus.

AETNA

Didactic poem on volcanic nature of Etna. Authorship unknown.

BIBLIOGRAPHY

TEXTS AND COMMENTARIES: TEXTS: *PLM*, vol. I, rev. F. Vollmer; J. Vessereau (Budé, 1923); W. Richter (Berlin 1963); F. R. D. Goodyear, in *Appendix Vergiliana* (OCT, 1966). COMMENTARIES: H. A. J. Munro (Cambridge 1867); R. Ellis (Oxford 1901); F. R. D. Goodyear (Cambridge 1965: with index).

STUDIES: E. Bickel, 'Apollon und Dodona. Ein Beitrag zur Technik und Datierung des Lehrgedichts Aetna', *Rh.M.* 79 (1930) 279–302; P. de Lacy, 'The philosophy of the Aetna', *T.A.Ph.A.* 74 (1943) 169–78; W. Richter, 'Lucilius, Seneca, und das Aetnagedicht', *Philologus* 96 (1944) 234–49; K. Büchner, in *RE* VIIIA (1955) 1136–55; F. Weissengruber, 'Zur Datierung der Aetna', *W.S.* 78 (1965) 128–38; J.-H. Waszink, *Gnomon* 41 (1969) 353–62 (review of edd. by Richter and Goodyear).

EPIGRAMS ASCRIBED TO SENECA AND PETRONIUS

Apart from various discountable items (*Anth. Lat.* 464–5, 667, 799, 804), three poems are transmitted under the name of Seneca (*Anth. Lat.* 232, 236–7) and sixty-seven ascribed to him by Scaliger and others (*Anth. Lat.* 396–463). There is nowadays much uncertainty, indeed scepticism, about the attribution of most of these pieces. So with Petronius. Five poems are transmitted under his name or cited as his by Fulgentius (*Anth. Lat.* 466, 476, 650–1, 690), fourteen are ascribed to him by Scaliger (*Anth. Lat.* 464–5, 467–75, 477–9), ten by Binet (*Anth. Lat.* 218, 691–9), who claims to take the ascription from a manuscript, and eight by Baehrens (*Anth. Lat.* 700–7). Great doubt attaches to the last two groups, but there are indications that some at least of the other pieces may be Petronian.

BIBLIOGRAPHY

TEXTS AND COMMENTARY: TEXTS: *PLM*, vol. IV; *Anth. Lat.* COMMENTARY: C. Prato, *Gli epigrammi attribuiti a L. Anneo Seneca* (Rome 1964).

STUDIES: O. Rossbach, *Disquisitionum de Senecae filii scriptis criticarum capita duo* (Breslau 1882); C. W. Krohn, *Quaestiones ad anthologiam latinam spectantes* (Halle 1887); A. Collignon, *Étude sur Pétrone* (Paris 1892) 362–76; E. Herfurth, *De Senecae epigrammatis quae feruntur* (Jena 1910); K. P. Harrington, 'Seneca's epigrams', *T.A.Ph.A.* 46 (1915) 207–15; H. Bardon, 'Les épigrammes de l'anthologie attribuées à Sénèque le philosophe', *R.E.L.* 17 (1939) 63–90; V. Tandoi, 'Il trionfo di Claudio sulla Britannia e il suo cantore', *S.I.F.C.* 34 (1962–3) 83–129, 137–68; idem, 'Sugli epigrammi dell' Antologia Latina attribuiti a Seneca', *S.I.F.C.* 36 (1964) 169–89.

PRIAPEA

Book of about eighty short poems, in hendecasyllables, elegiacs, and choliambs, addressed to or concerned with Priapus: has sustained some minor damage, but may otherwise be virtually complete. Commonly regarded as a collection of pieces by divers authors, assembled in or soon after Augustus' times, it is rather the work of a single poet, very possibly later than Martial.

BIBLIOGRAPHY

TEXTS: *PLM*, vol. III; F. Buecheler, *Petronii saturae et liber Priapeorum* (Berlin 1912); *PLM*, vol. II rev. F. Vollmer; I. Cazzaniga, in *Carmina ludicra Romanorum* (Turin 1959).

STUDIES: F. Buecheler, 'Vindiciae libri Priapeorum', *Rh.M.* 18 (1863) 381–415 = *Kleine Schriften* (Leipzig 1915) 328–62; H. Herter, *De Priapo*, *Rel. Vers. u. Vorarb.* 23 (Giessen 1932); R. Helm, in *RE* XXII (1954) 1908–13; V. Buchheit, *Studien zum Corpus Priapeorum*, Zetemata 28 (Munich 1962).

APOCOLOCYNTOSIS DIVI CLAUDII

Satire on the emperor Claudius, in a mixture of prose and verse. Of our three principal MSS two give the title *Ludus de morte Claudii* ('A sport on Claudius' death') and one *Divi Claudii apotheosis per satiram* ('The blessed Claudius' apotheosis, in satire'). The former may be an original title or sub-title, though this use of *ludus* is not attested in classical Latin, and in the latter *apotheosis* may be an explanatory gloss which has ousted an original title *apocolocyntosis*, preserved not by the direct tradition, but by Cassius Dio (60.35), who says, 'Seneca composed a piece which he called *apocolocyntosis*, a sort of deification as it were'. Most scholars accept that the work we have is that to which Dio refers as composed by Seneca. A minority hold that it is not the same and not necessarily Senecan, on the grounds (i) that neither *apocolocyntosis* itself nor Dio's explanation of the term fits the existing work, and (ii) that there are some indications that its attribution to Seneca in our medieval MSS has no great antiquity (see R. Roncali, *Belfagor* 29 (1974) 571–3). Whether Seneca's or another's the satire was probably written late A.D. 54, shortly after Claudius' death. Arguments for composition much later in Nero's principate have not carried conviction: see A. Momigliano, *C.Q.* 38 (1944) 96–100 = *Secondo contributo* (Rome 1960) 454–61.

BIBLIOGRAPHY

(for 1922–58, see M. Coffey, *Lustrum* 6 (1961) 239–71)

TEXTS AND COMMENTARIES: TEXTS: F. Buecheler and W. Heraeus, in *Petronii saturae* etc., 6th ed. (Berlin 1922); O. Rossbach (Bonn 1926). COMMENTARIES: O. Weinreich (Berlin 1923); C. F. Russo, 4th ed. (Florence 1964).

STUDIES: R. Helm, *Lucian und Menipp* (Leipzig 1906); R. Heinze, 'Zu Senecas Apocolocyntosis', *Hermes* 61 (1926) 49–78; A. Momigliano, *Claudius: the emperor and his achievement* (Oxford 1934); H. MacL. Currie, 'The purpose of the Apocolocyntosis', *A.C.* 31 (1962) 91–7; K. Kraft, 'Der politische Hintergrund von Senecas Apocolocyntosis', *Historia* 15 (1966) 96–122; H. Haffter, *Römische Politik und römische Politiker* (Heidelberg 1967) 121–40; K. Bringmann, 'Senecas Apocolocyntosis und die politische Satire in Rom', *A.&A.* 17 (1970) 56–69; G. Binder, 'Hercules und Claudius', *Rh.M.* 117 (1974) 288–317; M. Coffey, *Roman satire* (London – New York 1976) 165–77; M. T. Griffin, *Seneca: a philosopher in politics* (Oxford 1976) 129–33.

CONCORDANCE: in R. Busa and A. Zampolli, *Concordantiae Senecanae* (Hildesheim 1975).

PETRONIUS ARBITER

LIFE

Not certainly documented, but the author is plausibly identified with T. Petronius Niger, consul *c.* A.D. 62, d. 66. Sources: Tac. *Ann.* 16.17–19 (character sketch and account of his suicide); Pliny, *N.H.* 37.20; Plut. *Mor.* 60e; Macr. *Somn.* 1.2.8. See R. Browning, 'The date of Petronius', *C.R.* 63 (1949) 12–14; H. C. Schnur, 'The economic background of the *Satyricon*', *Latomus* 18 (1959) 790–9; Sullivan (1968, under *Studies* below) 21–33; Walsh (1970, under *Studies* below) 67–70, 244–7; K. F. C. Rose, *The date and author of the Satyricon, Mnemosyne* suppl. 16 (1971).

WORKS

Satyrica or *Satyricon libri*, not *Satyricon*, in at least sixteen books. We have fragments of bk 14, a long passage, the *cena Trimalchionis*, perhaps coextensive with bk 15, and fragments of bk 16 and probably later books too. Apparently written in second half of Nero's reign. Various pieces of verse, which may well be extracted from the *Satyrica*, are attributed to P. in the Latin Anthology and elsewhere.

BIBLIOGRAPHY

(see G. L. Schmeling and J. H. Stuckey (Leiden 1977))

TEXTS AND COMMENTARIES: TEXTS: F. Buecheler, 6th ed. (Berlin 1922); A. Ernout, 4th ed. (Budé, 1958); K. Müller (Munich 1961); K. Müller and W. Ehlers (Munich 1965). COMMENTARIES: *Cena Trimalchionis*: L. Friedländer (Leipzig 1891); W. D. Lowe (London 1905); W. B. Sedgwick (Oxford 1925); P. Perrochat (Paris 1939); M. S. Smith (Oxford 1975). *De bello civili:* F. T. Baldwin (New York 1911); G. Guido (Bologna 1976).

STUDIES: E. Klebs, 'Zur Komposition von Petronius' Satirae', *Philologus* 47 (1889) 623–55; A. Collignon, *Étude sur Pétrone* (Paris 1892); R. Heinze, 'Petron und der griechische Roman', *Hermes* 34 (1899) 494–519; W. Heraeus, *Die Sprache des Petronius und die Glossen* (Leipzig 1899), revised in *Kleine Schriften* (Heidelberg 1937) 52–150; R. Cahen, *Le Satiricon et ses origines* (Paris 1925); W. Süss, *De eo quem dicunt inesse Trimalchionis cenae sermone uulgari* (Dorpat 1926); H. Stubbe, *Die Verseinlagen im Petron, Philologus* suppl. 25 (1933); J. W. Duff, *Roman satire* (California 1936) 84–105; W. Kroll, in *RE* XIX (1937) 1202–14; E. Courtney, 'Parody and literary allusion in Menippean satire', *Philologus* 106 (1962) 86–100; A. Stefenelli, *Die Volkssprache im Werk des Petron im Hinblick auf die romanischen Sprachen* (Vienna 1962); P. Veyne, 'Le "je" dans le Satiricon', *R.E.L.* 42 (1964) 301–24; B. E. Perry, *The ancient romances* (California 1967); J. P. Sullivan, *The Satyricon of Petronius* (London 1968); A. M. Cameron, 'Petronius and Plato', *C.Q.* n.s.19 (1969) 367–70; A. Scobie, *Aspects of the ancient romance and its heritage, Beiträge zur klassichen Philologie* 30 (Meisenheim am Glan 1969); A. M. Cameron, 'Myth and meaning in Petronius: some modern comparisons', *Latomus* 29 (1970) 397–425; H. D. Rankin, 'Some comments on Petronius' portrayal of character', *Eranos* 68 (1970) 123–47; P. G. Walsh, *The Roman novel* (Cambridge 1970); P. Parsons, 'A Greek Satyricon?', *B.I.C.S.* 18 (1971) 53–68; F. I. Zeitlin, 'Petronius as paradox: anarchy and artistic integrity', *T.A.Ph.A.* 102 (1971) 631–84; G. Luck, 'On Petronius' bellum civile' *A.J.Ph.* 93 (1972) 133–41; P. A. George, 'Petronius and Lucan de bello civili', *C.Q.* n.s.24 (1974) 119–33; M. Coffey, *Roman satire* (London 1976) 178–203.

INDEX: I. Segebade and E. Lommatzsch (Leipzig 1898).

VELLEIUS PATERCULUS

LIFE

b. *c.* 20 B.C. Military tribune in Thrace and Macedonia; accompanied Gaius Caesar to the east A.D. 1; served under Tiberius in Germany and Pannonia for eight years. Quaestor A.D. 7, praetor A.D. 15. d. later than A.D. 30. Praenomen uncertain. Refs. to ancestors and career: Vell. 2.16.2, 69.5, 76.1, 101.2–3, 104.3, 107.1, 111.3–4, 113.3, 115.1, 121.3, 124.4. See Sumner (1970, under *Studies* below) 257–79.

WORKS

Outline history in two books, pubd A.D. 30. Bk 1 (mythological times to 146 B.C.) is largely lost: we lack the preface, but have the narration from near the beginning to the foundation of Rome; vast lacuna follows to 167 B.C. Bk 2 (146 B.C.–A.D. 29) is virtually complete. No other works known. V. says several times that he intends to write a major history, but apparently never did so.

BIBLIOGRAPHY

TEXTS AND COMMENTARIES: TEXTS: C. Halm (BT, 1876); F. Haase (BT, 1884); R. Ellis (Oxford 1898); F. W. Shipley (Loeb, 1924); C. Stegmann de Pritzwald (BT, 1933). COMMENTARIES: D. Ruhnken (Leiden 1779); F. Kritz (Leipzig 1840). 2.94–131: A. J. Woodman (Cambridge 1977).

STUDIES: H. Dodwell, *Annales Velleiani* (Oxford 1698); F. Milkau, *De Velleii Paterculi genere dicendi quaestiones selectae* (Regensburg 1888); C. Jodry, 'L'utilisation des documents militaires chez Velleius Paterculus', *R.E.L.* 29 (1951) 265–84; I. Lana,

Velleio Patercolo o della propaganda (Turin 1952); H. J. Steffen, *Die Regierung des Tiberius in der Darstellung des Velleius Paterculus* (Kiel 1954): A. Dihle, in *RE* VIIIA (1955) 638–59; J. Hellegouarc'h, 'Les buts de l'oeuvre historique de Velleius Paterculus', *Latomus* 23 (1964) 669–84; A. J. Woodman, 'Sallustian influence on Velleius Paterculus', in *Hommages à Marcel Renard* I (Brussels 1968) 785–99; G. V. Sumner, 'The truth about Velleius Paterculus: prolegomena', *H.S.C.Ph.* 74 (1970) 257–97 A. J. Woodman, 'Velleius Paterculus', in (ed.) T. A. Dorey, *Silver Latin* II (London 1975) 1–25; idem, 'Questions of date, genre and style in Velleius', *C.Q.* n.s.25 (1975) 272–306.

CURTIUS RUFUS, QUINTUS

LIFE

Unknown, except that he lived under the principate and that not long before he wrote his history the empire went through a period of trouble and anxiety (10.9.1–6). His work, which has been placed as early as Augustus and as late as Alexander Severus, was most probably written under Claudius or Vespasian. He has been identified (without foundation) with a rhetorician mentioned by Suetonius (*De gramm. et rhet.* p. 2 Brugnoli), with a governor of Africa (Tac. *Ann.* 11.20.3–21.3), and with a son of the latter.

WORKS

Historiae Alexandri Magni in ten books: first two lost and substantial gaps in 5, 6, and 10. Text transmitted in numerous MSS, but not in a very good state. No other writings known.

BIBLIOGRAPHY

TEXTS: E. Hedicke (BT, 1908); J. C. Rolfe (Loeb, 1946); H. Bardon (Budé, 1947); K. Müller (Munich 1954).

STUDIES: S. Dosson, *Étude sur Quinte-Curce, sa vie et son oeuvre* (Paris 1887); E. Schwartz, 'Curtius', in *RE* IV (1901) 1871–91; W. Kroll, *Studien zum Verständnis der römischen Literatur* (Stuttgart 1924) 331–51; F. Wilhelm, *Curtius und die jüngere Seneca* (Paderborn 1928); J. Stroux, 'Die Zeit des Curtius', *Philologus* 84 (1929) 233–51; H. Lindgren, *Studia Curtiana* (Uppsala 1935); W. W. Tarn, *Alexander the Great* II (Cambridge 1948) 91–122; W. Rutz, 'Zur Erzählungskunst des Q. Curtius Rufus. Die Belagerung von Tyrus', *Hermes* 93 (1965) 370–82; J. Blaensdorf, 'Herodot bei Curtius Rufus', *Hermes* 99 (1971) 11–24.

INDEXES: O. Eichert (Hanover 1893); J. Therasse (Hildesheim 1976).

TACITUS, PUBLIUS (or GAIUS) CORNELIUS

LIFE

b. *c.* 55 A.D., family origins uncertain. Entered public life under Vespasian. Betrothed to Agricola's daughter 77. Praetor and *XVvir* 88; abroad 90–3, but back in Rome during Domitian's last years. Consul *suffectus* 97; delivered funeral oration over Verginius Rufus. Prosecuted Marius Priscus, ex-governor of Africa, on extortion charge 100. Proconsul of Asia *c.* 112/13, d. not earlier than A.D. 116. Sources: Tac. *Agr.* 2–3, 45 (refs. to Domitian), 9.6 (marriage), *Dial.* 1.1–2, 2.1 (study of oratory), *Hist.* 1.1.3–4 (general statement of career), *Ann.* 11.11.1 (praetor, *XVvir*); Pliny, *Epist.* 2.1 (funeral oration), 2.11 (prosecution of Priscus), 1.6, 1.20, 4.13, 4.15, 6.9, 6.16, 6.20, 7.20, 7.33, 8.7, 9.10, 9.14, 9.23; *CIL* VI 10229 (= *ILS* 8379a: possibly paired with Pliny in a will); *OGIS* 487 (proconsul); Pliny, *N.H.* 7.76 (his father (?) a procurator in Gallia Belgica); *Hist. Aug. Tac.* 10.3 (his works ordered to be placed in libraries). See M. L. Gordon, 'The patria of Tacitus', *J.R.S.* 26 (1936) 145–51; R. Syme, *Tacitus* (Oxford 1958) 611–24; R. Hanslik, 'Die Ämterlaufbahn des Tacitus im Lichte der Ämterlaufbahn, seiner Zeitgenossen', *A.A.W.W.* 102 (1965) 47–60; E. Koestermann, 'Tacitus und die Transpadana', *Athenaeum* 43 (1965) 167–208; S. Borzsák, in *RE* suppl. XI (1968) 375–99; R. P. Oliver, 'The praenomen of Tacitus', *A.J.Ph.* 98 (1977) 64–70.

WORKS

Five works survive, in whole or part: *De vita Iulii Agricolae*, dating from A.D. 98, *De origine et situ Germanorum*, from the same year, *Dialogus de oratoribus*, probably later than 100, *Historiae* (12–14 bks), composed between *c.* 100–110, and *Ab excessu divi Augusti* or *Annales* (16–18 bks), later than *Hist.* and probably still being written in 116. Titles *Historiae* and *Annales* have little or no ancient authority, and, though these works are likely to have been first pubd separately, they also, from a date unknown, circulated in a joint edition of thirty books (see Goodyear on *Ann.* 1.1.1). Only *Agricola* and *Germania* (thus commonly known) remain intact. *Dialogus* is impaired by a lacuna of some size. Of *Historiae* we possess only 1–4, part of 5, and a few fragments. Of *Annales* we have 1–4, a small piece of 5, 6, part of 11, 12–15, and part of 16. Much controversy about number of books T. devoted to *Hist.* and *Ann.*: some favour distribution of twelve and eighteen, others of fourteen and sixteen. The only firm evidence (numeration of second Medicean MS) supports the latter view. The matter is further complicated by possibility that he did not live to complete the *Annales*. No other writings recorded.

BIBLIOGRAPHY

(see Borzsák (1968, under *Studies* (1) below); F. R. D. Goodyear, *G.&R., New surveys in the classics* 4 (Oxford 1970); H. W. Benario, *C.W.* 71 (1977) 1–32)

TEXTS AND COMMENTARIES: TEXTS: Minor works: E. Koestermann (BT, 1970); R. M. Ogilvie and M. Winterbottom (OCT, 1975). *Hist.*: C. D. Fisher (OCT, 1910); H. Heubner (BT, 1978). *Ann.*: C. D. Fisher (OCT, 1906); H. Fuchs (Frauenfeld 1946–9); E. Koestermann (BT, 1971); P. Wuilleumier (Budé, 1974–8). COMMENTARIES: *Agr.*: R. Till (Berlin 1961); R. M. Ogilvie and I. A. Richmond (Oxford 1967). *Germ.*: J. G. C. Anderson (Oxford 1938); R. Much, 3rd ed. rev. H. Jankuhn and W. Lange (Heidelberg 1967). *Dial.*: W. Peterson (Oxford 1893); A. Gudeman, 2nd ed. (Leipzig–Berlin 1914). *Hist.*: E. Wolff, vol. I, 2nd ed. (Berlin 1914), vol. II, 2nd ed. rev. G. Andresen (Berlin 1926); C. Heraeus, rev. W. Heraeus, vol. I, 6th ed. (Leipzig 1929), vol. II, 4th ed. (Leipzig 1927). Bks 1–2: A. L. Irvine (London 1952). Bks 1–4: H, Heubner (Heidelberg 1963–). Bk 3: K. Wellesley (Sydney 1972). *Ann.*: H. Furneaux, vol. I, 2nd ed. (Oxford 1896), vol. II, 2nd ed. rev. H. F. Pelham and C. D. Fisher (Oxford 1907); K. Nipperdey, rev. G. Andresen, vol. I, 11th ed. (Berlin 1915), vol. II, 6th ed. (Berlin 1908); E. Koestermann (Heidelberg 1963–8). Bk 1: N. P. Miller (London 1959). Bk 1.1–54: F. R. D. Goodyear (Cambridge 1972). Bk 1.55–81 and Bk 2: F. R. D. Goodyear (Cambridge 1981). Bk 14: E. C. Woodcock (London 1939). Bk 15: N. P. Miller (London 1973).

STUDIES: (1) GENERAL: F. Leo, *Tacitus* (Göttingen 1896) = *Ausg. kl. Schr.* II (Rome 1960) 263–76; G. Boissier, *Tacitus and other Roman studies* (London 1906); R. von Pöhlmann, 'Die Weltanschauung des Tacitus', *S.B.A.W.* 1910, 1; E. Fraenkel, 'Tacitus', *N.J.W.* 8 (1932) 218–33 = *Kleine Beiträge* II (Rome 1964) 309–32; F. Klingner, 'Tacitus', *Ant.* 8 (1932) 151–69 = *Römische Geisteswelt*, 4th ed. (Munich 1961) 490–513; M. L. W. Laistner, *The greater Roman historians* (Berkeley 1947) 103–40; C. W. Mendell, *Tacitus: the man and his work* (New Haven 1957); R. Syme, *Tacitus* (Oxford 1958); E. Paratore, *Tacito*, 2nd ed. (Rome 1962); V. Pöschl, 'Der Historiker Tacitus', *W.G.* 22 (1962) 1–10; R. Häussler, *Tacitus und das historische Bewusstsein* (Heidelberg 1965); A. Michel, *Tacite et le destin de l'empire* (Paris 1966); S. Borzsák, 'P. Cornelius Tacitus', *RE* suppl. XI (1968) 373–512; D. R. Dudley, *The world of Tacitus* (London 1968); R. T. Scott, *Religion and philosophy in the Histories of Tacitus, Papers and monographs of the American academy in Rome* 22 (Rome 1968); R. Syme, *Ten studies in Tacitus* (Oxford 1970); R. H. Martin, *Tacitus* (London 1981).

(2) MINOR WORKS: F. Leo, review of Gudeman's ed. of *Dial.*, *G.G.A.* 1898, 169–88 = *Ausg. kl. Schr.* II 277–98; R. Reitzenstein, 'Bemerkungen zu den kleinen Schriften des Tacitus', *N.G.G.* 1915, 173–276 = *Aufsätze zu Tacitus* (Darmstadt 1967) 17–120; E. Norden, *Die germanische Urgeschichte in Tacitus' Germania*, 3rd ed. (Berlin 1923); E. Wolff, 'Das geschichtliche Verstehen in Tacitus' Germania', *Hermes* 69 (1934) 121–64; R. Heinze, '*Urgentibus imperii fatis*', in *Vom Geist des Römertums* (Leipzig–Berlin 1938) 255–77; R. Güngerich, 'Der Dialogus des Tacitus und Quintilians Institutio Oratoria', *C.Ph.* 46 (1951) 159–64; K. Barwick, 'Der Dialogus de oratoribus des Tacitus, Motive und Zeit seiner Entstehung', *Ber. Sächs. Akad. Wiss.* 1954, 4; A. Michel, *Le 'Dialogus des Orateurs' de Tacite et la philosophie de Cicéron* (Paris 1962);

E. A. Thompson, *The early Germans* (Oxford 1965); H. Gugel, *Untersuchungen zu Stil und Aufbau des Rednerdialogs des Tacitus*, *Commentationes Aenipontanae* 20 (Innsbruck 1969); R. Häussler, 'Zum Umfang und Aufbau des Dialogus de oratoribus', *Philologus* 113 (1969) 24–67; A. Köhnken, 'Das Problem der Ironie bei Tacitus', *M.H.* 30 (1973) 32–50.

(3) PREDECESSORS AND SOURCES: T. Mommsen, 'Cornelius Tacitus und Cluvius Rufus', *Hermes* 4 (1870) 295–325 = *Gesamm. Schr.* VII (Berlin 1909) 224–52; P. Fabia, *Les sources de Tacite* (Paris 1893); E. Schwartz, 'Cassius Dio', *RE* III (1899) 1684–1722, esp. 1714ff.; H. Heubner, *Studien zur Darstellungskunst des Tacitus* (Würzburg 1935); F. Klingner, 'Die Geschichte Kaiser Othos bei Tacitus', *Ber. Sächs. Akad. Wiss.* 1940, 1 = *Studien* (Zurich 1964) 605–24; A. Briessman, *Tacitus und das flavische Geschichtsbild*, *Hermes Einzelschriften* 10 (1955); F. Klingner, 'Tacitus und die Geschichtsschreiber des ersten Jahrhunderts nach Christus', *M.H.* 15 (1958) 194–206; C. Questa, *Studi sulle fonti degli 'Annales' di Tacito*, 2nd ed. (Rome 1963); G. B. Townend, 'Cluvius Rufus in the Histories of Tacitus', *A.J.Ph.* 85 (1964) 337–77; R. H. Martin, 'Tacitus and his predecessors', in (ed.) T. A. Dorey, *Tacitus* (London 1969) 117–47; D. Flach, 'Tacitus und seine Quellen in den Annalenbüchern I–VI', *Athenaeum* 51 (1973) 92–108.

(4) HISTORIOGRAPHY: F. Leo, 'Die staatsrechtlichen Excurse in Tacitus' Annalen', *N.G.G.* 1896, 191–208 = *Ausg. kl. Schr.* II 299–317; P. S. Everts, *De Tacitea historiae conscribendae ratione* (Kerkrade 1926); F. Krohn, *Personendarstellungen bei Tacitus* (Leipzig 1934); C. W. Mendell, 'Dramatic construction in Tacitus' Annals', *Y.Cl.S.* 5 (1935) 3–53; J. Vogt, 'Tacitus und die Unparteilichkeit des Historikers', *Würzburger Studien* 9 (1936) 1–20; I. S. Ryberg, 'Tacitus' art of innuendo', *T.A.Ph.A.* 73 (1942) 383–404; D. M. Pippidi, *Autour de Tibère* (Bucharest 1944); J. Cousin, 'Rhétorique et psychologie chez Tacite, un aspect de la deinosis', *R.E.L.* 29 (1951) 228–47; B. Walker, *The Annals of Tacitus* (Manchester 1952); F. Klingner, 'Tacitus über Augustus und Tiberius', *S.B.A.W.*, Heft 7, 1953 = *Studien* 624–58; E. Koestermann, 'Die Majestätsprozesse unter Tiberius', *Historia* 4 (1955) 72–106; idem, 'Die Feldzüge des Germanicus 14–16 n. Chr.', *Historia* 6 (1956) 429–79; idem, 'Die Mission des Germanicus im Orient', *Historia* 7 (1957) 331–75; S. G. Daitz, 'Tacitus' technique of character portrayal', *A.J.Ph.* 81 (1960) 30–52; M. Fuhrmann, 'Das Vierkaiserjahr bei Tacitus', *Philologus* 104 (1960) 250–78; E. Koestermann, 'Der Eingang der Annalen des Tacitus', *Historia* 10 (1961) 330–55; J. Tresch, *Die Nerobücher in den Annalen des Tacitus* (Heidelberg 1965); D. C. A. Shotter, 'Tacitus, Tiberius and Germanicus', *Historia* 17 (1968) 194–214; D. Timpe, *Der Triumph des Germanicus* (Bonn 1968); K. Wellesley, 'Tacitus as a military historian', in (ed.) T. A. Dorey, *Tacitus* (London 1969) 63–97; S. Borzsák, 'Zum Verständis der Darstellungskunst des Tacitus', *A. Ant. Hung.* 18 (1970) 279–92; D. Flach, *Tacitus in der Tradition der Antiken Geschichtsschreibung* (Göttingen 1973); K. Gilmartin, 'Corbulo's campaigns in the East', *Historia* 22 (1973) 583–626; D. O. Ross, 'The Tacitean Germanicus', *Y.Cl.S.* 23 (1973) 209–27.

(5) LANGUAGE AND STYLE: E. Wölfflin, 'Jahresberichte über Tacitus 1–3', *Philologus*

25 (1867) 92–134, 26 (1867) 92–166, 27 (1868) 113–49, excerpted in *Ausg. Schr.* (Leipzig 1933) 22–102; A. A. Draeger, *Über Syntax und Stil des Tacitus*, 3rd ed. (Leipzig 1882); F. G. Moore, 'Studies in Tacitean ellipsis: descriptive passages', *T.A.Ph.A.* 34 (1903) 5–26; E. Courbaud, *Les procédés d'art de Tacite dans les Histoires* (Paris 1918); R. Ullmann, *La technique des discours dans Salluste, Tite-Live et Tacite* (Oslo 1927); E. Löfstedt, *Syntactica* II (Lund 1933) 276–90; N. Eriksson, *Studien zu den Annalen des Tacitus* (Lund 1934); G. Sörbom, *Variatio sermonis Taciti* (Uppsala 1935); H. Hommel, 'Die Bildkunst des Tacitus', *Würzburger Studien* 9 (1936) 116–48; E. Löfstedt, 'On the style of Tacitus', *J.R.S.* 38 (1948) 1–8; C. O. Brink, 'Justus Lipsius and the text of Tacitus', *J.R.S.* 42 (1952) 32–51; R. H. Martin, 'Variatio and the development of Tacitus' style', *Eranos* 51 (1953) 89–96; F. Klingner, 'Beobachtungen über Sprache und Stil des Tacitus am Anfang des 13 Annalenbuches', *Hermes* 83 (1955) 187–200; K. Seitz, *Studien zur Stilentwicklung und zur Satzstruktur innerhalb der Annalen des Tacitus* (Marburg 1958); A. Kohl, *Der Satznachtrag bei Tacitus* (Würzburg 1960); R. Enghofer, *Der Ablativus absolutus bei Tacitus* (Würzburg 1961); F. Kuntz, *Die Sprache des Tacitus und die Tradition der lateinischen Historikersprache* (Heidelberg 1962); B.-R. Voss, *Der pointierte Stil des Tacitus* (Münster 1963); N. P. Miller, 'Dramatic speech in Tacitus', *A.J.Ph.* 85 (1964) 279–96; R. H. Martin, 'The speech of Curtius Montanus: Tacitus, Histories iv, 42', *J.R.S.* 57 (1967) 109–14; F. R. D. Goodyear, 'Development of language and style in the Annals of Tacitus', *J.R.S.* 58 (1968) 22–31; N. P. Miller, 'Tiberius speaks', *A.J.Ph.* 89 (1968) 1–19; J. N. Adams, 'The language of the later books of Tacitus' Annals', *C.Q.* n.s.22 (1972) 350–73; idem, 'The vocabulary of the speeches in Tacitus' historical works', *B.I.C.S.* 20 (1973) 124–44; idem, 'Were the later books of Tacitus' Annals revised?', *Rh.M.* 117 (1974) 323–33.

LEXICA: W. Boetticher (Berlin 1830); P. Fabia, *Onomasticon Taciteum* (Paris–Lyons 1900); A. Gerber, A. Greef, C. John (Leipzig 1903).

PLINIUS CAECILIUS SECUNDUS, GAIUS

LIFE

b. A.D. 61/62 at Comum. On his father's death was brought up by the elder Pliny, his maternal uncle, and took his name when formally adopted by him in his will. At Rome studied rhetoric under Nicetes Sacerdos and Quintilian; began a long career in the law-courts. Held all the regular magistracies (consul *suffectus* 100), and other administrative posts: *praefectus aerari militaris*, *praefectus aerari Saturni*, *curator alvei Tiberis*. Governor of Bithynia *c.* 111, d. *c.* 112. Sources: Pliny, *Epist. passim*; *CIL* V 5262. See T. Mommsen, *Hermes* 3 (1869) 31–140 = *Gesamm. Schr.* 4 (Berlin 1906) 366ff; W. Otto, *S.B.A.W.* 1919, 10; M. Schuster, in *RE* XXI (1951) 439–45; R. Syme, *Tacitus* (Oxford 1958) 75–85; A. N. Sherwin-White, *The letters of Pliny* (Oxford 1966) 69–82.

WORKS

Two works survive: (1) the *Panegyricus*, P.'s expanded version of his speech of thanks to Trajan on becoming consul in A.D. 100, transmitted along with eleven much later speeches in the same vein (the so-called *Panegyrici Latini*), and (2) a collection of letters in nine books, dating apparently from about A.D. 97 to 108, and pubd in parts by Pliny A.D. 103–9 (in what parts exactly is still disputed). In addition there is a number of private and official letters to and from Trajan, written mainly *c.* 111 when P. was governor of Bithynia, pubd presumably after his death and added as a tenth book to P.'s collection. We hear from P. himself of several speeches which he revised and circulated (see, e.g., 1.8.2, 4.9.23, 5.20.2, 7.30.4, 9.13.1), of a laudatory biography (*Epist.* 3.10), and of verses in various metres. Of these nothing remains, except perhaps for the poem in *Anth. Lat.* 710. Specimens of P.'s versification in *Epist.* 7.4 and 7.9.

BIBLIOGRAPHY

TEXTS AND COMMENTARIES: TEXTS: Complete works: H. Keil (Leipzig 1870); M. Schuster, rev. R. Hanslik (BT, 1958); B. Radice (Loeb, 1969). *Epistulae*: 1–10, E. T. Merrill (Leipzig 1922); 1–9, A.-M. Guillemin (Budé 1927–8); 10, M. Durry (Budé, 1959); 1–10, R. A. B. Mynors (OCT, 1963). *Panegyricus*: E. Baehrens (BT, 1874); W. Baehrens (BT, 1911); M. Durry (Budé, 1959); R. A. B. Mynors (OCT, 1964). COMMENTARIES: *Epistulae* 1–10: A. N. Sherwin-White (Oxford 1966). Bk 6: J. D. Duff (Cambridge 1906). Bk 10: E. G. Hardy (London 1889). SELECTIONS: E. T. Merrill (London 1903); A. N. Sherwin-White (Oxford 1967). *Panegyricus*: M. Durry (Paris 1938).

STUDIES: H. Peter, *Der Brief in der römischen Literatur* (Leipzig 1901); A.-M. Guillemin, *Pline et la vie littéraire de son temps* (Paris 1929); M. Schuster, in *RE* XXI (1951) 439–56; R. T. Bruère, 'Tacitus and Pliny's Panegyricus', *C.Ph.* 49 (1954) 161–79; S. E. Stout, *Scribe and critic at work in Pliny's letters* (Bloomington 1954); J. Niemirska-Pliszczyńska, *De elocutione Pliniana* (Lublin 1955); H. W. Traub, 'Pliny's treatment of history in epistolary form', *T.A.Ph.A.* 86 (1955) 213–32; B. Radice, 'A fresh approach to Pliny's letters', *G.&R.* 9 (1962) 160–8; A. N. Sherwin-White, 'Trajan's replies to Pliny', *J.R.S.* 52 (1962) 114–25; A. D. E. Cameron, 'The fate of Pliny's letters in the late empire', *C.Q.* n.s.15 (1965) 289–98; F. Millar, 'Emperors at work', *J.R.S.* 57 (1967) 9–19; B. Radice, 'Pliny and the Panegyricus', *G.&R.* 15 (1968) 166–72; A. N. Sherwin-White, 'Pliny, the man and his letters', *G.&R.* 16 (1969) 76–90; H.-P. Bütler, *Die geistige Welt des jüngeren Plinius* (Heidelberg 1970); S. MacCormack, 'Latin prose panegyrics', in (ed.) T. A. Dorey, *Silver Latin* II (London 1975) 143–205.

INDEX: X. Jacques and J. van Ooteghem (Namur 1968).

SUETONIUS TRANQUILLUS, GAIUS

LIFE

b. *c.* A.D. 70. Birthplace uncertain. After practising as a lawyer devoted himself to writing. Declined a military tribunate; obtained (though childless) the *ius trium liberorum* from Trajan through Pliny. Appointed secretary under Trajan and Hadrian, but dismissed 121/122 along with Septicius Clarus (dedicatee of *De vita Caes.*). d. later, perhaps much later, than A.D. 122. Sources: Suet. *Cal.* 19.3, *Nero* 57.2, *Otho* 10.1, *Dom.* 12.2, *De gramm. et rhet.* 4.9 (background); Pliny, *Epist.* 1.18 (lawyer), 1.24 possibly a schoolmaster), 3.8 (tribunate), 5.10 (slow to publish), 9.34 (P. asks about public recital of his verses), 10.94–5 (*ius t.l.*); *Hist. Aug. Hadr.* 11.3 (secretary, dismissal); Ioh. Lyd. *De mag.* 2.6 (dedication to Clarus). See E. Marec and H. G. Pflaum, 'Nouvelle inscription sur la carrière de Suétone, l'historien', *Comptes rendus de l'acad. des inscr.* 1952, 76–85, *A.E.* 1953, no. 73; J. A. Crook, 'Suetonius ab epistulis', *P.C.Ph.S.* n.s.4 (1956–7) 18–22; R. Syme, *Tacitus* (Oxford 1958) 778ff.; G. B. Townend, 'The Hippo inscription and the career of Suetonius', *Historia* 10 (1961) 99–109.

WORKS

(1) *De vita Caesarum*: twelve biographies, from Julius Caesar to Domitian, in eight books, complete except for opening chs. of first life. Bk. 1, and possibly others, perhaps pubd 119–22. (2) *De viris illustribus*: numerous short biographies of persons eminent in literature and education, arranged in classes, perhaps (i) poets, (ii) orators, (iii) historians, (iv) philosophers, and (v) grammarians and rhetoricians. We have part of the section *De grammaticis et rhetoribus*, independently transmitted. Some lives from the *De poetis* are transmitted along with the poets themselves. Those of Terence, Horace and Lucan seem clearly Suetonian, and Donatus' life of Virgil contains at least some Suetonian material. Part of the life of the orator Passienus Crispus survives in the scholia on Juv. 4.81, part of the elder Pliny's accompanies his *Natural History*, and Jerome in his chronicle frequently draws on S. (3) Numerous treatises, some in Greek, on a wide range of subjects, such as critical signs, the Roman year, Roman customs, famous courtesans, and terms of abuse. Only occasional fragments remain. For further details see Schanz–Hosius III 58–64.

BIBLIOGRAPHY

TEXTS AND COMMENTARIES: TEXTS: C. L. Roth (BT, 1858). *De vita Caes.*: M. Ihm (BT, ed. mai. 1907, ed. min. 1908). *De gramm. et rhet.*: A. Reifferscheid (Leipzig 1860: also the fragments); A. Brugnoli (BT, 1960). COMMENTARIES: D. C. G. Baumgarten-Crusius (Leipzig 1816–18). *Julius*: H. E. Butler and M. Cary (New York–Oxford 1927). *Augustus*: E. S. Shuckburgh (Cambridge 1896); M. A. Levi

(Florence 1951). *Galba–Domitian*: G. W. Mooney (London 1930). *Vespasian*: A. W. Braithwaite (Oxford 1927). *De gramm. et rhet.*: R. P. Robinson (Paris 1925). *De poetis*: A. Rostagni (Turin 1944).

STUDIES: A. Macé, *Essai sur Suétone* (Paris 1900); F. Leo, *Die griechisch-römische Biographie nach ihrer litterarischen Form* (Leipzig 1901); D. R. Stuart, *Epochs of Greek and Roman biography* (Berkeley 1928); G. Funaioli, in *RE* IVA (1931) 593–641; G. d'Anna, *Le idee letterarie di Suetonio* (Florence 1954); F. della Corte, *Suetonio eques Romanus* (Milan–Varese 1958); G. B. Townend, 'The date of composition of Suetonius' Caesares', *C.Q.* n.s.9 (1959) 285–93; idem, 'The sources of the Greek in Suetonius', *Hermes* 88 (1960) 98–120; C. Questa, *Studi sulle fonti degli 'Annales' di Tacito*, 2nd ed. (Rome 1963) 95–123; W. Steidle, *Sueton und die antike Biographie*, 2nd ed. (Munich 1963); T. F. Carney, 'How Suetonius' lives reflect on Hadrian', *P.A.C.A.* 11 (1968) 7–24; B. Mouchova, *Studie zu Kaiserbiographien Suetons*, *Acta universitatis Carolinae phil. et hist.* 22 (Prague 1968); J. Gugel, 'Caesars Tod', *Gymnasium* 77 (1970) 5–22; K. Bringmann, 'Zur Tiberiusbiographie Suetons', *Rh.M.* 114 (1971) 268–85; S. Döpp, 'Zum Aufbau des Tiberius-Vita Suetons', *Hermes* 100 (1972) 444–60.

INDEX: A. A. Howard and C. N. Jackson (Cambridge, Mass. 1922).

FLORUS, JULIUS or L. ANNAEUS

LIFE

Unknown, unless the same as P. Annius Florus (next entry). The Bambergensis calls him Julius Florus, other MSS L. Annaeus Florus: both names suspect. Internal evidence (*praef.* 8 and 1.5.5–8) suggests *c.* A.D. 140 as earliest time for his writing, and admits a considerably later date. Occasional praise of Spain (e.g. 1.22.38) may indicate connexions with that province.

WORKS

Epitoma de Tito Livio bellorum omnium annorum DCC (so the MSS): this title, ancient but probably not F.'s, ill represents the contents; perhaps *tabella* (*praef.* 3) figured in F.'s title. B, marginally more authoritative than other MSS, divides the work into two books, the rest into four. The two books seem rather long, but this division makes some sense and may be tolerated.

BIBLIOGRAPHY

TEXTS: O. Jahn (BT, 1852); O. Rossbach (BT, 1896); E. S. Forster (Loeb, 1929); E. Malcovati, 2nd ed. (Rome 1972); P. Jal (Budé, 1967).

STUDIES: P. Monceaux, *Les Africains. Étude sur la littérature latine d'Afrique. Les païens* (Paris 1894) 193–209; F. Schmidinger, 'Untersuchungen über Florus', *N.J.Ph.* suppl. 20 (1894) 781–816; O. Hirschfeld, 'Anlage und Abfassungszeit der Epitome des Florus', *Sitzb. Berl.* 29 (1899) 543–54; O. Rossbach, in *RE* VI (1909) 2761–70; E. Norden, *Die Antike Kunstprosa*, 4th ed. II (Leipzig–Berlin 1923) 598–600; S. Lilliedahl, *Florusstudien, Acta Universitatis Lundensis* 24.7 (Lund–Leipzig 1928); R. Zimmermann, 'Zum Geschichtswerk des Florus', *Rh.M.* 79 (1930) 93–101; R. Sieger, 'Der Stil des Historikers Florus', *W.S.* 51 (1934) 94–108; E. Malcovati, 'Studi su Floro', *Athenaeum* 15 (1937) 69–94, 289–307, and 16 (1938) 46–64; A. Nordh, 'Virtus and Fortuna in Florus', *Eranos* 50 (1952) 111–28; A. Garzetti, 'Floro e l'età adrianea', *Athenaeum* 42 (1964) 136–56; R. Häussler, 'Vom Ursprung und Wandel des Lebensaltervergleichs', *Hermes* 92 (1964) 313–41; I. Hahn, 'Prooemium und Disposition der Epitome des Florus', *Eirene* 4 (1965) 21–38; P. Jal, 'Nature et signification politique de l'ouvrage de Florus', *R.E.L.* 43 (1965) 358–83; W. den Boer, *Some minor Roman historians* (Leiden 1972) 1–18.

LEXICON: M. L. Fele (Hildesheim 1975).

FLORUS, P. ANNIUS

LIFE

Poet and rhetorician from Africa who competed in Domitian's *ludi Capitolini* (A.D. 86 or 90 or 94). After some years became a schoolmaster in Spain. Here he places a dialogue in which he is himself a protagonist. Its dramatic date cannot be much before A.D. 100, its composition may be appreciably later. Many identify him with the preceding entry, explaining away discrepancies in nomenclature. He may also be identifiable with the next entry.

WORKS

Dialogue entitled *Vergilius orator an poeta.* Only the first few pages survive.

BIBLIOGRAPHY

Partly as for preceding entry. Add R. Hirzel, *Der Dialog* II (Leipzig 1895) 64–70.

FLORUS, (?) ANNIUS

LIFE

A poet known to Hadrian, as poems interchanged by them (*Hist. Aug. Hadr.* 16.3–4) attest, and probably the Annius Florus whose letters to Hadrian Charisius cites

(66.10 and 157.21 Barwick), and the author of several poems under the name Florus in the *Anthologia Latina*. Charisius' mention of the name Annius supports identification with the writer of the dialogue. The further identification with the writer of the epitome is at best uncertain. To coalesce epitomator, rhetorician, and poet into one provides a tempting solution to many problems, but not a solution readily acceptable, when the nomenclature offered by our MSS is so various. Two men of similar name could have been writing at much the same time.

WORKS

Short poems on various themes, and letters.

BIBLIOGRAPHY

Partly as for last entry but one. Add *Anth. Lat.* 1.1.119–21 and 200–2; J. W. and A. M. Duff, *Minor Latin poets* (Loeb, 1935) 423–35.

MELA, POMPONIUS

LIFE

Dates of birth and death unknown, but was writing during early part of Claudius' principate. From Tingentera in Spain (2.96).

WORKS

Geography, *De chorographia*, in three books. Completed late A.D. 43 or early 44 (3.49 conquest of Britain accomplished but Claudius' triumph still to come): see G. Wissowa, *Hermes* 51 (1916) 89–96. Apparently (1.2, though the passage has been interpreted otherwise), M. planned to write more fully on the same subject, but whether he did so is unknown: see P. Parroni, *R.F.I.C.* 96 (1968) 184–97.

BIBLIOGRAPHY

TEXTS AND COMMENTARY: TEXTS: G. Parthey (Berlin 1867); C. Frick (BT, 1880); G. Ranstrand (Göteborg 1971: with index). COMMENTARY: C. H. Tzschucke (Leipzig 1806–7).

STUDIES: E. H. Bunbury, *A history of ancient geography* II (London 1879) 352–70; H. Oertel, *Über den Sprachgebrauch des Pomponius Mela* (Erlangen 1898); A. Klotz, *Quaestiones Plinianae geographicae* (Berlin 1906); D. Detlefsen, *Die Geographie Afrikas bei Plinius und Mela und ihre Quellen* (Berlin 1908); F. Gisinger, in *RE* XXI (1952) 2360–411.

COLUMELLA, LUCIUS IUNIUS MODERATUS

LIFE

Dates of birth and death unknown, but was writing under Nero and before A.D. 65 (3.3.3, Pliny, *N.H.* 14.49–51); b. in Gades (Cadiz). Moved to Italy at some stage and owned estates in various regions. His work is used by the elder Pliny in his Natural History. He was probably advanced in years when he completed it, but this view rests partly upon a doubtful reading at 12.59.5. See further 1.7.3, 2.10.18, 3.9.2, 8.16.9, 10.185; *CIL* IX 235 (C. a military tribune); W. Becher, *De L. Iuni Moderati Columellae vita et scriptis* (Leipzig 1897).

WORKS

Two works survive: *Res rustica*, in twelve books (bk 10 in verse), and one book *De arboribus*. The *De arboribus* seems to be the second book (see its opening sentence) of a shorter and earlier treatise on agriculture in two or more books, and deals with the same material as books 3–5 of the larger work. Cassiodorus (*Inst.* 1.28.6) mentions sixteen books on agriculture by C. If the number is correctly transmitted, it may well relate to the longer and shorter treatises taken together. But the position is complicated by a reference in our MSS (*Res Rust.* 11, *ad fin.*) to a single book *De cultura vinearum et arborum* addressed to Eprius Marcellus. Interpretation and credibility of this notice are debatable. Perhaps it refers to the *De arboribus* and perhaps the whole shorter treatise was dedicated to Marcellus, as the larger is to Silvinus. C. tells us (11.1.31) of a work he wrote *Adversus astrologos* and (2.21.5–6) of his intention to write on lustrations and other sacrifices.

BIBLIOGRAPHY

TEXTS AND COMMENTARIES: TEXTS: V. Lundström, Å. Josephson, S. Hedberg (Uppsala–Göteborg 1897–1968); H. B. Ash, E. S. Forster, E. H. Heffner (Loeb, 1941–55). Bk 10: J. Häussner (Karlsruhe 1889); J. P. Postgate, in *Corpus poetarum Latinorum* II (London 1905). COMMENTARIES: J. M. Gesner, in *Scriptores rei rusticae veteres Latini* I (Leipzig 1735); J. G. Schneider, in *Scriptores rei rusticae veteres Latini* II (Leipzig 1794).

STUDIES: R. Reitzenstein, *De scriptorum rei rusticae libris deperditis* (Berlin 1884); H. Stadler, *Die Quellen des Plinius im 19. Buche der n.h.* (Munich 1891); E. Weiss, *De Columella et Varrone rerum rusticarum scriptoribus* (Breslau 1911); A. Kappelmacher, in *RE* X (1919) 1054–68; B. Baldwin, 'Columella's sources and how he used them', *Latomus* 22 (1963) 785–91; T. Janson, *Latin prose prefaces, Studia Latina Stockholmiensia* 13 (Stockholm 1964) 83ff.; K. D. White, *Roman farming* (London 1970) *passim*.

INDEX: G. G. Betts and W. D. Ashworth (Uppsala 1971).

PLINIUS SECUNDUS, GAIUS

LIFE

b. at Comum A.D. 23/24; of equestrian rank. Served in Germany under Pomponius Secundus at periods from *c.* 46; commanded cavalry squadron. On return to Italy 57/58 pursued rhetorical and grammatical studies, and active as lawyer at some stage. Procurator in Spain *c.* 73. d. during eruption of Vesuvius A.D. 79. Sources: Pliny, *N.H. passim*; Pliny, *Epist.* 3.5 (works, lifestyle), 6.16 and 20 (death); Suet. *De vir. ill.* p. 92 Reifferscheid; *CIG* III 4536. See K. Ziegler, in *RE* XXI (1951) 271–85; R. Syme, 'Pliny the procurator', *H.S.Ph.* 73 (1969) 201–36.

WORKS

Listed by the younger Pliny (*Epist.* 3.5.3–6), apparently in chronological order and sometimes with indication of date: *De iaculatione equestri*, *De vita Pomponi Secundi* (2 bks), *Bella Germaniae* (20 bks), *Studiosus* (training manual for orators; 3 bks), *Dubius sermo* (grammatical work 'on uncertainties of expression'; 8 bks), *A fine Aufidi Bassi* (continuation of Bassus' history; 31 bks), and *Naturae historiae* or *Naturalis historia* (37 bks). Only the last survives, apart from fragments, but the historical works were much used by later writers, including Tacitus.

BIBLIOGRAPHY

(see H. le Bonniec, *Bibliographie de l'Histoire naturelle de Pline l'Ancien* (Paris 1946))

TEXTS AND COMMENTARIES: TEXTS: J. Sillig (Hamburg–Gotha 1851–5); L. Jan (BT, 1854–65); D. Detlefsen (Berlin 1866–82); C. Mayhoff (BT, 1892–1909); H. Rackham, W. H. S. Jones, D. E. Eichholz (Loeb, 1938–63). *Dubii sermonis reliquiae*: J. W. Beck (BT, 1894). COMMENTARIES: A. Ernout and others (Paris 1947–). Bk 2: D. J. Campbell (Aberdeen 1936). See also K. Jex-Blake and E. Sellers, *The elder Pliny's chapters on the history of art* (London 1896); K. C. Bailey, *The elder Pliny's chapters on chemical subjects* (London 1929–32).

STUDIES: J. Müller, *Der Stil des aelteren Plinius* (Innsbruck 1883); C. F. W. Müller, *Kritische Bemerkungen zu Plinius' Naturalis Historia* (Breslau 1888); F. Münzer, *Beiträge zur Quellenkritik der Naturgeschichte des Plinius* (Berlin 1897); D. Detlefsen, *Untersuchungen über die Zusammensetzung der Naturgeschichte des Plinius* (Berlin 1899); E. Norden, *Die antike Kunstprosa*, 4th ed. (Leipzig–Berlin 1923) I 314–18; W. Kroll, *Die Kosmologie des älteren Plinius* (Breslau 1930); W. Kroll, K. Ziegler, H. Gundel, W. Aly, R. Hanslik, in *RE* XXI (1951) 271–439; J. André, 'Pline l'Ancien botaniste', *R.E.L.* 33 (1955) 297–318; A. Önnerfors, *Pliniana* (Uppsala 1956); A. della Casa, *Il Dubius Sermo di Plinio* (Genova 1969); K. G. Sallmann, *Die Geographie des älteren*

Plinius in ihrem Verhältnis zu Varro (Berlin 1971); T. Köves-Zulauf, 'Die Vorrede der plinianischen Naturgeschichte', *W.S.* 86 (1973) 134–84.

FRONTINUS, SEXTUS IULIUS

LIFE

b. *c.* A.D. 35. Praetor 70, consul *suffectus c.* 74. Legate of Britain *c.* 76–8; subdued Silures. Appointed *curator aquarum* by Nerva *c.* 96–7. Consul again in 98 and 100. d. 103 or 104. Sources: Frontin. *De aquis* 1 (*curator*), *Strat.* 4.3.14; Pliny, *Epist.* 4.8.3 (P. succeeds F. as augur; see Sherwin-White, *ad loc.*), 5.15, 9.19, *Pan.* 61–2 (thrice consul); Tac. *Agr.* 17.2 (in Britain), *Hist.* 4.39 (praetor); Mart. 10.58; Ael. Tact. *praef.*; Veget. *De re mil.* 2.3; *PIR*² I 322. See A. Kappelmacher, *RE* X (1919) 591–5.

WORKS

(1) EXTANT: *Strategemata* (4 bks), written between A.D. 83 and 96, and *De aquis* (1 or 2 bks), *c.* A.D. 98. (2) LOST: Works on surveying (fragments, or adaptations, in C. Thulin, *Corpus agrimensorum Romanorum* I 1 (BT, 1913)), and on the art of war (*Strat. praef.* and Veget. 1.8).

BIBLIOGRAPHY

TEXTS: *Strat.*: G. Gundermann (BT, 1888); G. Bendz, 2nd ed. (Berlin 1978). *De aquis*: F. Buecheler (BT, 1858); F. Krohn (BT, 1922); C. Kunderewicz (BT, 1973). Both works: C. E. Bennett (Loeb, 1925).

STUDIES: G. Bendz, *Die Echtheitsfrage des vierten Buches der Frontinischen Strategemata* (Lund 1938); N. Wood, 'Frontinus as a possible source for Machiavelli's method', *J.H.I.* 28 (1967) 243–8.

INDEX: G. Bendz (Lund 1938).

QUINTILIANUS, MARCUS FABIUS

LIFE

b. *c.* A.D. 35 at Calagurris in Spain. Taught at Rome by the orator Domitius Afer. At some time returned to Spain, and recalled by Galba 68. Active as teacher and advocate for twenty years; first rhetorician to receive public salary. Received *ornamenta consularia* for educating Domitian's two great-nephews. d. probably not before A.D. 95, perhaps years later. Sources: Quint. *Inst.* 1 *praef.* 1 (duration of teaching), 2.12.12 (retirement), 4 *praef.* 2 (tutor to Domitian's heirs), 5.7.7 (Afer; see Pliny, *Epist.*

2.14.9), 6 *praef.* (death of his wife and sons), 6.1.14 (possibly in Rome 57), and *passim*; Mart. 2.90 (tribute); Juv. 7.186–90 (Q.'s wealth); Auson. *Grat. act.* 7.31 (*ornamenta consularia*), *Prof. Burd.* 1.7. (birthplace); Jerome, *Chron. sub* A.D 68 (Galba) and 88 (salary). See Colson (under *Commentaries* below) ix–xx; M. L. Clarke, *G. & R.* n.s. 14 (1967) 24–37.

WORKS

Institutio oratoria (12 bks) alone survives: some details of composition in Q.'s prefatory epistle to his publisher Trypho. Pubd before Domitian's death, and probably not long before, but exact dating impossible. Q. had earlier pubd a treatise *de causis corruptae eloquentiae* (see *Inst.* 6 *praef.* 3 and 8.6.76), and one of his speeches, while versions of others were circulated without his consent (*Inst.* 7.2.24). Two extant collections of declamations are attributed to him. Some of them or some parts of them may be genuine, but there are very good reasons for doubt, particularly about the longer pieces (*declamationes maiores*).

BIBLIOGRAPHY

TEXTS AND COMMENTARIES: TEXTS: G. L. Spalding (Leipzig 1798–1816); C. Halm (BT, 1868–9); L. Radermacher (BT, 1907, 1935, rev. V. Buchheit 1959); M. Winterbottom (OCT, 1970); J. Cousin (Budé, 1975–). COMMENTARIES: Bk 1: F. H. Colson (Cambridge 1924). Bk 3: J. Adamietz (Munich 1966). Bk 10: W. Peterson (Oxford 1891). Bk 12: R. G. Austin (Oxford 1948).

STUDIES: K. Barwick, *Remmius Palaemon und die römische Ars grammatica*, *Philologus* suppl. 15.2 (1922); J. F. d'Alton, *Roman literary theory and criticism* (London 1931); J. Cousin, *Études sur Quintilien* (Paris 1936); W. Kroll, 'Rhetorik', in *RE* suppl. VII (1940) 1039–1138; S. F. Bonner, *Roman declamation* (Liverpool 1949); M. L. Clarke, *Rhetoric at Rome* (London 1953); H. I. Marrou, *A history of education in antiquity* (London 1956); G. Kennedy, 'An estimate of Quintilian', *A.J.Ph.* 83 (1962) 130–46; F. Kuehnert, 'Quintilians Erörterung über den Witz', *Philologus* 106 (1962) 29–59, 305–14; M. Winterbottom, 'Quintilian and the vir bonus', *J.R.S.* 54 (1964) 90–7; G. Kennedy, *Quintilian* (New York 1969); T. Gelzer, 'Quintilians Urteil über Seneca', *M.H.* 27 (1970) 212–23; M. Winterbottom, *Problems in Quintilian*, *B.I.C.S.* suppl. 25 (1970); M. L. Clarke, 'Quintilian on education', in (ed.) T. A. Dorey, *Silver Latin* II (London 1975) 98–118; M. Winterbottom, 'Quintilian and rhetoric', ibid. 79–97.

LEXICON: E. Bonnell (Leipzig 1834).

APPENDIX (declamations ascribed to Q.): TEXTS: *Declamationes maiores*: G. Lehnert (BT, 1905). *Declamationes minores*: C. Ritter (BT, 1884).

FRONTO, MARCUS CORNELIUS

LIFE

b. at Cirta, Numidia, probably *c.* A.D. 100, perhaps earlier. Leading orator in Rome and teacher of Marcus Aurelius and Lucius Verus. Consul *suffectus* 143. d. *c.* 167, perhaps considerably later. Sources: Fronto, *Epist. passim*; Marc. Aur. 1.11; Gell. 2.26, 13.29, 19.8, 10, 13; *Pan. Lat.* 8.14.2; Macr. *Sat.* 5.1.7; *PIR*² C 1364 (Stein). See Haines (Loeb ed.) xxiii–xliii; G. W. Bowersock, *Greek sophists in the Roman empire* (Oxford 1969) 124–6; E. Champlin, 'The chronology of Fronto', *J.R.S.* 64 (1974) 136–57.

WORKS

A collection of letters and essays, partially preserved in a 5th-c. palimpsest (nearly half lost and portions illegible). We have the remains of: letters to and from Marcus Aurelius (9 bks), Lucius Verus (2 bks), and Antoninus Pius (1 bk); letters to friends (2 bks); miscellaneous pieces. Securely datable items range from *c.* A.D. 139 to 166. Details of publication unknown: no indication that F. pubd the material himself; it is disordered and the merest ephemera are included. Of his speeches only fragments and titles survive.

BIBLIOGRAPHY

TEXTS: S. A. Naber (Leipzig 1867); C. R. Haines (Loeb, 1919–20); M. P. J. van den Hout (Leiden 1954). See also L. Pepe, *Marco Aurelio Latino* (Naples 1957).

STUDIES: T. Mommsen, 'Die Chronologie der Briefe Frontos', *Hermes* 8 (1874) 199–216 = *Gesamm. Schr.* IV (Berlin 1906) 469–86; H. Peter, *Der Brief in der römischen Literatur* (Leipzig 1901) 124–35; E. Norden, *Die antike Kunstprosa*, 4th ed. I (Leipzig–Berlin 1923) 362–7; M. D. Brock, *Studies in Fronto and his age* (Cambridge 1911); R. Hanslik, 'Die Anordnung der Briefsammlung Frontos', *C.V.* 1 (1935) 21–47; R. Marache, *La critique littéraire de langue latine et le développement du goût archaïsant au IIe siècle de notre ère* (Rennes 1952); idem, *Mots nouveaux et mots archaïques chez Fronton et Aulu-Gelle* (Paris 1957); S. Jannaccone, 'Appunti per una storia della storiografia retorica nel II secolo', *G.I.F.* 14 (1961) 289–307.

GELLIUS, AULUS

LIFE

b. *c.* A.D. 129, date of death unknown. Only source his own work: *praef.* (in Attica), 7.6.12 (youth in Rome), 12.11.1 (Athens), 12.13.1, 14.2.1 (*iudex* at Rome), 13.13.1 (ref. to beginning of his career), 13.18.2–3 (his tutor Sulpicius Apollinaris), 19.12.1

(hears Herodes Atticus in Athens), and *passim*. On date of birth, see P. K. Marshall, *C.Ph.* 58 (1963) 143–9.

WORKS

Noctes Atticae: learned miscellany in twenty books; beginning of Preface and all bk 8 (except ch. headings) lost. More projected (*praef.* 23–4) but apparently never written. Pubd not before A.D. 165 (*praef.* 1: children ref. to as adults) and perhaps appreciably later; see E. Castorina, *G.I.F.* 3 (1950) 137–45. No other works known.

BIBLIOGRAPHY

TEXTS AND COMMENTARY: TEXTS: M. Hertz (Berlin 1883–5); C. Hosius (BT, 1903); P. K. Marshall (OCT, 1968). Bks 1–10: R. Marache (Budé, 1967–78). COMMENTARY: Bk 1: H. M. Hornsby (Dublin–London 1936).

STUDIES: H. Nettleship, 'The Noctes Atticae of Aulus Gellius', *A.J.Ph.* 4 (1883) 391–415 = *Lectures and essays* (Oxford 1885) 248–76; M. Hertz, *Opuscula Gelliana* (Berlin 1886); C. Knapp, 'Archaism in Aulus Gellius', *Classical studies in honour of H. Drisler* (New York 1894) 126–71; C. Hosius, pref. to his ed., 16–59; idem, in *RE* VII (1912) 992–8; P. Faider, 'A. Gellii Noctium Atticarum praefatio', *M.B.* 31 (1927) 189–216; R. Marache, *La critique littéraire de langue latine et le développement du goût archaïsant au IIe siècle de notre ère* (Rennes 1952); idem, *Mots nouveaux et mots archaïques chez Fronton et Aulu-Gelle* (Paris 1957); S. Jannaccone, 'Cicerone in Gellio', *Ciceroniana* 3–6 (1961–4) 193–8; L. Gamberale, *La traduzione in Gellio* (Rome 1969).

THE LATER PRINCIPATE

GENERAL WORKS

(1) History of late antiquity

Bury, J. B., *History of the later Roman empire from the death of Theodosius I to the death of Justinian* (repr. London 1958).

Jones, A. H. M., *The later Roman empire*, 3 vols. (Oxford 1964; with maps).

Lot, F., *The end of the ancient world and the beginning of the middle ages* (New York 1932).

Mazzarino, S., *The end of the ancient world* (London 1966).

Rémondon, R., *La crise de l'empire romain: de Marc-Aurèle à Anastase* (Paris 1964).

Stein, E., *Histoire du bas-empire I: de l'état romain à l'état byzantin* (Paris 1959).

Walbank, F. W., *The awful revolution: the decline of the Roman empire in the West* (Liverpool 1969).

(2) Culture, religion and art

Entretiens XXIII: Christianisme et formes littéraires de l'antiquité tardive en occident (Fondation Hardt, Geneva 1977).

Bowder, D. *The age of Constantine and Julian* (London 1978).
Brown, P. R. L., *The world of late antiquity* (London 1971).
idem, *Religion and society in the age of St. Augustine* (London 1972).
Courcelle, P., *Late Latin writers and their Greek sources* (Cambridge, Mass. 1969).
Dodds, E. R., *Pagan and Christian in an age of anxiety* (Cambridge 1965).
Geffcken, J., *The last days of Greco-Roman paganism* (Amsterdam 1978).
Glover, T. R., *Life and letters in the fourth century* (Cambridge 1961).
Grabar, A., *The beginnings of Christian art, 200–395* (London 1967).
Marrou, H.-I., *Décadence romaine ou antiquité tardive? IIIe–IVe siècle* (Paris 1977).
Momigliano, A. D. (ed.), *The conflict between paganism and Christianity* (Oxford 1963).
Paschoud, F., *Roma aeterna: études sur le patriotisme romain dans l'occident latin à l'époque des grandes invasions* (Rome–Geneva 1967) 133–55.
Vogt, J., *The decline of Rome* (London 1967).

ANNIANUS, SEPTIMIUS SEVERUS, etc.

TEXT: E. Castorina, *I poetae novelli* (Florence 1941).

HADRIAN

TEXT: *FPL* 136.

NEMESIANUS, MARCUS AURELIUS OLYMPIUS

LIFE AND WORKS

Late 3rd c. A.D., from Carthage. Author of four *Eclogues*, once ascribed to Calpurnius (see M. Haupt, *De carminibus bucolicis Calpurnii et Nemesiani* (Berlin 1854)); *Cynegetica* (written *c.* 284, see vv. 63–5; 325 lines survive); and perhaps of two fragments *De aucupio*. Also wrote on fishing and sailing (*Hist. Aug. Carinus* 11.2) and projected an epic on Carinus and Numerianus (*Cyn.* 63–5).

BIBLIOGRAPHY

TEXTS: P. van der Woestijne (Bruges 1937); C. Giarratano, 3rd ed. (Turin 1943); P. Vopilhac (Budé, 1975).
STUDIES: J. Meurice, *Essai sur les Bucoliques de Némésien* (Liege 1935); W. Schmid, 'Tityrus Christianus', *Rh.M.* 96 (1953) 101–65; B. Luiselli, 'Il proemio del Cynegeticon di Olimpio Nemesiano', *S.I.F.C.* 30 (1958) 73–95.

REPOSIANUS

TEXT: *Anth. Lat.* 253; *PLM* IV 348ff.; U. Zuccarelli (Naples 1972).

STUDIES: J. Tolkiehn, 'Das Gedicht des Reposianus', *Jh.f.Kl.Phil.* 155 (1897) 615ff.; U. Zuccarelli, *Lessico di Reposiano* (Naples 1976).

PENTADIUS

TEXT: *Anth. Lat.* 234–5, 265–8; *PLM* IV 343–6, 358–9.

EPISTULA DIDONIS

TEXT: *Anth. Lat.* 83; *PLM* IV 271–7.

VESPA

TEXTS AND COMMENTARY TEXT: *Anth. Lat.* 199; *PLM* IV 326–30. COMMENTARY: F. Pini (Rome 1958: with tr.).

STUDIES: O. Weinreich, 'Zu Vespas iudicium coci et pistoris', *Hermes* 50 (1915) 315f.; V. Tandoi, 'Il contrasto del cuoco e del fornaio', *A. & R.* n.s.4 (1959) 198–215.

VERBA ACHILLIS IN PARTHENONE

TEXT: *Anth. Lat.* 198; *PLM* IV 322–5.

PERVIGILIUM VENERIS

Poem in ninety-three trochaic verses celebrating spring and the forthcoming festival of Venus; date and author unknown. Location of festival, v. 49: '*iussit Hyblaeis tribunae stare diua floribus*'. Of the three Sicilian cities called Hybla (Steph. Byz. s.v.) the reference is probably to Hybla Gereatis on the slopes of Etna, the modern Paterno, twelve miles east of Catania. Cf. Schilling *ad* v. 49.

BIBLIOGRAPHY

TEXT: R. Schilling (Budé, 1944: with brief notes).

TRANSLATION: J. Lindsay, *Song of a falling world* (London 1948) 64–8.

STUDIES: E. K. Rand, 'Sur le Pervigilium Veneris', *R.E.L.* 12 (1934) 83–95; P. Boyancé, 'Encore le Pervigilium Veneris', *R.E.L.* 28 (1950) 212–35; I. Cazzaniga, 'Saggio critico ed esegetico intorno al Pervigilium Veneris', *S.C.O.* 2 (1953) 47–101.

DISTICHA CATONIS

TEXT: M. Boas (Amsterdam 1952); *PLM* III 205–42.

STUDIES: F. Skutsch, *RE* V (1905) 358–70.

OPTATIANUS PORFYRIUS, PUBLILIUS

LIFE AND WORKS

Early 4th c. A.D., probably an African and to be identified with the *Praefectus urbi* in 329 and 333. Author of a collection of poems in acrostic and other highly contrived forms. Nos. 1–20 form part of a panegyric sent to Constantine 325/326. Sources: Optatianus 2.31; Jerome, *Chron.* A.D. 328; letter of Constantine quoted in prose preface to O.'s poems. Cf. *PLRE* I 649.

TEXTS AND COMMENTARY: TEXTS: L. Müller (BT, 1877); E. Kluge (BT, 1926). COMMENTARY: G. Polara, 2 vols. (Turin 1973).

TIBERIANUS

LIFE

Praetorian Prefect in Gaul A.D. 336–7 (Jerome, *Chron.* A.D. 335); earlier appointments in Africa and Spain (*Cod. Theod.* 3.5.6, 12.5.1; *Cod. Iust.* 6.1.6).

WORKS

Twenty trochaic tetrameters catalectic (*Amnis ibat*); twenty-eight hexameters on the evils of gold (attributed to T. by Serv. *ad Aen.* 6.136); other fragments preserved by Serv. *ad Aen.* 6.532, Fulg. *Myth.* 3.7 and *Expos. serm.* s.v. *sudum.*

BIBLIOGRAPHY

TEXT: *PLM* III 263–9.

TRANSLATION: J. Lindsay, *Song of a falling world* (London 1948) 61–4.

STUDIES: H. Lewy, 'A Latin hymn to the creator ascribed to Plato', *H.Th.R.* 31 (1946) 243–88; E. R. Curtius, *European literature and the Latin middle ages*, tr. W. R. Trask (London 1953) 196–200.

[LACTANTIUS], DE AVE PHOENICE

TEXT: *PLM* III 247–62; *Anth. Lat.* 731.

IUVENCUS, GAIUS VETTIUS AQUILINUS

LIFE AND WORKS

Spanish priest, fl. under Constantine. *Evangeliorum libri IV*: hexameter narrative of the gospel story. Sources: Jerome, *Chron.* A.D. 328, *De vir. ill.* 84; Juvencus 4.805.

BIBLIOGRAPHY

TEXT: J. Huemer, *CSEL* XXIV (Vienna 1891).

STUDIES: C. Wegman, 'Zu Iuvencus', *Beiträge zur Geschichte der christlich-lateinischen Poesie* (Munich 1926) 21–8; U. Moricca, *Studi di letteratura latina cristiana* II.2 (Turin 1928) 831ff.; H. H. Kievits, *Ad Iuvenci evangeliorum librum primum commentarius exegeticus* (Groningen 1940); J. de Wit, *Ad Iuvenci evangeliorum librum secundum commentarius exegeticus* (Groningen 1947); N. Hannson, *Textkritische zu Iuvencus, mit vollständigem Index verborum* (Lund 1950); R. Herzog, *Die Bibelepik der lateinischen Spätantike* I (Munich 1972) esp. 52–98.

AVIENIUS, POSTUMIUS RUFIUS FESTUS

LIFE

4th c. A.D. from Volsinii in Etruria.

WORKS

Descriptio orbis terrae: geography in hexameters based on Greek original by Dionysius Periegetes. *Ora maritima*: description in iambics of western and southern coasts of Europe (see 51ff.), written after *Descriptio* (*Ora mar.* 71); section on coast from Marseilles to Cadiz alone survives. *Aratea*, *Phaenomena* and *Prognostica*: expanded hexameter translations of Aratus. Sources: *CIL* VI 537 (= *ILS* 2944); *IG* III 635; inscription from Bulla Regia (*PLRE* I 336); Jerome, *In ep. ad Tit.* 1.12; Serv. *ad Aen.* 10.272 and 388 (poem on Virgilian legends and iambic epitome of Livy, possibly by Avianus).

BIBLIOGRAPHY

TEXTS AND COMMENTARIES: TEXTS: A. Holder (Innsbruck 1887). *Descriptio*: P. van de Woestijne (Bruges 1961). COMMENTARIES: *Ora maritima*: A. Schulten (Barcelona–Berlin 1922); A. Berthelot (Paris 1934).

STUDIES: J. F. Matthews, 'Continuity in a Roman family: the Festi of Volsinii', *Historia* 16 (1967) 484–509; A. Cameron, 'Macrobius, Avienus and Avianus', *C.Q.* n.s. 17 (1967) 385–99.

AUSONIUS, DECIMUS MAGNUS

LIFE

b. in Bordeaux A.D. 310. Taught there for thirty years, then summoned by Valentinian to be tutor to Gratian; joined them in campaigns in Germany 368–9. Praetorian Prefect in Gaul 378 and consul 379. On Gratian's murder in 383 retired to Bordeaux and d. 393/394. Sources: Auson. *praef.*; Symm. *Epist.* 1.13–43, 1.20, 22, 23; Auson. *Grat. act.* 2.11, 8.40; Auson. *Epist.* 27.90ff., 31.

WORKS

Following are likely dates of composition for those of A.'s works whose chronology can be established; few if any of them are certain. (Page refs. to Peiper's ed.) *c.* 335: *Epistula ad patrem de suscepto filio* (p. 255). 367–371: *Versus Paschales* (p. 17). 368: *Cento nuptialis* (p. 206). 369: *Bissula* poems (p. 114). 370–371: *Mosella* (p. 118), *Epist.* 4, 6, 7 (p. 232). 374: *Epist.* 12 (p. 238). 378–379: *Epicedion in patrem* (p. 21), *Precationes* (p. 24). 379: *Gratiarum actio* (p. 353), *Epist.* 11 (p. 236), *De herediolo* (p. 16), *Ordo urbium nobilium* (? 1st ed.; p. 144). 380: *Caesares* (p. 183), *Epist.* 2 (p. 222). 379–383: *Parentalia* (p. 28), *Epist.* 23, 25, 26 (p. 268). 383: *Technopaegnion* (p. 155). 380–389: *Commemoratio professorum Burdigalensium* (p. 48). 388–390: *Ordo urbium nobilium* (p. 144). 389–390: *Epitaphia* (p. 72). 390: *Ludus septem sapientium* (p. 169). Arguments on dating of A.'s poems are most clearly set out in Pastorino's ed., intr. 70–105. Cf. *PLRE* I 140–1.

BIBLIOGRAPHY

TEXTS AND COMMENTARIES: TEXTS: K. Schenkl (Berlin 1883); R. Peiper (BT, 1886); H. G. Evelyn White (Loeb, 1919); A. Pastorino (Turin 1971); S. Prete (BT, 1978). COMMENTARIES: *Mosella*: C. Hosius, 3rd ed. (Marburg 1926); W. John (Trier 1932); E. H. Blakeney (London 1933); A. Marsili (Turin 1957).

TRANSLATION: J. Lindsay, *Song of a falling world* (London 1948) 70–82 (select poems).

STUDIES: R. Pichon, *Les derniers écrivains profanes* (Paris 1906) 151–216, 297–319; A. Delachaux, *La latinité d'Ausone* (Neuchâtel 1909); S. Dill, *Roman society in the last century of the western empire*, 2nd ed. (London 1910) 167–86; J. M. Byrne, *Prolegomena to an edition of the works of Decimus Magnus Ausonius* (New York 1916); M. J. Pattist, *Ausonius als Christ* (Amsterdam 1925); Z. A. A. Jouai, *De magistraat Ausonius* (Nijmegen 1938); N. K. Chadwick, *Poetry and letters in early Christian Gaul* (London 1955) 47–62; S. Prete, *Ricerche sulla storia del testo di Ausonio* (Rome 1960); M. J. Hopkins, 'Social mobility in the later Roman empire. The evidence of Ausonius', *C.Q.* n.s.11 (1961) 239–49; A. Pastorino, 'A proposito della tradizione del testo di Ausonio', *Maia* 14 (1962) 41–68, 212–43; D. Korzeniewski, 'Aufbau und Struktur der Mosella des Ausonius', *Rh.M.* 106 (1963) 80–95; P. Courcelle, *Histoire littéraire des grandes invasions germaniques*, 3rd ed. (Paris 1964) 293–302.

EPIGRAMMATA BOBBIENSIA

On Naucellius, see Symm. *Epist.* 3.10–16; *Epigr. Bobb.* 2–4, 7; *PLRE* I 617–18.

TEXTS: F. Munari (Rome 1955); W. Speyer (BT, 1963).

STUDIES: W. Speyer, *Naucellius und sein Kreis* (Munich 1959), reviewed by W. Schmid, *Gnomon* 32 (1960) 340–60; S. Mariotti, *RE* suppl. IX (1962) 37–64.

CLAUDIANUS, CLAUDIUS

LIFE

b. *c.* A.D. 370 in Alexandria. Came to Rome *c.* 394 and became court poet under Honorius and his regent Stilicho. After moving to Milan (where he obtained senatorial status), returned to Rome in 400 and was honoured with a statue for his panegyric on Stilicho's consulate; in the same year married a noble African through influence of Stilicho's wife Serena. Probably d. in Rome 404. Sources: *CIL* VI 1710 (= *ILS* 2949) (honours); Suda s.v. Κλαυδιανὸς Ἀλεξανδρεύς; Claud. *Carm.* 39.20 (native of Alexandria), 42.14 (arrival in Rome); August. *C.D.* 5.26, Oros. 7.35 (religion).

WORKS

1: *In consulatum Olybrii et Probini* (395). 2–5: *In Rufinum* (395). 6–7: *De III consulatu Honorii Augusti* (396). 8: *De IV consulatu Honorii Augusti* (398). 9–10: *De nuptiis Honorii et Mariae* (398). 11–14: *Fescennina* (398). 15: *De bello Gildonico* (398). 16–17: *De consulatu Manlii Theodori* (399). 18–20: *In Eutropium* (399–400). 21–4: *De consulatu Stilichonis* (399–400). 25–6: *De bello Pollentino* (402). 27–8: *De VI consulatu*

Honorii Augusti (404). 29: *Laus Serenae* (?404). Unfinished epic *De raptu Proserpinae* and remaining poems not datable with certainty.

BIBLIOGRAPHY

TEXTS AND COMMENTARIES: TEXTS: T. Birt (Berlin 1892); J. Koch (BT, 1893); M. Platnauer (Loeb, 1922), COMMENTARIES: *De raptu Proserpinae*: J. B. Hall (Cambridge 1969). *In Rufinum*: H. L. Levy (Detroit 1971). *De IV consulatu Honorii*: P. Fargues (Aix-en-Provence 1936). *De nuptiis Honorii et Mariae*: U. Frings (Meisenheim am Glan 1975). *De bello Gildonico*: M. E. Olechowska (Leiden 1978). *De consulatu Manlii Theodori*: W. Simon (Berlin 1975). *In Eutropium*: P. Fargues (Paris 1933). *De bello Pallentino*: H. Schroff (Berlin 1927). *De VI consulatu Honorii*: K. A. Müller (Berlin 1938).

TRANSLATION: J. Lindsay, *Song of a falling world* (London 1948) 135–60 (selections).

STUDIES: P. Fargues, *Claudien: études sur sa poésie et son temps* (Paris 1933); T. Nissen, 'Historisches Epos und Panegyrikus in der Spätantike', *Hermes* 75 (1940) 298–325; N. Martinelli, 'Saggio sui carmi greci di Claudiano', *Miscellanea Galbiati II* (Rome 1957) 47–76; D. Romano, *Claudiano* (Palermo 1958); F. Paschoud, *Roma aeterna: études sur le patriotisme romain dans l'occident latin à l'époque des grandes invasions* (Rome–Geneva 1967) 133–55; A. Gualandri, *Aspetti della tecnica compositiva in Claudiano* (Milan 1969); P. G. Christiansen, *The use of images by Claudius Claudianus* (The Hague 1969); A. Cameron, *Claudian. Poetry and propaganda at the court of Honorius* (Oxford 1970); U. Keudel, *Poetische Vorläufer und Vorbilder in Claudians De consulatu Stilichonis* (Göttingen 1970); A. Cameron, 'Claudian', in (ed.) J. W. Binns, *Latin literature of the fourth century* (London 1974) 134–59.

PRUDENTIUS CLEMENS, AURELIUS

LIFE

b. A.D. 348 in Hispania Tarraconensis. Gave up a successful public career (provincial governorship, high office under Theodosius) to devote himself to writing Christian poetry. Sources: Prud. *praef.*; Gennadius, *De vir. ill.* 13.

WORKS

(1) IN LYRIC METRES: *Cathemerinon*: twelve hymns. *Peristephanon*: fourteen poems in praise of Christian martyrs. (2) IN HEXAMETERS: *Apotheosis*: on the doctrine of the Trinity. *Hamartigeneia*: on the origin of sin. *Psychomachia*: allegory on the Christian

virtues and pagan vices. *Contra Symmachum*: polemic against paganism in two books. *Dittochaeon*: on scriptural subjects from both testaments. Pubd together in 404 (Prud. *praef.* 1). Cf. *praef.* 34–42 (list of works, possibly chronological) and *PLRE* I 214.

BIBLIOGRAPHY

TEXTS AND COMMENTARY: TEXTS: J. Bergman, *CSEL* LXI (Vienna 1926); M. Lavarenne (Budé, 1943–51); H. J. Thomson (Loeb, 1949–53).; M. P. Cunningham, *CC* CXXVI (Turnhout 1966). COMMENTARY: *Cathemerinon* 1, 2, 5 and 6: M. M. Hijmans-van Assendelft (Groningen 1976).

TRANSLATION: J. Lindsay, *Song of a falling world* (London 1948) 96–106 (select poems).

STUDIES: I. Rodriguez-Herrera, *Poeta Christianus: Prudentius' Auffassung vom Wesen und von der Aufgabe des christlichen Dichters* (Speyer 1936); B. Peebles, *The poet Prudentius* (New York 1951); M. Lavarenne, *Études sur la langue du poète Prudence* (Paris 1953); I. Lana, *Due capitoli Prudenziani* (Rome 1962); C. Gnilka, *Studien zur Psychomachie des Prudentius* (Wiesbaden 1963); K. Thraede, *Studien zur Sprache und Stil des Prudentius* (Göttingen 1965); R. Herzog, *Die allegorische Dichtkunst des Prudentius* (Munich 1966); C. Witke, *Numen litterarum: the old and new in Latin poetry from Constantine to Gregory the Great* (Leiden–Cologne 1971) 102–44; M. Smith, *Prudentius' Psychomachia: a reexamination* (Princeton 1976).

RUTILIUS CLAUDIUS NAMATIANUS

LIFE AND WORKS

b. in Gaul late 4th c. A.D.; his father a distinguished public figure. *Magister officiorum* and *Praefectus urbi c.* 412 and 414. The surviving part (1, except beginning, to 2.65) of his elegiac poem *De reditu suo* describes his journey back to Gaul in 417 as far as Luna on the bay of La Spezia. Date of death unknown. Sources: Rutilius 1.20 (birthplace); 1.575ff. (father); 1.157 and 563 (offices); 1.167, 417, 466, 493, 542 (friends); 1.135–6 (date of poem; interpretations vary).

BIBLIOGRAPHY

TEXTS AND COMMENTARIES: TEXTS: J. Vessereau and F. Préchac (Budé, 1933; 2nd ed. 1961); P. van de Woestijne (Antwerp 1936). COMMENTARIES: J. Vessereau (Paris 1904); R. Helm (Heidelberg 1933); E. Castorina (Florence 1967), reviewed by E. J. Kenney, *C.R.* n.s.18 (1968) 238–9 and P. F. Hovingh, *Mnemosyne* 23 (1970) 324–5; E. Doblhofer, vol. 1 (Heidelberg 1972: bibliography and tr.).

STUDIES: A. Giannotti, *La metrica di Rutilio Namaziano* (Udine 1940); I. Lana, *Rutilio Namaziano* (Turin 1961); J. Carcopino, *Rencontres de l'histoire et de la littérature romaine* (Paris 1963) 233–70.

PAULINUS, MEROPIUS PONTIUS

LIFE

b. *c.* A.D. 355 at Bordeaux; pupil of Ausonius. After embarking on a public career, was baptized *c.* 390 and later settled in Nola, where he became bishop *c.* 410 and d. 431. Sources: Gennadius, *De vir. ill.* 48; Auson. *Epist.* 19–25; August. *Epist.* 34; Ambrose, *Epist.* 58.3; Paulinus, *Epist.* 1.10 (ordained priest at Barcelona 25 Dec. 394); ibid. 5 (settled at Nola 395); Uranii presbyteri *Ep. ad Pacatum* 12 (death). Cf. *PLRE* I 681–3.

WORKS

Thirty-six poems (mostly in hexameters) and fifty-one letters. On dating see Fabre (1948, under *Studies* below).

BIBLIOGRAPHY

TEXTS: W. Hartel, *CSEL* XXIX, XXX (Vienna 1894).

TRANSLATIONS: *Letters*: P. G. Walsh, 2. vols. (Westminster, Maryland 1967). Select poems: J. Lindsay, *Song of a falling world* (London 1948) 93–6.

STUDIES: R. Goldschmidt, *Paulinus' churches at Nola* (Amsterdam 1940); P. Fabre, *Essai sur la chronologie de l'oeuvre de Saint Paulin de Nole* (Paris 1948); N. K. Chadwick, *Poetry and letters in early Christian Gaul* (London 1955) 63–88; W. Meany, *The humanism of St. Paulinus of Nola* (Freiburg-im-Breisgau 1956); C. Pietri, *Saint Paulin de Nole* (Namur 1964); S. Prete, *S. Paolino di Nola e l'umanesimo cristiano* (Bologna 1964); J. Bouma, *Het Epithalamium van Paulinus van Nola* (Assen 1968); W. H. C. Frend, 'Paulinus of Nola and the last century of the western empire', *J.R.S.* 60 (1969) 1–11; R. P. H. Green, *The poetry of Paulinus of Nola: a study of his Latinity* (Brussels 1971); A. Esposito, *Studio sull' Epistolario di S. Paolino di Nola* (Naples 1971); C. Witke, *Numen litterarum: the old and the new in Latin poetry from Constantine to Gregory the Great* (Leiden 1971) 75–101; W. H. C. Frend, 'The two worlds of Paulinus of Nola', in (ed.) J. W. Binns, *Latin literature of the fourth century* (London 1974) 100–33; W. Erdt, *Christentum und heidnisch-antike Bildung bei Paulin von Nola* (Meisenheim am Glan 1976).

AVIANUS

Dates unknown, except that he probably dedicated his forty-two fables (see *praef.*) to Macrobius (*fl. c.* A.D. 410); see Cameron below. Possible author of a lost poem on Virgilian legends and an iambic epitome of Livy (Serv. *ad Aen.* 10.272 and 388).

BIBLIOGRAPHY

TEXT AND COMMENTARY: TEXT: A. Guaglianone (Paravia, 1958). COMMENTARY: R. Ellis (Oxford 1887).

STUDIES: L. Hervieux, *Les fabulistes latins* I (Paris 1894) 1–48; A. Cameron, 'Macrobius, Avienus and Avianus', *C.Q.* n.s.17 (1967) 385–99.

MEROBAUDES, FLAVIUS

LIFE

Spanish rhetorician, early 5th c. A.D. Court poet under Valentinian III and Aetius at Ravenna; in 435 honoured with a statue recording his merits as general and poet; see *CIL* VI 1724 (= *ILS* I 2950).

WORKS

Parts of prose and verse panegyrics on Aetius' consulates in 437 and 446; birthday-poem in hendecasyllables addressed to Aetius' son, modelled on Stat. *Silv.* 2.7; fragments of other court poems; thirty hexameters in praise of Christ.

BIBLIOGRAPHY

TEXT AND COMMENTARY: TEXT: F. Vollmer (Berlin 1905). COMMENTARY: F. M. Clover (Philadelphia 1971: with tr. and reprint of Vollmer's text).

SIDONIUS, GAIUS SOLLIUS APOLLINARIS

LIFE

b. in Lyons *c.* A.D. 431, of distinguished family. Delivered verse panegyrics to emperors Avitus (whose daughter he had married 451), Majorian and Anthemius (*Carm.* 7, 5 and 2); appointed *Praefectus urbi* by the latter 468. Consecrated bishop of Auvergne 471 and organized resistance to the Visigoths. Briefly imprisoned by Euric 475, then resumed his bishopric and d. 486. Sources: Sidonius, *Epist.* 1.5, 1.8, 4.25, *Carm.* 13.23

(birthplace); *Epist.* 5.16, 3.12, 5.9, 8.6 (family); *Epist.* 5.16 (marriage); *Epist.* 4.12, 5.11 (children); *Carm.* 8.8, 9.16 (statue in forum); *Epist.* 1.9 (Praefectus); *Epist.* 3.1, 6.1 (bishop); *Epist.* 8.9, 9.3 (prisoner of Euric); *Epist.* 5.9, 8.6, 9.16 (old age); Gennadius, *De vir ill.* 92.

WORKS

Carmina: twenty-four poems, including panegyrics, epithalamia and epistles, in various metres; pubd 469. *Epistulae*: nine books of letters dating from 455–60 to 482; dedicated to Constantius, priest of Lyons (*Epist.* 1.1, 7.18).

BIBLIOGRAPHY

TEXTS: C. Luetjohann (Berlin 1887); P. Mohr (BT, 1895); W. B. Anderson (Loeb, 1936–65); A. Loyen (Budé, 1960–70).

STUDIES: C. E. Stevens, *Sidonius Apollinaris and his age* (Oxford 1933); H. Rutherford, *Sidonius Apollinaris. Études d'une figure gallo-romaine du Ve siècle* (Clermont-Ferrand 1938); A. Loyen, *Recherches historiques sur les Panégyriques de Sidoine Apollinaire* (Paris 1942); idem, *Sidoine Apollinaire et l'esprit précieux en Gaule aux derniers jours de l'empire* (Paris 1943); idem, 'Sidoine Apollinaire et les derniers éclats de la culture classique dans la Gaule occupée par les Goths', *Settimane di studio del Centro Italiano di studi sull'alto Medioevo* 3 (1955) 265–84; K. F. Stroheker, *Der senatorische Adel im spätantiken Gallien* (Tübingen 1948); N. K. Chadwick, *Poetry and letters in early Christian Gaul* (Cambridge 1955) 296–327; P. Courcelle, *Histoire littéraire des grandes invasions germaniques*, 3rd ed. (Paris 1964) 166–80, 235–9; idem, *Late Latin writers and their Greek sources* (Harvard 1969) 251–62.

PAULINUS OF PELLA

LIFE

b. A.D. 376 at Pella in Macedonia. Grandson of Ausonius and educated by him in Bordeaux. After Gothic invasions of Bordeaux and Bazas, compromised with the Alans and held office under Attalus in 410. Lived near Marseilles for many years, and later returned to Bordeaux. Sources: *Eucharisticon, passim.*

BIBLIOGRAPHY

TEXTS: W. Brandes (Vienna 1888); H. G. Evelyn White, *Ausonius*, vol. II (Loeb, 1919); C. Moussy (Paris 1974); P. Courcelle, 'Un nouveau poème de Paulin de Pella', *V. Chr.* 1 (1947) 101–13.

TRANSLATION: J. Lindsay, *Song of a falling world* (London 1948) 190–9.

HISTORIA AUGUSTA

Collection of lives of emperors and pretenders from Hadrian to Numerian; lives of Nerva and Trajan probably lost. Addressed to Diocletian, Constantine and other contemporaries, and purportedly written from before 305 till after 324. Attributed to six otherwise unknown authors. On date and purpose see excursus below. Sources: *Avid. Cass.* 3.3, *Marcus Aurelius* 19.21, *L. Verus* 11.4, *Macrinus* 15.4, *Aelius* 1.1, *Severus* 20.4, *Pescennius Niger* 9.1 (dedications to Diocletian); *Geta* 1.1, *Heliogabalus* 2.4, *Alexander Severus* 65.1, *Claudius* 4.2, *Maximinus* 1.1, *Gordiani* 34.6 (dedications to Constantine); *Proculus* 12.6, *Saturninus* 11.4, *Aurelian* 10.1 (methods); *Capitolinus et Balbinus* 4.5, *Triginta tyranni* 11.6 (aims); *Avidius Cassius* 9.5, *Hadrian* 12.4, *Pertinax* 15.8 (Marius Maximus); *Clodius* 12.14 (Herodian); *Alexander Severus* 49.3, *Gordiani* 2.1 (Dexippus).

EXCURSUS ON THE NATURE AND DATE OF THE HISTORIA AUGUSTA

A certain disquiet regarding the obvious errors and inconsistencies of the *Hist. Aug.* was general in nineteenth-century scholarship, but there was no systematic attempt either to diagnose the peculiar features of these texts or to put forward a hypothesis to explain them. It was as a result of his work as editor of volume II of the *Prosopographia Imperii Romani* that Dessau in 1889 published a paper in which he mustered and analysed these errors and inconsistencies, and concluded that the work was a forgery, written by a single hand in the reign of Theodosius, drawing partly on the historical epitomes of Aurelius Victor and Eutropius, and containing veiled references to persons and events of the late fourth century.[1] The authors to whom the lives were attributed were creatures of the author's imagination. Historians who perforce made use of the *Hist. Aug.* were disconcerted to find the branch upon which they were sitting suddenly sawn off, and tried to save their sources from Dessau's destructive critique. This they could only do by supposing that texts of the Diocletianic or Constantinian periods had been worked over or edited by a later writer or writers. This was the view of Mommsen, who postulated a single editor in the Theodosian age.[2] The problem now became one of distinguishing original text and interpolations, a type of problem with which Mommsen's study of Roman law had made him familiar. Other scholars put forward similar hypotheses, sometimes involving more than one editor or reviser. This approach to the problem was pushed to its limit by von Domaszewski,[3] who postulated a series of editors who worked over the original text between the fourth and sixth centuries, 'bringing it up to date', rather as a standard legal text-book or Mrs Beeton's

[1] H. Dessau, 'Über Zeit und Persönlichkeit der Scriptores Historiae Augustae', *Hermes* 24 (1889) 337–92.

[2] T. Mommsen, *Gesammelte Schriften* VII (Berlin 1909) 302–62.

[3] A. von Domaszewski, *S.H.A.W.* 7 (1916) 7, 15; 8 (1917) 1; 9 (1918) 6; 11 (1920) 6.

Cookery Book is regularly revised and re-edited. The difficulty, however, is to see why anyone should have wanted to revise such a collection of imperial biographies once, let alone many times over the course of two centuries. Von Domaszewski's position was almost a *reductio ad absurdum* of the whole concept of an original text subsequently revised. For a time some scholars, of whom the most distinguished was Baynes, argued that the *Hist. Aug.* was indeed a forgery, but that it should be dated in 360–2, when it was allegedly written as propaganda for the emperor Julian.[1] This theory has now been generally abandoned. The alleged allusions to items of Julian's policy are not at all clear. Recently Momigliano[2] has re-examined the whole problem and come to the tentative conclusion that Dessau's original charges are not proven, and that the *Hist. Aug.* may be just what it purports to be. His very cautious fundamentalist position has not inspired much enthusiasm, and most scholars today adhere to some variant of Dessau's hypothesis. Among these may be numbered Hartke,[3] Chastagnol,[4] Straub,[5] and Mazzarino.[6] All these seek some public or political motivation for the forgery. Syme[7] has recently argued with great cogency that the work may rather be inspired by the delight in mystification and invention for its own sake, a theory which would bring the *Hist. Aug.* closer to such romantic works of history as the pseudonymous accounts of the Trojan war or the Alexander Romance. The controversy continues.[8]

BIBLIOGRAPHY

TEXT: E. Hohl, suppl. C. Seyfarth and I. Samberger (BT, 1965).

STUDIES: Works cited in the footnotes to the excursus and the following: W. Hartke, *Geschichte und Politik im spätantiken Rom. Untersuchungen über die Scriptores Historiae Augustae* (Leipzig 1940); H. Stern, *Date et destinataire de l'Histoire Auguste* (Paris 1953); *Bonner Historia-Augusta Colloquium* 1–4 (1964–70); E. K. Merten, *Zwei Herrscherfeste in der Historia Augusta* (Bonn 1968); R. Syme, *Ammianus and the Historia Augusta* (Oxford 1968); F. Kolb, *Literarische Beziehungen zwischen Cassius Dio, Herodian und der Historia Augusta* (Bonn 1972); K. P. Johne, *Kaiserbiographie und Senatsaristokratie* (Berlin 1976: good summary of history of the problem 11–46); T. D. Barnes, *The sources of the Historia Augusta* (Brussels 1978).

[1] N. H. Baynes, *The Historia Augusta. Its date and purpose* (Oxford 1926).

[2] A. Momigliano, 'An unsolved problem of historical forgery', *Journal of the Warburg and Courtauld Institutes* 17 (1954) 22–46 = *Studies in historiography* (London 1966) 143–80.

[3] W. Hartke, *Römische Kinderkaiser* (Berlin 1951).

[4] A. Chastagnol, *Recherches sur l'Histoire Auguste* (Bonn 1970).

[5] J. Straub, *Heidnische Geschichtsapologetik in der christlichen Spätantike* (Bonn 1963).

[6] S. Mazzarino, *Il pensiero storico classico* II (Bari 1966) 2 216–47.

[7] R. Syme, *Emperors and biography. Studies in the Historia Augusta* (Oxford 1971).

[8] Most recent survey of the literature by K. P. Johne, *Kaiser-biographie und Senatsaristokratie* (Berlin 1976) 11–46.

LATIN ALEXANDER ROMANCE

TEXTS: B. Kübler, *Iuli Valeri Alexandri Polemi Res Gestae Alexandri Macedonis* (Leipzig 1888); C. Müller, *Itinerarium Alexandri*, in F. Dübner, *Arriani opera* (Paris 1846); F. Pfister, *Der Alexanderroman des Archipresbyters Leo* (Heidelberg 1913).

DICTYS CRETENSIS

Origin and date of work: Dictys, *Epistula*.
TEXT: W. Eisenhut (BT, 1958).

DARES PHRYGIUS

TEXT: J. Meister (BT, 1873).

AUGUSTINUS, AURELIUS (see also p. 925)

WORKS

Confessions: thirteen books, written *c.* A.D. 397. See August. *Retract.* 2.32, *Epist.* 231.6.

BIBLIOGRAPHY

TEXT: M. Skutella, 2nd ed. by H. Juergens and W. Schaub (Stuttgart 1969).

TRANSLATION: F. J. Sheed (London–New York 1943).

STUDIES: E. R. Dodds, 'Augustine's Confessions: a study of spiritual maladjustment', *Hibbert Journal* 26 (1927–8) 459–73; P. Courcelle, *Recherches sur les Confessions de S. Augustin* (Paris 1950); idem, *Les Confessions de S. Augustin dans la tradition littéraire: antécédents et postérité* (Paris 1963); C. Mohrmann, 'S. Augustin écrivain', *Recherches augustiniennes* 1 (1958) 43–66; H.-I. Marrou, *S. Augustin et la fin de la culture antique*, 4th ed. (Paris 1958); M. Pellegrino, *Les Confessions de S. Augustin* (Paris 1960); R. J. O'Connell, 'The riddle of Augustine's Confessions: a Plotinian key', *International Philosophical Quarterly* 4 (1964) 327–72; P. L. R. Brown, *Augustine of Hippo* (Oxford 1967) 158–81.

IULIUS OBSEQUENS

TEXT: O. Rossbach, *T. Livi Periochae* (BT, 1910).

IUSTINUS, MARCUS IUNIANUS

Author (possibly 3rd c. A.D.) of an epitome of Pompeius Trogus' *Historiae Philippicae*; see *praef.*

TEXT: O. Seel (BT, 1972); idem, *Pompei Trogi fragmenta* (BT, 1956).

STUDIES: L. Castiglione, *Studi intorno alle Storie Filippiche di Giustino* (Naples 1925); O. Seel, *Die Praefatio des Pompeius Trogus* (Erlangen 1955).

ENMANN'S KAISERGESCHICHTE

STUDIES: H. Enmann, 'Eine verlorene Geschichte der römischen Kaiser und das Buch De viris illustribus urbis Romae', *Philologus* suppl. 4 (1884) 337–501; R. Syme, *Ammianus and the Historia Augusta* (Oxford 1968) 106ff.; idem, *Emperors and biography* (Oxford 1971) *passim*; W. den Boer, *Some minor Roman historians* (Leiden 1972) 21.

AURELIUS VICTOR, SEXTUS; ORIGO GENTIS ROMANAE; DE VIRIS ILLUSTRIBUS

LIFE OF AURELIUS

b. in Africa, probably *c.* A.D. 330. Rose from humble background to be appointed governor of Pannonia Secunda by Julian 361, and *Praefectus urbi* by Theodosius 389. Later details unknown. Sources: Amm. Marc. 21.10.6; Aur. Vict. *Caesares* 20.5; *CIL* VI 1186. Cf. *PLRE* I 960.

WORKS

Caesares: résumé of Roman history from Augustus to Constantine II, written 360; see Jerome, *Epist.* 10.3; Lyd. *De Mag.* 3.7. Later combined with *Origo gentis Romanae* (covering legendary period) and *De viris illustribus* (biographies of regal and republican figures), both of unknown date and authorship.

BIBLIOGRAPHY

TEXTS: F. Pichlmayr, corr. R. Gruendel (BT, 1966: includes *Origo* and *De vir. ill.*); P. Dufraigne (Budé, 1975). *De vir. ill.*: W. K. Sherwin (Norman, Oklahoma 1973: with tr.).

TRANSLATION: E. C. Echols, *Brief imperial lives* (Exeter 1962).

STUDIES: C. G. Starr, 'Aurelius Victor, historian of Empire', *Am. Hist. Rev.* 61 (1955/6) 574–86; E. Hohl, 'Die Historia Augusta und die Caesares des Aurelius Victor', *Historia* 4 (1955) 220–8; S. d'Elia, 'Per una nuova edizione critica di Aurelio Vittore', *Rendiconti dell'Accadamia di Archeologia, Lettere e Belle Arti di Napoli* 43 (1968) 103–94; W. den Boer, *Some minor Roman historians* (Leiden 1972) 19–113. *Origo*: A. D. Momigliano, 'Some observations on the Origo gentis Romanae', *J.R.S*, 48 (1958) 56–73; idem, 'Per una nuova edizione dell'Origo gentis Romanae', *Athenaeum* 36 (1958) 248–59; G. Puccioni, 'Tradizione e innovazione nel linguaggio dell'Origo gentis Romanae', *S.I.F.C.* 30 (1958) 207–54. *De vir. ill.*: L. Braccesi, *Introduzione al De viris illustribus* (Bologna 1973).

EUTROPIUS

LIFE

Accompanied Julian on Persian campaign A.D. 363 and was private secretary to Valens. Probably identical with E. who was proconsul of Asia 371–372, Praetorian Prefect of Illyricum 380–381, and consul 387. Sources: Nicephorus Gregoras, *Or. in Const. Magn.* in Lambecius, *Comm. de bibl. Vindob.* 8.136; *Scriptores Orig. Constantinopolitanae* 2.144; Amm. Marc. 29.1.36; Symm. *Epist.* 3.46–51; *Cod. Iust.* 1.54.4[a] etc.; *ILS* 5911. Cf. *PLRE* I 317.

WORKS

Breviarium ab urbe condita (10 bks): survey of Roman history from foundation of city to accession of Valens 364; see Eutrop. *Brev. praef.*; Suda s.v. Εὐτρόπιος.

BIBLIOGRAPHY

TEXT: H. Droysen (Berlin 1879); C. Santini (BT, 1979).

STUDIES: E. Malcovati, 'I breviari del quarto secolo', *Ann. Fac. Lettere e Filosofia Univ. Cagliari* 1 (1942) 23–65; W. den Boer, *Some minor Roman historians* (Leiden 1972) 114–72. *Greek translations*: Text in Droysen above. L. Baffetti, 'Di Peanio traduttore di Eutropio', *Byz. neugr. Jahrb.* 3 (1922) 15–36.

FESTUS

LIFE

b. Tridentum in Raetia. Governor of Syria late A.D. 360s, private secretary to Valens, and proconsul of Asia *c.* 372. Dismissed after Valens' death 378 and d. at Ephesus 380. Sources: Amm. Marc. 29.2.22–5; Liban. *Or.* 1.156–9; Eunap. *V.S.* 7.6.11–13. Cf. *PLRE* I 334–5.

WORKS

Breviarium rerum gestarum populi Romani: compendium of Roman history from foundation of city to reign of Valens, written 369; see Fest. *Brev.* 1, 2, 10.

BIBLIOGRAPHY

TEXT AND COMMENTARY: TEXT: C. Wagener (BT, 1886). COMMENTARY: J. W. Eadie (London 1967).

STUDIES: E. Malcovati, 'I breviari del quarto secolo', *Ann. Fac. Lettere e Filosofia Univ. Cagliari* 1 (1942) 23–65; W. den Boer, *Some minor Roman historians* (Leiden 1972) 173–223; B. Baldwin, 'Festus the historian', *Historia* 27 (1978) 192–217.

EPITOME DE CAESARIBUS

TEXT: In F. Pichlmayr, *Sextus Aurelius De Caesaribus*, corr. R. Gruendel (BT,1966).

STUDIES: J. Schlumberger, *Die Epitome de Caesaribus. Untersuchungen zur heidnischen Geschichtsschreibung des 4. Jahrhunderts n. Chr.* (Munich 1974); W. Hartke, *Römische Kinderkaiser. Eine Strukturanalyse römischen Denkens und Daseins* (Berlin 1951) 375ff.

EXCERPTUM VALESIANUM

TEXT: J. Moreau, rev. V. Velkov (BT, 1968).

AMMIANUS MARCELLINUS

LIFE

b. of Greek parents at Antioch *c.* A.D. 325–330. Served in the East and in Gaul under Ursicinus for seven years from 353/354, and joined Julian in his Persian campaign 363. Visited Egypt, Greece (366) and Antioch (371), and later settled in Rome. Date of death unknown. Sources: Amm. Marc. *passim*, esp. 19.8.6, 14.9.1, 14.115, 15.5.22, 16.2.8, 16.10.21, 17.4.6, 18.8.11, 19.8.12, 21.5.7, 22.15.1., 24.1.5, 24.2.1, 24.5.1, 24.8.4, 25.1.1, 25.2.1, 25.3.1, 29.1.24, 29.2.16, 30.4.4; Liban. *Epist.* 983 (recitals of parts of his history at Rome). Cf. *PLRE* 1 547–8.

WORKS

Res gestae: continuation of Tacitus, originally in thirty-one books (A.D. 96–378), of which only 14–31 survive (starting in 353); written from 360s until possibly 395;

see Amm. Marc. 31.16.9, 15.1.1, 16.1.3, 15.9.2, 28.1.2, 26.1.1, 27.2.11; Liban. *Epist.* 983.

BIBLIOGRAPHY

TEXTS AND COMMENTARIES: TEXTS: C. U. Clark (Berlin 1910–15); J. C. Rolfe (Loeb, 1935–40); A. Selem (Turin 1965); W. Seyfarth (Berlin 1968–71); E. Galletier, J. Fontaine, G. Sabbah (Budé, 1968–). COMMENTARIES: P. de Jonge (Groningen 1935–); J. Szidat, *Historischer Kommentar zu Ammianus Marcellinus Buch* XX–XXI (Wiesbaden 1977–).

STUDIES: (1) GENERAL: W. Ensslin, *Zur Geschichtsschreibung und Weltanschauung des Ammianus Marcellinus* (Leipzig 1923); E. A. Thompson, *The historical work of Ammianus Marcellinus* (Cambridge 1947); C. P. T. Naudé, *Ammianus Marcellinus in die lig van die antieke geskiedskrywing* (Leiden 1956); S. Jannaccone, *Ammiano Marcellino* (Naples 1960); A. Demandt, *Zeitkritik und Geschichtsbild im Werk Ammians* (Bonn 1965); P. M. Camus, *Ammien Marcellin. Témoin des courants culturels et religieuses à la fin du IVe siècle* (Paris 1967); A. Momigliano, 'The lonely historian Ammianus Marcellinus', *A.S.N.P.* 4 (1974) 1393–1407; Z. V. Udal'tsova, *Idejno-politicheskaya bor'ba v rannej Vizantii* (Moscow 1974) 7–82; F. C. Blockley, *Ammianus Marcellinus. A study of his historiography and political thought* (Brussels 1975: with bibliography); J. M. Alonso-Nuñez, *La visión historiográfica de Ammiano Marcellino* (Valladolid 1975: with bibliography). (2) PARTICULAR TOPICS: G. B. Pighi, *I discorsi nelle storie di Ammiano Marcellino* (Milan 1936); A. Cameron, 'The Roman friends of Ammianus Marcellinus', *J.R.S.* 54 (1964) 15–28; F. Paschoud, *Roma aeterna. Études sur le patriotisme romain dans l'occident latin à l'époque des grandes invasions* (Rome 1967) 33–70; R. Syme, *Ammianus and the Historia Augusta* (Oxford 1968); C. Samberg, 'Die "Kaiserbiographie" in den Res Gestae des Ammianus Marcellinus', *Klio* 51 (1969) 349–482; H. Drexler, *Ammianstudien* (Hildesheim 1974); G. A. Crump, *Ammianus Marcellinus as a military historian* (Wiesbaden 1975).

JEROME (HIERONYMUS)

WORKS

Chronicle: survey of world history, an expanded translation (A.D. 380) from Eusebius of Caesarea; see *praef.* and *ann. Abr.* 2342. *De viris illustribus*: 135 notes on Christian writers from Peter to J. himself, written 392; see *praef.*

BIBLIOGRAPHY

TEXTS: *Chron.* A. Schoene (Berlin 1866–75). *De vir. ill.* E. C. Richardson (BT, 1896); C. A. Bernoulli (Freiburg i. Br.–Leipzig 1895).

STUDIES: R. Helm, *Hieronymus' Zusätze in Eusebius' Chronik und ihre Wert für die Literaturgeschichte*, *Philologus* suppl. 21 (1929).

RUFINUS

WORKS

Ecclesiastical history: abbreviated translation from Eusebius of Caesarea, supplemented by two books covering 324–95; written A.D. 410s. See Gennadius, *De vir. ill.* 17.

TEXT: T. Mommsen, in E. Schwartz, *Eusebius' Kirchengeschichte* (BT, 1903) vol. II.

SULPICIUS SEVERUS

WORKS

Chronicle (2 bks): Christian history from creation to A.D. 400; see Gennadius, *De vir. ill.* 19, Sulp. Sev. *Chron.* 1.1.

BIBLIOGRAPHY

TEXTS: C. Halm (Vienna 1866); A. Lavertujon (Paris 1896–9).

STUDIES: N. K. Chadwick, *Poetry and letters in early Christian Gaul* (Cambridge 1955) 89–121.

AUGUSTINUS, AURELIUS (see also p. 920)

De civitate dei (22 bks): vindication of the Christian church, pubd A.D. 413–425; see *Retract.* 2.43.1.

BIBLIOGRAPHY

TEXTS: B. Dombart and A. Kalb (BT, 1928–9); G. E. McCracken (London 1957–72).

STUDIES: H.-I. Marrou, *S. Augustin et la fin de la culture antique*, 2nd ed. (Paris 1949); R. H. Barrow, *Introduction to St. Augustine*, '*The City of God*' (London 1950); J. Straub, 'Augustins Sorge um die regeneratio imperii. Das imperium als civitas terrena', *H.J.* 73 (1954) 36–60; F. G. Maier, *Augustin und das antike Rom* (Stuttgart 1955); P. L. R. Brown, *Augustine of Hippo* (London 1967) 299–329; F. Paschoud, *Roma aeterna. Études sur le patriotisme romain dans l'occident latin à l'époque des grandes invasions* (Rome 1967) 234–75.

OROSIUS

LIFE

b. in Spain *c.* A.D. 375–380. Went to Augustine in Hippo *c.* 410–412 and returned there after visiting Jerome in Bethlehem 415. Date of death unknown. Sources: Gennadius, *De vir. ill.* 39; Oros. *Hist.* 7.22.8; August. *Epist.* 166.2, 169.13; Braulio Caesaraugustensis, *Epist.* 44 (Migne, *PL* LXXX 698D); Avitus presbyter, *Ep. ad Balchonium* (Migne, *PL* XLI 806).

WORKS

Historiarum adversus paganos libri VII: anti-pagan Roman history, completed 417/418; see Hist. 1 *prol.* 1ff.; 7.43.19.

TEXT: C. Zangemeister (Vienna 1882).

TRANSLATION: I. W. Raymond (New York 1936).

STUDIES: J. Svennung, *Orosiana* (Uppsala 1922); G. Fink-Errara, 'San Augustin y Orosio', *Ciudad de Dios* 167 (1954) 455–549; B. Lacroix, *Orose et ses idées* (Paris 1965: with bibliography).

LATIN RHETORICIANS

TEXT: C. Halm, *Rhetores Latini minores* (BT, 1863).

STUDIES: M. L. Clarke, *Rhetoric at Rome*, 2nd ed. (London 1966); G. Kennedy, *The art of rhetoric in the Roman world* (Princeton 1972).

PANEGYRICI LATINI

LIVES

Latinius Pacatus Drepanius: *Pan. Lat.* 12.1.3 etc.; Sid. Apoll. *Epist.* 8.11; Auson. pp. 86, 155, 169 Peiper; *Cod. Theod.* 10.2.4[a], 9.42.13[a]. Cf. *PLRE* I 272.

Claudius Mamertinus: *ILS* 755; Amm. Marc. 21.8.1, 21.10.8, 21.12.25, 22.31, 26.55, 27.7.1. Cf. *PLRE* I 540–1.

Nazarius: Jerome, *Chron.* A.D. 324, 336; Auson. *Prof. Burd.* 15.7–10. Cf. *PLRE* I 618–19.

Eumenius: *Pan. Lat.* 5.1.1, 5.11.2, 5.14.1–3, 5.17.3–4. Cf. *PLRE* I 294–5.

BIBLIOGRAPHY

TEXTS: E. Galletier (Budé, 1949–55); R. A. B. Mynors (OCT, 1964); W. J. G. Lubbe, *Incerti panegyricus Constantino Augusto dictus* (Leiden 1955); H. Gutzwiller, *Die*

Neujahrsrede des Konsuls Claudius Mamertinus vor dem Kaiser Julian (Basel 1942); G. Barabino, *Claudio Mamertino. Il panegirico dell'Imperatore Giuliano* (Genoa 1965).

STUDIES: W. S. Maguinness, 'Some methods of the Latin panegyrists', *Hermathena* 47 (1932) 42–61; idem, 'Locutions and formulae of the Latin panegyrists', *Hermathena* 48 (1933) 117–38; E. Vereecke, 'Le corpus des panégyriques latins de l'époque tardive. Problèmes d'imitation', *A.C.* 44 (1975) 141–60.

SYMMACHUS, QUINTUS AURELIUS

LIFE

b. *c.* A.D. 345 of distinguished Roman family; studied rhetoric under tutor from Bordeaux. Governor of Bruttium 365, Proconsul of Africa 373–374, *Praefectus urbi* 384–385, consul 391. d. after 402. Sources: full refs. in *PLRE* I 865–70.

WORKS

Eight speeches, including two panegyrics addressed to Valentinian (369 and 370) and one to Gratian (369), and ten books of letters, written between 364 and 402 and pubd after his death; bk 10 (*Relationes*) comprises official reports sent by S. as *Praefectus urbi* to Valentinian II. See Socr. *Hist eccl.* 5.14; Symm. *Epist.* tit., 3.11, 5.85, 5.86; Macrob. 5.1.7; Prudent. *c. Symm.* 1.632; Sid. Apoll. *Epist.* 1.1.

BIBLIOGRAPHY

TEXTS: O. Seeck (Berlin 1883). *Letters*: J. P. Callu (Budé, 1972). *Relationes*: R. H. Barrow (Oxford 1973).

STUDIES: S. Dill, *Roman society in the last century of the western empire*, 2nd ed. (London 1910) 143–66; J. A. MacGeachy, *Q. Aurelius Symmachus and the senatorial aristocracy of the west* (Chicago 1947); D. Romano, *Simmaco* (Palermo 1955); F. Paschoud, *Roma aeterna. Études sur le patriotisme romain dans l'occident latin à l'époque des grandes invasions* (Rome 1967) 71–109; F. Canfora, *Simmaco e Ambrogio* (Bari 1970); R. Klein, *Symmachus* (Darmstadt 1971); idem, *Der Streit um den Victoria-Altar* (Darmstadt 1972); J. F. Matthews, 'The letters of Symmachus', in (ed.) J. W. Binns, *Latin literature of the fourth century* (London 1974) 58–99; idem, *Western aristocracies and imperial court AD 364–425* (Oxford 1975).

MACROBIUS AMBROSIUS THEODOSIUS

WORKS

Commentary on the dream of Scipio: discussion of dream recounted in Cic. *Rep.*; see *Comm.* 1.5.1. *Saturnalia* (7 bks; parts missing): purported account of symposium held during Saturnalia of 384; see *praef.*, 1.15. *De differentiis et societatibus graeci latinique verbi*: fragments in *GLK* v 599ff.

BIBLIOGRAPHY

TEXT: J. Willis (BT, 1963).

TRANSLATION: *Comm.*: W. H. Stahl (New York 1952).

STUDIES: T. Whittaker, *Philosophy, science and letters in the year 400* (Cambridge 1923); K. Mras, 'Macrobius' Kommentar zu Ciceros Somnium, ein Beitrag zur Geistesgeschichte des V. Jahrh. n.Chr.', *S.P.A.W.* 1933, 6.232–86; A. Cameron, 'The date and identity of Macrobius', *J.R.S.* 56 (1966) 25–38; P. Courcelle, *Late Latin writers and their Greek sources* (Cambridge, Mass. 1969) 13–47; J. Flamant, *Macrobe et le Néo-Platonisme latin à la fin du IVe siècle* (Leiden 1977).

MARTIANUS MIN(N)E(I)US FELIX CAPELLA

LIFE

Lived in Carthage, possibly a teacher of rhetoric; see *Nupt. Phil. et Merc.* 9.997, 6.577.

WORKS

De nuptiis Philologiae et Mercurii (9 bks): prose and verse encyclopaedia of the liberal arts, which are introduced allegorically as handmaids to Philologia at her marriage to Mercury, god of eloquence; see 1.3, 1.5.

BIBLIOGRAPHY

TEXT AND COMMENTARY: TEXT: A. Dick (BT, 1925). COMMENTARY: Bk 2: L. Lenaz (Padua 1975).

TRANSLATION: W. H. Stahl, R. Johnson, E. L. Burge (Columbia 1977).

STUDIES: H. W. Fischer, *Untersuchungen über die Quellen der Rhetorik des Martianus Capella* (Breslau 1936); G. Leonardi, *I codici di Marziano Capella* (Milan 1960);

P. Courcelle, *Late Latin writers and their Greek sources* (Cambridge, Mass. 1969) 211–19; W. H. Stahl, *Martianus Capella and the seven liberal arts* (New York – London 1971).

SACERDOS, MARIUS PLOTIUS

TEXT: *GLK* VI 415–546.

CHARISIUS, FLAVIUS SOSIPATER

TEXT: *GLK* I 1–296; C. Barwick (BT, 1925).

DIOMEDES

TEXT: *GLK* I 298–592.

DONATUS, AELIUS

LIFE

fl. A.D. 353; teacher of Jerome.

WORKS

Ars grammatica in two versions (*Ars minor* and *Ars maior*), and commentaries on Virgil (introduction survives) and Terence (extant version probably modified). Sources: Jerome, *Chron.* A.D. 353; *Comm. in Eccles.* 1; *Apol. adv. Rufin.* 1.16; *Prisc. GLK* III 281, 320 etc.

TEXT: *GLK* IV 355–402. *Comm. Ter.*: P. Wessner (BT, 1902–8).

MARIUS VICTORINUS AFER, GAIUS

LIFE

fl. mid-4th *c.* A.D. Jerome's teacher of rhetoric and intellectual leader of Roman Neoplatonists. Converted to Christianity in old age. Sources: Jerome, *De vir. ill.* 101, *Comm. in Galat. praef.*, *Chron.* A.D. 353.

WORKS

(Partly extant). *Ars grammatica*, four books on metre; translations of Greek philosophers; commentaries on Aristotle and Cicero's *De inventione* and *Topica*; Christian treatises, commentaries and poems. See August. *Conf.* 8.2; Cassiod. *Inst.* 2, *Rhet.* 10 (Halm p. 153); *PLRE* I 964.

BIBLIOGRAPHY

TEXTS: *GLK* VI 1–184; C. Helm, *Rhetores Latini minores* 153–304; T. Stangl, *Tulliana et Mario-Victoriana* (Munich 1888); Migne, *PL* VIII (Paris 1844); P. Hadot, *Marius Victorinus. Opera theologica* (Vienna 1971); P. Henry and P. Hadot, *Marius Victorinus. Traités théologiques sur la Trinité* (Paris 1960); A. Locher, *Marius Victorinus. Opera theologica* (BT, 1976).

STUDIES: P. Hadot, *Porphyre et Victorinus* (Paris 1968); H. Dahlmann, 'Zur Ars grammatica des Marius Victorinus', *Abh. Akad. Mainz* 1970, 2; P. Hadot, *Marius Victorinus. Recherches sur sa vie et ses oeuvres* (Paris 1971).

SERVIUS

LIFE

Unknown: his presence as a young man in Macrobius' *Saturnalia* (1.2.15, 6.6.1) is probably an anachronism.

WORKS

Commentary on Virgil, probably written A.D. 420s, surviving also in a version supplemented by material from other commentators (Servius *auctus* or Servius Danielis). See Prisc. *GLK* II 256.14, 515.23 etc.

BIBLIOGRAPHY

TEXTS: *GLK* IV 405–565; G. Thilo and H. Hagen (BT, 1889–1902); E. K. Rand et al., *Servianorum in Vergilii carmina commentariorum editionis Harvardianae*, vols. II–III (Lancaster, Pa. 1946–65).

STUDIES: J. F. Mountford and J. T. Schulz, *Index rerum et hominum in scholiis Servii et Aeli Donati tractatorum* (New York 1930); G. Funaioli, *Esegesi virgiliana antica* (Milan 1930); A. Cameron, 'The date and identity of Macrobius', *J.R.S.* 56 (1966) 25–38; G. P. Goold, 'Servius and the Helen episode', *H.S.Ph.* 74 (1970) 101–68; C. E. Murgia, *Prolegomena to Servius 5: the manuscripts* (Berkeley–Los Angeles–London 1975).

DONATUS, TIBERIUS CLAUDIUS

WORKS

Interpretationes Vergilianae: commentary on *Aeneid* in twelve books; see *praef.* and *PLRE* I 268–9.

TEXT: H. Georgii (BT, 1905–6).

NONIUS MARCELLUS

LIFE

African, probably active first half of 4th c. A.D.

WORKS

De compendiosa doctrina: lexicon of Republican Latin in twenty books (bk 16 lost); see *subscriptio* to *De comp. doct.* and *CIL* VIII 4878.

BIBLIOGRAPHY

TEXT: W. M. Lindsay (BT, 1903).

STUDIES: W. M. Lindsay, *Nonius Marcellus' dictionary of Republican Latin* (Oxford 1901); A. Coucke, *Nonius Marcellus en zijn De compendiosa doctrina* (Louvain 1936–7); F. Bertini and G. Barabino (edd.), *Studi Noniani* I–IV (Genoa 1967–77).

MATERNUS, IULIUS FIRMICUS

LIFE

Sicilian of senatorial rank; practised as advocate.

WORKS

Matheseos libri VIII: handbook of astrology, written 330s or 340s. *De errore profanorum religionum*: anti-pagan polemic attributed in MSS to Julius Firmicus Maternus, and possibly written by the author of the preceding.

BIBLIOGRAPHY

TEXTS AND COMMENTARY: TEXTS: *Math.*: W. Kroll, F. Skutsch, K. Ziegler (BT, 1897–1913). *De errore*: K. Ziegler (BT, 1908). COMMENTARY: *De errore*: C. Heuten (Leipzig 1908).

STUDIES: F. Boll, *Sphaera* (Leipzig 1903) 394ff.; F. H. Cramer, *Astrology in Roman law and politics* (Philadelphia 1954); T. Wilkström, *In Firmicum Maternum studia critica* (Uppsala 1935).

PALLADIUS RUTILIUS TAURUS AEMILIANUS

LIFE

4th c. A.D. Owner of estates in Italy and Sardinia (4.10.16 and 24).

WORKS

De re rustica (15 bks), comprising an introductory book, one book for each month of the year, a book on the care of farm-animals (*De veterinaria medicina*; first pubd by Svennung, see below), and a book in elegiacs on the cultivation of trees (*De insitione*).

BIBLIOGRAPHY

TEXTS: R. H. Rodgers (BT, 1975: with bibliography). *De vet. med.*: J. Svennung (Göteborg 1926: ed. princ.).

STUDIES: H. Widstrand, *Palladiusstudien* (Uppsala 1926); J. Svennung, 'De auctoribus Palladii', *Eranos* 25 (1927) 123–78, 230–48; idem, *Untersuchungen zu Palladius und zur lateinischen Fach- und Volkssprache* (Uppsala 1935); K. D. White, *Agricultural implements of the Roman world* (Cambridge 1967); idem, *Roman farming* (London 1970); idem, *Farm equipment of the Roman world* (Cambridge 1975); R. H. Rodgers, *An introduction to Palladius* (London 1975).

VEGETIUS RENATUS, FLAVIUS

WORKS

Epitoma rei militaris: four books on Roman military system, written between A.D. 383 (ref. to *divi Gratiani* 1.20) and 450 (revision made by Eutropius of Alexandria); dedicated to an emperor, probably Theodosius I. *Mulomedicina*: six books on veterinary science, attributed in MSS to P. Vegetius, probably identical with author of the *Epitoma*.

BIBLIOGRAPHY

TEXTS: *Epitoma*: C. Lang, 2nd ed. (BT, 1885; repr. 1967). *Mulomedicina*: E. Lommatzsch (BT, 1903).

STUDIES: D. Schenk, *Flavius Vegetius Renatus. Die Quellen der Epitoma rei militaris* (Leipzig 1930); A. Andersson, *Studia Vegetiana* (Uppsala 1938); F. Rayniers, *Végèce et l'instruction des cadres et de la troupe dans l'armée romaine* (Nancy 1938).

DE REBUS BELLICIS

TEXT AND COMMENTARY: E. A. Thompson, *A Roman reformer and inventor* (Oxford 1952).

ARNOBIUS

LIFE AND WORKS

b. *c.* A.D. 240; teacher of rhetoric and advocate from Sicca Veneria in Africa. After his conversion to Christianity in the early 4th c. wrote *Adversus nationes*, an attack on paganism in seven books. Sources: Jerome, *Chron.* A.D. 326 (possible year of death), *De vir. ill* 79, *Epist.* 58; Arnobius 1.1, 1.13, 2.71.

BIBLIOGRAPHY

TEXT: C. Marchesi (Turin 1934).

STUDIES: W. Kroll, 'Arnobiusstudien', *Rh.M.* 72 (1917) 63–112; F. Gabarrou, *Arnobe, son oeuvre* (Paris 1921); idem, *Le latin d'Arnobe* (Paris 1921); H. Hagendahl, *La prose métrique d'Arnobe* (Göteborg 1936); E. Rapisarda, *Arnobio* (Catania 1946).

APULEIUS

LIFE

b. *c.* A.D. 125 at Madauros (August. *C.D.* 8.14; *Epist.* 102.32). Educ. Carthage (*Flor.* 18.15) and Athens (*Apol.* 72.3, *Flor.* 18.15); visited Rome (*Flor.* 17.4). Arrived Oea 155–156 and married Pudentilla (*Apol.* 73ff.). Indicted for magic at Sabrata 158–159 (on the date, R. Syme, *R.E.A.* 61 (1959) 316f.). Subsequent life at Carthage as chief priest (*Flor.* 16.38); honorific statues to him (*Flor.* 16.1ff.). No evidence after 170.

WORKS

(1) EXTANT: *Apology* 158–159, *Florida c.* 160–170, *Metamorphoses*, date uncertain, probably after 160. Of the philosophical works (dates uncertain), *De deo Socratis* is undisputed, *De dogmate Platonis* and *De mundo* are probably A.'s, περὶ ἑρμηνείας is possibly his, but *Asclepius* is spurious. (2) LOST: Love-lyrics and satirical poetry in Catullan mode (*Apol.* 6.3, 9.12ff.); hymns (*Flor.* 17.18, 18.37ff.); other poetry (*Flor.* 9.27f., 20.6); speeches (*Apol.* 55.10, August. *Epist.* 138.19); *Hermagoras*, a romance (Prisc. *GLK* II 85 and Fulg. p. 122 Helm); *Eroticus*, anthology of love-stories (Lydus, *Mag.* 3.64); *Epitome historiarum* (? = collection of abbreviated stories; Prisc. *GLK* III 482); *Quaestiones convivales* (Sid. Apoll. 9.13.3 and Macr. *Sat.* 7.3.23); *De republica* (Fulg. p. 122 Helm); translation of *Phaedo* (Sid. Apoll. 2.9.5); *Quaestiones naturales* (*Apol.* 36ff.); *De proverbiis* (Charisius, *GLK* I 240); *Arithmetica* (Cassiod. *Arithm.*); *De musica* (Cassiod. *Mus.*); *De re rustica* (Palladius 1.35.9); *De arboribus* (Serv. *ad* Virg. *G.* 2.126); *Medicinalia* (Prisc. *GLK* II 203).

BIBLIOGRAPHY

(up to 1970, see Bursian 171 (1915) 147ff., 175 (1919) 1ff.; D. S. Robertson, *Y.W.C.S.* 1938, 94ff.; C. C. Schlam, *C.W.* 64 (1971) 285ff.)

TEXTS AND COMMENTARIES: TEXTS: Complete: R. Helm and P. Thomas, 1st–3rd edd. (BT, 1955–69). *Apol.* and *Flor.*: P. Vallette (Budé, 1960). *Philosophica*: J. Beaujeu (Budé, 1973: *De deo Socr.*, *De Platone*, *De mundo*). *Met.*: D. S. Robertson (Budé, 1940–5). COMMENTARIES: *Apol.*: H. E. Butler and A. S. Owen (Oxford 1914); B. Mosca (Florence 1974). *Met.*: Bk 1: A. Scobie (Meisenheim 1975). Bk 2: B. J. de Jonge (Groningen 1941). Bk 3: R. T. van der Paardt (Amsterdam 1971). Bk 4.1–27: B. L. Hijmans et al. (Groningen 1977). *Cupid and Psyche*: L. C. Purser (London 1910); P. Grimal (Paris 1963). Bk 11: J. G. Griffiths (Leiden 1975).

STUDIES: P. Junghanns, *Die Erzählungstechnik von Apuleius' Metamorphoses und ihrer Vorlage* (Leipzig 1932); M. Bernhard, *Der Stil des Apuleius von Madaura*, 2nd ed. (Amsterdam 1965); B. E. Perry, *The ancient romances* (Berkeley 1967); P. G. Walsh, *The Roman novel* (Cambridge 1970); (edd.) B. L. Hijmans and R. T. van der Paardt, *Aspects of the Golden Ass* (Groningen 1978); J. Tatum, *Apuleius and the Golden Ass* (Ithaca 1979). See also recent bibliographies in edd. of Beaujeu, Scobie and Griffiths above.

EPILOGUE

Bolgar, R. R., *The classical heritage and its beneficiaries* (Cambridge 1954).
idem (ed.), *Classical influences on European culture AD 500–1500* (Cambridge 1971).

de Ghellink, J., *Littérature latine au moyen age*, 2 vols. (Paris 1939).
idem, *L'essor de la littérature latine au XIIe siècle* (Brussels 1955).
Hagendahl, H., *Latin fathers and the classics* (Göteborg 1958).
Highet, G., *The classical tradition* (London 1949).
Laistner, M. L. W., *Thought and letters in western Europe, AD 500–900* (London 1931).
Manitius, M., *Geschichte der lateinischen Literatur des Mittelalters*, 3 vols. (Munich 1911–31).
Raby, F. J. E., *A history of secular Latin poetry in the middle ages*, 2 vols., 2nd ed. (Oxford 1957).
idem, *A history of Christian-Latin poetry*, 2nd ed. (Oxford 1953).

SENECA, LUCIUS ANNAEUS

LIFE AND WORKS

LIFE: b. of equestrian family at Corduba in Spain, probably in 50s B.C. Divided his time between Rome and Spain (dates uncertain). *Condiscipulus* and lifelong friend of Porcius Latro, but not a rhetorician himself. Three sons: Novatus (later Junius Gallio), Seneca (the philosopher), and Mela (Lucan's father). d. before A.D. 41. See Fairweather, under *Studies* below, 3–26. WORKS: (1) Extant: *Oratorum et rhetorum sententiae divisiones colores* (completed after A.D. 34 (*Suas.* 2.22), possibly in Caligula's reign): one book of seven *Suasoriae* (more were planned, *Contr.* 2.4.8), and ten, each with preface, of *Controversiae* (only bks 1–2, 7, 9–10 survive; 4th–5th c. abridgement supplies two missing prefaces and excerpts from lost books). (2) Lost: History from beginning of civil wars to his own times; see younger Seneca fr. 98 Haase.

BIBLIOGRAPHY

TEXTS AND COMMENTARY: TEXTS: A. Kiessling (BT, 1872); H. J. Müller (Vienna 1887); M. Winterbottom (Loeb, 1974). COMMENTARY: *Suas.*: W. A. Edward (Cambridge 1928).

STUDIES: H. Bardon, *Le vocabulaire de la critique littéraire chez Sénèque le Rhéteur* (Paris 1940); L. A. Sussman, *The elder Seneca* (Leiden 1978); J. A. Fairweather, *Seneca the elder* (Cambridge 1981).

SURVEYS: J. E. G. Whitehorne, *Prudentia* 1 (1969) 14ff.; forthcoming articles by Sussman and Fairweather in *ANRW*.

METRICAL APPENDIX

(1) BASIC PRINCIPLES

(A) STRESSED AND QUANTITATIVE VERSE

In metres familiar to speakers of English, rhythm is measured by the predictable alternation of one or more stressed syllables with one or more unstressed syllables (distinguished by the notation – and ᴗ, or ′ and ˣ). Consequently, it is word-accent that determines whether or not a word or sequence of words may stand in a certain part of the verse. Thus the word *classical* may occupy the metrical unit represented by the notation –ᴗᴗ by virtue of the stress imparted to its first syllable in everyday pronunciation. In contrast, the rhythms of classical Latin metres are measured by the predictable alternation of one or more 'heavy' syllables with one or more 'light' syllables (defined below, and distinguished by the notation – and ᴗ), so that in the construction of Latin verse the factor of primary importance is not word-accent but syllabic 'weight'. Thus the word *facerent*, although accented in normal speech on the first syllable, consists for metrical purposes of two light syllables followed by one heavy syllable, and for this reason can only occupy the metrical unit ᴗᴗ–. Verse constructed upon this principle is conventionally designated *quantitative*: it should be emphasized that this term refers to the quantity (or 'weight') of syllables, and that throughout this account such quantity is described by the terms 'heavy' and 'light' to distinguish it from the intrinsic length of vowels; unfortunately, both syllabic weight and vowel-length are still generally denoted by the same symbols, – and ᴗ.

(B) SYLLABIFICATION

A syllable containing a long vowel or diphthong is heavy (e.g. the first syllables of *pacem* and *laudo*).

A syllable containing a short vowel is light if it ends with that vowel (e.g. the first syllable of *pecus*), but heavy if it ends with a consonant (e.g. the first syllable of *pectus*).

To decide whether or not a short-vowelled syllable ends with a consonant (and thus to establish its quantity), the following rules should be observed:[1] (i) word-division

[1] The resulting division is practical only; for the difficulties involved in an absolute definition of the syllabic unit see Allen (1973) under (4) below, esp. 27–40.

should be disregarded; (ii) a single consonant between two vowels or diphthongs belongs to the succeeding syllable (thus *pecus*→*pe–cus*; *genus omne*→*ge–nu–som–ne*); (iii) of two or more successive consonants, at least one belongs to the preceding syllable (thus *pectus*→*pec–tus*; also *nulla spes*→*nul–las–pes*, though short final vowels are normally avoided in this position), except as allowed for below.

Note: for this purpose *h* is disregarded; *x* and *z* count as double consonants, 'semi-consonantal' *i* and *u* as consonants (except in the combination *qu*, regarded as a single consonant).

To (iii) there is an important exception. In the case of the combination of a plosive and liquid consonant (*p*, *t*, *c*, *b*, *d*, *g* followed by *r* or *l*), the syllabic division may be made either between the consonants (e.g. *pat–ris*) or before them (e.g. *pa–tris*), resulting in *either* a heavy *or* a light preceding syllable. However, when two such consonants belong to different parts of a compound or to two different words, the division is always made between them, giving a heavy preceding syllable (e.g. *ablego*→*ab–lego*, not *a–blego*; *at rabidae*→*at–rabidae*, not *a–trabidae*). Lastly, when, after a short final vowel, these consonants begin the next word, the division is nearly always made before them, giving a light preceding syllable (e.g. *plumbea glans*→*plum–be–a–glans*).

(C) ACCENT

The nature of the Latin word-accent (whether one of pitch or stress) and its importance in the construction of verse are both matters of controversy: for a clear discussion of the basic problems see Wilkinson under (4) below, 89–96, 221–36. By way of practical guidance in reading Latin verse, all that may be said is that for the present-day English speaker, accustomed to a naturalistic manner of reading poetry, it will sound as strange (and monotonous) to emphasize the heavy syllables of a metrical structure ('Quális Théseá iacuít cedénte carína') as it does to read Shakespearian verse with attention only to its iambic structure ('Now ís the wínter óf our díscontént'); furthermore that, even in giving stress to the word-accent in Latin verse, heavy syllables will generally coincide with accented syllables with sufficient frequency to ensure that the metre is not forgotten – particularly at the beginning and end of many metres, as in the hexameter quoted above. It should be remembered, however, that what sounds natural is not thereby authentic, and that poetic delivery is highly susceptible to whims of fashion, idiosyncrasy and affectation. Even now it is not uncommon criticism of a Shakespearian actor that he 'mutilates' the shape of the verse by reading it as prose, while recordings of Tennyson and Eliot reading their poetry already sound bizarre (in different ways) to the modern ear.

(2) TECHNICAL TERMS

Anceps ('unfixed'): term used to describe a metrical element which may be represented by either a heavy or a light syllable. The final element of many Latin metres is regularly of this nature, but not in certain lyric metres in which there is metrical continuity (*synaphea*) between as well as within lines.

Brevis brevians, or *the law of iambic shortening*: in comedy and other early Latin verse a heavy syllable may be lightened if it directly follows a light syllable and is adjacent to an accented syllable. See p. 87.

Caesura ('cutting') and *diaeresis*: division between words within a verse is termed *caesura* when occurring inside a metrical foot, or *diaeresis* when occurring at the end of a foot. The varied distribution of these plays an important part in avoiding monotony in the structure of verse; in particular, the caesura prevents a succession of words co-extensive with the feet of a metre (as found in Ennius' hexameter, 'sparsis hastis longis campus splendet et horret').

Elision and *hiatus*: a vowel (or vowel + *m*) ending a word is generally suppressed or *elided* when immediately preceding another vowel or *h*. When it is not elided in these circumstances (a phenomenon most frequently found in comedy), it is said to be in *hiatus*; by the rare process of *correption* a long vowel or diphthong in hiatus may be scanned short to make a light syllable. *Prodelision* (or *aphaeresis*) signifies the suppression of *e* in *est* after a final vowel or *m*, *hypermetric elision* the suppression of a vowel between lines (nearly always that of -*que*).

Resolution: the substitution of two light syllables for a heavy one.

(3) COMMON METRES

For the sake of simplicity only the most basic characteristics of each metre are given here. For the numerous divergencies regarding anceps, resolution, position of caesura etc., see Raven under (4) below.

(a) Stichic verse (constructed by repetition of the same metrical line)

Iambic senarius (or trimeter):

⏓–⏑– |⏓–⏑– |⏓–⏑⏓

(commonest dialogue metre in early Roman drama; also used in Seneca's tragedies, Phaedrus' *Fables*, and, in alternation with an iambic dimeter (= ⏓–⏑– |⏓–⏑–), Horace's *Epodes* 1–10)

Iambic septenarius (or tetrameter catalectic):

⏓–⏑– |⏓–⏑– |⏓–⏑– |⏑–⏓

(common dialogue metre of comedy)

Trochaic septenarius (or tetrameter catalectic):

–⏑–⏓|–⏑–⏓|–⏑–⏓|–⏑⏓

(very common dialogue metre in early Roman drama)

Hexameter:

–⏕|–⏕|–⏕|–⏕|–⏑⏑|–⏓

(regular metre for epic, satiric, pastoral and didactic poetry)

Pentameter:

–⏕–⏕–|–⏑⏑–⏑⏑⏓

(following the hexameter this forms the elegiac couplet, which is regarded as an entity and hence as stichic; regular metre for love-poetry and epigram)

Phalaecean hendecasyllables:

⏓⏒|–⏑⏑–|⏑–⏑–⏓

(i.e. first foot may be a spondee, iamb or trochee; used by Catullus, Martial and Statius)

(b) Non-stichic verse (constructed by combination of different metrical lines)

Alcaic stanza:	––⏑––|–⏑⏑–|⏑⏓	(twice)
	––⏑–––⏑–⏓	
	–⏑⏑–⏑⏑–|⏑–⏓	
Sapphic stanza:	–⏑––|–⏑⏑–|⏑–⏓	(three times)
	–⏑⏑–|⏓	(adonean)
Third asclepiad:	––|–⏑⏑–|⏑⏓	(glyconic)
	––|–⏑⏑––⏑⏑–|⏑⏓	(lesser asclepiad)
Fourth asclepiad:	––|–⏑⏑––⏑⏑–|⏑⏓	(lesser asclepiad, three times)
	––|–⏑⏑–|⏑⏓	(glyconic)
Fifth asclepiad	––|–⏑⏑––⏑⏑–|⏑⏓	(lesser asclepiad, twice)
	––|–⏑⏑–|⏓	(pherecratean)
	––|–⏑⏑–|⏑⏓	(glyconic)

(the First and Second asclepiad consist, respectively, of the lesser and greater asclepiad only; the latter = ––|–⏑⏑––⏑⏑––⏑⏑–|⏑⏓)

All the above found in Horace's *Odes*; some in Catullus and Statius.

(4) BIBLIOGRAPHY

Allen, W. S., *Vox Latina*, 2nd ed. (Cambridge 1978).

idem, *Accent and rhythm* (Cambridge 1973).

Raven, D. S., *Latin metre* (London 1965).

Wilkinson, L. P., *Golden Latin artistry* (Cambridge 1963) 89–134 and *passim*

WORKS CITED IN THE TEXT

Abel, K. (1967). *Bauformen in Senecas Dialogen.* Heidelberg.

Adams, J. N. (1973). 'The vocabulary of the speeches in Tacitus' historical works', *B.I.C.S.* 20: 124–44.

Ahl, F. M. (1976). *Lucan, an introduction.* New York.

Allen, W. (1972). 'Ovid's *cantare* and Cicero's *Cantores Euphorionis*', *T.A.Ph.A.* 103: 1–14.

Allen, W. S. (1973). *Accent and rhythm: prosodic features of Latin and Greek.* Cambridge.

Altevogt, H. (1952). *Labor improbus.* Münster, Westf.

Anderson, R. D., Parsons, P. J. and Nisbet, R. G. M. (1979). 'Elegiacs by Gallus from Qaṣr Ibrîm', *J.R.S.* 69: 125–55.

Anderson, W. B. (1933). 'Gallus and the Fourth Georgic', *C.Q.* 27: 36–45, 73.

Anderson, W. S. (1961). 'Venusina Lucerna. The Horatian model for Juvenal', *T.A.Ph.A.* 92: 1–12.

(1964). *Anger in Juvenal and Seneca.* Berkeley.

André, J. (1949). *Étude sur les termes de couleur dans la langue latine.* Paris.

André, J.-M. (1967). *Mécène. Essai de biographie spirituelle.* Paris.

Anliker, K. (1960). *Prologe und Akteinteilung in Senecas Tragödien.* Bern & Stuttgart.

Arnheim, M. T. W. (1972). *The senatorial aristocracy in the later Roman Empire.* Oxford.

Arnott, W. G. (1970). 'Phormio Parasitus', *G. & R.* n.s. 17: 32–57.

(1972). 'Targets, techniques, and tradition in Plautus' Stichus', *B.I.C.S.* 19: 54–79.

(1975). *Menander, Plautus, and Terence. Greece & Rome* New Surveys in the Classics IX. Oxford.

Arns, E. (1953). *La technique du livre d'après Saint Jérôme.* Paris.

Astin, A. E. (1967). *Scipio Aemilianus.* Oxford.

Auerbach, E. (1953). *Mimesis*, tr. W. R. Trask. Princeton.

Austin, R. G. (1961). 'Virgil, *Aeneid* 2.567–88', *C.Q.* n.s. 11: 185f.

(1964). (ed.). *P. Vergili Maronis Aeneidos Liber secundus.* Oxford.

Axelson, B. (1945). *Unpoetische Wörter.* Lund.

(1958). 'Der Mechanismus des ovidischen Pentameterschlusses: eine mikrophilologische Causerie', in Herescu (1958) 121–35.

(1967). *Korruptelenkult: Studien zur Textkritik der unechten Seneca-Tragödie Hercules Oetaeus*. Lund.

Aymard, J. (1951). *Quelques séries de comparaisons chez Lucain*. Montpellier.

Badian, E. (1966). 'The early historians', in T. A. Dorey (ed.), *Latin historians* 1–38. London.

(1970). *Titus Quinctius Flamininus: Philhellenism and Realpolitik*. Lectures in Memory of Louisa Taft Semple, Second Series. Cincinnati.

(1971). 'Ennius and his Friends', in *Ennius*, Entretiens Hardt XVII 149–208. Geneva.

Bailey, C. (1935). *Religion in Virgil*. Oxford.

Barchiesi, M. (1962). *Nevio epico*. Turin.

Bardon, H. (1940). *Les empereurs et les lettres latines d'Auguste à Hadrien*. Paris.

(1956). *La littérature latine inconnue*. II. *L'époque impériale*. Paris.

Barlow, C. W. (1938). (ed.). *Epistolae Senecae ad Paulum et Pauli ad Senecam quae vocantur*. Papers and Monographs of the American Academy X. Rome.

Barnes, J. W. B. and Lloyd-Jones, H. (1963). 'Un nuovo frammento papiraceo dell' elegia ellenistica', *S.I.F.C.* 35: 205–27.

Bayet, J. (1930). 'Les premières "Géorgiques" de Virgile', *R.Ph.* 3me sér. 4: 128–50; 227–47.

(1955). 'Un procédé virgilien: la déscription synthétique dans les Géorgiques', in *Studi in onore di G. Funaioli* 9–18. Rome.

Beare, W. (1964). *The Roman stage*. 3rd edn. London.

Beazley, J. D. (1951). *The development of Attic black-figure*. Berkeley.

Bentley, R. (1726). 'De metris Terentianis schediasma', in *P. Terenti Afri Comoediae* i–xix. Cambridge.

Besslich, S. (1973). 'Die "Hörner" des Buches. Zur Bedeutung von cornua im antiken Buchwesen', *Gutenberg-Jahrbuch* 44–50.

Bickel, E. (1950). 'De elegis in Maecenatem, monumentis biographicis et historicis', *Rh. Mus.* 93: 97–133.

Bignone, E. (1942–50). *Storia della letteratura latina*. 3 vols. Florence.

Birt, T. (1877). *Ad historiam hexametri latini symbola*. Diss. Bonn.

(1882). *Das antike Buchwesen in seinem Verhältniss zur Litteratur mit Beiträgen zur Textgeschichte des Theokrit, Catull, Properz und anderer Autoren*. Berlin.

(1913). *Kritik und Hermeneutik nebst Abriss des antiken Buchwesens*. Munich.

Blakeney, E. H. (1933). *Ausonius. The Mosella*. London.

Bolgar, R. (1954). *The Classical heritage and its beneficiaries*. Cambridge.

Bonner, S. F. (1949). *Roman declamation in the late Republic and early Empire*. Liverpool.

(1977). *Education in ancient Rome from the elder Cato to the younger Pliny*. London.

Bourgery, A. (1922). *Sénèque prosateur*. Paris.

Bowersock, G. W. (1971). 'A date in the Eighth Eclogue', *H.S.C.Ph.* 75: 73–80.

Bowra, C. M. (1929). 'Some Ennian phrases in the Aeneid', *C.Q.* 23: 65f.

(1933–4). 'Aeneas and the Stoic Ideal', *G. & R.* 3: 8f.

Boyancé, P. (1955). 'M. Fulvius Nobilior et le dieu ineffable', *R.Ph.* 29: 172–92.
(1970). *Études sur l'humanisme cicéronien.* Collection Latomus CXXI. Brussels.
Bramble, J. C. (1974). *Persius and the programmatic satire: a study in form and imagery.* Cambridge.
Brisset, J. (1964). *Les idées politiques de Lucain.* Paris.
Brooks, C. and Warren, R. P. (1960). *Understanding poetry.* 3rd edn. New York, Chicago, San Francisco, Toronto.
Brower, R. A. (1959). *Alexander Pope: the poetry of allusion.* Oxford.
Brunt, P. A. (1963). Review of H. D. Meyer, *Die Aussenpolitik des Augustus und die Augusteische Dichtung* (Cologne 1961). *J.R.S.* 53: 170–6.
Buchheit, V. (1962). *Studien zum Corpus Priapeorum.* Zetemata XXVIII. Munich.
Büchner, K. (1936). *Beobachtungen über Vers- und Gedankengang bei Lukrez. Hermes,* Einzelschrift 1. Berlin.
(1955). 'P. Vergilius Maro', *Real-Enzyclopädie* VIIIA. Sep. publ. 1956.
(1961). 'Überlieferungsgeschichte der lateinischen Literatur des Altertums', in *Geschichte der Textüberlieferung* I. Zürich.
(1964). *Cicero: Bestand und Wandel seiner geistigen Welt.* Heidelberg.
Bühler, W. (1960). *Die Europa des Moschos.* Wiesbaden.
Bulloch, A. W. (1973). 'Tibullus and the Alexandrians', *P.C.Ph.S.* n.s. 19: 85ff.
Burck, E. (1929). 'Die Komposition von Vergils Georgica', *Hermes* 64: 279–321.
Burr, V. (1959). 'Editionstechnik', *RAC* IV 597–610.
Butler, H. E. (1909). *Post-Augustan poetry from Seneca to Juvenal.* Oxford.
Cairns, F. J. (1969). 'Propertius 1.18 and Callimachus' *Acontius and Cydippe*', *C.R.* n.s. 19: 131–4.
(1972). *Generic composition in Greek and Roman poetry.* Edinburgh.
Callmer, C. (1944). 'Antike Bibliotheken', *Acta Inst. Rom. regni Sueciae* 10: 145–93.
Cameron, A. (1964). 'Literary allusions in the Historia Augusta', *Hermes* 92: 363–77.
(1970). *Claudian: poetry and propaganda at the court of Honorius.* Oxford.
(1976). *Circus factions. Blues and Greens at Rome and Byzantium.* Oxford.
Camps, W. A. (1954). 'A note on the structure of the *Aeneid*', *C.Q.* n.s. 4: 214f.
(1959). 'A second note on the structure of the *Aeneid*', *C.Q.* n.s. 9: 53f.
Cancik, H. (1969). 'Zur Geschichte des Aedes (Herculis) Musarum auf dem Marsfeld', *M.D.A.I.(R.)* 76: 323–8.
(1970). 'Die Statue des L. Accius im Tempel der Camenen', in M. von Albrecht and E. Heck (eds.), *Silvae: Festschrift für E. Zinn zum 60. Geburtstag* 7–17. Tübingen.
Canter, H. V. (1925). *Rhetorical elements in the tragedies of Seneca.* University of Illinois Studies in Language and Literature X.1. Urbana.
Caplan, H. (1954). (ed.). *Rhetorica ad Herennium.* Loeb. London & Cambridge, Mass.
(1970). *On eloquence.* Cornell.
Cavenaile, R. (1958). (ed.). *Corpus papyrorum Latinorum.* Wiesbaden.
Cèbe, J.-P. (1960). 'Le niveau culturel du public plautinien', *R.E.L.* 38: 101–6.

Cichorius, C. (1908). *Studien zu Lucilius*. Leipzig.
Cizek, E. (1972). *L'époque de Néron et ses controverses idéologiques*. Roma Aeterna IV. Leiden.
Clarke, M. L. (1953). *Rhetoric at Rome: a historical survey*. London.
Classen, C. J. (1968). 'Poetry and rhetoric in Lucretius', *T.A.Ph.A.* 99: 77–118.
Clausen, W. V. (1959). *A. Persi Flacci et D. Iunii Iuvenalis Saturae*. Oxford.
(1964). 'Callimachus and Latin poetry', *G.R.B.S.* 5: 181–96.
(1972). 'On the date of the First Eclogue', *H.S.C.Ph.* 76: 201–5.
(1976*a*). 'Virgil and Parthenius', *H.S.C.Ph.* 80: 179.
(1976*b*). 'Ariadne's leave-taking: Catullus 64.116–20', *Ill.Cl.S.* 2: 219–23.
(1976*c*). 'Catulli Veronensis Liber', *C.Ph.* 71: 37–43.
(1976*d*). 'Virgil and Juvenal', *H.S.C.Ph.* 80: 181–6.
Clift, E. H. (1945). *Latin pseudepigrapha*. Baltimore.
Coffey, M. (1957). 'Seneca tragedies, 1922–1955', *Lustrum* 2: 113–86.
(1976). *Roman satire*. London & New York.
Cole, A. T. (1972). 'The Saturnian verse', *Y.Cl.S.* 21: 3–73.
Coleman, R. G. G. (1962). 'Gallus, the Bucolics, and the ending of the Fourth Georgic', *A.J.Ph.* 83: 55–71.
Conington, J. (1881). *P. Vergilii Maronis Opera* I. London.
Costa, C. D. N. (1973). (ed.). *Horace*. London.
Crowther, N. B. (1971). 'Valerius Cato, Furius Bibaculus, and Ticidas', *C.Ph.* 66: 108–9.
Crump, M. M. (1920). *The growth of the Aeneid*. Oxford.
Dahlmann, H. (1951). 'Zur Überlieferung über die "altrömischen Tafellieder"', *A.A.M.* 17: 1191ff.
D'Alton, J. F. (1931). *Roman literary theory and criticism*. London.
Day Lewis, C. (1966). *The Eclogues, Georgics and Aeneid of Virgil*. (Trans.) Oxford.
De Decker, J. (1913). *Juvenalis declamans*. Ghent.
De Lacy, P. (1948). 'Lucretius and the history of Epicureanism', *T.A.Ph.A.* 79: 12–23.
(1957). 'Process and value: an Epicurean dilemma', *T.A.Ph.A.* 88: 114–26.
Derow, P. S. (1973). 'The Roman calendar, 190–168 B.C.', *Phoenix* 27: 345–56.
Devoto, J. (1954). *Tabulae Iguvinae*. Rome.
Dickinson, R. J. (1973). 'The *Tristia*: poetry in exile', in J. W. Binns (ed.), *Ovid* 154–90. London.
Dilke, O. A. W. (1960). (ed.). *Lucan book VII*. Revision of Postgate's edition (Cambridge 1913). Cambridge.
Doblhofer, E. (1966). *Die Augustuspanegyrik des Horaz in formalhistorischer Sicht*. Heidelberg.
Dorey, T. A. (1965). (ed.). *Cicero*. Studies in Latin literature and its influence. London.
Douglas, A. E. (1966). *M. Tullii Ciceronis Brutus*. Oxford.
(1968). *Cicero. Greece & Rome* New Surveys in the Classics II. Oxford.

(1973). 'The intellectual background of Cicero's Rhetorica: a study in method' in *ANRW* I.3 95–138. Berlin & New York.

Douglas, F. L. (1929). *A study of the Moretum*. New York.

Drabkin, I. E. (1930). *The Copa*. New York.

Drew, D. L. (1923). 'The Copa', *C.Q.* 17: 73–81.

(1925). 'The Copa – II', *C.Q.* 19: 37–42.

Drexler, H. (1932/3). *Plautinische Akzentstudien*. 2 vols. Breslau.

(1967). *Einführung in die römische Metrik*. Darmstadt.

(1969). *Die Iambenkürzung*. Hildesheim.

Duckett, E. S. (1925). *Catullus in English poetry*. Smith College Class. Stud. VI. Northampton, Mass.

Duckworth, G. E. (1952). *The nature of Roman comedy*. Princeton.

(1954). 'The architecture of the Aeneid', *A.J.Ph.* 75: 1f.

(1957). 'The *Aeneid* as a trilogy', *T.A.Ph.A.* 88: 1f.

(1959). 'Virgil's *Georgics* and the *Laudes Galli*', *A.J.Ph.* 80: 225–37.

(1962). *Structural patterns and proportions in Vergil's Aeneid*. Michigan.

(1969). *Vergil and classical hexameter poetry: a study in metrical variety*. Ann Arbor.

Due, O. S. (1962). 'An essay on Lucan', *Class. et Med.* 22: 68–132.

Duff, J. D. (1928). (ed.). *Lucan*. Loeb. London & Cambridge, Mass.

Du Quesnay, I. M. Le M. (1976). 'Vergil's Fourth *Eclogue*', *Papers of the Liverpool Latin Seminar 1976. ARCA* 2. Liverpool.

Dziatzko, K. (1899*a*). 'Buch', *RE* III 939–71.

(1899*b*). 'Buchhandel', *RE* III 973–85.

Eckhardt, L. (1936). *Exkurse und Ekphraseis bei Lucan*. Heidelberg.

Edwards, M. W. (1960). 'The expression of Stoic ideas in the *Aeneid*', *Phoenix* 14: 151f.

Eliot, T. S. (1927). Introduction to *Seneca his tenne tragedies translated into English*, edited by Thomas Newton, anno 1581. London & New York.

Elliott, R. C. (1960). *The power of satire, magic, ritual, art*. Princeton.

Ellis, R. (1891). *Noctes Manilianae*. Oxford.

Enk, P. J. (1918). (ed.). *Gratti Cynegeticon quae supersunt*. 2 vols. Zutphen.

(1919). 'De Lydia et Diris carminibus', *Mnemosyne* n.s. 47: 382–409.

(1953). 'The Latin accent', *Mnemosyne* 4.6: 93–109.

Enmann, H. (1884). *Eine verlorene Geschichte der römischen Kaiser und das Buch De viris illustribus urbis Romae. Philologus* Suppl. IV 337–501.

Erath, W. (1971). *Die Dichtung des Lygdamus*. Diss. Erlangen.

Ewbank, W. W. (1933). (ed.). *The poems of Cicero*. London.

Fairclough, H. R. (1934). (ed.). *Virgil* II: *Aeneid VII–XII and the minor poems*. Loeb. London & Cambridge, Mass.

Fedeli, P. (1972). 'Sulla prima bucolica di Virgilio', *G.I.F.* 24: 273–300.

Ferguson, J. (1975). *Utopias of the classical world*. London.

Fiske, G. C. (1920). *Lucilius and Horace*. Madison.
Fraenkel, E. (1922). *Plautinisches im Plautus*. Berlin.
(1927). 'Zur Vorgeschichte des *versus quadratus*', *Hermes* 62: 357–70.
(1928). *Iktus und Akzent im lateinischen Sprechvers*. Berlin.
(1937). Review of Pasquali (1936), in *J.R.S.* 27: 262ff.
(1951*a*). 'Additional notes on the prose of Ennius', *Eranos* 49: 50ff.
(1951*b*). 'The pedigree of the Saturnian metre', *Eranos* 49: 170f.
(1956). 'Catulls Trostgedicht für Calvus', *W.S.* 69: 279–88.
(1957). *Horace*. Oxford.
(1960). *Elementi plautini in Plauto*, tr. F. Munari. Florence. (Rev. version of *Plautinisches im Plautus*. Berlin 1922.)
(1964). *Kleine Beiträge zur klassischen Philologie*. 2 vols. Rome.
(1966). 'The Dirae', *J.R.S.* 56: 142–55.
(1968). *Leseproben aus Reden Ciceros und Catos*. Sussidi eruditi XXII. Rome.
Frank, T. (1928). *Catullus and Horace*. Oxford.
Fraser, P. M. (1972). *Ptolemaic Alexandria*. 3 vols. Oxford.
Friedländer, L. (1886). (ed.). *M. Valeri Martialis Epigrammaton Libri*. 2 vols. Leipzig.
(1908–28). *Roman life and manners under the early Empire*, tr. L. A. Magnus, J. H. Freese, A. B. Gough. 4 vols. London.
Friedländer, P. (1912). *Johannes von Gaza und Paulus Silentiarius*. Leipzig & Berlin.
Friedrich, W. H. (1933). *Untersuchungen zu Senecas dramatischer Technik*. Leipzig.
(1954). 'Sprache und Stil des Hercules Oetaeus', *Hermes* 82: 51–84. Repr. in Lefèvre (1972) 500–44.
Froesch, H. H. (1968). *Ovids Epistulae ex Ponto I-III als Gedichtsammlung*. Diss. Bonn.
Frost, R. (1946). *The poems of Robert Frost*. New York.
Furley, D. J. (1966). 'Lucretius and the Stoics', *B.I.C.S.* 13: 13–33.
Gabba, E. (1956). *Appiano e la storia delle guerre civile*. Florence.
Gaiser, K. (1970). 'Die plautinischen *Bacchides* und Menanders *Dis exapaton*', *Philologus* 114: 51–87.
(1972). 'Zur Eigenart der römischen Komödie: Plautus und Terenz gegenüber ihren griechischen Vorbildern', *ANRW* I.2 1027–1113.
Galinsky, G. K. (1975). *Ovid's Metamorphoses: an introduction to the basic aspects*. Berkeley & Los Angeles.
Galletier, E. (1920). *Epigrammata et Priapea*. Paris.
Garson, R. W. (1964). 'Some critical observations on Valerius Flaccus' *Argonautica*, I', *C.Q.* n.s. 14: 267–79.
Geffcken, J. (1911). 'Studien zur griechischen Satire', *Neue Jahrbücher für das klassiche Altertum* 27: 393–411, 469–93.
Gelzer, M. (1968). *Caesar*, tr. P. Needham. Cambridge, Mass.
Georgii, H. (1891). *Die antike Äneiskritik*. Stuttgart.
Getty, R. J. (1955). (ed.). *M. Annaei Lucani De bello ciuili Liber I*. Corr. repr. Cambridge.

Giancotti, F. (1959). *Il preludio di Lucrezio*. Messina, Florence.
Giardina, I. C. (1966). *L. Annaei Senecae tragoediae*. 2 vols. Bologna.
Gigon, O. (1938). 'Bemerkungen zu Senecas Thyestes', *Philologus* 93: 176–83.
Giussani, C. (1896). *Studi lucreziani*. Turin.
Gomme, A. W. (1937). 'Menander', in *Essays in Greek history and literature* 249–95. Oxford.
Goodyear, F. R. D. (1971). 'The *Dirae*', *P.C.Ph.S.* n.s. 17: 30–43.
Goold, G. P. (1970). 'Servius and the Helen Episode', *H.S.C.Ph.* 74: 101f.
Gossage, A. J. (1972). 'Statius', in *Neronians and Flavians: Silver Latin* I. Greek and Latin Studies, ed. D. R. Dudley. London.
Gow, A. S. F. (1950). (ed.). *Theocritus*. 2 vols. Cambridge.
(1952). (ed.). *Theocritus*. 2 vols. 2nd edn. Cambridge.
Gow, A. S. F. and Page, D. L. (1965). (eds.). *Hellenistic epigrams*. 2 vols. Cambridge.
(1968). (eds.). *The Greek Anthology. The Garland of Philip*. 2 vols. Cambridge.
Granrud, J. E. (1913). 'Was Cicero successful in the art oratorical?', *C.J.* 8: 234–43.
Grant, M. A. (1924). *Ancient rhetorical theories of the laughable*. Wisconsin Studies in Language and Literature XXI. Madison.
Green, P. (1967). *Juvenal, the sixteen satires*. (Trans.) Harmondsworth.
Grenade, P. (1950). 'Le mythe de Pompée et les Pompéiens sous les Césars', *R.E.A.* 52: 28–67.
Gresseth, G. K. (1957). 'The quarrel between Lucan and Nero', *C.Ph.* 52: 24–7.
Griffin, J. (1979). 'The Fourth Georgic, Virgil and Rome', *G. & R.* n.s. 26: 61–8.
Griffith, J. G. (1969). 'Juvenal, Statius, and the Flavian establishment', *G. & R.* n.s. 16: 134–50.
Grimal, P. (1949). 'L'episode d'Antée dans la Pharsale', *Latomus* 8: 55–61.
(1960). 'L'éloge de Néron au début de la *Pharsale*', *R.E.L.* 38: 296–305.
Grisart, A. (1959). 'La publication des "Métamorphoses": une source du récit d'Ovide (*Tristes* I, 7, 11–40)', in *Atti del convegno internazionale ovidiano* II 125–56. Rome.
Gronovius, J. F. (1661). (ed.). *L. Annaei Senecae Tragoediae*. Leiden.
(1682). (ed.). *L. Annaei Senecae Tragoediae*. 2nd edn. rev. J. Gronovius. Amsterdam.
Grube, G. M. A. (1965). *The Greek and Roman critics*. London.
Guillemin, A.-M. (1937). *Le public et la vie littéraire à Rome*. Paris.
(1951). 'L'inspiration virgilienne dans la *Pharsale*', *R.E.L.* 29: 214–27.
Gwynn, A. (1926). *Roman education from Cicero to Quintilian*. Oxford.
Haase, F. (1852). (ed.). *L. Annaei Senecae Opera quae supersunt*. 3 vols. Leipzig.
Haffter, H. (1934). *Untersuchungen zur altlateinischen Dichtersprache*. Berlin.
(1935). *Die altlateinische Dichtersprache*. Problemata X. Leipzig.
Hafner, G. (1968). *Das Bildnis von Q. Ennius*. Baden-Baden.
Haines, C. R. (1919). (ed.). *The correspondence of Marcus Cornelius Fronto*. Loeb. London & Cambridge, Mass.
Handley, E. W. (1968). *Menander and Plautus*. London.

Harder, R. (1929). 'Über Cicero's "Somnium Scipionis"', *Königsb. Abh.*, Geistesw. Kl. Heft III, 115–50 = *Kleine Schriften*, ed. W. Marg (1960) 354–95. Munich.
Harding, D. P. (1962). *The club of Hercules*. Urbana.
Haupt, M. (1875). *Opuscula* I. Leipzig.
(1876). *Opuscula* III. Leipzig.
Haury, A. (1955). *Ironie et humour chez Cicéron*. Leiden.
Helm, R. (1934). 'Die *Praetexta Octavia*', *Sitz.-Ber. Berlin* 283–347.
(1954). 'Praetexta', *RE* XLIV 1569–75.
Henry, J. (1873–89). *Aeneidea, or critical, exegetical, and aesthetical remarks on the Aeneis*. 4 vols. London, Edinburgh & Dublin.
Herescu, N. I. (1958). (ed.). *Ovidiana: recherches sur Ovide*. Paris.
Herington, C. J. (1961). 'Octavia praetexta: a survey', *C.Q.* n.s. 11: 18–30. Repr. in Lefèvre (1972) 376–401.
(1966). 'Senecan tragedy', *Arion* 5: 422–71.
Herrmann, L. (1924). *Le théâtre de Sénèque*. Paris.
Heseltine, M. (1913). (ed.). *Petronius*. Loeb. London & Cambridge, Mass.
Highet, G. (1954). *Juvenal the satirist*. Oxford.
(1972). *The speeches in Vergil's Aeneid*. Princeton.
Holleman, A. W. J. (1971). 'Ovid and politics', *Historia* 20: 458–66.
Hollis, A. S. (1970). (ed.). *Ovid, Metamorphoses Book VIII*. Oxford.
(1973). 'Aemilius Macer, Alexipharmaca?', *C.R.* n.s. 23: 11.
(1977). 'L. Varius Rufus, *De Morte* (Frs. 1–4 Morel)', *C.Q.* n.s. 27: 187–96.
Hornsby, R. A. (1970). *Patterns of action in the Aeneid*. Iowa.
Horsfall, N. M. (1969). 'Aclys and Cateia', *Class. et. Med.* 30: 297–9.
(1976). 'The *Collegium Poetarum*', *B.I.C.S.* 23: 79–95.
Hosius, C. (1893). 'Lucan und seine Quellen', *Rh. Mus.* 48: 380–97.
(1922). (ed.). *Octavia Praetexta cum elementis commentarii*. Bonn.
Housman, A. E. (1903–30). *M. Manilii Astronomicon Libri*. 5 vols. Cambridge. (Repr. in 2 vols. Olms 1972.)
(1972). J. Diggle and F. R. D. Goodyear. (eds.). *The classical papers of A. E. Housman*. 3 vols. Cambridge.
Hubaux, J. (1930). 'Une Epode d'Ovide', *Serta Leodiensia* 187–245. Liège.
Hughes, T. (1969). 'The Oedipus of Seneca' (poetic translation), *Arion* 7: 324–71.
Humbert, J. (1925). *Les plaidoyers écrits et les plaidoiries réelles de Cicéron*. Paris.
Hunt, H. A. K. (1954). *The humanism of Cicero*. Melbourne.
Ihm, M. (1893). 'Die Bibliotheken im alten Rom', *Centralbl. für Bibliothekswesen* 10: 513–32.
Immisch, O. (1923). 'Zur Frage der plautinischen *Cantica*', *Sitzungsberichte der Heidelberger Akademie* (Phil.-Hist. Kl.) 14: 7. Abhandlung 41.
Jahn, O. (1851*a*). (ed.). *Junii Juvenalis Saturarum libri V*. Berlin.
(1851*b*). 'Über die Subscriptionen in den Handschriften römischer Classiker', *Ber. d. sächs. Ges. d. Wiss. zu Leipzig* (Phil.-Hist. Kl.) 3: 327–72.

Jahn, P. (1908). 'Vergil und die Ciris', *Rh. Mus.* 63: 79–106.

Jal, P. (1963). *La guerre civile à Rome*. Paris.

Jellicoe, S. (1968). *The Septuagint and modern study*. Oxford.

Jocelyn, H. D. (1964). 'Ancient scholarship and Virgil's use of republican Latin poetry. I', *C.Q.* n.s. 14: 280–95.

(1969). 'The poet Cn. Naevius, P. Cornelius Scipio, and Q. Caecilius Metellus', *Antichthon* 3: 32–47.

(1972). 'The poems of Quintus Ennius', *ANRW* 1.2 987–1026.

(1973). 'Greek poetry in Cicero's prose writings', *Y.Cl.S.* 23: 61–111.

Johnson, W. R. (1973). 'The emotions of patriotism: Propertius 4.6', *California Studies in Classical Antiquity* 6: 151–80.

Jordan, H. (1860). *M. Catonis praeter librum de re rustica quae extant*. Leipzig.

Juhnke, H. (1972). *Homerisches in römischer Epik flavischer Zeit: Untersuchungen zu Szenennachbildungen und Strukturentsprechungen in Statius' Thebais und Achilleis und in Silius' Punica*. Zetemata LIII. Munich.

Kennedy, G. (1972). *The art of rhetoric in the Roman world, 300 B.C. to A.D. 300*. Princeton.

Kenney, E. J. (1963). Review of Buchheit (1962), in *C.R.* n.s. 13: 72–4.

(1965). 'The poetry of Ovid's exile', *P.C.Ph.S.* n.s. 11: 37–49.

(1970*a*). 'Doctus Lucretius', *Mnemosyne* 4.23: 366–92.

(1970*b*). 'Love and legalism: Ovid, *Heroides* 20 and 21', *Arion* 9: 388–414.

(1973). 'The style of the *Metamorphoses*', in J. W. Binns (ed.), *Ovid* 116–53. London.

(1976). 'Ovidius prooemians', *P.C.Ph.S.* n.s. 22: 46–53.

Kenyon, F. G. (1951). *Books and readers in ancient Greece and Rome*. 2nd edn. Oxford.

Keseling, P. (1941). 'Horaz in den Tragödien des Seneca', *Philologische Wochenschrift* 61: 190–2.

Kidd, D. A. (1977). 'Virgil's voyage', *Prudentia* 9: 97–103.

Kienast, D. (1954). *Cato der Zensor*. Heidelberg.

Kirkwood, G. M. (1961). 'The authorship of the Strasbourg Epodes', *T.A.Ph.A.* 92: 267–82.

Kleberg, T. (1967). *Buchhandel und Verlagswesen in der Antike*. Darmstadt.

Kleve, K. (1969). 'Lucrèce, l'épicurisme et l'amour', *Actes du viii Congrès G. Budé* 376–83.

Klingner, F. (1963). *Virgils Georgica*. Zurich & Stuttgart.

Klotz, A. (1947). 'Zur Verskunst des römischen Dramas', *Würzburger Jahrbücher für die Altertumswissenschaft* 2: 301–57.

Knauer, G. N. (1964). *Die Aeneis und Homer*. Göttingen.

Knight, W. F. Jackson (1939). *Accentual symmetry in Vergil*. Oxford.

(1966). *Roman Vergil*. 2nd edn. London.

Knoche, U. (1975). *Roman satire*, tr. E. S. Ramage. Bloomington.

Knowles, M. D. (1958). 'The preservation of the classics', in *The English library before 1700*. London.

Knox, B. M. W. (1968). 'Silent reading in antiquity', *G.R.B.S.* 9: 421–35.

Koep, L. (1954). 'Buch I (technisch)', *RAC* II 664–88.

Kost, K. (1971). *Musaios, Hero und Leander*. Bonn.

Krenkel, W. (1970). *Lucilius, Satiren*. Leiden.

Kroll, W. (1926). (ed.). *Historia Alexandri Magni* (*Pseudo-Callisthenes*) I: *Recensio vetusta*. Berlin.

(1929). *C. Valerius Catullus*. Stuttgart.

Kruuse, J. (1941). 'L'originalité artistique de Martial', *Class. et Med.* 4: 248–300.

La Cerda, I. L. de (1608). *P. Vergilii Maronis Bucolica et Georgica*. Frankfurt am Main.

Latte, K. (1960). *Römische Religionsgeschichte*. Munich.

Laughton, E. (1951). 'The prose of Ennius', *Eranos* 2: 35ff.

(1960). 'Observations on the style of Varro', *C.Q.* n.s. 10: 1–28.

Laurand, L. (1907; 4th edn. 1936–8). *Études sur le style des discours de Cicéron*. 3 vols. Paris.

Lawall, G. (1966). 'Apollonius' *Argonautica*: Jason as anti-hero', *Y.Cl.S.* 19: 116–69.

Leeman, A. D. (1963). *Orationis ratio*. Amsterdam.

Lefèvre, E. (1972). (ed.). *Senecas Tragödien*. Darmstadt.

Lejay, P. (1925). *Plaute*. Paris.

Lelièvre, F. J. (1958). 'Parody in Juvenal and T. S. Eliot', *C.Ph.* 53: 22–5.

Leo, F. (1878). (ed.). *L. Annaei Senecae Tragoediae*, I (*Observationes criticae*), II (critical text). Berlin.

(1897*a*). *Die plautinischen Cantica und die hellenistische Lyrik*. Berlin.

(1897*b*). 'Die Composition der Chorlieder Senecas', *Rh. Mus.* 52: 509–18.

(1906). 'Diogenes bei Plautus', *Hermes* 41: 441–6 (= *Ausgewählte Kleine Schriften* I, Rome 1960, 185–90).

(1912). *Plautinische Forschungen*. 2nd edn. Berlin.

(1913). *Geschichte der römischen Literatur* I: *Die archaische Literatur*. Berlin.

Levin, H. (1952). *Christopher Marlowe: the Overreacher*. Cambridge, Mass.

Lewis, C. S. (1936). *The allegory of love: a study in medieval tradition*. Oxford.

(1942). *A preface to Paradise Lost*. London, New York & Toronto.

Lewis, N. (1974). *Papyrus in classical antiquity*. Oxford.

Lindsay, W. M. (1904). *Ancient editions of Plautus*. Oxford & St Andrews.

(1907). *Syntax of Plautus*. Oxford.

(1922). *Early Latin verse*. Oxford.

Lişcu, M. O. (1937). *L'expression des idées philosophiques chez Cicéron*. Paris.

Longi, E. (1955). 'Tre episodi del poema di Lucano', in *Studi in onore di G. Funaioli* 181–8. Rome.

Lovejoy, A. O. and Boas, G. (1935). *Primitivism and related ideas in antiquity*. Baltimore.

Luck, G. (1959). *Die römische Liebeselegie.* Heidelberg.

(1968). (ed.). *P. Ovidius Naso. Tristia.* II. *Kommentar.* Heidelberg.

(1974). 'The woman's role in Latin elegiac poetry', in G. K. Galinsky (ed.), *Perspectives of Roman poetry* 23ff. University of Texas.

Ludwig, W. (1961). 'Die Anordnung des vierten Horazischen Odenbuches', *Mus. Helv.* 18: 1–10.

(1968). 'The originality of Terence and his Greek models', *G.R.B.S.* 9: 169–82.

Lyne, R. O. A. M. (1971). 'The dating of the *Ciris*', *C.Q.* n.s. 21: 233–53.

Maas, P. and Lloyd-Jones, H. (tr.) (1962). *Greek metre.* Oxford.

MacCary, W. T. and Willcock, M. M. (1976). (eds.). *Plautus, Casina.* Cambridge.

Mackail, J. W. (1930). *The Aeneid of Virgil.* Oxford.

MacKay, L. A. (1961). 'The vocabulary of fear in Latin epic poetry', *T.A.Ph.A.* 92: 308–16.

Magie, D. (1921–32). (ed.). *The Historiae Augustae.* 3 vols. London & Cambridge, Mass.

Malcovati, H. (1943). *Cicerone e la poesia.* Padua.

(1955). *Oratorum Romanorum fragmenta liberae rei publicae.* 2nd edn. (1st edn. 1930). 3 vols. Turin.

Mariotti, S. (1952). *Livio Andronico e la traduzione artistica.* Milan.

(1955). *Il 'Bellum Poenicum' e l'arte di Nevio.* Rome.

Marouzeau, J. (1949). *Quelques aspects de la formation du Latin littéraire.* Paris.

Marrou, H. I. (1956). *A history of education in antiquity*, tr. G. Lamb. London.

(1958). *Saint Augustin et la fin de la culture antique.* 4th edn. Paris.

Marti, B. (1945). 'The meaning of the *Pharsalia*', *A.J.Ph.* 66: 352–576.

(1968). 'La structure de la *Pharsale*', in *Lucain*, Entretiens Hardt XV 1–50. Geneva.

Martin, R. H. (1976). (ed.). *Terence, Adelphoe.* Cambridge.

Martini, E. (1933). *Einleitung zu Ovid.* Prague.

Marx, F. (1904). *C. Lucilii carminum reliquiae.* 2 vols. Leipzig.

Mason, H. A. (1959). *Humanism and poetry in the early Tudor period.* London.

(1963). 'Is Juvenal a classic?', in Sullivan (1963) 93–167.

Matthews, J. (1975). *Western aristocracies and Imperial court.* Oxford.

Maurois, A. (1957). *Les trois Dumas.* Paris.

Meillet, A. (1928: 4th edn. 1948). *Esquisse d'une histoire de la langue latine.* Paris.

Mendell, C. W. (1967). *Latin poetry: the age of rhetoric and satire.* Hamden.

Mette, H.-J. (1964). 'Die römische Tragödie', *Lustrum* 9: 5–212.

Meuli, K. (1955). 'Altrömische Maskenbrauch', *Mus.Helv.* 12: 206–35.

Meyer, W. (1886). 'Ueber die Beobachtung des Wortaccentes in der altlateinischen Poesie', *Abhandlungen der bayerischen Akademie der Wissenschaften* (Phil.-Hist. Kl.) 17: 3–120.

Michels, A. K. (1967). *The calendar of the Roman Republic.* Princeton.

Miniconi, P. J. (1951). *Étude des thèmes guerriers de la poèsie greco-romaine.* Publ. Fac. Lettr. Algér. II sér. 19. Paris.

(1962). 'La joie dans l'Éneide', *Latomus* 21: 503–11.

Mohrmann, C. (1961). *Études sur le latin des Chrétiens.* II: *Latin chrétien et médiéval.* Rome.

Momigliano, A. (1941). Review of B. Farrington, *Science and politics in the ancient world*, in *J.R.S.* 31: 149–57.

(1957). 'Perizonius, Niebuhr and the character of early Roman tradition', *J.R.S.* 47: 104–14.

(1962). (ed.). *The conflict between Paganism and Christianity in the fourth century.* Oxford.

(1969). 'Il trapasso fra storiografia antica e storiografia medievale', *Rivista storica italiana* 81: 286–303.

(1975). *Alien wisdom: the limits of Hellenization.* Cambridge.

Morford, M. P. O. (1967). *The poet Lucan.* Oxford.

Motto, A. L. (1970). *Seneca sourcebook: guide to the thought of Lucius Annaeus Seneca.* Amsterdam.

(1973). *Seneca.* New York.

Mountford, J. F. and Schultz, J. T. (1930). *Index rerum et nominum in scholiis Servii et Aelii Donati tractatorum.* Ithaca, New York.

Müller, G. (1953). 'Senecas Oedipus als Drama', *Hermes* 81: 447–64. (Repr. in Lefèvre (1972) 376–401.)

Müller, R. (1969). 'Lukrez V 1101ff und die Stellung der epikureischen Philosophie zum Staat und zu den Gesetzen', in O. von Jurewicz and H. Kuch (eds.), *Die Krise der griechischen Polis.* Berlin.

Münscher, K. (1922). *Senecas Werke: Untersuchungen zur Abfassungszeit und Echtheit. Philologus* Suppl.-Band XVI, Heft 1.

Mynors, R. A. B. (1958). (ed.). *C. Valerii Catulli carmina.* Oxford.

Nachmanson, E. (1941). *Der griechische Buchtitel. Einige Beobachtungen.* Gothenburg.

Nash, E. (1961–2). *A pictorial dictionary of ancient Rome.* London.

Nettleship, H. (1890). 'Literary criticism in Latin antiquity', *Journal of Philology* 18: 225–70.

Neumeister, C. (1964). *Grundsätze der forensischen Rhetorik.* Munich.

Newman, J. K. (1967). *Augustus and the New Poetry.* Collection Latomus LXXXVIII. Brussels.

Nisbet, R. G. M. (1963). 'Persius', in Sullivan (1963) 39–71.

Nisbet, R. G. M. and Hubbard, M. (1970). *A commentary on Horace: Odes Book I.* Oxford.

Norden, E. (1898; repr. Stuttgart 1973). *Die antike Kunstprosa.* 2 vols. Leipzig.

(1913). *Agnostos Theos.* Berlin.

(1915). *Ennius und Vergilius. Kriegsbilder aus Roms grosser Zeit.* Leipzig & Berlin.

(1916). (ed.). *P. Vergilius Maro Aeneis Buch VI.* Berlin.

(1926). (ed.). *P. Vergilius Maro, Aeneis Buch VI.* 3rd edn. Leipzig & Berlin.

(1939). *Aus altrömischen Priesterbüchern.* Lund.

Nougaret, L. (1943). 'La métrique de Plaute et de Térence', *Mémorial des études latines . . . offert . . . à J. Marouzeau* 123–48. Paris.

(1948). *Traité de métrique latine classique*. Paris.

Nowak, H. (1955). *Lukanstudien*. Diss. Vienna.

Ogilvie, R. M. (1965). *A commentary on Livy Books 1–5*. Oxford.

Ollfors, A. (1967). *Studien zum Aufbau des Hexameters Lucans*. Gothenburg.

Opelt, I. (1957). 'Die Seeschlacht vor Massilia bei Lucan', *Hermes* 85: 435–45.

(1969). 'Zu Senecas Phoenissen', in Lefèvre (1972) 272–85.

Otis, B. (1959). 'Three problems of *Aeneid* 6', *T.A.Ph.A.* 90: 165f.

(1963). *Virgil: a study in civilized poetry*. Oxford.

(1966). *Ovid as an epic poet*. Cambridge.

Packard, D. W. (1968). *A concordance to Livy*. 4 vols. Cambridge, Mass.

Page, D. L. (1940). (ed.). *Select papyri* III. Loeb. London & Cambridge, Mass.

(1950). (ed.). *Select papyri* III. *Literary papyri: poetry*. Revised repr. Loeb. London & Cambridge, Mass.

(1972). 'Early Hellenistic elegy', *P.C.Ph.S.* n.s. 18: 63–4.

Parks, E. E. (1945). *The Roman rhetorical schools as a preparation for the courts under the early Empire*. Diss. Baltimore.

Parsons, P. (1971). 'A Greek Satyricon?', *B.I.C.S.* 18: 53–68.

Pasquali, G. (1936). *Preistoria della poesia romana*. Florence.

Patin, H. J. G. (1883). *Études sur la poèsie latine*. 3rd edn. Paris.

Patzer, H. (1955). 'Zum Sprachstil des neoterischen Hexameters', *Mus. Helv.* 12: 77–95.

Pearce, T. E. V. (1966). 'The enclosing word-order in the Latin hexameter', *C.Q.* n.s. 16: 140–71, 298–320.

(1968). 'A pattern of word-order in Latin poetry', *C.Q.* n.s. 18: 334–54.

Pecchiura, P. (1965). *La figura di Catone Uticense nella letteratura latina*. Turin.

Peiper, R. and Richter, G. (1902). (eds.). *L. Annaei Senecae Tragoediae*. Leipzig.

Perry, B. E. (1965). *Babrius and Phaedrus*. Loeb. London & Cambridge, Mass.

Peter. H. (1901). *Der Brief in der römischen Literatur*. Leipzig.

(1914). *Historicorum Romanorum fragmenta*. 2nd edn. Leipzig.

Peterson, W. (1891). (ed.). *M. Fabi Quintiliani Institutionis oratoriae Liber decimus*. Oxford.

Petersson, T. (1920). *Cicero: a biography*. Berkeley.

Pfeiffer, R. (1968). *History of classical scholarship from the beginnings to the end of the Hellenistic age*. Oxford.

Phillips, O. C. (1968). 'Lucan's Grove', *C.Ph.* 62: 296–300.

Philp, R. H. (1968). 'The manuscript tradition of Seneca's tragedies', *C.Q.* n.s. 18: 150–79.

Pichon, R. (1906). *Les derniers écrivains profanes*. Paris.

(1912). *Les sources de Lucain*. Paris.

Pierleoni, G. (1906). 'Fu poeta Grattius?', *Rivista di Filologia e di Istruzione Classica* 34: 580–97.

Pighi, G. B. (1963). 'Seneca metrico', *Rivista di Filologia e di Istruzione Classica* 91: 170–81.

Platnauer, M. (1922). (ed.). *Claudian.* 2 vols. Loeb. London & Cambridge, Mass.

(1951). *Latin elegiac verse. A study of the metrical usages of Tibullus, Propertius & Ovid.* Cambridge.

Poncelet, R. (1957). *Cicéron traducteur de Platon.* Paris.

Portalupi, F. (1955). *Bruto e i neo-atticisti.* Turin.

Posch, S. (1969). *Beobachtungen zur Theokritnachwirkung bei Vergil.* Comm. Aenipont. XIX. Innsbruck.

Pöschl, V. (1950). *Die Dichtkunst Virgils: Bild und Symbol in der Aeneis.* Innsbruck; tr. G. Seligson, Michigan 1962.

Poultney, J. W. (1959). *The Bronze Tables of Iguvium.* A.P.A. Monograph XVIII.

Pound, E. (1918). In *The little review*, ed. M. Anderson. Chicago.

Préchac, M. (1934). 'La date de la naissance de Sénèque', *R.E.L.* 11: 360–75.

Putnam, M. C. J. (1960). 'Catullus 66. 75–88', *C.Ph.* 55: 223–8.

(1965). *The poetry of the Aeneid.* Harvard.

Questa, C. (1967). *Introduzione alla metrica di Plauto.* Rome.

(1970). 'Alcune strutture sceniche di Plauto e Menandro', in *Ménandre*, Entretiens Hardt XVI 181–228. Geneva.

Quinn, K. (1963). *Latin explorations.* London.

(1965). 'The Fourth Book of the *Aeneid:* a critical description', *G. & R.* n.s. 12: 16f.

Radford, R. S. (1928). 'Ovid's *Carmina furtiva*', *Phil. Quart.* 7: 45–59.

(1930). 'The *Culex* and Ovid', *Philologus.* 86: 18–66.

Rambaud, M. (1953). *Cicéron et l'histoire romaine.* Paris.

Raven, D. S. (1965). *Latin metre.* London.

Rawson, E. (1973). 'The interpretation of Cicero's "De Legibus"', *ANRW* I.4, 334–56. Berlin & New York.

Regenbogen, O. (1927/8). 'Schmerz und Tod in den Tragödien Senecas', *Vorträge der Bibliothek Warburg* VII 167–218. (Repr. as monograph with same title, Darmstadt 1963).

(1932). *Lukrez, seine Gestalt in seinem Gedicht.* Neue Wege zur Antike II.1 Leipzig & Berlin. (Repr. (1961) in *Kleine Schriften.* Munich.)

Reitzenstein, R. (1912). 'Zur Sprache der lateinischen Erotik', *S.H.A.W.* 12: 9–36.

Rennie, W. (1921). 'Satira tota nostra est', *C.R.* 35: 21.

Reynolds, L. D. (1965). *The medieval tradition of Seneca's letters.* Oxford.

Reynolds, L. D. and Wilson, N. G. (1974). *Scribes and scholars. A guide to the transmission of Greek and Latin literature.* 2nd edn. Oxford.

Rhys Roberts, W. (1901). (ed.). *Dionysius of Halicarnassus: the three Literary Letters.* Cambridge.

Ribbeck, O. (1865). *Der echte und der unechte Juvenal.* Berlin.

(1866). *Prolegomena critica ad P. Vergili Maronis opera maiora.* Leipzig.

Richter, W. (1957). (ed.). *Vergil, Georgica* (edn. with commentary).

Ricks, C. (1968). (ed.). *A. E. Housman.* New Jersey.
Rieth, C. (1964). *Die Kunst Menanders in den Adelphen des Terenz.* Hildesheim.
Rieu, E. V. (1950). *Homer, the Iliad.* (Trans.) Harmondsworth.
Rist, J. M. (1969). *Stoic philosophy.* Cambridge.
Roberts, C. H. (1954). 'The Codex', *P.B.A.* 40: 169–204.
(1956). *Greek literary hands 350 B.C.–A.D. 400.* Corr. repr. Oxford.
Robinson, R. P. (1923). 'Valerius Cato', *T.A.Ph.A.* 54: 98–116.
Rohde, E. (1914). *Der griechische Roman.* 2nd edn. Leipzig.
Rose, H. J. (1934). *A handbook of Greek literature.* London.
Rose, K. F. C. (1971). *The date and author of the Satyricon.* Leiden.
Ross, D. O. jr. (1969*a*). *Style and tradition in Catullus.* Cambridge, Mass.
(1969*b*). 'Nine epigrams from Pompeii (*CIL* 4.4966–73)', *Y.Cl.S.* 21: 127–42.
(1975*a*). *Backgrounds to Augustan poetry: Gallus, elegy and Rome.* Cambridge.
(1975*b*). 'The *Culex* and *Moretum* as post-Augustan literary parodies', *H.S.C.Ph.* 79: 235ff.
Rowell, H. T. (1947). 'The original form of Naevius' *Bellum Poenicum*', *A.J.Ph.* 68: 35ff.
Rudd, N. (1960*a*). 'Horace on the origins of Satire', *Phoenix* 14: 36–44.
(1960*b*). 'Patterns in Horatian lyric', *A.J.Ph.* 81: 373–92.
(1976). *Lines of enquiry: studies in Latin poetry.* Cambridge.
Russell, D. A. (1964). *'Longinus' on the sublime.* Oxford.
Rutz, W. (1965). 'Lucan 1943–1963', *Lustrum* 9: 243–340.
Sabine, G. H. and Smith, H. B. (1929). *Cicero on the Commonwealth.* Columbus, Ohio.
Saint-Denis, E. de (1956). *Virgile, Géorgiques* (Budé). Paris.
Sanford, E. M. (1931). 'Lucan and his Roman critics', *C.Ph.* 26: 233–57.
Sassoon, S. (1945). *Siegfried's journey 1916–1920.* London.
Scazzoso, P. (1956). 'Reflessi misterici nelle Georgiche', *Paideia* 11: 5–28.
Schanz, M. and Hosius, C. (1927). *Geschichte der römischen Literatur* I: *Die römische Literatur in der Zeit der Republik.* 4th edn. Munich.
Schmid, W. (1944). Review of J. Mewaldt, *Der Kampf des Dichters Lukrez gegen die Religion, Gnomon* 20: 97–100.
Schöpsdau, K. (1974). 'Motive der Liebesdichtung in Vergils Dritter Ekloge', *Hermes* 102: 268ff.
Schubart, W. (1921). *Das Buch bei den Griechen und Römern.* 2nd edn. Berlin & Leipzig.
Schulze, K. P. (1898). 'Ovid *Trist.* IV.10.43f.', *Rh. Mus.* 53: 541–6.
Schutter, K. H. E. (1952). *Quibus annis comoediae Plautinae primum actae sint quaeritur.* Groningen.
Scivoletto, N. (1966). 'Quando nacque Seneca?', *G.I.F.* 19: 21–31.
Scott, I. G. (1927). *The grand style in the satires of Juvenal.* Northampton, Mass.
Scriverius, P. (1621). (ed.). *L. Annaeus Seneca Tragicus.* 2 vols. Leiden.
Segal, C. (1966). 'Orpheus and the Fourth Georgic', *A.J.Ph.* 87: 307–25.

Seitz, K. (1965). 'Der pathetische Erzählstil Lucans', *Hermes* 93: 204ff.

Sellar, W. Y. (1889). *The Roman poets of the Republic*. 3rd edn. Oxford.

Shackleton Bailey, D. R. (1965–70). (ed.). *Cicero's Letters to Atticus*. 7 vols. Cambridge.

Sherk, R. K. (1969). *Roman documents from the Greek East: Senatus consulta and Epistulae to the age of Augustus*. Baltimore.

Sherwin-White, A. N. (1966). *The Letters of Pliny: a historical and social commentary*. Oxford.

Shipp, G. P. (1953). 'Greek in Plautus', *W.S.* 66: 105–12.

(1955). 'Plautine terms for Greek and Roman things', *Glotta* 34: 139–52.

Sifakis, G. M. (1967). *Studies in the history of Hellenistic drama*. London.

Skutsch, O. (1968). *Studia Enniana*. London.

Skydsgaard, J. E. (1968). *Varro the scholar*. Copenhagen.

Slater, D. A. (1912). 'Was the Fourth Eclogue written to celebrate the marriage of Octavia to Mark Antony?', *C.R.* 26: 114.

Sluiter, Th. H. (1949). (ed.). *Octavia fabula praetexta*. Leiden.

Small, S. G. P. (1959). 'The Arms of Turnus: *Aeneid* 7. 783–92', *T.A.Ph.A.* 90: 243f.

Smith, K. F. (1913). (ed.). *The Elegies of Albius Tibullus*. New York.

Solmsen, F. (1948). 'Propertius and Horace', *C.Ph.* 43: 105–9.

Sommer, R. (1926). 'T. Pomponius Atticus und Ciceros Werke', *Hermes* 61: 389–422.

Sonner, P. (1910). *De P. Vergili Maronis carminibus capita tria*. Diss. Halle.

Sparrow, J. (1931). *Half-lines and repetitions in Virgil*. Oxford.

Speyer, W. (1971). *Die literarische Fälschung im heidnischen und christlichen Altertum. Ein Versuch ihrer Deutung*. Munich.

Steele, R. B. (1933). *The Nux, Maecenas and Consolatio ad Liviam*. Nashville.

Steyns, D. (1906). *Étude sur les métaphores et les comparaisons dans les oeuvres en prose de Sénèque le philosophe*. Gand.

Stroh, W. (1968). 'Ein missbrauchtes Distichon Ovids', in M. von Albrecht and E. Zinn (eds.), *Ovid* 567–80. Darmstadt.

(1971). *Die römische Liebeselegie als werbende Dichtung*. Amsterdam.

Strzelecki, L. (1935). *De Naeviano 'Belli Punici' carmine quaestiones selectae*. Krakow.

Suerbaum, W. (1968). *Untersuchungen zur Selbstdarstellung älterer römischer Dichter, Livius Andronicus, Naevius, Ennius*. Hildesheim.

Sullivan, J. P. (1963). (ed.). *Critical essays on Roman literature. Satire*. London.

Summers, W. C. (1910). *Select letters of Seneca*. London.

Süss, W. (1965). 'Cicero: eine Einführung in seine philosophischen Schriften', *Abh. Mainz Geistes- und Sozialw. Kl.* 5: 210–385. Wiesbaden 1966.

Syme, R. (1939). *The Roman revolution*. Oxford.

(1958). *Tacitus*. 2 vols. Oxford.

Tandoi, V. (1969). 'Il ricordo di Stazio "dolce poeta" nella sat. 7 di Giovenale', *Maia* 21: 102–22.

Tarn, W. W. (1932). 'Alexander Helios and the golden age', *J.R.S.* 22: 135–60.

(1948). *Alexander the Great*. I *Narrative*; II *Sources and Studies*. Cambridge.

Taylor, L. R. (1937). 'The opportunities for dramatic performances in the time of Plautus and Terence', *T.A.Ph.A.* 68: 284–304.
(1949). *Party politics in the age of Caesar*. Berkeley & Los Angeles.
Thompson, L. and Bruère, R. T. (1968). 'Lucan's use of Virgilian reminiscence', *C.Ph.* 63: 1–21.
Thulin, C. (1906). *Italische sakrale Poesie und Prosa*. Berlin.
Till, R. (1936). *Die Sprache Catos*. *Philologus* Suppl.-Band XXVIII, Heft 2.
Tillyard, E. M. (1943). *The Elizabethan world picture*. London.
Townend, G. B. (1961). 'Traces in Dio Cassius of Cluvius, Aufidius, and Pliny', *Hermes* 89: 227–48.
(1964). 'Cluvius Rufus in the *Histories* of Tacitus', *A.J.Ph.* 85: 337–77.
(1969). 'Some problems of punctuation in the Latin hexameter', *C.Q.* n.s. 19: 330–44.
(1973). 'The literary substrata to Juvenal's satires', *J.R.S.* 63: 148–60.
Toynbee, J. M. C. (1971). *Death and burial in the Roman world*. London.
Traina, A. (1970). *Vortit barbare. Le traduzioni poetiche da Livio Andronico a Cicerone*. Rome.
Tränkle, H. (1967). 'Neoterische Kleinigkeiten', *Mus.Helv.* 24: 87–103.
Trendall, A. D. (1967). *Phlyax vases*. *B.I.C.S.* Suppl. XIX. 2nd edn. London.
Trillitzsch, W. (1971). *Seneca im literarischen Urteil der Antike. Darstellung und Sammlung der Zeugnisse*. 2 vols. Amsterdam.
Turner, E. G. (1968). *Greek papyri: an introduction*. Oxford.
(1971). *Greek manuscripts of the ancient world*. Oxford.
Tyrrell, R. Y. and Purser, L. C. (1933). *The correspondence of Cicero* VI. 2nd edn. Dublin.
Valéry, P. (1962). 'Variations sur les *Bucoliques*', *Oeuvres* I: 207–22.
van de Woestijne, P. (1929). 'Haud mollia iussa', *R.B.Ph.* 8: 523–30.
van Groningen, B. A. (1963). '"Εκδοσις', *Mnemosyne* 4.16: 1–17.
Van Rooy, C. A. (1965). *Studies in classical satire and related literary theory*. Leiden.
Van Sickle, J. (1975). 'The new erotic fragment of Archilochus', *Quadri Urbinati di cultura classica* 20: 123–56.
Vessey, D. W. T. C. (1970). 'Statius and Antimachus: a review of the evidence', *Philologus* 114: 118–43.
(1972). 'Aspects of Statius' epithalamion: *Silvae* 1.2', *Mnemosyne* 4.25: 172–87.
(1972–3). 'The myth of Falernus in Silius, *Punica* 7', *C.J.* 68: 240–6.
(1973). *Statius and the Thebaid*. Cambridge.
(1975). 'Silius Italicus: the shield of Hannibal', *A.J.Ph.* 96: 391–405.
Warmington, B. H. (1957). *Remains of Old Latin* III: *Lucilius, The Twelve Tables*. 2nd edn. Loeb. London & Cambridge, Mass.
Waszink, J.-H. (1950). 'The Proem of the *Annales* of Ennius', *Mnemosyne* 3. 3: 215–40.
(1972). 'Zum Anfangsstadium der römischen Literatur', *ANRW* 1.2, 869–927.

Watson, A. (1971). *Roman private law around 200 B.C.* Edinburgh.
Watts, W. J. (1971). 'The birthplaces of Latin writers', *G. & R.* n.s. 18: 91–101.
Welsford, E. (1935). *The Fool, his social and literary history*. London.
Wendel, C. (1949). *Die griechisch-römische Buchbeschreibung verglichen mit der des Vorderen Orients*. Halle.
(1954). 'Bibliothek', *RAC* II 664–88.
Wessner, P. (1929). 'Lucan, Statius und Juvenal bei den römischen Grammatikern', *P.Ph.W.* 49: 296–303, 328–35.
West, D. A. (1969). 'Multiple-correspondence similes in the *Aeneid*', *J.R.S.* 59: 40–9.
Westendorp Boerma, R. E. H. (1949). (ed.). *P. Vergili Maronis Catalepton*. 2 vols. (vol. II 1963). Assen.
(1958). 'Virgil's debt to Catullus', *Acta Classica* 1: 55f.
White, P. (1974). 'The presentation and dedication of the *Silvae* and the *Epigrams*', *J.R.S.* 64: 40–61.
Wiedemann, T. (1975). 'The political background to Ovid's *Tristia* 2', *C.Q.* n.s. 25: 264–71.
Wiesen, D. (1963). 'Juvenal's moral character, an introduction', *Latomus* 22: 440–71.
Wilamowitz-Moellendorff, U. von (1924). *Hellenistiche Dichtung*. 2 vols. Berlin.
(1928). *Erinnerungen 1848–1914*. Leipzig.
Wili, W. (1947). 'Die literarischen Beziehungen des Properz zu Horaz', *Festschrift Tièche*. Bern.
Wilkinson, L. P. (1955). *Ovid recalled*. Cambridge.
(1963). *Golden Latin artistry*. Cambridge.
(1969). *The Georgics of Virgil: a critical survey*.
Williams, G. W. (1956). 'Some problems in the construction of Plautus' *Pseudolus*', *Hermes* 84: 424–55.
(1958). 'Evidence for Plautus' workmanship in the *Miles Gloriosus*', *Hermes* 86: 79–105.
(1968). *Tradition and originality in Roman poetry*. Oxford.
Williams, R. D. (1960). (ed.). *Virgil, Aeneid V*. Oxford.
(1961). 'The function and structure of Virgil's Catalogue in *Aeneid* 7', *C.Q.* n.s. 11: 146–53.
(1962). (ed.). *Virgil, Aeneid III*. Oxford.
(1963). 'Virgil and the *Odyssey*', *Phoenix* 17: 266f.
(1972). 'The pageant of Roman heroes', in *Cicero and Virgil: Studies in honour of Harold Hunt*. Amsterdam.
Williamson, G. (1951). *The Senecan amble: prose form from Bacon to Collier*. Chicago.
Wimmel, W. (1960). *Kallimachos in Rom. Hermes* Einzelschrift XVI. Wiesbaden.
Wingo, E. O. (1972). *Latin punctuation in the classical age*. The Hague & Paris.
Winterbottom, M. (1974). (ed.). *The Elder Seneca. Declamations*. 2 vols. Loeb. London & Cambridge, Mass.

Wirszubski, C. (1950). *Libertas as a political idea at Rome during the late Republic and early Principate.* Cambridge.

Wiseman, T. P. (1969). *Catullan questions.* Leicester.

Wissowa, G. (1917). 'Das Prooemium von Vergils Georgica', *Hermes* 52: 92–104.

Wright, J. (1974). *Dancing in chains: the stylistic unity of the comoedia palliata.* Papers and monographs of the American Academy in Rome XXV. Rome.

Zetzel, J. E. G. (1972). *Latin textual criticism.* Unpubd diss. Harvard.

(1973). '*Emendavi ad Tironem*: some notes on scholarship in the second century A.D.', *H.S.C.Ph.* 77: 225–43.

Zieliński, Th. (1904). *Das Clauselgesetz in Ciceros Reden: Grundzüge einer oratorischen Rhythmik. Philologus* Suppl.-Band IX 589–875.

Zwierlein, O. (1966). *Die Rezitationsdramen Senecas.* Meisenheim am Glan.

INDEX

Main references are distinguished by figures in bold type. References to the Appendix (which should normally be consulted for basic details of authors' lives and works, and for bibliographies) are given in italic figures.